Economic Commission for Europe

ECONOMIC SURVEY OF EUROPE IN 1989-1990

Prepared by the
SECRETARIAT OF THE
ECONOMIC COMMISSION FOR EUROPE
GENEVA

NEW YORK, 1990

NOTE

The designations employed and the presentation of the material in this publication do not imply the expression of any opinion whatsoever on the part of the Secretariat of the United Nations concerning the legal status of any country, territory, city or area, or of its authorities, or concerning the delimitation of its frontiers or boundaries.

UNITED NATIONS PUBLICATION

Sales No. E.90.II.E.1

ISBN 92-1-116469-9
ISSN 0070-8712

PREFACE

The present *Survey* is the forty-third in a series of reports prepared by the secretariat of the Economic Commission for Europe to serve the needs of the Commission and to help in reporting on world economic conditions.

The *Survey* is published on the responsibility of the secretariat, and the views expressed in it should not be attributed to the Commission or to its participating Governments.

The pre-publication text of this *Survey* was completed on 20 March 1990 as a document for the 45th session of the Economic Commission for Europe. The final text, incorporating minor changes, was completed on 5 April 1990.

EXPLANATORY NOTES

The following symbols have been used throughout this *Survey*:

A dash (-) indicates nil or negligible;

Two dots (..) indicate not available or not pertinent;

An asterisk (*) indicates an estimate by the secretariat of the Economic Commission for Europe;

A slash (/) indicates a crop year or financial year (e.g., 1988/89);

Use of a hyphen (-) between dates representing years, for example, 1987-1989, signifies the full period involved, including the beginning and end years.

Unless the contrary is stated, the standard unit of weight used throughout is the metric ton.

The term "billion" signifies a thousand million.

References to dollars ($) are to United States dollars unless otherwise stated.

The following abbreviations have been used:

CMEA	Council for Mutual Economic Assistance
ECE	Economic Commission for Europe
EEC	European Economic Community
FAO	Food and Agriculture Organization of the United Nations
GDP	Gross domestic product
GNP	Gross national product
GSP	Gross social product
IMF	International Monetary Fund
NMP	Net material product
OECD	Organization for Economic Co-operation and Development
OPEC	Organization of the Petroleum Exporting Countries
SDR	Special drawing rights

CONTENTS

CHAPTER 1

The economic situation in the ECE region

1.1	SUMMARY OF CURRENT ECONOMIC DEVELOPMENTS	1
	(i) Western Europe and North America	1
	(ii) Eastern Europe and the Soviet Union	2
	(iii) East-west trade	3
1.2	ECONOMIC REFORM IN THE EAST: A FRAMEWORK FOR WESTERN SUPPORT	5
	(i) Introduction	5
	(ii) The long-term deterioration in the economic performance of the eastern countries	5
	(iii) The problems of conversion and post-war adjustment in western Europe	9
	(iv) The Marshall Plan	10
	(v) Is a 'Marshall Plan' needed for eastern Europe?	13
	(vi) Eastern reform and the environment	17
	(vii) Eastern reforms and international trade	18
	(viii) The pace of reform in the eastern countries	21
	(ix) Summary and conclusions	23

CHAPTER 2

Western Europe and North America

2.1	AN OVERVIEW OF 1989 AND THE OUTLOOK FOR 1990	27
	(i) Expansion continues in 1989	27
	(ii) The outlook for 1990	29
	(iii) The possible effects of a German monetary union	30
	(iv) The effects of the eastern reform process on the rest of the world	32
2.2	OUTPUT AND THE STRUCTURE OF DEMAND	35
	(i) Real GDP and domestic demand	35
	(ii) Industrial production and capacity utilization	39
	(iii) The components of demand	40
2.3	INTERNAL AND EXTERNAL BALANCE	50
	(i) Costs and prices	50
	(ii) Labour markets	61
	(iii) External balances	67

CHAPTER 3

Eastern Europe and the Soviet Union

3.1	GENERAL ECONOMIC DEVELOPMENTS	75
	(i) The background to economic developments	75
	(ii) Policy makers' expectations for 1989	77
	(iii) Economic performance in 1989	78
	(iv) Sectoral output growth	79
	(v) Domestic absorption in 1989	80
	(vi) Developments in foreign trade	80
	(vii) Reliability of statistics	81
	(viii) Outlook for growth in 1990	83

			Page
3.2	PRODUCTION		86
	(i)	General production trends	86
	(ii)	Developments in industry	96
	(iii)	Agricultural production	102
3.3	UTILIZATION OF OUTPUT AND DOMESTIC BALANCE		112
	(i)	Resource allocation by broad demand categories	112
	(ii)	Overall indicators of consumption	120
	(iii)	Investment policies since 1970 and the role of investment in restructuring	128
	(iv)	Domestic imbalances: open and repressed inflation	134
3.4	EXTERNAL BALANCE AND FOREIGN ECONOMIC RELATIONS		140
	(i)	Foreign trade and external balances	140
	(ii)	What role for the CMEA?	144
	(iii)	Lessons from history: a new EPU as a bridge-gap	147
3.5	THE BROADER POLICY FRAMEWORK FOR 1990 AND BEYOND		151
	(i)	The Polish stabilization programme	151
	(ii)	Towards stabilization in Hungary?	153
	(iii)	Unemployment and the safety net: a new problem	153
	(iv)	Perestroika and stabilization in the Soviet Union	154
	(v)	Late joiners: post-revolutionary economic policies	155
3.6	DEVELOPMENTS IN THE SERVICE SECTOR, 1970-1987		157
	(i)	The role and place of the service sector	157
	(ii)	General development of the service sector	159
	(iii)	Producer services	167
	(iv)	Consumer services	173
	(v)	Conclusions	182

CHAPTER 4

East-west economic relations

4.1	WORLD TRADE AND PAYMENTS		183
	(i)	Trade volumes	183
	(ii)	Trade prices and terms of trade	185
	(iii)	Exchange rate and monetary developments	186
	(iv)	Trade and current account balances of developed market economies	187
	(v)	External balances and debt problems of developing countries	188
	(vi)	Prospects	190
4.2	EAST-WEST TRADE		191
	(i)	Introduction and summary	191
	(ii)	Prices and terms of trade	194
	(iii)	Eastern exports	194
	(iv)	Eastern imports	199
	(v)	Eastern trade balances with the west	201
4.3	EAST-WEST FINANCIAL DEVELOPMENTS		202
	(i)	Eastern current account	202
	(ii)	Eastern indebtedness and debt burden	204
	(iii)	Financing of debt	206
	(iv)	Country by country financial summary	207
4.4.	INTERNATIONAL INITIATIVE IN SUPPORT OF EASTERN REFORMS		212
	(i)	Introduction	212
	(ii)	Institutional developments	212
	(iii)	Group-of-24 aid packages	215
	(iv)	Trade policy measures	216
	(v)	Financial measures in support of Poland and Hungary	219
	(vi)	Preliminary assessment of the international initiative	221
4.5	SOME IMPLICATIONS OF A GERMAN MONETARY UNION		224
4.6	PROSPECTS		227

CHAPTER 5

Economic reforms in eastern Europe and the Soviet Union

5.1 OVERVIEW 233
    (i) Extension of economic reforms 233
    (ii) Contents of economic reforms 234
    (iii) Varied options of political and economic reforms 234

5.2 ECONOMIC REFORM IN POLAND 237
    (i) Introduction 237
    (ii) Overview of the economic reforms in the 1980s 238
    (iii) Progress of economic reform in 1988 and the first half of 1989 239
    (iv) The 1990 stabilization programme 240
    (v) Prospects 242

5.3 ECONOMIC REFORM IN HUNGARY 244
    (i) Three decades of reforms: the results and their costs 244
    (ii) Explanations of the economic malaise 245
    (iii) The conceptual framework of the reform proposals 248
    (iv) Building blocks already in place 249
    (v) The uncharted road of transition 250
    (vi) Prospects 252

5.4 ECONOMIC REFORM IN THE SOVIET UNION 253
    (i) Introduction 253
    (ii) Economic reform in the second half of the 1980s 253
    (iii) Emergency adjustments to reform measures in 1988-1989 255
    (iv) The economic stabilization programme from 1990 onwards 257
    (v) Conclusions 258

5.5 ECONOMIC REFORM IN YUGOSLAVIA 261
    (i) Introduction 261
    (ii) Major aspects of the reform 261
    (iii) Introduction of an integral market 262
    (iv) Pluralism in the forms of ownership 262
    (v) Ownership rights in the social sector 263
    (vi) Integration in the international economy 264
    (vii) Independent economic management 264
    (viii) New legal framework for macro-economic policies 265
    (ix) Stabilization policies 266
    (x) Prospects 269

CHAPTER 6

Economic integration and the export performance of west European countries outside the EC

6.1 THE EFFECTS OF INTEGRATION 271
    (i) Introduction 271
    (ii) The expected effects of integration 272

6.2 CHANGES IN THE STRUCTURE OF EXPORTS 274
    (i) Market structure and product composition 274
    (ii) Structure and export performance 283

6.3 ASSESSING THE EFFECTS OF INTEGRATION 288
    (i) The effects of past trade liberalization 288
    (ii) Possible effects of 1992 290
    (iii) Conclusions 294

    APPENDIX 296
    (i) A note on the CMS analysis 296
    (ii) The method used to estimate the effects of integration 296

CHAPTER 7

Europe's trade in engineering goods: Specialization and technology

	Page
7.1 INTRODUCTION	299
(i) General background	299
(ii) Structure of the study	301
7.2 STRUCTURAL FEATURES OF ENGINEERING GOODS TRADE	302
(i) Importance of engineering goods in total trade of manufactures	302
(ii) Changes in the regional and country pattern of exports and imports	303
(iii) Inter-and intra-regional trade flows of engineering goods	305
7.3 INTER-INDUSTRY SPECIALIZATION IN ENGINEERING GOODS TRADE	312
(i) Some theoretical considerations	312
(ii) Measuring specialization patterns	313
(iii) A comparison of specialization patterns	314
(iv) Recent trends in specialization patterns	321
(v) A brief digression: Country specialization in machine-tools	326
(vi) A statistical analysis of RCA patterns	327
7.4 ENGINEERING GOODS TRADE BY GROUP OF TECHNOLOGY INTENSITY	336
(i) General background	336
(ii) Measuring technology intensity	340
(iii) Trade in engineering goods by group of technology-intensity	341
7.5 CONCLUSIONS	352
STATISTICAL APPENDICES	354
(A) Definitions	354
(B) List of 29 engineering commodity groups	354
(C) Classification of engineering goods by technology intensity	354
(D) Statistical Sources and Explanatory Notes	356

Statistical appendices

	Page
Appendix A. Western Europe and North America	373
Appendix B. Eastern Europe and Soviet Union	386
Appendix C. International trade and payments.	405

LIST OF TABLES AND CHARTS

Chapter 1

Chart

1.2.1	Real output per head in eastern Europe and the Soviet Union relative to that in the Federal Republic of Germany	8
1.2.2	The phasing out of direct controls in post-war Britain	22

Chapter 2

Table

2.1.1	Selected statistical indicators for the Federal Republic of Germany and the German Democratic Republic in 1989	28
2.1.2	Money supply in 1989: German Democratic Republic relative to the Federal Republic of Germany	31
2.2.1	Annual changes in real GDP, 1987-1990	35
2.2.2	Contribution to changes in real GDP, 1988-1989	37

Table		Page
2.2.3	Contribution to changes in real GDP, 1988-1989	36
2.2.4	Industrial production, 1988-1989	39
2.2.5	Capacity utilization rates in manufacturing industry, 1973-1989	40
2.2.6	Real private consumption expenditure, 1987-1990	41
2.2.7	Household savings ratios, 1987-1989	41
2.2.8	Real public consumption expenditure, 1987-1990	42
2.2.9	Total real fixed investment, 1987-1990	44
2.2.10	Real fixed investment by type of asset, 1987-1989	45
2.2.11	Real fixed investment in manufacturing industry, 1987-1989	47
2.2.12	Volume of trade in goods and services, 1987-1990	48
2.3.1	Contributions to the change in the GDP deflator, 1988-1989	58
2.3.2	Contribution to the change in the domestic demand deflator, 1988-1989	60
2.3.3	Labour market changes in western Europe and North America, 1980-1989	63
2.3.4	Growth rates of labour force, employment, and unemployment by sex in western Europe and North America	63
2.3.5	Changes in employment, by sector, 1975-1989	64
2.3.6	Participation rates, 1975, 1988, 1989	64
2.3.7	Share of women in labour force, employment and unemployment, 1980-1989	67
2.3.8	Share of young persons (less than 25 years old) in registered unemployment, 1985, 1988-1989	67
2.3.9	Trade volumes, 1987-1989	68
2.3.10	Terms of trade, 1987-1989	69
2.3.11	Real effective exchange rate indexes, 1987-1989	71
2.3.12	Trade and current account balances, 1987-1989	71
2.3.13	Southern Europe: trade and current account balances, 1987-1989	72

Chart		
2.2.1	Real GDP and the components of demand, 1980-1989	38
2.2.2	Contribution to changes in real GDP: Domestic demand and the net foreign balance	43
2.2.3	Manufacturing production by major branch, 1983-1989	43
2.2.4	Nominal and real investment output ratios and the relative price of investment goods	46
2.2.5	Investment output ratios by type of asset	46
2.3.1	Quarterly and monthly changes in consumer prices, 1980-1989	52
2.3.2	World market price of raw materials, in US dollars and ECUs, 1981-1989	53
2.3.3	Intermediate product prices and producer prices in manufacturing industries, 1988-1989	54
2.3.4	Changes in GDP deflator and labour costs, 1980-1989	55
2.3.5	Contribution of unit labour costs to the change in the GDP deflator, 1980-1989	56
2.3.6	Contribution of the non-labour component of GDP to the change in the GDP deflator, 1980-1989	57
2.3.7	Contribution of the change in the domestic demand deflator, 1980-1989	59
2.3.8	Labour market developments, 1975-1989	62
2.3.9	Unemployment rates in selected countries, 1970-1989	66

Chapter 3

Table		
3.1.1	Eastern Europe and the Soviet Union: Basic economic indicators, 1981-1990	77
3.2.1	Net material product (produced), 1981-1990	87
3.2.2	Net material product (NMP) and net value added, by sector, 1981-1988	91
3.2.3	Gross social product (GSP) and sectoral gross output, 1981-1990	92
3.2.4	Employment, total and in the material sphere, 1981-1989	93
3.2.5	Labour productivity and capital productivity, 1981-1990	93
3.2.6	Gross-social-product to net-material-production ratio	95
3.2.7	Industrial output, 1981-1990	97
3.2.8	Factor inputs in industry, 1981-1989	98
3.2.9	Selected efficiency indicators in industry, 1981-1989	98
3.2.10	Material intensity of industrial production, 1981-1988	100
3.2.11	Primary energy production, 1981-1989	101
3.2.12	Changes in energy consumption and energy intensity, 1981-1988	101
3.2.13	Gross agricultural production, 1981-1990	105
3.2.14	Main crop production, 1981-1990	106
3.2.15	Livestock numbers and livestock output, 1981-1990	107
3.2.16	Agricultural factor inputs, 1981-1988	109
3.2.17	Factor productivity, capital intensity and material costs, 1981-1988	110
3.3.1	Allocation of NMP used, 1981-1989	113
3.3.2	NMP levels by broad category of demand, 1981-1989	115
3.3.3	Output and standard of living, 1986-1990	116
3.3.4	Retail tade sales of main consumer durable goods, 1987-1989	117
3.3.5	Gross fixed investment, 1976-1990	118
3.3.6	Investment ratios	120
3.3.7	Comparison of work time required to purchase selected consumer goods in 1988	121
3.3.8	Retail trade relatives of selected consumer goods in 1988	121
3.3.9	Alternative channels of food supply in the Soviet Union	124
3.3.10	Direct budgetary subsidies in 1988	125
3.3.11	Saving deposits of households	126
3.3.12	Housing density	127
3.3.13	Dwellings constructed	127
3.3.14	Unfinished investment as a share of investment	128
3.3.15	Fixed capital brought into operation, 1971-1988	129
3.3.16	Gross fixed capital formation: Selected indicators, 1976-1988	130
3.3.17	Fixed assets under five years old, 1975-1988	131

Table		Page
3.3.18	Apparent retirement rates of fixed assets, 1971-1988	131
3.3.19	Replacement investment 1976-1988	132
3.3.20	Consumer price changes in eastern Europe and the Soviet Union, 1971-1989	136
3.4.1	Eastern Europe and the Soviet Union: Volume of foreign trade, by country, 1987-1989	141
3.4.2	Eastern Europe and the Soviet Union: Volume of foreign trade by direction, 1987-1989	141
3.4.3	Eastern Europe and the Soviet Union: Trade balances, 1985-1989	142
3.4.4	Eastern Europe and the Soviet Union: Change in foreign trade value and trade balances by partner region, 1987-1989	143
3.6.1	Services: employment, investment and fixed assets, 1970-1987	160
3.6.2	Factor inputs in the service sector, 1971-1987	163
3.6.3	Employment in material and non-material services, 1970-1987	166
3.6.4	Investment in the material and non-material services, 1971-1987	166
3.6.5	Transport and communications: share in output, employment, investment and fixed assets, 1971-1987	168
3.6.6	Volume of investment in transport and communications, 1976-1987	168
3.6.7	Efficiency indicators in transport and communications, 1971-1987	171
3.6.8	Freight transport services	171
3.6.9	Number of telephones in 1987	172
3.6.10	Trade sector: share in output, employment, investment and fixed assets, 1971-1987	173
3.6.11	Volume of investment in trade, 1976-1987	173
3.6.12	Efficiency indicators in trade, 1971-1987	174
3.6.13	Factor inputs in the non-material sphere, 1971-1987	175
3.6.14	Non-material sphere: share in output, employment, investment and fixed assets, 1971-1987	175
3.6.15	Volume of investment in housing, 1976-1987	177
3.6.16	Number of doctors per 10,000 persons, 1970-1987	180
3.6.17	Hospital beds per 10,000 persons, 1970-1987	180
3.6.18	Volume of investment in health services, 1971-1987	181

Chart		
3.2.1	Growth of net material product	88
3.2.2	Factor inputs and NMP growth	89
3.2.3	Growth rates of gross industrial output	99
3.2.4	Growth rates of gross agricultural output	104
3.3.1	Actual and planned NMP, gross fixed capital formation, and investment ratio (actual and planned), 1980-1990	119
3.3.2	Consumer supplies and purchasing power of the population	123
3.6.1	Factor inputs in services, 1971-1987	161
3.6.2	Employment in services and in the total economy, 1970-1987	162
3.6.3	Investment in services and in the total economy, 1970-1987	164
3.6.4	Employment in trade and transport, 1970-1987	169
3.6.5	Investment in trade and transport, 1970-1987	170
3.6.6	Employment in the health, education and housing sectors, 1970-1987	178
3.6.7	Investment in the health, education and housing sectors, 1970-1987	179

Chapter 4

Table		
4.1.1	World trade: Volume changes, 1986-1989	184
4.1.2	The Economist commodity price index, in terms of SDRs	185
4.1.3	Changes in international trade prices in US dollars and in SDRs	186
4.1.4	Trade and current account balances, 1987-1989	188
4.2.1	East-west trade: Value, volumes, prices and terms of trade, 1985-1989	192
4.2.2	East-west trade: Value and volumes, by eastern country, 1985-1989	196
4.2.3	East-west trade: Value by country group, 1985-1989	197
4.2.4	OECD imports of petroleum and petroleum products from eastern Europe and the Soviet Union, 1986-1989	198
4.2.5	East-west trade balances, east with western country groups, 1984-1989	200
4.2.6	East-west trade balances, by eastern country, 1984-1989	200
4.3.1	Eastern Europe and the Soviet Union: Estimated current account balance of payments with market economies, 1984-1989	203
4.3.2	Eastern Europe and the Soviet Union: Estimated convertible currency debt, 1983-1989	204
4.3.3	Eastern Europe and the Soviet Union: Ratio of net interest payments to exports to the market economies, 1984-1989	206
4.3.4	Eastern Europe and the Soviet Union: Ratio of net debt to exports to the market economies, 1984-1989	206
4.3.5	Eastern Europe and the Soviet Union: Medium- and long-term funds raised on the international financial markets	207
4.3.6	Eastern Europe and the Soviet Union: Gross debt vis-à-vis BIS and OECD reporting institutions, 1985-1989	208
4.3.7	Eastern Europe and the Soviet Union: Assets with BIS reporting banks and liquidity ratios, 1982-1989	209
4.4.1	Partial list of international financial commitments to Hungary and Poland, for 1990 and after	215
4.4.2	Value of financial assistance to become available to Poland and Hungary, by source and year of availability	221

Chart		
4.2.1	International trade of eastern Europe and the Soviet Union with the west	193

Chapter 6

Table		
6.1	The market structure of the six countries' total exports, 1963, 1972 and 1987	275
6.2	The share of each of the six exporting countries in regional markets, 1963, 1972 and 1987	276
6.3	Trade intensity coefficients, 1963, 1972 and 1987	277

Table		Page
6.4	Production composition of exports from the six countries, 1963, 1972 and 1987	280
6.5	Specialization coefficients, 1963, 1972 and 1987	281
6.6	A CMS decomposition of changes in market share, 1961-1973 and 1973-1985	284
6.7	A CMS decomposition of changes in market share, by market, 1961-1973 and 1973-1985	285
6.8	A CMS decomposition of changes in market share, by product, 1961-1973 and 1973-1985	286
6.9	The estimated effects of trade liberalization on the six countries' exports, by market, 1963-1972 and 1972-1985	290
6.10	The share of selected products in exports to the EC12 and EFTA, 1987	294

Appendix table

6.1	A market decomposition of the CMS analysis	297

Chart

6.1	Trade intensity coefficients for each country total export to the EC 6, the EC 3 and EFTA, 1963-1987	278
6.2	The estimated effects of trade liberalization on exports of the six countries, by market	291

Chapter 7

Table

7.2.1	Changes in world exports of engineering goods and total manufactures	302
7.2.2	The share of engineering goods in total trade of manufactured products	303
7.2.3	Regional shares of world trade in engineering goods	303
7.2.4	Major twelve exporters of engineering goods	305
7.2.5	Major twelve importers of engineering goods	305
7.2.6	Market penetration ratios: 1986	306
7.2.7	Origin and destination of engineering goods exports, 1987	307
7.2.8	Origin and destination of engineering goods imports, 1987	308
7.2.9	Trade intensity coefficients for engineering goods trade, 1987 and 1970	310
7.3.1a	The pattern of specialization in engineering goods exports	315
7.3.1b	The pattern of specialization in engineering goods exports	316
7.3.1c	The pattern of specialization in engineering goods exports	317
7.3.1d	The pattern of specialization in engineering goods exports	318
7.3.2a	Recent trends in RCA - indices: 1980-1987	322
7.3.2b	Recent trends in RCA - indices: 1980-1987	323
7.3.2c	Recent trends in RCA - indices: 1980-1987	324
7.3.2d	Recent trends in RCA - indices: 1980-1987	325
7.3.3	Machine tools (SITC, Rev.1: 715.1)	327
7.3.4	Country specialization in engineering goods exports	329
7.3.5	Indices of revealed comparative advantages: skill-intensive engineering goods	330
7.3.6	Diversification of comparative advantage	330
7.3.7	Correlations between world market shares in engineering goods exports and the RCA index in each country	331
7.3.8	Rank correlation coefficients between RCA indices of three major countries and the corresponding RCA indices of 25 countries	332
7.4.1	Composition of engineering goods trade, by group of technology intensity	343
7.4.2	Balance of trade in engineering goods, by class of technology intensity	346
7.4.3	World export market shares of engineering goods exports, by group of technology intensity	349
7.4.4	Indices of revealed comparative advantage, by class of technology intensity	350

Appendix table

7.1	The share of engineering goods in total trade of manufactures	357
7.2	Indices of revealed comparative advantage in engineering goods, by SITC groups, 1970	358
7.3	Indices of revealed comparative advantage in engineering goods, by SITC groups, 1980	360
7.4	Indices of revealed comparative advantage in engineering goods, by SITC groups, 1987	362
7.5	Indices of revealed comparative advantage in engineering goods, by SITC groups: Eastern Europe and the Soviet Union	364
7.6	Changes in specialization patterns: Regression analysis	365
7.7	Changes in specialization patterns: Regression analysis	366
7.8	Composition of engineering goods exports by group of technology intensity	367
7.9	Composition of engineering goods imports by group of technology intensity	368
7.10	Engineering goods exports: World market shares by group of technology intensity	369

Chart

7.3.1	Diversity of specialization patterns: RCA indices, by SITC groups, in 1987 for Japan, USA and the Federal Republic of Germany	333
7.3.2	Changes in RCA indices 1970-1987 in relation to RCA indices in 1970	334
7.4.1	World exports of engineering goods, by group of technology intensity	342

Appendix table   *Page*

Appendix A. Western Europe and North America

Appendix table

A.1	Gross domestic product	374
A.2	Private consumption	375
A.3	Public consumption	376
A.4	Gross domestic fixed capital formation	377
A.5	Volume of exports of goods and services	378
A.6	Volume of imports of goods and services	379
A.7	Current account balances	380
A.8	Industrial production	381
A.9	Consumer prices	382
A.10	Average hourly earnings in manufacturing	383
A.11	Total employment	384
A.12	Annual unemployment rates	385

Appendix B. Eastern Europe and Soviet Union

B.1	Net material product	387
B.2	Net material product used for domestic consumption and accumulation	388
B.3	Monthly nominal wages	389
B.4	Money incomes of population and volume of retail trade	390
B.5	Real wages and per capita real incomes	391
B.6	Consumer prices	392
B.7	Dwellings constructed	392
B.8	Total gross investment	393
B.9	Total gross fixed assets	394
B.10	Employment	395
B.11	Gross industrial production	396
B.12	Industry: Gross investments, gross fixed assets and employment	397
B.13	Gross agricultural output	398
B.14	Agriculture: Gross investments, gross fixed assets and employment	399
B.15	Export and import volumes	400
B.16	Energy production: Electricity, coal and crude oil	401
B.17	Steel production	402
B.18	Grain production	403
B.19	Saving deposits of the population	404

Appendix C. International trade and payments

C.1	World trade: Value, by region	406
C.2	World trade: Volume change, by region	407
C.3	Western Europe and North America: Trade volume change	408
C.4	Eastern Europe and the Soviet Union: Exports by main directions, 1970-1988	409
C.5	Eastern Europe and the Soviet Union: Imports by main directions, 1970-1988	410
C.6	East-west trade: Value of western exports, by country of origin	411
C.7	East-west trade: Value of western imports, by country of destination	412
C.8	East-west trade: Western trade balances by western country	413
C.9	East-west trade: Western exports, imports and balances by eastern country	414
C.10	Eastern Europe and the Soviet Union: Balance of payments in convertible currencies	415
C.11	Eastern Europe and the Soviet Union: Gross debt, assets and net debt in convertible currencies	416

Chapter 1

THE ECONOMIC SITUATION IN THE ECE REGION

1.1 SUMMARY OF CURRENT ECONOMIC DEVELOPMENTS

The economic performance of the *market economies* remained quite favourable in 1989, although on average the pace of expansion tended to moderate. This reflects largely the impact of tighter monetary policies designed to prevent inflation from accelerating. Output growth slowed down in North America and remained broadly unchanged in western Europe. There was also a deceleration in the pace of economic activity in Japan, although GDP growth is still higher there than in the other two regions. Growth differentials between these three regions tended to narrow in the course of 1989. Total output in the market economies grew on average by some 3½ per cent, compared with over 4 per cent in 1988.

Expectations for 1990 are for a continuation of relatively strong performance in the ECE market economies. There will be some slow-down in output growth, and this will tend to ease the strains which high activity levels have put recently on the utilization of available resources. Fixed investment will again be the major support for growth. In western Europe the forecast deceleration in output growth is small, except for the United Kingdom. The outlook for the United States is surrounded with some uncertainty, but growth in 1990 is most likely to be close to that expected for western Europe. Monetary policy will remain cautious and avoid any early reduction in interest rates. For the ECE market economies, combined GDP growth for 1990 is forecast at 2½ per cent, compared with 3 per cent in 1989.

In the *centrally planned economies* there was a substantial slowing of economic activity in 1989, which in several countries turned into a recession. In the Soviet Union, output growth fell to less than 2½ per cent, from 4½ in 1988. Output contracted in absolute terms in at least two of the six east European countries, and aggregate growth for the five which reported data was only half of one per cent.[1] The deceleration was thus general and in most cases ran counter to expectations.

In almost all countries, social or political upheavals played an important role in the downturn, although deteriorating macro-economic control, the effects of fiscal deficits and worsening internal market balance appear to have been the main causes. Apart from this, there is growing evidence that the impediments to the implementation of economic reforms or the costs of transition to a market system were underestimated. In the Soviet Union, the dismantling of central controls has not been paralleled by the development of institutional arrangements appropriate to the new circumstances. This could be a long process — either because reform has not been comprehensive enough, as in the Soviet Union, or because the new institutions cannot be created overnight.

The short-term outlook is for a deepening recession in the east European countries in 1990, and for sluggish growth at best in the Soviet Union. This reflects the progressive slowing of output growth during the course of 1989, which turned into contraction in the final quarter or the first months of 1990, the growing sense of economic crisis surrounding the policy discussions in several countries, and also the signs of a breakdown in the intra-CMEA trading system.[2]

(i) Western Europe and North America

In the ECE *market economies* the long upswing of the 1980s continued in 1989. Growth of actual output has been exceeding the expansion in potential output over the last two years in many countries and capacity utilization rates are very high. At this stage of the output cycle productivity reserves are largely exhausted and this has stimulated the demand for labour. Employment growth was about 1 per cent in western Europe and some 2 per cent in North America. Unemployment declined, both as a proportion of the labour force and in absolute size. Nevertheless, the average west European rate of unemployment is still very high at almost 8 per cent (down from some 8½ per cent in 1988). In the United States, despite the slow-down in

---

[1] No information is as yet available from Romania.

[2] See sections 3.1 and 3.4 below.

economic activity, the unemployment rate fell to just over 5 per cent, the lowest rate since 1973.

Consumer prices rose somewhat faster than in 1988, although the average increase of about 4½ per cent in 1989 conceals a stabilization or even deceleration in the second half of the year, helped by an easing of non-oil commodity prices and the restrictive stance of monetary policy.

Although the external imbalances of the main industrial countries remained large, there was nevertheless a further decline in the US deficits and the Japanese surpluses in 1989. In contrast, in the Federal Republic of Germany the trade and current account surpluses increased further.

Investment was the main driving force of domestic demand in the majority of countries, but private consumption remained strong. Strong domestic demand stimulated international trade, making for both considerable export and import growth in the various countries.

At the beginning of 1990 business and consumer confidence is quite high in western Europe and the outlook is for another year of relatively strong economic growth. With the tight stance of monetary policy — and excepting the impact of unforeseen factors — inflation rates are likely to stabilize in the neighbourhood of the rates observed in 1989. Business investment continues to be the major driving force of domestic demand, but private consumption will also provide a strong support for output growth.

In the United States a further slowing down in the expansion rate is expected in 1990, largely on account of lower growth of household demand and a further weakening of export performance.

There is no doubt that the changes under way in the economic systems and arrangements of the eastern countries will affect economic developments in the market economies in 1990, although it is virtually impossible to determine as yet their impact. Interest rates have risen recently in financial markets in anticipation of a large demand for capital needed to finance the transformation of the east European economies. Higher interest rates also reflect fears of inflation in the Federal Republic of Germany as a consequence of the imminent monetary union with the German Democratic Republic. While these reactions in the financial markets may be exaggerated, it is nevertheless clear that in the years ahead a significant part of world savings will flow to eastern Europe if they are offered a competitive rate of return. One danger is that financial flows will be diverted to the east to the detriment of the developing world. In these circumstances a steady reduction of the United States budget deficit could make an important contribution to easing the upward pressure on world interest rates and in maintaining — or even increasing — the flow of funds to developing countries.[3]

(ii) Eastern Europe and the Soviet Union

Aggregate net material product (value added in the material sphere) in the eastern countries rose by less than 2 per cent in 1989. Growth slowed throughout the year and output actually fell in most (possibly all) of the seven countries in the last quarter. To a certain extent, the weakness in production was spread through the CMEA trade network. In some cases, production shortfalls and transport bottlenecks in the Soviet Union spilled over into neighbouring countries. Industrial activity stagnated in eastern Europe and grew by less than 2 per cent in the Soviet Union, construction appears to have generally contracted, and agricultural output grew by less than 1 per cent.

The impact of production developments on domestic resource absorption was mitigated by foreign trade flows. In eastern Europe, the volume of exports fell by 2½ per cent while imports rose by 1 per cent. Although the terms of trade improved slightly for eastern Europe, there was some contraction of the overall trade surplus of these countries (from $7 billion to $6 billion). In the case of the Soviet Union, export volume stagnated while imports rose by an estimated 7 per cent. Together with a slight worsening of the overall terms of trade, this caused a $9 billion turnround of the Soviet trade balance, from a surplus of $3½ billion in 1988 to a $5½ billion deficit in 1989.

In the allocation of resources for domestic utilization, consumption was given priority over accumulation in all the eastern countries. The volume of investment fell by some 3 per cent in eastern Europe and increased only marginally in the Soviet Union.

Domestic imbalances persisted or, in most countries, worsened. Open inflation or inflationary pressures were fuelled by large fiscal deficits, the existence of which was revealed in a number of countries for the first time. In the Soviet Union the budget deficit reached 10 per cent of GNP in 1989. In Poland, the already high inflation accelerated to more than 240 per cent, year over year. In Hungary, consumer prices rose at 17 per cent. Inflation gathered momentum also in Bulgaria and the Soviet Union, although open inflation remained at the single-digit level.

Economic *reforms* under way in the eastern countries accelerated dramatically in 1989, together with political change. In the economic sphere, these aim, to one degree or another, at improving performance through increased use of markets and through closer integration into the world economy.

In the Soviet Union, and probably also in Bulgaria and Romania (where the formulation of objectives is still at an early stage), reforms basically envisage a transformation of the existing centrally planned system through the use of monetary and financial instruments and market channels to replace the "command" system of physical resource allocation and output determi-

---

[3] See section 2.1 below.

nation. Much increased enterprise autonomy, demonopolization of the enterprise structure, room for non-state economic activity alongside the dominant state sector, improved price systems (with better links to world market prices), and the "hardening" of financial constraints are expected to bring significant efficiency gains. All reforms include measures to achieve a substantial opening to the outside world, ranging from decentralization of the authority to trade abroad to liberalized provisions for the entry of foreigners into the domestic economic system (mainly in the form of joint ventures or free trade zones).

In Hungary and Poland, the reform agenda was extended radically in 1989, and now aims at the establishment of fully-fledged market economies in which the role of state planning is reduced to largely macroeconomic functions. Broadly similar aims came to the fore in Czechoslovakia after the political overturn at the end of the year, but are still in the course of being formulated. These countries now envisage a significant and rapid reduction of state-owned industries through privatization and a substantial role for foreign direct investment. The difficult issue facing these countries is how to manage the transition from centrally planned to market systems, and this — especially in Poland — in the face of sharply deteriorating economic performance. Poland has opted for a shock cure in the hope of thus shortening the transition period, whereas in the other two countries the appropriate pace is still to be decided.

Transition to a market system is also on the agenda in the German Democratic Republic, where until very recently not even minor reforms were considered necessary. However, in that country the issue is now largely one of how best to manage integration with an existing and strong market economy and not how to re-fashion a separate economic entity — a task which has its own difficulties, but should be incomparably easier.

The immediate prospects for eastern Europe and the Soviet Union are bleak. Governmental programmes for 1990 focus on the twin aims of transforming economic systems and stabilizing economies in disarray. These are tasks of a large order and frequently involve contradictory demands. Inflationary processes are likely to yield only slowly to moderate deflationary policy measures, and where policy is strong (as in Poland) the cost of a recessionary downturn will be high. Balance of payments constraints have increased for most countries, including now the Soviet Union, and this reduces the leeway for domestic policy.

Although the problems and prospects facing the eastern countries are fairly daunting, the ability to implement effective policies to deal with them and reap the longer-term benefits could be greatly increased by the adoption of consistent reform measures. In eastern Europe, the political legitimacy conferred on governments by free parliamentary elections, due to take place in most countries in 1990, and by a significant programme of technical and financial support by the western market economies should help in facing the costs of reform.

(iii) East-west trade

East-west trade in 1989 was characterized by a slackening of eastern export growth and a substantial pick-up in the volume of eastern imports. It evolved against the background of a rapid, although slowing, expansion of world trade and momentous changes in the political environment of east-west relations.

After a pick-up in 1988, the volume of *east European exports* to the west slowed again in 1989, expanding at some 3 per cent in the first nine months. Volume growth for the year as a whole is likely to be lower still as the political developments in the last quarter generally had a negative impact on the supply of exportables. In some countries — notably Czechoslovakia and Hungary — changes in the trade regime in the course of economic reform none the less appear to have favoured relatively strong export growth. East European *imports* from the west, which had stagnated in the preceding year, rose sharply — by 13 per cent — in the first nine months of 1989. This reflected mainly very strong import expansion in Hungary and Poland in consequence of the liberalization of trade régimes in these countries. Import growth seems to have slowed toward the end of the year, probably reflecting efforts to improve current accounts or hold down the growth of foreign debt.

Eastern Europe's *trade surplus* with the west appears to have nearly vanished in consequence of these changes, although the balance *in convertible currencies* with all market economies still remained positive. A substantial rise in the deficit on *invisibles* (from less than $3 billion in 1988 to $4½ billion) none the less caused the east European *current account in convertible currencies* to swing into a deficit again (estimated at some $2 billion). The aggregate *net indebtedness* of the east European countries rose by $1½ billion, from $76½ billion at the end of 1988 to almost $78 billion at the close of 1989.

The volume of *Soviet exports* to the west increased by some 3 per cent in the first nine months of 1989, after strong expansion in the preceding year. Export growth slowed substantially in the course of the year owing, at least in part, to supply difficulties originating in the Soviet fuels and transport sectors. Soviet *imports*, on the other hand, rose rapidly — by 13 per cent in volume in the first nine months — and at an accelerating pace, which seems to have continued into the last quarter when emergency imports of consumer manufactures began to arrive.

For the first time in several years, the *terms of trade* of the Soviet Union with the west improved in 1989 owing to the rise in world market fuels prices. However, the gains were not sufficient to prevent a sharp widening of the Soviet *trade deficit* with the west — from some $3 billion in 1988 to $6½ billion on the basis of Soviet data for the full year. The *current-account deficit* worsened even more, and estimated

Soviet *net indebtedness* increased by $10 billion in nominal terms, from $26½ billion to $36½ billion.[4]

All eastern countries are at various stages of implementing economic reforms with aims ranging from greater use of market instruments to improve economic planning to full transition from planned to market economies. Such reforms raise the possibility of overcoming the east's systemic weaknesses which have long held back the integration of these countries into the world economy. The positive impact of reform measures on the trade of a number of eastern countries during the past several years gives some cause for optimism. On the other hand, the poor initial state of the eastern economies and the disruptions caused by reforms themselves or the upheavals of transition from one economic system to another has in some cases cut exports and increased the pressure to import.

Together with higher international interest rates and their implications for debt service burdens, these factors will tend to augment current-account deficits at a time when commercial banks are becoming increasingly cautious about extending new funds to the east (in part because of the uncertainty raised by the process of economic reform and political changes).

This lends additional importance to the international support initiatives launched by western governments and multilateral financial institutions.[5] These measures should meet the financial needs of Hungary and Poland during the current year, but are likely to be much less immediately supportive for the other east European countries now in the first stages of elaborating transition or reform programmes. In addition to financial relief, the international initiatives address the various objectives of economic reform: macro-economic stabilization, modernization and restructuring of the domestic economy, raising income levels, and integrating these countries into the world economy. Altogether, these developments are a major step forward in cementing economic and political relations in the region.

---

[4] Newly reported Soviet data indicate higher levels of gross debt than are used for these estimates, but are not yet sufficiently detailed to permit a review of changes over time (see section 4.3).

[5] See section 4.4 below.

1.2 ECONOMIC REFORM IN THE EAST: A FRAMEWORK FOR WESTERN SUPPORT

(i) Introduction

The extraordinary — and it must be added, totally unexpected — developments in eastern Europe and the Soviet Union in 1989 constitute a major turning point in Europe's post-war history. Most of the peoples of eastern Europe have made it clear — in one way or another — that they want a radical and decisive change in the way their political and economic affairs are conducted. Most of these countries are now moving, at varying rates of progress, towards pluralist forms of government and decentralized, market economies.

Recent developments, however, have created massive uncertainty in the eastern countries and this is likely to exacerbate economic problems in the short run. The authority of the old political systems has been rejected in eastern Europe while the legitimacy of the new awaits confirmation in a series of parliamentary elections which begin, in the German Democratic Republic, in mid-March. Political change may often be very rapid, but economic adjustment is generally much slower: the certainties of the central planning system have been eroded more quickly than the alternative mechanisms of the market can be put in their place. Disappointment with the progress of economic reforms was an important factor in accelerating the pace of change in 1989.

Eastern economic performance in 1989 was probably the worst since the immediate post-war period: apart from Czechoslovakia and the German Democratic Republic, output in eastern Europe fell or stagnated; in the Soviet Union it rose, but by much less than in 1988 and considerably less than planned. Domestic imbalances were also worse than at any time since the post-war recovery. Economic problems were partly responsible for — and were certainly compounded by — widespread social unrest which took a variety of forms ranging from strikes to large-scale emigration.

In 1990 the eastern countries are faced with a formidable array of problems. Policy makers are currently preoccupied with restoring political and social stability, and with implementing economic stabilization programmes which will impose heavy burdens on the population in the immediate future. At the same time they have to introduce fundamental reforms which will lead to the replacement of central planning by decentralized market systems. All this must be done against the background of a short-run economic outlook for the eastern economies which is far from encouraging.[6] However, despite the sombre outlook for 1990, a social consensus has already emerged in some countries and formal economic stabilization programmes have been (or are being) put into place. Moreover, for the first time ever, the western market economy countries have clearly stated their willingness to support the process of reform in the east. This opening chapter of the *Survey* therefore focuses on the form that such assistance could take.

In order to place the current programmes of reform in context, the chapter begins with a brief summary of eastern economic performance over the last few decades in section (ii). As many observers have called for a new "Marshall Plan" to help the east, this suggestion is examined in some detail: first the situation of western Europe in 1948 and then the main features of the Marshall Plan are discussed in sections (iii) and (iv), followed by an assessment of the relevance of a similar plan to the present situation in the east in section (v). Various issues which are important both for the reform process itself and for the structure of any western programme of support — the environment, international trade, the pace of the reform process — are discussed in sections (vi) to (viii). The final section pulls together the main elements which the secretariat thinks should be given priority in any programme of western assistance to the east.

(ii) The long-term deterioration in the economic performance of the eastern countries

The present economic situation in eastern Europe and the Soviet Union is not so much a cyclical or short-term phenomenon as the most recent stage in a general deterioration in performance which stretches back over two decades or more. Economic growth rates had been very high in the 1950s and the 1960s, and to a large extent they reflected a successful recovery from the destruction and dislocation of the Second World War. Although a slow-down in such "recovery" rates of growth might be regarded as normal, planners in the eastern countries introduced in the late 1960s the notion of a transition from *extensive* to *intensive* growth as a means of maintaining rapid rates of expansion. These were required in order to close the gap in levels of economic development between the east and the west. The possibility of extensive growth, i.e., growth based on a simultaneous expansion of labour and capital, had diminished as the available reserves of labour became fully employed. Growth would therefore become intensive, based on a more efficient use of the available resources.

---

[6] The current economic situation in the eastern countries is discussed in detail in chapters 3 and 4 of this *Survey*.

Rates of fixed capital formation did in fact accelerate and from the mid-1960s investment ratios were often higher than envisaged in the five-year plans. As a ratio to net material product, gross fixed investment in the seven[7] eastern countries averaged about one third in the first half of the 1970s and about 30 per cent in the first half of the 1980s. In the early 1970s fixed investment was rising at double-digit annual rates in eastern Europe, but slowed sharply thereafter and actually fell between 1979 and 1982 as a result of the adjustments that followed the second oil shock and the accompanying international debt crisis. In the Soviet Union the fluctuation was less volatile than in eastern Europe, but there was still a sharp fall in the rate of investment. There was some recovery in the latter half of the 1980s, but compared with the 1970s fixed investment was relatively modest in all seven countries.[8]

Despite the considerable expansion of investment, especially in the 1970s, the secular slow-down in rates of output growth was not reversed (except for a brief period in the late 1960s and early 1970s in eastern Europe) and the growth of labour productivity fell steadily from the early 1970s. Capital productivity has fallen persistently in all seven countries since 1976 and in most of them since 1971.[9] In the first half of the 1980s the contribution of changes in total factor productivity to the growth of NMP was generally smaller than in the early 1970s.[10]

There are many reasons for the inefficiency of investment: lead times are long and have tended to increase in the 1980s (i.e., the proportion of unfinished, non-performing investment projects in gross fixed investment has risen); the latter is partly due to a systemic tendency for enterprises to start an excessive number of new investment projects in order to get them "into the plan" and so lay a claim on future investment funds; equipment is often out of date by the time it is actually installed and operating; there appear to be widespread co-ordination failures in balancing supplies of labour, material inputs and productive capacities; and material and energy consumption per unit of output is very high in comparison with the market economies, in part owing to a structural bias in the development process which favoured the nurturing of the upstream sectors of "heavy" industry, but also reflecting generally lower levels of efficiency and technology throughout the productive process. Imports of western capital goods do not appear to have eased these problems to any significant degree. Indeed, it seems that the eastern economies have found it difficult to absorb western technology and improve their economic performance: this is in marked contrast to the newly industralized economies (NIEs) of south east Asia where imported western technology appears to have had a significant impact in raising general levels of efficiency and export competitiveness.[11] These and other factors, such as inadequate transport and communications systems, all point to a general systemic inefficiency which has been increasing over time.

The consequences of this long-run deterioration in productive efficiency on domestic consumption, which originally had to be restrained to make room for the rise in fixed investment and for high levels of expenditure on defence, were partly attenuated by rising import surpluses throughout the 1970s. Financed by cheap and easily available loans from the west, eastern Europe had trade and current account deficits, in convertible currency, in every single year of the decade. However, this situation could not be sustained after the second oil shock in 1979. The policy response of the market economies to this shock was very different from that to the first shock in 1973: as a result of a severe tightening of monetary policy in all the major market economies, real interest rates rose to unprecedented levels and the world economy moved into its most severe recession since the Second World War. Eastern Europe's debt servicing burden increased dramatically, particularly in Hungary and Poland, as did the group's deficit on the invisibles account. Lending from the west virtually ceased, and with a general weakening of export markets the east European countries had no alternative to a massive squeeze on domestic demand. Domestic consumption actually fell in 1982 (especially in Poland), but most of the adjustment was borne by fixed investment. The policy succeeded in turning the east European trade balance from a convertible currency deficit of $5 billion in 1979 to a surplus of some $7 billion in 1984. Since then there has been some relaxation of policies and a renewed deterioration of the trade and current accounts in most east European countries.[12] In contrast, the Soviet Union benefited from the second oil price shock in 1979 and was able to support a large increase in the volume of imports in the first half of the 1980s.[13] With the subsequent fall in oil prices the volume of Soviet imports from the west was cut sharply in 1986 and 1987 and the 1985 level had still not been

---

7 Bulgaria, Czechoslovakia, the German Democratic Republic, Hungary, Poland, Romania and the Soviet Union. The convention followed throughout this *Survey* is to use "eastern Europe" to refer to this group *excluding* the Soviet Union.

8 See United Nations Economic Commission for Europe, *Economic Survey of Europe*, New York. Each issue has a separate section on fixed investment in the eastern countries and relevant tables in Statistical Appendix B.

9 United Nations Economic Commission for Europe, *Economic Survey for Europe*.

10 United Nations Economic Commission for Europe, *Economic Survey of Europe in 1987-1988*, New York, 1988, table 3.4.3. For a more detailed discussion of the productivity slow-down in the eastern economies see "Productivity trends in eastern Europe and the Soviet Union, 1970-1983", *Economic Survey of Europe in 1985-1986*, New York, 1986, pp.209-223.

11 See United Nations Economic Commission for Europe, "East-west trade in investment goods, 1970-1987", *Economic Bulletin for Europe*, vol.41, New York, 1989, pp.91-97.

12 On the present situation (and on revisions to previously published official data), see below, section 3.4(i).

13 The net inflow of real resources from the west into the Soviet Union between 1980 and 1985 was considerable, some $63 billion at 1975 prices. See United Nations Economic Commission for Europe, *Economic Survey for Europe in 1987-1988*, New York, 1988, pp.298-301.

regained at the end of 1989 despite a strong recovery in exports.

Although the adjustment policies in the east have led to some reduction in debt burdens, some countries are still faced with high levels of foreign debt which constrain future policy options and which carry implications for the nature of any western programme of financial assistance. The debt burden is particularly heavy in Poland, Hungary and Bulgaria, which together account for nearly three quarters of eastern Europe's total gross debt of around $100 billion. Net debt is 3½ (Hungary) to 4½ (Poland) times larger than export earnings and debt servicing in 1989 was equivalent to some 42 per cent (Hungary) to 56 per cent (Poland) of hard currency export earnings.[14]

Although the export performance of most eastern countries had improved during the first half of the 1970s, all of them subsequently experienced a secular decline in competitiveness. Since the mid-1980s east European exports have lagged behind the dynamic growth of world trade. Their deterioration reflects the influence of many factors including the competitive success of the NIEs in world markets but especially in western Europe,[15] the large cuts in eastern imports of western machinery, interruptions to imports of essential intermediate goods and so on. In addition eastern export performance has been more generally undermined by the systemic inefficiencies of the eastern economies (see below).

Internal imbalances in the eastern countries have also worsened over the last decade or so. Hidden or repressed inflation has been a pervasive phenomenon for some time and can be inferred from the widespread queues for goods and services, from forced substitution (where private consumers and enterprises are forced to buy certain products *faute de mieux*), and from the extensive bottlenecks throughout the productive system.[16] More recently open inflation has become apparent in the price statistics of some of the eastern countries. In Poland open inflation has accelerated rapidly, reaching over 240 per cent in 1989. Inflation has also picked up sharply in Hungary (from 4½ per cent in 1986 to 17 per cent in 1989) and in Bulgaria (some 9 per cent in 1989).[17]

Internal imbalance is also evident in the large government deficits which have only recently been revealed in a number of countries. For example, in the Soviet Union the 1989 budget deficit is now stated to have reached 92 billion roubles or some 10 per cent of GDP, leaving the domestic national debt at over 400 billion roubles. In Hungary the 1989 budget deficit was 55 billion forints, or 3-4 per cent of GNP. Hungary's domestic national debt is now some 65 per cent of GDP, one of the highest ratios in Europe. The correction of these deficits, which are partly due to attempts to maintain domestic price stability in the face of external shocks, is now a high priority of the various stabilization programmes which are in place or being prepared in the eastern countries.[18]

Open unemployment is still virtually non-existent in the eastern economies, although at the turn of the year some has been officially revealed as a result of restructuring in the German Democratic Republic, Hungary, Poland and the Soviet Union. Full employment was a prime objective and a characteristic feature of the centrally planned economies of eastern Europe in the post-war period, and of the Soviet Union since the late 1920s. However, labour hoarding (disguised unemployment) is widespread in enterprises, and it is this which produces a general situation of labour shortage. Full employment was essentially a consequence of the rapid rates of fixed investment and output growth set by the central planners and an incentive structure encouraging over-employment as an insurance against being caught "short-handed" in an emergency. The lack of even open frictional unemployment reflects the "soft-budget constraints"[19] on individual enterprises, which ensure that penalties for cost over-runs are not severe and bankruptcies rarely occur. Consequently full employment in the eastern economies is secured at the cost of considerable inefficiency in the use of labour. As economic reforms lead to a market economy structure of incentives for both labour and capital, frictional and structural unemployment can be expected to rise.

The long-term weakness of economic performance in the eastern economies has meant that little progress has been made in closing the gap between their levels of development and those of western Europe and North America. That gap cannot be estimated with any great precision. Real income comparisons among countries with *similar* economic systems are fraught with problems of measurement and interpretation, and these are compounded by differences in economic structure and pricing systems in the case of east-west comparisons. Nevertheless, serious attempts have been made to estimate international differences in real GDP levels and, although subject to large margins of error, they can provide a rough idea of the magnitude of the task involved in trying to raise eastern levels of output and income to those prevailing in the west.

---

14 For further details, see below, chapter 4.3.

15 Eastern export performance has been the subject of many studies in the *Economic Bulletin for Europe* and the *Economic Survey of Europe*, both annual publications of the Economic Commission for Europe. For an overview see "Exports of manufactures from eastern Europe and the Soviet Union to the developed market economies, 1965-1981", *Economic Bulletin for Europe*, vol.35, No.4, Pergamon Press for the United Nations, 1983. On competition between the eastern countries and southern Europe see "The effects of west European integration on imports of manufactures from eastern and southern Europe", *Economic Survey of Europe in 1988-1989*, New York, 1989, pp.64-86.

16 See. J. Kornai, *Economics of Shortage*, Amsterdam, 1980 and J. Kornai, "The Hungarian Reform Process", *Journal of Economic Literature*, 24:4, 1986.

17 For detailed statistics and discussion, see below, section 3.3(iv).

18 For details, see below, section 3.3(iv).

19 See Kornai, 1980, *op.cit*.

CHART 1.2.1

Real output per head [a] in eastern Europe and the Soviet Union relative to that in the Federal Republic of Germany, 1950-1985
(Federal Republic of Germany = 100)

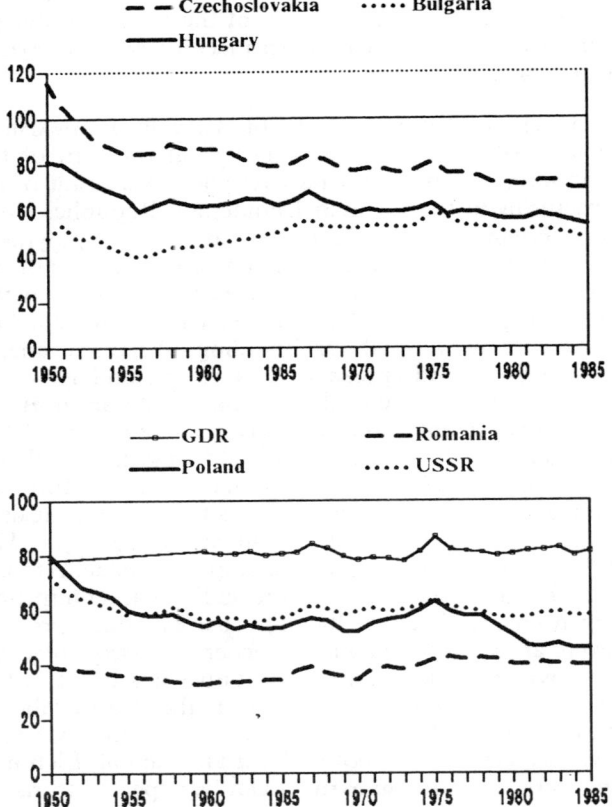

Source: Based on data in Robert Summers and Alan Heston, "A New Set of International Comparisons of Real Product and Prices: Estimates for 130 countries, 1950-1985", *The Review of Income and Wealth*, Series 34, No 1, March 1988.

[a] Real gross domestic output per head.

In chart 1.2.1 estimates of real output per head in the eastern countries are compared with that in the Federal Republic of Germany, which is widely regarded as the "core" economy of western Europe. Real output per head in the east is not only considerably lower than in the Federal Republic of Germany, but for most eastern countries the gap has tended to widen during most of the period since 1950, and especially since 1975.[20] In 1985 real output per head in the east, on average, was more than 40 per cent below the level prevailing in the Federal Republic of Germany, with individual countries ranging from 60 per cent below (Romania) to nearly 20 per cent below (German Democratic Republic). It must be stressed, however, that considerable uncertainty surrounds all estimates of this kind.[21] The estimates of real output per head are obviously not secure enough to bear a heavy weight of interpretation. Nevertheless, despite their variance, they all point to very large differences in development levels between the eastern countries and the western market economies. More importantly, there does not appear to have been any significant narrowing of these differences in the last 30 years or so.

From the above brief sketch of economic developments in eastern Europe and the Soviet Union it is apparent that they are suffering from chronic structural disequilibria as well as short-run stabilization problems. The former differ, at least conceptually, from the latter in that their correction requires fundamental changes in economic structures and in the behaviour of economic agents: they usually imply a complex and long-term process of positive structural adjustment and often require important political changes as well. The limited success of the eastern economies in achieving a more "intensive" growth path reflects, essentially, a failure of the planning process to react effectively to important changes in the economy, such as the exhaustion of labour reserves, and inability to integrate meaningfully within the CMEA and with the western economies via east-west trade. The reactions to the exogenous shocks of the 1970s and 1980s were no better: it is true that trade deficits were corrected fairly quickly, but this is not very difficult to achieve if the adjustment is concentrated on domestic demand. It was not accompanied by the structural changes and supply-side reforms that occurred in the western economies in the late 1970s and early 1980s.

The distinction between short-run and long-run adjustment problems is important for the discussion of the types of assistance that might be provided by the international community to support the process of change in the east; it is also relevant to the question of whether reforms should be implemented quickly or gradually (see below, section (viii)). However, although the distinction is clear in principle, in practice the two types of problem may interact. A failure to deal with short-run disequilibria promptly and effectively may exacerbate structural problems. Foreign exchange constraints may increase inflationary pressures by restricting the imports required to increase a country's productive potential; and, *ceteris paribus,* the failure to change economic and social behaviour will diminish the impact of a given volume of imports (or investment) on productive capacity. Thus any attempt to break out of relative stagnation may be foiled by a rapid expansion of current account deficits and inflation. It is to avoid such an outcome — of stagflation and a progressive decline in relative levels of economic development — that an increasing number of commentators and policy makers, both in the west and the east, have sug-

---

20 In contrast, the gap between the Federal Republic of Germany and the United States narrowed considerably over the same period. According to Summers and Heston, the Federal Republic of Germany was 40 per cent of the United States' level in 1950 and about 85 per cent in 1985. See Robert Summers and Alan Heston, "A new set of international comparisons of real product and prices: estimates for 130 countries, 1950-1985", *The Review of Income and Wealth*, No.1, March 1988.

21 Thus, a United Nations study implies that real output per head in Hungary and Poland in 1985 was 43 per cent and 33 per cent respectively of the level in the Federal Republic of Germany, as compared with 54 per cent and 46 per cent respectively in the Summers and Heston data. See United Nations Statistical Commission and Economic Commission for Europe, *International Comparisons of Gross Domestic Product in Europe, 1985*, New York, 1988.

gested that some kind of a new "Marshall Plan" might be an appropriate way to support the process of economic and political reform in eastern Europe. Since *Marshall Plan* is in danger of becoming a hackneyed synonym for throwing large amounts of money at large problems, it will be useful to take a closer look at the original Marshall Plan and the problems to which it was addressed before suggesting the outlines of a programme of western support for eastern reform.

(iii) The problems of conversion and post-war adjustment in western Europe

At the end of the Second World War most countries in western Europe were faced with a combination of problems that bear a strong resemblance to those facing many of the eastern economies today. There are also very important differences in the two situations, and these will be discussed at the end of the next section.

In the immediate post-war years western Europe consisted for the most part of highly regulated economies. Some degree of regulation dated from the protectionist policies of the 1930s but it was mainly the legacy of the need to use direct controls to mobilize resources for wartime objectives: it was considered that monetary and fiscal policies alone would be inadequate to ensure the necessary supplies of military equipment and to avoid open inflation. Some controls, especially on international trade, reinforced restrictions which had been introduced during the inter-war period of depression. In the United Kingdom, for example, the government controlled the level and composition of production through a battery of direct controls on imports, on the allocation of foreign currency and transport facilities, and on the allocation of raw materials.[22] Fixed investment in machinery and equipment was steered through the government's control of raw material allocation and the capital market; construction was subject to licensing and the controls on raw materials allocation. The government also had direct control over output and investment in the nationalized industries.

On the demand side,[23] Government controls included consumer rationing and price controls, and these were reinforced by the other schemes for controlling imports, allocating materials, etc. In addition, all the items in the balance of payments were controlled via foreign exchange and import regulations.[24]

Thus the wartime economy of the United Kingdom — and many of its characteristics were shared in varying degrees by other European countries — was a tightly controlled, planned system in which all production, consumption and investment decisions were subordinate to the objectives set by the government. The system of centralized controls was not used to set detailed targets for individual enterprises, as is (or was) the case in the centrally planned systems of eastern Europe and the Soviet Union; but the government did fix prices, allocate factors of production, and determine the composition of output by the use of direct controls rather than market forces.

Although there was some academic discussion at the end of the war as to whether some direct controls (especially on imports) might need to be retained indefinitely in order to maintain full employment, the general consensus was for a return to a decentralized market economy: the problem that preoccupied policy makers was not whether controls should be abandoned but how fast and in what order. This question is taken up below, but it can be noted here that the major preoccupation of governments was to avoid a repetition of the inflation that had followed the rapid removal of controls after the First World War.

The range and seriousness of the problems facing western Europe after the war were considerable and are comparable to some of those confronting the east European economies today. First was the immediate problem of "conversion", of restructuring the production system so that it could meet civilian instead of military needs. But the productive system was in poor shape: although the wartime destruction of machinery and equipment was much less than originally feared, maintenance and replacement had been neglected during the war years and in many industries, especially those producing consumer goods, investment had been very low or non-existent. Thus capital stocks were run-down, old and ill-adapted to the new, emerging structure of demand. Much of the transport and communications network had been destroyed, especially in Germany, and most of that which remained was run-down and inefficient, also because of a lack of investment and adequate maintenance.

Housing was also in a bad condition. In many countries there were severe shortages of accommodation, since large amounts of the housing stock had been destroyed by bombing. That which remained was often in poor condition and many people lived in cramped and over-crowded conditions. Supplies of food, energy and other consumer goods had been sharply curtailed in favour of military production during the war, but shortages continued for some years after 1945, partly because of lags in the "conversion" process but also because of balance-of-payments problems.

In trying to solve this array of supply-side problems, the post-war governments of western Europe also had to deal with a number of other constraints on the

---

22 Certain consumer durables (private cars, vacuum cleaners, etc,) simply disappeared from the market because the necessary materials were not supplied for their production. The British Government's overall planning did not require detailed intervention in all product markets and enterprises.

23 These controls were not aimed solely at restraining demand. The various rationing schemes were also intended to ensure an equitable distribution of essential goods in short supply.

24 For a detailed account of the United Kingdom's system of wartime controls (including several not mentioned above) see Peter Wiles, "Pre-war and wartime controls", in G.D.N. Worswick and P.H. Ady, *The British Economy 1945-1950*, Oxford, Clarendon Press, 1952, and J.C.R. Dow, *The Management of the British Economy 1945-1950*, Cambridge University Press, 1965, ch.vi.

long-run adjustment process. Among the most prominent of these was the "dollar shortage". During the war reserves of gold and foreign currencies had been greatly reduced in most countries and there were limited opportunities for exporting to North America which, because of the world-wide disruption caused by the war, was the major source not only of manufactured goods but also of food and raw materials. Western Europe was faced with a large, structural balance-of-payments deficit with the dollar area. Since most of their currencies were inconvertible,[25] the European countries were restricted in their ability to finance imports from one another or from non-dollar sources outside Europe. This of course encouraged them to maintain their wartime (and pre-war) controls on imports and domestic demand, thereby reinforcing the bilateral nature of intra-European trade.

Another major concern was the threat of inflation. As a result of the controls and other constraints on private consumption and business fixed investment, many countries were faced with a large "overhang" of household and corporate savings which had been accumulated during the war.[26]

This "excess saving" of the war years threatened to become the "excess demand" of the immediate post-war period. Some countries dealt with this problem by implementing currency reforms which incorporated some confiscation of wartime savings (Belgium and Germany, for example). The solution adopted in the United Kingdom was to remove direct controls only gradually and thereby "spread" the excess demand over a number of years.[27]

To summarize briefly, western Europe in the immediate aftermath of the Second World War was a collection of highly regulated economies faced with considerable problems of reconstruction and restructuring. Their attempts to find effective solutions were hampered by large current-account deficits, the correction of which was impeded by overvalued and inconvertible currencies, and by a network of bilateral trading relationships which restricted the growth of intra-European trade and the development of specialization on the basis of comparative advantage. Many countries were concerned at the threat of open inflation and some had high levels of foreign debt. Moreover, after the privations of wartime there were fears that the post-war expectations of the population would rise faster than the economic capacity to satisfy them, thereby increasing the risks of social unrest and political instability.

(iv) The Marshall Plan

When US Secretary of State George C. Marshall made his famous speech at Harvard University on 5 June 1947 the economic outlook in western Europe was not encouraging. Following the severe winter and fuel shortage of 1946-1947, the rapid recovery of output in 1946 appeared to have come to an end. Shortages of raw materials were widespread and the immediate flows of dollar aid after the end of hostilities had been quickly exhausted with, apparently, little to show for them in terms of permanent economic improvement. In its first economic *Survey* of Europe, written in early 1948, the United Nations Economic Commission for Europe concluded that "progress in the coming year" was unlikely to be as substantial as in 1946.[28] Thus, significant advance in solving the problems described above seemed unlikely, a prospect which appeared to be reinforced by the deteriorating outlook for political stability in Europe.

Secretary Marshall drew a picture of Europe where the entire fabric of its economy had been dislocated by the war, where machinery was in disrepair or obsolete, and where the "breakdown of the business structure ... was complete".[29] Moreover, funds required for reconstruction were being rapidly used up by the need to supply the population with essential commodities. The purpose of Marshall's proposal for American assistance to Europe was to break this vicious circle wherein long-run structural adjustment was frustrated by intractable short-run problems. Marshall emphasized that United States assistance was meant to provide a cure, not a palliative.

At a broader level, the Marshall Plan was a belated recognition that policy makers had been far too optimistic about the time required for the system of world trade and payments to return to some sort of "normality". By this was meant a return to a system of multilateral settlement and free trade, as incorporated in the rules of the new Bretton Woods organizations which would provide the basic architecture of the post-war economic system. The initial post-war optimism that this new structure could be rapidly put into place evaporated in a series of European dollar crises and in the premature and brief adoption of Sterling convertibility in 1947.[30]

The Marshall Plan recast the post-war adjustment process into a more realistic time-frame: it set 1952 as

---

25 Only Sweden, Switzerland and the United states had convertible currencies at this time.

26 Despite high rates of taxation, households in Britain were saving around 25 per cent of their disposable incomes during the war compared with less than 5 per cent before the war. Worswick and Ady, *op.cit.*, p.22.

27 Another solution would have been to impose a capital levy when the war was over. This was actually suggested by J.M. Keynes in his *How to Pay for the War*, Macmillan, 1940.

28 Economic Commission for Europe, *A Survey of the Economic Situation and Prospects of Europe*, United Nations, Geneva, 1948, p.4. It should be remembered, in view of remarks made below, that the lags in the availability of statistics were much worse than they are now. The latest (and preliminary) output data in this first *Survey*, which was issued in April 1948, was for the third quarter of 1947.

29 The text of Secretary Marshall's speech is reproduced in OECD, *From Marshall Plan to Global Interdependence*, Paris, 1978, pp.227-229.

30 A condition of the 1945 loan from the United States to Britain was that the latter would, immediately and unilaterally, implement the various clauses of the

the date by which internal and external balance would be re-established, i.e., some six years after the end of the war. The recipients of aid were expected to take special measures to boost intra-European trade as a step towards restoring a "working" world economy based on multilateralism and a liberal trading system. In the transition period the United States effectively allowed the west European countries to discriminate against American imports in order to conserve their dollar balances. The programme also emphasized the need to boost output and productivity growth, and to develop economic co-operation and integration within western Europe.

A key feature of the European Recovery Programme (ERP) — as the Marshall Plan was termed officially — was that each recipient had to draw up a four-year outline plan for recovery. Each plan had to include estimates of output, import requirements and expected exports, and it had to demonstrate how the recipient country expected to achieve adjustments and economic balance by the end of the four-year period. In order to co-ordinate these plans and the allocation of aid, the 16 European countries which finally accepted the United States' offer of assistance established a Committee for European Economic Co-operation (CEEC) which was quickly converted into the more permanent Organisation for European Economic Co-operation (OEEC) in April 1948. This framework reflected Marshall's insistence that the European countries themselves should assess their requirements for aid and take the initiative in making proposals for action, and that there should be a degree of united and co-operative effort among the Europeans themselves.[31]

As part of its objective to raise output and productivity levels in Europe, the ERP included a technical assistance programme whose purpose was to demonstrate to Europeans the value of American production techniques and management-labour relations, and to persuade participating countries to set up national productivity centres. The most prominent element of this programme was the sending of teams of personnel from European industrial enterprises to visit their counterparts in the United States, the idea being that direct experience was an effective way of gaining insight into the methods which gave the United States higher levels of productivity. European managers and technical personnel were also sent to the United States for special training and American experts were posted to Europe.

However, the technical assistance element of the Marshall aid programme was actually quite small and was little more than a "fairly modest informational programme".[32] Nevertheless, this is a part of the ERP which should not be ignored when its relevance to current problems is assessed.

Another feature of the ERP which should be noted is the use of counterpart funds. These were the national currency equivalent of Marshall aid grants and their domestic use was subject to approval by the ECA. The ECA tried to use them to influence the composition of fixed investment, but its success appears to have been limited. Not all European governments used the funds for fixed investment (Norway and the United Kingdom used them entirely for debt retirement), and in those that did they played "a useful but by no means indispensable role".[34] The use of counterpart funds tends to be a two-edged sword from the point of view of recipient governments: on certain occasions they can strengthen the government's hand in overcoming domestic opposition to certain projects which the government considers worthwhile or essential; but in others the authorities may be weakened by the charge of permitting too much external interference in domestic affairs. There is also the risk that counterpart funds may distort the market indicators of relative scarcities.[33]

Marshall aid officially ran for just under four years, from April 1948 until the end of 1951, after which the programme merged into the defence-related assistance provided under the Mutual Security Act. Over that four-year period $12.4 billion[35] were allotted to the 16 west European member countries of OEEC. Most of it was in the form of grants and there was also a large grant element in the loans, which were usually for 35 years at 2½ per cent interest with repayments starting in 1952. Marshall aid was also used to finance the two intra-European Payments Agreements of 1948-1949 and 1949-1950, and the European Payments Union which ran from late 1950 to the end of 1959.

As a proportion of United States' GNP, Marshall aid averaged just over 1 per cent for the four-year period, although it was as high as 2.4 per cent in 1949. For the recipient countries, ERP aid averaged just over 2 per cent of GNP, although there was considerable variation among countries and from year to year. In the first year of the programme Marshall aid "was an important addition to national income in all the recipi-

---

proposed IMF. Implementation was in fact delayed for one year following Congressional ratification of the IMF legislation in June 1946, but it still led to the convertibility crisis of the July-August 1947.

31 In the United States, the ERP was established by the Economic Co-operation Act of 1948, which entered into force on 3 April 1948, and was administered by the Economic Co-operation Administration (ECA). In October 1951 the ECA Act was superseded by the Mutual Security Act and the ECA was replaced by the Mutual Security Agency (MSA). In practice officials of the ECA played an influential role in the preparation of the European proposals and in advising on what would be acceptable to the Administration and to Congress.

32 Imanuel Wexler, *The Marshall Plan Revisited*, Greenwood Press, 1983, pp.92-93.

33 In the Federal Republic of Germany the ERP counterpart fund still exists (*ERP Sondervermögen*) and is administered by the Kreditanstalt für Wiederaufbau. Resources from this fund are now being used to finance projects in the German Democratic Republic. According to press reports (*Neues Deutschland*, Berlin, 21 February 1990) DM 6 billion (roughly $3.5 billion) is to be made available over three years for projects in the German Democratic Republic. These funds, of which DM 2 billion are earmarked for environmental protection, DM 700 million for the promotion of tourism, and DM 1.3 billion as start-up funds for new enterprises, will be directed at private enterprise and will consist of 15-20 year loans at a fixed rate of interest and with a five-year grace period on repayments. Austria also has substantial funds in ERP counterpart accounts. According to the Mayor of Vienna, some Schillings 10-20 billion (roughly $0.8-1.7 billion) could be easily mobilized to support eastern investments with preferential credits - as reported in *Nepszabadsag*, Budapest, 22 November 1989.

34 Alan S. Milward, *The Reconstruction of Western Europe 1945-1951*, Methuen, 1987, pp.107-112.

35 Wexler, *op.cit.*, p.249.

ent countries except Belgium and Sweden" — as a proportion of national income it ranged from 2.4 per cent in the United Kingdom to 14 per cent in Austria.[36] The largest shares of total Marshall aid were received by Britain and France (23 and 21 per cent, respectively), a reflection of the fact that the principal criterion for distribution was the size of the recipient's dollar deficit: the larger the deficit, the larger the country's share of total aid. The Federal Republic of Germany's share of Marshall aid was relatively small (about 10 per cent), but it received considerable sums under the GARIOA programme.[37]

In trying to assess the relevance of the Marshall Plan experience to current problems, it is clearly important to have some idea of what it achieved, of whether it attained its objectives or not. However, this is not a simple task since the whole question is now a matter of considerable controversy among economic and diplomatic historians. For many years the standard account was that Marshall aid overcame the problems and avoided the dangers described by Secretary Marshall in his 1947 address: it succeeded in lifting Europe out of the post-war morass into which it had fallen and even if all the specific objectives had not been achieved by 1952 it had created the conditions for sustained growth in Europe and, more generally, for viable market economies and stable democratic institutions.

The extent to which this interpretation should be revised is the subject of the controversy mentioned above. One view is that, while accepting that the Marshall Plan cannot be given all the credit for the post-war recovery and reconstruction of Europe, it "provided the 'crucial margin' that made European self-help possible. It facilitated essential imports, eased production bottlenecks, encouraged higher rates of capital formation, and helped to suppress inflation ...".[38] A different interpretation accepts that Marshall aid enabled western Europe to finance its dollar deficit, but argues that the deficit was due to the strength of the recovery in European output and that the recovery would have continued even if Marshall aid had not been forthcoming.[39]

Without going into the details of this argument, the assertion that a strong recovery was already under way in western Europe in 1947 and 1948 is clearly important in deciding what might be expected from similar large scale programmes of aid: there is clearly a difference between easing constraints on a growing and dynamic economy and restoring a broken-down and non-functioning system to working order. The evidence suggests that post-war Europe fell into the first category rather than the second and that fairly rapid progress was being made through domestic initiatives in solving many of the problems described in the previous section. Nevertheless, Marshall aid helped to ensure that the recovery would continue without being checked by balance-of-payments constraints. By lowering the risk of widespread bottlenecks and general shortages of materials, it helped to maintain business confidence and, thereby, the growth of fixed investment.

The setbacks of early 1947 proved to be temporary and by the time Secretary Marshall was making his speech at Harvard, progress was actually being resumed at "the same momentum as before".[40] European industrial production, excluding the Federal Republic of Germany, rose 13.6 per cent in 1947 and 13 per cent in 1948; including the Federal Republic of Germany, the average increases were 15.3 and 15.7 per cent respectively. By 1947 pre-war levels of output had been regained in most countries, but instead of slowing down as post-war reorganization came to an end, west European industry continued to grow at a fairly uniform annual rate of around 13 per cent up to 1951. This prolonged performance was partly due to the longer delay in the recovery of the Federal Republic of Germany, which helped to maintain the growth of total activity when other countries were approaching full capacity.

Part of the explanation for the rapid post-war recovery in output is that the damage to industrial machinery and equipment was much less than thought at the end of the hostilities. In fact, Europe's industrial capacity in 1945 was greater than before the war and in some respects, for example, the increased size of the engineering industries, was actually well placed to meet post-war needs. Nevertheless, the need for replacement investment and the profitable opportunities presented by post-war shortages led to a rapid recovery of fixed investment. By 1947 the volume of fixed investment in most of western Europe had regained the pre-war level and in all countries except the United Kingdom the share of investment in national output was higher than before the war.[41]

The rapid recovery and strength of fixed investment is evidence that morale and business expectations quickly improved at the end of the war. It also shows that the structures of the market economy in western Europe were still essentially intact despite their suspension or dilution during the six years of war. The most

---

[36] Milward, op.cit. p.96.

[37] "Government Aid and Relief in Occupied Areas". Between July 1946 and March 1950 the value of goods financed under this programme was $1.62 billion, slightly more than the Federal Republic of Germany received in Marshall aid. See Manfred Knapp, "Reconstruction and West-Integration: the Impact of the Marshall Plan on Germany", *Zeitschrift für die gesammte Staatswissenschaft*, 137:3, September 1981.

[38] Michael J. Hogan, *The Marshall Plan*, Cambridge University Press, 1989, p.432.

[39] Alan S. Milward, op.cit., especially chapter II.

[40] United Nations Economic Commission for Europe, *Economic Survey of Europe in 1948*, New York, 1949, p.5. For the OEEC countries as a whole, GNP in 1948 was about 9 per cent higher (in volume terms) than in 1947. Between 1947 and 1951 the average growth rate was 7.7 per cent a year. See OEEC, *Statistics of National Product and Expenditure 1938, 1947 and 1952*, Paris, 1954, p.31.

[41] See United Nations Economic Commission for Europe, *Economic Survey of Europe since the War*, Geneva, 1953, chapter 5. The lower figure for the United Kingdom was due to a lower volume of house-building: business investment had increased as in the rest of Europe.

critical problem facing the post-war European economy was its huge balance-of-payments deficit, most of it with the dollar area. This was a global, structural problem which could not be solved quickly. The Marshall Plan therefore played an important role in enabling western Europe to maintain high rates of growth of output and investment without it being forced to accept cuts in living standards which, although improving, were still relatively low. The austerity which was later to be associated with short-run stabilization programmes subject to IMF conditionality was therefore avoided or, at least, greatly reduced. This may well have helped to reinforce political stability in post-war Europe although, by the nature of things, it is difficult to test such statements with any confidence.[42]

(v) Is a 'Marshall Plan' needed for eastern Europe?

The Marshall aid programme provided 16 west European countries with some $12.4 billion over four years or $3.1 billion a year. In 1989 prices[43] this is equivalent to $65.4 billion, or $16.4 billion a year.

In order to provide some scale to the numbers involved, suppose that a western aid programme for the eastern countries were based on this figure of $42 per head. Then, on the basis of 1989 estimates of population, total aid for the six east European countries would be around $4.8 billion a year: if the Soviet Union were included the total would be nearly $16.7 billion a year. This last figure is thus only slightly higher than the original Marshall aid programme adjusted for price changes.

Recently the President of the Commission of the European Communities provided some idea of the scale of aid that he thought might be provided by the European Community to eastern Europe.[44] He suggested that if the six east European countries were given the same support as provided by the Community to its own depressed regions, then the Community's budget would require an additional ECU 14 billion a year for the next 5-10 years, depending on the pace of transformation in the eastern countries. In addition a further ECU 5 billion a year would be needed for the European Investment Bank. Such a level of assistance would amount to roughly $23 billion a year, which is nearly 5 times larger than the Marshall Plan equivalent for the six countries quoted above. In fact the EC proposal would be more than one third larger than the Marshall Plan equivalent for *all* the eastern countries (i.e., including the Soviet Union). Since the programme suggested by the EC President could run for 5-10 years, his proposal for the six east European countries would be some 6 to 12 times larger than the original Marshall Plan adjusted for price changes.

In terms of western GDP/GNP these are not very large numbers: $16.4 billion, the Marshall Plan at US prices of 1989, is about 0.3 per cent of either US GNP or the European Community's GDP — for the United States, the EC and Japan combined it would be just over 0.1 per cent of GDP. Mr. Delors' proposal of $23 billion would amount to some 0.45 per cent of the Community's GDP in 1989.

However, the important question is not so much whether the western countries can afford a "Marshall Plan" on this scale, but whether the eastern economies can absorb it. Throughout the 1970s, the eastern countries borrowed heavily from the west, gross debt rising by some $64 billion in eastern Europe between 1970 and 1981 and in the Soviet Union by over $27 billion. This inflow of resources, which for eastern Europe, on an annual basis, is considerably less than the sum suggested by Mr. Delors, appears to have had little impact on structural change and productive efficiency in the eastern economies.[45] One of the objectives of the radical changes now under way in the political and economic systems of the eastern countries is, of course, to obtain a marked improvement in economic performance. This will require, *inter alia*, a greatly increased capacity to adopt new technologies throughout their economies. However, improving such absorptive capacities requires fundamental changes in economic structures and in the behaviour of economic agents. These changes take time and there is no reason to suppose that the capacity of the eastern economies to absorb western resources on the scale described above has radically improved in the last year or so.

A crucial and fundamental difference between the transformation problems facing west European countries in 1945 and those facing the eastern countries today is that the former did not have to reconstruct market economies from first principles. Although the free workings of the market mechanism were overridden or suspended in many countries for part or most of the war, it was generally quite clear that this was a temporary state of affairs based on pragmatic considerations about how to focus activity on achieving a number of well-defined and limited objectives. A clear system of property rights remained in place and after the war enterprises were free to seek access to foreign markets. Although there was argument over the extent to which governments should intervene to correct deficiencies in the workings of the market mechanism, there was a

---

[42] It has been argued that the Marshall Plan had an important positive effect on business expectation in the Federal Republic of Germany. See the work of Borchardt and Buchheim, quoted in Alan S. Milward, "Was the Marshall Plan Necessary", *Diplomatic History*, 13:2, Spring 1988, p.240. Manfred Knapp, *loc.cit.*, p.421, argues that for the Federal Republic of Germany the Marshall Plan was not simply an economic aid programme but also "an instrument for political rehabilitation".

[43] Based on the change in the US GNP deflator between 1948-1951 and 1989.

[44] Address by Jacques Delors to the European Parliament, "Presenting the Commission's Programme for 1990", Strasbourg, 17 January 1990 (EC press release).

[45] For this reason, and despite the need to re-equip industry, a cautious approach to foreign borrowing in the future has been advocated in the Soviet Union. Eduard Gostev, Deputy Chairman of Vneshekonombank, noted in early 1989 that some of the equipment purchased years ago by the Soviet Union had not even been installed. He also stated that some 2.7 billion roubles ($4.4 billion) worth of goods purchased with convertible currencies had been wasted in recent years. *International Herald Tribune*, 31 January 1989.

general consensus that the wartime planning systems would not be able to cope with the multifarious demands of a decentralized system in which consumers are ultimately sovereign. It should also be noted that the basic incentive structure of the market system was constrained but not eliminated by wartime planning in the market economies: entrepreneurs still had incentives to improve efficiency and this contributed to the savings overhang at the end of the war. It also helps to account for the rapid response of domestic investment to the bottlenecks and other shortages of the immediate post-war years.[46]

The basic system of economic organization which has prevailed in the Soviet Union since the late 1920s and in eastern Europe from the early 1950s is very different. The main features of that system may be recalled briefly: the central plan is the main instrument of policy and basically decides what individual enterprises should produce. Prices are determined bureaucratically and are used very little as an instrument of planning: producer prices have little influence on resource allocation, and the level and pattern of investment is allocated according to the priorities of the plan rather than the perceptions of enterprises as to profitable opportunities; consumer prices pay some attention to demand insofar as turnover taxes are supposed to be set at rates which would adjust demand to available supplies, which are determined by the central plan. Prices are based on average rather than marginal costs and therefore are unreliable as indicators of true social costs. Moreover, in practice, prices have remained unchanged for long periods and this has contributed to severe shortages. In the traditional model trade policy was essentially autarkic and foreign trade, which was monopolized by the state, was seen as meeting the residual needs of the system. The whole system was enclosed in a state where party, state and economic hierarchies were intermeshed but where one-party supervision was predominant.

The incentive structure of this system is such that micro-inefficiency is widespread and responsible for the endemic shortage which characterizes the centrally planned economies.[47] More fundamentally, enterprises will not be active in adopting new technologies and raising efficiency simply because there is no strong incentive to do so. The incentive structure, which reflects the restricted, non-allocative role of prices, also means that new enterprises cannot be set up in response to profitable opportunities and the failures of established concerns. Entry and exit of firms is controlled by the plan and industrial structures tend to be dominated by large, inefficient and inflexible enterprises. In general, the widespread failures on the supply side have provided enterprises with strong incentives to meet their own needs for intermediate goods; this, in turn, has led to a lack of specialization, overstocking (hoarding) of materials etc., and a lowering of efficiency throughout the productive system.

Attempts to remedy the deficiencies of this basic model have been made more or less continuously since the late 1950s. At first — and in some countries still — reform was focused on improving the traditional model, especially in regard to improving enterprise incentives (for example, replacing gross output targets with various bonus-setting indicators or even some degree of profit), but the basic sovereignty of the planners over the price mechanism was not in question. More radical reforms have been introduced in some east European countries since the the late 1960s, and especially by Hungary which in 1968 introduced a significant degree of decentralization into the economic system. However, all these reforms failed to alter significantly the behavioural patterns of enterprises.[48] Most of the reforms before 1989 still left the central authorities with considerable powers to control and influence the economic behaviour of individual enterprises.[49] Because of the close relationship between the political and economic structures, reforms were always checked at the point where any further change in the system of economic management would challenge the established interests of the party hierarchy. This is why the events of 1989 represent a radical break with the past: the end of one-party rule opens up the possibility of establishing decentralized market economies where the principal (but not necessarily only) economic role of government is to pursue macro-economic goals using the indirect methods of fiscal and monetary policy. This is now a stated objective in Czechoslovakia, the German Democratic Republic, Hungary and Poland.

The transformation of a centrally planned economy into a decentralized market economy of the western (or, more broadly, the OECD) variety is both a precise and a vague concept: it is precise in terms of the general direction which is to be pursued, but vague as to the precise destination. Indeed, from both the policy and analytical points of view the whole transformation issue is largely uncharted territory. It is often overlooked, even by many economic agents in the market economies, that the actual functioning of markets and market economies depends on a detailed infrastructure of property rights, corporate and non-corporate law, an extensive array of specialized financial institutions, regulations and regulatory bodies, labour law and procedures for settling disputes, and so on. Much of this infrastructure is embodied in institutions, but important elements are embedded in cultural and social traditions and in the conventions of business practice. Although all the leading market economies today share a number of basic characteristics, especially concerning the role of the price mechanism and decentralized decision

---

[46] The rapid recovery of fixed investment was noted above. Worswick (Worswick and Ady, *loc.cit.*, pp.7-8) also points to productivity gains and to improvements in the quality of management which were stimulated by the acute labour shortage during the war.

[47] Kornai, *op.cit.*, (1980); cf. "Whole sectors of industry are producing things in which no-one is interested, while the things we need are in short supply". President Václav Havel, in his New Year's address (English version published BBC, *Summary of World Broadcasts*, Nr. EUR/06, 1 March 1990).

[48] See Kornai, *op.cit.* and T. Bauer, "Reform policy in the complexity of economic policy", *Acta Oeconomica*, volume 34, 1985. The latter points to the lack of competition and the maintenance of monopolies as reasons for the limited effects of the Hungarian reforms.

[49] In most eastern countries in mid-1989, management appointments to enterprises were still controlled by the party authorities.

making, the ways in which they arrange the details of the market infrastructure vary both as to style and to the relative importance attached to the different elements. Moreover, most of the market economies have shown considerable capacity to adapt their institutions and behavioural conventions to changing circumstances. Beyond a number of core elements, there is no single, homogeneous model of a market economy. Thus, as a policy objective, the transformation of a centrally planned economy into a market economy is more a statement of general principle than a detailed programme of action. The latter requires a detailed specification of how institutions should be changed or constructed, and how the behaviour of individuals and enterprises should be adapted.

This discussion suggests that if policy makers are considering the Marshall Plan as a model for western assistance to the reforming countries the appropriate thing to do would be to turn it upside down. The entire structure of institutions and economic incentives in the eastern countries today is radically different from those in western Europe in 1948 and the capacity of the east to absorb new capital and technology has been recently shown to be very limited. Whereas the Marshall Plan was long on grant aid and short on technical assistance, western aid to eastern Europe, at least initially, should reverse their relative importance.

Detailed proposals for technical assistance could be drawn up by the eastern countries themselves in the light of the particular arrangements that they consider will best suit their own preferences and traditions. In this the western countries should perhaps follow the wisdom of the Marshall Plan in leaving it to the recipient country to draw up a programme for its transition to a market economy and to indicate the types of technical assistance required. In practice, assistance from western experts or international institutions may be desirable in preparing these programmes: not only can they help in identifying worthwhile projects but they can also advise on the appropriate presentation of submissions to western governments and international bodies (ECA staff played a similar role in the formulation of requests for Marshall aid). Such programmes could also indicate needs for financial assistance, although it would be necessary to show that it could be effectually absorbed. By establishing some links between absorptive capacity, technical assistance and financial aid it might be possible to avoid one of the weaknesses of the Marshall aid programme, namely, that it did not do enough to strengthen incentives to better performance. Such links would also mean that the need for financial assistance would be derived from a coherent programme for solving specific problems rather than the sort of contingent arithmetic presented earlier.

Many suggestions have already been made as to the types of technical assistance that need to be provided to the east: management training and expertise in specific technologies are most often mentioned. However, what is less frequently referred to — but which the discussion above suggests should be given priority — is the infrastructure of market behaviour. The transformation of a planned economy into a market economy requires a major change in the rules according to which a society conducts its economic activity. The people who are expert in analysing such rules and assessing their impact on economic behaviour are not businessmen[50] or technologists, but economists, political theorists, anti-trust lawyers and some central bankers. The market economies and the international economic organizations are relatively well-endowed with such people and their advice and assistance in the early stages of the transformation process could be invaluable. Western specialists who are also familiar with the systemic problems of the eastern economies could make an especially valuable contribution.

The assistance and advice of such western experts is important because they are the people who are also most familiar with the nature and causes of market failure[51] in the market economies.

In the public discussions of the possibilities of market economies in eastern Europe it is not always emphasized enough that the efficiency gains of a decentralized market system depend on the degree of competition in product, capital and labour markets. In the traditional neo-classical theory the superiority of market solutions to economic problems rests on perfect competition and Pareto optimality.[52] Since real-world markets are usually far from satisfying the optimality conditions of perfect competition, it follows that government intervention to improve the efficiency of markets can never be excluded on *a priori* grounds. In practice western governments have adopted numerous policies to deal with market failure, ranging from nationalization to competition policy. Since the early 1970s, however, the emphasis has been on making markets more competitive.

These are not academic points which can be brushed aside in the urgency of "getting things done". The east European economies at the present time, and irrespective of their location on the path towards a market economy, are characterized by numerous distortions: markets are segmented and inefficient; market structures tend to be monopolistic or, at best, oligopolistic; market and economic information is sparse and/or inaccurate. Given the large suppressed demand for consumer goods, these are ideal conditions for domestic (and foreign) enterprises to make supernormal profits once the price system is freed from control.[53] These might be tolerated as a short-run

---

50 A businessman *qua* businessman is no more an expert on the rules of a market economy than is a chauffeur on the physics of the internal combustion engine.

51 Market failure principally arises from the presence of monopolies, externalities or public goods.

52 The Austrian school's case for the market rests more on its superiority as a co-ordinating mechanism in a situation of uncertainty and imperfect information. As represented by Hayek, the school's case for markets also rests on libertarian value judgements.

53 For foreign enterprises such profits might help to offset the risk of exchange rate adjustment, especially when the rate is generally agreed to be too high.

phenomenon while a competitive market framework was being constructed, but there will always be a risk of strong social reactions to "profiteering" which could harm the process of reform. Such reactions were evident last year in the Soviet Union where there was considerable popular criticism of the prices charged and profits made by some co-operatives.

Similar caution is in order when rapid rates of privatization are proposed. The analysis of western experience in this area stresses the crucial importance of competition in the relevant sector in order for the potential gains in efficiency to be realized.[54] A change in ownership may simply transform a public monopoly into a private one, although the private managers will probably be better paid than when they were in the public sector. In the eastern countries there are major problems in establishing correct estimates of net worth when there are no efficient capital markets and when accounting rules bear little relation to those in a functioning market economy. In such circumstances there is a considerable risk that social assets will be sold off at prices which would imply large transfers of wealth either to the old managers and to former members of the *nomenklatura* or to newcomers from the west.

Foreign enterprises can play an important role in increasing the level of competition in the sectors in which they operate, in transferring technology, modern management techniques and so on. Many eastern governments recognize the advantages of opening their economies to foreign companies and are seeking to attract them by changing joint-venture and other relevant legislation. However, the rush to attract foreign investment into eastern Europe could be premature if a competitive market framework is still far from completion. It is a mistake to believe that all market economy enterprises require a *competitive* market economy in which to operate. As long as they have security of title to their assets and guarantees of profit repatriation, foreign enterprises, like sportsmen, will be happy to play according to whatever the rules are in place. If markets are not competitive, there can be no presumption that the activities of foreign companies will automatically contribute to a more efficient use of resources.[55]

Many of the "supply-side" policies adopted by the market economies in the 1970s were focused on deregulation and increasing competition. There is considerable expertise on these matters, both in official (national and international) institutions and in the law and economics faculties of the universities, on which the eastern countries can easily draw. There is also a variety of experience among the market economies which increases the chance of individual eastern countries finding policies and techniques which are in line with their own particular preferences and situation. A technical assistance programme could easily set up ways for the east to obtain expert advice in this area. It will not be expensive and the long-run returns could be very high. Following OECD experience in this area, it can be very useful to discuss, compare and monitor the structural adjustment policies in individual countries in an international forum which can bring together all the donors and all the recipients of assistance.

Technical assistance will also be needed to set up a variety of financial institutions (clearing and investment banks, insurance companies and pension funds) which are vital for the efficient working of a market economy. There is an abundance of specialized technical expertise in all these areas in the west, upon which the east may easily draw. However, because the possibilities are numerous, it might be wise to use first the more general advisers mentioned in the previous paragraphs to obtain guidance as to the types of institutions and financial expertise which are likely to be best suited to the particular needs and circumstances of individual eastern countries.

Another area which should be given high priority, because of its importance to the efficient functioning of a market economy, is statistics. The state of eastern statistics has been the subject of much comment, both in eastern and western publications.[56] Much of this comment has focussed on the poor coverage or inaccuracy of the published figures. The extent to which the latter is due to biases in the reporting systems, to defective methodologies or to deliberate falsification is difficult to determine. The fact is that there are major deficiencies in the existing set of official statistics: these shortcomings have recently been officially acknowledged in many of the eastern countries.[57] However, an efficient market economy needs not only accurate statistics but different types of statistics from a centrally planned economy. In the first place, macro-economic policy in a market economy relies in the main on various instruments of fiscal and monetary policy, rather than direct controls, and, as such, requires a different data set to that used by a central planner: some of these statistics, particularly in the monetary field, will only be generated, of course, after the relevant institutional changes have occurred. Secondly, reliable statistics (as well as other economic and commercial information) become essential to individual enterprises as they move from a command system to one where they must take their own decisions on output and investment in response to market signals. In the west, private enterprises often invest in collecting their own data based on

---

[54] For an analysis of the experience of privatization in the United Kingdom see George Yarrow, "Privatization in theory and practice", *Economic Policy*, No.2, April 1986.

[55] The role of multinational companies in the process of integrating the eastern economies in the world economy should be given explicit consideration because of their relative independence from national government constraints. For a discussion of some of the key issues in the context of the European Community, see M. Panic, *The Impact of Multinational on National Economic Policies*, University of Cambridge, Department of Applied Economics, Working Paper No.8905 (1989).

[56] See, for example, United Nations Economic Commission for Europe, *Economic Survey of Europe in 1988-1989*, New York, 1989, pp.120-122; and this *Survey*, section 3.1(vii), below.

[57] See below, chapter 3, for more details on this issue.

sample surveys but a considerable amount of market information is culled from official statistics.[58]

The reforming economies of eastern Europe will also require statistics to monitor their progress towards a market economy and to track the adjustment of economic behaviour to the new systems of incentives. Such data will be necessary for the effective adjustment of particular policies, but they may also be required by foreign donors of financial aid and technical assistance. In this context the institution of business surveys, as conducted by business organizations or research institutes in the west, could make a useful contribution.[59]

It should be emphasized that the provision of comprehensive and reliable economic statistics is not simply a service to the business sector but a public good which makes a crucial contribution to the optimal working of a market economy.[60] Moreover, the provision of such statistics is essential for the closer integration of the eastern countries in the world economy: not only are they required for conducting international business at the enterprise level, but they are also a condition of membership of the Bretton Woods institutions.

Statistics (including market research and related activities for enterprises) is thus another priority area where a technical assistance programme could be speedily effective in helping to meet the requirements of the eastern countries. Once the needs for technical assistance are clear, a well-defined programme of financial assistance could easily follow (perhaps to provide PCs, computer software, etc.).

To summarize this section: it has been argued that despite a number of close similarities between the problems facing the western countries in 1945-1948 and those confronting the reforming eastern economies in 1990, the differences in the infrastructure of the two economic systems and in their capacity to absorb foreign financial aid are so large that it would be a mistake to assume that a repeat of the 1948 Marshall Plan would be a suitable western response to current eastern problems. For present purposes the structure of the original Marshall Plan should be turned upside down so that technical rather than direct financial assistance becomes the major component. The Marshall Plan could be imitated by encouraging recipient countries to draw up their own list of assistance needs in a coherent programme, but it is suggested that high priority should be given to technical advice and assistance for (a) constructing the legal, financial and institutional infrastructure essential for a competitive market system and (b) providing a comprehensive and reliable statistical service for both government and enterprises in their new roles in a decentralized market economy. It is not suggested that these two priority areas for technical assistance should "crowd out" or delay other innovations.

Institutional reform must clearly proceed on a fairly broad front: for example, the decentralization of investment decisions from the central plan to individual enterprises will obviously require the creation of capital markets and stock exchanges. Similarly, it will not be difficult to draw up long lists of candidates for technical assistance, from training and education in subjects such as economics, accountancy and statistics to the essentials of marketing and selling. But it is because the list of desirable projects is long that choices will have to be made, if for no other reason than not everything can be done at once. The two priorities mentioned here were selected because not only are they necessary conditions for *efficient* market systems but in the market economies they are so taken for granted that they are frequently overlooked.

Before turning to the question of international trade and payments, it will be useful to consider briefly the environmental issue since it brings together some of the points already discussed.

(vi) Eastern reform and the environment

This brief section is not intended to review environmental issues and policy but to suggest how they might fit into the discussion of the previous section. It was noted there that market economies were subject to a number of cases of market failure, associated for the most part with public goods, externalities and monopolies. One of the most prominent examples of market failure is the problem of pollution. One explanation of this failure points to ill-defined property rights: environmental pollution is caused by over-exploitation of resources either because resources are owned in common or because nobody owns them. Because property rights are badly defined, it is difficult for environmental spillover effects to be internalized into the pricing system or the costs of enterprises. One way of dealing with this problem, which is being given increased attention in many market economies, is to introduce market-based incentives to modify the workings of the free market. Basically this means that there has to be some central decision about the value of environmental resources and then that value has to be introduced into the market prices of goods and services. For an economy switching to a decentralized market system it might be appropriate to consider incorporating such incentives from the start. Similarly it might be advantageous to consider early adoption of particular western schemes, such as those for road-use pricing to limit urban congestion: the introduction of such user fees now would forestall potential opposition from future car owners and producers in eastern Europe. For the same reason, the eastern economies might be well advised to develop policies to deal with spillover effects at the

---

[58] Some idea of the ways in which public statistics are put to use in private enterprise can be obtained from the papers in Statistics Users' Council, *UK International Trade Statistics*, London, December 1988. The United Kingdom government's "visible trade statistics are among the most widely used of all business statistics" (p.163).

[59] This type of survey has already been introduced in Hungary with the assistance of the Institut für Wirtschaftsforschung (IFO) of Munich.

[60] "Perfect information", it will be recalled, is one of the optimality conditions of the neo-classical argument for the market economy. A respectable "free market" case can therefore be made for subsidizing the price at which official statistics are sold.

same time as they introduce market pricing. This would, *inter alia*, provide a useful signal to western companies which might be tempted to avoid western environmental controls by relocating plant in the east. The early adoption of high environmental standards should not be regarded as a "luxury" which can be postponed until high levels of output are achieved. The increasing consciousness of environmental issues on the part of western consumers and the adoption of various environmental and anti-pollution measures by most western governments means that environmental standards will be an important component of international competitiveness in the 1990s.[61]

The above refers in the main to future developments. Meanwhile "planning failures" in the eastern countries have led to major problems of pollution, emanating in particular from a range of heavy industries. The damage to air and water resources, and also to the health of the population, is already extensive. This is perhaps one area where significant financial assistance and a "Marshall Plan" spirit might be most effectively deployed. There are signs that a number of west European countries, for evident reasons of self-interest, are ready to finance environmental clean-ups in the east. In the absence of an efficient pricing system, however, there will presumably be cases where instead of clean-up there should be a shut-down of certain industrial plants in the east. Because they are closely connected with the way markets work (or fail to work), it is suggested that western assistance (and east-west collaboration) on environmental problems should be closely co-ordinated with the proposed technical assistance in market infrastructure and regulation.

(vii) Eastern reforms and international trade

In the traditional, centrally planned economy, foreign trade was seen as a source of uncertainty which, mainly because of unexpected changes in foreign demand and the terms of trade, was liable to upset the calculations of domestic resource balances in the plans. Consequently trade in the eastern countries was largely motivated by the need to meet residual needs, to supply the goods for which there were no adequate domestic substitutes. Thus, although a major feature of the eastern countries, particularly of some of the smaller economies of eastern Europe, is their relatively low levels of trade in relation to economic size and national output, reductions in imports can have severe effects on domestic output and supply.

Trade performance is affected by the different arrangements for trade with the western, convertible currency countries and with the other eastern countries within the CMEA. CMEA members account for some 40-80 per cent of east European countries' total trade, although most of this consists of bilateral exchanges with the Soviet Union rather than trade among the smaller economies. Since eastern currencies are not freely convertible most of the intra-CMEA trade has remained bilateral and subject to five-year and annual negotiations between governments. The prices actually used in these transactions have usually been negotiated around a moving average of past prices in the world markets. The arrangements for intra-CMEA trade are now the subject of considerable controversy among CMEA members, both as to the prices used in this trade and the consequences of past investment decisions which, by giving priority to bloc needs, may not have been in line with the comparative advantages of individual countries. It is widely asserted that most member countries give low priority to their CMEA trade commitments and there are frequent complaints that the goods supplied are of low quality, are delivered late, etc. The existence of such "soft" markets — soft not only in currency terms but also in the product and distribution standards demanded — has done little to improve the competitiveness of the eastern countries in world markets as a whole.

Despite the autarkic tendencies inherent in the traditional centrally planned economy, trade with the western economies has grown rapidly at various times over the past few decades. Nevertheless their share of western markets remains quite small and their export competitiveness appears to have deteriorated considerably and fairly steadily over the last decade or so. On western markets, the eastern countries have been overtaken by the newly industrialized economies of South East Asia and also, within the European Community, by the countries of southern Europe.[62]

Because of the way import requirements are set in the traditional planning system, and because domestic prices do not reflect real resource cost, eastern exports to the west have generally been subject to quotas and other quantitative restrictions. These are seen by western countries as legitimate attempts to compensate for the difference between the trading régimes of the eastern countries and those who trade according to GATT rules. One result of these differences between market and planned economies is that eastern exports have become one of the main targets for anti-dumping actions by the European Community.[63] However, only 12 per cent of these actions led to anti-dumping duties being imposed — and insofar as the other actions may have encouraged a closer alignment of export prices with real cost, they may have been to the benefit of the eastern exporters.

---

61 If the eastern economies were able to deal with some of their major environmental problems in a market economy context, it could have a powerful demonstration effect in the developing countries.

62 See United Nations Economic Commission for Europe, "The effects of west European integration in imports of manufactures from eastern and southern Europe", *Economic Survey of Europe in 1988-1989*, New York, 1989, chapter 2.5. See also chapter 7 below.

63 Between 1980 and 1988, 41 per cent of all anti-dumping cases initiated by the EC were against state-trading countries, a proportion which is 4.5 times larger than their share of EC imports. Yugoslavia accounted for another 7 per cent of the total number of cases. See Rolf Wiedemann, "The Anti-Dumping Policy of the European Communities," *Intereconomics*, January/February 1990.

Although western trade restrictions may have affected eastern exports of particular products,[64] the declining competitiveness of the east is essentially an external manifestation of the domestic problems at which the whole process of reform is directed. Eastern enterprises, faced with excess demand on their domestic markets, have little incentive to incur the additional costs and effort of developing export markets. In any case, design and marketing skills, which are important elements in successful exporting, have been long neglected by eastern enterprises.[65] The enterprise in the centrally planned economy has been traditionally insulated from direct contact with foreign markets by the state monopoly of foreign trade. Consequently their marketing skills and their market information systems are weak and these contribute to their inability to respond quickly to developments in world markets. Moreover, given the system of setting domestic prices and fixing exchange rates, many eastern enterprises probably have only rudimentary knowledge of those areas in which they might have a competitive advantage in world markets. Also, the residual approach to imports, as well as the complex systems of import controls and licensing in the east, has not only removed the competitive effect of imports on domestic enterprises but has also deprived them of one of the principal sources of economic "information" by which market economies identify the areas in which they have (or may have) an international comparative advantage. The nature of the eastern trading régimes generally prevents the development of long-term international relationships between enterprises which, in western Europe, have underpinned the rapid development of intra-industry trade. In contrast to western Europe in general and the European Community in particular, the members of CMEA have not achieved a high degree of international specialization through trade. Intra-industry exchange among the eastern countries is very much lower than among the market economies[66] and especially so in the smaller economies of eastern Europe, which implies a considerable sacrifice of the efficiency gains which could have been obtained via increased specialization.

The radical reforms proposed already and under way in the eastern countries will address a considerable number of the factors behind this deteriorating export performance. However, marketing, including the collection and use of market intelligence, and the whole range of skills required to compete effectively in world markets is an obvious area for international technical assistance to the east. These are areas which have been neglected for many years but are crucial for improving export performance.

However, the emphasis on *radical* reforms is particularly relevant for international trade since the west has made the removal of quotas and other restrictions on imports subject to continued progress in economic *and* political reform.[67] If such progress were to stop, the restoration of quotas might very well be amplified by what happens after 1992. As yet this issue has not been settled, but existing national quotas, which are not in fact applied by all member countries, might be replaced by a single quota which could be more restrictive than the existing (national) ones. If the transformation to decentralized, market economies is maintained, then the control of the EC's quantitative restrictions after 1992 by the Commission rather than the member countries is likely to work in favour of the eastern countries: the collective western objective of supporting the process of economic and political reform will be less likely to be compromised by sectional interests in individual EC countries.

Nevertheless, if all the eastern economies embark on roughly the same path of radical reform, approximately the same concessions will have to be granted to all. This could pose some adjustment problems in parts of western Europe and it might therefore be necessary either to set a timetable for the gradual elimination of all restrictions[68] or to increase the available funds for restructuring and/or regional assistance. Since the immediate supply responses in the eastern countries may not be very rapid, a gradualist approach on the western side may be implemented quite easily.

Western countries will also expect the state monopoly of eastern trade to be replaced by commercial policy, but a process of gradual and much longer structural adjustment will be required in the east. In order to implement a gradual adjustment, the present system of restricting imports in the eastern countries will need to be transformed into the more transparent devices of tariffs and quotas. Once that is achieved, a programme can be drawn up for their reduction and eventual elimination. The gradual adjustment of restrictions on imports not only reflects an element of the post-war Marshall Plan but is well-founded in the classical tradition of economics.[69]

---

64 The importance of supply-side factors is shown by the fact that many EC quotas on imports from the east are not fully taken up.

65 This is part of the lack of incentives to innovate in "shortage" economies. Although COCOM controls have restricted eastern imports of certain advanced technologies from the west, the main reasons for eastern imports being dominated by medium and low technology goods (see below, chapter 7) are to be found in the structure of enterprise incentives.

66 See Z. Drabek and D. Greenaway, "Economic Integration and Intra-Industry Trade: the CMEA and EEC compared", *Kyklos*, 37, 1984.

67 The Commission of the EC has recently persuaded Community Foreign Ministers to agree to the accelerated removal of quotas on imports from Hungary and Poland, subject to the above-mentioned condition.

68 This would have to be precise and strictly adhered to in order to avoid endless postponements being obtained by special interest groups.

69 Adam Smith accepted that the sudden abolition of trade barriers could lead to serious unemployment especially if labour mobility was low. "Humanity may in this case require that the freedom of trade should be restored only by slow gradations, and with a good deal of reserve and circumspection". (Adam Smith, *The Wealth of Nations*, edited by R.H. Campbell and A.S. Skinner, Oxford, vol.1, 1976, p.469). Smith also considered the effect on the owner of specific capital goods: "The equitable regard ... to his interest requires that changes of this kind should never be introduced suddenly, but slowly, gradually, and after a very long warning". (Adam Smith, *ibid*, p.471). Ricardo agreed with this approach and recommended that Britain's corn law duties should be phased out over a ten-year period from 1846 (see M. Panic, *National Management of the International Economy*, 1988, p.124).

Ever since 1949, 17 western countries, acting together in the Co-ordinating Committee for Multilateral Export Controls (COCOM), have restricted the supply of certain technologies to the eastern countries. It is not clear whether or not these controls, intended to protect the strategic defence interests of the west, have seriously constrained the economic development of the east: it was suggested above that the more binding constraints might be domestic in origin and especially those which reduced or removed the incentives for eastern enterprises to innovate. However, if the various programmes of reform are successful in weakening such systemic constraints, the bite of existing COCOM controls could become sharper and affect the development of strategic sectors, such as telecommunications. This sector illustrates some of the problems involved. It is generally accepted that the telecommunications systems of eastern Europe are inadequate: they employ out-of-date technology and provide less than reliable service to a minority of the population. It is clear that they constitute a potentially serious obstacle not only to the restructuring of industry and the emergence of new service industries, such as tourism, but also to the development of other activities, such as financial services and the dissemination of accurate and up-to-date economic information, which, as argued in section (v) above, are essential for the efficient working of a decentralized market system. Since the western countries now perceive that they also have a strategic interest in the success of economic and political reform in eastern Europe, plans to relax a proportion of COCOM controls are already under discussion and could be ready for implementation in the summer.[70] It will be useful to monitor more closely the effects of COCOM controls on the reforming eastern economies and to provide for more rapid review procedures whenever serious constraints on the reform process are identified.

If the reform process continues on radical lines and if market access to the west is not obstructed by quantitative restrictions, the prospects for eastern exports to the west will be greatly improved. A fairly rapid expansion of exports might be possible within a few years and some of the market share lost to the NIEs regained. The outcome of the Uruguay Round may also benefit eastern exports in the longer run, especially if progress is made in reducing barriers to trade in textiles, clothing and agricultural products. Reduced barriers to trade in services are unlikely to have much effect on eastern exports for some time, since eastern financial infrastructures are still very underdeveloped. Some activities, such as computer software services might develop quite quickly in some countries but others, especially tourism, will first require large fixed investments and the development of auxiliary services.[71]

Eastern export performance may also be enhanced by foreign direct investment and other forms of co-operation with western companies. In this context one alleged failing of eastern exports, their technological backwardness, should be treated with some reserve. As shown elsewhere in this *Survey*, most of the trade in engineering goods of most west European countries consists of products of medium levels of technology intensity. The key point is not the level of technology *per se*, but correct pricing and the quality of the product and of its marketing. It should be remembered that there are thriving world markets for goods at all levels of technological intensity: the principle of comparative advantage suggests that the successful exporting country will be the one that selects the technologies most appropriate to its endowments of natural resources, capital and human skills.

However, the creation of internationally competitive enterprises is a slow process, and the eastern countries will have to do this at a time when the competitive pressures in western Europe will be increasing as the detailed programme for 1992 is put into place. Moreover, the process is complicated by the need for such a large number of interrelated reforms in the economic systems in which eastern enterprises currently operate. As noted above, the CMEA has not led to a high degree of specialization among its member countries and has failed to meet many of its original objectives and to provide a stimulus to sustained growth in its member countries. Relations among the CMEA members are strained at present because of problems in clearing trade among themselves which, in part, are due to increasing divergencies in the pace and extent of the various programmes of reform. Some of the east European members appear to be turning away from the CMEA altogether. Nevertheless, it is worth considering whether some reform of intra-CMEA economic relations is possible in order to provide an intermediate but temporary stage between the rigid bilateralism of the present CMEA and full integration in a world economy of multilateralism and free trade. Again, some lessons can be drawn from the post-war reconstruction of western Europe — this time from the European Payments Union which was established with the help of Marshall aid.

After the war, trade among the west European countries was severely hampered by inconvertible currencies and a network of bilateral agreements. To conserve hard currency each country applied a range of quotas and other direct controls on trade. Since the liberalization of trade required a reform of the payments system, after two earlier schemes, the European Payments Union was set up in 1950. Within the union, bilateral surpluses were offset by bilateral deficits and only net positions came up for settlement with the central clearing authority (which was backed by Marshall aid funds). The scheme minimized members' payments in gold and convertible currency (the dollar) and effectively made all member currencies mutually convertible within the Union. This, as well as the provision of automatic credit facilities up to certain limits, helped to encourage the removal of quantitative

---

[70] See *Financial Times*, 17 February 1990.

[71] See United Nations Economic Commission for Europe, "A note on recent developments in east-west trade in services", *Economic Bulletin for Europe*, vol.41, New York 1989. The number of hotel rooms in the whole of eastern Europe and the Soviet Union in 1987 was only slightly higher than the total for Austria (*ibid*, p.65).

restrictions on trade between the members of the Union. (In fact, trade liberalization was an indispensable corollary to the multilateralization of payments, because there is no point in freeing payments without also freeing transactions.) As a result of EPU, competition and trade were stimulated among the west European countries and the allocation of resources was more closely adapted to the underlying patterns of comparative advantage. By 1958, most of the countries of western Europe had re-established convertibility in the sense of Article VIII of the IMF. During the transition period, the union gave some protection to members against dollar imports and encouraged the reconstruction of enterprises capable of producing substitutes for dollar imports. Considerable and rapid progress was made in liberalizing intra-European trade and the momentum of this process continued in the 1960s with European integration and the global rounds of tariff reduction under the GATT.

Could an arrangement similar to EPU perform a similar role for the reforming countries in the east? This question is discussed in some detail in chapter 3 below (section 3.4), where it is concluded that the creation of a Central European Payments Union (CEPU) is worth serious consideration as an intermediate stage in the transition towards a fully multilateral system of trade and payments. Such a scheme would require western assistance, but the sums involved do not appear to be very large and they would be provided in a way which would minimize interference in the emerging structure of market-based incentives in the reforming countries.

In suggesting such an institution two considerations are thought to be especially relevant. First, even if the existing members of the CMEA wished to switch all or most of their present CMEA trade to western partners, they could only do so at a very great cost since their existing stocks of physical and human capital would have to be radically transformed or written off before they could meet the demands of western markets. If such a reorientation of trade was extended over time, there would still be a need for large volumes of intra-CMEA trade in order to maintain the remaining capital stocks — mainly of eastern origin — in working order. Second, reforming the present system of intra-CMEA trade relations is a much greater task than simply removing obstacles to trade: what is required is fundamental reform in the micro-foundations of that trade, so that its level, product composition and market structure is changed in line with comparative advantages based on efficient market prices. To obtain the latter it is necessary to have convertible currencies. To achieve all this in circumstances of foreign exchange shortage is a considerable task. Convertibility could be introduced suddenly — the "big bang" approach — but this would appear to assume that the various structural adjustments would occur quickly, that the "supply responses" would be large and rapid. Most eastern countries appear to be sceptical as to the possibility of such rapid responses and are clearly in favour of more gradual adjustment. A CEPU would meet the demands for gradualism while at the same time providing a central authority with the means to ensure that gradualism was not pursued to the point of undermining progress towards the ultimate objective of full convertibility.

Membership of a CEPU might at first be attractive only to the radical reformers of eastern Europe — Hungary, Poland, Czechoslovakia — but other countries could easily join when they felt that their market-oriented reforms needed extra support. One complication arises from present CMEA relations with the German Democratic Republic: these economic links are strong and CMEA trade with the German Democratic Republic could not be placed on a convertible currency basis at short notice after unification of the two Germanies. It would therefore be important to find ways of including these trade links within the payments union even if they become incorporated in the trade of a united Germany. The precise modalities of a CEPU would have to be explored in much greater detail by specialized working groups: the aim of the present discussion (see chapter 3) is to argue that the suggestion should not be dismissed out of hand. A CEPU offers the possibility of gradual but disciplined adjustment in the trade and payments systems of the reforming countries and, as such, could make a significant contribution to the success of the various programmes of reform.

(viii) The pace of reform in the eastern countries

An underlying theme of the previous sections is that the transformation of centrally planned economies into decentralized market economies is a much more difficult task than the reconversion of the west-European economies from wartime controls. The basic structures of the market economy have to be largely created in the east, whereas in the west they were never completely abandoned or destroyed during the period of wartime planning. Nevertheless, the process of post-war adjustment in western Europe was for the most part a gradual one as governments sought to avoid creating inflationary shocks in the economy. The strategy was to retain various direct controls, mainly on consumer demand, until rising supply made them redundant: as can be seen in chart 1.2.2, the phasing-out period in the United Kingdom, for example, stretched into the late 1950s, although the process was fairly rapid once it got under way and for the most part was well advanced by the early 1950s. In contrast, and in very different circumstances, the monetary reform in the Federal Republic of Germany in 1948 was a carefully prepared "shock" reform which had rapid and positive effects on domestic output. But, again, it must be emphasized that the Federal Republic of Germany in 1948 still had the basic structures and traditions of a market economy, as well as a large capital stock which had been very much less damaged by the war than had been previously thought. Domestic supply was therefore highly responsive to the reform. Nevertheless, the return to a market economy in the Federal Republic of Germany was not as abrupt as is sometimes claimed: after the currency reform, price controls and rationing persisted for a wide range of basic foodstuffs and raw materials; price controls were maintained on important consumer goods such as textiles and shoes and in addi-

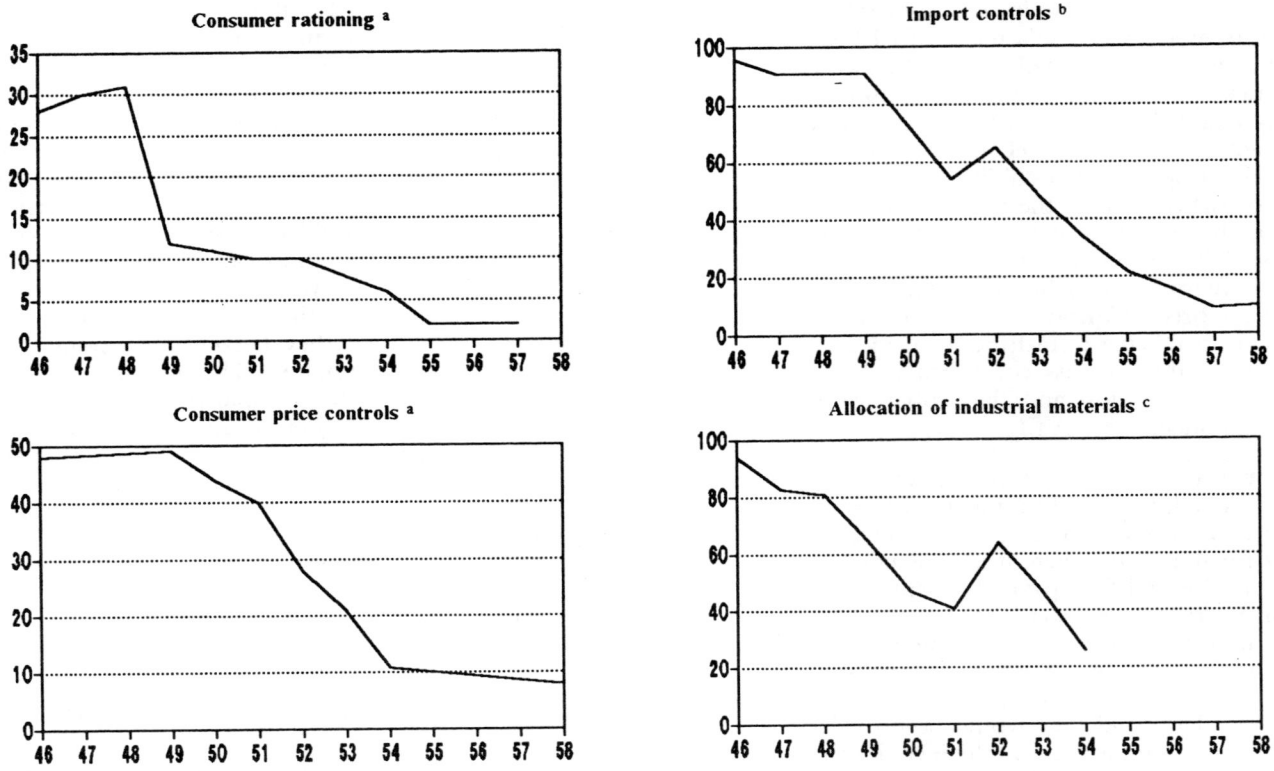

CHART 1.2.2

The phasing out of direct controls in post-war Britain, 1946-1958
(Per cent)

Source: Based on data in J.C.R. Dow, *The Management of the British Economy 1945-60*, Cambridge University Press, 1965, tables 6.3-6.6.

  a Expenditure on controlled items as a proportion of total consumers expenditure. (Coal rationing continued until 1958.)
  b Controlled imports (government imports *plus* restricted private imports) as a proportion of total imports, each category weighted by the value of imports in 1955.
  c Materials distributed under government allocation schemes as a proportion of total "industrial inputs" of materials. Coal rationing continued until 1958; apart from this, allocation schemes were not important after 1954.

tion the authorities continued to control imports. All these controls were eventually phased out as a series of other measures (tax reforms, etc.) were introduced. Altogether the return to the market economy was gradual and carefully planned.[72]

Efficient markets do not simply spring to life on the retreat of central planners and bureaucratic controls: they require a complex infrastructure of law, financial systems, as well as certain habits of economic behaviour (as regards competition, risk-taking, financial probity, etc.). Markets also require a certain size distribution of enterprises, a degree of openness to the world economy, and a measure of supervisory regulation if they are to be competitive and to encourage innovation and economic adaptability. It is because so many of these features are missing or underdeveloped, albeit in varying degrees between individual countries, that doubt is cast on the ability of the eastern countries to absorb large amounts of financial assistance at the present time. Hence, the emphasis on programmes of technical assistance. However, this emphasis is not meant to imply that there is no place at all for financial assistance. On the contrary: one area where financial assistance could play a strategic role in raising the efficiency of markets is transport and telecommunications. The importance of the latter has already been mentioned, but communications in general have a vital role to play in the functioning of markets. Poor communications in the eastern countries are frequently cited by western businessmen as one of the major obstacles to conducting business in the east. Financial assistance to improve the communications infrastructure would not only support the development of efficient domestic markets but would also increase the scope for productivity gains via the classical route of an effective increase in the extent of the market.

Since changes in economic structure and behaviour occur only with a certain delay, it follows that the arguments presented point to a more evolutionary approach to the reform process than the rapid, shock treatment suggested by some observers. Those who advocate a rapid rate of reform would appear to be

---

[72] See Hans Möller, "Die deutsche Währungsreform von 1948", in Deutsche Bundesbank, *Währung und Wirtschaft in Deutschland 1876-1975*, Frankfurt-am-Main, 1976 pp.433-483, and Rudolf Stucken, *Deutsche Geld- und Kreditpolitik 1914-1963*, 3rd edition, Tübingen, 1964, p.209.

fairly optimistic about the speed with which competitive markets can be established. They might be right in their assumptions, in which case there would be little need for any sort of "Marshall Plan". The "evolutionists", however, not only see the establishment of competitive markets as a difficult process requiring time and careful intervention by governments, but they are also concerned at the consequences of the market "optimists" being proved wrong. The expectations of the population are always raised by the possibilities of reforms and to add to this the prospect of rapid fulfilment is to risk an explosive social situation if the optimism proves ill-founded.

The argument over whether reform should be rapid or gradual is sometimes obscured by the mixing up of macro- and micro-economic considerations and of long-run structural changes with macro-economic stabilization issues. All the reforming countries need to implement sound macro-economic policies, based on monetary and fiscal instruments, since macro-economic instability is likely to be a major reason for micro-economic reforms being reversed or rendered ineffective (this has been a common experience in some developing countries). Those eastern countries with very high rates of inflation or pent-up imbalances and large external deficits must clearly move quickly in order to contain and correct these disequilibria, but that is a different matter from implementing a programme of rapid structural reform.[73] The latter may be desirable, but the reality is that macro-economic stabilization in some of the eastern countries is likely to be complicated by obdurate supply-side problems for some years to come. In this situation western assistance efforts could be especially helpful in allowing these countries to concentrate on their structural problems — in some countries by easing pressures on the balance of payments and reducing the problems of high levels of inherited foreign debt. "Marshall aid" type assistance could be especially important here.

The argument that the legal and financial infrastructures of the market economy must be put in place *before* markets can perform as expected suggests that the *order* in which reforms are introduced may be more important than the pace of reform. Encouraging large inflows of foreign investment, for example, while there are still considerable distortions in domestic markets may lead to serious misallocation of investment, as well as to upward pressure on the real exchange rate when the opposite might be appropriate. (This point recalls the more familiar discussion of whether a developing country should liberalize the capital account of the balance of payments before the trade account, or vice versa.)

One of the most important determinants of success in reforms is whether the government is able to create and maintain credibility in its programme. Economic reforms and liberalization measures usually generate political resistance because the immediate costs of the changes are usually seen more clearly by the population than the long-run benefits. This is even more so when reforms are extensive and interrelated. It is particularly true for the east European countries where the latest reforms are moving into the *terra incognita* of transition from one economic and social system to another. There is also at present a great deal of mistrust and suspicion on the part of the population towards the authorities which will have to be overcome — in some countries this may be easier to do after the elections which are due to take place later this year. Credibility, however, is not simply a question of providing information about the ultimate benefits, but of presenting a coherent programme of reforms. Coherent here means a credible *sequence* of reforms in the sense that the implementation of A before B increases the probability of success for both A and B, whereas the opposite sequence may raise expectations that either or both will fail or be reversed. If economic agents expect a reversal of policy they will act accordingly and undermine the policy before the government has time for second thoughts.

Although the incorporation of expectations and credibility effects into the analysis of policy questions has been an important development in the market economy countries in recent years, there is no simple or universal formula which will show governments how to secure credibility for their programmes. In the end, the structure of an agenda for reforms will have to be determined on the basis of pragmatic or *ad hoc* considerations. But it needs to be recognized that the question of credibility and its relation to the sequence of reforms may be one of the most important factors determining whether or not a process of radical structural reform can be sustained. The various processes of reform in the eastern countries therefore need to be coherent in this particular sense and any programme of western assistance, to be effective, should be structured to reinforce that coherence. The preparation of such coherent programmes is perhaps another area where technical assistance from western macro-economists, especially those who also have knowledge of the eastern systems, could make a useful contribution.

Once a reform programme gains credibility — and it must be admitted that this requires not just economic but political skill of a high order — the question of gradualist versus shock or "big bang" approaches becomes secondary. In practice, given the range and scale of the structural problems faced by the eastern countries, progress is likely — but not certain — to be difficult and gradual. But that may not matter very much so long as there is progress and so long as it does not diverge too much from the rising expectations of the population.

(ix) Summary and conclusions

The tasks facing the eastern reformers are enormous. To transform their economies into efficient market economies they must embark on a programme

---

[73] Structural reform in countries with high rates of inflation will anyway tend to be difficult because investment propensities tend to weaken in the face of the associated increase in relative price uncertainty.

of institutional changes on a very broad front. These changes, *inter alia,* include: reforms of the price setting mechanism and of the tax system, the introduction of a two-tier banking system and the setting up of capital markets, the introduction of private property rights, the construction of social security systems (which should provide a safety net for those who lose their present jobs in the restructuring process), and a radical transformation of the mechanisms for conducting foreign trade. Plans must also be made for moving towards currency convertibility and more realistic exchange rates. All this must be started in most countries against a background of severe, short-run stabilization problems, the solutions to which are likely to make heavy demands on the population. The extent to which these demands will be accepted without breaking the social consensus will depend in part on the degree to which there is confidence and credibility in the longer-run programme for radical structural reform.

This chapter has suggested the basic outlines of how the western market economies might support the various programmes of reform in the eastern economies. Although it is not complete and many elements need to be examined in much greater detail, it has tried to identify some of the main priorities and to provide a framework for assessing and monitoring both the eastern reform process and western programmes to support it. The discussion has been focused on general principles and has deliberately avoided consideration of the detailed circumstances of individual countries: these vary considerably, as does the scope of the various reform programmes and the extent to which they have been implemented. In Hungary, for example, some of the building blocks of a fully-fledged market economy are already in place, but elsewhere progress is less advanced.[74] In Poland, the legitimacy conveyed by the 1989 parliamentary election has enabled the Solidarity-led government to impose the sacrifices of a consistent and very tough stabilization policy which elsewhere is still beyond the reach of governments.

Similarly, western support for the eastern reform process is also under way principally, but not exclusively, under the auspices of the Group of 24. So far, most of the financial support is debt-creating, although the G-24 programme clearly recognizes the need for technical assistance. However, the scale of the latter is modest. Current support programmes also include funds for environmental purposes, but so far the amounts involved are small in relation to the scale of the problems.[75]

The "basic" reform programme which is implicit in the discussion is one which explicitly aims to replace bureaucratic central planning with a decentralized market economy, where the central authorities are responsible for stabilization and co-ordination using macro-economic policies, and ultimate economic sovereignty is transferred from planners to consumers. Intermediate stages between the two systems are not considered: these are more difficult to specify and, at present, are unlikely to qualify for western assistance.

Because it is frequently suggested that the Marshall Plan provides an appropriate model for large-scale assistance to the east, section (iii) above looked at the problems of post-war reconstruction and adjustment in western Europe and the contribution made by Marshall aid. The conclusion drawn is that although there are a number of similarities between the problems faced by the west then and the east now, the differences in basic economic structures are so large that a simple repetition of the Marshall Plan would not be appropriate in present circumstances. Nevertheless, the Marshall Plan experience does provide a number of valuable lessons which could be put to good use.

Marshall aid consisted for the most part of grant aid with a relatively small proportion of technical assistance. Given the nature of the structural problems in the eastern countries, it is suggested that these proportions need to be reversed in any assistance programme for the east. In other words, the Marshall Plan should be turned on its head, especially in the short run. This does not mean that there is no case for financial aid, only that the possibilities for its effective absorption are at present limited by the lack of many complementary factors, not the least of which is an institutional infrastructure appropriate to a market economy. Effective technical assistance will increase the eastern capacity to absorb new capital funds and technology, although the more successful the assistance the less will be the need for *grant* aid and the greater the attraction for private capital. Nevertheless, there is still a need for financial assistance in the immediate future, and especially for grant aid which would avoid any addition to existing debt levels. It is suggested that the priority objectives for such financial aid should be:

— radical improvement of transport and telecommunications systems;

— the rapid reduction of environmental pollution.

Financial assistance may also play a useful role in breaking other well-defined bottlenecks, particularly when their removal will support or speed up the process of establishing efficient markets. However, it is essential that any financial assistance should avoid the mistakes of the 1970s when western banks stepped up their lending with apparently little appreciation of the micro-economic distortions and inefficiencies imbedded in the eastern economies. Foreign direct investment may play a role in the transformation process but this is likely to be limited until a number of reforms are implemented and the eastern countries can produce an internationally competitive rate of return. Anyway, as suggested in section (viii), inflows of foreign investment could lead to serious misallocation problems if domestic market distortions are still prevalent.

---

[74] Details of the various programmes will be found below in section 3.5.

[75] For a more detailed discussion of western support programmes, and of recent developments in trade policies, see chapter 4 below.

There is also a need for currency stabilization loans (already agreed by the G-24 for Poland) and for balance-of-payments support. In particular it is necessary to ensure that progress in the reform process is not checked or swallowed up by the burdens on some countries of servicing their foreign debt.

The recent Paris Club rescheduling of Poland's official debt, together with the postponement of interest payments in 1990, will save some $5 billion in scheduled hard-currency payments this year. This sum, which dwarfs the current assistance of the G-24, obviously relieves Poland of a major obligation in the early stages of a very tough stabilization programme. However, the relief is only temporary and it seems probable that ways will have to be found to provide more permanent relief through debt reduction either within the framework of the 1989 Brady Plan or through some other arrangement. Debt reduction is a sensitive topic among western officials and bankers, largely because of the demonstrative effect it might have on other borrowers in other parts of the world — but it may be essential in order to maintain the momentum of reform in countries such as Poland, Hungary and, eventually, Bulgaria. If the initial gains from tough stabilization measures and restructuring were to go into servicing foreign debt rather than domestic investment and the personal consumption of the long-suffering working class in countries such as Poland, the social consensus for reform could be seriously threatened. The question of debt relief has not been treated in any detail in this chapter because it is widely discussed elsewhere; nevertheless, it should be considered as the third key element in the framework suggested here.

One proposal made in section (vii) would also require financial assistance, namely:

— the creation of a Central European Payments Union to facilitate the eastern countries' transition to a system of free trade and multilateral settlements.

This suggestion, which is discussed in more detail in section 3.4 below, is inspired by the successful experience of the west European countries in the European Payments Union, which was set up with the help of Marshall aid.

The constituents of any technical assistance programme will depend on the particular circumstances of each recipient country, but it is suggested that a number of elements should be given priority since they will play an important role in creating credibility in the reform programmes and calibrating the expectations of economic agents with a realistic pace of structural reform (see section (viii)). The suggested priorities for technical assistance are:

— the creation of the legal, financial and institutional framework essential for the operation of a competitive market system (section (v));

— the provision of comprehensive and reliable statistical and economic information services for both government and enterprises in their new decision-making roles in a decentralized market economy (section (vi));

— the development of the various marketing skills required for boosting exports to world markets (section (vii)).

Improvements in eastern competitiveness should not be frustrated by import barriers abroad and, indeed, changes in commercial policy, both by western importers and by the eastern countries themselves, could help to encourage and maintain such improvements. The steps which might usefully be taken are, by the western countries:

— the elimination of all quotas and other quantitative restrictions on imports from reforming eastern countries according to a precise timetable (section (vii));

— a closer monitoring of the effects of western COCOM controls on the eastern economies and a more rapid review process whenever constraints on the eastern reforms process are identified (section (vii));

and by the eastern countries:

— a conversion of the present administrative controls on eastern imports into the more transparent devices of tariffs and quotas and the drawing up of a timetable for their gradual elimination (section (vii)).

In developing a programme of assistance to the eastern countries, a number of other features of the Marshall aid experience might be followed. Among these are:

— the needs for assistance should be identified by the recipient countries themselves;

— recipient countries should produce coherent programmes showing how they intend to reach their structural adjustment objectives;

— adjustment programmes should be specified and assistance committed over a reasonable period of time: Marshall aid was originally committed for an estimated four-year period of adjustment, but the time required for current eastern programmes could be much longer;

— the needs of the various recipients should be co-ordinated by a technically qualified international institution, which could help to identify and clarify those needs as well as monitoring progress and providing a forum for exchanging ideas and knowledge of the various national programmes.

The existing institutional framework for international assistance programmes is now very different from that which existed at the time of the Marshall Plan. In 1948 there was one donor, sixteen European recipients and one newly-created international, co-ordinating institution. Today there are at least twenty four potential donors, six or seven potential recipients, and at least seven major international institutions already involved in various forms of international aid and co-operation. The present structure has a number of advantages for the eastern countries, especially insofar as an extensive international framework for technical assistance already exists and the considerable experience accumulated since the war can be utilized. Nevertheless, the problems of co-ordination, both of assistance itself and the monitoring of progress, are much greater, especially as there is only one international economic institution which currently includes all the eastern countries and the western market economies in its membership. Although particular sub-programmes may be efficiently co-ordinated by institutions with less comprehensive membership, it may be valuable to use a more broadly based institution for overall review and co-ordination, perhaps within the framework of the Conference on Security and Co-operation in Europe (CSCE).

The need for close monitoring and review of both the eastern reform process and the effectiveness of western programmes of support is especially important given the uncertainties surrounding the entire venture. As mentioned earlier, the transformation of a centrally planned into a market economy is a journey into largely unknown territory. Past experience, such as post-war adjustment in western Europe, or even the earlier attempts at reform in the east, provides some lessons and many warnings, but little in the way of precise guidance as to the best path to follow. In such circumstances, policy makers, both in the east and the west, will need to be willing and able to make frequent and speedy policy adjustments in the light of experience. To be able to do this, close and accurate monitoring of developments is essential. Similarly, the suggestions made here as to the relative importance of technical and financial assistance were made in the light of certain fundamental characteristics of markets on the one hand, and an assessment of the structural problems of the eastern economies on the other. But there is no dogma in this: the relative importance of the two types of assistance should also be subject to revision in the light of experience and the circumstances of individual countries.

Finally, it is worth remembering that although the eastern countries have embarked on a difficult and, probably, long process of reform and adjustment, the international economy is now much stronger than when the Marshall aid programme was introduced (indeed, one of the objectives of that programme was to strengthen the working of the global economy itself). After recovering from the various shocks of the 1970s, growth in the market economies has been sustained at relatively high rates throughout the 1980s. In western Europe, supported by expectations about the benefits of "1992", the underlying trend appears set to continue, perhaps even more strongly, in the 1990s. Against such a background of sustained growth in the world economy, not only should the burden of assistance programmes prove to be relatively light, but so should the adjustment costs of dismantling protectionist barriers against imports into the market economies. At the same time, a buoyant world economy provides the eastern economies with an opportunity to develop outward-oriented policies and thereby underpin the process of their transformation into competitive market economies.

Chapter 2

WESTERN EUROPE AND NORTH AMERICA

2.1 AN OVERVIEW OF 1989 AND THE OUTLOOK FOR 1990

This section provides a brief summary of the main economic developments in 1989 which are discussed in greater detail in sections 2.2 and 2.3. After a discussion of the macro-economic outlook for 1990 there is a review of some of the possible effects of a German monetary union and, more generally, of the impact of the eastern reform process on the rest of the world.

(i) Expansion continues in 1989

The long upswing of the 1980s continued in 1989, although at a slightly less rapid pace than in 1987 and 1988. In western Europe, real GDP rose on average by 3.3 per cent, compared with 3.6 per cent in 1988. For 1989 as a whole, GNP in the United States grew by about 3 per cent (4.4 per cent in 1988), although in the last quarter of the year the seasonally adjusted annual growth rate had fallen to 0.9 per cent. In western Europe the slow-down was quite sharp in the United Kingdom (even when allowance is made for interruptions to oil production), but in the other three major economies the deceleration was quite small. (In the Federal Republic of Germany real GNP, i.e., including net factor incomes from abroad, increased by 4.1 per cent in 1989, more than GDP (3.6 per cent) and more than GNP in 1988.) In the smaller west European economies, GDP growth, on average, accelerated in 1989, especially in Ireland, the Netherlands and Norway. In southern Europe there was a sharp slow-down in Greece and Turkey, but domestic output growth remained buoyant in Spain and Portugal. In Yugoslavia, after two years of severe recession, there was a small increase in gross social product.

Although estimates of capacity output are uncertain, it seems likely that the growth of actual output has been exceeding the expansion in potential output since the second half of 1987. Fears were already being expressed in early 1988 that capacity limits were being approached in some countries and when inflation rates began to accelerate there was a rapid response from the monetary authorities. Monetary policy was tightened in early 1988 in the United States and the United Kingdom, the two countries which were ahead of the other market economies in terms of the output cycle, and somewhat later in the year in the other main European economies. Short-term interest rates in the United States rose progressively from under 7 per cent in the first quarter of 1988 to 9.6 per cent in the second quarter of 1989, after which there was some decline in response to a moderate easing in monetary policy. In western Europe, short-term interest rates rose more steeply than in the United States and there was no reversal in the second half of 1989 (nor in the first quarter of 1990). In Japan the rise in interest rates in 1988 was quite small, but there was a sharp increase through the second half of 1989 in response to rising inflation. Fiscal policy, in general, continued to have little impact on short-run activity in the market economies.

The tightening of monetary policy has helped to slow the pace of domestic output growth in the United States, with private consumption and business investment actually falling in the last quarter of 1989. GDP growth has also fallen sharply in the United Kingdom, although one of the notable features of developments in 1989 has been the slow response of consumer spending to high interest rates. In the other west European countries activity was still relatively buoyant at the end of 1989. In the Federal Republic of Germany GNP in the fourth quarter was 1 per cent higher than in the previous quarter and 4 per cent higher than a year earlier. This sustained rate of growth in the Federal Republic was still based on fixed investment and exports, although the latter appear to have slowed down from the first half of the year, but, in contrast with the earlier quarters, private consumption growth accelerated. This appears to have been due in part to the large inflow of immigrants in the last quarter of 1989[76] and the associated increase in spending; but an-

---

[76] Altogether 720,900 immigrants arrived in the Federal Republic in 1989, an addition of 1.2 per cent to the total population. Of these, some 343,900 were from the German Democratic Republic and two thirds of them arrived in the last quarter. The others came from other eastern countries and were spread more evenly over the year.

TABLE 2.1.1

Selected statistical indicators for the Federal Republic of Germany and the German Democratic Republic in 1989

			Germany, Federal Republic of	German Democratic Republic
I.	Population [a]	Million	62.5*	16.4
	Employment	Million	23.2	8.5*
II.	Private households			
	1. Disposable income [b]	Billion DM/Mark	1 404.1	167.5
	2. Savings	Billion DM/Mark	190.4	9.3 [c]
	3. Savings ratio [d]	Per cent	13.6	5.6
	4. Financial assets [a,e]	Billion DM/Mark	2 685 *	195 *
	of which:			
	Very liquid assets	Billion DM/Mark	820 [f]	177.0 [g]
	Savings deposits	Billion DM/Mark	693.6 [h]	160.5
	5. Per caput monthly disposable income	DM/Mark	1 872	850
	6. Very liquid assets per capita		13 120	10 793
	7. Ratio: very liquid assets/disposable income		0.58	1.06
III.	Money supply			
	1. Currency in circulation	Billion DM/Mark	146.9 [i]	16.5
	2. Currency in circulation, per capita	DM/Mark	2 350	1 006
	3. Currency in circulation/disposable income		0.10	0.10
	4. M1 [a]	Billion DM/Mark	450.6	..
	M2 [a]	Billion DM/Mark	776.4	177.0 [g]
	M3 [a]	Billion DM/Mark	1 255.4	..

Sources: ECE, Division of Economic Analysis and Projections based on national statistics and ECE secretariat estimates.

a End of year.
b For the German Democratic Republic net money incomes of the population.
c Changes in savings deposits and changes in money in circulation.
d Savings as a per cent of disposable incomes – see also b above.
e Federal Republic of Germany: money in circulation, deposits in banks and insurance companies, securities. German Democratic Republic: money in circulation plus savings deposits.
f Money in circulation, sight deposits, time deposits below 3 months, savings deposits with statutory notice.
g Money in circulation plus saving deposits.
h Including non-profit organizations.
i Excluding banks cash balance.

ticipation of the tax cuts, scheduled for 1 January 1990 and which give a significant boost to net income growth, may have also been a factor.

The slow-down in 1989 was generally less than expected in western Europe at the start of the year, the main reasons for this being the continued strength of fixed investment and an acceleration, rather than the expected slow-down, in international trade. Fixed investment rose by more than 6 per cent in 1989, after increases of 7.5 per cent and 4¼ per cent in 1988 and 1987. Business investment in machinery and equipment increased by some 8½ per cent in 1989, only slightly less than in 1988. In the United States total investment decelerated much more sharply, but investment in machinery and equipment still rose by more than 6 per cent.

The strength of fixed investment has been a major feature of the current upswing and in western Europe it has been the strongest component in the growth of domestic demand for the last two years. Although the high rates of capacity utilization in western Europe provide some stimulus to investment in new capacities, the strength of investment activity appears to be based on broader features of the economic environment in the 1980s. The general success in controlling inflation and lowering inflationary expectations was crucial in this regard. Continued wage moderation, widespread deregulation, and lower burdens of taxation have all contributed to raising profit shares in national income and raising the rates of return on fixed capital. To some extent the investment boom of the mid and late 1980s has been making up for the "lost" investment of the 1970s and the recession of 1980-1982. But the propensity to invest is also widely believed to have increased as a result of the planned completion of the internal market of the European Community by the end of 1992. This has encouraged investment from both within the Community and from outside as enterprises take steps to meet the increase in competition expected from the removal of national barriers to intra-regional business. More generally, there is much greater confidence in the ability of governments to maintain a favourable environment for growth and business activity.

That confidence was probably reinforced by the prompt tightening of monetary policy in 1988 and 1989 in response to rising inflationary expectations. Inflation rates did increase in 1989: in western Europe from an average 3.1 per cent in 1988 to 4.5 per cent, and in the United States from 4.1 per cent to 4.8 per cent. However, most of the acceleration was in the first half of the year; in the second half rates stabilized in western Europe and fell slightly in North America. Much of the rise in consumer prices in 1989 was due to indirect taxes, in the Federal Republic of Germany for example, and higher interest rates, which in the United Kingdom added nearly two percentage points to the rise in consumer prices. Underlying rates of inflation – consumer prices excluding food and energy – did not in fact rise very much in western Europe. On average the increase in the GDP deflator accelerated from 3.7 per cent in 1988 to 4.1 per cent in 1989, much less than the acceleration in consumer prices and in the domestic demand deflator (which includes the impact of higher import prices).

In North America, however, the GDP deflator accelerated more strongly (from 3.4 per cent to 4.2 per cent) than the domestic demand deflator reflecting the effect of the appreciation of the dollar on the latter. Thus, while the main reason for the acceleration of inflation (as measured by the domestic demand deflator) in western Europe in 1989 was the increase in import prices, in North America this was mainly due to unit labour costs which rose much faster than in 1988.[77] In general, monetary policy appears to have been successful in checking inflationary expectations: long-term interest rates were falling in the United States through 1989 and, although they rose in western Europe, the gap between long- and short-term interest rates has narrowed in the wake of tighter monetary policies. The general expectation, which is reflected in most of the short-term forecasts for 1990, is that inflation will not reach very high levels and in most of the major economies will start decelerating from around mid-year. The main exceptions to this are Japan, where inflation could accelerate through 1990 as a result of the recent depreciation of the yen, and the United States where, although inflation is unlikely to increase, it seems likely to remain at around 4-4½ per cent.

The recovery in the labour markets continued in both western Europe and North America in 1989. Employment growth was 1.1 per cent in western Europe and 2.2 per cent in North America. Also, unemployment rates fell in both regions, although they still remain high in Canada and in many west European countries. Labour supply pressure weakened considerably in western Europe but increased in North America. Despite falling unemployment rates, tighter labour markets and further increases in profits, wage inflation in the majority of countries was again more moderate than expected. Furthermore, thanks to surprisingly large gains in productivity (particularly in western Europe), the rise in unit labour costs was less than the forecast in the majority of countries.

The foreign trade of the market economies continued to expand strongly in 1989 as a result of the sustained growth in output. West European export volumes rose over 7 per cent (national accounts basis), mainly due to intra-European trade although exports to eastern Europe and the Soviet Union, Japan and the developing countries also increased. Although the expansion of United States' exports slowed down considerably from 1988, growth of some 11 per cent in volume made a significant contribution to sustaining the levels of world trade. The investment boom in the market economies led to a rapid expansion of international trade in machinery and equipment in 1989.

Rapid import growth accompanied the growth of output in most European economies, so the net stimulus to output tended to be negative except in the Federal Republic of Germany and in the United States.

Although the trade figures have been exceptionally volatile in 1989, especially in the United States, some progress was made in reducing the large current account imbalances among the major market economies. The United States deficit and the Japanese surplus both decreased, while the large surplus of the Federal Republic of Germany is largely offset by the deficits of its west European partners. The Federal Republic's trade surplus peaked in August and declined thereafter. Strong import growth in the closing months of 1989 and in early 1990 may also reflect the increased expenditure of visitors and immigrants from the east. However, the adjustment of global imbalances tended to slow down during the year as the effects of earlier dollar depreciation and yen appreciation began to wear out. The dollar was appreciating until mid-year, the effect of the relatively tighter monetary policy in the United States for most of 1988 and the first half of 1989, while the weakness of the yen in 1989 has raised fears of the trade surplus increasing again and provoking a fresh wave of protectionism in other market economies. Since the last quarter of 1989, the Deutschmark has strengthened and this at least will support the process of adjusting global imbalances. Nevertheless, continuing uncertainty about exchange rates and current account adjustments seem likely to persist in 1990.

(ii) The outlook for 1990

The outlook for the market economies in 1990 is still quite favourable despite the effects of tight monetary policies. In contrast to all other output expansions in post-war history, inflation in the current upswing has remained moderate. Unless particular external external shocks occur during the course of 1990, most national and international forecasters expect a gradual slowdown in demand combined with the modest increase in unit labour costs which may be largely absorbed by profit margins as in 1989. However, current official forecasts indicate only a slight fall in inflation rates of 1990 — on average, the rise in the west European GDP deflator is expected to fall from 4.1 per cent in 1989 to 3.7 per cent in 1990. The monetary authorities, especially in western Europe, are therefore likely to remain cautious and avoid any early reduction in interest rates. This is particularly true for the Federal Republic of Germany where the January tax cuts and developments in the east have raised fears of a *short-run* increase of inflationary pressure. Inflationary pressures may be eased by falling non-oil commodity prices and by relatively stable oil prices, although the net impact on domestic inflation will depend on changes in the exchange rate between the dollar and European currencies.

With capacity utilization rates at their highest levels for many years, and with signs of overheating in a number of countries, especially in the markets for skilled labour there could be increased pressure on

---

[77] See below, section 2.3(i).

prices from labour costs in 1990. Recent outbursts of labour militancy suggest that continued wage moderation is not assured, especially given the increased inflation of last year and the continued buoyancy of profits. However, productivity gains may still be large enough to offset a large proportion of the increase in wages.

Output growth in the market economies is expected to slow down in 1990 although, apart from the United Kingdom and some of the smaller European countries, the deceleration is not very great. Current forecasts by governments point to GDP growth in western Europe of some 2.7 per cent compared with 3.3 per cent in 1989. Gross domestic fixed capital formation will again be the main support for growth, rising by a little over 4 per cent, somewhat less than the roughly 6½ per cent in 1988. However, business investment in manufacturing industry expected to remain strong and rise by the same amount as last year.

Forecasts made at the end of 1989 for the Federal Republic were pointing to broadly the same growth rate of real GDP as in 1989 (some 3 to 3.5 per cent). This conceals, however, an important shift in the underlying sources of growth, with domestic demand taking over as the main driving force. After a weak performance in 1989 there will be a strong recovery of private consumption due to the reduction of income taxes at the beginning of 1990, which − in the aggregate − will lower the tax burden on wage and salary earners by some DM 22 billion. Further strong support comes from the inflow of immigrants, which are to add some 0.5 to 0.75 percentage points to private consumption growth. Investment in housing will also remain strong, with demand supported by government subsidy schemes adopted in autumn 1989. Export growth should decelerate, a reflection of the general slow-down in world trade and the recent appreciation of the Deutschmark.

With the sources of growth shifting primarily to domestic demand, economic activity in the Federal Republic in 1990 should give a strong boost to imports, while exports will be increasingly constrained by capacity. Such a development will mainly benefit the exports of other west European countries and reduce their trade deficits with the Federal Republic.

The outlook for the United States is somewhat more uncertain. The underlying rate of growth is now under 2 per cent and given that involuntary stockbuilding was the main support to domestic demand in the last quarter there could be a further slow-down in the first half of 1990. Private consumption is likely to weaken further, but lower interest rates could check the decline in private housebuilding and moderate the slow-down in business investment. Also, the appreciation of the dollar in 1988 and early 1989 will weaken export prospects and strengthen import growth in 1990, although these effects will eventually be offset by the recent decline in the dollar. Although private forecasts[78] are suggesting growth of less than 2 per cent in 1990, it is possible that it could remain above that if de-stocking is not too large and if there is a further depreciation of the dollar.

Given the expected slow-down in output growth, the increase in employment is likely to be smaller in 1990 than last year. However, as the working age population will continue its long-term downward trend in western Europe and since participation rates usually adjust more slowly than the demand for labour to changes in output, unemployment rates may stabilize at their present levels or even fall slightly. In the United States, however, unemployment is more likely to increase given the more dynamic supply of labour and the expected faster slow-down in demand.

The economic outlook is always surrounded by a variety of risks and uncertainties. At the present time, however, a new element which could alter the outlook for the market economies is the prospect of radical transformation in the economies of eastern Europe and the Soviet Union.

(iii) The possible effects of a German monetary union

In an attempt to halt the tide of people emigrating from the German Democratic Republic to the Federal Republic of Germany, the authorities of the Federal Republic on 7 February proposed the creation of a monetary and economic union with the German Democratic Republic. This proposal, which took many observers and commentators by surprise and has since been widely discussed, reverses the process originally envisaged, whereby monetary union would have been the culmination of an adjustment process in the German Democratic Republic which would have taken place over a period of several years, at the end of which the German Democratic Republic would have begun to approach the productivity levels prevailing in the Federal Republic of Germany. The process would have started with a basic re-orientation of economic principles towards a market economy system, including the creation of the required legal and institutional framework, and a new independent currency. In such an approach the exchange rate was expected to play the role of a shock absorber which, via devaluation, would enable price competitiveness to be improved during the process of removing various rigidities and solving other adjustment problems.

The now imminent formation of an economic and monetary union, which is expected to be followed in the near future by the political unification of the two German states, will have considerable repercussions on their respective economies. At the same time there will be growth and other economic effects which will spill over to western Europe as a whole, as well as other parts of the world.

The technical modalities of the introduction of the Deutschmark in the German Democratic Republic are not yet known. This notably concerns the conversion

---

[78] See *Economic Forecasts*, Vol.7, No.2, February 1990.

rate between the DM and the Mark of the German Democratic Republic.

It is evident that the choice of the conversion rate is of prime importance, since it will determine the point of departure for firms and households in the ensuing adjustment process. In fact, the introduction of the Deutschmark will take away the "veil" behind which the German Democratic Republic economy has so far been operating. All variables that can be expressed in money terms will become immediately comparable to those prevailing in the Federal Republic and other market economies. This will be especially important for wage costs and productivity levels.

At the same time it is clear that the introduction of the Deutschmark will have to be accompanied by reforms of the legal and institutional framework in which the economy is operating. These pertain, *inter alia* to private property rights and the involvement of foreign firms in economic activity, notably as regards takeovers. Also the Bundesbank will need to extend the Federal Republic's capital market and two-tier banking system to the east in order to maintain control of monetary policy. In addition there is a need for price and tax reform and a revision of the legal provisions with regard to the labour market and the control of monopoly power.

A particular cause for concern has been the implications for monetary policy and price stability in the Federal Republic. The introduction of the Deutschmark in the German Democratic Republic will inevitably lead to an increase in the money supply. But this will — at least partly — be matched by the production capacity of the German Democratic Republic. How much of this capacity is economically viable once assets, debts, costs and prices are denominated in Deutschmarks remains an open question, hence the crucial importance of the conversion rate.

The choice of conversion rate will also determine the immediate inflationary consequences for the Federal Republic. The total money supply in the German Democratic Republic (defined as money in circulation plus savings deposits) is estimated at about Mark 177 billion at the end of 1989 (table 2.1.1). If converted at parity this would correspond to 14 per cent of the M3 money supply in the Federal Republic, but only 4.7 per cent at a rate of 1:3 (table 2.1.2). The indications are that the Federal authorities will opt for a rate of 1:1 but will introduce accompanying measures (temporary freezing of savings deposits, etc.) which will dampen the impact on the money supply.

Another open question is the size of the possible monetary overhang in the German Democratic Republic. Given distorted prices and the fact that supply was often unable to meet demand — notably for consumer durables and motor cars — part of the accumulated savings may have been forced, i.e., individuals are holding more financial assets than they actually desire. Indicators of such an inflationary overhang are not easy to derive, but it appears from table 2.1.1 that the order of magnitude involved is probably not very large. The average household saving ratio in the German Democratic Republic has been much lower than in the Federal Republic: in 1989 it was 5.6 per cent in the former but 13.6 per cent in the latter. The ratio of very liquid assets to household disposable income, in contrast, was about twice as high in the German Democratic Republic. This reflects, however, the fact that it is virtually impossible for households in the German Democratic Republic to acquire financial assets such as bonds and shares, which are of considerable importance in the portfolios of private households in the Federal Republic. On the other hand, the ratio of currency in circulation to disposable income is the same (0.10) in both countries. These indicators thus provide no clear-cut evidence for the existence of an inflationary overhang: if it exists, it is unlikely to be very large. A considerable part, in any case, may be syphoned off by a price reform which would lead to a once-for-all increase in the average price level. It has also been suggested that households be given the possibility to acquire assets such as company shares or housing. Another factor that will prevent households from spending their savings rapidly will be the general uncertainty concerning job security during the restructuring of the German Democratic Republic economy. Although "forecasts" of massive unemployment overdramatize the situation, the changing economic environment in the German Democratic Republic and the accompanying uncertainty is likely to be reflected in cautious spending behaviour. Thus, it appears unlikely that the creation of an economic and monetary union *per se* will have a significant effect on inflationary pressure.

It is also appropriate in this connection to recall an obvious fact, namely, that the gap between supply and demand in the German Democratic Republic will be closed by inflows of goods not only from the Federal Republic but also from firms in other countries. The strengthening of demand in the German Democratic Republic will divert FRG exports away from other countries and this will contribute to reducing the large trade surplus. Also monetary union will not lead to the sudden death of all German Democratic Republic companies — a considerable number of them will continue to produce, although many will have to adjust production processes and products to the changing pattern of demand. Apart from this there are financial implications for the Federal budget of supporting the

TABLE 2.1.2

Money supply in 1989: [a] German Democratic Republic relative to the Federal Republic of Germany
(Percentages)

	Money supply definition (Federal Republic of Germany)		
	M1	M2	M3
Conversion rate (DM/Mark)			
1:1	39.3	22.8	14.1
1:2	19.6	11.4	7.0
1:3	13.1	7.6	4.7

Sources: ECE, Division of Economic Analysis and Projections.

[a] End of year.

adjustment process in the German Democratic Republic.[79] These pertain to social security expenditures such as unemployment benefits and old age pensions, transfer payments to companies and households and public sector investments (e.g., in roads and railways, etc.).

At present there is hardly any serious estimate of the order of magnitude of the financial flows that might be involved. These will partly depend on the dynamics of the economic adjustment process in the German Democratic Republic since economic recovery will itself generate part of the funds needed to finance public expenditures. Also, there already exist considerable transfer payments from the Federal budget to border regions in the Federal Republic, which had been cut off from their "natural" economic space in the east, and to West Berlin which could be diverted to investment projects in the German Democratic Republic. The main role in the adjustment process, however, will have to be played by private capital. The accumulated net capital exports of the Federal Republic of Germany in 1988 and 1989 amounted to nearly DM 250 billion. Given a competitive rate of return, these flows could be re-channelled to investment projects in the German Democratic Republic. In any case, it is important to emphasize that the process of economic transformation will take time and that attempts to estimate the costs of this process are as uncertain as estimates of the benefits.

The introduction of the Deutschmark will also reveal the competitiveness of German Democratic Republic firms. Considerable importance attaches to the wage level that will prevail in the German Democratic Republic after the introduction of the Deutschmark. If converted at par, average gross monthly wages in industry in the German Democratic Republic would be about 40 per cent of the FRG level. Data on average labour productivity suggest that the output per worker is about 50 to 60 per cent of the corresponding figure in the Federal Republic. A rate of 1:1 appears as a floor needed to maintain the average real purchasing power of workers. Any lower rate would probably increase the number of migrants to the west. The authorities may also find it necessary to support the real income levels of households by means of temporary transfer payments, e.g., for housing and the use of infrastructure such as telephones. Such transfers could be gradually reduced with the increase in productivity. Given the average productivity difference between the two Germanies, a conversion rate of 1:1 would not appear to conflict with the objective of making investment and production profitable in the German Democratic Republic. Again the complexities are in the dynamics of the wage determination process. Current wage levels in the German Democratic Republic do not always reflect relative skills and productivity levels and there will be corresponding adjustments that will tend to raise wages in several branches above the floor rate.

It is virtually impossible at this moment to predict with much hope of accuracy the consequences of economic and monetary union on the economy of the Federal Republic in 1990. Much, of course, will depend on the date when it becomes effective. Given the outcome of the elections in the German Democratic Republic on 18 March 1990, it seems likely that the movement towards union will accelerate. Given the high demand, especially for consumer and investment goods, in the German Democratic Republic, capacity utilization rates in the Federal Republic of Germany will probably rise to their ceiling and exports to other countries may be cut back in favour of deliveries to the German Democratic Republic. At the same time the demand for imports from other countries will rise in both German states, thus providing a stimulus to economic activity abroad, notably in western Europe. Quantitative estimates of the effects of such linkages are difficult to make, given the uncertainty concerning the pace of economic transformation in the German Democratic Republic and the difficulty of predicting the reactions of economic agents. In technical terms there are simply no data on past behaviour, and consequently no econometric equations, that would enable a reasonable prediction to be made of what lies ahead. Nevertheless, it does not appear to be particularly reckless to expect a relatively strong recovery of the German Democratic Republic economy in the medium term.

(iv) The effects of the eastern reform process on the rest of the world

The underlying objective of the economic reforms in the eastern economies is to raise their productivity levels and standards of living to something approaching those in western Europe. As noted in chapter 1.2, real output per head in the countries of eastern Europe in the mid-1980s was on average some 40 per cent lower than in the Federal Republic of Germany — and given the uncertainty surrounding such estimates, the true figure could be much lower than that. Moreover, their relative position has almost certainly deteriorated since then. The population of the six countries of eastern Europe is roughly equal to that of France and the United Kingdom combined, while that of the six plus the Soviet Union is only about three per cent lower than the population of OECD Europe. Clearly, if these countries were to succeed in significantly narrowing the gap between them and the west, even at a more modest rate than western Europe has narrowed the economic distance between it and the United States in the postwar period, then they would constitute a significant source of growth in the world economy. Moreover, since such a development would be accompanied by the gradual insertion of the eastern countries into the global, multilateral trading system, it could make an important contribution to world-wide utility through a more efficient allocation of global resources.

However, all that is for the long run. As discussed at length in chapter 1, the problems facing the reforming economies are immense and their solution will take

---

[79] At the beginning of March the Bundestag passed a supplementary budget of DM6.5 billion largely directed towards supporting the German Democratic Republic's economy. This puts the planned borrowing requirements of the central government for 1990 at DM 34.5 billion or some 1.5 per cent of GNP.

time and require considerable assistance from the west. Nevertheless, once the process of reform is under way, east-west trade is likely to receive a major boost. Although west European investment in the east may eventually replace some investment in the west, in the short to medium term it is likely to depend on capital goods produced in the west. This is a development which is likely to get under way during the 1990s. The unification of Germany will also provide a separate boost to domestic investment in the early 1990s insofar as unification leads to a re-organization of production in both economies.

Improved growth and the entry of the eastern countries into the multilateral trading system will also improve the prospects for trade between the reforming economies and the developing countries. However, it is likely that improved competitiveness will enable the countries of eastern Europe to regain some or all of the market share they have lost to the newly industrialized economies of South East Asia, especially in the west European market for manufactured goods. The east Europeans' competitiveness will also benefit eventually from their being gradually drawn into the more specialized division of labour within an integrated European economy. (This refers to the spontaneous integration that is likely to occur among geographically close, industrialized (or industrializing) economies. Special institutional arrangements between the eastern countries and the EC or EFTA would, of course, accelerate the process.) This, again, is a development which could get under way during the 1990s.

The more immediate concern of some developing countries is that financial resources will be diverted from them to eastern Europe and the Soviet Union. Since commercial bank lending to the developing countries is already low or non-existent and is unlikely to expand in eastern Europe, their concern is mainly to do with foreign direct investment by private companies and with official grant aid. It is probable that there will be some switch of western private investment to eastern Europe, although on what scale is impossible to say at present. However, the switch to the east may be as much at the expense of western Europe and North America as the developing countries. Again, such a switch is likely to develop slowly, at least at first. Foreign enterprises will remain cautious about investing significant sums in eastern Europe until the various reform processes are firmly established and until progress has been made in the areas of property rights, convertible currency regimes, and so forth. Only when progress has been made in these areas will it be possible to obtain reasonable ideas of rates of return on investments in the east.

The matter of grant aid is likely to be the more immediate issue for developing countries. The acting administrator of the United States Agency for International Development has said explicitly that aid for eastern Europe will have to be at the expense of developing countries[80] and his remarks have been echoed by a senior director of the Canadian International Development Agency.[81] The President of the Commission of the European Communities has suggested that aid to the six east European countries would require a large *addition* to the Community's budget,[82] but as yet it is not clear whether member countries would support such an increase. Fiscal policy in the market economies is still dominated by the objectives of lowering budget deficits and cutting the size of public expenditure. In this context the member countries of the OECD have not made any special effort to reallocate public expenditure so as to be able to meet the OECD development aid target of 0.7 per cent of GNP. Unless specific measures to the contrary are taken, it would appear that the fears of developing countries about the diversion of foreign aid are not without foundation.

The most immediate effect on the rest of the world, and on the developing countries in particular, could be higher interest rates. Bond yields in the Federal Republic of Germany have already risen by more than one percentage point as a result of fears that unification of the two German states will boost inflation and, because of the close integration of the European economies, this has already had a generally hardening effect on west European interest rates in general.

Some of the fears about the effects of unification may well be exaggerated, as noted above, but the essential point about German unification in particular and the eastern reform process in general is that there is bound to be an increase in the demand for investible funds. In recent years the main international sources of loanable funds have been Japan and the Federal Republic itself. If real rates of return are high in eastern Europe then foreign private capital will switch from countries such as the United States (and in Europe from France, Italy, the United Kingdom and southern Europe). In the event of German unification, the Federal Republic's current account surplus will effectively be invested at home rather than abroad. This does not mean that German interest rates have to remain high. Bond yields have risen because of the perception that Federal Government expenditure will increase as a result of the transition costs after unification (social security support, subsidised training, housing, etc.) and, given the anti-inflationary stance of monetary policy, this will have to be financed by government borrowing. But if rates of return to private investment in the east prove to be as high as some observers think, then private capital will take on most of the task of restructuring. Insofar as this attracts private capital from the rest of the world German interest rates could fall while the exchange rate remains firm. However, countries such as the United States, which have to attract foreign capital with high interest rates in order to finance a large budget deficit, may be forced to raise interest rates still further in order to compete with higher rates of return

---

80 "We are in a zero-sum game in foreign aid and no-one gets more unless someone gets less", as quoted in the *Financial Times*, London, 12 December 1989.

81 *Ibid.*

82 See chapter 1.2(v) and footnote (44) in the same section.

elsewhere. Thus, the reduction of the United States budget deficit, a process which may now be helped by large cuts in defence expenditure, could help to relieve the upward pressure on world interest rates. This will directly benefit the indebted developing countries and will ensure that an increasing proportion of world savings can be employed in the development of eastern Europe and the developing countries.

2.2 OUTPUT AND THE STRUCTURE OF DEMAND

In western Europe strong economic growth continued in 1989. The major driving forces, as in 1988, were business investment and exports. The favourable course of developments has bolstered confidence of consumers and firms, and the upswing is increasingly sustained by domestic demand. The margins of unused capacity have dwindled away over the last two years and this has partly acted as a constraint on output growth but also as a spur to investment. In contrast to western Europe there was a marked slow-down of economic activity in North America in the course of 1989. This section reviews changes in output and the major components of demand in western Europe and North America.

(i) Real GDP and domestic demand

Brisk economic activity has continued in western Europe in 1989.[83] After the virtual stagnation of real GDP in 1981 — when activity was still falling in several countries — there has now been a period of eight years during which output has risen continuously (see chart 2.1.1). On the basis of preliminary data, real GDP for the 18 west European countries is estimated to have grown by 3.3 per cent in 1989, only marginally lower than the increase of 3.6 per cent in 1988 (table 2.2.1).

These growth rates are considerably above the rates at which potential output is estimated to have been expanding in recent years.[84] Although estimates of potential output are always surrounded by a considerable margin of uncertainty, it is clear that rapid economic expansion has reduced considerably the margins of unused capacity in the market economies of the ECE region. With the recent strengthening of fixed investment, which is itself partly a response to higher utilization rates, there has probably been some acceleration in the growth of potential output, but this was not been sufficient to prevent a further narrowing of the gap between actual and potential output. In many countries output levels are now close to capacity ceilings. This entails a very intense utilization of productive resources and raises the question of the sustainability of the current pace of expansion. In some sectors of industry, however, output appears be moving in step with changes in productive capacities.

The overall buoyancy of demand is also reflected in labour markets (see section 2.3(ii) below). Total employment has increased further in 1989 and unemployment rates have been falling in the majority of countries. The demand for skilled labour has been encountering increasing shortages and overtime work is now a regular feature of productive activity.

Domestic demand continued to rise faster than domestic output in western Europe (chart 2.2.2). Among the major components of domestic demand fixed investment was the most dynamic, but private consumption also remained strong (chart 2.2.1).

The overall buoyancy of domestic demand spilled over to the foreign trade sector. As in 1988, imports constituted a considerable leakage from the circular

TABLE 2.2.1

Annual changes in real GDP, 1987-1990 [a]
(Percentage change over previous year)

	1987	1988	1989 [b]	1990 [c]
France	1.9	3.5	3.3	3.0
Germany, Fed.Rep. of	1.8	3.7	3.6	3.5
Italy	3.0	3.9	3.4	3.2
United Kingdom [d]	4.8	4.5	2.4	1.2
Total 4 countries	2.7	3.9	3.2	2.8
Austria	1.9	4.2	4.0	3.0
Belgium	2.0	4.3	4.5	3.4
Denmark	-0.6	-0.2	1.2	1.7
Finland	4.0	5.2	5.0	2.5
Ireland	4.9	3.7	5.7	4.7
Netherlands	1.1	2.8	4.2	3.0
Norway	3.4	1.1	2.3	1.5
Sweden	2.9	2.3	2.0	1.1
Switzerland	2.0	3.0	3.0	2.2
Total 9 countries	2.1	2.9	3.4	2.4
Total 13 countries	2.6	3.6	3.3	2.7
Greece	-0.1	4.0	2.3	2.0
Portugal	4.6	4.2	4.8	4.2
Spain	5.5	5.0	4.9	4.1
Turkey	7.4	3.4	1.1	5.7
Yugoslavia [e]	-1.1	-1.7	0.8	..
Southern Europe	4.3	3.6	3.4	4.2 [f]
Total 18 countries	2.8	3.6	3.3	2.7 [f]
Canada	4.5	5.0	2.8	2.0
United States	3.8	4.4	3.0	2.3
North America	3.9	4.5	3.0	2.3

Sources: National statistics and estimates of official and private institutions and ECE.

[a] At market prices. [b] Preliminary estimates. [c] Forecasts.
[d] Output measure of GDP at factor cost. [e] Gross Social Product.
[f] Excluding Yugoslavia.

---

[83] In this section the term western Europe is used for the aggregate of 18 countries listed in table 2.2.1.

[84] See e.g. Raymond Torres and John P. Martin, *Potential output in the seven major OECD countries*, OECD, Working Papers No. 66, May 1989, Paris; Bernd Görzig, "Wie hoch sind die Kapazitätsreserven der deutschen Wirtschaft?", *DIW Wochenbericht*, 47/89, Berlin, 23 November 1989.

TABLE 2.2.2

Contributions to changes in real GDP, 1988-1989
(Percentage points)

	Private consumption	Public consumption	Fixed investment	Stocks	Total domestic demand	Exports	Imports	Gross domestic product	Memo item: net foreign balance
France									
1988	1.7	0.4	1.6	0.2	4.0	1.5	-2.0	3.5	-0.5
1989	1.5	0.5	1.2	-	3.1	1.9	-1.8	3.3	0.1
Germany, Federal Republic of									
1988	1.5	0.4	1.2	0.4	3.6	1.7	-1.7	3.7	0.1
1989	0.9	-0.2	1.6	0.3	2.7	2.9	-2.0	3.6	0.9
Italy									
1988	2.4	0.5	1.1	0.5	4.5	1.3	-1.9	3.9	-0.6
1989	2.2	0.4	1.2	0.4	4.2	1.4	-2.2	3.4	-0.8
United Kingdom									
1988	4.3	0.1	2.4	0.7	7.4	0.2	-3.7	4.0	-3.4
1989	2.4	-	1.0	0.2	3.6	1.3	-3.0	2.0	-1.6
Four major countries									
1988	2.4	0.4	1.6	0.4	4.8	1.2	-2.2	3.7	-1.0
1989	1.6	0.1	1.3	0.2	3.3	2.0	-2.2	3.1	-0.2
Nine smaller countries [a]									
1988	1.0	0.1	1.5	-	2.6	3.4	-3.1	2.9	0.3
1989	1.4	0.2	1.4	-	3.0	3.8	-3.5	3.4	0.2
Five south European countries [a]									
1988	2.2	0.6	1.8	-0.1	4.5	1.8	-2.8	3.6	-0.9
1989	2.7	0.5	2.1	0.1	5.4	1.3	-3.4	3.4	-2.1
Total 18 countries									
1988	2.1	0.3	1.6	0.3	4.3	1.8	-2.5	3.5	-0.7
1989	1.7	0.2	1.4	0.2	3.5	2.3	-2.6	3.2	-0.3
Canada									
1988	2.4	0.6	3.1	-0.4	5.7	3.1	-4.2	5.0	-1.1
1989	2.2	0.4	2.2	1.2	5.9	-0.2	-2.5	2.8	-2.8
United States									
1988	2.2	0.1	1.0	0.1	3.4	1.7	-0.7	4.4	1.0
1989	1.8	0.5	0.3	-0.1	2.5	1.2	-0.7	3.0	0.5
North America									
1988	2.2	0.1	1.2	0.1	3.6	1.8	-1.0	4.5	0.8
1989	1.8	0.5	0.5	-	2.8	1.1	-0.9	3.0	0.2

Source: ECE, Division of Economic Analysis and Projections, estimates based on data in Appendix A tables.

Note: For the United Kingdom the growth rates of GDP shown above are based on the expenditure measure of GDP. They differ from the figures shown in table 2.2.1, which are calculated from the output measure of GDP. The latter is usually considered to be the most reliable measure of short term changes in GDP. Accordingly, there is a statistical discrepancy between the change in the output measure of GDP and the sum of the growth contributions given above. For 1988 (1989) this discrepancy amounts to 0.5 (0.4) percentage points.

[a] For individual country data see table 2.2.3.

flow of domestic incomes, while exports were a major support to output growth. Export growth was broadly based but in some countries it was limited by production capacities, which were insufficient to meet both higher domestic and foreign demand.

The investment boom was reflected in long order books and high activity levels in the west European investment goods industries, notably the machine-tool sector. A country like the Federal Republic of Germany, with an export structure that is specialized on these goods, tended to benefit especially from such a demand pattern[85] and the foreign trade surplus rose to a record level. The concomitant strength of exports and imports in western Europe is indicative of the intensive trade links that have been developed between the individual countries. Trade is more and more characterized by the exchange of similar goods, i.e., the so-called intra-industry trade. A major reason for this is to be found in the exploitation of economies of scale, which allows reductions in unit costs and improvements in price competitiveness.

Within this overall picture of sustained growth, there has emerged a striking contrast between developments in the United Kingdom and in the market economies of continental Europe (table 2.2.1). The United Kingdom had recorded very high growth rates in 1987 and 1988 which also stimulated — via foreign trade — economic activity in the other west European countries, but this country now appears to have passed the peak of the current cyclical upswing and has thus moved out

---

[85] For a detailed analysis of specialization patterns in engineering goods industries, see chapter 7.

TABLE 2.2.3

Contribution to changes in real GDP, 1988-1989
(Percentage points)

	Private consumption	Public consumption	Fixed investment	Stocks	Total domestic demand	Exports	Imports	Gross domestic product	Memo item: net foreign balance
Nine smaller countries									
Austria									
1988	1.7	0.1	1.3	1.5	4.7	3.7	-4.2	4.2	-0.5
1989	2.1	0.2	1.5	-0.4	3.4	4.8	-4.3	4.0	0.5
Belgium									
1988	1.6	-0.1	2.6	0.3	4.4	6.4	-6.5	4.3	-0.1
1989	2.2	-0.1	2.5	0.2	4.8	6.8	-7.1	4.5	-0.3
Denmark									
1988	-0.9	-0.2	-0.9	-0.1	-2.2	2.5	-0.4	-0.2	2.0
1989	-0.3	-0.1	-0.3	0.9	0.2	2.5	-1.4	1.2	1.0
Finland									
1988	2.8	0.5	2.3	0.9	6.5	1.1	-3.4	5.2	-2.3
1989	2.2	0.7	3.1	0.7	6.7	0.5	-3.1	5.0	-2.6
Ireland									
1988	1.9	-0.7	-0.3	-0.7	0.1	6.3	-2.7	3.7	3.6
1989	3.1	-0.4	2.2	-0.7	5.5	7.2	-7.0	5.7	0.3
Netherlands									
1988	0.7	-	2.0	-0.5	2.2	4.8	-4.2	2.8	0.6
1989	2.1	0.2	1.5	0.4	4.2	4.0	-4.0	4.2	-
Norway									
1988	-1.1	-	0.4	-1.8	-2.4	2.4	1.1	1.1	3.5
1989	-0.8	0.4	-1.0	-2.8	-4.2	6.4	0.1	2.3	6.5
Sweden									
1988	1.3	0.4	1.1	0.4	3.1	1.1	-1.7	2.5	-0.6
1989	0.6	0.5	1.7	-	2.9	1.4	-2.1	2.2	-0.7
Switzerland									
1988	1.4	0.4	1.9	-0.3	3.4	2.1	-2.5	3.0	-0.4
1989	1.5	0.5	1.5	-	3.6	2.4	-3.0	3.0	-0.5
Five south European countries									
Greece									
1988	2.6	0.9	1.4	-0.9	4.0	2.0	-2.0	4.0	-
1989	2.1	0.8	1.2	-0.1	4.1	1.1	-2.8	2.3	-1.8
Portugal									
1988	4.3	0.8	4.3	1.0	10.4	2.9	-9.1	4.2	-6.2
1989	2.6	0.5	3.4	-	6.5	5.4	-7.1	4.8	-1.7
Spain									
1988	2.8	0.7	3.1	0.4	7.1	1.3	-3.4	5.0	-2.1
1989	3.5	0.8	3.5	0.1	7.9	0.9	-3.9	4.9	-3.0
Turkey									
1988	1.9	0.2	-0.3	-0.8	1.0	3.6	-1.3	3.4	2.4
1989	2.2	-	-0.7	-0.3	1.3	1.2	-1.4	1.1	-0.2
Yugoslavia									
1988	-0.6	-	-1.1	-1.0	-2.8	0.9	0.2	-1.7	1.1
1989	0.5	-0.1	0.1	1.8	2.3	1.0	-2.4	0.8	-1.5

Source: ECE, Division of Economic Analysis and Projections, estimates based on data in Appendix A tables.

Note: See also table 2.2.2.

of phase with the rest of western Europe. In 1989 there was a sizeable slow-down in the pace of economic activity, which reflects the impact of a tightening of policies started in 1988 to reduce inflation and curb the soaring deficit on the foreign account. It should, however, be noted that the data do not provide an accurate picture of the underlying strength of the UK economy because of a series of disruptions in oil production, which depressed exports.

In the other three major economies growth rates of GDP remained broadly unchanged from 1988 (table 2.2.1). It is noteworthy that in the Federal Republic of Germany the growth of *real GNP* was 4.1 per cent, much higher than the estimated increase of about 3.6 per cent for *real GDP*.[86] As can be seen from table 2.2.1, the majority of smaller countries grew faster than the west European average in 1989. It is noteworthy that output growth resumed in Denmark after two years of

---

[86] Gross national product (GNP) is defined as the sum of GDP and net factor incomes from abroad. In 1989 there was a very large increase in the Federal Republic's investment income from abroad.

CHART 2.2.1

Real GDP and the components of demand, 1980-1989
(Indices 1980 = 100, semi-logarithmic scale)

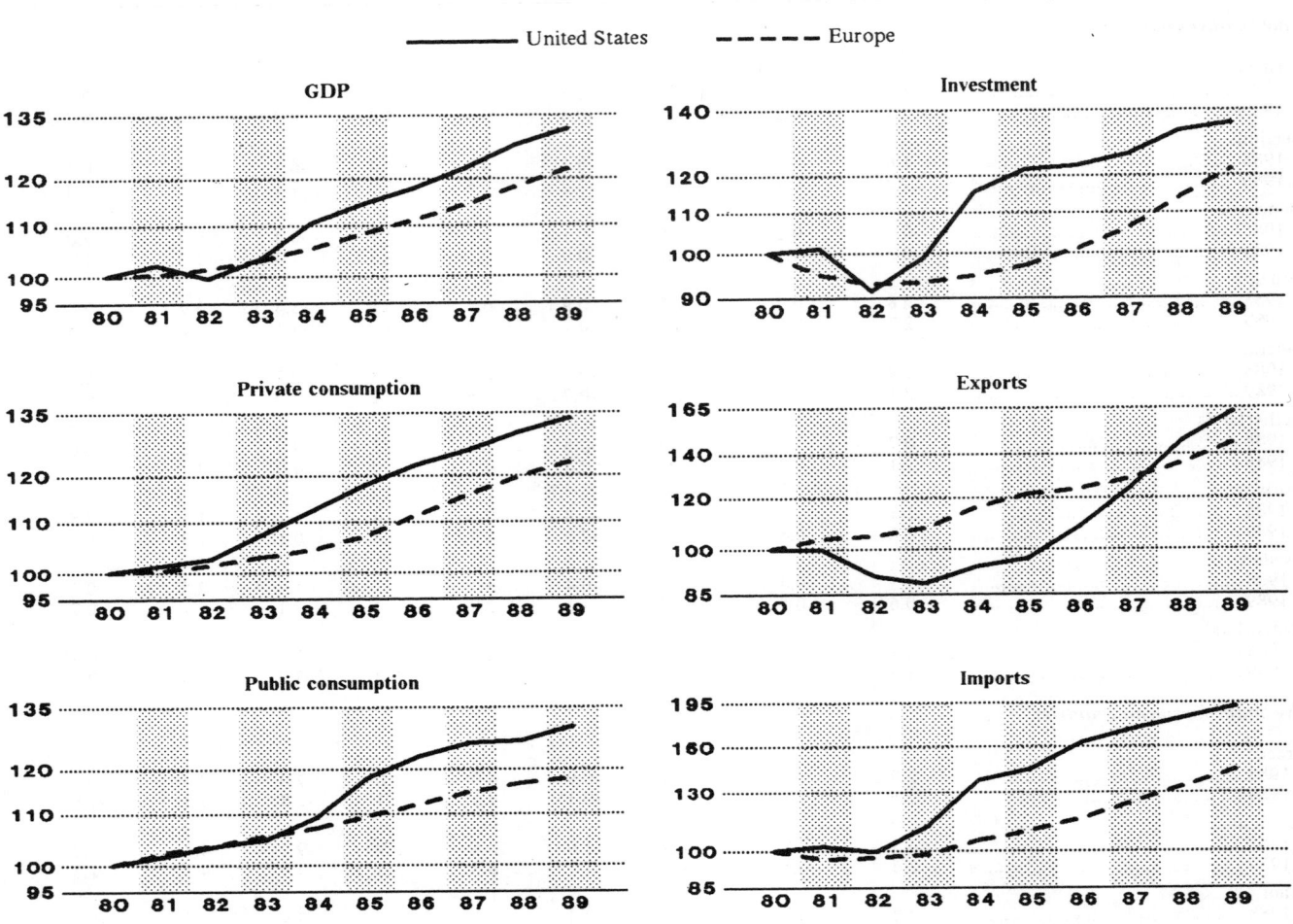

Source: ECE, Division of Economic Analysis and Projections.

successive declines following the tightening of policies to dampen domestic demand and reduce the large current account deficit. GDP growth also picked up in Norway, although — as in 1988 — this conceals a decline for the aggregate of activities not related to oil and gas production. Fiscal policy shifted in 1989 to an expansionary stance in order to contain rising unemployment and this has supported domestic demand.

Among the five south European countries economic growth remained on average extremely buoyant in Spain and Portugal, reflecting strong domestic demand and export growth. Economic policies have been tightened to contain inflationary risks and to reduce high import growth.

In contrast to western Europe there was a notable weakening of economic growth in North America in the course of 1989 (table 2.2.1). Although the slow-down is considerable, the annual growth rate was only slightly below the west European average. In the United States, real GDP rose by 3 per cent in 1989, down from an increase of 4.4 per cent in 1988. Tight monetary policies in response to mounting cost and price increases on account of the intense utilization of productive resources dampened domestic demand. Export growth remained strong but there was a sizeable deceleration compared with 1988, as the competitive gains from the depreciation of the dollar after 1985 began to wear off. The still high annual growth rate conceals a marked slow-down in economic activity in the final quarter of 1989.

There was also a slow-down in consumption and fixed investment in Canada, partly owing to the tightening of fiscal and monetary policies. Growth in total domestic demand remained broadly unchanged, supported notably by fixed investment and strong stockbuilding. The primary cause for the lower growth rate of GDP was the net foreign balance: exports fell mainly because of the weakening of demand from the United States, while imports continued to rise strongly although less so than in 1988.

(ii) Industrial production and capacity utilization

Boosted by strong demand for goods both at home and abroad, industrial production maintained the momentum gained in 1988. Higher production in the course of last year was increasingly inhibited by the lack of spare capacity, despite firms making large additions to their capital stock over the last two years (see further below). There were also reports of shortages in the market for skilled labour.

For the west European countries combined, total industrial production rose by some 4 per cent in 1989 only slightly below the 4.5 per cent increase currently estimated for manufacturing production (table 2.2.4). Actual output growth has started to be constrained by the limits of existing production capacity. This goes some way towards explaining the slow-down in manufacturing production, e.g., in Italy and Switzerland, and the below-average growth rate in Sweden.

TABLE 2.2.4

Industrial production, 1988-1989 [a]

(Percentage change over previous year)

	Total industry [a]		Manufacturing industry	
	1988	1989 [b]	1988	1989 [b]
France	4.6	4.5	5.0	4.7
Germany, Fed.Rep. of	3.6	4.9	4.1	5.2
Italy	6.9	2.3	5.1	3.0
United Kingdom	3.6	0.8	7.1	4.8
Total 4 countries	4.5	3.4	5.1	4.6
Austria	4.4	5.4	5.6	5.7
Belgium	5.7	3.0	6.3	3.3
Denmark	..	..	..	..
Finland	4.0	3.0	3.7	3.6
Ireland	10.9	12.5	12.7	12.9
Netherlands	-	5.0	4.9	4.6
Norway	5.1	16.3	-1.0	-
Sweden	2.7 [c]	2.7 [c]	3.5	2.6
Switzerland	6.7	2.0	6.7 [d]	3.0 [d]
Total 9 countries	4.0	5.7	5.1	3.6
Total 13 countries	4.4	3.9	5.1	4.4
Greece	5.1	1.3	5.1	2.0
Portugal	6.2	4.5	5.7	1.8
Spain	3.1	5.1	3.3	5.0
Turkey	..	..	..	..
Yugoslavia	-1.0	1.9	-1.0	1.9
Southern Europe	2.4	3.9	2.7	3.8
Total 18 countries	4.2	3.9	4.8	4.3
Canada	6.2	0.9	6.1	1.8
United States	5.7	3.3	6.0	3.9
North America	5.8	3.2	6.0	3.7

Source: OECD, *Main Economic Indicators*, Paris, and national statistics. National data are aggregated by means of weights derived from GDP originating in industry, expressed at 1985 US dollar exchange rates.

[a] Industrial production covers the following sectors: mining and quarrying, manufacturing, electricity, gas and water.
[b] Preliminary estimates.
[c] Refers to mining and manufacturing.
[d] Industry less electricity, gas and water.

On average, the growth rates of total industrial production and manufacturing output have not differed significantly in the large majority of countries. As can be seen from table 2.2.4, the major exceptions are the United Kingdom and Norway. In the first country industrial production was depressed because of the interruptions to oil production since the middle of 1988. In contrast, the very strong rise in total production in Norway in 1989 is entirely due to the energy sector. Manufacturing output was unchanged from its average level of 1988, largely on account of weak domestic demand.

Within manufacturing industry the output of the machinery and equipment producing firms showed in general a particularly strong growth on account of the persistently strong demand for investment goods (see chart 2.2.3). But it can also be seen from chart 2.2.3 that the expansion of manufacturing output has been broadly based over the last few years: there has also been considerable expansion in the intermediate goods — notably in 1988 — and in the consumer goods industries.

Manufacturing output in western Europe in 1989 was, on average, some 10 per cent above its level in

TABLE 2.2.5

Capacity utilization rates in manufacturing industry, 1973-1989
(Per cent)

	Previous peaks [a]		Yearly averages		1988	1989				
						Quarterly rates: [b]				
	1973/1974	1979/1980	1988	1989	QIV	QI	QII	QIII	QIV	
France	87.8	85.3	85.7	87.8	86.4	87.1	87.7	88.2	88.2	
Germany, Federal Republic of	88.1	86.0	85.0	88.1	86.5	87.7	87.7	88.4	88.6	
Italy	78.8	77.3	77.6	80.0	79.0	79.9	79.2	80.0	80.8	
United Kingdom	90.6	87.6	93.7	91.4	93.9	94.3	92.5	90.4	88.3	
Total 4 countries	86.6	84.4	85.3	87.1	86.4	87.2	86.9	87.1	87.0	
Austria [c]	89	86	84	87	84	..	..	..	87	
Belgium	85.4	79.1	78.7	80.3	79.7	79.0	79.3	80.5	82.2	
Finland [d]	..	90.1	89.0	88.5	89	89	89	88	88	
Ireland	..	68.1	74.0	74.3	76.5	74.0	73.4	73.3	76.4	
Netherlands	86.0	83.0	84.4	85.8	85.1	85.2	86.1	85.7	86.1	
Sweden	..	83.7 [e]	88.9	89.3*	89.7	90.0	89.1	89.1	89.1*	
Switzerland	89.5	87.0	87.7	89.2	88.6	89.2	89.6	88.6	89.4	
Total 7 countries	87.4 [f]	83.9	85.0	86.3	85.7	86.1	86.2	86.1	86.7	
Total 11 countries	86.7 [f]	84.3	85.2	86.9	86.3	87.0	86.8	86.9	86.9	
Canada	93.3	87.3	83.4	82.0	82.8	82.6	82.3	81.7	81.5*	
United States	87.7	86.5	83.5	83.8	84.4	84.4	84.4	83.9	82.5*	

Sources: Belgium, France, Federal Republic of Germany, Ireland, Italy, United Kingdom: Commission of the European Communities, *European Economy*, supplement B, November 1989, Table 7; Sweden: Statistiska Centralbyrån, *Statistiska Meddelanden* (Industrins Kapacitetsutnyttjande I 13 SM 8904); United States: OECD, *Main Economic Indicators*, Paris; Austria: Oesterreichisches Institut für Wirtschaftsforschung, *Monatsberichte*, 1/1990 and previous issues; Switzerland: Bundesamt für Statistik, *Wirtschaftsspiegel*, various issues; and *La vie économique* 2/1990 and previous issues; Canada: *Statistics Canada*,. Finland: *Bank of Finland*, direct communication.

a Quarterly high. For the United States monthly high.
b Quarterly rates are seasonally adjusted.
c Data refer to November of each year.
d Only semi-annual data are available.
e No data are available for 1979.
f Aggregate of countries for which data are available.

1987. Although firms have stepped up considerably their expenditures on machinery and buildings over this period in order to add to the existing capacity, this has not been sufficient to prevent actual output from either catching up with capacity output or coming quite close to it.[87] The significant rise in utilization rates has been accompanied by mounting cost pressures, as more firms introduce overtime to accommodate new orders. Some increasing flexibility in the production process may have been gained in recent years by the widespread introduction of electronic data processing equipment and flexible manufacturing systems; however, quantitative evidence on this issue is hard to come by. In any case, *capacity utilization rates* in manufacturing have tended to rise in the course of 1989 or to remain at the high levels attained at the end of 1988 (table 2.2.5). The intense use of available resources can be seen from the fact that in a number of countries these utilization rates are now above the high values recorded at the last major cyclical peak in 1973-1974. The major exception to this general pattern appears to be the United Kingdom, where utilization rates peaked in 1988 and declined apparently quite sharply in the course of 1989, although this may be doubted.[88]

Manufacturing output in the United States stabilized at a high level in the second half 1989. The strong average growth rate for 1989 (an increase of 4 per cent) is thus largely due to a statistical carry-over effect. In the final quarter of last year manufacturing output was only 2 per cent higher than in the corresponding period of 1988. The deceleration of manufacturing activity is also reflected in the capacity utilization rates, which remained broadly unchanged from the final quarter of 1988 to the second quarter of 1989, but fell somewhat thereafter. Overall, however, these data indicate that the level industrial activity in the United States is still quite high. It can be seen from chart 2.2.3 that the expansion of manufacturing output has been as broadly based as in western Europe.

(iii) The components of demand

(a) Private consumption

Private consumption, as in 1988, was a major support of domestic demand in 1989. For the 18 west European countries combined real private household expenditures rose by 2.8 per cent in 1989, about half a percentage point less than in 1988. This deceleration in the aggregate, however, is primarily accounted for by the developments in the Federal Republic of Germany and the United Kingdom, where there were marked slow-downs in consumer expenditures (table 2.2.6).

---

[87] See United Nations Economic Commission for Europe, *Economic Survey of Europe in 1988-1989*, New York, 1989, pp.22-24.

[88] The utilization rates for the United Kingdom are estimated by the European Community on the basis of business survey data pertaining to the percentage of firms operating at full capacity. The strong fall of the utilization rates in the course of 1989 is somewhat puzzling when seen in relation to developments recorded for actual production. It may be surmised that the EC estimates for the growth of production capacity are biased upwards and that, consequently, the magnitude of the fall in the capacity utilization rate is providing a somewhat distorted picture of actual changes. It should be noted that another estimate of capacity utilization in UK manufacturing actually shows a rise from 1988 to 1989. See *National Institute Economic Review*, 4/89, table 6, p.15.

TABLE 2.2.6

Real private consumption expenditure, 1987-1990
(Percentage change over previous year)

	1987	1988	1989 a	1990 b
France	2.7	2.8	2.5	2.5
Germany, Fed.Rep. of	3.5	2.7	1.6	3.5
Italy	3.9	3.8	3.4	2.8
United Kingdom	6.1	6.9	3.7	1.2
Total 4 countries	4.0	3.9	2.7	2.5
Austria	3.0	3.0	3.7	3.3
Belgium	2.9	2.4	3.4	3.0
Denmark	-1.7	-1.7	-0.5	1.7
Finland	5.7	5.0	4.0	2.5
Ireland	2.5	3.2	5.2	3.7
Netherlands	3.1	1.2	3.5	3.2
Norway	-0.8	-2.3	-1.7	2.0
Sweden	4.6	2.5	1.2	1.4
Switzerland	2.1	2.2	2.5	2.5
Total 9 countries	2.6	1.7	2.5	2.6
Total 13 countries	3.7	3.4	2.6	2.6
Greece	0.9	3.7	3.0	2.0
Portugal	6.8	6.5	3.8	3.5
Spain	5.5	4.5	5.5	3.7
Turkey	6.5	2.6	3.1	4.0
Yugoslavia	0.3	-1.3	1.0	..
Southern Europe	4.7	3.5	4.2	3.6
Total 18 countries	3.8	3.4	2.8	2.8
Canada	4.9	4.3	3.9	2.1
United States	2.8	3.4	2.7	2.2
North America	2.9	3.4	2.8	2.2

Sources: National statistics and estimates of official and private institutions and ECE secretariat.

a Preliminary.   b Forecasts.

TABLE 2.2.7

Household savings ratios, a 1987-1989
(Per cent of disposable income)

	1987	1988	1989 b
France	11.5	12.4	12.5
Germany, Fed.Rep. of	12.3	12.6	12.0
Italy c	22.1	22.7	22.5
United Kingdom	6.2	4.4	4.0
Austria	12.3	12.6	14.4
Belgium	11.9	13.3	13.9
Denmark	1.5	2.8	1.5
Finland	3.5	-0.1	-
Ireland	18.4	15.9	14.4
Netherlands	13	12.5	12.0
Norway	-5.0	-2.8	-0.5
Sweden	-3.4	-5.3	-3.2
Switzerland	8.7	9.8	10
Greece	16.2	20.4	22.5
Portugal c	24.8	22.8	21.3
Spain	8.0	8.8	7.7
Canada	8.5	8.2	10.1
United States	3.2	4.2	5.5

Sources: ECE, Division of Economic Analysis and Projections, based on national and international statistics.

a Savings as percentage of disposable incomes.
b Preliminary.   c Gross ratio.

The general feature, however, is for somewhat higher or broadly unchanged growth rates of real household expenditures. Higher employment and favourable growth in earnings were the main factors behind higher expenditures on goods and services. Inflation rates, on average, were only slightly higher than in 1988 so that real disposable income growth also remained rather strong. Lower tax payments provided a substantial boost to household purchasing power in Austria and Ireland, though in the former this leaked primarily into higher savings (see table 2.2.7). There is, however, no systematic pattern in the changes estimated for savings ratios between 1988 and 1989. In a number of countries the average propensity to save declined to accommodate larger expenditures, while in others the savings ratio rose (table 2.2.7). Consumer demand in western Europe was particularly buoyant for long-life consumer durables, notably passenger cars. But demand for services has also been quite strong.

Among the four larger west European economies, the sizeable deceleration in the growth of household demand in the United Kingdom mainly reflects the stabilization of the savings ratio, which had fallen sharply in 1988, and the slow-down in employment growth. In contrast, in the Federal Republic of Germany the weakening of real private consumption is entirely due to higher inflation: nominal disposable incomes rose at about the same rate as in 1988 and there was even a small decline in the savings ratio.

Among the smaller countries the predominant feature was for a higher growth of consumer expenditures in comparison with 1988 (table 2.2.6). Private consumption continued to decline in Denmark and Norway, although in the course of the year demand started to strengthen. In Norway this partly reflects the expansionary fiscal policy measures adopted in Spring 1989. In Sweden strong growth in factor incomes would have allowed for a higher levels of expenditure, but instead there was a considerable increase in the saving ratio — the first since the credit market deregulation in 1985. Among the five south European countries, there was a notable weakening of consumer demand in Portugal in 1989. This reflects the impact of restrictive policy measures adopted in order to curb inflation and reduce import growth. There was a large drop in imported passenger motor cars, which had increased by 72 per cent in 1988, and almost entirely accounted for the strong growth in private consumption in that year.

Consumer demand in the United States slowed down to a growth rate of 2.7 per cent, the lowest annual increase since the present upswing began. Preliminary estimates point to only very small growth in the fourth quarter after a flare-up in the third quarter, which reflected special factors. Higher employment and favourable real earnings growth supported consumer demand but there was a major offset from the rise in the household saving ratio, from 4.2 per cent in 1988 to 5.5 per cent in 1989. Part of this increase may be explained by higher interest rates which have made savings more attractive since 1987. To some extent it may also be due to the large rise in farm proprietors' incomes following a return of crop output to normal levels after the drought. It may be surmised that the larger part of this income increase was saved.

(b) Public consumption

Public consumption remained a subdued component of domestic demand in western Europe in 1989. For the 18 countries combined the yearly growth rate for 1989 was only about 1 per cent in comparison with an already very modest increase of 1.8 per cent in 1988 (table 2.2.8). In fact, the increase in 1989 was the smallest since 1960. Correspondingly, the contribution of public consumption to overall GDP growth remained very modest, amounting to 0.2 percentage points only (table 2.2.2). The explanation for this virtual stagnation continues to be the overriding objective of consolidating government budgets by tightly controlling expenditure growth. A widespread factor behind the higher expenditure in 1989 was the rising wage and salary bill for public sector employees on account of somewhat higher employment and/or wage increases. The absolute fall in real public consumption in the Federal Republic of Germany is due to special factors: there has been a reform of the public health system, which led private households to bring forward into 1988 on a massive scale purchases of medical services and goods in anticipation of reduced reimbursements in 1989. The decline in real expenditures in Ireland is fully accounted for by a large increase in the price of public services. In nominal terms, public consumption rose by about 4 per cent. And in Sweden, the low growth of this demand component is partly due to the very tight labour market, which makes it very difficult to increase public sector employment as desired. In Norway, the recovery of government expenditures reflects the expansionary shift in fiscal policy in order to limit unemployment.

In the United States, government expenditures picked up somewhat after sluggish growth in 1988.[89] This reflects mainly the steady expansion of state and local government expenditures and a smaller reduction of the inventories held by the Commodity Credit Corporation than in 1988. These inventories had fallen significantly in the course of 1988 as a result of the drought. In contrast, defence expenditures have continued to decline at about the same rate as in 1988, namely by about 1-2 per cent.

(c) Fixed investment

Over the last two years fixed investment has been the most buoyant component of domestic demand in western Europe. For the 18 countries combined the annual growth rate in 1989 is estimated to have been about 6.5 per cent, compared to 7.7 per cent in 1988 (table 2.2.9).

The vigour of fixed capital formation reflects an overall economic environment which has become very conducive to business investment. Apart from strong

TABLE 2.2.8

Real public consumption expenditure, 1987-1990
(Percentage change over previous year)

	1987	1988	1989 [a]	1990 [b]
France	3.0	2.3	2.4	2.3
Germany, Fed.Rep. of	1.5	2.2	-0.8	1.0
Italy	3.6	3.0	2.4	2.2
United Kingdom	1.1	0.4	-0.3	0.2
Total 4 countries	2.1	1.9	0.7	1.4
Austria	0.4	0.7	1.0	0.5
Belgium	1.3	-0.7	-0.6	-
Denmark	2.5	-0.9	-0.5	-1.0
Finland	4.5	2.5	3.4	3.0
Ireland	-3.8	-4.3	-2.5	-1.0
Netherlands	2.0	-0.1	1.2	-
Norway	4.5	0.1	2.1	4.0
Sweden	1.3	1.0	1.2	1.7
Switzerland	1.8	3.2	3.6	3.8
Total 9 countries	1.9	0.5	1.2	1.2
Total 13 countries	2.0	1.6	0.8	1.3
Greece	1.8	5.6	5.0	3.0
Portugal	2.0	4.5	2.7	2.5
Spain	8.7	5.0	5.5	3.5
Turkey	5.0	2.1	0.3	4.9
Yugoslavia	-1.5	0.1	-1.0	..
Southern Europe	5.9	4.2	4.0	3.5
Total 18 countries	2.3	1.8	1.1	1.5
Canada	0.7	3.1	2.3	0.9
United States	2.7	0.4	2.6	1.9
North America	2.5	0.6	2.6	1.8

Sources: National statistics and estimates of official and private institutions and ECE secretariat.

[a] Preliminary. [b] Forecasts.

output growth and favourable sales expectations, the rate of return on capital has risen considerably over the last few years. Profits in many countries have outpaced labour costs as a result of the overall wage moderation in western Europe.[90] Profit shares in a number of countries are at very high levels. Strong profits growth has also strengthened the ability of enterprises to finance investment projects from their own funds. Against this background, the tightening of monetary policies and the ensuing rise in interest rates do not appear to have affected investment significantly in 1989, although lagged reactions cannot be excluded for 1990.

Against a background of very high capacity utilization rates, there has been a rise in the proportion of investments undertaken to increase production capacity. The brisk investment in 1989 has consequently eased some of the tensions emerging from the intensive use of existing productive resources in a number of countries.

Nevertheless, rationalization of the production process and the introduction of new processes and products has in general remained a dominant motive for business investment. A considerable part of the overall investment continues to be undertaken in anticipation

---

[89] Note that in contrast to west European countries, public consumption data in the United States includes public sector investment expenditures.

[90] See below, section 2.3(i).

CHART 2.2.2

Contribution to changes in real GDP : Domestic demand and the net foreign balance
(Percentage points)

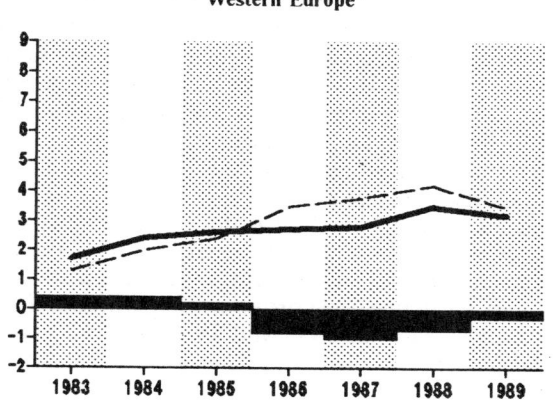
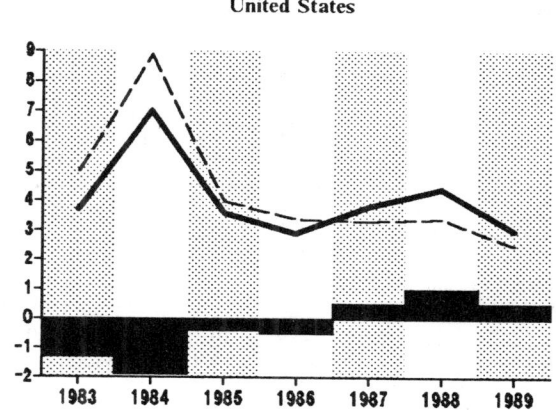

Source: ECE/DEAP
[a] 18 countries. See tables 2.2.2 and 2.2.3.

CHART 2.2.3

Manufacturing production by major branch, 1983-1989
(Indices 1985 = 100)

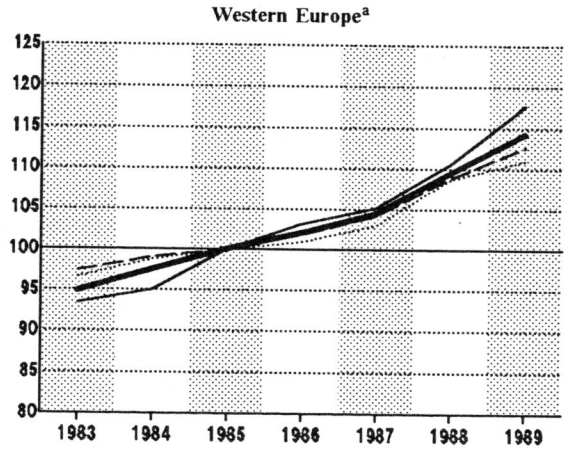
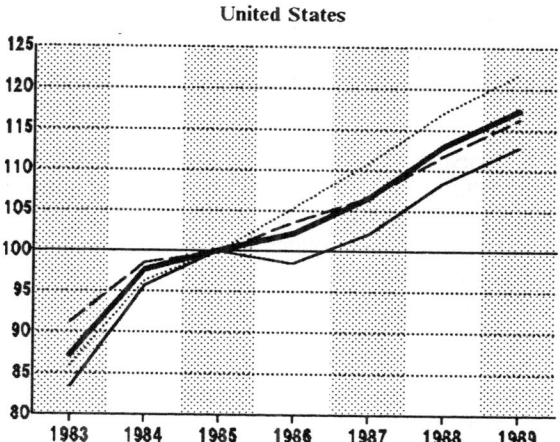

Source: ECE/DEAP.
[a] France, Federal Republic of Germany, Italy, United Kingdom.

TABLE 2.2.9

Total real fixed investment, 1987-1990
(Percentage change over previous year)

	1987	1988	1989 a	1990 b
France	3.7	7.8	5.4	4.5
Germany, Fed.Rep. of	2.2	5.9	7.9	6.0
Italy	6.8	4.9	5.4	5.0
United Kingdom	8.5	13.7	5.2	1.7
Total 4 countries	4.7	7.8	6.2	4.5
Austria	2.9	5.8	6.5	3.7
Belgium	5.2	16.0	14.1	8.1
Denmark	-7.4	-4.8	-1.5	-0.5
Finland	5.4	9.8	12.6	3.0
Ireland	-1.9	-1.7	11.2	11.0
Netherlands	0.7	9.7	6.9	1.7
Norway	-0.5	1.9	-4.3	-18.7
Sweden	7.6	6.4	5.6	2.5
Switzerland	7.4	6.9	5.3	2.7
Total 9 countries	2.9	6.9	6.3	1.6
Total 13 countries	4.3	7.5	6.2	3.8
Greece	-7.9	10.1	8.4	6.0
Portugal	20.2	16.0	11.5	9.7
Spain	14.6	14.0	14.6	11.7
Turkey	5.6	-1.3	-3.4	7.0
Yugoslavia	-5.1	-5.8	0.5	..
Southern Europe	8.8	8.7	9.5	10.4
Total 18 countries	4.8	7.7	6.6	4.2
Canada	11.7	13.2	8.5	3.4
United States	2.6	5.8	1.8	3.3
North America	3.6	6.7	2.6	3.3

Sources: National statistics and estimates of official and private institutions and ECE secretariat.

a Preliminary. b Forecasts.

of the completion of the EC's internal market by the end of 1992 and, in particular, the perceived need to prepare for intensified competition in a larger market.

Within total fixed investment, both major components, viz. machinery and equipment, as well as construction, generally grew strongly (table 2.2.10). Among machinery and equipment goods electronic products, notably for information processing and communication, continued to expand at above average growth rates.

Overall investment growth decelerated considerably in the United Kingdom, largely on account of declining private residential investment and a moderation of investment in the business services sector after a very high growth rate of about 34 per cent in 1988. Among the south European countries investment growth remained buoyant in Greece, Spain and Portugal, propelled by strong domestic demand and the need to modernize and adjust the composition of the capital stock as a consequence of entry to the EC. Foreign capital inflows, private and EC-funds, continue to be a strong support for domestic investment activity. The decline in fixed investment in Turkey reflects a large reduction in public sector expenditures on investment projects; but private sector investment growth weakened also. In Yugoslavia total fixed investment appears to have stabilized in 1989 at a low level: for the year as a whole it was 20 per cent below its level in 1983.

The increase of existing production capacities often requires the extension of existing or the erection of new buildings — this was a major factor in business investment in many European countries and has given a strong support to *construction investment* (table 2.2.10). Within this aggregate *housing investment* was also relatively strong, reflecting existing shortages and improved profitability. Higher real incomes appear to have stimulated the demand for larger and better quality accommodation. To some extent this also reflects the impact of government subsidy schemes. Housing investment has been particularly vigorous in Belgium and Finland, with growth rates in 1988 and 1989 above 20 per cent. In the Federal Republic of Germany the large inflow of immigrants from eastern Europe led the authorities in October 1989 to enhance the existing support schemes in order to accelerate the creation of additional housing. In the United Kingdom private residential investment declined under the impact of rising mortgage rates and was only slightly cushioned by an increase in public housing investment, which had fallen in 1988. There was also a sharp fall in housing investment in Norway in 1989, a consequence of high borrowing costs and the heavy household debt burden (table 2.2.10).

Given the strong growth of production, notably in the investment goods sector, and the very high capacity utilization rates, the strength of investment in *manufacturing industry investment* is no surprise (table 2.2.11). It is noteworthy that in many countries investment by manufacturing industry was much more vigorous than in the other business sectors. On average, industrial investment in western Europe rose by about 9 per cent in 1989, broadly the same as in 1988. The slackening of manufacturing investment in the United Kingdom (table 2.2.11) is much less pronounced when leased assets are taken into account.[91] Manufacturing investment growth in 1989 was extremely buoyant in Finland and Ireland. In the latter country, investment expenditures over the last two years have risen by nearly 75 per cent.[92] Manufacturing investment in Norway has fallen in 1989 owing to weak domestic demand but the large decline in the total is largely due to developments in the oil refining sector.

In the United States, the growth of total fixed investment slowed down to a mere 2 per cent, the lowest annual rate of the current upswing (table 2.2.9). De-

---

[91] Including leased assets, real fixed capital formation in the UK manufacturing industry rose by 5.5 per cent in 1989, following an increase of 12 per cent in 1988. Note that in the national accounts fixed assets are allocated to the sectors which own the investment goods, which are not always those which actually use them.

[92] Note that the strong decline in manufacturing investment shown for Finland in 1988 (table 2.2.11) does not reflect a sharp deterioration of actual investment performance, but rather the statistical treatment in the national accounts of sales of real estate from manufacturing companies to pension foundations and real estate firms owned by the manufacturing companies themselves. In pure accounting terms this reduces the capital stock of manufacturing industry (i.e., there is disinvestment) and increases the capital stock of the services sector. Total investment in the country is, of course, not affected by these accounting changes.

TABLE 2.2.10

Real fixed investment by type of asset, 1987-1989
(Percentage change over previous year)

	Machinery and equipment			Construction					
				Total			Housing		
	1987	1988	1989 [a]	1987	1988	1989 [a]	1987	1988	1989 [a]
France	4.3	9.0	7.0	3.3	6.2	3.8	0.6	3.4	..
Germany, Federal Republic of	5.6	7.5	8.8	-0.3	4.7	7.2	-1.5	4.8	6.0
Italy	14.1	6.0	7.0	-0.4	3.7	3.5	-1.6	-0.2	..
United Kingdom	7.0	18.6	10.3	10.0	6.7	-1.4	6.8	7.7	-10.0
Total 4 countries	7.5	9.8	8.3	2.5	5.4	3.9	0.4	3.8	..
Austria	0.9	5.6	10.0	4.9	5.9	3.0	..	..	..
Belgium	8.6	14.0	16.0	5.5	12.0	9.0	7.1	21.4	20.8
Denmark	-14.9	-6.9	4.6	-0.8	-3.1	-5.5	-8.6	-10.0	-5.0
Finland	12.1	10.6	13.5	0.9	9.3	12.0	0.7	16.6	20.0
Ireland	2.7	2.8	14.5	-6.7	-6.8	7.0	..	..	..
Netherlands	1.3	4.9	9.8	0.7	13.0	4.3	2.0	13.9	2.7
Norway	4.7	18.2	-1.1	-2.4	-4.5	-5.7	3.6	-4.2	-16.6
Sweden	10.1	7.9	8.8	5.4	4.9	2.8	11.9	11.4	3.2
Switzerland	11.3	7.9	5.0	5.4	6.4	5.5	..	..	..
Total 9 countries	3.8	7.1	9.4	2.2	5.9	3.6	2.7	10.1	..
Total 13 countries	6.6	9.2	8.5	2.5	5.5	3.8	0.8	4.9	..
Canada	16.5	22.2	13.7	8.8	7.3	4.7	16.3	4.6	4.1
United States [b]	8.1	11.5	5.2	-2.7	-0.2	-2.3	-0.5	-0.4	-2.7
North America	8.9	12.7	6.2	-1.0	1.0	-1.1	1.5	0.3	-1.8

Sources: National statistics and estimates of official and private institutions.

[a] Preliminary.
[b] Private sector investment only.

mand for machinery and equipment remained strong, although the growth rate halved in comparison with 1988 (table 2.2.10). But both non-residential and residential construction expenditures fell, continuing the weak performance observed already in 1988. Manufacturing investment (table 2.2.11) appears to have increased by some 7 per cent in 1989.[93] Although capacity utilization rates in the US manufacturing industry have fallen somewhat in the course of 1989, they are, nevertheless, still high and this seems to have encouraged investment. Also, US firms may have again been more fully exposed to stronger international competition as the beneficial effects of the dollar depreciation began to peter out. This may have triggered higher investment aimed at modernizing and rationalizing product lines and production processes.

As in 1988, fixed investment was the mainstay of economic growth in Canada in 1989. Machinery and equipment remained the most buoyant component of domestic demand. Manufacturing investment rose by some 11 per cent, continuing the strong growth rates of the last few years.

With the recent strengthening of fixed investment, there has been a partial reversal of the long-run decline in the *investment-output ratio* in western Europe (chart 2.2.4). This indicator is often employed to gauge the relative strength of investment and it is therefore important to understand the factors which underly its movements. Changes in this indicator in the 1980s reflect two specific developments: one is the rapid growth of machinery and equipment compared with construction investment; the other is the depressing effect of changes in the relative price of investment goods on the nominal investment-output ratio (i.e., the ratio expressed at current prices).

It was only in 1987 that nominal investment expenditures started again to grow faster than nominal output in western Europe (chart 2.2.4). The nominal investment-output ratio is now close to its value in 1981, but this is still far below the values that prevailed in the early 1970s. It can be seen from chart 2.2.4 that the real investment-output ratio (i.e., the ratio between the two variables expressed at constant prices) had already started to rise again in 1986 and that in 1989 it was somewhat above its level in 1980. The gap between the constant and current price ratios that has opened up since 1982 reflects the change in the relative price of investment goods, i.e., the price of investment goods relative to the price of all goods in the economy. This relative price was more or less stable in the 1970s, but it has fallen steadily – although not by very much – since 1981. In 1989 there was no change compared with 1988.

This tendency for a change in the relative price of investment goods to drive a wedge between the nominal and the real investment-output ratios was much more pronounced in the United States in the 1980s (chart 2.2.4). In fact, at constant prices, the ratio is now close

---

[93] This figure is derived from business surveys of new plant and equipment expenditure. Note that survey data differ in concept and coverage from the national accounts series on fixed investment.

CHART 2.2.4

Nominal and real investment output ratios and the relative price of investment goods
(Indices, 1980 = 100)

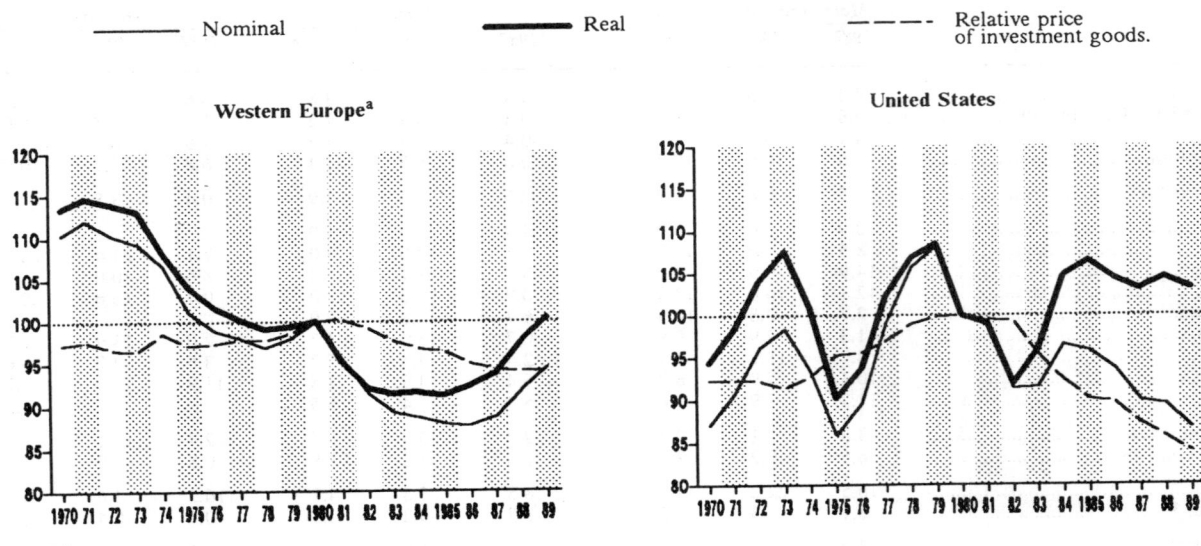

Source: ECE/DEAP.

Note: Ratio of gross fixed capital formation to GDP. Investment data for the United States cover only private sector expenditures. The relative price of investment goods is defined as the ratio of the implicit deflator of fixed investment over the implicit GDP deflator.

[a] 18 countries.

CHART 2.2.5

Investment output ratios by type of asset
(Indices, 1980 = 100)

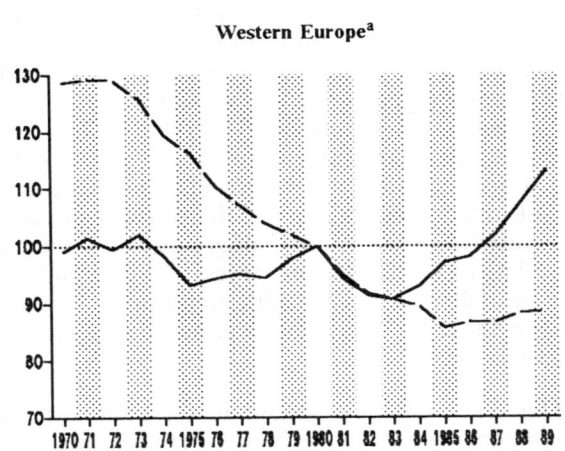

Source: ECE/DEAP.
Note: See chart 2.2.3.
[a] 13 countries; excluding southern Europe.

TABLE 2.2.11

Real fixed investment [a] in manufacturing industry, 1987-1990
(Percentage change over previous year)

	1987	1988	1989	1990 [b]
France	3.4	13.1	8.7	12.0
Germany, Fed.Rep. of	5.6	3.5	11.1	8.5
Italy	12.3	10.1	12.2	11.5
United Kingdom	7.4	12.0	1.8	2.0
Total 4 countries	7.1	8.8	9.3	9.0
Austria [c]	-0.4	-3.0	5.0	10.5
Belgium	7.5	18.0	12.0	15.0
Denmark	8.9	5.9	10.7	11.0
Finland [c]	20.5	-16.1	34.0	4.5
Ireland	-0.9	45.0	31.0	10.0
Netherlands	-	-6.9	-2.0	8.0
Norway	11.7	-13.3	-28.0	-5.0 [c]
Sweden [c]	13.1	5.4	13.0	7.0
Total 8 countries	7.1	7.5	7.8	8.0
Total 12 countries	7.1	8.5	9.0	9.0
Canada	18.8	14.5	10.7	..
United States	3.8	11.7	7.3	1.5
North America	5.1	11.9	7.6	1.5*

Sources: Compiled from national sources and from the Commission of the European Communities, *European Economy*, Supplement B. No.1, January 1990.

[a] Excluding leased assets. [b] Forecasts. [c] Includes mining.

to the high levels of 1973-1974, whereas the nominal ratio is close to the very low values for 1975 and 1970. This reflects the steep fall in the relative price of investment goods by 16 per cent between 1980 and 1989. Thus an increase in the real investment output ratio by 3 percentage points between these two years was accompanied by a decline in the nominal ratio by 13 per cent (chart 2.2.4). This fall in the aggregate relative price of investment goods in the United States was largely due to machinery and equipment, the relative price of which fell by nearly 25 per cent between 1980 and 1989, whereas the relative price of structures fell by only 3 per cent.

As can be seen from chart 2.2.4, the relative price of investment goods in western Europe in the 1980s fell much less than in the United States. It should also be noted that for the west European countries on average, the relative price of both types of assets roughly declined by the same amount: machinery and equipment by 7 per cent and construction by some 4.5 per cent.

Against this background it is interesting to note that the change of the aggregate *real* investment-output ratio conceals strikingly different trends for the two major types of assets, viz. machinery and equipment on the one hand and construction (structures) on the other hand (chart 2.2.5).

During every year of the current upswing, real expenditure on machinery and equipment has grown faster than real GDP in western Europe, so that in 1988-1989 the machinery-output ratio reached its highest value for the last twenty years (chart 2.2.5). In sharp contrast to these changes is the development of the other major component of fixed capital formation, namely construction. After reaching a peak in the early 1970s, the ratio of construction investment to output did not stop falling until 1985; in that year it was one third below its peak values in 1971-1972. Although there has been some recovery since then, the relative performance of structures, compared with machinery and equipment, has had a depressing effect on the overall real investment-output ratio.

In the United States the two ratios have been much more volatile than in western Europe (chart 2.2.5). The trends in the 1980s, however, are strikingly similar to those in Europe. In 1989 the ratio of machinery to output reached its highest value in twenty years, whereas for construction this ratio is lower than at any other time in period since 1970.

Altogether, for the market economies, the share of machinery and equipment in total real capital formation has been rising. At the same time, however, the relative price of this most dynamic component of investment has fallen, which has tended to depress the nominal aggregate investment-output ratio.

The sluggishness, until recently, of construction investment relative to machinery and equipment reflects the interplay of several factors which can only be briefly mentioned here. A marked feature of economic policies since the early 1980s has been the concern to consolidate budget deficits and to contain the growth of public expenditures. To a large extent this overall restraint on expenditures has fallen on public investment because of its more discretionary nature. This has been one factor depressing construction investment. Another important factor is the influence of the rather sluggish economic growth over many years after the two oil price shocks which dampened the growth expectations of firms. In such an environment, their main concern was to rationalize production rather than to expand capacity. Those years were characterized by relatively large excess capacity and so the demand for new industrial buildings was rather modest. It is only in the more recent years, when output has moved quickly towards the limits of capacity, that investment in new industrial structures has recovered significantly.

(d) Stockbuilding

Stockbuilding provided only a modest support for higher output growth in 1989 (tables 2.2.2 and 2.2.3). For the 18 European countries combined the contribution to final domestic demand amounted to some 0.2 percentage points, slightly less than in 1988.[94] With buoyant demand for manufactured goods the level of stocks of finished and semi-finished goods remained at relatively low levels. Only in a few countries (Austria, Ireland, Norway, Turkey) did inventory changes actually subtract from final demand growth. The conspicuously large offset to final demand originating from stocks in Norway is explained by changes in the volume

---

[94] Detailed short-term data on stockbuilding is in general not available for the majority of countries. The aggregate stock change is often derived as a residual and includes therefore a statistical discrepancy between the change in total GDP and its major components.

TABLE 2.2.12

Volume of trade in goods and services, [a] **1987-1990**
(Percentage change over previous year)

	Exports				Imports			
	1987	1988	1989 [b]	1990 [c]	1987	1988	1989 [b]	1990 [c]
France	3.0	7.6	8.4	6.3	7.7	8.1	7.1	5.7
Germany, Fed.Rep. of	0.4	5.6	9.4	6.5	4.1	5.9	6.9	6.5
Italy	3.3	5.9	6.1	5.8	10.1	7.2	8.1	6.0
United Kingdom	5.1	0.8	4.7	6.2	7.6	12.4	9.2	1.2
Total 4 countries	2.6	4.7	7.5	6.3	6.9	8.3	7.8	4.8
Austria	2.4	8.8	10.9	6.7	4.7	10.0	9.6	7.0
Belgium	7.1	8.2	8.4	6.9	9.3	8.3	8.7	7.0
Denmark	4.8	6.7	6.2	4.7	-2.2	1.2	4.0	3.2
Finland	2.6	3.9	1.7	3.5	9.0	11.5	9.6	3.5
Ireland	13.4	8.7	9.5	8.0	5.0	3.9	10.0	8.2
Netherlands	4.1	7.7	6.2	5.8	6.1	7.1	6.5	5.7
Norway	3.5	4.8	12.1	3.0	-6.6	-2.7	-0.3	1.4
Sweden	3.8	3.3	4.0	3.0	7.2	5.8	6.0	4.0
Switzerland	1.7	5.2	6.1	4.1	5.5	5.4	6.4	5.3
Total 9 countries	4.6	6.7	7.3	5.4	5.3	6.3	6.9	5.5
Total 13 countries	3.3	5.5	7.4	5.9	6.3	7.5	7.5	5.1
Greece	15.9	7.7	4.0	4.0	16.5	6.5	9.0	6.0
Portugal	10.8	7.1	13.0	8.5	26.4	17.3	12.0	9.5
Spain	5.9	6.3	4.3	5.2	20.4	15.2	15.8	10.7
Turkey	26.0	17.2	5.0	5.0	17.4	5.0	5.5	7.2
Yugoslavia	0.5	4.9	4.9	..	-6.9	-0.9	13.2	..
Southern Europe	9.7	8.2	5.4	5.5	16.6	11.0	12.5	9.4
Total 18 countries	3.8	5.7	7.3	5.7	7.1	7.8	7.9	5.5
Canada	6.5	9.5	-0.7	1.6	9.0	13.9	7.8	2.1
United States	15.0	17.7	10.9	7.3	6.3	5.1	5.2	6.1
North America	12.8	15.7	8.1	6.0	6.8	6.7	5.7	5.3

Sources: National statistics and estimates of official and private institutions.

[a] National accounts basis.   [b] Preliminary.   [c] Forecasts.

of oil platforms under construction. Stockbuilding may have been an important factor behind the turnround in domestic demand recorded in Yugoslavia for 1989, consumption and fixed investment remaining weak. But this is obscured by a possible statistical discrepancy.

Also in the United States stockbuilding did not add to the growth of final demand. Preliminary data indicate a small, negative effect on growth. There was a small increase in farm inventories after two years of successive falls, but this was more than offset by changes in the non-farm sector. In contrast, stockbuilding in Canada added a considerable 1.2 percentage points to final demand growth. This was entirely due to the recovery of agricultural inventories, which had been run down in the wake of the drought in 1988. In 1989 crop yields improved and agricultural inventories were replenished.

(e) Foreign balances

Domestic economic activity in the market economies received a strong boost from foreign demand last year. At the same time the rapid expansion of domestic demand also stimulated import growth. The expansion of trade was broadly based, but the investment boom has led notably to a surge of international trade in machinery and equipment. Trade flows in 1989 were another illustration of the close relations that exist between the European market economies; at the same time they were indicative of the high degree of complementarity in specialization patterns between the various countries.

For the 18 west European countries combined, real exports of goods and services in 1989 rose by about 7.5 per cent in comparison with 5.7 per cent in 1988. Aggregate real imports rose by 8 per cent, roughly the same as in 1988 (table 2.2.12). In general, the growth rates for real exports and imports were quite similar for individual countries in 1989.

The impact of changes in the real foreign trade balance on GDP growth differed a lot between individual countries (tables 2.2.2 and 2.2.3). For the 18 European countries in aggregate the stimulus to domestic activity from higher exports was less than the negative effect of increased imports. Consequently the real foreign balance lowered GDP growth in 1989 on average by some 0.3 percentage points (table 2.2.2). This is considerably less than during the period 1986-1988 (chart 2.2.2).

Among the four larger economies the change in the real foreign balance added significantly to GDP growth only in the Federal Republic of Germany (a contribution of 1 percentage point). Apart from their strong specialization on investment goods, German exporters benefited from increasing price competitiveness. The

Deutschmark not only depreciated against the dollar but also, in real terms, within the EMS. In Italy and the United Kingdom the real foreign balance was a considerable drag on domestic output growth (table 2.2.2). In the latter country this was partly because of the disruptions to oil production which have depressed oil exports since 1988.

Among the 14 smaller economies the contribution of the net foreign balance to growth was generally negative (table 2.2.3). The offset to GDP growth was particular large in Finland, Greece, Portugal, Spain and Yugoslavia. In contrast, in Norway the favourable changes in the foreign account turned a decline in domestic demand into an increase of real GDP.

In the United States, export growth slowed down after the exceptionally rapid expansion in 1988. The average growth rate for 1989 was about 11 per cent, following an increase of nearly 18 per cent in 1988. This may be partly explained by the fact that the stimulus given to price competitiveness by the sharp depreciation of the dollar is beginning to wear off. In fact, this tendency was somewhat reinforced by the strengthening of the US dollar in the foreign exchange markets in 1989. Overall the US economy has been able to take considerable advantage of the dollar depreciation: real exports in 1989 were 50 per cent above their level in 1986. With import growth unchanged from 1988 (an increase by about 5 per cent) and again much lower than the increase in exports, the deficit on the foreign account in real terms was reduced by about $22 billion, to $80.7 billion, in 1989.[95] The combined effect of these changes in exports and imports has been to reduce the positive impact of the net foreign balance on domestic output growth from 1 percentage point in 1988 to 0.5 percentage points in 1989 (table 2.2.2 and chart 2.2.2).

In contrast, in Canada the real foreign balance was a considerable drag on output growth in 1989, lowering the increase in GDP by nearly 3 percentage points. Exports to the United States, which account for 75 per cent of all Canadian merchandise exports, declined as a result of the combined effects of weaker domestic demand in the US and a relatively strong appreciation of the Canadian dollar. Exports to other regions rose but were not sufficient to compensate for the lower shipments to the United States. In the event, the total volume of exports fell by about 1 per cent in 1989.

---

[95] This is the real trade deficit excluding net factor incomes and is the appropriate variable to look at when examining changes in GDP rather than GNP. It may be recalled that the latter is calculated by adding net factor incomes from abroad to GDP. It is noteworthy, that the receipts of factor incomes by US residents are still significantly higher than payments of factor incomes to foreign residents. In 1989 net factor incomes from abroad amounted to about $28 billion, the same as in 1989. Correspondingly, the deficit on the real foreign balance falls to $53 billion in 1989 when these flows are taken into account.

2.3 INTERNAL AND EXTERNAL BALANCE

This section reviews changes in the internal and external balance of the market economies in 1989. Rates of inflation picked up in 1989, but the rise in consumer prices was partly due to increases in indirect taxes and interest rates, both measures intended eventually to reduce inflation. Underlying rates of inflation generally rose only modestly (section (i)). The sustained growth of output led to further increases in employment and lower unemployment (section (ii)), and to a continued expansion of world trade (section (iii)). There was also progress in reducing the large current account imbalances among the market economies, although the pace of adjustment tended to slow down in the second half of 1989.

(i) Costs and prices

(a) Introduction

Inflation in 1989, for the year as a whole accelerated both in western Europe and in North America. Measured by the consumer price index, the average inflation rate was 4.5 per cent in western Europe and 4.8 per cent in North America compared with 3.1 per cent and 4.1 per cent in 1988 respectively. However, most of the acceleration occurred in the first half of the year. In the second half, helped by an easing in non-oil commodity prices and a more restrictive monetary policy stance, the rate of change more or less stabilized in western Europe and decelerated in North America. Inflation continued to be much more severe in the south European countries, although there were much larger differences among these countries than in the rest of the region. The rate of inflation in Spain, which accelerated in 1989, was still lower than the UK rate while the hyperinflation in Yugoslavia gained further momentum.

The higher inflation rates of 1989 were to a large degree due to special factors, such as increases in indirect taxes and public service charges in some countries and external factors such as the significant recovery in oil prices which was further aggravated for the west European countries by the depreciation of their currencies against the US dollar. In fact the rate of change in the GDP deflator in western Europe, which is the broadest measure of inflation and which reflects mainly the changes in domestic factor costs, accelerated much less than the domestic demand deflator which reflects also the change in import prices. The increase in the GDP deflator was 3.7 per cent in 1988 and 4.1 per cent in 1989, while the rate of change of the domestic demand deflator, increased on average from 3.4 per cent to 4.2 per cent. In contrast, the rate of change of the GDP deflator in North America accelerated more strongly (from 3.4 per cent to 4.2 per cent) than the domestic demand deflator (from 3.4 per cent to 4.0 per cent). This difference between the two regions mainly reflects the fact that import price inflation more than tripled to an annual rate of 6.1 per cent in western Europe in 1989, while it more than halved to an annual rate of 1.2 per cent in North America.

Wage inflation (here measured by the rate of change in compensation per employee) which accelerated in late 1988 continued in 1989, although at much more modest rates than were expected in the majority of the countries given the further tightening of labour markets and the large and well publicized increases in profit margins during the last few years. Furthermore, thanks to surprisingly large productivity gains, especially in western Europe, the rise in unit labour costs was also lower than foreseen in the majority of the countries at the start of 1989. In real terms (i.e., deflated by the GDP deflator) unit labour costs fell again for the eighth consecutive year in western Europe (on average by some 0.5 per cent). However, there also continued to be large differences between countries: increases in unit labour costs reached a 9-year high in the United Kingdom and Sweden, while in the Netherlands they fell. In North America unit labour costs accelerated much more strongly than the west European average and in real terms they increased by nearly a percentage point, the largest rise since 1985. The less favourable development in North American unit labour costs was due to smaller gains in productivity (0.9 per cent versus 2.1 per cent in western Europe); the rise in compensation per employee in both regions were rather similar on the average (6.0 per cent versus 5.7 per cent), but in North America relatively weaker output growth (3.0 per cent versus 3.3 per cent) was combined with a much larger rise in employment (2.0 per cent versus 1.2 per cent).

The acceleration in the GDP deflator in 1988 was mainly due to large gains in unit profits, but in 1989 the main factor behind the modest acceleration was unit labour costs in the majority of the countries and indirect taxes in others. Nevertheless, overall profit performance, as indicated by, as yet, incomplete and provisional estimates for the year as a whole, was still favourable, and particularly in western Europe during the second half of the year.

Despite some marked differences between countries and regions, considering that 1989 was the seventh year of the present upswing with very high capacity utilization rates, tighter labour markets *and* a significant increase in external cost pressures, overall price developments in the developed market economies of the ECE region in 1989 were surprisingly favourable. While the tighter stance of monetary policies throughout the year and falling non-oil commodity prices during the second half were important, it was especially because wages did not greatly respond to the earlier acceleration of prices, that 1989 was another year of sustainable and job-creating growth. Wage restraint is to some extent a function of the tightening of policy, but there is evidence that there has been a change in underlying wage behaviour in recent years which, in turn, has eased the burden on monetary policy in securing stability.[96] The contribution of the slow-down in wage growth to the disinflation process during the 1980s in western Europe and the United States is considered in more detail below in section (e).

(b) Consumer prices

Inflation measured by the consumer price index increased from 3.1 per cent in 1988 to 4.5 per cent in 1989 for the west European countries on average[97] (Appendix table A.9). In North America, the increases were 4.1 per cent and 4.8 per cent respectively. Part of this faster inflation in 1989 was due to external and special factors such as the higher world price of oil, amplified in the west European countries by the stronger dollar, and a rise in indirect taxes in some countries (Belgium, Federal Republic of Germany, Italy, Canada). Much of the acceleration was in the first half of the year: the average (year-on-year) rate increased from 3.5 per cent in the last quarter of 1988, to 4.5 per cent in the second quarter of 1989 in western Europe and from 4.3 per cent to 5.2 per cent in North America. In order to prevent any risk of a sustained acceleration of inflation rates and the generation of a new price-wage spiral, monetary policy took a more restrictive stance in May and short-term interest rates started to rise. In addition, world food prices, which contributed significantly to the rise in consumer prices during the early months of the year, fell by nearly 15 per cent (year-on-year basis) during the second half of 1989. Consequently, the average inflation rate in western Europe during the second half of 1989 stabilized around 4.5 per cent. In the United states, during the same period, there was a fall in the rate (chart 2.3.1) reflecting to a large extent the weakening of economic activity. From September onwards, the year-on-year inflation rate in the United States fell below the west European rate: in December it was 4.2 per cent in the United States compared with 4.6 per cent in western Europe and 5.1 per cent in Canada. It was only in France (3.6 per cent), the Federal Republic of Germany (3 per cent), Austria (2.9 per cent), Belgium (3.6 per cent) and the Netherlands (1.3 per cent) that the December inflation rates were below the US rate.

In western Europe annual rates of inflation were highest in the United Kingdom (7.8 per cent), Finland, Italy and Sweden (all three at 6.6 per cent).[98] The inflation rate also accelerated in 1989 in the traditionally low inflation countries, namely, the Federal Republic of Germany, Austria, Belgium and Switzerland, but to much lower levels (between 2.5 and 3 per cent). In the former three countries the rate stabilized during the second half of the year; in Switzerland, however, inflation accelerated considerably throughout the year to reach 5 per cent in December (year-on-year), due to a unusually large increase in unit labour costs, a weaker currency and the effect of higher interest rates on rents in the last quarter. The lowest annual rate of inflation in 1989 was again in the Netherlands (1.1 per cent) and only in Norway did it actually fall, from 6.7 per cent in 1988 to 4.6 per cent in 1989, thanks to strong growth in productivity and domestic production of oil.

In 1989, the problem of inflation was again much more severe in the south European countries than in the other market economies of the ECE region. However, inflation rates and trends differed considerably among these countries. In Greece the inflation rate in 1989 (13.7 per cent) was only marginally higher than in 1988: despite large falls in productivity and soaring unit labour costs, prices were restrained by support for the drachma, a policy which led to high interest rates. Both in Portugal and Spain inflation accelerated strongly: from 9.6 per cent in 1988 to 12.6 per cent in 1989 in Portugal and from 4.8 per cent to 6.8 per cent in Spain. During 1989 the monthly trends in both countries were similar to those elsewhere in west European countries, that is, most of the acceleration occurred during the first half of the year: during the second half the rate fluctuated around 7 per cent in Spain and decelerated in Portugal. The year-on-year rate of change in Portugal in December 1989 was 11 per cent, nearly one percentage point lower than that of a year earlier. In Turkey the inflation rate, which was over 75 per cent in 1988, started to slow down during the final months of 1989 as a result of the sharp slow-down in the economic activity, an anti-inflationary exchange rate policy, and the relatively restricted monetary and fiscal policy stance maintained during the year. For 1989 as a whole the rate was 69.6 per cent. In January 1990, the year-on-year change was 60 per cent compared with 68.7 per cent in the preceding month. In Yugoslavia, the hyperinflation of the last three years gathered further momentum during 1989. In December, the year-on-year rate of change reached 2,720 per cent; for the year as a whole, the increase was 1,252 per cent compared with 194 per cent in 1988. In Cyprus the inflation rate accelerated slightly from 3.4 per cent in 1988 to 3.7 per cent in 1989. In Malta, the inflation rate fluctuated between 2 and 3 per cent during the first half of 1989 but in the second half consumer prices fell slightly; for the year as a whole the rate was just below 2 per cent, compared with 0.9 per cent in 1988.

As the prices of food and energy are relatively more sensitive to seasonal and other exceptional factors than other items in the consumer price index, a better indi-

---

[96] See Commission of the European Communities, *European Economy*, Supplement A, November 1989.

[97] Weighted average of 13 developed market economies of western Europe. See Appendix A for the list.

[98] In the United Kingdom, the retail price index includes mortgage interest rates. Thus, an anti-inflationary tightening of monetary policy has a direct, positive effect on the index. In December 1989 the UK retail price index excluding mortgage rates was 6.1 per cent higher than in 1988; including the mortgage rate, the increase was 7.7 per cent. Central Statistical Office, *Retail Prices Index and Tax and Price Index in December*, Press Release, 19 January 1990.

CHART 2.3.1

Quarterly and monthly changes in consumer prices[a], 1980-1989
(Percentage change over corresponding period of preceding year)

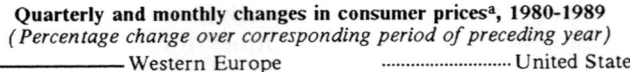
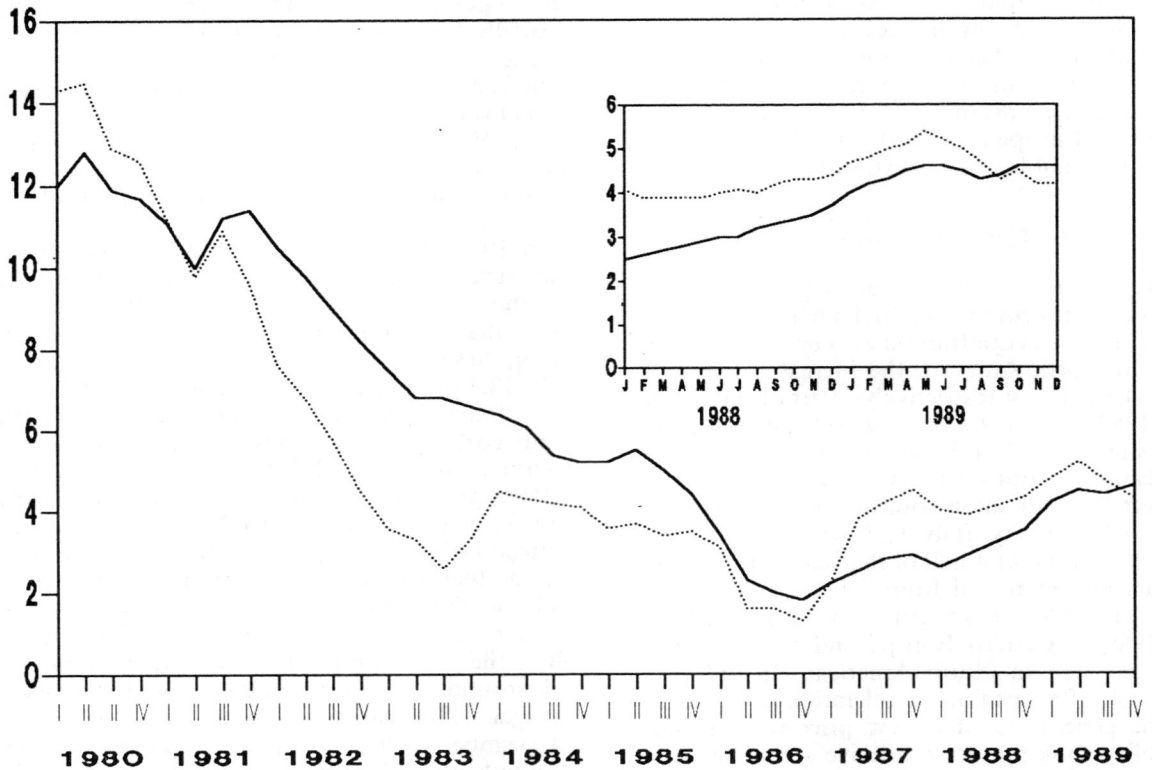

Source: National sources.

a Weighted average of 13 countries.

cator of the "core" inflation can be obtained by excluding these two items from the index. Except in the oil and gas producing countries (the United Kingdom, Norway and the Netherlands) and Canada, where the exchange rate appreciated strongly, this "core" rate of inflation increased at lower rates than overall inflation rates in 1989 as in 1988; however, there was still a significant acceleration in "core" rates in Austria, Ireland, Switzerland, the Federal Republic of Germany, Italy and Belgium. In the latter three countries this is partly explained by the increase in indirect taxes at the beginning of the year. It was only in France and Norway and, to a lesser extent, in Denmark that the "core" inflation rate fell in 1989 compared with 1988. In the United Kingdom the acceleration in the "core" rate was much more significant than in the overall index: increasing from 4.1 per cent in 1988 to 8.2 per cent in 1989. This difference may be explained in part by the inflation restraining effect of the appreciation of sterling on the import prices of food in the first half of 1989.[99]

Within the consumer price index, both in western Europe and North America, the prices of services increased faster than those for manufactured goods (excluding food and drink). However, the latter accelerated much more: service prices increased by 4.6 per cent in 1988 and 4.8 per cent in 1989 in western Europe[100] and by 4.6 and 4.9 per cent respectively in the United States. The increase in manufacturing prices, however, accelerated from 2.4 per cent in 1988 to 3.7 per cent in 1989 in western Europe and from 3.2 per cent to 4.1 per cent in the US. This greater acceleration in manufacturing prices can be explained to a large extent by the larger impact of higher energy prices on goods production, very high capacity utilization rates

---

99 The "core" rate quoted here for the United Kingdom includes interest payments on home mortgages.

100 Unweighted averages of Belgium, Denmark, France, the Federal Republic of Germany, Italy, Norway and Switzerland.

and the tighter labour market for skilled workers in the manufacturing sector.

(c) Primary commodity prices

The rise in non-energy commodity prices since mid-1987 came to an end early in 1989 (chart 2.3.2).[101] Dollar prices at the end of 1989 were nearly 11 per cent below their levels at the end of 1988.[102] On an average annual basis, dollar prices increased by half of a percentage point in 1989 compared with 21.3 per cent in 1988. However due to the appreciation of the US dollar against the European currencies, non-energy commodity prices in ECUs increased by 9.5 per cent for 1989 as a whole,[103] although on a quarterly basis there were considerable variations in dollar prices and the dollar-ECU exchange rate.[104] In contrast to the previous two and a half years, non-energy commodity prices in the second half of 1989 ceased to exert pressure on the overall inflation rate in western Europe and were a disinflationary factor in the United States. The main reasons for this were the effect of the relative slow-down in economic activity during a period of excess supplies on basic metals prices (excluding lead and gold) and the collapse of international agreements for coffee and cocoa. Further falls in commodity prices were avoided because of poor harvests and very low stock levels in grains, sugar and meat. In December 1989, dollar prices for food and industrial raw materials were 17 per cent and 13.5 per cent respectively below their levels of a year earlier.

Although OPEC has been consistently producing over its agreed quota[105] stronger than expected world demand for oil[106] and a succession of disruptions in non-OPEC supply, led to *oil prices* being a major factor in the faster rate of inflation both in US and more so in western Europe since the closing months of 1988. Brent crude, which fell just below $12 a barrel at the beginning of October 1988, reached $20 at the end of 1989. The Alaskan oil spill at the end of March, the explosion at a North sea oil platform in mid-April (which is estimated to have reduced British crude oil output by one quarter), the shortage of hydroelectrical output due to the summer drought in southern Europe, and the exceptionally cold winter in North America during the closing weeks of 1989 and the beginning of 1990, pushed oil prices to new heights. On the supply side, there was also a fall in US oil production (some 6

CHART 2.3.2

World market prices of raw materials, in US dollars and ECUs, 1981-1989
(1980 = 100, semi-logarithmic scale)

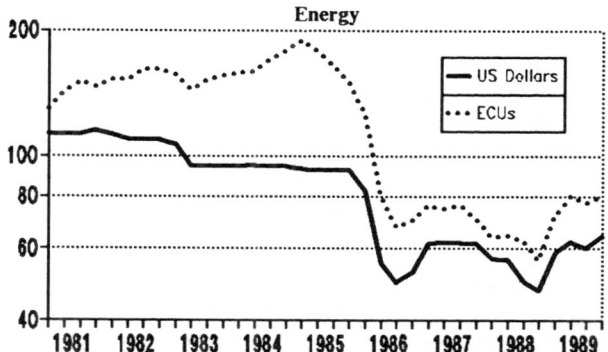

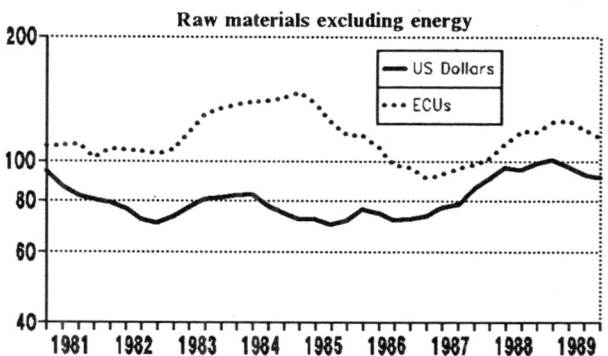

Source: Dollar index is published by HWWA (Hamburg) in *Intereconomics*. The conversion to ECUs was made by the ECE secretariat on the basis of the US dollar-ECU exchange rate published in IMF, *International Financial Statistics*, Washington, D.C.

per cent) and a significant decline in net Soviet oil exports. The latter was caused by the increase in domestic demand for oil which was due to significantly reduced coal production and regional strife which affected both the production and the distribution of crude oil. *World energy prices*[107] increased by 17.5 per cent in dollar terms and 27.3 per cent in ECU terms in 1989.

---

[101] As measured by the HWWA index. Produced by the HWWA Institute for Economic Research, Hamburg, this index weights world market prices (in dollars) by the relevant commodity shares in total imports of the western industrialized countries in 1974-1976.

[102] Because of the volatility of commodity prices in recent years it may be misleading to compare changes solely on an annual (i.e., year-on-year) basis.

[103] Against the ECU the US dollar appreciated by 11.4 per cent during the first half of 1989 and 5.4 per cent during the second.

[104] During the first quarter, on a year-on-year basis, non-oil commodity prices increased by 11.4 per cent in dollars and by 22 per cent in ECUs. In the second quarter dollar prices stabilized, whereas the ECU prices increased by a further 14.2 per cent. In the second half of the year dollar prices fell by 5 per cent and ECU prices were nearly stable.

[105] While the official OPEC ceiling on production increased from 18.5 million b/d in the first quarter to 20.5 million b/d in the fourth, OPEC supply accelerated from 20.5 million b/d to 23.5 million b/d, its highest level since the first quarter of 1981.

[106] Demand projections for oil were repeatedly understated during 1989. Not only was OECD demand stronger than expected, but the largely neglected increased demand in the developing world has played an important part in sustaining prices above the level expected. In 1989 world demand for oil (excluding the east European countries) increased by 2 per cent compared with 3.2 per cent in 1988. While the rate of growth in demand for oil in the OECD area is estimated to decelerate to 1.1 per cent in 1989 from 2.8 per cent a year earlier, developing country consumption (equivalent to 28 per cent of total world demand) grew by 4.5 per cent to an average of 14.5 million b/d in 1989.

[107] The weight of oil in the total energy component of the HWWA index is 91.3 per cent.

CHART 2.3.3

Intermediate product prices and producer prices in manufacturing industries,[a] **1988-1989**
(Change over corresponding month of the previous year)

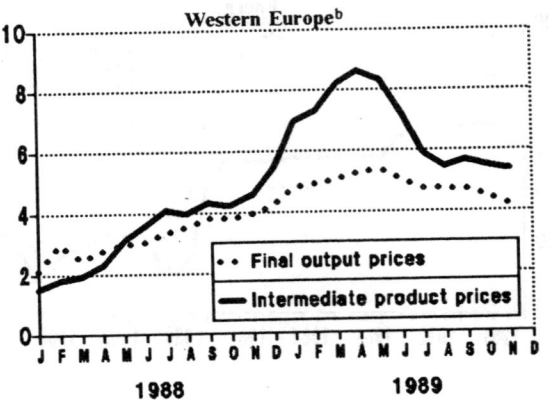
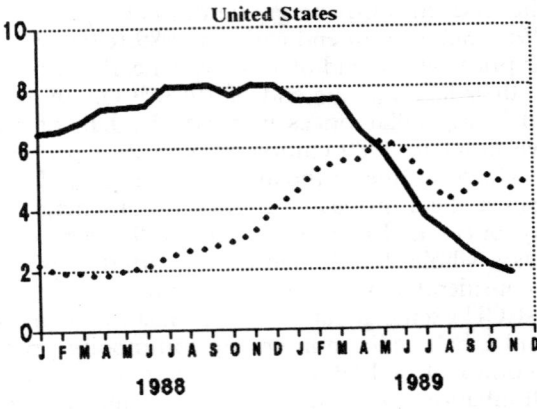

Source: ECE secretariat common data base, based on national sources.

[a] For definitions of indices, see United Nations Economic Commission for Europe, *Economic Survey of Europe in 1982*, New York, 1983, pp. 32-33.
[b] Unweighted average of 13 countries.

The increase *during* the year was still larger: world energy prices at the end of 1989 were 27.6 per cent in US dollars and 29.4 per cent in ECUs above their levels at the end of 1988.

(d) Intermediate goods and producers' prices in manufacturing industry

In western Europe,[108] intermediate goods prices continued to rise with further momentum, in 1989 (chart 2.3.3). In April the year-on-year increase of 8.6 per cent was the largest in five years. This was mainly the effect of higher import prices which on a national accounts basis, and for western Europe as a whole, increased by 6.1 per cent in 1989 compared with 1.9 per cent in 1988. During January-November 1989 intermediate goods prices were, on average, nearly 7 per cent higher than in the same period in 1988, more than double the rate for 1988 during the same period. Producer prices of manufactures in western Europe also continued to rise in 1989, although at much lower rates: in January-November they were nearly 4.5 per cent higher on average than in the same period in 1988. Changes in both intermediate goods and output prices of manufacturing industry in western Europe decelerated in the second half of the year. The difference between the changes in these two price indices, which indicates the pressure of material input costs on output prices reached some 3.5 percentage points in April 1989.[109] This difference decreased significantly after April, although it did not disappear until the end of the year.

In the United States, the prices of intermediate goods decelerated throughout 1989, thanks mainly to falls in non-oil commodity prices and the dampening effect of an appreciating dollar on other import prices (rate of increase in import prices decelerated from 3.3 per cent in 1988 to 1.5 per cent in 1989). During the January-November period, average annual rate of change was 4.8 per cent in 1989 compared with 7.5 per cent in 1988 during the same period. In November 1989 the year-on-year increase was just below 2 per cent, down from 8.1 per cent in the same month of 1988. On the other hand, producers' prices in the United States continued to accelerate until mid-1989: there was some easing during the summer months but since September they have fluctuated with no definite trend. During the January-November period, the average annual rate of change was 5.1 per cent in 1989 compared with 2.5 per cent in 1988 during the same period. The difference between the two indices, which started to enlarge in mid-1987, disappeared in May 1989. Since May it has been steadily widening again but this time due to higher rates of change in producers' output prices. In Canada intermediate goods prices, which had fallen strongly since the second quarter of 1988, started to increase in March 1989 and accelerated over the year. In contrast, the deceleration in producers' prices continued with further momentum in 1989. In October 1989, the year-on-year increases were 6.9

---

[108] Unweighted average of 13 west European countries.

[109] The rate of change in intermediate goods prices minus the rate of change in producers' output prices.

CHART 2.3.4
Changes in the GDP deflator and labour costs, 1980-1989
(Annual percentage changes)

— Deflator of GDP at market prices
– – – Nominal labour cost per employee
········ Real labour cost per employee
—■— Real unit labour cost[a]

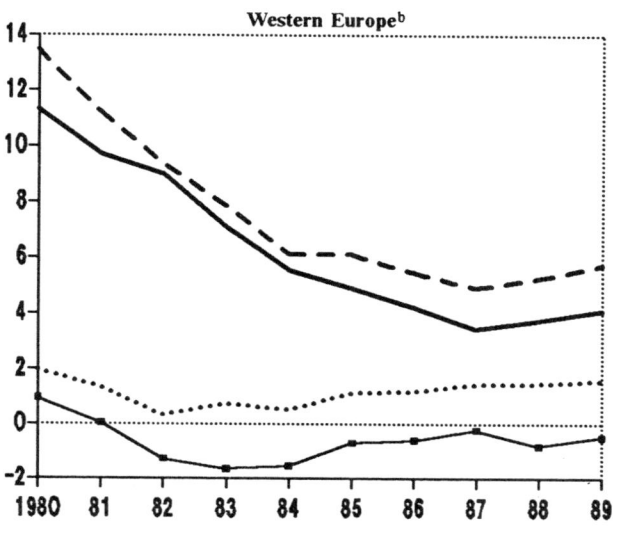
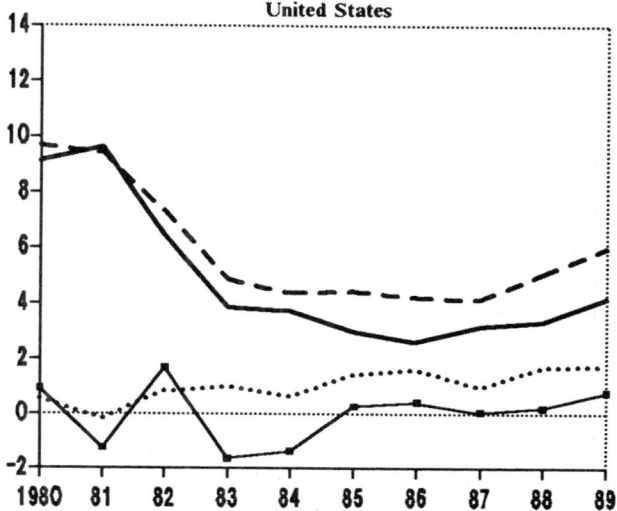

Source: National accounts.

[a] Nominal unit labour costs deflated by the GDP deflator at market prices.
[b] Weighted average of 13 countries.

per cent for intermediate goods and 1.2 per cent for producer goods.

Thus in western Europe, largely due to higher import prices, input costs maintained pressure on output prices in 1989 whereas in the United States the stronger dollar played an important role not only in containing the overall inflation rate but also, given the increase in unit labour costs, in preventing a further squeeze on unit profits, particularly during the second half of the year.

(e) Domestic and external inflationary pressures

In the last three years, not only output growth but also inflation has been much more favourable than expected. In 1989, the seventh successive year of economic expansion in the western industrialized world, in spite of stronger than expected demand growth and falling unemployment, inflation (measured by the GDP deflator) again remained moderate: it averaged just above 4 per cent both in western Europe and the United States, thanks to surprisingly large productivity gains and relatively modest wage rises. In fact the disinflation of the 1980s and the more recent job-creating investment led growth were strongly supported by the slow-down in nominal and real wage increases. Real unit labour costs, which measure the gap between real labour cost per employee and labour productivity, fell 6 per cent in western Europe and 1.5 per cent in the United States between 1983 and 1989. Moreover, this moderation in labour costs was achieved without an adverse effect on demand since the purchasing power of earnings (i.e., nominal compensation per employee deflated by the change in consumer prices) improved throughout the period 1983-1989 by an average of 1.6 per cent a year in western Europe and 1.1 per cent in the United States. Hence, strengthened consumer demand, combined with large gains in terms of trade due to much weakened primary commodity prices in the mid-1980s, allowed strong growth in both output and profits while inflation rates remained moderate in most countries during the late 1980s.

In western Europe, the increase in the GDP deflator, the broadest measure of inflation, fell steadily from 11.3 per cent in 1980 to 3.4 per cent in 1987 (chart 2.3.4). During the same period the rate of increase in nominal compensation per employee fell from 13.5 per cent to 4.9 per cent. Since 1987, this downtrend in

CHART 2.3.5

Contribution of unit labour costs to the change in the GDP deflator, 1980-1989
(Percentages)

——— Deflator of GDP at market prices
– – – Contribution of unit labour costs
········ Contribution of labour cost per employee
▒▒▒▒ Effect of productivity[a]

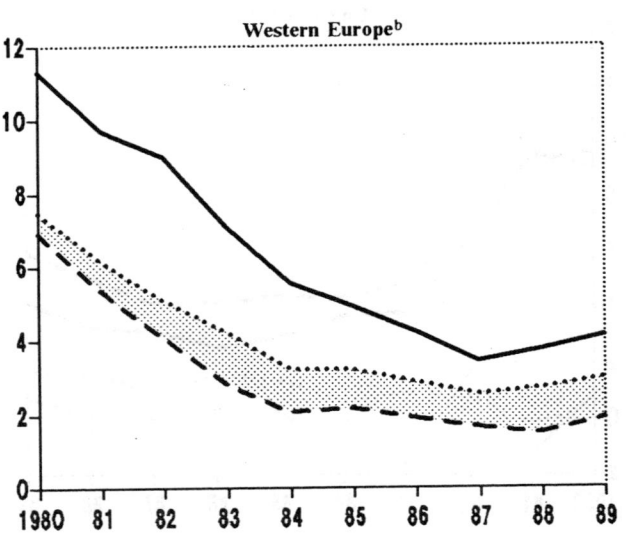
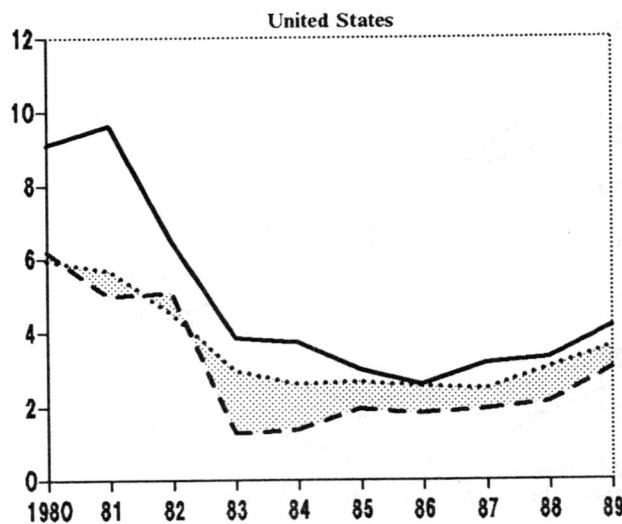

Source: National accounts.
[a] Effect of the change in labour productivity on the GDP deflator. If the shaded area is below the dotted line, it is having a negative effect on the deflator; if it is above, the effect is positive.
[b] Weighted average of 13 countries.

compensation per employee and inflation has been partly reversed, but both the GDP deflator and labour costs increased by less than one percentage point during the following two years to reach 4.1 per cent and 5.7 per cent respectively in 1989. In the United States the increase in the GDP deflator came down from 9.6 per cent in 1981 to 2.6 per cent in 1986, well below the lowest annual rate achieved in western Europe during the 1980s. During the following three years, however, inflation in the United States accelerated faster than in western Europe, reaching 4.2 per cent in 1989. The rise in the compensation per employee in the United States fell from 9.7 per cent in 1980 to 4.1 per cent in 1987; but it also accelerated faster than in western Europe during the following two years to reach 6 per cent in 1989.

The fact that the nominal wage increases have adjusted to the fall in inflation and that real wages have increased persistently less than the growth of productivity means that profits have been allowed to rise significantly while at the same time disinflation has continued. Unit profits (operating surplus per unit of value added) increased by 7.4 per cent a year in western Europe and 5.1 per cent in the United States between 1980 and 1988. This favourable profit performance is one of the factors behind the recent strong growth in fixed investment and employment.

Contributions to the growth in the GDP deflator give a clearer view of developments in domestic costs in the economy as a whole. The relative contribution of unit labour costs in western Europe fell each successive year from nearly 7 points in 1980 to 1.5 percentage points in 1988 (chart 2.3.5), a reflection of both diminished contributions from the rise in compensation per employee and large productivity gains. In 1989 the contribution of unit labour costs increased slightly (to 1.9 percentage points) as the somewhat slower productivity growth could not totally offset the uptrend in compensation per employee. In the United States, on the other hand, unit labour costs' contribution to the rise in the GDP deflator did not follow a continuous trend during the 1980s. After falling precipitously from 5 percentage points in 1982 to less than 1.5 points in 1983-1984, their contribution remained around 2 points for the following four years. In 1989 there was nearly a percentage point jump in the unit labour cost contribution in the United States: one third was due to the

CHART 2.3.6
Contribution of the non-labour component of GDP to the change in the GDP deflator, 1980-1989
(Percentages)

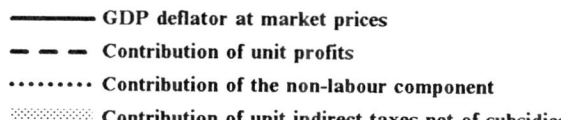
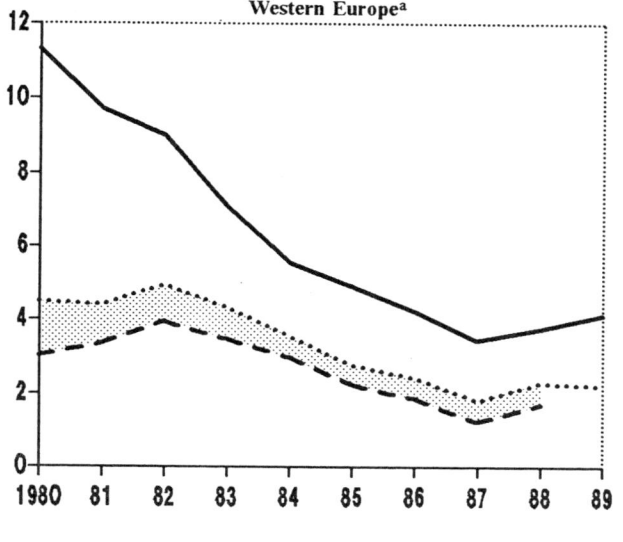
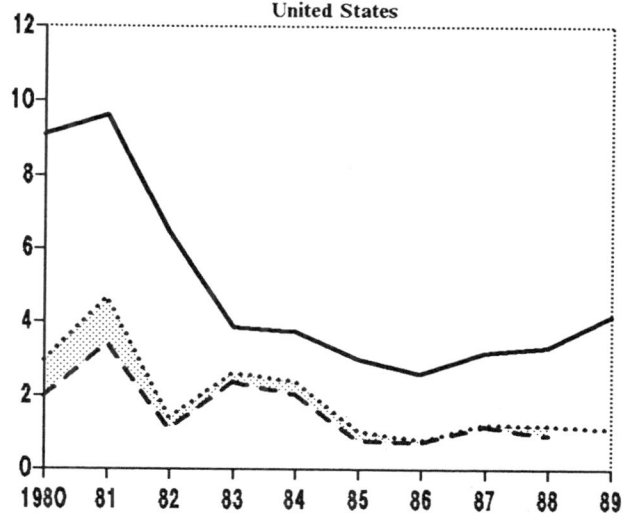

Source: National accounts.
a Weighted average of 13 countries.

productivity slow-down and the rest due to higher compensation per employee.

While the contribution of unit labour costs slowed down throughout the period 1980-1988 in western Europe, the contribution of unit profits to inflation fell without interruption only between 1983 and 1986 (chart 2.3.6). The faster increase in the GDP deflator in 1988 was due to the acceleration in unit profits which increased by 4.7 per cent and accounted for nearly one half of the total increase in the deflator. For 1989, the data on current price GDP at factor cost were not available for most countries during the preparation of this *Survey*. Nevertheless, given the slight slow-down in the rate of change in the non-labour component[110] of the GDP deflator, and taking into account the indirect tax increases in some countries in 1989 (the Federal Republic of Germany, Belgium, Italy), it is likely that the rate of change in unit profits decelerated and their contribution to the change in the GDP deflator was smaller in 1989 than in 1988.

In the United States, both the rise in unit profits and their contribution to the rise in the GDP deflator did not show any clear trend during the 1980s. They fluctuated strongly around very high average rates during the first half of the decade; between 1985 and 1988 their growth was between 2.5 and 3.5 per cent a year and they did not account for more than one third of the rise in the GDP deflator. In 1989, the contribution of the non-labour costs component in the United States did not change (1.1 per cent both in 1988 and 1989). Since there were no new indirect taxes during the year it may be concluded that the contribution of unit profit to the rise in the GDP deflator remained more or less the same as in 1988 and that the entire acceleration in the GDP deflator in 1989 was due to the faster rise in unit labour costs, as in western Europe. However, while more than the two thirds of the increase in the GDP deflator in 1989 was due to unit labour costs in the United States, it was less than one half in western Europe.

Among the west European countries, however, there were large differences, in both the increase of the GDP deflator and its components (table 2.3.1). The rise in the GDP deflator ranged from 1.1 and 2.2 per cent in the Netherlands and the Federal Republic of Ger-

---

[110] The non-labour component of GDP consists of gross profits (operating surplus) and indirect taxes net of subsidies.

TABLE 2.3.1

Contributions to the change in the GDP deflator, 1988-1989

(Annual percentage change)

	Change in the GDP deflator [a]	of which due to:				
		Unit labour costs			Unit profits [c]	Unit indirect taxes net of subsidies
		Total	Compensation per employee [b]	Labour productivity		
France						
1988	3.1	0.7	2.2	-1.5	1.5	0.9
1989	2.9	1.3	2.4	-1.1	1.6	
Germany, Fed. Rep. of						
1988	1.5	0.1	1.7	-1.6	1.3	-
1989	2.2	0.6	1.7	-1.1	1.0	0.6
Italy						
1988	6.0	2.9	4.1	-1.1	1.8	1.3
1989	6.0	2.8	3.9	-1.0	3.1	
United Kingdom [d]						
1988	6.5	3.7	4.1	-0.4	1.8	1.0
1989	7.2	4.0	4.5	-0.5	3.2	
Austria						
1988	2.0	-0.2	1.7	-1.9	2.1	0.2
1989	2.6	2.0	3.4	-1.3	0.5	
Belgium						
1988	1.9	-0.5	0.9	-1.5	2.4	-
1989	3.3	0.4	2.2	-1.8	2.9	
Denmark						
1988	4.2	2.2	2.2	-0.1	1.8	0.3
1989	3.8	1.4	2.4	-1.1	2.4	
Finland						
1988	6.9	2.4	5.4	-2.9	2.7	1.8
1989	6.5	3.5	5.3	-1.7	2.1	0.9
Ireland						
1988	2.9	0.3	1.7	-1.4	2.3	0.3
1989	4.9	-	3.0	-3.0	4.1	0.8
Netherlands						
1988	1.8	-	0.8	-0.8	1.7	-
1989	1.1	-0.3	1.1	-1.5	1.3	0.1
Norway						
1988	4.4	3.4	4.5	-1.0	1.6	-0.5
1989	5.3	2.1	5.3	-3.1	3.3	
Sweden						
1988	6.6	4.0	4.5	-0.5	2.6	0.1
1989	7.3	5.1	5.5	-0.3	2.1	
Switzerland						
1988	2.5	1.7	2.8	-1.1	0.7	0.1
1989	3.5	2.4	3.6	-1.1	1.0	
Western Europe [e]						
1988	3.7	1.5	2.7	-1.2	1.7	0.6
1989	4.1	1.9	3.0	-1.1	2.2	
Canada [d]						
1988	4.1	2.1	3.0	-0.9	1.3	0.8
1989	5.0	3.0	3.4	-0.4	2.0	
United States						
1988	3.3	2.1	3.0	-0.9	0.9	0.3
1989	4.2	3.0	3.6	-0.6	1.1	

Source: National accounts. Small discrepancies are due to rounding.

a GDP at market prices.
b Wage and non-wage costs per person employed.
c Includes capital consumption.
d Based on data for three quarters.
e Weighted average of 13 countries.

many to more than 7 per cent in Sweden and the United Kingdom. Not only the size but also the direction of change differed among countries: in France, Denmark, Finland and the Netherlands, the rate of change in the deflator decelerated in 1989, while in Italy it was the same as in 1988. In the Federal Republic of Germany, if indirect taxes had not been increased, the rise in 1989 would have been 1.5 per cent, the same as in 1988. (In the Federal Republic of Germany the slow-down in unit profits nearly offset the relatively

CHART 2.3.7

Contributions to the change in the domestic demand deflator, 1980-1989
(Percentages)

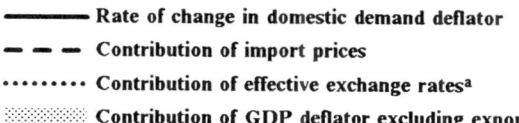

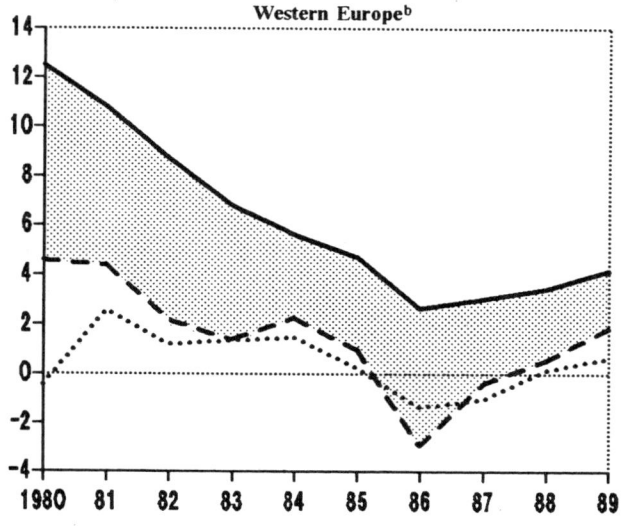
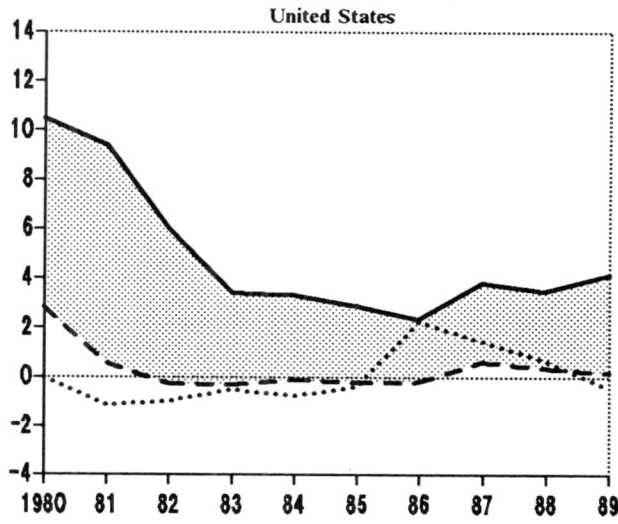

Sources: National accounts and IMF, *International Financial Statistics*, Washington, D.C.
a Reciprocal of IMF MERM rates.
b Weighted average of 13 countries.

large rise in unit labour costs caused by the slow-down in productivity.) In Denmark, the slow-down in inflation was due to the favourable productivity performance in 1989 as the GDP rose for the first time since 1986. In France and Finland the deceleration of inflation in 1989 was due to a significant slow-down in the rate of change of the non-labour component of the GDP deflator, whereas in the Netherlands there was also a fall in unit labour costs (0.6 per cent) thanks to accelerated productivity growth.

Unit labour costs contributed largely to the acceleration in inflation in 1989 in Austria, Sweden, Switzerland and, to a much lesser extent, in Belgium. In the latter two countries, this was due to a significant acceleration in compensation per employee while in the former two the productivity slow-down also had an unfavourable effect. The largest increase in compensation per employee were in Finland, Sweden, Norway, Italy and the United Kingdom (between 8 and 10 per cent). However, in Norway productivity increased by nearly 5.6 per cent and so unit labour costs could still decelerate from 6.2 per cent in 1988 to 3.8 per cent in 1989. In the other countries, unit labour costs accelerated strongly reaching 8.8 per cent in Sweden, 7.3 per cent in the United Kingdom, and 6.6 per cent in Finland. In Italy they rose by 6.2 per cent, just below the rate in 1988. The contribution of unit labour costs in 1989 was smaller than in 1988 only in Denmark, Ireland and Norway, while in the Netherlands they actually pulled down the overall inflation rate. In all four countries this was due to large productivity gains. In the Federal Republic of Germany, Italy and Finland the relative contribution of compensation per employee was the same as in 1988 but in the latter two it was still very large, nearly two thirds and four fifths respectively of the total increase in the GDP deflator.

Thus while the acceleration of inflation in 1988 was mainly due to gains in unit profits, in 1989 the main factor behind the acceleration in the GDP deflator was unit labour costs (only in Ireland and Norway, was the acceleration of inflation in 1989 due to profit push). Furthermore, if productivity gains had been less favourable, then inflation in some west European countries would have been considerably higher.

Inflation, as measured by the GDP deflator, also accelerated in all the south European countries in 1989. The increases ranged from 7.2 per cent in Spain to 73.8 per cent in Turkey (data are not available for Yugoslavia). While the rates differed, the sources of inflation were similar. In all four countries both unit labour costs and unit profits contributed to the acceleration in inflation in 1989. The rate of change in compensation per employee increased in all four while, except in Portugal, productivity growth slowed down: consequently there was a significant acceleration in unit labour costs.

Domestic inflation rate in western Europe as a whole, measured by the change in the domestic demand

TABLE 2.3.2

Contribution to the change in the domestic demand deflator, 1988-1989
(Annual percentage change)

	Change in domestic demand deflator	Changes in GDP deflator excluding exports [a]	of which due to: Import prices Total	Exchange rates [b]	Export prices of suppliers [c]
France					
1988	2.8	2.4	0.5	0.4	-
1989	3.3	1.7	1.6	0.5	1.1
Germany, Fed. Rep. of					
1988	1.3	0.9	0.4	0.2	0.2
1989	2.9	1.5	1.3	0.5	0.9
Italy					
1988	5.7	4.9	0.7	0.7	-
1989	6.0	4.6	1.4	-	1.3
United Kingdom [d]					
1988	5.5	5.7	-0.2	-1.4	1.2
1989	5.6	4.6	1.0	0.9	0.1
Austria					
1988	1.7	1.1	0.6	0.4	0.2
1989	3.8	2.0	1.8	1.0	0.9
Belgium					
1988	1.7	-0.1	1.7	0.6	1.1
1989	3.2	-1.2	4.4	1.1	3.4
Denmark					
1988	5.1	4.4	0.8	0.5	0.3
1989	4.6	3.6	2.1	1.3	0.8
Finland					
1988	5.6	5.3	0.3	-0.2	0.5
1989	5.5	4.8	0.6	-0.5	1.2
Ireland					
1988	3.6	-	3.5	0.4	3.1
1989	4.6	-0.5	5.1	1.8	3.3
Netherlands					
1988	1.3	1.4	-0.1	0.1	-0.2
1989	1.1	-2.5	3.6	1.2	2.4
Norway					
1988	7.1	5.0	2.0	0.1	1.9
1989	7.8	4.8	3.0	0.5	2.4
Sweden					
1988	6.1	4.8	1.3	-	1.3
1989	6.9	5.0	1.9	0.3	1.7
Switzerland					
1988	2.8	1.4	1.4	0.5	0.9
1989	4.2	1.3	2.8	2.6	0.2
Western Europe [e]					
1988	3.4	2.9	0.5	0.1	0.4
1989	4.2	2.5	1.7	0.6	1.1
Canada [d]					
1988	3.2	4.0	-0.9	-1.4	0.5
1989	3.2	3.6	-0.4	-1.5	1.0
United States					
1988	3.5	3.1	0.4	0.7	-0.3
1989	4.1	4.0	0.2	-0.4	0.6

Source: National accounts and IMF, *International Financial Statistics*, Washington, D.C. Small discrepancies are due to rounding.

[a] Calculated as a residual of the change in the domestic demand deflator minus the contribution of the change in import prices.
[b] Effective exchange rates (reciprocal of IMF MERM rates).
[c] These are the prices of imports in terms of the national currency of the country of origin.
[d] Based on data for three quarters.
[e] Weighted average of 13 countries.

deflator[111] fell through most of the 1980s, from 12.5 per cent in 1980 to 2.6 per cent in 1986 (chart 2.3.7). This down-trend was partly reversed after 1986 and the rate of domestic inflation accelerated to 3 and 3.4 per cent respectively in 1987 and 1988 and to 4.2 per cent in 1989. The rate accelerated in all countries except the

---

[111] Inflation measured by the GDP deflator excludes, by definition, the effect of changes in import prices and includes the effect of changes in export prices. Hence, overall inflationary pressure in the domestic economy is better indicated by the change in the domestic demand deflator. The extent to which domestic inflation is home made or imported can then be seen by decomposing the change in the domestic demand deflator into the contribution coming from the

United Kingdom, Finland, Denmark and the Netherlands. The highest rates were in Italy, Norway and Sweden (between 6 and 8 per cent) and the lowest in the Netherlands (1.1 per cent). In the Federal Republic of Germany, even though the rate more than doubled (to 2.9 per cent), it was still much lower than the regional average.

After falling sharply in 1986 (by 10.7 per cent) and to a much lesser extent in 1987 (1.3 per cent), import prices in western Europe rose by 1.9 per cent in 1988 and started to exert an upward pressure on domestic prices. In 1989, mainly due to the marked increase in dollar price of oil and the depreciation of most European currencies against the dollar, average annual import price inflation more than tripled to 6.1 per cent — significantly higher than the GDP deflator both including and excluding exports (4.1 and 3.3 per cent respectively). Import price inflation was between 7 and 9 per cent in the majority of countries. The smallest increase in import prices was in Finland (2.5 per cent) thanks to a 2 per cent increase in the effective exchange rate of the markka.

Hence, the acceleration in the average rate of west European domestic inflation in 1989 was due to import prices, the increase in prices for home consumed domestic production being smaller than in 1988 (table 2.3.2). It was only in the Federal Republic of Germany and, to a much lesser extent, in Sweden that the change in the GDP deflator excluding exports also contributed to the acceleration in domestic inflation in 1989. Nevertheless, while their effect diminished, nearly three fifths of domestic inflation in western Europe in 1989 was still due to domestic factor costs and indirect taxes. Within the import price contribution, one third was due to exchange rate movements and the rest due to higher suppliers' prices in general.

Domestic inflation in the United States fell from 10.5 per cent in 1980 to 2.3 per cent in 1986 (chart 2.3.7). After a significant acceleration in 1987 (3.8 per cent) it slowed marginally in 1988 (3.5 per cent) thanks to a much smaller depreciation of the dollar than in 1987 and the continued decline in overseas suppliers' prices. In 1989, despite the favourable effect of the appreciation of the dollar (4.1 per cent in MERM effective exchange rate terms) on import prices, domestic inflation in the United States increased virtually at the same rate as in western Europe in general. However, contrary to western Europe, the acceleration in the United States rate was entirely due to a large rise in the GDP deflator excluding exports. In Canada domestic inflation rose by 3.2 per cent, the same as in 1988, thanks to a further strong exchange rate appreciation (5.7 per cent in MERM effective exchange rate terms). Canada was the only market economy in the ECE region where the change in import prices pulled down the overall domestic inflation rate in 1989.

(ii) Labour markets

The recovery in the labour markets continued in both western Europe and North America in 1989. Employment growth was 1.1 per cent in western Europe and 2.2 per cent in North America.[112] As in the recent past, employment creation has been dominated by employment in services which, to a large extent, consists of part-time jobs for females. Also the unemployment rates fell in both regions, although they still remain high in Canada and in many west European countries. Labour supply pressure weakened considerably in western Europe while in North America it gained further momentum, increasing nearly as fast as demand. In 1989, female and youth unemployment remained particularly high. Furthermore despite its decline in the last two years, the proportion of long-term unemployment remained high, particularly in those countries where the overall unemployment rates were above the regional average.

(a) Recent changes in demand for labour

The present upswing of employment in western Europe has been continuing since 1984 (chart 2.3.8). In the first quarter of 1989, high levels of economic activity contributed to further gains in employment, but the upward trend appears to have lost strength in the late spring. While most countries in western Europe reported brisk output growth, particularly in the first half of 1989, tighter monetary policies, especially in the United Kingdom, have put a brake on output and employment growth. As a result, the rise in employment in western Europe in 1989 was less than in 1988 for the year as a whole: 1.1 per cent versus 1.4 per cent in 1988 (table 2.3.3). Nevertheless 1.4 million additional jobs in 1989 brought the total increase in the number of employed persons between the last cyclical trough in 1983 and 1989 to 6.6 million.[113] Variance between the countries in 1989 remained considerable, both in terms of employment growth rates and trends. The strongest growth and largest acceleration in employment was in the Federal Republic of Germany and the Netherlands (2.2 per cent in both). The rate decelerated in the United Kingdom (from 3.2 per cent to 1.4 per cent) and to a lesser extent in Denmark and Switzerland. Employment shrank slightly in Italy and by more than 3 per cent in Norway.

---

change in the GDP deflator excluding exports and the change in the import deflator. This is essentially an accounting exercise and cannot itself say anything about the causes of inflation.

[112] Unless otherwise stated, data in this section are from labour force surveys and hence may differ from the national accounts data presented in the Appendix tables.

[113] The figures reported here do not take account of the results of the 1987 census in the Federal Republic of Germany. The Statistical Office of the Federal Republic reports a discrepancy in the monthly employment series between 1986 and 1987 of just over one million (1,12 million). The new series, which replaced the old in 1987, thus starts at a higher level of employment and, at the moment, leaves a discontinuity in the time series. (Statistisches Bundesamt, Fachserie 1, *Bevölkerung und Erwerbstätigkeit*, Reihe 4.3, *Erwerbstätigkeit und Arbeitsmarkt*, Wiesbaden, December 1989). Total employment in western Europe, including the new census figures for the Federal Republic of Germany was therefore just over 126 million in 1989, compared with 125 million in the old series.

CHART 2.3.8

Labour market developments, 1975-1989
A. *Millions*

Employment [a]   Unemployment

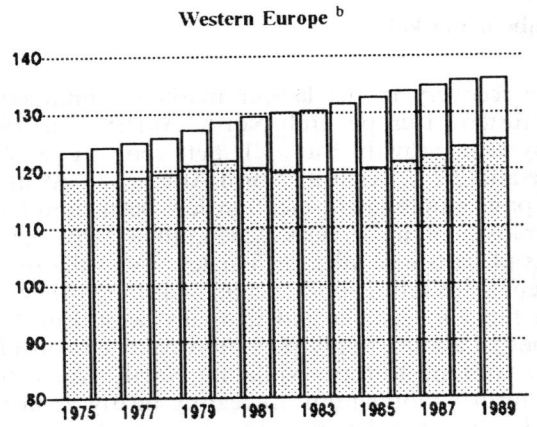
Western Europe [b]

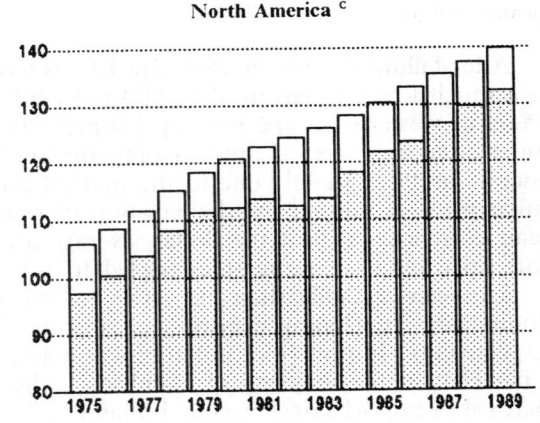
North America [c]

B. *Annual percentage changes*

— Labour force growth [a]   --- Employment growth

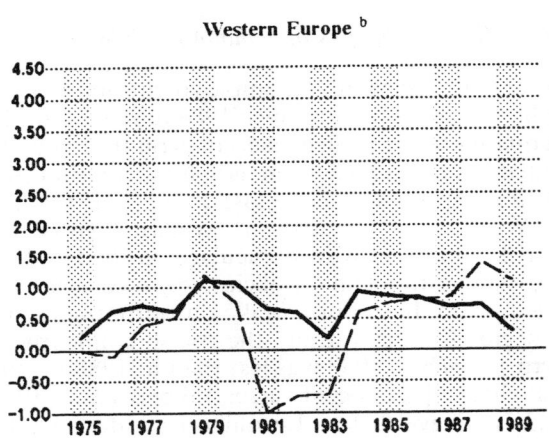
Western Europe [b]

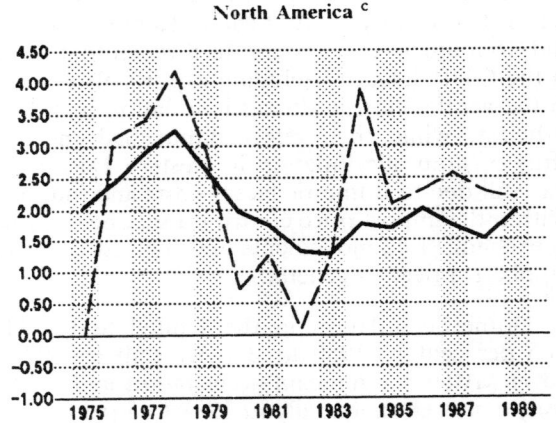
North America [c]

Source: National statistics and ECE secretariat estimates.

[a] Includes the armed forces.
[b] Weighted average of 13 countries.
[c] Weighted average of Canada and the United States.

Employment growth slowed down for both sexes (table 2.3.4), although the rate of growth in female employment was again much higher than that for males (1.4 per cent versus 0.9 per cent respectively).

Despite a stronger slow-down in economic activity during the second half of the year, demand for labour in North America in 1989 was again much more dynamic than in western Europe. Employment increased by 2.2 per cent (twice the west European rate) only slightly slower than in 1988, due to a fall in the Canadian rate. In 1989, there were 2.8 million additional jobs in North America, bringing the rise in the number of employed persons since the last cyclical trough in 1982 to 20 million. Contrary to western Europe, male employment in 1989 rose at the same rate as in 1988 (1.8 per cent) and the slight deceleration in total employment was due to a relatively smaller increase in the female employment (2.6 per cent versus 2.8 per cent in 1988).

Partial data (table 2.3.5), which are not strictly comparable with the data used elsewhere in this section, indicate that in western Europe[114] the growth of service

---

[114] Weighted average, excluding Belgium for which data were not available.

TABLE 2.3.3

Labour market changes in western Europe and North America, 1980-1989

	Western Europe			North America		
	Labour force	Employment	Unemployment	Labour force	Employment	Unemployment
Annual average change (thousands)						
1980-1982	995	-403	1379	2021	317	1673
1983-1986	965	427	538	2152	2765	-628
1987	909	1015	-106	2297	3178	-881
1988	980	1663	-683	2050	2895	-845
1989	391	1359	-968	2692	2840	-148
Average annual growth rate (per cent)						
1980-1982	0.8	-0.3	18.5	1.7	0.3	20.2
1983-1986	0.7	0.4	4.9	1.7	2.4	-5.4
1987	0.7	0.8	-0.9	1.7	2.6	-9.3
1988	0.7	1.4	-5.5	1.5	2.3	-9.8
1989	0.3	1.1	-8.3	2.0	2.2	-1.9

Sources: National statistics and ECE secretariat estimates.

TABLE 2.3.4

Growth rates of labour force, employment, and unemployment by sex in western Europe and North America, 1987-1989
(Annual percentage change)

	Labour Force		Employment		Unemployment	
	Men	Women	Men	Women	Men	Women
Western Europe						
1987	-	1.6	0.2	1.8	-1.8	0.3
1988	0.5	1.1	1.2	1.7	-7.1	-3.8
1989	0.1	0.6	0.9	1.4	-10.3	-6.1
North America						
1987	1.2	2.4	2.0	3.4	-9.3	-2.7
1988	1.0	2.1	1.8	2.8	-11.1	-9.3
1989	1.6	2.4	1.8	2.6	-1.9	-1.9

Source: National statistics and secretariat estimates.

sector employment decelerated in 1989. Nevertheless it was again the main source of additional jobs in the economy. After declining for more than a decade, industrial employment recovered slightly in the last two years (some 200,000 additional jobs). There were falls in industrial employment in 1989 only in Italy, the Netherlands (0.8 per cent in both), in Norway (6.9 per cent) and for the third successive year in Denmark (3.2 per cent). There was also a strong deceleration in the United Kingdom (from 1.9 per cent in 1988 to 0.5 per cent in 1989) due to a significant slow-down in manufacturing output growth since the spring of 1989. On the other hand, there were relatively large gains in industrial employment in France, the Federal Republic of Germany, and some of the smaller countries of the region. Agricultural employment in western Europe continued its long-term decline. Employment in all three broad sectors rose faster in North America compared with western Europe. Employment growth in the service sector was the highest among the three sectors and accounted for 85 per cent of the total increase in North American employment. The expansion of industrial employment also slowed in North America (from 1.9 per cent in 1988 to 1.1 per cent in 1989) but, nevertheless, there were 374,000 additional industrial jobs in this sector compared with 82,000 in western Europe in 1989.

Since the mid-1970s, employment creation has been dominated by employment in services and to a large extent by female part-time jobs. At present, in the four major economies of western Europe, about 72 per cent of workers in the service sector are women, which is considerably higher than the ratio for the economy as a whole. In North America, the share of women in the service sector is currently around 53 per cent, and has been growing steadily in recent years. Female employment growth in the sector was still higher than the rapid growth of male employment leading to an increase in the share of women in services throughout the region. As the share of young people in the labour force has declined, so the service sector has focused on the growing female labour force as well as older workers to meet its needs for labour, a process which can be observed in some countries.

During the present upswing over three quarters of new jobs were female and nearly two thirds of the increase was part-time. Including males, part-time employment accounted for three quarters of the increase

TABLE 2.3.5

Changes in employment, by sector, 1975-1989
(Average annual percentage change)

	1975-1979	1980-1982	1983-1986	1987	1988	1989
Western Europe [a]						
Agriculture	-2.3	-3.0	-2.3	-2.7	-3.3	-3.2
Industry	-0.5	-2.2	-1.6	-0.6	0.3	0.2
Service	3.0	1.4	1.8	1.9	2.4	1.2
North America						
Agriculture	0.4	0.2	4.9	1.1	-2.1	1.0
Industry	1.9	-3.8	1.8	0.6	1.9	1.1
Service	3.4	1.8	3.0	3.5	2.6	2.7

Sources: National statistics and ECE secretariat estimates.

[a] Belgium is not included in the figures for 1988 and 1989 due to lack of data.

in total employment during this period. The share of part-time female workers in total female employment in 1988-1989 was highest in the United Kingdom, Denmark and Sweden (between 40-43 per cent). In the Netherlands, the share was nearly one-third and in France, Germany and Canada, nearly one quarter. According to a household survey taken in October in the United States, 17 per cent of total male and female employment is part-time and nearly one quarter of these part-time jobs are involuntary which may suggest that the fall in unemployment has been somewhat overestimated. Nevertheless, increase in part-time employment also indicates a more flexible labour market which has helped job creation in recent years.

(b) Recent changes in labour supply

The long term downward trend in the rate of growth of the population of working age in western Europe (table 2.3.3) continued with increased momentum in 1989 and labour force growth slowed significantly (from 0.7 per cent in 1988 to 0.3 per cent in 1989). However, there were large differences between the countries: it fell in Italy and the United Kingdom (by 0.5 per cent in both) and in Norway (1.3 per cent), whereas it increased faster than in 1988 in France, the Federal Republic of Germany[115] and some smaller countries of the region. In 1989, participation rates increased in most countries as a result of a strong output growth and improved prospects for employment (table 2.3.6). These rates fell only in Norway, Sweden, Switzerland and to a much lesser extent in the Federal Republic of Germany. Therefore, as in 1988, the deceleration in the labour force growth in western Europe in 1989 was the result of the continued slow-down in the growth of the working age population due, in the majority of the countries, to the aging of population. In 1989, the female labour force growth rate halved to 0.6 per cent (table 2.3.4), but this rate was still much higher than the growth of the male labour force (0.1 per cent down from 0.5 per cent in 1988). Thus in 1989, 86 per cent of the rise in the total labour force (391,000) in western Europe was female and women's share in the labour force increased slightly to 40.4 per cent (table 2.3.7).

TABLE 2.3.6

Participation rates: 1975, 1988, 1989
(Per cent)

	1975					1988					1989
	All	Male	Female	Male 15-19	Male 55-64	All	Male	Female	Male 15-19	Male 55-64	All
France	67.0	84.3	51.1	30.0	68.9	65.5	77.0	57.2	15.5	47.3	65.8
Germany, Federal Republic of	67.9	87.0	49.6	55.0	68.1	66.8	80.8	52.8	48.3	56.5	66.5
Italy [a]	54.2	79.6	29.9	28.9	42.4	60.2	77.2	43.6	28.0	36.5	60.2
United Kingdom	73.6	92.1	55.1	62.5 [b]	87.6	77.3	88.7	65.8	77.8 [b]	68.4	78.0
Austria [c]	63.8	81.3	47.6	62.3	88.9	66.9	81.0	53.1	49.0	78.1	67.5
Belgium [d]	63.8	83.5	44.0	30.8	61.1	63.7	75.2	52.0	-	-	63.7
Denmark [e]	76.8	89.8	63.5	56.7	83.7	81.6	87.2	75.9	74.0	69.6	81.6
Finland	72.5	79.7	65.6	52.0	65.6	76.9	80.8	73.0	40.9	45.2	77.0
Ireland [f]	62.6	89.9	34.5	50.9	83.8	61.6	84.3	38.4	33.9	75.1	61.8
Netherlands	57.3	83.2	31.0	30.9	72.2	59.1	75.2	42.7	26.1	38.5	59.3
Norway	70.7	88.8	53.3	44.2 [b]	84.1	81.8	89.0	74.4	53.7 [b]	75.6	80.3
Sweden	78.5	88.9	67.6	59.0 [b]	82.0	85.8	88.9	82.6	45.2 [b]	74.9	82.4
Switzerland	74.8	96.2	51.9	-	-	71.3	89.8	54.6	-	-	70.8
Canada	68.1	85.2	50.0	54.6	79.4	76.4	86.8	67.2	58.5	66.6	76.8
United States	69.1	85.1	53.2	59.9 [b]	74.6	77.7	87.4	68.3	57.2 [b]	66.4	78.4

Source: OECD, *Labour Force Statistics*, Paris, national statistics, and ECE secretariat estimates.

Note: The participation rate for all ages is the ratio of the total labour force to the total population aged 15-64. The participation rate for an age group is the ratio of the labour force in that age group to the total population of the age group.

[a] Age range 14-19, 60-64. [b] Age range 16-19. [c] Age range 15-20, 50-60. [d] 1977, 1987. [e] 1976, 1987. [f] 1987.

---

[115] In the Federal Republic of Germany this was due to the arrival of 720,000 immigrants during 1989.

During the 1980s not only the demand for labour has been but also the rise in the supply of labour was much more dynamic in North America than in western Europe. In 1989 labour force growth accelerated to 2 per cent in North America (from 1.5 per cent in 1988), nearly seven times the west European rate. Both faster growth in the working age population and the rise in participation rates played a role in adding 2.7 million more people to the work force. Although both the male and female labour forces increased, the rate of increase in the latter (2.4 per cent) was considerably higher than the former (1.6 per cent). Women's share in the labour force increased to 44.5 per cent and they contributed 54 per cent of the rise in total labour force.

As frequently noted in previous *Surveys*, the increased participation of women in the work force has been a notable development in the market economies since the early 1970s. Table 2.3.6 compares participation rates by sex[116] in 1975 and 1988. Disaggregation of participation rates by sex indicates that female rates rose considerably between 1975 and 1988 in all countries of western Europe and North America, while male rates declined in most countries (except in the Nordic countries excluding Denmark, and North America).

This decline in male participation rates in the last 15 years is due to the downward trend in the rates for young workers and older males. Table 2.3.6 shows also the changes in the participation rates for 15-19 year olds and 54-65 year old males between 1975 and 1988. The decline in the participation rates of these two groups is common to both western Europe and North America, with a few exceptions for young males (the United Kingdom, Denmark, Norway and Canada). The fall in youth participation is explained partly by the increase in the number of young people in full-time education and, until recently, by "discouraged" withdrawals from the labour market due to sluggish labour market conditions. A similar pattern is observed for young women, but the decline in their participation was offset by the increase in the participation of women in the prime age groups.

Although labour shortages are expected as the growth of the female labour force slows down and as the aging of the population continues in the future, the alternative sources of labour supply are hard to identify. Increasing longevity is observed in most countries in western Europe and North America: raising the participation rate of older male workers would appear to be one possible source. However, it may be difficult to reverse the current trend of decreasing participation rates of older male workers within the existing retirement systems in many countries. Current social security and pension systems often encourage early retirement. A strong influence of social security and private pension plans on the timing of retirement and on labour force participation has been reported in the United States.[117] Although there is a high proportion of part-timers among older male workers in most countries in western Europe and North America, older workers still face a choice between full-time jobs or withdrawing from the labour force altogether, because of the unattractive conditions of part-time employment, which usually pays relatively low wages and provides very few benefits. Hence, some early retirements are probably due to the lack of good part-time employment opportunities.[118]

(c) Unemployment

The decline in unemployment, both as a proportion of the labour force and in absolute size, continued for the third successive year in 1989 in western Europe (table 2.3.3 and chart 2.3.9).[119] Only in Italy was the rate unchanged from 1988 and in Denmark and Norway it continued to increase, largely due to a fall in employment in the latter. Nevertheless, the average west European unemployment rate of 7.9 per cent (down from 8.6 per cent in 1988), representing 10.7 million persons (968,000 persons less than in 1988), was still much higher than in 1979 (its previous cyclical trough, at 5 per cent). In 1989, unemployment rates varied between 0.5 per cent in Switzerland to 11.8 per cent in Italy and 16.5 per cent in Ireland. Apart from Switzerland, the rate was lowest in Sweden (1.4 per cent) Austria and Finland (3.3 per cent in both). One important aspect of the changes in the west European labour market during the last two years is that, for the first time since 1979, the United Kingdom unemployment rate pulled down the west European average. The United Kingdom unemployment rate fell from a peak of 11.5 per cent in 1986 to 6.5 per cent in 1989, well below the west European rate. Both in 1988 and 1989 the unemployment rate fell nearly 2 percentage points per year. The fall in the numbers unemployed in the United Kingdom was 564,000 in 1988 and 509,000 in 1989, equivalent to 82 per cent and 53 per cent of the total decline in western Europe in the last two years respectively.

In North America, the fall in unemployment slowed down in 1989 due to both accelerated growth in labour supply and a high but stable rate of change in demand for labour. Nevertheless, the unemployment rate of 5.4

---

[116] The female participation rate is measured as the ratio of the total female labour force to the female working age population (15-64 years old). International comparisons of statistics on female labour force should be treated with more caution than that for males as women are more likely to be omitted from the labour statistics than men when unemployed. See for example, A. Dale and J. Glover, "Women at work in Europe: The potential and pitfalls of using published statistics", in the Department of Employment, *Employment Gazette*, June 1989.

[117] For example, see L. J. Kotlikoff, D. A. Wise, "Employee retirement and a firm's pension plan", D. A. Wise (ed.), *The economics of aging*, National Bureau of Economic Research, Chicago, USA, 1989; M. Hurd and M. Boskin, "The effect of social security on retirement in the early 1970s", *Quarterly Journal of Economics*, November 1984; also R.P. Hagemann and G. Nicoletti, "Population aging: Economic effects and some policy implications for financing public pensions", OECD, *Economic studies*, No.12/Spring 1989. This last article reports the simulation results of raising the retirement age in several west European countries and considers raising it as an option to secure funds for social security.

[118] D.E. Herz and P.L. Rones, "Institutional barriers to employment of older workers", Department of Labor, *Monthly Labor Review*, April 1989.

[119] The unemployment rates reported here are not standardized rates and hence not strictly comparable between the countries. Total labour force, including the armed forces, is used as the denominator.

CHART 2.3.9

Unemployment rates in selected countries, 1970-1989
(Per cent of total labour force)

——— Total employment   - - - Female employment

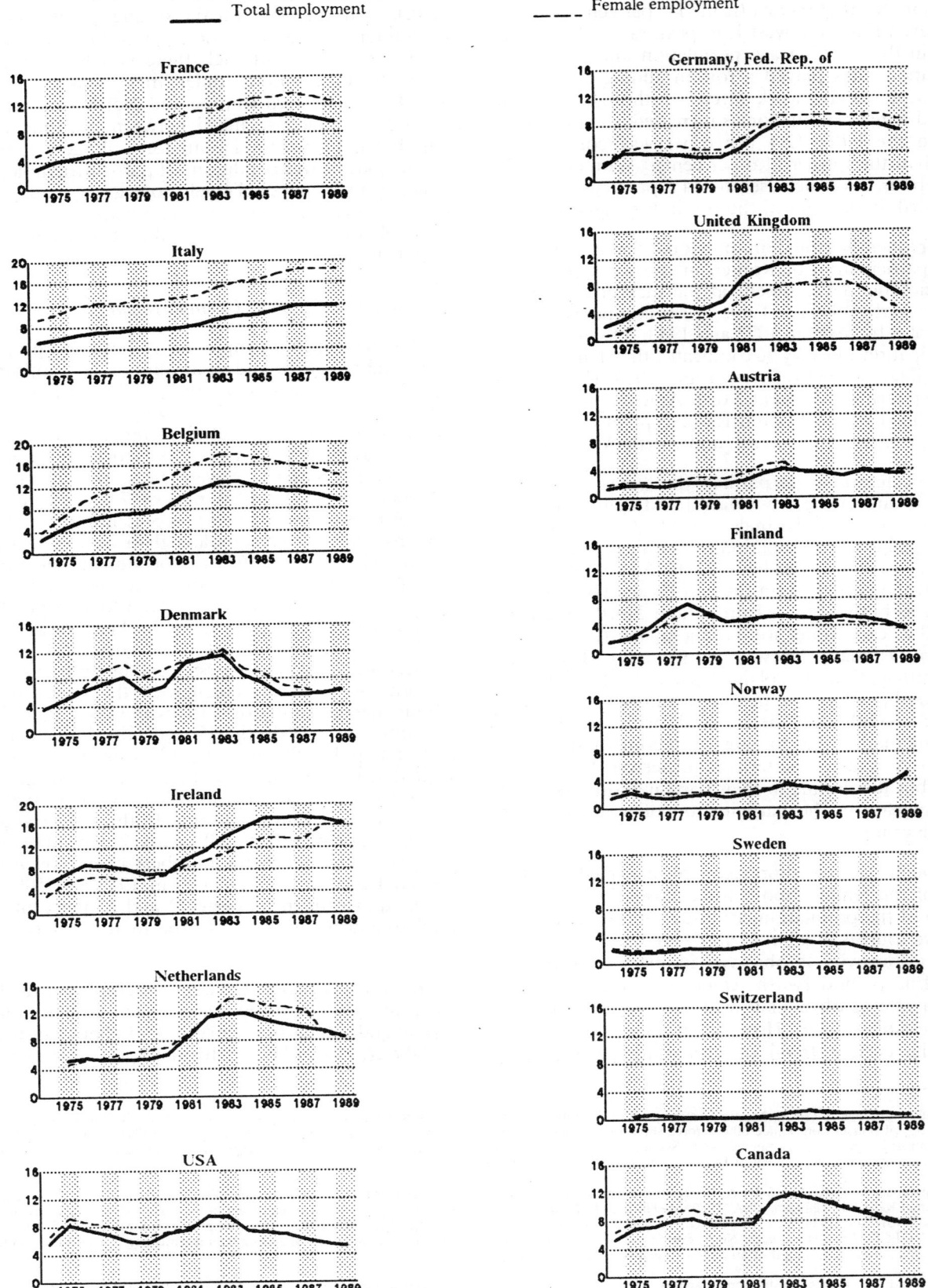

Sources: National labour force surveys and secretariat estimates. Labour force includes the armed forces.

TABLE 2.3.7

Share of women in labour force, employment and unemployment, 1980-1989
(Per cent)

	Labour force	Total employment	Unemployment
Western Europe			
1980-1982	38.2	37.6	46.3
1983-1986	39.0	38.5	44.8
1987	40.1	39.5	46.6
1988	40.3	39.6	47.5
1989	40.4	39.7	48.6
North America			
1980-1982	41.9	41.7	44.5
1983-1986	43.1	43.1	42.3
1987	44.0	44.0	44.9
1988	44.3	44.2	45.6
1989	44.5	44.4	45.7

Sources: National statistics and ECE secretariat estimates.

TABLE 2.3.8

Share of young persons (less than 25 years old) in registered unemployment, 1985, 1988-1989
(Per cent)

	1985	1988	1989
France	38.4	29.5	27.0
FR Germany	24.4	19.7	16.8
Italy	46.8	41.9	42.6
United Kingdom	37.7	31.2	28.4
Austria	..	26.7	23.5
Belgium	34.9	29.5	27.4
Denmark	24.7	23.2	22.5
Finland [a]	28.2	24.0	23.7
Ireland	31.0	27.7	25.9
Netherlands	37.6	30.3	43.4
Norway [a]	45.1	47.8	40.6
Sweden [a]	32.3	34.0	43.9
Switzerland	..	27.2	23.2
Canada [a]	35.6	31.6	29.6
United States [a]	38.6	37.2	37.0

Sources: National statistics and ECE secretariat estimates.

[a] Unemployed persons according to labour force surveys.

per cent (down from 5.6 per cent in 1988) was the lowest rate for a decade and a half. In North America the number of unemployed in 1989 was 7.6 million, 4.6 million below the previous peak in 1983. In the United States, despite the slow-down in economic activity, the number of unemployed declined by 133,000 in 1989 and the rate fell from 5.4 per cent in 1988 to 5.2 per cent (the lowest rate since 1973, at 4.8 per cent).

As in the recent past, the fall in unemployment was unevenly distributed between males and females in most countries (table 2.3.4). In western Europe, the number of unemployed males fell by 10.3 per cent (the rate of male unemployment fell to 7.9 per cent from 10.3 per cent in 1988) against a 6.1 per cent decline in unemployed females (the rate of female unemployment fell to 9.5 per cent from 10.1 per cent in 1988). In the United States also, male unemployment fell faster than female unemployment (2.3 per cent versus 1.6 per cent). Only in Canada, Switzerland and the United Kingdom, did the fall in female unemployment significantly exceed that of males. Thus, in most countries, the share of women in total unemployment continued to expand. Women's share of total unemployment in western Europe was 48.6 per cent in 1989 compared with 47.5 per cent in the previous year (table 2.3.7). In North America, women's share of unemployment in 1989 was 45.7 per cent, much the same as in 1988. Table 2.3.8 shows that the share of *young workers*[120] in total unemployment has been falling fairly steadily in most countries in western Europe. According to the registered unemployment statistics, the average share of youths in total unemployment was 30.9 per cent in 1989, 1.3 percentage points lower than in 1988. Compared with 1985, the share of young people in unemployment in the four major European countries fell by 6.6 percentage points. This trend is apparent in all the individual countries where the data are available. In North America, young workers accounted for 36.1 per cent of total unemployment in 1989, 0.3 percentage points lower than in 1988. Between 1985 and 1989, the share of young workers in total unemployment has fallen 2.1 percentage points. Despite the persistent decline in its share of total unemployment, the youth unemployment rate still remains very high, at about twice the total unemployment rate in the majority of the countries.

Among the various groups of the unemployed, in addition to females and young people, the proportion of *long-term unemployed*, defined as those unemployed for one year or more, remains high. The share of this "hard core" in total unemployment increased considerably between 1983 and 1985. During 1986-1987 the rate remained more or less stable but at very different levels in individual countries depending on their overall unemployment levels. During 1988 and, more strongly, in 1989, the share of long-term unemployment in total unemployment fell in the majority of the countries. The significant declines were in those countries where employment growth has been strongest in recent years: the Federal Republic of Germany, the United Kingdom and Finland. However, the rate in 1989, according to preliminary and partial data, still remained around 45 per cent in the Federal Republic of Germany and 42 per cent in the United Kingdom. In Finland the rate fell to some 7 per cent. In 1989, as in 1988, the rate continued to increase in Belgium and Italy, reaching three quarters and two thirds of the total unemployed respectively. From much lower levels it also increased further in France, the Netherlands and Norway. In the rest of the smaller countries of western Europe and North America the rate continued to fall in 1989.

---

[120] Young people are defined as workers below the age of 25, the lower bound varying across countries.

TABLE 2.3.9

Trade volumes, 1987-1989
(Percentage change over previous year)

	Export volumes			Import volumes		
	1987	1988	1989 [a]	1987	1988	1989 [a]
France	3.7	8.7	8.9	7.1	6.7	7.7
Germany, Federal Republic of	3.0	7.4	7.8	5.5	6.6	7.2
Italy	2.0	6.0	9.3	9.5	6.9	10.6
United Kingdom	5.2	1.1	6.3	6.9	13.6	9.2
Total 4 countries	3.5	6.0	8.0	6.9	8.4	8.5
Austria	2.5	12.1	13.0	5.1	8.3	12.5
Belgium	8.3	8.5	8.5	7.2	10.0	10.3
Denmark	2.0	5.9	6.5	5.1	-1.0	0.7
Finland	3.0	-1.0	4.8	13.2	-0.8	7.0
Ireland	14.2	7.0	10.0	6.2	4.7	11.9
Netherlands	5.8	7.3	4.4	6.7	6.3	4.3
Norway	13.7	6.5	15.0	-1.7	-9.7	-7.5
Sweden	3.9	2.8	-0.9	7.7	4.5	2.6
Switzerland	1.0	7.0	5.1	6.4	6.8	5.5
Total 9 countries	6.0	6.7	6.6	6.4	5.3	5.9
Total 13 countries	4.4	6.3	7.5	6.8	7.3	7.6
Canada	4.8	9.4	-1.7	8.9	15.8	12.0
United States	13.0	18.0	11.4	2.6	3.8	6.3
North America	10.4	15.4	7.7	3.8	6.2	7.5
Total above	6.2	9.1	7.6	5.6	6.8	7.6
Japan	0.4	4.4	5.8	9.0	16.6	7.5
Total above	5.3	8.4	7.3	5.9	7.8	7.6

Sources: IMF, *International Financial Statistics*, March 1990; OECD, *Monthly Statistics of Foreign Trade*, Series A, Paris, February 1990; OECD, *Economic Outlook*, No.46, December 1989; national statistics and ECE estimates. Weights for aggregation are US dollars trade shares in 1985.

[a] Preliminary or estimates.

(iii) External balances

In the market economies of the ECE region, the rapid growth of foreign trade continued in 1989, stimulated by the sustained expansion of economic activity. The trade and current account deficits of the United States and the surpluses of Japan have fallen for the second year running, due in part to the lagged effects of the large change in relative price competitiveness caused by the steep fall of the dollar in 1986-1988 (although this trend was partly reversed during 1989). In contrast, the large surpluses on both the trade and current accounts of the Federal Republic of Germany tended to increase until the final quarter of 1989, largely because of growing imbalances in intra-European trade. In all the other major west European economies — the United Kingdom, France and Italy — there were large external deficits in 1989. The evolution of trade balances reflected mainly changes in trade volumes, since movements in the terms of trade of the market economies in 1989 were relatively small, although negative, except for a few countries with relatively large exports of primary commodities.

(a) Recent developments in trade volumes

There was a further strengthening in the volume growth of exports in western Europe in 1989, with high growth rates in the first half of the year, followed by somewhat lower rates in the second half. For the 13 countries combined the increase for the whole year is estimated at 7½ per cent, following 6½ per cent growth in 1988 (table 2.3.9). This acceleration was due to much faster export growth in the four large European market economies (about 8 per cent, against 6 per cent in 1988). In the Federal Republic of Germany exports grew by almost 8 per cent, with most of the acceleration in the first three quarters of 1989 (there was no increase in export volume in the final quarter in relation to the fourth quarter of 1988). Export volumes in Italy and France increased by some 9 per cent and in the United Kingdom by 6 per cent.

These developments can be largely attributed to substantial increases in intra-EC trade, and conform with the trend observed in the enlarged European Community since 1982. "From 1982 to 1988, intra-EC export volumes increased on average by more than 5 per cent per annum, while extra-EC export volumes remained virtually stagnant."[121] In 1986 and 1987, there were absolute declines in extra-EC export volumes, associated with the depreciation of the US dollar. There followed a slight recovery of these exports in 1988 and growth of 7.3 per cent is estimated for 1989. A growing proportion of extra-EC exports has been going to the EFTA countries: in the case of industrial goods the share has increased from about one fifth to more than

---

[121] Commission of the European Communities, *European Economy*, November 1989, p.208.

TABLE 2.3.10

Terms of trade, [a] **1987-1989**
(Percentage change over previous year)

	1987	1988	1989 [b]
France	0.7	0.7	-0.9
Germany, Fed.Rep. of	3.7	-0.3	-2.5
Italy	2.5	1.5	-1.4
United Kingdom	1.5	1.2	1.8
Total 4 countries	2.3	0.6	-1.0
Austria	1.8	1.1	-1.1
Belgium	0.7	-0.5	-0.2
Denmark	2.7	-0.7	-0.1
Finland	3.3	2.4	2.8
Ireland	0.1	0.6	-0.9
Netherlands	-3.4	1.6	-
Norway	-5.3	-7.0	2.3
Sweden	-0.3	-0.5	1.8
Switzerland	7.8	-0.1	-1.6
Total 9 countries	0.4	-0.1	0.2
Total 13 countries	1.7	0.4	-0.6
Canada	0.9	5.0	5.1
United States	-5.1	2.1	0.6
North America	-3.9	2.8	1.6
Japan	1.7	3.2	-2.5

Sources: Compiled from IMF, *International Financial Statistics*, March 1990; OECD, *Monthly Statistics of Foreign Trade*, Series A, January 1990; and national statistics.

[a] Ratio of unit value index of exports to that of imports.
[b] Preliminary or estimated.

a quarter during the 1980s.[122] In 1989, however, there were also high rates of export growth from the EC, as well as from other west European countries, to eastern Europe, the Soviet Union, Japan and the developing economies.

Although the growth of merchandise exports from the United States slowed down to some 11½ per cent in 1989, the continued expansion of US trade contributed significantly to sustaining the rapid pace of world trade. Between 1987 and 1989, the volume of US exports rose by almost 50 per cent. However, in Canada, export volume declined in 1989, partly because of the earlier strong appreciation of the Canadian dollar against the US dollar. A deceleration of export growth was already evident in the second half of 1988. The volume fall, however, has been compensated by rising export prices and a considerable improvement in the terms of trade.

Japan's export growth remained relatively moderate in 1989 (close to 6 per cent), notwithstanding its acceleration for the second year running.

For the market economies of western Europe (excluding southern Europe), North America and Japan combined, the growth of exports exceeded 7 per cent but was lower than in 1988. Exports of manufactured goods from the developed market economies increased by 10.1 per cent, on average, in the first three quarters of 1989: 10 per cent for western Europe, 11.3 per cent for North America and 9.1 per cent for the other developed market economies.[123]

The strong export growth in the market economies was accompanied by a sustained expansion of imports (table 2.3.9). For 13 countries of western Europe, the imports grew by about 7½ per cent, slightly more than in 1988. The average growth rate in the four larger west European economies was much the same as in 1988, but this was mainly because of a sharp slow-down in the United Kingdom: in the other three countries there was an acceleration which was particularly strong in Italy (from 6.9 per cent to 10.6 per cent). In the smaller economies import growth, boosted by strong domestic demand, varied from 10 to 12½ per cent in Ireland, Austria and Belgium, and from 4½ to 7 per cent in the Netherlands, Switzerland and Finland. There were much smaller increases in Sweden and Denmark and a large decline in Norway.

In North America imports accelerated to 7½ per cent as a result of opposite trends in Canada and in the United States. Rapid import growth of around 12 per cent in Canada was, however, slower than in 1988. On the other hand, in the United States a faster, 6 per cent growth was registered, despite a negative impact on imports of a deceleration in internal demand and some appreciation of the US dollar in 1989 (table 2.3.11).[124]

After expanding rapidly in the last three years, Japan's imports decelerated sharply in 1989 but still rose by 7½ per cent.

Thus, for the 16 developed market economy countries as a group, the growth of import volume in 1989 was 7½ per cent, slightly more than the increase in exports.

(b) Trade and current account balances

Trade balances in 1989, as in 1988, were largely determined by the underlying volume changes described above, since changes in the terms of trade were relatively small. However, in contrast to 1988, the terms of trade deteriorated in most of the market economies, mainly because of strong commodity prices and a recovery in the price of oil.[125] Those market economies of the ECE region with a significant share of oil, metals, forest products or cereals in their exports — Canada,

---

[122] *Op.cit.*, p.31, 208, 211, 213.

[123] See United Nations *Monthly Bulletin of Statistics*, New York, December 1989, p.254.

[124] The above volume growth estimates of US exports and imports in 1989 should, however, be treated with caution. They were derived from the reported value growth rates of merchandise exports and imports (f.a.s. customs basis), equal, respectively, to 13.0 and 7.2 per cent, and the implicit price deflators (1.4 and 0.8 per cent), obtained from growth indices of US merchandise export and import values, expressed in current and constant (1982) dollars, adjusted on a balance of payments basis. See *US Department of Commerce News*, 27 February 1990. According to another source, however, US export and import prices increased by 2.6 and 9.9 per cent, respectively, in 1989, which would imply, in particular, a negative growth of import volume and a large deterioration in terms of trade. See IMF, *International Financial Statistics*, March 1990, pp.80-81.

[125] For more details see chapter 4, section 4.1.

the United Kingdom, Finland, Norway and Sweden — benefited from these price developments. But in the other main industrial economies — the Federal Republic of Germany and Japan — the terms of trade deteriorated by some 2-3 per cent (table 2.3.10).

Exchange rate movements in the course of 1989 were not, in general, favourable to the reduction of foreign imbalances. Both the Deutschmark and the yen depreciated against the US dollar, although developments in the second half of the year, particularly in the final quarter, moderated the rate of effective appreciation of the dollar. The levelling out of the dollar exchange rate was due *inter alia* to diminishing interest rate differentials caused by a rise in European and Japanese interest rates. The latter rose sharply in October, while in the United States there was a continued softening of the monetary stance, provoked by signs of a slow-down in economic activity. Interest rate differentials diminished somewhat in January 1990 as the US Federal Reserve tightened policy in response to a stubborn inflation rate. Interest rates generally remained high because of increased inflationary pressures.

Although the external imbalances of the main industrial countries remained large there was nevertheless a further diminution of the US deficits and the Japanese surpluses in 1989. In the Federal Republic of Germany the trade and current account surpluses, expressed in national currency, increased further, mainly as a result of larger surpluses with other west and south European countries, and in particular with the United Kingdom (table 2.3.12). These trends were pronounced during the first ten months of the year but there seems to have been some reversal in November and December. The trade deficit of the United States narrowed by $14 billion, on a balance-of-payments basis, following a $32 billion reduction in 1988. Most of the reductions occurred in the first half of the year, and especially the first quarter when the deficit fell by $5 billion. The adjustment in real terms was larger than that implied by the nominal figures. The slow-down in the pace of adjustment in the trade balance can be partly explained by a worsening in the competitive position of US products, associated with an increase in the value of the dollar, as well as strong internal demand, particularly in the first half of the year. A gradual slackening of overall economic activity and a weakening of the dollar in the fourth quarter relieved some of the pressures on the trade account and led to some improvement in American competitiveness. There were large falls in the United States' bilateral deficits with other developed countries (Canada, Japan, western Europe) as well as with the newly industrialized economies in the Far East in 1988 and 1989. However, the US deficit with oil-producing and other developing countries increased.

In Japan, after a small decrease in the preceding year, the trade surplus was considerably reduced in the course of 1989, from $95 billion to $77 billion. Thus the strong appreciation of the yen after 1985 (notwithstanding some reversal, notably in the second and third quarters in 1989) has finally brought about some adjustment in the trade balance and contributed to a shift towards sustainable — as is believed in Japan — domestic demand-led growth.[126]

The trade surplus of the Federal Republic of Germany rose in the first and third quarters of 1989, but fell sharply in the final quarter, possibly because of the surge in internal demand associated with the inflow of visitors and immigrants from the German Democratic Republic. The reported trade surplus (f.o.b.-c.i.f.), reached DM134.7 billion. This amounts to an estimated DM147 billion (about $78 billion) on an f.o.b.-f.o.b. basis, as compared with $78.7 billion in 1988.[127] Growth rates of values were higher for imports than exports because of worsening terms of trade but, due to the large difference in their levels, the absolute increase in imports, in national currency, was once again larger than the increase in exports. Because of the depreciation of the Deutschmark between 1988 and 1989, from some 1.76 to 1.88 Deutschmarks per dollar, there was a small decrease in the trade surplus in dollar terms, contrary to earlier projections based on developments in the first three quarters. Nevertheless, the trade surplus of the Federal Republic of Germany in 1989 was, for the first time, higher than that of Japan. Eighty five per cent of this was accumulated in trade with other EC countries, notably the United Kingdom, France, Italy and Spain. Large and growing surpluses were also evident in trade with EFTA countries, particularly Switzerland and Austria. In contrast, the Federal Republic of Germany's trade surplus with the United States fell for the third consecutive year, to DM84 billion, while the deficit with Japan remained more or less unchanged (at about DM16 billion).

The total trade surplus was due to a persistent surplus in manufactures, notably in capital goods.[128] The surplus in the latter has fluctuated around DM160 billion a year for the previous five years, i.e., around a level some 25 to 45 per cent higher than the total trade surplus. A large part of the surplus was associated with direct foreign investments of German firms, particularly in the south European member countries of the EC — Greece, Portugal and Spain — but also in the United Kingdom, France and Italy.

The trade deficit of the United Kingdom increased to £23.1 billion in 1989, against £20.8 billion in 1988 (about $37.6 billion and $37 billion respectively, at average exchange rates). However, while for the first three quarters the visible trade deficit grew from £14.5 billion to £18.7 billion (balance of payments basis, seasonally adjusted), it declined in the final quarter (from £6.3 billion in 1988 to £4.4 billion in 1989). This change was due to an acceleration of export growth (of both oil and non-oil products) and a decrease in imports of manufactures.

---

[126] See H. Okumura, "A new phase of development", *Financial Times*, 3 January 1990.

[127] See *Statistische Beihefte zu den Monatsberichten der Deutschen Bundesbank*, Reihe 3, *Zahlungsbilanzstatistik*, No.1, January 1990; *Wall Street Journal*, 12 February 1990.

[128] Products of investment good-producing enterprises, defined according to the national trade nomenclature, *ibid*, p.305.

TABLE 2.3.11

Real effective exchange rate indexes,[a] 1987-1989
(1985 = 100)

	1987	1988	1989 [b]	1989 QI	QII	QIII	QIV
France	108.6	106.3	103.9	103.1	102.8	103.4	106.2
Germany, Federal Republic of	119.2	118.4	116.3	115.6	114.8	115.4	119.3
Italy	105.7	101.9	101.7	100.5	100.7	102.4	103.1
United Kingdom	92.7	97.7	94.3	98.6	95.2	93.4	90.1
Austria	121.4	120.0	117.0	116.4	115.4	116.1	120.1
Belgium	111.2	110.1	108.4	108.1	107.5	107.9	110.0
Denmark	117.6	115.7	111.1	110.6	109.4	110.2	114.2
Finland	106.6	107.5	109.8	107.6	110.4	110.1	110.9
Ireland	107.4	106.6	103.5	103.1	102.3	102.8	105.6
Netherlands	118.8	118.6	115.8	115.4	114.7	115.0	118.1
Norway	96.3	96.0	94.6	94.9	94.9	94.3	94.7
Sweden	102.2	102.2	101.3	101.3	101.3	101.5	101.2
Switzerland	121.4	119.8	111.6	113.2	109.2	111.6	112.3
Canada	90.0	95.2	101.0	99.1	100.9	102.0	102.0
United States	72.2	68.0	71.0	69.0	72.1	72.3	70.5
Japan	136.9	151.8	145.2	154.0	146.6	141.9	138.2

Sources: IMF, *International Financial Statistics*, February 1990, Washington, D.C.

a Based on weights derived from the IMF's Multilateral Exchange Rate Model.

TABLE 2.3.12

Trade and current account balances, 1987-1989
(Billion US dollars)

	Trade balances			Current account balances		
	1987	1988	1989 [a]	1987	1988	1989 [a]
France	-8.7	-8.1	-10.5	-4.4	-3.5	-3.3
Germany, Federal Republic of	69.9	78.7	77.9	45.6	48.6	52.7
Italy	-0.1	-0.8	-12.3	-1.7	-5.5	-11.7
United Kingdom	-18.0	-37.0	-37.6	-6.4	-26.1	-34.1
Total 4 countries	43.2	32.8	17.5	33.1	13.5	3.6
Austria	-5.1	-6.3	-7.2	-0.4	-0.5	-
Belgium	-0.2	1.1	1.9	2.8	3.4	3.5
Denmark	0.8	1.8	2.3	-3.0	-1.8	-1.3
Finland	1.4	1.1	-1.3	-1.8	-3.0	-4.2
Ireland	2.6	3.8	3.7	0.4	0.7	0.5
Netherlands	5.2	8.2	7.5	3.5	5.2	5.0
Norway	-0.8	-0.1	4.9	-4.2	-3.7	2.0
Sweden	4.5	4.7	3.7	-1.2	-2.5	-5.0
Switzerland	-5.4	-4.6	-5.6	6.3	8.3	5.0
Total 9 countries	2.9	9.8	9.9	2.3	6.2	5.5
Total 13 countries	46.0	42.7	27.4	35.4	19.7	9.1
Canada	9.1	8.9	4.0	-7.1	-8.3	-14.0
United States	-158.9	-126.8	-113.3	-143.1	-126.2	-105.9
North America	-149.8	-117.9	-109.3	-150.2	-134.5	-119.9
Total above	-103.8	-75.2	-81.9	-114.9	-114.8	-110.8
Japan	96.4	95.0	77.1	87.0	79.6	57.0
Total above	-7.4	19.8	-4.8	-27.9	-35.2	-53.8

Sources: IMF, *International Financial Statistics*, February 1990, Washington, D.C.; OECD, *Economic Outlook*, No.46, December 1989; national statistics and ECE secretariat estimates.

a Preliminary or estimated.

Also in France, there was a reduction in the trade deficit in the fourth quarter. Nevertheless, the annual deficit of FF67.25 billion was almost one third higher than in 1988.[129]

---

[129] *Le Monde*, 16 February 1990.

TABLE 2.3.13

Southern Europe: trade and current account balances, 1987-1989
(Billion US dollars)

	Trade balances			Current account balances		
	1987	1988	1989 a	1987	1988	1989 a
Greece	-5.5	-6.1	-6.9	-1.2	-1.0	-2.5
Portugal	-3.4	-5.1	-5.6	0.6	-0.6	-1.0
Spain	-13.0	-18.0	-27.0	-0.2	-3.8	-11.6
Turkey	-3.2	-1.8	-4.0	-1.0	1.5	0.8
Yugoslavia	0.1	0.8	-1.5	1.2	2.5	2.3
Total above	-25.0	-30.2	-45.0	-0.6	-1.4	-12.0

Sources: IMF, *International Financial Statistics*, February 1990, Washington, D.C.; OECD, *Monthly Statistics of Foreign Trade*, Series A, February 1990; OECD, *Economic Outlook*, No.46, December 1989.

a Preliminary or estimated.

Current account balances generally moved in the same direction as the trade balances. In the United States a reduction in the current account deficit (to below 2.5 per cent of GNP) was larger than that in the trade balance (due to a 41 per cent rise in the surplus in services), although both deficits ran quite close to each other in 1988 and 1989. A deterioration in net investment income in the first half of the year, was reversed in the second half, and particularly in the final quarter, when the relative weakening of the dollar increased the nominal value of income from abroad in terms of US dollars. In Japan, the current account surplus was reduced to $57 billion (28.4 per cent lower than in 1988), due to an 18 per cent reduction in the merchandise trade balance and a 31 per cent rise in the deficit on services. Both Japan and the Federal Republic of Germany — where the current account surplus increased further — continued to offset their surpluses with large capital transfers to other countries, notably the United States and the United Kingdom. The counterpart of the external surplus of the Federal Republic of Germany is located mainly within the EC, although only in part in the relatively less developed countries and regions of the Community.[130] Increases in the current account deficits of the United Kingdom and Italy, and in the trade deficit of France, in the first three quarters of 1988, were due mainly to internal factors, namely, a decline in competitiveness, and a rapid growth of domestic demand. These deficits were already beginning to fall in the last quarter of 1989: this tendency should continue as a result of a slackening in the growth of internal demand, as well as adjustments in real interest rates and exchange rates in the final quarter of 1989 and in the first quarter of 1990 (e.g., a devaluation of the Italian lira by 3.1 per cent against the ECU on 5 January 1990). In France, in particular, the current account deficit diminished slightly in national currency terms, from FF21.3 billion in 1988 to FF21.1 billion in 1989 (despite increasing deficits on trade and unilateral transfers accounts), due to a large growth of the positive balance of services.

(c) External balances in southern Europe

In the five countries of southern Europe, the trade gap widened considerably in 1989 (in total, by about $12 billion), due to a moderate growth of export volume (some 6 per cent) and a rapid acceleration in the growth of imports, to almost 16 per cent. In value terms, the differences in the growth of imports and exports were less pronounced because of favourable movements in the terms of trade. The largest increase in the trade deficit was in Spain, where it reached $26 billion (table 2.3.13), $8 billion more than in 1988 and double the 1987 deficit.

These trends in trade volumes reflect a number of factors, including strong domestic demand (although there was some slow-down in economic activity in 1989, particularly in Turkey and Portugal), continued inflationary pressures, buoyant foreign investment, liberalization of imports, and a loss of competitiveness due to rising labour costs and effective appreciation of national currencies in 1988 and 1989 (notably the Spanish peseta, the Portuguese escudo and the Greek drachma).

Deepening trade deficits were accompanied by similar changes in the current accounts. The total current account deficit of the five countries of southern Europe increased by some $10.5 billion, to some $12 billion in 1989. Only Yugoslavia and Turkey had surpluses, although they were smaller than in 1988. The largest deficit, in absolute terms, was in Spain — $11.6 billion or, about 3 per cent of GDP. In relative terms, however, the current account deficit of Greece (equivalent to 5 per cent of the GDP) was higher. A large part of the trade deficits of southern Europe was counterbalanced by growing receipts from tourism and emigrants' remittances (except in Greece, where these receipts fell in 1989, following a steep rise in 1988). But interest payments abroad were also growing, a result of high levels of external debt and rising interest rates. In Turkey, for instance, the debt service (including rescheduled

---

130 "To the extent that the surpluses find their counterpart in the deficit of the less favoured countries, the imbalances can be seen as contributing to the catching-up process of the latter where there is a need for increasing investment. The sum of the current account deficits of Spain, Portugal and Greece in 1989, however, is equivalent to about 1.25 per cent of the GDP of the Federal Republic of Germany, i.e., the combined deficits of these countries explain less than one quarter of the German surplus. Therefore, the present level of the disequilibria goes beyond what could be justified by these considerations. Excessive imbalances, via the inevitable real adjustment, could become a danger for the continuation of growth, investment and job creation." Commission of the European Communities, *European Economy*, No.11, November 1989, p.16.

debt payments) amounted to some $7.5 billion, equivalent to about 40 per cent of current account earnings. The continued worsening in the external accounts, however, did not create financial problems, since the recent growth in the trade deficits was, to a large extent, associated with direct foreign investment and non-debt creating transfers from the ECs' development funds (notably to Spain and Portugal).[131]

The gross foreign debt of the five south European countries, which amounted to about $127 billion at the end of 1988, decreased somewhat — in dollar terms — in the first half of 1989, mainly because of the appreciation of the US dollar against the Deutschmark and ECU, and presumably increased again in the second half of the year. About 55 per cent of the total debt of the five countries was due to Turkey and Spain.

---

[131] See Commission of the European Communities, *European Economy*, No.42, November 1989, Part B.

Chapter 3

EASTERN EUROPE AND THE SOVIET UNION

3.1 GENERAL ECONOMIC DEVELOPMENTS

Economic growth slowed sharply in the Soviet Union and came to a standstill in eastern Europe in 1989. At the turn of 1990, most of the eastern countries appear headed into a recession. The economic downturn comes on a background of profound political changes and in many countries sharp shifts in the objectives of economic reforms. This section provides a broad overview of these developments, which are reviewed in greater detail in sections 3.2 to 3.5 and in chapter 5.

In all respects 1989 was an extraordinary year for eastern Europe[132] and the Soviet Union. Event pushed event in the political sphere throughout the year, starting with the "Round Table" negotiations between the established party government and the barely legitimized opposition in Poland and the lively parliamentary elections in the Soviet Union in the early months. By mid-year, the political environment in the Soviet Union had already been transformed by the remarkably disputatious opening session of the new Congress of People's Deputies, a new parliament dominated by the opposition was in session in Poland, the barbed wire had been removed at Hungary's western frontier and citizens of the German Democratic Republic started to move through the opening in large numbers. A new constitution declaring the country a "market economy" was in the making in Hungary and a new government was in charge in Poland before the end of the third quarter, the latter the first in the post-war period not led by the Communist party. Before the year was out, party and/or government leadership had also changed — peacefully except in Romania — in all the other east European countries, and the new governments were all committed to one degree or another to far-reaching change in the economic as well as the political systems of their countries.

These political events and their repercussions will exert a powerful influence on the economic, political and social make-up of the area. The extraordinary character of these developments has been perhaps most forcefully underlined by the rapid settlement in principle of the German issue, though not yet its problems, and the promise that by year's end the closing chapter of the Second World War may finally have been written.

The situation in early 1990 is, therefore, fluid. Although the changes ahead are likely to be far-reaching, they are bound to be less spectacular than the events of late 1989 and early 1990. None the less, they are certain to alter profoundly many features of the European economic landscape.

(i) The background to economic developments

As far as economic developments are concerned, these events are bound to have widespread ramifications for the current economic performance of the eastern ECE countries and their ability to regain stability and sustainable growth. In terms of growth, the short-run impact is likely to be negative. The radical changes in economic management systems being pursued — or currently envisaged — in all countries of the group and in the ways in which these countries will henceforth formulate and implement their economic policies cannot but affect also the channels and forms of their relations with other parts of the world economy.

Arguably the central focus of economic policies in this group of countries, particularly since mid-1989, has been the search for dependable anchors of economic policy. This is motivated by two broad sets of concerns. One is how to maintain stability in domestic and external economic relations, including the linkages in the CMEA framework or some alternative. The other is how to conduct at the same time far-reaching, market-oriented economic reforms. These preoccupations were reinforced during the year by set-backs to ongoing reforms which were largely systemic in origin

---

[132] Bulgaria, Czechoslovakia, the German Democratic Republic, Hungary, Poland and Romania.

and by a number of new shocks which threatened economic stability.

In most cases, disappointing progress with system reforms was more a cause than an effect of the socio-political transformations that occurred in the course of the year. The much more sluggish pace of socio-economic reform than had earlier been envisaged stemmed, by and large, from the inability of economic and political leaderships to carry out the tasks established in the reform blueprints. In the economic sphere, the resulting drift created imbalances which appeared increasingly impervious to piecemeal responses. Moreover, the degree of disappointment and frustrations with system reforms felt among wide layers of society rose markedly because the intended course proved in practice to be inhibited by intrinsic contradictions in the aims as well as the means of the reform process. Of particular importance has been the lack of success with Soviet *perestroika*. In fact, by late 1989 the Soviet leadership openly admitted that the country was in severe economic crisis, partly because of worsening internal imbalances, and was in need of a "recovery" programme.[133]

Unanticipated events increased the need to regain a greater measure of economic, political and social stability. These included social unrest in several forms. One was large-scale emigration, particularly from the German Democratic Republic,[134] but also from Bulgaria[135] and the Soviet Union.[136] There were also various types of labour friction, including strikes, particularly in Poland in the first half and in the Soviet Union in the latter part of 1989. In the Soviet Union, the consequences of the massive earthquake in Armenia in late 1988 and the civil strife and regional antagonisms (such as the blockade of much of Armenia by Azerbaijan) exerted a negative effect on production levels, in part through their impact on an already strained transport infrastructure. On a different plane, the sudden erosion of the dominant role of the Communist parties throughout eastern Europe, leading to their abrupt collapse in several countries at the end of the year, is also relevant here. Although in several countries new policy-making structures were rapidly put in place, in others there were no ready substitutes in the short run, and the resulting policy vacuum did not contribute to the stability of these economies.[137]

In consequence, the economic environment in eastern Europe and the Soviet Union in 1989 was further burdened by rising uncertainty. This manifested itself in several ways, including — apart from the deterioration of macro- and micro-economic performance — also in growing obstacles to the functioning of the traditional trade and payments régime for intra-CMEA transactions. Uncertainty continues to weigh heavily on the socio-economic situation at the beginning of 1990, particularly with respect to the way in which system reform will be undertaken, the costs that will need to be borne, how quickly this adjustment burden will have to be absorbed and how equitably and by what criteria it will be apportioned over the various layers of society. The distribution of that cost and the speed at which it will have to be borne pose questions to which, for lack of a firm socio-political consensus, the systems in place have found it very difficult to provide answers.

Events in the course of 1989 and early 1990 were almost a textbook illustration of what may go awry with system reform. They suggested once again that economies that have been managed for a long time by way of highly centralized administrative methods may require a period of stabilization before serious systemic change can be attempted with a reasonable expectation of success.

Such stabilization has to address several issues. The most obvious is the imbalances inherited from the administrative economic model, perhaps best epitomized by the so-called "monetary overhang."[138] Another is the the need to formulate and put into place an operational alternative co-ordination mechanism to central planning. Even with these issues resolved, economic reform can be pursued only at a cost, the size of which depends to a large extent on the aims of the reform and the specific problems that policy makers are trying to address.

---

133 See Prime Minister N. Ryzhkov's report to the second session of the Congress of People's Deputies on "Measures for the recovery (*po ozdorovleniyu*) of the economy ...", *Ekonomicheskaya gazeta*, No.51, December 1989.

134 Total emigration into the Federal Republic in 1989, largely in the second half of the year, was over 340,000 (according to data of the Statistisches Bundesamt, Wiesbaden). These were largely able-bodied, young, and quite skilled individuals. The trend continues in 1990. In the first two months alone, some 114,000 individuals left for the Federal Republic and the outflow is continuing at a rate of more than 1,000 per day (*Frankfurter Allgemeine Zeitung*, 6 March 1990).

135 This emigration was essentially by the Moslem minority, with perhaps 380,000 individuals leaving Bulgaria primarily for Turkey in 1989; in late August, Turkey felt compelled to close its border with Bulgaria. The Bulgarian Government has since taken measures to restore the rights of the Moslem minority and some 80,000 of the migrants returned. Those still in refugee camps in Turkey may in the end seek to return to Bulgaria as well.

136 In 1989, 228,600 people — more than twice the number in the preceding year — emigrated permanently from the Soviet Union (*Pravda*, 14 January 1990), chiefly to Israel and the United States.

137 This applies especially to those countries where existing governments formed under the old power arrangements are likely to be replaced after elections in the near future, as in Hungary and the German Democratic Republic, and possibly also in Bulgaria and Romania. Only in Czechoslovakia does the interim government appear to have the social support that might survive the coming elections. In this waiting period, governmental decisions are bound to lack firmness or the enforceability that stems from the likelihood of policy continuity over a longer time horizon. See, e.g., the statements of L. Bokros, board member of the National Bank, and L. Antal, a Government advisor, on the paralysis of decision-making and the disintegration of governmental control over the economy in Hungary reported in *Financial Times*, 14 March 1990.

138 This is usually understood as the volume of liquid assets that households hold in cash and call savings accounts for lack of desired goods and services. These assets are largely in local currency, but in some countries (notably the German Democratic Republic, Hungary and Poland) sizeable convertible currency balances are held by the population. These convertible currency balances are especially important in influencing the velocity of money circulation. The potential of "unsatisfied demand" suddenly descending upon newly released market forces is a phenomenon that obviously also applies to "forced substitution" by economic agents. They are most likely to reverse their second-best choice once the allocation mechanism permits more flexible adjustments between demand and supply, including for leisure.

TABLE 3.1.1
Eastern Europe and the Soviet Union: Basic economic indicators, 1981-1990
(Average annual and annual growth rates, in percentages)

Country or group, indicator	1981-1985	1986-1990 Plan	1986-1989	1986	1987	1988	1989 Plan	1989 Actual
Eastern Europe								
Net material product	2.2	5.3	2.6 a	4.6	3.2	3.1	4.5	0.5 a
Industrial output b	2.8	4.4	2.7 a	4.6	3.5	3.5	4.0	0.3 a
Agricultural output b	1.1 c	2.7 c	1.0 a	5.3	-0.8	1.4	3.0	1.0 a
Gross investment	-0.7	3.4	3.1 a	3.9	4.7	2.6	..	-2.7 a
Exports	4.8	..	0.7	0.3	1.2	3.9	..	-2.4
Imports	0.6	..	2.7	5.3	1.8	3.0	..	0.8
Soviet Union								
Net material product	3.2	4.3	2.7	2.3	1.6	4.4	5.7 d	2.4
Industrial output b	3.6	4.6	3.4	4.4	3.8	3.9	4.5 d	1.7
Agricultural output b	1.1 c	2.7 c	1.8	5.3	-0.6	1.7	6.5 d	0.8
Gross investment	3.3	4.3	4.9	8.3	5.7	6.2	4.1 d	0.6
Exports	1.5	..	4.4	10.0	3.3	4.8	..	-0.3*
Imports	5.8	..	0.8	-6.0	-1.6	4.0	..	7.1*

Source: Secretariat of the United Nations Economic Commission for Europe, based on national statistical publications, plans and plan fulfilment reports.

a Excluding Romania.
b Gross output.
c Annualized change in the five-year average production levels from the average of the preceding five years.
d Increase from the *actual* level of the preceding year. In national documents, plan targets are stated against the *planned* level of the preceding year (see United Nations Economic Commission for Europe, *Economic Survey of Europe in 1987-1988*, New York, 1988, pp.143-145).

Pervasive uncertainty thus remains a central feature of these economies at the beginning of 1990. Finding a feasible reform variant for the erstwhile centrally planned economy and ensuring steady and rapid transition toward the desired reform state will require time and considerably more effort than has thus far been expended on the venture.

(ii) Policy makers' expectations for 1989

The objectives that the countries of eastern Europe and the Soviet Union had laid down in their respective national economic plans for 1989 envisaged an acceleration of *NMP growth,* from an average 3 per cent reported for eastern Europe in 1988 and the 4½ per cent registered in the Soviet Union to some 4½ per cent and 6 per cent, respectively.[139] These targets were predicated on the expectation of substantial efficiency gains and fairly strong output growth in industry as well as in agriculture throughout the area.

Policy targets on the *utilization* of national output (domestic absorption) tended towards austerity in eastern Europe, while in the case of the Soviet Union the policy stance appears to have been still fairly permissive. By late 1988, when these plans were being formulated, inflationary pressure — and the state budget deficit which was feeding it — had become a serious policy concern in the Soviet Union, yet policy makers still found it very difficult to face up to the full dimensions of the problem.[140] In most of the east European countries (apart from Hungary and Poland), the inflationary problem and its monetary policy and public deficit origins were still kept under wraps in the policy statements for 1988-1989,[141] but the evident worsening of balance-of-payments constraints (in part also revealed in the public statistics only after the changes in the power structure)[142] forced the hand of policymakers.

The precise intentions of policy makers in the *allocation* of national income are not always easily discernible from the available information, but generally *consumption* appears to have been favoured relative to

---

[139] Growth targets cited for the Soviet Union are ECE estimates reflecting an effort to translate the official plan figures, stated as growth over the preceding year's *plan* target, into planned change from that year's *actual* level. See also footnote (162) below.

[140] In the initial presentation of the state budget of the Soviet Union in October 1988, the largest component of the anticipated public sector deficit — some 64 billion roubles — was still shown as an element of government revenues (albeit under the entry "income from the loan fund"); a few months later — largely under the pressure of the economics profession — the true size of the planned borrowing requirement (initially 99 billion roubles, which was later raised to 121 billion roubles, or some 13½ per cent of GNP) was freely admitted also in official statements.

[141] The existence of sizeable state budget deficits was admitted (and interpreted as part of the economic problem) in Bulgaria, Czechoslovakia, the German Democratic Republic and Romania only *after* the government changes in the last quarter of 1989. None of these were reflected in the official statistical publications published a few months earlier.

[142] Notably in the case of the German Democratic Republic, whose official statistics had claimed a $0.1 billion convertible-currency *surplus* for 1988 (*Statistisches Jahrbuch der DDR 1989*, p.241, and report to the United Nations Statistical Office of October 1989), whereas revised data now indicate a $1 billion *deficit* for the same year (direct communication from the GDR Statistical Office to the ECE secretariat).

accumulation in the plans for 1989. Targets for average wages and retail sales volume − the usual proxies for government intentions in the consumption sphere − indicate that fairly high growth was aimed at in Bulgaria, the German Democratic Republic, Poland and the Soviet Union, whereas a more restrictive stance prevailed in Czechoslovakia, Hungary and Romania. *Investment* targets, by contrast, were restrictive (negative or below planned NMP growth) in Czechoslovakia and the Soviet Union, but appear to indicate that some rise in the investment rate may have been intended in a number of other countries (Hungary, Poland, Romania). However, given the tense situation in consumer markets combined with the priority assigned by policy makers to consumption to ease social tensions, as well as balance-of-payments pressures, the leeway for investment outlays was evidently quite narrow everywhere. Also, policy makers have been trying to shift capital funds towards modernization rather than expansion in breadth.

Regarding the overall pace of output growth, the policy stance for 1989 varied substantially among countries (see table 3.2.1). In eastern Europe, the countries most actively engaged in economic reform − Hungary and Poland, and also Czechoslovakia, anticipated some slowing of NMP growth, whereas in Bulgaria, the German Democratic Republic and Romania the targets implied a pronounced upswing from the 1988 performance. In all countries, efficiency gains were to feed this expansion, as indicated by sectoral targets, formulated in *gross* output terms, which generally were lower than those for NMP.

In the east European countries, in fact, no acceleration was expected in the growth of *industrial gross output* except in Romania (see table 3.2.7 below); it was the high target of the latter country which raised the group's planned growth to 4 per cent, as against 3½ in 1988. The Soviet Union, by contrast, had sought to accelerate industrial growth significantly in 1989, to 4½ per cent as compared with less than 4 per cent obtained the previous year, aiming at the same time at a substantial shift in its structure (consumer goods output was to rise by 7 per cent and that of producer goods by 2½ per cent). The *construction* sector in most countries was affected negatively by the shift in investment priorities.

Good performances in *agriculture* were also anticipated. The countries that had done comparatively poorly in 1988 forecast a rapid acceleration in gross output, whereas those that had recorded a good performance, especially Czechoslovakia and Hungary, anticipated not only that it could be repeated but improved upon. As a result, the east European group reckoned on an increase in agricultural output of some 3 per cent as against the 1½ per cent recorded the previous year; the corresponding data for the Soviet Union are 6½ per cent for 1989 as against almost 2 per cent in 1988.

At the same time, most countries hoped to gain some flexibility in the *foreign trade* sector by placing a tight lid on levels of domestic absorption and by boosting exports. This was to enable countries to continue with their external adjustment efforts, first introduced in the early 1980s, as well as with structural change and economic reform.

In all countries but Hungary and Poland, policy makers were still making an effort to position economic targets for 1989 in the context of the *five-year plans for 1986-1990*. Reaching the targets of those programmes, however modest they were in some cases, would have required an extraordinary coincidence of favourable developments: good luck with the weather, no deterioration in the terms of trade with convertible currency partners,[143] solid trade performance based on a rapid shift of production capacity into exports and otherwise positive developments in the foreign trade accounts, constraints on domestic absorption and considerable gains in total factor productivity.

(iii) Economic performance in 1989

As anticipated in last year's *Survey*,[144] the growth objectives for 1989 over a wide range of output and consumption targets proved, in retrospect, to have been overly optimistic. In early 1989, the ECE secretariat suggested that a target of 3½ per cent aggregate growth for the group as a whole would be more realistic. Official growth rates were deemed to be too ambitious, in part because of prevailing internal market imbalances and difficulties with the reform programmes in countries that had already put them in train. It was already evident that the constraints on intra-CMEA trade were tightening, largely because of adverse changes in the Soviet Union's terms of trade at a time of slowing or declining Soviet export supplies. This in turn would restrict the ability of eastern Europe to export and, in some cases, to operate near full capacity. In the east-west context, the outlook for buoyancy of trade with the market economies was not considered good as a result of an anticipated slow-down in the world economy and lingering external payments problems in many countries of the group.

Even that judgement in the end proved to have been optimistic (table 3.1.1 and chart 3.2.1). In eastern Europe, aggregate NMP growth in 1989 at best came to a standstill, and may have turned negative.[145] Country performances ranged from 1-2 per cent growth in

---

143 The formula underlying CMEA transaction prices for 1989 yielded a gain in east European terms of trade with respect to the Soviet Union. That country stood to lose owing to the weak world prices of energy in the mid-1980s: transferable rouble reference prices − around which actual transaction prices are negotiated (but at times with wide margins) − for 1989 were to be the world market prices of 1984-1988, as opposed to 1983-1987 the previous year.

144 See United Nations Economic Commission for Europe, *Economic Survey of Europe in 1988-1989*, New York, 1989, p.2. It should be noted that many of the data reported there for years prior to 1988 differ from those utilized here because of significant revisions of national statistics released since that issue of the *Survey* was written, especially the very substantial revisions in the national accounts for the Soviet Union published in late 1989.

145 Full data are not yet available as *Romania* will not report its performance for 1989 until the end of March 1990, too late to be included in this *Survey*. It is

Czechoslovakia and the German Democratic Republic to a 2 per cent fall in Hungary (see table 3.2.1). Two countries (Bulgaria and Hungary) reported a fall in NMP produced. In Poland it stagnated. In the event, only Czechoslovakia almost succeeded in reaching its 1989 aggregate output target.[146] In the Soviet Union, growth in 1989 slowed to less than 2½ per cent.

On the whole, the 1989 output results were arguably the worst since the post-war stabilization. In addition to the two countries actually in recession (defined as a fall in net output), several others were clearly close to it, as indicated by the downward trend of output in successive quarters of 1989, current expectations for 1990 and the results for the first months of the current year. In this context it should be noted, however, that conclusions about recent trends are somewhat hazardous owing to the large changes in statistical reporting practices now occurring in the region. The downturn in a number of countries may in fact have occurred earlier but have been hidden by deceptive statistics (see section 3.1(vii) below).

The slow-down at the aggregate level reflects weak performance throughout the main economic sectors in most countries. The socio-political events of 1989 were only in part responsible for the economic deterioration. Labour disputes, demonstrations and chaotic emigration obviously contributed to the slow-down. But the current weakness had deeper roots in the continuing inability of policy makers in eastern Europe and the Soviet Union to regain a growth path with sustained significant increases in output per head. The paltry gains in average labour productivity reflected largely low capital- and resource-use efficiency. This is a phenomenon of long standing in all the economies that used to rely mainly on detailed central planning for resource allocation.

Eastern Europe and the Soviet Union have experienced a secular decline in output performance since the early 1970s, albeit with considerable year-to-year variations.[147] In 1979-1982, output in eastern Europe had increased only marginally, with falls in per head output levels officially registered in at least one year in several countries (and probable, although concealed, in others). There had been a substantial rebound in eastern Europe during 1983-1985, which was taken as a signal that developments could be reversed in the latter part of the 1980s. Although the Soviet Union had also experienced some development difficulties in the first half of the 1980s, it none the less had maintained positive growth throughout the period.

For the latter part of the 1980s, policy makers in eastern Europe had anticipated a more balanced development path with a steady, if not spectacular, pace of output growth. The priority of restraining absorption was maintained, owing largely to the continued and pervasive scarcity of foreign exchange. In the Soviet Union, however, the five-year plan had been launched together with the first steps of *perestroika*. Initially, this restructuring of the economy was envisaged to run parallel with an acceleration *(uskorenie)* of output growth, particularly in the engineering sectors.

The five-year planning period 1986-1990 had started rather promisingly, except in Hungary. Since then, however, substantial difficulties have compounded the continuing tightness in the external accounts for most of eastern Europe and, owing to adverse terms-of-trade developments, also the Soviet Union. The sluggish performance of 1987-1988 turned into recession or near-recession in several east European countries in 1989 and, at best, to an unimpressive performance in the Soviet Union.

(iv) Sectoral output growth

Aggregate *industrial output* stagnated or declined in eastern Europe in 1989. In the Soviet Union it grew by less than 2 per cent, the lowest growth rate registered in the post-war period; however, the output of consumer manufactures ("sector B") advanced faster than industry as a whole, by 4½ per cent — a reflection of the high priority that the Soviet leadership has recently been placing on improving consumer market supplies.

The weakness of aggregate east European industrial production reflected a significant contraction of output in Hungary and Poland (-2 per cent) and near stagnation in Czechoslovakia (see table 3.2.7 and chart 3.2.2). Only Bulgaria and the German Democratic Republic reported real growth in 1989 (above 2 per cent), in both countries in spite of a substantial outflow of skilled workers since mid-year and the disorganization caused by political disturbances later in 1989. The cumulative effect of these factors, however, was increasingly felt in both countries in the last quarter.

Generally, industrial production deteriorated throughout the year. In the last quarter, output fell in absolute terms in the German Democratic Republic, Hungary, Poland, the Soviet Union, almost certainly in Romania and probably also in Bulgaria. The downturn deepened in a number of countries in the first months of 1990. In January, output was below the level of a year earlier by 4 per cent in Czechoslovakia, 6 per cent in the German Democratic Republic, 8 per cent in Hungary and more than 20 per cent in Poland and Romania. An absolute downturn appears to have occurred also in the Soviet Union in January 1990.[148]

---

probable, however, that slow growth at best was achieved through the first 9-10 months of the year. The disturbances of late 1989 must have severely cut output levels in Romania, so that for the year as a whole a downturn is likely. The other five countries jointly registered a rise in NMP of 0.5 per cent.

[146] Economic performance in Czechoslovakia undoubtedly benefited from the peaceful and extraordinarily rapid transitions in the political leadership in November 1989. Furthermore, the "revolution of the *Magic Lantern*" had unfolded without emigration or substantial social tensions. None the less, output stagnated in November and declined in December.

[147] For a more detailed examination, see United Nations Economic Commission for Europe, *Economic Survey of Europe in 1986-1987*, New York, 1987, pp.209-211.

[148] According to a statement of Prime Minister N. Ryzhkov: " ... output produced in the national economy is at a rate of 1 per cent lower than in January of

Preliminary data for February indicate that the falls generally have not been arrested.

Agricultural performance also remained well below expectations in 1989. Both for eastern Europe and the Soviet Union, preliminary estimates indicate growth of less than one per cent. The best performance in eastern Europe was 2 per cent in the case of Poland. Elsewhere in the group — except Hungary, where a contraction was recorded after the strong 1988 performance — output rose by ½ to 1½ per cent. In spite of fairly good harvests reported by Bulgaria, Poland and the Soviet Union, setbacks in crop output in 1988 and tightening external payments constraints undoubtedly contributed to holding down livestock production, which was weak or declining throughout the region; Czechoslovakia was the only exception.

Although estimates for *construction* activity are still sketchy, data on investment activity in 1989 suggest that the sector must have been running well below capacity and probably registered a fairly sharp contraction. Bottlenecks in *transportation* and distribution in many countries accounted for the weak performances in those sectors.

(v) Domestic absorption in 1989

Foreign exchange constraints have limited policy choices throughout the eastern countries almost continuously since the late 1970s. The intensity of the constraint has been much larger in countries with a sizeable foreign debt, such as Hungary and Poland. But it was also very severe in Romania, which for its own domestic reasons had resolved to repay its foreign debt ahead of time. Foreign exchange problems have recently also curtailed policy flexibility in the Soviet Union, owing largely to worsening terms of trade and capacity limitations on output, notably in the fuels sector. Because access to fresh funds from abroad was either closed to the heavily indebted countries or not sought by the others, domestic absorption throughout the group has expanded sluggishly for several years.

Information on actual developments in national income uses in 1989 is still sketchy. There is, however, little doubt that intentions regarding *absorption levels* could not be implemented in most countries. In Hungary and Poland, austerity was maintained — as originally planned — but at levels of aggregate absorption sharply lower than intended. Elsewhere in eastern Europe and in the Soviet Union, however, widening consumer market imbalances and measures to improve supplies to ease social tensions resulted in worsening external balances — in some cases by sizeable margins — in spite of cut-backs in investment outlays.

Aggregate *consumption* grew very little in real terms in most countries, or contracted — as in Hungary, Poland and most likely Romania. Efforts to improve consumer markets were not always successful, in part because of wage and income policies that conflicted with that goal. Though rising fast in nominal value, retail sales in real terms increased only marginally in several of these economies. Money incomes generally grew more rapidly than nominal retail sales, which further aggravated domestic market imbalance. This occurred in spite of efforts to boost production for the domestic market, to increase consumer imports and encourage savings through more differentiated interest rates.

An especially large increase in retail sales was reported by the Soviet Union, in part as a result of efforts to stem popular discontent with the inability of *perestroika* to improve significantly the domestic output situation. A substantial share of the overall rise stemmed, however, from the rapid increase in the sale of alcoholic beverages, an item that had deliberately been placed under official supply constraints for social reasons in the mid-1980s, with deleterious consequences for macro-economic balance.[149] Though part of the increase was made possible by the earmarking of defence industry capacities and inventories for civilian uses, emergency imports — which contributed to a sharp deterioration of the external accounts — also had to be called upon. None the less the consumer markets remained severely disturbed throughout the year, as is suggested by the rapid spread of local rationing schemes and other non-market arrangements to "distribute the shortages."

The volume of *gross investment* (and in some cases nominal investment outlays) clearly contracted in eastern Europe in 1989; in the Soviet Union it grew only marginally. This marked a sharp break with the trends of the last three years, when investment volume growth outpaced the expansion of total output. Policy makers in several countries, including the Soviet Union, have been looking for ways of curtailing investment outlays. In that sense, the results of 1989 must have been encouraging. However, the micro-economic aims associated with the easing of the investment ratio — improved efficiency in the investment process and in the use of capital — were not achieved.[150] Moreover, in the reforming countries the hoped-for replacement of budget financing by enterprise financing does not appear to have improved investment discipline. This has been mainly due to chronic rigidities in the distribution system for investment goods and unabated administrative controls over investment activity.

---

last year ... The country as a whole produced output worth 75,000 million roubles." Television interview with Dmitrii Biryukov on 23 February 1990, quoted in BBC, *Summary of World Broadcasts*, No.SU/0698, 26 February 1990, p.B.1.

149 Because about 90 per cent of the retail price of alcoholic beverages is accounted for by excise taxes, and given that consumption of these products in 1984 amounted to roughly 14 per cent of consumption outlays, the steep reduction of the official sales of these products deprived the state budget of substantial amount of revenues, which contributed significantly to the rapid rise of the budgetary deficit of the Soviet Union.

150 For example, in the Soviet Union the authorities could not even meet the target for commissioning priority projects as less than half of the 359 capacities with "state order" status planned to be put on stream actually materialized (see *Pravda*, 28 January 1990).

(vi) Developments in foreign trade

The foreign trade sector remained a constraining factor in all countries of the group in 1989. Although import volume in most countries increased faster (or fell less) than export volume, which eased domestic market imbalances, balance-of-payments concerns generally held this in fairly narrow boundaries. None the less, the external balances deteriorated in both eastern Europe and – substantially – the Soviet Union (see sections 3.4 and 4.3 below).

In CMEA relations, the trade-constraining tendencies inherent in a structure of predominantly bilateral arrangements appear now to be moving the system into a downward spiral. At its origin is the deterioration of the Soviet terms of trade vis-à-vis eastern Europe which stemmed from the lagged introduction of world market prices into the CMEA trade price structure and caused the Soviet trade balance with eastern Europe to swing into deficit in the second half of the 1980s. In 1989 and early 1990 several east European countries (notably Hungary and Poland) took special measures to curb rouble exports in an attempt to stave off sizable surpluses in transferable roubles. The Soviet Union, on the other hand, introduced export constraints of its own on manufactured consumer goods to protect the supply to domestic markets. In addition, Soviet deliveries of fuels and raw materials fell short of commitments owing to production and, probably, transport difficulties. In the event, the volume of Soviet exports to eastern Europe appears to have contracted slightly in 1989 – by perhaps 1-2 per cent – while Soviet imports from eastern Europe fell somewhat more steeply – by 2-3 per cent; none the less, the Soviet trade deficit rose from 2½ billion roubles to over 4 billion roubles.[151]

External payments constraints were largely responsible for the weak trade performance with non-CMEA partners. Imports from these partners increased in both eastern Europe and the Soviet Union, in some cases as a consequence of the deliberate choice of policy makers around mid-year to improve domestic supplies through consumer goods imports. As a result, the trade balance of the Soviet Union with the convertible currency area registered a $6 billion turnround, swinging from surplus to a deficit of about $1½ billion. A substantial proportion of the contraction – roughly $2 billion – was on account of a declining surplus with the developing countries. Matters were less dramatic in eastern Europe's relations with third partners. None the less the trade surplus of $3 billion with the market economies in 1988 contracted to some $2½ billion.

(vii) Reliability of statistics

The recent political changes in eastern Europe and the Soviet Union have been accompanied by numerous official revelations of serious problems with past statistical reporting, ranging from tampering with reports by the now deposed leadership, as in Bulgaria, the German Democratic Republic and Romania, to systematically biased methodological approaches, as in the case of the Soviet Union (see box 3.1).

As reported in earlier issues of this *Survey*,[152] public scepticism about the reliability of official statistics had grown rapidly in recent years. In the Soviet Union, it had found increasing reflection in the economic literature and also in statements of policy makers unhappy about the quality of the information reaching them.[153] Until the end of 1989 there was none of this, however, in those east European countries whose data practices had long been the most problematic – Bulgaria, the German Democratic Republic and, notably, Romania.

Statistical deficiencies clearly touched all areas of reporting, from physical indicators – which could be miscounted, mismeasured, or simply falsified[154] – to the more complex aggregate measures of production, consumption and investment, including the national accounts.[155] Methodological shortcomings affected especially the aggregate measures, including price statistics, but a desire to mislead certainly underlay the data distortions in other areas, especially politically sensitive ones such as fiscal deficits, foreign trade flows and balances and external debt.

In the last months of 1989 and at the beginning of 1990, substantial corrections were published to the statistics of almost all the eastern countries, and data never before released were made available in some cases. Earlier information on NMP growth was reduced by as much as almost 4 percentage points (in the case of Bulgaria for 1988) and by lesser amounts in other countries (see box 3.1 for the Soviet Union), the existence of fiscal deficits of significant proportions (more than one tenth of NMP in Bulgaria in 1988, for instance) was for the first time revealed in a number of east European countries, external debt data were published for the first time or revised (by $3 billion in the case of Hungary), and new foreign trade returns were

---

[151] Hungary was in the vanguard of trying to hold down exports to the Soviet Union. Yet it ended up with a trade surplus and doubled the current account surplus on transferable rouble account.

[152] Last year's *Survey* (pp.98-99) raised the question of the accuracy of recent Soviet aggregate output statistics, as well as (pp. 120-122) broader aspects of output reporting. Whereas numerous data, including aggregate output statistics for 1985-1987, were recently revised, Soviet aggregate output data for 1988 were not. But doubt remains justified. Similar questions were raised with regard to a number of east European countries – especially the output data of Bulgaria (*ibid.*, p.96) and the foreign trade data of the German Democratic Republic and Romania (pp.159-163).

[153] For a useful recent review of the overall issues, see E.G. Yasin, "Perestroika i statistika" (*Perestroika* and statistics), *Ekonomika i matematicheskie metody*, (1989), pp.773-781. A more detailed survey of what has to be done with Soviet statistics is summarized in "Krugly stol redaktsii" (Editor's round table), *Ibid.*, pp.900-931.

[154] For some striking examples, see the article by V.N. Kirichenko, *Kommunist*, 1990, No.3, from which an excerpt is given in box 3.1.

[155] Key problems of the Soviet national accounts are examined in G.N. Zoteev, "O printsipakh perestroiki statistiki natsionalnogo dokhoda SSSR" (Regarding principles of the restructuring of USSR national income statistics), *Ekonomika i matematicheskie metody*, No.5 (1989), pp.789-800.

BOX 3.1

New thinking about national statistics

USSR

The head of the Soviet statistical office, Goskomstat, observes in response to recent criticism of official statistics: *"The most unreasonable thing to do ... would be to attempt to save the 'honor of the uniform' by claiming that in spite of occasional shortcomings, which are being overcome, the situation on the whole and in general is not bad. Society in any case would not believe such assertions. And not without reason: they do not correspond to reality."*

"In truth, for decades the prevailing stance has been to demonstrate successes and advantages, to keep silent about difficulties and negative features in the development of the country and its regions. Statistics, as well as theory, was assigned a perverted ideological function of forming the illusion of the well-being and infallibility of the command-administrative system. This 'lacquering' approach found expression in the very methodology of the calculation of indicators (growth rates of social production, dynamics of prices, level of consumption of products, effectiveness and losses), in tendentious revisions of the methodology of data preparation which were hidden from the public. There has been no safeguarding of comparability with standards, indicators and methods for their preparation which have been accepted in the statistical practice of developed countries and the international economic organizations. The distorted data on growth rates, levels and proportions of the socio-economic development of the country did not constitute a reliable basis for decision-making on the most important socio-economic issues."

"Of course, many shortcomings of statistical information were connected with exaggerated reporting and outright cheating. The battle with these phenomena requires unflagging attention. Yet, the main casualties to the credibility of statistical data were inflicted by the imperfections (or tendentiousness) of the methodology of computations, its subordination to current political tasks. Here are some examples:"

"It was not in faraway times, but in the years of perestroika already, that corrections were made in the ... data for 1985-1987 on GNP, GSP, national income and the real incomes of the population, to eliminate the impact on the dynamics of these indicators of the cut in the production and sales of alcoholic drinks. As a result, the growth of national income (NMP) in 1985 and 1986 was about doubled. In actuality NMP produced did not rise by 3.5% in 1985 but by only 1.6%, and in 1986 not by 4.1% but by 2.3%. It is obvious that such data are not suitable for an analysis of the situation and the taking of well-based decisions. The USSR Goskomstat has now eliminated these shortcomings... ". [1]

Bulgaria

From an editorial under the title "The entire truth" in the daily of the Bulgarian Central Committee:

"Real data on the situation in the country have been carefully hidden from the broad public and the mass media, covered by a veil of secrecy. Not a few of us tried to uncover what is behind the veil. But this intention proved ever unrealizable as the real data contained a charge which could have been destructive for the command-administrative system. And it was in the interest of the peace and quiet of that very system that the population was so generously supplied with calming reports..."

"It is time that the Central Statistical Office turns itself into an autonomous, wholly independent organ which maintains itself from the budget, but has full assistance in the collection and full freedom in the dissemination of information." [2]

Romania

Editorial under the title: "Statistics must be the servant of the truth and nothing but the truth" in the first issue of the new Romanian statistical information bulletin.

"As is known, excessive limitation of access to statistical data constituted the main modality for hiding the truth and denying the real situation of the Romanian economy. Statistical 'secretomania' had assumed such dimensions that the only source of information at the disposal of economists, researchers, teaching staff, engineers, doctors and other categories of specialists requiring the utilization of statistical data for their activities were the speeches of the dictator, the annual plan fulfilment reports, as well as the Statistical Yearbook of the RSR containing ever less significant information."

"To this must be added the fact that until the Revolution precisely the statistics destined for publication were continuously subjected to an intense process of pollution from the side of the dictatorship in order to 'underpin' the theses of the regime. The quality of the data suffered above all under the pressures exercised by the leaders of the party organs to present information not in conformity with reality. Their arrangements regarding the 'level of realization' resolved to a large degree the problems of implementing unrealistic plans dictated by the 'supreme leadership' and, in consequence, masked their incompetence."

"Under the new conditions, the workers of the central and territorial apparatus of the National Commission for Statistics, in agreement with the entire people, consider that all conditions have been created for Romanian statistics to reflect the truth ... " [3]

---

[1] Vadim N. Kirichenko, "Vernut' doverie statistike" (To render credibility to statistics), *Kommunist*, No. 3, 1990, pp.22-33.
[2] Yu. Popov, "Tsyalata istina" (The entire truth), *Rabotnichesko delo*, 22 November 1989, p.1.
[3] Comisia nationala pentru statistica, *Buletin de informare publica*, No. 1, 1990 (February 1990), p.1.

published which revealed the old ones to have been outright constructs (the German Democratic Republic), to mention only a few.

This issue of the *Survey* reflects some of the corrections in the previously published misleading statistics.[156] It should be noted, however, that while the most recent data quite evidently reflect the effort to improve public information, they are frequently not accompanied by corresponding revisions of data for prior periods. Any analysis based on the available mixture of revised and unrevised data is therefore always in danger of missing crucial developments or arriving at a wrong identification of the turning points.

(viii) Outlook for growth in 1990

Policy objectives for 1990 for most countries of the area are not yet crystallized at the time of writing. Only the Soviet Union has an explicit annual plan that is still being adhered to. In late 1989, Czechoslovakia adopted a plan that aimed at continuing the slow growth path of the past several years. But the new government has abandoned even these modest goals and is now formulating an alternative that better reflects what appears to be feasible at this stage, pending the introduction of market-oriented economic reforms. Also Romania adopted a formal plan prior to the December 1989 events. The goals set there were very ambitious — in fact, unrealistic — and it is certain that it will be replaced. For the time being, the new Government of Romania is operating with an emergency quarterly plan that later in the year will be replaced by a revised plan for the year as a whole. However, little information on the contents of the first quarter plan is available.[157] Hungary and Poland no longer have explicit plans. The debates about plan formulations in Bulgaria[158] and the German Democratic Republic[159] have not so far resulted in the parliamentary adoption of plans in the old sense, though current operations of these economies undoubtedly proceed still largely under the guidance of the old planning institutions.

Although the explicit policies usually embodied in formal output and distribution plans and budget statements, and the discussions around them, are not available for 1990 for most countries, the fluidity of the socio-political situation throughout the area makes it likely that the medium-term commitment of policy makers to steady growth is not very strong.

The information available indicates that current economic policy is dominated by preoccupations about regaining economic, social and political stability, often in conjunction with preparations for systemic change. In some countries, a social consensus already prevails, and formal economic stabilization programmes are being placed at the heart of short-run economic policy. Regaining order in monetary and fiscal affairs is a prerequisite for moving towards a more market-oriented environment. In other countries, particularly Bulgaria and Romania, such a sharp policy turn will have to await the outcome of the political development. Finally, in view of the rapid erosion of economic, social and political stability in the German Democratic Republic at the beginning of the year and the prospect of unification with the Federal Republic, policy deliberations other than those about the modalities of unification have a very short horizon.

Parliamentary elections are scheduled in all east European countries for 1990, beginning with the German Democratic Republic and Hungary in the second half of March. All will be contested by multiple parties as the constitutional prerogatives of one-party rule have been abolished in all these countries.[160] In most countries, the outcome is likely to result in the formation of coalition governments made up by the strongest parties in the electoral contests. The horizon of the present political leadership, under the circumstances, is rather short. Priority in policy making is gravitating towards many issues other than those required to manage the economy according to plan. In some countries, this stems from concerns about the imminent elections. In others, as in Romania, it follows from the fact that the top priority is to improve the appallingly low standard of living of the population without aggravating imbalances too much.

The national economic plan of the Soviet Union for 1990 intends a "large-scale structural manoeuvre" with two main aims: the implementation of "priority measures to reduce the social tensions in the country" and recovery of the country's monetary-fiscal balance. On the output side this means an acceleration of growth "almost entirely on account of growth of the consumption sphere of the economy with simultaneous stabilization and in a number of cases reduction of productive resources."[161]

The overall growth aim may be an acceleration to as much as 4-5 per cent for NMP and 3½ per cent for industrial output, with a pronounced structural shift: the output of producer goods ("sector A") is expected

---

[156] The *"some"* should be stressed: revisions of official data appeared in such volume throughout the early months of 1990, the time of writing of this publication, that not all could be included in the tables or the analysis. This is important for the stricture made in the text above.

[157] The existence of such a plan and of a newly-created National Institute of Economic Research entrusted with the task of formulating a feasible reform blueprint were announced by the Romanian Prime Minister Petre Roman in a speech to the National Salvation Front on 4 January 1990 (see BBC, *Summary of World Broadcasts*, EE/0657, 9 January 1990, pp.B/6-8).

[158] A plan is due to be submitted in March to the National Assembly for discussion and ratification (see interview with Belcho Belchev, Minister of Finance, in *Narodna armiya*, 12 January 1990, pp.1,3).

[159] In the first quarter, the economy was being steered on an *ad hoc* basis. Deputy Prime Minister and Minister of Economics Christa Luft expects a contraction in aggregate output of 4-5 per cent with a sizeable external deficit. *Neues Deutschland*, 6 February 1990, pp.1, 2.

[160] They are now under review in the Soviet Union too. But a final decision has to await the next session of the Congress of People's Deputies.

[161] Prime Minister N.I. Ryzhkov, *Ekonomicheskaya gazeta*, No. 51, December 1989, p.9.

to expand hardly at all, whereas consumer goods production ("sector B") is to rise by almost 7 per cent.[162] The provision of goods to consumer markets is to rise by 66 billion roubles (18 per cent over the expected 1989 level).[163]

One key objective of economic policy in 1990 is to increase domestic supplies of manufactured consumer goods well over levels observed in 1989. For the same reason, overall investment activity is to be curtailed sharply, possibly by as much as 10 per cent, after stagnating in 1989.[164] Apart from its macro-economic impact of freeing resources for consumption, the cut of investment expenditures also serves the second priority aim, the re-establishment of fiscal balance, as a large part is still financed from the state budget.

With respect to foreign trade in 1990, the outlook is not very encouraging for intra-CMEA relations. Intragroup trade flows continue to be hampered by capacity constraints in Soviet deliveries of fuels and raw materials, some of which have already been cut well below agreed volumes. Thus, Bulgaria, Czechoslovakia, Hungary[165] and Poland[166] disclosed substantial cuts in Soviet oil delivery plans for the first quarter of 1990, ranging from 20 per cent in the case of Czechoslovakia[167] and one third in the case of Poland to 50 per cent in that Bulgaria.[168] Another important obstacle on the horizon is the problem of bilateral imbalances on transferable rouble accounts, for which a solution is not yet in sight. Early in 1990 Hungary decided to revoke all licences for exports denominated in transferable roubles[169] in an effort to come to check what threatened to become a run-away transferable rouble surplus[170] and to impose greater selectivity in export production.[171] Some enterprises have already been severely hurt by this measure.[172] Discussions are currently under way on how to reform quickly the key elements of the trade and payments régimes of these countries (see sections 3.4 and 3.5).

Economic developments in the east-west context in the course of the year will be a function of two interrelated factors. One is the ability of the east European countries and the Soviet Union to emerge from their current economic recession and to redirect resources towards export sectors. Prospects are not particularly good in that respect, as several countries already expect a fall in output. The other critical factor, in the case of the east European countries attempting to rebuild their institutions as market economies, will be the amount of assistance provided by western countries under the programmes now being co-ordinated under the auspices of the Commission of the European Communities (see section 4.4).

Much of what happens in 1990 in the economic domain will be the outcome of system reforms under way in some countries, especially in Hungary and Poland, in conjunction with stabilization measures. These envisage major transformations that will subject economic processes much more to the discipline of

---

[162] Intentions of the Soviet Union regarding the growth course in 1990 — whether the annual plan aims at an easing or at acceleration — are somewhat obscured by the fact that all plan figures are expressed relative to five-year plan targets for 1989. On this basis, NMP produced is to grow 1.1 per cent, NMP-used 2.6 per cent, industrial output 2.1 per cent, with the growth of group "A" (producer goods) of 0.5 per cent, and of group "B" (consumer goods) of 6.7 per cent (later corrected to 0.8 per cent and 7.6 per cent for "A" and "B", respectively — Prime Minister N.I. Ryzhkov, loc. cit.), and real income per capita 1.3 per cent. It is known that the five-year plan target for 1989 was not achieved, and hence rates of planned increase over 1989 actual must be much higher — but in many instances it is not known what the original FYP target for 1989 was, nor whether the original or a revised target was used for the 1990 plan calculations. The figures given in the text are the ECE estimates of the change relative to the actual 1989 levels implied by these targets.

[163] In his address to the second session of the Congress of People's Deputies in December 1989, Prime Minister Ryzhkov observed: "It must be said that this number — 66 billion roubles — evokes doubts as to its realism in some people. Indeed, this is a large increment. But one must ask: can we under the present conditions of deficits on the consumer market tackle the issue in a different manner? We considered the pros and cons and took the decision to utilize the capacities of the entire economy to attain this goal. In one word, comrades, enough vacillation, now it is time to direct the emotions into the stream of practical matters." Ryzhkov, loc.cit.

[164] The 1990 plan provides for investment outlays "from all sources" of 196.9 billion roubles (Pravda, 11 November 1989), as against actual outlays in 1989 "at estimate prices" of 219.4 billion roubles (Pravda, 28 January 1990). If the two figures are expressed at the same prices, the intended contraction in investment volume would be over 10 per cent. According to Prime Minister Ryzhkov, investment activity is to remain frozen at this level also in 1991-1992 (statement to the second session of the Congress of People's Deputies, Ekonomicheskaya gazeta, No.51, December 1990). The impact on net investment in the economy (increase in the stock of fixed assets) should be smaller if accompanying measures, including a new tax on enterprise investment activity, leads to accelerated commissioning of new objects and a rapid reduction of the stock of unfinished projects.

[165] In 1989, Soviet oil deliveries to Hungary are reported to have been 150,000 tons or 2.3 per cent short of the agreed volume. For the first quarter of 1990 the authorities expect a shortfall of about 400,000 tons (Heti Világgazdaság, 24 February 1990). However, this may not necessarily be indicative of the change for the year as a whole, as shifts in committed deliveries over the four quarters are not unusual. There is none the less little doubt that overall deliveries are likely to fall short of those specified in the long-term commitments made earlier. It should be noted that the annual trade protocol for 1990 was, in contrast to past practice, still under negotiation in March 1990.

[166] Again, this may be simply on account of redistribution of quarterly deliveries. Thus, because of supply constraints in the Caucasian fields, Poland expects to receive 25 per cent less oil from the Soviet Union than originally envisaged (Zycie Warszawy, 12 January 1990, p.2 and Zycie Warszawy, 7 February 1990). The Polish-Soviet trade agreement for 1990, which also was not yet signed in March, apparently foresees deliveries of 13 million tons of crude oil (Zycie Warszawy, 7 February 1990) — marginally less than in 1988 (13.09 million tons). However, it is not clear whether the expected overall volume for 1990 includes petroleum products, which amounted to another 2.2 million tons in 1988.

[167] Rudé právo, 3 February 1990, p.2.

[168] Financial Times, 14 February 1990, p.2.

[169] This came into force on 18 January 1990 (see Magyar Hirlap, 19 January 1990, p.1).

[170] During the first two weeks of January alone, a surplus of 220 million roubles on current account was reported (Heti Világgazdaság, 27 January 1990).

[171] The revocation was also aimed at cutting sharply the ability of firms with open-ended licences to procure funds through exports to the transferable rouble area, because of the immediate cash payment system applied there.

[172] Firms whose output used to be destined chiefly for the Soviet market are in especially deep trouble. For example, the bus manufacturer Ikarus felt compelled to close several plants, with a labour force of over 10,000, on 16 February 1990 for 3 to 7 weeks because of problems with transferable rouble exports (see International Herald Tribune, 17-18 February 1990, p.17 and Magyar Nemzet, 17 February 1990).

market relations, something that had been all but excluded under central planning during the past forty years. By their very nature, such far-reaching economic transformations affect both the micro- and the macro-economic domains.

In the micro-economic sphere, major changes in property rights, pricing, labour remuneration, enterprise financing and autonomy of firms will come to the fore. At the macro-economic level, these countries need to put in place adequate instruments and institutions to implement policies yet to be designed that will, in due course, provide greater stability in monetary and fiscal affairs and replace the central planning mechanism as traditionally understood with co-ordinated monetary and fiscal policies. Given that most of the societies in question retain a strong preference for egalitarianism and social security, there may also be a need to formulate proper price and incomes policies, in conjunction with measures to stabilize the economy and implement market-oriented reforms.

The transformations in economic systems are also bound to leave a lasting imprint on the mechanisms and channels through which these countries interact with each other, as well as with third partners, through trade, payments and foreign assistance. Furthermore, the reshaping of the international economic relations of the majority of these countries is bound to affect the course of regional integration efforts in Europe. Their probable consequences will need to be taken into account as the European economy is being reshaped.

With respect to the ECE region, the changes in eastern Europe and the Soviet Union in early 1990 are having significant implications for east-west trade and finance, and the position of the east European countries *vis-à-vis* the regional economic integration schemes in western Europe. The assistance efforts of the Group of 24, co-ordinated by the Commission of the European Communities (see section 4.4) will involve the western countries in the eastern reform process.

3.2 PRODUCTION

Production growth in 1989 was disappointing in eastern Europe and the Soviet Union. Aggregate domestic output (NMP produced) of the seven countries taken together grew less than 2 per cent compared with 4 per cent in 1988 and with 5½ per cent implied by the plan targets for 1989. Economic reforms and their short-run costs in the form of disruptions of established economic linkages affected the outcome. This was particularly the case in the Soviet Union, but also in Hungary and Poland. But weakening economic performance reflected mainly accumulated internal and external imbalances. These were exacerbated by new supply constraints and transport bottlenecks. Serious discontinuities also appeared in intra-CMEA trade. Political upheavals disturbed production at the end of the year in several countries.

The deceleration in domestic output growth was shared by all seven countries, with absolute contractions of NMP produced in some. A strong deceleration in industrial output growth contributed significantly to the slow-down of overall net output. Agricultural performance was modest and remained substantially below the annual plans. Domestic output and efficiency changes are examined in section (i), industrial developments in section (ii) and agricultural outcomes in section (iii).

(i) General production trends

(a) Growth of national output

In 1989, the east European countries and the Soviet Union experienced a sharp deceleration in rates of economic growth. For the seven countries combined, real growth of NMP produced fell from 4 per cent in 1988 to less than 2 per cent in 1989. A sharp deceleration in the rate of NMP growth was registered both in eastern Europe[173] and the Soviet Union (see table 3.2.1). The deceleration was substantial and indeed the worst since 1982. Three countries (Bulgaria, Hungary and Poland) recorded falls in, or zero growth of, output. In most countries the deterioration in the course of the year continued into the early months of 1990.

Domestic output performance in 1989 reflected a number of factors, from changes in the availability of factor inputs and in the efficiency with which they are used to different policy objectives, including those concerning economic reform. Worsening supply bottlenecks in several critical sectors, slow progress in improving the use of production inputs and balance of payments constraints all contributed significantly to the deceleration of domestic output.

Among the factors contributing to the slow-down in economic growth in 1989 were some which could hardly have been anticipated when the annual plans for that year were prepared. Strikes in the Soviet Union led to raw material and energy shortages which were exacerbated by bottlenecks in the Soviet transport system. These appeared to spill over into neighbouring economies via reduced export deliveries. Renewed unrest in some Soviet republics also worsened inter-sectoral imbalances. Labour shortages appeared as a result of large-scale emigration, particularly from Bulgaria and the German Democratic Republic.

Policy objectives for 1989 called for an acceleration of economic growth in most countries under review. Only Hungary expected zero NMP growth though Czechoslovakia also planned only a modest increase. In the other countries, NMP growth expectations ranged from 4 per cent in the German Democratic Republic to 8½ per cent in Romania (table 3.2.1). The Soviet NMP target for 1989 of not quite 4 per cent growth over the *planned* output level in 1988 implied an increase of almost 6 per cent over the actual level in 1988. As pointed out in the previous issue of this publication,[174] these output targets were very optimistic given developments in the last 15 years and the economic situation in the countries concerned.

Events in 1989 again confirm the conclusion that the forces which were expected to determine output growth in 1986-1990, particularly those pertaining to improvements in efficiency, were not strong enough to offset a number of braking factors. Among them were an obsolete and aging capital stock (section 3.3(iii) below), inefficiencies and rigidities stemming from centralized management and planning systems, underdeveloped incentive systems both for enterprises and the work force and disturbances arising from political and economic reform.

Several countries took specific measures to reduce overall demand and thereby cope with endemic shortages due to the unrealistic price structures imposed under central planning (sections 3.3(ii) and (iv) below).

---

[173] Statistical data on the economic development of Romania in 1989 were not available in the time of writing. Aggregates for eastern Europe in 1989 hence refer to the other five east European countries.

[174] United Nations Economic Commission for Europe, *Economic Survey of Europe in 1988-1989*, New York, 1989, p.88. The ECE secretariat estimated that a reasonable growth forecast for eastern Europe and the Soviet Union combined was about 3½ per cent in 1989.

TABLE 3.2.1
Net material product (produced), 1981-1990
(Annual percentage change)

	1981-1985	1986	1987	1988	1989	Plan 1989	Plan 1990	1986-1989	Plan 1986-1990
Bulgaria	3.7	5.3	5.1	2.4	-0.4	6.2	-3.7 a	3.1	5.4
Czechoslovakia	1.8	2.6	2.1	2.4	1.3	1.4	2.2	2.1	3.4
German Dem.Rep	4.5	4.3	3.3	2.8	2.0	4.0	..	3.1	4.6
Hungary	1.3	0.9	4.1	0.3	-2.0 *	- *	..	0.8	2.8-3.2
Poland	-0.8	4.9	1.9	4.9	-	4.2	..	2.9	3.0-3.5
Romania	4.4	7.3	4.8	3.2	..	8.5	9.5	..	10.3
Eastern Europe	2.2	4.6	3.2	3.1	0.5 b	4.5	..	2.6 b	5.3
Soviet Union	3.2	2.3	1.6	4.4	2.4	5.7 c	4.4 c	2.7	4.2
Eastern Europe and Soviet Union	2.9	3.0	2.1	4.0	1.8*	5.3	..	2.7*	4.6

Source: ECE secretariat Common Data Base, based on national statistics, plans and plan fulfilment reports and direct communication to the ECE secretariat. National data are aggregated by means of weights derived from CMEA investigations.

a National forecast.
b Excluding Romania.
c Official plan targets are expressed as growth over the preceding year's *plan* level. Figures shown are ECE estimates of implied growth over the *actual* level of that year.

While the sluggishness of economic activity in 1989 was shared by all countries, performance none the less differed.

For the first time in post-war history, *Bulgaria* reported an absolute decline in NMP produced in 1989. This indicates not only difficulties in the Bulgarian economy, but perhaps also an improvement in statistical reporting.[175] A significant weakening of domestic output performance began in 1988 and continued into 1989. Growing imbalances in the national economy stemming from mismanaged planning as well as events specific to 1989 contributed to the downturn. The latter include notably labour shortages due to emigration and socio-political disturbances. These were manifested at the end of the year, when industrial output declined strongly (by 12.7 per cent in December 1989 compared with its year-earlier level). External constraints, particularly those which appeared in intra-CMEA trade, also held back economic growth.

Bulgarian performance in 1989 was also disappointing relative to the very ambitious annual plan, which had expected growth of over 6 per cent in NMP produced. The comparison of the 3 per cent average annual NMP growth in 1986-1989 with the five-year plan target of 5½ per cent for 1986-1990 indicates that unrealistic expectations were embodied in both annual and five-year plans.

In *Czechoslovakia*, policy objectives for 1989 called for a moderation of economic growth, improved internal balance and a faster pace of economic reform. It was assumed that developments in the external sector, policies aimed at improving domestic balances and the transition to a new economic mechanism would all have constraining effect on short-term output growth.

Outcomes in 1989 confirm these assumptions. Reported growth of NMP produced slowed to just over 1 per cent, but may in fact have been weaker.[176] While the slowing was in line with the annual plan, this outcome was substantially below what had been envisaged by the original five-year plan target (table 3.2.1). The sluggish expansion of domestic output since the mid-1980s has thus continued. NMP growth in 1989 was affected by falling exports to CMEA countries, declining transport output and the stagnation of the trade sector. However, more deeply-rooted forces also underly poor economic performance. These are generally linked with the management and planning systems, which led to an aging of the capital stock, obsolete infrastructure and environmental damage.[177]

Over a medium-term perspective, no noteworthy results have been recorded in Czechoslovakia in either growth or structural change. Economic growth in the 1980s has averaged less than 2 per cent annually, with a moderate upswing in 1984-1985 following zero growth in 1981-1982. On the other hand, relative macro-economic stability has been maintained so far.[178]

In the *German Democratic Republic,* growth slowed for the third year in 1989. While in the past the German Democratic Republic reported relatively high and stable rates of NMP growth, this changed after 1986

---

[175] Doubts shared by many analysts concerning the inflation of Bulgarian output statistics were confirmed by the revised figure for the growth of NMP produced in 1988 provided in the plan fulfilment report for 1989. The 1988 increase had originally been reported as 6.2 per cent, but this has now been reduced to 2.4 per cent. See *Rabotnichesko delo*, 30 January 1990, p.4.

[176] As pointed out in the report of the Federal Statistical Office on Czechoslovak social and economic development in 1989, existing methods of calculating price statistics do not reflect certain price rises and real NMP growth was therefore lower than reported. See *Mladá fronta*, 10 February 1990, p.3. In the same spirit, Prime Minister M. Calfa pointed out in a recent speech to the Federal Assembly that, taking into account hidden inflation, it is doubtful whether there was any growth at all. See BBC, *Summary of World Broadcasts*, EE/0701, 1 March 1990, p.C/4.

[177] A critical assessment of the economic situation in Czechoslovakia was made by the Prime Minister in his speech to the Federal Assembly, *Rudé právo*, 20 December 1989, p.2.

[178] See *PlanEcon Report*, No.52, 29 December 1989.

CHART 3.2.1
Growth rates of net material product
(Annual percentage change)

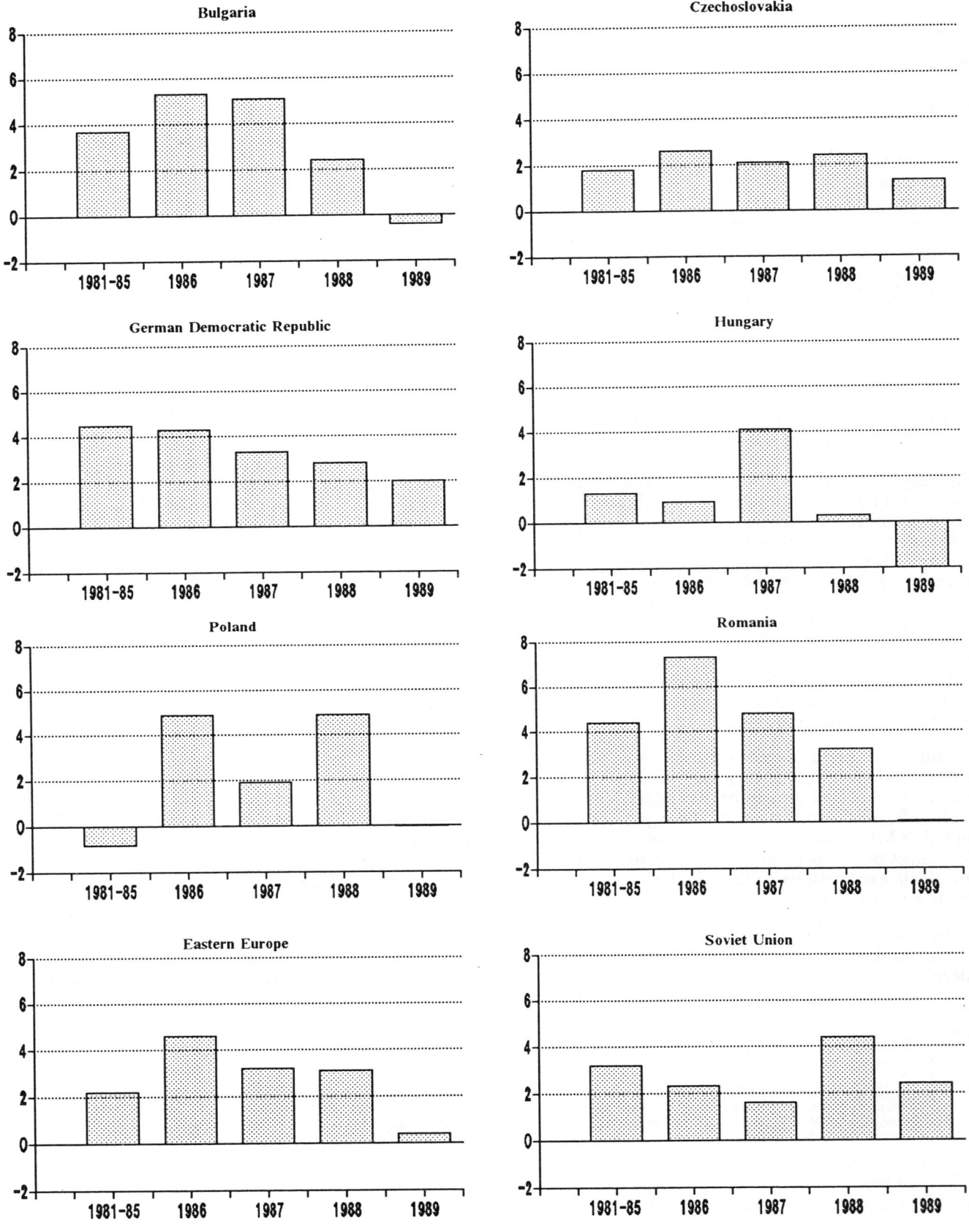

Source: ECE secretariat Common Data Base.

Production

CHART 3.2.2

Factor inputs and NMP growth
(*Indices, 1970 = 100*)

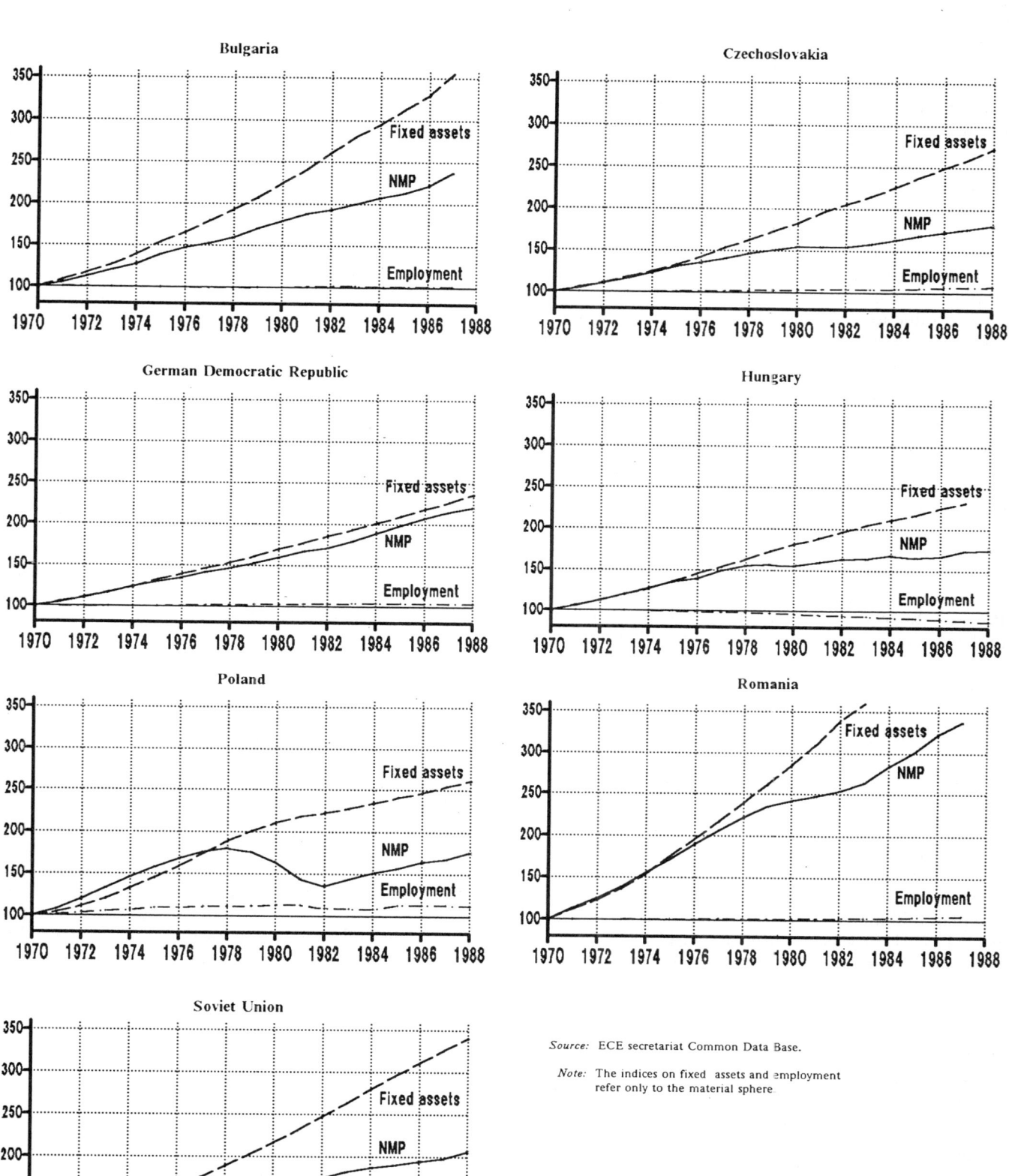

Source: ECE secretariat Common Data Base.

Note: The indices on fixed assets and employment refer only to the material sphere.

(table 3.2.1). Actual performance in 1989 lagged substantially behind the 4 per cent annual plan target and was the worst since 1961. Output performance deteriorated dramatically in the last quarter of 1989, when NMP produced fell by 3 per cent in comparison with the corresponding period of the preceding year. This was mainly due to large-scale losses in the labour force from emigration and caused growing tension in the domestic market.

In *Hungary*, economic developments in 1989 were mixed. Domestic output, measured in terms of gross domestic product (now the main national output measure which includes gross value added both in the material and non-material spheres),[179] fell by 1-2 per cent, although the annual plan envisaged no change in output. Thus, 1989 was the second successive year when production contracted. Constraints on the demand side resulting from restrictive domestic policies were mainly responsible.

In *Poland*, NMP stagnated in 1989 even as political and economic reform accelerated. A 4 per cent increase had been planned, which would have permitted re-attainment of the pre-crisis level last reached in 1978. Recovery from the 1979-1982 recession had initially been rapid, but began to stall two years ago. Structural change in 1989, however, was significant: a fall in the net output of the socialized sector (by 2½ per cent) was accompanied by a rapid expansion (by some 11-12 per cent) in the output of the private sector. None the less, Poland's huge overall external indebtedness, its accumulated internal imbalances and hyperinflation represented serious constraints on output expansion. An additional factor affecting the 1989 outcome was the deteriorating energy and material input supply situation. Domestic coal output declined while imports of energy, raw and other materials decreased. Further, the freeing of agricultural prices led to a fall in the supply of inputs of agricultural origin, which had adverse consequences for the food-processing industries.

A worrying feature of Polish economic development in 1989 was the continuous decline of output performance in the course of the year. Moreover, as stated in the plan fulfilment report, published figures on changes in real NMP produced must be considered provisional due to the possible understatement of price changes.[180]

The *Romanian* economy is in a state of serious crisis, with huge domestic imbalances and an obsolete and aging capital stock both in the material sphere and in the non-material sphere infrastructure. Though no statistical data had been reported for 1989 at the time of writing, it can be assumed that the dramatic political developments in December 1989 were reflected in falling output levels.

In the *Soviet Union*, the 2½ per cent growth of NMP produced was 2 percentage points less than in the preceding year and some 3 percentage points below planned growth (table 3.2.1).[181] Gross national product, calculated on the basis of the United Nations methodology of national accounts (SNA), which is now also reported in Soviet publications, increased by 3 per cent. Thus value added in the *non-material sphere* must have grown faster than that of the material sphere, which attests to a growing role of services in Soviet domestic output growth. Judging from the performance of the main sectors of the material sphere (industrial growth of less than 2 per cent and agricultural growth of less than 1 per cent, both in gross output terms), it seems that the trade sector, in contrast with preceding years, contributed significantly to measured NMP growth.[182]

The plan target for 1989 was known to be "taut" and to be dependent on very significant efficiency gains.[183] It is possible that the annual plan for 1989 was too ambitious and did not take fully into account the forces likely to hold back domestic output growth. Some of them were difficult to foresee, since they stemmed from the political and economic transformation now under way in the Soviet Union. To this group of factors can be attributed strikes and inter-ethnic conflicts which caused shortages in raw material and energy supplies and transport bottlenecks. The activities most severely hit were the fuel, energy and metallurgical complexes, but other sectors and branches also suffered indirectly. However, it seems that disturbances arising from the transition to a new economic management system and growing supply shortages were mainly responsible for poor output performance. There have, for example, been conflicts between greater enterprise independence and continuing central management and control.[184] To find the right balance between the pace of economic growth, external adjustment and economic reform appears to have been more difficult than originally assumed.[185]

---

179 See footnote 219 below.

180 See "Statystyka Polski," supplement to *Rzeczpospolita*, 1 February 1990.

181 The 1989 annual economic plan called for a 3.8 per cent increase in NMP over the level *planned* for 1988 (*Pravda*, 29 October 1988). ECE secretariat estimates indicate this means a 5.7 per cent increase over the actual NMP level of that year.

182 This is confirmed by V. Kirichenko, Chairman of the Soviet State Committee for Statistics, who noted that the expansion of consumer goods imports and increased production and sale of alcoholic beverages significantly contributed to the growth of NMP produced. Net value added in enterprises in the material sphere, which eliminates the impact of the net contribution of foreign trade and turnover tax changes to NMP produced, increased by only 1.5 per cent in 1989. See *Pravitel'stvennyi vestnik*, No.4, January 1990.

183 See the statement by USSR Gosplan Chairman Yu. Maslyukov, *Pravda*, 28 October 1989.

184 See the interview with N. Petrakov, *Financial Times*, 19 February 1990, p.18.

185 Prime Minister N.I. Ryzhkov in his report to the second Congress of People's Deputies singled out four groups of causes of the present serious economic situation in the Soviet Union. *First*, the deeply-rooted factors linked with past developments — an outdated industrial structure and obsolete fixed assets with resulting low overall efficiency and slow technological progress. *Second*, shortcomings in the implementation of economic reform. *Third*, miscalculations in some respects, such as the anti-alcohol campaign or the fight against non-labour incomes. *Fourth*, radical changes which have led to unfavourable phenomena

TABLE 3.2.2

Net material product (NMP) and net value added, by sector, 1981-1988

	Annual percentage change				Percentage contribution of the sectors to NMP growth			
	1981-1985	*1986*	*1987*	*1988*	*1981-1985*	*1986*	*1987*	*1988*
Bulgaria								
NMP	3.5	4.3	6.8	..	100.0	100.0	100.0	..
Industry	6.9	5.7	5.6	..	103.0	75.7	47.6	..
Construction	5.4	2.0	4.7	..	14.8	4.7	6.8	..
Agriculture	-3.9	22.4	-14.6	..	-15.7	59.3	-28.6	..
Transport and communications	4.1	3.8	4.8	..	9.5	7.3	5.8	..
Trade	-3.2	-17.7	55.7	..	-10.9	-40.6	63.3	..
Other branches	-0.9	-9.9	14.4	..	-0.8	-6.5	5.2	..
Czechoslovakia								
NMP	1.7	2.6	2.1	2.4	100.0	100.0	100.0	100.0
Industry	1.6	3.1	3.9	3.3	55.7	71.1	110.6	85.7
Construction	1.0	0.6	2.9	1.7	6.8	2.5	15.6	8.0
Agriculture	-0.6	2.3	-3.3	-1.5	-2.8	6.5	-11.9	-4.4
Transport and communications	2.3	3.9	-0.2	0.7	6.7	7.6	-0.6	1.5
Trade	4.1	1.3	-2.1	1.1	37.7	8.6	-16.5	7.7
Other branches	-11.1	23.3	12.0	6.7	-4.1	3.7	2.9	1.6
German Democratic Republic								
NMP	4.5	4.3	3.6	2.8	100.0	100.0	100.0	100.0
Industry	5.1	5.2	4.1	4.0	70.1	76.3	73.3	93.0
Construction	4.6	6.2	4.2	4.6	7.2	10.3	8.4	12.1
Agriculture	3.8	-0.6	-0.1	-8.0	10.2	-1.7	-0.2	-31.6
Transport and communications	3.3	2.3	2.0	3.4	4.1	3.0	3.1	6.5
Trade	2.8	4.0	3.9	4.2	5.7	8.1	9.5	13.3
Other branches	3.5	5.1	6.0	5.2	2.8	4.1	5.9	6.7
Hungary								
NMP	1.3	0.9	4.1	0.3	100.0	100.0	100.0	100.0
Industry	2.7	-1.3	5.2	1.5	94.9	-64.7	59.0	239.5
Construction	-2.0	0.8	3.4	-2.3	-17.9	9.2	8.5	-77.6
Agriculture	0.5	4.5	-3.0	5.7	7.5	87.4	-13.5	329.0
Transport and communications	0.7	3.2	6.5	1.9	5.0	32.2	14.8	60.8
Trade	0.3	0.5	7.9	-9.9	2.8	7.2	26.5	-467.1
Water economy	6.7	14.9	9.9	2.2	7.9	28.7	4.9	15.4
Poland								
NMP	-0.9	4.9	1.9	4.9	100.0	100.0	100.0	100.0
Industry	-1.1	4.5	3.3	4.8	63.9	44.0	82.5	48.7
Construction	-3.6	4.3	2.1	6.2	54.1	10.5	12.9	15.2
Agriculture	3.7	6.3	-7.8	1.3	-58.3	20.1	-64.1	3.9
Transport and communications	-0.2	5.0	6.1	4.7	1.3	5.3	16.3	5.2
Trade	-1.9	5.3	5.7	7.0	38.3	17.8	48.6	25.0
Other branches	-0.4	6.5	3.9	5.1	0.8	2.5	3.9	2.1
Romania								
NMP	4.4	7.3	4.8	..	100.0	100.0	100.0	..
Industry	5.4	7.5	6.7	..	69.5	60.4	82.9	..
Construction	3.5	3.3	1.0	..	6.9	3.9	1.7	..
Agriculture	2.8	13.1	2.5	..	10.2	27.4	8.4	..
Transport and communications	1.8	7.1	1.9	..	2.6	5.8	4.7	..
Trade	4.2	1.7	2.0	..	10.9	2.6	4.7	..
Soviet Union								
NMP	3.2	2.3	1.6	4.4	100.0	100.0	100.0	100.0
Industry	2.8	0.9	4.3	6.7	49.5	20.9	117.4	84.0
Construction	3.2	12.0	5.3	8.0	10.4	54.2	38.1	21.4
Agriculture	-0.4	6.3	-1.8	2.8	-1.4	26.6	-11.1	6.1
Transport and communications	3.0	3.4	0.8	5.8	5.7	9.1	3.2	7.9
Trade	6.7	-1.3	-4.2	-5.0	35.8	-10.6	-47.5	-19.4

Source: National statistics, ECE secretariat estimates and direct communication to the ECE secretariat.

Note: The figures on NMP growth were obtained by summing net output of main sectors of the material sphere. Therefore they do not always coincide with NMP changes as reflected in table 3.2.1. In Romania and the Soviet Union "other branches of the material sphere" are included in the trade sector.

Deteriorating performance in the course of 1989 also gave cause for concern. Quarterly output figures indicate that good performance in the first quarter (a 4 per cent increase in NMP produced compared with year-earlier levels) was followed by sharply decelerating rates of growth in the second quarter (the half-yearly increase was 2.5 per cent). This tendency continued into the second half of the year.

---

such as strikes, inter-ethnic conflicts, a decline in labour discipline and the failure of enterprises to fulfil their obligations. *Ekonomicheskaya gazeta*, No.51, December 1989, p.8.

TABLE 3.2.3

Gross social product (GSP) and sectoral gross output, a 1981-1990
(Annual percentage change)

	1981-1985 b	1986	1987	1988	1989	Plan 1989	Plan 1990	1986-1989	Plan 1986-1990 b
Bulgaria									
GSP total	4.0	4.5	5.2	4.3	..	..	..	..	..
Industry	4.3	4.0	4.2	5.0	2.2	5.0	..	3.8	4.9
Agriculture	1.2	11.7	-5.1	-0.1	0.4	8.9		1.6	1.6-1.9
Construction	3.9	0.3	4.0	2.4	1.5	..	..	..	..
Czechoslovakia									
GSP total	1.7	2.8	1.9	2.2	1.7	1	2.0	2.1	..
Industry	2.7	3.2	2.5	2.1	1.0	1.9	3.0	2.2	3.1
Agriculture	1.9	0.6	0.9	2.9	1.1	0.3	2.2	1.4	1.3
Construction	-0.4	2.6	2.1	0.1	1.7	..	..	1.6	1.9
German Democratic Republic									
GSP total	2.7	2.9	2.6	2.6	2 *	..	..	2.5*	..
Industry	4.1	3.7	3.1	3.2	2.3	3.5	..	3.1	3.9
Agriculture	1.7	-	-0.1	-2.9	1.5	1.5	..	-0.3	1.5
Construction c	2.9	2.8	2.2	3.0	-0.4	..	..	1.9	3.0
Hungary									
GSP total	2.0	2.8	2.0	0.5	-1.7*	..	..	0.9*	..
Industry	2.0	1.9	3.5	-0.7	-2.0	-0.5	..	0.7	2.7-3.0
Agriculture	2.2	2.4	-2.0	4.3	-2.0	0.5	..	0.7	1.4-1.9
Construction	-2.2	0.7	3.8	-3.2	1 *	..	..	0.5*	2.2-2.8
Poland									
GSP total	-	4.9	2.6	4.6	-1.2*	..	..	2.7*	..
Industry	0.4	4.7	3.4	5.3	-2.0	4.2	..	2.8	3.0
Agriculture	-0.5	5.0	-2.3	1.2	2.0	2.8	..	1.4	2.0
Construction	-2.6	3.6	2.1	6.2	-2.0	..	..	2.4	..
Romania									
GSP total	3.2	4.1	6.5	3.0*	..	..	..	..	..
Industry	4.0	7.7	4.5	3.6	..	6.5	7.1	..	7.9
Agriculture	2.0	12.8	2.3	2.9	..	5.0-5.5	..	..	6.1-6.7
Construction	2.6	4.4	2.3	2.9	..	..	..	..	..
Soviet Union									
GSP total	3.3	3.3	2.6	3.5	2.2	..	..	2.9	..
Industry	3.6	4.4	3.8	3.9	1.7	4.5 d	3.4	3.4	4.6
Agriculture	1.1	5.3	-0.6	1.7	0.8	6.5 d	..	1.8	2.7
Construction	1.9	7.8	5.2	4.3	..	..	..	..	..

Source: ECE Secretariat Common Data Base, based on national or CMEA statistical, plans and plan fulfilment reports and direct communication to the ECE secretariat.

a Both indicators include intermediate material costs.
b For agriculture, annualized changes between five-year totals of the period shown as compared with the previous five-year period.
c Building output in centrally and locally administered construction industries.
d Calculated on the basis of annual plan targets for 1986, 1987, 1988 and 1989 and actual growth in 1986-1988.

As already noted,[186] official data on Soviet NMP growth for the period since 1985 have recently been significantly revised, with sharp downward adjustments for all years but 1988.[187] On the basis of the revised figures, NMP growth in the first four years of the current five-year plan was 2.7 per cent per annum, and it is quite obvious that the target of 4.2 per cent average annual growth for 1986-1990 is now well out of reach. Moreover, the revised data indicate that Soviet NMP growth in recent years has been unstable (chart 3.2.1).

The contribution of the main sectors to NMP growth is shown in table 3.2.2. *Industrial expansion* was the main contributor in all the countries under review, though there were some exceptions such as Hungary in 1986 (where net industrial output declined by 1.3 per cent) and the Soviet Union in 1986 (when the industrial sector contributed only 20 per cent of NMP growth). The importance of industry in fueling economic growth can also be seen from the fact that in some years industry generated the whole of the increment in NMP produced.

Construction contributed substantially less than industry, but made a positive contribution to NMP growth except for Hungary in 1981-1985 and 1988. However, its performance shows stronger variations than industry. In the Soviet Union, construction has played an important role in recent years. In 1986, 1987

---

[186] See section 3.1(vii) above.

[187] Growth for that year continues to be shown at the 4.4 per cent originally reported. However, some Soviet economists estimate that in 1988 NMP produced virtually stagnated — and that there was even an absolute decline in domestic output in 1989. See an interview with V. Selyunin in *Sotsialisticheskaya industriya*, 31 December 1989. Again, it is believed that the data on output growth are inflated due to inaccurate price statistics. The Soviet State Committee for Statistics has begun to calculate a composite index of consumer prices for goods and services according to the "shopping basket" principle. Previously the price index was calculated on the basis of list prices and average group prices. This method underestimated real price rises. See *Izvestiya*, 11 January 1990.

TABLE 3.2.4

Employment, total and in the material sphere, 1981-1989
(Annual percentage change)

	Total employment						Employment in the material sphere					
	1981-1985	1985	1986	1987	1988	1989	1981-1985	1985	1986	1987	1988	1989
Bulgaria [a]	0.4	-0.1	0.5	-	..	-2.8	0.2	-0.3	0.2	-0.1	-0.2	-3.5
Czechoslovakia	0.7	1.0	1.3	0.6	0.6	0.4	0.4	0.6	1.0	0.5	0.1	-
German Democratic Republic [b]	0.5	0.2	-	0.2	0.3	..	0.2	-0.2	0.1	-0.2	0.2	-0.8
Hungary	-0.6	-0.5	-0.3	-0.5	-0.6	..	-1.2	-1.2	-1.3	-1.4	-1.6	-1
Poland	-0.2	1.0	0.6	0.2	0.6	-4.0	0.7	0.5	0.3	-0.6	-1.6	-5.0
Romania	0.4	0.7	0.8	0.5	0.4	..	0.2	0.5	0.7	0.7	0.6	..
Soviet Union	0.7	0.6	0.5	-0.2	-1.6	-1	0.5	0.3	0.5	-0.3	-2.7	0.1

Source: As for table 3.1.1.

[a] Total employment refers to workers and employees only. Employment in the material sphere was estimated from growth of NMP produced and NMP produced per employee in the material sphere.
[b] Employment at 30 September (excluding apprentices).

TABLE 3.2.5

Labour productivity and capital productivity, 1981-1990
(Annual percentage change)

	Labour productivity [a]							Capital productivity [b]			
	1981-1985	1986	1987	1988	1989	1986-1989	Plan 1986-1990	1981-1985	1986	1987	1988
Bulgaria	3.5	5.2	5.0	2.6	3.2	4.0	6.4	-2.9	0.2	-2.6	-4.3
Czechoslovakia	1.1	2.5	2.1	2.4	1.3	2.1	3.2	-3.6	-2.0	-2.1	-2.1
German Democratic Republic	4.3	4.5	3.6	3.0	2.8	3.5	4.1-4.4	0.2	0.1	-0.2	-1.2
Hungary	2.1	2.3	5.5	1	..	..	4.7-5.1	-2.2	-2.7	1.1	..
Poland	-0.1	4.6	1.9	6.4	5	4.5	2.7-3.1	-3.4	2.7	-1.2	2.2
Romania	4.2	6.8	4.1	2.6	..	..	..	-4.2	-0.3	-2.1*	..
Soviet Union	2.7	1.9	1.9	7.3	2.3	3.3	3.7-4.2	-3.1	-2.8	-3.4	-0.6

Source: National statistics, ECE secretariat estimates and direct communication to the ECE secretariat.

[a] Net material product per employee in the material sphere.
[b] Net material product per unit of fixed assets in the material sphere.

and 1988 it accounted for 54, 38 and 21 per cent of the total increment of NMP produced.

The role of *agriculture* in overall output growth can be clearly seen in table 3.2.2. In some years (for example 1986) the contribution of net agricultural output to NMP growth was relatively high. In Bulgaria and Hungary, it accounted for 60 and 87 per cent of the NMP increment in 1986. However, agricultural performance in most years was poor and the sector acted as a brake on NMP growth. The negative impact of agriculture was strong in 1987, with a resulting deceleration of NMP growth in all the countries reviewed except Hungary (chart 3.2.1).

Given the weight of *transport and communications* in NMP produced (it varied between 5-9 per cent in recent years) and taking into account the fact that on average net output of these sectors grew at rates close to those of NMP, it is not surprising that in most cases the contribution of transport and communications to the NMP increment did not exceed 10 per cent, with the exception of Hungary in 1986-1988.

The share of the *trade sector* in NMP produced (10-16 per cent) ranks second after industry among the material-sphere sectors. However, its contribution to NMP growth differed widely by countries and years.

This can be explained by the fact that the trade sector includes retail and wholesale trade, public catering, procurement of agricultural products and foreign trade. Besides the performance of these sub-sectors, the methodology of calculation of net output, particularly with regard to foreign trade, may have affected the results. Thus, the trade sector made a negative contribution to Soviet NMP growth in 1986-1988 and contributed significantly to the slow-down of domestic output growth in this period, irrespective of the fact that retail sales increased.

Developments in 1989 can be assessed only tentatively on the basis of figures on changes in the gross output of the main material sphere sectors (table 3.2.3). Judging from the fact that industrial gross output stagnated in the east European countries, and grew at rates lower than those of NMP produced in the Soviet Union, it seems that industry, together with the moderate rise in agricultural production, was mainly responsible for the sharp downswing of NMP growth in 1989. However the picture is incomplete, since figures on the performance of other sectors are missing. Partial information on *transport performance* indicates that, as already noted, transport bottlenecks contributed significantly to weakening overall output performance in most countries in 1989. In Bulgaria, the German Democratic Republic, Hungary and the Soviet Union the volume of goods transported (in tons) declined by 4, 1.8, 2.5 and 2 per cent, respectively, against the 1988 level. In Czechoslovakia too, freight transport decreased considerably. Although the transport intensity of NMP produced declined by 5 per cent, it is still considered excessive. Poland recorded the steepest fall in the transport of goods since 1982 (by 12 per cent in the socialized sector). This was only partly compensated by rapid expansion of transport in the private sector. As shown in section 3.6, the transport and communications sectors were very often neglected in past resource allocation and their underdevelopment constitutes an important constraint on economic growth.

The narrow definition of NMP in the material product system (MPS) used in the east European countries and the Soviet Union (summation of net output in the material sphere sectors only) does not permit any analysis of the growing importance of non-material services. This topic is taken up in section 3.6.

(b) Factor inputs and efficiency

The economic strategy of transition from predominantly "extensive" to "intensive" (i.e., resource-efficient) economic growth has been repeatedly formulated and stressed in national plans and official policy documents. The need for it reflected a changed situation with regard to the availability of production inputs. Important constraints appeared, particularly in the field of energy, raw and other material inputs. Since production factors are limited, efficiency in their use was required in order to maintain and certainly accelerate economic growth. Although there are always difficulties in measuring total factor productivity changes (which combine labour and capital productivities and also changes in the material intensity of production into one synthetic indicator) and their contribution to economic growth, movements in partial efficiency indicators suggest that no decisive turnround in this respect occurred in the period 1986-1989. Changes in output and in the main production inputs in the period 1970-1988 can be seen in chart 3.2.2. The slowing growth of NMP produced was accompanied by stagnant or moderately declining employment growth in the material sphere in most countries under review. However, data for 1988 indicate a growing outflow of labour from the material sphere. This tendency strengthened substantially in 1989 in most countries for which data are available. It seems that the consequences of economic restructuring and reform have begun to be reflected in higher mobility of the labour force. In Bulgaria and the German Democratic Republic, large-scale emigration of workers was mainly responsible for this (table 3.2.4).

The picture with regard to *labour productivity* change is mixed. A clearly decelerating trend between 1986 and 1989 can be seen in Bulgaria, the German Democratic Republic and Romania. Very slow growth, with a deceleration in 1989, was recorded for Czechoslovakia. In other countries there have been big fluctuations over the years (table 3.2.5). However, a comparison of developments in 1986-1989 with the preceding five-year period indicates an improvement in labour productivity growth in most of the countries reviewed. A slow-down was registered in the German Democratic Republic and probably in Romania (1989 figures are not yet available).

Capital productivity generally continued to decline over the 1980s, although at decelerating rates in most countries. In Poland, its level even increased in 1986 and 1988 as a response to low investment and a consequent slow expansion of fixed assets in the material sphere. However, it should be borne in mind that the accuracy of statistical data in the field of investment and fixed assets can also be questioned in most countries — particularly as regards the price deflators used to estimate volume data. Figures on changes in fixed assets could be inflated and the declines in capital productivity thereby overstated.

Although the *material intensity* of output fell in most countries in 1988 (particularly in Hungary and the Soviet Union), incomplete information on developments in 1989 suggests that these positive changes were of short-term duration (table 3.2.6). Insufficient progress in reducing the energy and material intensity of production was reported by most countries for 1989. The high share of material-intensive sectors and branches in total output and the slow modernization of fixed assets in favour of energy-saving technologies were mainly responsible for this. In Czechoslovakia, the material intensity of output, measured by the ratio of gross social product to NMP, increased. In the German Democratic Republic, intermediate consumption (including depreciation charges) grew in 1989 at the same rate as NMP produced. In the Soviet Union, the material intensity of output only improved slightly. Preliminary Polish figures on NMP and sectoral gross output changes in 1989 indicate a possible improvement in this respect.

Altogether, it is likely that in 1986-1989 the contribution of total factor productivity to economic growth did not change significantly in most countries in comparison with the poor results reached in this respect in the preceding five-year period. The economic strategies embodied in the five-year plans for 1986-1990 called for important improvements in the use of factor inputs. The failures of the centrally planned economies to increase overall factor efficiency are apparent and in part explain the political and economic changes under way in the east European countries and the Soviet Union.

(c) Short-term outlook

Given the rapid political and economic changes currently under way in the east European countries and the Soviet Union, which have accelerated substantially in recent months, estimates of output growth for 1990 are difficult. All countries but the Soviet Union have abandoned the traditional system of annual plans with quantified output targets. Thus the aggregate target for NMP growth for the seven countries combined, which even in the past was not very meaningful, cannot now be calculated. Given sharply declining output growth in 1989, particularly at the end of the year, existing constraints on both the supply and demand sides and

TABLE 3.2.6

Gross-social-product to net-material-product ratio [a]
(Annual percentage change)

	1981-1985	1985	1986	1987	1988	1989
Bulgaria	0.2	0.4	-0.8	-1.5	-1.7	..
Czechoslovakia	0.6	-	0.2	-0.2	-0.2	0.4
German Dem.Rep.	-1.5	-2.4	-1.3	-0.7	-0.2	..
Hungary	0.3	1.2	1.4	-0.9	-3.9	0.3
Poland	2.1	-0.2	1.0	0.7	-0.3	-1.2
Romania	0.7	-2.4	-	1.5	-0.2	..
Soviet Union	-0.4	-0.1	1.0	1.0	-0.9	-0.2

Source: National statistics and CMEA statistical yearbooks, various issues.

a Calculated from the ratio of the index of gross material product divided by the index of net material product.

disturbances likely to arise from rapid political and economic changes, the short-term prospects are not very bright.

Difficulties in intra-CMEA trade, large domestic imbalances, the obsolete capital stock inherited from the past and disturbances linked with the transition period, are likely to continue to adversely affect the pace of output expansion. Inflationary pressures, budget deficits, constraints on the side of foreign trade due to high indebtedness and growing social tensions may also hold back output growth.

Policy objectives for 1990 as outlined in the annual plans and other policy documents offer a variety of macro-economic objectives and the means by which they are to be implemented.

No official annual plan for 1990 has been adopted by *Bulgaria*. This results from the critical economic situation of the country. NMP is expected to fall by 3.7 per cent in 1990.[188] The new government proclaimed an anti-crisis programme with the objective of stabilizing the economy and to prevent a sharp decline in living standards. To this end, a restrictive budgetary policy and measures to promote production, particularly of consumer goods and exports, are to be taken. A comprehensive economic reform on the basis of market principles is to be adopted in the near future.[189]

For *Czechoslovakia*, official information on the annual plan for 1990 is scanty.[190] NMP produced is expected to grow by 2.2 per cent — the same as achieved on average in the previous four years. In comparison with 1989, the planned output target means an acceleration of economic growth. Economic strategy stresses improvements in internal balance and more rapid structural change. However, it can be assumed that developments in the external sector, policies aiming to improve domestic balances and to accelerate the transition to a new economic system characterized by a reduced role for government, increased reliance on decentralized decision-making and the market mechanism, and a more outward-looking orientation, will all have constraining effects on short-term output growth. Thus, the plan targets embodied in the annual plan for 1990 can be considered optimistic.[191]

In *the German Democratic Republic*, the main objective of economic policy for 1990 is seen to be the stabilization of the economic situation, which has been disrupted by disturbances from strikes, continued emigration and radical political and economic changes. No annual plan for 1990 has been announced. Stagnating production levels in 1990 as compared with 1989 were envisaged by the official forecast.[192] A projection dating from the beginning of this year indicates a possible 4-5 per cent fall of total output in 1990.[193] However, all forecasts are risky, since the approaching unification of the two Germanies and the economic measures which are to be taken in this respect (see section 4.5) will have important implications for the future economic development of the German Democratic Republic.

In *Hungary*, the traditional annual plan approach has been abandoned. The National Planning Office has prepared only an economic programme for 1990, which is designed to serve as a guideline for economic policies. Structural adjustment and international solvency through restrictive monetary and fiscal policies are seen as the main objectives of this programme. No significant overall output change is expected. However, apparent stagnation in output is expected to be accompanied by accelerated structural change.

Short-term growth prospects for the *Polish* economy are not bright, since the present situation is characterized by falling output and large domestic and external imbalances. Economic policy will aim to implement two groups of measures. The first relates to far-reaching systemic changes and the second includes measures to achieve rapid stabilization.[194] Despite their mutual interdependence, preference is to be given to stabilization measures, particularly those for curbing inflation and improving domestic balances. The process of halting hyperinflation will entail social costs and

---

[188] Statement by Finance Minister B. Belchev during his budget presentation to the National Assembly on 5 March 1990, as cited in BBC, *Summary of World Broadcasts*, No. EE/7070, 8 March 1990, p.C1/1.

[189] See speech by Prime Minister A. Lukanov to the Bulgarian National Assembly, BBC, *Summary of World Broadcasts*, EE/0685, 10 February 1990, p.B/3.

[190] Basic macro-economic figures were given in an article written by M. Jurceka, Deputy Chairman of the State Planning Commission, *Hospodárské noviny*, No.49, 8 December 1989.

[191] As announced, the falling output levels of December 1989 continued into January 1990, mainly due to reduced output of the defence industry and smaller-than-envisaged deliveries of Soviet oil, which adversely affected the chemical branch. See *Rudé právo*, 16 February 1990, p.3.

[192] See the statement of Prime Minister H. Modrow in the National Assembly, *Neues Deutschland*, 12 January 1990.

[193] See *Svet hospodárství*, No.19, 13 February 1990, p.1.

[194] The government programme on economic policies in 1990, which replaces the traditional annual plan, was published in *Rzeczpospolita*, 15 December 1989, pp.5-6. However, no macro-economic figures were reported on expected developments in the Polish economy in 1990.

a drop in real incomes. Thus the backing and involvement of all social forces will be necessary to speed up the transition to a market economy. Poland faces a critical period, since fundamental restructuring will be implemented in very unfavourable conditions. A 5 per cent fall in industrial output was projected for 1990, but much steeper decline, as already noted, occurred in the first two months.

The *Romanian* economy is in serious crisis. Domestic imbalances increased in 1989 and were exacerbated by energy shortages and by political and social turmoil in the winter months. The former government adopted an annual plan for 1990 containing traditionally unrealistic output targets (9.5 per cent for NMP growth), but this plan has been abandoned. Given the present complex situation and the uncertainties linked with radical political and economic transformation, the new government approved an emergency stabilization programme for the first quarter of 1990. High priority is given to improving supplies of energy, raw and other material inputs, but also to increasing deliveries of consumer goods to domestic markets. Higher imports of fuel, energy and consumer goods, which are possible owing to the low level of foreign debt, will work to the same end. Central controls continue to be applied in allocating scarce resources and a new plan for 1990 is under preparation by the provisional government. However, rigid planning is to be transformed into a more flexible system of "indicative" planning and the number of plan indicators is to be drastically reduced.[195] Further decentralisation is envisaged as the economic situation improves.

In the *Soviet Union*, stabilization and the reorientation of the economy to reduce social tensions are the main economic policy objectives envisaged for 1990. The interpretation of output growth targets is once again complicated by the fact that the annual plan targets are expressed relative to the *plan* levels for the previous year. As already noted (section 3.1(viii) above), the official NMP target for 1990 of 1 per cent growth in fact indicates growth of some 4½ per cent relative to the *actual* levels attained in 1989, and possibly more.[196] The 1990 objective is ambitious in view of the internal and external imbalances.

A striking feature of the Soviet annual plan for 1990 is its stress on accelerated structural change. In particular, production of consumer goods is to increase by some 8 per cent while the output of producer goods is set to rise by only 1-2 per cent.[197] The defence industry is to be partly directed into production of equipment for the light and food-processing industries and for the production of consumer durables. Investment is to be shifted into branches producing consumer goods or into the social sphere.

The implementation of the annual plan for 1990 is to be supported by an economic recovery programme adopted by the second Congress of People's Deputies of the Soviet Union in December 1989. The programme contains measures to be introduced gradually over the period 1990-1995, with the aim of creating a socialist market economy. In the first stage (1990-1992), central planning and control is to be combined with the gradual introduction of some market mechanisms.

Altogether, a decline in aggregate output in eastern Europe and at best very moderate expansion in the Soviet Union seem to be a reasonable prognosis for 1990. However, the differences between countries can be wide and the margins of error in such an estimate are large.

A pessimistic short-term outlook for economic growth in eastern Europe and the Soviet Union is supported by reported figures on industrial output change for January 1990. As already noted (section 3.1), gross industrial output had fallen from the year-earlier level in the five east European countries for which this information is available as well as in the Soviet Union. Thus evidence is mounting that the eastern countries are moving into a recession, which could prove very deep in some of them.

(ii) Developments in industry

(a) Growth of industrial output

Industrial output growth decelerated sharply in 1989. In the five *east European countries* reporting, output virtually stagnated in 1989 compared with a 3½ per cent rise in 1988.[198] It was the worst performance since 1981, when an 11 per cent fall in Polish output dragged down the seven-country average. Annual plans for 1989 called for a 4 per cent rise in industrial production, and the difference between plans and reality is thus very apparent.

In the *Soviet Union* industrial output growth slowed from 3.9 per cent in 1988 to 1.7 per cent in 1989. Such poor performance has never been recorded in previous years and was well below the annual plan target of 4.5 per cent (table 3.2.7).

The sharp deceleration of industrial output growth had several causes. *First*, industrial growth and structural change were intertwined with the scope and speed of economic reforms. Disruptions during the transition period were reflected in slower growth or even in a contraction of output in some industrial branches.

---

[195] As announced by the Minister of the National Economy, General V. Stanculescu, the plan for 1990 comprises 12-14 economic-financial indicators and some 400 physical product indicators instead of 100 economic-financial positions and 1,800 products in the old plan. See *Tribuna economica*, No.6, 9 February 1990, pp.7-8.

[196] Since the 1989 *plan* level used in the calculations of Soviet policy-makers is unknown, a substantial error margin is inherent in this estimate. See also footnote (162).

[197] See footnote (204) below.

[198] No data are available as yet for Romania.

TABLE 3.2.7

Industrial output, 1981-1990
(Annual percentage change)

	1981-1985	1984	1985	1986	1987	1988	1989	Plan 1989	Plan 1990	Plan 1986-1990
Bulgaria	4.3	4.2	3.2	4.0	4.2	5.0	2.2	5.0	..	4.9
Czechoslovakia	2.7	4.0	3.5	3.2	2.5	2.1	1.0	1.9	3.0	3.0
German Democratic Republic	4.1	4.2	4.4	3.7	3.1	3.2	2.3	3.5 [a]	..	3.7-4.1 [a]
Hungary	2.0	3.2	0.7	1.9	3.5	-0.7	-2.0	-1.0	-	2.7-3.0
Poland	0.4	5.2	4.5	4.7	3.4	5.3	-2.0	4.2	-5 [b]	3.0
Romania [a]	4.0	6.7	4.9	7.7	4.5	3.6	..	6-7	7.1	7.5-8.3
Eastern Europe	2.8	4.8	4.1	4.6	3.5	3.5	0.3 [c]	4.0	..	4.4
Soviet Union	3.7	4.1	3.4	4.4	3.8	3.9	1.7	4.5	3.4	4.6
Eastern Europe and Soviet Union	3.4	4.3	3.6	4.4	3.7	3.8	1.3	4.3	..	4.5

Source: ECE secretariat Common Data Base, derived from national statistics, plans and plan fulfilment reports.

[a] Marketable production.
[b] Projection.
[c] Excluding Romania.

Second, policies calling for a restoration of balance on domestic markets also resulted in declining output growth. *Third*, restrictive policies domestically and constrained intra-CMEA trade externally acted as brakes on industrial expansion in most east European countries. *Finally*, the above developments were exacerbated by a variety of country-specific social factors, already described in section (i) above. The industrial slow-down in 1989 was common to all countries and was a culmination of a decelerating trend which began in 1986 (chart 3.2.3).

A striking feature of industrial developments in 1989 was decelerating output performance over the course of the year. Thus, in all east European countries for which information is available, industrial production fell in absolute terms in the last quarter compared with year-earlier levels. The fall was exceptionally strong in December 1989 and, as noted, continued into January 1990.

As in previous years, industrial performance varied between countries. In *Bulgaria*, industrial output growth decelerated strongly from 5.0 per cent in 1988 to 2.2 per cent in 1989. Given the reported 3.5 per cent rise in industrial output for the first three quarters of 1989, most of the fall was concentrated in the fourth quarter. In December industrial output decreased by 12.7 per cent in comparison with the corresponding month of 1988. Political turmoil, strikes and emigration contributed to these developments. Bulgaria finds itself in a very critical situation which could persist into 1990.

In *Czechoslovakia*, a strong deceleration of industrial output growth occurred in 1989. The 1 per cent rise in output is the lowest since the mid-1960s and similar to that in 1982. Although the annual plan for 1989 envisaged a slow-down in industrial growth (to 1.9 per cent), results are far behind expectations. It seems that important deviations from the planned targets took place in engineering, which was badly hit by a sharp drop in Czechoslovak exports of machinery and equipment to socialist countries and particularly to the Soviet Union. The conversion of the defence industry into civilian uses also contributed to the slow-down. In December, industrial output declined to 4½ per cent below its year-earlier level.

The *German Democratic Republic* reported a 2.3 per cent rise in marketable industrial production in 1989 – the lowest since 1950. This was substantially less than envisaged by the annual plan (3.5 per cent) and was poor when considered against the background of reported stable and relatively fast industrial growth in the first half of the 1980s (above 4 per cent annually). A sharp 2 per cent fall in industrial output occurred in the last quarter of 1989 compared with the final quarter of 1988. The causes were identical with those mentioned earlier in connection with changes in NMP produced.

In *Hungary*, industrial output in the socialist sector fell by more than 3 per cent. There was more dynamism in the private sector, but it could not compensate for the decline in the state and co-operative sectors. Thus, 1989 is the second successive year in which industrial production contracted. The slow-down was even greater than envisaged by the annual plan for 1989 (from zero to minus 1 per cent). Contributory factors were the process of restructuring itself, falling exports to the Soviet Union and restrictive policies which constrained domestic demand. Sales on domestic markets and exports to the socialist countries both fell by 6-7 per cent. A worrying feature of 1989 was the progressive output decline throughout the year: zero growth in the first half of the year compared with year-earlier levels and falls of 3.9 and 9 per cent in the third and fourth quarters, respectively. In December, industrial production was 16 per cent below the level of the corresponding month of the previous year.

In *Poland,* gross industrial output fell by about 2 per cent in 1989. The decline in output (measured by sales) in the socialized sector was even stronger (3.4 per cent). The difference between these figures reflects the vigorous expansion of the private industrial sector, where production increased by about 26 per cent. However, given the small share of private activity in the

TABLE 3.2.8

Factor inputs in industry, 1981-1989
(Annual percentage change)

	Bulgaria	Czechoslovakia	German Dem.Rep.	Hungary	Poland	Romania	Soviet Union
Employment							
1981-1985	0.7	0.4	0.7	-1.8	-1.6	1.5	0.6
1986	1.3	0.4	-0.3	-0.2	0.2	1.0	0.3
1987	1.1	-	-0.4	-0.7	-0.5	1.4	-0.2
1988	0.9	-	0.1	-1.9	-1.6	0.3	-2.0
1989	-1.1	-0.7	-0.8	-4 [a]	-4.5	..	-1.3
Fixed assets							
1981-1985	7.1	5.5	4.9	4.6	3.0	9.0	6.5
1986	5.9	4.8	4.9	5.7	2.2	8.7	5.1
1987	10.6	4.3	4.1	3.7	3.6	7.2	4.8
1988	..	4.8	4.5	..	2.4	..	4.2
Gross fixed capital formation							
1981-1985 [b]	6.3	0.1	2.1	-3.2	-10.8	1.6	3.5
1986	11.7	1.6	5.6	-6.5	6.8	4.7	8.4
1987	8.6	10.1	12.9	5.3	4.7	-3.3	5.7
1988	..	6.7	9.0	-7.4	4.3	..	6.0

Source: ECE secretariat Common Data Base, derived from national statistics and plan fulfilment reports.

Note: Due to differences in coverage of industrial sector, figures in this table may differ slighly from officially reported data.

[a] Socialist sector only.
[b] Annualized rates of growth between the five-year total of the five-year period shown and that of the previous five-year period.

TABLE 3.2.9

Selected efficiency indicators in industry, 1981-1989
(Annual percentage change)

	Bulgaria	Czechoslovakia	German Dem.Rep.	Hungary	Poland	Romania	Soviet Union
Labour productivity [a]							
1981-1985	3.7	2.2	3.6	3.9	1.8	2.4	3.2
1986	2.7	2.7	4.3	2.4	4.2	6.6	5.0
1987	3.1	2.5	4.4	5.2	4.3	3.1	4.3
1988	4.1	2.1	3.9	1.2	6.5	3.3	6.0
1989	3.3	1.7	3.7	1	2.6	..	3.1
Capital productivity [b]							
1981-1985	-2.6	-2.6	0.3	-2.5	-2.7	-3.4	-2.5
1986	-1.8	-1.6	0.3	-3.6	2.2	-1.1	0.1
1987	-5.8	-1.7	-	-0.2	0.1	-0.4	-0.7
1988	..	-2.6	-0.5	..	2.3	..	-0.3

Source: ECE secretariat Common Data Base, derived from national statistics and plan fulfilment reports.

[a] Gross industrial output per employee.
[b] The ratio of industrial gross output to fixed assets.

total, this dynamic performance did not fully offset the decline in the socialized sector.

Industrial output has been steadily slipping in the course of the year. Thus in the first quarter of 1989 industrial production increased by 3 per cent but in the following quarters it fell by 0.9, 6.6 and 8.3 per cent, respectively, below year-earlier levels. Fuel and energy were hit hard (declines of 5 per cent), and also metallurgy (decrease of 5.5 per cent) and food-processing (an 8.4 per cent fall). The resulting energy and material input shortages spilled over into other industrial branches.

Beside the disruption due to rapid political and economic change, which strengthened in the second half of the year, the deteriorating supply of energy, raw and other material inputs (both of domestic origin and from imports) was mainly responsible for poor performance. The situation was exacerbated by the energy- and material-intensive structure of industrial output and outdated industrial plant.

In the *Soviet Union,* as noted, industrial output growth of 1.7 per cent in 1989 was the lowest since 1950 and far below the annual plan target which had already been revised downward from 4.5 to 3.0 per cent. Almost all major industrial complexes failed to meet their

CHART 3.2.3

Growth rates of gross industrial output
(Annual percentage change)

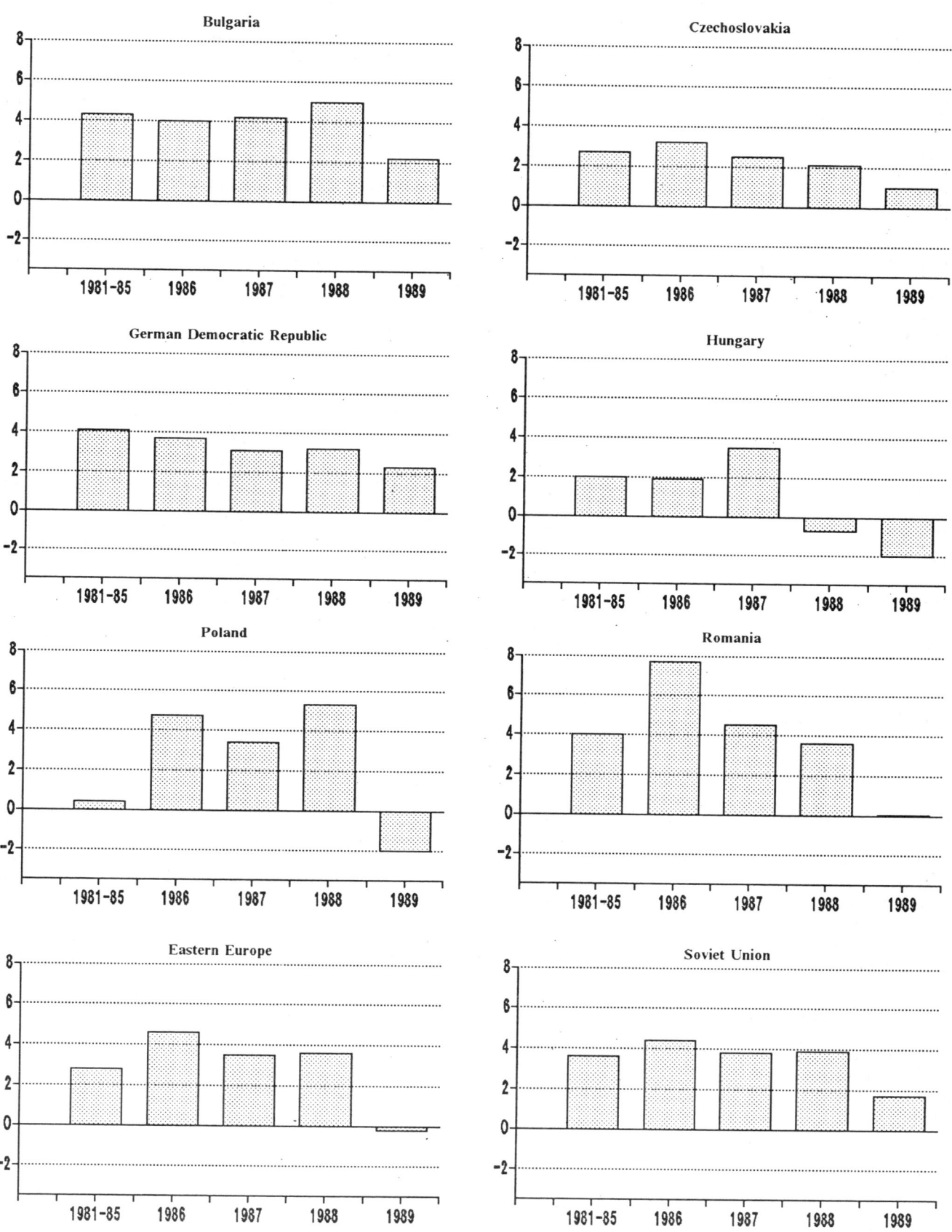

Source: ECE secretariat Common Data Base.

TABLE 3.2.10

Material intensity of industrial production, 1981-1988
(Annual percentage change)

	Gross output	Net output	Implied material intensity [a]
Bulgaria			
1981-1985	4.3	7.0	-2.5
1986	4.0	5.7	-1.6
1987	4.2	5.6	-1.3
1988	5.0	5.1	-0.1
Czechoslovakia [b]			
1981-1985	1.5	1.6	-0.1
1986	3.6	3.1	0.5
1987	2.4	3.9	-1.4
1988	2.3	3.3	-1.0
German Democratic Republic [b]			
1981-1985	4.1	5.1	-0.9
1986	3.7	5.0	-1.2
1987	3.1	3.8	-0.7
1988	3.2	3.8	-0.6
Hungary [b]			
1981-1985	2.0	2.7	-0.7
1986	1.9	-1.3	3.2
1987	3.5	5.2	-1.6
1988	-0.7	1.5	-2.2
Poland [b]			
1981-1985	0.4	-1.1	1.5
1986	4.6	4.5	0.1
1987	3.0	3.3	-0.3
1988	5.1	4.8	0.3
Romania [b]			
1981-1985	3.4	5.3	-1.8
1986	7.1	7.5	-0.4
1987	4.5	6.7	-2.1
1988	..	..	..
Soviet Union [c]			
1981-1985	3.6	2.8	0.8
1986	4.4	0.9	3.5
1987	3.8	3.5	0.3
1988	3.9	6.7	-2.6

Source: National statistics.

[a] Calculated from the ratio of gross output index to net output index.
[b] Based on national accounts statistics.
[c] Data on net output changes are taken from CMEA statistical yearbooks, various issues.

output targets. Industrial performance worsened in the course of the year. While industrial output growth in the first half of 1989 reached 2.7 per cent, it declined to less than 1 per cent in the second half. Taking into account the sharp deceleration in the rate of growth of industrial output in 1989 and the 3.4 per cent average annual rate achieved in 1986-1989, it is clear that the five-year plan target (4.6 per cent) is out of reach.

(b) Industrial efficiency changes

The decline in industrial employment in most of the seven countries reviewed started in 1987 and gathered pace in 1989 judging from the sketchy information yet available (table 3.2.8). The shift of employment from industry to services, which has been observed in the developed market economies for a long time, was delayed in the centrally planned economies due to continued stress on industralization. Substantial declines in industrial employment in Hungary and Poland in 1989 reflected economic restructuring. The decrease in industrial employment in the German Democratic Republic occurred in the last three months of 1989 and was caused by emigration. Nevertheless, the declines in industrial employment were not transformed into accelerated *labour productivity* growth. On the contrary, industrial labour productivity decelerated in 1989 in comparison with 1988 in all six countries for which data are available and rose by less than in any other year during 1986-1989, except in Bulgaria (table 3.2.9). Both the supply and demand factors constraining industrial growth contributed to this outcome. The long-standing problems of low micro-economic efficiency stemming from central planning and control, slow technological progress, obsolete and aging fixed assets, worked to the same end.

Industrial fixed asset growth accelerated moderately in Czechoslovakia and the German Democratic Republic and decelerated in Poland and the Soviet Union in 1988 (the last year for which data are available). This was translated into bigger declines in industrial *capital productivity* in the two former countries and some improvement in the latter two. Poland even recorded a 2.3 per cent increase in industrial capital productivity in 1988. Developments in 1989 can be only tentatively estimated. Given the relatively small changes in the rates of growth of industrial fixed assets on a year-to-year basis and the sharp deceleration of industrial output growth in 1989, it can be assumed that industrial capital productivity fell further.

The material intensity of industrial production, calculated as the differential between gross and net industrial output growth, fell in all countries but Poland. The contraction of material intensity in 1988 ranged from 0.1 per cent in Bulgaria to 2.6 per cent in the Soviet Union (table 3.2.10). However this measure has many deficiencies and its reliability should not be overestimated.[199] Sketchy information on this aspect of industrial efficiency in 1989 indicates that no noteworthy results in reducing the material intensity of industrial output were attained. In Bulgaria, material expenditures are reported to have declined by 1 per cent per unit of industrial output.[200] In Czechoslovakia, the material intensity of industrial production declined by 0.4 per cent and in the German Democratic Republic it remained unchanged in comparison with 1988.

(c) Energy production and consumption

The overall energy situation in the region became serious in 1989. Because winter conditions were mild in 1988 and 1989, energy supplies in some countries did not constitute an important constraint on NMP and industrial growth. However, fuel and energy shortages appeared in Poland, Romania and the Soviet Union

---

[199] For a discussion of this topic see United Nations Economic Commission for Europe, *Economic Survey of Europe in 1988-1989*, New York 1989, pp.104-105.

[200] However, in *real* terms material intensity of industrial production stagnated at the 1988 level. See *Rabotnichesko delo*, 30 January 1990, p.4.

TABLE 3.2.11

Primary energy production, 1981-1989
(Annual percentage change)

	1981-1985	1981	1982	1983	1984	1985	1986	1987	1988	1989
Bulgaria	0.9	-1.2	9.4	1.6	-	-4.6	11.7	4.4	-4.4	0.4
Czechoslovakia	0.5	-0.5	1.1	1.5	1.2	-0.8	0.6	0.8	-1.4	-3.9
German Democratic Republic	4.0	3.6	3.2	1.7	6.4	4.9	0.4	-0.6	0.5	-2.7
Hungary	1.4	-0.3	3.7	-1.2	2.4	2.5	-3.6	1.4	-6.3	-1.9
Poland	0.6	-14.2	13.9	1.7	2.0	1.5	1.4	1.3	-	-6.7
Romania	1.9	4.2	0.2	3.5	1.8	-0.3	-	-2.2	-1.2	..
Eastern Europe	1.5	-4.2	6.3	1.9	2.6	1.3	0.9	0.3	-0.8	-3.8 [a]
Soviet Union	2.5	1.8	2.8	2.3	2.8	2.7	4.5	3.2	2.7	-0.7
Eastern Europe and the Soviet Union	2.3	0.7	3.4	2.2	2.8	2.4	3.9	2.7	2.1	-1.2 [a]

Source: CMEA statistical yearbooks, national yearbooks and plan fulfilment reports.

Note: Data on primary energy production calculated by the ECE secretariat in standard coal equivalent (coefficients vary across countries). Figures for 1989 based on national plan fulfilment reports and ECE estimates.

[a] Assuming zero change in Romania.

TABLE 3.2.12

Changes in energy consumption [a] and energy intensity, [b] 1981-1988
(Annual percentage change)

	1981-1985	1981	1982	1983	1984	1985	1986	1987	1988
Bulgaria									
Energy consumption	1.8	1.5	3.5	1.4	1.1	1.3	-1.8	3.7	..
Energy intensity	-1.9	-3.4	-0.6	-1.5	-3.4	-0.5	-6.7	-1.2	..
Czechoslovakia									
Energy consumption	0.5	-1.0	-1.1	1.4	0.9	2.6	1.2	1.6	-0.9
Energy intensity	-1.2	-0.9	-1.3	-0.9	-2.5	-0.4	-1.4	-0.5	-3.2
German Democratic Republic									
Energy consumption	1.2	0.1	-0.2	-0.1	4.3	2.1	0.6	0.8	-3.1
Energy intensity	-3.1	-4.4	-2.7	-4.5	-1.1	-2.9	-3.5	-2.7	-5.7
Hungary									
Energy consumption	-1.0	-0.8	0.1	-1.2	-5.1	2.2	-0.3	3.0	-1.4
Energy intensity	-2.3	-3.2	-2.7	-1.5	-7.5	3.6	-1.2	-1.1	-1.7
Poland									
Energy consumption	0.8	-5.9	1.8	1.4	3.8	3.0	0.5	3.1	-2.0
Energy intensity	1.6	6.9	7.7	-4.3	-1.7	-0.4	-4.2	1.1	-6.5
Romania									
Energy consumption	1.2	0.8	-1.4	1.4	3.4	1.7	1.5	0.4	..
Energy intensity	-3.1	-1.3	-4.0	-2.2	-3.9	-3.9	-5.4	-4.2	..
Soviet Union									
Energy consumption	3.0	2.3	2.9	2.0	3.3	4.5	2.5	3.0	1.5
Energy intensity	-0.2	-1.0	-1.0	-2.1	0.4	2.8	0.2	1.3	-2.8

Source: ECE Energy Data Bank, based on country submissions to ECE and national statistics.

Note: Data for 1988 are taken from national statistical yearbooks and may not be fully comparable with data for 1981-1987.

[a] Gross primary energy consumption in tons of oil equivalent.
[b] Ratio of gross primary energy consumption to NMP produced in constant prices.

— particularly at the end of the year — and contributed to a sharp fall in production. Although the rates of growth of primary energy production in the seven countries combined decelerated significantly in recent years (from 3.9 per cent in 1986 to 2.1 per cent in 1988), it even fell (by 1.2 per cent) in 1989 by comparison with 1988 (table 3.2.11). As usual, the decisive role in aggregate production was played by the *Soviet* fuel and energy branches. Soviet primary energy production fell by 0.7 per cent after a 2.7 per cent rise in 1988. Electricity and natural gas production increased in 1989 by 1 and 3 per cent, respectively, while oil and coal output decreased by 3 and 4 per cent, respectively. Oil deliveries were 13 million tons short of the plan target and the fall in coal production reached 32 million tons compared with 1988. There were various reasons for poor performance in the Soviet fuel and energy sector. Among them were shortages of new equipment, transport bottlenecks, strikes and mismanagement in enterprises. Moreover, nuclear power production lagged substantially behind plan targets.

Aggregate primary energy production of the six *east European countries*, which fell by 0.8 per cent in 1988, decreased further in 1989 (by 3.8 per cent).[201] This was mainly caused by a sharp decline in Poland (6.7 per cent), Czechoslovakia (3.9 per cent) and the German Democratic Republic (2.7 per cent). Coal production in 1989 fell by 4.3 per cent in the five east European countries for which data are available. Since coal extraction accounts for 79 per cent of primary energy output in the six east European countries combined, the reduction of coal consumption, particularly in old thermal power stations, can contribute to an improved environment.[202] In *Bulgaria*, electricity production fell by 1.7 per cent and coal extraction increased by a moderate 0.5 per cent. In *Czechoslovakia*, total electricity generation increased by 2.2 per cent (in nuclear power stations by 5.5 per cent), but coal production declined by 5 per cent. In *Poland*, the output of hard coal in 1989 was 8 per cent below the 1988 level. Electricity generation increased by 0.8 per cent. For *Romania*, no figures for 1988 and 1989 are available. However, it seems that very poor energy output performance in this country persisted. Energy shortages had a strong negative impact on Romanian industrial growth and living standards.

Efficiency gains in the use of energy, which have become an important element of overall intensification strategies in eastern Europe and the Soviet Union, have so far lagged behind demanding energy-saving targets. Developments in 1986-1988 offer a mixed picture (table 3.2.12). Bulgaria succeeded in sharply reducing the energy intensity of NMP in 1986, but in 1987 the results were only moderate. Czechoslovakia, the German Democratic Republic, Poland and the Soviet Union substantially reduced the energy intensity of NMP in 1988, but this was mainly due to a mild winter. However, a slow-down in the output of energy-intensive branches was also a contributing factor. Developments in 1989 are difficult to estimate. Mild weather in some countries could have contributed to a further improvement, but the sharp deceleration of NMP growth acted in the opposite direction. In Hungary, total energy consumption fell by 1.3 per cent in 1989. Given a similar rate of decline in NMP, the energy-intensity of output will have remained more or less stable. A 0.7 per cent decline in the energy intensity of Soviet NMP was reported in the plan fulfilment report for 1989.

Altogether it appears that the transition towards a less energy-intensive path of development will be a more difficult and longer-term process than originally expected in the five-year plans for 1986-1990.

(d) Industrial policy objectives for 1990

Only a few countries published annual plans with quantified targets for industrial production — and in some cases these no longer represent policy. Generally, it can be assumed that the factors shaping industrial growth on both the supply and demand sides will brake industrial expansion in 1990.

Industrial growth and structural change are interwined with the scope and speed of economic reforms. The disruptions during the transition period of reform are likely to be reflected in slower growth, or even a contraction of output, in most east European countries. In *Czechoslovakia,* the official forecast is for 3 per cent growth, while in *Hungary* output is expected to remain unchanged and in *Poland* a fall by 5 per cent is forecast to result from the constraints on demand that are part of the anti-inflation policy package.[203]

The annual plan of the *Soviet Union* for 1990, as already noted, aims at a significant restructuring of industrial output in favour of consumer goods production — the latter is to rise by some 8 per cent, about 5 times as fast as producer goods output.[204] This industrial strategy is part of the endeavour to improve very rapidly the huge imbalances on the domestic consumer goods market. It relies in part on the re-profiling of defence industry enterprises and on priority production assignments to other industrial branches, including those not significantly engaged in consumer goods production.

For the fuel and energy sector, the annual plan includes rather ambitious targets. The output of electricity, oil, gas and coal is planned to reach 1,792 billion kWh, 598 million tons, 845 billion m^3 and 771 million tons, respectively. This implies rates of change of 4.1, *minus* 1.5, 6.2 and 4.2 per cent, respectively, over 1989 levels. However, in the case of coal production, the planned increase is to compensate for the fall in 1989. Thus, the energy balance in 1990 is expected to remain tight.

Given recent economic difficulties as well as the disruptions likely to arise from the policy changes and economic adjustments linked with the process of transition from centrally planned to market economies in a number of countries, the prospects are for a drop in industrial output in eastern Europe and probably only moderate growth in the Soviet Union in 1990.

---

201 Under the assumption that no changes in Romanian primary energy production occurred in 1989 as compared with 1988, which is rather optimistic given the energy situation in the country.

202 It is likely that the fall in coal production will continue into the future in Czechoslovakia, the German Democratic Republic and Poland. This will have a positive impact on the environment. Fuel and energy savings and structural changes in industry are expected to play a crucial role in offsetting reduced output levels.

203 See *Zycie gospodarcze*, No.7, 18 February 1990, p.11.

204 Targets stated in the 1990 plan law are for an increase of 0.5 per cent in the industrial output of means of production (group "A") and 6.7 per cent in the production of consumer goods (group "B") over the *five-year plan* levels for 1989 (which themselves are not known). See *Pravda*, 11 November 1989, p.2. Since the 1989 plan was not achieved, the intended growth relative to the 1989 *actual* levels must also be rather higher. One Soviet estimate communicated to the ECE secretariat gives the intended growth from the 1989 actual as 1.6 per cent for group "A" and 8.2 per cent for group "B", with total industrial growth of 3.4 per cent.

(iii) Agricultural production

(a) Growth of agricultural output

The majority of *east European* countries recorded a rise in agricultural production in 1989, though it declined in Hungary (chart 3.2.4). No data have yet been published for Romania. The increase in the other five east European countries taken together was about 1 per cent (table 3.2.13) – roughly the same as in the *Soviet Union*. Crop production rose in all the eastern countries except Hungary, but livestock output fell in several.

The generally declining trend of agricultural production in *Bulgaria* in the second half of the 1980s continued. After a 5 per cent decline in 1987 agricultural output has virtually stagnated during 1988-1989 as a whole. In 1989, *Czechoslovakia* continued the slow but stable growth of the preceding three years. In the *German Democratic Republic*, three successive years of decline were followed by a modest 1.5 per cent rise in 1989, but average annual production levels in 1986-1989 were lower than in 1981-1985. In *Hungary*, a 2 per cent decline in 1989 marked a further swing in a period of irregular agricultural production growth, which averaged only a half percentage point annually over the past four years. The further increase in output recorded in *Poland* in 1989 wiped out the big drop in 1987 and brought the average growth between 1981-1985 and 1986-1989 to 1.4 per cent annually. Generally favourable weather conditions must have assisted performance in *Romania*. In the *Soviet Union*, the past three years as a whole yielded only a slight increase following the strong advance in 1986. Average annual growth of 1.8 per cent achieved between 1981-1985 and 1986-1989 as a whole was nevertheless the highest among the eastern countries.

As compared with the five-year plan targets for the current quinquennium (expressed as the change compared with the five-year average of output in the preceding quinquennium), output in 1986-1989 was in line with or above targets in Czechoslovakia, the German Democratic Republic, Poland and probably Romania. Although the significance of the five-year plan targets has changed considerably in all east European countries following recent political and economic changes in the region, it is perhaps worthy of note that, if the five-year targets are to be met, agricultural output growth in 1990 will need to accelerate in Bulgaria, Hungary and the Soviet Union.

With the exception of Hungary, total *crop output* grew in all east European countries and the Soviet Union in 1989. After two years of contraction, its growth was particularly strong in Bulgaria and Poland. The *grain harvest* was good in all seven countries (table 3.2.14). Bulgaria, after several unfavourable agricultural years, recorded the second best in its history. This helped to bring the annual average of production in 1986-1989 to the same level as in the previous quinqennium. Czechoslovakia enjoyed its sixth good harvest in succession within the 11-12 million ton range; average grain production in 1986-1989 was more than 7 per cent higher than in 1981-1985. Stable growth in grain output in the German Democratic Republic since the early 1980s was interrupted in 1988 but recovered in 1989. The average 1986-1989 harvest was almost 5 per cent above the 1981-1985 level. Grain production in Hungary has remained high and stable in the 14.5-15.0 million ton range since 1985; the average 1986-1989 outturn was almost unchanged relative to the first half of the decade. Poland harvested a record grain crop in 1989, exclusively due to higher yields.[205] The excellent 1989 harvest followed three good agricultural years and brought the average in 1986-1989 to a level 16 per cent above that in the first half of the 1980s. According to official statistics, which have been strongly criticized within the country, the average grain harvest in Romania in 1986-1988 exceeded annual production in 1981-1985 by almost 45 per cent. No data are available for 1989.

The good Soviet grain harvest of 1989 brought average output in 1986-1989 to 207 million tons (191 million tons on an internationally comparable basis) which is 15 per cent higher than the 1981-1985 average. But this is about 40 million tons short of the five-year plan target for 1986-1990. Grain shortages are exacerbated in the Soviet Union by large scale losses and waste. Harvesting, transport and storage losses alone amount to about 30 million tons annually and those due to vermin, disease and weed infestation to an additional 40 million tons (20 per cent of output). About 5 million hectares of the area sown annually to grain are used to pasture cattle, and losses caused by the need to re-sow winter-killed grains rose from 16 per cent of the area under winter grains in 1971-1975 to about 20 per cent in 1986-1987. With a seeding rate of 2 quintals per hectare, the losses due to extra seed requirements alone amount to 1.5-2 million tons annually.[206] Although low in protein, grain is extensively fed to cattle in default of alternative feed supplies in the Soviet Union. It is estimated that the excessive feeding of grain in nutritionally unbalanced rations wastes a further 30 million tons.[207]

The *area sown to grain* has contracted in recent years (mainly in favour of fodder crops and oilseeds) in Czechoslovakia, the German Democratic Republic and the Soviet Union. It also fell in Hungary in 1989 as

---

[205] CMEA, *Statisticheskii byulleten'*, January-December 1989, Part 1, Moscow, March 1990.

[206] E. Sosnin, "Kak razvivaetsya zernovoe khoziaistvo strany" (How the country's grain sector is developing), *Planovoe khozyaistvo*, No.10, October 1989, pp.34-41.

[207] The share of grain in compound feed has increased by 16 per cent over the past 20 years and in 1988 stood at 68 per cent of total compound feed output by volume. In the United States, the share of grain does not exceed 48 per cent, in the Federal Republic of Germany and France – 45 and in Holland – 29 per cent. The use of oilseed cake and meal in the Soviet Union constitutes only one third of the quantities used in the United States and France and a quarter of its use in the Federal Republic of Germany and Holland. The share of oilseed cake and meal in compound feed production varies in these countries from 18 to 27 per cent which makes possible considerable economies of grain. See "Vsemu nachalo – khleb" (Bread – the beginning of everything), interview with Yegor Stroyev, Secretary of the CPSU Central Committee, *Pravda*, 28 December 1989.

CHART 3.2.4

Growth rates of gross agricultural output
(Annual percentage change)

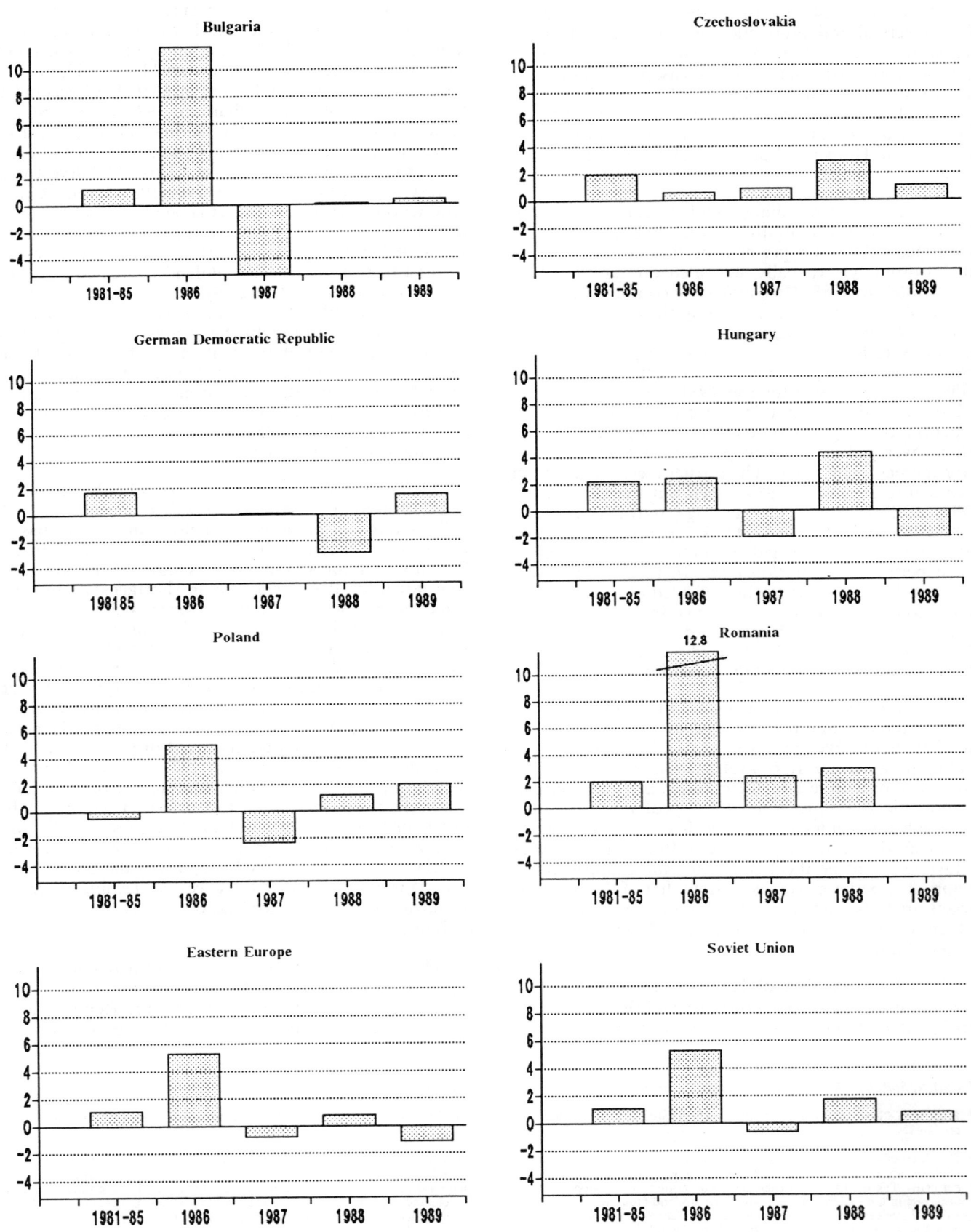

Source: ECE secretariat Common Data Base.

TABLE 3.2.13

Gross agricultural production, 1981-1990
(Annual percentage change)

	1981-1985 a	1985	1986	1987	1988	1989	Plan 1990	Plan a 1986-1990
Bulgaria								
Total	1.2	-12.3	11.7	-5.1	0.1	0.4	..	1.6-1.9
Crop	0.2	-22.5	22.7	-8.8	-0.3	4.1	..	..
Animal	2.4	-2.9	3.7	-1.9	0.4	-2.6	..	..
Czechoslovakia								
Total	1.9	-1.6	0.6	0.9	2.9	1.1	2.3	1.3
Crop	2.5	-4.1	-2.5	1.8	4.0	0.2	..	1.5-1.7
Animal	1.4	0.4	2.9	0.3	2.1	1.7	..	1.0-1.2
German Democratic Republic								
Total	1.6	3.7	-	0.1	-2.9	1.5*	..	1.5*
Crop	2.7	6.0	-3.7	-0.8	-6.3	2.4 b	..	1.7 b
Animal	1.0	1.9	3.0	-0.9	-	..	..	1.4
Hungary								
Total	2.1	-5.5	2.4	-2.0	4.3	-2	..	1.4-1.9
Crop	1.8	-5.4	3.7	-5.5	7.5	-2	..	1.3-1.4
Animal	2.4	-5.6	1.1	1.5	1.5	-2	..	..
Poland								
Total	-0.5	0.7	5.0	-2.3	1.2	2.0	..	2.3
Crop	1.2	-2.0	6.3	-2.0	-0.3	4.0	..	2.1-2.5
Animal	-2.0	4.0	3.2	-2.7	3.2	-1.0	..	2.3
Romania								
Total	2.0	0.1	12.9	2.3	2.9	..	..	6.1-6.7
Crop	2.5	-1.5	19.9	-0.2	2.9	..	..	..
Animal	1.1	2.5	2.9	3.3	2.9	..	..	..
Eastern Europe								
Total	1.1	-1.1	5.3	-0.8	1.4	1.0 c	..	2.7
Crop	1.9	-3.1	6.8	-1.9	0.9	2.2 c	..	..
Animal	0.4	1.1	2.9	-0.3	2.0	..	..	..
Soviet Union								
Total	1.1	0.1	5.4	-0.6	1.7	0.8	6.6	2.7
Crop	0.7	-0.9	6.1	-2.6	-1.4	0.2	..	..
Animal	1.4	0.9	4.5	1.2	4.1	1	..	..
Eastern Europe and Soviet Union								
Total	1.1	-0.3	5.3	-0.7	1.6	0.8 c	..	2.7
Crop	1.0	-1.7	6.4	-2.2	-0.6	..	..	..
Animal	1.1	1.0	3.9	0.7	3.4	..	..	..

Source: ECE secretariat Common Data Base, based on national and CMEA statistics; national plan and plan fulfilment reports.

a Average annualized percentage change as compared with average output in the previous five-year period.
b Grain units.
c Excluding Romania.

---

grain production became less profitable due to rapidly rising prices for non-agricultural inputs. In Bulgaria, Poland and Romania, the area under grain generally expanded in the second half of the 1980s.

All countries have recently achieved *higher grain yields*. The highest, almost 50 quintals per hectare, were recorded in Czechoslovakia and Hungary. This is comparable, for example, with average 1986-1988 yields in Austria and Denmark, but is 7 quintals lower than in France and the United Kingdom and 15 quintals below the Netherlands. The 1989 yield in the German Democratic Republic, at about 45 quintals, was 10 quintals below the 1986-1988 average in the Federal Republic of Germany. A yield of about 40 quintals per hectare in Bulgaria is comparable with Italy. A record 32 quintals achieved in Poland was 5 and 7 quintals lower than the 1986-1988 averages for Norway and Sweden, respectively. At 19 quintals per hectare, grain yields in the Soviet Union remain by far the lowest in the region. Moreover, in 1988 one hectare in three yielded less than 10 quintals.

Domestic production of grain is less than requirements in all east European countries but Hungary, and also in the Soviet Union. The Soviet Union has been a particularly big importer of grain throughout the 1980s, purchasing 36 million tons in 1989 — one million tons more than in 1988.[208]

---

[208] See "Ekonomika strany: itogi goda" (Economy of the country: results of the year) and Report of the State Committee on Statistics of the USSR on the social and economic development of the country in 1989, *Pravda*, 28 January 1990. However, the Soviet Union has not always been such a big importer of cereals. Russia exported about 10.5 million tons of wheat, rye, barley and oats annually in 1909-1913. Grain exports in 1928-1929 were insignificant, but two years later they had grown to 5 million tons annually. During the period 1932-1942, grain exports fluctuated between 0.3 and 2 million tons a year. The grain exported at the beginning of the 1930s, during severe famine in the grain-producing regions of the country, earned hard currency to pay for equipment imported

TABLE 3.2.14

Main crop production, 1981-1990
(Thousand tons)

	Bulgaria	Czechoslovakia	German Dem.Rep.	Hungary	Poland	Romania	Soviet Union
Grain							
1981-1985 [a]	8 276	11 079	10 479	14 599	22 544	21 927	180 301
1985	5 456	11 983	11 740	15 028	24 178	23 344	191 674
1986	8 576	11 017	11 766	14 546	25 510	30 694	210 068
1987	7 363	11 996	11 314	14 442	26 572	31 702	211 401
1988	7 913	12 153	9 926	14 966	25 069	32 600	195 058
1989	9 766	12 278	10 903	15 000	27 573	..	211 078
1990 Plan (million tons)	..	11.4-11.6 [b]	..	..	..	..	236.5*
Oilseeds							
1981-1985 [a]	538	308	320	784	707	1 166	5 705
1985	406	343	397	858	1 082	1 105	5 995
1986	549	378	459	1 078	1 304	1 554	6 251
1987	454	415	379	1 010	1 192	1 814	7 288
1988	398	461	435	932	1 206	..	7 644
1989	479	481	434	971	1 599	..	..
Coarse fodder [c]							
1981-1985 [a]	3 405	11 198	9 414	4 710	17 349	5 881	194 483
1985	3 139	12 111	10 300	4 630	16 661	4 128	218 339
1986	3 682	11 789	10 116	4 165	16 542	..	209 295
1987	3 544	12 294	11 946	4 377	17 368	..	238 017
1988	3 096	12 832	10 978	4 112	16 681	..	228 037
Vegetables							
1981-1985 [a]	1 625	1 117	1 723	1 637	4 622	5 103	29 225
1985	1 506	1 092	1 955	1 769	4 370	5 769	28 050
1986	1 488	1 093	1 852	1 733	5 345	6 908	29 783
1987	1 600	1 196	1 924	2 042	5 582	6 719	29 249
1988	1 618	1 129	1 771	2 092	5 576	..	29 330
1989	1 611	1 146	1 897	2 065	5 436	..	28 494
Potatoes							
1981-1985 [a]	431	3 591	10 116	1 446	36 594	5 869	78 351
1985	439	3 450	12 350	1 378	36 546	7 294	73 009
1986	491	3 512	9 997	1 264	39 037	9 106	87 186
1987	316	3 072	12 228	1 077	36 252	7 572	75 908
1988	358	3 659	11 546	1 407	34 707	..	62 705
1989	538	3 124	9 083	1 301	34 390	..	71 987
Fruits							
1981-1985 [a]	2 101	800	977	2 515	2 273	3 580	17 807
1985	1 822	638	1 219	1 986	2 190	3 010	16 434
1986	2 002	886	1 019	2 513	2 757	4 824	18 338
1987	1 775	588	767	2 142	1 036	3 371	14 321
1988	1 789	945	1 099	2 401	2 168	5 125	14 938
1989	1 756	1 010	1 047	2 040	2 078	..	14 900

Source: ECE secretariat Common Data Base, based on national and CMEA statistics plan; and plan fulfilment reports.

[a] Annual average.
[b] Five-year plan target.
[c] Natural, annual, perennial hay and silage maize (converted into feed units at 0.4 per kg), plus feed roots (converted into feed units at 0.2 per kg). Hungarian data include pastureland hay.

Fodder crop production increased in all eastern countries except Bulgaria in recent years. To achieve better balanced animal feed, priority was given to *oilseed* cultivation in the majority of east European countries. The area under *coarse fodder* declined in recent years in almost all of them but output increases were achieved from higher yields.

Output of meat and other *livestock products* rose in almost all east European countries and the Soviet Union in recent years, but in Poland there was a slight fall in milk and egg production (table 3.2.15). This was paralleled by a decline in the number of cattle and, especially, of cows in all east European countries. Pig herds also contracted in Hungary and Poland. In the Soviet Union, the increase in cattle herds was accompanied by a drop in the number of milking cows while the pig herd expanded.

Meat production rose in all of the seven countries reviewed except Hungary between 1981-1985 and 1986-1988. The rise ranged between 8-9 per cent of the level in the first half of the decade in Bulgaria, Czechoslovakia, the German Democratic Republic and Romania to 16 per cent in the Soviet Union and 21 per cent in Poland. In Hungary output stagnated. In most

from western countries. The state was unable during those years to secure long-term loans from abroad to cover imports considered necessary for industrialization. In the post-war period, large scale exports resumed in 1948 and continued up to the mid-1970s within a range of 3-9 million tons annually. The main purchasers of Soviet grain in those years were the east European countries. See interview with D.A. Klimov, chairman of Eksportkhleb, in *Sel'skaya zhizn'*, 9 December 1989.

TABLE 3.2.15

Livestock numbers and livestock output, 1981-1990

	Bulgaria	Czecho-slovakia	German Dem.Rep.	Hungary	Poland	Romania	Soviet Union
Livestock numbers (*thousand livestock units*)							
1981-1985 [a]	4 562	7 052	9 527	5 796	17 520	13 995	154 851
1985	4 410	6 885	9 585	5 397	17 597	14 680	156 824
1986	4 419	6 966	9 529	5 582	17 066	..	158 351
1987	4 359	7 046	9 374	5 360	16 658	..	156 496
1988	4 343	7 115	9 325	5 312	16 635	..	156 568
Meat production (*thousand tons*)							
1981-1985 [a]	826	1 501	1 954	1 726	2 587	1 803	16 227
1985	843	1 547	2 077	1 745	2 792	1 889	17 131
1986	886	1 563	2 116	1 704	3 121	1 965	18 057
1987	883	1 607	2 144	1 783	3 119	1 976	18 926
1988	912	1 689	2 145	1 765	3 172	..	19 680
1989	940	..	2 162	..	..	..	20 000
Milk production (*thousand tons*)							
1981-1985 [a]	2 475	6 456	7 370	2 764	15 983	5 313	94 579
1985	2 537	6 942	7 910	2 729	16 446	5 941	98 608
1986	2 600	7 075	8 123	2 778	15 790	5 818	102 173
1987	2 590	6 982	7 976	2 833	15 543	5 827	103 745
1988	2 570	7 024	7 968	2 886	15 491	..	106 754
1989	2 503	..	8 223	..	..	..	108 100
Eggs (*millions*)							
1981-1985 [a]	2 577	5 247	5 718	4 351	8 186	7 229	73 409
1985	2 742	5 499	5 596	4 228	8 636	7 866	76 337
1986	2 820	5 558	5 634	4 290	8 304	8 535	79 892
1987	2 829	5 544	5 680	4 237	7 966	8 612	81 917
1988	2 740	5 596	5 720	4 695	8 103	..	84 181
1989	2 650	..	5 926	..	..	..	84 600

Source: ECE secretariat Common Data Base, based on national and CMEA statistics; plan fulfilment reports.

[a] Annual average.

countries the share of grain-feed-intensive poultry production in total meat output rose, as did the share of pork. This continued to stimulate demand for grain and oilseeds which could not be satisfied without continuing imports. In the Soviet Union, most of the rise in meat output was due to poultry, but the share of beef in the total also increased.

Milk production grew between 1981-1985 and 1986-1988 in all the east European countries except Poland. Czechoslovakia and the German Democratic Republic both recorded a 9 per cent increase. The rise was about 5 per cent in Bulgaria and 3 per cent in Hungary and as much as 10 per cent in the Soviet Union. In Poland, milk output fell by over 2 per cent between the same two periods. Incomplete information for 1989 suggests that Czechoslovakia, the German Democratic Republic and the Soviet Union recorded further increases in milk output in that year. In contrast, Bulgaria registered a 2.5 per cent decline.

These developments should be viewed against continuing reductions in the number of milking cows in all east European countries and the Soviet Union, which point to increasing animal productivity. Indeed, *milk yields* continued to grow in 1988 in all the seven countries under study. By 1988 they were highest in Hungary (nearly 5,000 kg per cow), followed by the German Democratic Republic (nearly 4,000 kg) and Czechoslovakia (3,900 kg). Bulgaria and Poland had the lowest milk yields in eastern Europe with up to 3,500 kg, but they were still lower in the Soviet Union (2,500 kg).

Egg production also increased between 1981-1985 and 1986-1988 in most eastern countries. The sole exception was again Poland. The highest growth was recorded in the Soviet Union and the lowest in the German Democratic Republic. Egg production in Bulgaria has declined since 1985 but in 1986-1989 the annual average remained higher than in the previous five-year period.

(b) Agricultural inputs and efficiency

Continuous growth in the use of *material inputs* of non-agricultural origin in agricultural production was recorded in the second half of the 1980s in all east European countries for which data are available. The rise exceeded the growth of gross agricultural output in all of them – particularly in Bulgaria, Czechoslovakia and Poland, where higher gross agricultural production growth was achieved. Changes in the quantity of material inputs to the agricultural sector recorded in the German Democratic Republic and Hungary were roughly similar in 1986-1988, but were associated with a decrease in production in the former country and stagnation in the latter. In the Soviet Union, the growth of material input use slowed down in recent years to rates comparable with those of output growth; in the previous five-year period, they had been considerably higher.

The rise in *material inputs per unit of gross output* recorded in the 1986-1988 period in Bulgaria, Czechoslovakia, the German Democratic Republic and Poland indicate that agricultural production in these countries continues to depend on increasing supplies of production inputs in volume terms (table 3.2.17). In other words, attempts to check the growth of material input use has usually had a negative impact on production growth.

Agricultural *profits* are also being squeezed. This arises from the continuing non-equivalent exchange between the products which the state purchases from the farms and the mixed feed, fertilizers, equipment, building materials, repairs, etc., which are sold to them — the "price scissors". The cause of the widening price difference is well-known.[209] Branches with a high degree of production monopoly and a rapidly changing product list — which is the case for the engineering, chemicals, construction and other branches which supply agricultural inputs — can easily raise prices, particularly now that the central authorities have only limited possibilities for verifying producers' justifications for doing so. But such price rises do not always reflect real improvements in the quality or performance of the product. Disproportionate increases in the prices of new machinery relative to its productivity creates "creeping inflation" with regard to agricultural inputs.[210]

In agriculture on the other hand, as in other raw-material-producing branches where only a small number of basic products are involved for which the quality specification changes little if at all, the monitoring of prices "from above" is relatively effective. Thus the prices of non-agricultural inputs and services used in the agricultural sector are running ahead of agricultural producer prices. In 1988, for example, agricultural machinery prices grew in the Soviet Union by 34 per cent compared with only an 8 per cent increase in the purchase prices of crops.[211] As a consequence, agriculture periodically becomes a low-profit or even an unprofitable operation. Indeed, it is difficult to see how Soviet agricultural production can be profitable when farms must, for example, sell much of their grain at a low price and then buy it back, in the form of mixed feeds, at a price two to three times higher. This is why large periodic one-time price increases become necessary.

Agricultural profitability is also being squeezed in Hungary and Poland and for similar reasons. As countries travel farther in the direction of market-oriented reform, the more pressing becomes the need to break up the monopoly position of suppliers of agricultural inputs and of the agencies responsible for the purchase of farm products.

Agricultural *employment* decreased in Bulgaria, Czechoslovakia, Hungary, Poland and the Soviet Union in the second half of the 1980s (table 3.2.16). In these countries the trend of the previous quinquennium continued. Most noteworthy were the declines in agricultural employment in Bulgaria and Hungary. This created shortages of agricultural manpower in Bulgaria, where schoolchildren, students, industrial workers and administrative personnel from agro-industrial complexes had to assist in the 1989 harvest.[212] Such practices have also been common for decades in the Soviet Union. In the German Democratic Republic, agricultural employment grew throughout the 1980s — although at decreasing rates in the 1985-1987 period — but the year 1988 marked the first fall. Agricultural employment did not change significantly in Romania.

Agricultural *labour productivity*, calculated on a net output basis, behaved irregularly in the 1986-1988 period (table 3.2.17) as a result of variations in output growth. An absolute decline in labour productivity (more than 3 per cent annually in 1986-1988) was registered in the German Democratic Republic. In Czechoslovakia, it declined in 1988 for the second successive year, but it increased in all the other countries. Its growth was most pronounced in Hungary, Romania and the Soviet Union and smallest (about 1 per cent) in Bulgaria and Poland.

Growth in *capital intensity* (fixed assets per worker) was much stronger than the increases in labour productivity during the same period (table 3.2.17), varying between an annual average of 3 per cent in the German Democratic Republic and about 7 per cent in Bulgaria and Romania. Capital intensity growth also considerably exceeded increases in gross agricultural production in all east European countries and the Soviet Union. As touched upon earlier, the causes of the disproportionately low growth in gross output relative to increases in inputs stem not only from inadequate overall use of resources by farms. Complaints about the low quality of agricultural machinery, for example, reflect the fact that the annual cost of Soviet agricultural machinery maintenance is about 6-8 billion roubles. This is equivalent to about 20 per cent of annual investment allocations to agriculture. The labour force engaged in agricultural machinery repair is estimated at 1.3 million workers — more than the total employed in agricultural machinery production. The lifespan norm for Soviet tractors is no more than 8-10 years — 50 per cent lower than in the United States. About 300,000 Soviet tractors are scrapped every year, one quarter of which *within* this already short active lifetime norm. Almost all newly-produced tractors are replacements and do

---

[209] See for example Nikolai P. Shmelev, "Rethinking price reform in the USSR," *Soviet Studies*, 1988, 4, pp.319-327.

[210] For example, the price of the new Soviet "Don" harvester, which helps to reduce losses during harvesting, is 43,000 roubles. This compares with 11,000 roubles charged for the old "Niva" harvester. The productivity of the two machines is 600 and 270 tons per shift respectively. Thus, a doubling of productivity has been accompanied by a quadrupling of price. The reliability of the new harvester is also rather low — 10-20 hours of work between breakdowns — which means that during the harvesting period the machine has a serious breakdown every day. See "Kombainy *Don* prodayut i obsluzhivayut dilery" (Dealers sell and service *Don* harvesters), *Izvestiya*, 19 January 1990.

[211] F. Bogomolov, "Anatomiya poter'" (Anatomy of losses), *Ekonomicheskaya gazeta*, No.47, November 1989, p.10.

[212] Interview with Agriculture and Forestry Minister Georgi Menov, *Rabotnichesko delo*, as cited in BBC, *Summary of World Broadcasts*, 17 July 1989.

TABLE 3.2.16

Agricultural factor inputs, 1981-1988
(Annual percentage change)

	Bulgaria	Czechoslovakia	German Dem.Rep.	Hungary	Poland	Romania	Soviet Union
Employment							
1981-1985 [a]	-2.1	-0.8	0.6	-0.1	..	-2.0	-0.3
1985	-2.5	-	0.7	-4.1	0.1	-0.3	-0.5
1986	-2.1	-0.6	0.5	-4.6	-1.2	0.1	-0.9
1987	-3.4	-0.8	0.4	-3.9	-0.8	0.1	-0.4
1988	..	-1.3	-0.2	-3.0	-2.6	..	-0.7
Investment							
1981-1985 [a]	-0.1	3.2	-3.6	-2.4	-6.7	5.8	1.9
1985	8.0	7.8	-5.7	-7.0	-1.9	10.7	1.3
1986	-12.1	3.1	5.8	6.9	0.4	-3.2	6.4
1987	13.0	-1.5	8.6	21.4	3.6	-2.4	2.3
1988	..	0.4	9.1	-22.5	3.5	..	6.3
Fixed assets							
1981-1985 [a]	4.8	6.1	4.6	4.1	4.1	8.4	6.5
1985	3.5	6.4	3.2	2.1	2.4	8.6	4.3
1986	4.4	5.4	2.9	1.7	1.6	7.5	4.4
1987	3.8	5.2	3.0	2.5	2.1	7.1	4.2
1988	..	5.4	3.1	..	2.1	..	2.9
Material inputs							
1981-1985 [a]	6.1	4.9	1.2	2.2	-0.5	5.1	2.2
1985	-4.7	4.4	3.5	-3.7	1.0	-0.7	3.5
1986	3.7	2.5	0.4	1.1	3.7	11.4	4.0
1987	3.4	2.0	0.2	0.1	2.4	-1.9	-0.3
1988	..	2.1	0.3	1.3	1.5	..	1.1

Source: ECE secretariat Common Data Base, based on national and CMEA statistics.

[a] Average annualized percentage change as compared with the average in the previous five-year period.

not increase the country's tractor park.[213] The excessively high maintenance costs implied by the above comments are one important reason for the disparities in rates of output growth and material input use in agriculture.

Agricultural *investment* grew in the 1986-1988 period in three of the seven eastern countries – the German Democratic Republic, Poland and the Soviet Union (table 3.2.16). In the first two this reversed the trend of the first half of the 1980s. Agricultural investment in the Soviet Union experienced steady, almost uninterrupted growth throughout the past decade. Wide year-to-year fluctuations in agricultural investment occurred in Bulgaria and Hungary in 1986-1988. Its level remained practically unchanged in Czechoslovakia and declined in Romania.

Agricultural *fixed assets* continued to grow in all east European countries and the Soviet Union in the second half of the 1980s (table 3.2.16). The annual average rates of growth were, however, lower than in the 1981-1985 period in all of them. In the German Democratic Republic, Hungary and Poland – the countries where agricultural investment declined in 1981-1985 – only moderate rises in fixed assets occurred in 1986-1988. An increasing share of newly-installed machines were needed to replace aging equipment. Stagnating agricultural investment in Bulgaria in 1981-1985 and fluctuating investment in 1986-1987, together with relatively high rates of fixed asset growth, point to an aging of the country's agricultural fixed assets. In Czechoslovakia and the Soviet Union, the increase in agricultural fixed assets was continuous and rather high. It also remained high in Romania, despite the negative growth rates of agricultural investment recorded since 1986. This reflects in part the prolongation of the service life of fixed assets, and a consequent aging of the capital stock, in these countries also.

Capital productivity, calculated on the basis of net agricultural output, deteriorated in 1986-1988 in all the countries for which data are available (table 3.2.17). Continued growth of fixed assets, paralleled by much lower increases in gross output and rising costs, explain the generally declining trend in agricultural capital productivity. The drop was particularly big in Czechoslovakia and the German Democratic Republic in 1986-1988 (about 6 per cent annually). It was less pronounced but still visible in all the other countries.

(c) Policy objectives for 1990

In the coming years, the east European and Soviet agricultural sectors will have to adapt to new economic conditions and notably the transition to market principles. Only two countries – Czechoslovakia and the Soviet Union – have published plan targets for agriculture in 1990.

---

[213] F. Bogomolov, *op.cit.*

TABLE 3.2.17

Factor productivity, capital intensity and material costs, a 1981-1988
(Annual percentage change)

	Bulgaria	Czecho-slovakia	German Dem.Rep.	Hungary	Poland	Romania	Soviet Union
Labour productivity							
1981-1985 b	-1.3	0.5	1.9	1.3	-0.5	1.1	-0.3
1985	-18.6	-6.4	3.5	-2.3	-	1.4	-4.4
1986	25.0	2.9	-1.1	9.5	7.5	13.0	7.3
1987	-11.6	-2.5	-0.4	0.9	-7.1	2.4	-1.4
1988	..	-0.1	-7.8	8.9	4.1	..	3.5
Capital productivity							
1981-1985 b	-7.8	-6.0	-1.9	-2.8	-4.4	-8.6	-6.6
1985	-23.3	-12.0	1.1	-8.2	-2.2	-6.9	-8.8
1986	17.2	-3.0	-3.4	2.7	4.6	5.2	1.8
1987	-17.7	-8.1	-3.0	-5.3	-9.7	-4.3	-5.8
1988	..	-6.5	-10.7	..	-0.7	..	-0.1
Capital intensity							
1981-1985 b	7.1	6.8	3.9	4.2	4.1	10.7	6.8
1985	6.2	6.4	2.5	6.4	2.2	8.9	4.8
1986	6.7	6.0	2.4	6.6	2.8	7.4	5.4
1987	7.5	6.1	2.6	6.6	2.9	7.0	4.6
1988	..	6.8	3.3	..	4.8	..	3.6
Material inputs per unit of gross output							
1981-1985 b	6.9	1.5	-0.4	0.1	-	2.7	1.2
1985	8.6	2.9	-0.2	2.0	0.2	-0.8	3.4
1986	-7.2	-0.2	0.4	-1.3	-1.2	-0.7	-1.3
1987	8.9	1.2	0.2	2.2	4.8	-1.9	0.6
1988	..	0.6	3.1	-2.9	0.3	..	-0.6

Source: ECE secretariat Common Data Base, based on national and CMEA statistics.

a Based on net output.
b Average annualized percentage change as compared with the average in the previous five-year period.

In *Czechoslovakia*, a further 2.3 per cent increase in agricultural production is planned for 1990. This would bring agricultural output above the level envisaged in the 1986-1990 five-year plan. Checking the rising costs of production without threatening its stable growth will be a main longer-term policy issue. On average, state farms make a loss of about Kcs 263 per hectare of land.[214] Higher productivity will also require improvements in fixed assets. According to national experts, agricultural equipment in Czechoslovakia is at best at the qualitative level of the 1960s or 1970s compared with western countries.[215]

In the *Soviet Union*, gross agricultural production is planned to grow in 1990 by 6.6 per cent. Agriculture is singled out as the most important priority in the 1990 plan.[216] This will clearly also be the case in the years beyond 1990 and the plan embodies demanding targets.

Per capita annual consumption of food products by 1995 is planned at 80 kg for meat and meat products, 400 kg for milk and milk products, and for eggs – 285 units. Assuming that the population grows by more than 20 million people up to that year, the targets would represent a 25 per cent increase in meat and milk production and a 10 per cent increase for eggs relative to 1989. Grain output is planned to reach 250-255 million tons in the same year.[217] It is clear that simply increasing the inflow of resources to agriculture will not be sufficient to achieve these targets. Stress is currently being placed on restructuring the economic mechanism in such a way that full equality of different forms of agricultural ownership – collective or state farms, small co-operatives, personal plots or family farms – is achieved. To this end leaseholding will be encouraged.[218] Leasing is expected to act as a barrier to the wasteful practices now customary at many state and

---

214 Speech by J. Haman at the Unified Agricultural Co-operative Conference, 14 October 1989, as cited in BBC, *Summary of World Broadcasts*, EE/0591, 19 October 1989, p.B/3.

215 CTK in English, 9 August 1989, as cited in BBC, *Summary of World Broadcasts*, EE/W0091, p.A/9.

216 Interview with Prime Minister N. Ryzhkov, with Moscow Home Service, 1 November 1989, as cited in BBC, *Summary of World Broadcasts*, SU/0605, p.C/4.

217 E. Sosnin, "Kak razvivaetsia zernovoe khozyaistvo strany" (How the country's grain sector is developing), *Planovoe khozyaistvo*, No.10, October 1989, pp.34-41.

218 Leaseholding was given the force of law in February 1990, when the Supreme Soviet adopted the Law on Land which allows Soviet citizens to lease land and bequeath it to their children. In order to prevent local authorities from blocking the grant of leases or making available only poor land, the Presidium of the USSR Council of Ministers decided on 5 December 1989 to write off 73.5 billion roubles of farm debts, but only for those farms which agree to offer leasehold contracts. Moreover, debt will only be written off proportionally to the share of leaseholding in the total activity of the farm. It will also apply only to those collectives which grant leasehold agreements for a period of not less than five years. If a collective gives up leasehold operation within that period, it will

collective farms, to check the growth of unwarranted expenditure and to force people to relate expenditures to receipts — which has not been the case with traditional state and collective farms.

---

again be liable for its debts plus the interest accrued during the time during which no repayment had been made. Moscow radio interview (6 December 1989) with Valentin Pavlov, USSR Minister of Finance, as cited in BBC, *Summary of World Broadcasts,* SU/W0107, p.A/8.

3.3 UTILIZATION OF OUTPUT AND DOMESTIC BALANCE

This chapter examines developments in the level and allocation of resources in eastern Europe and the Soviet Union. Section (i) reviews recent changes in the major demand categories. Section (ii) outlines indicators of consumption and analyses consumer prices, together with some physical aspects of real consumption levels in recent years. Section (iii) assesses recent and medium-term developments in investment and investment efficiency together with their implications for the state of the capital stock on the eve of economic restructuring.

This is used as background for a discussion of investment prospects in the context of recent resource allocation policies, the requirements of economic restructuring and the possibilities for western aid programmes to assist in this process. Section (iv) summarizes recent price changes, the emergence in some countries of hyperinflation and of budget deficits and examines the links between inflation and the implementation of reform programmes.

(i) Resource allocation by broad demand categories

(a) Developments in 1989

The stagnation of net output (NMP produced) in the countries of *eastern Europe* in 1989 was probably accompanied by an only slightly less pronounced deceleration in the growth of net absorption (NMP used). In the *Soviet Union*, the sharp rise in the trade deficit may have cushioned the impact of the slowing of output growth on aggregate absorption. However, few data are available on the changes in NMP used domestically and its allocation in 1989, and probable trends must be deduced from the behaviour of various proxy variables — gross investment, retail sales, real wages and the external balance — which are not always very reliably correlated with the changes in domestic absorption and its components. On the basis of such observations, it appears that *accumulation* absorbed the brunt of the retrenchment in most countries. Gross investment generally stagnated or declined, and *net fixed asset formation* is likely to have been affected even more severely.

In eastern Europe, *Czechoslovakia* was the only exception, with NMP used rising some 2 per cent in volume, or twice the rate of growth of NMP produced; most of this increase seems to have been absorbed by consumption, though there was a definite slow-down in investment. In contrast, falling investment levels were reported by all other east European countries. In *Bulgaria*, most of the decline in output seems to have been concentrated on investment outlays. In the *German Democratic Republic*, slightly rising retail trade and a sizeable but smaller investment decline indicate a similar shift against a background of a small output increase. In *Hungary*, the estimated fall in NMP used[219] exceeded the decline in output growth; private consumption fell, but government consumption and accumulation fell even more. In *Poland*, consumption fell against a background of marginal output growth; accumulation in fact rose as a result of a second successive year of heavy stockbuilding, but investment growth was negative. No data on 1989 are available for *Romania*, but statistics for the month of January 1990 indicate that while retail sales were above, and the provision of paid services below, year-earlier levels, investment had declined by a massive 62 per cent. In the *Soviet Union*, fast rising net imports seem to have done little to ease domestic shortages which are now reaching crisis dimensions. It is likely that most of the modest rise in production was allocated to consumption; investment rose only fractionally, there was a sizeable shift within industry towards the production of consumer goods (see section 3.2) and the average earnings of the Soviet labour force again rose strongly — indeed outpacing the growth in the supply of consumer goods.

The events of 1989 have seen an intensification of pressures apparent in eastern Europe and, to a lesser extent, in the Soviet Union during most of the current decade. All east European countries spent the first years of the 1980s in adjusting their domestic resource allocation patterns to cut back the growth of, or to begin repaying, external indebtedness. This shift of resources, achieved mainly by import restrictions rather than by export expansion, was accompanied by slowdowns in output growth.

In the Soviet Union, developments were rather different during the early 1980s. No great restraint on the growth of imports proved necessary throughout the first half of the decade and NMP growth rates were not significantly below those recorded in the late 1970s. The situation changed with the fall in oil prices at the end of 1985, since when the Soviet Union has also been compelled to shift a greater proportion of its resources abroad to pay for its imports.

---

[219] Departing from earlier traditions, the 1989 report of the Central Statistical Office of Hungary did not provide any information either on NMP produced or used and all data were estimated according to the SNA methodology. See *A Központi Statisztikai Hivatal tájékoztatója a társadalom és a gazdaság 1989. évi helyzetéről* (Communiqué of the Central Statistical Office on the state of the society and the economy in 1989), manuscript, Budapest, 2 February 1990.

TABLE 3.3.1

Allocation of NMP used, 1981-1989

Country/period	Percentage change in volume terms [a]		Percentage shares [b]			
				Consumption		Accumulation
	Consumption	Accumulation	Total	Personal	Social	total
Bulgaria [c]						
1981-1985	3.7	2.4	67.1	..	..	33.4
1986	3.6	23.8	65.2	..	..	36.3
1987	4.6	-10.7	67.9	..	..	32.3
1988	3.6	4.1	67.8	..	..	32.4
1989	..	..	..	..	..	..
Czechoslovakia						
1981-1985	2.0	-7.3	0.2	56.9	23.2	19.8
1986	3.4	12.2	79.7	55.2	24.5	20.3
1987	3.6	-1.1	81.2	55.8	25.4	18.8
1988	4.3	-9.8	82.7	55.8	25.4	17.3
1989	2.3*	1.3*	..	..	..	..
German Democratic Republic [d]						
1981-1985	2.4	-2.9	77.8	61.6	16.1	22.2
1986	4.5	3.4	78.7	62.6	16.0	21.3
1987	3.8	6.5	78.3	62.1	16.2	21.7
1988	3.6	2.3	78.5	62.3	16.1	21.5
1988	..	..	..	..	..	..
Hungary						
1981-1985	1.4	-13.6	80.8	70.0	10.8	19.2
1986	2.0	21.4	80.9	69.9	11.0	19.1
1987	3.1	2.7	80.2	69.6	10.7	19.8
1988	-3.5	-2.5	80.4	68.7	11.7	19.6
1989	-2 *	-3 *	..	..	..	..
Poland						
1981-1985	-0.8	-4.0	77.8	65.7	12.1	22.2
1986	4.8	5.4	73.0	60.5	12.5	27.0
1987	2.8	-2.4	73.0	60.6	12.5	27.0
1988	2.9	12.8	68.1	56.7	11.4	31.9
1989	..	..	..	..	..	..
Romania [e]						
1981-1985	6.6	-	72.7	..	..	27.4
1986	4.7	4.6	..	..	..	..
1987	..	..	..	..	..	..
1988	..	..	..	..	..	..
1989	..	..	..	..	..	..
Soviet Union						
1981-1985	3.0	3.7	74.0	63.4	3.3	26.0
1986	3.3	-1.3	74.2	63.1	3.6	25.8
1987	3.3	-3.0	75.4	63.8	3.9	24.6
1988	5.4	6.6	75.2	63.5	4.0	24.8
1989	..	..	..	..	..	..

Source: National statistics. Figures do not necessarily add up to 100 due to rounding (Romania), the separate repricing of time series (Bulgaria) or as a consequence of the ommission of reported losses and statistical discrepancies (Czechoslovakia).

[a] Current prices for Romania and the Soviet Union.
[b] Current prices for Czechoslovakia, Hungary, Poland and the Soviet Union.
[c] 1962 prices.
[d] 1985 prices.
[e] 1977 prices.

If the timing and causes of the economic slow-down in the 1980s were different within eastern Europe and the Soviet Union, its effects on the allocation of resources were similar throughout the seven countries. All of them have held back the growth of resources for domestic use (NMP used) to rates less than those of total output (NMP produced) during the whole of the present decade.

In Hungary and Poland, the level of NMP used was lower than in 1980 in most years of this decade. The countries in which the NMP produced growth rate exceeded that of NMP used by most since 1980 are the German Democratic Republic, Hungary, Romania (for which data are only available up to 1985) and, some way behind, Czechoslovakia (table 3.3.2). The difference, however, was very small in Bulgaria, and only slightly bigger in Poland and the Soviet Union. In all countries but Czechoslovakia, however, NMP used has grown at rates much closer to those of NMP produced since 1985. This broadly confirms the evidence of trade data in volume terms.[220] These show shrinking deficits

---

[220] The difference between the growth rates of NMP produced and NMP used is not, however, a completely reliable indicator of movements in the foreign balance. The difference between NMP produced and NMP also includes losses and "errors and omissions". Moreover visible trade balances alone exclude by

(or rising surpluses) for most countries in the post-1980 period as a whole. In Bulgaria, however, the trade deficit (in 1985 prices) was higher in 1986-1988 than at the beginning of the decade. Previously improving trends were also reversed, though not so sharply, in Czechoslovakia and the German Democratic Republic.

For 1989, trade data in value terms indicate that the east European countries recorded smaller net inflows or bigger net outflows of resources from and to abroad compared with 1988. The exceptions were Czechoslovakia and probably Romania, whose trade surpluses fell. In the Soviet Union, the large surplus of 1988 was replaced by a deficit of almost twice that size in 1989.

These resource shifts — which contrast with a net inflow of credit-financed resources in the majority of the east European countries during the 1970s — have not prevented a considerable rise in the net hard currency indebtedness of all of them except for the German Democratic Republic and Romania between 1980 and 1988 — most of which occurred since 1985. This partly represents terms-of-trade losses. Poland has been quite unable to expand its net exports — despite, or because of, its crippling import cutbacks and attempts to avoid even deeper cuts in consumption than those imposed to date.

Regarding the components of NMP used, *consumption* grew uniformly faster over the decade — or, in Hungary and Poland, fell by less — than *accumulation*. The year 1989 was thus the culminating year of a long period within which investment activity had been curtailed in favour of the maintenance of current consumption. Indeed, in Czechoslovakia, the German Democratic Republic, Hungary, Poland and Romania the absolute level of accumulation fell substantially after 1980. The extent of the decline between 1980 and 1985 ranged between 14 and 52 percentage points in these five countries. Despite some recovery thereafter, it had not been made good by 1988 and the fall resumed in most countries in 1989.

It is clear that policies over the last decade have largely been dictated by short-term expediency. No boost to factor productivity has materialized in producing sectors and indeed output growth rates have decelerated markedly in the 1980s. The poor quality of production and the consequent further decline in export competitiveness has meant that debt servicing and repayment has had to be achieved by restricting imports rather than by raising exports. Scarce imports of industrial supplies has further constrained output growth. Under these circumstances, policy was dominated by attempts to avoid the social turmoil experienced in Poland from the beginning of the decade and in most of the other countries in 1989. In the majority of countries, a deterioration of the capital stock (section (iii) (a) below) has been tolerated in preference to cuts in consumption levels as a now long-term aspect of resource allocation policy. This has continued even into the most recent years for which data are available.

The task for the policy-makers of the future is complicated by the very small room for manoeuvre now available for choosing alternative resource allocation options. The high level of foreign debt in several countries will call for the further allocation of scarce resources to foreign creditors. Living standards are still well below those in the developed market economies. There is a clear need for the refurbishment of basic health and other social services. Productivity levels and the quality as well as the quantity and range of goods produced are falling progressively behind world market standards. Problems on this scale call for a large investment effort. This is at present constrained not only by resource shortfalls but also by the fact that in none of the countries concerned is the full range of mechanisms yet in place to ensure that investment resources are used more rationally than in the past (section (iii) (b) below). Education and training budgets alone will need to be expanded considerably if a new generation of managers in all spheres of business life are to operate satisfactorily under the new conditions now facing them.

(b) Standard of living in 1989 and early 1990

When the pace of NMP growth continued to slacken in 1989 much more strongly than envisaged in the annual plans, two distinctly *different policy options* were implemented in the seven countries reviewed here. The perceptible underfulfilment of the main output targets (NMP) in Bulgaria and the German Democratic Republic was immediately reflected in slower growth in the quantitative indicators of living standards (table 3.3.3). By contrast, wage and income growth in Hungary, Poland and the Soviet Union were allowed to remain unchanged or even continue rising despite stagnating or falling production levels. These reported income gains were to a large extent inflationary in Poland and the Soviet Union. In the case of Hungary, their unplanned rise was caused by particular circumstances. (The developments in these three countries will be discussed in more detail below.) In Czechoslovakia, rather weak output growth was anticipated by the annual plan and no special actions were required to adjust consumption downward. At the time of writing only scanty information was available about developments in Romania for the years 1988-1989. Judging from the data released on wages and retail sales at current prices, it is almost certain that real incomes must have fallen or at the best stagnated in the last two years.

Although figures in table 3.3.3 are assumed to reflect real changes for all countries, in the case of the Soviet Union and Poland the underlying price deflators are rather questionable. As explained at greater length in section (iv) below, the Soviet statistical authorities still do not possess measurement methods or the necessary observation network to monitor price changes. An additional deficiency recently revealed is that the nominal retail trade aggregate includes a sizeable amount of

---

definition the balances on invisibles, which are included in the NMP produced/NMP used difference. In some cases too, differences may reflect varying approaches to the calculation of main statistical aggregates. In the Soviet Union, for example, visible trade balances do not coincide with either the sign or the direction of change in the difference between NMP used and NMP produced for many of the years since 1970. This indicates that the differences in coverage mentioned above are not the only source of discrepancies.

TABLE 3.3.2
NMP levels by broad category of demand, 1981-1989
(Indices, 1980 = 100)

	Average 1981-1985	1985	1986	1987	1988	1989
Bulgaria						
Accumulation	112	113	140	125	130	..
Consumption	113	122	126	132	137	..
NMP used	113	120	130	130	135	..
NMP produced	113	120	126	133	136	135
Czechoslovakia						
Accumulation	71	68	77	76	69	..
Consumption	105	110	114	118	124	..
NMP used	97	100	105	108	110	112
NMP produced	104	109	112	114	117	119
German Democratic Republic						
Accumulation	85	86	90	95	98	..
Consumption	106	113	118	122	126	..
NMP used	101	106	110	115	119	..
NMP produced	114	125	130	135	139	141
Hungary						
Accumulation	68	48	59	60	59	57 *
Consumption	105	107	109	113	109	107 *
NMP used	98	96	99	102	99	96
NMP produced	106	107	108	112	112	110
Poland						
Accumulation	74	82	86	84	95	..
Consumption	92	96	101	103	106	..
NMP used	87	92	97	99	103	104
NMP produced	90	96	101	103	108	108
Romania						
Accumulation	76	75	..	..	..	..
Consumption	106	116	..	..	..	..
NMP used	96	101	..	..	..	..
NMP produced	112	124	133	140	144	144
Soviet Union						
Accumulation	.. (128)	.. (138)	.. (137)	.. (133)	.. (144)	..
Consumption	.. (114)	.. (121)	.. (124)	.. (128)	.. (135)	..
NMP used	110 (117)	115 (125)	117 (127)	118 (129)	123 (136)	..
NMP produced	111 (117)	117 (125)	120 (127)	122 (130)	127 (137)	130

Source: ECE/DEAP Common Data Base based on national statistics.

Note: All data in constant prices except those in brackets (Soviet Union only) which are in current prices.

a 1980 figure was negative (i.e., a balance of trade deficit) but was positive in later years/period shown.

goods actually sold to enterprises, institutions and co-operatives. If this component is eliminated, the *nominal* growth of retail sales to the household sector in 1989 falls to 4.5 per cent (as against the 10.2 per cent reported for total sales),[221] which in real terms (deflated at the official price index) means an increase of some 2 per cent — i.e., 5 percentage points less than shown in table 3.3.3.

In Poland, the problems derived not so much from measurement techniques but from the combined effects of rampant inflation and growing shortages on consumer markets. In 1989, as price inflation accelerated, nominal wages temporarily rose faster than the cost of living index. In reality this meant little for Polish consumers because of the overall deterioration in the supply situation. The 9 per cent reported real wage growth may be arithmetically correct as a reflection of the increased potential purchasing power of wages,[222] but amidst growing shortages this was not a realisable welfare gain. Remnants of rationing and absolute shortages continued to hold down consumption rather than prices, most of which continued to be controlled in 1989. The real value of the resulting forced savings, on the other hand, was rapidly absorbed by the continuing inflation.

In Hungary, the apparent contradiction between negative output growth and rising real incomes is explained by an increase in social benefits which overcompensated for inflation. In 1989, the cost of living rose by 17 per cent, whilst pension payments, family and child allowance grew by 21, 44 and 21 per cent respectively. Beyond this registered rise in real incomes, there is another element of consumption which is officially estimated, but does not appear in the national accounts. The indicator of *consumption of the Hungarian population* is a net estimate which makes allowance both for the consumption of foreigners in Hungary (which is excluded) and for the purchases and the con-

---

[221] V. N. Kirichenko, "Vernut' doverie statistike" (Give back credibility to statistics), *Kommunist*, 1990, No.3. p.23.

[222] With accelerating inflation, precise measurement of price changes becomes increasingly difficult since the reported figures (a 254 per cent rise the cost of living and a 286 per cent increase in nominal wages) are subject to bigger measurement errors.

TABLE 3.3.3

Output and standard of living, 1986-1990
(Annual percentage change)

	1986	1987	1988	1989	Plan/ National projection 1990
Bulgaria					
NMP produced	5.3	5.1	2.4	-0.4	..
Real wages [a]	1.6	4.3	3.7	-1.2	..
Real incomes [b]	2.8	4.0	3.4	-2.4	..
Retail trade sales	3.5	3.9	2.0	0.3	..
Czechoslovakia					
NMP produced	2.6	2.1	2.4	1.3*	2.2
Real wages [a]	1.1	1.9	2.1	3.8	0.9*
Real incomes [b]	2.6	3.6	3.7	1.6	..
Retail trade sales	1.7	2.9	4.7	2.3	..
German Dem.Rep.					
NMP produced	4.3	3.6	2.8	2.0	..
Real wages [a]	3.5	5.4	2.9	1.6	..
Real incomes [b]	5.7	4.6	4.1	..	..
Retail trade sales	4.1	3.6	3.9	1.5	..
Hungary					
NMP produced	0.9	4.1	0.3	-2 *	-*
Real wages [a]	1.9	-0.4	-4.9	-	-(2.0-2.5)
Real incomes [b]	2.4	0.7	-0.9	2	-(1.0-1.5)
Retail trade sales	3.7	5.3	-6.5	-2.3	..
Poland					
NMP produced	4.9	1.9	4.9	-	..
Real wages [a]	2.7	-3.5	14.4	9.1	..
Real incomes [b]	1.7	0.8	13.2	..	..
Retail trade sales	5.7	5.0	5.2	-7.1	..
Romania					
NMP produced	7.3	4.8	3.2	..	9.5
Real wages [a]	1.1	0.6	2.6 [c]	..	..
Real incomes [b]	..	..	..	..	..
Retail trade sales	2.3	2.8	0.5 [c]	1.6 [c]	..
Soviet Union					
NMP produced	2.3	1.6	4.4	2.4	4
Real wages [a]	1.0	1.8	5.9	6.7	..
Real incomes [b]	0.1	0.9	3.2	..	5.8
Retail trade sales	0.5	0.9	4.9	7.6	10.1 [c]

Source: National statistics.

Note: Retail trade measured at constant prices unless otherwise indicated.

a As defined in Appendix table B.5.
b Per capita.
c Nominal.

As noted in an earlier edition of this publication, a substantial improvement has occurred since 1980 in most of the seven countries reviewed with respect to the stock and supply of *consumer durables*.[224] For 1989 a varied picture appears when annual retail sales figures are compared (table 3.3.4). In Czechoslovakia, the supply of cars and television sets fell slightly, while in Poland there were improvements in these categories. It should be mentioned, however, that in some countries a considerable private import of western cars, televisions and refrigerators occurred in 1989 which is not reflected in the table. Hungarian citizens, for example, imported 68,000 cars in 1989 alone.[225] This type of import, not registered within the domestic retail trade statistics, has played an important role in Poland for many years. Very recently, private purchases of western cars began to play a role in the German Democratic Republic as well.

In the first two months of 1990, imbalances on consumer markets have increased considerably in the German Democratic Republic, Romania and the Soviet Union. In these countries *wages and incomes* rose very fast and the supply of goods did not keep pace. Nor could it have done, even under normal circumstances. This applies first of all to the Soviet Union, where cash incomes reportedly grew by 14-15 per cent in the first two months of the year.[226] By contrast, the first two months saw *production on the decline* in these countries. In Romania, for example, capacity utilization was only 80 per cent in January. Output definitely fell in the German Democratic Republic and a contraction in key areas of the Soviet economy cannot be excluded. The natural response was panic buying, financed from *dissavings* (depletion of saving accounts). All these developments mutually reinforced their individually detrimental impact on the markets.

In the German Democratic Republic, money incomes and retail sales rose by more than 10 and 8 per cent respectively in early 1990 in comparison with their level a year earlier. The stock of savings fell by 1 per cent relative to the 1989 end-year figure. Further wage rises, totalling 3.6 billion marks, effective from 1 March 1990, have been announced.

In Romania, the authorities injected 38 billion lei of additional purchasing power into the economy in the form of wage and income adjustments in January 1990, and another 22 billion lei was added in February 1990.[227] In the light of previously accumulated imbalances, these new measures are potentially inflationary — a fact which seriously worries the Romanian authorities.[228] As far as the present state of the consumer

sumption of Hungarian tourists *abroad*. As it happened, the "private imports" of Hungarian tourists in 1989 attained unprecedently high levels. These purchases, or more precisely that part which was declared to the customs offices, was added to the volume of domestic consumption of the Hungarian population.[223] Thus the official estimates indicate that *total* consumption of the Hungarian population rose by about 2 per cent in 1989 — even while there was a contraction of *domestic* retail sales.

---

223 In line with accepted practices among the CMEA countries, Hungarian national accounts reflect *domestic* production and utilization only.

224 Romania may be an exception, but no figures are available for this country to measure changes since 1980. For a review of developments in the other countries in the 1980-1986 period, see United Nations Economic Commission for Europe, *Economic Survey of Europe in 1987-1988*, New York, 1988, pp.187-189.

225 *Népszabadság*, 15 February 1990.

226 This figure was disclosed by Professor N. Petrakov, economic adviser to President Gorbachev. *Financial Times*, 17 March 1990, p.2.

227 Statement by General V. Stanculescu (Minister of the National Economy), BBC, *Summary of World Broadcast*, 10 February 1990.

228 As explained by I. Iliescu (Chairman of the Provisional National Unity Council), strategy is based upon the assumption that increased monetary incentives will help to boost production at a faster rate than prices. "The economy cannot offer enough commodities to absorb the population's larger incomes. We also

TABLE 3.3.4

Retail trade sales of main consumer durable goods, 1987-1989
(Thousands)

Country/years	Cars	TV sets	Washing machines and driers	Refrigerators
Bulgaria				
1987	56.0	303	222	124
1988	44.1	287	220	122
1989	..	..	..	..
Czechoslovakia				
1987	110	517	360	526
1988	135	577	370	571
1989	134	507	..	..
German Dem.Rep.				
1987	161	527	369 [a]	622
1988	163	594	374 [a]	639
1989	166	..	..	649 *
Hungary				
1987	140	487	455	484 [b]
1988	128	407	430	417 [b]
1989	136	395 *	400 *	551 *
Poland				
1987	163 [c]	785	1 274	916
1988	165 [c]	908	1 215	974
1989	170 [c]	1 068	1 186	830
Romania				
1987	..	..	..	..
1988	..	..	..	..
1989	..	..	..	..
Soviet Union				
1987	1 790 [d]	8 190	5 168	4 597
1988	2 014 [d]	8 409	5 536	4 793
1989	..	8 830	6 034	5 224

Source: *Statisticheskii ezhegodnik stran-chlenov SEV 1989*, (CMEA statistical yearbook), Moscow, 1989, pp.323-329. National sources for 1989.

[a] Excluding driers.
[b] Excluding deep freezers.
[c] Excluding cars sold for convertible currencies ("internal export").
[d] Including second-hand cars.

markets is concerned, the figures released for January 1990 probably give an indication of the shortages which had previously prevailed. In aggregate terms, retail sales rose by 10 per cent (presumably at current prices). The supply of certain key products, such as veal, sugar, butter and cheese, was increased by 60-80 per cent in comparison with January 1989. This was achieved by withholding exports and increasing imports. With respect to milk, bread and eggs and other staples, little or no improvement was reported.[229]

The state of the domestic food market deteriorated also in Bulgaria at the beginning of 1990. In the first two months of the year, shortages of meat and meat products were strongly felt.[230]

In Poland, administrative price control was gradually lifted in the course of 1989. A last push was given to this process in January 1990, when subsidies were almost entirely eliminated in the production and consumption sphere alike. Within weeks, the purchasing power of the population was reduced by 20-30 per cent in real terms. This was sufficient (temporarily at least) to liquidate excess demand on the consumer markets. What had been a sellers' market for decades became a buyers' market.

(c) Investment in 1989

As noted above, investment expenditures since the mid-1970s have come under considerable pressure from a combination of decelerating output growth rates, shifts in real resources to the foreign balance to offset deteriorations in the terms of trade and increasing debt servicing obligations. They were further squeezed by decisions to maintain certain social priorities and hence to avoid, to the extent possible, cuts in the standard of living. This has not always been avoided — notably in Poland, but also in Hungary — and, as far as can be seen from the incomplete data available, in Romania.

These developments were only partly anticipated. Almost all countries planned slower investment growth in 1981-1985. However, absolute levels fell certainly in four east European countries and probably in five (table 3.3.5 and chart 3.3.1). Actual performance, in fact, reflected a bigger impact of resource constraints than had been expected — especially in Hungary and Romania.

The volume of investment expenditures fell in all east European countries but Czechoslovakia in 1989, as already noted. In the Soviet Union, it rose by about half of one per cent only. The slump followed what can now be considered a short-lived recovery in most countries since 1985.[231]

Investment data for Bulgaria, which are available only in nominal terms, in fact show capital formation rising steadily during most of the 1980s at rates averaging some 4-5 per cent annually. However, at least part of this may have been absorbed by price changes. The downturn in 1989 by 8 per cent in nominal value represents an abrupt break in this trend. In Czechoslovakia, despite a slow-down compared with 1988, investment is still growing considerably faster than in the first half of the decade. In the German Democratic Republic, the recovery after the middle years of the decade appears to have come to an end. In Hungary, where investment declined in almost every year since 1979, a further fall in 1989 leaves the level some 15 per cent below the previous peak year of 1979. In Poland, a fairly strong recovery since the middle years of this decade leaves investment still some 20 per cent below the peak year of 1978. In Romania, investment growth has been very low since 1983 even in current prices and

---

took certain measures to boost prices for foodstuffs so as to stimulate the agricultural sector. Certainly, this accentuates inflationist phenomena. Nevertheless we count of a growing volume of foodstuffs". Interview in *Romania Libera*, 27 February 1990, as summarized in BBC *Summary of World Broadcast*, 1 March 1990.

[229] Comisia Nationala pentru Statistica, *Buletin de informare publica*, 1990, No.1.

[230] Press conference of Minister for Trade and Services E. Marinova, as reported in BBC, *Summary of World Broadcasts*, 15 March 1990.

[231] It is, however, difficult to document the underlying trends in Bulgaria and Romania because the publication of constant price series was discontinued for the years after 1983.

TABLE 3.3.5

Gross fixed investment, 1976-1990 a

(Annual percentage change)

	1976-1980	1981-1985	1986-1989	1988	1989	Plan 1989	Plan 1990	Five-year plan 1981-1985	Five-year plan 1986-1990
Bulgaria	6.8	4.5	5.1	2.4	-7.7	..	..	2	6.1
Czechoslovakia	5.8	-0.4	2.2	4.1	2.1	-3.5	-4.1	-1	2.1
German Dem.Rep.	4.9	-0.1	3.6	8.2	-4.0	..	..	-0.6	1.4
Hungary	5.5	-2.0	0.7	-7.2	-2.0	1.5	..	-	0.8
Poland	6.5	-7.4	5.7	5.4	-2.0	5.2	..	..	4.4
Romania	10.9	1.3	1.2	-1.3	..	4.2	12.4	5.2	3.6
Eastern Europe	6.9	-1.3	2 *	2.6	-2.7 b	..	..	1.7 c	3.4
Soviet Union	5.2	3.4	5.5	6.2	0.6	4.1	-10*	2.1	4.3
Eastern Europe and Soviet Union	5.6	1.9	4.9*	5.3	-0.1	..	..	2 b	4.1

Source: ECE secretariat Common Data Base, based on national statistics, plans and plan fulfilment reports and direct communication to the ECE secretariat. National data are aggregated by means of weights derived from CMEA investigations.

a All data on sub-periods refer to the annualized change between the annual average in the period indicated relative to the annual average of the preceding five years.
b Excluding Romania.
c Excluding Poland.

it is likely that this cloaks a considerable fall in real terms; in January 1990, it was was reported that investment stood at only 38.1 per cent of its level twelve months earlier.[232] Soviet capital expenditures, which also grew fairly strongly during the early 1980s, accelerated during the early years of *perestroika*, but this upswing did not persist into 1989.

In general, the decline in eastern investments in 1981-1985 was reversed in 1986-1989 as a whole, which witnessed a somewhat faster than planned investment growth in most countries. However, this was accompanied by a noticeable acceleration in investment goods imports from the OECD countries. An attempt was made to raise the previously falling share of imports in total machinery and equipment investment which occurred from the late 1970s in most of the seven countries concerned. In fact, in the earlier years of this decade only the Soviet Union and Hungary had succeeded in maintaining this share at the same level as in the early 1970s.[233] Even in those countries, and especially in the Soviet Union, it has fallen away in the last few years.[234] Rising investment goods imports from the west appear to have been one of the main elements in the further rise of east European hard currency debt since the middle of this decade and as such proved to be unsustainable in the absence of any improvement in export performance.

The investment ratio (gross fixed investment as a share of NMP produced) fell sharply in all east European countries but Bulgaria during the 1980s; it remained constant in the Soviet Union. The declines in most east European countries were reversed in the middle of this decade, but not enough to offset the preceding falls (table 3.3.6). The steepest declines between 1980 and 1985 were in Hungary and Romania (9 percentage points), followed by the German Democratic Republic (8 percentage points), Poland (6 percentage points) and Czechoslovakia (5 points). While the recovery in investment after 1985 reversed the declining trend of the investment ratio, it is still considerably lower in eastern Europe as a whole than in the 1970s. Only Bulgaria and the Soviet Union have succeeded in maintaining the investment effort more or less in line with the growth of total resources.

The distinct deceleration and even decline in investment activity in eastern Europe and the Soviet Union in 1989 represents in part the slower growth of output and available resources, in part difficulties in adjusting to new conditions of doing business but also, perhaps for the first time, confidence factors. The few countries which have published annual economic plans (except Romania, the plan for which was produced by the previous government) indicate a further decline in 1990. In the Soviet Union the fall could be as much as 10 per cent if the target given in the plan document for 1990 is taken at face value.[235] The new situation involves considerable uncertainty as to the likely future appropriateness of new investments — notably with regard to the supply situation in the next few months or even years, as well as the future movement of prices and hence of enterprise profitability. For the first time,

---

[232] *Buletin de informare publica*, 1990, No.1.

[233] Investment goods imported from the OECD countries in 1986-1987 accounted for about one third of Hungarian investment in machinery and equipment in 1987, 6-7 per cent in the Soviet Union and probably no more than 3-4 per cent in Romania where the fall in such imports from the late 1970s has been very large. The Hungarian share probably represents an upper limit for other east European countries; the German Democratic Republic is probably on a par with Hungary given that its *per capita* imports of such goods are the same ($111). In Czechoslovakia, investment goods imports amounted to $101, in Bulgaria to $79, in Poland and the Soviet Union to $29 and in Romania to $12 *per capita*, all at 1980 prices. See United Nations Economic Commission for Europe, *Economic Bulletin for Europe*, Vol.41, New York, 1989, pp.78 and 83 (table 4.5).

[234] United Nations Economic Commission for Europe, *Economic Bulletin for Europe*, vol.41, New York, 1989, pp.80 (table 4.3) and 84 (chart 4.2).

[235] The plan law refers to a figure of 196.9 billion roubles (*Pravda*, 11 November 1989). This compares with outlays in 1989 of 219.5 billion roubles at "estimate prices" of 1 January 1984 (*Pravda*, 28 January 1990).

CHART 3.3.1

Actual and planned NMP, gross fixed capital formation, and investment ratio (actual and planned), 1980-1990
(Indices, 1978-1982 = 100)

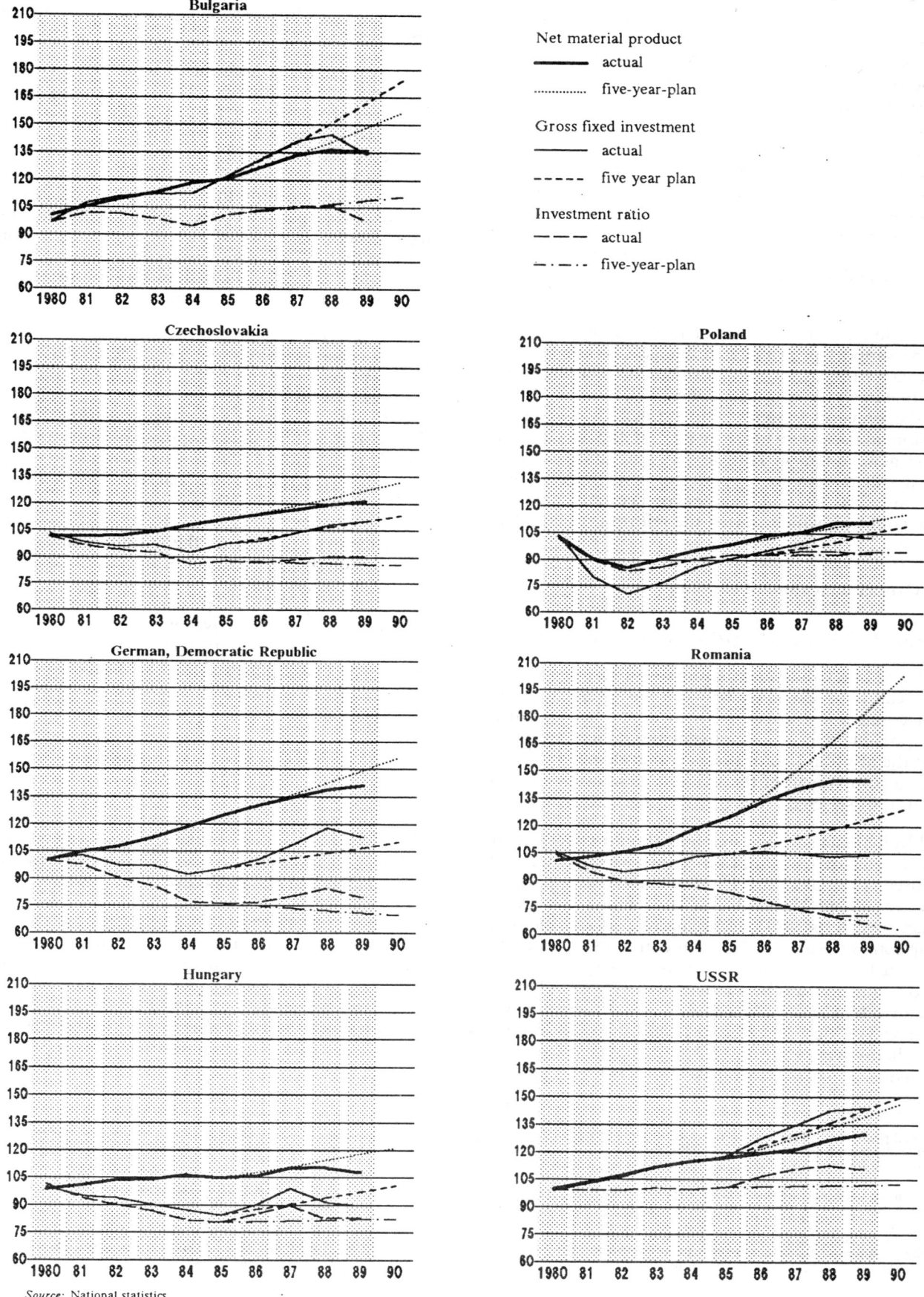

Source: National statistics.

TABLE 3.3.6

Investment ratios [a]

(Per cent)

	1980	1985	1989	Plan [b] 1990
Bulgaria	33.9	35.5	34.4	38.8
Czechoslovakia	36.2	31.4	32.5	30.6
German Dem.Rep.	33.9	25.9	27.0	23.8
Hungary	38.1	28.8	28.7	29.5
Poland	32.1	25.8	26.0	26.3
Romania	43.8	34.5	29.3	26.1
Soviet Union	30.6	30.3	33.4	30.8

Source: ECE secretariat Common Data Base.

[a] Ratio of gross fixed investment to NMP produced in constant prices.
[b] Based on five-year plan figures assuming constant rates of growth of investment and NMP between 1985 and 1990.

it is no longer guaranteed that loss-making enterprises will be supported by the state budget. While the pace of progress towards a market-oriented economy is not the same in all the countries concerned, in none of them has the previous system of investment financing and decision making remained intact. If the implications of the new system in Hungary, Poland and the Soviet Union still remain to be perfected and then digested, there are even fewer guidelines for decision makers in those countries which started the reform process later.

(ii) Overall indicators of consumption

(a) Levels of consumption and consumer prices

No fully reliable direct comparison of consumption levels can be made either between the seven east European countries or between them and other countries. One possible way to circumvent the difficulties arising from the arbitrariness of prices and exchange rates is to make a comparison of the working time needed to buy one unit of selected types of consumer goods.

Ideally, such an investigation should cover a common basket of consumption goods which could then be used to make direct inter-country comparisons. However, there are problems in defining a common basket which is also representative, given that consumption patterns vary between countries — either because of local tradition or because of large differences in consumption levels. This is clearly a problem between western and eastern countries, but there are likely to be wide differences also between the eastern countries themselves. In any case, data availability limits the scope of such an exercise for most of the seven eastern countries. The limited exercise undertaken here rests on the indicators presented in table 3.3.7. The data included are incomplete and their precision and inter-country comparability cannot always be guaranteed. They are however, adequate for the purpose of illustration.[236]

As expected, the amount of work required to purchase selected consumer goods is considerably higher in all the eastern countries than it is in the Federal Republic, with the notable exception of bread. This commodity is traditionally inexpensive in the socialist countries, due to the symbolic value attached to it. By contrast, other commodities, which are often considered luxuries, such as coffee, colour television, motor cars and petrol, are priced in a discriminatory manner, meaning that the average worker has to labour disproportionally longer for them than the countries' overall development level would imply.

Another often mentioned impediment to cross-country comparisons is the great dissimilarity of the relative price structures between eastern and western countries. In order to illustrate this, the retail price of 1 kg of pork was taken as unity and the prices of all other commodities were expressed as a fraction or multiple of it (table 3.3.8).[237] The table shows that relative price structures differ not only in comparisons between eastern and western countries, but also among eastern countries themselves. Relative to pork, bread is rather inexpensive in all the countries under review, and particularly so in Czechoslovakia. Considerable country variation can also be seen in the relative prices of processed agricultural produce, such as tea, coffee and cigarettes. The relative price of certain consumer durables (motor car, colour television or washing powder) is extremely high in Poland, both in comparison with the Federal Republic and with the other eastern countries.[238]

(b) Origins of new imbalances

The first part of the following analysis limits itself to the presentation of some of the main sources of imbalances on consumer markets. Two conventionally applied indicators will be used as a proxy for measuring excess demand at the retail level.

They are, first, the *ratio of money incomes to retail trade turnover*, which shows how much money remains in the hands of the population each year over and above the amount spent in retail trade, and second, the *ratio of saving deposits to annual retail sales*, which indicates the accumulated purchasing power of the population. In fact, these indicators measure *potential* excess demand only.

---

[236] Retail prices were taken from official statistics whenever possible. The gaps were filled by reasonable estimates provided by country experts. In all cases, when officially quoted prices allowed for multiple choice reflecting quality differentials, the cheapest quality product was always taken into account. ILO data were used data for the hours of work (see footnote to table 3.3.7).

[237] As in the previous case, the Federal Republic of Germany was chosen as the comparator country. The reservations expressed concerning the data in table 3.3.7 also apply here and the conclusions suggested by this comparison should therefore also be treated with caution.

[238] One Polish author argues that in past decades these disproportions of relative prices (as compared with other countries) contributed substantially to the general disequilibrium of Polish consumer markets, attributing it to an excessively low absolute level of consumer prices. See L. Podkaminer, "Estimates of Disequilibria in Poland's Consumer Markets, 1965-1978", *The Review of Economics and Statistics*, 1982, vol.64. pp. 423-431.

TABLE 3.3.7

Comparison of work time required to purchase selected consumer goods in 1988

(Hours of work required to buy 1 unit of consumer good in the Federal Republic of Germany = 1.0)

Item	Unit	Bulgaria	Czecho-slovakia	German Democratic Republic	Hungary	Poland	Soviet Union	Yugoslavia	Federal Republic of Germany
Food									
Pork	kg	4.1	3.4	1.3	2.4	2.0	2.7	4.7	1.0
Beef	kg	5.9	3.7	1.0	2.6	1.7	3.0	6.2	1.0
Chicken	kg	5.4	4.7	2.8	3.5	2.8	5.5	5.4	1.0
Egg	piece	5.5	3.8	2.4	2.6	6.6	4.2	5.4	1.0
Milk	litre	2.7	2.0	0.5	1.8	0.7	2.9	3.1	1.0
Butter	kg	6.0	3.6	1.9	2.5	3.5	4.0	6.9	1.0
Bread (white)	kg	0.9	0.5	0.4	0.5	0.5	0.8	0.6	1.0
Sugar	kg	7.1	3.3	1.4	3.2	3.6	4.5	4.7	1.0
Potato	kg	3.7	1.1	0.3	3.2	..	1.6	6.5	1.0
Apple	kg	1.6	1.6	1.2	1.4	..	7.1	2.6	1.0
Wine	litre	2.9	5.8	0.5	2.8	10.6	13.4	2.5	1.0
Beer	litre	3.8	2.0	1.3	2.7	7.0	2.7	8.4	1.0
Coffee	kg	18.2	10.4	6.8	7.2	17.8	11.3	8.5	1.0
Tea	kg	..	3.2	1.0	0.7	0.7	2.4	..	1.0
Cigarettes	box	1.7	1.0	1.7	0.7	0.6	1.4	..	1.0
Non-food									
Men's suit (winter)	piece	2.2	5.4	2.0	2.5	3.7	3.1	..	1.0
Men's shoes (leather)	pair	1.2	1.2	1.2	1.8	2.0	1.7	2.4	1.0
Motor car	piece	4.0	2.5	2.4	2.3	9.2	3.6	..	1.0
Colour television	piece	5.3	6.6	5.6	4.0	13.4	4.6	..	1.0
Heating oil	litre	8.4	..	..	5.7	..	..	..	1.0
Washing powder	kg	1.5	..	2.6	4.1	5.1	4.2	..	1.0
Petrol for cars	litre	8.1	7.0	2.6	5.7	5.0	4.0	..	1.0

Source: ECE secretariat estimates based on national statistics (wages and prices); ILO, *Yearbook of labour statistics 1988* and secretariat estimates (hours of work).

TABLE 3.3.8

Retail price relatives of selected consumer goods in 1988

(Price of 1 kg of pork = 1.00)

Item	Unit	Bulgaria	Czecho-slovakia	German Democratic Republic	Hungary	Poland	Soviet Union	Yugoslavia	Federal Republic of Germany
Food									
Pork	kg	1.00	1.00	1.00	1.00	1.00	1.00	1.00	1.00
Beef	kg	1.33	1.0	0.73	0.98	0.75	1.01	1.21	0.92
Chicken	kg	0.63	0.65	1.00	0.68	0.64	0.93	0.54	0.47
Egg	piece	0.03	0.03	0.04	0.03	0.07	0.04	0.03	0.02
Milk	litre	0.08	0.07	0.04	0.08	0.04	0.12	0.07	0.11
Butter	kg	1.20	0.87	1.20	0.85	1.40	1.18	1.18	0.81
Bread (white)	kg	0.09	0.06	0.13	0.09	0.11	0.12	0.05	0.41
Sugar	kg	0.31	0.17	0.19	0.24	0.31	0.29	0.18	0.18
Potato	kg	0.08	0.03	0.02	0.12	..	0.06	0.13	0.09
Apple	kg	0.10	0.13	0.25	0.15	..	0.69	0.15	0.27
Wine	litre	0.25	0.61	0.14	0.42	1.83	1.73	0.19	0.35
Beer	litre	0.17	0.11	0.18	0.20	0.61	0.17	0.32	0.18
Coffee	kg	7.50	5.22	8.75	5.09	14.53	6.92	3.04	1.67
Tea	kg	..	3.70	3.00	1.11	1.32	3.46	..	3.88
Cigarettes	box	0.16	0.11	0.50	0.10	0.11	0.19	..	0.37
Non-food									
Men's suit (winter)	piece	16.67	50.00	48.75	32.27	57.13	34.92	..	31.30
Men's shoes (leather)	pair	4.17	4.78	12.50	10.45	13.85	8.48	7.02	13.87
Motor car	piece	1 667	1 256	3 125	1 632	7 547	2 249	..	1 687
Colour television	piece	187	283	612	241	943	242	..	144
Heating oil	litre	0.06	..	..	0.07	..	..	..	0.03
Washing powder	kg	0.13	..	0.69	0.59	0.85	0.52	..	0.34
Petrol for cars	litre	0.19	0.20	0.19	0.22	0.23	0.14	..	0.09

Source: See table 3.3.7.

It can be seen that annual money incomes of the population in 1970-1989 have regularly exceeded the value of goods purchased in the course of the year by a margin of 20-40 per cent (chart 3.3.2). Of course, not all of this can be considered as excess demand, since a wide range of goods is sold to the population outside the retail trade network. In addition, savings constitute a normal part of a complex allocation system. However, major ups and downs in the rates usually indicate abnormal tensions. The chart depicting Polish developments supports this argument. With this exception, the ratio of money incomes to retail sales shows considerable stability in the other countries. It is worth noting, however, that the ratio has an upward drift in all countries save Bulgaria and Hungary.

The accumulated unspent purchasing power of households (saving deposits) relative to the value of annual retail trade sales has also tended to rise. In this respect Poland constitutes a notable exception for reasons explained later. The magnitude of the savings-related ratio is in fact more important than the ratio of money incomes to retail trade turnover in determining the size of potential excess demand. It is very large in the German Democratic Republic and Bulgaria, and it has also been growing steadily in the Soviet Union. In contrast, it appears to be less significant, even stable or decreasing, in Hungary and Poland.

These inter-country variations suggest that generalizations should be cautious. It appears, for example, that up to late 1989, reasonable market balance prevailed in the German Democratic Republic, though the importance of accumulated purchasing power as compared with the other countries has indicated a *potential* threat for several years.[239] Similarly, while current money incomes in Czechoslovakia exceed the value of annual retail sales by as much as in the Soviet Union, the magnitudes of excess demand in the two countries are clearly not the same.

The actual size of excess demand – and consequently the extent of shortages on retail trade markets – is also influenced by factors other than those depicted in chart 3.3.2. Firstly, it is obvious that the *price expectations* of households are of crucial importance – a point that will be taken up later in the context of the recent developments. Secondly, the size of the consumer market outside the scope of the retail trade system also influences the development of excess demand. In this respect two factors appear to have been important: the market for paid services and the market for privately-owned dwellings, reflecting development levels in general and the level of urbanization in particular. Since these aspects have already been analysed in earlier editions of this publication,[240] there is no need to repeat these findings.

During the past two years, however, additional forces have influenced the size of excess demand. Liberalization of travel regulations and the accompanying relaxation in foreign exchange regulations and parities had major effects on spending behaviour first in Poland, then in Hungary and more recently in the German Democratic Republic. Spending behaviour was influenced by at least three different motives. Firstly, the liberalization of travel regulations increased expenditures related to travel itself. Secondly, citizens of the three above-mentioned countries spent large amounts of convertible currencies, attracted by a wider range of goods than they were accustomed to, frequently at lower prices. Finally, the motive of capital flight has to be mentioned. Part of it was legal, in that the convertible currency equivalent of domestic money was deposited within the home country of the citizens, but significant amounts may simply have disappeared into illegal channels.

As inflation has gathered momentum amidst the circumstances of acute shortages on consumer markets, new issues have been emerging for which the traditional centrally planned system has no tested remedies. They include the growing importance of outlets for the disposal of consumer goods outside the traditional retail trade system, the appearance of cash shortages which affected the settlement of internal payments, including wages, and the elimination of consumer subsidies as well as of some credit subsidies – notably for housing construction. These new issues are discussed below.

In the Soviet Union, the proportion of goods distributed outside the regular retail trade network has increased constantly. Table 3.3.9 displays the results of a public opinion survey carried in the second half of 1989, suggesting that as much as two fifths of food supplies might be provided in this way. Although the report from which the data have been taken did not indicate the size and composition of the sample or the methods of data collection, the figures are sufficient to indicate the approximate size of these alternative trade outlets.

The *segmentation of markets* has an important regional and therefore political aspect, too. As a reaction to growing shortages, various administrative measures were introduced in the three Baltic republics to protect local markets from tourists from the other republics coming to shop. Latvians, for example, have to show a special card before they may buy goods and food on a special list. A similar system has recently been introduced in Lithuania, while in Estonia such a system came into force as early as January 1989. Byelorussia subsequently followed suit. In Leningrad, the second largest city of the Soviet Union after Moscow, proof of domicile has been needed for shopping since January 1990.[241]

---

[239] This was noted in an earlier edition of this publication. See United Nations Economic Commission for Europe, *Economic Survey of Europe in 1987-1988*, New York, 1988, p.191.

[240] See *op.cit.*, pp.191-193.

[241] *Izvestiya*, 16 August 1989. (See BBC *Summary of World Broadcasts* 17 August 1989, 2 and 9 February 1990). These restrictions parallel those introduced in late 1988 and 1989 in each of the east European countries, banning exports of key consumer goods by individual visitors and tourists.

CHART 3.3.2

Consumer supplies and purchasing power of the population

- - - Ratio of money incomes of the population to retail trade turnover

——— Ratio of savings deposits to annual retail trade turnover

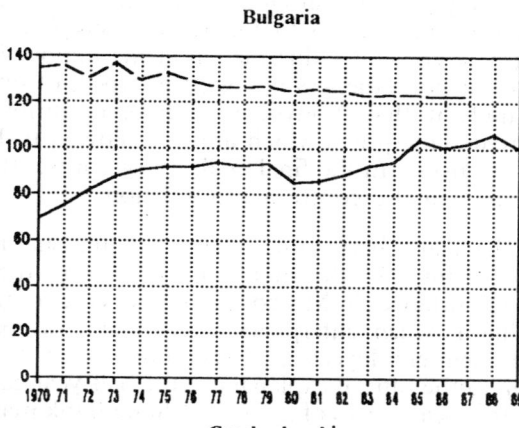
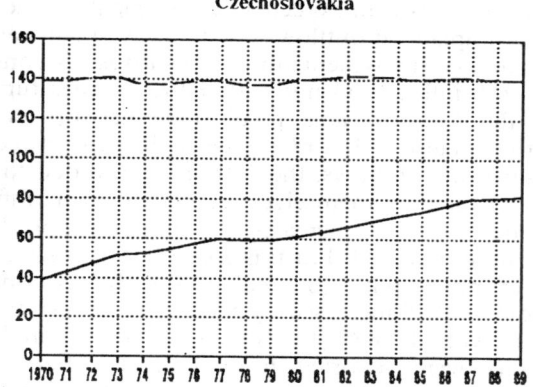
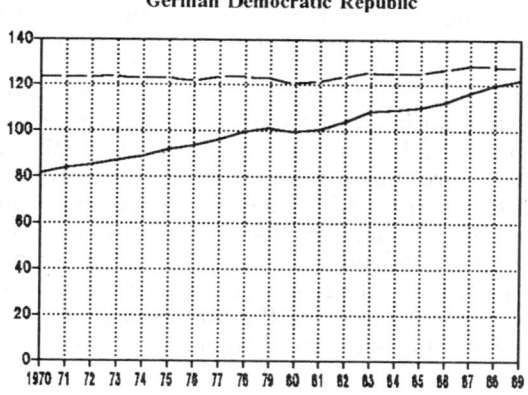
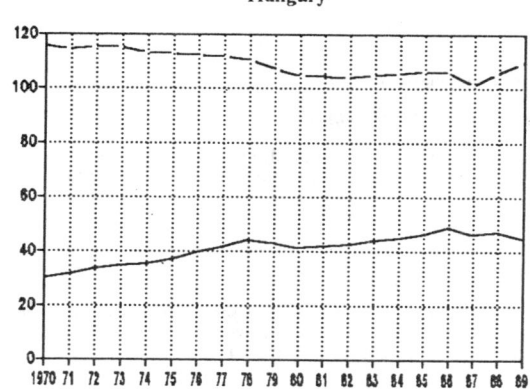
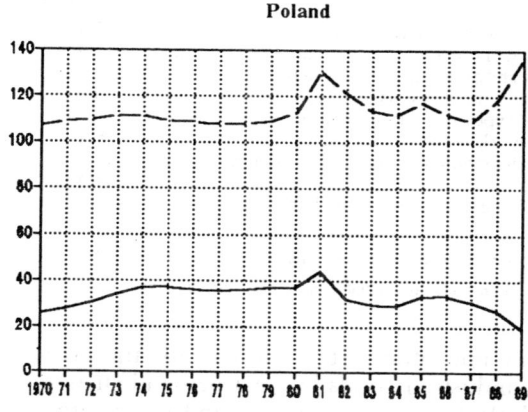
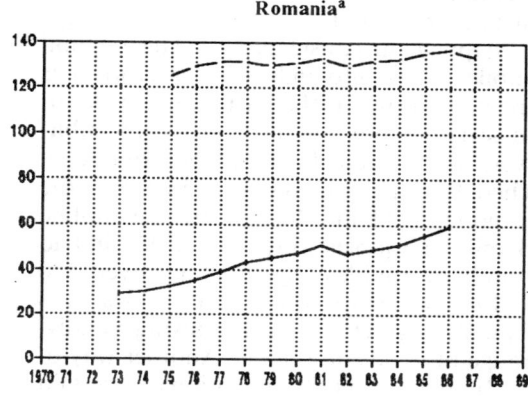
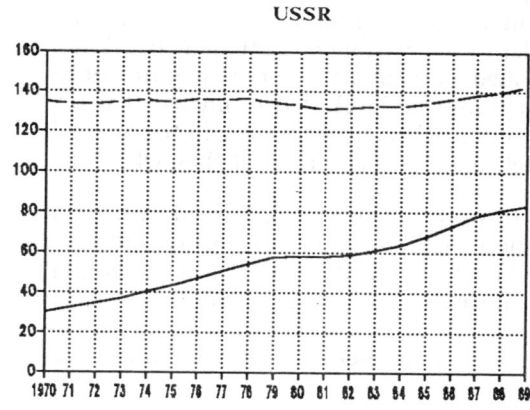

Source: ECE secretariat, based on national and international (CMEA, IMF) statistics.

[a] Money incomes cover the socialist sector only.

TABLE 3.3.9

Alternative channels of food supply in the Soviet Union
(Answer to a public opinion survey, in percentages)

Questions: Where and how do you buy food?	Share a
Advance orders at work place	7.4
Sales facilities at work place	15.9
In limited access shops at place of residence serving war veterans, invalids, etc.	9.0
Through various types of rationing cards distributed at work place	6.1
Rationing cards distributed at place of residence	18.2
Other channels	11.4
Not using any of the above-mentioned channels	40.7

Source: VTSIOM public opinion survey, published in *Ogonyek*, No.5, 1990.

a The figures do not add up to 100 due to the possibility of multiple choice.

In Moscow and other urban settlements, the practice of selling industrial goods in great demand such as footwear and clothing, television sets and refrigerators through out-of-store trade outlets (*vyezdnaya torgovlya*) has stepped up considerably. The method of sending mobile shops into industrial enterprises is certainly not new, although in the past quantifiable information was scarce or non-existent. A recent publication, however, sheds some light on the volume of goods dispatched through this system. In 1986, the total value of goods sold in Moscow by the mobile shops was 83 million roubles only. By 1987, it had risen to 200 million roubles, by 1988 to over 600 million and in 1989 it reached 1.6 billion roubles. It is not only the quantity which has been growing rapidly, but also the range of goods on offer.[242] Another way of selling goods is by issuing special invitations to certain big stores which are closed to other shoppers for those few hours. The proliferation of alternative distribution systems parallel to the existing retail trade network has, effectively, created as many as twenty new forms of rationing. At nation-wide level, it is estimated that one third of total sales reached the consumer in the first half of 1989 through these non-commercial channels.[243]

There are obvious advantages and disadvantages in these distribution methods. On the positive side, the equity aspect used to be mentioned. It was hoped that these various forms of rationing would better target certain social groups (e.g., factory workers in key industrial enterprises, war veterans). In addition, it was believed that rationing is a good way of minimizing corruption and speculation.[244] As far as the negative effects are concerned, Soviet experts usually emphasize two things. First, the resort to extraordinary measures in trade is in itself an additional impetus to panic purchases by the population at large. Once indiscriminate purchasing sets in,[245] any actual increase in supplies, as in the case of consumer durables, remains unnoticed. A smaller but none the less noteworthy aspect of out-of-store trade it that it involves additional turnover costs to trade enterprises which are not allowed to be reflected in prices. In the final analysis, of course, this cost increase will also contribute to inflation.

There have also been some other, quite unusual resulting problems. In the middle of 1989, e.g., there were several instances in Moscow and other cities of the Soviet Union, when enterprises were unable to pay wages to their employees as *banks ran out of cash*. According to the official explanation, the half-year cash plans for the local offices of the USSR State Bank made no provision for two unexpected developments. These were, first, unplanned outflows due to above-plan wage increases and cash payments to co-operatives. Second, planned cash inflows did not materialize as sales turnover in the Moscow area retail trade network was smaller than planned. In order to close the gap between cash inflows and outflows, the authorities reverted to a solution which they themselves recognized as harmful in the long run: they increased the money supply by printing more money.[246] For this and other reasons, the amount of money put into circulation in the economy as a whole in 1989 increased by more than 50 per cent compared with 1988.[247] In November 1989, similar phenomena were reported from Poland. Farmers waiting for payments for grain and meat met with with empty tills in the local banks. As farmers could not draw any money, they were prevented from paying their taxes on time, which reduced state budget receipts.[248]

Considerable consumer and other subsidies are one of the main vehicles used to achieve price stability on the consumer markets under central planning although their relative size differs from country to country. In 1988, the first year for which data with a certain degree of comparability became available, the German Democratic Republic, Poland and the Soviet Union appear to have particularly high degrees of consumer price subsidization (see table 3.3.10; no relevant data are available for Bulgaria and Romania).[249] Now, both

---

[242] For a detailed analysis of this phenomenon, see E. Kolesnikova, "Vyezdnaya torgovlya ... vsya vlast' talonam" (Out-of-store trade ... all power to the rationing cards), *Pravitel'stvenny vestnik*, No.6, 1990, pp.6-7.

[243] *Ibid*.

[244] In recent discussions, however, this second assumption was frequently questioned. See, e.g., E. Kolesnikova, *loc. cit*.

[245] The value of jewellery sales, for example, rose from 212 million roubles in 1985 to 1.8 billion roubles in 1989 (*ibid*.).

[246] See the text of a letter to the Moscow City Trade Union Council from A. Vlasov, Chairman of the RSFSR Council of Ministers. *Moskovskaya Pravda*, 27 July, 4 and 8 August 1989, as reported in BBC *Summary of World Broadcasts*, 25 August 1989 and *Trud*, 28 July 1989, as reported in BBC *Summary of World Broadcasts*, 11 August 1989.

[247] See Kirichenko, *op.cit*.

[248] See BBC *Summary of World Broadcasts*, 28 November 1989.

[249] In the Soviet Union, regular statistical coverage for such data still does not exist and figures quoted here from secondary sources should be treated with caution. In the German Democratic Republic, the expenditure side of the central budget has been published regularly for many years in a very detailed form. Moreover, the planning authorities used every opportunity to praise the practice of subsidization as an integral part of their welfare policy.

TABLE 3.3.10

Direct budgetary subsidies in 1988

	Czechoslovakia a	German Dem. Rep.	Hungary	Poland	Soviet Union
(1) Total value of consumer subsidies financed from central budget b	..	..	44.5	4 196.8	..
of which:					
(2) Food and non-food products	45.0	49.8	..	..	86.3
(3) Food	35.0	31.9	15-20 *	1 438.4	41.3 c
(4) Value of retail trade b					
of which:					
(5) Food and non-food products	341.2	162.6	679.4	13 155.4	366.4
(6) Food	152.9	38.2	161.5	3 714.1	54.0 c
(7) Value of paid services b	..	7.8	203.9	2 651.2	..
(8) Budgetary price support as percentage of:					
Total sales (1):(4+7)	..	..	6.5	31.9	..
Food and non-food products sales (2):(5)	13.2	30.6	..	..	23.6
Food sales (3):(6)	22.9	83.7	9-12	38.8	76.5

Source: National statistical yearbooks (German Democratic Republic, Hungary and Poland), Soviet Union: *Argumenty i fakty* no.37, 1989, p.3; Czechoslovakia: *Rudé pravo*, 21 February 1990; Hungary: *Valóság*, No.10, 1989.

a 1989.
b Billions of national currency units.
c Meat, meat products, fish, milk and milk products and sugar only.

countries are considering urgent measures to *eliminate consumer subsidies*, but the road from decision to action appears to be more difficult than envisaged. As far as the Soviet Union is concerned, there is widespread agreement among economic experts that sound economics necessitate the abolition of price subsidies, but for social and other reasons such a move is not politically feasible at present.[250] An additional argument frequently advanced is that this would require a long period of preparation.

Until very recently, similar views were also widely held in the German Democratic Republic. Under the pressure of economic and political circumstances, however, the government adopted a new approach in early 1990. First, subsidies on children's clothing and shoes were eliminated. The ensuing price rises, estimated at 2 billion marks, were fully compensated by an increase in the state child benefits. It was subsequently decided that food subsidies, which had kept the prices of basic items at the low 1952 level, would be abolished after the mid-March elections. They would be replaced by payments of 150 marks a month to each of the country's 16.4 million citizens. As the figures in table 3.3.10 indicate, the elimination of 32 billion marks in subsidies should raise the price level of foodstuffs by over 80 per cent.[251] The indirect impact — i.e., the price rise in the rest of the economy — can hardly be quantified as the expectations of economic agents (enterprise managers, households, government) will be influenced by other economic and political developments as well.

Given the particular circumstances prevailing in the German Democratic Republic, the experience of other countries cannot help either.

In addition to consumer goods subsidies, *subsidized bank loans* were also granted to the population to a varying extent in different countries. This issue has recently become acute in Hungary, where about 3 million subsidized construction loans were outstanding at the end of the 1980s. The total amount outstanding of these easy-term loans — carrying a 3 per cent interest on average, as compared with an overall inflation rate of some 10 per cent per year during the 1980s — amounted to some 300 billion forints. As long as inflation remained low, the interest rate subsidy paid from the central budget to the National Savings Bank was of negligible importance. However, as going market rates rose to 10 and later to 20 per cent (always somewhat ahead of inflation), such subsidies became a crippling burden on central finances. In 1987, interest rate subsidies cost only 10 billion forints, but in 1989 the total rose to 37 billion forints — i.e., from 0.8 per cent to 2.3 per cent of GDP.[252] In December 1989, Parliament decided to introduce a special "interest tax" on outstanding mortgages in order to remedy the situation. As soon as the government's intention became known, debtors rushed to the bank and within a few days an estimated 15 billion forints were paid back ahead of schedule. To put this figure into perspective, the average repayment of loans ahead of the contracted period was only 2-3 billion forints in past years. Early repay-

---

[250] In a newspaper interview published in Hungary, Academician A. Aganbegian acknowledged that in 1986-1987 leading economic advisers had missed the right moment to call for an elimination of food prices subsidies. They had hoped that conditions would be more favourable later on. At that time, the argument continues, shortages on the consumer markets were only partial and a change in relative prices would not have left consumers without alternatives. By the middle of 1989, shortages had spread into every segment of the market and the population became nervous. In such a situation, Mr. Aganbegian said, new price rises could lead to social disruption. In his view, 3-4 years will be needed to stabilize the market and hence the elimination of subsidies will have to be postponed until this goal is achieved. *Élet és Irodalom*, 2 June 1989.

[251] *Neues Deutschland*, 20 and 23 February 1990.

[252] *Heti Világgazdaság*, 10 March 1990.

ment of these loans short-circuited government plans — including issues which had already been settled with the IMF — because the government was compelled to pay an additional 15 billion forints to the Savings Bank as interest rate compensation.[253]

(c) Savings behaviour

Personal monetary savings in eastern Europe and the Soviet Union are either deposited in savings banks or held in cash. The stock of savings deposits is regularly reported in national statistical yearbooks and/or in CMEA and IMF publications, but only a few countries publish estimates of private cash holdings.[254] Savings in the form of financial investments are non-existent or still embryonic (Hungary, Poland, Soviet Union); thus, changes in savings deposits could serve as a proxy for changes in savings overall.

In *nominal* terms, the flow of savings (i.e., the annual change in savings deposits in 1989) was positive in all six countries for which data were available at the time of writing (see Appendix table B.19). However, the impact of inflation must also be taken into account. In the last decade, the erosion of the *real purchasing power of savings* was most pronounced in Poland as inflation, shortages and insufficient incentives to keep money in these accounts effectively halved their real value. From the point of view of depositors, the situation worsened dramatically in 1989. Slowly but steadily, inflation has also eroded the purchasing power of Hungarian personal savings deposits. Despite considerable growth in nominal terms, the inflation-adjusted real value of Hungarian saving deposits is only 20 per cent above its 1980 level. The case of the Soviet Union represents the other extreme. Since 1980, the real value of these assets adjusted for inflation rose by nearly 90 per cent, exerting pressure on the already shaken balance between the flow of consumer incomes and supplies.

Changes in savings behaviour can also be related to changes in nominal money incomes (Panels B and C of table 3.3.11). It can be observed that the *savings ratios* in the countries reviewed range between 3 and 8 per cent of money incomes.[255] They were also relatively stable, but tended to rise in Poland and the Soviet Union. The high and rising ratios in these two countries also indicate a deterioration in the supply situation.

The *marginal savings ratio* relates the annual increase in incomes to changes in savings, i.e., that percentage of the *increment* in money incomes which is added to savings. In the Soviet Union, for example, it appears that a rise in monetary income of 100 roubles

TABLE 3.3.11
Saving deposits of households

	1986	1987	1988	1989
Panel A: Value at constant prices [a]				
(1980 = 100.0)				
Bulgaria...............	145.2	153.3	162.8	154.0
Czechoslovakia......	137.5	147.2	155.0	159.7
German Dem.Rep. ..	132.5	142.1	151.8	157.1
Hungary...............	130.1	128.9	123.1	116.7
Poland.................	88.6	83.8	78.4	49.6
Romania..............	130.5	..	..	..
Soviet Union.........	144.5	156.0	169.5	188.1
Panel B: Savings ratio [b]				
(Percentage ratio)				
Bulgaria...............	3.0	4.4	..	..
Czechoslovakia......	3.7	3.8	3.0	2.5
German Dem.Rep. ..	5.2	6.1	6.0	5.0
Hungary...............	5.9	3.3	4.2	4.0
Poland.................	6.1	4.4	7.5	7.7
Romania..............	3.6	..	..	..
Soviet Union.........	5.1	5.3	6.1	7.2
Panel C: Marginal savings ratio [c]				
(Percentage ratio)				
Bulgaria...............	-122.4	37.4	..	..
Czechoslovakia......	5.2	6.4	-16.7	-11.4
German Dem.Rep. ..	23.0	25.7	3.3	-27.4
Hungary...............	21.3	-27.8	11.2	3.1
Poland.................	-0.5	-1.8	11.2	7.8
Romania..............	-1.0	..	..	..
Soviet Union.........	18.3	12.6	13.7	16.5

Source and Notes: See Appendix tables B.4, B.6. and B.19.

[a] Nominal value of saving deposits, deflated by the consumer price index.
[b] Ratio of increment in savings deposits to money incomes of the population.
[c] Ratio of annual increments in savings to annual increase in money incomes.

in 1989 led to 17 roubles of extra savings. Like most marginal indicators, the marginal savings ratio shows wide year-to-year fluctuations. The figures for the German Democratic Republic and Hungary, for instance, indicate that sudden behavioural changes occurred in these countries in 1989. In both cases, changes in the marginal savings ratio clearly show that households reacted to the growing danger of inflation and (perhaps more importantly) to the increased opportunities for spending money abroad.

(d) Provision of housing

The provision of housing continues to remain at the centre of public interest in all the seven countries. Since 1970, most of these countries have probably improved

---

[253] In March 1990, the newly created Constitutional Court found the law on interest tax and the accompanying degrees unacceptable on constitutional grounds. This means that a new solution will have to be found. *Népszabadság*, 15 March 1990.

[254] In Hungary and Poland, the volume of cash in circulation amounts to about 50 per cent of savings deposits. In the German Democratic Republic the amount of cash in the hands of the population was around 10 per cent at the end of 1989 — a figure similar to those reported for earlier years (*Statistisches Jahrbuch der Deutschen Demokratischen Republik 1989*, p.51). In the Soviet Union, the same indicator was estimated at 40-70 billion roubles — 13-23 per cent of the stock of savings at the end of 1988, in a statement by Yu. D. Maslyukov, Chairman of the State Planning Committee, to the the USSR Supreme Soviet (*Pravda*, 5 August 1989, p.3). No data are available for the other countries.

[255] This ratio is low by international standards, but not excessively so. In western Europe, the savings ratio is above 10 per cent in some countries, but in the Nordic countries and in the United Kingdom it was about the same or even lower than in eastern Europe and the Soviet Union in 1988. See United Nations Economic Commission for Europe, *Economic Survey for Europe in 1988-1989*, New York, 1985, p.24.

TABLE 3.3.12

Housing density
(End of period)

	1970	1975	1980	1985	1988
Number of inhabitants per dwelling					
Bulgaria	..	3.47	3.12	2.83	2.70
Czechoslovakia	3.35	3.09	2.90	2.73	2.66
German Dem.Rep.[a]	2.82	2.61	..	2.44	2.38
Hungary	3.22	2.97	..	2.77	2.68
Poland	3.90	3.66	3.56	3.42	3.39
Romania	..	..	..	..	..
Soviet Union	..	..	..	..	3.36

Source: United Nations Economic Commission for Europe, *Annual Bulletin of Housing and Building Statistics for Europe*, national statistics and direct communication from the Central Statistical Office of the USSR.

[a] Dwellings in residential buildings only.

TABLE 3.3.13

Dwellings constructed

	1976-1980	1981-1985	1986-1988	1989
Panel A: Per 1,000 inhabitants				
Bulgaria	8.0	7.7	6.8	4.3
Czechoslovakia	8.6	6.3	5.2	5.6
German Dem.Rep.	6.7	7.1	5.7	5.0
Hungary	8.5	6.9	5.6	4.9
Poland	7.5	5.2	5.0	3.9
Romania	7.7	6.3	4.7	..
Eastern Europe	7.7	6.3	5.4	..
Soviet Union	7.8	7.3	7.7	7.6
Eastern Europe and Soviet Union	7.8	7.0	7.1	..
Panel B: Per 1,000 marriages				
Bulgaria	890	1 032	950	..
Czechoslovakia	990	822	668	747
German Dem.Rep.	797	920	687	636
Hungary	994	981	864	777
Poland	813	641	748	585
Romania	863	832	..	..
Eastern Europe	875	810	..	..
Soviet Union	745	729	802	..
Eastern Europe and Soviet Union	778	748	..	..

Source: National statistics.

ventional measures. (In the past, Soviet data applied only to the dwelling stock in urban areas, and even this figure was expressed in square meters of useful floor space and not in the unit conventionally used in international comparisons.)[256] In the light of this figure, the Soviet housing situation appears to be worse than the east European average (Romania excluded), but slightly better than in Poland.

Some country-specific aspects of the housing situation are reviewed below. Panel A of table 3.3.13 displays the conventional indicator (new dwelling construction per 1,000 inhabitants), while Panel B compares the number of newly-built dwellings with the number of marriages.[257]

It should be mentioned that in January 1990 the statistical authorities of the German Democratic Republic published a substantial downward revision of their housing data for the period 1985-1988. Figures on annual new dwelling construction published earlier, including those which appeared in the last (1989) edition of the national statistical yearbook, were scaled down by 20 per cent.[258] However, no explanation was given, nor is it clear whether the figures for the preceding years will also be revised or whether they can still be regarded as accurate. In spite of this downward revision, the housebuilding efforts of the last 20 years were recently singled out as the prime cause of the (so far unreported) state budget deficit.[259] None the less, assuming that the figures for the pre-1985 period remain unchanged, the *Wohnungsbauprogramm* seems to have been fulfilled, even after allowing for the latest revisions. During the three quinquennia, from 1976 to 1990, the commissioning of 2.8-3.0 million new or modernized dwellings was planned.[260] This target had already been met by 1989. This does not yet mean, however, that the programme reached its substantive objective of "solving the housing question".

As far as the east European countries are concerned, *new construction* decelerated in 1986-1989 in all countries. This is the more important because of the slowdown in 1981-1985 relative to the previous five-year period; this was most pronounced in Bulgaria and Poland. In 1989, only in Czechoslovakia was the downward trend halted. In Poland less than 150,000 new homes were completed in 1989, the lowest absolute figure since 1963. In the German Democratic Republic, some 80,000 new dwellings were built, less than in any year since 1973. Bulgarian performance was worse than in any year since systematic data collection started in 1956. Most probably the final Romanian results will be similar, as a downward trend in housebuilding was clearly present during the previous ten years. The ex-

their housing situation. Housing density (the number of individuals per dwelling) has declined in all countries for which comparable figures exist (table 3.3.12). But data available in this respect are not complete, and nor are they wholly comparable. For the first time in recent years, the Soviet Union officially communicated data to the ECE secretariat on its housing stock using con-

---

[256] See various past editions of the United Nations Economic Commission for Europe, *Annual Bulletin of Housing and Statistics for Europe* and United Nations Economic Commission for Europe, *Economic Survey of Europe in 1987-1988*, p.190.

[257] Absolute figures on dwelling construction are given in Appendix table B.7.

[258] See Staatliche Zentralverwaltung für Statistik, "Mitteilung zur wirtschaftlichen und sozialen Entwicklung der DDR im Jahre 1989," manuscript, Berlin, 23 January 1990.

[259] See the interview with Finance Minister E. Höfner, *Neues Deutschland*, 16 November 1989.

[260] See Akademie de Wissenschaften der DDR, Zentralinstitut für Geschichte, *DDR: Werden und Wachsen* (GDR – Living and Growing), Dietz Verlag, Berlin 1974, p. 547 and W. Junker, "Das Wohnungsbauprogramm der DDR für die Jahre 1976 bis 1990" (The housebuilding programme of the GDR for the years 1976-1990), *Neues Deutschland*, 4 October 1973.

planation of this poor performance is straightforward; in the centrally planned economies, where the annual performance of enterprises and individuals are customarily assessed on the basis of the fulfilment of end-year targets, production is notoriously subject to strong seasonality. As it happened, the wave of political turmoil sweeping through eastern Europe reached Bulgaria, the German Democratic Republic and Romania in the last two months of 1989. Thus disruption of production discipline meant that the customary end-year rush failed to occur, resulting in an unprecedently low rate of housing completions.

In contrast, developments in the Soviet Union were somewhat more favourable. In 1986-1988, performance improved slightly though there was a relatively minor drop in 1989. Nation-wide, the annual plan was fulfilled by 97 per cent. It is of interest that the republics singled out in the plan fulfilment report for particularly poor performance were those which were most affected by regional and other types of political unrest (Georgia, Lithuania, Moldavia, Armenia and Estonia).[261]

The data in panel B of table 3.3.13 set dwelling construction figures in a different perspective. For obvious reasons, housing needs are sensitive to demographic changes. One way of taking account of this factor is to compare the number of new dwellings with the number of new marriages. In this perspective, the relative position of individual countries looks different from those shown in the upper panel of the table. In 1981-1985, the numbers of house completions were above or close to the number of new marriages in several countries. In the next three years the situation clearly worsened in this respect. Soviet housing construction appears relatively good by east European standards in *per capita* terms: but if needs arising from new marriages are considered, the current Soviet situation is worse than in two of the five reporting east European countries. The official plan fulfilment report gives further evidence for this: in urban areas, it reported that 10 per cent of married couples live as paying sub-tenants of other families. More than 2.5 million young couples are on the waiting list for new apartments — and one third of them have already been waiting for 5-10 years.[262]

None of the east European countries have indicated the number of *new dwelling completions planned* for 1990. On the basis of the poor outcome in 1989, it is likely that the carry-over effect may improve results in 1990. However, given the political uncertainties in many countries, the behaviour of private or semi-private builders is unpredictable. By contrast, the Soviet plans are rather ambitious in this respect, with a targeted 12.4 per cent real increase in dwelling construction.

---

[261] *Pravda*, 28 January 1990. p.2.

[262] *Loc. cit.*

(iii) Investment policies since 1970 and the role of investment in restructuring

(a) Investment efficiency and the state of the capital stock

The investment slow-downs planned in all of the seven countries for the first half of the 1980s reflected a new policy element. This was to improve the efficiency of the investment process itself by cutting investment lead times, to speed up the implementation of new projects, and, ultimately, to adjust economic planning and management within the centrally planned system by improving enterprise efficiency and reducing the resource intensity of output.

In fact, even the first step in this process demands major changes in the planning system. Reductions in investment lead times and the allocation of resources in line with real supply and demand can only occur if there is a rational price framework — and if the usual penalties for wrong decisions, and rewards for right ones, apply: this has not been the case. Investment lead times therefore remain overly long and commercially viable opportunities have not been grasped. While cuts in the growth of investment were achieved, no improvements in the efficiency of the investment process occurred to offset them.

TABLE 3.3.14

Unfinished investment as a share of investment
(Per cent)

	1970	1975	1980	1985	1988
Bulgaria	87	101	103	115	115
Soviet Union:					
Unfinished construction as a share of:					
- total investment	73	75	87	78	78
- construction investment	112	121	158	169 [a]	..
Uninstalled machinery as a share of machinery and equipment investment:					
- total	19	16	25	20 *	..
- imported	6	5	11	8 *	..

Source: Statististicheski godishnik NRB 1988, p.122, *Narodnoe khozyaistvo SSSR*, 1984, pp.376, 382, 387 and 1987, p.299, *Kapital'noye stroitel'stvo SSSR*, 1988, p.32.

[a] 1984.

The improvement of investment efficiency means accelerating the rate at which new capacity is commissioned and thereby increasing in the short term the amount of production from a given volume of investment. To the extent that the resulting reduction of current investment lead times also reduces the volume of unfinished projects, it also brings quantitative gains in new capacity at only marginally extra investment cost. Further gains of the same kind can be achieved by shifting away from new projects and towards the re-equipment and modernization of existing plant; this reduces construction costs, increases the share of the "active" component (machinery and equipment) in

TABLE 3.3.15

Fixed capital brought into operation, 1971-1988
(Per cent of gross fixed capital investment)

	1971-1975	1976-1980	1981-1985	1986-1988	1986	1987	1988
Bulgaria [a]							
Total economy	84	88	89	89 [b]	78	100	
Industry	81	84	82	88 [b]	66	108	
Czechoslovakia							
Total economy	98	94	99	98	102	93	96
Industry	103	96	104	101	110	93	84
German Democratic Republic [c]							
Total economy	..	..	101	..	..	..	
Industry	..	..	98	..	..	..	
Hungary							
Total economy	89	91	99	100 [c]	131	107	102
Industry	94	85	95	119 [c]	131	107	102
Poland [a]							
Total economy	82	84	82	80	79	80	75
Industry	80	84	77	78	76	79	71
Romania							
Total economy	..	82	93	..	..	..	..
Industry	..	76	89	..	..	..	..
Soviet Union							
Total economy	93	93	97	94	94	95	88
Industry	..	..	94	89	88	90	83

Source: National statistics.
[a] Current prices. [b] 1986-1987. [c] 1980 prices.

total investment and thereby also increases the value of production from a given volume of investment. Together, these policy aims were expected to help offset decelerations in the availability of investment resources.

The "hidden reserves" which could be exploited in this way were, in fact considerable. Investment lead times are known to be 2-3 times those generally considered acceptable in the west. Construction backlogs are thus very high. In the Soviet Union for instance, unfinished construction was 160 per cent higher than total investment expenditures on construction in the 1980s, and in Bulgaria unfinished investment was about 15 per cent higher than the value of investment as a whole (table 3.3.14).

Recent data for the Soviet Union also show hold-ups in the installation of machinery and equipment, with non-installed machinery and equipment rising from about a fifth of total machinery and equipment investment in 1970 to a quarter in 1980.

Only two countries out of the seven reviewed here have regularly published such figures. But although the volume of unfinished construction projects, and of backlogs of an installed machinery and equipment relative to the total investment effort, cannot be directly estimated for the other countries, it is possible to indicate the direction of change. This can be done by calculating the ratio between newly-commissioned fixed assets and investment expenditures (table 3.3.15). A rise in the ratio indicates a slow-down in the pace at which the backlog of uncompleted investment is rising, but not a fall in its level unless the ratio exceeds 100. The ratios show significant improvements since the early 1970s only in Bulgaria and Hungary. But improvements in the latter country, especially in the first half of the 1980s, resulted from slowly growing or falling investment (the denominator of the ratio). In the Soviet Union, where little or no investment slow-down occurred in the 1980s, there was no improvement. Neither was there any in Czechoslovakia and Poland *despite* the investment slow-down. More importantly, apart from Hungary in 1986-1988 and in Czechoslovakia in 1986, the ratio was generally less than 100 — indicating a continuously rising backlog of unfinished investment. Policy to cut investment lead times has thus not resulted in any detectable success in most countries.

The share of machinery and equipment in total investment rose quite sharply, in contrast, in most east European countries (table 3.3.16). The exceptions were Poland and, most probably, Romania — the only country to have ceased publishing the relevant information in recent years. This share also rose only modestly in the Soviet Union.

Despite the improvement in this single indicator of investment efficiency, there is no other indication that policies to improve investment efficiency which were followed throughout the 1970s and the 1980s were generally successful. All in all, the attempts to reduce the number of investment projects by central "fiat" were not able to overcome the tendency of enterprises to play safe by over-investment, nor induce them to oversee more closely the speed and quality of the installation work. The funds committed were, in any event, overwhelmingly state funds (i.e., they did not belong to the enterprises concerned), their misuse in-

TABLE 3.3.16

Gross fixed capital formation: Selected indicators, 1976-1988
(Annual percentage volume changes and per cent of totals)

	1976-1980	1981-1985	1986-1988	1986	1987	1988
Bulgaria			[a]			
Machinery and equipment investment	8.3	6.2	16.6	10.1	16.9	..
- per cent of total	33	36	41	39	42	..
Engineering output	11.7	7.9	10.1	7.3	8.8	..
Investment in buildings etc.	6.2	3.7	5.9	6.4	1.2	..
Investment goods imports from OECD [b]	1.1	8.9	1.7	-5.5	-12.7	..
Czechoslovakia						
Machinery and equipment investment	8.1	0.5	7.8	6.0	12.4	6.7
- per cent of total	38	39	46	43	47	48
Engineering output	7.7	5.0	6.5	4.9	4.0	2.9
Investment in buildings etc.	4.6	-1.0	-1.4	-1.8	-1.6	1.8
Investment goods imports from OECD [b]	2.9	-3.7	9.0 [a]	-	3.5	..
German Democratic Republic						
Machinery and equipment investment	4.2	0.9	9.3	11.7	14.4	11.1
- per cent of total	45	48	55	53	56	57
Engineering output	6.9	6.5	4.7	5.5	6.2	6.1
Investment in buildings etc.	5.6	-0.9	-1.5	-1.0	0.9	4.5
Investment goods imports from OECD [b]	4.3	-1.3	16.9 [a]	41.9	19.3	..
Hungary						
Machinery and equipment investment	7.2	-3.3	3.9	7.9	16.0	-9.7
- per cent of total	43	42	48	47	49	4.8
Engineering output	6.3	2.7	4.2	3.4	4.1	0.4
Investment in buildings etc.	5.4	-2.6	-4.2	-3.3	6.6	-7.0
Investment goods imports from OECD [b]	8.5	0.5	-1.3 [a]	-8.8	-0.8	..
Poland						
Machinery and equipment investment	6.5	-10.1	14.1	7.9	6.8	6.4
- per cent of total	36	31	32	32	33	33
Engineering output	11.0	0.4	9.1	7.3	7.2	8.0
Investment in buildings etc.	6.5	-6.1	9.9	3.8	3.1	5.0
Investment goods imports from OECD [b]	1.0	-17.6	2.6 [a]	-10.7	-10.4	..
Romania			[a]			
Machinery and equipment investment	15.5	2.1	..	..	..	..
- per cent of total	45	44	..	..	..	..
Engineering output	15.1	7.1	12.4	7.7	4.7	..
Investment in buildings etc.	7.6	3.6	..	..	..	..
Investment goods imports from OECD [b]	1.2	-19.9	-21.5	-12.7	-57.1	..
Soviet Union						
Machinery and equipment investment	8.4	5.0	6.0	7.0	1.4	5.2
- per cent of total	36	39	38	39	38	37
Engineering output	9.7	6.5	8.4	6.7	5.6	5.3
Investment in buildings etc.	3.6	2.4	7.5	9.3	8.4	6.8
Investment goods imports from OECD [b]	10.5	2.0	-9.9 [a]	-5.0	-22.6	..

Source: ECE secretariat Common Data Base and UN COMTRADE.

Note: Percentage changes between periods are annualized changes between the annual average in the period shown compared with the average in the previous period.

[a] 1986-1987.
[b] OECD-reported data.

volved no tangible financial penalty which could not be covered by state guarantees of solvency to the enterprises concerned, and had no traceable ill effects on the remuneration of enterprise managers or workers.

The investment slow-downs or absolute cuts in the level of investment in most countries in 1981-1985 and also, in most, cuts in investment goods imports, must themselves have contributed to the lack of success in the above aspects of investment policy in most countries. They clearly had a major effect in Poland, where many projects had to be deliberately frozen under the emergency conditions of the early to middle years of this decade. They also had other deleterious effects, notably on the quality of the capital stock.

The first of these is the very sharp decline in the share of new fixed assets in total productive capacity. The steady deterioration in the age structure of the capital stock began in the mid-1970s and gathered pace in the 1980s (table 3.3.17). The fall was smallest, though still considerable, in Bulgaria and the Soviet Union (about 20 per cent), where investment cutbacks were smaller than in the other countries. But in

TABLE 3.3.17

Fixed assets under five years old, 1975-1988 [a]
(Percentage shares)

	Material sphere				Industry			
	1975	1980	1985	1988	1975	1980	1985	1988
Bulgaria	47	45	41	39 [b]	52	49	46	45 [b]
Czechoslovakia	31	32	25	23	31	32	25	23
German Democratic Republic	30	29	23	22	30	30	26	24
Hungary	31	32	23	21 [b]	41	41	28	24 [b]
Poland	34	31	17	19	42	35	17	19
Romania	51	53	38	34 [b]	51	53	37	33 [b]
Soviet Union	44	41	35	35	45	40	35	36

Source: ECE secretariat Common Data Base.

[a] Cumulated investment over the previous five years as a share of fixed assets in years.
[b] 1987.

TABLE 3.3.18

Apparent retirement rates of fixed assets, 1971-1988 [a]
(Per cent)

	Material sphere				Industry			
	1971-1975	1976-1980	1981-1985	1986-1988	1971-1977	1976-1980	1981-1985	1986-1988
Bulgaria	2.9	3.1	2.8	2.9 [b]	3.9	3.5	3.4	3.2 [b]
Czechoslovakia	1.4	1.3	0.4	0.5	1.5	1.4	0.2	0.1
German Democratic Republic	1.1	1.5	0.8	0.6	0.8	1.7	1.0	0.6
Hungary	0.8	1.8	1.5	1.1 [b]	2.0	2.5	1.7	0.4 [b]
Poland	0.6	-0.1	1.0	1.5	1.0	0.3	0.7	1.0
Romania	2.1	3.5	0.7	0.4 [b]	1.3	3.3	0.5	-0.4 [b]
Soviet Union	2.4	2.5	1.9	2.6	2.6	2.3	1.7	2.8

Source: ECE secretariat Common Data Base.

[a] Investment in periods shown minus absolute increment of fixed assets between last year of period shown and final year of preceding period expressed as an annualized percentage of fixed assets in the periods shown.
[b] 1986-1987.

Poland, the share of new fixed assets has fallen by half since 1975 — and by a quarter to a third in the other east European countries. Another element also played a role: the reaction of enterprises to shortages of investment funds was to prolong the service life of existing but obsolete fixed assets.

There has always been a tendency to hold on to existing equipment under central planning, a fact that has been regularly cited in the literature of most of the countries concerned. Under conditions where the main indicator of enterprise profits was, as noted, the attainment of output targets, it was clearly important to keep a reserve of equipment in case new equipment did not do the job — for instance, if working-up periods were unduly prolonged, if breakdowns could not be put right for lack of spare parts or in case of unexpectedly high output demands from planners. Several western commentators have described the disruptive effects of new equipment on long-established procedures at enterprise level. But one of the most pointed descriptions, originating in Poland, details the institutional factors which actually induced managers to *oppose* the installation of new, more productive equipment.[263] At all events, and for whatever reasons, the last two decades have seen a marked fall in the write-off rates of old equipment which has further contributed to the aging of the capital stock (table 3.3.18).

It is recalled that the general line of investment policy in the 1970s and 1980s was to ensure that, in effect, reductions in "excessive" investment were compensated by "better" investment. The final results of these developments can be shown in terms of the share of the relationship between investment and the expansion of the capital stock (table 3.3.19). First, it is clear that the bulk of investment expenditure continued to be devoted to expanding the capital stock, and the share of this component of investment grew consistently and steadily between the early 1970s until the first half of the 1980s in all countries without exception. It grew further, moreover, in 1986-1988 in all countries except for Hungary and the Soviet Union. The policy of streamlining the stock of fixed assets by replacing obsolete with new fixed assets — thereby reducing the rate of growth of fixed assets and minimizing unit costs —

---

[263] Jan Winiecki, *The Distorted World of Soviet-type Economies*, Routledge, London and New York, 1988, p.179.

was not achieved. The stock of fixed assets deteriorated — partly because obsolete plant and equipment were not weeded out — in qualitative terms.

This highlights failure to implement the central investment strategy of the four successive five-year plans for the period 1970-1990. The sought-for improvements in investment efficiency were simply not achieved and, with only a few exceptions, the indicators tabulated above worsened. The capital stock in all the seven countries is without exception in a worse qualitative state on the eve of economic restructuring than it was two decades ago, and the share of investment resources available domestically for its renewal is, moreover, at at a historically low level.

(b) Economic restructuring and investment prospects

This section surveys some of the main issues relevant to the restructuring of investment decision-making now being discussed in some countries.

It should be borne in mind that, while Hungary and Poland have gone far along the road to a complete abandonment of the centrally planned economic model, blueprints for change in the other countries are unclear. Apart from the above two countries, the Soviet Union had advanced the fastest up to the autumn of 1989. However, rapid political change in Bulgaria and Czechoslovakia has already rendered out of date the more modest reform programmes proposed in those countries before the 1989 upheavals. In Romania and the German Democratic Republic, these upheavals toppled previous governments which had expressed no intention of carrying out economic restructuring. Even in the German Democratic Republic, where the present situation is now dominated by the prospect of unification, no detailed information is yet available concerning the more market-oriented economic systems likely to be adopted. In fact, no details of the future course of reform are available for any of these four countries.

In the Soviet Union, economic reform strategies are currently circumscribed by the need for stabilization policies to redress domestic and foreign trade imbalances which have worsened in recent years. This can be attributed in part to difficulties in adjusting traditional behavioural patterns to new conditions as well as to the lack of institutions appropriate to the new circumstances. There is a risk, however, that the stabilization policies themselves are essentially reverting to past "administrative" patterns of economic management (section 5.4 below). The Soviet reform process so far can and has been criticised as a series of half measures which do not yet add up to real progress towards a market system. This is highlighted by the failure as yet to address the reform of price formation or monopolistic practices, and the far from whole-hearted commitment to a new system of property relations detectable in the law adopted by the Supreme Soviet in March 1990. Developments in the Soviet Union contrast sharply with those in Hungary and Poland, where the solution even of negative economic phenomena, including inflation and unemployment, which are likely to be initial accompaniments of reform, is being left to market forces rather than to administrative intervention.

TABLE 3.3.19

Replacement investment 1976-1988 [a]

(Per cent of investment)

	1976-1980	1981-1985	1986-1988	1987	1988
Material sphere					
Bulgaria	47	44	32 [b]	21	..
Czechoslovakia	42	20	15	20	13
German Dem.Rep.	34	23	21	26	24
Hungary	35	12	26 [b]	36	..
Poland	30	-61	37	24	40
Romania	51	34	5 [b]	4	..
Soviet Union	42	37	39	39	44
Industry					
Bulgaria	51	49	29 [b]	12	..
Czechoslovakia	44	20	11	18	10
German Dem.Rep.	31	32	21	39	25
Hungary	45	12	9 [b]	28	..
Poland	29	-71	30	4	41
Romania	47	32	-5 [b]	-3	..
Soviet Union	42	37	41	47	42

Source: ECE secretariat Common Data Base.

[a] Calculated as 100 *minus* the percentage share of the increment in fixed assets between the final year of the period shown and the final year of the preceding period relative to total investment in the year or period shown. Negative signs show the extent by which fixed assets grew faster than investments, e.g., through the recommissioning of plant previously scrapped.

[b] 1986-1987.

Bearing in mind some of the difficulties encountered in the analysis of investment developments, and at the risk of considerable over-simplification, it seems clear that a first priority in any of the new programmes should be to improve the mechanisms and the criteria for selecting investment projects. This will be especially important during any period of transition to a market system. If it is not done, there is a high risk that decisions based on unreliable price signals will continue to be taken for an undetermined period following the date on which decisions to reform have been taken. This is currently the case for the Soviet Union.

If domestic price reform is a pre-condition of a successful investment policy, it is equally clear why this aspect of reform is currently causing the biggest headaches in the eastern countries. Eastern Europe has made all its investment decisions for the last 40 years in the absence of rational price signals, a process that has been going on for 70 years in the Soviet Union. Therefore many past investments may not have been efficient from the point of optimal resource allocation. A rapid transition to market prices will bring this to the surface in the form of bankruptcies on the one hand and windfall profits on the other. But without price reform, the longer-term goal of external convertibility cannot be attained, and without convertibility, the screening of investment decisions in the light of international comparative costs cannot be undertaken either.

Market price formation is also the essential basis for decentralized decision making. Enterprise independence itself is currently a less controversial aspect of the reform programmes — though it is far from clear what kind of change in property rights will be needed to achieve this goal. Decentralization is closely linked with the responsibility of the enterprise to cover its outgoings (by supplying goods which are needed and by minimising costs) and to make profits which it can use to finance the repair and renewal of plant and the expansion of its activities investment. This replaces the old system under which profits were paid over to the centre and then redistributed in the form of grants together with instructions for new investment. (In fact, many of these grants were used not for investment but as subsidies to loss-making firms.)

In this context, the question of how to introduce prices which can truly reflect real supply and demand must also be addressed at an early stage. Decentralized decisions based on the wrong price signals can be just as irrational as central resource allocation in a similar environment. Moreover, competitive markets are not possible under present circumstances because of the virtual monopoly situation of many large state-owned firms. Much of industry in the seven countries is concentrated in this way — the legacy of the time when they were created, when size was viewed solely in terms of the economies accruing from large-scale production, rather than in the cost-and price-controlling context of competition.[264]

The Soviet Union has opted for a cautious approach — that is, on a transitional period of intermediate length for the move from central planning to a market system. It is possible that Bulgaria and Romania, where there is no tradition of industrial life outside the context of central planning, may do likewise. It may be that this represents less a lack of conviction than a realistic appraisal of the time required to develop the human resources necessary to build up a comprehensive institutional framework without which a market system of even the most elementary kind cannot operate.

The creation of functioning markets will involve setting up a whole range of legal and financial structures for which trained personnel are not available in any of the eastern countries. These institutions are essential for the optimal selection and implementation of investment decisions. The problem for the eastern countries is that investment decisions are needed now, and perhaps more urgently than ever given the increasing technological lag which they must confront. But such decisions will only be optimal if they are well-founded upon information provided by efficient markets.

A final point concerns the ownership of productive capacity. At present prospects under the reformed economies are still unclear as to the degree to which private ownership of the means of production will be permitted. In some countries, including Bulgaria and the Soviet Union, the practice of issuing interest-bearing bonds for purchase by workers in the firms issuing them has already begun on a small scale. But there are as yet no possibilities for their sale or purchase on an open market. In Hungary, this is now accepted. Even before the latest political changes, it had also been accepted that private ownership in Hungarian small-scale manufacturing, services and construction could ultimately embrace around 40 per cent of total output. A figure of 15-20 per cent has been mentioned for the Soviet Union.[265] In Czechoslovakia, the German Democratic Republic, Hungary and Poland, the advent or the likelihood of non-communist governments has seen the principle extended much farther. Without rapid change in this direction, it is difficult to envisage that investment based on entrepreneurial decision-making considerations — with all the flexibility and speed of response to new conditions that characterize them — can take root in the seven countries.

In the unique case of the German Democratic Republic, private firms from the Federal Republic are likely to play an extensive role in transforming the economy. But there has also been an upsurge of western interest in joint ventures with the other eastern countries — some 3,500 had been established in the eastern countries by end-February 1990 compared with 165 two years earlier.[266] This demonstrates the possibilities offered by the new perceptions of self-interest embodied in the eastern countries' restructuring programmes.

One of the most important set of policy concerns for the countries of eastern Europe will be the conditions under which western aid may be made available to support the reform process. Basic concerns will be the relative size and composition of technical as against financial assistance and the choice and timing of individual projects. There is a distinction to be made between private finance — direct investment in the countries concerned which could range from the creation of wholly foreign-owned productive capacity to joint ventures or take-overs of existing eastern firms — and official aid through the provision of finance for balance of payments or stabilization programmes, direct investment to reduce pollution, etc. No comprehensive decisions have been taken on the size or final sectoral or other destinations of such assistance has yet been taken, although disbursements for specific purposes have already begun.

Private financial assistance, on the analogy of other countries which have developed their manufacturing

---

[264] No bankruptcy of a large firm has yet been recorded in Hungary or Poland, though it is officially acknowledged that plant closures will begin on a substantial scale in 1990. Some of these firms are now being considered for sale — or, in Hungary, have already been sold — to domestic or foreign private interests.

[265] *Moscow News*, 7 January 1990.

[266] ECE secretariat estimates. The total capitalization of east-west joint ventures established in the eastern countries now stands at some $3 billion. The capitalization of the ten biggest Soviet projects varies between $30-50 million, and from $1-6 million in Poland. With Hungary, these countries alone account for over 95 per cent of all eastern-domiciled joint ventures concluded between eastern Europe and the Soviet Union with western firms. While the average capitalization averaged only about $1 million and many of the agreements represented little more than pilot projects to sound out future possibilities, others could be of considerable size. Four projects in the Soviet chemicals sector, apparently not yet finalised and hence excluded from the above summary figures, are stated to be worth a total of $14-$15 billion. See *The Economist*, 3 March 1990, pp.67-68.

industries on the basis of imported capital and expertise, can have immediate and noticeable effects on the development of recipient countries — not only in terms of the development of productive capacity but in the in-house training of local managers and ultimately of business leaders. In the final analysis, the opening of the east European and Soviet economies is not the least among the principal objectives of the reform process as a whole.

With regard to official assistance, no comprehensive decisions had yet been made available on its size or on the breakdown between different types of financial assistance now being prepared by the Group of 24 western countries to support economic reform in eastern Europe are available (see chapter 4 below). The PHARE programme, which is at the most advanced stage of implementation, applies only to Hungary and Poland; no information is available on the extent of aid packages for the other east European countries, and the Soviet Union has so far not been included as a possible recipient.

The most general statement is that a total aid package of up to $23 billion annually for the next 5-10 years could be appropriate for the six east European countries.[267] In concrete terms, this represents nearly four times the total of east European imports of investment goods from the OECD countries in 1986-1987.[268]

While relatively small compared to the total resources of possible donor countries (about 0.2 per cent of their aggregate GNP) and hence perfectly feasible,[269] the main question is how best such sums could be put to use by recipient countries.

The purpose of these comparisons is not to suggest that financial assistance should be confined to investment activity. Indeed, as suggested in earlier paragraphs of this section and in chapter 1 above, the lack of adequate price indicators for the evaluation of new projects, the poor state of knowledge of the present situation in the eastern economies, the absence of institutions and personnel qualified to take decisions reflecting the true comparative advantages of the economies concerned, as well as their poor performance in absorbing credit-financed purchases of western technologies in the 1970s, all suggest the need for caution in disbursing large amounts of financial assistance directly for investment purposes in the immediate future. Moreover the narrow room for manoeuvre with regard to overall resource allocation policy (section 3.3(i) above) in these countries, combined with low levels of consumption and the constraining effect of debt servicing, suggest that the claims of other sectors in the restructuring process may be equally pressing in the short term.

The logical conclusion to these comments is twofold. In general, the presence of skilled but low-cost labour forces situated close to the large west European market offers considerable potential for east-west cooperation within a European and indeed within a wider framework. On the one hand, and to the extent that more or less obvious areas for investment assistance can be identified — the modernization of the transport, communications, education and training infrastructure, the provision of funds for environmental improvement and the reduction of industrial pollution, for example — there is room for immediate financial assistance for investment purposes. On the other hand, the broader concepts of building up a viable manufacturing sector and the development of competitive export industries as a basis for long-term economic stability and development involve much more sophisticated decisions not only at the strategic but, in particular, at the microeconomic or enterprise level. The dynamic for this can only come, in the long run, from indigenous sources, from an appropriately trained managerial establishment and within the framework of an economic system which has in place appropriate mechanisms for the mobilization and rational allocation of investment resources.

(iv) Domestic imbalances: open and repressed inflation

Imbalances in domestic markets in 1989 were the worst since post-war stabilization. The causes include the disappointing progress of economic reform, the need to service a sizeable external debt in some east European countries or to earn sufficient revenue to pay for necessary imports, and unanticipated problems in CMEA trade relations. These gaps continue to affect policy-making in 1990.

The reforms under way in some countries and those being envisaged in others will have to address the prevailing imbalances, as well as a range of issues pertaining to the attainment of higher levels of efficiency and the incentives and other stimuli which will needed if they are to be achieved. It is important that aggregate economic imbalances, or even those arising in partial markets, are placed in their proper context. Frequently they are seen as an inevitable concomitant of reform. Upon closer scrutiny, however, this is not necessarily so.[270] It would, therefore, be useful to keep apart as much as possible the various forces in play. To do so, it will be instructive to review theoretical issues of open and repressed inflation and their relationships with detailed central planning, as well as the actual record on price increases in eastern Europe and the Soviet Union.

---

[267] Address by M. Jacques Delors to the European Parliament presenting the Commission's Programme for 1990, Strasbourg, January 17 1990 (EC mimeo). The implications of an assistance programme of this size are discussed in chapter 1 of the present publication.

[268] See United Nations Economic Commission for Europe, *Economic Bulletin for Europe*, Vol.41, New York, 1989, pp.78 (table 4.1).

[269] See chapter 1 of the present publication.

[270] For a comprehensive analysis, see "Inflation, stabilization and economic reform in China, eastern Europe, the Soviet Union and Viet Nam — aspects of the political economy of transition", *World Economic Survey, 1990* (United Nations publication No. E.90.II.C.1, 1990), chapter 6.

(a) Open inflation and inflationary pressures

In a market environment, imbalances between demand and supply give rise to price adjustments and, perhaps after some lags, to changes in demand and supply. In the traditional planned economies of eastern Europe and the Soviet Union, however, the response to imbalances has been mixed. The logic of that type of planning dictated that quantum changes in supply to remove current shortages or surpluses should be resolved within the planning framework, usually during the subsequent planning cycle. These countries have adhered to substantial domestic price autonomy and the administrative setting of prices to ensure plan stability (as in the case of wholesale prices) and social welfare (as in the case of consumer prices). Thus open inflation can occur only when the strict planning framework is relaxed or when "fiat" prices are recomputed with the explicit intention of achieving better market balance. Otherwise, inflationary pressures find their expression in so-called "repressed" inflation, meaning essentially that these imbalances are resolved by means other than price adjustments. These can take many different forms, including changes in the length of queues, rationing, the emergence of the second economy,[271] involuntary savings, quality deterioration, the substitution of goods and services in the official economy and concealed price adjustments — such as increases in the price of ostensibly "new" products.

Overt price inflation has manifested itself in several of the east European countries that have pursued flexible price policies for some time, even though relative prices there as a rule do not yet reflect true scarcities. In others, imbalances have essentially given rise to changes in one or more of the non-monetary indicators mentioned above. Even in these countries, however, the authorities have increasingly been paying closer attention to inflation in all its forms. In the case of the Soviet Union, for example, though official measurements of open price inflation for 1989 came to about 2 per cent, imputations of price movements that would have been required to equilibrate markets have officially yielded an inclusive inflation rate of 7.5 per cent.[272]

The acceleration of open inflation in several of the economies under review in 1989 was most evident for Hungary and Poland. Especially in the latter, spectacular open inflation erupted in the course of the year, but it had been gathering considerable momentum throughout the decade, albeit with some oscillations. Since 1988, the pace of inflation has picked up sharply in Hungary.

With decisions to seek far-reaching reforms having been taken throughout this group of countries, the spectre of sizeable open inflation, or of strong but suppressed inflationary pressures, has emerged as a key policy issue looming at least on the horizon. It is essential to clarify the causal links between market-oriented reforms and inflation. More often than not, the burst of inflation experienced during the first phases of such a reform is simply the response to repressed pressures built up over a number of years prior to the enactment of system modifications. In fact, it may have constituted one policy concern that played a major role in what determined the emergence and the conceptualization of the reform. Inflationary pressure may, however, also stem from unbalanced macro-economic policies or from the adjustment of relative prices.

As argued below in section (c), it is useful to distinguish among these various determinants of inflation in order to design appropriate policy corrections. Only then will it be possible to interpret correctly the degree of similarity between the causes of inflationary pressures in planned and market economies and to isolate them from the other multiple differences stemming from the institutional and organizational features of these economies.

As shown in table 3.3.20, changes in officially measured[273] consumer prices in eastern Europe and the Soviet Union have been very uneven across countries as well as over time. The various experiences fall essentially into three groups. Those countries (especially the German Democratic Republic and the Soviet Union) that have by and large adhered to fixed prices, perhaps with the intermittent re-setting of relative prices, have maintained a considerable degree of price stability. The second group (especially Bulgaria before 1989 and Czechoslovakia) have also maintained price stability in the short run, but have also resorted periodically to often sizeable "fiat" price adjustments. Romania's experience has been a mixture of these two groups. Finally, Hungary and Poland have been permitting substantial price changes since the early 1970s.

It is evident from the table that most countries have maintained a considerable degree of price stability over the years. Hungary and Poland are the two notable exceptions, and as such deserve to be examined in slightly greater detail. But something needs to be said also about Bulgaria, because it now acknowledges having experienced considerable inflation over the past decade, and the Soviet Union, because price pressures have become a core issue on the agenda of policy makers and a worrisome concern of the population at large.

The emergence of open inflation in *Poland* coincided roughly with the organizational reform introduced in 1972. At the same time, the authorities adopted a new industrialization strategy, aiming, among other things, at a relative opening up of the Polish economy in the early 1970s. This effort in fact coincided with the

---

[271] These, of course, help to improve market balance, although they are not reflected in most official statistical measurements.

[272] See V.I. Kirichenko, "Trudnye shagi ekonomiki" (Difficult steps of the economy), *Pravitel'stvenny vestnik*, No.4 (1990), p.3. Such an estimate would have been unheard of even as recently as one year ago. In Czechoslovakia, hidden increases in prices were estimated at 3-4 per cent annually. See statement by Prime Minister M. Calfa at a meeting with trade unions, BBC, *Summary of World Broadcast*, 17 February 1990.

[273] The policy debates in the past few months, as noted below, have unleashed an intense inquiry into the statistical probity of a whole range of data released earlier by the statistical authorities in several of the countries concerned.

TABLE 3.3.20

Consumer price changes in eastern Europe and the Soviet Union, 1971-1989 [a]
(Average annual and annual percentage changes)

	1971-1975	1976-1980	1981-1985	1986-1989	1986	1987	1988	1989
Bulgaria	0.2	4.0	0.9	3.5	3.4	-	1.3*	9.2*
Czechoslovakia	0.1	2.0	1.8	0.6	0.4	0.1	0.2	1.5
German Democratic Republic	-0.2	0.1	-	0.5	-	-	-	2
Hungary	2.8	6.3	6.8	11.5	5.3	8.6	15.7	17
Poland	2.4	6.8	32.5	69.7	17.3	25.5	59.0	244
Romania	0.5	1.4	4.8	..	-0.1	0.2*	..	..
Soviet Union	-	0.6	1.0	2.1	1.9	1.9	2.3	2.3

Source: based on official national statistics and other sources.

[a] Note that official measures differ in methodology and definition among the various countries. Moreover, statistical accuracy leaves something to be desired as sampling and weighting procedures are not always disclosed. See also notes to Appendix table B.6.

severe inflation in world markets. Beginning in 1975, these world market disturbances were gradually phased into the intra-CMEA trade pricing formula. Because of the partial opening-up of the economy, these upward drifts in trade prices were to some degree funnelled into the domestic price equation as well. With unaltered macro-economic policy stances, inflationary pressure emerged as an endemic problem, which was seriously exacerbated in the 1980s. Even the massive revision of consumer and producer prices in early 1982 did not suffice to stem the inflationary tide. Macro-economic policy stances, including those envisaged in the various reform blueprints of the 1980s, which were partially implemented, permitted wages to chase prices and at times even to outpace them. With these fiscal and monetary imbalances, it became impossible to cope with the sizeable external debt and restore domestic price stability. The resulting pressure erupted into hyper-inflation in the second half of 1989.

Since the end of 1988, the Polish authorities have introduced a series of large price increases for a wide variety of products, ranging from fuel to medicines. This has been driving up the cost of living well beyond the planners' short-term intentions. Thus, policy makers sought to contain the retail price increase on average to some 20 per cent in 1989, that for foodstuffs being limited to about 15 per cent.[274] Matters changed dramatically for the worse in the course of the year, however. The decision to lift several key price controls over the foodstuff sector in August 1989 triggered the hyper-inflation that gripped Poland for the rest of the year.[275] But even before that change in policy, the pace of inflation could not be contained within the plan target because the central authorities failed to live up to their own pricing commitments.

The inflation phenomenon in Poland has many other origins that in fact go back to the end of the 1970s. These include unfavourable terms-of-trade developments, sizeable debt-servicing requirements at a time of restricted output capabilities, lax monetary policy, inadequate wage restraint policies for socio-political reasons, currency devaluation, structural problems in agriculture and other factors,

In Hungary, there has also been a steady increase in prices for virtually all kinds of goods and services since the introduction of the New Economic Mechanism in 1968. The underlying assumption was that economic adjustment requires greater income differentiation. Because the authorities thought that nominal wages could be adjusted only upwards, a decision was made to accept moderate wage inflation in combination with periodic price increases to control household demand.

The upward price drift in Hungary, none the less, remained comparatively small — in the range of an annual 2-5 per cent — until 1979, when the authorities decided to seek broadly-based adjustments in prices. From then until 1986, the cost of living increased in the range of 5-8 per cent per year. In 1987-1989, however, prices rose relentlessly. Whereas in 1987 inflation was still at 8 per cent, in 1989 it reached about 18 per cent.

Since early 1988, inflation has been at the top of the policy agenda in the Soviet Union for two reasons. It began to manifest itself openly as some firms adjusted their input and output plans in response to the newly gained freedom for autonomous decision-making. Furthermore, extra money, over and above commodity coverage, was put into circulation and tended to exert pressure on prices, particularly those that were not narrowly circumscribed by administrative fiat.[276] Although the situation in 1988 as such was unique, the phenomenon of inflation certainly was not. This observation has been increasingly emphasized in recent months, in conjunction with complaints that the measurement of inflation by the statistical authorities leaves very much to be desired.

---

274 See Trybuna Ludu, 15 December 1988, p.1.

275 During the first seven months of the year, retail prices rose by some 10 per cent on average on a month-over-month basis. In August and September however, the pace accelerated to the 30-40 per cent range, and remained near 30 per cent on average through the last quarter (i.e., at an annual rate of some 2,000 per cent).

276 The problem in 1988 was not endemic, as it became in 1989. See R. Lokshin, "K razrabotke balansov denezhnykh dokhodov i raskhodov naselenia" (On the preparation of population money income and expenditure balances), Planovoe khozyaistvo, No.1 (1990), p.74.

Statistical measures of inflation in the Soviet Union have traditionally supported the claims made concerning the stability of wholesale and retail prices over the long haul — a basic foundation of Soviet central planning. True, these fixed administrative prices were revised from time to time, some prices being lowered while others were raised. But rarely was a pronounced upward trend discernible either from official statistical releases or from academic research and related inquiries in the Soviet Union.[277] Both claims have met with great scepticism in western literature on Soviet economic development, however. More recently, basically since *glasnost'* and *perestroika*, very probing questions about inflation have also been raised in the Soviet Union by academic researchers and government officials as well as by the broader public.[278] As new qualitative and quantitative information surfaced, similar critical questions have been re-examined in the western literature.[279]

There is as yet no consensus on the precise measure of inflation in the Soviet Union, when it was most intense, or on the chief institutional and policy mechanisms by which it has been driven, controlled or suppressed. Indeed, reliable quantitative indicators of inflation are not available; there is, for example, no official retail price index as yet. Moreover, implicit deflators, such as are embodied in official aggregate output indicators or the national accounts, have come under sharp criticism from Soviet observers, thereby belatedly echoing the findings of academic researchers in the west. There is now broad agreement that earlier claims about price stability under orthodox central planning need to be re-examined in more than one respect.

The controversy on what needs to be measured and the methodology to be adhered to, given the features of repressed inflation, continues. Price statistics are now considered to be one of the least reliable statistical measures collected, compiled and disseminated by the official statistical authorities (especially *Goskomstat*, the USSR State Committee on Statistics).[280] Because of the unsatisfactory nature of official measurements[281] and the growing public concern about inflation, various Soviet organs and private researchers have recently released their own estimates, which vary considerably. For 1989, estimates range from the near-official 2 per cent to over 10 per cent.[282] The situation has become so unsatisfactory that, in November 1989,[283] the Supreme Soviet instructed the State Committee on Statistics in conjunction with the State Committee on Prices to devise during the first quarter of 1990 a comprehensive methodology for calculating reliable price and inflation indices.

At this stage, there is little dispute over the fact that there has been considerable inflationary pressure at least since the early 1970s, although its intensity has fluctuated over time. This manifestation of profound imbalances in the economy is partly related to Soviet domestic and trade performance, but also to macro-economic policy stances. In serious dispute is how best to measure the degree of inflation that appears in the form of supply shortages and non-price changes of the type mentioned earlier.

Elsewhere in eastern Europe, the problem of inflation is among the top priorities of policy makers. Open inflation in Czechoslovakia, the German Democratic Republic and Romania in recent years has remained rather low. A recent estimate for Bulgaria indicates that the pace of inflation, including imputed price changes to take account of repressed inflation, was about 9 per cent annually during the past decade.[284] Underlying inflationary pressures of the non-price kind are believed to have been more moderate in Czechoslovakia than in any of the other countries. With a decisive move towards a market-oriented economy, however, the existence of pent-up repressed inflation is a cause for concern because it could turn into open inflation.

(b) Fiscal deficits and national debt levels

A priority area of concern, the intensity of which rose measurably in 1989, has been the ability of macro-economic policy to ensure stability, particularly in government finances. The existence of substantial deficits in state budgets became public knowledge for the first time in a number of countries. This initiated the search for effective and far-reaching fiscal and price

---

[277] For a perceptive note on the reason for this, see Anders Åslund, *Gorbachev's Struggle for Economic Reforms*, Pinter, London, 1989, pp.3-8.

[278] For two recent Soviet analyses of inflation under central planning and beyond, see Yury Yakovets, "Inflyatsionnaya volna: prichiny, sledstvia, protivodeistvie" (The inflationary wave: causes, consequences and countermeasures), *Voprosy ekonomiki*, Moscow, 1989, No.9, pp.26-33, and Ruslan Grinberg, "Inflyatsia v sotsialisticheskikh stranakh: zakonomernosti i osobennosti" (Inflation in socialist countries: regularities and specific features), *Voprosy ekonomiki*, Moscow, 1989, No.9, pp.67-76.

[279] For two recent inquiries with useful references, see Vladimir G. Treml, "*Perestroika* and Soviet statistics," *Soviet Economy*, 1988, No.1, pp. 65-94; and "J. Vanous' 'Dark side of glasnost' revisited," *Comparative Economic Studies*, 1989, No.4, pp.95-109.

[280] See *Ekonomicheskie nauki*, 1989, No.6, pp.64-72.

[281] Statistics in general have come under sharp criticism under the impulse of relentless probing by a growing number of Soviet researchers and commentators. The questions raised range from the accuracy of measurements as such to the collection and computation of data of direct use to decision makers in government, industry and academia.

[282] The more optimistic estimates are usually prepared on the basis of official statistical releases. These are felt to understate by wide margins the imbalances incurred since the launching of *perestroika*. The higher estimates take into account changes in a broader pattern of consumer prices, reflecting the more rapidly escalating prices in co-operative outlets, as well as in the pattern of consumption and changes in the quality of goods and services being measured. The higher number is from M. Panova and Yu. Yakutin, "Mery chrezvychainye, no neobkhodimye" (extraordinary but necessary measures), *Ekonomicheskaya gazeta*, 1989, No.47, p.9.

[283] *Pravda*, 29 November 1989, pp.1 and 3.

[284] *Rabotnichesko delo*, 26 December 1989, p.4.

policies. Cutting down military and administrative expenditures, narrowing the scope of large-scale state-financed investment projects, eliminating a sizeable part of budget subsidies and resort to certain price controls were among the remedies proposed or adopted by decision makers.

A striking measure of *glasnost'* in 1989 in this respect was the disclosure of the substantial fiscal deficits that have built up over the years into considerable domestic debts. Revelations have been especially startling in the case of the Soviet Union, where the budget deficit in 1989 reached 90 billion roubles — roughly 10 per cent of GNP[285] — adding to a domestic national debt[286] of over 400 billion roubles.[287] This has traditionally been financed chiefly through loans from the central bank. In part, this amount of lending was covered by increases in savings deposits. But some proportion was provided through the issuance of money, thereby exacerbating any lingering inflationary pressures in the economy.[288] Under the current stabilization effort, the budget deficit is due to be slashed severely to 60 billion roubles.

In Bulgaria, a 4 billion leva deficit (14 per cent of budget expenditures and 13 per cent of NMP) in the 1988 budget was belatedly revealed in the 1990 budget presentation. This was still 1.3 billion leva (4.6 per cent of NMP) in 1989, and is to be reduced to a 1.0 billion leva deficit (3.7 per cent of expenditures) in 1990.[289]

In the case of Hungary, the budget deficit in 1989 amounted to 55 billion forints. This made a further contribution to a total domestic national debt of 1,100 billion forints or about 65 per cent of GDP — among the highest in Europe. It is estimated that domestic debt-service alone will claim roughly 15 per cent of fiscal revenues in 1990. In the context of stabilization efforts, that deficit is now due to be slashed to at most 10 billion forints.

In November 1989, the authorities of the German Democratic Republic expected the state budget deficit for the year to reach 55 billion Marks. In the light of events in the last quarter, the final figure is likely to have been higher. The domestic debt was reported as 130 billion Marks, equivalent to about 48 per cent of national income.[290]

(c) The relationship between inflation and economic reform

As a manifestation of aggregate imbalances, the pressures determining the degree of open inflation in reforming economies may arise from a variety of factors. For diagnostic purposes, it is useful to distinguish, conceptually at least, among three main forces, since the policy response to each differs in important respects. The first is the stock phenomenon: as a rule, reforms are launched in an attempt to come to grips with chronic domestic or external imbalances, or both, that policy makers no longer feel able to remedy through traditional central planning. Economic agents — consumers in the first instance — have involuntarily built up savings or substituted less desirable goods and services for those in short supply. Once market adjustments are permitted, many agents will revert to their original preferences, including dissaving, thereby aggravating imbalances at least in the short run.

Closely related are the imbalances generated in the process of moving from central planning to an environment in which economic decisions need to be co-ordinated through macro-economic policy instruments and the institutions which will replace central planning as the pivotal organizing principle. One of the most common and predictable causes of this type of imbalance is the *primitive macro-economic policy setting* in place at the outset of reform. Also, policy errors are bound to be committed as ambitious reforms through indirect means open up vast uncharted territory. If central authorities embarking on reform fail to maintain budgetary discipline or monetary policy fails to rein in credit demand, the already existing, pent-up excess demand must inevitably be exacerbated.[291]

Finally, the creation of market incentives forms the essence of effective economic decentralization. Market determination of relative prices, including interest rates, wage norms, exchange rates and the other parameters which affect economic behaviour is indispensable for that purpose. Because marketization requires the elimination of most retail price subsidies, upward pressure on the price level in the short run is bound to manifest itself. The elimination of subsidies on basic goods and services is unlikely to be offset by any reduction of turnover taxes.

---

[285] Earlier expectations had placed the deficit at roughly 100 billion roubles or 11 per cent of GNP (Yury Borozdin, "Ekonomicheskaya reforma i tovarno-denezhnye otnoshenia" (Economic reform and commodity-money relations), *Voprosy ekonomiki*, 1989, No.9, p.17).

[286] There is also growing concern about the proper definition of the debt. Thus, some argue it ought not be restricted to the simple nominal sum of money, but should include a value for what the government has failed to do (such as waste in output and unfinished investment, pollution, the undermining of people's health and other "deficits"). See S. Dzarasov, "Reforma i rubl" (Reform and the rouble), *Planovoe khozyaistvo*, 1989, No.12, p.26.

[287] S. Dzarasov, *loc.cit.*

[288] See R. Lokshin, *op. cit.*, p. 74.

[289] Finance Minister B. Belchev in his presentation of the 1990 draft budget to the National Assembly, as reported in BBC, *Summary of World Broadcasts*, No. EE/0707, 8 March 1990, p.C1/1. Budgetary revenues in 1990 are expected to total 24.9 billion leva and public outlays will run at 25.9 billion leva.

[290] See J. Gurtz, "Was bedeuten 130 Milliarden Mark Innenverschuldung?" (What does a 130 billion Mark domestic debt mean?), *Finanzwirtschaft*, 1990. No.1-2. pp.32-33.

[291] There is considerable controversy in the literature about whether the "monetary overhang", in other words the entire stock of imbalances, is of recent vintage, or whether it was generated in the process of transition toward a reformed economy at a time when macro-economic control has not yet been refined sufficiently to ensure stability. For a lucid characterization of the two points of view, but with the latter one favoured, see Padma Desai, "*Perestroika*, prices, and the rouble problem," *The Harriman Institute Forum*, November 1989, No.2.

Because eastern Europe, and perhaps also the Soviet Union, find themselves at the threshold of radically new developments, the opportunities for reform should be evaluated carefully. Past reform efforts have demonstrated that the emergence of open inflation — or the acceleration in its pace — when genuine decentralization is attempted, evokes reactions of a diametrically opposed nature. Some reformers may wish to avoid eroding social welfare levels or to forestall open inflation, and perhaps unemployment too. They will, therefore, seek to defer price reform or at least prolong the process of realigning relative prices with underlying market-oriented scarcities well into the future. This necessarily debilitates the movement towards greater efficiency through economic devolution.

Others see this phase as a necessary adjustment period for the transition towards an environment in which a clear-cut separation exists between macro-economic policy and largely autonomous decision-making by economic agents. It will take some time to put in place the institutions and policy instruments necessary to ensure indirect economic co-ordination. It is also necessary to experiment in order to work out the most promising macro-economic mechanisms for a reforming planned economy, to redefine societal priority tasks and to adjust expectations in line with feasibility.

3.4 EXTERNAL BALANCE AND FOREIGN ECONOMIC RELATIONS

Exports of the east European countries and the Soviet Union declined in volume in 1989. Imports into eastern Europe stagnated, but those of the Soviet Union rose rapidly. Trade balances deteriorated for most countries — strongly so for the Soviet Union. Falling trade among the European CMEA countries reflected in part a general weakening of the CMEA trade and payments system. Current developments in foreign trade are summarized in section (i) below. Section (ii) explores the role of the CMEA in the context of the economic reforms under way in the eastern countries, and section (iii) develops the idea of a "payments union" on the EPU model as one possibility to ease the transition to a reformed foreign trade system.

(i) Foreign trade and external balances

The slowing in the foreign trade activity of the eastern ECE countries noted in the first half of 1989[292] became more accentuated in the second half of the year — as was true for economic activity in these countries in general. After expanding by over 4 per cent in 1988, exports of the area fell by more than 1 per cent in 1989. Imports increased by less than 4 per cent, entirely on the strength of rapid import growth in the Soviet Union. The feebleness of these trade flows contrasts sharply with the continued buoyancy of world trade in 1989. A 2 per cent downturn in intra-CMEA trade (which absorbs almost three fifths of the foreign trade of these countries) was at the heart of the weakness in foreign trade performance, though exports to the developed and developing market economies also declined. The only strong element in 1989 was the 13 per cent growth of eastern imports from the market economies.

Trade price developments were favourable overall for the eastern countries, though only marginally so for the Soviet Union. In eastern Europe, improving terms of trade in intra-CMEA transactions produced a rising nominal trade surplus even though export volume contracted faster than that of imports. East European terms of trade with the market economies also improved, but not enough to offset the effect of stagnant export and rising import volume, and the nominal trade surplus declined. The terms-of-trade and trade-balance changes of the Soviet Union in the CMEA market of course mirrored the east European ones with reversed sign. In trade with the market economies, Soviet terms of trade improved, but in the face of stagnant export volume and a very strong upturn of imports, the Soviet trade balance deteriorated alarmingly.

Changes in the overall volume of trade, in trade prices and the terms of trade, and in external balances will be reviewed in succession below.[293] Thereafter, some aspects of changes in trade among the European centrally planned economies will be examined. East-west trade is considered in greater detail in chapter 4.

The focus of this review is on trade *volume* changes wherever feasible, even though this involves a substantial amount of estimation concerning developments in the most recent year.[294]

(a) Trade volumes

Exports from the eastern countries, as noted, fell by more than 1 per cent. This reflects stagnant exports of the Soviet Union and, in eastern Europe, steep falls in the exports of Bulgaria and Romania,[295] contraction also in Czechoslovakia and Poland, and stagnation or only weak growth in the remaining countries (table 3.4.1). The feebleness of exports was thus broadly

---

[292] See Economic Commission for Europe, *Economic Bulletin for Europe*, vol.41, New York, 1989, chapter 1.

[293] For reasons of data availability for the last year under review, in particular as concerns the estimation of volume and structural changes, the breakdown of trade partners used in the text and tables of this section differs somewhat from that employed normally in UN statistics and especially in sections 4.2-4.3 below (see table 3.4.4., note a). Exceptionally, and following the practice of the national statistical sources of the European centrally planned economies, Yugoslavia is here included in the data on trade with "socialist economies". Trade with the "market economies" refers to trade with all developed and developing countries not included in the "socialist trade" aggregate.

[294] Information on changes in trade *value* is shown, for reference purposes, in table 3.4.4 (see also Appendix tables C.4 and C.5, which provide information on trade levels, 1970-1989, in a somewhat different breakdown of trade partners). For the sake of comparability with other value data in this *Survey* and other international publications, the aggregate data shown here generally reflect values measured in US dollars even for trade flows largely conducted in other currencies (e.g., intra-CMEA trade conducted in roubles, in particular). Consequently, value changes will differ — often substantially — from those shown in national sources. More significantly, owing to large differences between countries in exchange rate adjustments against the dollar and the rouble (and the resulting cross-rate variations), this procedure tends to reduce the cross-country comparability of value changes in rouble area trade flows. These are therefore shown in rouble terms in several of the tables below.

[295] *Romania* is the only east European country that does not publish any within-year foreign trade returns; together with the *German Democratic Republic* — which at least provides quarterly figures — it makes public only data on the sum of exports and imports at the most aggregate level expressed in national currency. Through 1985, the Romanian statistical yearbook reported data on the value of bilateral trade flows, but for 1986-1987 these have been omitted in that publication (see *Anuarul statistic al RSR 1988*, with data through 1987; no statistical compendium covering 1988 has been published so far). In the absence of data on trade flows by origin and destination, the appraisal of Romanian trade performance for 1986-1989 here reflects ECE secretariat calculations based on changes recorded in the statistics of the main CMEA and OECD trade partners, and very rough estimates of likely changes in trade with the remaining — mainly developing — countries. Accordingly, these estimates involve a considerable error margin.

TABLE 3.4.1

Eastern Europe and the Soviet Union: Volume of foreign trade, by country, 1987-1989
(Annual percentage change)

	Exports			Imports		
	1987	1988	1989 [a]	1987	1988	1989 [a]
Bulgaria	1.8	2.0	-9.5*	-1.4	6.0	-9.3*
Czechoslovakia	3.4	3.2	-3.1*	4.3	2.9	2.6*
German Democratic Republic	-0.7	1.0	1.7*	3.4	3.3	2.8*
Hungary	4.0	5.1	-	3.3	-2.0	1.0
Poland	4.8	9.1	-0.7	4.5	9.4	-0.7
Romania	-4.3*	7.4*	-8.2*[b]	-6.3*	-5.8*	0.8*[b]
Eastern Europe	1.2	3.9	-2.4	1.8	3.0	0.8
Soviet Union	3.3	4.8	-0.3*	-1.6	4.0	7.1*
Eastern Europe and the Soviet Union	2.3	4.4	-1.3	0.2	3.5	3.7

Source: Appendix table B.15.

[a] Preliminary national data or ECE secretariat estimates.
[b] January-September.

TABLE 3.4.2

Eastern Europe and the Soviet Union: Volume of foreign trade by direction, 1987-1989
(Annual percentage change)

	Exports			Imports		
	1987	1988	1989 [a]	1987	1988	1989 [a]
Eastern Europe, to or from:						
World	2	4	-2	2	3	1
Socialist economies	3	5	-2	2	-	-2
Market economies	3	2	-1	-3	4	3
Soviet Union, to or from:						
World	3	5	-	-2	4	7
Socialist economies	1	1	-	-	1	-1
Market economies	6	6	-1	-3	9	22

Source: ECE secretariat estimates. For explanation of country groups, see footnote (293).

[a] Preliminary.

based in the region and differentiates the experience of these countries from that of practically all industrial market economies in 1989 on the export side and, perhaps more to the point, also with regard to their import volume growth (see Appendix table C.3) which for the eastern countries expresses potential export demand. In general, the downturn directly or indirectly reflected supply side problems, ranging from disturbances in the production and distribution systems for exportables (especially fuels in the case of the Soviet Union) to quasi-mercantilistic policies aiming to protect domestic supplies by inhibiting the export of products "in deficit" (mainly in intra-regional and soft-currency relations).

Imports into the eastern countries rose by almost 4 per cent in volume in 1989. This reflects almost solely the rapid expansion − at some 7 per cent − in the imports of the Soviet Union, entirely on account of imports from the market economies. In most east European countries import volume stagnated or contracted (table 3.4.1). Only Czechoslovakia and the German Democratic Republic[296] appear to have been able to sustain a moderate level of import growth.

The pace of trade flows varied between the two *trading areas:* "socialist" trade, dominated broadly by intra-CMEA trade flows, and trade with the developed

---

[296] Foreign trade returns of the *German Democratic Republic* have long posed a puzzle owing to obscure valuation methods (in *valuta marks,* an accounting unit, at only implicitly revealed conversion coefficients) and inadequately detailed publication practices. Thus, for the last decade and a half, only country-group aggregates of exports and imports were published, while bilateral flows were reported in "turnover" terms (i.e., as the sum of exports and imports − a useless magnitude for analytical purposes). However, beyond this *concealment* of information there must also have been some outright distortions. Thus, when revalued data in "valuta mark equivalent values" (at a conversion rate of VM 8.14 to the US dollar and VM 4.40 to the Deutschmark as against VM 2.90 per dollar and VM 1 per Deutschmark used previously for the 1988 trade flows) were published early in 1990 "because the currency parities used previously were obsolete" (*Dokumentationen zur Aussenwirtschaft,* No.10, 7 March 1990), it was not only the *level* of reported trade that changed, but also the *sign* of the trade balance. Thus, a small surplus claimed for 1988 in "non-socialist" trade only a few months earlier (*Statistisches Jahrbuch der DDR 1989,* p.241) turned into a $1 billion deficit − something a mere revaluation at less obsolete conversion coefficients could not have achieved. The data for 1988 and 1989 shown in this publication reflect the revision, but those for prior years are still part of the old reporting practice (see footnote *(c)* to table 3.4.4). It should be noted that even the new data are still inadequate, as so far only aggregate trade flows (at the level of country groups) have been reported on the new definitions, but not bilateral flows and commodity details − only that type of detail will permit the confirmation of official returns against trade-partner-reported information normal in trade analysis.

TABLE 3.4.3

Eastern Europe and the Soviet Union: Trade balances, 1985-1989
(Billion US dollars or transferable roubles)

	1985	1986	1987	1988	January-September 1988	January-September 1989	1989
Eastern Europe with:							
World	4.9	0.7	4.1	7.1	6.4	6.7	6.1
Socialist countries (billion TR)	0.7	-1.4	0.8	4.4	2.3	3.3	4.5
Developed market economies	2.2	0.4	1.0	0.2	2.3	1.5	0.9
Developing countries	2.3	1.7	2.3	2.7	1.9	1.6	1.7
Soviet Union with:							
World	3.9	8.1	11.7	3.4	1.8	-5.0	-5.4
Socialist countries (billion TR)	2.0	3.8	2.1	-0.5	-0.6	-2.4	-2.4
Eastern Europe (billion TR)	0.9	2.6	0.1	-2.4	-1.2	-2.9	-4.1
Developed market economies	-0.9	-3.9	0.5	-2.7	-2.2	-4.6	-6.5
Developing countries	2.4	6.6	7.9	6.9	4.9	3.4	5.0

Source and country groups: As for table 3.4.4.

and developing market economies in 1989. However, on the side of exports this difference was much less than in past years, whereas in imports the contrast was pronounced (table 3.4.2).

Exports of the *Soviet Union* to the *market economies* are estimated to have declined slightly in 1989, after quite substantial volume growth in the preceding two years. A fall in the volume of fuels exported was probably the main factor in this decline.[297] A substantial rise in world market fuel prices more than compensated for this decline and permitted Soviet export revenues from the market economies (measured in US dollars) nonetheless to rise by 5½ per cent (table 3.4.4).

Soviet exports to the *developed* market economies may have increased some 2-3 per cent in volume for the year as a whole, substantially less than the 10 per cent rise registered in the preceding year, with revenues rising some 8 per cent (data for the first nine months are analyzed in detail in chapter 4 below). Soviet exports to the *developing* countries probably fell in volume again, with a value increase of only 2 per cent in 1989.[298]

The 7 per cent rise in the volume of Soviet imports in 1989, as noted, stems entirely from trade with the *market* economies. After a 16 per cent contraction in 1986-1987, these imports had turned up sharply in 1988, and in 1989 rose by a further 22 per cent in value and probably also in volume, thus again surpassing the 1985 level. Imports from *developed* and *developing* market economies rose at similarly high rates (table 3.4.4) and at a pace which accelerated in the later part of the year.[299]

Soviet trade with *socialist* countries contracted slightly in volume in 1989. This reflects predominantly the course of trade with the east European CMEA countries conducted in rouble terms, which turned down somewhat more — by 1-2 per cent in the case of Soviet exports and 2-3 per cent in that of Soviet imports. Prices in rouble trade in 1989 continued to reflect the lagged adjustment of CMEA prices to past world market price changes, including in particular the oil price collapse of 1986; hence the rouble price for fuels was still declining in 1989 (by some 10 per cent), in contrast to its rise on world markets.[300] Soviet terms of trade in consequence continued to decline, and Soviet export revenues fell more steeply than export volume.

East European trade with the *market* economies was characterized by a small contraction of export volume and a small rise in imports. In both cases the contracting component was trade with the *developing* countries. Exports of the east European countries to developing country markets fell steeply — by 14 per cent — in value, and east European imports contracted at about half that rate. Trade with the *developed* market economies, by contrast, rose, but relatively slowly — perhaps 5 per cent in volume in the case of both exports and imports.[301]

---

[297] The 1 per cent fall in Soviet primary energy production (table 3.2.11) and a 7 per cent decline in Soviet petroleum and product exports to OECD countries in the first nine months of 1989 (table 4.2.4) are undoubtedly related. The share of fuels in the value of Soviet exports to the market economies has fallen to 39 per cent in 1988 (from a peak of 59 per cent in 1984), but remains large enough to exert powerful leverage on Soviet export earnings and terms of trade.

[298] Analysis of Soviet exports to the developing countries continues to be impeded by the fact that over one half of the total reported flow is *not specified by country of destination* in Soviet statistics. This component for the first time in many years rose more slowly than exports to specified countries in 1989 — by a mere 1 per cent in dollar terms, as against the 4 per cent increase for the remainder.

[299] The difference between the 22 per cent volume growth of Soviet imports from the market economies registered here and the 13 per cent rise of Soviet imports in east-west trade in the first nine months shown in table 4.2.1 below reflects this acceleration rather than a discrepancy between eastern and western data. Soviet trade returns also showed a 13 per cent rise in value for that period.

[300] Because of these differences in price movements, the presentation of changes in intra-CMEA trade value and trade balances (in tables 3.4.3 and 3.4.4) in rouble terms appears more useful than a presentation in dollar terms, which would impute the slight depreciation of the rouble against the dollar in 1989 to these flows and exaggerate the fall in Soviet export revenues.

[301] As noted in section 4.2 below, western data for the first nine months indicate a much stronger increase in east European imports.

TABLE 3.4.4

Eastern Europe and the Soviet Union: Change in foreign trade value and trade balances by partner region, 1987-1989
(Growth rates in percentages; trade balances in billion US dollars or billion transferable roubles)

Country and trade partner groups a	Growth rates						Trade balance, in billion US dollars		
	Exports			Imports					
	1987	1988	1989 b	1987	1988	1989 b	1987	1988	1989 b
Bulgaria									
World	12.1	9.1	-7.3	6.3	3.4	-10.9	-0.3	0.6	1.2
Socialist countries (in TR terms)	2.6	6.5	-3.8	1.9	-5.4	-10.8	0.1	1.1	1.6
Developed market economies	9.6	3.3	4.8	5.5	4.4	-1.7	-1.4	-1.5	-1.4
Developing countries	20.7	-3.5	-37.5	-36.1	81.3	-20.4	1.0	0.3	-0.1
Czechoslovakia									
World	13.2	8.5	-2.9	11.1	4.4	-2.1	-0.3	0.7	0.2
Socialist countries (in TR terms)	5.6	5.1	0.9	0.5	0.2	6.4	-0.1	0.5	-0.1
Developed market economies	12.3	13.6	10.9	18.8	9.8	-1.6	-0.5	-0.4	0.1
Developing countries	-13.0	-1.2	0.1	0.2	5.7	17.0	0.4	0.3	0.2
German Democratic Republic									
World	8.7 c	2.6 c	4.3	6.2 c	2.7 c	2.1	0.9 c	-0.8	-0.4
Socialist countries (in TR terms)	1.3 c	1.3 c	-0.2	-2.6 c	-0.1 c	-3.3	0.4 c	0.3	0.7
Developed market economies	4.9 c	2.2 c	9.5	8.0 c	5.1 c	6.7	-0.1 c	-1.2	-1.0
Developing countries	0.5 c	-9.4 c	-0.2	-17.6 c	-10.7 c	5.3	0.4 c	0.2	0.2
Hungary									
World	4.5	4.3	-1.7	2.8	-4.9	-3.1	-0.3	0.6	0.8
Socialist countries (in TR terms)	0.7	7.9	-5.0	1.6	0.2	-7.3	0.2	0.9	1.1
Developed market economies	20.0	14.9	12.6	11.9	0.4	10.8	-0.6	-0.1	-
Developing countries	11.9	11.8	-6.2	5.6	7.5	-11.7	0.2	0.3	0.3
Poland									
World	1.2	13.3	-7.0	-3.2	12.8	-7.6	1.4	1.6	1.6
Socialist countries (in TR terms)	8.9	3.2	3.9	1.4	-3.9	0.9	0.3	1.3	1.7
Developed market economies	24.2	18.5	5.2	16.6	30.1	6.3	0.8	0.4	0.4
Developing countries	-18.1	14.0	-6.7	9.7	12.9	-8.0	0.4	0.5	0.5
Romania									
World	6.4*	9.5*	-8.4*	-3.1*	-6.8*	-1.9*	2.7*	4.4*	3.0*
Socialist countries (in TR terms)	-4.2*	5.3*	-4.1*	-7.3*	-3.4*	6.6*	-0.1*	0.4*	-0.5*
Developed market economies	10.2*	4.2*	-6.9*	-19.1*	-6.6*	-10.9*	2.9*	3.1*	3.0*
Developing countries	-0.9*	27.2*	-9.9*	-7.4*	-22.0*	-7.3*	-0.1*	0.9*	0.5*
Eastern Europe									
World	8.5	7.1	-4.0	5.0	2.7	-3.6	4.1	7.1	6.1
Socialist countries (in TR terms)	3.3	4.5	-0.7	-0.3	-1.8	-0.8	0.8	4.4	4.5
of which: Eastern Europe	4.3	5.4	-2.1	4.2	5.1	-1.2	-	-	-
Soviet Union	3.2	3.2	-2.2	-4.3	-6.5	-5.2	0.6	3.8	4.6
Developed market economies	12.1	8.9	6.4	9.6	8.8	4.3	1.0	0.2	0.9
Developing countries	-0.9	7.2	-14.0	-10.1	4.2	-5.8	2.3	2.7	1.7
Soviet Union									
World	11.0	2.7	-1.3	8.0	11.6	6.9	11.7	3.4	-5.4
Socialist countries (in TR terms)	-3.1	-3.0	-1.5	0.7	3.0	3.0	2.1	-0.5	-2.4
Developed market economies	20.4	7.8	7.8	-2.6	22.6	21.1	0.5	-2.7	-6.5
Developing countries	13.7	2.2	2.0	7.9	17.4	26.0	7.9	6.9	5.0

Source: Secretariat of the United Nations Economic Commission for Europe, based on national foreign trade statistics. Figures for 1989 are in some cases ECE secretariat estimates based on trade data for the first 9-11 months, supplemented by trade partner statistics and trend analysis; these may be subject to substantial error margins and should therefore be considered first approximations only.

Note: Growth rates and trade balances are based on trade values in terms of US dollars in the case of total trade and trade with the market economies, and on trade values in terms of transferable roubles (TR) in the case of trade among socialist countries; growth rates may therefore differ from those shown in national statistics. National data are converted to dollars at the conversion coefficients used for statistical purposes. In most—but not in all—cases these are time-weighted averages of the official "basic" exchange rate against the dollar, as announced by national banks or other authorities.

a The partner country grouping follows the practice of the national statistical sources, which differs from the breakdown usually employed in United Nations publications. Thus, "socialist countries" includes Yugoslavia and Cuba, in addition to the east European countries, the Soviet Union, and the Asian centrally planned economies. "Eastern Europe" refers to the six east European countries-members of the CMEA shown separately in the table.

b Preliminary. All entries marked with an asterisk are based on January-September data.

c Based on unrevised value data. The foreign trade statistics of the German Democratic Republic were under revision at the beginning of 1990. Preliminary results indicate that changes from data reported earlier will be very substantial, especially as regards trade balances. However, revised data were available at the time of writing only for 1988 and 1989, and only at the most aggregate level. It can be expected that data for earlier years will also revised in time.

In contrast to the broadly similar features of the intra-CMEA trade development in all east European countries, the evolution of trade with the market economies differed substantially among countries. *Bulgaria* and *Romania*[302] were at one end of the scale, with very steep contraction of exports to the market economies (22 per cent and 11 per cent in value terms) and slightly less severe falls of imports (see table 3.4.4). Exports of *Poland* to the market economies stagnated while imports expanded at some 4 per cent in volume. The remaining east European countries managed to raise exports at some 5-8 per cent in volume; the *German Democratic Republic* and *Hungary* also increased their imports at similar rates, while imports of *Czechoslovakia* expanded slowly.

(b) External balances

In 1989, for the first time since the mid-1970s, the trade balance of the *Soviet Union* swung into an overall deficit, as the remaining surplus with developing countries is no longer large enough to offset the rising deficits with the developed market economies and the countries of eastern Europe. The balance with the market economies swung from a $4 billion surplus into a $1.5 billion deficit, a $5.5 billion turnaround, and the deficit with socialist countries deepened by almost 2 billion roubles, most of this in trade with the countries of eastern Europe (table 3.4.3). As noted earlier (section 3.1) and discussed further below, the rouble area imbalance, because of the absence of convenient means to "convert" these claims into goods, is proving a powerful impediment to the development of intra-CMEA trade.

A deterioration also took place in the aggregate trade surplus of the east European countries as well as the joint trade surplus of these countries with the convertible currency area. However, this change primarily reflects an estimated contraction in the oversize convertible currency surplus of Romania. Except for Bulgaria, which has been sliding towards serious payments difficulties for a number of years, the remaining east European countries appear to have held their trade balances with the market economies on an approximately even level. However, their balance-of-payments position with the convertible currency area worsened, owing to growing deficits on the invisibles accounts (see section 4.3 below).

(ii) What role for the CMEA?

Because of the rapid pace of changes in eastern Europe, the once buoyant trade among the CMEA countries has been crumbling, as have the efforts to bring about genuine production integration. The regionwide transformations have also immobilised the CMEA in a number of respects. This outcome is in marked contrast to earlier expectations of intensifying institutionalized economic co-operation in the course of 1989.

Steps towards further refinement and the gradual implementation of fundamental changes in the integration strategy and mechanism, which have been under elaboration since late 1986, were scheduled to be taken in 1989, the fortieth anniversary of the CMEA. These measures were to have been approved by the third economic summit of the 1980s[303] and the regular summer Council Session. The new summit was first slated to be convened in Prague in March 1989, but it failed to materialize. After several attempts to call it to order in April and May, it was postponed indefinitely. The 45th Council Session, initially set for June, was first deferred until October and subsequently to December.[304] The meeting was finally convened on 9-10 January 1990 in Sofia.

Instead of commemorating forty years of economic co-operation and socialist integration, 1989 was marked by indecision and recrimination. Friction within the group has been mounting for several years and this has led to two kinds of action that are detrimental to group co-operation. One has taken the form of additional unilateral constraints on regional mobility of goods, services and people.[305] These measures were intended to avert private arbitrage exploiting the large price and supply differences among the various countries, thereby aggravating already strained domestic market balances in some countries. In early 1989, even the Soviet Union found it necessary to impose export controls on a wide range of foodstuffs in normal commerce.[306] These restrictions have since been extended to a whole range of consumer manufactures.

The other type of action consisted of constraints on regular commercial transactions. These became more acute in the course of 1989 for two reasons. One reflected the inability of the Soviet Union to offset the losses in its CMEA terms of trade sustained over the past several years by increasing export volumes of fuels and raw materials at the traditional transferable rouble prices in order to maintain balanced trade. The other derived from the reluctance of trade partners to honour agreed export volumes where this involved incurring substantial current account surpluses in transferable roubles, which are difficult to mobilize, even over time, and so constitute involuntary, quasi interest-free loans

---

302 Information for Romania stems from trade partner data for the first nine months.

303 The first two were held in Moscow in June 1984 and November 1986.

304 See *Rudé právo*, 30 October 1989, p.1.

305 Institutional arrangements for capital mobility in the CMEA have always been rather limiting. As a result, capital flows, other than for short-term trade financing at the time of shocks and for officially designated integration projects, have been only of limited magnitude.

306 Constraints on private arbitrage have been in effect since February 1988.

to the partners in deficit.[307] The result has been a gradual contraction of intragroup trade at a time when imports from convertible-currency countries were already constrained. Also the interest in pursuing production specialization, perhaps by continued adherence to the integration programmes hammered out in the 1980s, has waned considerably.

However unsettling these events have been for maintaining intragroup exchanges and hence domestic economic stability, the CMEA malaise actually runs much deeper. The probability of any major change being enacted in support of stabilization and economic growth for the group as a whole is rather slim at this juncture. Support for seeking a solution through CMEA reform has been rapidly evaporating in recent months for a variety of reasons. For one thing, the Soviet Union has become so enmeshed in its domestic problems that the priority of revitalizing the CMEA has been downgraded. Moreover, several eastern European economies are seriously questioning the very *raison d'être* of the CMEA. A central issue here is that bilateral trade and payments agreements and their co-ordination — so far the pivots of CMEA relations — have become highly unsuited to promoting the reforms envisaged by the most ambitious CMEA members.

The need to review CMEA economic relations has at least three dimensions. The first involves the clearing of regular trade and financial flows. Some CMEA members are presently exploring the possibility of shifting their trade accounting to current world market prices and to clearing trade in convertible currency, instead of the orthodox transferable rouble price and accounting systems. If applied generally these changes will entail major shifts in the level, commodity composition and geographical distribution of intragroup trade. Simulations of what may eventually occur have already aggravated tensions that may in the end be more harmful to maintaining within-group goodwill than the undoubtedly beneficial medium- to long-term effects that can be anticipated from "marketizing" the CMEA.

The second revolves around the implications of CMEA trade and payments reforms for the non-European members, all of which in the past have benefited from substantial economic assistance through the typical CMEA trade and payments régimes. There is little doubt that with the genuine commercialization of economic decisions in the European CMEA members, the real cost of development assistance to the non-European members is henceforth going to be carefully scrutinized. In view of the palpable internal and external economic imbalances, the chances of holding development assistance at its present level, let alone of raising it, are not promising. In fact, several eastern European countries have already announced that they will not be in a position to continue the kind of price and tariff subsidies that were granted during the past decades.

The third reason for the plight of the CMEA is the redrawing of east-west economic co-operation lines, particularly in Europe. Aside from autonomous structural adjustments that would have been undertaken in any case by one country or another, the fractionalization of the CMEA is bringing additional pressure to bear on these economies, if only because there is now greater urgency in establishing a viable niche in world markets in competition with developing countries. This is not perforce an undesirable outcome, provided competition is waged chiefly on the basis of underlying economic strengths. With much of eastern Europe enmeshed in protracted economic adjustments, however, there is every likelihood that, for some time, during the transition phase pressure to export as such will gain ascendancy over the need to export profitably.

Because of the difficulties in CMEA co-operation over the past decade or so, CMEA members have been pondering reforms of their regional integration infrastructure for a long time, so far largely in vain.[308] The sequence of official deliberations about CMEA reform is very long. With the failure to agree on reforms on the occasion of the most recent (45th) Council Session in Sofia the question of what can be done with the CMEA and whether serious efforts should be initiated to ensure its survival is being posed with increasing frequency.[309]

However, the CMEA is a complex of regional trade and payments linkages, and in spite of serious difficulties in maintaining trade volumes, all CMEA countries continue to depend on each other for between 40 and 80 per cent of their total trade.[310] Seen from this practical angle, the CMEA is likely to be maintained in some form. Foregoing such commercial ties would require massive diversion of trade and considerable structural changes in the member economies. The required adjustments would be so severe that the already taut social fabric of these countries could well be stretched beyond its limits.

Although a rational allocation of resources would certainly lead to a very different level, geographical direction and commodity composition of trade from that

---

[307] Such interest claims are claims against the members of the settlement mechanism of the International Bank for Economic Co-operation as a whole. By contrast, a trade surplus with respect to the region, even though kept in multilateral accounts, is in fact broken down on a country by country basis. Such claims are directly imputable, which interest claims are not.

[308] "... It cannot be said that the inevitability of radical changes in the forms and methods of co-operation in the CMEA framework has been recognized only now. But up to the most recent period we have in reality managed to implement only some organizational changes, including the reduction of the Council organs from 36 to 19 and the cutting of the Secretariat posts by approximately one third. However, these measures yielded no notable benefits since the realization of fundamental decisions, relating to changes in the economic mechanism of co-operation itself, effectively did not move forward." L. Krasnov (Deputy Permanent Representative of the USSR to CMEA), "SEV: poisk novykh putei" (CMEA: the search for new approaches), *Pravitel'stvennyi vestnik*, No.8, February 1990.

[309] For a detailed analysis of the recent evolution of the integration debate, see *World Economic Survey, 1989* (United Nations publication No.E.89.II.C.1, 1989), pp.113-131.

[310] Trade data at official exchange rates, especially of reporter countries that still adhere to official or notional commercial exchange rates, tend to overstate the CMEA share. But even if correction is made for that distortion, eastern Europe is highly dependent on intra-CMEA commercial exchanges.

observed during the post-war period, it would not suppress intraregional trade altogether. In other words, there are significant comparative advantages embodied in the resource endowments of the individual economies that, with the proper institutions and policies, could be exploited more fully to the benefit of welfare levels in the region and elsewhere.

The debate on what might be the proper economic mechanism of regional integration in the eastern part Europe has been going on now for a long time. Various proposals for change were tabled over the past several years. The 45th Council Session, in fact, was to have examined the proposals worked out by a special reform commission established in 1987. These recommendations were deemed to be no longer relevant in early 1990, given the new constellation of political forces and economic priorities. As a result, a new reform commission has been entrusted with the formulation of "radical CMEA reform" measures by the end of the first quarter of 1990. These recommendations are subsequently, sometime in mid-1990, to be taken up at the ministerial or summit level.

Pending significant reforms in trade and payments régimes, regional trade is going through an unnecessarily sharp contraction, and its harmonization with the newly-emerging interests of the reforming economies is impeded. For that reason, some of the reforming economies now would like to reduce gradually the share of CMEA relations in their total trade. This sentiment is buttressed by the advice offered by international economic organizations and by the Commission of the European Communities in particular, both in the context of the assistance effort co-ordinated on behalf of the Group of 24 as well as in its own right.

This raises two different questions. One concerns how to accomplish this trade diversion, given the importance of intragroup linkages and the need to radically restructure much of the knowledge and technology in place. Even if these countries wanted to incur the full adjustment cost arising from pronounced trade diversion, it could be absorbed only over time. There would, therefore, remain a considerable demand, for example, for spare parts, components and maintenance services to keep the appropriate machine park running to supply at least the other CMEA members.

Even if a drastic change in the geographical distribution of trade were to be a policy objective in its own right, in the interim the paramount technical issue that remains to be addressed is how to facilitate that level of CMEA trade that needs to be maintained in the short run until either the CMEA integration mechanism can be reformed or the reforming members can redirect a substantial part of their trade to market economies.

The other question is much more fundamental and rests on the existence of static comparative advantages within the region, and the potential for building up dynamic comparative advantages as well, if only because of growth through national economic reforms. From a technical economic point of view, these opportunities should be fully exploited. For that, anchoring appropriate institutions, trade policies and commercial policy instruments within the framework of regional co-operation of an institution like the CMEA is an urgent priority.

To reconcile the orthodox trade and payments régimes of the CMEA as they operate today with the aspirations of the reforming economies, gradual accommodation of economic structures and processes through economic discipline is required. On that basis, productive processes that are really not warranted on economic grounds should be phased out as quickly as circumstances permit. Others that ought to be fostered, for reasons of static and dynamic comparative advantage, are in need of more suitable accommodation than has thus far been possible for them to have.

Placing intra-CMEA exchanges on a more solid economic footing has ramifications for the trade and payments régimes; in fact, the success of such an objective may depend on first modifying these régimes.

Regarding the trade régime, a three-phased approach could usefully be explored. At the core stands the question of how best to ensure that domestic economic decision-making, especially in the micro-economic sphere, will not be overburdened and possibly derailed by the irrational prices and administrative commercial regulations so pervasive in CMEA economic relations. Central authorities that have signed formal trade and payments agreements may well feel impelled to discharge these obligations for now. To do so, equalization payments in the form of *ex post* subsidies and taxes need to be instituted to ensure that the transition to domestic pricing and entrepreneurial decision-making based on competition, national and international, is not obstructed or undermined. Differences between transferable rouble and domestic prices (or prices that are geared towards those of world markets) should be absorbed through taxes and subsidies by the central budget. That trade yields essentially a net fiscal revenue or expenditure, very much like the price-equalization account used to operate in the orthodox planned economy.[311]

The second step towards accommodation should ensure that the next sequence of trade and payments arrangements is negotiated as much as possible on the basis of the micro-economic efficiency guidelines that are developing in the internal economy. Practical reasons may necessitate that these agreements be negotiated bilaterally by high-level representatives from various ministries, rather than the enterprises that will eventually undertake these exports or imports. Even so, these negotiations need to be guided as much as possible by the emerging parameters, especially prices in the wide sense, of a more rational allocation pattern. Those adopted for reasons of state should be subsidized from the general state budget or, as the case may be, be subjected to a levy that accrues to the general

---

[311] For a detailed description of how this operates under alternative economic models, see "Economic reforms in the centrally planned economies and China," *World Economic Survey, 1988* (United Nations publication No.E.88.II.C.1, 1988), pp.96-98.

budget. Regarding the bulk of trade, however, government negotiators would need to ensure that the commitments into which they enter reflect as much as possible the direct interests of enterprises in exporting to or in importing from CMEA markets.

The final step consists in working towards the reform of CMEA economic relations from within the trade and payments régimes in place. This could take several forms. One would be outright replacement of the orthodox administrative integration mechanism with one much more closely related to economic efficiency indicators. Another would be to take advantage from within of the growing sentiment for CMEA reform. This applies even to countries whose economies continue to be steered largely by central planning institutions and instruments. Thus, direct enterprise relations across national frontiers would be encouraged. If enterprises from a reforming economy can take advantage of the non-scarcity prices maintained through administrative regulation in partner countries, there is no reason why such exchange should be discouraged by the reforming economy. Micro-economic rationality dictates that the enterprise has identified a temporary niche that yields arbitrage or other economic benefits. There is, therefore, no technical micro-economic reason to discourage that firm from exploiting such opportunity. If a macro-economic or meta-economic reason exists, it should be dealt with through appropriate policy instruments, rather than a simple injunction against the exchange.

(iii) Lessons from history: a new EPU as a bridge-gap

It needs to be recognized that there are now several east European countries that have wedded themselves to radical economic reform centreing around the institutionalization of markets for goods, services, labour and capital. Relations among these countries are likely to be increasingly based on simple market relations, provided a solution can be found for the prevailing imbalances and those likely to emerge during the transition towards fully-fledged marketization.

Negotiations about quantities and prices of tradeable goods, in most cases, can best be left to the discretion of the economic agents most directly concerned in international trade. If guidance is needed, for example because domestic prices are still being restructured, current relative world market prices could be adopted as the starting point for negotiations. But in due course, some divergences from world market prices to suit local demand and supply relations could emerge. Settlements of such transactions and the correction of temporary as well as structural imbalances, however, are matters for which central authorities must assume full responsibility. If enterprises, for example, were to decide to trade at world prices in convertible currency, the question of the exchange rate would be a purely domestic affair. By definition, there would be no technical problem of what to do with imbalances since they are settled in convertible currency. The latter, however, must be funded somehow, and this raises the issue of reforming the orthodox CMEA payments system.

The critical problem for the reforming economies in maintaining their reciprocal economic relations is twofold. One is the chronic shortage of convertible currency. Likewise, external pressures are such that these countries are extremely reluctant to use this limited foreign exchange for making payments that used to be denominated in transferable roubles and cleared in some fashion through the settlements mechanism entrusted to the International Bank for Economic Cooperation.

Short of a CMEA-wide "big bang" approach, it is useful to consider the experience of the west European economies after the Second World War. Whether the course adopted at that time was wise, in retrospect, is not at issue.[312] Policy makers at the time committed themselves to pursue stability and the gradual reintroduction of fully-fledged market relations. In the foreign context, the latter were made contingent on regaining domestic stability through various policy measures.

Externally, these countries faced a severe dollar shortage. They therefore decided to enforce bilateralism and a range of related foreign exchange and trade controls so as to avoid chronic payments problems. These controls tended to exacerbate the dollar shortage experienced immediately after the war because of generally overvalued exchange rates in Europe. They also worked to inhibit the recovery of intra-European trade.

The solution adopted at the time was the creation of the European Payments Union (EPU).[313] The core objective of that clearing mechanism was to promote intragroup trade through the gradual elimination of bilateralism. Another essential ingredient was that the starting capital, expressed in dollars, was made available by the United States in the context of its European Recovery Programme. By requiring that intragroup payments be increasingly made in fungible assets managed through the EPU, the countries of western Europe regained convertibility in the sense of Article VIII of the International Monetary Fund, with some, rather inconsequential, exceptions, by 1958.

The central task of alleviating the constraints on intra-CMEA trade differs slightly from what was the root economic motivation of the EPU. The core short-run task is not so much bolstering the opportunities for trade as obtaining support for re-structuring intragroup trade. This needs to be aligned with the principles and mechanisms of economic rationality that

---

[312] Revisionist economic historians argue that Europe was already well on its way to recovery before Marshall Plan aid became available, that Marshall Plan aid accrued in particular in support of current-account deficits rather than on account of capital goods imports facilitating private investment, and that countries with endemic balance-of-payments problems were thereby dissuaded from revising the pervasive administrative controls and interferences, including in foreign trade. Some of the latter were remnants of the economic nationalism that prevailed in the 1930s or were imposed during the Second World War. There were, however, also restraints adopted for balance-of-payments reasons.

[313] This and the European Coal and Steel Community constituted the twin pillars of sustained recovery and movement towards integration in Europe. The argument is developed at length in Alan S. Milward, *The Reconstruction of Western Europe, 1945-51*, London, Methuen & Co. Ltd, 1987.

are being sought in the domestic economies and in east-west economic relations. Such changes themselves must be subject to co-ordination according to explicit macro-economic policies, aided by appropriate institutions and policy instruments. One obstacle to bringing about such a transition is the shortage of foreign exchange.

Efficient market relations in support of domestic and foreign economic reforms cannot be obtained without a decisive movement towards the establishment of currency convertibility in virtually all trade relations. Such a bold move could be realized either through the "big bang" approach to convertibility, as currently adopted by Poland, or through a more gradual approach. Several CMEA countries have expressed a clear preference for the latter, but the commitment to gradualism may get dissipated under force of circumstance.

A clearing institution with some supervisory authority could offer a route towards obtaining convertibility. For want of a better title, this may be called the Central European Payments Union (CEPU). Membership might initially be confined to the central European countries, including the German Democratic Republic for reasons to be explained below — hence the suggested name. But it need not remain exclusive as more countries in the region seek to implement broad-based market-oriented reforms in an effort to enhance their integration into the world economy.

Whereas the main task of the CEPU, therefore, differs slightly from that of the EPU, the mechanisms involved are much the same. The central technique is to accommodate bilateral imbalances by transforming them into multilateral ones and ensuring that the net surpluses or deficits *vis-à-vis* the participating group as a whole remain manageable. Manageable in this context means that the clearing agency should have sufficient funds to finance the imbalances, perhaps initially through loans,[314] and ample supervisory powers to guide members of the Union into mutually reinforcing behaviour. At the same time, it could be conceived in such a way that, on balance, the requirements for resources of the central fund decrease over time as a steadily rising proportion of the imbalances is paid in convertible currency.

How long would it take to reach convertibility? What conditions need to be met to ensure that the clearing agency can operate in a stable environment? What should be done with the fund's capital base when convertibility is reached? These are some of the many questions that would need to be addressed.

Regarding the duration of the clearing mechanism, everything depends on how quickly these countries will be able to place their trade on a convertible currency basis. This may be more difficult than was the case for western Europe in the 1950s, owing to the fact that eastern Europe and the Soviet Union not only need to introduce market-oriented reforms but also to restructure their external trade and payments. The task of maintaining the volume of trade, while at the same time effecting major changes in its commodity composition and geographical direction in line with comparative advantage, is a daunting one. When it is realized that the latter can proceed only by revising the traditional pricing system and ensuring that the necessary links between the domestic and trade sectors are created, the tasks ahead become even more complex, even under very favourable developments of both the domestic economy and international trade. It could take as much as a decade to achieve all this.

Regarding the technical aspects of the clearing fund and the dangers against which it needs to be safeguarded in order to prevent its premature demise, considerable experience is available from earlier clearing schemes (including the EPU, the sterling area, the French franc zone and the Belgian-Luxemburg clearing area). A foremost concern is that any clearing scheme suffers from a fundamental theoretical weakness. To require in principle that all countries balance their current account within the clearing system is tantamount to assuming that they balance at the same time their accounts with countries outside the system. Without this, participants will be tempted to use their surplus with clearing partners to offset their deficits with outside trade partners; countries in deficit *vis-à-vis* the clearing partners will not want to repatriate their surpluses with outside partners into the clearing arrangement.

In the case of the EPU, this temptation was not very significant for several reasons. One was the size of the intragroup trade. Most participants conducted the bulk of their external commerce among themselves once the process of sustained economic recovery was under way. Furthermore, these countries had enjoyed a considerable degree of mutual political trust and there was a general understanding that all stood to gain from scrupulously observing the rules. As a result, each was willing to pay some price for making the EPU and the transition towards currency convertibility work. Some, such as the Benelux countries, had already embarked on creating considerable regional economic and political cohesion, which helped in reaching consensual solutions to otherwise intractable technical problems. Also, trade and payments with non-participating countries were overwhelmingly with the United States and hence, conducted in the vehicle currency. The United States had been one of the main sponsors of the EPU and had little interest in draining its own currency from the fund.

Are these conditions likely to be met in the case of the eastern countries? Given the present disarray in the CMEA, it is difficult to envisage these countries as a group being imbued with a great deal of trust and confidence at this juncture, although this could change once the uncertainty about objectives begins to dissipate. This lack of confidence is much less pronounced for some of the smaller east European countries. Thus, a clearing agency for the central European countries, to

---

[314] If the fund were to be small, it might be useful to let surplus countries acquire convertible currency loans repayable to the fund. Deficit countries would then provide the additional funding after meeting certain agreed-upon rules on deadlines and magnitudes of tolerable imbalances.

be joined later by other reforming countries, would reflect similar political interests and commitments "to making it work".

The prospect of German unification raises special problems. For one, the German Democratic Republic is the second largest trade partner of most CMEA members. Its industrial prowess, while lagging significantly behind that of most developed market economies, is none the less intimately linked to the needs of the present CMEA partners. This holds in particular for most countries of central Europe, but also for the Soviet Union. At the very least, these CMEA partners will continue to require parts, components, and maintenance of their existing machine park, which is overwhelmingly of CMEA origin, and to a significant degree from the German Democratic Republic. These exchanges can be maintained only if the integration of the eastern part of Germany into the more developed western part does not forcibly exclude them. If only for this reason, it would be important to ensure that part of the trade of a united Germany be conducted through the CEPU, for the CMEA members would in all likelihood find it impossible to place the trade formerly conducted with the German Democratic Republic on a convertible currency basis in the very short run.

Perhaps a solution can be found by recognizing the potential obstacles arising from other technical issues. One concerns the currency unit of the CEPU. Another revolves around the exchange rates to be used in the process. There is no readily identifiable optimal solution, given that convertible currency exchange rates are flexible, that the present currencies of the CMEA countries are inconvertible and that there is simply no ideal — let alone fixed — exchange rate that could be selected for the CEPU members. A pragmatic proposition could be studied: for example, the ECU could be placed at the heart of the CEPU scheme.

The ECU is the most attractive currency unit because it is increasingly being used as the invoicing currency of much of eastern Europe's trade with western Europe. It is also more stable than most other currencies and, of course, fully convertible. Furthermore, it is a currency unit that does not depend solely on any one country's national monetary policy and would, therefore, be better suited to guide international commerce. Also, the aid that is being channelled through the European Communities into eastern Europe is denominated in ECUs.

The members themselves would have to take care, for the time being, of managing the rates at which their external trade gets translated into domestic currencies. This solution would not only invite the CEPU members gradually to manage their foreign exchange régime in tandem with that of the European Monetary System (EMS): it would also subject them to the discipline of the EMS. Of course, such a choice would invite the European Communities to assume a major role in financing the CEPU and seeing to its success over a fairly protracted period of time by, in effect, allowing the members of the CEPU to discriminate against the key western partners. This discrimination is not, however, implemented through standard commercial policy instruments, such as tariffs and quotas, but through preferential access to funds, as was done at the time of the EPU arrangements.

Severe payments problems, especially those of Hungary and Poland, may undermine the scheme from the very beginning. It would, therefore, be useful to find a way that would permit these countries, at least in the short run, to focus on current trade, while the apparently insoluble problems caused by their inherited external debts are resolved through other means.[315] The experience of dealing with severe debt problems during the 1980s in the developing countries is not very encouraging, however. But the east-west assistance efforts coming to fruition under the aegis of the European Communities may well embody a greater degree of political and commercial interest in ensuring the separability of the stock of debt from current payments for trade and services other than debt service.

The major commercial interchanges of these countries are likely to be mainly with non-participants in the CEPU. On the one hand, the key partner in the CMEA is the Soviet Union, with whom trade is still conducted in transferable roubles.[316] On the other hand, western Europe is the key western partner and that trade is conducted in convertible currency. This might tempt participants to erode the clearing fund's base by appropriating surpluses to pay for convertible currency deficits. Only concerted action on the part of the major convertible currency partners, who, as noted, may initially have to finance the clearing scheme, could help to stem that tide.

It is easiest to think about what could usefully be done with the capital fund, when the clearing agency loses its *raison d'être*. In the case of the EPU, once the outstanding clearing credits and debits were transformed into long-term loans, the capital fund was appropriated for development loans and grants to the least developed areas of southern Europe. Something similar could be envisaged for the CEPU. But various other worthwhile purposes could be readily identified. Thus at the time of closing the capital fund, assets could be appropriated to retire frozen debts, encourage the fight against pollution, assist the least developed countries and many others. Allocating the ultimate capital fund, from the moment it is committed to the least developed countries would be a concrete step towards assuaging — albeit not in the short run — the anxiety of devel-

---

[315] The recent agreement reached for Poland in the context of the Paris Club (see *International Herald Tribune*, 17-18 February, p.15) is particularly encouraging in this regard.

[316] As noted, Hungary and Poland have expressed an interest in conducting their trade with the Soviet Union on the basis of world prices and in convertible currency. Agreements to that effect have been under negotiation with the intention of stepping over to such trading and payments arrangements in 1991. Hungary and Poland themselves had intended to be able to do so earlier, perhaps from the start of 1990. This switch has been giving rise to considerable anxieties about potential imbalances to be settled in convertible currency, however. It is, therefore, not at all sure whether the agreements will be put in place as originally envisaged and for all trade.

oping countries about commercial and official financial flows being diverted to eastern Europe.

In the context of the assistance currently being provided, for example by the Group of 24 (see chapter 4), it might be useful to explore the possibilities of setting up a capital base from which the CMEA countries, or at least a subgroup thereof, could find support for moving towards currency convertibility in a comparatively brief period of time. The sums involved are not large. Intragroup trade of the European CMEA countries expressed at official exchange rates amounted to some $75 billion in 1989, with the absolute sum of bilateral imbalances totaling some $5 billion, largely on account of the Soviet Union. If the scheme were to be mounted initially for the most reform-oriented countries, the volume of trade among Czechoslovakia, the German Democratic Republic, Hungary and Poland in 1989 was roughly $7.7 billion with absolute imbalances vis-à-vis the group amounting to $288 million. The volume of imbalances actually to be financed would be even smaller, owing to offsetting service imbalances and other factors. True, the lifting of bilateral constraints to trade among these countries would in all likelihood initially entail greater intragroup imbalances, but not necessarily larger absolute claims on the clearing region.

However, earmarking some of the assistance, already committed through the multilateral financial institutions and the Group of 24 — say, a quarter — for the purpose of reinforcing the trade relations of the reforming countries would be ample. Not only would it support the CMEA reform process from within and strengthen intragroup relations; it would also provide assistance in a form that would least interfere with the emerging economic incentives for micro-economic agents and the market-oriented macro-economic framework being elaborated.

3.5 THE BROADER POLICY FRAMEWORK FOR 1990 AND BEYOND

As discussed in section 3.1(viii), the prospects for positive growth in eastern Europe and the Soviet Union in 1990 are not very good. Indeed, policy priorities are on economic stabilization and putting in train market-oriented reforms rather than on growth *per se*. The policy setting is none the less very different for Hungary and Poland, both of which are pursuing stabilization, and the other countries. Among the latter, the policy framework being put together in Czechoslovakia, while maintaining slow growth in the short run, differs markedly from that of the other economies, all of which are in a state of economic crisis for which solutions still have to be formulated.

(i) The Polish stabilization programme

In early 1990, Poland introduced an exceedingly tight austerity programme. Its central aim is twofold. The immediate objective is to bring rampant inflation under control through orthodox macro-economic policies, that is, the reduction of domestic absorption and the reallocation of resources towards the tradeable sectors. The more structural task is to enforce market orientation for all economic agents through a variety of policy instruments and institutions to be created in part to apply the new government policies.

Among the many measures introduced,[317] the following are the most critical. A ceiling has been placed on wages and pensions for at least the first half of the year, and the programme foresees that the "line be held" for the rest of the year. Strict financial rules are being enforced for enterprises. The government is committed to pursue rapid privatization of a substantial share of state assets and to encourage private property formation from new savings, domestic as well as foreign. Most prices of goods and services have been deregulated. An active anti-monopoly policy aims to keep them under the discipline of competition. At the same time, economic agents are held to see to their own revenues, which are now a binding constraint rather than a flexible one which can be loosened through transfers of one kind or another.

In addition to domestic competition, firms are to be exposed to effective competition from abroad, in the first instance from market economies but also increasingly from the reforming CMEA partner economies, with which liberalized bilateral trade and payments regimes are to be introduced (see section 3.4). To foster this, the exchange rate of the zloty was devalued massively, roughly to the level observed in secondary markets.[318] Access to foreign exchange has been very much broadened by instituting internal currency convertibility. Although at present the government is maintaining a fixed exchange rate, this is seen as a point of orientation only for the first phase — perhaps the first quarter of 1990 — of the transformation. The exchange rate is then to be adjusted according to a basket of convertible currencies in line with developments in international financial markets and changes in domestic and international trade prices.

Micro-economic efficiency is to be enforced through tight monetary policy that will bring about positive real interest rates by the end of the first quarter and tolerate only commercially oriented lending by the decentralized banks. This policy stance is supported by the elimination of subsidies for most retail goods and services.[319] Unprofitable firms will be forced to close as bankruptcy proceedings are becoming effective. These policies regarding micro-economic enterprise management and bankruptcy are bound to result in substantial unemployment, for which a comprehensive social safety net is to be established (see section (iii) below).

Alongside monetary policy, the entire fiscal system is to be restructured around a value-added tax, a personal income tax and a uniform corporate tax. Putting all these measures in place will take time, however.

Finally, considerable efforts are made to establish the infrastructure required for genuine financial intermediation. This extends from commercial, merchant and investment banking, to pension funds, insurance schemes and an active stock exchange. Such an infrastructure obviously can also be set up only gradually.

This policy package aims at stabilization along several lines. Private consumption will be compressed by large cuts in the real value of wages and other monetary incomes, especially during the first half of 1990. Investment demand is to be constrained by monetary policy instruments, including positive real interest rates and restrictions on the money supply. Credit demand is to be actively rationed by commercial banks on the

---

[317] For a detailed exposition of the rationale of the stabilization policy and the key measures, see "Zalozenia polityki spoleczno-gospodarczej na 1990 r." (Fundamentals of the socio-economic policy for 1990), *Rzeczpospolita*, 15 December 1989, pp.5-6. See also section 5.2 below.

[318] When introduced in early January (9,500 zloty per dollar), the official rate exceeded the free market rate for the first time in the post-war period.

[319] The share of all subsidies in the budget is to be reduced from 31 per cent in 1989 to 14 per cent in 1990. Subsidies are retained at present to check the rise in rents and the prices of some public transport, energy, bread and some dairy products.

basis of economic merit. The devaluation of the currency, it is hoped, will in time boost exports, especially to convertible-currency partners, for which reason the implicit rouble-dollar exchange rate prevailing has been further devalued to about 4.52 roubles to the dollar.[320] A drastic reduction in the budget deficit, by eliminating all kinds of overt and concealed consumer price and enterprise subsidies, will compress consumption and investment demand. This radical, "big bang" stabilization programme is being enacted with the support of multilateral and bilateral donors (for more details see section 4.4).

When the stabilization package was introduced, policy makers were open about the adverse impact which was bound to ensue during the first few months. Thus, they anticipated price increases ranging from 25 per cent to 50 per cent a month during the initial stage of the programme as firms losing subsidies would raise prices to survive. For January 1990 alone, the rate of inflation was expected to be 45 per cent, due largely to the elimination of subsidies for staples and other goods.[321] Real incomes as a result would be reduced in a short period of time by an average of 20 per cent.[322] Aggregate output was expected to fall by 2 to 3 per cent, owing largely to an anticipated drop of 5 per cent in industrial production. The level of unemployment was expected to rise sharply to perhaps 300,000 workers or about 1½ per cent of the work force.[323] On the positive side, inflation was expected to abate to a few per cent a month by mid-1990.

Although the Polish government hopes that the stabilization programme will arrest inflation by mid-1990 and then begin to encourage positive growth, serious doubts remain whether the hyperinflationary situation prevailing at the end of 1989 can be turned round that quickly at a socially acceptable cost. The impact of the initial "corrective" price and exchange rate adjustments, intended to provide a sound base for the further development, clearly exceeded anticipations. In January 1990, factory sales prices were 110 per cent and consumer prices almost 80 per cent above the December 1989 level. In consequence, interest rates — at 38 per cent per month — were negative in real terms to a much larger degree than expected. However, already in February they may have turned positive, depending on which sector of the economy one considers.[324] On a daily basis, nominal money incomes of the population in February were 57 per cent above the December 1989 level, but 30 per cent below that level in real terms. The fall was even steeper for the average wage — some 47 per cent. This had a pronounced impact on consumer demand. Consumer spending on goods and services in February 1990 was 22 per cent above the December 1989 level in nominal terms — and some 45 per cent below the December level in real terms.

Economic activity in the first two months of 1990 contracted very rapidly.[325] Industrial production in the socialized sector declined by almost one third relative to the same period of 1989 (but remained at roughly the January level in February), a fall that was only partly offset by a rise in private activities for which statistical accounting is yet to be completed. Government spokesmen placed the overall contraction in industry at perhaps 15 per cent — far worse than anticipated. The fall mainly reflected the sharp contraction of consumer real incomes and purchasing power. Output of the main consumer goods branches (the light industry and food processing sectors) fell by over 40 per cent.

In the process, levels of unemployment soared to some 152,000 at the end of February, while the number of announced job vacancies fell from more than 250,000 at the end to 1989 to about 20,000.[326]

After an initial steep fall of both exports and imports in January, exports picked up in February as enterprises began to search for outside markets to replace the fall in domestic demand.[327] Many firms complain that they are uncompetitive at the fixed exchange rate introduced,[328] owing in part to the very sharp increase in the cost of raw materials and especially of fuels. Apparently, the large cut in real incomes forced people to convert their dollar savings into zloty which may have provided a somewhat artificial prop to the chosen fixed exchange rate.

In spite of the considerable political goodwill enjoyed by the present Solidarity-led government, the se-

---

320 In early 1989, the Polish cross rate had been 2.20 roubles per dollar. This was raised rapidly in the course of 1989 — in mid-year it stood at 2.50, in September at 3.00, and in December at 3.60. These rates contrast sharply with the rouble/dollar exchange rate — roughly 0.65 in December 1989 — quoted by the International Bank for Economic Co-operation in Moscow, which is entrusted with managing transferable rouble transactions, and the official exchange rate against the dollar of the Soviet State Bank (0.61 roubles per dollar in December 1990).

321 Coal, gasoline and other energy prices alone were raised five- to sevenfold in early 1990. Subsidies for public transportation were slashed and tariffs increased by some 250 per cent.

322 At the same time, it was hoped that the programme would quickly eliminate pervasive shortages. The real effect of the cut in incomes on levels of well-being would, therefore, be somewhat less than the magnitude of the real income effect.

323 Estimates made by the International Monetary Fund reportedly placed expected unemployment at about three times that level, with nearly 1 million individuals or 5 per cent of the labour force out of work by year's end. *Rzeczpospolita*, 8 February 1990, p.2.

324 Producer prices rose only 7 per cent over January levels, while consumer prices increased some 24 per cent, most of this reflecting the impact of price increases introduced in the course of January. Interest rates for February had been reduced to a rate of some 20 per cent per month.

325 Key quantitative indicators are reported in *Rzeczpospolita*, 8 February 1990, p.2 and 23 March 1990, pp.7-8.

326 See *Rzeczpospolita*, 23 March February 1990, p.7.

327 Total exports fell by 1½ per cent in volume in the first two months while imports declined by 13 per cent. In rouble trade, exports declined by 3½ per cent and imports by 19 per cent, whereas in convertible-currency trade exports stagnated in the first two months while imports fell by 6½ per cent. The rouble trade surplus increased 1.5 fold and the surplus in convertible-currency trade by 20 per cent. *Rzeczpospolita*, 23 March 1990.

328 For commentary, see *Rzeczpospolita*, 8 February 1990, p.2 and *Zycie gospodarcze*, No.7 (1990), p.11.

verity and abruptness of the austerity programme led to some strikes, albeit brief, in key sectors, including coal mining. The confusion and even panic that occurred during the first weeks of the programme have since given way to less pained responses, if not calm and order, on the part of households and enterprise managers.

Certainly, developments in two months cannot be indicative of the eventual overall success of the stabilization programme. Whereas price increases have abated signifcantly in February and early March, there are structural problems in the Polish economy that do not augur well for limiting the contraction of output. One is the shortage of liquidity which may be putting out of business firms that otherwise would be perfectly sound. This applies also to the financing of agriculture for both inputs (such as fertilizer) and outputs (such as the grain crop). Inadequately developed financial structures are also hampering exports and the rapid introduction of small and medium-sized firms on which the Polish authorities have placed great hopes.

(ii) Towards stabilization in Hungary?

Hungary has also been trying to put into place a stabilization programme, in the first instance to come to grips with external imbalances,[329] but also to control accelerating inflation. Although stabilization measures have been debated at great length and some have been agreed upon, if only to contain the growth of the external debt (about $20 billion with convertible currency partners), there is not as yet a comprehensive, internally consistent programme in place.

Without refinancing of the external debt, the ongoing reform efforts could be nipped in the bud. The necessary foreign support could be mustered only by working out a new medium-term agreement with the International Monetary Fund.[330] Apart from gaining fresh funds through such a programme from the IMF and the World Bank, it was expected to provide a seal of approval for the country's creditworthiness and hence the co-operation of international banks in, at least *de facto*, debt rescheduling. Although a firm agreement with the IMF had not yet been signed,[331] in December 1990, the authorities adopted a short-term deficit-reduction programme that in part reflected the Fund's conditions to be embodied in any future agreement. This programme is being implemented since January 1990.

The programme comprises a cut in budget subsidies for basic foodstuffs and services (including housing and transport), privatization of part of state assets, the introduction of positive real interest rates, reducing growth of the money supply, a decrease in the trade surplus with CMEA partners as long as this cannot be turned into convertible currency, and a reduction of inflation. To boost exports, there was a further 10 per cent devaluation of the forint in late December 1989. Price subsidies are to be slashed by Ft 40 billion, although social expenditures will be raised in an effort to ease social tensions. Bank loans are to be reduced below their 1989 nominal level and savings are to be encouraged through positive real interest rates.[332]

This stricter policy is expected to lead to a rate of inflation of 20 per cent in 1990, on account of the forint devaluation[333] and the sharply reduced price subsidies. In the process, real wages are being lowered by an anticipated 2.5 per cent, the expected inflation being substantially offset through nominal wage increases of about 17 per cent. Unemployment is to rise to 50,000 or 1 per cent of the labour force, but a moderate social safety net is in place. By creating greater competition, in part through accelerated privatization, inflationary pressures are expected to be held in check. But one main cause of pressure will be the commitment to abolish substantial elements of the remaining rigidities of the price system and effectively linking domestic to world prices as soon as circumstances permit.

There is, however, broad agreement among policy makers and economists in Hungary that much more needs to be done to reverse the crippling fiscal deficit and to come to deal with the sizeable domestic debt, and the substantial external debt in convertible currency, to regain a competitive position in world markets, restructure the economy along market-oriented lines and regain a faster but sustainable pace of growth. Under current circumstances, action will in all likelihood be taken only after the general election in March.

(iii) Unemployment and the safety net: a new problem

As already noted, policy makers in the countries pursuing stabilization and far-reaching economic reforms are aware of the possible emergence of sizeable levels of unemployment — an altogether new phenomenon for eastern countries. This raises two difficult issues. One has to do with the social aspects of unemployment. It may be very difficult for society to accept substantial unemployment levels, if only because the

---

[329] In late 1989, Hungarian policy makers were facing a precarious balance-of-payments outlook, owing in part to the fact that for 1990 the country needed $1.5 billion for interest payments and $1.9 billion for repayments of principal — about 10 per cent of GDP.

[330] *Népszabadság*, 20 December 1989. pp.1 and 4.

[331] A letter of intent was signed on 14 February 1990 (*Neue Zürcher Zeitung*, 15 February 1990, p.35). A full-scale agreement may be reached perhaps as early as March.

[332] Perhaps the most difficult compromise had to be reached for housing subsidies. In 1989, in support only of the interest rate differential between the contracted mortgage rate and the going market rate, these claimed Ft 45 billion. Rents for state-owned apartments were increased. Also the rate on "old" mortgages was retroactively increased through a special "interest tax".

[333] Smaller devaluations of about 2 per cent were enacted twice during the first three weeks of February. Central banking authorities have made it clear that frequent devaluations — and possibly revaluations — will be pursued in the coming months.

right to a job has been so deeply ingrained in the psychology of the population at large. Under the post-war framework, everybody has a constitutional right to a job from which dismissal is possible only under rather rigid rules. Without agreed new rules on acquired rights, tough stabilization policies open the door to all kinds of arbitrary decisions. This appears already to be causing discontent in Poland, for example. Phenomena such as unemployment and unexpected price changes are difficult to reconcile with political expectations, as in Poland, where Solidarity — at root a trade union — has been in the vanguard of moving towards greater pluralism in decision-making.

The other problem is whether society should come to grips with unemployment by instituting a broad social safety net, including explicit provisions for unemployment allowances, and to what degree, relative to prior earnings, this security should be pursued and for how long. Hungary put in place such a programme in 1989[334] and Poland introduced its version in February 1990.[335] In Poland, the unemployed receive 70 per cent of their most recent wages for three months, 50 per cent for the next six months and 40 per cent thereafter without any time limit. But refusal to take up a job offer will reduce the benefits to zero. In addition to direct income transfers, the safety net also includes an elegant incentive scheme to encourage job creation and job retraining and relocation benefits.[336] It remains to be seen what will be the impact on the budget of these provisions at a time of rapid escalation of unemployment levels.

The Hungarian unemployment provisions are less generous: beginning in 1990,[337] for one year, the unemployed can obtain unemployment benefits amounting to 55 to 70 per cent of their gross average monthly earnings of the last 12 months of employment; for the next 12 months, the unemployed automatically qualify for an unemployment allowance amounting to 75 per cent of the last month's unemployment benefits.[338] There are also retraining grants for firms and individuals,[339] public works programmes organized by local government, low-interest state loans for private ventures by the unemployed, and other provisions. The number of unemployed has remained low, however.[340]

(iv) Perestroika and stabilization in the Soviet Union

After nearly five years of vacillating reform with growing imbalances, the Soviet leadership now appears determined to deal with the crises that are perceived to immobilize the Soviet economy in general and to penalize the consumer in particular. Certainly, the government tried earlier to implement measures to curb inflation and stabilize the economy, but neither had a sizeable impact. At present, there is broad agreement that bold initiatives need to be taken.

As a result of the rapidly deteriorating economic situation since mid-1989, stabilization also ranks high on the policy agenda in the Soviet Union, where it is now perceived as the necessary first step towards laying the foundations upon which genuine *perestroika* can be pursued in the 1990s. This does not yet signal a prelude to fully-fledged marketization, however.[341] But what precisely needs to be done, in what form, and how quickly stabilization should be pursued as a precondition for making headway with genuine decentralization, remain key issues in the ongoing discussions of reform. The first economic priority at present, however, is to reduce the budget deficit by a sizeable amount, increase supplies of consumer goods and foodstuffs, convert decommissioned military installations and equipment to civilian uses and reactivate the inadequate transportation sector.

With a rapidly worsening economic situation in 1989 in key consumer markets, an effective stabilization policy became an urgent need. In late 1989, Deputy Prime Minister Leonid I. Abalkin tabled a complementary draft to *perestroika*, including a detailed stabilization programme for 1990 which was to be the foundation stone for moving swiftly ahead with *perestroika* thereafter.[342]

The stabilization package was built around three themes. First, it envisaged a deficit-reduction programme, a tight-money policy, a major effort to improve the supply of consumer goods and services, the gradual elimination of virtually all loss-making firms by

---

[334] An unemployment scheme introduced in 1957, which allowed Ft 600 per month for six months, remained in legal force until the mid-1980s. Because it was apparently never applied, the provision was completely forgotten when the need arose to put in place a safety net (*Heti Világgazdaság*, 24 December 1983).

[335] Also the German Democratic Republic has recently introduced unemployment benefits to offset the involuntary layoffs due to the large emigration wave, which, as noted, has led to considerable industrial disorganization. Unemployment in early February 1990 amounted to roughly 50,000 (interview with Deputy Prime Minister Christa Luft, in *Neues Deutschland*, 6 February 1990, p.5). Unlike in Hungary and Poland, the number of advertised job vacancies for now remains very high, however.

[336] For the text of the law, see *Rzeczpospolita*, 5 January 1990, pp.3-4.

[337] When first introduced in 1989, this safety net provided for unemployment benefits for one year only.

[338] *Heti Világgazdaság*, 27 January 1990.

[339] These were first introduced in 1983 (*Figyelö*, 27 October 1983).

[340] At the end of September 1989, the number was less than 15,000. Some 5,000 individuals qualified for benefit payments, 4,600 were employed by local government in public works, 370 asked for retraining and less than 600 applied for "restart loans". For details, see *Figyelö*, 11 January 1990.

[341] Early in 1990, it was not even clear whether the Soviet Union eventually aims at anchoring its economy to market decision-making co-ordinated through orthodox macro-economic policies. For a discussion of the ambivalence on this issue, see A. Bachurin, "Kakoi rynok nam nuzhen" (What kind of market do we need?), *Planovoe khozyaistvo*, No.1 (1990), pp.42-51.

[342] See *Izvestiya*, 22 September 1989, p.3. The post-stabilization part of the programme consists of the start-up of genuine reform during 1991-1992, the introduction of the new system throughout the economy during the next three years and the full realization of the programme during the second half of the 1990s.

transferring assets to other property forms, and a range of measures to reduce gradually the monetary overhang. This package would constitute one of the prerequisites for launching new wholesale prices in 1990 and genuine wholesale trading, with firms themselves determining prices and quantities, as opposed to the present overwhelming use of state orders. The second component consisted of the adoption of laws and regulations on the new banking system, economic stabilization through macro-economic policy and anti-monopoly measures as the legislative basis for new economic measures.

This moderately ambitious programme could have helped to redress the worst imbalances in the Soviet economy. But it failed to elicit the full support of the leadership and the parliamentary organs, which instead adopted a much less radical set of measures aimed at protecting real incomes and state enterprises, in part by spreading the adjustment of prices over a longer period of time. In its resolution of 20 November 1989,[343] the Supreme Soviet adopted a package of anti-inflation measures that include the temporary suspension of legal provisions which permitted enterprises to set contract prices for basic foodstuffs and certain non-food goods in wide use as well as a similar suspension of the right of enterprises to export on their own initiative (i.e., outside the plan) consumer goods and basic raw materials for their production. At the same time, the government implemented measures to prevent the removal of cheap mass products from production and to forestall further hidden price rises for "new products": both measures are aimed at stabilizing consumer markets.[344] The programme seeks to spread stabilization over a multi-year period. Moreover, measures are being prepared to compensate some strata of the population for the erosion of fixed incomes. Finally, several initiatives were endorsed to bolster production and destocking of consumer goods, including from the military sector, and increase the sale of houses and apartments.

At the same time, the government was mandated to accelerate the implementation of radical economic reforms, set in train measures for financial recovery, stabilize money circulation and satisfy consumer demand during 1990-1992. This period would also be used to work out new methods of macro-economic management, including commercial, fiscal and monetary policies. Furthermore, during 1990, draft laws on ownership, including of land, on the autonomy of republics and regions, on the banking sector, on regulating investment activity, on employment and on related reform matters should be finalized.

The above steps may not suffice to stabilize the economy fully, however. But the broad debate on how to reform the Soviet economy since the inception of *glasnost'* is now polarizing into the mainstream view that genuine economic reform with balanced macro-economic policies will take a long time. Prior to changing the economic system in a major way, economic stabilization policies need to be formulated and implemented in order to pull the country out of stagnation. Policy makers still hope that such stabilization can be achieved largely by increasing the supply of goods and services and increasing the range of assets that households and firms can hold. Price reform is now planned to be carried out only gradually, starting with wholesale and procurement prices from 1991 and much later retail prices.

(v) Late joiners: post-revolutionary economic policies

In the other eastern countries, short-run priorities diverge considerably from each other as well as those just discussed. As noted earlier, the preoccupation in the *German Democratic Republic* at this stage is with its status as a sovereign economy and state, and perhaps with the terms at which its economy might be absorbed into that of the Federal Republic, rather than with economic growth.

Czechoslovakia is committed to a firm course of societal reforms, including the transition to a fully-fledged market economy. Instead of a "big bang" approach, however, the leadership appears to aim at a gradual phasing out of the planning system with all its ramifications of administratively fixed prices, enterprise subsidies, generous lending policies, state ownership of the means of production and other features of central planning. In the short run, policy makers are bent on putting together a viable package of reforms while at the same time keeping the economy on the slow, but stable growth path experienced for the last decade. The new Czechoslovak government is engaged in the creation of the legislative and organizational prerequisites,[345] with the aim of dismantling the monopolistic position of big enterprises and to increase competition. Further steps are to include liberalization of prices, cutting of subsidies and opening the economy towards the world.[346] Policy makers hope, however, that the loosening of constraints on markets over a period of three to four years, with unemployment amounting to perhaps 2 per cent of the labour force and some rise in inflation as subsidies are gradually eliminated, will make possible at the same time a slight acceleration in economic growth after 1990.[347]

---

[343] *Pravda*, 29 November 1989, pp.1 and 3. The Congress of People's Deputies also addressed the issues at stake in December and issued instructions to the government (see *Pravda*, 22 December 1989, pp.1, 2).

[344] As of 1 January 1990, the price of "new" consumer products can be augmented at most by 30 per cent.

[345] Laws on the state enterprise, on private enterprises and on shareholding companies are to be adopted by the Federal Assembly in the early part of 1990. See *Financial Times*, 26 February 1990, p.18.

[346] Speech of Prime Minister M. Calfa to the Federal Assembly, cited in BBC, *Summary of World Broadcasts*,, No.EE/0701, 1 March 1990, pp.C/1-C/7.

[347] Interviews with Deputy Prime Minister Valtr Komárek, *Neue Zürcher Zeitung*, 8 February 1990 and BBC, *Summary of World Broadcasts*, No.EE/0683, 8 February 1990, p.B/5. An anti-inflation programme is being worked out, according to Minister of Finance Václav Klaus. *Svet hospodářství*, 9 February 1990, pp.1, 2.

In Bulgaria and Romania, the socio-political situation was rather unstable in the early months of 1990, and the further path of these economies was only being mapped out. Both countries face elections later in the year. In both, authorities in the meantime appear to aim at reforms that more resemble the Soviet combination of central planning with market co-ordination than the transformations sought in the other east European countries.

In *Bulgaria,* first concerns are with an "anti-crisis" economic policy which is to arrest the recession, curtail inflation fed by the fiscal deficit, and deal with the parlous balance-of-payments situation. This is to go hand in hand with the creation of instruments for an effective social protection of the economically weak strata of the population. The measures to be taken to this end are to be viewed as the first step towards and at the same time the pre-condition for a radical economic reform.[348] The medium-term aim is the building of a "socially oriented mixed market economy," where the term "mixed" refers both to property forms and to the economic mechanisms. Planning may continue, but will not be binding on enterprises. In a first stage, already in 1990, there will be some deregulation of economic activity; the creation of the legal bases for decentralized economic activity is envisaged for a second stage reaching to 1995, and full marketization for the second half of the 1990s.[349]

Top priority in *Romania* at the beginning of 1990 was the establishment of an emergency programme to overcome the "blockage of the entire economic mechanism" and to revive the economy.[350] Industrial production in the first months of 1990 was 70 per cent of the preceding year's level, and inflation was rising.[351] Under these circumstances, management of the economy continues to rely largely on the central administrative apparatus in place, though with increased autonomy of sectoral ministries and large enterprises,[352] with planning on an *ad hoc* or a very short-term (quarterly) basis. Some steps have been taken towards a limited liberalization of markets, including the authorization of small-scale private economic activity (up to 20 employees),[353] and considerations are being given to the issue of on what terms to admit foreign investment. However, although the authorities of the provisional government foresee a movement towards a more decentralized economy with larger elements of market co-ordination and a pluralized (mixed) property structure, at present the concessions in this direction seem rather grudging.[354] If only for these reasons, a decisive move towards a more decentralized, market economy environment is so far a matter for the long-term, not of short-term economic policy.

---

[348] "Deklaratsiya na Pravitelstvoto," (Government declaration), *Rabotnichesko delo,* 9 February 1990.

[349] Interview with Minister for Problems of Economic Reform Stefan Stoilov, in *Narodna armiya,* as cited in BBC, *Summary of World Broadcasts,* No.EE/0700, 28 February 1990, p.B/2.

[350] See speech of Prime Minister Petre Roman to the National Salvation Council on 4 January 1990, as reported in BBC, *Summary of World Broadcasts,* No.EE/0657, 9 January 1990, pp.B/8-10. In a later speech, the Prime Minister compared the state of the economy to "that of a ropewalker, the distance between the rope and the floor getting smaller at times and greater at other times". Rompres, 5 February 1990, as cited in BBC, *Summary of World Broadcasts,* No.EE/0682, 7 February 1990, p.B/7.

[351] Interview of the Chairman of the Provisional National Unity Council Ion Iliescu in *Romania libera,* as cited in BBC, *Summary of World Broadcasts,* No.EE/0701, 1 March 1990, p.B/2.

[352] Centrally determined allocation of resources has been reduced from 100 plan indicators and 1,800 commodities of the previous administration to 12-14 indicators and 400 commodities. See "Economia in centrul preocuparilor" (The economy at the centre of preoccupations), report on a press conference of General V. Stanculescu, Minister of the National Economy, in *Tribuna economica,* 1990, No. 6, 9 February 1990.

[353] "Decret-lege privind organizarea si desfasurarea unor activitati economice pe baza liberei initiative" (Decree-law on the organization and conduct of certain economic activities on the basis of free initiative), *Adevarul,* 7 February 1990.

[354] Discussions of decentralization often stress that it will not be "brutal," but cautious, and the issue of privatization frequently comes up in the context of what is *not* suitable for this form – large enterprises and large state farms, for instance. See, e.g., Iliescu, *loc. cit.*

3.6 DEVELOPMENTS IN THE SERVICE SECTOR, 1970-1987

The analysis of the east European and Soviet economies in the Economic Survey of Europe has traditionally concentrated on developments in agriculture, industry, investment, living standards and foreign trade. The growing role of services in domestic activity as well as in international trade justifies a closer review of the evolution of this sector as well. This section offers a survey of the development of services between 1970 and 1987 in the eastern Europe and the Soviet Union. Section (i) examines the role and place of services in the national economies, while section (ii) analyses the development of the service sector as a whole and its quantitative importance within the total economy. Two basic sub-groups are also examined: section (iii) focuses on producer services (transport, communications and trade), while the evolution of consumer services is discussed in section (iv). Conclusions are given in section (v).

(i) The role and place of the service sector

While services have emerged as one of the most important and most dynamic sectors in the developed market economies, in the centrally planned economies development priorities were generally given to the rapid expansion of the material sphere of the economy, particularly industry. The overall level of development of the countries concerned played an important role in the allocation of resources.[355] But for historical and doctrinal reasons, in particular the excessive significance attached to the so called "productive" – i.e., material – sphere, services have tended to be neglected and had lagged behind the growing demand for them.[356] However, the picture is not uniform between countries or between different time periods. With the maturing of economies, which was reflected in the diversification of demand and economic activity, a more complex division of labour and the diffusion of science and technology, the growing importance of the service sector has become apparent. The service sector, as shown in several previous issues of this publication, has absorbed a growing share of the economically active population. Employment in the material sphere, dominated by branches producing goods, either stagnated or even fell somewhat during the 1980s in most countries.

Developments in services in the developed market economies suggest that a large macro-economic structural change in favour of the service sector could be an important driving force in the future economic development of eastern Europe and the Soviet Union. It has also become increasingly apparent that without a better understanding of the dynamics and functioning of services within national economies and internationally it will be difficult to foresee the direction of change in modern societies.[357]

A detailed analysis of the factors causing an extension of the service sector in most contemporary economies goes beyond the framework of this section. But it seems that the following elements underlying the growing role of services can be singled out:

– changes in demand patterns, which include a shift from the consumption of goods to services as incomes rise;

– the shortening of working hours, which provides more free time for leisure activities (further education, sport, culture and tourism);

– the development of many branches producing goods (industry, construction and agriculture) increasingly requires the strengthening of corresponding producer services (transport, communications and trade). A variety of additional services has appeared in this field which have become essential for the smooth functioning and increased efficiency of the economy, such as business and professional services. Moreover, the economic reforms promulgated in most east European countries and the Soviet Union, and the greater independence of enterprises in both domestic and external activities, now call for specialization in fields such as banking, insurance, marketing, legal and information services and consultancy;

– the increasing role played by services in international trade. Besides services which are complementary with trade in goods (transport, marketing etc.), other types of services such as transnational banking, international market in-

---

[355] As indicated in some studies, the link between development level of the whole economy and the development of services (infrastructure) is fairly strong. See, for example, E. Ehrlich, *Services. An International Comparison, 1960-1983*. Paper written for the Fifth Annual Seminar on the Service Economy, PROGRES, Services World Forum, Geneva, May 1989.

[356] S.A. Shalayev, Chairman of the Soviet All-Union Central Council of Trade Unions, stated that among the reasons why services lagged behind other sectors of the national economy was a deeply-rooted planning practice according to which a "residual approach" to the social sphere, including the service sector, predominated. Speech at the 19th Conference of the CPSU, *Pravda*, 3 July 1988.

[357] In this respect see Orio Giarini, *The Emerging Service Economy*, Pergamon Press, Services World Forum, 1987.

formation services, telecommunications and tourism have expanded very rapidly;[358]

— science and technology, especially information technology and the application of computers, have led to the creation of new computer-related services and broader utilization of telecommunications;

— the increasingly important role in the development of the service sector played by social preferences in eastern Europe and the Soviet Union. The increasing share of total consumption financed from public and collective funds, particularly in spheres such as housing, science, education and health in some countries, may also have promoted a shift towards services.

The service sectors perform a wide range of functions indispensable for the operation of a modern economy and the improvement of its efficiency. The service sectors create employment opportunities in both a quantitative and a qualitative sense (e.g., through development of knowledge-intensive services, linked with information technology). Improvements in the standard of living at the present stage of development in the countries under review depend to a great extent on expanded provision of personal and social services — housing, health, education, culture, tourism, sport, etc. Last but not least, increased trade in services (for example tourism) is often a cost-effective way to provide additional foreign-exchange earnings.[359] For all these reasons, the role of services in development and policy issues has attracted increased attention of economists and policy makers in eastern Europe and the Soviet Union in recent years.

The traditional partition of activities into "productive" and "non-productive" lines, which used to be the basis for classifying economic sectors and branches into the material and non-material spheres under the systems of national accounting used in the seven countries reviewed here, has come under challenge. However, no comprehensive theory on the service economy exists in the east European countries or the Soviet Union. Discussions on this topic, and recent changes in statistical and planning practices in some of these countries, indicate recognition of the need to deal more comprehensively with this subject.[360]

The term "services" is not easy to define, since it includes a variety of activities (often classified differently in different countries) with varying characteristics. Some commonly accepted characteristics of services (immateriality, non-storability and simultaneity of production and consumption) which distinguish them from goods are only relative and can be changed by technological developments (such as the computerized storage of data flows). Moreover, the complex character of modern production processes, notably their interlinkages between different activities, makes it difficult to separate the production of goods from producer services. In addition to conceptual and methodological problems there are major difficulties in compiling statistical information on services. There is still no internationally agreed definition on what constitutes services, and the very concept thus varies from country to country.[361]

For practical reasons this study is based on statistics and classifications available from east European and Soviet sources. Lack of data restricts possibilities for a comprehensive examination of the service sector. This is particularly the case with regard to the output of the sector, measurement of which is inherently difficult and for which only limited systematic aggregated data are available. Another obstacle is posed by the different classification systems used by individual countries, and notably differences among the seven countries reviewed in the attribution of particular activities to material production and to the non-material sphere.[362]

The main classification difference between the countries examined is that in Czechoslovakia and the Soviet Union, passenger transport and communications serving the population are included in the non-material sphere, whereas in the other countries of eastern Europe they are classified as belonging to the material sphere. There are also others: for example, in Czechoslovakia, the output of laundries, cleaners, independent computer centres, etc., is not included in the material sphere, whereas geological research work, the water economy and others are treated as part of material production.

The incomplete statistical record of services also poses a problem. Some services are hidden in goods-producing branches. Thus design or repair and main-

---

358 A discussion on trade in services in the world economy and also in eastern Europe and the Soviet Union can be found in UNCTAD, *Trade and Development Report, 1988*, United Nations, New York, 1988. In its report on international trade in 1988-1989 the GATT underlined the growing importance of services in the world economy. Growth in services trade has outstripped that of merchandise exports for much of this decade. It now stands at slightly less than 20 per cent of total trade in goods and services for both developed and developing countries. See GATT, *International Trade 88-89*, Geneva, 1989. See also United Nations Economic Commission for Europe, *Economic Bulletin for Europe*, vol.41, New York, 1989.

359 It should be noted that tourism benefited in recent years from improved east-west relations and expanded significantly, particularly in Hungary, Czechoslovakia and Poland. This brought about a welcome increase in hard currency earnings. Some east European countries have announced their intention to reinforce the expansion of tourism in the years to come. In the Soviet Union, the reform of tourism is seen as an integral part of overall economic reforms. However, shortages of hotels and the lack of other services have appeared as important constraints. International co-operation (joint ventures) in this field can bring about good results. See *Pravda*, 25 August 1989.

360 See for example *Hospodarske noviny*, No. 25, 23 June 1989, p.3. The resolution of the USSR Congress of People's Deputies requires that statistical indicators of economic development be presented in accordance with international practice. *Pravda*, 25 June 1989.

361 See United Nations Economic and Social Council (Statistical Commission), *Service statistics*, E/CN.3/1989/7, 5 October 1988. See also United Nations Economic Commission for Europe, *Economic Bulletin for Europe*, vol.41, New York, 1989.

362 For a discussion on the distinction between the sphere of material production and the non-productive sphere, together with a list of activities belonging to the material and the non-material spheres, see United Nations Economic Commission of Europe, *Economic Survey of Europe in 1984-1985*, New York, 1985, pp.154-156.

tenance work carried out by industrial enterprises themselves is usually not differentiated from the production activity of the industrial sector. Service occupations in the goods-producing sectors are thus not included in service sector employment. The picture on the performance of the service sector would be different, moreover, if the black (shadow) economy were taken into account, but such activities are by definition not registered at all.[363] Thus, not only is it difficult to draw a precise dividing line between services and other activities, but also a large part of service activities evade statistical measurement.

Bearing these problems in mind, the service sector is defined, for the purposes of this study and for practical reasons, as a complex including all activities of the national economy outside agriculture, forestry, construction and industry.

The data for the service sector as a whole were accordingly calculated by grouping together some sectors of the material sphere (transport, communications and trade – referred to as *producer services*) and all sectors of the non-material sphere (*consumer services*). Again, inter-country differences in classification and methodology mean that data for these two highly aggregated spheres are not always fully comparable.[364]

A constant problem in analysing developments in eastern Europe and the Soviet Union is price formation. Under central planning prices were not necessarily related to demand or to scarcity. Thus, services are generally priced low or provided free of charge to stimulate social consumption; their share in the economy – including the share of the producer service branches in NMP – thus tends to be understated Even such variables as investment, fixed assets or the remuneration of service sector employees may be priced low, relative to, say, consumer goods, to encourage enterprises to invest. Similar biases may also exist between different types of investment goods in order to influence the structure of investment. Moreover, differences in such price relatives are not necessarily uniform between countries.

(ii) General development of the service sector

Developments in the service sector of eastern Europe and the Soviet Union in 1970-1987 were strongly influenced by the general macro-economic environment, particularly changes in the pattern of demand and of input availabilities. When the structure of total demand shifted towards services, the availability of inputs has appeared as a constraining factor – particularly over the last decade. The general slow-down in economic growth, under deteriorating external conditions and with policy priorities designed to protect consumption, substantially reduced investment possibilities. Moreover, employment in the service sector was affected by demographic changes which slowed the growth of the labour supply (table 3.6.1 and chart 3.6.1).

The share of services in total *employment* grew steadily in all countries under review. In 1970, this share was below 30 per cent in all countries but Czechoslovakia and the Soviet Union. By 1987 (the last year for which data are available) it had reached about 40 per cent in Czechoslovakia, the German Democratic Republic and Hungary and a somewhat higher level in the Soviet Union. In Bulgaria and Poland the service shares were close to one third in 1987. Romania registered the lowest share (around a quarter in 1987).

The share of services in total employment can be interpreted as an indicator of overall development levels. In this sense the high share of the Soviet Union among the seven countries reviewed seems surprising as, judging by other indicators, including internationally estimated *per capita* GDP levels, the Soviet Union is not the most developed country of the group.[365] The sectoral breakdown of service employment indicates that the high service share in the Soviet Union stems above all from employment in science and education.[366]

Comparisons with the developed market economies indicate that the share of the service sector in total employment in the seven countries is low relative to their overall level of economic development.[367] Inversely, these countries thus employ relatively high shares of the

---

[363] Soviet economists estimate employment in the shadow economy at about 20 million persons (15 per cent of total employment). If true, this would increase the share of services in total employment from 42 to almost 50 per cent in 1987. The output of the black economy is believed to have been 70-90 billion roubles in 1987 – about 5 per cent of Soviet GNP. *Hospodarske noviny*, No.42, 21 October 1988, p.11.

[364] Moreover, the unspecified or "other" branches of the material sphere, which include a variety of activities belonging either to goods-producing sectors and or to services, are treated variously in individual countries. In the national statistics of Romania and the Soviet Union they are grouped in a "trade and other" category, and are thus treated in this section as part of the service sector.

[365] According to ECE estimates, *per capita* gross domestic product in the countries reviewed amounted in 1973 to $3,301 in the German Democratic Republic, $3,117 in Czechoslovakia, $2,776 in the Soviet Union, $2,507 in Bulgaria, $2,482 in Poland, $2,433 in Hungary and $2,082 in Romania. See United Nations Economic Commission for Europe, *Economic Bulletin for Europe*, Vol.31, No.2, New York, 1980, p.31. Similar estimates for more recent years are also available for Hungary and Poland. Other sources indicate the same ranking. See, for example, Yu.N. Belayev, *Strany SEV v mirovoi ekonomike* (CMEA countries in the world economy), Moscow, 1984, p.50.

[366] In a data set of more restricted coverage than that used here (total employment in the state and co-operative sector), the "science and education" share in 1987 was over 14 per cent in the Soviet Union, as against 7 to 11 per cent in the east European countries. See *Statisticheskii ezhegodnik stran-chlenov SEV 1988* (CMEA statistical yearbook 1988), Moscow 1989, pp. 415, 419, 426.

[367] The share of the tertiary sector (used as an approximation for the service sector) in total employment in 1985 was 44 per cent in southern Europe, 55 per cent in Japan, 59 per cent in western Europe, 64 per cent in northern Europe and 70 per cent in North America. Equivalent shares for the centrally planned economies were 42 per cent in the Soviet Union, 39 per cent in Czechoslovakia, the German Democratic Republic and Hungary, 33 per cent in Poland and Bulgaria, and 27 per cent in Romania. See A.M. Vacic, "Eastern Europe and the Soviet Union: agricultural employment and related issues, 1960-1985," *Ost-Europa Wirtschaft*, 1988, No.2, pp.161-163.

The relative labour endowment of the service sector in the European centrally planned economies in comparison with 14 developed market economies has also been measured by the number of persons employed in services per thousand inhabitants. In 1985, this indicator was 180 per thousand in the centrally

TABLE 3.6.1

Services:[a] employment, investment and fixed assets, 1970-1987
(Percentage shares, total economy = 100)

	Bulgaria	Czecho-slovakia	German Dem.Rep.	Hungary	Poland	Romania	Soviet Union
Employment							
1970	25.2	33.8	35.2	29.7	26.8	19.9	36.4
1975	29.8	35.7	36.6	32.9	28.6	23.2	39.0
1980	31.8	37.8	37.1	35.5	29.2	26.3	40.9
1985	32.8	39.3	37.9	38.3	31.0	26.6	41.9
1987	33.3	39.4	38.4	40.2	31.5	26.6	42.1
Investment [b]							
1971-1975	43.6	48.7	33.2	45.6	39.4	33.5	41.1
1976-1980	44.6	45.4	34.5	44.0	39.5	32.1	40.3
1981-1985	43.0	41.0	33.2	46.5	45.0	29.5	41.4
1986-1987	40.3	39.9	32.9	47.9	45.8	28.0	42.3
Fixed assets							
1970	54.3	56.8	44.5	63.2	66.0	50.2	55.5
1975	51.9	55.8	42.5	59.3	60.7	43.1	53.3
1980	50.5	53.6	41.9	56.2	56.3	40.5	51.4
1985	50.1	51.9	41.4	55.5	55.4	38.5	50.3
1987	49.2	51.5	41.0	55.3	55.5	37.1	50.5

Source: ECE secretariat Common Data Base, derived from national statistics.

a Transport, communications, trade and all non-material branches of the national economy.
b Five-year totals and for the years 1986-1987 two-year totals.

labour force in the primary (agriculture, forestry and fisheries) and secondary (mining, manufacturing, construction and handicrafts) sectors.[368] For most developed market economies, the share of employment in services rose from 40-50 per cent in 1960 to 55-66 per cent in 1985.[369] In the United States, the service sector has generated almost all the new jobs created since 1970 (29 million out of 30 million) and now accounts for some 70 per cent of total employment, compared with 60 per cent in 1970. Small businesses, together with a high proportion of the newly self-employed, were the main source of new employment.[370] However, comparisons with the developed market economies need to be made with caution, for several reasons. *First,* such rapidly developing services as computers, consultancies, repairs and certain transport services, among others, have become specialized in the developed market economies and thus separated from other activities, while in the centrally planned economies they mostly remained within the enterprises of the goods-producing sectors. *Second,* the relative growth and importance of the service sector in the developed market economies is probably exaggerated by the growth of part-time employment. *Third,* services linked with the functioning of the market (banking, insurance, finance and advertising) have remained underdeveloped under central planning. *Finally,* it can be assumed that the "black" or underground economy plays a more important role in services in the seven countries examined than in the developed market economies.

Nevertheless, the rates of growth of employment in services surpassed those in the economy as a whole in all countries reviewed (chart 3.6.2). The difference in the growth rates of total and service sector employment was significant in Bulgaria, Hungary and Romania. In contrast, in the German Democratic Republic, service sector employment outpaced employment in the total economy only moderately. The average annual rate of growth of employment in services in the whole period 1970-1987 reached almost 2 per cent in the seven countries combined and varied between 1 per cent in the German Democratic Republic and about 2 per cent in Bulgaria, Poland, Romania and the Soviet Union.[371] However, employment growth in the service sector decelerated strongly towards the end of the 1970-1987 period (table 3.6.2). This was linked with the demographic situation which led to a decelerating supply of labour overall. Moreover, the outflow of labour from the agricultural sector decelerated during the 17 years in

---

planned economies, as against 304 per thousand inhabitants in the developed market economies, a difference of almost 70 per cent. See *Wiadomosci statystyczne,* Warsaw, No.6, 1989, p.5.

368 In this connection, it was noted by a Czechoslovak analyst that Czechoslovakia and the German Democratic Republic, with shares of employment in the secondary sector reaching almost 50 per cent, are the "most industrialized countries" in the world. See *Hospodarske noviny,* No.16, 21 April 1989, p.8.

369 OECD, *National Accounts Statistics, 1960-1985,* Paris, 1987.

370 *The OECD Observer,* No.152, June/July 1988, pp.9-10.

371 It should be noted that, in the same period, the average annual rate of employment growth in the service sector surpassed 2 per cent in the majority of developed market economies. In three expansionary periods (1967-1973, 1975-1979 and 1982-1988) the average annual rate of growth in services employment was rather stable and close to 3 per cent for the OECD countries as a whole. However, it differed widely across countries. See OECD, *Labour force statistics 1967-1987* (June 1989 tape) and *OECD Economic Outlook,* No.45, June 1989, p.125.

Developments in the service sector, 1970-1987　　161

CHART 3.6.1

Factor inputs in services, 1971-1987
(Percentage shares, total economy = 100)

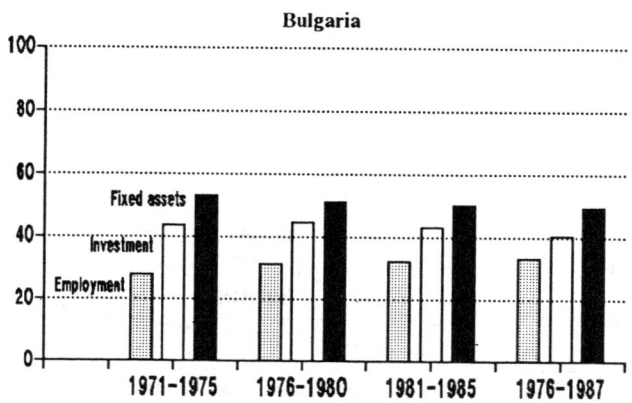

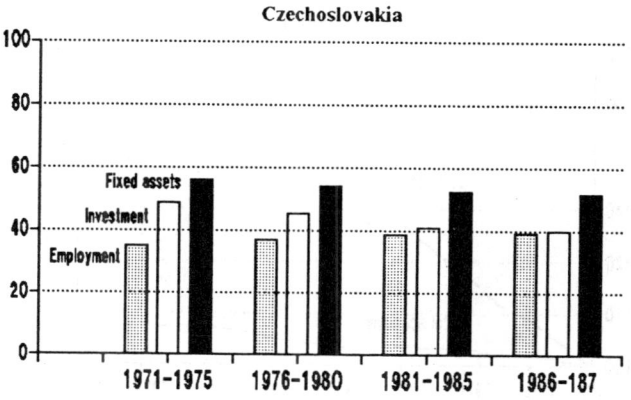

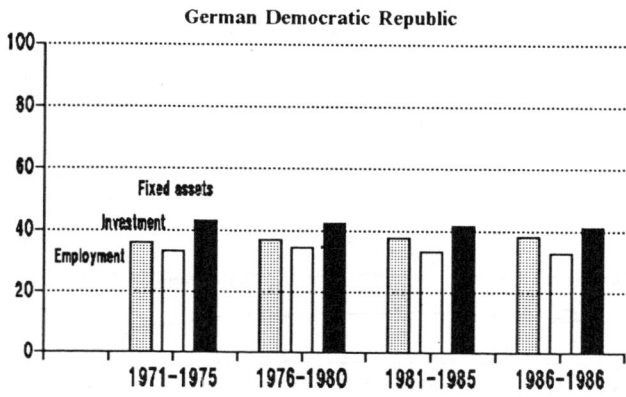

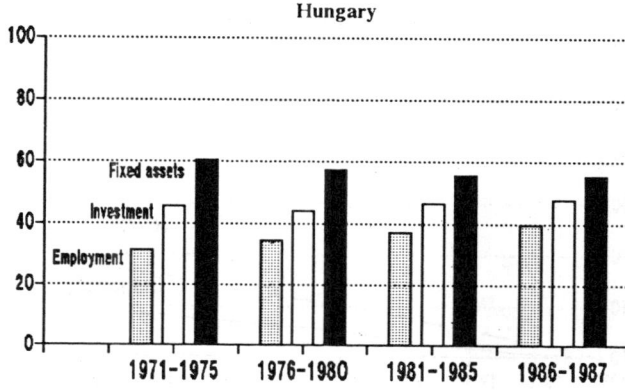

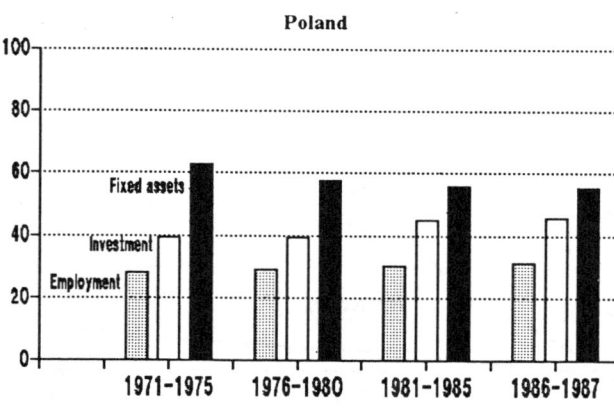

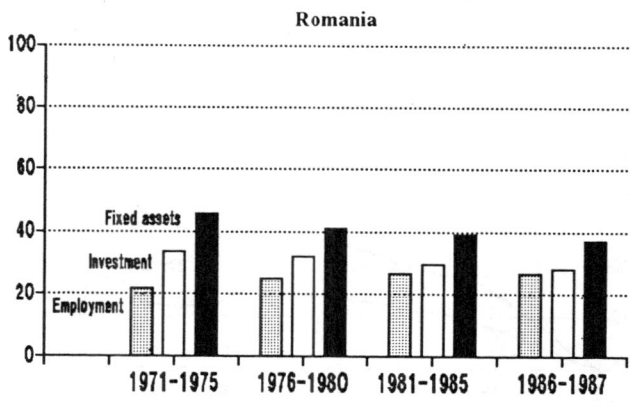

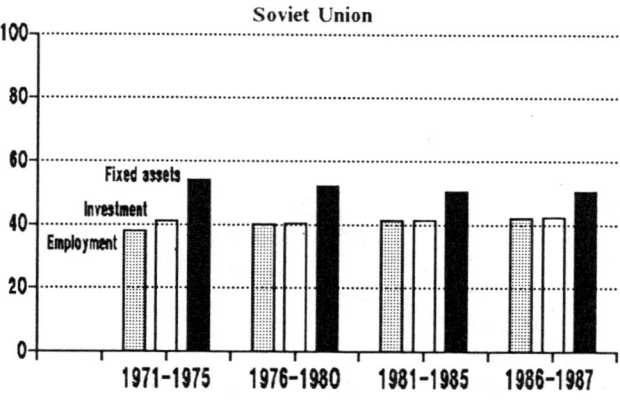

Source: ECE secretariat Common Data Base.

CHART 3.6.2

Employment in services and in the total economy, 1970-1987
(Indices, 1970 = 100)

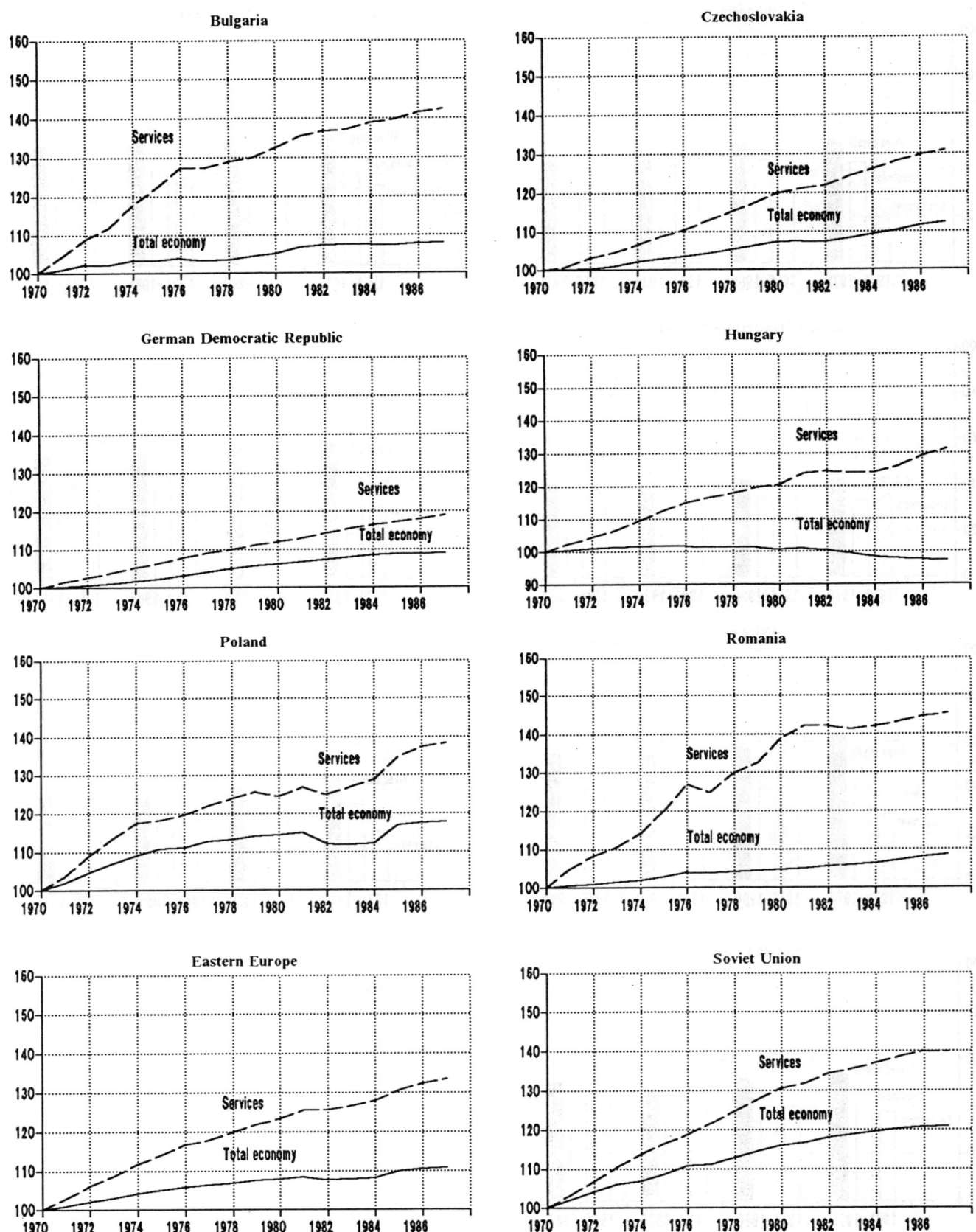

Source: ECE secretariat Common Data Base.

all of the seven countries but Hungary (where agricultural employment in 1986-1987 declined by more than 4 per cent annually). The German Democratic Republic even registered an increase in agricultural employment in the course of the 1980s. Industrial employment continued to grow in most countries, albeit at substantially slower rates in the 1980s as compared with the 1970s. But its absolute level has declined in Hungary since 1975, in Poland between 1978-1983 and, in 1986-1987, in the German Democratic Republic and the Soviet Union. Altogether, there has been almost no net outflow of labour from the goods-producing sectors to services in recent years in eastern Europe and the Soviet Union, the only exception being Hungary.[372] However, there is some evidence of greater mobility of labour between sectors in some countries as a result of economic reforms. This is the case for Hungary, but also for Poland and the Soviet Union where in 1987 industrial employment declined absolutely. These decreases accelerated in 1988.

Investment growth rates in the service sector were high in the second half of the 1970s, varying between 4.5 per cent in Czechoslovakia and the Soviet Union and almost 10 per cent in Romania. However, the situation changed drastically in the first half of the 1980s. Except for Bulgaria and the Soviet Union, where investment growth in the service sector was maintained at an average of 4 per cent annually, it was negative in all other countries, with the average annual rate of decline ranging between a 0.5 per cent in Romania to almost 5 per cent in Poland. This was related to the specific difficulties and peculiarities of this period — deceleration of economic growth, an outflow of resources due to the repayment of external debt and efforts to maintain overall levels of consumption. These led to drastic cuts in investment overall. The service sector was hit more strongly than the economy as a whole in the majority of countries (chart 3.6.3). Nevertheless, over the whole period 1970-1987, investments in services outpaced those in the total economy only in Hungary and Poland.

The revival of investment growth in the service sector in 1986-1987 which occurred in all countries was thus a response to the slow-down of investment growth and even real declines in investment levels in the preceding five-year period. The upswing was very strong in Poland and the Soviet Union, where it exceeded 10 per cent annually. Notwithstanding the efforts made, aging of fixed assets in the economy as a whole, but particularly in the service sector, has not yet been halted. The deterioration of the services sector's infrastructure which took place in the first half of the 1980s was on such a scale that the improvements linked with the modernization and re-equipment of the main service branches will need both time and huge investments. However, it should be noted that the many negative phenomena in this sphere cannot be treated by investment activity alone.

Investment priority of the service sector as a whole, indicated by its share in total investments (table 3.6.1), shows a clearly declining trend in Czechoslovakia and Romania. In Bulgaria and the German Democratic Republic the share began to decline since 1976-1980. The opposite tendency appeared in Poland and, since 1976-1980, in Hungary and the Soviet Union.

Changes in *fixed assets* in the services sector more or less followed investment trends. The share in total

TABLE 3.6.2

Factor inputs in the service sector, 1971-1987
(Average annual percentage change)

	Bulgaria	Czechoslovakia	German Dem.Rep.	Hungary	Poland	Romania	Soviet Union
Employment							
1971-1975	4.1	1.7	1.3	2.4	3.4	3.7	3.2
1976-1980	1.6	2.0	1.0	1.4	1.1	3.0	2.3
1981-1985	1.1	1.4	0.9	0.9	1.6	0.6	1.2
1986-1987	1.0	1.1	0.7	2.1	1.3	0.7	0.4
Investment [a]							
1976-1980	7.3	4.4	5.7	5.0	6.7	9.9	4.7
1981-1985	4.0	-2.7	-0.8	-1.0	-4.7	-0.5	3.9
1986-1987	6.5	1.2	3.3	1.9	10.7	0.2	10.1
Fixed Assets							
1971-1975	6.9	5.0	4.4	4.5	3.3	6.2	7.0
1976-1980	7.0	5.0	4.6	4.3	4.2	7.7	6.0
1981-1985	6.8	4.2	4.2	3.5	2.2	7.2	5.6
1986-1987	5.5	4.0	3.6	3.3	2.9	4.7	5.4

Source: ECE secretariat Common Data Base, derived from national statistics.

a Annualized rates of growth based on levels in the period shown as compared with those in the previous five-year period.

---

[372] In most west European countries there has been an apparent outflow of labour force from the industrial sector in the last decade or so, but this has not occurred in the United States, Japan or Canada.

CHART 3.6.3

Investment in services and in the total economy, 1970-1987
(Indices, 1970 = 100)

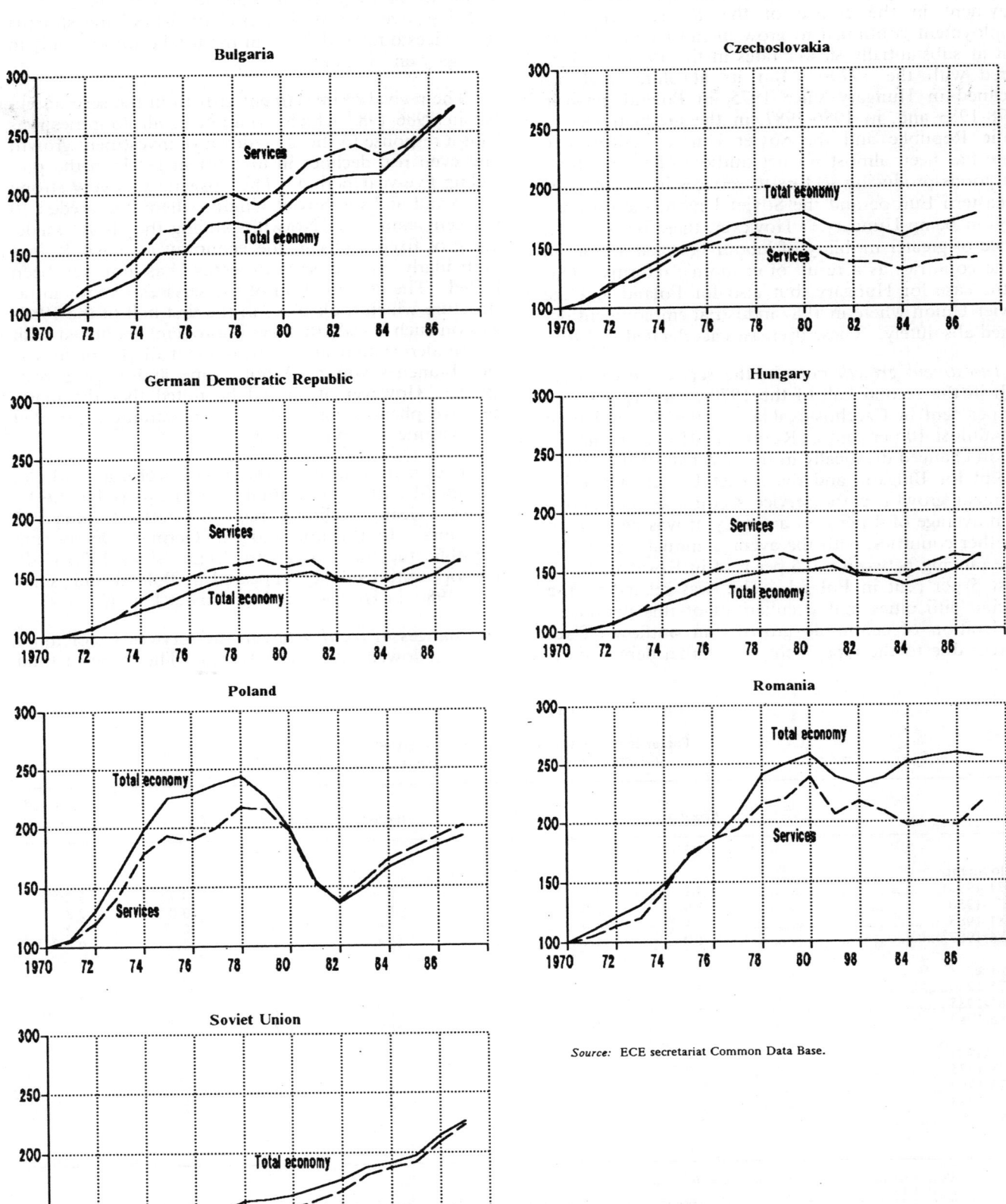

Source: ECE secretariat Common Data Base.

fixed assets of fixed assets in services declined in the course of the review period in all countries. These shares are substantially higher than those for employment, which indicates the relatively high capital intensity of certain service activities. In six countries out of the seven, the share of services in total fixed assets exceeded or was close to 50 per cent. It was lowest in Romania, reflecting the low overall level of development of this country and the priorities given in economic policy to industrial development.

In addition to their declining shares in total fixed assets, the technical and qualitative level of fixed assets of the service sector is generally low. Given the rapid scientific and technological development of services in the developed market economies (computerization, telecommunications, introduction of modern equipment), larger investment allocation will certainly be needed to modernize and re-equip this sector of the economy. Due to the importance of roads, housing, schools, hospitals, transport and communication facilities, hotels, etc., and their contribution to economic and social development, demand for such investment in the 1990s is likely to be much greater than in the past.

A dividing line can be drawn within the service sector between *producer (material)* and *consumer (non-material) services*.[373] A common feature of producer services is the fact that the objects of these services are usually tangible goods (although there are some exceptions to this rule and some differences exist between countries). In the centrally planned economies, producer services have been treated as part of the material sphere. The typical representatives of this group of branches are transport, communications and trade. Consumer services arise from the activities of the non-material sphere and satisfy personal or social needs (housing, science, education, health and social care, sport, tourism, culture, insurance, banking and administration). An examination of the allocation of inputs between producer and consumer services indicates the direction and priorities of economic policy in the countries reviewed (tables 3.6.3 and 3.6.4).

In examining *employment changes* in the period 1970-1987, a shift of employment in favour of consumer as against producer services is apparent in six of the seven countries under review (table 3.6.3).[374] The exception is Romania, where the faster rate of growth of employment in the consumer services started later and was interrupted in 1986-1987. It can be assumed that the development of personal and social services in that country lags substantially behind needs. Assignment of a high priority to the consumer services is clearly observable in the German Democratic Republic and Hungary. In these two countries the share of consumer in total services increased by more than 5 percentage points between 1970 and 1987. The relatively high share of employment in the consumer services in Czechoslovakia and the Soviet Union in part reflects different classification of activities belonging to the material and consumer spheres (passenger transport and communications serving the population being included in the consumer sphere while in the other countries they are treated as branches of the material sphere). The share of employment of consumer in total services has in recent years exceeded 50 per cent in most countries. A recalculation of the shares for Czechoslovakia (by shifting passenger transport and communications serving the population to the material sphere) suggests that the share of employment in consumer services came to over 56 per cent of the total service sector in 1987, still the highest share among the east European countries. (A similar recalculation cannot be carried out for the Soviet Union.)

The rate of growth of employment in both groups of services decelerated, but it remained faster in consumer services (with the exception of Romania). The Soviet Union was the only country in which an absolute decline in employment in producer services occurred (in 1986-1987); the continuing efforts to develop the consumer sphere under conditions of diminishing overall labour supplies contributed to this outcome.

Investment allocations to the producer and consumer services did not follow the same trend in all countries (table 3.6.4). While in Bulgaria and Czechoslovakia the shares in total investments in the service sector were more or less stable, in the German Democratic Republic and Poland the share of producer services tended to decline up to 1983-1984 and partially recovered thereafter. A very sharp drop in the share of producer services in total investment in services occurred in Poland, where it fell from the peak level of 32 per cent in 1975 to only 19 per cent in 1982 – though it rose regularly thereafter. It is likely that insufficient investment in transport, communications and trade adversely affected the overall performance of Polish economy. In Romania and the Soviet Union, preference was given to producer services up to 1983, but this tendency was then reversed. In Hungary, the share of producer in total investment in services showed a declining tendency, particularly in the last decade or so.

Altogether, it can be said that in the second half of the 1970s the rates of growth of investment in the ser-

---

[373] The classification of services used in this study is somewhat arbitrary and is based on the classification of activities in the material product system (MPS). In fact, the distinction between producer (material) and consumer (non-material) services stems from the object of services and not from the criterion of where the service is used (whether in the production or consumption spheres). According to the latter criterion, producer services are intermediate inputs in the production process, while consumer services are marketed, or provided free of charge, directly to the consumer. However, there are considerable problems with this classification, since many services do not fall completely into either category. Moreover, it should be borne in mind that the definition of producer and consumer services in the market economies differs from that in the centrally planned economies due to a broader conception of the sphere of production in the former group of countries. Thus, producer services in the market economies include, besides trade, communications and transport and also financial, insurance and business and professional services, since they largely satisfy intermediate demand and their output is mainly purchased by other enterprises or by governments. The distinction between the two groups of services is thus not always clear cut.

[374] Although the data are not fully comparable, a similar tendency was observed in the developed market economies. A study examining the changes in the structure of employment in the service sector in 1960-1981 came to the conclusion that employment in retail and wholesale trade, transport and communications has been declining in relative importance throughout the period in all countries of western Europe for which relevant data were available. See United Nations Economic Commission for Europe, *Economic Survey of Europe in 1982*, New York, 1983, p.80.

TABLE 3.6.3

Employment in material and non-material services,[a] 1970-1987

	Shares, total services = 100					Annual rates of growth			
	1970	1975	1980	1985	1987	1971-1975	1976-1980	1981-1985	1986-1987
Bulgaria									
Material	48.0	47.3	46.5	45.7	45.6	3.8	1.3	0.7	0.9
Non-material	52.0	52.7	53.5	54.4	54.4	4.4	1.9	1.4	1.1
Czechoslovakia									
Material	38.1	38.9	37.8	37.3	36.7	2.1	1.4	1.1	0.2
Non-material	61.9	61.1	62.2	62.7	63.3	1.4	2.4	1.5	1.6
German Democratic Republic									
Material	51.6	49.8	48.1	46.4	46.2	0.5	0.3	0.2	0.5
Non-material	48.4	50.2	51.9	53.6	53.8	2.0	1.7	1.6	1.0
Hungary									
Material	52.1	51.4	49.8	48.4	47.0	2.1	0.7	0.3	0.7
Non-material	47.9	48.6	50.2	51.6	53.0	2.7	2.1	1.5	3.4
Poland									
Material	50.2	50.4	50.4	48.2	47.8	3.5	1.1	0.7	0.9
Non-material	49.8	49.6	49.6	51.8	52.2	3.3	1.0	2.5	1.6
Romania									
Material	42.9	45.0	48.8	47.6	48.1	4.7	4.7	0.1	1.3
Non-material	57.1	55.0	51.2	52.4	51.9	2.9	1.6	1.1	0.2
Soviet Union									
Material	45.3	45.3	44.7	44.1	43.5	3.1	2.0	0.9	-0.2
Non-material	54.7	54.7	55.3	55.9	56.5	3.1	2.6	1.4	1.0

Source: ECE secretariat Common Data Base, derived from national statistics.

a Material (producer) services include transport, communications and trade, while the non-material services are identical with the activities in the non-material sphere of the national economy. Since the classifications applied in individual countries differ, the coverage is only broadly comparable across countries.

TABLE 3.6.4

Investment in the material and non-material services, 1971-1987

	Shares, total services = 100 [a]				Annual rates of growth [b]		
	1971-1975	1976-1980	1981-1985	1986-1987	1976-1980	1981-1985	1986-1987
Bulgaria							
Material	33.2	35.4	33.3	31.5	8.7	2.7	3.5
Non-material	66.8	64.6	66.7	68.5	6.6	4.6	8.0
Czechoslovakia							
Material	21.1	21.8	21.2	22.8	5.1	-3.2	4.8
Non-material	78.9	78.2	78.8	77.2	4.2	-2.5	0.1
German Democratic Republic							
Material	37.8	36.3	32.2	35.4	4.9	-3.1	8.2
Non-material	62.2	63.7	67.8	64.6	6.2	0.5	0.8
Hungary							
Material	35.5	36.5	33.8	31.9	5.6	-2.5	-1.1
Non-material	64.5	63.5	66.2	68.1	4.6	-0.1	3.4
Poland							
Material	30.3	25.1	21.2	24.3	2.7	-8.0	18.8
Non-material	69.7	74.9	78.8	75.7	8.2	-3.8	8.5
Romania							
Material	40.8	41.3	45.3	41.0	10.2	1.4	-4.7
Non-material	59.2	58.7	54.7	59.0	9.7	-1.9	4.1
Soviet Union							
Material	32.6	36.0	36.5	33.8	6.8	4.2	6.0
Non-material	67.4	64.0	63.5	66.2	3.6	3.8	12.4

Source: ECE secretariat Common Data Base, derived from national statistics.

a Calculated from five-year and two-year totals.
b Annualized rates of growth derived from the levels in the period shown as compared with those in the previous five-year period.

vice sector were rather high, and preference was given to producer services in most of the countries concerned.

The situation dramatically changed in 1980-1985 when the development of both groups of services was hit hard by the economic slow-down and restricted investment allocations. Although both groups suffered, producer services were affected more strongly (except in Romania and the Soviet Union). The recovery which took place in recent years has been very strong in the case of producer services in the German Democratic Republic and Poland and in the case of the consumer services in the Soviet Union. However, the expansion and modernization of service infrastructures was generally neglected in the countries under review.

(iii) Producer services

The review of changes in the principal variables of the service sector can be supplemented by a more detailed examination of the basic characteristics of individual branches. In this section, a distinction will be made between transport and communications on the one hand and trade on the other. The information on these major branches of producer services is broader than that on consumer services, as data are also available on the output of these branches. The analysis can therefore also take into account their performance in terms of labour and capital productivity and of capital intensity.

(a) Transport and communications

Transport and communication services have been closely linked with the overall economic development of the countries under review, the availability of transport and communication facilities constituting an important determinant of their industrial and economic growth. In general, the *output* of transport and communication services expanded quickly between 1970-1975. In the second half of the 1970s, transport growth slowed down in line with lower rates of overall economic growth. Higher fuel prices obviously played a role in this. This tendency continued into 1981-1985, probably owing to constraints on the investment allocated to transport and communications. Moreover, fuel saving became an important element of transport policy in that period. The adaptation of the transport system to changing conditions was rather slow and this contributed to emerging disproportions between demand for transport and the capacities of the sector which became a constraint on overall economic growth. Developments in recent years indicate a certain recovery in transport and communication services. Recent performance should not be overestimated, however, since it is too early to judge whether the improvement is likely to be lasting.[375]

The changing role of the transport and communications sector is shown on the basis of its share in NMP and production inputs during the period 1971-1987 (table 3.6.5 and charts 3.6.4 and 3.6.5). The consequences of such changes for the labour and capital productivities of the branches concerned is discussed below (table 3.6.7).

The share of transport and communications[376] in NMP produced varied in recent years between 5-6 per cent in five out of the seven countries examined. In Bulgaria and Hungary, however, it exceeded 8 and 9 per cent respectively.[377] Given the small weight of transport and communications in NMP produced, and taking into account the fact that these sectors on average grew slower than or almost the same as NMP, it would appear that their contribution to overall output growth has been insignificant. However, it should be noted that the importance of transport and communications is probably understated by their share in NMP measured at transaction prices owing to the significant subsidization of the sector's services.[378] Its real importance stems from its position in the production chain, where shortfalls in services to other sectors and branches of the economy can influence the overall performance of the economy. This is evident from reports of output losses stemming from an inadequate transport and communication infrastructure. These can be rather high, for example, in the agricultural sector or in severe winter conditions. However, these indirect effects are hard to quantify and become very visible only when acute bottlenecks in transport and communication services emerge.[379]

As can be seen in table 3.6.5, the share of *employment* in the transport and communication sectors in the total material sphere labour force has tended to rise. This contrasts with their falling share in investment in all countries except the Soviet Union. Rates of growth of *investment* allocated to transport and communications decelerated significantly in 1981-1985 in all countries. In four of them, investments declined absolutely compared with the average level in the preceding five-year period (table 3.6.6). In 1986-1987, investment growth accelerated in all countries but Romania, representing some recovery from the depressed investment levels in the previous five-year period and attempts to remedy emerging bottlenecks and reverse the aging of fixed assets in this sector. Insufficient investment in the transport and communication systems

---

[375] Recent disturbances in rail transport and substantial output losses stemming from them in the Soviet Union once again confirmed the importance of the smooth transport of goods to overall economic performance.

[376] The transport and communication services are examined together in this study, since separate data for the two branches are available only in two countries. Moreover, the share of communications in the main macro-economic indicators is negligible (its share in NMP produced in Bulgaria and Czechoslovakia, for instance, is about 1 per cent). As already mentioned, the comparability of data between countries is affected by differing classifications.

[377] In most developed market economies the share of transport, storage and communication in GDP was close to 6½ per cent in 1987. See OECD, *National Accounts*, 1975-1987, Paris, 1989.

[378] Distortions in the price system of course also affect the measured contribution to NMP of other sectors of production (most notably in understating those of agriculture and the extractive industries). It is therefore difficult to establish the net impact of this factor on any given sector.

[379] Thus, in Hungary, it was estimated that under the present conditions the annual losses on transport operations have reached 70-80 billion forints (6.5 per cent of the value of GDP in 1987). *Summary of World Broadcasts*, BBC, EE/W0039, London, 18 August 1988, p. A/12.

TABLE 3.6.5

Transport and communications: share in output, employment, investment and fixed assets, 1971-1987
(Percentage shares, total material sphere = 100)

	Bulgaria	Czecho-slovakia [a]	German Dem.Rep.	Hungary	Poland	Romania	Soviet Union [a]
Net output							
1971-1975	6.5	4.6	6.2	9.5	4.0	7.1	6.0
1976-1980	8.3	4.8	6.2	9.3	4.4	6.7	6.1
1981-1985	8.5	5.3	5.8	9.1	5.0	6.5	6.0
1986-1987	8.2	5.1	5.4	9.4	5.3	5.9	5.8
Employment							
1971-1975	7.1	5.0	9.2	8.9	7.3	5.2	11.8
1976-1980	8.1	4.9	9.4	9.7	7.6	6.3	12.7
1981-1985	8.1	5.0	9.3	9.9	7.4	8.0	13.3
1986-1987	8.2	5.1	9.4	10.4	7.3	8.0	13.0
Investment							
1971-1975	16.1	9.2	11.5	17.5	12.6	12.3	15.0
1976-1980	17.3	8.9	11.5	16.5	11.0	12.9	16.1
1981-1985	15.6	7.7	10.6	16.2	10.4	13.4	16.6
1986-1987	13.8	7.8	11.4	17.1	12.4	11.2	16.0
Fixed assets							
1971-1975	24.1	12.0	15.5	35.8	14.5	17.8	21.4
1976-1980	23.2	10.9	14.7	31.1	13.9	17.0	20.8
1981-1985	22.5	10.5	13.8	28.2	12.7	17.4	20.5
1986-1987	21.3	10.2	13.4	26.9	12.1	..	20.6

Source: ECE secretariat Common Data Base, derived from national statistics.

[a] Excluding transport and communications serving the population.

led in most countries to a decline in infrastructure, inadequate road and rail conditions and slow expansion of telephone networks. In addition, there was a generally slow introduction of innovative specialized services based on a convergence of computer and telecommunication technologies (high-speed data transmission, teleconferencing, video services, facsimile and various forms of electronic mail).

In examining the basic efficiency indicators (labour and capital productivities and capital intensity), transport and communications emerge as a low productivity sector. The level of labour productivity is below the material sphere average (table 3.6.7). Capital productivity varies between one half and one third of the material sphere average, while capital intensity is 1.5-2.6 times higher. The high capital intensity of this sector in a period of investment constraint is probably one of the main factors in its slow development in the last decade or so — particularly as far as the modernization and speeding up of technological change are concerned. The lag behind developments in the developed market economies in this area is apparent. However, relative capital intensity decreased substantially (in comparison to the material sphere average) during the review period and relative capital productivity improved slightly. This reflected first of all slower rates of growth of fixed assets in transport and communications as compared with the material sphere and hence a falling share in the fixed assets of the material sphere as a whole (table 3.6.5).

Factors contributing to below-average efficiency originate in the low and declining share of transport and communications in NMP produced (possibly affected by the system of prices and tariffs) and in the internal structure of transport services where low value-added bulk products — such as coal, iron ore, wood, cement, heavy chemicals and rolled metals — predominate.

TABLE 3.6.6

Volume of investment in transport and communications, 1976-1987
(Average annual percentage change) [a]

	1976-1980	1981-1985	1986-1987
Bulgaria	8.5	2.6	4.1
Czechoslovakia	6.1	-2.3	4.4
German Democratic Republic	4.5	-1.9	9.0
Hungary	5.1	-3.3	1.5
Poland	3.1	-9.8	20.2
Romania	12.1	2.7	-6.0
Soviet Union	7.3	3.9	5.6

Source: ECE secretariat Common Data Base, derived from national statistics.

[a] Annualized rates based on levels in the period shown as compared with those in the previous five-year period.

The *transport intensity of production* in the centrally planned economies is judged excessive by international standards.[380] This is a consequence of several decades of extensive economic development in eastern Europe and the Soviet Union, which has resulted in particularly high material and energy intensity of output. The fast

---

[380] As stated by Prime Minister Adamec in his report "On the development of the national economy and present tasks", the transport intensity of output in Czechoslovakia is approximately twice as high as in comparable developed market economies. *Rude pravo*, 21 June 1989, p.4.

CHART 3.6.4

Employment in trade and transport, 1970-1987
(Indices, 1970 = 100)

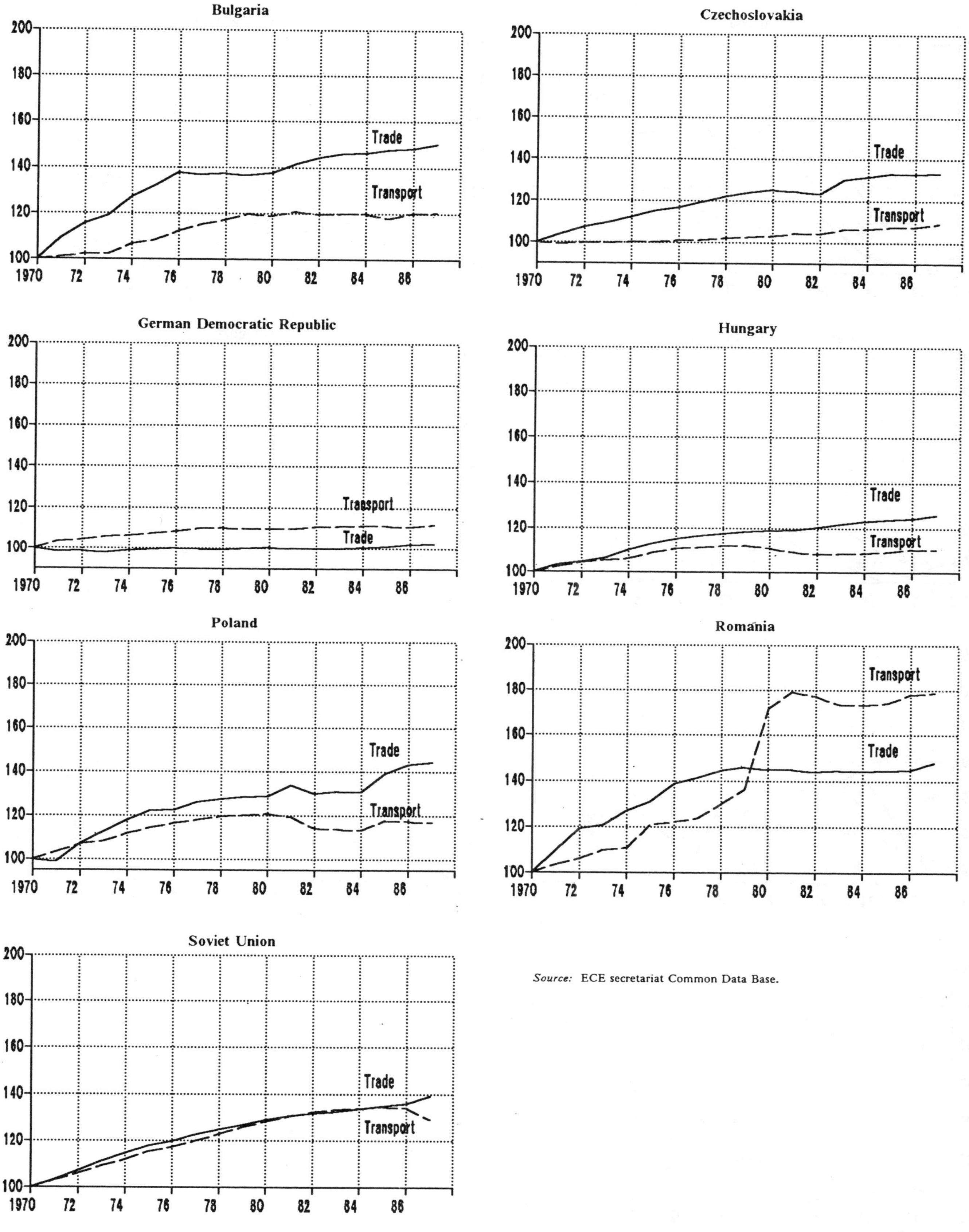

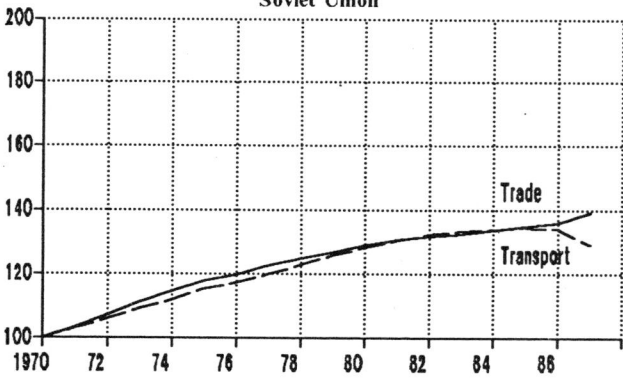

Source: ECE secretariat Common Data Base.

CHART 3.6.5

Investment in trade and transport, 1970-1987
(Indices, 1970 = 100)

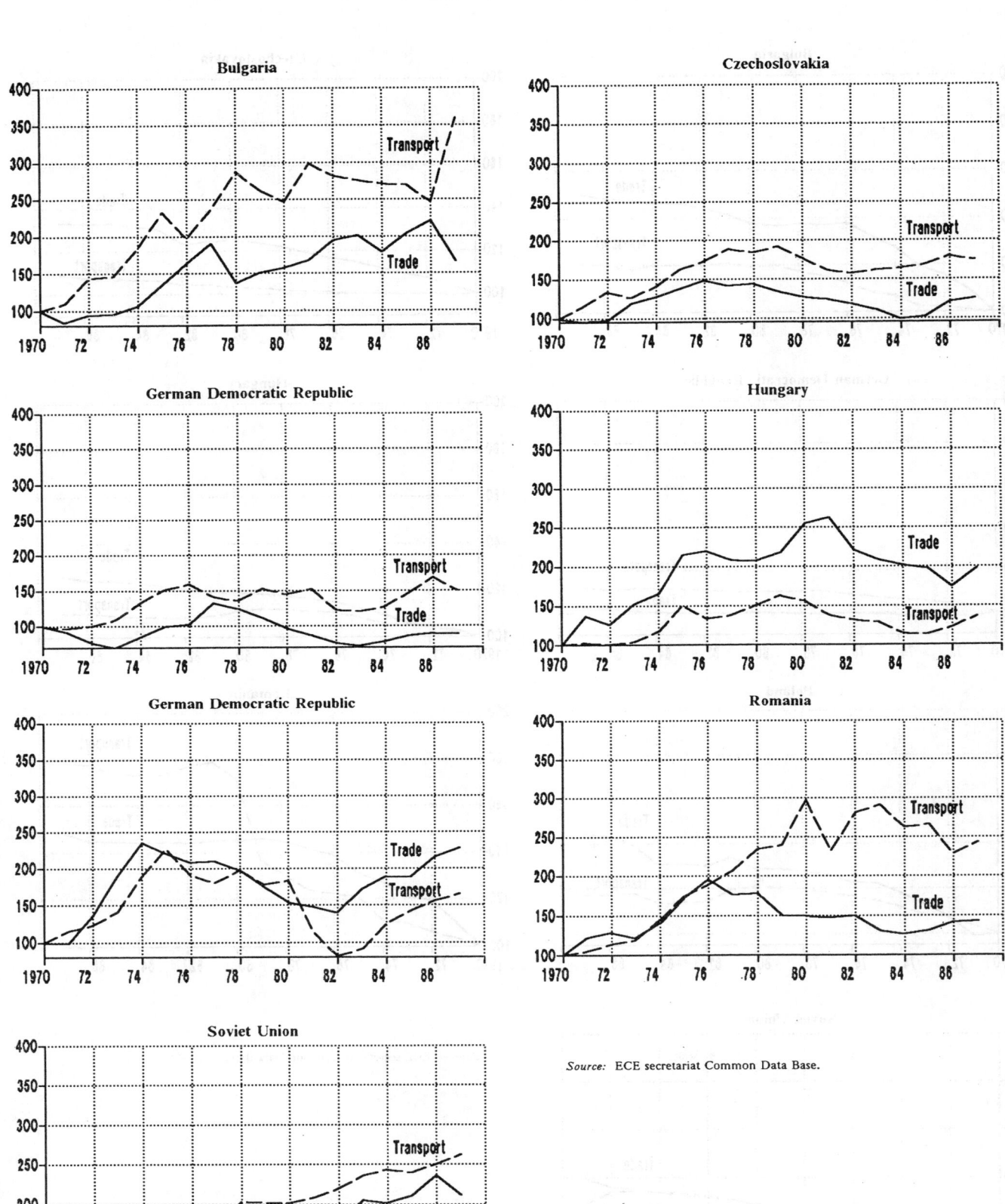

Source: ECE secretariat Common Data Base.

TABLE 3.6.7

Efficiency indicators in transport and communications, 1971-1987
(Relative levels, total material sphere = 1)

	Bulgaria	Czecho-slovakia [a]	German Dem.Rep.	Hungary	Poland	Romania	Soviet Union [a]
Labour productivity [b]							
1971-1975	1.05	0.93	0.67	1.07	0.54	1.38	0.51
1976-1980	1.03	0.98	0.66	0.96	0.59	1.06	0.48
1981-1985	1.05	1.03	0.62	0.93	0.68	0.80	0.45
1986-1987	1.00	1.01	0.57	0.90	0.72	0.74	0.44
Capital productivity [c]							
1971-1975	0.31	0.38	0.40	0.27	0.27	0.40	0.28
1976-1980	0.36	0.45	0.42	0.30	0.32	0.40	0.29
1981-1985	0.38	0.50	0.42	0.32	0.40	0.37	0.29
1986-1987	0.38	0.50	0.40	0.35	0.43	-	0.28
Capital intensity [d]							
1971-1975	3.37	2.45	1.68	4.00	1.98	3.44	1.81
1976-1980	2.87	2.21	1.57	3.22	1.84	2.68	1.64
1981-1985	2.77	2.06	1.48	2.86	1.70	2.16	1.54
1986-1987	2.61	2.00	1.43	2.58	1.65	-	1.58

Source: ECE Secretariat Common Data Base, derived from national statistics.

a Only freight transport and communications serving production.
b Net output in transport and communications per employee.
c Ratio of net output in transport and communications to fixed assets.
d Fixed assets in transport and communications per employee.

expansion of the extractive and heavy industries (mining, metallurgy, chemicals), and the resulting effects on transport demand of fast growing output of bulk products was very often too much for the limited capacities of the transport system. This caused considerable economic losses. In addition, the high degree of centralized output allocation added to growing transport requirements, while the system of prices and tariffs did not exert sufficient pressure to lower the transport intensity of output.

TABLE 3.6.8

Freight transport services [a]
(Average annual percentage change)

	1971-1975	1976-1980	1981-1985	1986-1987
Bulgaria	3.3	6.6	-1.2	5.6
Czechoslovakia	2.1	3.0	0.6	-0.9
German Dem.Rep.	3.4	0.0	-1.0	10.1
Hungary	5.7	3.6	-0.2	2.1
Poland	10.3	3.4	-5.1	3.5
Romania	9.1	3.6	1.9	..
Soviet Union	6.2	3.5	1.5	2.3

Source: Statisticheskii ezhegodnik stran-chlenov SEV (CMEA yearbook), 1988, p.283.

a Based on tonne/kilometres for all modes of traffic excluding air freight transport.

Macro-economic data on transport and communications can be supplemented by figures in physical terms, which give a partial indication of performance in this sector. The growth of *transport performance* in ton-kilometres, an indicator which takes into account the length of haul, followed a decelerating trend between 1970-1985, with a subsequent upswing in most countries in 1986-1987 (table 3.6.8). While in the 1970s transport performance was more or less correlated with output growth measured as gross material product (including intermediate inputs), in 1981-1985 this was probably not the case. A sharp deceleration in transport performance occurred in that period, with falls in absolute terms in four countries. On first view, the sharp deceleration of output growth at that time appears as an explanatory factor. However, a comparison of transport performance in ton-kilometers with output growth indicates that the deceleration in the growth of freight traffic was in fact substantially steeper than that of output. It is likely therefore that bottlenecks and disruptions in the transport system were among the factors contributing to weak output performance in this period. Increased oil prices and reduced deliveries of Soviet oil were partly responsible. Transport performance substantially improved in 1986-1987 in most countries except in Czechoslovakia.[381]

Inland freight traffic concentrated on two modes — rail and road. As far as the volume of transport of goods (in tons) is concerned, in 1987 the share of *rail* transport was highest in Poland (almost 70 per cent) and the German Democratic Republic (62 per cent). It was still substantial in Czechoslovakia and Romania (40-45 per cent), much smaller in the Soviet Union and Hungary (about 33 per cent) and least in Bulgaria (18 per cent). In all countries except the German Democratic Republic, the weight of rail haulage in the total transport of goods had declined over the course of the period examined. The share of *road* transport had correspondingly increased, accounting for the bulk of freight in most countries under review. In Bulgaria and

---

[381] No data are available for Romania.

Hungary it accounted for over 70 and over 60 per cent respectively, and in the Soviet Union, Czechoslovakia and Romania for 50-55 per cent of the total volume of transported goods in 1987. Only in the German Democratic Republic and Poland is its role substantially smaller (25 and 17 per cent, respectively). The fast development of road traffic in the 1970s was facilitated by relatively cheap oil imported from the Soviet Union. However, in 1981-1985 higher oil prices, accompanied by reduced quantities of oil imported from the Soviet Union, led to energy-saving measures. This strongly constrained the performance of the highly energy-intensive transport sector.

In terms of ton-kilometres, however, rail transport still dominates the structure of freight transport performance, and railways are thus still the backbone of the region's inland transport system. Important features of the review period are the emergence of *pipeline* transport and the growing volume of *maritime* transport — though both modes account for only a small part of the total tonnage carried. In this connection, it may seem surprising that the share of inland waterways — the most energy-efficient transport mode — in total inland transport performance made only moderate progress. This may have reflected the already intensive use of river transport, as well as the high capital cost of extending inland waterways.

Development of the *communications sector* was rather rapid in the 1971-1987 period, although it was not sufficient to satisfy growing demand. The number of telephones installed increased substantially (table 3.6.9).

TABLE 3.6.9

Number of telephones in 1987

	Index 1970 = 100	Per 100 inhabitants
Bulgaria	471	25
Czechoslovakia	215	25
German Democratic Republic	185	23
Hungary	195	15
Poland	247	12
Soviet Union	321	12

Source: *Statisticheskii ezhegodnik stran-chlenov SEV*, (CMEA Yearbook), 1988, Moskva, p.303.

The number of telephones per hundred inhabitants varies between 12 in Poland and the Soviet Union and 25 in Czechoslovakia and Bulgaria.[382] The west European average is close to 40 subscribers per hundred inhabitants. The lag in this sphere is very apparent. However, growing recognition of the importance of this sector can be seen in some countries. For example, Hungary, which has a low telephone density (only 15 per hundred inhabitants), has sharply stepped up investment in its telephone system and in other parts of the telecommunication network. The share of telecommunications in total investment increased from an annual average of 1.6 per cent in 1980-1982 to 2.6 per cent in 1985 and 4 per cent in 1987. Similar intentions to increase the share of investment in the communication sector in the near future, and in this way to improve communication services, have been announced by Czechoslovakia and Poland.[383]

(b) Trade

The trade sector as discussed in this section includes retail and wholesale trade, public catering, procurement of agricultural products and foreign trade.[384] The trade sector generally fulfills the distribution function (with the exception of part of public catering, which also includes the production of goods), but it is classed as a sector of the material sphere. In the course of the period examined, the trade sector underwent important changes (table 3.6.10).

The trade sector contributes from 10 to 16 per cent of NMP produced and ranks second (after industry) among the material-sphere sectors. In the period under review its share in NMP tended to rise in most countries (with the exception of the German Democratic Republic and Hungary). While its growing share in output is clear, its role as a recipient of production factors is not so apparent: employment in trade generally grew faster than total material-sphere employment, but its share of investment has lagged behind others sectors. The inflow of labour has not met growing demand; comparisons with the developed market economies indicate that the trade sector in the centrally planned economies is significantly understaffed. However, the situation differs between countries, with trade having the highest share of total employment in the material sphere of the seven countries in Czechoslovakia and Hungary (14 and 13 per cent, respectively) and the lowest in Romania (7 per cent) in the years 1986-1987.

Low, and in a majority of countries declining, shares of investment in trade (varying between 2.5 per cent in Romania and 5.6 per cent in Hungary in 1986-1987) indicate serious neglect of this sector, which requires comprehensive re-equipment in most countries to bring it up to modern technical standards. This can also be documented by changes in the volume of investment allocated to trade (table 3.6.11).

After satisfactory investment growth in 1976-1980 (except in Poland), investment levels declined absolutely in 1981-1985 compared with the average level of the preceding five-year period in five out of seven countries. This lag was partially made good in 1986-1987, though not in Hungary. The Soviet Union is the only country where the rates of investment growth in the trade sector accelerated in the course of

---

[382] Figures for Romania are not available.

[383] See *Rude pravo*, 21 June 1989, p.4; *East European Markets*, Vol.9, No.12; *Financial Times*, London, 16 June 1989, p.7.

[384] A detailed study on the role and function of retail trade in the centrally planned economies can be found in United Nations Economic Commission for Europe, *Economic Survey of Europe in 1988-1989*, New York, 1989, pp.166-177.

TABLE 3.6.10

Trade sector: share in output, employment, investment and fixed assets, 1971-1987
(Percentage shares, total material sphere = 100)

	Bulgaria	Czecho-slovakia	German Dem.Rep.	Hungary	Poland	Romania [a]	Soviet Union [a]
Net output							
1971-1975	5.6	12.9	9.7	14.6	14.9	5.6	12.5
1976-1980	8.2	14.2	9.6	14.9	16.1	9.7	14.9
1981-1985	9.8	16.3	9.0	13.8	17.0	11.6	16.9
1986-1987	9.6	16.2	8.7	13.9	16.9	10.7	16.5
Employment							
1971-1975	8.4	12.3	13.0	10.3	8.9	5.9	10.7
1976-1980	9.7	13.4	12.8	11.5	9.5	6.9	11.4
1981-1985	10.0	14.0	12.7	12.4	10.1	6.8	11.7
1986-1987	10.3	14.2	12.9	13.3	10.7	6.8	12.1
Investment							
1971-1975	4.3	7.6	4.3	5.5	3.8	4.7	3.6
1976-1980	4.8	6.5	4.6	5.7	3.1	3.5	3.4
1981-1985	4.5	5.1	3.3	6.5	4.3	2.6	3.9
1986-1987	3.8	5.3	3.3	5.6	4.7	2.5	3.9
Fixed assets							
1971-1975	4.1	6.9	3.6	3.0	3.1	1.8	5.9
1976-1980	4.1	7.2	3.6	3.7	2.9	2.2	5.8
1981-1985	3.9	7.1	3.7	4.2	2.9	2.1	5.6
1986-1987	4.0	7.0	3.7	4.5	2.9	-	5.6

Source: ECE secretariat Common Data Base, derived from national statistics.

[a] Trade and "other material branches".

the period examined — a result of a policy re-orientation towards consumer demand.

TABLE 3.6.11

Volume of investment in trade, 1976-1987
(Average annual percentage change) [a]

	1976-1980	1981-1985	1986-1987
Bulgaria	9.2	3.4	1.1
Czechoslovakia	3.8	-4.4	5.3
German Democratic Republic	6.0	-6.7	5.5
Hungary	6.8	-0.3	-7.8
Poland	1.4	-2.4	15.1
Romania [b]	4.4	-4.2	1.7
Soviet Union [b]	4.8	5.9	7.4

Source: ECE secretariat Common Data Base, derived from national statistics.

[a] Annualized percentage changes between period shown and the previous five-year period.
[b] Trade and "other material branches".

Labour productivity levels in the trade sector (table 3.6.12) are close to the material sphere average in three countries (in Bulgaria, Czechoslovakia and Hungary); in Poland, Romania and the Soviet Union they are 1.5 times higher. However, inter-country differences in the coverage and methodology used to calculate net output in trade (particularly in foreign trade) influence the comparability of results.

Another striking feature of the trade sector is its high capital productivity. In most countries reviewed it is 2.5-3 times higher than the average for the material sphere as a whole — and is exceptionally high in Poland and Romania (by more than 5 times). This is linked with very low capital intensity and the small share of trade in total investments and fixed assets. The combination of high labour and capital productivities thus indicates above average total factor productivity and hence significant potential for a positive contribution to economic growth and overall efficiency from transfers of resources towards this more productive sector.

(iv) Consumer services

Consumer services (personal and social) are rendered by a complex of branches which, according to the general economic theory up to now current in eastern Europe and the Soviet Union, do not create new *value*. Whereas according to the system of national accounts applied in western countries the output (services) produced by these branches is included in GDP on the same basis (market value, wherever applicable, or cost) as more "tangible" products, according to the material product system applied in eastern Europe and Soviet Union the work performed in this sphere is not considered "production" and the value added in these branches is not included in net material product (NMP), the main aggregate measure of domestic output.[385] Professional discussions under way in the countries concerned on the role and place of the

---

[385] For definitions, classifications and an analysis of developments in this sphere up to the year 1983, see United Nations Economic Commission for Europe, *Economic Survey of Europe in 1984-1985*, United Nations, New York, 1985, pp.154-165.

TABLE 3.6.12

Efficiency indicators in trade, 1971-1987
(Relative levels, total material sphere = 1)

	Bulgaria	Czechoslovakia	German Dem.Rep.	Hungary	Poland	Romania	Soviet Union
Labour productivity [a]							
1971-1975	0.66	1.05	0.74	1.43	1.67	0.95	1.17
1976-1980	0.85	1.06	0.75	1.30	1.68	1.41	1.30
1981-1985	0.98	1.16	0.71	1.11	1.68	1.69	1.47
1986-1987	0.93	1.14	0.67	1.04	1.58	1.58	1.45
Capital productivity [b]							
1971-1975	1.37	1.88	2.67	4.82	4.76	3.05	2.12
1976-1980	2.00	1.96	2.66	4.01	5.62	4.36	2.56
1981-1985	2.50	2.28	2.40	3.28	5.93	5.44	3.03
1986-1987	2.40	2.31	2.37	3.08	5.76	-	2.98
Capital intensity [c]							
1971-1975	0.48	0.56	0.28	0.30	0.35	0.31	0.55
1976-1980	0.43	0.54	0.28	0.32	0.30	0.32	0.51
1981-1985	0.39	0.51	0.29	0.34	0.28	0.31	0.47
1986-1987	0.39	0.49	0.28	0.34	0.27	-	0.47

Source: ECE secretariat Common Data Base, derived from national statistics.

[a] Net output in trade sector per employee.
[b] The ratio of net output in trade to fixed assets.
[c] Fixed assets in trade per employee.

non-material sphere as a whole in the socialist economies will certainly result in a reappraisal of present doctrines and also of statistical and planning practice. But statistical time series on output, and hence on the overall performance of the non-material sphere, are missing in most countries. For this reason the role of the non-material sphere in the centrally planned economies can only be discussed in terms of factor inputs and their changing shares in total factor allocations.

The allocation of factor inputs to the non-material sphere (table 3.6.13) was characterized first by relatively fast (as compared with the average for the material sphere) but, in most countries, declining rates of employment growth. Second, the allocation of investment was very uneven — fast growth in 1976-1980 as compared with the previous five-year period, followed by a sharp deceleration in the first half of the 1980s (except in the Soviet Union). This was followed by a revival in 1986-1987 which was very pronounced in most countries. Thus, although the rates of growth of investment in the non-material sphere generally lagged behind those in the material sphere, in the 1970s and the first half of the 1980s it outstripped that of the material sphere in Hungary, Romania and the Soviet Union. It is likely that in some countries this changed pattern of investment allocation indicated greater preference in favour of non-material sphere activities in general.

Employment in the non-material sphere grew faster than in the material sphere (table 3.6.14). However, the consequent rise in the share of the non-material sphere in total employment was insufficient by international standards, and demand remained unsatisfied. Among the causative factors was the general underestimation of the role of the non-material sphere in overall economic development and in improving living standards in particular. A worrisome feature of factor input allocation can be seen in the decelerating rates, and in four countries even falling levels, of *investment* in consumer services in 1981-1985. This was linked, as already discussed, with general constraints on investments under conditions of decelerating economic growth and an outflow of resources due to the repayment of external debt in the east European countries. These developments resulted in an aging of fixed assets, constrained capacity increases and slow technical modernization in most branches of the non-material sphere.

The growing shares of the non-material sphere in total employment are clearly observable in the period 1971-1987 in all countries under review. The increases were highest in Hungary (5.7 percentage points) and lowest in Romania (1.7 percentage points). In the latter country, the share of the non-material sphere in total employment was already the lowest among the seven countries. It is likely that the ranking of countries in this respect generally coincides with their overall level of economic development. As already noted, the relatively high shares shown for employment in the non-material sphere in Czechoslovakia and the Soviet Union also reflect the fact that passenger transport and communications serving the population are included in this sphere, whereas in the other countries they are classified in the material sphere. This also affects data on investment and fixed assets.

The share of *investment* in the non-material sphere in total investments is generally higher than that of employment. However, the direction of change has not been uniform. While in the German Democratic Republic and and Poland (up to 1985) and in Hungary and the Soviet Union (in 1976-1987) the share of investment allocated to the non-material sphere in total investment was generally on the rise, it declined in the

TABLE 3.6.13

Factor inputs in the non-material sphere, 1971-1987
(Average annual percentage change)

	Bulgaria	Czechoslovakia	German Dem.Rep.	Hungary	Poland	Romania	Soviet Union
Employment							
1971-1975	4.4	1.4	2.0	2.7	3.3	2.9	3.1
1976-1980	1.9	2.4	1.7	2.1	1.0	1.6	2.6
1981-1985	1.4	1.5	1.6	1.5	2.5	1.1	1.4
1986-1987	1.1	1.6	1.0	3.4	1.6	0.2	1.0
Investment [a]							
1976-1980	6.6	4.2	6.2	4.6	8.2	9.7	3.6
1981-1985	4.6	-2.5	0.5	-0.1	-3.8	-1.9	3.8
1986-1987	8.0	0.1	0.8	3.4	8.5	4.1	12.4
Fixed assets							
1971-1975	5.9	5.0	4.5	4.9	2.8	4.9	6.5
1976-1980	6.8	4.8	4.7	4.8	3.9	6.1	5.6
1981-1985	7.0	4.1	4.6	4.1	2.4	6.0	5.2
1986-1987	6.2	4.1	3.4	3.8	3.1	-	5.5

Source: ECE secretariat Common Data Base, derived from national statistics.

[a] Annualized percentage changes between period shown and the previous five-year period.

TABLE 3.6.14

Non-material sphere: share in output, employment, investment and fixed assets, 1971-1987
(Percentage shares, total economy = 100) [a]

	Bulgaria	Czechoslovakia [b]	German Dem.Rep.	Hungary	Poland	Romania	Soviet Union [b]
Employment							
1971-1975	14.5	21.4	17.9	15.2	14.3	12.1	20.8
1976-1980	16.5	22.8	18.9	17.1	14.6	13.4	22.1
1981-1985	17.4	24.3	20.0	19.3	15.5	13.8	23.1
1986-1987	18.1	24.9	20.6	20.9	16.4	13.8	23.8
Investment							
1971-1975	29.1	38.5	20.6	29.4	27.4	19.9	27.7
1976-1980	28.8	35.5	21.9	27.9	29.6	18.9	25.8
1981-1985	28.7	32.3	22.5	30.7	35.4	16.1	26.3
1986-1987	27.6	30.8	21.2	32.7	34.6	16.5	28.0
Fixed assets							
1971-1975	34.9	45.8	29.8	35.5	54.9	32.4	37.1
1976-1980	33.0	44.1	29.3	34.5	49.1	27.1	34.7
1981-1985	32.3	42.4	29.2	34.4	47.6	24.4	33.1
1986-1987	32.5	41.6	29.0	34.8	47.5	-	32.8

Source: ECE secretariat Common Data Base, derived from national statistics.

[a] Calculated from five-year and two-year totals.
[b] Including passenger transport and communications serving population.

other countries. Investment allocation to the non-material sphere strongly depends on the general economic environment and macro-economic policies. But it is clear that in the recent periods of economic slowdown and growing imbalances in the national economy (both internal and external), investments in the non-material sphere have very often been restricted more severely than those for the material sphere. As in the case of some producer services, discussed above, this reflected an underestimation of the role of consumer services in economic and social development and the high priorities attached to output growth reflected in NMP produced.

In recent years the approach to the non-material sphere has been changing in some of the countries reviewed. Thus, an upswing in the shares of investment in the non-material sphere occurred in 1976-1987 in Hungary and the Soviet Union. In the latter country, recent economic strategies strongly emphasize the need for faster development of the "social sphere" and a further shift of resources in this direction is envisaged in the years to come. In the next five-year period (1991-1995), the share of investment in the social and cultural spheres is to reach 34 per cent of total investment, compared with only 26 per cent in the current five-year period. These investment are to rise by 50 per cent (8.4 per cent yearly) in 1991-1995 compared with their average level in the preceding five-year period.[386] Although no definition of the "social sphere" is given, the context in which these figures are mentioned indicates that it refers to the non-material sphere.

The non-material sphere's shares in total *fixed assets* were substantially higher than those of employment and markedly higher than those of investment. This reflects the fact that buildings and structures — notably housing — predominate in the non-material sphere assets and these have substantially a longer lifetime than machinery and equipment. At all events, the data indicate the relatively high capital intensity of non-material sphere activity. The share of fixed assets ranged from 24 per cent of the total capital stock in Romania to 47 per cent in Poland. However, there has been a clearly decreasing tendency in this share in all the countries examined which is not paralleled by changes in investment shares. This development can be partly explained by the relatively slower rates of liquidation of obsolete and very old fixed assets in the non-material sphere.

Developments in the supply of main inputs to the non-material sphere can be explained less in terms of its own requirements than as a reflection of developments in the material sphere. A "residual approach" was often applied in the centralized allocation of resources to the non-material sphere. Systematic aggregated data on *the output side* are not available for the non-material sphere in most of the countries under review. Hungary, uniquely, has regularly reported data on GDP — i.e., national output including that of the non-material sphere — since 1968. In recent years Poland and the Soviet Union have started to supplement traditional macro-economic indicators based on the material product system (MPS) by the indicators calculated on the basis of the UN system of national accounts (SNA). However, time series in constant prices are missing in most countries. Thus no consistent analysis of the performance of the non-material sphere in terms of GDP or, hence, of derived indicators on labour and capital productivity can be offered. Difficulties in measuring the output of services are, in any case, well known — particularly in such branches as education, health and administration. Other methodological problems, including differences in the classification of activities or in the pricing of output (in the centrally planned economies many non-material sphere services are provided free and are therefore not priced at all) and statistical recording have already been touched upon in section (i) above. International comparisons must therefore be interpreted with caution.[387] Notwithstanding the above difficulties and constraints, an attempt to assess the significance of the non-material sphere in terms of output and resulting factor productivities is offered here for three countries.

In *Hungary,* the share of the non-material sphere in GDP (at 1981 prices) increased from 12.4 per cent in 1970 to 14.5 per cent in 1988. The rates of growth of output in both the material and non-material spheres changed significantly in the course of the review period: while in the 1970s output measured by value added grew virtually at the same rate in both spheres, in the period 1981-1988 output growth in the non-material sphere was twice as high as that of the material sphere — a clear indication of the growing role of services in recent years.

In *the Soviet Union,* the economic importance of the non-material sphere can be analysed on the basis of recently published figures on gross national product (GNP) calculated according to the SNA methodology of the United Nations. Available data indicate that in 1987 the non-material sphere of the Soviet Union accounted for 19 per cent of total GNP.[388] A comparison of the rates of growth of NMP and GNP suggests that the non-material sphere's share in domestic output (GNP) has also risen in the Soviet Union.

A similar conclusion can be drawn for *Poland,* where the share of the non-material sphere in total GNP was between 14-15 per cent in the years 1985 and 1986. Changes over the 1980-1986 period indicate a faster rate of growth of real value added in the non-material sphere as compared with that in the material sphere, although rather strong annual fluctuations can be observed.[389]

Comparisons of the share of the non-material sphere in GNP in the above three countries and in total employment and total fixed assets suggest lower than average labour and capital productivity than for the material sphere as a whole. Thus, a shift of resources in favour of services would not, *prima facie,* lead to improved overall efficiency.[390] However, some important considerations need to be taken into account to explain the relatively low level of these two efficiency indicators. *First,* the output of the non-material sphere is not adequately reflected in GNP due to low-priced or free services provided by many non-material sphere

---

[386] Speech of Prime Minister Ryzhkov at the USSR Congress of People's Deputies, *Pravda,* 8 June 1989, p.3.

[387] The available data indicate that the contribution of the service sector (including both producer and consumer services) to the creation of GDP in the centrally planned economies is substantially smaller than in the developed market economies. Thus, while in the latter group of countries this contribution is close to 60 per cent, in Hungary (the only country for which such data are available) it reached no more than 32 per cent in 1987. See *Statisztikai Evkonyv 1988* (Statistical yearbook of Hungary 1988), Budapest, 1989, p.57.

[388] In 1987, the material and non-material spheres contributed 668 and 157 billion roubles to GNP respectively (*Narodnoe khozyaistvo SSSR v 1987 g.,* Finansy i statistika, Moscow, 1988, p.15). The methodology of calculating Soviet GNP is described in *Vestnik statistiki,* No.7, 1988, pp.32-38.

[389] *Rocznik statystyczny 1988,* Warsaw, 1988, pp.89-91.

[390] However, this conclusion contradicts the experience of the developed market economies where a comparison of the share of services in total GDP and total employment indicates higher-than-average labour productivity in the service sector as compared with the goods-producing sectors. In recent years, modern services activities such as telecommunications and banking have demonstrated spectacular productivity gains. See *The Emerging Service Economy, op.cit.,* p.137.

organizations.[391] *Second*, the motivation of service enterprises to give higher performance is low due to the absence of market criteria such as prices and profits. The free provision of some services (education, health) obviously leads to the neglect of economic criteria in their supply and costing. For instances, wages in the non-material sphere are generally lower than those in the material sphere. Motivation of the labour force is thus low. *Third*, the recent rapid development of science and technology (computers, information technology, modern technical equipment in medicine, etc.) and their growing application in the non-material sphere, are changing the traditional concept of the service sector. Activities which were formerly labour intensive, are now becoming capital intensive.

Available information indicates that the material intensity of services is generally lower than in the material sphere. The relatively low energy- and material-intensity of services is important, given existing constraints on energy and material input supplies in eastern Europe and the Soviet Union. Little further information exists of the kind necessary to extend the analysis by examining the performance and efficiency of individual branches of the non-material sphere, which can differ considerably. Since there is considerable heterogeneity in services, structural change within the non-material sphere can also significantly affect total efficiency in this sphere. To highlight this, an attempt is made in the following paragraphs to examine developments in three non-material branches — *housing, education* and *health* — on the basis of employment and investment changes and by also taking into account selected indicators in physical terms.

(a) Housing

Housing is perceived in the centrally planned economies as an integral part of social welfare policy. The "right" of each family to adequate housing is frequently referred to as the main objective in this domain in policy documents. The predominant attitude to housing is based on the assumption that dwellings under socialism do not belong to the group of commodities for which prices are determined by the market. This is reflected in low, highly-subsidized rents and state allocation of housing. At the same time it subjects the provision of housing to centralized decision-making, where the allocation of resources to this sector has to compete directly with the requirements of other economic goals.

While improvements in housing were generally made in the 1970s, the situation changed in the course of the 1980s, when rising costs (both investment and current), together with slower economic growth, held back the resources needed for new housing construction. In the east European countries generally, the number of dwellings completed rose in the 1970s, but the picture changed drastically in the 1980s. For eastern Europe as a whole, the number of completed dwellings increased from 657,000 in 1970 to 864,000 in 1979 (the peak year), but subsequently declined to only 606,000 in 1988 (30 per cent less than in 1979 and 8 per cent less than in 1970). However, the situation differs between countries. The German Democratic Republic recorded the best results in this sector: the peak level was attained in 1983 (123 thousand completions) when it was almost twice as high as in 1970, which was followed by only a slight slow-down (to 110,000) in 1988 (charts 3.6.6 and 3.6.7). Drastic reductions in the number of dwellings completed occurred in Hungary (from 89 to 55,000 completions) and in Romania (from 198 to 104,000 in 1980 and 1988).

Development were different in the Soviet Union. Between 1970 and 1975 the number of dwellings completed stagnated, while thereafter it declined up to 1981. The subsequent upturn in 1986-1987 was strong (from an average annual 6 per cent rate of increase in 1981-1985 to more than 9 per cent in 1986-1987). This was linked with policies to shift resources in favour of the social sphere, but insufficient to cure the long-term shortages.

Changes in the number of dwellings completed reflected trends in investment in housing. But the relationship is not perfect because of changes in the quality of housing. This has led to rising investment costs per unit of housing (table 3.6.15). The decline in housing investment in most east European countries during the 1980s is thus a worrying feature. In both eastern Europe and the Soviet Union, the housing situation remains unsatisfactory with regard not only to new dwelling construction but also to repairs and the renovation of the existing housing stock.

TABLE 3.6.15

Volume of investment in housing, 1971-1987 [a]

(Average annual percentage change)

	1971-1975	1976-1980	1981-1985	1986-1987
Bulgaria	8.2	7.6	3.0	3.8
Czechoslovakia	5.2	0.0	-2.1	-0.4
German Dem.Rep.	10.4	7.5	3.2	-0.9
Hungary	9.0	-0.1	-2.0	-4.8
Poland	11.7	2.5	-2.8	0.0
Romania	11.2	6.4	-8.8	..
Soviet Union	3.9	2.1	5.8	9.4

Source: Statisticheskii ezhegodnik stran-chlenov SEV (CMEA statistical yearbook), various issues.

[a] Average annual compound growth rates between the final year of the period shown and the final year of the previous period.

Discussion of economic reforms indicate that more flexible housing policies (notably the mobilization of private finance for the construction, maintenance and repair of housing and rent reform) are being considered in all countries.

---

[391] An important impact on service efficiency stems from the operation of unprofitable enterprises. In the Soviet Union, 23 per cent of all state enterprises in the service sector were subsidized.

CHART 3.6.6

Employment in the health, education and housing sectors, 1970-1987
(Indices, 1970 = 100)

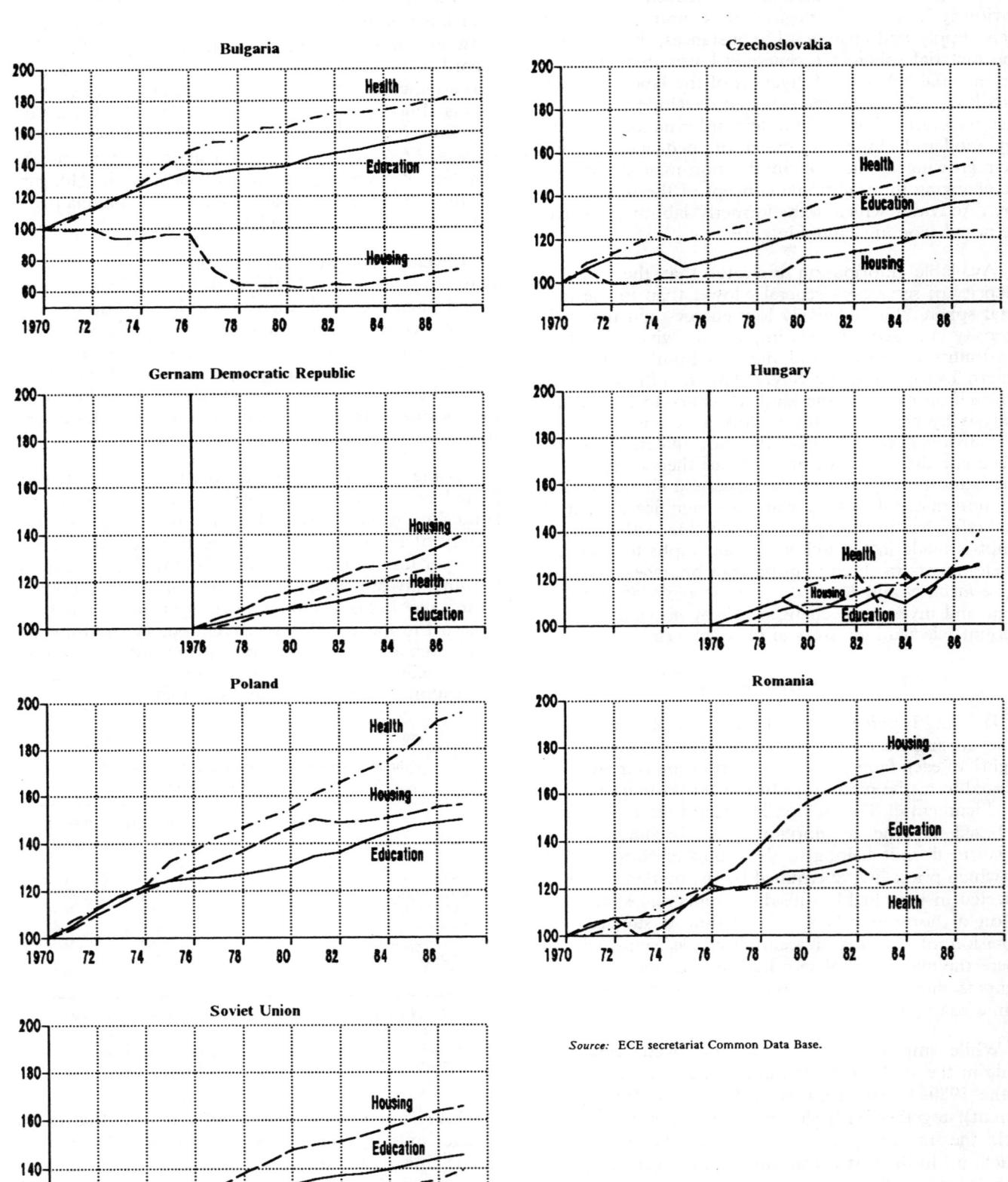

Source: ECE secretariat Common Data Base.

CHART 3.6.7

Investment in the health, education and housing sectors, 1970-1987

(Indices, 1970 = 100)

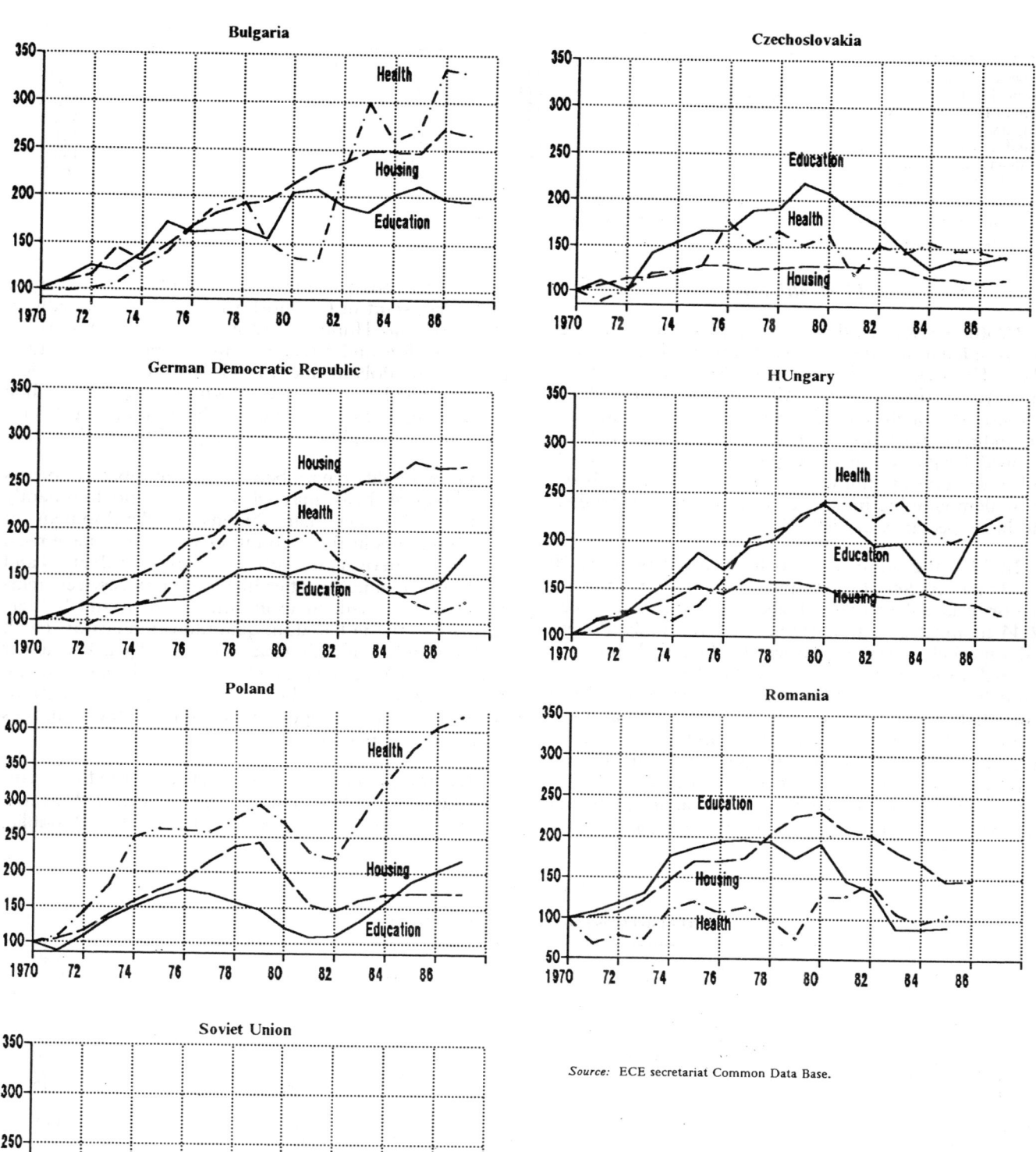

Source: ECE secretariat Common Data Base.

TABLE 3.6.16

Number of doctors ^a per 10,000 persons, 1970-1987

	1970	1975	1980	1985	1987	1987 (Indices, 1970=100)
Bulgaria	22.0	26.0	30.0	35.0	37.0	168.2
Czechoslovakia	23.0	27.0	32.0	36.0	37.0	160.9
German Democratic Republic	20.0	34.0	26.0	30.0	32.0	160.0
Hungary	22.0	25.0	28.0	32.0	32.0	145.5
Poland	19.0	22.0	23.0	24.0	25.0	131.6
Romania	15.0	16.0	18.0	21.0	21.0	140.0
Soviet Union	27.0	33.0	38.0	42.0	44.0	163.0

Source: *Statisticheskii ezhegodnik stran-chlenov SEV* (CMEA statistical yearbook), various issues.

a Including dentists.

(b) Health care

Health services in the centrally planned economies are considered an important component of social policies. The right to adequate free health care is a basic objective in this sphere. Although it is difficult to measure accurately the performance of the health sector, indirect indications can be derived from data in physical terms, for instance those showing the availability of services (number of doctors, hospital beds) or by demographic indicators such as infant mortality, and life expectancy at birth.[392]

In 1970 the number of doctors ranged between 20 and 27 per 10,000 of the population. By 1987, this indicator was substantially higher and varied between 32-44 in most countries (table 3.6.16). Only Poland and, especially, Romania lagged significantly behind the regional average, while the Soviet Union remained markedly above it.[393] With regard to hospital care, a somewhat different picture emerges. Substantial inter-country variations existed in 1970, and these widened over the 1970-1987 period (table 3.6.17). Thus, Poland had two-thirds of the number of hospital beds per 10,000 inhabitants of the Soviet Union in 1970, but only 53 per cent in 1987. While the average number of hospital beds per 10,000 inhabitants remained more or less constant in Czechoslovakia, it rose markedly in Romania and Hungary and even more quickly in the Soviet Union and Bulgaria. In contrast, the number declined in Poland and the German Democratic Republic. The latter country, which occupied the leading position among the seven countries reviewed in this respect in 1970, had fallen to third place by 1987.

Growing differences between the number of doctors and hospital beds may also indicate predominantly "extensive" rather than "intensive" development of health services in those countries where they have risen fastest. Moreover, the low motivation of doctors and medical personnel to offer higher quality services, reinforced by an inadequate incentive system and by performance criteria based on quantitative indicators (such as the number of visits) has undoubtedly led to lower standards and quality of medical care in some cases. On the other hand, shortfalls in hospital accommodation have been reported in some of the countries concerned — particularly in the larger cities.

On the *factor input side,* a steady growth of employment in the health sector can be seen in Bulgaria, Czechoslovakia, the German Democratic Republic,

TABLE 3.6.17

Hospital beds per 10,000 persons, 1970-1987

	1970	1975	1980	1985	1987	1987 (Indices, 1970=100)
Bulgaria	77.0	86.0	91.0	94.0	98.0	127.0
Czechoslovakia	100.0	99.0	100.0	102.0	102.0	102.0
German Democratic Republic	111.0	108.0	103.0	102.0	101.0	91.0
Hungary	79.0	81.0	84.0	90.0	93.0	117.7
Poland	74.0	75.0	72.0	70.0	70.0	94.6
Romania	81.0	89.0	90.0	89.0	93.0	114.8
Soviet Union	109.0	118.0	125.0	130.0	131.0	120.2

Source: *Statisticheskii ezhegodnik stran-chlenov SEV* (CMEA statistical yearbook), various issues.

---

392 Selected demographic indicators reflecting changes in infant mortality rates and life expectancy at birth (males and females) in the period 1970-1990 can be found in *World Economic Survey 1989,* United Nations, New York, 1989, pp.214-220. However, it should be noted that there is a significant but not necessarily simple or direct relationship between the changes in such demographic indicators and health services.

393 However, the definition of doctors is not the same in all countries. In the Soviet Union it also includes dentists with special vocational training.

Poland and the Soviet Union (charts 3.6.6 and 3.6.7).[394] In three countries (Bulgaria, Czechoslovakia and Poland), the inflow of manpower into the health services was the fastest among the three major non-material sphere sectors shown in the chart. Only in Romania (since 1976) and Hungary (between 1980-1985) has the number of persons employed in health services failed to increase.

Investment allocations to the health services have followed a different path in different countries (chart 3.6.7). Priority treatment was given to health in Bulgaria, Poland and Hungary up to 1980. But the volume of health investments remained constant in Romania for virtually the whole of the 1970-1987 period, and this was also the case for Czechoslovakia (since 1977) and Hungary (since 1980). rather sharp rise during 1970-1978 was followed by a significant fall, as a result of which the volume of investment in the health sector in 1987 was approximately the same as in 1974 (table 3.6.18). This partially reflected the priority given to housing construction.

However, the above quantitative indicators alone do not shed much light on the quality of medical services, which is frequently judged to be low by international standards. The standard of medical equipment and the conditions of building has also been found unsatisfactory by commentators in the countries concerned.[395]

TABLE 3.6.18

Volume of investment in health services,[a] 1971-1987 [b]
(Average annual percentage change)

	1971-1975	1976-1980	1981-1985	1986-1987
Bulgaria	7.0	-0.6	14.9	10.1
Czechoslovakia	5.2	4.8	-2.0	-2.4
German Dem.Rep.	4.9	8.0	-8.0	0.0
Hungary	5.7	12.9	-3.6	4.6
Poland	21.2	0.7	6.7	6.2
Romania	3.7	1.1	-3.7	..

Source: Statisticheskii ezhegodnik stran-chlenov SEV (CMEA statistical yearbook), various issues.

[a] Including social care, sport and tourism.
[b] Average annual compound growth rates between the final year of period shown and the final year of the previous period.

(c) Education

The overall economic slow-down and lower than expected efficiency gains over the period 1970-1987 also affected the development of education in the countries concerned. While employment in this sector[396] tended to rise in all the countries reviewed, its rate of growth was generally slower than employment growth in the health sector (in Bulgaria, Czechoslovakia, Hungary and Poland) or in housing (in the German Democratic Republic, Romania and the Soviet Union). In the German Democratic Republic and Poland, employment growth in education was the slowest among the three major non-material sectors, which reflected primarily demographic changes (chart 3.6.6).

Investment allocations were generally on the rise up to the end of the 1970s but declined thereafter (Czechoslovakia, Romania, Hungary and Poland) or they stagnated (Bulgaria and the German Democratic Republic). The Soviet Union was the only country where investment in education grew continuously; it has continued to accelerate in recent years.

International comparisons in the area of education based on physical indicators indicate the relatively good standing of eastern Europe and the Soviet Union.[397] This reflects free education at all levels. All seven countries have developed extensive *pre-school facilities*. Indeed, this service is an important pre-condition of the high participation of women in the work force which characterizes all of them. Thus, the number of children attending pre-school establishments in the early 1970s varied between two out of ten in Poland and Romania and five out of ten in the German Democratic Republic. Between that year and 1987, this ratio increased in all the countries and reached five or more out of ten in all countries but Poland.[398] By far the most advanced country in this respect is the German Democratic Republic, where the ratio increased from 5 to nearly 9 between 1970 and 1987.[399]

The *number of people receiving education* is another indicator of services provided in this area. The number of students in higher educational establishments (including universities) per 10,000 of the population increased between 1970/1971 and 1987/1988 in Bulgaria (from 108 to 133), Czechoslovakia (from 91 to 109) and Hungary (from 78 to 93). In contrast, the ratio declined in the German Democratic Republic (from 84 to 80), Poland (from 101 to 91) and the Soviet Union (from 188 to 177).[400] The Soviet Union thus occupies the leading position in this respect. These developments can be partially explained by demographic changes. The low number of students per 10,000 of the population registered in the German Democratic Republic, in particular, can be explained in terms of the atypical demographic age structure of that country. Nevertheless, inter-country differences remain rather wide.

---

[394] The data quoted refer to health and social care together with sport and tourism.

[395] See Ye. I. Chazov, USSR Minister of Health, speech at the 19th All-Union CPSU Conference, *Pravda*, 30 June 1988. A similar assessment can be found in the statement of J. Prokopec, Minister of Health and Social Affairs of the Czech Socialist Republic, *Rude pravo*, 16 October 1989, p.5.

[396] Including science and culture.

[397] See E. Ehrlich, *op.cit.*

[398] No figures have been published for Romania.

[399] See *Statisticheskii ezhegodnik stran-chlenov SEV 1988* (CMEA statistical yearbook 1988), Moscow 1988, p.430.

[400] *Op.cit.*, p.436. No figures are available for Romania.

Several European centrally planned economies have started to *reform their education systems*. Under conditions of rapid world-wide technological advance, improvements in the qualifications of teaching staff and in education and training systems are particularly important. The contribution of education to economic growth, although difficult to measure, is significant, but improving the motivation of teachers and increased investment — particularly in computers and modern teaching equipment — are seen as important pre-conditions for implementing the programmes announced.

(v) Conclusions

Over the long-term, the service sector of the east European countries and the Soviet Union has very often been disadvantaged in the process of resource allocation and has thus lagged behind the growing demand for services. Development priorities were generally focused on the expansion of goods-producing sectors, particularly heavy industry and a "residual" approach was applied to the allocation of resources to the service economy. This worsened lags in this sector relative to the production of goods. International comparisons indicate that the endowment of the service sector in terms of both capital and labour, and consequently the performance of this sector, was much lower than seems appropriate in relation to the overall level of economic development of the countries concerned. This resulted in unsatisfied demand for consumer services and also in large losses in production due to the underdevelopment of producer services — particularly transport and communications.[401]

A critical assessment of the present situation in many of the seven countries was followed by the announcement of intentions to develop the service sector more rapidly in the years to come. However, its future development will depend to a great extent on proper resource allocation. The prospects for redeploying labour from goods-producing sectors to services appear to be fairly good, due to overemployment in industry, agriculture and construction. However, the prospects for redirecting investment to satisfy vast infrastructural needs are less clear since investment allocations to goods-producing sectors will have to continue at high levels if the aging of fixed assets is to be reversed and past slow progress in re-equipment and modernization is to accelerate.

Under these circumstances, economic reform and policy changes can play an important role, particularly those which leave more room for enterpreneurial initiatives, dismantle the monopolistic position of state institutions in providing services, promote competition through the participation of smaller enterprises, co-operatives and the private sector, and introduce more flexible price policies.

Policy makers also need to be made aware that any major structural change in favour of the service sector presupposes considerable technical and technological shifts, improved economic information, radical changes in performance criteria and incentive systems, training and re-training of manpower, promotion of innovations in services and the reinforcement of international co-operation and trade in services.[402] All these represent a considerable challenge, and some time will be needed to bring about substantial improvements in this increasingly important domain.

---

[401] Although difficult to measure, there are clear indications of unsatisfied demand for services, which are reflected in such phenomena as transport difficulties, crowded shops and long shopping times, waiting lists for telephones, shortages of hotel accommodation, the low standard and quality of health services and poor repair and maintenance of housing stock. On the other hand, the high demand for services indicates substantial possibilities for developing this sphere and enhancing rates of economic growth and living standards.

[402] A sizeable share of the joint ventures established between European centrally planned economies and western countries will operate in the service sector. Some perspectives for international co-operation in general in east-west trade in services are given in United Nations Economic Commission for Europe, *Economic Bulletin for Europe*, vol.41, New York, 1989.

Chapter 4

EAST-WEST ECONOMIC RELATIONS

4.1 WORLD TRADE AND PAYMENTS

Fast expansion of world trade volume continued in 1989, although some slow-down against the preceding year was registered. Average non-oil commodity trade prices remained strong, despite a descending tendency in the second half of the year, while oil prices tended to recover. Terms of trade moved in favour of commodities as against manufactures, but non-oil developing countries were on balance net losers. Trade and current account surpluses of Japan and the deficits of the United States diminished further during the year. Some progress was achieved towards attenuating the international debt crisis.

In 1989 the volume of world merchandise trade increased by approximately 7 per cent, somewhat less than in the boom year of 1988. Fast and sustained growth of international trade accompanied a generally good economic performance in many world regions in 1987-1988, resulting in a growth of world trade volume by almost a quarter over the last three years.

Although the US trade deficit diminished further, the problem of the external imbalances of the main industrial countries persisted in 1989. Appreciation of the dollar, which was particularly pronounced from May to mid-October, did not favour the adjustment of the US external balance. The strengthening of the dollar was due, *inter alia*, to the buoyancy of the United States economy, uncertainties in other world regions, and to the rise in US interest rates. A tighter monetary stance was also adopted by many other industrial countries to curb the threat of resurgent inflation, to defend their currencies against further depreciation and to improve the balance of payments.

The brief Wall Street crisis of mid-October 1989 brought about some corrections to these trends, checking the rise of the dollar and provoking some easing in the monetary policy of the United States. Nonetheless, a substantial increase in average nominal and real interest rates around the world in 1989 against 1988 and, more so, against 1986-1987, has affected the external position of the indebted countries, increasing their debt service obligations and the capital outflow towards industrial countries, as well as wiping out the gains of primary commodity producers from the recovery of real prices of their export products. The need for new approaches to the international debt problem has been recognized more widely and new initiatives in this field have been undertaken.

The year 1989 was the second successive year of improvement in the terms of trade of primary commodities *vis-à-vis* manufactured products, and the second since 1984 of simultaneous recovery of the real prices of non-oil primary commodities. The dollar prices of non-fuel primary commodities continued to rise in the first half of 1989 under the impact of strong demand in the industrial countries, but fell in the second half of the year. On the other hand, oil prices, which had started to recover at the end of 1988, fluctuated at a level well above the 1988 average.

(i) **Trade volumes**

Statistical data on the foreign trade of individual countries in 1988 and 1989 have been subject to considerable delays and to many revisions concerning, in particular, the split of the increase in trade values into volumes and prices, and the evaluation of the volume growth of the trade of developing countries.[403] In 1988 the volume of world merchandise trade rose by more than 8 per cent, the fastest growth in this decade since 1984.

From still less than complete information it can be concluded that the rapid expansion of trade continued in 1989. For the year as a whole, the pace decreased, however, to some 7 per cent. Sustained economic growth of the developed market economies, combined

---

[403] The delays in the recording and publication of foreign trade data in 1988 and 1989 were partly due to the introduction by a number of countries of a new commodity classification system, the "Harmonized Commodity Description and Coding System", a switch to a new revised SITC classification (Rev.3) and the introduction by the EC at the beginning of 1988 of a new standardized customs document, adopted also by EFTA.

with strong investment, was largely responsible for the high growth of world trade volume in 1989 (table 4.1.1).

It was the increase in volume of west European exports and imports (by some 7½ per cent), as well as of US exports (above 11 per cent) and Japanese imports (7½ per cent), which contributed most to maintaining the high growth rate of world trade.[404] The acceleration of west European trade, after respectable growth in 1988, was due to intra-regional trade, as well as to large increases in imports from the United States (a lagged effect of the earlier depreciation of the dollar), the oil-producing countries and some newly industrialized Asian economies.

The volume of exports from Japan, which had stagnated in 1986-1987 (due to sharp appreciation of the yen) and had risen by 4½ per cent in 1988, grew at almost 6 per cent in 1989.

The volume of total exports from the developing countries, having grown by more than one third over the 1986-1988 period (and at two-digit rates in 1987 and 1988), increased at a rate close to the world average in 1989. Exports of oil-producing countries, after a strong recovery in 1988, rose by about 6 per cent in 1989, and those of other developing countries by about 7 per cent (table 4.1.1).[405] Rapid export expansion in some newly-industrialized economies of Asia and Latin America (Argentina, Brazil) came to a halt, however, or continued at slower rates than in 1988. The aggregate export volume of Latin America and the Caribbean remained virtually stationary in 1989.[406] Growing domestic absorption and currency appreciation as well as protectionist pressures from developed economies were partly responsible for this slow-down.

Imports of developing countries were also among the most dynamic segments of world merchandise trade in 1989. The aggregate import volume of non-oil developing countries continued its fast recovery, particularly in countries benefiting from higher commodity prices and relatively diversified export patterns. In the developing Asian-Pacific region, for instance, the growth of imports has tended to accelerate.[407] On the other hand, in a number of Latin American economies there were sharp reductions in imports as a result of economic recession and adjustment programmes, e.g., in Argentina, Nicaragua, Peru and Venezuela. In some other economies of the region (Brazil, Mexico, Costa Rica) imports went up significantly, stimulated by the economic recovery and import liberalization measures.[408] There was also a modest recovery of import demand in the oil-exporting countries, an upturn which had already started in 1988, after a protracted period of decline (imports fell by almost a half between 1982 and 1987).

In contrast to developments in the market economies, there was a decrease in export volume in eastern Europe and the Soviet Union in 1989. East European imports stagnated, while those of the Soviet Union rose by 7 per cent.

The lack of buoyancy in east European and Soviet trade reflects above all an absolute contraction in the volume of intra-group trade (including a 2 per cent fall in the volume of Soviet deliveries to eastern Europe) and of exports to developing countries. Exports to market economies appear to have stagnated or declined in volume, after substantial growth in 1988, whereas

TABLE 4.1.1
World trade: volume changes, 1986-1989
(Percentage change from previous year)

	1986	1987	1988	1989 [a]
Exports				
Developed market economies	1.6	5.5	8.2	7.3
North America	1.7	10.4	15.4	7.7
Western Europe	2.4	4.4	6.3	7.5
Southern Europe	-3.1	8.3	2.5	6.0
Japan	-0.6	0.4	4.4	5.8
Developing countries	8.9	11.1	11.0	6.6
Oil exporters [b]	11.3	1.5	11.6	5.9 [c]
Non-oil exporters	8.0	15.0	10.7	6.8 [c]
Eastern Europe and the Soviet Union	5.1	2.2	4.4	-1.3
Eastern Europe	0.3	1.2	3.9	-2.4
Soviet Union	10.0	3.3	4.8	-0.3
Total above	3.7	6.5	8.5	6.3
Imports				
Developed market economies	8.2	6.6	7.4	8.5
North America	11.1	3.8	6.2	7.5
Western Europe	5.7	6.8	7.3	7.6
Southern Europe	12.1	17.2	7.1	15.8
Japan	10.5	9.0	16.6	7.5
Developing countries	-4.4	5.7	10.2	8.7
Oil exporters [b]	-20.7	-8.3	3.4	5.1 [c]
Non-oil exporters	1.6	9.8	11.9	9.5 [c]
Eastern Europe and the Soviet Union	-0.3	0.2	3.5	3.7
Eastern Europe	5.3	1.8	3.0	0.8
Soviet Union	-6.0	-1.6	4.0	7.1
Total above	4.7	5.8	7.7	8.1

Sources: IMF, *International Financial Statistics*, March 1990; OECD, *Monthly Statistics of Foreign Trade*, Series A, February 1990; and ECE secretariat estimates for the developed market economies; IMF, *World Economic Outlook*, October 1989 for developing country groupings; ECE secretariat calculations, based on national sources for the European centrally planned economies. Weights for aggregation are US dollar trade shares in 1985.

a Preliminary or estimated.
b OPEC members, except Ecuador and Gabon, plus Oman.
c IMF estimates for full year.

---

[404] See United Nations *Monthly Bulletin of Statistics*, January 1990; OECD, *Monthly Statistics of Foreign Trade, Series A*, February 1990.

[405] IMF forecasts for the whole year. See IMF, *World Economic Outlook*, October 1989, p.93.

[406] See United Nations Economic Commission for Latin America and Caribbean, *Preliminary Overview of the Economy of Latin America and the Caribbean 1989*, LC/G.1586, Santiago, Chile, 29 December 1989, pp.9-11.

[407] See United Nations Economic and Social Commission for Asia and the Pacific, *Review of Economic Performance and Prospects of the Developing Asian-Pacific Region and the end of 1989*, Bangkok, 22 December 1989, p.10.

[408] For more details see United Nations Economic Commission for Latin America and Caribbean, *Preliminary Overview of the Economy of Latin America and the Caribbean 1989, op.cit.*, pp.9-11.

imports from the developed and developing market economies expanded by some 13 per cent. The fall in the volume of exports was due, *inter alia,* to supply constraints in some sectors (e.g., transport, energy and agriculture), growing domestic demand, rising inflation, as well as industrial unrest and slackening output growth in countries of the east.

(ii) Trade prices and terms of trade

After an overall upturn in the second half of 1987 and a widespread increase in non-fuel commodity prices in 1988,[409] most commodity prices remained firm or — in terms of SDRs — were still growing moderately in the first half of 1989. This reflected the influence of continued, although slowing, economic expansion in the industrialized countries, strong demand and tight supplies in many developing countries, low stocks and weather-related supply factors.

However, the price trends flattened during the year (table 4.1.3). Since June the value of the UNCTAD non-oil commodity price index has been close to or lower than in the corresponding months of 1988. For the whole year the UNCTAD index, in terms of SDRs, increased by 4.9 per cent, while in terms of US dollars it remained at its 1988 level. In the final quarter of 1989 this index decreased, however, by 6.5 per cent and 2.2 per cent respectively. For many commodities, after a sharp rise, there was volatility or a decline from peak levels — e.g., aluminium, nickel and silver. Copper prices, having risen by about 45 per cent in 1988, increased further in the first half of 1989 (by about 20 per cent, in dollar terms) and fell again in the second half. The prices of zinc and tin were booming, despite a fall in the final quarter. Food prices, in terms of SDRs, stayed firm in the first half, but fell below their 1988 level during the second half of the year (table 4.1.2). The aggregate index, however, contains divergent price developments for individual commodity groups and products. Depressed prices of tropical beverages (especially cocoa and coffee) were due to structural oversupply. A recovery in crops of soybeans and cereals (maize), after the severe drought in 1988 in North, Central and South America, led to price falls in the second half of 1989. Cereal stocks were depleted in 1987-1988 and remain at generally low levels. Sugar prices, after a rise of 50 per cent in 1988, strengthened further during 1989. Prices of agricultural raw materials, which rose sharply in 1987-1988, also registered some growth in 1989, at least in terms of SDRs, *inter*

TABLE 4.1.2

The Economist commodity price index, in terms of SDRs
(1985 = 100)

	30 Dec. 1986	29 Dec. 1987	28 Dec. 1988	27 June 1989	3 Oct. 1989	2 Jan. 1990
All items	81	99	121	112	105	94
Food	83	87	92	91	79	74
Industrials						
All	76	107	150	132	131	114
Non-food agricultural	88	97	103	111	110	104
Metals	68	111	182	147	146	121

Source: Various issues of *The Economist,* London.

alia as a result of price increases for cotton, jute and sisal.[410]

In 1989, in contrast to 1988, rising non-oil commodity prices coincided with a substantial upturn in the fuel market with respect to both trade volumes and prices. The recovery commenced after the OPEC agreement of November 1988 on a production ceiling for 13 members of 18.5 million barrels a day for the first half of 1989, which constituted a substantial cut-back in OPEC's output, then estimated at some 22 million barrels a day. Oil prices were also affected by reductions in oil production and exports in other oil exporting countries as well as by a higher than expected rise in world oil consumption. It had reached 22.7 billion barrels in 1988 (the highest level since 1980) and increased somewhat faster in 1989 than the earlier forecast of 2 per cent.[411]

Strong world demand for oil, as well as pressures from exporting countries, pushed OPEC to increase the agreed production quotas up to 19.5 million barrels per day early in 1989, and later (in September) to 20.5 million barrels per day. Actual oil output rose in September to 22.4 million barrels per day and in October to 22.9 million barrels per day. On 28 November 1989 OPEC agreed to raise the production ceiling again, up to 22 million barrels a day, with a "minimum" reference price of $18 a barrel. This limit, however, was surpassed as well. In December 1989, OPEC's average daily output was equal to 24.5 million barrels, and in the first half of January 1990 to 23.7 million barrels.[412]

The average spot market price of Brent (UK), Dubai and Alaskan North Slope — representing light, medium and heavier crude oil — which had bottomed at $11.5 a barrel in October 1988 and recovered to $12.4 in the fourth quarter of 1988 (for a 1988 average of $14.2),[413] rose to $16.4 in the first quarter of 1989 and

---

[409] In 1988 the UNCTAD index of dollar prices of non-fuel primary commodities exported by developing countries rose by 18 per cent, and in terms of SDRs, by 14 per cent (see table 4.1.3). Of the 40 commodity prices in the UNCTAD index, 37 increased. UNCTAD, *Monthly Commodity Price Bulletin,* January 1990. Still higher growth was evidenced by the IMF world index of non-fuel primary commodities, which rose in 1988 by 34.4 per cent, in dollar terms, and by 18.9 per cent, in terms of SDRs. In purchasing power terms (relative to export unit values of manufactures), non-fuel commodity prices increased by 16.6 per cent. See IMF, *Primary Commodities. Market Developments and Outlook,* July 1989, Washington, D.C., p.1-2.

[410] See UNCTAD, *Monthly Commodity Price Bulletin,* January 1990.

[411] See United Nations, *World Economic Survey 1989,* chapter V, pp.94-95; WEFA, *World Economic Outlook,* October 1989, p.2.5.

[412] *Financial Times,* 26 September 1989, 18 September 1989, 29 November 1989; *Wall Street Journal,* 19-20 January 1990.

[413] This average corresponds roughly to the average of the seven crude oils included in the basket for the OPEC reference price, set at $18 a barrel as of 1 February 1987 (the official crude oil prices were, however, *de facto* abandoned in the first half of 1988). See IMF, *World Economic Outlook,* April 1989, p.107.

TABLE 4.1.3
Changes in international trade prices in US dollars and in SDRs
(Percentage change from previous year)

					1989	
	1986	1987	1988	Jan.-March	April-June	July-Sept.
Manufactures [a]						
In US dollar terms.....................	20	13	6	-	-2	4
In terms of SDR........................	3	2	2	4	6	8
Fuels and related materials [b]						
In US dollar terms.....................	-37	7	-12	-7	4	21
In terms of SDR........................	-46	-3	-15	-3	12	25
Non-oil commodities [c]						
In US dollar terms.....................	4	3	26	11	2	-4
In terms of SDR........................	-10	-7	21	15	10	-1

Source: United Nations, *Monthly Bulletin of Statistics,* December 1989 and UNCTAD, *Monthly Commodity Price Bulletin,* January 1990.

a Export unit value index for manufactures of developed market economies.
b Unit value of the developed market economies' imports of mineral fuels.
c UNCTAD index of market prices of principal commodity exports of developing countries, using weights proportional to the value, in terms of US dollars, of exports from developing countries in the years 1984-1986.

$17.6 in the second quarter (i.e., close to the 1987 average level of $17.8). After some decline in the course of the year (from $18.8 in April to $16.0 in August) the average spot price firmed again in the final quarter and fluctuated close to the target level of $18 a barrel. Thus in 1989 the average spot price of crude oil ($17.2 a barrel) was 21 per cent higher than in 1988.[414] The changes in the UN index of unit values of developed market economy countries' imports of mineral fuels were more moderate and lagged behind the changes in the crude oil spot prices (see table 4.1.3).

For the whole of 1989, dollar oil prices, represented by the export unit values of the twelve major oil exporters, were forecast by the IMF to increase by 18.5 per cent.[415]

In the first three quarters of 1989 prices of manufactures exported by developed market economies rose by less than one per cent, while free market prices of non-oil commodities grew by almost 3 per cent in terms of current US dollars.[416]

On the basis of the forecasts and preliminary figures, it can be concluded that the terms of trade of industrial countries deteriorated slightly in 1989, for the first time since 1981, and those of developing countries showed an improvement. However, among the latter group, the net energy importers — whose terms of trade improved in 1988 — have now been net losers. On the other hand, the terms of trade of fuel exporters have improved substantially in 1989. However, these tendencies represent only a modest recovery in the real prices of primary commodities, which is not expected to endure in 1990. Actually, in view of the prospect of a slow-down in overall economic activity in the industrial countries, further weakening of non-oil primary commodity prices — in nominal and real terms — is envisaged for 1990.[417]

(iii) Exchange rate and monetary developments

Exchange rate movements in 1989 were marked by an upward trend of the US dollar, which had started in December 1988 after some appreciation and downturns earlier in 1988. Nonetheless, the average annual value of the US dollar, in terms of SDRs, was still about 4 per cent lower in 1988 than in the preceding year and by one fourth lower than in 1985. However, in the 12 months from the end of 1987, the dollar had appreciated by 5.4 per cent against the SDR. During successive quarters of 1989 the dollar rose, in relation to the SDR, by 3.8, 7.3, 2.8 and 4.5 per cent as compared with the corresponding periods of 1988.[418]

In 1989 the US dollar strengthened, on average, by 4.6 per cent against the SDR. Nominal appreciation of the US dollar was most pronounced against the pound sterling (8 per cent) and the Japanese yen (7.1 per cent). On the other hand, the US currency depreciated by 6.7 per cent against the Canadian dollar, which was favoured by rising commodity prices. In relation to the major EMS currencies, the US dollar appreciated by about 6.5 per cent. The average real effective appreciation of the US dollar amounted to 3 per cent in 1989, which followed its depreciation by almost 6 per cent in 1988. The yen depreciated by 4.3

---

414 IMF, *International Financial Statistics,* October 1989, p.84; UNCTAD, *Monthly Commodity Price Bulletin,* January 1990, p.11.

415 See IMF, *World Economic Outlook,* October 1989, *op.cit.*

416 See UNCTAD, *Monthly Commodity Price Bulletin,* January 1990, p.1; UN, *Monthly Bulletin of Statistics,* December 1989, p.252.

417 See IMF, *loc.cit.* See also UNCTAD, *Trade and Development Report, op.cit.,* pp.61-62, 213-214.

418 See IMF, *International Financial Statistics,* February 1990, pp.21; UNCTAD, *Monthly Commodity Price Bulletin,* January 1990, p.19.

per cent, in real terms, in 1989, having appreciated by nearly 11 per cent in the preceding year.[419]

Among the factors underlying the sharp recovery of the dollar was the widespread conviction that the growth of the US economy would continue, although at a more moderate pace, in 1989 and 1990, without triggering inflation, and that relatively high interest rates would be maintained. Political and economic uncertainties in other parts of the world also increased the attraction of the US dollar and of foreign investment in the US economy. The position of the Federal Reserve Board and the orientation of international monetary policy, co-ordinated to some extent within the Group of Seven, were also partly responsible for the situation on international financial markets. But financial markets remained very nervous and sensitive to current political and economic events, as well as to short-term developments, such as quarterly or monthly reports on changes in the trade balances of the United States and other major industrial economies.

The easing of monetary policy after the stock market crash of October 1987, reflected in the lowering of interest rates and in the expansion of money supply in many developed market economies — which provided a considerable boost to economic activity — lasted into the early part of 1988. Later in that year, however, the booming economy and the signs of rising inflation, particularly in the United States and in the United Kingdom (augmented by the effects of exceptional factors, e.g., the drought in the United States) led to a tightening of the monetary stance in those and other industrial countries.

In 1989, monetary conditions remained firm, with short-term interest rates generally high.[420] Some decline in US rates during the second and the third quarter, induced by signs of a possible economic slow-down, was not sufficient to alter substantially the upward trend of the dollar. The associated rise in dollar-denominated prices of oil and some other commodities increased general concern about inflation and overheating in other industrial countries. The resilience of the dollar to massive and repeated interventions of Group of Seven banks and the reluctance of the Federal Reserve Board to reduce US interest rates, led other industrial countries to increase their rates (in September and October) and thus to narrow the rate differentials. The decision of the Bundesbank on 5 October to raise its discount rate from 5 to 6 per cent[421] was soon followed by similar increases in the United Kingdom, France, Switzerland, Japan and in other countries.

In these circumstances a fall of 6.9 per cent in the Dow Jones industrial index on 13 October 1989 triggered a fall in the value of the dollar and some reduction in short-term interest rates. Concerted action by the central banks and governments of the Group of Seven contributed to a rapid, although partial, recovery of financial markets.[422] Volatility of exchange rates and steep falls in stock prices were also registered in the course of the final quarter of 1989 and the first quarter of 1990. The Japanese yen continued its slide against the US dollar, reaching the three year lowest rate (more than 153 yen to the dollar) on 19 March 1990. Sharp drops in stock prices on the Tokyo stock exchange were linked to inflationary pressures, stock arbitrage and current political and economic developments. An expected growth of interest rates materialized after a one percentage point rise (to 5.25 per cent) in the official discount rate of the Bank of Japan on 20 March 1990. Risks and uncertainties associated with the proposed monetary union of the Federal Republic of Germany with the German Democratic Republic were weakening west German bond prices and the Deutschmark, which appreciated, however, after the victory of conservative parties in the German Democratic Republic's elections of 18 March 1990. In the United Kingdom fears of a possible rise in inflation — with little room left for an increase in interest rates — were depressing the pound sterling. Thus the US dollar, supported by firm interest rates, again tended to strengthen.

(iv) Trade and current account balances of developed market economies

The aggregate merchandise trade deficit of the developed market economies widened again in 1989, with large deficits or surpluses of individual industrial countries persisting or, in some cases, increasing during the year. The aggregate current account deficit of the developed market economies rose also in 1989. But this information is not particularly meaningful as the substantial statistical discrepancy between the aggregate surpluses and deficits in the global balance of payments persists.[423]

The US trade deficit, which fell substantially in the first quarter (by about $5 billion, compared with the same period of 1988), diminished further during the year, although with a slowing pace.[424]

---

[419] See IMF, *International Financial Statistics*, February 1990.

[420] E.g., the average value of LIBOR on three-month dollar deposits which amounted to 8.4, 6.9, 7.2 and 8.0 per cent per annum, respectively, in successive years of the 1985-1988 period, reached 9.3 per cent in 1989. See IMF, *International Financial Statistics*, February 1990.

[421] The discount rate of 6 per cent was maintained through the end of 1989. For comparison, the level of this rate amounted to 4 per cent in 1985, 3.5 per cent in 1986, 2.5 per cent in 1987, 3.5 per cent in 1988 and 4 per cent in the first quarter of 1989.

[422] The Dow Jones industrial average which had reached a value of 2722 on the Wall Street stock market on 25 August 1987 and then bottomed at 1739 on 19 October 1987 ("Black Monday"), recovered thereafter to a record level of 2791 on 9 October 1989, to plunge to 2569 on Friday 13 October. It fell further (to about 2520) on Monday morning, 16 October, and then rebounded during the day, to 2657 at closure. *International Herald Tribune*, 16 October 1989; *Wall Street Journal*, 17 October 1989.

[423] See IMF, *World Economic Outlook*, October 1989, pp.59-63; *IMF Survey*, 8 January 1990, pp.1-12.

[424] See *Wall Street Journal*, 19 February and 14 March 1990.

TABLE 4.1.4

Trade and current account balances, 1987-1989
(Billion US dollars)

	Trade balances			Current account balances		
	1987	1988	1989	1987	1988	1989
Developed market economies	-33	-9	-51	-38	-48	-82
North America	-150	-118	-109	-150	-135	-120
Europe	21	13	-18	35	18	-3
Japan	96	95	77	87	80	57
Australia and New Zealand	-	1	-1	-10	-11	-16
Developing countries	55	43	47	5	-10	-11
Oil exporters	37	28	41	-6	-15	-2
Non-oil exporters	18	15	6	11	5	-9
Eastern Europe and the Soviet Union [a]	11	7	-	9	3	-6
Eastern Europe [a]	3	3	2	1	-	-2
Soviet Union [a]	8	4	-2	8	3	-3
Total above	33	41	-4	-24	-55	-99

Sources: IMF, *International Financial Statistics*, February 1990, Washington, D.C.; OECD, *Economic Outlook*, No.46, December 1989; national statistics and ECE secretariat estimates. Small discrepancies are due to rounding.

[a] With market economies.

There were large falls in the United States' bilateral deficits with other developed countries (Canada, Japan, western Europe) as well as with the newly industrialized economies in the Far East in 1988-1989. On the other hand, the US deficit with oil-producing and other developing countries increased.

The US deficit on current account also showed a significant improvement in 1989.[425]

Japan's trade surplus, after narrowing slightly in 1988 — for the first time since 1982 (in terms of US dollars) — diminished by $18 billion in 1989. The value of imports rose considerably faster than that of exports (by 11½ and 6½ per cent, respectively). The substantial growth in the value of Japanese imports reflected rising oil and commodity prices, as well as a booming internal demand. Japan's current account surplus in 1989 narrowed even more (by $22.6 billion).

In 1989 the problems of external imbalance became more severe for several European market economy countries. However, the aggregate current account surplus of the group with the rest of the world is close to disappearing (see table 4.1.4).

The trade and current account surpluses of the Federal Republic of Germany rose further in national currency terms in 1989. In dollar terms the changes were not so significant. The surplus on the current account widened by 8½ per cent (in dollar terms), due in part to a change in the balance on services. The surplus on the trade account increased, in Deutschmarks, but slightly decreased in terms of US dollars. The growth of import volume was, for the whole year, almost as fast as that of exports (close to 8 per cent), and the terms of trade deteriorated by some 2.5 per cent. For the second consecutive year the surplus rose significantly in trade with the other countries of western Europe, both of the EC and EFTA, as well as with the Soviet Union and eastern Europe. The trade surplus with the United States narrowed further, while the deficit with Japan increased, and that with non-oil developing countries of Asia and Latin America diminished.[426]

Three other large European industrial countries — the United Kingdom, France and Italy — have registered important trade and current account deficits for the last three years. The largest were reported for the United Kingdom, where the trade deficit rose from $18 billion in 1987 to $37 billion in 1988 and almost $38 billion in 1989, the current account deficit reaching some $34 billion last year. The deterioration of the United Kingdom trade balance was due to the substantially faster growth of imports than of exports (respectively about 9 and 6½ per cent in volume in 1989), while the terms of trade were improving. Imports from North America and the developing countries, and exports to the EC, were the most dynamic elements of UK visible trade.

Among the other European market economy countries, deficits were recorded in the three south European countries which had joined the EC in this decade. The trade deficit of Spain was the most pronounced and rapidly growing.

---

[425] The US current account deficit declined from $65.5 billion in the first half of 1988 to $61.4 billion in the corresponding part of 1989. However, the deficit on non-merchandise transactions increased from $0.8 billion to $5.3 billion. This trend was reverted in the second half of the year, and notably in the final quarter, due to some depreciation of the dollar which augmented the nominal value of receipts of income on US assets abroad, in terms of US dollars. For the whole year the US current account deficit diminished to $105.9 billion.

[426] See *Statistische Beihefte zu den Monatsberichten der Deutschen Bundesbank*, No.2, February 1990.

(v) External balances and debt problems of developing countries

The merchandise trade of developing countries, which expanded very rapidly in 1988, was also particularly dynamic in 1989, notwithstanding a slow-down in growth rates. The increase in the value of imports appears to have exceeded that of exports, both in 1988 and 1989, and the aggregate trade balance of the developing countries deteriorated again, after a marked improvement in 1987. Behind the aggregate figures of trade and trade balances there are considerable differences between balances of individual countries, regions and economic groups of developing countries.

According to the IMF statistics, the aggregate trade balance of the developing countries swung into a small deficit again in 1988 ($2 billion), after a surplus of around $30 billion in 1987. The trade surplus of oil-exporting countries fell from $36 billion in 1987 to $32 billion in 1988, and the deficit of non-oil developing countries grew from $5 billion to $30 billion. Exports and imports of the latter groups expanded by 18 and 23 per cent, while the export value of oil-exporting countries rose only slightly in 1988 and their imports increased by 10 per cent.[427]

In the first half of 1989, total exports and imports of developing countries increased by 12 and 15 per cent in dollar terms (compared with 15 and 21 per cent in 1988). The value of exports of oil-exporting countries rose by some 8 per cent, and that of non-oil developing countries by 12 per cent. Imports of the two country groups increased by about 1 and 18 per cent respectively. This resulted in a further rise in their aggregate trade deficit (to some $12 billion in the first half of 1989, with a $30 billion deficit of non-oil developing countries).[428]

In these circumstances, and in view of increased interest rates, the improvement in the current account balances of non-oil developing countries, which had resulted in small surpluses in 1987 and 1988 (of $6-7 billion), may have been reversed in 1989.[429] In the case of oil-exporting countries, the deficit on current account, close to $12 billion in 1988, probably disappeared in 1989. The aggregate current account balance of the developing countries, which was in surplus in 1987 and 1988, turned into a small deficit in 1989.[430] The external debt of developing countries, which was reported by the IMF to have declined slightly in 1988 (to $1,197 billion, from $1,200 billion in 1987) for the first time in at least 20 years, remained practically unchanged in 1989 and is expected to start increasing again.[431]

The temporary stabilization of the debt in 1987-1989 and a decline in debt-to-export ratios were due to the evolution of trade balances as well as to such factors as successive reductions in external borrowing, valuation adjustments stemming from the appreciation of the US dollar, and progress in the application of debt-to-equity conversions and other debt-reducing techniques,[432] implemented after the Toronto Summit of the Group of Seven in June 1988. In March 1989 an international initiative on debt was launched by the US Secretary of the Treasury (the "Brady Plan").[433] This envisaged the use, in a flexible way, of different options for debt reduction, on a case-by-case basis. It implies co-ordinated action by commercial banks, international financial institutions (supposed to grant new loans and funds for collateral) and debtor countries' governments (responsible for effective adjustment programmes).

The preliminary agreement under this plan was reached with Mexico in July 1989 and signed, in a final form, by the Mexican Minister of Finance and representatives of the Advisory Committee of commercial banks on 4 February 1990. The agreement covered $48.5 billion of medium- and long-term bank debt. It offered lending banks three options: swapping of debt for 30-years bonds at 65 per cent of face value, at a floating interest rate of 0.81 per cent over LIBOR; swapping bonds at full face value but with a fixed — 6¼ per cent interest rate; and rescheduling of debt maturities from 1989 to 1994, together with granting new long-term loans over four years, equal to 25 per cent of a bank's credit exposure, with an interest rate of 0.81 per cent over LIBOR. In addition, Mexican authorities agreed to permit US $1 billion in debt-to-equity conversion per year until 1992. All these operations will reduce the Mexican debt by some $20 billion.[434] Other debt reduction agreements based on the Brady Plan were reached with commercial banks by the Philippines (in the summer of 1989) and by Costa Rica (in November 1989). A rescheduling agreement with the Philippines offered banks a larger variety of market options. Wider use was made by the Philippines of the opportunity to buy back its own debt at a discount, with recourse to resources from the international financial institutions.

---

[427] On a customs basis, see IMF, *International Financial Statistics*, January 1990, pp.76-79. According to other IMF statistics, on a balance of payments basis, the trade balance of the developing countries was, however, in surplus of $59 and $43.5 billion, respectively, both in 1987 and 1988. See *IMF Survey*, 8 January 1990, p.10.

[428] See IMF, *International Financial Statistics*, January 1980, pp.76-79.

[429] *IMF Survey*, 8 January 1990, pp.9-13.

[430] In 1987 and 1988 the surpluses were equal to $26.6 and $28.4 billion, respectively (adjusted for statistical discrepancies). According to unadjusted data, there was a small current account surplus ($2.6 billion) in 1987 and a deficit of $4.7 billion in 1988. *IMF Survey*, 8 January 1990.

[431] IMF forecasts. See IMF, *World Economic Outlook*, October 1989, p.107 and *IMF Survey*, 8 January 1990.

[432] See IMF, *World Economic Outlook*, April 1989, chapter iv, pp.54-57.

[433] See United Nations, *World Economic Survey 1989, op.cit.*, pp.67-79; IMF, *Annual Report 1989*, Washington, D.C., 1989, pp.23-27.

[434] See *The Economist*, 12 August 1989; *Journal de Genève*, 5 February 1990.

The agreement with Costa Rica, which covered $1.5 billion of medium-term bank debt and $325 million of arrears, provided for reduction of the debt or of the service thereon, giving incentives for large-scale buybacks at a price of about 16 per cent of the nominal value. Other Latin American indebted countries, including Venezuela, Argentina, Ecuador and Uruguay, also initiated negotiations with their commercial bank creditors aiming at debt reduction arrangements based on the Brady Plan, while Bolivia — through two buyback transactions, carried out in 1988 and in May 1989 — retrieved about two thirds of its outstanding bank debt.

In 1989 around $30 billion of official funds were committed for debt reduction purposes, by the IMF and the World Bank ($12 billion each) and by Japan (at least $6 billion).[435] However, effective application of the Brady Plan on a wider scale requires raising much more funds from international financial institutions and other sources than has hitherto been possible.[436] Nevertheless, the international search for and adoption of flexible approaches to the external debt problem has become indispensable for significantly reducing the debt burden and thereby lowering the risk of future shocks and tensions within the world economy.[437]

(vi) Prospects

The expansion of international trade is likely to slow further in 1990, in line with overall economic activity in the United States and most other developed market economies. Nevertheless, a 6 per cent rate of increase in the volume of world merchandise exports appears probable. Total exports of the industrial countries are expected to grow slightly faster and imports somewhat slower than total world trade, in line with the probable changes in export and import volumes of the United States and western Europe. The growth of Japanese imports in 1990 is again likely to exceed substantially the growth of exports. On the other hand, the imports of the developing countries, and especially of oil exporters, will grow faster than their exports, and faster than the volume of world trade. Similarly, the imports of the east European countries and of the Soviet Union will increase more than their exports.

The growth of oil prices is expected to be small and the rising trend in non-oil commodities to be reversed in 1990. Hence, the long-term trend for prices of manufactures to rise relative to those of primary commodities is likely to resume. However, changes in the terms of trade of the major country groups are unlikely to be large. This applies, in particular, to the industrial countries. Some deterioration is likely in the terms of trade of the developing countries.

The external imbalances of the main industrial countries will stay large, with further growth in the US current account deficit not unlikely. The total debt of the developing countries will increase again, notwithstanding a wider use of debt reduction techniques, in consequence of the high level of interest rates attained in 1989 which are not expected to decline significantly until fears of increasing inflation are eased. The US dollar is likely to fluctuate around or fall somewhat below its average level in 1989 in the face of the persistent US current account deficit and the diminution of international interest rate differentials. The so far undertermined modalities of the German currency unification imparts some uncertainty to the outlook for currency relations. The large trade and current account imbalances among the west European market economies which started to diminish at the end of 1989 are not likely to increase substantially in the course of 1990.

---

[435] See United Nations Economic Commission for Latin America and Caribbean, *Preliminary Overview of the Economy of Latin America and the Caribbean 1989*, op.cit. pp.11-13.

[436] "Although a total of 39 countries have been discussed as potential users of the plan, if one just considers the 15 countries that are commonly grouped together as a sample of heavily-indebted countries, it is clear that of $29 billion already committed to the Brady Plan could support no more than a very partial reduction of the debt overhang." United Nations, *World Economic Survey 1989*, op.cit., p.75.

[437] According to a statement of US Treasury Undersecretary David C. Mulford, an agreement based on the Brady Plan could also be reached with Poland after the Polish economic reform programme is approved by the IMF. See *Rzeczpospolita*, 4 January 1990.

4.2 EAST-WEST TRADE

East-west trade in 1989 was characterized by a slackening of eastern export growth and a substantial pickup of the volume growth of eastern imports. Similar trends prevailed in the western trade of the Soviet Union and of the east European countries. The Soviet trade deficit with the west increased sharply, and the east European surplus dwindled. In consequence, current-account balances of the eastern countries worsened and debt increased. Sections 4.2 and 4.3 present a review of these developments in east-west trade and financial relations.[438]

Beyond short-term trade trends, east-west relations were profoundly transformed in 1989 by the fundamental political changes in all eastern countries, leading inter alia to an intensification in the search for economic reform solutions and in several countries to a commitment to the more radical endeavour of a full systems change. Some implications of these developments are taken up in section 4.4, which provides an assessment of western initiatives to support the transition endeavours in eastern Europe, and section 4.5, which surveys the issues posed by of German monetary unification. Finally, section 4.6 offers a brief discussion of the outlook for east-west trade.

(i) Introduction and summary

East-west trade developed unevenly last year. Eastern exports slowed from 8 per cent in 1988 to only 3 per cent in the first three quarters of 1989, owing primarily to tightening supply constraints in the eastern countries.[439] By contrast, the pace of eastern imports quickened to some 13 per cent in volume, the result of a combination of governments' decisions to compensate for domestic shortages and to liberalize their trade régimes. As a result there was a sharp deterioration in eastern trade and current account balances and a concomitant rise in the area's external indebtedness. Overall these developments in the foreign sector mirror the worsening state of the domestic economies discussed in chapter 3.

East-west trade and finance evolved against the background of momentous political and systematic changes in 1989. Hungary and Poland embarked on the path to a fundamental transformation of their economies. Later in the year, changes of leadership in other countries in the area paved the way for the acceleration of the reform process, with far-reaching implications for future economic relations in the region.

The volume of *Soviet exports* to the west increased by some 3 per cent in the first nine months of 1989, after strong expansion in the preceding year. Export growth slowed substantially in the course of the year, and on scattered data appears to have turned down further in the final quarter. Supply difficulties stemming from developments in fuels production and in Soviet transport are the likely cause of this slow-down. Soviet *imports,* on the other hand, rose rapidly — by 13 per cent in the first nine months — and at an accelerating pace. This trend is likely to have strengthened in the last quarter as emergency imports of consumer manufactures decided upon in the second half of the year (but not yet captured in the data used here) began to arrive.

Though the *terms of trade* of the Soviet Union with the west improved in 1989 owing to the rise in world market fuels prices, the gains were not sufficient to prevent a sharp widening of the Soviet *trade deficit* — from some $3 billion in 1988 to $6½ billion on the basis of Soviet data for the full year. The current-account deficit worsened even more, and Soviet *net indebtedness* increased by an estimated $10 billion in nominal terms, from $26½ billion to $36½ billion.

After a pickup in 1988, the volume of *east European exports* to the west slowed again in 1989, expanding at some 3 per cent in the first nine months. Volume growth for the year as a whole is likely to be lower still as the political developments in the last quarter generally had a negative impact on production and supplies. However, performance varied widely between countries; in some — notably Czechoslovakia and Hungary — changes in the trade régime in the course of economic reform appear to have resulted in relatively strong export growth. East European *imports* from the west, which had stagnated in the preceding year, rose sharply — by 13 per cent — in the first nine months of 1989. This reflected mainly very strong import expansion in Hungary and Poland in consequence of the liberalization of trade régimes in these countries. On the basis of national data, import growth appears to have been slowing somewhat in the last quarter, probably reflect-

---

[438] The terms "west", or "western", or "developed market economies" as used here refer to the countries of western Europe (including Turkey and Yugoslavia), North America and Japan. This grouping is intended only for statistical convenience. The term "eastern Europe" refers to Bulgaria, Czechoslovakia, the German Democratic Republic, Hungary, Poland and Romania taken together. The term "east" or "eastern countries" refers to eastern Europe and the Soviet Union.

[439] Unless otherwise noted, growth rates are for the first nine months of 1989 relative to the same period in 1988.

TABLE 4.2.1

East-west trade: Value, volumes, prices, and terms of trade, 1985-1989
(Percentage change over the same period of previous year)

From/To:	Eastern exports					Eastern imports				
	1985	1986	1987	1988	1989 QI-III	1985	1986	1987	1988	1989 QI-III
Values (in US dollars)										
Eastern Europe and the Soviet Union	-8	-1	12	5	7	2	6	4	12	12
of which:										
Eastern Europe	-2	10	13	7	5	8	18	13	6	11
Soviet Union	-11	-10	10	2	9	-1	-3	-3	18	13
Volumes										
Eastern Europe and the Soviet Union	-4	10	3	8	3	3	-13	-4	5	13
of which:										
Eastern Europe	-1	1	-	6	3	7	-1	2	-	13
Soviet Union	-7	21	7	9	3	-	-20	-9	9	13
Prices (in US dollars)										
Eastern Europe and the Soviet Union	-4	-11	7	-1	3	-1	20	9	8	-1
of which:										
Eastern Europe	-2	9	13	2	1	1	20	11	7	-1
Soviet Union	-5	-26	2	-6	5	-2	20	7	8	-
Values and volumes										
Memorandum item:										
Total western imports/exports										
Values	4	12	19	13	8	4	16	18	14	8
Volumes	6	8	7	7	9	4	2	6	8	7

Eastern terms of trade (1975 = 100)

	1983	1984	1985	1986	1987	1988	1989 QI-III
Eastern Europe and Soviet Union	152	153	146	109	108	98	102
of which:							
Eastern Europe	115	114	111	101	103	98	100
Soviet Union	190	198	191	117	112	97	102

Sources: United Nations commodity trade data base (COMTRADE); OECD, *Statistics on Foreign Trade,* Series A, Paris; IMF, *Directions of Trade* and *International Financial Statistics,* Washington, D.C.; Statistisches Bundesamt, *Warenverkehr mit der Deutschen Demokratischen Republik und Berlin (Ost),* Reihe 6, Wiesbaden; United Nations, *Monthly Bulletin of Statistics* (volume indices of total western exports to and imports from the world); national statistics.

Note: Price and volume indices: for the methodology and derivation, see United Nations Economic Commission for Europe, *Economic Bulletin for Europe,* vol.31, No.1, New York, 1979.

These data reflect the trade of 23 western reporting countries (Appendix table C.6 contains a list of the countries included). The same data are used in chart 4.2.1.

ing efforts to improve current accounts or hold down the growth of foreign debt.

The *trade surpluses* of the east European countries with the west and *in convertible currencies* still remained roughly unchanged. However, a substantial rise in the deficit on *invisibles* (from less than $3 billion in 1988 to $4½ billion) caused the east European *current account* to swing into a deficit again (estimated at some $2 billion). The aggregate *net indebtedness* of the east European countries rose by $1½ billion, from $76½ billion at the end of 1988 to almost $78 billion at the close of 1989.

In order to increase Hungary's and Poland's chances for a successful transition to a market system, western governments and multilateral financial institutions launched a series of support initiatives in 1989 which are now gathering pace. The unprecedent scope of the intended reforms was seen as ample justification for exceptional assistance. The agreed measures involve material and financial aid and a liberalization of trade policy that has set the stage for the eventual normalization of east-west economic relationships.

Given the deteriorating state of the Hungarian and, especially, Polish economies, the first priority for their governments was to elaborate credible economic stabilization programmes acceptable to the IMF. The aim was to eliminate macro-economic imbalances, implement far-reaching economic reforms and, with the assistance of other organizations, adopt measures to quicken structural change. The Polish and Hungarian governments' implementation of these programmes is a cause for optimism in that it shows a willingness to address fundamental problems. The experience gained may well be applicable to other highly-indebted countries which choose to embark on the path to reform.

The international initiative signals an increasing role for official multilateral and bilateral financing of the eastern economies. The new role stems from the recognition that without support certain countries will find it difficult or impossible to obtain new private credits. Also there is an emerging structure of institu-

CHART 4.2.1

International trade of eastern Europe and the Soviet Union with the west

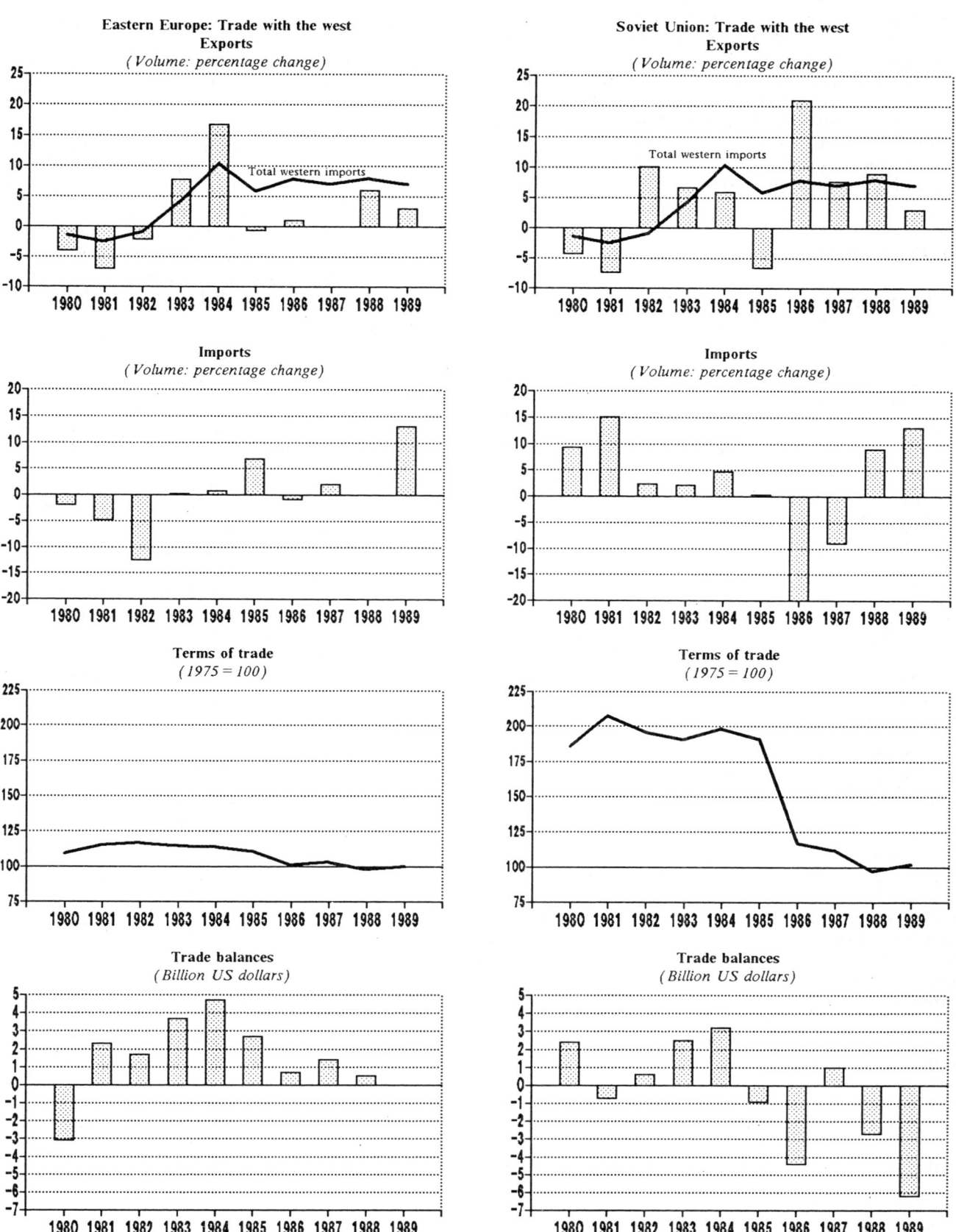

Source: As for table 4.2.1; trade balances from table 4.2.5, Panel B.

tional relations which includes the creation of the European Bank for Reconstruction and Development (EBRD), the prospective membership of Bulgaria and Czechoslovakia and the reactivation of Romania's participation in the Bretton Woods institutions. Their role, together with official credit agencies and other sources of aid, may be crucial given that, for a variety of reasons, commercial banking institutions are taking an increasingly cautious view of lending toward the east. Included among these is the uncertainty associated with the reform process itself.

(ii) Prices and terms of trade

The prices of manufactures and of key commodities in east-west trade, measured in US dollars, moved in opposite directions in the first three quarters of 1989.

Manufactured goods prices reported by west European countries, which jointly account for the bulk of the developed market economies' trade in manufactures with the east, declined by 4 per cent in dollar terms, reflecting the appreciation of the US dollar.[440]

Amongst commodities, *fuel* prices, led by *petroleum products* and *crude oil*, rebounded in 1989. The prices of the latter two commodities increased by some 16 per cent and 12 per cent respectively in the first three quarters of the year.[441] The rises have been attributed in part to lower Soviet sales in world markets.[442] Natural gas prices recovered in the course of the first three quarters of the year 1989, although the average was still some 10-20 per cent below the level of the same period in the previous year. The directions of change of other primary commodity prices were mixed. *Cereals and metals* prices weakened as the year progressed, but still showed an increase on a year-on-year basis, as did most *natural fibres*, the prices of which strengthened again. By contrast, prices of other *crude agricultural materials* declined.[443]

As a consequence of these commodity price movements, the *average prices* of east European trade with the west and of Soviet imports, measured in US dollars, changed little in the first nine months of 1989 (table 4.2.1). By contrast, Soviet export prices, reflecting the high fuels component, rose by some 5 per cent during the same period. This resulted in an upturn in the Soviet Union's *terms of trade* with the west, the first improvement since the early 1980s. For most of the decade, the country had experienced steep and continuous losses in its terms of trade, owing chiefly to the decline in fuel prices.

(iii) Eastern exports

According to western statistics, *east European and Soviet* export volume growth to the west slowed from to 8 per cent in 1988 to some 3 per cent in the first three quarters of 1989 (charts 4.2.1 and tables 4.2.1 and 4.2.2).

After the sharp pickup in 1988, *east European* export growth slackened to 3 per cent in the first three quarters of 1989. The area nonetheless registered its strongest export performance since the export boom of 1983-1984. However, it still lagged behind the growth of western import demand, which quickened from 7 per cent in 1988 to 9 per cent in the first three quarters of the year. Import growth behaved similarly in western Europe, the largest western market for eastern goods (table 4.1.1). While buoyant western markets undoubtedly facilitated eastern export growth, this cannot be the main explanation for the recent expansion of eastern deliveries since, in preceding years, western trade had also boomed, but east European exports stagnated. Supply factors appear to have been more important.

It should be noted at the same time that there are marked discrepancies in the growth rates of east-west trade in 1989 as measured by eastern national trade returns and by western statistics reported in international data sources (see box 4.2.1). Because eastern trade data, especially for the most recent period, generally are available only at the most aggregate level (total trade by major country groups), if at all,[444] and generally provide no commodity detail, this section and its tables are based, as usual, upon western reported statistics. For 1989 these tend to show a more rapid development of east-west trade than eastern data, particularly on the side of eastern imports. However, the discussion also draws upon eastern statistics when appropriate.

In terms of *individual countries*, the expansion of east European exports was uneven in the first three quarters of 1989 (table 4.2.2). Bulgarian, Czechoslovakian and Hungarian exports accelerated to 5-13 per cent in volume. Bulgarian exports to the west, which had been declining in volume for several years, appear to have risen by 9 per cent in the first three quarters.[445] For Hungary, 1989 constitutes the third consecutive year of export growth. This is notable since no east European country was able to mount a sustained export drive during the first half of the 1980s. Polish exports had also shown a period of strong expansion in 1987-1988. Western data show further

---

[440] Since manufactured goods are largely invoiced in currencies other than the US dollar, the appreciation of the US currency (9 per cent against the ECU in the first three quarters of 1989 relative to the same period in 1988) reduced trade prices measured in US dollars.

[441] IEA, *Energy Prices and Taxes*, Third Quarter, Paris, 1989 and IEA, *Oil Market Report*, January 1990.

[442] *International Herald Tribune*, 31 October 1989.

[443] See the review of commodity markets in section 4.1 above.

[444] No within-year trade returns are provided by the German Democratic Republic and Romania; the latter country has also not reported annual data since 1986.

[445] The contrast between western data and national trade returns is particularly striking in this case: Bulgarian data show the dollar value of exports to the west rising by a mere 0.9 per cent in January-September 1989, which would imply a further fall in the volume (see box 4.2.1).

BOX 4.2.1

East-west trade, January-September 1989:
Comparisons of eastern and western reported statistics
(Percentage change from previous year)

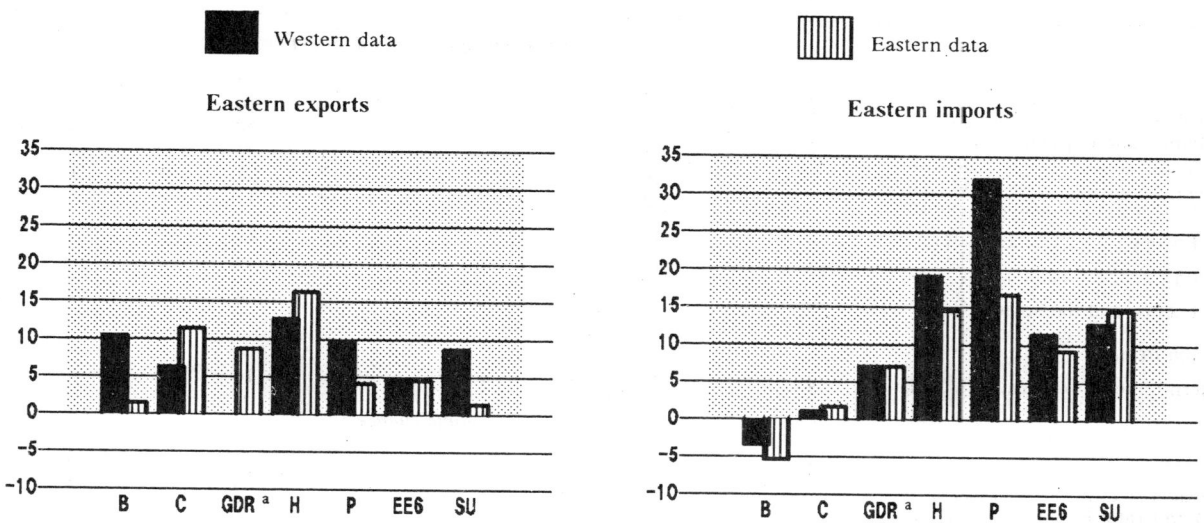

Source: As for table 4.2.1 and table 3.4.1.

Note: B = Bulgaria, C = Czechoslovakia, GDR = German Democratic Republic, H = Hungary, P = Poland, SU = Soviet Union.

[a] Non-socialist.

For reasons mainly of data availability, especially as regards commodity detail, the secretariat's analysis of developments in east-west trade is based primarily upon the statistics of 23 western reporting countries. These data are regularly compared with the national statistics of five eastern countries which make such information available. Ideally, the trade flows reported from the two sides ("mirror statistics") should be identical. In practice, there are differences, the reasons for which have received attention in the literature. [1]

In the first three quarters of 1989 differences arose between the two sets of statistics which were not only unusually large but, more importantly, lead to rather different conclusions about the development of certain east-west trade flows. Polish and Soviet national statistics show a deceleration of exports during the year and value growth rates in the first three quarters which imply declines in volume (see chart). By contrast, western-reported mirror statistics point to the continuation of strong export expansion with perhaps some slowing. Data for Bulgaria show similar discrepancies in growth rates. At the level of the east European aggregate, however, the country differences cancel out. [2]

On the side of eastern imports, the major discrepancy concerns Poland. Western data yield a growth rate twice that derived from national statistics and, unlike the national data, does not indicate a deceleration of purchases. The differences for Hungary are smaller, having diminished sharply from those recorded in the first half of the year. [3]

---

[1] See, for example, Paul Marer, "Toward a solution of the mirror statistics puzzle in east-west commerce," in F. Levcik, (ed.), *International Economics Comparisons and Interdependence*, Vienna Institute for Comparative Economic Studies, 1978. It should be stressed that the "mirror statistics" problem is not limited to east-west trade flows. They arise from lags in recording trade transactions in partner countries, the particular treatment of middleman trade, and differences in recording trade (i.e., general or specialized).

[2] These comparisons are limited to the five countries which publish current statistics on their trade with the west. No such reports are available for the German Democratic Republic and Romania. Since the trade statistics for these two countries are by necessity constructed from western-reported data, there is no basis for comparison.

[3] Western data for the first half of 1989 showed Hungarian imports from the west increasing 15 per cent, compared to only 8 per cent reported in the Hungarian trade returns. Economic Commission for Europe, *Economic Bulletin for Europe*, vol.41, New York, 1989.

TABLE 4.2.2

East-west trade: Value and volume, by eastern country, 1985-1989

(Percentage change)

From/To:	Eastern exports					Eastern imports				
	1985	1986	1987	1988	1989 [a]	1985	1986	1987	1988	1989 [a]
	Value change (in US dollars)									
Bulgaria	-2	3	3	4	10	26	17	7	1	-4
Czechoslovakia	-5	15	10	6	6	8	19	18	7	1
German Democratic Republic	-3	14	11	5	-	1	27	23	4	7
Hungary	2	13	21	11	13	11	21	11	1	19
Poland	1	7	16	15	10	7	7	16	21	32
Romania	-7	5	12	1	-4	4	17	-24	-7	-11
Eastern Europe	-2	10	13	7	5	8	18	13	6	11
Soviet Union	-12	-10	10	2	9	-2	-3	-3	18	13
Eastern Europe and the Soviet Union	-8	-1	12	5	7	2	6	4	12	12
Memorandum item:										
Total western imports/exports	4	12	19	13	8	4	16	18	14	8
	Volume change									
Bulgaria	-1	-7	-9	4	9	25	-4	-4	-3	-3
Czechoslovakia	-4	1	-2	3	5	7	-3	6	1	3
German Democratic Republic	-1	6	-3	4	-1	-	8	10	-1	8
Hungary	5	-1	7	7	13	8	1	-1	-5	21
Poland	1	-6	8	9	8	10	-12	8	12	33
Romania	-3	7	-5	5	-8	5	2	-30	-12	-11
Eastern Europe	-1	1	-	6	3	7	-1	2	-	13
Soviet Union	-7	21	7	9	3	-	-20	-9	9	13
Eastern Europe and the Soviet Union	-4	10	3	8	3	3	-13	-4	5	13
Memorandum item:										
Total western imports/exports	6	8	7	7	9	4	2	6	8	7

Source: As for table 4.2.1.

[a] January-September.

strong growth of Polish exports in the first three quarters of 1989, but Polish statistics show much weaker growth and a downturn in volume in the second half of the year.[446] After some recovery in the previous year, the German Democratic Republic's exports appear to have come to a standstill in the first three quarters of 1989, prolonging the stagnation which has characterized this country's export performance in the second half of the 1980s.[447] Romania's deliveries to the west also recovered in 1988, but contracted again in the first three quarters of 1989.[448]

The overall picture, giving more weight to the eastern data, is of faltering export growth, Czechoslovakia's, Hungary's and possibly the German Democratic Republic's performances being the chief exceptions.

The expansion of east European exports was fairly broadly based in terms of commodities in the *first half* of 1989, the sales of most *major commodity groups* increasing.[449] The exceptions were fuels and consumer goods exports, the value of which fell. Engineering goods sales rose by some 10 per cent, which reflects increases by all countries except Czechoslovakia. Czechoslovakia's machinery sales to the west have declined for a number of years. Overall, eastern Europe's engineering goods export performance somewhat exceeded the growth of western reporting countries' overall imports in this commodity group. All east

---

[446] Polish data show the value of exports to the convertible currency area increasing by only 1.8 per cent for the full year of 1989, and volume declining by 0.7 per cent.

[447] The German Democratic Republic's data show exports to the non-socialist area increasing by 8.5 per cent in nominal US dollars, which implies a slightly lower rise in volume. It is useful to bear in mind that the German Democratic Republic's trade statistics are being revised and should be considered provisional.

[448] On the basis of western data. No national trade returns are available for Romania.

[449] This cursory review of east-west trade by commodity is based upon the trade returns of a sample of western countries for which commodity data were available for the first half of 1989 and for the same period in 1988: all west European countries (except Denmark, Greece, Spain, Turkey and Yugoslavia) plus Japan and the United States. Romania has been excluded from this review since the sample was not sufficiently representative of the country's total trade with the west. The sources of these data are United Nations Statistical Office, COMTRADE, Quarterly trade data, "Series D"; Statistisches Bundesamt, *Warenverkehr mit der Deutschen Demokratischen Republik und Berlin (Ost)*, Reihe 6, Wiesbaden.

TABLE 4.2.3

East-west trade: Value, by country group, 1985-1989
(Percentage change of value in US dollars)

	Eastern exports					Eastern imports				
	1985	1986	1987	1988	1989 a	1985	1986	1987	1988	1989 a
Eastern Europe and Soviet Union with:										
Developed market economies	-8	-1	12	5	7	2	6	4	12	12
Western Europe	-7	-2	11	3	7	7	10	7	7	12
of which:										
EC	-8	-1	13	4	7	5	13	13	7	14
EFTA	-4	-9	13	-1	4	8	14	8	8	8
North America	-10	-1	5	21	-	-24	-32	-5	63	31
Japan	-10	22	31	30	4	10	16	-14	19	-9
Eastern Europe with:										
Developed market economies	-2	10	13	7	5	8	18	13	6	11
Western Europe	-1	12	14	6	6	9	19	14	6	13
of which:										
EC	-	15	16	6	7	14	23	15	5	15
EFTA	1	4	14	9	2	4	20	22	7	8
North America	-5	-2	4	11	-14	-15	1	-11	20	13
Japan	-28	12	47	43	2	15	21	5	8	-24
Soviet Union with:										
Developed market economies	-11	-10	10	2	9	-1	-3	-3	18	13
Western Europe	-11	-13	9	-1	8	4	2	-	9	11
of which:										
EC	-14	-13	9	2	7	-3	2	10	10	11
EFTA	-7	-16	11	-9	5	10	11	-1	9	8
North America	-26	2	6	58	43	-26	-41	-2	82	37
Japan	-4	24	28	26	5	9	15	-19	22	-5

Source: As for table 4.2.1.

Note: Appendix tables C.6 and C.7 contain similar data for all western countries.

a January-September.

European countries managed to increase their sales of semi-manufactures. Within this category, chemicals — especially from Bulgaria — were the most dynamic. Several countries also boosted iron and steel exports, those from Poland rising by over one half in volume. All east European countries' sales of consumer goods grew only weakly or declined, although within this group exports of household appliances did well. Most countries increased the sales of food, which accounted for the bulk of the growth of their primary goods exports. The value of fuel sales rose, the increase in prices more than offsetting somewhat lower deliveries of petroleum products (see table 4.2.4).

To the extent that the relatively rapid expansion of eastern engineering goods exports in the first half of 1989 is confirmed by more complete data, it would imply a more favourable commodity pattern of growth than in 1988. In that year, the dynamism of overall east European exports had derived primarily from various semi-manufactures, which consist largely of comparatively low value-added goods. Engineering goods exports also lagged in 1988, despite the investment boom in the west. As a result there was little progress in improving the commodity structure of exports, including those of the countries at the forefront of the reform movement. The slowness of restructuring has frequently been deplored in policy discussions in the east.

Aside from buoyant western market demand, factors having a positive impact on the growth of east European exports include, most prominently, changes in the management of foreign trade. It is noteworthy that Hungary and Poland, the two countries where reforms have been the most far-reaching, have achieved the fastest and most sustained expansion of exports during the past few years. These reforms, among others, include an active exchange rate policy. Another factor is improved differential rewards for exporting enterprises introduced in several east European countries. The Czechoslovak authorities have attributed that country's good export growth in 1989 to incentives provided to enterprises by the introduction of convertible currency retention accounts.[450] The sharp increase in the number of enterprises exercising foreign trade rights in that country is also believed to have contributed. However, the new instruments of trade management do not always appear to have been used appropriately. In Poland, an appreciation of the real effective exchange rate of the zloty (already overvalued at the official rate) from the end of 1988 through the third quarter of 1989, may have contributed to the

---

450 *Rudé Právo*, 20 September 1989.

TABLE 4.2.4

OECD imports of petroleum and petroleum products from eastern Europe and the Soviet Union, 1986-1989
(Million tons and percentage change)

	National sources				IEA data [a]					
	1986	1987	1988	1988 Per cent	1986	1987	1988	Jan.-Sept. 1988	Jan.-Sept. 1989	1989 Per cent
Eastern Europe										
Crude oil	..	..	..	..	1.8	0.1	0.1	0.1	0.1	-6.1
Products	..	..	..	..	17.5	19.9	19.1	14.5	14.0	-2.9
Total	..	..	..	..	19.4	20.0	19.2	14.5	14.1	-2.9
Soviet Union										
Crude oil	38.1	43.8	55.3	26.3	45.7	39.9	49.9	37.0	30.4	-17.7
Products	40.4	40.8	42.9	5.1	32.2	42.7	43.0	31.5	33.3	5.7
Total	78.6	84.5	98.2	16.2	77.9	82.6	92.9	68.4	63.7	-7.0
Memo item:										
Soviet imports of crude oil [b]	14.6	14.0	19.8	41.4	..	..	..	..	..	..

Source: IEA/OECD, *Monthly Oil and Gas Statistics*, Paris, January 1990 and previous issues, for quantities of petroleum and petroleum products, *Vneshnyaya torgovlya SSSR v 1987 godu* (Moscow: Finansy i statistika, 1988), and *Vneshnye ekonomicheskie sviazy SSSR v 1988 godu* (Moscow: Finansy i statistika, 1989).

Note: Starting in 1987 the IEA classifies refinery feedstocks in the "products" category, whereas previously they were included in "crude oil".

[a] Excludes imports from Yugoslavia.
[b] Soviet imports from OPEC countries.

---

slowing of Polish export growth in 1989.[451] Subsequently this policy was reversed. In general, it is difficult to differentiate between the impact of reform measures and the exercise of the traditional centralized administrative measures on trade.

Hungary's efforts to meet the targets set in its austerity programme, which included a stringent current account target, contributed to boost exports. Measures were probably also taken to quicken export growth to compensate for the deterioration in the travel component of the current account (see below).

A country's capacity to export should benefit from a more ample supply of imports. However, a cursory country-by-country examination reveals no clear relationship between recent east European export and import growth. Poland's industry appears to have benefited from the rapid rise in imports over the past few years. Nonetheless, exports fell in the second half of 1989. Czechoslovakia achieved an export push without any increase in the volume of imports.

Several adverse factors tended to hold back exports. Industrial production in most countries stagnated and some of them experienced shortfalls in planned imports of energy and raw materials. In particular, this may have contributed to the decline in the deliveries of petroleum products to the west.

After expanding relatively rapidly during 1986-1988, the growth rate of *Soviet exports* appears to have slowed noticeably to only 3 per cent in the first three quarters of 1989, judging on the basis of western data.[452] The slackening in the pace appears due to the downturn in petroleum and petroleum products deliveries and recalls similar difficulties in 1985, which caused the total volume of Soviet exports to the west to contract.

According to western *commodity* trade statistics, a significant part of the increase in Soviet exports to the west in the first half of 1989[453] was due to primary goods, particularly non-ferrous metals and, to a lesser extent, ores and minerals. The sales of semi-manufactures (above all iron and steel) and various types of consumer goods rose comparatively rapidly. On the whole, the value and volume of Soviet engineering goods exports declined somewhat, but those of motor vehicles expanded very quickly. The volume of Soviet fuel exports declined, although there was a small increase in value due to the rise in fuel prices.[454] IEA statistics show a 7 per cent decline in the combined volume of OECD imports of crude oil and petroleum products from the Soviet Union in the first three quarters of the year (table 4.2.4), a sharp decline in crude oil imports offsetting an increase in those of petroleum products.[455] Soviet natural gas deliveries to the west

---

[451] IMF, *International Financial Statistics*, February 1990.

[452] It should be noted that these data show the Soviet Union's exports rising by some 9 per cent in *value* in the first three quarters of 1989 and 3 per cent in *volume*. However, Soviet data only show a 1 per cent increase in value for the same period (see box 4.2.1) and imply a decline in the quantity of exports of some 3 per cent.

[453] See footnote (449). The commodity data are for the first half of 1989.

[454] Overall these results are consistent with the Soviet plan fulfilment report. Soviet exports of machinery and equipment, crude oil and some other commodities significantly fell short of the export plan (*Pravda*, 28 January 1990).

[455] IEA/OECD, *Monthly Oil and Gas Statistics*, Paris, January 1990 and previous issues. These data point to a faltering of Soviet crude petroleum exports as the year progressed. Soviet re-exports of Middle East crude to the west, in principle not included in the IEA data, also appear to have fallen. Soviet trade data

appear to have increased. EC statistics show that imports of Soviet gas into this major market rose by nearly 15 per cent in the first half of the year, markedly faster than the 2.5 per cent rise in gross inland consumption in the EC.[456]

As already noted, the Soviet Union's capacity to export oil and oil products was reduced in 1989 owing to shortfalls in domestic oil production, which declined by some 17 million tons to 607 million tons.[457] The deterioration of oil production has been attributed by the Soviet authorities to, among other things, shortages of oilfield equipment and transport bottlenecks.[458] Indirectly, strains in the overall energy balance — a fall in coal output (by 32 million tons), the slow-down in the commissioning of nuclear power stations, and a slackening pace of gas production — may have also curtailed oil export potential (see section 3.2). Moreover, as already noted, Soviet re-exports of Middle Eastern crude, an important component of the country's export receipts, declined in value and volume.

(iv) Eastern imports

After turning upwards in 1988, the growth of the combined import volume of *eastern Europe and the Soviet Union* accelerated in the first three quarters of 1989. This was due to the upturn in east European import growth to 13 per cent and the faster pace of Soviet imports (see chart 4.2.1. and tables 4.2.1 and 4.2.2). In general it appears that imports were stepped up to ease growing domestic imbalances, but some countries also liberalized their trade régimes. This pace constitutes the most rapid expansion in eastern purchases since the mid-1970s. It markedly exceeds the growth of western exports to the world, and implies some gain in the importance of the east as a market for western goods.

Eastern Europe's imports from the west surged by 13 per cent in the first three quarters of 1989, after stagnating during 1986-1988. The upturn in 1989 reflects revival in import growth into the German Democratic Republic and Hungary and the continuing expansion of Poland's purchases. Western data indicate growth rates for these countries of 8 per cent in the German Democratic Republic, 21 per cent in Hungary and 33 per cent in Poland. It should be noted that national statistics for Hungary and, especially, Poland yield lower growth rates (see box 4.2.1). On the basis of either set of statistics, the German Democratic Republic, Hungary and Poland are responsible for the expansion. By contrast, Bulgaria's and Czechoslovakia's purchases stagnated.[459] Romania curtailed imports further during the first three quarters of the year, very deep cuts in the first half of the year being only partially offset by some recovery in purchases in the third quarter.

In terms of *commodities,* the boom in *east European* imports from the west was due to sharply higher purchases of engineering goods and, to a lesser extent, primary products.[460] As in 1988, Hungary, the German Democratic Republic and Poland were responsible for the entire increase in *engineering goods* imports, with the latter two boosting purchases by over one-half. Imports of engineering goods appear to have been reduced slightly in Bulgaria and Czechoslovakia and sharply in Romania. The increase in *primary products* imports owes chiefly to higher purchases of *food* by all countries except Romania, which trimmed these imports further during the first half of 1989.

Imports of *semi-manufactures* required for industrial production sagged, with all countries except Hungary and Poland cutting back. *Consumer goods* imports also weakened, reductions by Czechoslovakia, the German Democratic Republic and Romania offsetting higher purchases by the other countries.

The growth of food imports continued to be important in the first half of 1989. The heightened importance of engineering goods imports in 1989 contrasts with developments in 1988, when there was a marked shift in composition toward food and consumer goods. At that time, the value increment of imports of these two products accounted for over 60 per cent of the increase in the value of the area's imports.[461]

Changes in imports of the individual east European countries in 1989 reflect different policy priorities and the shift in some countries away from a highly centralized control of imports. As in 1988, Bulgaria appears to have restrained imports to contain its trade deficit and the rise in indebtedness, which increased sharply nonetheless. In Czechoslovakia, the system whereby enterprises rely increasingly upon their own convertible currency funds (i.e., the retention account system) to finance imports is reported to have led to a more cautious attitude towards imports. This tendency on the enterprise level was presumably reinforced by the long-standing Czechoslovak policy now applying only to the

---

for the first nine months of the year indicate that the country's imports from Algeria, Iraq, Iran and Libya declined by 31 per cent in value, which implies an even larger fall in volume.

[456] Eurostat, *Energy Statistics*, Luxembourg, No.10, 1989.

[457] According to J. Petrium, First Vice Chairman of Soyuznefteexport, direct exports of crude oil and oil products, including exports to the CMEA countries, had dropped by 10 million tons in 1989. This reflected efforts to co-operate with OPEC as well as transport difficulties. *Financial Times,* 15 February 1990.

[458] First Deputy Minister for Oil and Gas Vladimir Filanovsky attributed faltering oil production to a combination of staff cuts, decentralization, and a failure to supply new equipment to the industry. Summary of an interview with *Sotsialisticheskaya industriya* in *Financial Times,* 28 September 1989.

[459] These statistics record only a part of the rise in Hungary's merchandise imports from the west. Goods purchased abroad privately by Hungarian travellers (e.g. consumer electronics and automobiles) are not included in the customs statistics. However, these expenditures are partially reflected in the deterioration of the tourism item in the country's balance of payments.

[460] See footnote (449). The commodity data are for the *first half* of 1989.

[461] United Nations Economic Commission for Europe, *Economic Bulletin for Europe,*, vol.41, New York, 1989, p.34.

TABLE 4.2.5
East-west trade balances, east with western country groups, 1984-1989
(Billion US dollars, f.o.b.-f.o.b.)

	1984	1985	1986	1987	1988	1988 Jan.-Sept.	1989 Jan.-Sept.	1989 [a]
(A) Western data								
Eastern Europe and the Soviet Union with:								
Developed market economies	6.4	2.0	-0.8	2.1	-0.9	0.6	-1.3	-2.5
Western Europe	11.4	6.2	2.1	3.7	2.1	2.6	1.4	1.2
of which:								
EC	10.1	6.7	3.9	4.2	3.7	3.4	2.4	2.4
EFTA	1.8	0.9	-0.7	-0.4	-1.2	-0.6	-0.9	-1.2
North America	-3.6	-2.4	-0.9	-0.7	-2.1	-1.5	-2.6	-3.1
Japan	-1.4	-1.9	-2.1	-0.9	-0.9	-0.5	-0.1	-0.5
Eastern Europe with:								
Developed market economies	3.8	2.1	1.0	1.2	1.6	1.7	0.6	0.6
Western Europe	3.2	1.6	0.6	0.6	0.8	1.1	0.2	-0.1
of which:								
EC	2.5	1.2	0.5	0.6	0.9	1.2	0.3	-
EFTA	0.5	0.4	-	-0.2	-0.2	-0.1	-0.3	-0.4
North America	0.7	0.8	0.8	0.9	1.0	0.7	0.4	0.6
Japan	-0.1	-0.3	-0.4	-0.3	-0.1	-0.1	0.1	0.1
Soviet Union with:								
Developed market economies	2.5	-0.2	-1.8	0.9	-2.5	-1.1	-2.0	-3.0
Western Europe	8.2	4.6	1.5	3.2	1.3	1.5	1.2	1.3
of which:								
EC	7.6	5.6	3.4	3.7	2.8	2.2	2.1	2.4
EFTA	1.4	0.6	-0.7	-0.1	-1.0	-0.5	-0.6	-1.8
North America	-4.3	-3.2	-1.7	-1.6	-3.0	-2.2	-3.0	-3.7
Japan	-1.3	-1.6	-1.7	-0.7	-0.8	-0.4	-0.2	-0.6
(B) Eastern data								
Eastern Europe and the Soviet Union with:								
Developed market economies	7.9	1.8	-3.8	2.2	-2.0	0.2	-3.6	-5.0 [b]
of which:								
Eastern Europe	4.7	2.7	0.6	1.2	0.7	2.3	1.5	1.4 [b]
Soviet Union	3.2	-0.9	-4.4	1.0	-2.7	-2.1	-5.1	-6.4 [b]

Source: As for table 4.2.1.
Note: Section A is based on western data which have been adjusted to an f.o.b.-f.o.b. basis by the ECE secretariat; section B is based on eastern national sources.
[a] Extrapolated on the basis of January-September data for exports and imports.　　[b] Full year data.

TABLE 4.2.6
East-west trade balances, by eastern country, 1984-1989
(Billion US dollars, f.o.b-f.o.b)

	1984	1985	1986	1987	1988	1988 Jan.-Sept.	1989 Jan.-Sept.	1989 [a]
Bulgaria	-0.8	-1.2	-1.5	-1.6	-1.7	-1.3	-1.2	-1.5
Czechoslovakia	0.8	0.4	0.4	0.1	0.1	0.3	0.5	0.4
German Democratic Republic	0.9	0.7	0.2	-0.5	-0.4	-0.1	-0.5	-0.6
Hungary	-0.1	-0.3	-0.6	-0.3	0.1	-	-0.2	-0.2
Poland	0.8	0.6	0.7	0.8	0.7	0.6	-0.1	-0.3
Romania	2.2	1.9	1.9	2.7	2.8	2.2	2.1	2.8
Eastern Europe	3.9	2.1	1.0	1.2	1.6	1.7	0.6	0.6
Soviet Union	2.5	-0.2	-1.8	0.9	-2.5	-1.2	-2.0	-3.0
Eastern Europe and the Soviet Union	6.4	2.0	-0.8	2.1	-0.9	0.6	-1.3	-2.5

Source: As for table 4.2.1. ECE secretariat estimates based upon western data.
[a] Extrapolated on the basis of January-September data for exports and imports.

allocation of centrally controlled funds aiming at limiting external indebtedness.

The rise in Hungary's purchases is due in part to the liberalization of the trade régime, as a result of which the share of liberalized imports from the convertible currency area increased to 40 per cent. This favoured increased inflows of machinery and equipment and semi-manufactures. Import growth from the convertible currency area (of which the west as defined here is only a part) exceeded the plan by some 3-4 percentage points.[462]

Confronted with falling export revenues, the former Romanian leadership seems to have cut imports during the first nine months (despite large internal needs) in order to maintain a large trade surplus and further reduce net debt.

The *Soviet Union's* western imports increased strongly, by 9 per cent in volume in 1988 and 13 per cent in the first three quarter of 1989. However, the volume of Soviet imports was still below the 1985 level. During 1986-1987, the Soviet authorities had scaled back the volume of imports by almost 30 per cent, partially in response to balance-of-payments pressures.

In the *first half* of 1989, the bulk of the growth in the value of Soviet imports from the west was due to increased purchases of food.[463] Imports of various types of engineering goods, especially machinery, office and telecommunications equipment, also rose rapidly. By contrast, Soviet purchases of semi-manufactures, particularly iron, steel and chemicals, were reduced. Consumer goods imports from the west appear to have been scaled back as well in the first half of the year, but this is likely to have changed as a special import programme to ease consumer market problems began to be implemented.

(v) Eastern trade balances with the west

After moving into deficit with the west in 1988, the combined trade balance of *eastern Europe and the Soviet Union* continued to deteriorate in the first three quarters of 1989 (table 4.2.5), the growth of imports outpacing exports.

Eastern Europe's trade surplus with the west had risen slowly during 1987-1988, but remained in the $1-2 billion range (table 4.2.5 and 4.2.6). In the first three quarters of 1989, by contrast, the surplus contracted sharply and, for the entire year, is likely to amount to less than $1 billion.

The weakening of the area's trade balance in 1989 is due to the worsening trade positions of the *German Democratic Republic, Hungary and Poland* for which western data register small trade deficits (table 4.2.6).[464] During the first three quarters of the year, *Bulgaria* incurred another comparatively large deficit and *Romania* another (estimated) surplus of of some $2 billion. *Czechoslovakia's* surplus with the west widened marginally. If trends in the first three quarters of the year continued for the remainder of 1989, all of these countries would have posted full-year trade balances of roughly the same magnitude as in the first nine months.

In 1989, the major change in the geographical distribution of eastern Europe's trade balance was the reduction in its trade surplus with western Europe, owing chiefly to a narrowing of a trade surplus with the EC and a larger deficit with EFTA countries. The area's surplus with North America also contracted.

Western data indicate that the *Soviet Union's* trade deficit with the west continued to widen in the first nine months of 1989. Since the pace of imports is known to have quickened in the final quarter, the trade deficit is bound to have been larger in 1989 than the $3 billion extrapolated from January-September trends in the western data shown in table 4.2.5 Panel A. Soviet national statistics, which are available for the entire year (see table 4.2.5, panel B) register a larger deficit of $6.4 billion. As noted above, exports fell below plan and imports were increased rapidly to ease domestic shortages. The Soviet Union's deficit would have been even greater if the country had not benefited from the generally unexpected rises in oil prices and in the value of the US dollar in 1989, both of which boosted Soviet terms of trade. This would be the largest imbalance since the mid-1970s, when the Soviet Union pursued a policy of import-led growth, causing annual deficits of $3-4 billion.

Western data in table 4.2.5, Panel A show that most of the deterioration in the Soviet trade account for the first nine months resulted from changes in trade flows with North America. This stems from a 37 per cent increase in Soviet imports, much of which appears to reflect the higher price of grain in 1989 and larger Soviet purchases.

---

[462] Hungarian imports from the convertible currency area had been planned to grow by 3-4 per cent in volume in 1989.

[463] See footnote (449).

[464] Polish data show a narrowing surplus.

4.3 EAST-WEST FINANCIAL DEVELOPMENTS

(i) Eastern current account

The *east's* current account in convertible currencies deteriorated sharply in 1989, swinging from a surplus of $3 billion to a deficit of $6 billion (table 4.3.1).[465] This constitutes the area's largest deficit since 1981, and owes to unfavourable movements in the accounts of both eastern Europe and the Soviet Union.

After posting current-account surpluses in 1987-1988, *eastern Europe* swung to a deficit of over $2 billion in 1989. The accounts of all countries except Czechoslovakia deteriorated to various extents, and all countries except Czechoslovakia and Romania registered deficits. Trade balances generally deteriorated and most countries experienced higher net interest payments, owing to rising country stocks of debt and higher interest rates.

Bulgaria's current-account deficit is estimated to have reached an all time high of $1.7 billion in 1989, the result of further deterioration in the trade and investment income items. Secretariat estimates show an improvement in *Czechoslovakia's* current account to a balanced position.[466]

The *German Democratic Republic's* current account appears to have deteriorated marginally in 1989 to a deficit of nearly $1 billion.[467] Attention is drawn to the fact that, for the first time, the GDR authorities released data on the country's current account. They report a $2.4 billion deficit in 1989,[468] substantially larger than the secretariat's $1 billion estimate.

After two consecutive years of improvement, *Hungary's* current-account deficit in convertible currencies deteriorated sharply in 1989, from around $800 million to some $1.4 billion. As a consequence the $400-500 million deficit target was missed. The trade surplus of $554 million was marginally above plan and the best performance since 1984. Net interest payments rose to $1.4 billion ($400 million above plan) and there was a sharp deterioration in the travel item. Hungary's traditional tourism surplus, reduced to $20 million in 1988, swung to a deficit of $420 million in 1989. Much of the turnaround can be attributed to the population's use of travel entitlements for the private import of consumer goods.[469] In April, the Hungarian authorities tightened customs regulations on these imports in order to stem the deterioration in the current account and in November curtailed travel allowances sharply for the same reason.

Higher net interest obligations and a significantly smaller trade surplus caused *Poland's* current-account deficit to widen to $1.9 billion. The $126 million trade surplus was lower than the $1.2 billion target for 1989 and the $1 billion surpluses achieved in recent years. Of the G-24 pledges of assistance made last year (see section 4.4) some $300 million in food shipments financed by official transfers are reflected in Poland's current account for 1989.

For *Romania*, the $3.7 billion current-account surplus estimated by the secretariat derives entirely from a trade surplus. It is likely to exceed the actual figures because of the methods of estimation and the particular dynamics of Romanian trade. Also, exports of food and possibly other goods appear to have been suspended and imports boosted following the revolution in December.

According to official data for all of 1989, the *Soviet Union* posted a trade deficit with the market economies of over $2 billion, which implies a current-account deficit of more than $3 billion. In trade with the developed market economies alone, which is conducted on a cash basis, the Soviet Union posted a deficit of $6.4 billion. The Soviet Union continued to run a surplus in trade

---

[465] The data on convertible currency transactions for Hungary, Poland and, until 1986, Romania are based upon national sources; they include convertible currency transactions with socialist countries. It should be noted that the Polish balance of payments data reported here are on a cash basis. They differ somewhat from those reported previously by the secretariat, which were on a financial settlements basis. This latter series is reported in the tables in Appendix C. Revised data for 1988 and 1989 recently released by the German Democratic Republic statistical authorities have led to revisions in the trade balance component of the current account.

As an approximation to the trade balance component of the convertible currency current accounts of the remaining eastern countries, eastern data on the trade balance with developed and developing market economies are used here. Beyond the west as defined in this section, this group also includes the developed countries of the southern hemisphere and the developing countries, most of which conduct trade on a convertible currency basis. The trade balance data shown thus include, on the one hand, balances on clearing accounts (about which, in general, very little is known especially for the current year), and, on the other, exclude balances of convertible currency transaction among the socialist countries. See Appendix table C.10 for estimates of the eastern current account in convertible currencies covering the period 1970-1989.

[466] According to officials of the Czechoslovak State Bank, the country ran a $300 million surplus in 1989.

[467] The estimated current-account *deficit* of $0.6 billion in 1988 represents a revision from a *surplus* of nearly the same magnitude. The change derives entirely from a revision of official trade figures which now yield a $1 billion non-socialist trade deficit for 1988, as opposed to the previously reported balanced trade position.

[468] Reported by Minister of Economics Christa Luft, *Financial Times*, 4 January 1990.

[469] The liberalization of convertible currency travel entitlements was instituted already in 1988.

TABLE 4.3.1

Eastern Europe and the Soviet Union: Estimated current account of the balance of payments with market economies, 1984-1989

(Billion US dollars)

	Trade balances [a]		Net services plus transfers [b]		Current account
	Total	of this: DME [c]	Total	Investment income	
Bulgaria					
1984	0.6	-0.4	0.1	-0.1	0.7
1985	-0.1	-0.8	0.1	-0.1	-
1986	-1.1	-1.4	-0.1	-0.3	-1.2
1987	-0.4	-1.4	-0.1	-0.3	-0.5
1988	-1.2	-1.5	-0.1	-0.4	-1.3
1989 [d]	-1.4	-1.3	-0.3	-0.6	-1.7
Czechoslovakia					
1984	0.9	0.4	-0.2	-0.3	0.7
1985	0.7	0.2	-0.2	-0.2	0.5
1986	0.4	-0.1	-0.2	-0.2	0.2
1987	-0.1	-0.4	-0.1	-0.2	-0.2
1988	-0.1	-0.4	-0.2	-0.2	-0.3
1989 [d]	0.3	0.1	-0.3	-0.3	-
German Democratic Republic					
1984	1.0	0.9	-	-0.8	0.9
1985	1.1	0.9	-	-0.7	1.1
1986	0.4	0.1	0.2	-0.8	0.6
1987	0.3	-0.2	0.6	-0.7	0.9
1988	-1.0	-1.2	0.5	-0.8	-0.6
1989 [d]	-0.9	-1.1	0.2	-1.1	-0.7
Hungary [e]					
1984	0.9	0.2	-1.8	-0.8	0.1
1985	0.1	-0.5	-1.0	-0.8	-0.8
1986	-0.5	-0.7	-1.0	-1.0	-1.5
1987	-	-0.5	-0.9	-1.0	-0.9
1988	0.5	-	-1.3	-1.1	-0.8
1989 [d]	0.6	0.3	-2.0	-1.4	-1.4
Poland [e]					
1984	1.5	1.1	-2.2	-2.5	-0.7
1985	1.2	0.7	-1.7	-2.4	-0.5
1986	1.1	0.5	-1.7	-2.6	-0.6
1987	1.0	0.9	-1.4	-2.8	-0.4
1988	0.9	0.6	-1.5	-2.9	-0.6
1989 [d]	0.1	0.3	-2.0	-3.1	-1.9
Romania [e]					
1984	2.2	2.6	-0.6	-0.7	1.5
1985	1.4	2.3	-0.5	-0.6	0.9
1986	1.9	2.2	-0.5	-0.6	1.4
1987	2.4	2.9	-0.2	-0.3	2.1
1988	3.9	3.2	-0.1	-0.2	3.8
1989 [d]	3.7	3.1	-	-	3.7
Eastern Europe					
1984	6.9	4.7	-3.8	-5.3	3.2
1985	4.4	2.7	-3.2	-4.9	1.2
1986	2.3	0.6	-3.2	-5.4	-0.9
1987	3.3	1.2	-2.2	-5.3	1.1
1988	3.0	0.7	-2.8	-5.6	0.3
1989 [d]	2.4	1.4	-4.5	-6.5	-2.0
Soviet Union					
1984	6.7	3.2	-	-1.2	6.7
1985	0.7	-0.9	-0.1	-1.3	0.6
1986	1.4	-4.4	-0.5	-1.7	0.9
1987	8.1	1.0	-0.3	-1.5	7.8
1988	3.5	-2.7	-0.4	-1.7	3.1
1989 [d]	-2.3	-6.4	-0.9	-2.2	-3.2
Eastern Europe and Soviet Union [f]					
1984	13.6	7.8	-4.1	-6.9	9.5
1985	5.2	1.8	-3.7	-6.6	1.5
1986	3.7	-3.7	-4.0	-7.4	-0.3
1987	11.4	2.4	-2.8	-7.2	8.6
1988	6.5	-2.0	-3.5	-7.6	3.0
1989 [d]	0.1	-5.0	-5.7	-9.2	-5.5

Sources: National sources for Hungary and Poland; Romania (1984-1986 only); and ECE secretariat estimates.

[a] Trade balance f.o.b.-f.o.b. except for Hungary's trade balance with the developed market economies which is reported f.o.b.-c.i.f.
[b] Invisibles balances are ECE secretariat estimates, except in the cases of Hungary (1984-1988), Poland (1984-1989) and Romania (1984-1986). Investment income (inflows) for the other eastern countries reflect only estimates of interest earned on assets held at BIS reporting banks.
[c] Developed market economies (see definition in footnote (438) above).
[d] For most countries trade balances for 1989 are based upon full year data. Romanian trade balances for 1989 are extrapolations from nine month western returns (see table 3.4.4).
[e] Current account in convertible currencies.
[f] Includes estimated net interest payments of the CMEA banks.

TABLE 4.3.2

Eastern Europe and the Soviet Union: Estimated convertible currency debt, 1983-1989 [a]
(Billion US dollars, end-of-year)

	1983	1984	1985	1986	1987	1988	1989 [a]
Gross debt							
Bulgaria	2.4	2.1	3.5	4.9	6.2	7.7	9.0
Czechoslovakia	3.5	3.1	3.3	3.9	5.1	5.2	5.1
German Democratic Republic	12.1	11.6	13.6	16.1	19.1	20.2	20.6
Hungary [b]	10.7	11.0	14.0	16.9	19.6	19.6	20.6
Poland	26.3	26.9	29.3	33.5	39.2	39.2	39.9
Romania	8.9	7.2	6.6	6.4	5.7*	3.1*	1.4
Eastern Europe	63.9	61.9	70.3	81.7	94.9	95.0	96.5
Soviet Union and CMEA Banks	26.9	25.6	31.4	37.4	40.3	41.7	50.6
Eastern Europe and the Soviet Union	90.8	87.5	101.6	119.0	135.1	136.8	147.1
Net debt [c]							
Bulgaria	1.2	0.7	1.4	3.5	5.1	5.9	7.7
Czechoslovakia	2.6	2.1	2.3	2.7	3.5	3.5	3.1
German Democratic Republic	8.7	7.1	7.1	8.6	10.1	10.7	11.0
Hungary [b]	9.4	9.4	11.7	14.8	18.1	18.2	19.5
Poland	25.1	25.4	28.1	31.8	36.2	35.6	36.5
Romania	8.4	6.6	6.3	5.8	4.3	2.3	-0.1
Eastern Europe	55.5	51.2	56.4	67.1	77.3	76.3	77.7
Soviet Union and CMEA Banks	16.0	14.2	18.3	22.5	26.1	26.5	36.4
Eastern Europe and the Soviet Union	71.4	65.4	74.7	89.7	103.4	102.7	114.1

Sources: National data for Hungary, Poland, and for Romania until 1986; BIS/OECD, *Statistics on External Indebtedness, Bank and Trade-Related Non-Bank External Claims on Individual Borrowing Countries and Territories*, various issues, Paris and Basle: for Bulgaria, Czechoslovakia, German Democratic Republic (adjusted here to include claims of the Federal Republic of Germany arising from clearing exchanges), Soviet Union (including CMEA banks). These data exclude any indebtedness to countries outside the BIS/OECD reporting area (e.g., all developing market economies).

a Preliminary estimates except for Hungary, the German Democratic Republic and Poland.
b Revised series.
c Gross debt less eastern assets with BIS reporting banks only.

with the developing countries. However, since part of its exports to this area are financed by long-term credits they yield little cash which can be used to offset deficits elsewhere. Net interest payments rose but receipts from tourism probably increased as well.

(ii) Eastern indebtedness and debt burden

According to the data set presented in table 4.3.2, the combined gross indebtedness of *eastern Europe and the Soviet Union* increased from $137 billion in 1988 to over $147 in 1989 and net debt by a similar increment to $114 billion. Incomplete *official data* show higher levels of gross debt — some $147 billion in 1988 rising to an estimated $159 billion in 1989 (box 4.3.1).

Given the flux in the state of statistics on eastern indebtedness, the secretariat has decided to present two sets of data. Those data presented in table 4.3.2 are the "traditional" set, a mixture of official and western reported statistics and estimates for the most recent year. Virtually all eastern countries released official debt statistics during the past year, but in some cases only for a single year. Since these data invariably show levels above western estimates, they have been treated separately — see box 4.3.1. In order to allow comparisons of total eastern debt in 1988 and 1989 as reported incompletely in official sources, some secretariat estimates have been incorporated into the totals for both years.

Unlike in recent years, the movement of exchange rates had little impact on the nominal US dollar value of the eastern debt. During the first half of the year, the US currency appreciated, lowering the level of the eastern liabilities, measured in US dollars, by some 5-7 per cent. In the second half of the year, the trend was reversed and, by the end of 1989, the impact on the nominal debt amounted to a reduction of only 1-2 per cent relative to end-1988.

In 1989, most countries borrowed for balance of payments support, thereby raising their liabilities. The exceptions were Romania, which continued to liquidate debt, and possibly Czechoslovakia. On the basis of western reported data (table 4.3.2), Soviet gross debt rose from $42 in 1988 to an estimated $51 billion at the end of 1989; net debt increased from $26½ billion to an estimated $36½ billion during the same period. Official data (see box 4.3.1) shows Soviet gross debt at $49.4 billion at the end of 1988. The secretariat estimates it to have risen to $58.5 billion in 1989.

In general the eastern countries' debt burdens rose in 1989 (tables 4.3.3 and 4.3.4). The *interest-payments ratios* of all countries except Romania increased, owing to the rise in interest rates and, in many cases, a growing stock of debt. Most eastern countries' *net debt-export* ratios decreased marginally. However the rapid increase in Bulgaria's debt caused its debt export ratio to rise sharply, placing it in the ranks of higher indebted countries. The debt-export ratios for Hungary and Poland continue to indicate high debt burdens, al-

BOX 4.3.1

Comparison of data on eastern gross debt and eastern financial indicators, 1989
(Billion US dollars, end of year and per cent)

Country	Gross debt Western estimates 1988	Gross debt Official data 1988	Gross debt Official data 1989	Net debt [a]	Net-debt exports	Debt service ratio	BIS deposits	Exports credits [b]
Bulgaria	7.7	7.8	10.6	9.3	397	79	1.3	3
Czechoslovakia	5.2	7.3 [c]	7.7	5.8	95	18	1.9	7-8
German Democratic Republic	20.2*	20.2*	20.6	11.0	109	44	9.6	..
Hungary	19.6 [d]	19.6 [d]	20.6 [d]	19.5	342	42	1.1	3.8
Poland	39.2 [e]	39.2 [e]	39.9 [e]	36.5	457	56	3.4	2.0
Romania	3.1*	3.1*	1.4*	-0.1	-	7	1.5	3
Eastern Europe	95.0	97.2	100.5	82.0	214	..	18.8	..
CMEA Banks [f]	4.0*	-	-	-	-	..	-	-
Soviet Union [f]	37.7*	49.4 [g]	58.5*	44.3	94	21	14.2	144 [h]
Eastern Europe and the Soviet Union	136.8	146.6	159.0	126.3	149	..	33.0	..

Sources: Western estimates, as for table 4.3.2; national sources.

a   Official gross debt less BIS deposits.
b   Reflects convertible-currency claims on partner countries.
c   The official data for 1988 are higher than originally announced because of the incorporation of foreign borrowing by joint ventures.
d   Revised official data.
e   Official data.
f   Estimates based upon a reported total Soviet and CMEA bank debt of $41.7 billion.
g   This figure reflects $46.2 billion in convertible currency debt and $3.2 billion in clearing account deficits, cumulated chiefly with Yugoslavia and Finland.
h   Includes non-convertible currency claims.

New debt information

With the exception of Hungary and Poland, the eastern countries traditionally have not provided data on their external financial position. As a result, analyses of east-west economic developments have relied upon a combination of "mirror" financial statistics compiled by various western multilateral economic organizations and analysts' estimates — see, for example, tables 4.3.1 (current account) and 4.3.2 (debt).

It has always been understood that western estimates of eastern debt, such as compiled jointly by the BIS and the OECD, provide lower bounds of overall eastern convertible currency liabilities since they reflect only eastern obligations vis-à-vis private and official institutions in countries reporting to those two organizations. These estimates have excluded, or have only partially taken into account, convertible currency bank liabilities vis-à-vis non-reporting western countries (e.g., Turkey and Yugoslavia), the developing countries (e.g., Arab banking centres), the CMEA countries and banks, or those arising from clearing accounts arrangements. The latter are a central features of the Soviet Union's trade agreements with Finland and Yugoslavia and of the Federal Republic of Germany-German Democratic Republic bilateral trade agreement. Also, aside from limitations of geographical coverage, eastern bonds, à forfait instruments and other claims held by individuals, enterprises and western non-bank financial institutions not reporting to the BIS or the OECD are not covered by these debt estimates. Similar strictures apply to estimates of eastern assets.

The advantages of the western series have been consistency, broken occasionally as the coverage of reporting countries and institutions has broadened, and reasonably timely reporting. In recent years, changes in financial stocks have also been made available on an exchange-rate-adjusted basis (see table 4.3.6), increasing the analytical value of the series.

Recently, most eastern countries have released official data on their external indebtedness in convertible currencies, but generally only for a single year. These official data are shown along with western estimates in the table above. While the official data have clearly increased understanding of the east's financial situation, the availability of only single points has also presented certain difficulties.

In some cases the exact coverage of the official data is unclear and statistics for two consecutive years, when available, may not be fully consistent. It has been confirmed in all cases that the western estimates have been too low, thus underlining the importance of regular reporting in the future. Also, the absence of even short series has precluded the analysis of recent trends and presentation of time series in tables. In these circumstances, the secretariat has retained, for the time being, the traditional estimates on eastern debt and the indicators derived therefrom (debt/export ratios, net interest payments, etc.) shown in the text tables and in Appendix table C.11.

TABLE 4.3.3

Eastern Europe and the Soviet Union: Ratio of net interest payments to exports to the market economies, 1984-1989
(Per cent)

	Previous peak (Level, year)	1984	1985	1986	1987	1988	1989 [a]
Bulgaria	16.7 (1978)	3.7	2.9	10.1	9.8	13.1	24.2
Czechoslovakia	8.6 (1981)	5.1	4.3	4.6	4.3	4.3	5.1
German Democratic Republic	23.2 (1981)	9.2	7.9	8.9	7.4	9.5	11.2
Hungary	28.0 (1981)	17.5	19.0	21.0	20.2	18.8	24.6
Poland	52.9 (1981)	43.1	43.7	43.2	42.4	36.8	41.7
Romania	14.7 (1982)	10.1	10.0	10.2	5.2	2.8	0.6
Eastern Europe	23.4 (1981)	15.1	14.7	16.2	15.0	14.7	17.7
Soviet Union	5.2 (1978)	2.8	3.7	4.8	3.8	4.0	4.9
Eastern Europe and Soviet Union [b]	13.3 (1981)	8.3	8.9	10.4	9.0	8.9	10.7
Memo item: ratio including goods and invisibles [c]							
Hungary	19.4 (1981)	12.6	13.2	15.2	13.7	12.7	16.8
Poland	39.7 (1981)	39.5	29.5	30.7	28.9	25.0	28.9
Romania	13.5 (1982)	9.4	9.5	9.0	4.6	2.5	1.4

Source: As for table 4.3.1. Export data used refer to goods only and thus exclude service and transfer receipts.

[a] Preliminary estimates. [b] Includes net interest payments of CMEA banks. [c] Exports reflect all receipts in convertible currency.

TABLE 4.3.4

Eastern Europe and the Soviet Union: Ratio of net debt to exports to the market economies, 1984-1989
(Per cent)

	Previous peak (Level, year)	1984	1985	1986	1987	1988	1989 [a]
Bulgaria	255 (1976)	21	44	140	178	205	321
Czechoslovakia	67 (1979)	42	50	53	66	62	51
German Democratic Republic	217 (1978)	78	78	91	104	123	115
Hungary	240 (1978)	221	307	374	396	349	342
Poland	455 (1982)	433	503	534	545	458	456
Romania	151 (1982)	93	97	100	70	33	-1
Eastern Europe	201 (1978)	149	173	204	219	205	204
Soviet Union	77 (1976)	25	40	55	54	54	72
Eastern Europe and the Soviet Union [b]	139 (1978)	84	108	132	136	127	136
Memo item: ratio reflects receipts from goods and invisibles [c]							
Hungary	189 (1978)	160	213	270	268	236	234
Poland	418 (1982)	340	366	381	371	312	325
Romania	139 (1982)	87	92	88	62	30	-1

Source: As for tables 4.3.1 and 4.3.2; ECE secretariat estimates. Net debt is calculated using only deposits of these countries with BIS reporting banks. Incorporation of other assets would lower these ratios (see Appendix table C.11), as would service and transfer receipts in exports.

[a] Preliminary estimates. [b] Includes debt of CMEA banks. [c] Exports reflect all receipts in convertible currency.

though in both cases they have fallen somewhat below the peak levels recorded in 1987.

(iii) Financing of debt

In 1989, the east raised $4.2 billion in the *international financial markets*, marginally less than in 1988 (table 4.3.5). Although its credit takings contracted markedly, the Soviet Union remained the largest single borrower. It was followed in this respect by Hungary and Bulgaria, both of which were more active in these markets than in 1988. As in recent years, Hungary's borrowing was concentrated in the bond markets.

As regards borrowing conditions, the east encountered a significant stiffening of terms in 1988 and 1989. The average margin (basis points over LIBOR) eastern countries paid more than doubled from 24 points in 1987 to 52 points in 1989.[470]

Several reasons for the tightening terms on new credits and for banks' increasing caution towards lending to the east, especially since the end of 1989, can be cited:

---

[470] OECD, *Financial Market Trends*, February 1990, p.32. At the same time, however, the average maturity on new loans lengthened marginally to 8 years 6 months.

TABLE 4.3.5

Eastern Europe and the Soviet Union: Medium- and long-term funds raised on the international financial markets, 1984-1989
(Million US dollars)

	1984	1985	1986	1987	1988	1989
Bulgaria	-	475	45	260	194	580
Czechoslovakia	-	100	279	242	330	334
German Democratic Republic	936	1 173	81	209	-	-
Hungary	1 166	1 642	1 315	1 951	1 016	1 334
Poland	260	-	-	30	-	163
Romania	-	150	-	-	-	-
Eastern Europe	2 362	3 540	1 720	2 692	1 540	2 411
Soviet Union	867	1 508	1 821	1 003	2 679	1 679
CMEA Banks	140	250	400	20	75	75
Total above	3 369	5 289	3 941	3 716	4 294	4 165
of which:						
Bank loans a	2 676	4 200	2 664	2 144	1 050	1 410
Foreign bank loans b	358	339	404	729	1 652	464
Other c	295	250	733	288	232	35
Bonds	41	447	291	555	1 360	2 256

Source: OECD, *Financial Statistics Monthly*, Part I, various issues.

a International bank loans in Eurocurrencies, excluding offically guaranteed loans and rescheduling of debt.
b In domestic currency of lending countries, excluding guaranteed loans.
c Other bank facilities, including bankers' acceptances.

— rapid increase in the indebtedness of some countries, particularly to commercial banks;

— recent poor economic performance and uncertain prospects in the light of accelerating reforms;

— possible loosening of financial authorities' control over debt because of decentralization of borrowing; and

— the movement toward democracy raises questions about the authorities' capability to implement strong adjustment measures to control external imbalances.

International bank lending to the east picked up sharply in 1989. During the past few years commercial banks have become the east's preferred source of funds. The recent large rise in borrowing appears to have contributed to the hardening of conditions already noted. Data for the *first three quarters* of the year show eastern liabilities rising by over $7 billion (adjusted for exchange rate movements), compared to about $5 billion in the same period in 1988 (table 4.3.6).[471] The Soviet Union's bank liabilities rose by over $6 billion, the largest recorded increment in bank debt for this country. Bulgaria's heavy borrowing boosted its bank obligations by another $0.8 billion. Most other east European countries posted smaller increases. Romania continued to liquidate its liabilities.

The east's *non-bank financial obligations* (official bilateral credits, guaranteed non-bank trade credits etc.) turned upward in the *first half* of 1989, increasing by nearly $2 billion (adjusted for exchange rate effects — see table 4.3.6). Most eastern countries, particularly the Soviet Union, raised their non-bank liabilities. In preceding years there had been a pronounced shift in eastern borrowing away from non-bank sources of finance towards pure commercial bank credits, and the volume of eastern non-bank obligations had actually declined. The reasons for this were the lower costs of commercial credits and a trend in eastern borrowing policy towards greater transparency in trade and financing transactions, better achieved by decoupling the two activities. It has often been noted that the prices of goods financed with official credits tend to be higher than if the two transactions are not linked.

The *asset* positions of the eastern countries, measured here by their deposits with BIS reporting banks, remained broadly unchanged in the first three quarters of 1989 at nearly $33 billion (table 4.3.7). Romania improved its position by $0.7 billion, those of Czechoslovakia and the German Democratic Republic strengthening somewhat less. All other countries drew down deposits marginally, Bulgaria posting the largest reduction. The *liquidity ratio* of the eastern trading area remained high, declining marginally to somewhat less than 5 months' import coverage. All countries except Hungary have assets coverage in excess of three months' imports, the minimum generally considered prudent.

(iv) Country by country financial summary

Bulgaria has run comparatively large current-account deficits for several years, resulting in a rapid increase in debt. In 1989 the deficit reached an all time high, estimated at $1.7 billion, in result of higher trade

---

[471] It should be noted that aside from direct bank-to-bank lending, the BIS statistics also reflect any eastern bonds, commercial paper and syndicated loans held in the portfolios of BIS reporting banks. Most eastern countries have generally preferred bank-to-bank borrowing to publicized credit syndications and bond issues as means of raising funds.

TABLE 4.3.6

Eastern Europe and the Soviet Union: Gross debt vis-à-vis BIS and OECD reporting institutions, 1985-1989

(Changes in million US dollars at constant exchange rates)

		By Institution:	
Country	Total debt (1)	Bank (2)	Non-bank (3)
Bulgaria			
1985	856	886	-30
1986	595	452	143
1987	584	677	-94
1988	1 768	1 774	-6
1989 [a]	771	691	80
1989 [b]	..	803	..
Czechoslovakia			
1985	-193	-55	-138
1986	57	25	32
1987	572	636	-59
1988	471	554	-40
1989 [a]	-	89	-89
1989 [b]	..	307	..
German Democratic Republic			
1985	365	996	-631
1986	364	161	203
1987	620	875	-255
1988	2 092	2 376	-284
1989 [a]	475	418	39
1989 [b]	..	416	..
Hungary			
1985	792	763	29
1986	204	220	-16
1987	671	759	-87
1988	-181	-133	-48
1989 [a]	338	296	42
1989 [b]	..	456	..
Poland			
1985	-1 294	-166	-1 128
1986	1 293	-831	2 123
1987	1 628	-526	2 154
1988	-2 195	-689	-1 505
1989 [a]	-62	-600	538
1989 [b]	..	-722	..
Romania			
1985	-674	-511	-163
1986	-471	-536	65
1987	-1 014	-665	-349
1988	-2 195	-689	-1 505
1989 [a]	-335	-330	-5
1989 [b]	..	-401	..
Eastern Europe			
1985	-148	1 913	-2 061
1986	2 042	-509	2 550
1987	3 149	1 739	1 310
1988	149	2 287	-2 104
1989 [a]	1 169	564	605
1989 [b]	..	859	..
Soviet Union			
1985	1 728	3 718	-1 990
1986	1 977	3 607	-1 631
1987	-2 260	549	-2 854
1988	4 525	5 387	-862
1989 [a]	6 162	4 802	1 359
1989 [b]	..	6 391	..

Sources: BIS and OECD, *Statistics on External Indebtedness*, New Series, Basle and Paris, January 1990 and previous issues. ECE secretariat estimates for 1985 and January-June 1986 are based on data found in the prior series of the same source and adjusted for valuation effects. BIS, *International Banking Developments*, Basle, February 1990.

Note: Changes are from end-December of the previous year; Total debt excludes any liabilities vis-à-vis institutions outside the BIS/OECD reporting area and multilateral finanical institutions. The figures also exclude claims of the Federal Republic of Germany on the German Democratic Republic.

[a] First half of 1989.
[b] First three quarters.

TABLE 4.3.7

Eastern Europe and the Soviet Union: Assets with BIS reporting banks and liquidity ratios, 1982-1989
(Levels, changes at constant exchange rates, in billion US dollars; ratio in per cent)

	1982	1983	1984	1985	1986	1987	1988	1989-QIII
Bulgaria								
Assets (billion)	1.0	1.2	1.4	2.1	1.4	1.1	1.8	1.3
Changes (billion)	0.2	0.2	0.3	0.5	-0.9	-0.5	0.7	-0.4
Liquidity ratio (per cent)	35.2	44.7	52.9	63.4	38.2	33.4	44.2	36.2
Czechoslovakia								
Assets (billion)	0.7	0.9	1.0	1.0	1.2	1.6	1.7	1.9
Changes (billion)	-0.3	0.2	0.2	-0.1	0.1	0.2	0.2	0.3
Liquidity ratio (per cent)	16.8	22.8	25.7	25.6	25.8	29.5	28.5	35.9
German Democratic Republic								
Assets (billion)	1.9	3.4	4.5	6.5	7.5	9.0	9.9	9.6
Changes (billion)	-0.2	1.4	1.5	1.4	0.1	0.4	1.6	0.4
Liquidity ratio (per cent)	27.5	44.0	55.9	81.1	81.3	87.4	101.2	91.5
Hungary								
Assets (billion)	0.7	1.3	1.5	2.3	2.1	1.5	1.4	1.1
Changes (billion)	-0.2	0.5	0.3	0.4	-0.4	-0.8	-0.1	-0.2
Liquidity ratio (per cent)	16.5	30.0	37.4	56.7	47.6	30.8	27.3	22.3
Poland								
Assets (billion)	1.0	1.2	1.5	1.6	1.7	3.0	3.6	3.4
Changes (billion)	0.3	0.2	0.4	-0.1	-	1.0	0.8	-0.1
Liquidity ratio (per cent)	24.2	30.4	35.8	34.1	35.8	54.6	53.2	48.1
Romania								
Assets (billion)	0.3	0.5	0.6	0.4	0.6	1.4	0.8	1.5
Changes (billion)	-	0.2	0.2	-0.3	0.3	0.7	-0.6	0.7
Liquidity ratio (per cent)	6.2	12.9	15.2	8.5	16.8	37.9	22.1	61.7
Eastern Europe								
Assets (billion)	5.6	8.6	10.7	13.9	14.6	17.6	19.2	18.8
Changes (billion)	-0.1	2.8	2.8	1.8	-0.9	1.1	2.7	0.6
Liquidity ratio (per cent)	20.5	31.9	39.0	48.9	47.5	54.7	54.5	53.6
Soviet Union								
Assets (billion)	10.0	10.9	11.3	13.1	14.8	14.1	15.3	14.2
Changes (billion)	2.0	0.7	1.7	0.9	0.8	-1.9	1.7	-0.2
Liquidity ratio (per cent)	25.6	28.8	31.0	36.1	44.6	43.2	38.9	30.1
Eastern Europe and the Soviet Union								
Assets (billion)	15.6	19.5	22.1	26.9	29.4	31.7	34.4	33.0
Changes (billion)	1.9	3.4	4.5	2.7	-0.1	-0.9	4.4	0.7
Liquidity ratio (per cent)	23.5	30.1	34.4	41.7	46.0	48.9	46.3	40.1

Source: BIS *International Banking Developments - Quarterly Reports*, Basle. ECE secretariat estimates.

Note: *Asset* positions refers to the end of the period; *changes* are from end-December of the previous year; *liquidity ratios* relate assets to annual imports from all developed and developing market economies.

and invisibles deficits. The $10.6 billion gross debt[472] constitutes a very heavy burden, given the magnitude of Bulgaria's convertible current exports, and places it in the ranks of highly indebted countries. The debt service ratio is reported to have risen from nearly 47 per cent in 1984 to 79 per cent in 1988-1989.[473] Despite drawings upon reserves in the early part of the year, Bulgaria's BIS deposits amounted to $1.3 billion at the end of September, or over 4 months' import coverage.

After several years of running deficits, *Czechoslovakia* achieved a balanced current account in 1989. Nonetheless, the country's gross indebtedness in convertible currencies rose to $7.7 billion.[474] The bulk of the increase was due to borrowing by joint ventures ($270 million), and banks, enterprises and foreign trade organizations ($170 million).[475] Czechoslovakia has not made much use of official government credits, and the country's debt-service ratio remains below 20 per

---

[472] *Ikonomicheski zhivot*, 24 January 1990. Former President Zhivkov had stated that Bulgaria's gross debt stood at $7.8 billion at the end of 1988. The $2.8 billion increase in debt in 1989 far exceeds the requirements for financing the current-account deficit.

[473] *Ibid.*

[474] Communication from the State Bank of Czechoslovakia.

[475] *Rudé Právo*, 1 March 1990. The article gives a somewhat higher debt figure of $7.9 billion for end-1989.

cent.[476] By the end of September 1989, deposits with BIS banks had risen to a historical high of nearly $2 billion. Total assets reached $7-8 billion, of which some $2 billion are non-convertible currency obligations of the Soviet Union. Approximately $1.5 billion in claims on developing countries have been classified as uncollectable.[477]

There is some confusion concerning the recent development of the *German Democratic Republic's* external financial position. As noted above, the recently released official current-account statistics show a deficit of $2.4 billion, much larger than then secretariat's $1 billion estimate. The deficit in 1989, regardless of its exact dimensions, should be mirrored in the country's indebtedness. However, western reported financial data for the first three quarters of 1989 show no increase in the German Democratic Republic's net debt.[478]

One explanation for this is that the entire deficit was concentrated in the last quarter of the year. In this case the financing of the German Democratic Republic's current account should only show up in data for the full year. Alternatively, credits may have been raised outside of the western financial reporting area (e.g., Arab banking centres).

It may be noted that the *revised* trade *statistics for 1988*, which yield a trade deficit of $1 billion (instead of a balanced trade account as claimed earlier) and a small estimated current-account *deficit*, are consistent with the small increase in the German Democratic Republic's net liabilities registered in western financial sources.

Earlier estimates of the ECE secretariat, using the *unrevised* data, yielded current-account *surpluses* of the German Democratic Republic of cumulatively almost $2 billion for the period 1986-1988; however, the separately estimated net debt of the country *vis-à-vis* western creditors *increased* by $1.4 billion, instead of declining as would be expected.[479] This lack of consistency between the estimated current and capital accounts has been often commented upon. The "unaccounted for" borrowing has been typically explained as the German Democratic Republic's financing of, among other things, exports to developing countries.[480] However, it is possible that eventual revisions of the German Democratic Republic's trade data for years prior to 1988 will cause the reconciliation problem to disappear entirely.

Recently the German Democratic Republic authorities placed the country's convertible currency gross debt at $20.6 billion for end-1989.[481] This is close to western estimates and implies that the country acquired few liabilities outside the western reporting area. In this respect, the German Democratic Republic's position differs from that of other eastern countries, the official debt estimates of which show or imply more significant obligations toward the developing countries and other creditors not covered by the western reporting system.

The German Democratic Republic's assets are officially reported in the range of $7-9 billion at the end of 1989,[482] which compares to $9.6 billion in deposits registered by the BIS for the end of September.

The *Hungarian* financial authorities have recently revised the data on the country's debt upward by over $2 billion to nearly $21 billion.[483] The new higher debt series has been incorporated into tables 4.3.2 and 4.3.4, the latter showing the net-debt export ratio. This is seen to have peaked in 1987 and subsequently declined as export growth exceeded the accumulation of debt. Similarly, the country's debt-service ratio declined to a figure reported in the range of 42-44 per cent. Hungary's assets with BIS reporting banks continued to decline in the first nine months of the year.

As in recent years, *Poland's* current-account deficit in 1989 was financed almost entirely through the postponement of interest obligations on official debt. Most scheduled interest payments on commercial debt were met. A small rise in indebtedness and weak export growth resulted in little change in the country's debt-export ratio, which remains below the peak level of 1987.

Since the early 1980s the *Romanian* authorities had resolutely pursued a policy to eliminate external indebtedness. Large trade surpluses were attained chiefly through radical reductions in imports, exports having more or less stagnated. By the end of 1988, the authorities had managed to reduced the gross debt to some $3 billion and in April 1989 it was announced that the country's foreign liabilities had been fully re-

---

[476] *Rudé Právo*, 23 February 1990.

[477] *Ibid.*

[478] BIS data for the first three quarters of the 1989 show no change in the German Democratic Republic's net debt: its bank liabilities and assets both rose by $0.4 million on an exchange rate adjusted basis (table 4.3.6 and table 4.3.7). Data on the German Democratic Republic's non-bank liabilities compiled by BIS/OECD show only a marginal rise in the first half of the year (table 4.3.6).

[479] See United Nations Economic Commission for Europe, *Economic Bulletin for Europe*, vol.41, New York, 1989, table 2.17.

[480] Borrowing for this reason is also believed to have been common among other eastern countries, but eastern claims on many of the customers (largely developing countries) are now uncollectable.

[481] Statement of Christa Luft, Minister of Economics, as reported in the *Financial Times*, 4 January 1990.

[482] *Ibid.*

[483] According to the National Bank, the revision stems from an overall re-evaluation of balance sheets. "The difference compared to previous figures was inherited from the second half of the seventies, when a decision was made by the political leadership to present a lower foreign indebtedness as a consequence of not including loans from non-reporting banks and some trade related obligations.". National Bank of Hungary, *Hungary's external debt in convertible currencies*, Mimeo, November 1989.

paid.[484] Although western creditors continued to report some claims on Romania, the country's foreign reserves increased to $1.5 billion at end-September 1989. Therefore, on a net basis, the country's debt has been effectively liquidated.

It has been reported that the Romania has external claims worth nearly $3 billion, much of which was not being serviced because of financial difficulties of the debtors. It appears that some governments were willing to repay their obligations to Romania in foodstuffs, clothing and medicines, but the former government's policy was to accept payment only in convertible currency. This policy has been changed and negotiations with debtors have resumed for repayment in goods.[485]

On the basis of western reported data (table 4.3.2), Soviet gross debt (including the liabilities of CMEA banks) rose from $42 billion in 1988 to an estimated $51 billion at the end of 1989; net debt increased from $26½ billion to an estimated $36½ billion during the same period. This $10 billion rise in current dollars is nearly the same if adjusted for exchange rate movements.[486] In 1988, Soviet net debt remained roughly constant at some $26 billion, but at constant exchange rates — a better measure of net borrowing — net debt rose by some $3 billion. On the basis of official data (see box 4.3.1) Soviet gross debt was $49.4 billion at the end of 1988. The secretariat estimates it to have risen to $58.5 billion in 1989.

The Soviet Union has in the past followed a policy of tight restraint on the growth of external indebtedness. Borrowing has been selective, undertaken mainly to cushion the impact of internal and external economic shocks (poor harvests, terms of trade losses, production shortfalls, etc.). Whenever the external balance came under pressure, adjustment measures were always implemented rapidly — exports were raised and/or imports reduced — to nudge the trade account back toward balance. Thus in the two years 1986-1987 which followed the collapse of oil prices, exports were boosted and western imports were cut by some 28 per cent in volume. Gold sales of around $8 billion supported these measures, and according to western data, net indebtedness rose by less than $1 billion (on an exchange rate adjusted basis).[487] Also, in years when food imports had risen, purchases of other goods, including capital goods, tended to be scaled back to limit the overall import bill.

Developments in 1988-1989 no longer fully fit into this general pattern. The Soviet Union experienced another sharp terms-of-trade shock in 1988; in response it sold gold worth some $3.7 billion and borrowed more widely, raising indebtedness by nearly $3 billion (on an exchange rate adjusted basis). However, in these last two years there has been no evidence of trade adjustments to narrow the deficit that had opened up with the west. Imports were allowed to advance rapidly and, in fact, accelerated in the final quarter of 1989. At the same time there was no acceleration in the volume of export growth as in the past, but on the contrary data for the second half of 1989 show a deceleration of export growth. As a result the Soviet Union posted a $6½ billion trade deficit with the developed market economies in 1989 and an even larger estimated increase in external debt, as noted.

Though it is perhaps too early to conclude that this pattern signals a fundamental shift in Soviet policy priorities regarding external balance and debt, the change from earlier patterns is significant. It has to be seen against the background of the deteriorating domestic balance, both as regards production and consumer market supplies, which required the acquisition of additional imports at the same time as the supplies of tradeables became constrained. It should be borne in mind that, in real terms, 1989 Soviet imports from the west still fell short of the 1985 level.

Despite the rapid increase in the Soviet Union's liabilities and various indicators of debt burden, overall indebtedness remains moderate. Foreign currency reserves remain high and the country is believed to maintain large gold stocks, the value of which has recently been increasing as the price of gold has risen.[488] However, faltering export performance, if not reversed, would be a source of concern in the longer term.

---

[484] Statement of the then President Ceausescu to the Romanian Parliament, *Scinteia*, 17 April 1989.

[485] BBC, *Summary of World Broadcasts*, EE/W0113, 1 February 1990, quoting Rompres.

[486] It may be noted that the $10 billion increase in the Soviet Union's net debt exceeds the financing requirement for its $6.5 billion trade deficit with the developed market economies. For the first three quarters of 1989, Soviet debt *vis-à-vis* BIS/OECD reporting countries rose by some $7.7 billion (table 4.3.6) but the trade deficit with the west was only $4.6 billion.

[487] Economic Commission for Europe, *Economic Bulletin for Europe*, vol.40, No.3, Pergamon Press for the United Nations, December 1988, chapter 2. At current exchange rates, Soviet net debt rose by some $8 billion in 1986-1987 (see table 4.3.2), owing chiefly to the depreciation of the US dollar.

[488] The Soviet Ministry of Finance has recently released data concerning Soviet financial claims on partner countries. Of a total of R85.8 billion ($143.3 billion at the official exchange rate of $1.67 per rouble), roughly one half is exposure towards socialist countries (including R34.1 billion *vis-à-vis* Cuba, Vietnam, and Mongolia) and the balance towards the developing economies. Presumably these amounts represent a combination of claims denominated in roubles and in convertible currencies. The article suggests that a large share of the assets is considered uncollectable. See "Unikal'nyi dokument. Komu my dali 'v dolg' 85,800,000,000 rublei" (A unique document: to whom we gave "on loan" 85.8 billion roubles), *Izvestiya*, 1 March 1990, p.3.

4.4. INTERNATIONAL INITIATIVE IN SUPPORT OF EASTERN REFORMS

(i) Introduction

In this section recent developments in western economic policy towards eastern Europe and the Soviet Union are reviewed.[489] The focus is on the emerging international support initiative for eastern economic and political reforms. It was originally undertaken, in response to appeals from Hungary and Poland, both of which had formally requested support for the transformation of their economies. The initiative was subsequently extended to other east European countries as their political situations evolved. Offers of material assistance have not been made to the Soviet Union, nor has the country requested any.[490] The initiative is complex and dynamic, comprising a formal aid programme (PHARE), government actions undertaken unilaterally, bilaterally, and through official and semi-official international organizations. Multilateral economic organizations (IMF, World Bank) have played an increasing role and various private organizations have become involved.

New institutional developments are discussed in section (ii), Group of 24 aid packages in section (iii), recent trade policy measures in section (iv), and financial measures in support of Hungary and Poland in section (v). The presentation ends with a preliminary assessment of the support initiative in section (vi).

(ii) Institutional developments

A key feature of the international support initiative is the growth of new east-west institutional linkages and the increasing involvement of international economic institutions in the process of eastern reform. Several developments deserve special mention. The starting point was the creation by the G-24 of the PHARE programme itself, co-ordinated by the EC. Progress has continued on the conclusion of bilateral agreements between the EC and all individual eastern countries; a new financial institution, the European Bank for Reconstruction and Development (EBRD) is being created to focus on the needs of the eastern countries; European Investment Bank (EIB) facilities have been extended to Hungary and Poland and consideration is being given to making those of the European Coal and Steel Community (ECSC) available as well; the IMF and the World Bank have played important advisory and financial roles in the Hungarian and Polish reforms. This role will be extended to other eastern countries as they become members of these organizations.[491]

At the July 1989 Economic Summit (G-7), participating Heads of State responded to the quickening political and economic reform in Hungary and Poland, and to these countries' requests for assistance by launching an international aid programme, which was given the name PHARE.[492] The main objectives of the programme have been to improve Hungary's and Poland's chances for a successful transition to a fully-fledged market economy and to foster further liberalization of their political systems. The Commission of the European Communities (EC) was given responsibility for co-ordinating the efforts of 24 western countries (Group of 24) which had agreed to participate.

Five working groups were set up to co-ordinate measures in the following areas:

— emergency food supplies to Poland;

— management and vocational training;

— investment and joint ventures;

— environmental co-operation;

---

[489] This section complements and updates the secretariat's review of "Support for eastern reforms", in United Nations Economic Commission for Europe, *Economic Bulletin for Europe*, vol.41., New York, 1989, chapter 2(iv), pp.48-56 and section 1.2 above. No claim is made to be comprehensive, which in any case would be difficult given the multitude of changes and initiatives.

[490] Soviet analysts have, however, reflected upon the forms which western assistance for *perestroika* could take, some of which are similar to the proposals advanced by Hungary and Poland (market access, training of cadres, support for joint ventures, relaxation of COCOM controls, etc.). Additional proposals include, for example, joint research groups of Soviet and western experts to elaborate models for the transformation of the Soviet economy; association with and eventual membership in the international economic organizations (GATT, International Monetary Fund, and World Bank); and conversion of military industry to civilian use. See, for example, M. Maximova, "How can the west contribute to *perestroika* (A Soviet economist's perception)", paper presented to the Malente Symposium VII, in *On the Way to Stronger East-West Economic Relations – Opportunity and Challenge*, Malente, Federal Republic of Germany, 16-18 October 1989.

[491] Early in 1990, Mr. Lari, the World Bank's director for Europe, raised the possibility that the World Bank would provide at least $5.5 billion to eastern Europe over the period 1990-1995. This would include $2.5 billion for Poland, $1 billion for Hungary, $2 billion for Romania and additional funds when the other east European countries became members. *Financial Times*, 24 January 1990. Lari's statement gave a prospective lending of $7.5 billion, which also includes $2 billion for Yugoslavia.

[492] "PHARE" stands for "Pologne Hongrie: Assistance à la Restructuration Economique". The members of the group are the G-7, the other members of the Communities, the EFTA countries, Turkey, New Zealand and Australia. It was decided at the 1 August 1989 meeting that each country would prepare a separate note on the measures which they had already taken, or might take, bilaterally in support of Hungary and Poland.

— access to western markets.

At a meeting in December 1989, the G-24 representatives responded to the political changes in Bulgaria, Czechoslovakia and the German Democratic Republic and to the announcements by their new leaderships that the countries would move toward more market-oriented and pluralist political systems with an invitation to submit requests for assistance.[493] The six countries did so at the fourth co-ordinating meeting of the G-24 in February 1990.[494] The formal decision on their participation in the enlarged PHARE programme is scheduled to be made in June.

The G-24's task requires the development of an aid strategy, determination of the level of aid required, where and how it should be channelled, and elaboration of a system for monitoring its use. It also requires the co-ordination of the activities of governments, multilateral financial institutions, international economic organizations, and private institutions operating in a combination of bilateral and multilateral settings. The lack of paradigms as a guide for finding the best approach to the transformation of a centrally planned economy into a market economy has complicated the entire undertaking.

In the wake of the 1988 Joint Declaration on *EC-CMEA relations*,[495] the Communities had concluded an agreement on industrial co-operation with Czechoslovakia (December 1988) and broader trade and co-operation agreements with Hungary (September 1988), Poland (November 1989), and the Soviet Union (December 1989). An accord with the German Democratic Republic was initialled in early March 1990.[496] Negotiations on the completion of trade and economic co-operation agreements with Bulgaria are nearing conclusion.[497] Czechoslovakia and the EC have decided to negotiate an extension of the existing limited agreement on trade in industrial products. A meeting of the EC-Romania joint committee is awaited before the EC decides whether to enlarge the 1980 agreement still in force which covers only trade in industrial products. Negotiations with Romania on a broader accord had been suspended in April 1989 owing to political disagreements.

These bilateral arrangements vary in scope and detail, but typically call for mutual granting of MFN treatment, abolition of certain quantitative restrictions applied by the EC, improved access for EC companies to the eastern partner's market (i.e., "effective reciprocity") and economic co-operation in the areas of environment, science and technology, industry and transport. The agreements with Hungary and Poland contain timetables for the removal by the EC of specific quantitative restrictions by 1994-1995. This schedule was moved up to 1 January 1990 as part of PHARE initiative. In the case of the Soviet Union, the EC is to eliminate a first set of specific quantitative restrictions on Soviet industrial goods in 1990. Further liberalization is foreseen for mid-1992, after which a joint committee is to review progress and agree upon a timetable for ending most of the remaining obstacles by 1995.[498] The agreements under negotiation with Bulgaria, Czechoslovakia and the German Democratic Republic are reported to be similar and are likely also to include provisions for the removal of quantitative restrictions prior to 1992.

Looking beyond these "second generation" accords and addressing the increasing attraction of the EC for the countries of eastern Europe, the EC Commission has proposed new individual association agreements. They would cover trade, technical assistance, financial support, joint infrastructure projects, cultural co-operation and political dialogue. Each association agreement would be tailored to suit the individual east European country's state of development. However, the agreements would not include a commitment to eventual EC membership, although in this regard the German Democratic Republic might be a special case.[499] Previous EC association agreements with Greece and Turkey contain explicit membership commitments.[500] According to the EC, the eastern countries' advance towards association agreements will be conditional upon the demonstration of progress in political and economic reform.

Negotiations have progressed on the establishment of a *European Bank for Reconstruction and Development* (EBRD). Proposed at the meeting of EC Heads of Government Summit in November, the bank's aim will be "to promote, in consultation with the IMF and the World Bank, productive and competitive investment in

---

[493] Romania was added to the list of eligible countries in January. Yugoslavia was also included in the list of countries invited to request support.

[494] The Czechoslovak government has set out a number of aid priorities: education and training; environmental protection; and restructuring and reducing the scale of heavy industry and metallurgy. Romania's requests for support focus on the tourism, energy and heavy industry sectors plus additional food deliveries. *Agence Europe*, 3 March 1990.

[495] Joint Declaration on the establishment of official relations between the European Economic Community and the Council for Mutual Economic Assistance, done at Luxembourg, 25 June 1988.

[496] This step was undertaken independently of the work on German monetary union and reunification. A 10-year agreement was originally planned, but now the accord will govern EC-German Democratic Republic economic relations until German unification. *Agence Europe*, 22 February and 14 March 1990.

[497] *Agence Europe*, 6 March 1990.

[498] *East European Markets*, 15 December 1989.

[499] According to President Delors of the EC Commission, the German Democratic Republic's special relationship with the Federal Republic of Germany means that it should be able to start negotiating entry into the EC before 1992, either as an independent state or as a part of a united Germany. *International Herald Tribune*, 2 February 1990.

[500] According to Commission sources, the EC could not envisage admitting east European countries for at least 10 years because the of institutional complications of such a move and the poor state of some of these economies. *International Herald Tribune*, 2 February 1990.

the States of central and eastern Europe; to reduce, where appropriate, any risks related to the financing of a market-oriented economy; to speed up the necessary structural adjustments, support economic recovery and modernization in eastern Europe".[501] The bank is to be modelled on existing multilateral regional development banks (e.g., Asian Development Bank).

Membership will consist of at least 34 countries (the Group of 24, eastern Europe, the Soviet Union, Cyprus, Israel and Malta), the European Commission and the European Investment Bank, making it the first institution owned jointly by eastern and western governments. The bank will provide finance on both concessional terms and at market interest rates. It is expected to be capitalized at ECU 10 billion ($12.2 billion). Members will have the right to bid on bank-financed projects.[502]

Agreement appears to have been reached on several key issues. The nations and institutions of the European Community would hold slightly over 50 per cent of the bank's capital (capital shares determine voting power) and the United States and the Soviet Union possibly some 10-11 per cent and 6 per cent, respectively. The Soviet Union would be eligible to borrow up to a ceiling expressed, among other things, in terms of a maximum percentage of total loans.[503] An unresolved issue is whether the bank should lend only to the private sector, as favoured by the United Kingdom and the United States, or whether loans to state enterprises and for infrastructure would also be allowed. A possible compromise mentioned recently would limit lending for roads, bridges, telecommunications and other infrastructure investment to 40 per cent of the total.[504] In the light of the anticipated curtailment of international bank lending to the east (see section 4.6), the EBRD is likely to become a major source of new funds for these countries.

In a move extending the resources of the Communities' institutions to Hungary and Poland, the European Community has formally approved *European Investment Bank* (EIB) lending of up to ECU 1 billion over a three-year period. Practical arrangements for the selection of infrastructure and industrial projects are being finalized, with private sector projects receiving priority.[505] Co-operation and possibly co-financing with the World Bank is to be an important feature of the operation. Release of funds to Hungary and Poland has been made conditional upon each country reaching formal agreement with the IMF on a stabilization programme.

It seems that the EIB is to act as a pathfinder for the new EBRD (which is not expected to be in operation until the end of the year). After the initial loan of ECU 1 billion, financing of east European operations would be the task of the EBRD.[506]

The European Commission has also considered making Hungary and Poland eligible for *European Coal and Steel Community* (ECSC) credits. An upper limit of ECU 200 million is under discussion. These credits would be earmarked for industrial projects in the coal and steel sectors and for infrastructure projects.[507] Originally ECSC credits were intended for modernizing coal and steel facilities in the EC, but, in recent years, operations have been extended to infrastructure projects outside the Community with the proviso that EC steel be used. This condition would also apply to any loans made to eastern Europe.[508]

Various measures have been taken to establish the basis for foreign direct investment in the east, starting with the enactment of legislation in the eastern countries allowing join ventures and other forms of equity participation. Governments have started to conclude *bilateral investment protection agreements* and, in certain cases, western governments have extended their *investment guarantee programmes* to the eastern countries. In the EC a proposal has been made to create an OPIC-like investment guarantee institution which would also provide coverage in eastern Europe.[509]

The Soviet Union has formally requested observer status in the *GATT*,[510] a move which has recently received broad support in the west. Poland, which acceded to the GATT in 1967, has asked for a change in the terms of membership to reflect the country's transition to a market economy.[511] It's protocol of accession did not guarantee the country MFN treatment. Instead of adopting a tariff schedule at the time, Poland

---

[501] Proceedings of the European Summit in Strasbourg, 8-9 December 1989. Summarized in *East-West (Fortnightly Bulletin)*, 13 December 1989.

[502] It is this privilege which has prompted countries beyond the initial 34 to seek membership. So far these include Egypt, Lichtenstein, Morocco and the Republic of Korea.

[503] *International Herald Tribune*, 10-11 March 1990.

[504] *Ibid*. The exact political and economic conditionality to be attached to the bank's lending also remains to be decided.

[505] *Financial Times*, 10 October 1989 and 21 January 1990; *Agence Europe*, 24 November 1989.

[506] According to Mr. M. Orbanados, a Vice-President of the EIB, reported in the *Financial Times*, 20 January 1990.

[507] *Agence Europe*, 24 November, 1989.

[508] *Financial Times*, 22 November 1989. The loans would be guaranteed by, but not a direct charge on, the EC budget.

[509] This proposal was made by EC finance ministers in October. *Agence Europe*, 17 October 1989. OPIC stands for the United States' Overseas Private Investment Corporation, which, among other things, insures private firms' investments against political risk.

[510] *International Herald Tribune*, 10-11 March 1990. The issue has arisen whether the Soviet Union should be admitted as an observer before or after the termination of the current round of trade talks in December.

[511] *Financial Times*, 25 January 1990.

TABLE 4.4.1

Partial list of international financial commitments to Hungary and Poland, for 1990 and after
(Million US dollars)

	Bilateral credits		Investment and credit guarantees		Grants and assistance for 1990		
	Hungary	Poland	Hungary	Poland	Hungary	Poland	Announced objectives
Australia................	..	151	..	..	..	..	
Austria...................	..	83	..	146	1.3 [a]	1.3 [a]	
Belgium..................	..	..	85	85	6	6	Training programmes for three years
Canada...................	14	..	..	17	8	8	Fund for private projects
Denmark................	..	46	..	153	23 [a]	23 [a]	East European industrial fund
Finland..................	100	..	..	..	0.2	15.9 [a]	Training; environmental protection for Poland
France...................	348	..	..	678 [b]	..	16 [a]	Technical aid and training
Germany, Fed.Rep.of...	587	..	493 [c]	1614	14	12 [a]	Training for Hungary
Greece...................	..	..	..	..	..	..	
Iceland...................	..	..	..	..	..	..	
Ireland...................	..	40	..	..	..	..	
Italy......................	219 [a]	40 [d]	..	446 [e]	1	9	Training; medical aid for Poland
Japan.....................	500	500 [a]	400	350 [a]	24 [a]	51 [a]	
Luxembourg.............	..	..	..	..	..	0.6	
Netherlands.............	..	..	..	..	2	5	Medical supplies for Poland; training for Hungary
New Zealand............	..	..	..	..	0.2	0.2	Training and environmental protection
Norway...................	..	..	..	23	..	3	Training and environmental protection for Poland
Portugal..................	..	..	..	..	..	..	
Spain.....................	..	..	100	..	..	..	Training
Sweden...................	150	..	..	..	..	49 [a]	Environmental protection for Poland
Switzerland..............	..	..	..	..	50 [a,f]	99 [a]	Technical, economic and humanitarian aid
Turkey....................	..	..	108	100	0.8	0.8	Training, grant in local currency for investment
United Kingdom........	..	..	..	..	33 [a]	66 [a]	Know-how fund
United States...........	..	..	40	200	92 [a]	321 [a]	
Nordic countries........	..	..	..	..	..	47	Environment
Sub-total.................	1917	920	1226	3811	253	732	
EEC.......................	1000	..	..	..	150 [a,j]	716 [a,g,j]	
EIB........................	527 [a,i]	675 [a,i]	..	..			
ECSC[h]..................	105 [a,i]	135 [a,i]	..	..			
IMF.......................	208	723	..	..			
World Bank[k]..........	990 [a]	2527 [a]	..	..			
Sub-total.................	2830	4060	..	..	150	716	
Total above..............	4748	4880	1226	3811	403	1448	

Sources: ECE secretariat estimates, based on official communiqués and newspaper reports, using exchange rates as of 5 March 1990.

a Commitments for 1990 and the next 2-4 years.
b From this FF900 million for the creation of an investment fund in France.
c Current exposure, no restriction on further cover.
d For the creation of a specialized bank in Italy.
e $180 million for individual projects, $180 million for Italian firms, $80 million for co-financing with the World Bank.
f Open for other east European countries.
g Including $275 million food and agricultural aid.
h European Coal and Steel Community.
i Assuming that credits will be disbursed according to IMF quota proportions.
j Excluding any share of the ECU 1.85 billion under consideration for all east European countries 1991-1992.
k Including $27 million for the International Finance Corporation.

committed itself to increase imports by 7 per cent annually.

(iii) Group-of-24 aid packages

Member countries responded to the G-24 initiative in favour of Hungary and Poland with "aid packages" which addressed not only the original priorities of PHARE, but often included measures that went far beyond the scope of the original exercise. The aid packages vary considerably, but generally include new credits, credit and investment guarantees, food grants, technical assistance, etc. The largest G-24 countries — France, Japan, the Federal Republic of Germany, the United States, Italy — and the EC have made the largest material commitments. These have been classified, by type of aid, in table 4.4.1 along with the pledges of other G-24 members.

France's assistance to Hungary consists chiefly of bilateral trade credits. For Poland, France has allocated mostly investment and credit guarantees and has created a $150 million investment fund.

New bilateral credits worth nearly $600 million and $500 million in export credit guarantees constitute the major part of the *Federal Republic of Germany's* assistance to Hungary. Support for Poland consists of $1.6 billion in insurance coverage for exports destined for the Federal Republic's joint ventures in Poland. The Federal Republic has also forgiven a part of Poland's debt (see below).

The *United States* Congress approved an aid package worth $938 million, of which $852 million is earmarked for Poland and $86 million for Hungary. The first instalment of the three-year allocation, amounting to $533 million, is to be made in 1990. Overall, Poland is to receive $125 million in emergency food aid, $240 million in grants for the support of private enterprise, $25 million to modernize Polish telecommunications, and $200 million for the stabilization fund (see below). The breakdown of the package for Hungary is similar, but the amounts are smaller.[512]

Japan's package includes the equivalent of a $150 million low-interest loan and $25 million in food aid to Poland. The country's Export-Import Bank is to offer credit lines each amounting to $500 million over three years (beginning April 1989) to Hungary and Poland. The Japanese government will extend coverage of trade insurance up to $350 million for Poland and $400 million for Hungary (up from the current $200 million) over a two-year period. In Poland's case this represents a resumption of insurance coverage.[513] Japan is prepared to transfer technology worth about $25 million to both countries over the next few years. It has also offered to receive trainees and send experts in business management and the environment.[514]

Late in 1989 *Switzerland* elaborated a SF 200 million programme in favour of Hungary and Poland. Subsequently this amount was raised to SF 250 million and extended to all reforming east European economies.[515]

The amount of aid which the EC intends to make available to eastern Europe over the next few years is still undetermined. In January, the President of the EC noted that if the six east European countries were to be given support on the scale currently extended to the Communities' depressed regions, an additional ECU 14 billion ($16.8 billion) a year for the next 5-10 years and a further ECU 5 billion a year from the European Investment Bank would be required.[516]

More recently it has been proposed that the EC devote ECU 2.35 billion ($2.9 billion) out of its own budget to eastern Europe over the next three years.[517] The total includes the ECU 300 million for Hungary and Poland for 1990 decided by the Commission last year[518] and a further ECU 200 million proposed by the Commission for the five other eastern countries qualifying for G-24 assistance. Allocations of ECU 850 million for 1991 and ECU 1 billion for 1992 are envisaged.

The G-24 countries have only started to consider the extension of multiyear support packages to the east European countries aside from Hungary and Poland.

Food shipments have been limited to Poland and Romania, both of which experienced internal shortages. Some $300-400 million in food has been pledged to Poland for delivery in 1990, which comes in addition to shipments of similar magnitude made in 1989.[519] In the wake of the change in leadership in Romania, millions of dollars of official and private aid (including clothes and medical supplies) were provided by foreign donors. EC ministers of agriculture have approved ECU 40 million ($48 million)[520] and the United States' administration $80 million in food aid.[521]

The importance of *technical assistance* and the *environment* has also been recognized in the aid initiative. Grants to Hungary and Poland for various types of training amount to around $200 million, some of which will be spread out over several years (see table 4.4.1).[522] G-24 governments have committed similar sums for environmental protection.[523]

---

512 *East-west (Fortnightly Bulletin)*, p.4, 27 November 1989.

513 Japan had suspended insurance on trade with Poland in 1984 after the latter had rescheduled its debts.

514 *Financial Times*, 10 January 1990 and 6 March 1990.

515 *Neue Zürcher Zeitung*, 7 March 1990.

516 Address of Mr. J. Delors, President of the European Commission to the European Parliament presenting the Commission's Programme for 1990, Strasbourg, 17 January 1990 (EC Press Release).

517 Mr. P. Schmidhuber, EC Budget Commissioner. The amounts proposed fall within the overall planned budget ceilings negotiated by EC leaders in 1988. *Financial Times*, 22 February 1990.

518 The European Commission has decided on the first financing under this allocation. Fifty million ECU will be spent on plant health products (pesticides) intended to protect the next agricultural harvest in Poland. Applied before the next sowing, this is estimated to safeguard crops worth some ECU 300 million. *Agence Europe*, 22 February 1990. ECU 20 million has been allocated to the Tempus training programme.

519 Only approximate amounts are given here because of lack of information about pledges and the timing of deliveries.

520 Earlier, as a condition for EC food aid, the EC had asked that Romania halt the export of food for the foreseeable future. *Financial Times*, 15 January and 24 January 1990.

521 *Bulletin of the United States Mission*, Geneva, 15 March 1990. The food aid package has two components – a $60 million donation of surplus food and a $20 million 25-year, low-investment loan which allows Romania to purchase food on a concessional basis.

522 EC, *PHARE – Indicative Financial and Aid Commitments and Near Commitments in Favour of Poland and Hungary*, Mimeo, Brussels, updated 12 December 1989.

523 *Ibid*.

(iv) Trade policy measures

Various measures concerning tariff and quantitative restrictions have been taken or are planned to liberalize east-west trade.[524]

Eastern exports already receive *Most Favoured Nation* (MFN) treatment in most western nations.[525] In the United States only Hungary, Poland and Romania have enjoyed these benefits. Hungary was granted MFN status in 1974, but subject to annual review; permanent MFN status was conferred on it in October 1989.[526] Romania renounced these privileges in July 1988, but it is expected that Romania's MFN status will be restored shortly.[527] The United States has undertaken to restore MFN status to Czechoslovakia and to extend this benefit to the Soviet Union, provided that these countries pass legislation liberalizing emigration. Poland regained MFN treatment in the United States, after a suspension during the period 1982 to 1987.

Most EC and certain other G-24 member countries have recently extended the application of their *General System of Preferences* (GSP)[528] régimes to Hungary and Poland as of January 1990.[529] GSP treatment was one of the original requests put forward by Hungary and Poland to the members of the Group of 24. Prior to this only Romania had received these privileges from the west. In the latter case GSP was withdrawn by the United States in July 1988 and by the EC in late October 1989. Both grantors cited the political situation in Romania as their justification for their actions. The EC plans to reinstate GSP treatment for Romania.[530] In the case of the United States, GSP would be restored along with MFN.[531] Bulgaria's access to the EC's GSP is an issue in the current negotiations on a bilateral trade and co-operation agreement.[532]

In November 1989, the EC decided to lift specific (discriminatory) *quantitative restrictions* on Polish and Hungarian goods as of the beginning of 1990. This measure advanced the timetable set in the bilateral trade and economic co-operation agreements which had initially scheduled the removal of these restrictions for 1994 and 1995. However, non-discriminatory quantitative restrictions were to remain in place and products subject to sectoral agreements — textiles, steel and agriculture — were not to be affected. Subsequently, the EC Commission proposed additional liberalization measures:[533] a one-year suspension of remaining quantitative restrictions on such products as passenger cars, footwear and toys; granting significant increases in quotas on imports of textiles above levels agreed within the framework of the Multifibre Arrangement;[534] finalization of a new agreement with the two countries on steel products, which would pave the way for the eventual elimination of the quantitative restrictions applied by a number of EC countries.

In a separate initiative, the European Community agreed to a 15 per cent enlargement in steel imports quotas for Bulgaria, Czechoslovakia, Hungary, Poland and Romania.[535] Earlier, the United States had increased Hungary's steel quota by 30 per cent.[536]

The EC has also agreed to provide more favourable treatment for some of Hungary's and Poland's agricultural products, including in some cases tariff rebates as of 1990.[537]

---

[524] The economic reforms undertaken in certain eastern countries have involved major changes in their systems of foreign trade management. This subject, which is beyond the scope of this review, is addressed in sections 5.2 to 5.5.

[525] Austria extended MFN status to Hungary in 1988 and is expected to grant it to Poland. *Business Eastern Europe*, 30 October 1989. The eastern countries formally grant MFN privileges to their western trade partners. However, in general, tariffs have not played an important, or any economic, role in these countries.

[526] The change in United States legislation was based upon conditions set out in Section 40 of the Trade Act of 1974 (Jackson-Vanik Amendment). These were met when the Hungarian Parliament modified legislation on the transborder movement of individuals.

[527] *Financial Times*, 27 December 1989.

[528] The GSP is a system of tariff preferences accorded by developed economies to assist developing country exports, each industrial country elaborating its own system of preferences. In general, textiles, footwear, agricultural products and some steel products are excluded from the régimes.

[529] Previously only New Zealand had accorded GSP treatment to both countries; and Hungary had also received GSP status from Austria and Japan. Hungary became eligible for United States' GSP treatment in early November 1989. *Népszabadság*, 3 November, 1989. Canada granted GSP to Hungary and Poland from 1 December 1989. For Poland, these preferences apply to all manufactures and semi-finished goods, but a selected list of textile products, footwear and certain electronic goods are excluded; some agricultural goods are also covered. BBC, *Summary of World Broadcasts*, 4 January 1990.

[530] *East-West (Fortnightly Bulletin)*, No.472, 15 January 1990.

[531] *Financial Times*, 22 December, 1989.

[532] *East-West (Fortnightly Bulletin)*, No.472, 15 January 1990.

[533] *East-West (Fortnightly Bulletin)*, 27 November 1989, p.2; *Financial Times*, 24 November 1989.

[534] In a move also affecting textiles, the Swedish Parliament voted to abolish all quantitative restrictions on textiles from Poland as of 1 August 1991. Swedish statement to the 38th Session of the ECE Committee on the Development of Trade, December 1989.

[535] It has been estimated that this measure could result in an increase of 350,000 tons in the EC's steel imports, which is roughly the equivalent of a small EC steelmaker's annual production. The move also increased quotas for Brazil and eliminated those on exports from the Republic of Korea and Venezuela. *International Herald Tribune*, 4 March 1990.

[536] Statement of Secretary of Commerce R. Mosbacher, *Bulletin of the United States Mission*, Geneva, 18 September 1989.

[537] *Agence Europe*, 8 November 1989.

The overall quantitative impact of the trade measures taken by western countries is difficult to assess.[538] Even the estimation of static gains is problematic because eastern exports have often been constrained more by supply factors than by western policies, although this has varied from sector to sector. Quotas have sometimes gone unfilled because sales have failed to be profitable for eastern producers. Hence, the lifting of certain Western restrictions does not automatically imply an increase in eastern exports. However, various studies have shown that MFN tariff treatment has had a strong impact on some eastern exports. In the longer term, the eastern countries could derive large benefits from the dynamic effects of trade liberalization if the reforms succeed in improving the competitiveness of eastern manufactures and result in a more world market-oriented trade policy.

No comprehensive assessment of the impact of the recent trade liberalization measures is presently available. However, a few examples of the estimated benefits to exporters stemming from specific measures may be given. It is estimated that the EC's GSP represents a potential gain of some ECU 100 million for Hungary and Poland combined.[539] Tariffs applied to their industrial goods (presently in the range of 8-22 per cent) will be lifted totally.[540] The Communities' concessions on textiles are estimated to be worth approximately ECU 80 million to Poland and ECU 50 million to Hungary.[541] For Hungary alone, it has been estimated that the EC's concessions on industrial products could yield an additional $60-80 million annually in export revenues.[542] As regards measures taken by the United States, Czechoslovak officials estimate that restoration of MFN by the United States could raise export revenues by some $100-$400 million.[543] The benefits for Romania could be lower because of its smaller share of manufactures in exports. The significance to Hungary of the recent United States move has been largely symbolic, although the reduction of uncertainty stemming from permanent MFN states may encourage additional trade between the two countries in the long term.

The US administration estimates that GSP treatment will result in the elimination of tariffs on some $110 million of Hungarian exports to the United States,[544] raising Hungarian export receipts by some $5-6 million.[545] Poland will face lower tariffs on some 4,100 products currently included in the United States GSP programme.[546]

The recent measures signal an important shift away from post-war western policy of discriminatory treatment of eastern goods. That policy has been justified in the west as a legitimate attempt to compensate for the differences between the trading régimes of the state-trading countries and those whose institutions make possible trade according to GATT rules.

The shifts in western policy have been motivated, first of all, by the desire to provide assistance to the reforming economies. However, as the eastern countries move toward a market system with prices reflecting scarcities and with tariffs and quotas replacing administrative measures as instruments of trade policy, the western case for trade discrimination should disappear completely.[547]

The importance which the west attaches to the support initiative is reflected in its willingness to increase market access even in the traditionally "sensitive" product areas — textiles, steel, agriculture — despite resistance from some governments and interest groups.[548] Concern about the potential influx of eastern goods into western Europe in conjunction with PHARE was already being voiced by labour and industrial groups in 1989.[549]

Steps have also been taken to liberalize the long-standing western system of *export controls*. Instituted after the Second World War to prevent the transfer of strategic technologies, the COCOM system, at the same time, denied countries certain advanced goods required for modernization. Responding to the recent events in the east,[550] the 17 members of COCOM adopted new

---

[538] It should be borne in mind that the list of measures listed here is not exhaustive.

[539] *Neue Zürcher Zeitung*, 13 October 1989.

[540] *Ibid.*

[541] *East-west (Fortnightly Bulletin)*, 27 November 1989, p.2; *Neue Zürcher Zeitung*, 13 October 1989.

[542] *Figyelő*, 4 January 1990.

[543] Direct communication to the ECE secretariat.

[544] Statement of Secretary of Commerce R. Mosbacher, *Bulletin of the United States Mission*, Geneva, 18 September 1989.

[545] *Népszabadság*, 3 November 1989.

[546] *Bulletin of the United States Mission*, Geneva, 5 January 1990.

[547] In the light of the changes in its system of economic management, Hungary has formally asked the EC to be removed from the latter's list of state trading nations, but EC officials felt it was too early (interview with J. Maslen, *Figyelő*, 16 November 1989). This request was repeated at the December 1989 G-24 meeting by Foreign Minister Gy. Horn (*Figyelő*, 4 January 1990).

[548] For example, the EC had initially proposed a higher (18 per cent) increase in steel quotas than was eventually approved, but even the smaller liberalization was resisted by some governments and the steel industry. *International Herald Tribune*, 4 March 1990.

[549] See, for example, *Le Monde Diplomatique*, October 1989.

[550] At various times in the recent past all eastern countries have called for a relaxation of COCOM controls to reflect the new politico-economic situation.

measures to enhance eastern access to western technology for civilian purposes in February 1990.[551]

Their decisions included:

— reduction from 12 to 8 weeks of the time COCOM takes to process the so-called "exceptions" applications required to export goods on its control list. This provision will take place immediately, but is considered the least important part of the accord;

— to shorten by mid-year the list of restricted micro-computers, precision machine tools and telecommunications equipment. It is estimated that these three categories account for roughly one half of the 1,500 applications for exceptions processed by COCOM each year;

— meanwhile, east European countries will be offered special treatment provided that they institute their own system of controls and agree to on-site verfication to prevent transshipment of sensitive goods to third countries;

— the recent agreement was a first step to an even wider review of strategic export controls which will study the possible liberalization of other products on the list (e.g., civil aircraft). The study will be discussed at the next high level meeting at mid-year and serve as a basis for any proposals for a future round of liberalization.

(v) Financial measures in support of Poland and Hungary

Poland and the *IMF* reached agreement at the end of December 1989 on the Polish government's economic stabilization programme (see section 5.2). The arrangement authorizes drawings on a standby credit of up to $723 million over 13 months and triggers a host of other western credits,[552] including $215 million of a $500 million bridge loan from the *Bank of International Settlements* (BIS).[553] The BIS loan, requested by Poland, was assembled by a group of industrialized countries and was finalised at the end of December 1989.

The agreement with the IMF also gives Poland access to of *World Bank* funds. Some $1.0-1.4 billion has been earmarked by the Bank for disbursement in 1990 and $2.5 billion during 1990-1992.[554] Some $360 million became available in early 1990 to fund projects intended to foster industrial exports and help modernize the agricultural sector. A $150 million loan for the modernization of the country's railway rolling stock is under consideration.

Poland's signature of the IMF letter of intent cleared the way for negotiations with official bilateral creditors *(Paris Club)*, the members of which hold some two thirds of the country's $40 billion debt. Agreement among western governments on a new rescheduling was reached unusually quickly in February 1990.[555]

At issue are $9.4 billion in interest and principal, payment of which is to be made over 14 years with an 8-year grace period. This amount includes debt service arrears of $3.4 billion from 1989 and $6 billion in interest and repayments falling due until the end of March 1991 (some $5 billion in 1990 alone).[556] It should be borne in mind that although the rescheduling is a crucial element of Poland's stabilization programme (see below), the country has not serviced this component of its debt for some years. Consequently, the formal rescheduling implies no *de facto* change in Poland's actual servicing of financial obligations *vis-à-vis* Paris Club members.

At the completion of the Paris Club accord, member governments stressed that they expected commercial banks (*London Club*) to make an equally exceptional gesture toward Poland in their forthcoming negotiations.[557]

If the commercial banks were to postpone all of Poland's interest payments in 1990 — interest payments on commercial debt have been running some $1 billion annually — Poland would effectively realize a $1 billion inflow on capital account and enjoy a substantial loosening of its balance of payment constraint. In an earlier accord with Poland, bank creditors agreed to reschedule or roll over into a revolving trade credit facility about $200 of principal falling due in 1989-1990. Therefore it is possible that Poland will not face any

---

[551] *International Herald Tribune*, 17 February 1990 and *Financial Times*, 17 February 1990 and 6 March 1990.

[552] *Financial Times*, 27 December 1989, and IMF *Press Release*, No.90/6.

[553] Such credits are sometimes used to bridge the gap between an agreement with the IMF and the actual disbursement of IMF and World Bank funds, which are in turn used to repay the BIS.

[554] *Financial Times*, 24 January and 23 February 1990.

[555] See comments of Mr. Jean-Claude Trichet, Chairman of the Paris Club, as reported in the *International Herald Tribune*, 17-18 February 1990. The agreement is also considered exceptional because it involves the largest sum yet rescheduled by the Paris Club. This was motivated by a consensus on the importance of helping Poland as much as possible during a time of enormous political and economic change.

[556] The accord comes close to meeting Poland's initial request for complete relief from its Paris Club obligations to the end of 1992. Poland has also requested a moratorium on repayments of principal coming due over the next decade.

[557] *International Herald Tribune*, 10 February 1990. It should be noted that commercial banks have never agreed to include in a formal rescheduling accord the postponement of all interest payments as the Paris Club has done. In October 1989, the Polish authorities announced a unilateral decision to pay commercial banks only 15 per cent of interest payments on medium- and long-term obligations due in the final quarter of 1989. Poland undertook to make the overdue payments of about $150 million in the first half of 1990. Economist Intelligence Unit, *Poland*. No.4, 1989.

debt service obligations at all (i.e., neither commercial nor official) in 1990.[558]

The $1 billion *Stabilization Fund*, intended to provide Poland with a supplemental line of reserves to support its new foreign exchange régime was completed at the end of December 1989. The régime is a key element of the country's market-oriented reform and includes, as of the beginning of the year, internal zloty convertibility for most current-account transactions. Under the new system exporters must sell all of their export earnings to the state banks for zlotys, but have the right to repurchase foreign exchange as needed, at a uniform exchange rate. The fund, of which $300 million was made available to Poland immediately, will allow the authorities to intervene in the market to stabilize the currency at the new level of 9,500 zloty per US dollar.[559]

Participants extending low cost loans to the fund include Austria ($20 million), Canada ($25 million), the Federal Republic of Germany ($250 million), Japan ($150 million), France, Italy and the United Kingdom ($100m each), Portugal ($5 million), Spain ($20 million) Switzerland ($30 million) and the United States (a $200 million grant), and Turkey, ($0.75 million). The Federal Reserve Bank of New York is serving as administrator of the fund.[560]

Group of 24 governments and international financial institutions have committed some $6.3 billion in new credit facilities and grants to Poland (see table 4.4.1).[561] This includes some $1.4 billion worth of food deliveries, grants and miscellaneous assistance; bilateral credits of $0.9 billion and various multilateral facilities amounting to $4.1 billion. About $3 billion will be available to Poland in 1990, chiefly to fund specific programmes or projects. In addition, debt relief of some $5-6 billion has been decided upon for 1990. Altogether this represents a potential net inflow of resources of $8-9 billion in the current year, nearly all of which could be debt creating.

Several initiatives are under way which will reduce or hold out the possibility of reducing Poland's convertible currency debt. The Federal Republic of Germany cancelled DM 760 million in arrears on a DM 1 billion loan made in 1975. Future payments on this loan amounting to DM 570 million are to be converted into zlotys for financing German/Polish projects. Debt-equity swaps are also in store. For example, in Austria, plans have been announced to create an East-West Fund, which is to act as a bank and provide risk insurance for Austrian firms prepared to get involved in debt-equity swaps in eastern Europe. The undertaking concerns Poland, whose obligations to Austria amount to over 35 billion schillings ($2.9 billion).[562] The Polish authorities have requested extension of the Brady Plan to Poland, with the aim of obtaining a reduction in the country's commercial debt.

Hungary has been putting a stabilization programme into place (see section 5.3) which received formal approval from the *IMF* on 14 March. The Agreement will release a new a one-year SDR 159 million ($208 million) standby credit. SDR 32 million can be drawn immediately, an equivalent amount in end-May and the remaining three tranches in quarterly instalments.[563] However, owing an unscheduled repayment of SDR 150 million[564] and another SDR 90 million in maturities falling due, Hungary will be a net *creditor vis-à-vis* the IMF in 1990. Nevertheless, the agreement is crucial for a number of reasons, including gaining access to World Bank, various bilateral and other financing which contains cross-conditionality clauses. These funds are important if Hungary is to maintain solvency in a period of high-scheduled debt repayments.

In an exceptional gesture toward a third country, the *EC Commission* has proposed granting an $1 billion loan to Hungary to "support its structural development".[565] The loan will be available for five years in three tranches, the first of which would become available in April 1990. The credit is subject to three conditions: that agreement be reached with the IMF, that the loan constitute additional funds rather than substitute for commercial credits, and that economic reforms be actively pursued. The latter should involve progress in restructuring, elimination of monopolies and the gradual elimination of subsidies. Progress in these areas is a condition for the disbursement of the second and third tranches.

Financial commitments of G-24 governments and international financial institutions to Hungary total $4.8 billion (table 4.4.1). Of this amount, some $1.9 billion is bilateral credit lines and the balance multilateral facilities. In 1990, some $1.7 billion will become available, mostly in support of specific projects and World Bank programmes (table 4.4.2) and will complement

---

558 The Polish authorities have also requested a moratorium to 1 January 1993 on interest payments and the suspension of capital repayments on commercial debt coming due in this decade. *Financial Times*, 16 December, 1989.

559 This compares with a 1989 average of 1,440 zloty per dollar and and end-December level of 6,600 zloty per dollar.

560 *Bulletin of the United States Mission*, Geneva, 4 January, 1990; *Agence Europe*, 14 December 1989.

561 This excludes the $1 billion earmarked for the Stabilization Fund.

562 *Heti Világgazdaság*, 7 December 1989.

563 Announced by Mr. A. Cseres, an official of the National Bank of Hungary. (*Heti Világgazdaság*, 10 March 1990).

564 *Ibid*. The repayment was made according to IMF rules governing faulty or false reporting (see the comments on Hungary's debt in section 4.3), in which case the borrower is obliged to return credits obtained during the preceding two years. The repayment was a condition for access to the new standby credit.

565 *Agence Europe*, 7 December 1989; *Financial Times*, 7 December 1989; and *Heti Világgazdaság*, 23 December 1989; Hungary had requested the loan in September 1989.

funds which Hungary has obtained in the international credit markets.

G-24 governments have also made credit and investment guarantees available to western enterprises as incentives to make direct investments in Hungary and Poland (table 4.4.1). Coverage amounts to $1.2 billion for Hungary and $3.8 billion for Poland.[566]

(vi) Preliminary assessment of the international initiative

A very preliminary assessment of the international initiative as applied so far to Hungary and Poland may be useful since the same or a similar approach will be extended to other eastern countries interested in participating in the programme. Also, beyond aiding the reforms, the initiative is an instrument for enhancing east-west economic integration and eastern economic development and should be examined from those perspectives.

The G-24 action plan was initially conceived to provide support for the transformation of the Hungarian and Polish economies to a market system. As other parts of this *Survey* clearly demonstrate, this is an extremely complex undertaking which involves several interrelated tasks: economic stabilization, restructuring, closing income gaps between east and west, and the integration of the east into the world economy. The implications of the initiative for each of the tasks are commented upon briefly below.

The initiatives for Hungary and Poland give priority to the re-establishment of *macro-economic equilibrium*. As discussed in chapter 3, these countries have experienced major imbalances which have been reflected in accelerating inflation, growing budget deficits, and deteriorating current account balances. With the assistance of the IMF, both countries have implemented economic stabilization programmes which also contain measures to reinforce the process of economic reform[567] and promote structural adjustment. IMF approval of the austerity programmes is a condition not only for the release of the accompanying standby credits, but also activates a host of other credit facilities. This cross-conditionality had raised the stakes to Hungary and Poland of designing acceptable stabilization packages. In both cases, it appears that the funds to be made available through the initiative are adequate to meet the country's financing needs during this year.

A number of international financial operations have been closely linked with and are crucial to the success of the stabilization programmes. At Poland's request, members of the G-24 established the $1 billion currency

TABLE 4.4.2

Value of financial assistance to become available to Poland and Hungary, by source and year of availability
(Million US dollars)

	Poland	Hungary
Relief measures proposed for 1990		
Food deliveries a	300	-
Other grants, including technical assistance	300	40
Sub-total	600	40
New credits:		
IMF medium-term programme	723	166
World Bank programme	1 000	330
IFC	27	-
From G-24 governments	300	600
EEC banks and funds	300	600
Sub-total	2 350	1 696
Debt relief measures 1990:		
Paris Club (official creditors)	5 000	-
London Club (commercial banks)	100-1 200	-
Medium-term assistance for 1991-1992		
Other grants, including technical assistance	400	50
New credits:		
From G-24 governments	500	1 300
ECE banks and funds	500	1 000
IMF medium-term programme	..	..
World Bank programmes	1 500	660
Sub-total	2 500	2 690
Memorandum item:		
Credit and investment guarantees b	3 811	1 226
Federal Republic of Germany debt forgiveness	800	..
Contributions to stabilization funds c	1 100	-
BIS bridge-loan	500	..

Source: As for table 4.4.1.

a Partly delivered already in 1989.
b Provided by western governments to western companies investing in Poland and Hungary.
c Provided in the form of grants or loans at concessional rates by the G-24 governments.

stabilization fund, which has been available to support the Polish currency after the introduction of internal convertibility. The rescheduling of Poland's Paris Club obligations, some debt relief from the London Club of commercial creditors and new bilateral credits will substantially loosen Poland's payments constraint and reduce the pressure of interest payments on the domestic budget. This additional financing will be necessary in the event that Poland's production and exports falter over an extended period and additional imports are required. In Hungary's case, new multilateral facilities and bilateral credits from G-24 members and normal commercial borrowing should ensure sufficient financing for the country's anticipated current account deficit and heavy amortization schedule (see section 4.6). The west has also taken steps to liberalize its markets to increase the potential export earnings of both countries.

The discussion so far shows that a country-by-country approach has been adopted. The EC, in its capacity as the G-24 co-ordinator, has stated that this will also apply to other eastern countries seeking sup-

---

[566] It appears that so far little of the DM 2.5 billion ($1.6 billion) coverage offered by the Government of the Federal Republic of Germany (Hermes) last year to encourage German firms to investment in Poland has been used.

[567] These reform measures are important, but have not always been a part of stabilization programmes. For example the adjustment undertaken by Romania in the 1980s relied entirely on the exercise of traditional central planning techniques. Such an approach may successfully achieve short-term macro-economic adjustment, but without the accompanying change in the economic mechanism needed to improve the longer-term allocation of resources. See M. Lavigne, *Eastern European Countries and the IMF*. Paper prepared for the IEA Conference on East-West Economic Relations in the Changing Global Environment, Budapest-Vienna, 8-12 October 1984.

port.[568] A differentiated strategy would seem appropriate given the vastly different situations prevailing in the eastern countries. Major differences in foreign indebtedness are perhaps the most important in this regard. Owing to their high debt levels, only Poland and Hungary have sought IMF standby agreements and only Poland has needed to deal with the London and Paris Clubs. Bulgaria may eventually find itself in a similar position. Most other eastern countries retain access to international multilateral bank financing. This and the large differences in income levels are likely to be taken into account by the G-24 countries to determine the relative amounts and types of aid.

From the very beginning, G-24 governments have made their assistance conditional upon the introduction of fundamental *economic reforms*, a stance which has been in agreement with IMF and World Bank approaches. Economic reform is largely an internal undertaking, but it can be supported with finance and technical assistance. It has been argued in chapter 1 that given the particular challenges facing reforming eastern economies — rebuilding the institutions and training economic agents essential to the functioning of a market economy — will require considerable technical assistance which, at this stage, may be more important than large infusions of funds. The eastern countries have already received advice on designing and implementing reforms from various sources, including, in certain cases, the international economic organizations. The need for various types of technical assistance is clearly recognized in the G-24 programme and has been promised by virtually all western participating countries. Overall, however, it appears that a more systematic and comprehensive approach is required (see chapter 1) and that the financial commitments made so far may fall far short of the task at hand. G-24 commitments to Hungary and Poland for this purpose appear to amount to only about $200 million and it is not clear whether the training covers the most important areas.[569] It also appears that little formal assistance has been forthcoming for the re-establishment of commercial, financial and legal institutions.

The combination of the reforms, machinery and equipment purchased using new credit facilities and inflows of foreign direct investment should spur the pace of modernization and *restructuring*. The IMF approved programmes, accompanied by standby credits, already contain some measures aimed at promoting these objectives. However, by and large, restructuring is a longer-term process which, in addition to the countries' own resources, will be supported by the World Bank, EIB, ECSC, EBRD and bilateral credit facilities. As noted above, these are largely linked to specific industrial projects intended to contribute to enterprise growth, new infrastructure, energy savings and new export capacity.

Foreign direct investment is seen as a key instrument for increasing output, introducing new product lines, and creating a more competitive domestic market. All eastern countries have passed legislation allowing joint ventures, in most cases permitting majority foreign ownership. Western governments have also sought to promote western enterprise investment in the east by providing various credit and investment guarantees, offering services to facilitate the establishment of joint ventures and concluding bilateral investment protection treaties. The complementary initiatives to upgrade eastern telecommunications and transport infrastructure are also necessary to improve the attractiveness of the eastern countries as domiciles for foreign investment. Similarly, the recent trade concessions made by the western countries may serve as an important incentive for foreign investments in certain products which are very sensitive to the degree of market access.

Much of the equipment required for modernization and restructuring is available chiefly in the west where it is often subject to COCOM controls. With a view toward meeting eastern needs in these areas, some relaxation of the restrictions is envisaged.

Raising *standards of living* in the eastern countries — for humanitarian and strategic reasons alike — is a general policy objective. Eastern and western governments both recognize that the long-term stability in Europe may hinge upon their success in narrowing the income gaps. Successful reforms would put these economies on higher growth paths, but it would still take some time for them to approach western income levels. The process could be accelerated with the injection of additional foreign resources, provided that the reforms increase the absorptive capacity of the economies.

Foreign direct investment is expected to play a role in this regard, but at this time, inflows large enough to have a perceptible impact on economic growth in the next few years are foreseen only for the German Democratic Republic. Grants could also be very important, but western governments have only started to debate long-term financial commitments to eastern Europe. For example, the EC President has mentioned support levels proportional to EC spending in its depressed regions — i.e., some ECU 19 billion a year for the next 5-10 years. But much lower allocations — some ECU 1 billion per year during 1991-1992 have been proposed by the Budget Commissioner, as noted. Some countries, of course, have scope for further borrowing from a variety of sources and all are eventually expected to be eligible for official multilateral credits.

Improving the environment would also raise the standard of living. However, huge investments, far beyond the present economic capacity of the eastern countries, will also be required. The G-24 countries have individually proposed funds for this purpose — perhaps some $200 million — so far only for Hungary and Poland. Given the scale of the problem, this level of resources would appear insufficient, even if some of

---

568 Statement of Commissioner Andriessen, as reported in *Agence Europe*, 15-16 January 1990, p.5. The differentiated approach is, of course, also reflected in the absence of a food programme for Hungary since food shortages have not been a problem.

569 EC, *PHARE — Indicative Financial and Aid Commitments ...*, op.cit.

the project lending under consideration has a favourable environmental impact (e.g., energy savings).

The international initiative also contains numerous measures to foster the *integration* of the eastern countries into the world economy. It is of the utmost importance that they increase specialization and exploitation of scale economies if their foreign sectors are to function as engines of economic growth. The dismantlement of many discriminatory trade obstacles by the west, whatever their original justification, demonstrates a long-term commitment to improve trade ties. Other trade promoting measures — direct investment, financial support for export-oriented projects, relaxation of controls on technology, investment in infrastructure, various technical assistance — should also foster integration.

In general, it appears that trade with the west would be favoured by these developments. Aside from immediately boosting the eastern countries' potential export revenues, the liberalization of western trade should reorient some eastern trade to the convertible currency area. Foreign enterprises will need to export there to earn profits which can be repatriated. The countries themselves are under pressure to redirect their trade in order to service their hard currency obligations.

While eastern integration into the world economy should be fostered,[570] it is also worth considering the potential benefits of a broader integration strategy in which the rejuvenation of trade between reforming eastern economies would be undertaken *in parallel*. Special arrangements would be required in which the west could play some role. The conditions and arguments for creating a trade area of reforming economies supported by a payments union are examined in chapters 1 and 3.

This assessment suggests that even though the international initiative is in its entirety a loosely co-ordinated effort involving numerous governments and international and private institutions, a clear strategy toward the east is emerging. To some extent this may simply be the outcome of broad agreement on certain key issues among the Group of 24 on the one hand and between the G-24 and the reforming eastern countries on the other: the need for profound economic reform and political liberalization; the necessity to move towards a marketization of the economies; the importance of private enterprise (although opinions vary on the dimensions) and a role for foreign direct investment; and recognition of the interdependence of benefits from commercial enterprises and modern infrastructure.

Policy discussions indicate that there is also a consensus in the west on avoiding open-ended lending to the east, as occurred in the 1970s. The present high debt levels of some eastern countries are a constant reminder that in the past they often borrowed to avoid necessary economic adjustments to external shocks, or to boost domestic consumption. Even when credits went to finance western machinery and equipment, this was generally poorly absorbed.[571] In short, eastern borrowers viewed credits as a substitute for economic reform rather than an instrument to advance it.

Given these experiences, it is not surprising that the conditions being attached to new credit facilities and the types of assistance being offered by the G-24 essentially aim to channel foreign resources into potentially productive activities and to ensure that these projects come to fruition. The economic reforms, the IMF-approved stabilization programmes and the associated restructuring initiatives are all intended to improve macro-economic efficiency. Importantly, G-24 governments have specifically linked the disbursement of EIB, ECSC, EBRD and most new bilateral credit lines (and, in the case of Poland, access to the stabilization fund) to the conclusion of agreements with the IMF. The bilateral and multilateral credit facilities are largely project-oriented and intended to improve micro-economic efficiency.[572] In most cases, the projects are to be subject to expert review and monitoring including those financed from bilateral sources. The encouragement of foreign direct investment is based upon the premise that investing enterprises will commit themselves only to profitable activities. Finally, the range of technical assistance being offered, in particular the training of economic agents in market know-how and skills, is also intended to promote an efficient use of resources.

The commitments for financial support made so far all address critical needs, but the bulk is debt-creating. Poland's debt is already excessive. Rescheduling repayments and interest obligations will increase debt further without itself creating any increase in export capacity. Hungary's overall debt burden is high, the share of interest payments in exports of goods and services is rising and the country will be faced with a heavy repayment schedule in the first half of the 1990s. The financial burden will become even greater unless the aid and the reforms stimulated strong export growth. The prospective IMF programmes and much of the new project-oriented financial support is intended to accomplish precisely that. However, the extent to which export growth can be achieved will depend, among other things, on the changing economic environment in which the new investments will function.

---

[570] It is useful to recall that before and immediately after the Second World War the degree of integration between the eastern and western countries was considerably higher than it is today. See "Changing intensity of east-west trade, 1955-1984", Economic Commission for Europe, *Economic Bulletin for Europe*, vol.37, No.4, Pergamon Press for the United Nations, December 1985, chapter 3.

[571] The west's concern about the east's absorptive capacity was recently demonstrated in the EC Parliament when questions arose whether the ECU 1 billion per year being sought for eastern Europe was excessive. *Financial Times*, 22 February 1990.

[572] Only a small proportion of the promised credits are untied — i.e., available without restriction for general balance of payments support.

4.5 SOME IMPLICATIONS OF A GERMAN MONETARY UNION

Among the consequences of the developments in eastern Europe in recent months, few issues have attracted as much attention as that of the unification of the two Germanies. While the completion of that process is still a matter for the future, the prospect of a single German state has given urgency to a number of concerns.

The most immediate issue is how to stem the tide of emigrants from the German Democratic Republic into the Federal Republic of Germany, where they acquire automatic access to various social welfare entitlements, as well as much better paying jobs for the skilled and able-bodied. In spite of the prospect of unification, the flow of migrants into the Federal Republic has in fact risen and is continuing at the time of writing this *Survey*. The resulting demands on the resources (housing, education, hospitals, medical care, other social welfare entitlements and so on) of the Federal Republic is placing considerable strain on the capacity of social and other services. It may also have started to place pressure on wages.

Another issue is how to merge the two economies, a matter that will give rise to a range of intricate problems. Some are social and political, but there is also a substantial number of technical economic issues. It has been agreed that the two Germanies will settle the terms (including the form, pace, timeframes and other conditions) of unification themselves, although in the context of a four-power arrangement.

There has been widespread apprehension about the impact of such an economic and monetary union. Many observers have cautioned against creating such a union before the introduction of far-reaching economic reforms in the German Democratic Republic. These reforms will eventually need to be made, if not through policy design, then through the operation of market forces. But in any case it is likely that monetary and economic unification will be pursued in tandem with radical changes in the economic structure of the German Democratic Republic.

It is impossible to state with any degree of precision what the various economic effects may be in the two Germanies and indeed in the two integration groupings to which they belong until the concrete details of the union have been negotiated. However, because the proposed unification essentially resembles the rapid formation of a customs union, the various effects and their signs, although not their precise magnitudes, can be sorted out. These observations are, of course, separate from the question of whether economic and monetary union will succeed in stemming the flow of immigrants into the Federal Republic.

Basically two kinds of effect are bound to occur. In the medium to long term, the unification of Germany is bound to lead to substantial growth of incomes in the eastern part as it catches up with the high productivity levels of the west. Because consumption of manufactured goods has been greatly restricted, the income elasticity of demand for them is likely to be high. Both effects are similar to the process observed in the post-war period as Germany and Japan caught up with the rest of western Europe and the United States.

High income growth in the eastern part of a united Germany will have spillover effects that will benefit, in particular trading partners in the European Community. Provided the CMEA countries can restructure their economies, they would also be well placed to benefit. The enlarged pool of labour resources may hold back wage demands in Germany, thereby further increasing Germany's competitive edge in world markets. Unification may also lead to significant changes in the allocation of world savings, if there is a large movement of capital from the western to the eastern part of Germany.

The dynamic economic effects of German unification are likely to be significantly positive because there are sizeable resources inside Germany that can be reallocated to more productive uses under the impulse of market forces. These effects are likely, on balance, to be trade-creating, thus generating income growth also outside the preferential trade area. Because of Germany's position in the European Communities, and also its pre-eminent role in the trade of the the EFTA countries, the longer-term economic benefits for Europe can be expected to be quite favourable.

All these conjectures are, of course, contingent on the market economy taking root in the eastern part of Germany so as to let these forces emerge and exert their impact on resource allocation. There is, however, a number of short-term effects to be evaluated beforehand. These can be assessed from the points of view of each of the two Germanies and of the two integration groupings to which these countries now belong. There may also be a significant impact of these changes on other countries, developed as well as developing.

The largest impact for other developed countries will be through the exchange rate, interest rates and capital flows. Inasmuch as the Federal Republic's surplus on current account in 1989 amounted to almost $53 billion, any substantial diversion to "domestic" use of that surplus would exert pressure on the financing of the US current account and budget deficit, imbalances that the United States has so far been able to support without severely restricting economic activity.

As regards the developing countries, a significant impact will be on foreign direct investment from the Federal Republic. Rather than moving new investments into, say, the NIEs, German transnationals may opt for developing the eastern part of Germany. Installations in place in the developing countries will of course not be scrapped and may even be expanded to the most efficient scale.

Economic and monetary union by definition means that there will be only one currency, the Deutschmark. Moreover, that currency must be controlled by a single monetary authority, namely the Bundesbank. The German Democratic Republic will therefore lose its autonomy over the money supply and monetary policy in the widest sense. This will severely curtail the economic autonomy of the country.

A uniform monetary policy poses the question of how the financial institutions in the German Democratic Republic can be brought under the institutional and instrumental umbrella of the Bundesbank. It may be assumed that the Bundesbank will want to avoid having to support expansion of the money supply in order to finance public and corporate deficits in the east. To assure this in practice and through the institutions at hand, there will be an urgent need for technical training, since the banking system in the German Democratic Republic has been catering to different needs and through the use of very different instruments from those prevailing in the Federal Republic.

More important in the short run will be the rate of conversion between the *Mark der deutschen Notenbank* and the *deutsche Mark*. Regarding wealth effects in the German Democratic Republic, the size of the stock of savings and of claims on future monetary transfers, such as pensions, will be determined by the conversion rate at which the Federal Republic takes over these state liabilities. There does not have to be a unique conversion rate: there could well be differential rates for wages, savings, pensions, companies' assets and debts and so on.

Prices of goods and services, including wages, in the German Democratic Republic would have to be aligned with those of the Federal Republic. Nominal wages may in fact have to be brought close to parity with wage levels in the western part, adjusted for differences in productivity levels. This poses numerous problems, given the large disparities in relative prices and levels of productivity between the two Germanies. Clearly, if the real wage in one part of the country diverges from the real wage in the other part by more than the perceived cost of moving, migration will not be halted. But how large the actual differential should be is still unclear. On the other hand, if real wages in the eastern part were to increase rapidly, indigenous firms would quickly go bankrupt and considerable unemployment could result. This in turn would call for substantial transfers from the Federal Republic.

Wealth held in real goods (houses, land, equipment) is likely to appreciate significantly after the above price changes have occurred. There may well be a case for a special wealth tax for some layers of society to offset the adverse consequences of unification sustained by the majority of people.

Currency conversion for the Federal Republic requires the issuance of money. Private households and firms in the eastern part will have to be given access to transactions balances immediately, and the problem for the Bundesbank is how to avoid an excessive growth in the money supply.[573] But a judicious combination of immediate encashment of liquid assets with claims on future resources could substantially mitigate any potentially adverse effects. A variable exchange rate could be used to postpone the conversion of savings balances into Deutschmarks.

There are also likely to be implications for the Federal Republic's budget. Supplementary appropriations in support of the German Democratic Republic have already been requested and approved. Much more may be required if the Federal Republic feels impelled to enact a favourable exchange rate and to transfer immediately substantial subsidies to the eastern part. Although private capital may be attracted eastwards by comparatively low real wages, some income transfers from the west may still be necessary to check emigration from the east. The consequent budget deficits which, in the short-run, could significantly exceed the currently planned budget deficit of the central government for 1990 (DM 34.5 billion, or 1.5. per cent of GNP), could be financed through increased debt, higher taxes or by increasing the money supply. The latter would be inflationary and lower the exchange rate. The former is likely to raise interest rates, which in turn may lead to some repatriation of German assets held abroad. Failing that, it will tend to depress levels of economic activity.

A rapid exchange of liquid assets at a generous conversion rate is bound to have implications, through inflation, interest and exchange rate movements, for the position of the Deutschmark in the EMS. Inasmuch as the German currency has been the *de facto* anchor of the EMS, its weakening could set the EMS adrift, although that eventuality would seem rather remote at this stage. On the other hand, anti-inflation policy in Germany may impose greater fiscal and monetary restraint in the rest of Europe and elsewhere than would be required if the technical aspects of unification were settled on purely economic grounds.

Preoccupation with German unification and the potential disturbances that may ensue from putting together economic and monetary union in a very rapid manner could conceivably delay the completion of Europe's internal market. That would be a set-back not only for western Europe but also for the further

---

[573] The whole known money supply of the eastern part converted at a rate of 1-to-1 amounts to 14 per cent of the entire money supply (M3) of the Federal Republic in 1989. See also section 2.1 above.

integration of eastern Europe into the integrated western economy, a priority of the most radically reforming eastern European countries.

Finally, inasmuch as the German Democratic Republic has been a very important partner in the CMEA, German economic and monetary union is bound to have a major impact on that grouping as well (see section 3.4).

Regarding trade, the implicit preferences extended to the CMEA would disappear as the commercial régime in the eastern part of Germany would have to be abolished and replaced by the commercial policy of the Federal Republic. Most CMEA countries have MFN status in the Federal Republic, but their traditional exports to the eastern part of Germany consist of foodstuffs and agricultural products, as well as manufactured products (clothing, textiles, footwear, metals, chemicals and so on), imports of which into the European Communities are restricted.

It may also be noted that a considerable number of foreign workers, largely from the Asian CMEA countries, are employed in the German Democratic Republic on a normal basis (as opposed to those on training programmes). The rise of unemployment, which is likely to be a short-run consequence of German unification, would probably affect these workers first in any restructuring programme.

For trade relationships with the CMEA, the monetary effects of German unification are very serious: not so much because of the replacement of transferable rouble prices by world market prices (this is scheduled to occur in CMEA in any case) but because of the need for payments in convertible currency. Given the tight external payments situation of most CMEA countries, there is no scope for placing eastern Europe's trade with the German Democratic Republic on a convertible currency basis. Inasmuch as the bulk of Soviet exports to the German Democratic Republic consist of goods that can be easily marketed at prevailing world prices, the problem of maintaining Soviet trade with the eastern part of Germany is not as acute as it is for eastern Europe. In the short run, unification will lead to a shrinkage in trade and will complicate the supply of spare parts and components for much of eastern Europe's stock of machinery and equipment.

Under the circumstances, it might be useful to devise means whereby the trade of the German Democratic Republic with the CMEA countries could be maintained through some kind of clearing arrangement. The CMEA countries, whose capital stock is dependent on the industrial output of the eastern part of Germany, would obviously benefit. But Germany as a whole could also gain from an adaptation of the commercial and technical links which have been developed over more than forty years by the German Democratic Republic in the context of the CMEA. The creation of a Central European Payments Union (see section 3.4) could meet many of these concerns, at least for the more reform-oriented members of CMEA.

4.6 PROSPECTS

The historic process of political and economic transformation embarked upon by eastern countries injects a larger than usual element of uncertainty into the prospects for east-west trade and finance. The process will vary considerably in terms of depth and speed. Poland and Hungary have advanced furthest in this respect (see chapter 5); in other countries key systematic changes will be undertaken only after the scheduled elections.

Although one of the aims of the reforms is to establish the basis for *export growth*, in the immediate future they may have the opposite effect. The transition from centrally planned to market-co-ordinated systems before all of the legislation, institutions and human capital necessary for the functioning of market economies are firmly in place poses risks. Indeed, output has already faltered in some countries and several anticipate recessions in the current year. Even those countries which manage some increase in output will, at least for some years, continue to be confronted with the factors which have traditionally held back eastern exports — poor commodity structure, declining competitiveness of manufactures and capacity constraints.

Western demand for eastern goods is expected to remain buoyant in 1990. Prospects are for some easing of growth in the developed market economies, perhaps to somewhat less than 3 per cent (see chapter 2). In western Europe, the largest western market for eastern goods, some deceleration is also foreseen, to a growth rate of about 2¾ per cent. During the past few years, imports have grown 2-3 times faster than output in this market. Such a relatively rapid expansion of western import demand can be expected to continue, providing additional market opportunities for eastern exporters. For Hungary and Poland, a further boost should result from the liberalization of western trade régimes as of the beginning of 1990 (see section 4.4). Later in the year, exports from Czechoslovakia should receive MFN treatment from the United States.

East European capacity to export to the west may also be affected by recent developments in intra-CMEA trade. One of these stems from the recent improvement in eastern Europe's terms of trade *vis-à-vis* the Soviet Union. In order to curtail undesired increases in the resulting rouble-trade surpluses, some east European countries have taken measures to reduce exports to the Soviet Union.[574] In principle, this could pave the way for diverting exports to convertible currency markets. In practice there is only limited scope for such a shift in the short run because most east European goods produced for intra-eastern trade are not easily sellable in the west. In these circumstances, the implications for certain industries oriented to the rouble market are unfavourable. Yet the very pressure on enterprises generated by declining orders should reinforce their efforts to modify and shift their manufactures to world markets.

With the tightening of Soviet fuel and raw material supplies, deliveries to at least some east European countries have fallen behind schedule.[575] This development has accentuated trade imbalances and increased pressure for the types of adjustments described above,[576] including boosting exports to the west. On the other hand, shortfalls of Soviet crude may reduce east European deliveries of petroleum products to the convertible currency area. To compensate, these countries may choose to purchase Middle Eastern crude for refining.[577] However, unless obtained on a barter basis, this would entail additional expenditures of convertible currency. Regardless of whether the east European countries choose to reduce petroleum product exports to the west or to maintain them by refining crude imported from the Middle East, their convertible currency trade accounts will come under pressure.[578]

---

[574] Eastern countries aim to avoid such surpluses which, because of their inconvertibility, can be considered interest-free credits to the partner in deficit. See chapter 3 above and "Note on adjustment in intra-eastern trade and its implications for east-west trade", in United Nations Economic Commission for Europe, *Economic Survey of Europe in 1988-1989*, New York, 1989, section 4(vi). Reduction of the rouble surplus is also an objective in the agreement concluded by Hungary with the IMF.

[575] According to east European officials, Soviet deliveries of oil and gas to Bulgaria, Czechoslovakia, Hungary and Poland had fallen sharply behind schedule in early 1990, at least in part because of supply difficulties in early 1990. In some cases the Soviet Union has promised to make up the shortfalls later in the year. *International Herald Tribune*, 20-21 January 1990, and *Financial Times*, 25 January 1990 and 14 February 1990. On the other hand, Soviet officials complain of shortfalls in east European deliveries of contracted consumer goods. They are not optimistic that these will be made up later in the year: "The east European countries have simply lost interest in our market.". Interview with Y. Kostrov, Director-General of the Raznoeksport Foreign Trade Association, in *Pravitel'stvennyi vestnik*, No.7, February 1990.

[576] Hungary's response has been to suspend all licences for exports denominated in roubles. Poland was considering a similar move, at least for some engineering and electronics items. *Financial Times*, 31 January 1990.

[577] For example, it has been announced that Hungary intends to import 200,000-250,000 tons of crude and 30,000 tons of petroleum products from convertible currency markets in January for home consumption. BBC, *Summary of World Broadcasts*, EE/W0110 A/8, 11 January 1990.

[578] Clearly, these potential losses should be distinguished from probable losses in east European terms of trade if the CMEA shifts to a system of world market prices and clearing in convertible currencies.

Nearly all *east European* countries expect their *imports* to increase in 1990. Moreover, governments will presumably be under pressure from the population and enterprises to ease import constraints, and this may be difficult for the new régimes to resist. The same would apply to convertible currency allocations for travel. Since the availability of new credits appears to be linked chiefly to specific projects, machinery and equipment purchases may be particularly buoyant, but this will depend on the way the countries allocate the total of convertible currency funds at their disposal. In the Soviet Union, balance-of-payments may force a curtailment of import growth in 1990, but its trade balance with the west will probably remain in deficit.

Oil prices are expected to soften further in the second quarter of the year despite pledges by OPEC ministers to adhere better to production quotas. An oil price in the range of $17-18 per barrel, as is now foreseen for the whole of 1990, would represent no change from 1989. However, it should be borne in mind that the probability of oil price increases is rising, the result of growing world demand and the increasing role of OPEC supply at the margin. *Cereals* prices have softened, although, they also remain high. The recent depreciation of the US dollar, together with rising domestic prices in western Europe, imply increases of several percentage points in the nominal dollar prices of traded manufactures. Overall, these price movements would imply little change, perhaps some loss, in east European and the Soviet Union *terms of trade* with the west.

Persistence of the high *interest rates* experienced in early 1990, including on the non-dollar currencies in which the eastern countries have traditionally maintained a large share of their external debt, will continue to place pressure on eastern current accounts. A percentage point increase in the average rate of interest raises eastern Europe's *net interest* obligations by nearly $1 billion, which, it might be noted, offsets the benefits of the support measures discussed above.

Overall, it appears likely that the east will run another comparatively large *current-account* deficit in 1990. A number of highly indebted eastern countries will need to finance balance of payments deficits and repayments of debt coming due in 1990, in Poland's case without any recourse to commercial bank credits. This eventuality had been anticipated in the international support initiative (see section 4.4). Financial elements of that programme, together with the prospective membership of several eastern countries in multilateral financial institutions, will make major new sources of finance accessible.

All east European countries will have access to European Bank for Reconstruction and Development (EBRD) credits, although perhaps not before 1991, and European Investment Bank (EIB) credits should be accessible to Hungary and Poland by mid-year. Official export credits are expected to remain available[579] and in several cases will serve as key sources of new finance. The IMF and World Bank plan to step up lending to eastern Europe. Both institutions are already creditors to Hungary and have recently started to lend to Poland. It is anticipated that relations with Romania, already a member, will be normalized. Czechoslovakia and Bulgaria are in different stages of applying for membership. A large role for both institutions can be expected in Bulgaria.

Overall, official and multilateral sources of finance may play an increasing role in most of the east European countries, especially as commercial banks have become more cautious about lending to this area. The financial press notes a reluctance of banks to extend new loans to the eastern countries for any purpose except specific project lending, and then at harder terms. Little new funding can be expected for general balance of payments support,[580] apparently even for the low-to-moderately indebted eastern countries.[581]

Moves by private banking institutions to restrain lending may in certain cases be reinforced by official measures. An example of this is the Bank of England's new guidelines on how banks should treat doubtful loans. British banks will now have to make provisions for loans to countries with poor economic performance (previously a country had to default on its loans or delay its interest payments before banks had to take action). Factors like a high ratio of debts to GDP, failure to meet targets set by the IMF, or high dependency on a single source of income will now be sufficient to trigger this requirement. Countries likely to be penalized are those with poor economic records which have nevertheless met all of their debt service obligations.[582]

Further borrowing by the Soviet Union will have to rely increasingly upon official government credits, particularly if the supply of commercial credit tightens. In the foreseeable future, the Soviet Union will probably not have access to multilateral funding, except possibly from the EBRD.

The G-24 programme contains a host of measures and new instruments to encourage foreign direct investment and privatization in the east. This will provide a new source of non-debt creating finance to foster modernization and restructuring. At this time the role of foreign capital in the eastern countries is marginal and its future rate of growth is uncertain. Recent trends

---

[579] According to the OECD, the official export credit institutions of most OECD countries have been undertaking a reassessment of the risks of lending to eastern Europe. While the trend is to take a more cautious view of lending to the region, most of these institutions remain willing to support domestic exports to the eastern countries (except in some cases, to Poland and Romania). OECD, *Financial Market Trends*, February 1990, pp.33-34.

[580] See, for example, *Financial Times*, 1 March 1989.

[581] The reasons for this lack of differentiation – including a higher perception of risk attached to all reforming economies – have been discussed above in section 4.3.

[582] On these points, see *The Independent*, 30 January 1990.

in the formation of joint ventures have not been altogether favourable. The number of new joint ventures has increased rapidly in Hungary and Poland but only in Hungary have equity investments become a non-negligible source of external finance. However, large investments in the German Democratic Republic are foreseen, above all by companies in the Federal Republic. As noted above, in 1990 the G-24 support initiative is likely to have a significant impact only on the economies of Hungary and Poland.

Review by country

Given *Bulgaria's* accelerating inflation, high current-account deficits and heavy debt burden, it is probable that the authorities will have to adopt a stabilization programme in the near future.[583] Even if Bulgaria's poor export performance improves dramatically, imports will have to be scaled back sharply. The country has formally applied for membership in the IMF and the World Bank, which should eventually facilitate economic adjustment and the management of its foreign debt.

Czechoslovakia has managed to avoid the large macro-economic disequilibria experienced by most other eastern countries. As a result it can focus its efforts on economic reform without having to deal with the additional complication of a stabilization programme. With a debt of nearly $8 billion, the country has the capacity to sustain much heavier borrowing to modernize its antiquated capital stock. As regards centralized foreign currency funds, the authorities have opted for a cautious borrowing stance until a clearer picture of enterprise performance emerges. Recent changes in the system of enterprise management have occasionally resulted in production difficulties. On the other hand, the recent external borrowing by joint ventures and certain enterprises, the latter typically very conservative because of their legal responsibility for servicing convertible currency obligations, may imply a strong response to perceived export opportunities; hence, at least for the time being, the recent rise in debt may be viewed as a positive development. Czechoslovakia's exports are eventually expected to benefit from MFN treatment in the United States (see section 4.4).

Given the new situation resulting from the prospective unification of Germany, the outlook for the *German Democratic Republic's* trade with the west is necessarily highly speculative. It is at least possible that the German Democratic Republic will remain a trading entity for the time being and that present regulations governing its trade with western trade partners will continue to apply.[584] It is likely that the German Democratic Republic's capacity to export to the west will suffer from the exodus of manpower and the expected downturn in production. However, imports are bound to rise sharply and create a larger trade deficit with the convertible currency area in 1990. The German Democratic Republic's consumer goods purchases should rise when monetary union with and income maintenance transfers from the Federal Republic of Germany occur. Imports of machinery and equipment should increase, financed by inflows of direct investment (predominantly from the Federal Republic of Germany), and funds available through the European Recovery Programme (see section 1.2).[585] Higher levels of other types of aid from the Federal Republic of Germany — investments in infrastructure, payments for services, protection of the environment etc. — would also raise the German Democratic Republic's import capacity.[586] The German Democratic Republic has a financial cushion in the form of deposits at BIS banks which, at the end of September, amounted to over $9 billion.

In the external sphere, the tasks set out in *Hungary's* austerity programme are a sharp reduction in the current-account deficit and maintenance of access to foreign financial resources.[587] The stabilization plan recently approved by the IMF (accompanied by a $208 million one-year standby credit) foresees a reduction in the current-account deficit from $1.4 billion to $550 million. This is to be achieved in part through a boost in exports to the convertible currency area by 8-9 per cent and by holding import growth to 5-6 per cent. The latter figures apparently reflect the government's intention further to liberalize the import regime. The new measures would raise the share of products for which import licences and quotas would be abolished from 40 per cent to 60 per cent of convertible currency imports.[588] A policy of tight demand management and periodic devaluation of the forint is to be pursued.[589]

---

[583] Recently Mr. P. Mladenov, the Bulgarian Party leader, announced that the country's rate of inflation would run into three digits unless a "sensible" relationship between prices and incomes is worked out. *Financial Times*, 13 December 1989.

[584] It should be borne in mind that intra-German trade is governed by bilateral agreements which set, among other things, quotas on exports of certain goods to the Federal Republic of Germany and restrictions on the re-export of these goods to EC countries. The German Democratic Republic's exports to other EC countries are subject to the EC trade regime. Improvement in the German Democratic Republic's access to this market is the subject of the current negotiations on a bilateral trade and economic co-operation agreement, see section 4.4.

[585] According to press reports (*Neues Deutschland*, 21 February 1990), DM 6 billion ($3.5 billion) is to be made available over three years for projects in the German Democratic Republic. DM 2 billion are to be earmarked for environmental protection, DM 700 million for the promotion of tourism and DM 1.3 billion as start-up funds for new enterprises. These funds will be directed at private enterprises and will consist of 15-20 year loans at a fixed rate of interest with a five-year grace period on repayments. See also note (33) above, chapter 1.2).

[586] It has been reported that the Federal Republic of Germany has allocated some DM 5 billion emergency aid for the German Democratic Republic, but apparently an undisclosed amount will be spent in the Federal Republic of Germany to relocate new arrivals. The Federal Republic of Germany is also to contribute about $540 million for 17 environmental improvement projects in the German Democratic Republic. *International Herald Tribune*, 14 December, 1989.

[587] See chapter 5 for more detailed discussion of Hungary's and Poland's stabilization programmes.

[588] The liberalization concerns chiefly additional intermediate goods imports for industry.

[589] The forint was devalued by 10 per cent in late December 1989 and by another 2 per cent in early February 1990. The banking authorities have indicated that further changes in exchange rates will be made in the coming months as necessary.

Also the tourism balance is to improve to a surplus of $200 million (from a deficit of some $400 million in 1989), chiefly as a result of the new lower individual travel allowances introduced in November 1989.

If the current-account target is achieved, the growth of Hungary's debt would slow and the debt burden decline.[590] Financing requirements will remain high — some $3 billion in 1990 — which includes scheduled repayments of medium- and long-term debt of some $1.6-$1.8 billion.[591] Hungary has maintained access to the commercial credit markets, but it appears that its reliance upon this source of loans will diminish. Instead, the importance of multilateral (IMF, World Bank and EIB) and bilateral sources (see section 4.4) and direct investment flows will rise. Hungary will also have access to the first tranche of the $1 billion structural adjustment loan from the EC.

At present, the external financial targets for 1990 included in *Poland's* IMF-approved stabilization programme (see section 5.2) have not been released. However, key policy measures — an initial large real devaluation of the zloty, unification of exchange rates, institution of internal convertibility and a reduction in internal demand — are intended to reverse the recent decline in exports. Exports to the convertible currency area are expected to rise by 2 per cent and imports by 13 per cent, which would yield the first trade deficit in many years.[592] As a result the country would run a current-account deficit in 1990 larger than the $1.9 billion in 1989, and perhaps as high as $3 billion. Significantly, financing for the programme is to be made available through the international assistance measures reviewed in section 4.4. These include multilateral credits (IMF, World Bank and EIB) official transfers (funding for emergency food deliveries, aid to agriculture, etc.), new bilateral credit lines and relief on the official and commercial debt. Since most of the financial assistance is debt-creating, including the postponement of interest payments, Poland's external liabilities will continue to rise.[593]

Early returns for January-February 1990 are not favourable, showing a higher than expected drop in production, a fall of 3 per cent in exports and an even larger one in imports (relative to January-February 1989) with the convertible currency area.[594]

One of the main priorities of *Romania's* new government is to improve the domestic supply situation. To this end, cuts in exports (at least for food) and higher imports, including emergency food and medical aid provided by western donors, have been announced. With a large current-account surplus in 1989, there was considerable scope for such measures without recourse to heavy borrowing. A small current-account deficit may be expected in 1990. (The authorities expect a $300 million deficit in the first quarter.)[595] In the longer term, the decline in exports needs to be reversed. The rich agricultural potential of the country may contribute in this regard if measures taken by the new government are effective. Increases in imported inputs and spare parts — western imports had been cut by some 75 per cent since the early 1980 — could loosen bottlenecks and, in combination with an improved social climate, strengthen production and exports. The exact state of the capital stock is an unknown factor. It was allowed to deteriorate over the past 10-15 years, as reflected in low investment and deep cuts in purchases of western equipment.

In January 1990, the value of Romanian convertible currency exports was down by 31 per cent and that of imports up by 10 per cent relative to January 1989.[596]

Romania is well positioned to increase borrowing for a multitude of internal needs. The country is the least indebted in the east and its reserves have reached an all time high of $1.5 billion. The change in leadership has opened the way for improved relations with all international financial institutions and a resumption of borrowing from the IMF and World Bank. The availability of commercial credits and G-24 support will be conditional upon the re-establishment of mutual confidence and progress toward a pluralist political system.

The prospects for the *Soviet exports*, which continue to depend heavily upon petroleum products and crude oil, are uncertain. Soviet officials have stated that both production and exports will be maintained at roughly 1989 levels, with exports in the 170-180 million ton range.[597] However, production and exports of crude petroleum fell again last year, and some Soviet and foreign observers believe further drops in exports are possible.[598] Indeed, oil and coal production were down

---

[590] Hungary's debt service ratio is expected to fall slightly from some 41-42 per cent in 1989. National Planning Office, *Economic Policy Programme of the Hungarian Government for 1990*, Budapest, January 1990.

[591] *Ibid.*

[592] *Rzeczpospolita*, 14 December 1989.

[593] According to Deputy Finance Minister J. Savicki, Poland's gross external debt is to rise by over $3 billion in 1990. BBC, *Summary of World Broadcasts*, EE/0685, 10 February 1990, p.B/4.

[594] *Financial Times*, 8 March 1990.

[595] Direct communication to the ECE secretariat.

[596] Comisia Nationala pentru Statistica, *Buletin de Informare Publica*, no.1/1990.

[597] According to G. Pertumin, First Vice-Chairman of Soyuznefteexport, responding to speculation that Soviet exports of crude oil and oil products would drop in 1990. *Financial Times*, 15 February 1990. According to the article, civil unrest in Azerbaijan had disrupted the oil equipment and service industry, but this now appeared to be recovering. Also, the Ministry of Oil is taking over certain factories from the Ministry of Defence and plans to transfer production of oil field equipment to more tranquil areas.

[598] For example, A. Arbatov of the Soviet Academy of Sciences points to the poor state of the country's energy infrastructure. See *The Economist*, 25 November

in January-February 1990,[599] which might be attributed at least in part to the impact of a cold spell, transport bottlenecks and shortages of critical inputs in Siberia earlier in the year.[600]

Given its great need for convertible currencies, the Soviet authorities will be under pressures to shift oil exports as much as possible from traditional soft currency customers to western markets. Increased gas exports to the west may be an option, but the scope for this will depend on western demand and the domestic energy balance. The latter has been under strain, with shortfalls in coal production requiring the substitution of petroleum products for coal in power generation. In the past, Soviet raw materials and manufactures exports have been boosted when the current account came under pressure. However, worsening shortages on the domestic market have recently led the Soviet authorities to impose restrictions on certain types of transactions which had been intended to serve as incentives to boost exports. The new rules include a ban on bartering or selling any food products, coal, oil products, timber, fertilizers and construction materials above the limits laid down in the state plan for 1990.[601]

The Soviet Union's need for *imports* is expected to remain large. This includes foodstuffs, despite an improved grain harvest of 211 million tons last year. A scheme to reduce dependence on food imports by paying state farms in convertible currencies for above-plan production has so far not had much impact.[602] Potential internal demand for imports of a wide range of consumer goods and industrial inputs should remain high owing to domestic market imbalances. In general, there is a large need for capital goods imports to modernize the economy, but the problem of absorption persists. For this reason, the leadership has aimed to reduce investment outlays and to encourage more selective foreign equipment imports so as to reduce the stock of uncommissioned equipment. The demand of many enterprises has been tempered by new regulations requiring self-financing of western machinery imports, either with repayable bank loans or from their own retained export earnings.

A continuation of Soviet import growth would result in a further deterioration in the country's current-account balance and further increases in indebtedness since little change is expected in Soviet terms of trade and the volume of exports to the west. Given the internal needs, the more relaxed attitude towards external borrowing suggested by recent increases in external liabilities may continue in the near future, despite some opposition to such a policy. It nonetheless appears that import growth will have to be curbed at a point,[603] particularly if the cost of new credits continues to rise and that the spending of borrowed funds comes under closer scrutiny. There may be more pressure to limit borrowing only to those cases where it directly or indirectly creates new capacity to service additional debt.

Soviet gold stocks are believed to be high (the price of gold has risen in recent months), $14 billion is on deposit at BIS reporting banks, and indebtedness remains moderate.

All eastern countries are in various stages of implementing economic reforms. Reforms raise the possibility of overcoming the east's systemic weaknesses which have long held back the development of east-west trade. The positive impact of reform measures on the trade of a number of eastern countries during the past several years gives some cause for optimism. On the other hand, the poor state of the eastern economies and the dislocation to production caused by the implementation of new reforms has in some cases cut exports and increased the pressure to import. These factors, together with higher international interest rates and debt servicing will tend to increase current-account deficits at a time when commercial banks are becoming increasingly cautious about extending new funds to the east. This latter development lends additional importance to the international support initiatives launched by western governments and multilateral financial institutions. The measures should meet Hungary's and Poland's financial needs during the current year. However, the financial implications for the other countries will be much smaller and will depend on the speed at which their relations develop with the various multilateral financial institutions. In addition to financial relief, the international initiative addresses the various objectives of economic reform: macro-economic stabilization, modernization and restructuring of the domestic economy, raising income levels and integrating these countries into the world economy. Altogether, these developments are a major step forward in cementing economic and political relations in the region.

1989 and *Financial Times*, 8 November 1989. The International Energy Agency expects a decline in total crude and petroleum products exports from the Soviet Union in 1990. *Financial Times*, 10 January 1990.

[599] *Financial Times*, 16 March 1990.

[600] *Financial Times*, 15 January 1990.

[601] *Financial Times*, 30 December 1989.

[602] Purchases under the programme in 1989 came to only 223,000 tons of grain, less than 1 per cent of total state purchases. *Financial Times*, 30 January 1990.

[603] Alluding to the growing imbalance in Soviet trade, Deputy Prime Minister S. Sitaryan, who is responsible for economic relations, has stated that imports need to be reduced, in particular "such an unjustified scale of rolled ferrous metals, pipes and tubes and, in the shortest possible time we have to put an end to this practice altogether". *Financial Times*, 3 November 1989.

Chapter 5

ECONOMIC REFORMS IN EASTERN EUROPE AND THE SOVIET UNION

5.1 OVERVIEW

This chapter offers first a brief summary of the ongoing reform processes as a whole, in section (i). The three subsequent sections give a more detailed survey of reforms in Hungary, Poland and the Soviet Union. Section (v) discusses the economic reforms in Yugoslavia — a country which is not normally categorized as a centrally planned economy but shares certain historical experiences with the other countries discussed here. The rationale for including this country is to take into account not only the most recent but also the long-term experience of Yugoslavia and thus to contribute to the identification of alternative economic reform options.[604]

(i) Extension of economic reforms

The economic reforms that took place during the 1960s practically faded away during the 1970s in all eastern countries with the exception of Hungary and Yugoslavia. In the early 1980s, after the profound economic crisis, the process of economic reform began again in Poland, and from the mid-1980s attempts of radical economic reform were begun in the Soviet Union. Until recently, however, none of these developments were regarded as leading to a fundamental reappraisal of the overall social and economic system, nor to a questioning of their close mutual economic relations, institutionalized in the Council of Mutual Economic Assistance (CMEA). Economic reforms were really meant to be *reforms* and were not meant to alter the social and economic order.

During 1989, however, the process of reform gathered momentum and proceeded in a way radically different from any change seen since the Second World War. In Poland, after the conclusion of the Round Table negotiations between the government and the ruling party on one side and the formerly outlawed opposition on the other early in the year, the aim of the reform shifted profoundly when the opposition (Solidarnosc) took over the leading role in a new government. In Hungary, political parties emerged in 1988 and in 1989. But the process of change, which was relatively slow until the autumn of 1989, accelerated rapidly in early October 1989, when the Hungarian Socialist Workers Party decided to dissolve itself and a new Hungarian Socialist Party was formed, with only a fraction of the membership of its predecessor. Political changes also gathered momentum in the Soviet Union, albeit in a different and in many respects more complicated manner, reflecting deeply-rooted institutions of the traditional centrally planned economy in Soviet society, the heterogeneous national composition of the Soviet Union, combined with substantial differences in the levels of economic development in individual Soviet republics.

Nevertheless, although the changes in Poland, Hungary and the Soviet Union were unprecedented and greatly exceeded expectations, the whole process of mutations in the centrally planned economies took a completely new direction when abruptly, spontaneously and politically-uncontrolled public unrest broke out in the remaining four east European countries between mid-October and end-December 1989. Since the beginning of 1990, the overall political framework, not only in the eastern countries but in Europe as a whole, has become radically different from that which existed over the last four decades.

The political changes, which have taken place in all the east European countries but Albania, have raised widespread expectations that economic reforms — earlier restricted because of political constraints — will now go faster and in more or less the same way in all countries. However, such expectations fail to grasp the

---

[604] For earlier treatment of the economic reforms in ECE publications see United Nations Economic Commission for Europe, *Economic Survey of Europe in 1986-1987*, New York, 1987, pp.226-227; *Economic Survey of Europe in 1987-1988*, New York, 1988, pp.268-278; and *Economic Reforms in the European Centrally Planned Economies*, New York, 1989.

origins of these reforms, the different nature of the various programmes in individual countries and the problems of their implementation.

The proposed reforms in eastern Europe and the Soviet Union are rooted in serious and chronic economic problems that most of the countries have now recognized to be insoluble within the traditional economic and political framework. These problems, largely rooted in the inherent inefficiencies of the centrally planned economic system, were briefly summarized in chapter 1.2.

One question is why the reform movements of 1989 did not happen earlier. In general terms, it is now clear that political and ideological considerations were behind the faltering of economic reforms in the late 1960s and the beginning of the 1970s. Had international markets remained unchanged, a new wave of economic reforms would probably have been unavoidable already in the mid-1970s. The two oil price shocks, however, substantially improved the terms of trade of the Soviet Union and, to a lesser but still significant degree, of eastern Europe with western countries. The high dependence of the east European countries on Soviet shipments of energy and raw materials acted in the same direction. Political and ideological considerations also played a role, and few people imagined that economic reforms in any east European country could lead to a change in its social and economic system, let alone its separation from the CMEA or the Warsaw Pact. Once the Soviet terms of trade turned the other way, however, domestic economic weakness could no longer be offset by rising real net imports and the situation inevitably became ripe for radical change in the Soviet Union, and, subsequently, eastern Europe.

(ii) Contents of economic reforms

The initial point of departure for the reforms in all east European countries and the Soviet Union was the same — an entirely centrally planned economy based on development priorities decided upon by central authorities, broken down into mandatory physical planning indicators to enterprises. This was earlier referred to as a *traditional socialist economic system* and is now frequently labelled as an *administrative command system*. Departures from that economic system have been various, to the extent that in some countries it is still the basic operational model while in others it has already been considerably altered. Moreover, the assessment of that economic system originally varied from country to country.

In some countries, until very recently, the intended aim of economic reforms was to improve the traditional socialist economic system. After the recent wave of changes, however, it seems clear that such limited approaches will no longer suffice and that more radical departures from the traditional centrally planned economy will be made. For almost all of these countries the objective now includes a shift to a fully-fledged market economy.

Moreover, in some of the eastern countries the reforms now under way — at least as regards announcements and implied intentions — envisage such profound changes in the existing economic system that alterations in the social and economic order would seem inevitable. Views on the possibility of such far-reaching changes vary considerably between and within individual countries.

A major factor in designing and implementing reforms at present is the *current economic situation*. The accumulation of long-term economic problems in eastern Europe and the Soviet Union have now resulted in an economic situation which in most countries is qualified as one of *crisis* or even *near collapse*.

Particular problems vary from country to country. In some they include a rising open inflation (Hungary, Bulgaria and the Soviet Union) and even, until recently, hyperinflation (Poland and Yugoslavia). Recent data suggest that a list of countries with high open inflation must soon be extended (the German Democratic Republic and Romania). In several countries (Bulgaria, Hungary and Poland) a prominent aspect of the economic crisis is high external indebtedness, which has required or will soon result in tough stabilization policies. In Romania, the policies of earlier years have brought the population to its lowest standard of living in the last several decades. In addition, the Soviet Union and several east European countries have recently reported budget deficits, which are considerable in both absolute and relative terms, as well as high levels of public debt. Finally, serious external and internal imbalances have recently been unveiled even in countries where economic developments were previously described as being among the most successful (the German Democratic Republic) or the most stable (Czechoslovakia) of the eastern countries.

Although current economic problems may have helped to trigger the latest wave of economic reforms, they may also act to limit or postpone them. Given the inevitable redistribution effects of economic restructuring, this limit is present in every reforming country. But its significance may be especially high in those countries where — because of limited earlier departures from the traditional system — the redistributive effects of abrupt economic reforms may be so great that they may not be supported either socially or politically. Such limits to economic reform seem to be most constraining in the Soviet Union, where the traditional centrally planned economic system is of the longest standing and is deeply rooted among the population. Thus a significant proportion of the Soviet population, even after five years of rather hesitant reform, does not appear to be ready to accept any change which would seriously compromise the usual understanding of equity as incorporated in the traditional centrally planned economy.

(iii) Varied options of political and economic reforms

At the beginning of 1990 there was a considerable variety of political and economic reforms in the eastern countries. Moreover, the situation has been changing rapidly with economic and political reforms playing rather different roles and alternating in relative importance. Thus only very brief profiles of the various countries can be given at this stage.

In *Hungary,* a series of economic reforms over a long period have gradually dismantled its traditional centrally planned economic system. However, since no consistent new economic system has emerged from these reforms, economic developments have been marked by various internal and external imbalances. Although these have not basically compromised the movement for reform, the imbalances indicated that Hungary had reached a point where a more radical approach was necessary. But this required a broad national consensus on the type of new economic, and possibly social, system to be adopted. This has not emerged so far but could develop after the general elections in March 1990. Details of the Hungarian reforms are given in section 5.3.

In *Poland,* despite the deep economic crisis at the end of the 1970s and the beginning of the 1980s, the population, until recently, refused any radical economic reforms proposed by the existing governments which could entail steep reductions of its living standard. In 1989, a completely new framework was created, representing, more or less proportionally, all the forces in Polish society. Irrespective of the fragile external and internal economic situation, the population seems to have been ready to endorse genuine economic reforms even at the cost of a further, but temporary, fall in the standards of living. This complex picture is described in more detail in section 5.2.

In the *Soviet Union,* after changes in the leadership of the country, it was accepted that the Soviet economic system, even in the mid-1980s, was essentially the same as that introduced at the end of the 1920s, and that despite many marginal changes it could no longer continue to function along the same lines. Hence, as early as 1986, the new leadership called for *radical* economic reform. However, the extensive internal and external imbalances have proved to be a major obstacle to any substantial let alone radical economic reform. Consequently, alterations in the economic system have so far been partial, inadequate, and to a large extent, inconsistent. The overall functioning of the economy has considerably deteriorated. Since the lack of political support for any genuine economic reform was increasingly seen as one of the major obstacles to economic reform, the Soviet authorities decided to extend restructuring *(perestroika)* to the social and political areas as well. Nevertheless, despite strong support for such a programme, restructuring has so far proved to be a very difficult process.

As a reflection of these difficulties, the Soviet authorities have shifted the emphasis from economic to political reforms. These have indeed gathered substantial momentum, to the extent that some of the cornerstones of the existing social and economic order, such as the dominant role of central planning, the rejection of the market economy, the leading role of the Communist Party, etc., are now questioned and subject to potentially fundamental change. However, because of a very difficult economic situation — which has turned out to be much worse than was generally assumed both in the country and abroad — it was judged that abrupt radical economic reforms at the present moment would carry unacceptable economic and social risks. Hence by the end of 1989 a compromise programme was adopted by the Supreme Soviet, aimed at an improvement of the Soviet economy by means of a mixture of traditional and more economic policy instruments. This programme is expected to pave the way for more fundamental economic reforms and a completely new development strategy for the 1990s. But this approach remains controversial and there are calls, by some top national leaders, for immediate radical economic reforms. A more detailed analysis of Soviet economic and political reforms is also presented in section 5.4.

The situation in Bulgaria, Czechoslovakia, the German Democratic Republic and Romania has certain common features while there are also considerable differences. On the one hand, all have explicitly rejected the previous leadership which maintained that their economic and political systems did not require substantial change. On the other, at least judging by the declarations of the new leaderships now installed in these countries, all of them are now aiming not only at real economic reform but also at substantial changes in their political and juridical systems. In most of these countries, however, these programmes were in the process of elaboration at the time of writing of this *Survey,* so that only brief preliminary assessments can be attempted.

Of the four countries, *Czechoslovakia* seems to be not only the most reform-oriented but also the one where the prospects for the implementation of economic and political reform appear to be brightest. The popular momentum for change was so strong in the autumn of 1989 that substantial changes in the political system quickly occurred, including changes in practically all the leading posts of authority in the country. Because of this, although operational reform programme are still at the drafting stage, it seems evident that Czechoslovakia is now moving towards a radical change of its economic institutions and mechanisms. The establishment of a decentralized market economy now seems likely, which would place Czechoslovakia in the same category as Hungary and Poland.

Similarly, abrupt political changes in the *German Democratic Republic* suddenly transformed a seemingly calm situation into one of turbulent change. There are two dominant issues. One is the enormous outflow of people from the German Democratic Republic to the Federal Republic of Germany which has become a problem for both countries. The second issue is the sudden emergence of the possibility of an early unification of the two Germanies, a development which has completely changed the outlook for economic and political developments in the German Democratic Republic.

In spite of frequent claims to be a reforming country, economic changes in *Bulgaria* during the 1980s were largely cosmetic. The change in the political leadership of the country in early November 1989 opened the way to potentially far-reaching reforms. However, the determination of the aims to be adopted is proving difficult. On the one hand, the traditional centrally planned economic system, including the social values implied by this system, appears to be much more deeply rooted than is commonly assumed. In this respect, Bulgaria is comparable to the Soviet Union. Immediately after the change in the leadership, Bulgaria opted for a reform of the traditional socialist economic system, real and significant, but not of a degree alter it fundamentally. At the beginning of 1990, however, it was already clear that this was not sufficient for the more reform-oriented members of the new leadership. Hence in February 1990, programmatic reports submitted to the Extraordinary 14th Congress of the Communist Party, as well as the first declarations of the new government, indicated that Bulgaria may now move much further away from a centrally planned economy, the new aim being a *social* market economy. The time table for these changes, however, is very cautious, anticipating a fundamental transformation of the economy only in the second half of the 1990s.

The internal economic situation in *Romania* has turned out to be even more disastrous than was generally assumed before the overthrow of the dictatorial régime in December 1989. In the present economic situation the first concern of the national authorities is to ensure the daily supply of basic commodities to the population. However, a national consensus on a new political and economic systems for Romania may prove very difficult to attain. Until political stability is restored it is difficult to envisage the nature of the economic system which a newly-elected government might seek to establish.

Yugoslavia, as already mentioned, ceased to be a centrally planned economy long ago. For this reason its development has long been analyzed in this publication in the context of the review of the market economies of Europe. If the abolition of mandatory physical planning indicators is used as a criterion, Yugoslavia ceased to be a centrally planned economy in 1953. Thereafter it gradually developed into a special type of market economy, combining this with indicative planning and various schemes of worker participation and self-management. Remnants of the traditional socialist economic system nevertheless persisted, and there were even some departures from the market system during the 1970s. After prolonged, painful and largely unsuccessful adjustments during the 1980s, a comprehensive package of economic reform and stabilization policies was put together at the end of 1989, which reflected a critical examination of the entire post-war experience of the country.

5.2 ECONOMIC REFORM IN POLAND

(i) Introduction

At the threshold of the 1990s, Polish economic reform entered a new stage aimed at the rapid formation of "a market system akin to the one found in the industrially developed countries".[605] Recent developments follow a decade-long reforming process triggered by the deep economic crisis and social and political changes of August 1980.

Economic reform ventures in Poland have, however, a much longer history, as well as a theoretical background reaching back to the works of O. Lange and M. Kalecki and the policy recommendations of the Economic Council established after the political changes that occurred in October 1956.

Pressure for economic reforms, exerted mainly by intellectuals, continued in the 1960s. They were directed at the re-orientation of development objectives and investment policies and at fuller use of market instruments. In economic policy, however, a tendency towards recentralization and a traditional extensive development pattern still prevailed. The role of international specialization and comparative advantage from trade was more widely recognized. Some accounting methods for the evaluation of economic efficiency of foreign trade and investment under conditions of central allocation of resources and biased prices were developed and brought into practice. Concepts of "selective development" of certain industrial branches and elimination or reduction of other activities were launched in the late 1960s. This policy failed when drastic food price rises brought about wide social unrest and a subsequent political crisis in December 1970.

In the 1970s, new political leaders tried to find a substitute for economic reforms in organizational and administrative changes, accompanied by a massive inflow of foreign technologies financed by western credits, as well as in further concentration and centralisation of the economy (establishment of "large economic organizations" — the WOGs, conversion of co-operatives into *de facto* state organizations subject to central planning). This policy resulted in over-investment, waste of resources, accumulation of considerable foreign debt and internal political tensions. At the same time the theory of economic planning and management was developed further, with an emphasis on the fuller use of economic parameters and synthetic measures (e.g., profit rate) for the evaluation of economic efficiency of enterprises, and on a need to abandon the comprehensive, quantitative planning for a system of economic regulation using few central indicators.

In the second half of the 1970s alternative political and economic movements appeared in Poland. They prepared the ground for the more radical reform programmes of the 1980s.

Since the late 1950s, the economic reforms in Poland had a stop-and-go character. Notwithstanding the evolution of the political and economic environment, various reform projects have had much in common, although their objectives and means of implementation were perceived differently.

Reforms, generally, aimed at granting greater autonomy to enterprises, establishment of a "self-management" system, rationalization of price setting and bringing the price structure closer to the world price pattern, formulation of an adequate system of various economic and monetary parameters (exchange rates, interest rates, etc.), and fuller use of economic regulators instead of commands and central distribution of resources; replacement of detailed, directive quantitative planning and control by use of a few global targets and synthetic measures for the evaluation of the activity of economic entities; application of a more liberal, transparent and stable fiscal policy; enlargement of the scope and the provision of better treatment for the economic activity of the non-socialized sector (first of all, in the spheres of agriculture, handicrafts, small industry and services).

In spite of numerous partial and complex economic changes, all the past reform projects until 1989 remained within the system of the centrally planned socialist economy. The projects of systemic changes were, in general, combined with proposals for changes in the strategy of long- and medium-term economic development aimed at easing tensions on the consumer market, decreasing the capital and material intensity of the growth pattern and securing a better balance of the economy with more emphasis on the development of agriculture, food-processing, light industries, housing and services.

The initially declared objectives, however, were always — under the pressure of influential industrial and political lobbies — successively abandoned in favour of further extensive growth of resource-intensive sectors such as mining, energy, and metallurgy.

This traditional development pattern, accompanied by recentralization and step-wise restrictions on or withdrawal of liberal economic and political reform measures, generally led to a new crisis after five to ten years, and then to a commencement of a new reform

---

[605] *Outline of Poland's Economic Programme*, Warsaw, October 1989 (submitted by the Polish delegation to the thirty-eighth session of the ECE Committee on the Development of Trade, Geneva, 4-8 December 1989). Published in Polish in *Rzeczpospolita*, 12 October 1989.

cycle (or a new round of the reform spiral) — a new reform programme starting, however, from a different position, characterized by a better social knowledge of economic and political premises and consequences of the reform and, importantly, by a growing awareness of the need for joint implementation of economic and democratic political reforms to safeguard the continuity of the reform process.

The recent political and economic changes introduced in Poland since late 1989 by the government of Mr. T. Mazowiecki are far more radical than any reforms conceived earlier. They change the substance of the hitherto existing system and aim at a transformation of the Polish economy into a fully-fledged market economy. To understand better their content it is necessary to look in more detail at reform attempts earlier in the 1980s, when the process of departure from the traditional centrally planned economy began.[606]

(ii) Overview of the economic reforms in the 1980s

In 1981 an outline of a new economic reform was elaborated. Basic legislative acts were prepared and entered into force on 1 January 1982.[607] Alternative reform programmes were also proposed and discussed. Some partial reforms were introduced already in 1981, e.g., changes in the economic system of state farms and some curtailment of central economic administration. This economic reform was based on the principles of self-management, self-financing and autonomy of enterprises, although under martial law (imposed in December 1981) these principles were not thoroughly implemented.

The reform, initiated in the midst of the crisis, was hindered by numerous internal and external constraints. Radical solutions, which might have caused an even stronger decline in output and living standards and could have endangered the interests of the industrial lobbies, were on the whole avoided. Nevertheless, the scope of central planning was considerably reduced. Central plans lost their obligatory character for economic organizations. Their implementation had to be secured mostly by use of indirect economic policy measures. Nevertheless, the economic effects of enterprise activity were largely dependent on access to scarce material and financial resources (including foreign exchange) which remained in part centrally allocated or tied up with the realization of government contracts or "operational programmes" in a few selected areas.

Prices were classified into three categories: centrally set official (administrative) prices; regulated prices (shaped according to some mostly cost-based price formulae) and free (contractual) prices. Some consumer goods (such as meat and sugar) were rationed. Functioning of the market mechanism was also limited by persistent monopolisation, connected, *inter alia,* with activities of reorganized (on a compulsory or voluntary basis) producers' associations and "communities", in particular in mining, energy and other base industry sectors, as well as with maintenance of rigid administrative structures within the co-operative sector, e.g., in agriculture, food processing, construction, small industry and trade. Some competition and flexibility was brought into the economy by small foreign firms established on the basis of the law passed on 6 July 1982, and by joint ventures with foreign capital, first admitted by the law enacted on 23 April 1986.[608]

Substantial changes were introduced in the sphere of foreign economic relations, especially with regard to trade with convertible-currency countries. Apart from the abolition of directive central planning, they included organizational changes, resulting in a rapid increase in the number of economic agents that could conduct foreign trade activities independent of administrative organs. For example, the number of permit holders grew from 245 in 1982 to 597 in 1987 and 905 in 1988.[609]

Since 1982, a policy of flexible adjustments in the rate of exchange of the national currency had been adopted, with a view to securing the profitability of 75-85 per cent of the value of exports to both convertible and non-convertible currency areas. (According to the 1987 reformulation of the principle, the levels of exchange rates was to assure profitability of at least 80 per cent of exports to both payment areas. This target was approached in the fourth quarter of 1987.) Although the pace of zloty devaluation often lagged behind the actual rate of inflation, and a vast class of official prices remained in use, the scope of the latter category was successively reduced in favour of contractual prices shaped under the impact of the prices paid or received in foreign currencies at current exchange rates.

Since 1982, exporters have, in principle, been eligible to retain a part of their receipts in foreign exchange and to use it to finance imports of intermediate inputs and capital goods. (In fact, the technical structure of the system was more complicated than this, and evolved over time.) In spite of its shortcomings, the system of retention quotas generated real impulses for bolstering export-oriented production. It was gradually

---

[606] The government objectives were characterized as follows by the Prime Minister, Mr. T. Mazowiecki in his Parliament statement on 18 January 1990: "Since January we have been implementing a very difficult economic programme which should eliminate a long-term, heavy crisis. For the first time in the post-war history of our country, it is not a programme of improvement of the system. We want to change the economic system, we want to build a market economy in Poland; let us add — a social market economy. The market economy should be created from the bottom and developed by individual or group activity of people. We consciously restrict the government role in the economy". *Rzeczpospolita,* 19 January, 1990.

[607] A more detailed review of Polish economic reform in the period up to 1988 is given in L. Balcerowicz, "Polish economic reform, 1981-1988: An overview" in United Nations Economic Commission for Europe, *Economic Reforms in the European Centrally Planned Economies,* Economic Studies No.1, New York, 1989.

[608] See *East-West Joint Ventures: Economic, Business, Financial and Legal Aspects,* United Nations, New York, 1988.

[609] GUS, *Rocznik statystyczny handlu zagranicznego,* various issues.

supplemented by the organization of foreign exchange auctions which enabled exporters to sell their hard-currency assets (or their rights to purchase foreign currencies) in quasi-exchange markets. This latter arrangement segmented into separate sub-markets for specific categories of participants serviced by different banks.

A rather marginal but growing part of imports was also financed by foreign currency credits granted mainly by the Foreign Trade Bank (Bank Handlowy) and — since 1987 — a new Export Development Bank. Preferential terms were established for export-oriented investments.

Notwithstanding many changes in the economic system introduced in the period up to 1987, the main objectives of the reform were not achieved. There was no substantial improvement in economic efficiency. Neither structural biases in the prices of goods, services and production factors, nor the monopolistic position of many producers, accompanied by persistent shortages, nor central allocation of resources were eliminated. Economic pressure for structural changes remained too weak to produce effects capable of overcoming the crisis and ensuring sustainable growth. This was also due to the dominance of the traditional economic policy mix — soft budget and monetary constraints combined with massive fiscal redistribution of revenues.

Preference was given, for social and political reasons, to maintaining the attained levels of consumption, of social benefits and of output as well as full employment. This was, however, in contradiction with the exigencies of economic efficiency and the need for deep structural changes. However, when assessing the progress of implementation of the Polish economic reform in the first half of the 1980s, account should be taken of adverse external constraints: growing debt service obligations and unavailability of new western credits and, on the other hand, deteriorating terms of trade with and limited possibilities for import growth from the Soviet Union and other CMEA countries, as also dysfunctional economic and financial mechanisms within the CMEA.

After some aborted attempts at recentralization, the government was reshaped and a second — more radical — stage of the economic reform was declared in 1987. It was based, *inter alia,* on the principle of equal legal treatment of economic agents of the state, co-operative and private sectors. Proposals for the implementation of an austerity programme, including sharp price rises, tougher monetary policy and accelerated structural adjustments, found no backing, however, in a referendum organized in November 1987. A more moderate variant of the second stage of the reform was then selected for implementation. A negative social response to the "price and income operation" of spring 1988 again resulted in governmental changes.

The government formed in the second half of 1988 by Mr. Rakowski prepared a "Plan for the Consolidation of the National Economy" (approved by the Parliament in January 1989) and passed a number of liberal economic laws, including more radical measures than those envisaged in the programme of the second stage of the reform. The remnants of the rationing system for private consumers were abolished (e.g., coupons for meat and gasoline) and subsidies on consumer products were reduced. Some unpopular restructuring decisions were taken. They concerned closing inefficient plants or those particularly harmful to the environment (e.g., metallurgical and chemical plants and shipyards). On 1 August 1989, most consumer prices, including food, were freed, accelerating manifold the rate of overt inflation. The Solidarity-led government which took over in August 1989 inherited a particularly difficult economic situation: three-digit inflation, general market shortages, stagnating output, large budget deficit and high debt-service obligations. Due to wide public support and perspectives of external economic assistance, the new government was able to launch a radical medium-term economic programme aimed at rapid stabilization of the economy, accomplishment of substantial ownership changes (partial privatisation), deregulation and establishment of western-type market relations and institutions. After some corrections, the programme was approved by the Parliament and agreed with the International Monetary Fund. It entered the phase of intensive implementation only at the beginning of 1990.

(iii) Progress of economic reform in 1988 and the first half of 1989

The main reforms and economic policy actions undertaken in 1988 and in the first half of 1989 are briefly reviewed below. Some laws enacted in this period have, however, been amended or replaced by new regulations passed by the Parliament in December 1989.

In the "Plan for the Consolidation of the National Economy" the following priority objectives were set:

(a) Acceleration of the development of the spheres vital for living conditions of the population, viz.:

— agriculture and food production,
— housing,
— protection of the environment.

(b) Wider opening of the economy by way of development of efficient exports.

The functions of central economic administration were reformulated — instead of control, limits and concessions, an emphasis was put on the stimulation of business activity, initiative and entrepreneurship of the economic actors in all sectors of ownership. This attitude was reflected in the package of economic laws enacted in December 1988 and in the first quarter of 1989. The three most important were:

(a) The Law on Economic Activity (of 23 December 1988) which introduced the principle of equal treatment of all ownership sectors and abolished restrictions on the founding of private firms. Except for some spheres of activity (where concessions were required), registration became sufficient to establish a firm and to engage in foreign trade. The employment limits for private companies were abolished.

(b) The Law on Economic Activity with Participation of Foreign Parties (of 23 December 1988), which replaced the Law on Joint Ventures of 1986, created more advantageous legal and financial conditions for foreign investment in Poland, especially with regard to taxes and possibilities for repatriation of capital. The upper limit for the share of foreign capital was lifted.[610]

A Foreign Investment Agency was established. The number of joint ventures which had increased from 13 to 129 during 1987, reached 657 by mid-October 1989, of which 605 have been registered under the 1988 investment law.[611]

(c) The Currency Law (of 15 February 1989) which legalized foreign currency transactions among Polish citizens and introduced the principle that exporters own their foreign currency revenues. They were, however, obliged to sell a part of their export earnings at an official rate of exchange to the National Bank. They could keep the rest of the revenues (10 to 50 per cent, depending on the kind of activity) in their bank accounts or sell it at foreign exchange auctions. These rules have, however, now been changed by the amendments to the Currency Law enacted in December 1989 which prepared the ground for the introduction of the internal convertibility of the zloty on 1 January 1990.

The above laws were supplemented by a number of other legal acts and financial regulations aimed at stimulating the restructuring processes and general economic activity.

The Bank Law (introduced on 31 January 1988) established a two-level bank hierarchy, with the National Bank of Poland (NBP) as a central bank and an expanding network of commercial banks. Apart from five already existing specialized banks, nine new regional banks were created in April 1989.

An Export Development Fund was also established (by a law of 15 February 1989 which entered into force on 1 March 1989) for the promotion of structural changes in exports.

A new customs tariff, based on the Harmonized Commodity Description and Coding System, was introduced on 1 January 1989. The tariff is also applicable to trade with socialist countries. Relatively higher duties were kept on imports of processed goods, except for capital goods needed for the development of sectors to which a priority has been given. For instance, *ad valorem* import tariffs on investment goods necessary for the modernization of industry and agriculture were reduced from 20-40 per cent to 10-25 per cent.[612]

(iv) **The 1990 stabilization programme**

Guidelines for the economic programme elaborated by the Government headed by Mr. Mazowiecki in the autumn of 1989, with the assistance of the IMF and some western economists envisaged two types of action: rapid stabilization of the economy, and transformation of the economic system. According to the main author of the economic programme, Deputy Prime Minister and Minister of Finance, L. Balcerowicz, " ... curbing inflation is the main political and economic objective for 1990".[613]

The average annual rate of inflation, as measured by an official consumer price index, increased from 25 per cent in 1987, 62 per cent in 1988 and 81 per cent in the first half of 1989, to 244 per cent for the whole of 1989. Between December 1988 and December 1989 consumer prices grew by 640 percent. In the last three months of 1989 consumer prices were rising by 55, 20 and 14.5 per cent respectively, prompted by the cutting of subsidies, wage indexing and devaluation of the currency.[614]

The official exchange rate against the US dollar, which had been 503 zlotys at the end of 1988, was raised continuously during 1989, reaching 1,800 zlotys on 28 September, 2,400 on 30 October, 3,800 on 27 November and 6,000 zlotys on 18 December 1989. Finally, on 1 January 1990 a new rate of exchange (9,500 zlotys per dollar) was fixed.[615] During 1989 the zloty was also progressively devalued against the transferable rouble, although much less than *vis-à-vis* the dollar (from 230 zlotys per rouble at the end of 1988 to 1,450 zlotys on 18 December 1989 and 2,100 zlotys on 1 January 1990).[616] Hence during the year, the implicit rouble/dollar cross rate changed from 2.19 to 4.52 roubles/dollar.

---

610 See *East-West Joint Venture Contracts*, United Nations, New York, 1989, pp. 121-132.

611 See *Financial Times*, 9 December 1989. By the end of 1989 about 800 joint ventures were permitted, with capital approaching $1 billion (according to Mr. M. Swiecicki, Minister of Foreign Economic Relations), *Rzeczpospolita*, 18 December 1989.

612 See *Raport o systemie kierowania handlem zagranicznym Polski w 1988 roku*, IKCHZ, Warsaw, 1989, p.224.

613 *Rzeczpospolita*, 12 December 1989.

614 See *Rocznik statystyczny 1989* and *Rzeczpospolita*, December 1989 (various issues), *Zycie Gospodarcze*, 28 January 1990.

615 *Rocznik statystyczny handlu zagranicznego 1989* and *Rzeczpospolita*, various issues.

616 *Ibid.*

In 1989, the zloty was devalued at a rate faster than the pace of inflation. The gap between the market exchange rates of foreign currencies and the official rates closed markedly in November and December 1989, whereas even in the second half of October, for example, the market rate of the dollar had been about four times higher than the official one.

In January 1990, subsidies on fuel and energy were substantially reduced. Prices of coal and electric energy were raised 5-7 times, resulting in a resurgence of inflation in January which exceeded expectations.

At the same time, a stricter wage control has been imposed, as required by the IMF (the elasticity-type wage indexing coefficient against the consumer price index was decreased from 0.7 to 0.3 in January 1990), budgetary financing of the non-material sphere was restricted, and a tougher monetary stance was adopted, with a base interest rate of the National Bank of Poland (set monthly) higher or close to the projected rate of inflation.[617]

According to the 1990 budget act, the budget deficit is to be eliminated by the end of the year. At the end of 1989, about 14 per cent of the central budget outlays were not covered by budgetary receipts. The share of subsidies in budget outlays would decline from 31 per cent in 1989 to 14 per cent in 1990.[618]

Government spending will no longer be financed by zero-interest "credits" granted by the National Bank to the Ministry of Finance, i.e., by issuing empty money.[619] Instead, treasury bonds are to be issued.

The government intends to proceed quickly with privatisation of state assets. This will supplement budgetary incomes with revenues from sales of shares of state enterprises in industry, construction and trade, from sales of land and apartments. Capital markets are to be created. The establishment of private banks has been authorized. Foreign banks have also been admitted.

Tax relief and credit preferences have been largely eliminated or reduced, including those connected with the development of export-oriented production and investment, agriculture, housing, etc.

Uniform income tax schemes have been introduced for all economic organizations irrespective of their form of ownership. Tax rates range from 20 to 50 per cent in individual classes of income, with an upper tax ceiling set at 40 per cent of the total income. A special tax on wage fund increments has been reintroduced. The base rate of the turnover tax has been raised from 15 to 20 per cent, and the scope of this tax has been widened, covering, for example, imports of some goods by individuals.

The customs law has also been amended. A uniform tariff — with regard to both commercial and non-commercial traffic — will be applied.

The book value of fixed assets in the national economy has been raised about 11-fold on average, with depreciation allowances rising 13-fold, to reflect the growing nominal values of fixed assets and changed depreciation rates.

More radical de-monopolisation measures will be applied, in particular with respect to producer "communities" in the fuel sector and to managing bodies of co-operative groupings, for example in the food-processing industry, trade, construction, etc.

The currency law of February 1989 was amended on 28 December 1989 to enable the introduction of the internal convertibility of the zloty from 1 January 1990. The changes aim at strengthening the national currency, eliminating foreign currencies from domestic transactions and abolishing their function as anti-inflationary hedges.

Economic organizations are again obliged to sell all their foreign exchange earnings to authorized banks at uniform exchange rates. At the same time they were given the right to purchase, without limitation, at official rates from specialized banks all the foreign exchange necessary for financing imports and covering other external obligations. Foreign exchange auctions have been abolished. All legal persons are, however, allowed to dispose freely of the foreign exchange assets accumulated in their capital accounts until the end 1989. The regulations concerning foreign currency accounts of Polish individuals have not been substantially changed.

In domestic settlements foreign currency can no longer be used unless specifically authorized. Compulsory currency exchange quotas for foreign tourists have been lifted.

Economic organizations which had earlier been permitted to sell goods and render services in Poland for foreign currency (e.g., *Pewex,* or many private firms and joint-stock companies, also with the participation of foreign capital) will lose these rights at the end of 1990, and in the meantime will have to offer their products for Polish currency as well after 1 July 1990.

The laws on joint ventures of December 1988, as well as that on the activity of small foreign firms in Poland of July 1982, were adjusted to reflect the amendments to the currency law and to general tax and credit regulations adopted for all business organizations active in Poland.

On 20 December 1989 the Parliament, approved — with some amendments — government guidelines on

---

[617] For January 1990, however, the base interest rate of 36 per cent was set at a lower level than the expected rate of inflation, probably to alleviate the shock due to the sharp devaluation and energy price increase.

[618] See *Rzeczpospolita,* 15 and 21 December 1989.

[619] However, some government borrowing on commercial terms is still envisaged for the first three quarters of 1990, to be repaid from central budget receipts during the fourth quarter.

agricultural policy. These envisage *inter alia* the establishment of an Agricultural Market Agency. Purchases and sales of agricultural products at market prices and a buffer stock policy are to constitute the principal instruments of central intervention in this sector. Minimum or guaranteed prices would no longer be established. This part of the government programme raised many objections and fears concerning the adaptability of Polish agriculture to sharply changing market conditions with rising production costs and, in spite of relatively low level of consumption, falling demand for food and agricultural products.[620]

The implementation of the austerity programme is expected to lead to numerous bankruptcies and restructurings of enterprises as well as increased unemployment. A system of social support has been conceived to give help to some 400,000 unemployed projected for 1990.[621] A Labour Fund has been established to finance professional education and retraining schemes and the allowances to be paid to the unemployed. A new labour law, introduced on 1 January 1990, extended the right to some social security benefits, with certain restrictions, also to Polish citizens re-entering the country after temporarily working abroad.[622]

(v) **Prospects**

The implementation of the stabilization programme is officially expected to reduce inflation sharply: from 45-50 per cent (on a monthly basis) in January and 15 per cent in February to 5-8 per cent in March, 3-5 per cent monthly in the second quarter, and similar or lower rates in the second half of 1990. The consumer price index of December 1990 is projected to be 140 per cent higher than in December 1989.[623] Although the official projections, because of the considerable risks and uncertainties involved, may be too optimistic, it is widely recognized that there was no alternative to the severe austerity measures proposed by the government.[624]

The scope and radicality of the deflationary actions create an opportunity for rapid stabilization of the economy which, however, is to remain under steady control of the government and to be the subject of monthly checks by the IMF. Tougher monetary measures, wage freezes, etc., are to be taken if necessary.[625] In any case, the social costs of the planned policy are expected to be substantial.[626]

According to the "pessimistic" variant of a set of economic simulations presented by the Central Planning Office, net material product might fall by 5 per cent in 1990, following stagnation registered in 1989. In two other variants, stabilization of the NMP level or growth of 2.8 per cent were projected.[627] However, it was pointed out during a meeting of the Social Planning Council that the "pessimistic" variant should rather be considered an overly optimistic one.[628] Other official forecasts expect real incomes of population to fall by one fourth by the end of the year against December 1989, and unemployment to reach up to 5 per cent of the labour force.[629]

The perspective of a steep fall in the standard of living and of other negative social consequences of the austerity programme provoked fears among the population and critical remarks from some economists, even those closely linked with Solidarity.[630]

When assessing the economic situation of Poland at the threshold of a new decade, and notably possible consequences of the expected recession in output and consumption, it should be borne in mind that in 1988 and 1989 the level of net material product was lower than in 1978 and that of individual consumption per capita only slightly higher than in 1978, but still below the 1980 level. On the other hand, in 1988 the share of gross fixed capital formation in gross material product reached 26 per cent, and total accumulation (including the increase in material inventories) exceeded 37 per cent at current prices.[631]

Although in the 1980s Poland only partially serviced its hard-currency debt, the total debt service over the period 1981-1989 amounted to $19.1 billion. Foreign

---

[620] *Rzeczpospolita*, 13, 15 and 20 December 1989; *Trybuna Ludu*, 15 and 29 December 1989.

[621] This contrasts with some 0.9 million vacancies and only about 5,000 persons registered as seeking employment at the end of 1989. However, by the end of February 1990 there were already 152,200 unemployed (*Rzeczpospolita*, 23 March 1990).

[622] *Trybuna Ludu*, 13 and 15 December 1989; *Rzeczpospolita*, 15 December 1989.

[623] According to statements of representatives of the Ministry of Finance. *Trybuna Ludu*, 13 December 1989; *Zycie Warszawy*, 16-17 December 1989; *Rzeczpospolita*, 6-7 January, 1990. Actual growth of the consumer price index (relative to the preceding month) amounted to 79 per cent in January, 24 per cent in February, and some 6 per cent in March. *Rzeczpospolita*, 23 March 1990.

[624] See the report of the first session of the Economic Council with the participation of eminent foreign economists. *Zycie gospodarcze*, 10 December 1989. See also *Polityka*, 28 October and 4 November 1989, *Tygodnik Solidarnosc*, 15 and 22 December 1989 and *Rzeczpospolita*, 19 December 1989.

[625] See the interview with Mr. M. Dabrowski, Deputy Minister of Finance, *Trybuna Ludu*, 13 December 1989.

[626] "If the programme does fail, outsiders should not be surprised. Few countries have ever eliminated hyperinflation at the first attempt. A history of failure may be needed before people are willing to accept the necessary sacrifices." "Poland on probation", *The Economist*, 2 December 1989.

[627] *Zycie Warszawy*, 9-10 December 1989.

[628] Statement by Professor M. Nasilowski. *Trybuna Ludu*, 9-10 December 1989.

[629] See *Rzeczpospolita*, 14 and 18 December 1989.

[630] See, for example, J. Mujzel, "Plan Balcerowicza: plusy i minusy", *Tygodnik Solidarnosc*, 15 December 1989.

[631] GUS, *Rocznik statystyczny 1989*; GUS, *Dochod narodowy i dochody ludnosci w 1988 r.*

credits over the same period came to $8.5 billion.[632] Hence the net outlow of capital from Poland in the last nine years reached $10.6 billion. In the first ten months of 1989 Poland paid about $1 billion in interest on her debt.[633]

By the end of 1989 the foreign debt of Poland amounted to about $40 billion (as compared to $39.2 billion a year earlier) and to 5.9 billion of transferable roubles (against 6.5 billion roubles at the end of 1988). The surplus in *convertible currency* trade diminished to some $742 million in 1989 (the smallest since 1981), after a second consecutive year in which imports had grown faster than exports. On the other hand, the trade balance in *non-convertible currency* trade reached a record surplus of 2.1 billion roubles, with the volumes of both imports and exports falling (by 3.6 and 1 per cent respectively) in 1989.[634]

External conditions are of vital importance for the overall economic situation and the effects of economic reform and the stabilization policy in Poland. This concerns, for instance, changes in interest rates and in the terms of trade, availability of foreign credits, access to foreign markets and technologies, possibilities and conditions of supplies of fuel, basic materials and other commodities (especially from the Soviet Union), and relations with the international financial institutions.

External support for the reform was a pre-condition for the introduction of internal convertibility of the zloty on 1 January 1990. On 23 December 1989, after two-month long consultations with the IMF negotiators, Polish officials signed a letter of intent pledging to follow the IMF-approved adjustment programme. Earlier in December, Mr. M. Camdessus, the Managing Director of the IMF, on a visit to Poland, stressed that the programme had not been forced upon Poland by the IMF, but had rather been conceived by the government of Poland.[635] Nonetheless, some bargaining on the harsher steps of the austerity programme took place before the letter of intent was signed.[636] The signing of the letter opened the way to a bridging loan to Poland of $215 million from the Bank for International Settlements already in 1989 and to a standby loan from the IMF as well as to credits and grants from other international and national, public and private sources in 1990, including a $1 billion stabilization loan.[637]

Co-ordination of the international aid for Poland with the internal stabilization measures and systemic changes aimed at "establishment of the basis for the market economy with features similar to those of the systems functioning in highly developed countries"[638] increased the probability of a successful implementation of the governmental economic programme in that it made possible relief on debt service payments and improved prospects for a gradual inflow of capital. A further reduction of the debt service *vis-à-vis* all creditors is envisaged in the guidelines on social and economic policy for 1990.[639] The trade balance with convertible currency countries is expected to turn into a deficit in 1990. The policy outline anticipates that repayments of principal can be postponed until after the year 2000 and partial payments of interest can be delayed until 1993.

Improved conditions of access for Polish exports to western markets (owing, for example, to elimination by the EC of specific quotas on imports from Poland and suspension of some other trade restrictions, granting of the GSP, etc.) were also indicated in the government programme as an important factor which would enable the growth of exports indispensable for restructuring the economy and the future servicing of the external debt.[640]

Recent political and economic changes in other east European countries might also create new opportunities for development of Poland's trade and economic cooperation with the European CMEA countries, based on direct market relations between economic organizations, gradual liberalization of trade including extended operations in convertible currencies in their mutual shipments and fuller integration of the respective countries into the European and world economy. But the crucial battles for a successful implementation of the stabilization programme and further economic reforms have to take place on Polish ground.

---

[632] According to Mr. W. Baka, the President of the National Bank of Poland. *Rzeczpospolita*, 18 December, 1989.

[633] *Zycie gospodarcze*, 10 December 1989.

[634] According to official estimates in *Rzeczpospolita*, 15 December 1989, 16 January 1990 and 1 February 1990.

[635] *Zycie Warszawy*, 12 December 1989. *Rzeczpospolita*, 28 December, 1989.

[636] *International Herald Tribune*, 18 December 1989.

[637] For more details see chapter 4.

[638] "Zalozenia polityki spoleczno-gospodarczej na 1990 r.", *Rzeczpospolita*, 15 December, 1989.

[639] *Ibid.*

[640] *Ibid.*

5.3 ECONOMIC REFORM IN HUNGARY

(i) Three decades of reforms: the results and their costs

For more than three decades Hungary has been in the vanguard of economic reforms among the centrally planned economies, in part because it has been an open economy, but also because the country aimed at a further growth in global economic participation. In comparison with other east European countries, Hungary has had the most outward-looking economy. Whatever was done on the domestic front worked quickly through the system, and the result immediately precipitated an improvement or worsening of the country's external position. This gave a reliable gauge into the hands of the planners, helping and forcing them to draw the necessary conclusions.

Politics aside, the problem facing the country at the beginning of the 1990s is similar to those that triggered all the previous waves of reforms and major institutional changes. Urgent measures were required to cope with balance-of-payment crises and to come to grips with the foreign indebtedness on two occasions in the mid-1950s (1953, 1955), once in the first half of the 1960s (1963-1964) and twice in the 1980s (1982, 1989). At the same time it has always been clear to decision makers and to the population at large that the real problems are rooted in more fundamental issues, such as high costs and low quality of production, cumulating domestic imbalances, etc., which at best can be cured only in the medium term.[641]

As in the other socialist countries, the reform measures were always initiated from the top. The leaders of the ruling party, the most influential enterprise managers and government officials were driven by their own growing dissatisfaction with the overall performance of the economy. In fact, there were two different levels of dissatisfaction. First, *operational dissatisfaction*, meaning the discontent of managers with the irrationalities of the existing economic system. Second, *performance dissatisfaction*, which relates to the national leaders' discontent with the overall growth performance and the country's external position. What made the Hungarian case unique was the fact that this dissatisfaction was openly stated by many politicians, and hence criticism and problem-oriented analysis produced by social scientists, writers and journalists were tolerated and even encouraged for decades.[642]

In a way, the reform measures initiated at these turning points of the Hungarian economic history were successful:

— The country remained solvent and has continued to service its debt. Slowly but steadily, Hungary became more integrated into the world economy. In 1950 the value of exports to the non-socialist countries amounted to 14 per cent of NMP produced; in 1988 the corresponding figure was above 21 per cent. After a spectacular rise in the last two years, the volume of direct capital investment from the west was estimated at $1 billion.[643] In addition to merchandise trade and capital flows, liberalization measures as well as large-scale investments permitted a gradual rise in tourism, both outward- and inward-bound. The number of Hungarian citizens travelling to non-socialist countries increased from 35,000 in 1960 to over 1.2 million in 1988; the rise of the counter-movement was equally remarkable — from 50,000 to over 3 million.

— Living standards improved. Between 1952 and 1987, *per capita* incomes and consumption in real terms increased every year without exception, with an annual average growth of some 4 per cent for the period.[644] First and foremost, the food supply of the population has been guaranteed from domestic sources since the early 1970s. For many years good quality food has been readily available without queuing and rationing. The grain harvest (mostly in the state and co-operative sector) rose from less than 8 million tons in 1967 to 14 million tons by 1980

---

641 It should be noted, however, that in the past the population and the outside world was generally not informed about the severity of these short-term external constraints. What was publicly acknowledged and also felt at the time was the temporary deterioration in the supply situation, hitting producers and consumers alike. From recently released archive materials, memoirs, interviews and other secondary sources, however, it can be clearly established that the decision makers of the time acted under the pressure of extreme balance-of-payments constraints. For a detailed account on the state of affairs in the mid-1950s, see the chapter entitled "The Question of National Indebtedness to Foreign Countries" in a book by Imre Nagy, the late Prime Minister of Hungary (*On Communism (In Defence of the New Course)*, Thames and Hudson, London, 1957, pp.184-193).

For a well-documented description of the situation in the mid-1960s, when recurring balance-of-payment strains were generated by massive grain imports, see T.I. Berend, *Gazdasági útkeresés, 1956-1965* (Searching the new path), Magvető Könyvkiadó, Budapest, 1983, pp.416-418.

642 For more arguments along these lines, see I. Major, "Two Aspects of Economic Reform in the Centrally Regulated Economies" (Paper presented at the Annual Congress of the European Economic Association, Augsburg (FRG), September 1989) and T. Bauer, "Reforming or Perfecting the Economic Mechanism in Eastern Europe", European University Institute Working Paper No. 86/247, Florence, 1986.

643 *Heti Világgazdaság*, 27 January 1990. Secretary of State I. Dunai of the Ministry of Trade put this figure at $1.1 billion, comprising direct investments worth $600 million and western equipment worth $500 million, acquired through leasing agreements. (*Figyelő*, 1 February 1990.)

644 *Statisztikai Évkönyv 1988* (Statistical yearbook), p.17.

and then stabilized at that level. In the period 1967-1984, annual meat production doubled. The 1968 economic reform, the New Economic Mechanism (NEM), gave a strong boost to the rise of consumer services (mostly in the private sector). Between 1971 and 1980, the consumption of goods increased by 2.8 per cent on average, while the volume of services grew by 4.8 per cent. Even in the period 1980-1988, when there was a relatively low increase of commodity consumption (0.6 per cent), consumption of services rose at annual rate of 2.6 per cent.[645]

— The volume of consumer goods imports from the developed market economies has been very significant, perhaps exceeding what the country's overall development would have justified. Among the six countries of eastern Europe, this figure was higher in per capita terms only in the German Democratic Republic. Between 1965 and 1986, the average annual percentage rise of this type of import (in real terms) was close to 10 per cent, higher than in any other country of the region.[646] The development level and the size of the retail trade network was also satisfactory in a region-wide comparison.[647] Undoubtedly, occasional shortages have continued to vex the consumers, but on the whole the situation was better, or at least as good as in other socialist countries.

— Until very recently, unemployment has never been a serious issue. The demand for labour has invariably surpassed the supply. Even in 1988, when the labour market became slightly tighter, only 16,000 people were dismissed nationwide, while 240,000 employees quit their jobs voluntarily.[648] Income differentials appear to have decreased at least until 1987. The number of people living below the poverty line was falling up to that year.[649]

— Before 1978, the annual rate of inflation was always below 5 per cent. But even later, when the price rises came very close to 20 per cent (1988-1989), the process still remained within the target range of the annual plans. Nevertheless, by the end of 1989 inflation became an issue of serious concern.

The other side of the coin is that Hungary has been living on borrowed time and money. In the last ten years the pace of economic growth — 1.3 per cent per annum[650] — was very slow. The qualitative aspect of economic growth was not altogether encouraging. From the very beginning the CMEA markets were the focus of all major development programmes. The lack of competition on and the low quality requirements of the east European and the Soviet markets[651] had a feather-bedding effect on the Hungarian producers for which macro-economic policy failed to provide a cure. But more importantly, it had a feedback into the development programmes themselves. Factories and entire industries were created to meet the "soft" requirements of the CMEA markets with obsolete production patterns and technologies. As a result, exports to convertible currency markets were insufficiently stimulated.

Between 1970 and 1989, the gross hard-currency debt rose sharply — from $1 billion to $21 billion.[652] A good part of this sum was used to build new industrial capacities geared toward the CMEA markets. As the external constraint became more and more pressing, the share of accumulation in NMP used fell from 25-28 per cent in the mid-1970s to 10-12 per cent by the end of the 1980s. Consequently the nation's capital stock became more and more obsolete. In industry, for example, the share of assets less than five years old declined from 41 per cent in 1975 to 24 per cent in 1987.[653] Moreover, the nation's aging capital stock was poorly maintained. This is a type of hidden internal debt affecting both the material and the non-material sphere. At the same time, it is a very dangerous form of "borrowing" because of its invisibility and the lack of quantitative information about it.[654]

---

[645] All these figures are expressed in per capita terms, at constant prices. The data are from official statistics, which means that the volume of services produced and consumed in the unregistered "second economy" was not taken into account.

[646] For more details, as well as for methodological explanations, see United Nations Economic Commission for Europe, "Eastern consumer goods imports from market economies, 1962-1986" in *Economic Survey of Europe in 1987-1988*, New York, 1988, pp.253-267.

[647] See "Retail trade in Eastern Europe and the Soviet Union, 1960-1987" in United Nations Economic Commission for Europe, *Economic Survey of Europe in 1988-1989*, New York, 1988, pp.166-177.

[648] *Statisztikai Évkönyv 1988*, p.53.

[649] For an analysis based on household surveys for the period 1962-1987, see R. Andorka, "Szegénység Magyarországon", *Társadalmi Szemle*, vol. 45. 1989. No. 12.

[650] Growth of real GDP in the period 1980-1989.

[651] In 1988, more than 60 per cent of the Hungarian exports directed to the CMEA markets were in fact sold to one country — the Soviet Union. The share of the east European countries was about 38 per cent. The role of the markets of the developing socialist countries (Cuba, Vietnam, Mongolia) was insignificant.

[652] Before 1970, the total value of Hungary's foreign indebtedness was thus incomparably smaller than today. But so were the country's export revenues. Before 1965, there was not a single year when the value of exports to the developed market economies surpassed the $300 million mark. According to Berend (*op.cit.*), in 1963 the debt was close to $350 million. In this perspective, the $60 million deficit in 1955 and the $80 million in 1964 must have appeared alarmingly high indeed.

[653] See table 3.3.17 above.

[654] Both aspects were emphasized by J. Vanous, "Privatization in Eastern Europe: Possibilities, Problems and the Role of Western Capital", *PlanEcon Report*, 30 September, 1989.

(ii) Explanations of the economic malaise

As mentioned, operational and performance dissatisfaction with the existing economic management system appeared at a relatively early stage of development of the Hungarian economy. This widely shared feeling called for rational explanations. In the course of three decades, various reasons were given to describe the origins of the economic malaise. Although these alternative approaches had some explanatory power, none of them was fully acceptable to the economic profession.

Five major lines of arguments were advanced:

— excessive directive and mandatory planning indicators;

— the vicious circles created by unsound industrial development;

— the "extensive" character of economic growth;

— the interpretation of the world-wide consequences of the 1973 oil crisis;

— the invariable behaviour of the Hungarian economy as an "economy of shortage".

(a) After the failure of the first five-year plan (1950-1954), the first reproach against the system of *centralized mandatory planning* was based on the argument that the system was ineffective owing to too many centrally-set plan targets.[655] This criticism implied that decision-making should be decentralized to enterprises and lower-level organs in general and the number of mandatory plan targets should be significantly reduced, possibly replaced by profits as a single synthetic indicator. By 1968, after several years of animated dispute, profit was widely accepted as a pivotal guide for economic activity. This led to the total abolition of mandatory plan indicators and later to the stepwise decoupling of enterprises from the state and the party (1977, 1984, 1989).

(b) Another lesson soon learned was that economically unsound, gigantic investment projects have a long-lasting impact upon the entire economy. First there is an obvious short- and medium-term crowding-out effect experienced during the construction phase of these projects. For the sake of the early completion of a few major industrial production units, the development of other sectors (e.g., communications, housing) had to be neglected. In later years, however, the units already commissioned required huge complementary investments for reasons of technology and/or capacity utilisation. The planners found themselves in a *vicious circle*. The dilemma they repeatedly faced was to choose between scrapping and writing off these colossal investments (often encompassing entire sectors of industry) or pouring more money into them in order to make them at least technologically viable. It took several decades to realize that the objectives of the development strategy themselves had never been derived from any rational macro-economic considerations. Their rationale was deeply imbedded in a complex system of political objectives, reflecting the interests and the ideology of the ruling party.[656]

(c) The distinction between *extensive* and *intensive* growth was one of the most often used means to justify economic reforms. According to this view, the development strategy and the methods applied in economic planning have to be different at various stages of building socialism. In the first part, when the foundations were laid down — i.e., in the 1950s, in the case of Hungary — both the strategy and its execution were basically correct. In the light of this analysis, the country had been originally rich in resources: there were abundant domestic labour reserves (mostly in agriculture) and the Soviet Union stood behind the country to satisfy all raw material needs at low cost. Later, however, the theory held, the country's own labour reserves became exhausted and the Soviet Union's delivery capacities became constrained. Thus, a transition to a more resource-intensive growth path had to be put on the agenda. In 1968, the economic justification of the NEM was totally based on this concept.[657] In later years, the demand for transition from extensive to intensive growth was repeatedly formulated in various government and party documents. In the absence of any agreed method to define and quantify the precise content of these concepts, politicians have continued to use this justification in a broad, all-inclusive sense.[658] The process of intensification was started, it was claimed, and the task on the agenda was to accelerate it.[659] In fact, it seems likely that in the period concerned (1970-1983) the contribution of pro-

---

[655] In 1953 the number of mandatory planning indicators approved by the Council of Ministers was close to 6,000. Twice as many were ordained by the ministries themselves. See I.T. Berend, *A magyar gazdasági reform útja* (The road of the Hungarian economic reform), Közgazdasági és Jogi Könyvkiadó, Budapest, 1988, p.39.

[656] See I. Pető, and S. Szakács, *A hazai gazdaság négy évtizedének története, 1945-1985* (The history of four decades in the domestic economy,1945-1985), Közgazdasági és Jogi Könyvkiadó, Budapest, 1985, and L. Antal, *Gazdaságirányítási és pénzügyi rendszerünk a reform útján* (Our economic and monetary system on the road of the reform), Közgazdasági és Jogi Könyvkiadó, Budapest, 1985, p.33.

[657] This can be illustrated by a short quotation, taken from the introductory part of the famous 1966 decree of the Hungarian Socialist Workers' Party (HSWP) which first announced the plan of the NEM. "The reform is justified by economic and political reasons. Its economic necessity is rooted, in the final analysis, in the fact that important sources and reserves of past economic growth have been largely exhausted. In the future, the possibility of fast economic growth is contingent upon the more intensive exploitation of the internal reserves of the economy and the acceleration of technical progress." (*Népszabadság*, 29 May 1966.)

[658] It is worth quoting the views of a leading expert on these issues. "The term *intensive stage* is a concept more of empirical economic economic policy than one of a theory or analysis of growth. In this sense it denotes the period when economic policies cede priority to the increase of productivity and efficiency as against the quantitative source of growth." See Z. Román, *Productivity and economic growth*, Akadémiai Kiadó, Budapest, 1982, p.171.

[659] Still in 1985, an important party document defining the tasks ahead used the following formulation: "In the coming years economic development has to be quickened. The intensive methods have to assert themselves in a strong and comprehensive manner by way of cost reduction and more efficient use of reserves in order to achieve balanced growth. This, in turn, will strengthen the equilibrium, permit the gradual and broad renewal of the material-technical fundaments

ductivity growth to overall economic expansion was declining or stagnating rather than increasing. In the material spheres of the economy the share of extensive factors (labour and capital) stood at 35 per cent in 1970-1975 period, but then increased to 57 per cent by 1983.[660]

(d) The *international oil crisis in 1973* and its aftermath had a double impact on the Hungarian economy and reform thinking. First, there was a short-term effect: in two years the terms of trade in convertible currencies transactions deteriorated by 20 per cent. The acceleration of inflation in the market economies and the ensuing deflationary period came at the worst time for Hungary. In 1972 the government had opted for an expansionist policy. At about the same time, strong conservative political opposition arose against the NEM. This largely carried the day, on the argument of the need to align the country's economic mechanism with that of the other (non-reforming) CMEA countries.[661] Thus, as the strain built up efforts were concentrated on neutralising the unfavourable effects in order to keep the promises made, both for investments and living standards. The terms-of-trade losses and the "normal" costs of the ongoing expansionist programme were covered by foreign borrowing. Between 1974-1978, this net resource import was equal to 6 per cent of GDP.[662] The effect of imported inflation was suppressed through increased price subsidies. The medium-term effect of these external shocks was also important. When international oil prices suddenly surged again in 1979, the country's industrial development policy was drastically changed. The domestic energy sector became a priority area. Between 1980 and 1988, more than 40 per cent of all industrial investments were allocated to the energy-related branches at the expense of all others.[663]

After a few years, however, during which government officials had repeatedly said that the "crisis" in the West would not spill over into Hungary, a full turn-round in policy became unavoidable. The ideological underpinning for the austerity measures and the changes in the system of management and planning was delivered by a new school in the reform camp. For them, the 1973 oil crisis and its after-effects marked the beginning of a *new epoch in the world economy*. They saw fundamentally new questions coming to the forefront (e.g., entirely new technologies in the developed countries, food shortages in the Third World, and world-wide concern over the environment).[664] The losses the country had already incurred were presented in a dramatic manner. According to a widely publicized estimate, the cumulated terms-of-trade loss between 1973-1983 was equal to the value of the assets Hungary had lost in the Second World War.[665] The beginning of the new epoch was also pictured as a major reclassification exercise among the countries participating in the development race. The issue at stake was formulated in this way: if Hungary adjusts to the requirements of the new epoch, there is a chance of catching up with the industrialized countries; if not, it will fall back in the group of Third World countries. In sum, these authors called for economic reforms in general — and within this for an *export-oriented growth strategy* — as an adjustment measure to the new circumstances.

(e) Professor Kornai's ideas on the *shortage economy* became known in the second half of the 1970s.[666] In a decade his ideas became part of common wisdom both in the Hungarian economic profession and in administration circles. This impact is well exemplified by the fact that in March 1989 the then ruling party, the Hungarian Socialist Workers' Party (HSWP), fully incorporated this concept into its new programme as a matter of course. The document stated that the main economic objective is a "consistent transition from an economy of shortages to a market economy" and everything else (e.g., property reform, convertibility, CMEA reforms) is contingent upon or derived from this task.[667]

For understandable reasons, only a rudimentary summary of Kornai's views can be given here. His main thesis holds that shortages are inevitable consequences of the traditional, non-reformed socialist system. Shortages are universal, chronic, self-generating and intensive. This does not mean, however, that there is always a shortage of everything. Nevertheless, they appear everywhere: on the market of consumer goods and services, in the production and investment process, in the sphere of foreign trade. Shortages are chronic — i.e., the efforts to eliminate them never bring more than a temporary attenuation. Shortages are self-generating. Shortage breeds shortage. The phenomenon is

---

of the economy and provide basis for increasing living standards." See *A Magyar Szocialista Munkáspárt XIII. Kongresszusa* (13th Congress of the Hungarian Socialist Workers' Party), Kossuth Könyvkiadó, Budapest, 1985, p.194.

660 See "Productivity trends in Eastern Europe and the Soviet Union, 1970-1983" in United Nations Economic Commission for Europe, *Economic Survey of Europe in 1985-1986*, New York, 1986, p.216.

661 In the course of 1974-1975, the party and government officials who had stood behind the NEM were removed from their positions. Among others, Central Committee Secretary R. Nyers as well as Prime Minister J. Fock and his two deputies were replaced.

662 According to the recollections of B. Csikós-Nagy, a key figure in the economic policy formation of these years, this was "the *best* solution for preventing any attack" by the anti-reformist forces. *Hungarian Business Herald*, No.4, 1989, pp.14-19.

663 In the previous 15 years the share of the energy-related industrial branches in total industrial investments had (on average) always been below 30 per cent. *Statisztikai Évkönyv 1988* (Statistical yearbook), p.25.

664 See, e.g., J. Bognár, "Strukturális váltásunk társadalmi-gazdasági összetevői és ellentmondásai" (The origins and the contradictions of our structural changes), *Közgazdasági Szemle*, 1980, No.7-8.

665 I.T. Berend, *Szocializmus és reform* (Socialism and reform), Akadémiai Kiadó, Budapest, 1986, pp.135-136.

666 Preceded by some articles and lectures, the Hungarian version of Kornai's book was published in 1980. For an English edition, see J. Kornai, *The Economics of Shortage*, 2 vols., North-Holland, Amsterdam, 1980.

667 *Népszabadság*, 11 March 1989.

intensive, meaning that it has forceful repercussions upon every single sector of the economy.

In the final analysis, the explanation of the phenomenon goes back to the problem of property rights. According to Kornai, shortages originate in the state enterprise sector. These enterprises have an insatiable demand for resources because they operate under a "soft budget constraint". Knowing that the government will always bail them out, they act accordingly. They are not really sensitive to prices or profits. Given their dependence on the state bureaucracy, they look more often in this direction, rather than at their own market. The conclusion is straightforward: as long as the state enterprises remain closely attached to the state bureaucracy, shortages will never cease to exist.

(iii) The conceptual framework of the reform proposals

Between the 1950s and the fundamental constitutional changes in the autumn of 1989, publicized reform proposals were necessarily self-limited. It was assumed that the country's constitutional set-up (including issues related to property rights, the role of the communist party, etc.), as well as its ties with the Soviet Union and the other east European countries, could not and need not be changed. Thus, the predominance of state ownership was never questioned by most economists.[668] The multiple links between economic policy decisions and the suggestions for changes in the economic mechanism were always conceived within this double constraint. An example can be useful to elucidate the nature of the second constraint.

At the time of the preparation of the NEM it was assumed that the transition would be facilitated by a stand-by loan agreement from the IMF and long-term investment credits from the World Bank. This would have permitted the liberalisation of imports and the external convertibility of the forint. According to the recollections of Hungarian bank officials,[669] confidential preliminary negotiations had been successfully concluded in November 1967. Then, however, the Hungarian political leadership shrank back. It was decided that the reform should be implemented on the basis of "self-reliance". For understandable reasons, such a decision — made at the very last moment — necessitated *ad hoc* solutions, some of which were counterproductive from a longer perspective.

In Hungary, as well as in many other socialist countries, the main idea behind the successive waves of economic reforms was the concept of *market socialism*. Although until very recently it was never formulated in such crude form,[670] this complex and sometimes very sophisticated concept, having its roots in the literature of the 1930s,[671] can be summarized in the form of an equation:

Market socialism = state property + market co-ordination.

The equation describes a behavioural norm for the the entire (or the predominant part) of the economy. Enterprises remain state property, but they should behave as *if* they were profit-seeking private agents of a market economy. In practice, the theoretical concept of market socialism was never fully accepted by policy makers. First, there has always been a considerable amount of mistrust *vis-à-vis* market co-ordination as such. Major investment decisions were always regarded as a prerogative of central planners.[672] Neither was the labour market ever left uncontrolled.[673] This was the reason why the theoretical discussions, as well as the reform documents, preferred to talk about the unity of *plan* and *market*.

The successive reforms followed three main avenues to make room for market co-ordination to work. First, great attention was paid to form enterprises of optimal size and output assortment. In the name of this objective, mergers and separations were ordered. In industry, for example, the number of state enterprises was gradually reduced, from 1,451 in 1957 to 699 in 1980. Later the process moved in the opposite direction. In 1988, state industry was made up of 1,143 units. Another area where the state authorities felt themselves obliged to act was the sphere of material incentives. Between 1957 and 1989, a dozen schemes (and hundreds of sub-versions) were tried to find the "optimal" link between enterprise performance and staff remuneration. Wages and bonuses were — sometimes

---

[668] In fact, there was one author, Tibor Liska, who liberated himself from this constraint. He openly questioned the economic rationality of the existing property relations and called for fundamental changes in this respect. Although his views were known to the profession, he remained marginalized for more than two decades. His book advocating an entrepreneurial society, which was written in 1964, was not published until 1988. He thought that property rights should be vested in citizens on a competitive basis. See T. Liska, *Ökonosztát* (The self-regulating economy), Közgazdasági és Jogi Könyvkiadó, Budapest, 1988.

[669] See E. Bakó, "Konvertibilis viszonylatú hitelfelvételi politikánkról a felszabadulástól napjainkig" (The history of our borrowing in convertible currencies from 1945 to the present), *Bankszemle*, 1989, vol.33, No.1, and an interview with J. Fekete in *Mozgo Világ*, vol.15, 1989, No.11, p.24.

[670] See J. Kornai, *Indulatos röpirat a gazdasági átmenet ügyében* (Passionate pamphlet on economic transition), Heti Világgazdaság Kiadói Részvénytársaság, Budapest, 1989, p.27.

[671] See, e.g., O. Lange, "On the Economic Theory of Socialism," *Review of Economic Studies*, October 1936 and February 1937. For a detailed overview of the debate on socialist planning, see D. Lavoie, *Rivalry and central planning. The socialist calculation debate reconsidered*, Cambridge University Press, Cambridge, 1985.

[672] In this respect, the Hungarian proponents of economic reforms have been — for a very long time — directly influenced by the views of the Polish economist Wlodzimierz Brus. He made a sharp distinction between investments serving simple and expanded reproduction. Brus thought that the first type of investments could be decentralized, while major investment decisions should remain centrally planned. For a detailed account of this Polish-Hungarian link see L. Szamuely (ed.), *A magyar közgazdasági gondolat fejlődése, 1954-1978* (The rise of Hungarian economic thought), Közgazdasági és Jogi Könyvkiadó, Budapest, 1986, p.51.

[673] The first time that unemployment was seriously considered was during the preparation of the NEM. According to the recollections of the deputy prime minister of that time, the implementation of a moderately rigorous profit regime was seen as endangering an estimated 150-200,000 jobs. Thus various "transitory" measures were taken to prevent such a development. See M. Timár, *Szürke pénzügyek* (Boring money matters), Magvető, Budapest, 1989, p.53.

directly — linked to the level of profit or to the change of this indicator. Later more and more sophisticated schemes were introduced, allowing for differences among the staff (workers and managers), in branch affiliation, etc. Last but not least, the efforts to correct the price system should be mentioned. Leaving aside minor modifications in relative prices, which occurred nearly every year, there were four major overhauls in the entire system of price formation (1959, 1968, 1980, 1988).

As noted, all reform efforts were induced and driven by two types of dissatisfaction shared by the leadership. After three decades of nearly uninterrupted changes in the economic mechanism it is little wonder that a third type of dissatisfaction was born. The economic profession and the public at large became *dissatisfied with reforms as such*. In the light of a deeper analysis it is possible to show that the changes in the economic mechanism were often hastily initiated and then worked at counterpurpose to the overall logic of earlier reforms. It is also true that the public was sometimes misled, as when minor corrections or irrelevant actions were presented as part of the reform process. At the beginning of the 1990s there is a widespread belief that everything has already been tried to make market socialism work, but nothing has helped. This is one of the primary reasons which led the ruling political party — the legal successor of the HSWP which had governed the country since 1956 — to opt for the transition to a market economy system[674] and to enshrine this view in the country's constitution.[675]

(iv) Building blocks already in place

The transition from a centrally planned economy to a fully-fledged market system will bring about seminal changes. Whether it requires a bold leap or a cautiously calibrated ponderous process remains to be seen. Instead of discussing the general problems which concern any country that engages itself in such a task, the analysis below (in this section and section (v)) is focused upon issues specific to the Hungarian case.

From the perspective of a smooth transition towards a market economy, the Hungarian reforms of the past three decades were not altogether in vain. Important building blocks of a fully-fledged market system have gradually emerged.

— The germs of private ownership are already present. Apart from industry, where the share of private activities is still insignificant, a small but fast-growing private sector is operating in the other branches of the economy. Almost 40 per cent of the agricultural produce comes from private farmers. Two thirds of the newly commissioned dwellings are built by small private firms or by the owners themselves. In retail trade, the share of private shopkeepers in total turnover is about 12 per cent. In public catering their weight is close to 30 per cent. In road transport, at least 10 per cent of lorries are owned privately.[676] These facts are corroborated by the 1988 tax returns. They showed that the number of taxpayers drawing a secondary income was close to 700,000. This is about 14 per cent of those gainfully employed. It is also important that a good part of the population has a relatively important stock of accumulated wealth. According to the 1985 household survey, more than 70 per cent of active households live in their own homes, nearly 40 per cent of them have their own car, and 6 per cent have a secondary home as well.[677] Some 200,000 individuals possess hard-currency accounts with various domestic financial institutions.

Earlier limitations on land property and real estate in general were recently abolished. Since 1 July 1989, Hungarian citizens can have as many houses or as much land as they can afford.[678] Members of agricultural co-operatives will soon have the right to leave the co-operative and regain full property rights over the land that they, or their ancestors, had brought in.[679]

The relatively wide-scale proliferation of private activities had a strong influence on the values and morale of the population. The emerging differentiation in incomes and wealth met with some opposition, but the principle that hard work and risk-taking have to be rewarded is generally accepted. If there is any resentment against the "new rich," it is mostly directed against the highly-paid managers of the state sector and the bureaucracy, and not against private entrepreneurs.

— The price and wage systems, although far from free of anomalies, do give reasonable guidance. Two factors explain this. First, the fact that prices have been used in controlling the entire agricultural sector since 1956, when the compulsory delivery system was abolished. Second, the openness of the Hungarian economy: price relatives, together with the system of interest and exchange rates, could not have remained totally arbitrary in an economy where

---

[674] See the "Programme of the Hungarian Socialist Party", *Népszabadság*, 10 October 1989.

[675] Article 9 of the amended constitution, which came into force on 23 October 1989, declared that "the economy of Hungary is a market economy, availing itself of the advantages of planning, where public and private ownership are equal and equally protected".

[676] Figures in this paragraph refer to 1988. See *Statisztikai Évkönyv 1988*, pp.26, 122, 158 and 159; *Belkereskedelmi Statisztikai Évkönyv 1988*, p.35.

[677] *Háztartásstatisztika 1985* (Family budget statistics 1985), KSH, Budapest, 1986, pp.28-31.

[678] This was made possible by an amendment to the 1987 Act on Land approved on 1 June 1989.

[679] This was made possible by a further amendment to the 1987 Act on Land, passed on 26 January 1990.

foreign trade and tourism has been allowed to develop to such an extent as in Hungary.

— Since 1989 the country has a modern company law.[680] This opened the possibility for citizens to found limited liability or shareholding companies. The act aims to promote competition, taking the nature of activity as the basis of regulation and not the form of organization or the sectoral adherence of those taking part in an association.[681] Domestic private firms may now have up to 500 employees. A new law on strikes, passed in March 1989, regulates the handling of industrial conflicts. In April 1989, the "socialist emulation movement" — the institutionalized form of campaigns to stimulate plan overfulfilment at the shop-floor level — was officially declared defunct and the relevant statutory provisions were revoked. Rights, guarantees and privileges of foreign investors are protected by a special act providing a legal framework for the activities of partly of fully owned foreign economic units.[682]

— A comprehensive banking reform was launched already in the second half of the 1980s. First the central bank's monopoly for credit extension was eliminated (1985). Enterprises were given the right to extend commercial credit to one another and to citizens as well. Two years later a two-tier banking system replaced the traditional mono-bank system. Legislation regulating the activities of the stock exchange was passed early in 1990. Since 1981, a great variety of new forms of savings instruments have appeared on the securities market such as bonds, shares, treasury bills, certificates of deposits and commercial bills. The former segmentation of the money market with its strict administrative separation of the households' financial transactions from those of the enterprises was thus abolished in most respects.[683]

— Public finance has been put on solid legal foundations, subject to approval by Parliament.[684] In the production sphere, taxation follows the logic of a value-added tax (VAT) system. Individuals are taxed upon their personal incomes.[685] Profits generated in the sphere of production by enterprises or private entrepreneurs are taxed in a uniform manner (entrepreneurial tax). From 1 January 1990, a newly created authority, the State Audit Office, supervises all financial aspects of the Government's activity.

— Substantial changes occurred in the regulation of trade denominated in convertible currencies and its financing. In 1989, 35-40 per cent of the convertible-currency imports were freed of licencing obligations.[686] As of 1 January 1990, six major commercial banks were allowed to finance convertible-currency transactions in foreign trade.[687] Four banks, all with foreign participation, were authorized to participate in credit and loan operations on western markets.[688]

— An Economic Deregulation Council started operation in September 1989. This new body of independent experts scrutinizes all proposed legislative actions. Earlier legislative documents issued by ministries shall cease to have effect from May 1990 unless the ministry concerned is able the convince the Council of the usefulness of the statutory provision.

— Hungary has a developed statistical system and maintains a broad public dissemination of related information. Unlike other east European countries, it has published national accounts data closely following the United Nations system (SNA) since 1968.[689] Great care and attention is paid to the measurement of inflation — a highly sensitive issue in all countries of the region. It is believed that — within the boundaries of measurement errors — the published figures correctly reflect the underlying trends.

(v) The uncharted road of transition

At the beginning of 1990 Hungary was administered by a *de facto* caretaker government. Major decisions, therefore, cannot be expected before the parliamentary

---

[680] "Act on Economic Associations", Ministry of Finance, *Public Finance in Hungary*, No.45, 1988.

[681] Thus, treatment under the law is the same whether the participants are state-owned, co-operative or private enterprises.

[682] "Act on Investments of Foreigners in Hungary", Ministry of Finance, *Public Finance in Hungary*, No.49, 1989.

[683] However, the level of interest rates for the two sectors was still different in 1989.

[684] Before 1988 such issues were regulated by decrees of the Council of Ministers or ordinances directly sent to the enterprises. Thus taxation rules were subject to arbitrary decisions of the bureaucracy.

[685] "Tax Reform in Hungary"; "Act on the General Turnover Tax"; "Act on Personal Income Tax"; Ministry of Finance, *Public Finance in Hungary*, No.39, 39/a, 39/b, 1987.

[686] This figure is an official estimate, based on the 1988 trade returns (see *Heti Világgazdaság*, 28 January 1990). The 1989 list of products which can be freely imported was published in the official gazette. Two thirds of the items figuring in the list are investment goods or components and spare parts for them.

[687] Transferable rouble deals with the CMEA countries and some special bilateral clearing agreements remain in the hand of the central bank.

[688] For the time being, fully Hungarian-owned commercial banks cannot borrow abroad without the approval of the National Bank (*Figyelő*, 11 January 1990).

[689] A World Bank check concluded that Hungarian GDP estimates were very close — within one half per cent — of what they would be if they followed a pure United Nations System of National Accounts (SNA) methodology. See *World Bank Staff Working Papers*, No.775 (1985).

elections, now scheduled for late March 1990. There are at least three areas where urgent decisions are required. These critical issues are the following: the scope and the methods of privatization of the larger state-owned units in industry and in the service sector, the future of the loss-making industrial firms, and the re-assessment of the future of the Hungarian agriculture and coal mining sectors.

— As a consequence of the political changes in 1989, the economic *raison d'être* of state property has now come into question. What is more, there is a broad consensus among the major political parties that the present weight of the state-owned sector is intolerably high and that large scale *privatization* is a pre-condition for the transition to a functioning market economy. However, the specific difficulty that Hungary has to face stems from the fact that, in some sense of the word, the state enterprises have been already "privatized". The roots of the problem go back the past legislation on the status of state enterprises. The 1977 Act on Enterprises already granted *autonomy* to them. Later, in the course of a half-hearted reform wave (1984-1985), 70 per cent of enterprises were transformed into *self-management* units. Apart from certain exceptions in the defence-related enterprises and public utilities, management rights were put into the hand of an elected body, the Enterprise Council.[690] Finally, a recently enacted piece of legislation, the 1989 Conversion Act,[691] opened the way for the enterprise councils to *change the legal status of their enterprises*. This means that the council can decide to turn the firm into a corporation and then partly or entirely sell it to any domestic or foreign buyer.

Needless to say, these laws were elaborated at times when the political environment was totally different from the realities of the years 1989-1990. Earlier, the legal "autonomy" of the enterprise was constrained by various formal or informal channels of political control. Thus, the central authorities were always in the position to keep an eye on major changes and block almost anything that they did not want. Now, the political events in 1989 — the introduction of a real multi-party system and the exclusion of all political parties from the work places[692] — removed these protective fences around the law. Although there were certain built-in legal guarantees to protect the interest of the state, the *de jure* owner of these firms, in practice it proved very difficult to bring them to bear effectively. Six months after the Conversion Act went into effect, an important and potentially valuable part of the state sector was already in the hands of foreign companies and private individuals. This process was particularly rapid in the activities related to tourism and the media (newspapers, publishing houses). There is concern among the political parties, shared by many experts both in the economics profession and in the administration, that by the time the new democratically-elected government assumes power, little will remain to be privatized. As a temporary measure — from 1 March 1990 — a newly established organization, the State Wealth Agency will monitor the process of privatization. The aim is to guarantee fair competition, realistic prices and to protect the interests of the central budget.

— Parliament passed a new law on *bankruptcy* in 1986. It was believed that at least 100 companies would be liquidated every year. In reality, however, there were not more than ten cases in the three years that followed. The reasons are rather straightforward. Given the monopolistic structure of the internal market, creditors themselves are at the mercy of their debtors. If they enforce liquidation, they will lose their most important or only clients. Moreover, under the present accounting rules it is more advantageous for the creditor (be it a bank or another enterprise) to carry illiquid claims on the books than to write off losses. If they did the latter, the losses would reduce current profits and the value of total assets to which wage and bonus payments are still linked according to a centrally prescribed formula.

At the end of 1989, some 41 large companies were in default, whose illiquidity blocked the normal financial flows in the entire economy. Altogether the number of firms which had shown a deficit for several years was put at 200. Other firms, good and bad alike, were waiting for their money, estimated at about ft 200 billion. This figure is close to the total value of short-term credit supplied by the banking sector (ft 232 billion).[693] Thus, in the absence of real bankruptcy, enterprises can create money for themselves by simply not paying their suppliers and creditors. Under such circumstances, strict monetary control — one of the measures practised by the present government and recommended to the future government by the international banking community — has little practical impact.

— Hungarian *agriculture* was known as one of the success stories of the post-1968 developments, whereas *coal mining* was always a trouble spot. In both sectors, production is largely determined by natural conditions. The emotional importance attached to these two sectors is also a common factor.

As mentioned, domestic food production experienced a spectacular growth between 1960 and 1980. By now the country's own needs are fully covered and one third of output goes for export. However, the prices on external markets for Hungarian agricultural exports have been depressed for a very long time — partly because they are determined by various forms of institutionalized interventions of the major producer countries. Between 1981 and 1987, Hungarian export prices, expressed in dollar terms, fell by 35 per cent. In order to maintain the interest of the Hungarian pro-

---

[690] The guidelines for these measures were defined in a Party resolution. For an English translation of this document, see *Acta Oeconomica*, vol.32, 1984, pp.363-474.

[691] The full title of the law is Act on the Conversion of Economic Organizations and Economic Associations.

[692] This latter decision was approved by a nation-wide referendum, the first in Hungarian history, on 26 November 1989.

[693] *Népszabadság*, 8 December 1989; *Heti Világgazdaság*, 16 December 1989; *Figyelő*, 4 January 1990.

ducers in exporting despite the fall in world market prices and the (partly unjustifiable) increase in the costs of production, the government was forced to pay heavy compensation. It is estimated that the total subsidy burden for the food sector (including price support for exports and the price reduction of inputs) amounts to 40 per cent of the value of output. In international comparison, the level of relative subsidization is not very high (lower than the average in western Europe). However, given the high share of agriculture in total output, the annual subsidy burden in 1987 was equivalent to about 9 per cent of GDP.[694]

Hungarian *coal mining* cannot pride itself on its production figures. In 1988 the volume of production was 3 per cent less (in caloric value terms) and the number of employees 2.5 per cent more than in 1951. In other words, in 40 years, despite the continuous pouring of investment resources into this branch, labour productivity actually fell. In the neighbouring socialist countries, output per man was higher by 45 per cent in Romania, 60 per cent in Bulgaria, and 350-500 per cent in Poland, Czechoslovakia and the German Democratic Republic.[695] It is rather evident that these differences largely reflect the poor resource endowment of Hungary. However, in this case little economic justification remains for the continuation of this activity. On the other hand, there are two factors which certainly make a radical solution very arduous. First, such a measure would be against the interest of 70,000 well-organized miners. Second, the substitution of this amount of energy will be difficult and costly, at least in the short run.

(vi) Prospects

At the time of writing, the present Parliament and the Government of Hungary have less than 60 days to remain in office. Nevertheless, in the framework of an earlier political agreement with the parties of the opposition, important pieces of legislation are planned to be passed before this deadline. According to the intention of the Government, these new laws are to serve one aim — a peaceful and co-ordinated transition from a centrally planned regime to a market economy system.

There is a growing consensus in the economic profession that the transition is inevitable and that it will require a painful stabilization policy. For political reasons, however, this requirement had not been articulated in the past and the necessary actions were postponed. In the course of painful adjustments to a new situation, when Hungarian performance will be measured on highly competitive markets, unemployment, volatile changes in prices and a fall in average standards of living seem more than likely. In addition, social conflicts will openly come to the surface. In order to shorten the length and to minimize the welfare losses of the transition period, determined and coherent economic policies will have to be formulated and implemented rapidly.

---

[694] I. Illés, "Válságkép zöldben-feketében" (The green and the black crisis), *Valóság*, vol.32, 1989, No.10.

[695] I. Illés, *op.cit.*

5.4 ECONOMIC REFORM IN THE SOVIET UNION

Economic reform in the Soviet Union is an integral part of the overall restructuring of society *(perestroika)*. The main objective of the reform is the creation of independent economic organizations operating on the basis of various types of property, financial autonomy, entrepreneurship and, in the public sector, self-management. This requires a radically new economic system, the engine of which will be market mechanisms, in contrast with the old one which was based on mandatory central directives. The transition from a centrally planned to a market economy is to be aided by the development of a flexible system for regulation of the economic activity of enterprises. However, the reforms implemented so far failed to achieve tangible results as the dismantling of the old command system was not accompanied by the creation of any consistent new co-ordination mechanism. The resulting economic crisis coupled with pronounced social tensions requires much more comprehensive reforms in addition to an efficient stabilization policy.

(i) Introduction

Soviet economic reforms have a long history. Even if the new economic policy (NEP), introduced in 1921 and terminated in 1929 is put aside, as early as in the 1950s serious shortcomings of the over-centralized economic mechanism introduced in the 1930s had motivated two attempts at partial reforms. The resolution on changes in agricultural policy, adopted at the September 1953 Plenum of the Soviet Communist Party, was the first. This was followed by a reform of the branch-based central management in 1957, which resulted in the abolition of most industrial ministries and the formation of 104 regional economic councils — *sovnarkhozy*.[696]

This new variant of a centralized management did not produce the expected results, and broad economic debate in the first half of the 1960s led to a more ambitious economic reform in 1965. Its major provisions included the re-creation of the industrial ministries, a reduction in the number of mandatory planning indicators, changes in the price formation system, an extension of the financial autonomy of enterprises and the introduction of some elements of market co-ordination.

This reform brought some improvements, including some acceleration of economic growth, but both proved short-lived.[697] The short-run economic effects of the 1965 reform thus were rapidly consumed. In the second half of the 1970s the pace of expansion slowed further and the country was poised for a new reform.

In July 1979 a joint decree of the Central Committee of the CPSU and the USSR Council of Ministers on improving planning and reinforcing the economic mechanism to raise production efficiency and the quality of work was adopted, which might be interpreted as a new reform attempt, albeit less ambitious than that of 1965.[698] The principal objectives of the decree were: to enhance responsibility at all levels of management and improve the efficiency of investment through the self-financing of enterprises, to strengthen plan fulfilment incentives by linking labour remuneration more closely with production results; to increase the share of enterprises in profits and to use a considerable part of these for incentive funds; to replace the multiplicity of performance indicators by three only — labour productivity, the quality of the output and the degree of fulfilment of deliveries agreed in supply contracts.

In the first half of the 1980s, new regulations were introduced to strengthen the 1979 dispositions. These included measures to reinforce bank monitoring of enterprise finance, more realistic interest rates, the greater use of bank credits instead of budgetary grants, increases in the power of local bodies with regard to land use, environmental protection, construction, the use of labour resources, production of consumer goods and so on.[699]

However, all these attempts failed to alter the traditional economic mechanism as they did not touch the basic principles of the administrative and command system. They also failed because they were based neither on any democratization of society nor corresponding political reform. In fact, even in the economic domain they had a half-hearted character and were largely cosmetic. Moreover, the apparatus running the administrative and command system opposed even these weak attempts to reform the centralized system of economic management set up in the 1930s which remained, to all intents and purposes, untouched.[700]

---

[696] Abbreviation of *sovety narodnogo khozyaistva*, councils of national economy.

[697] Average annual rates of growth in 1966-1970 were: NMP produced — 7.8 per cent; gross industrial output — 8.5 per cent; gross agricultural output — 4.2 per cent. This compares with 6.5, 8.6, and 2.3 per cent, respectively, in 1961-1965. In 1971-1975, the growth rates of the same variables declined considerably — to 5.7, 7.4, and 0.8 per cent, respectively. See *Statisticheski ezhegodnik stran-chlenov SEV* (CMEA yearbook), 1988, p.34.

[698] *Ekonomicheskaya gazeta*, No.32, Moscow, 1979.

[699] *Izvestiya*, 29 March 1981.

[700] According to a Soviet economist " ... the state bodies ruined the ideas of the 1965 economic reform. Those who ruined the reform were numerous, and their

(ii) Economic reform in the second half of the 1980s

Comprehensive economic reforms in the Soviet Union started only in 1985. In February 1986 the XXVII Congress of the Soviet Communist Party called for a reconstruction of the whole system of management in the economic area.[701] The main elements of the reform were to be as follows: the concentration of central planning bodies on strategic development tasks and targets; transformation of enterprises and associations into viable, self-financing organizations on the basis of cost-accounting; transition to economic management at all levels and sectors of the national economy; reconstruction of the supply, price formation, finance and credit systems.

The report stressed that the key element of economic reform was the economic independence of state enterprises and associations together with the broader introduction of economic methods of management. The Congress also gave the green light to co-operative forms of ownership and individual (private) activities.

In November 1986, a Law on individual (private) activity was adopted. The Law specified 29 categories of activity where private enterprise was to be allowed. The Law essentially provided for the formation of a new, if still small, private (usually called "individual" or "co-operative") sector of the national economy. In practical terms, it acknowledged that private property is not just a remnant of the past — as had been the earlier position — but also a necessity for the present and the future and provided a basis for the establishment of lasting private and co-operative activity.

Economic reforms initiated by the XXVII Congress of the CPSU have been thereafter continued by new legislation, but their implementation proved to be much more difficult than expected.

In contrast with previous attempts, the series of economic reforms in the 1980s has been termed "radical". There have been four stages:

— a preparatory stage, from April 1985 to June 1987;

— an early, juridical implementation stage, from mid-1987 to mid-1988;

— a period of growing imbalances in the national economy, from mid-1988 to mid-1989;

— a period of increasing social tension and the adoption of extraordinary measures, from mid-1989 to the present.

The *preparatory* stage was linked with the formulation of a theoretical and political framework for the radical restructuring of the economic management system. The main landmark in this period was the decision of the XXVII Party Congress, which was accompanied by comprehensive discussion on the conceptual problems of economic reform.

The crucial point in the *second stage* of the reform process was the June 1987 Plenum of the Soviet Communist Party, which adopted the "Basic Provisions for the Radical Restructuring of Economic Management". The main goal of this document was to create favourable conditions for enterprises and associations to consolidate their economic independence and responsibilities, to transform economic growth from a predominantly resource-based (extensive) to a resource efficient (intensive) pattern, to orient production to meet consumer demand, to promote the comprehensive development of human resources and to achieve the technological advances essential for intensive economic growth. The main elements of the economic reform formulated in this document were as follows: a considerable extension of enterprise operations based on profitability, full cost accounting and self-financing; the limitation of centralized economic management to fundamental issues concerning the strategy of national economic development; thorough reform of the planning, price formation, finance and credit mechanisms; transformation of an excessively centralized command system of management to democratic procedures based on self-administration and involving considerable changes in the working methods of party, local government and central economic bodies.

In line with the principles of the economic reform, two juridical acts were adopted: the Law on the state enterprise (association) in June 1987 and the Law on co-operatives in June 1988.

The *Law on the state enterprise (association)* was expected to constitute the core document for the economic reform as a whole. The 25 articles of this law specified the rights and obligations of state enterprises. The fundamental principle was the financial autonomy of enterprises and their responsibility for production, sales and the use of income. The role of competition and the possibility of bankruptcy were also expressly mentioned. The principle that "everything is permitted which is not prohibited" was adopted. The law defined five "principles of enterprise activity" (article 2): conformity with the state plan, economic accountability (*khozraschet*) and self-financing, self-management, economic competition, and adherence to the law. The mutual relationships between enterprises and their superior branch organizations (state bodies) were directed along four major channels: central planning targets (non-mandatory), state orders, stable long-term economic norms and limits (the relation between the volume of state capital expenditures and other centrally distributed material resources on the one hand and output on the other). In addition, enterprises were to conclude contracts with other enterprises for the implementation of their plans and for the disposal of production exceeding planned targets. The law on the

---

addresses are well-known — for example, the Ministry of Finance. The root of the reform was the independence of the enterprise. This was vitiated by all the bodies concerned, each of which pursued only its own interest.". V. Krivosheev, *Izvestiya*, 17 June 1988.

[701] *Politicheskii otchet tsentral'nogo komiteta KPSS 27 S'ezdu Kommunisticheskoi partii Sovetskogo Soyuza* (Political report of the CPSU Central Committee to the 27th Congress of the Communist Party of the Soviet Union), Moscow, 1986.

state enterprise (association) came into effect at the beginning of 1988.

The *Law on co-operatives* defined the economic, social, organizational and legal conditions for the operation of these organizations and for the role of the co-operative sector in the national economy as a whole. According to the Law, the co-operative is an independent organization of citizens, associated to conduct economic and other activities based on property legally belonging to them, rented by them, or leased to them by the public (state) sector. The Law calls for the autonomy, self-management and self-financing of such co-operatives. Their creation is not contingent on any permission from central organs. They are considered to exist from the moment their statute — the fundamental document regulating their activities — is registered with local government (Soviets) after adoption by a general meeting of all members. Operating according to principles of full financial autonomy and self-financing, the co-operatives define the thrust of their activity, the scale and structure of production; they implement production planning, organization and output of goods or services. Their economic activities are implemented solely on a contractual basis between them and suppliers or clients.[702]

At the same time as legislation to increase the economic independence of production units was introduced, a special resolution to improve the wage and salary structure (including the introduction of new wage tariffs in the material sphere) was also adopted.[703] The resolution came into effect in 1987 and affected 75 million employees (two thirds of the number employed in the material sphere). Its main objective was to raise wages, to widen earnings differentials and to transfer to enterprises certain rights in setting bonus rates and payments.[704] The minimum wage in the material sphere was raised from 70 to 80 roubles per month. The average wage rate was planned to increase by 20-25 per cent and the wages of highly qualified workers and engineers were to rise by 40-45 per cent in 1986-1990. Simultaneously, salaries in non-material sphere sectors were also increased substantially.

But there has been a big lag between intention and reality in the implementation of economic reforms,[705] which has led to criticisms of the reform measures taken so far, and implicitly of the reform programme altogether.[706] These criticisms culminated at the Plenary Session of the Central Committee of the Soviet Communist Party in February 1990.[707] The leadership of the country nonetheless did not consider that the economic reform should be stopped, let alone abandoned, but rather found that it was impossible to proceed with it without a far-reaching political reform and, in particular, a wide-ranging restructuring of the role of the party. A platform for restructuring the party was adopted in early 1990 and substantial changes in the constitutional system of the country are expected already during the current year.

(iii) Emergency adjustments to reform measures in 1988-1989

After the attempts to reform the management of the Soviet economy, as early as in 1988 the economic situation was marked by higher inflation rates and a worsening in state finances. The rate of growth of money incomes accelerated strongly and exceeded that for the two previous years combined. Nominal wages in industry, construction, agriculture and railway transport grew faster than labour productivity. The relationship between the growth of earnings and production deteriorated. The internal financial position of the country substantially worsened — the state budget deficit amounted to 120 billion roubles in 1988 alone — and the situation in the consumer markets became very tense. The growth of incomes exceeded the ability of the production system to meet higher demand.[708]

Official data show a strong volume increases in 1988 of GNP, NMP and other indicators, but there are indications that these data include an element of price inflation.

In the course of 1989 the overall real socio-economic situation in the country deteriorated further. Almost all the main economic indicators were below planned targets and some of them were below the previous year's level (see section 3.1 above).

Social unrest has also had substantial economic costs. Losses of working time for unjustified reasons in industry and construction alone increased by 30 per cent and reached more than 40 million man-days. Losses of working time due to strike action amounted to more than 7 million man-days.

---

[702] Many observers point out that this law is clearer and less ambivalent than the Law on the state enterprise. See, for example, P. Bunich, "Soyuzniki i konkurenty" (Allies and Competitors), *Ogonyek*, No.16, 1988. It has even been suggested that the Law on co-operatives be taken as a model for improving the Law on state enterprise. B. Kurashhvili, "Prava i ogovorki" (Rights and Reservations), *Moscow News*, No.16, 1988.

[703] *Pravda*, 3 November 1986.

[704] *Ekonomicheskaya gazeta*, No.34, 1987.

[705] For instance, average earnings increased by much more than envisaged by the legislation. As a result, earnings have grown much faster than labour productivity and consumer goods supplies. This has provoked serious imbalances on the consumer markets and a deepening economic crisis (see chapter 3, above).

[706] See summary of a speech by Academician L. Abalkin in BBC, *Summary of World Broadcasts*, London, 23 November 1989. See also *Moscow News*, No.2, 1990.

[707] In his speech to the Plenary Session, the secretary of the Leningrad party branch, B. Gidaspov, said that destabilization in the country was growing every day and that the reform of the Party proposed by Mr. Gorbachev "does not give cause for optimism". *Pravda*, 6 February 1990.

[708] Despite these inflationary pressures, official data reported that the index of retail prices in state and co-operative trade grew less than 1 per cent in the year 1988 as a whole. *Narodnoe khozyaistvo SSSR v 1988 gody*, Moscow, 1989, p.125.

In part, losses of potential real output have been exacerbated by inter-ethnic clashes, which have assumed considerable proportions and have begun to disturb seriously the restructuring process.[709] Money incomes went up by almost 13 per cent — much faster than the increase in expenditures on goods and services, labour productivity and/or production of consumer goods. According to official reports, in the last four years money incomes exceeded expenditures for purchases of goods and services by more than 160 billion roubles. As a result, personal savings increased 50 per cent,[710] but even that did not help and imbalances on the consumer markets widened further. In many regions of the country rationing was introduced for a number consumer goods. Plans for the construction of housing, schools and hospitals were not fulfilled.

Furthermore, not only did overall output growth slow down between 1988 and 1989, but the quarterly rates in 1989 decreased progressively. In fact, for the first time in Soviet history, excluding the war periods, all the main production complexes of the national economy registered negative growth in the last quarter of 1989 compared with levels a year earlier.[711]

The economic events of 1989 reflect the fact that economic reform was, in general, implemented slowly and inconsistently. On the one hand, a very important decree on the leasing of land and other state or collective property was adopted by the Presidium of the Supreme Soviet of the USSR in April 1989. Moreover, the Second Congress of People's Deputies adopted a special Law on leasing in December 1989, which has considerably extended the room for leasing of state owned means of production to co-operatives and thus pushed toward the frontiers of economic reform. Amendments were also introduced into the Law on state enterprises (associations) which were intended to extend further the economic independence and self-financing rights and responsibilities of enterprises. On the other hand, however, some administrative measures of a mandatory character, which act contrary to the logic of the economic reform, were also adopted. In October 1989 the USSR Supreme Soviet adopted a special law amending the previously adopted Law on co-operatives, which imposed upper limits for the prices and tariffs of basic consumer goods and services produced and sold by them. State monitoring of prices for some products manufactured under contract was also established. Simultaneously, the trading and purchasing activities of co-operatives were seriously limited.[712]

In November 1989, a decree of the USSR Supreme Soviet laying down additional measures for stabilizing consumer markets and strengthening state control of prices was adopted.[713] According to the decree, some articles of the Law on the state enterprise (association) — in particular those introducing the enterprise's right to establish contract prices for some goods, to export consumer goods etc. — were suspended. Simultaneously, new measures to strengthen state price controls were introduced (the prices of certain goods were frozen, measures were taken against the withdrawal of cheap goods from the market, and state orders were placed for low-priced essential goods).

Drastic restrictions were also imposed on the export of a wide range of food, consumer goods and raw materials. Export licensing and rationing now apply to all Soviet participants in foreign trade, and quotas have been set for each Soviet republic for the export of consumer goods and raw materials needed for processing goods in 1990. In connection with the existing shortage of goods in the domestic market, the USSR Council of Ministers adopted a decision "On measures to regulate consumer goods exports from the USSR" on 30 August 1989. It restricts, *inter alia*, exports of goods from the USSR by foreign citizens.

In August and September 1989, the USSR Supreme Soviet adopted a resolution on the taxation of the wage and salary funds of state enterprise and co-operatives engaged in the production of goods and services, leaseholders and organizations and enterprises of other public organizations. It was decided that, in the last quarter of 1989 and in 1990, state enterprises and co-operatives must pay into the budget of their place of registration a tax on any increases in the wage fund of more than 3 per cent. These resolutions replaced previously mandatory normative ratios between the growth of labour productivity and the growth of the wage and salary fund. The adoption of an extensive package of important Laws on land ownership, taxation and price formation was postponed until early March 1990; it was decided instead to introduce a series of special measures by the replacement of the state procurement system by wholesale trade advanced very little. Altogether, economic reform went slowly.

There were, nonetheless, some positive developments. Inter-enterprise exchanges based on contracts increased considerably. The number of co-operative and private firms and other forms of economic activity independent of the state rose considerably.[714] Nevertheless, as a whole, the question of whether it is possible to reconstruct a long-established command economy, to change deeply-rooted attitudes and release entrepreneurial initiative has received increasingly pessimistic answers in 1989. The reform proposals seem to have

---

[709] *Pravda*, 28 January 1990.

[710] *Pravda*, 28 January 1990, 8 February 1990.

[711] *Argumenty i fakty*, No.4, 1990.

[712] *Pravda*, 21 October 1989.

[713] *Pravda*, 25 November 1989.

[714] Between 1 January 1989 and 1 January 1990, the number of co-operatives, for example, increased from 135,600 to 250,500 and employment in them rose from 1.4 to 5.5 million. *Izvestiya*, 5 March 1990.

underestimated the nature of the country's economic problems and that is one of the main reasons why the restructuring process has not yet gone very far. Moreover, prominent economists and political personalities claim that it is because of the half-hearted measures adopted so far that overall effects of economic reforms have been counterproductive.[715] Occasionally, the poor economic results and notably the imbalances on the consumer markets have even been directly linked by public opinion to *perestroika*.

It is clear that the pace of economic reform has lagged behind the schedule originally adopted. Many enterprises, ministries and departments have continued to work according to previous routines and apparently new forms in fact cloak an old content. At the upper levels of the economy, there is apprehension about letting go the levers of control. At lower levels, and especially on the shop floor, there is a fear of losing wages and even jobs.

Finally, the fact is that the country began the process of restructuring with an unclear blueprint as to how the levers of economic management and legal norms should work, with an insufficiently thought-out institutional structure and with inadequately prepared personnel. This also explains why the restructuring has only replaced bad by weak economic management and has resulted so far in widespread social dissatisfaction requiring real reforms combined with stabilization policies.

(iv) The economic stabilization programme from 1990 onwards

In August 1989 a new governmental Commission on economic reform was formed jointly by the government and the Supreme Soviet. This commission, headed by Deputy Prime Minister Academician L. Abalkin, began to prepare a stabilization programme and a new reform package. The draft was ready by early autumn and was discussed in a preliminary way at a Conference on economic reform convened in November 1989. The final text of the programme was presented by Prime Minister Ryzhkov to the Second Congress of the People's Deputies in December. The main goal of this programme was the creation of a new economic system within the framework of socialist preferences. The main features of this system are as follows:

— a variety of forms of ownership of productive resources, their equal treatment by the law and competition between them as the fundamental basis of economic freedom. This is understood as a lasting feature of the economy and a key point of reference in the creation of incentives for enterprises and workers to improve productivity, to boost scientific and technological progress and for the attainment of an optimal economic structure.

— the use of the market as the main force for co-ordinating the activities of producers. The creation of internal markets is to be based on the variety of forms of ownership and presupposes the existence of normal economic competition and free prices. Important elements are to be financial and manpower markets, since only through the creation of markets in these areas can the necessary mobility of production resources be ensured.

— measures to ensure equal development possibilities for everybody and to improve the environment.

— macro-economic regulation of the national economy primarily by means of economic levers and indirect economic and social planning; the placing of state orders on a competitive basis; selected and limited state investment and subsidies; flexible regulation of prices, taxes and sanctions; the regulation of money circulation and credit; the use of state stocks of goods for market and price stabilization; legal regulation of economic activities including the break-up of monopolistic production structures; the promotion of competition and the defence of consumers.

— remuneration of labour be strictly according to real results, implying dependence of a company's wage funds on sales and profits and a close linkage between individual wages and performance of individual workers and workers teams.

It is considered that the implementation of this programme means not just the improvement or repair of the existing economic mechanism, but its dismantling and its substitution by a completely new model of economic organization.[716]

Hand in hand with this new model, the economic stabilization programme envisages the transition to a market economy; the creation of a multi-sector in place of a single state economy through a thorough-going revision of the Law relating to property; the introduction of regional as well as enterprise autonomy; and the maintenance of full social guarantees.

The second Congress of Peoples Deputies adopted the governmental programme of economic stabilization and the proposed timetable for the various stages of economic reform. Two stages are envisaged.

---

[715] Such views, for instance, are present ina summary of the debates in the Congress of Deputies and the Plenary session of the Central Committee of the CPSU in March 1990, as reflected in *Izvestiya*. 13 March 1990, p.2, and *Pravda*, 18 March 1990.

[716] "It is not repair of old buildings, but the pulling down of the administrative command system and its substitution by a qualitatively new model of the socialist economy." Academician L. Abalkin, "Radikalnaya ekonomicheskaya reforma: pervoocherednye i dolgovremennye mery" (The radical economic reform: priority and long-term measures), *Ekonomicheskaya gazeta*, No.47, 1989.

The first stage is scheduled for implementation in 1990-1992. In this period, a complex of special measures to liquidate the budgetary deficit and imbalances on consumer markets is to be applied. In practice, the implementation of these measures had already begun in 1989 by means of a reduction of investment in the material sphere, the redistribution of NMP used in favour of consumption, rigid wage and salary control in the latter part of the year, a reduction of military production and the improvement of consumer goods production and services. The price and tax reforms were postponed to 1991, which is a departure from earlier schedules.

The economic stabilization programme provides for a re-orientation of economic development in favour of individual and collective needs and also in favour of the general welfare. Of special significance are the special measures envisaged for 1990 to reduce social tension. The whole increment in NMP used is to be absorbed by increases in consumption and in residential and other non-productive construction projects, which are to increase by 6.5 per cent. Industrial output is to increase by 2.6 per cent, but a 7.6 per cent rate of growth has been retained for group B (mainly consumer goods) and only 0.8 per cent for group A (mainly producer goods). The growth of engineering output is set at 4.2 per cent, 30 per cent of which is accounted for by consumer goods. A similar increase in the production of goods is expected from the conversion of the defence complex. More than 100 defence industrial enterprises are scheduled to be transferred to the production of consumer goods in 1990.[717] Some 500,000 defence industry workers are to transfer to civilian production in 1990.[718] Besides these, the annual increase in paid services is targeted at 10-12 per cent.

The beginning of 1990 also saw the introduction of a number of new measures designed to bring prices more into line with real scarcities. On 1 January 1990, the tariffs on diesel oil, electricity and freight transport increased considerably. These will give rise to serious difficulties for many state enterprises and organizations (especially in the spheres of trade and culture) and will affect their development. Special taxation of wage and salary funds also continued. All these measures could exacerbate social tensions which in their turn may led to further postponement of the reform measures and leave in place certain special, "administrative" type actions.

The February 1990 Plenary Session of the Central Committee of the Soviet Communist Party adopted the draft programme to be presented to the XXVIII Party Congress, which indicated the main areas of further economic reform. During 1990-1992 the legal and normative basis of the new system is to be introduced. In particular, a package of fundamental laws to regulate economic activity is to be prepared in spring 1990. It includes legislation on ownership, land, self-management, self-financing at local and enterprise levels, based on a unified taxation system and on the independent status of socialist enterprises. Especially important will be the reform of the price formation and the taxation systems, in parallel with anti-monopoly and anti-inflationary legislation and provisions to ensure the social protection of the population.

The second stage covers the years 1993-1995. After the period characterized by special measures and the introduction of the reformed framework of economic regulation, a more actively functioning market is to be encouraged on the basis of changes in the ownership structure and land tenure (including leasing). It is expected that this will result in a fully-functioning market (including markets for labour, capital goods, and a stock market), combined with overall state regulation. For the latter, a second package of laws and decrees is to be formulated, covering a unified tax policy, banking, investment activity, employment and so on. An important part of the new model is to be the system of social guarantees (minimum standard of living, indexation of incomes, etc.).

Thus, 1993-1995 is to be a period in which the country will develop under the conditions of the new economic mechanism. The programme envisages the transition of 20 per cent of all Soviet enterprises to leasing by co-operatives and individual entrepreneurs and a rise in the share of the co-operative sector to 15-20 per cent of total output (it is currently 2 per cent only).[719]

Altogether the new programme seems to be far more radical and comprehensive than that of June 1987, which was virtually silent on ownership rights and focused primarily on the decentralization of decision-making in state enterprises only. New ownership rights are the centre-piece of the new approach, and the final goal is clearly a competition-oriented market economy. On the other hand, the programme is far less radical than economic reforms now under way in some east European countries and lags behind the proposals of some Soviet economists.[720]

(v) Conclusions

The new Soviet programme of economic reforms and stabilization policy goes beyond any earlier similar attempts but nevertheless remains very cautious. It envisages the preservation of central control over the economy and postpones crucial restructuring measures, including the reform of price formation and direct taxation. This is a result of several factors. Not least is the opposition of the officials running the system who will not easily relinquish their power. Moreover, the pro-

---

[717] *Pravda*, 14 December 1989.

[718] *Pravda*, 29 December 1989.

[719] *Moscow News*, 7 January 1990.

[720] See, e.g., statement of B. Eltsin in *Pravda*, 7 February 1990, and also the article by G. Popov in *Ogonek*, No.10, March 1990.

gramme pays too little attention to the detail of reform. As noted at the February 1990 Plenum of the Central Committee of the CPSU, the economic reform is being implemented in an over-simplistic manner and is lagging behind the schedule envisaged earlier. None of the necessary economic regulators have been introduced and the new principles of labour remuneration are being implemented inconsistently.[721]

The main criticisms of the latest reform and stabilization programme may be summarized as follows:

— the present reform programme is still an attempt to carry out the economic reforms from the top instead of the bottom, at the enterprise level ("with the consent of the masses");

— the reform is being implemented very slowly and inconsistently; there is a the possibility that it may be further disrupted by strikes, ethnic or other unrest, which could derail the whole process of economic reform and feed existing social tensions;

— some planned targets are vague, others unrealistic (for instance, the target for increasing consumer goods production in 1990 by 66 million roubles);

— old command methods of management are still kept in many areas, as was reflected in the increased share of state orders in general volume of output in 1989. This will delay market creation and strengthen centralizing tendencies;

— the reform with regard to agriculture has been half-hearted in respect of the extention of room for the private sector;

— only three economic laws have been adopted until early March 1990 (the Law on leasing, the Law on the economic autonomy of the Baltic republics and Byelorussia and the Law on property rights). The adoption of other laws has been postponed;

— the reform of management is partial, inconsistent and in many respects superficial.

The new programme did not reflect many apparently workable ideas and proposals put forward by some Soviet economists, including the following:

— to begin with reform in the agricultural sector and to follow that by the reform of services and consumer goods production;

— to create immediately a two-level economy embracing the state and non-state sectors, to introduce markets and competition among the sectors, to restrict the role of the state sector to heavy industry;

— to create an internal market and implement the reform of price formation and introduce a modern taxation system;

— to dismantle the old system of planning and state management and eliminate a number of ministries;

— to reduce the share of state orders in the national output;

— to give land to peasants who wish to withdraw from state or collective farms;

— to restore positive real interest rates throughout the economy and to sell off state-owned assets on a large scale in order to restore monetary and consumer goods market balances;

— to produce large numbers of cars and other consumer durable goods of high quality for which there is an enormous demand;

— to establish firm technological and economic links with western firms for entering the world market (joint ventures, free economic zones, etc.), and to create a powerful export sector in industry;

— to introduce a convertible rouble;

— to implement regional accounting in a rational manner which will not compromise the functioning of the Soviet economy as a whole.

Overall, the fifth post-war attempt to implement economic reform in the Soviet Union has, so far, failed to achieve tangible results. Partly because of unfavourable external conditions and internal tensions, but also due to its slow and inconsistent implementation, the economic situation in the country has worsened to the extent that it is frequently qualified as an open crisis — both abroad and at home.[722] The government is trying to remedy the crisis but it appears that outdated administrative measures can no longer help. The gap between expectations and reality in economic development has thus increasingly widened.

A significant lag between the dismantling of the old command mechanism of managing the economy and the creation of a new system seems to be a common denominator of all the weaknesses of the present situation. The inertia of the old economic mechanism, which is characterized by the non-market nature of the economy and a lack of interest among workers and collectives of state enterprises in the result of their labour, is still very strong. However, the Soviet authorities are increasingly aware that substantive reform

---

[721] *Pravda*, 8 February, 1990.

[722] See, e.g., the Platform of the Central Committee of the CPSU for the XXVIII Party Congress in *Ekonomicheskaya gazeta*, No.8, 1990.

must be carried out in a consistent and controlled manner. The February 1990 Plenary Session of the Central Committee of the CPSU indicated that strong political support is being put together for such reforms — a reason to hope that during the 1990s they may be more successful than in earlier decades.

5.5 ECONOMIC REFORM IN YUGOSLAVIA

(i) Introduction

After the Second World War, Yugoslavia was the first east European country to introduce the traditional centrally planned economic system, and did so of its own accord; but it was also the first country to question that economic system. Indeed, the departure from that system, both in theoretical and practical terms, was so decisive that for several decades the Yugoslav economic system has not been classified as a centrally planned economy. Yugoslavia did not restore a fully-fledged market system, but instead tried to combine the basic principles of a market economy with relatively extensive indicative planning and with the participation of employees in management. Because of the latter feature, the system became known as one of "self-management". The combination of these three elements brought about a kind of *socialist market economy*, a term often used to indicate a third way between the traditional centrally planned socialist system and the decentralized market economy.

Although the Yugoslav system enjoyed a period of international popularity, the reality was never as positive as it appeared at first glance. For many years the remnants of the traditional socialist system remained and occasionally re-emerged with surprising strength, while the orientation towards the market economy was in many respects hesitant and inconsistent. Conceptual and political debates – which were largely dominated by ideological rather than pragmatic considerations – coupled with strong centrifugal forces at the beginning of the 1970s, turned Yugoslavia away from the market economy and towards a hybrid which was difficult to describe as an economic *system*. The economic effects of this "system" were concealed by huge external borrowing during the 1970s, but by 1980 the limits of this safety valve had been reached. In spite of a fairly accurate analysis of the problems and a way out suggested by the long-term stabilization programme prepared in 1982, the lack of political consensus led to an open social and economic crisis by the mid 1980s.

Although internal political disagreements are still profound, the new Yugoslav Federal Government installed in early 1989 acted decisively. At the end of 1989, the Federal Parliament passed an ambitious package of economic reforms combined with comprehensive stabilization policies. The aim is to establish a multisectoral, fully-fledged market economy, beginning with immediate convertibility of the dinar. Although it carries some risk and is still controversial in Yugoslavia, the package has been carefully prepared – including an unprecedented build-up of foreign exchange reserves – and there is a good chance that it will be successful.

(ii) Major aspects of the reform

During the 1970s and the 1980s Yugoslavia was beset by a number of unsolved and worsening problems. These included:

– an inefficient economic system in which market forces were weak or non-existent and where macro-economic co-ordination was ineffectual;

– an outdated political system in which the League of Communists of Yugoslavia (LCY) dominated developments in the country;

– a federal constitutional system where, in practice, each of the six republics and two autonomous provinces could at any time veto any decision of the Federal Parliament;

– a mission to conduct macro-economic policy at the federal level which is entrusted to the Federal Executive Council (FEC), but which in practice the council has few means of implementing;

– an external debt which was excessive and was serviced mainly through domestic currency creation by the National Bank of Yugoslavia;

– rising inflation which at the end of 1989 reached some 60 per cent per month;

– mounting social and ethnic tensions.

Attempts to cure these and other problems during the 1980s failed, mainly because no political agreement could be reached on a radical reform of Yugoslavia's institutional structure. The contradiction between a situation which urgently required radical changes, on the one hand, and a lack of support for such changes at the federal level, on the other, led to the resignation of the Federal Government in late 1988. Several months elapsed before a new government was created in spring 1989.

As a condition of accepting office, the new prime minister insisted on three crucial changes: that all inter-republican committees be abolished and that the government carry out its duties without supervision by representatives of republics and provinces; that the government be freed of interference by various political bodies and left to act according to the constitution and in close co-operation with the Federal Parliament;

finally, that the members of the government, while chosen from candidates proposed by the republics and provinces, be selected by the prime minister elect and that, after approval by the Parliament, they should act independently rather than as representatives of their republics or provinces.

During 1989 the government pursued three main objectives: to maintain external credibility of the country by increasing the foreign exchange reserves to a level required for an effective stabilization policy and to prepare a stabilization programme which would lower inflation to a one-digit monthly rate during the first half of 1990; to prepare proposals for substantial economic reforms aimed at the introduction of an efficient, decentralized market economy; to design constitutional changes necessary to enable federal authorities to conduct an effective macro-economic policy in an open, decentralized market economy.

Despite the rapid acceleration of inflation during 1989, this programme has been largely fulfilled and a comprehensive package of economic reform and stabilization policies was ready for implementation at the beginning of 1990.[723] There are six basic elements of the latest Yugoslav programme, which is not confined to purely economic matters. These are:

— the introduction of a fully-fledged market economy;

— the establishment of pluralistic forms of ownership — public, collective, mixed and private — and their equal subjection to the law and competition policy;

— a clear identification of ownership rights in the social (public) sector;

— full integration of the Yugoslav economy into the international division of labour on the basis of an open market economy;

— a complete separation of economic management at all decision making levels from political tutelage;

— consistent application of the rule of law, ensuring legal guarantees of the autonomy of economic entities and their property and defining a completely new role of the state, appropriate to a market economy.

Each of these elements is briefly summarized below.[724]

(iii) Introduction of an integral market

Although Yugoslavia opted for a market-oriented economy in the late 1950s, this was limited to markets for goods. During the 1960s and the 1970s, a limited financial market was gradually introduced, although this innovation was accompanied by ideological disputes as to the compatibility of a capital market with a self-management economy. The latter was always regarded as being incompatible with a labour market, although a constrained and distorted form of such a market did emerge in the mid-1960s.

The new economic legislation opts for a fully-fledged market economy, with capital and labour markets. Capital transfers — including takeovers — are accepted not only within but also between the private, co-operative and public sectors. Commercial banks (independent from the central bank for more than a quarter of a century) are now completely separated from local authorities and turned into profit-oriented joint-stock companies. Foreign exchange and domestic bond markets are gradually expanding, and the first stock exchange — after a break of fifty years — was re-opened in Belgrade at the beginning of March 1990. Moreover, legislation on the "social capital" allows public enterprises to sell their capital to other enterprises, whether public or private, domestic or foreign, and to allow corresponding changes in their management, where the decisive role is transferred to the owners.[725]

(iv) Pluralism in the forms of ownership

When the socialist order was established in Yugoslavia in 1946, three forms of property were allowed — state, co-operative and private. Subsequently, the state property gradually evolved into a special type of public property which, in principle, belonged to society as a whole. In practice, the means of production included in this type of property were used by enterprises and controlled through various combinations of state and enterprise management and by multiform schemes of participation and/or self-management. In Yugoslavia this type of property has for decades been called *social* (*drustvena*). Co-operative property, after initial efforts to extend it to agriculture, gradually faded away, either becoming private or, in most cases, social. Private property has always been regarded unfavourably and was both legally constrained and economically discriminated against. Moreover, the Constitution adopted in 1974 did not envisage the continued existence of private property at all. Instead, some "independent personal work using means in the property of citizens" was allowed in some branches and even then it was limited

---

[723] For more details on this, see *Borba*, 19 December 1989, pp.1, 4-6.

[724] A complete set of the new legislation introducing these reforms was published in *Ekonomska reforma i njeni zakoni* (Economic Reform and its Legislation), Federal Executive Council, Federal Secretariat for Information, Belgrade, January 1990. It also contains a condensed presentation of economic policies for 1990.

[725] A recent interview with Federal Finance Minister V. Vukotic qualified the rather brief enactment introducing such a possibility as "an earthquake of ten articles". *Borba*, 3 January 1990, p.1 and 3.

as to the extent to which labour could be hired, and was subject to both general and discriminatory taxes.[726]

The legislation adopted in 1989 puts an end to the biased treatment of the non-social sectors. The new law on enterprises envisages four types of property — social, co-operative, mixed and private. Enterprises in all these sectors will "have the same position, rights and responsibilities in the market place" and are to conduct business under the same rules, as prescribed by the law, and good business practice. Within each category of property, various forms of organization are possible, of which some, such as shareholding and limited liability companies, are common to all of them. Management arrangements will vary considerably, depending on the way resources are used. However, all include elements of employee participation, which has now become a well-known feature and an established part of Yugoslav society. Nevertheless, even in the social sector, the management, however organized, will be ultimately responsible for success, which will be measured above all in terms of profits. Depending on the ownership of the capital, enterprise managers are to be elected by employees or owners or by some combination of both.

(v) Ownership rights in the social sector

The clear identification of the owners of socially-owned capital is a peculiarly Yugoslav problem.

Given the ideologically-based opposition to private property, and the experience of Soviet-type state ownership of productive property, the doctrine laid down in the Yugoslav constitution of 1974 aimed at the abolition of all property.[727] Hence, the basic principles of the Constitution of 1974 include the provision that "nobody has property rights to the social means of production" and that "nobody — neither a socio-political community, an organization of associated labour, nor a group of citizens nor individuals — can on the basis of property rights appropriate the product of social work, administer or dispose of the social means of production and labour or arbitrarily decide upon distribution arrangements".

One consequence of this is that after 1974 it was no longer possible to identify the owner of public land, factories, public utilities, etc., as the term *property* in the constitution is used only for the ownership of individual citizens. In practical terms this meant that Yugoslavia, as a federal state, does not own anything (except objects belonging to the Yugoslav National Army and to federal institutions necessary for their own work) and that social property is represented by republics and provinces. But even the competence of the latter was unclear and vague, with the consequence that nobody took responsibility for the care of public capital. In fact, enterprises could, and did, use that capital in order to achieve the highest wages possible, but in most cases at the expense of a falling value of social means of production. The social or public character of the means of production would become relevant only when an enterprise was close to bankruptcy — then *society* would be called upon to meet the losses caused by bad management and the waste of resources. *Society*, as represented by local governments or republics and provinces, in most cases proved sensitive to such appeals and regularly diverted resources from successful to unsuccessful enterprises, thereby weakening, if not destroying, the incentives for hard work and professional management.

The Yugoslav reform emphasizes the identification of the owners of the capital in the social sector itself. But this is very difficult to do: on the one hand, rapid privatization has not proved possible, while, on the other, not all enterprises can be transformed into clearly defined public ones.

The law on banking provides one solution to this problem in its provisions relating to transactions in social capital, by opening the way to a gradual transformation of enterprises working with social capital into other types of enterprise without putting into question the acquired rights of the employees.

Put simply, the law continues to call the capital employed by enterprises in the social sector *social*, but in practical terms it treats its employees as the collective owner. The workers' council of an enterprise, together with its individual or collective managers, uses the capital of the enterprise to make profits, and is expected to do so efficiently since external resources to cover losses will be very difficult to obtain after the new law is passed. What the employees cannot do is sell the capital and distribute it among themselves. Nevertheless, they can sell part or all of the social capital employed in their enterprise, but under three conditions: (a) that the market value of the capital be determined in a fair manner; (b) that the resources acquired in this way go to a Development Fund which will be formed at the level of republics and provinces, and which will finance new projects; and (c) that the buyers of the enterprise's social capital be given securities, issued by the Fund, which will give them the right to participate in the management of the enterprise.

Given that securities against social capital may be acquired in this way by other social, co-operative, mixed and private enterprises, as well as by foreign companies, this sort of capital market opens the way to privatization of social capital, to the inclusion of the

---

[726] At constant 1972 prices the share of the private sector in the Yugoslav gross social product (GDP excluding services) amounted to 38 per cent in 1947, 35 per cent in 1957, 21 per cent in 1967, 16 per cent in 1977 and 14 per cent in 1989. *Statisticki godisnjak Jugoslavije* (Statistical yearbook of Yugoslavia) 1977, p.81; *Index*, 1990, No.2, p.4; *Saopstenje* (Communiqué), Federal Statistical Office, No.526, 20 December 1989, p.3. Regular data on employment, investment, fixed assets, etc., are not available for the private sector. There are, however, partial data on paid employment, for example, but not for either total employment or self employment. These data are not sufficient to reconstruct a complete time series for employment in the private sector as a whole in Yugoslavia.

[727] E. Kardelj is usually cited as the most influential ideologue of this doctrine both at home and abroad; he is also thought of as the main figure behind the controversial Yugoslav Constitution of 1974. For more details on his views see E. Kardelj, *Slobodni udruzeni rad* (The Free Associated Labour), Radnicka stampa, Belgrade, 1978. A condensed presentation of his views, in English, can be found in B. Boskovic, D. Dasic (eds.), *Socialist Self-Management in Yugoslavia*, Belgrade, Socialist Thought and Practice, 1980, pp.379-399.

foreign capital into the domestic capital market and also for extension of the presently thin security market. Thus transformed, an enterprise is thereafter owned by the new buyers of the enterprises' capital (including the possibility that they own 100 per cent of that capital), or jointly by them and the workers — which is therefore reflected in the management of the enterprise. Assuming that employees may be unwilling to sell the social capital of their enterprise, the law allows that the same fund may issue securities for those employed in the enterprises, up to an amount equivalent to six months wages.

(vi) Integration in the international economy

The economic reform in Yugoslavia envisages the full integration of the Yugoslav economy into the world economy. To this end, all the special conditions previously attached to international operations have been abolished and all enterprises — social, co-operative, mixed and private — are allowed to undertake such operations once they have been registered to undertake foreign economic business. Moreover, for all foreign operations related to their own domestic activity, such as selling their own products, buying products for processing, assembling their products abroad, providing credits, etc., enterprises registered for domestic business activities are automatically allowed access to international markets.

Openness to the world economy also applies to flows in the opposite direction. Foreign companies are allowed to set up businesses in Yugoslavia under the same conditions as Yugoslav firms. They can also purchase existing Yugoslav companies — including social firms (with some exceptions, for example, in the defence sector) — either partly or entirely. They can invest in existing or new Yugoslav companies with full rights to repatriate profits and their capital, as well as to include Yugoslav companies in their business in third countries.

In order to facilitate these operations, the new legislation fully liberalizes foreign exchange transactions. Both individual citizens and legal entities are allowed to have foreign exchange accounts with Yugoslav banks and are completely free to dispose of their foreign currency as they wish. Furthermore, in order to encourage citizens to deposit their foreign exchange in banks, interest on foreign currency deposits is paid in the currency deposited, at the rates existing in the corresponding foreign country. Given such arrangements, the law forbids any contracts or payments between domestic economic agents to be settled in foreign currencies and at the same time outlaws all transactions in foreign exchange with outside banks. To support these arrangements, the new legislation also allows foreigners to own foreign exchange or saving accounts with Yugoslav banks, and substantially encourages joint ventures.[728] These measures are expected to have a special impact on almost a million Yugoslavs employed abroad, who are estimated to hold some $20 billion outside Yugoslavia.[729] It is hoped that at least part of these resources will now be placed in Yugoslavia.

(vii) Independent economic management

Effective implementation of the economic reforms listed above requires the complete separation of economic management at all levels from all kinds of political interference. This is not an easy task since there are many channels for such influence.

For many years before 1989, political influence was maintained through dual membership of certain personnel in the prominent bodies of the League of Communists of Yugoslavia (LCY) and the various state and economic organs. To curtail such practice, all holders of dual posts were required in 1989 to give up membership of any high-level LCY body if they also held a similar position on the administration side. Another link between party and administrative functions were the LCY bodies at company or other levels of organization: these tended to influence decision making not only on strategic but also on daily issues. Taking into account the political pluralism re-emerging in the country, LCY organizations have now been abolished in many enterprises and organizations. A third channel of political influence, although not very strong, used to be the united trade unions to which almost all those employed belonged by tradition. That situation has also changed and the trade unions are now looking for a different, independent role of their own, rather than being subservient to the LCY.

Irrespective of purely political influences on economic management, one of the most difficult reforms will be the separation of management from the self-management system. The economic system introduced by the Constitution of 1974, and developed further by the Associated Labour Act of 1976, not only removed the basis for any ownership of social capital, but also merged management into self-management functions. Put simply, this law first broke down all earlier enterprises into small "basic organizations of associated labour" (BOALs) in which an assembly of all employees was established as the main management organ. At the same time this law made all management functions in the enterprise and possibly at higher levels dependent on the BOAL's decisions. Since all management functions and decisions had to be covered by corresponding self-management procedures (self-management agreements), the whole system became excessively bureaucratic and inflexible, with little possibility of ever becoming efficient.

---

[728] According to Yugoslav sources, e.g., *Borba*, 17 January 1990, p.9, during 1989, 569 new joint ventures contracts were signed — 200 more than during the 22 previous years since this possibility was first open.

[729] The source cited above puts Yugoslav deposits abroad at between $10 billion and $30 billion. According to the Deutsche Bundesbank, quoted in the same source, Yugoslav accounts in the Federal Republic contained the equivalent of $7.5 billion in 1987.

Although the deficiencies of self-management were identified very soon after the system was inaugurated, and despite many attempts to cure them, the logic of the system is still present in many Yugoslav institutions. Many organizations still refer to the violation of their self-management rights whenever new reforms are proposed or when their debtors call for their liquidation. It is therefore significant that Prime Minister Markovic, has emphasized the importance of "drawing a line between management and a redefined self-management".[730] This is of fundamental importance for market-oriented business operations in a reformed Yugoslav economic system. A special problem in this respect may arise from the fact that the provisions for "redefined self-management" in the new Act on Enterprises are vague and some elements of the earlier system still exist — for example, the right to participate in the management of an enterprise on the basis of employment. Thus the crucial issue is still to draw a clear distinction between the roles to be played by owners and employees, as the latter retain their right to participate in management whether 100 per cent of the capital is in co-operative, mixed or private property. The whole issue is further complicated by the fact that excess employment in the social sector is estimated to be about one sixth of the total of some 6.7 million people employed in the sector: increased efficiency will therefore require large employment cuts, in addition to many bankruptcies. Thus the new, liberal approach to the roles to be played by other sectors — co-operatives, mixed and private — partly reflects the hope that they will provide a significant increase in new jobs.

(viii) New legal framework for macro-economic policies

The sixth complex area of current Yugoslav economic reforms is the creation and consistent implementation of a a law-governed state system. The significance of this reform cannot be understood without some awareness of the problems Yugoslavia faced during the 1970s and the 1980s.

These problems included a lack of any juridical security for conducting business. Being in many respects utopian, the principles of the Yugoslav economic system introduced in the first half of the 1970s were never worked out in an operational system of legislation. Indeed, the Associated Labour Act of 1976 never reached the stage of a technically closed enactment which could regulate business operations in a clear and non-controversial manner. In many instances it just repeated or further elaborated in descriptive terms the constitutional principles. Many of its articles therefore end with an instruction that further details of the functioning of the economy should be defined by self-management agreements and social compacts enacted by the organizations of associated labour. Since the number of basic organizations of associated labour is more than 20,000, the number of working organizations (the economic entities comparable to enterprises in the market economy) some 15,000, and for their normal functioning each of them had to adopt about 60 self-management enactments, it appears that the economic activity of Yugoslav firms had to be regulated by millions of normative acts. Although many organizations never succeeded in completing their own legislation, it is obvious that in such circumstances business operations cannot be conducted efficiently. Furthermore, it subsequently turned out that the state courts declared themselves incompetent to interpret and implement specific self-management legislation, so that a new type of court had to be introduced (the "associated labour courts").

Another problem of the legal system is the lack of sufficient legislative competence on the part of the federal authorities even in areas such as monetary and fiscal policy. An additional problem arises from the nature of decentralization in a country which deprives the federal authorities of any real power in monitoring the implementation of federal legislation and ensuring its uniform application throughout the country. Put simply, since the federal organs, the FEC included, have no administrative framework of their own, the implementation of federal legislation could only be ensured by local and/or republic and provincial governments. But, in many cases, they implemented the federal legislation according to their own preferences and sometimes simply ignored it. Thus even the single Yugoslav market — one of the fundamental principles of the Yugoslav Federation since its creation — has never functioned as such: local, provincial and republican governments used many legal, semi-legal or arbitrary rules and procedures to prevent the free movement of people, capital and even goods within the Federation.[731] It is not surprising therefore that already at the beginning of the 1980s both national and international sources found that the Yugoslav economy could no longer continue to function within the existing framework.[732] Although the nature of Yugoslavia's economic problems has been accurately diagnosed, the lack of a political consensus to alter the constitutional system prevented the required reforms from being implemented throughout the 1980s. This is why many prominent

---

[730] *Vjesnik*, 19 December 1989, p.5.

[731] According to Yugoslav sources, after the Constitution and the Associated Labour Act were passed in 1974 and 1976, respectively, there has been a clear tendency in the six Yugoslav republics and two provinces towards the creation of their own "national economies". At present only about one third of Yugoslav output, on average, circulates between the republics and provinces, the other two thirds being limited to their own territories. As for capital movements, national estimates put the trans-republican-provincial flows at some 2 per cent of total capital formation flows. For more details about regional developments in Yugoslavia see *Dokumenti Komisije za probleme dugorocne ekonomske stabilizacije* (Documents of the Commission for Problems of Long-term Economic Stabilization), vol.4., Belgrade, 1983, pp.143-179.

[732] "Yugoslavia's system of regional and enterprise level decentralization allowed rapid economic growth and accommodated the desire for autonomy of the country's diverse ethnic and linguistic groups. After two decades of increasing economic and political decentralization, however, the system had to be re-evaluated. Its fundamental failure was the lack of macro-economic control, manifested in accelerating inflation, burgeoning balance-of-payments difficulties, persistent interregional disparties in income, and a decline in the efficiency of investment." P.T. Knight, *Economic Reforms in Socialist Countries — The Experience of China, Hungary, Romania and Yugoslavia*, World Bank Staff Working Papers No.579, World Bank, Washington, D.C., 1983, p.105.

scholars qualified the Yugoslav economic crisis as a primarily political problem.[733]

The new Federal Government installed in the spring of 1989 from the very beginning included constitutional reform as an essential component of its programme for economic reform and stabilization. The government sought three basic alterations: first, that the Federation be given the necessary competence for functioning in a modern market economy by corresponding amendments to the Federal Constitution of 1974; second, that the competence of the Federal Government (FEC) and other federal institutions, such as the Yugoslav National Bank, be extended accordingly and, third, that changes be made in other legislation concerning the economic functions of the Federation and their implementation, including the right of federal institutions to monitor and ensure uniform application of federal legislation.

Although proposals for such constitutional amendments were prepared at the same time as those concerning the economic reforms and stabilization policies, and were submitted with them to the Federal Parliament, no changes so far have taken place or seem to be in sight. The reason is very simple: the Yugoslav constitution cannot be amended without the agreement of all the republics and provinces and, as yet, there is no unanimity on the changes required to cure the Yugoslav social and economic crisis. While some republics and provinces claim that the amendments proposed do not sufficiently strengthen the federal authorities, others claim that further decentralization is needed to turn Yugoslavia into a confederation.

(ix) **Stabilization policies**

Between 1979 and 1988 the foreign trade deficit was reduced from $7.2 to $0.6 billion and the current account changed from a deficit of $3.4 billion into a surplus of $2.5 billion. However, the level of external debt increased from $15.2 billion in 1979 to $22 billion in 1987, so that several reschedulings were needed. Meanwhile, there was a considerable deterioration of the internal situation. During the 1980s, gross material product contracted in four out of ten years and in 1989 was only 7 per cent above its level in 1979. Given the natural increase of the population, there was no increase in per capita domestic production during that decade. As a good portion of that production had to be diverted to increasing net exports in order to service debt, real incomes fell in eight out of ten years, and were 30 per cent lower in 1989 than in 1979. Due to the considerable importance of the subsistence economy and the increasing share of the "grey" economy, private consumption fell less, but in per capita terms it also contracted significantly. The same was true for public consumption. Gross fixed investment was also greatly affected and in 1989 was less than 60 per cent of its level in 1979.

In spite of these cuts in domestic absorption, inflationary pressures did not diminish. Instead, the rate of increase in retail prices steadily accelerated, to an annual rate of 1,225 per cent in 1989. Thus, in contrast to earlier reforms which were instigated by external pressures, in 1989 the main pressure for reform was the domestic hyperinflation. Furthermore, the situation required that the economic reforms be implemented in parallel with a comprehensive stabilization programme. However, in contrast to earlier attempts at stabilization where the principal adjustment was of the exchange rate, this time the approach was based on fixing, for a certain period, the exchange rate of the dinar against the Deutschmark and attacking the domestic origins of the inflation. In addition, the whole stabilization programme was put together in a comprehensive manner and organized under four major headings — the external sector, income and monetary policies, fiscal policy and prices. Each of these is briefly summarized below.

(a) Adjustment in the external sector

In many respects the most important and positively the most publicized single measure of the new stabilization programme has been the rapid introduction of convertibility of the Yugoslav dinar. Since 1 January 1990 the dinar is fully convertible in all foreign transactions and citizens are guaranteed the right to buy foreign currency at official exchange rates from commercial banks. Given the importance of the Federal Republic of Germany in Yugoslavia's external transactions, and the simultaneous conversion of the old dinar at 10,000 to 1 new dinar, a fixed exchange rate of 7 dinars to the Deutschmark was set for at least the first six months of 1990. The dinar's exchange rate against other currencies is linked to their cross rates with the Deutschmark. It is assumed that the foreign exchange reserves will be sufficient to cushion fluctuations in the set period.

The introduction of the convertible dinar — a first such attempt in the post-war history of Yugoslavia — has been the subject of some controversy in Yugoslavia. But there were a number of considerations behind the measure.

First, a dramatic measure was required in order to deflate the rapid escalation of inflationary expectations during 1989. The linking of the dinar to one of the most stable international currencies not only introduces a strong anti-inflationary discipline into the Yugoslav economy but it also has a strong psychological impact. Due to the strong economic ties between the Federal Republic of Germany and Yugoslavia, in particular because many Yugoslavs are employed in the Federal Republic, the Deutschmark is by far the best known foreign currency in Yugoslavia. In fact, before the introduction of convertibility, many domestic transactions were being carried out in Deutschmarks because of the lack of confidence in the dinar. Last but not the

---

[733] According to the Yugoslav press (*Ekonomska politika*, No.1681, 18 June 1984, p.14), the main message of the fourth congress of Yugoslav political scientists, held in mid-1984, could be summarized as follows: "The main cause and hence the main feature of the crisis of Yugoslav society is the crisis in the ideological and political spheres; the share of the economic crisis is the smallest one.".

least, the Yugoslav authorities hope to attract into commercial bank deposits the considerable amounts of convertible currency that many Yugoslavs keep at home and, to some extent, abroad. The Federal Government expects the net inflow of convertible currencies to increase so that by the end of 1990 foreign exchange reserves will have risen by about one third, to $8 billion.

The effects of these measures so far have been very positive: during the first two months of 1990 the net inflow into foreign exchange deposits of Yugoslav citizens has been about three times larger than expected and the foreign exchange reserves have increased to some $7.4 billion. This has strengthened the self-confidence of the Federal Government, which raised the expected level of foreign exchange reserves for the end of 1990 to $9 billion.

The level of foreign debt was reduced in both 1988 and 1989, altogether by some $3.4 billion, and debt servicing has declined from almost 40 per cent of current account earnings in 1986 to some 23.5 per cent in 1989. However, debt servicing will substantially increase after 1995 when the grace period of the last rescheduling expires. Because of the accumulation of serious structural problems during the 1980s, the foreign debt problem can only be solved by an energetic new development strategy. The foreign exchange reserves are needed, of course, to maintain the stabilization programme and are not available for debt repayment. The government, therefore, intends to initiate a policy to boost investment, starting in the second half of 1990.

To this end, some $3.6 billion will be needed during 1990-1991 from foreign commercial banks and international financial sources. There are already signs that the Yugoslav government will receive the support of major international financial institutions for the implementation of its programme.

Special measures will be applied to minimise the distorting — including the inflationary — effects of the ill-financed chronic surpluses with the foreign exchange clearing area and mainly with the Soviet Union. As in the case of other east European countries, the National Bank of Yugoslavia used to value all exports to the Soviet Union as soon as delivered in dinars at the official rate — irrespective of whether the price was in fact paid in foreign exchange. Given that the cumulated current account surplus over the last four years amounted to some $1.7 billion, this has exerted strong inflationary pressure on domestic markets and, at the same time, compromised efforts to boost exports to the convertible currency area, where the bulk of Yugoslav external debt is concentrated.

The Yugoslav authorities have for years sought ways and means of lessening these distorting effects and although no effective direct measures were implemented until the end of 1989, Yugoslav surpluses with the Soviet Union have been shrinking ever since 1987. In fact, the surplus in merchandise trade between the countries fell from almost $0.5 billion in 1986 to a negligible $10 million in 1989. The balance on the services side was volatile but in 1989 was still some $0.4 billion, and concerned primarily construction and transportation. To prevent further excessive surpluses, the National Bank of Yugoslavia will, as from 1 January 1990, only pay for those Yugoslav exports for which the corresponding eastern partner has already paid in the clearing-account currency and dinars. If the Yugoslav exporter does not require that currency, the NBY will, on request, issue securities in the same clearing currency, which can be either used to make further payments to foreign partners willing to accept them or be sold to other Yugoslav companies at market value. It is expected that this approach will soon balance Yugoslav and Soviet economic transactions while not putting Yugoslav companies interested in exporting to the Soviet Union at a disadvantage or creating problems for Soviet partners.

As for the unsettled surpluses cumulated over previous years — reported at some $700 million at the end of 1989[734] — the Yugoslav government now envisages several possibilities: the extension of the gas pipelines in Yugoslavia by Soviet companies; increases in imports of Soviet gas; investment of the Yugoslav surplus in Soviet enterprises producing goods which Yugoslav companies are especially interested in importing on a joint venture basis; the purchase of some Yugoslav debt before maturity through the convertible currency conversion of Yugoslav lending in the clearing area; the financing of additional imports of Soviet equipment using the Yugoslav surplus; special arrangements between the National Bank of Yugoslavia and the companies concerned; and the construction of special investment projects by Soviet enterprises in Yugoslavia.

(b) Income policies

In contrast to earlier stabilization programmes where the main emphasis was on freezing prices, this time the Yugoslav government has introduced strict control of wage increases. Wages are to be fixed at their level in November 1989 (as paid until 15 December that year), and increases will be allowed only to the extent of movements in the exchange rate of the dinar against the Deutschmark.

Implementation of this decision, however, has proved much more difficult than expected, for several reasons. First, within the economic system described above, it is extremely difficult to apply an effective income policy across the entire country. Second, many companies made retroactive increases in their salaries for November 1989 even after the wage ceiling was introduced. However, the government has reiterated its determination to maintain controls until the end of June 1990, as otherwise the whole stabilization package could be endangered.[735] After the end of June 1990, when the direct Deutschmark exchange rate should be-

---

[734] *Ekonomska reforma i njeni zakone*, op.cit., p.33.

[735] See, e.g., the statement made in this respect by Z. Pregl, Deputy Prime Minister of Yugoslavia, in *Borba*, 15 January 1990, p.5.

come flexible, incomes policy will be liberalized — assuming that meanwhile monetary and fiscal policies will have been strengthened sufficiently to prevent an excessive growth of wages.

In order to achieve a lasting basis for sound wage and income policies, wage determination arrangements will be introduced during 1990. In addition to macro-economic policies concerning total domestic demand and its individual categories, their main feature will be that collective contracts be signed between trade unions and the regionally organized economic chambers. In turn, this will require the rapid abolition of trade union dependence on governments and the LCY and their transformation into real employee unions for the protection of their members' economic interests and social status. The economic chambers — which are organized, with several communes participating, at the republican and provincial levels, and at the federal level — must also be freed of their parastatist functions and be transformed into independent macro-economic agents representing, in the first place, the views of enterprise managers and/or employers.

(c) Monetary policies

Another crucial aspect of current stabilization policies is a restrictive monetary policy.[736] The main dimensions of that policy — against the background of a convertible but stabilized dinar and a projected annual inflation rate for 1990 of 13 per cent — are as follows:

— net domestic portfolios of the commercial banks should not increase by more than 7 per cent; this is the backbone of the monetary policy for 1990, and assumes that the increase can be kept under control via mandatory reserves with the central bank;

— an increase in the domestic portfolio of the National Bank of Yugoslavia by 3 per cent only; allowing for a substantial decline in the velocity of circulation, the monetary mass is supposed to increase by rather more, but still within the limits of the restrictive policy;

— both the active and passive interest rates of the commercial banks are wholly liberalized, i.e., they are left to market conditions and the discount rate policy of the National Bank of Yugoslavia;

— the discount rate policy of the National Bank of Yugoslavia will of course support the objectives of the stabilization policy, i.e., it will be largely restrictive;

— the National Bank of Yugoslavia will not provide any more credits to the Federation, following a strict separation between the functions of the National Bank of Yugoslavia as a central bank on the one hand and the federal budget on the other.

If such policies are consistently implemented, it is assumed that the earlier practice of uncontrolled deficit spending at all government levels, as well as by enterprises, will cease and that, in consequence, direct controls on wages will no longer be needed.

(d) Fiscal policies

The fourth aspect of the stabilization package is the attempt to introduce a coherent fiscal policy at the national level. In the past, a number of deficiencies in the economic system made such a policy impossible.

As already mentioned, the Federal Government itself used the the National Bank of Yugoslavia to print money in order to meet its deficit and this was one of the major sources of accelerating inflation. One reason for the country's excessive public deficits in the first place is that the Federation had hardly any control over taxation in the republics and provinces, or even in local governments areas. Last but not least, the Federal Government had no influence on levies imposed on enterprises by some 7,000 "self-management interest communities" — parafiscal bodies, introduced in 1974, to finance expenditures on health, education, culture, etc. Thus, the excessive number of independent tax collectors (federation, six republics, two provinces, some 530 communes, 7,000 communities mentioned above) made it impossible to control the tax burden. This has been increasing for a decade or so, with serious adverse effects on capital formation by enterprises. Of all the tax collectors, the Federation was in the worst position, as its expenditure was only partly financed by its own revenues: a good deal of it was financed through contributions by republics and provinces — one of the reasons why the federal budget on several occasions was only adopted by the Federal Parliament with considerable delays.

In order to curtail any further inflationary financing of public expenditure and to reduce the overall tax burden on the economy, the Federal Government has taken or proposed the following measures:

— its own revenues are to be substantially increased (mainly through the federal turnover tax and customs duties), to about 92 per cent of its total expenditure;

— a detailed review and reorganization of the Federation's revenue and expenditure will be undertaken in 1990;

— it is proposed that the self-management interest communities be liquidated in the foreseeable future, so that the authority to levy taxes will be limited to the Federation, republics, provinces and communes (local governments);

---

[736] The likely effectiveness of this policy has been greatly increased by the upgrading of the authority of the Central Bank. Before the latest law on the National Bank of Yugoslavia was passed in 1989, the consensus voting required of the Council of Governors, composed of the Governor of the National Bank of Yugoslavia and governors of the six republican and two provincial banks, prevented it from exercising proper control over monetary policy.

— republican, provincial and local governments are asked to review their own revenue and expenditure accounts and to balance their budgets, since they will no longer be able to count on easy credits from the local commercial banks (which previously had been informally controlled by the local authorities);

— once the proposed constitutional amendments are adopted, the Federal Government will propose a completely new fiscal system for the country, based on a uniform taxation scheme at the country level and a co-ordination of the fiscal policies of the federation, republics, provinces and local governments. This is expected to bring about "a fiscal reintegration of all kinds of public consumption, as well as the introduction of a single (synthetic) tax on total income of individuals, coupled with the creation of a corresponding information system necessary for taxation of citizens".[737]

Once all this is achieved, macro-economic policies will be restored to the position which they occupy in all the other market economies of western Europe. However, given the problem described above, it is obvious that achieving this objective will be difficult and time consuming.

(e) Price policies

Unlike most earlier anti-inflationary packages, the latest stabilization programme in Yugoslavia excludes a general price freeze. Instead, after some adjustment in relative prices, the Federal Government decided in mid-December 1989 to freeze a range of public sector and major raw material prices (electricity, coal and coke, oil and oil derivates, railway and PTT services, basic chemicals and medicaments, ferrous and non-ferrous metallurgy). Taking into account the other stabilization measures described above, it is expected that before the end of the period concerned, major internal imbalances will be corrected and that by mid-1990 the producers of these and other goods will not need to seek the enormous price increases which followed earlier price freezes. A more balanced market situation might even require some of them to reduce rather than increase their prices.

With such views in mind, the government preferred to let all other prices be formed by market forces, reserving the right to intervene with selected imports of consumer goods if domestic producers abuse the transitional period of high price expectations to make unjustifiably high profits at the expense of consumer incomes. After mid-1990, the liberal price régime will be further extended. Nevertheless, an active price policy based on the same mechanisms as in other market economies, such as indirect control of public utility tariffs or other prices particularly important for the overall development of the economy, as well as specific mechanisms for agricultural produce and other primary products, will continue after the selective price ceilings introduced at the end of 1989 are lifted.

Developments at the beginning of 1990 indicate that this option of price policies may bring considerable results. After the record 58.8 per cent increase in December 1989, retail prices — the main inflationary indicator in Yugoslavia — decelerated in January to 41.5 per cent and decreased further to 13.6 per cent in February. Moreover, if allowance is made for the carry-over of the price increase of late December into January (regular monthly price records are made by the Federal Statistical Office on the 21st day of each month), the situation will be even better. Measured in terms of end-month changes, retail prices in Yugoslavia increased in January by 17.3 per cent and in February by 8.4 per cent. Expectations are for zero growth or a fall in March according to the both measures. Hence, although it is not certain whether the government will succeed in bringing down the annual rate of increase in consumer prices to only 13 per cent, it is obvious that the downturn in the Yugoslav inflation rate has already taken place — another reason to expect that the whole reform and stabilization package could well succeed.

(x) Prospects

The economic reforms introduced in Yugoslavia at the end of 1989 seem to be better designed than previous reform programmes. The stabilization policies have already had significant effects on both external balance and domestic inflation. Although there are inevitable costs to be paid in terms of a temporary fall in output and a large increase in unemployment, the prospects for the success of the Yugoslav economic reform have brightened considerably since the beginning of 1990.

For many years after it had abandoned central planning, Yugoslavia had strong political leadership but failed to implement any radical economic reforms. The present situation is the reverse of this: an independent Federal Government has produced a coherent programme of economic reform and stabilization policies, but its destiny depends on developments in the political sphere. However, the success of the economic reforms so far may help to rally the Yugoslav people behind the objectives of establishing an open market economy and a democratic State ruled by Law.

---

[737] *Ekonomska reforma i njeni zakoni ...*, op.cit, p.29.

Chapter 6

ECONOMIC INTEGRATION AND THE EXPORT PERFORMANCE OF WEST EUROPEAN COUNTRIES OUTSIDE THE EC

The completion of the internal market of the European Community, planned for the end of 1992, is likely to have important consequences for the patterns of intra-European trade. The direction and magnitude of the changes will depend not only on the removal of remaining barriers to intra-EC trade, but on whether the obstacles to trade between members and non-members are lowered and on whether liberalization also occurs among the non-members. This paper does not attempt to predict the effects of "1992" on non-members' trade; instead it looks at the possible effects of earlier stages in the process of west European integration and draws some relevant lessons from that experience to provide some insight into the possible consequences for non-EC members' exports of a closer integration of the EC economies in the 1990s.

6.1 THE EFFECTS OF INTEGRATION

(i) Introduction

Although the term "economic integration" has been interpreted in a variety of ways, in the theory of "customs union" it usually refers to a reallocation of production across three or more countries as a result of their removal of restrictions on each others' trade with each country specializing in the products or lines of production in which it has a comparative advantage. In western Europe, such improvements in the international division of labour have been brought about not only by the liberalization of trade but also by removing restrictions on the free movement of labour and capital.[738]

Other things being equal, the formation of the EC and EFTA as two separate entities (in 1957 and 1960 respectively) is likely to have strengthened trade within each group and to have weakened it with other partners, including the members of the other free trade organization.[739] The accession of the United Kingdom and Denmark to the EC in 1973 and the subsequent establishment of Free Trade Agreements (FTAs) between the EC and the EFTA members may have led to some strengthening of trade between the two areas and a stabilization or weakening of trade with other partners, including the original members of the EC and the former members of EC and EFTA. Moreover, if trade liberalization leads to a more rational division of labour across borders, there is a presumption that the countries concerned will specialize further in the products or lines of production in which they have a comparative advantage.

The purpose of this study is to highlight statistically the extent to which the developments hypothesized above are present in the export performance of the west European countries that are not EC members. The analysis covers the past two and a half decades and specifically refers to Austria, Finland, Norway, Sweden and Switzerland. Denmark was a founding member of EFTA, but joined the EC in 1973. Given its size, level of development and close links with the other Nordic countries, it seemed useful to include it in the analysis in order to compare the developments there with those in the other five countries which remained outside the Community. In the following text this sample of countries is variously referred to as "the six countries" or "the selected countries".

The analysis of past trends may be useful in assessing the possible effects of the completion of the EC's Internal Market. If the EC's attempt to tackle non-

---

[738] C.T. Saunders (ed.), *Regional Integration in East and in West*, Macmillan Press Ltd., 1983.

[739] The European Economic Community (EC) was formed in 1957 by six European countries, namely Belgium, Luxembourg, France, the Federal Republic of Germany, Italy and the Netherlands. The European Free Trade Association (EFTA) was constituted in 1960 by seven other countries: Austria, Denmark, Norway, Portugal, Sweden, Switzerland and the United Kingdom; Finland was an associate member and Iceland became a member in 1970.

tariff barriers leads to the re-emergence of two west European trading entities, trade patterns will be shaped in much the same way as after the formation of the EC and the EFTA. But if the abolition of the remaining barriers to trade applies also to EFTA members, the patterns of trade are likely to develop differently: to the extent that these barriers are presently hampering trade both inside and between each area, their removal would probably lead to a reinforcement of west European trade in general.

The "expected" effects of trade liberalization are discussed further below. Section 6.2(i) describes changes in the regional and product composition of the countries' exports; in section 6.2(ii) the impact of export structure on export performance is analysed by means of the "constant market share" method; section 6.3 provides tentative estimates of the effects of earlier trade liberalization and discusses the possible effects of the completion of the EC Internal Market; this is followed by an attempt to draw some conclusions.[740]

(ii) The expected effects of integration

The European Community's integration programme, as laid down in the Treaty of Rome in 1957, aims at the free movement of goods, services, labour and capital. Until recently, however, the implementation of this programme was limited to the abolition of tariffs and quotas on trade in goods: a number of technical barriers, and restrictions on trade in services and primary factor movements were left in place.

The removal of tariffs and quotas on intra-EC trade significantly affected the Community's west European neighbours, whose exports to the EC market remained subject to tariffs. The formation of EFTA in 1960 was a response to this discrimination. In 1973, two EFTA members, the United Kingdom and Denmark, left the Association and joined the EC, together with Ireland. The remaining EFTA countries then obtained Free Trade Agreements (FTAs) with the EC, thereby contributing to the freeing of the west European goods market.

Tariffs on intra-EC and intra-EFTA trade were practically abolished in the late 1960s. The liberalization of trade between the EC and EFTA started in April 1973 and by the end of the 1970s trade in industrial products inside western Europe was virtually free of tariffs.[741]

Until recently, "economic integration" in western Europe was largely confined to the liberalization of trade in industrial goods. It is well known that the removal of obstacles to trade inside a given area tends to intensify trade among the countries involved. This reinforcement of intra-regional trade results from a replacement of home production by imports (trade creation) and/or from a displacement of imports from outside the free trade area in favour of imports from within it (trade diversion).

A simple numerical example may illustrate this.[742] Let A be the home country, B the free trade partner and C the rest of the world.

	A	B	C	A	B	C
	Before tariff cut			After tariff cut		
Production costs	35	26	20	35	26	20
100% Tariff in A	-	26	20	-	-	20
Price in A	35	52	40	35	26	40

Before the freeing of trade with B, consumers in A would only buy the home-produced good; after free trade was established, tariff free imports from B would reach consumers in A at a price that would displace the home-produced good. This is the case of "trade creation".

If the initial tariff were 50 per cent, a different situation would emerge:

	A	B	C	A	B	C
	Before tariff cut			After tariff cut		
Production costs	35	26	20	35	26	20
50% Tariff in A	-	13	10	-	-	10
Price in A	35	39	30	35	26	30

Prior to the tariff cut, demand in A would be entirely met by imports from C, but after the formation of a free trade area with B, consumers would replace imports from C by imports from B. This is the case of "trade diversion".

Consequently, the strengthening of trade within a free trade area may occur at the cost of trade with third countries. Viner, who first discussed these effects, concluded that if the balance was in favour of trade creation, the free trade area would be generally advantageous.[743]

The effects described above refer to imports. Identification of the *export effects* is more complicated. Firstly, they are the sum of the import effects in partner countries: as a result of the freeing of trade inside a given area, exports from a given member country may increase because they replace home production in member countries and/or because they displace imports from countries outside the free trade area. This increase in exports may be obtained through the switching of domestic sales to the foreign market (export creation)

---

[740] The basic trade data refer to total exports excluding oil and oil products. For section 6.2 the data were extracted from the United Nations' COMTRADE data base. The computations reported in section 6.2(i) were carried out by the ECE secretariat. In these calculations, exports from the OECD plus Yugoslavia were taken as a proxy for world exports. The "constant market share" calculations in section 6.2(ii) were carried out at the University of Aalborg, Denmark. This kind of analysis had been carried out before at the Institute for Production of the University of Aalborg and the relevant computer programme was already available there. In these calculations total OECD exports plus non-OECD exports to OECD were taken as a proxy for world exports.

[741] See the United Nations Economic Commission for Europe, *Economic Survey of Europe in 1988-1989*, New York, 1989, section 2.5.

[742] The example is taken from R.C. Hine, *The Political Economy of European trade — An introduction to the Trade Policies of the EEC*, Sussex, 1985.

[743] J. Viner, *The Customs Union Issues*, New York, 1950.

and/or by diversion of exports from third markets to fellow members (export diversion).

Moreover, in the case of the formation of two separate trading entities, exports from members of both blocs may be affected by import diversion in the other. The reduced export opportunities faced by a member of a free trade area with respect to its exports to a separate trading group have been called "export impedance".[744]

Thus, following the formation of the EC and EFTA the diversion in the EC's imports from the five countries studied here outweighed the benefits they derived from the creation of EFTA. After the establishment of the FTAs with the EC, their exports to the EC are likely to have increased at the cost of third countries and, perhaps, of the original EFTA members. To the extent that the liberalization of trade contributed to a more rational division of labour across borders, the six countries may have specialized further in goods or lines of production in which they had a comparative advantage. These presumptions will be tested against the empirical data for the past two and a half decades.

---

[744] See EFTA Secretariat, *The Trade Effects of EFTA and the EEC, 1959-1967*, Geneva, June 1972.

6.2 CHANGES IN THE STRUCTURE OF EXPORTS

(i) Market structure and product composition

The regional and product patterns of the countries' exports are analysed here with reference to 1963, 1972 and 1987. These years broadly delimit two different periods in the liberalization of west European trade, the first covering the initial development of the EC and EFTA and, the second, the agreements between the EC and EFTA.

(a) Regional patterns

The analysis of regional trade structures is based on the shares of different markets in the six countries' exports, the countries' shares of foreign markets and "trade intensity coefficients". The latter measure the share of a given market in a country's exports, relative to the share of that market in world exports.

The breakdown of markets were as follows: the original *EC6* (Belgium, the Federal Republic of Germany, France, Italy, Luxembourg and the Netherlands), the countries that joined the EC in 1973, *EC3* (the United Kingdom, Denmark and Ireland), the remaining *EFTA* (Austria, Finland, Iceland, Norway, Sweden and Switzerland), the *south European* countries that have become members of the EC (Greece, Portugal and Spain), *eastern Europe* (Bulgaria, Czechoslovakia, the German Democratic Republic, Hungary, Poland, Romania and Yugoslavia), the *USSR, North America* (the United States and Canada), *Japan* and the *"rest of the world"*.[745]

Market orientation

Table 6.1 shows the share of each of these nine markets in the six countries' exports.

Inside western Europe, the *market* orientation of the six countries changed differently in 1963-1972 and in 1972-1987. *In the first period,* the share of EC6 in their exports fell, while that of EFTA, including the countries that later became EC members, rose considerably. *After 1972,* the share of the EC6 recovered (although not entirely for Finland and Sweden), but that of the countries which joined the EC in 1973 fell sharply. In 1987 the twelve members of the EC absorbed a smaller part of the countries' exports than in 1963, except for Austria and Switzerland. The share of the remaining EFTA countries remained practically unchanged for Norway and Sweden but decreased in the other countries, particularly for Austria and Switzerland.

The proportion of the six countries' exports going to eastern Europe and the Soviet Union fell in most cases in both periods. The North American market also accounted for a decreasing share of exports from most of the countries. But the Japanese market absorbed a growing share of exports from all of them. The share of the "rest of the world" rose sharply in Norway and Denmark, but was relatively unchanged in the other countries.

In 1987, the EC and EFTA together absorbed nearly three quarters of Austrian exports, around 70 per cent of exports from Norway, Sweden and Denmark and slightly less than two thirds from Finland and Switzerland. The share of the EC market was larger for Austria and Switzerland than for the Nordic countries (including Denmark), while the EFTA market was relatively more important for its Nordic members than for those in Austria and Switzerland.

The relative importance of markets outside western Europe varied between countries. The east European market remained important for Austria, as did the Soviet market for Finland. North America took less than 10 per cent of the countries' exports, except for Sweden where it accounted for almost 13 per cent. The share of the "rest of the world" was relatively large in exports from Switzerland and Norway.[746] Japan absorbed a relatively small proportion of the countries' exports: slightly less than 4 per cent for Switzerland and Denmark and between 1 and 2 per cent for the others.

Market shares

The shares of each exporting country in the different regional markets are indicated in table 6.2. These *market shares* changed more or less in line with the changes in market orientation described above.

In the *west European markets* a distinction can be made between the periods 1963-1972 and 1972-1987. In the first period, the countries' shares of the EC6 market declined and their shares of the EFTA market, including the countries that joined the EC in 1973, increased (except for Finland and Denmark, whose share in the latter markets fell). In 1972-1987 the countries' shares of the EC6 market recovered, but their shares in EC3 fell, in some cases quite dramatically. By 1987 only Austria and Switzerland had larger shares in EC12 than in 1963. Except for Finland, the countries' shares of the remaining EFTA market also declined from

---

[745] In most ECE studies Yugoslavia is considered as part of southern Europe. However, its position *vis-à-vis* the EC and EFTA is closer to that of the east European countries than to that of southern Europe.

[746] In the case of Norway, this may reflect increased exports of second-hand ships, much of which actually corresponds to "flagging out".

TABLE 6.1

The market structure of the six countries' total exports, 1963, 1972 and 1987
(Percentage shares)

Exporters / Markets	EC12 EC6	EC12 EC3	EC12 Southern Europe	EC12 Total	EFTA [a]	Eastern Europe [b]	Soviet Union	North America	Japan	Rest of the world	Total
Austria											
1963	49.8	5.4	2.4	57.6	10.9	12.8	4.7	4.5	0.4	9.2	100.0
1972	38.8	10.1	2.6	51.5	18.3	12.3	2.4	5.8	0.7	8.9	100.0
1987	54.7	5.9	2.8	63.4	11.2	8.5	2.5	4.4	1.2	9.0	100.0
Finland											
1963	29.8	25.3	1.7	56.8	7.0	5.0	16.1	5.4	0.3	9.4	100.0
1972	20.9	22.7	2.6	46.2	24.7	2.9	12.4	5.5	0.5	7.8	100.0
1987	23.9	15.5	2.2	41.6	21.9	1.9	15.5	6.4	1.4	11.3	100.0
Norway											
1963	27.5	24.7	2.3	54.5	17.2	3.7	1.2	10.6	0.4	12.5	100.0
1972	23.8	26.1	5.2	55.1	20.1	2.7	0.6	8.4	0.9	12.3	100.0
1987	27.3	19.3	2.4	48.9	20.1	1.2	0.7	8.6	2.1	18.5	100.0
Sweden											
1963	32.2	21.5	2.7	56.4	18.6	2.9	1.7	6.5	0.5	13.4	100.0
1972	25.9	24.3	3.1	53.3	20.6	3.4	1.0	8.6	0.9	12.3	100.0
1987	29.8	17.7	2.9	50.3	20.8	1.9	0.7	12.6	1.5	12.3	100.0
Switzerland											
1963	42.1	8.2	4.1	54.3	8.9	3.1	0.5	10.7	2.5	20.0	100.0
1972	36.6	9.7	4.6	50.9	11.6	4.4	1.0	10.2	3.1	18.8	100.0
1987	43.8	8.9	3.0	55.6	7.4	2.9	1.1	9.8	3.8	19.5	100.0
Denmark											
1963	28.9	23.7	1.5	54.1	22.3	3.3	1.6	7.4	0.5	10.7	100.0
1972	22.9	20.1	2.2	45.2	29.1	3.0	0.6	9.4	0.9	11.9	100.0
1987	32.7	11.6	2.8	47.1	24.1	1.2	0.4	8.0	3.8	15.4	100.0

Source: ECE secretariat, based on data from the United Nations' COMTRADE data base.

[a] Austria, Finland, Iceland, Norway, Sweden and Switzerland.
[b] Bulgaria, Czechoslovakia, the German Democratic Republic, Hungary, Poland, Romania and Yugoslavia.

1972. At the end of the period only Finland and Austria had larger shares of the present day EFTA than in the early 1960s.

Performance in the markets outside western Europe varied considerably from country to country. In the *east European and Soviet markets,* the shares of Austria and Finland declined in the first period, but recovered in the second; the Swiss shares rose steadily in both periods; and those of the other Nordic countries fell.

In the *North American market,* the positions of Norway, Switzerland and Denmark weakened, while that of Sweden improved in 1972-1987. In general, all the countries gained share in the *Japanese market* and in the "rest of the world" (except for the Swedish share in the "rest of the world" from 1972).

By 1987 the six countries' shares of imports into the EC12 were relatively small, ranging from about 1 per cent (Finland and Norway) to 3-3.5 per cent (Sweden and Switzerland). In the EFTA market, their shares were between 2 and 3 per cent, except for Denmark and Sweden with 4.2 and 6.5 per cent, respectively. Finland supplied 15 per cent of Soviet imports (from the OECD plus Yugoslavia), while Austria and Switzerland accounted for 9 and 5 per cent, respectively, of imports into eastern Europe. In the non-European markets the shares of Austria, Finland and Norway were around 0.5 per cent, whereas those of Denmark, Sweden and Switzerland varied from 1 to 3 per cent.

Trade intensity coefficients

The export and market shares discussed above are quite sensitive to demand and supply conditions. In fact, the share of a given market in a country's exports may increase because import demand is expanding there at a faster pace than in the rest of the world; in the same way, a country's share of a given market may rise because the country is generally benefiting from favourable supply conditions.

Developments in bilateral relations are better described by *relative* trade shares, commonly known as "trade intensity coefficients".[747] These coefficients relate the share of a market in a country's exports to the share of the same market in world exports. If the market itself is expanding, both the numerator and the denominator of the ratio will change in the same direction, the

---

[747] For a more detailed discussion of these coefficients, see United Nations Economic Commission for Europe, *Economic Bulletin for Europe,* vol.24, No.2, New York, 1973; Economic Commission for Europe, *Economic Bulletin for Europe,* vol.36, No.4, and vol.37, No.4, Pergamon Press for the United Nations, 1984 and 1985.

TABLE 6.2

The share of each of the six exporting countries in regional markets, a 1963, 1972 and 1987
(Percentages)

Markets Exporters	ECI2				EFTA b	Eastern Europe c	Soviet Union	North America	Japan	Rest of the world	Total
	EC6	EC3	Southern Europe	Total							
Austria											
1963	2.4	0.8	1.3	2.0	1.6	7.4	4.8	0.4	0.2	0.4	1.4
1972	1.7	1.7	1.2	1.7	2.9	6.2	2.4	0.4	0.3	0.5	1.4
1987	2.8	1.1	1.4	2.4	2.2	9.1	3.3	0.4	0.6	0.6	1.6
Finland											
1963	1.3	3.3	0.8	1.7	0.9	2.5	14.3	0.4	0.1	0.4	1.2
1972	0.7	2.9	0.9	1.1	2.9	1.1	9.3	0.3	0.1	0.4	1.0
1987	0.9	2.1	0.8	1.1	3.1	1.5	14.9	0.4	0.5	0.6	1.2
Norway											
1963	1.1	2.9	1.0	1.5	2.0	1.7	1.0	0.8	0.1	0.5	1.1
1972	0.9	3.6	1.9	1.5	2.6	1.1	0.5	0.5	0.3	0.6	1.1
1987	0.7	1.7	0.5	0.9	1.9	0.6	0.5	0.4	0.5	0.6	0.8
Sweden											
1963	3.8	7.8	3.5	4.7	6.6	4.1	4.2	1.4	0.5	1.5	3.3
1972	2.5	9.1	3.1	3.8	7.2	3.9	2.1	1.4	0.8	1.7	3.0
1987	2.5	5.2	2.3	3.0	6.5	3.2	1.4	1.7	1.2	1.4	2.6
Switzerland											
1963	3.7	2.2	3.9	3.4	2.4	3.2	0.9	1.7	2.0	1.7	2.5
1972	2.8	2.9	3.7	2.9	3.2	4.0	1.8	1.3	2.2	2.0	2.4
1987	3.8	2.7	2.5	3.5	2.4	5.2	2.4	1.4	3.1	2.3	2.7
Denmark											
1963	2.0	5.0	1.1	2.6	4.7	2.7	2.4	0.9	0.3	0.7	1.9
1972	1.1	3.7	1.1	1.6	5.0	1.7	0.7	0.7	0.4	0.8	1.5
1987	1.5	1.9	1.2	1.6	4.2	1.2	0.5	0.6	1.6	1.0	1.5

Source: As for table 6.1.

a Proxied by the regions' imports from the OECD.
b Austria, Finland, Iceland, Norway, Sweden and Switzerland.
c Bulgaria, Czechoslovakia, the German Democratic Republic, Hungary, Poland, Romania and Yugoslavia.

coefficient remaining broadly unchanged. For exporting country i and market j the coefficient is defined as:

$$T_{ij} = X_{ij}/X_{i.} \,/\, X_{.j}/X_{..} \qquad (1)$$

where

X_{ij} = exports from country i to market j
$X_{i.}$ = total exports from country i
$X_{.j}$ = world exports to market j, and
$X_{..}$ = total world exports.[748]

The coefficient equals unity whenever the share of a market in the country's exports is the same as the share of that market in world exports (or the share of the country in a given market is the same as the share of that country in the world market).[749] A coefficient smaller (larger) than unity indicates a weaker (stronger) trade link between countries i and j than could be expected on the basis of their shares of world trade.

At any given time, the value of the "trade intensity coefficients" between two countries is a reflection of differences in production structures, the geographical distance between them and historical ties. Changes in the value of the coefficient are assumed to reflect mainly changes in "economic distance", particularly those arising from alterations in trade policies. Hence, these ratios are more suitable than simple trade shares for assessing structural changes due to trade liberalization.[750]

---

[748] These coefficients also measure the share of a country in a given market relative to the share of that country in the world market. In this case, if the country's export performance is affected by supply factors, the shares in both the numerator and the denominator will change, the ratio staying more or less unchanged. In this case, the ratio is:

$$T_{ij} = X_{ij}/X_{.j} \,/\, X_{i.}/X_{..} \qquad (2)$$

[749] As already mentioned, exports from the OECD and Yugoslavia were taken as a proxy for world exports.

[750] Savage and Deutsch, *inter alia* developed these coefficients for the analysis of integration on trade flows (I.R. Savage and K.W. Deutsch "A Statistical Model of the Gross Analysis of Transactions Flows", *Econometrics*, vol.28, No.3, July 1960). Other authors using these coefficients include: H.R. Alker, Jr. and D. Puchala, "Trends in Economic Partnership: The North Atlantic Area, 1928-1963", in J.D. Singer (ed.), *Quantitative International Politics: Insights and Evidence*, The Free Press, New York, 1968; R.W. Chadwick and K.W. Deutsch, "International Trade and Economic Integration: Further Development in Matrix Analysis to estimate the Effects of Background Conditions *versus* Political Controls", Harvard University (mimeo) 1971; H. Thiel, *Economics and Information Theory*, North Holland Publishing Company, Amsterdam, 1967, chapter 10; United Nations Economic Commission for Europe, *Economic Bulletin for Europe*, vol.24 No.2, New York, 1973 and *Economic Survey of Europe in 1987-1988*, New York, 1988, chapter 2; A. Utne, "Reinforced Trade Links

TABLE 6.3

Trade intensity coefficients,[a] 1963, 1972 and 1987
(Percentages)

Exporters / Markets	EC12 EC6	EC12 EC3	EC12 Southern Europe	EC12 Total	EFTA [b]	Eastern Europe [c]	Soviet Union	North America	Japan	Rest of the world	Total
Austria											
1963	1.78	0.60	0.94	1.46	1.19	5.48	3.55	0.29	0.11	0.31	1.00
1972	1.24	1.25	0.86	1.22	2.11	4.60	1.77	0.31	0.20	0.39	1.00
1987	1.74	0.66	0.84	1.45	1.35	5.59	2.02	0.23	0.34	0.39	1.00
Finland											
1963	1.07	2.79	0.67	1.44	0.76	2.15	12.15	0.36	0.09	0.32	1.00
1972	0.67	2.79	0.87	1.09	2.85	1.10	9.00	0.29	0.14	0.34	1.00
1987	0.76	1.76	0.64	0.95	2.64	1.26	12.61	0.34	0.42	0.49	1.00
Norway											
1963	0.98	2.72	0.94	1.38	1.87	1.58	0.92	0.70	0.12	0.42	1.00
1972	0.76	3.20	1.72	1.30	2.32	1.02	0.45	0.45	0.25	0.54	1.00
1987	0.87	2.18	0.68	1.12	2.42	0.79	0.58	0.46	0.60	0.81	1.00
Sweden											
1963	1.15	2.37	1.08	1.43	2.03	1.25	1.29	0.43	0.16	0.46	1.00
1972	0.83	2.98	1.03	1.26	2.37	1.28	0.70	0.46	0.26	0.54	1.00
1987	0.95	2.00	0.86	1.15	2.50	1.23	0.54	0.67	0.44	0.53	1.00
Switzerland											
1963	1.51	0.90	1.60	1.37	0.97	1.31	0.37	0.71	0.83	0.68	1.00
1972	1.17	1.19	1.52	1.20	1.34	1.65	0.73	0.54	0.90	0.83	1.00
1987	1.39	1.00	0.90	1.27	0.89	1.89	0.86	0.52	1.12	0.85	1.00
Denmark											
1963	1.04	2.61	0.59	1.37	2.44	1.43	1.24	0.48	0.16	0.36	1.00
1972	0.73	2.48	0.72	1.07	3.36	1.13	0.46	0.50	0.25	0.52	1.00
1987	1.04	1.31	0.82	1.08	2.90	0.79	0.35	0.42	1.12	0.67	1.00

Source: As for table 6.1.

[a] The share of a given region in each country's exports relative to the share of the same region in OECD's exports.
[b] Austria, Finland, Iceland, Norway, Sweden and Switzerland.
[c] Bulgaria, Czechoslovakia, the German Democratic Republic, Hungary, Poland, Romania and Yugoslavia.

"Trade intensity coefficients" for exports from the six countries to the various markets are presented in table 6.3. The coefficients for exports to the EC and EFTA are also shown in chart 6.1. These coefficients changed more or less in line with the export and market shares described above, suggesting that the developments in those trade shares were largely a reflection of trade policies.

The data in chart 6.1 show clearly that, up to the early 1970s, there was a general weakening of exports to the EC6 and a relative strengthening of those to the original EFTA members (the main exception is Denmark, where trade with the EC3 weakened somewhat). From then until 1987 there was a recovery in trade relations with the EC6, which largely mirrored a weakening of exports to the countries that joined the EC in 1973. In the case of Austria and Switzerland there was also a distinct weakening of exports to the remaining EFTA countries, but this was not so in the case of Nordic countries.

The intensity of exports to Japan and to the "rest of the world" tended to increase for all countries, while the patterns of change in exports to eastern Europe, Soviet Union and North America were less uniform.

In 1987, the intensity coefficients for exports from Finland, Norway and Sweden to the EC6 were below unity, indicating that their relations with the EC6 were weaker than might be expected on the basis of the EC6 share of world exports. On the other hand, exports from the Nordic countries have been strongly oriented towards EFTA and the EC3, a feature that is much less pronounced for Austria and Switzerland.

The "intensity" of exports to eastern Europe was often stronger (particularly in the case of Austria) than could be anticipated on the basis of the share of this region in OECD exports. Exports to other markets were relatively weak, except for Finnish and Austrian exports to the Soviet Union and for Swiss and Danish exports to Japan.

Briefly, the data show that the countries' regional patterns of exports have changed largely in line with the "expected" effects of integration: up to the early 1970s, reflecting the formation of the EC6 and EFTA as two separate trading entities, there was a decline in exports to the EC6 and a strengthening of those to EFTA; following the accession of the United Kingdom, Denmark and Ireland to the EC and the establishment of

in Western Europe", *EFTA Bulletin*, 1/85, Geneva, 1985; M. Ponte Ferreira, "Structural Changes in Norway's Trade: The Impact of Integration", Norwegian Institute of International Affairs (NUPI), *Report* No.139, 1990.

CHART 6.1

Trade intensity coefficients for each country total export to the EC 6, the EC 3 and EFTA, 1963-1987

——— EC 6   — — — EC 3   ·········· EFTA

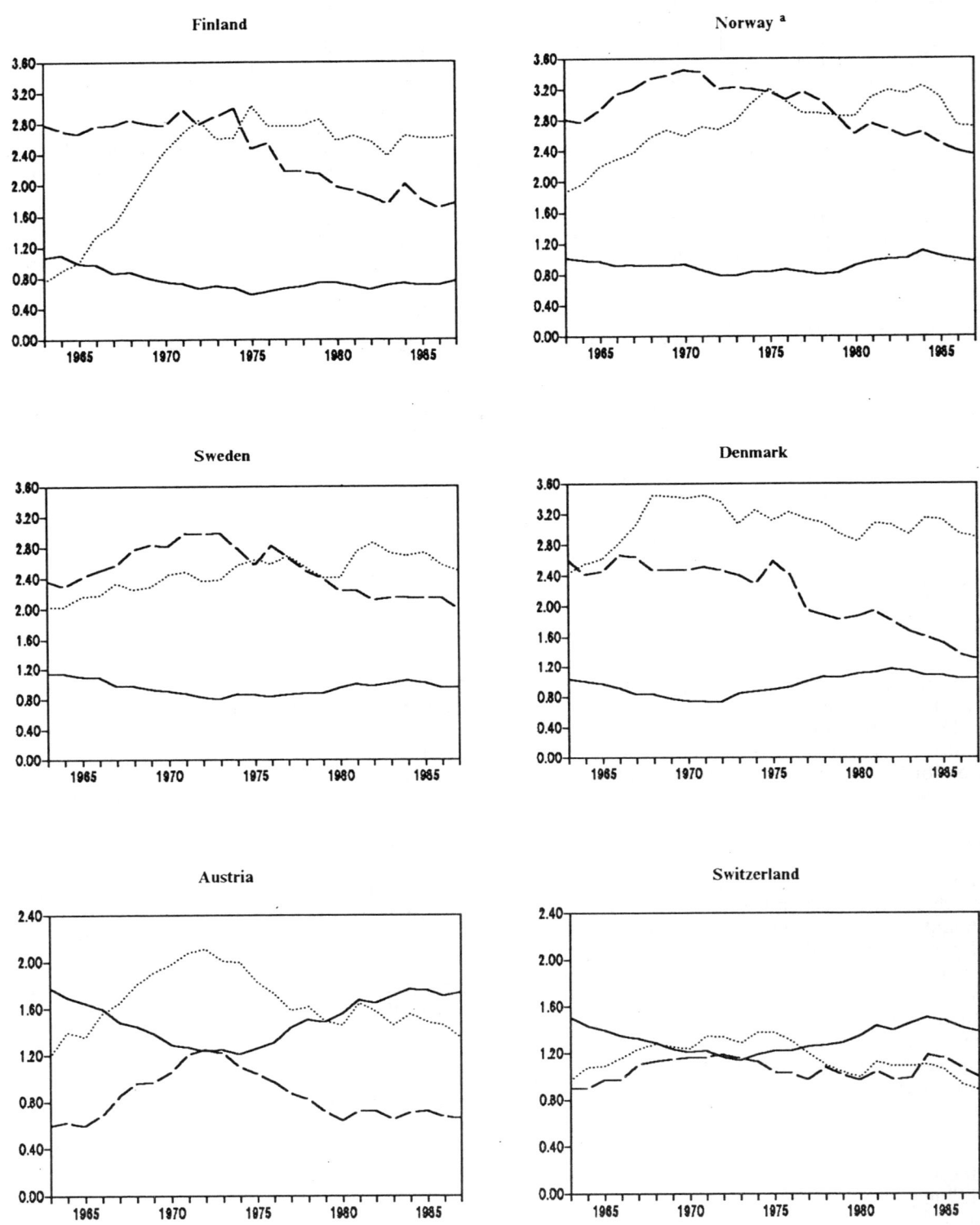

Source: As for table 6.1

[a] Exports excluding oil, ships and oil platforms.

trade agreements between the EC and the remaining EFTA countries, exports to the EC6 recovered, partly at the expense of exports to the initial EFTA members, and partly those that joined the EC.

(b) Product composition

The commodity structure of exports from the six countries will be reviewed here in terms of product shares and specialization coefficients, the latter being the share of a country in world exports of a given product normalized by the share of that country in world exports.

Product shares

Shares of twelve product groups in exports from the six countries are shown in table 6.4. A feature common to all six countries is that, in 1963, their exports were relatively concentrated in a few groups. In the Nordic countries and, to a lesser extent, in Austria, the main export goods were often resource and/or energy intensive: pulp, paper and wood products represented more than 70 per cent of Finnish exports; food, pulp, paper and metals accounted for half of Norwegian exports; pulp, paper, wood products and ferrous metals made up 43 per cent of exports from Sweden and about one third of those from Austria; and nearly half of Danish exports were food products. In Switzerland, in contrast, two thirds of manufactured exports were machinery and chemicals.

In the Nordic countries and Austria, product concentration was even higher in exports to the twelve members of the Community; exports to EFTA, on the other hand, were more diversified, with chemicals, machinery and transport equipment representing a larger share than in exports to the EC. In Switzerland, the shares of machinery and chemicals in exports to the EC were larger than the average, while textiles were a relatively high proportion of exports to EFTA.

Between 1963 and 1987 there were large changes in export structures: the share of traditional products declined and that of chemicals, machinery and transport equipment increased (except for the falling share of machinery in Swiss exports). This applies both to exports to the EC12 and to EFTA.

Specialization coefficients

Did these changes arise from specific developments in national production structures or did they follow a general trend in world trade? In other words, did the patterns of comparative advantage change for the countries under review?

A useful tool in the analysis of this issue is the coefficient of "revealed" comparative advantage.[751] It is based on the assumption that comparative advantage determines the structure of exports, the commodity pattern of trade reflecting relative costs and differences in non-price factors. For the purpose of international comparison, a country's share in world exports of a given commodity is normalized by its share in world exports of all commodities.

These normalized shares, which have also been called "specialization coefficients", are defined for exporter i and commodity k as:

$$s_{ik} = X_{ik}/X_{.k} / X_{i.}/X_{..} \qquad (3)$$

where:

X_{ik} = country i's exports of product k
$X_{.k}$ = world exports of product k
$X_{i.}$ = country i's total exports
$X_{..}$ = total world exports.

A coefficient larger than unity indicates that a country's specialization in that good is relatively high, while a value between zero and the unity suggests a relatively low specialization. The more concentrated the export structure of a country, the greater will tend to be the variance of the individual coefficients. This is reflected in table 6.5 where the high product concentration results in high "specialization" coefficients for the main export products (pulp and wood products in Finland, pulp and aluminium in Norway, food in Denmark, wood products in Austria, pulp and wood in Sweden and chemicals and machinery in Switzerland).

Between 1963 and 1987 the countries' specialization tended to decline in goods where they had an obvious comparative advantage in the early 1960s and to rise in those where no advantage was apparent, notably chemicals and machinery (except for Switzerland). Despite the latter increases, the coefficients for these goods remained relatively low. Some countries, however, specialized further in traditional exports (food, ferrous metals and aluminium in Norway, pulp and paper in Austria).

Did these changes occur in exports to both EFTA and to the EC?

In exports to EFTA (table 6.5) *in the years that followed its formation,* a number of countries specialized further in products were they had a clear advantage in the early 1960s (wood products in Austria and Sweden, food and aluminium in Norway, aluminium in Switzerland, food in Denmark); in other cases, new comparative advantages emerged (transport equipment in Finland, aluminium in Sweden, pulp and paper in Switzerland).[752] Austria, Finland, Switzerland and Denmark increasingly specialized in textiles and/or clothing. Some of these countries were already relatively specialized in these goods in 1963, but the tariff cut may have given them an increased advantage in the EFTA market, their textiles replacing domestic production or imports from other suppliers.

---

[751] B. Balassa. "Trade Liberalization and 'Revealed' Comparative Advantage", *The Manchester School*, XXXIII, 1965 and "Revealed Comparative Advantage Revisited: An Analysis of Relative Export Shares of the Industrial Countries, 1953-1971", *The Manchester School,*, XLV, 1977.

[752] The analysis of the specialization coefficients for exports to the EC in this period is somewhat misleading because the data in table 6.5 include exports to the United Kingdom and Denmark, which were then EFTA members.

TABLE 6.4

Product composition of exports from the six countries, 1963, 1972 and 1987

(Percentages)

	Austria			Finland			Norway			Sweden			Switzerland			Denmark		
	1963	1972	1987	1963	1972	1987	1963	1972	1987	1963	1972	1987	1963	1972	1987	1963	1972	1987
Total exports [a]																		
Food products	5.1	4.0	2.2	3.4	3.8	1.4	15.6	12.7	12.7	2.8	2.2	1.1	2.5	1.9	1.2	48.5	32.2	25.5
Pulp and paper	6.6	5.9	6.6	48.8	35.9	31.0	16.9	9.3	8.6	22.1	15.5	15.1	0.7	0.9	1.5	0.6	0.9	1.2
Wood products	10.1	6.5	4.2	23.8	14.4	8.5	1.1	1.2	1.1	7.8	7.0	4.7	0.4	0.4	0.5	1.4	1.4	1.6
Ferrous metals	14.7	9.9	7.5	1.4	3.0	4.9	8.8	8.0	6.1	13.1	11.0	6.8	0.7	0.7	1.4	0.9	1.2	1.8
Aluminium	2.2	0.9	1.6	0.1	0.3	0.3	9.0	9.2	10.9	0.2	0.5	0.6	1.1	0.9	1.1	0.1	0.3	0.6
Non-metallic minerals	4.4	3.8	3.4	0.4	0.8	1.5	0.7	0.9	0.7	0.7	0.9	1.2	2.7	2.1	4.8	1.2	1.6	1.3
Chemicals	3.4	5.2	9.1	1.4	3.0	5.6	9.0	7.3	12.6	3.2	4.3	7.3	19.4	22.4	22.0	4.7	6.5	9.5
Machinery	19.6	26.2	31.8	7.1	11.7	22.2	7.2	11.4	14.6	22.2	27.4	29.6	48.4	45.4	43.9	16.8	23.6	24.2
Transport equipment	2.6	3.1	4.0	6.2	7.0	6.6	7.6	18.8	15.4	13.6	15.7	17.3	0.2	0.4	1.4	5.4	4.5	3.7
Textiles and leather	10.6	10.8	7.1	2.8	4.3	3.9	5.2	3.3	2.5	3.1	2.6	2.0	9.9	7.9	5.3	4.2	6.0	5.7
Clothing	3.2	3.3	3.6	0.3	5.8	3.5	1.0	0.6	0.5	0.8	1.2	0.9	1.9	1.4	1.1	1.6	3.3	3.1
Other	17.4	20.4	19.0	4.3	10.1	10.9	18.0	17.2	14.5	10.2	11.8	13.7	12.2	15.5	15.9	14.8	18.5	21.9
Total	100.0	100.0	100.0	100.0	100.0	100.0	100.0	100.0	100.0	100.0	100.0	100.0	100.0	100.0	100.0	100.0	100.0	100.0
Exports to EC12																		
Food products	8.0	6.4	2.2	4.0	3.1	0.7	13.8	11.2	13.9	3.5	2.7	0.8	3.4	2.7	1.8	67.8	43.0	32.9
Pulp and paper	7.7	6.2	7.2	53.4	45.1	45.8	23.8	12.6	11.3	30.2	22.3	21.4	1.0	0.9	2.1	0.6	1.1	1.4
Wood products	15.7	9.5	5.0	34.3	25.2	13.1	1.2	1.5	1.1	11.9	11.0	6.1	0.6	0.7	0.8	1.2	1.7	1.8
Ferrous metals	13.5	9.0	6.8	1.1	2.4	5.7	12.0	10.0	7.4	6.8	7.3	7.8	0.9	0.9	2.0	0.4	0.9	1.9
Aluminium	2.7	1.1	1.8	0.0	0.2	0.2	8.7	11.7	18.5	0.1	0.4	0.8	1.4	1.0	1.4	0.1	0.3	0.8
Non-metallic minerals	4.6	4.1	2.6	0.3	0.4	1.1	0.4	0.4	0.7	0.7	1.0	1.0	3.7	2.9	5.3	0.6	1.2	0.9
Chemicals	2.3	3.1	8.0	0.9	2.2	3.7	8.9	6.0	11.4	2.9	3.5	7.4	17.3	21.1	20.1	2.5	4.5	7.0
Machinery	15.1	24.9	32.7	1.3	5.4	14.3	5.4	8.7	12.8	16.1	21.5	26.9	43.9	40.8	40.3	10.7	21.0	21.6
Transport equipment	1.3	2.2	4.2	0.2	3.0	2.1	3.4	20.0	5.3	6.1	11.2	13.7	0.3	0.5	1.4	0.9	2.9	3.7
Textiles and leather	9.4	10.2	7.6	1.4	3.8	3.8	3.9	2.8	2.7	2.6	2.1	2.1	10.3	8.1	6.6	2.7	5.5	4.7
Clothing	3.5	3.2	3.9	0.0	1.9	1.7	0.9	0.4	0.5	0.7	0.8	0.5	2.1	1.4	1.4	0.4	1.1	1.6
Other	16.4	20.1	18.0	3.1	7.4	7.9	17.7	14.7	14.5	18.4	16.2	11.6	15.3	19.2	16.9	12.3	16.9	21.7
Total	100.0	100.0	100.0	100.0	100.0	100.0	100.0	100.0	100.0	100.0	100.0	100.0	100.0	100.0	100.0	100.0	100.0	100.0
Exports to EFTA																		
Food products	2.4	1.3	1.6	5.3	1.9	0.9	12.0	10.3	10.1	1.3	1.9	1.4	0.7	0.4	0.6	17.8	13.4	7.4
Pulp and paper	3.0	4.0	4.9	12.2	8.5	10.7	1.7	2.1	4.5	4.7	5.9	7.1	0.7	1.9	2.6	0.8	1.1	1.7
Wood products	5.0	5.0	5.6	23.0	5.6	6.1	2.1	1.5	2.4	4.2	4.4	5.7	0.3	0.5	0.9	2.5	1.6	2.3
Ferrous metals	16.7	8.8	6.2	5.9	6.0	5.3	7.2	7.9	5.3	6.3	5.8	5.2	1.1	1.7	1.7	2.8	2.6	2.8
Aluminium	1.5	0.6	1.8	0.1	0.5	0.4	4.0	4.4	7.3	0.7	1.2	0.7	2.1	2.0	2.1	0.3	0.7	0.6
Non-metallic minerals	4.2	2.7	3.3	2.0	1.5	1.2	0.6	1.1	1.5	0.9	0.9	2.3	1.0	1.3	1.2	2.0	2.1	1.8
Chemicals	4.1	4.1	7.7	4.2	3.4	5.0	14.3	12.4	15.2	4.4	6.6	8.2	16.3	14.7	15.0	7.0	8.6	9.7
Machinery	19.9	21.4	24.7	14.6	20.5	27.3	13.1	19.5	20.0	25.5	27.6	29.0	42.1	35.5	41.5	22.7	24.4	27.1
Transport equipment	3.2	5.1	4.7	5.2	14.3	15.0	12.6	8.9	8.1	33.4	19.3	12.3	0.3	1.0	1.7	10.0	3.4	2.7
Textiles and leather	17.6	17.0	7.8	11.3	6.2	3.8	7.5	5.6	3.2	3.6	4.8	2.8	19.9	18.8	9.7	7.1	8.8	7.0
Clothing	4.5	6.9	7.0	1.3	15.1	7.1	2.3	1.3	1.1	2.1	3.1	2.9	2.5	4.3	1.9	5.7	8.9	9.1
Other	17.9	23.2	24.7	15.0	16.5	17.6	22.7	25.1	21.4	13.0	18.4	22.6	12.9	18.0	21.4	21.4	24.3	28.0
Total	100.0	100.0	100.0	100.0	100.0	100.0	100.0	100.0	100.0	100.0	100.0	100.0	100.0	100.0	100.0	100.0	100.0	100.0

Source: As for table 6.1.

[a] Excluding oil and oil products.

TABLE 6.5

Specialization coefficients,[a] 1963, 1972 and 1987

(*Percentages*)

	Austria			Finland			Norway			Sweden			Switzerland			Denmark		
	1963	1972	1987	1963	1972	1987	1963	1972	1987	1963	1972	1987	1963	1972	1987	1963	1972	1987
Total exports[b]																		
Food products	0.5	0.5	0.4	0.4	0.5	0.3	1.6	1.7	2.3	0.3	0.3	0.2	0.3	0.3	0.2	5.0	4.2	4.7
Pulp and paper	1.7	1.9	2.1	12.4	11.7	9.8	4.3	3.0	2.7	5.6	5.1	4.8	0.2	0.3	0.5	0.2	0.3	0.4
Wood products	4.9	3.7	3.2	11.5	8.2	6.6	0.5	0.7	0.8	3.8	4.0	3.7	0.2	0.2	0.4	0.7	0.8	1.3
Ferrous metals	2.2	1.6	1.9	0.2	0.5	1.3	1.3	1.3	1.6	2.0	1.8	1.8	0.1	0.1	0.4	0.1	0.2	0.5
Aluminium	2.5	1.2	1.7	0.1	0.4	0.4	10.2	12.3	11.7	0.3	0.6	0.7	1.3	1.2	1.2	0.1	0.5	0.6
Non-metallic minerals	2.3	1.6	1.5	0.2	0.4	0.5	0.3	0.4	0.3	0.3	0.4	0.5	1.4	0.9	2.2	0.6	0.7	0.6
Chemicals	0.4	0.6	0.8	0.2	0.3	0.5	1.1	0.8	1.1	0.4	0.5	0.7	2.4	2.5	2.0	0.6	0.7	0.6
Machinery	0.8	1.0	1.1	0.3	0.4	0.7	0.3	0.8	0.5	0.9	1.0	1.0	2.0	1.7	1.5	0.7	0.9	0.9
Transport equipment	0.3	0.2	0.3	0.6	0.5	0.4	0.7	1.3	1.0	1.3	1.1	1.1	0.0	0.0	0.1	0.5	0.3	0.8
Textiles and leather	1.1	1.6	1.5	0.3	0.6	0.9	0.6	0.5	0.5	0.3	0.4	0.4	1.2	1.2	1.1	0.4	0.9	0.2
Clothing	2.1	1.7	1.7	0.2	3.0	1.7	0.7	0.3	0.3	0.5	0.6	0.4	0.7	0.7	0.5	1.1	1.7	1.5
Other	0.8	1.0	1.0	0.2	0.5	0.6	0.8	0.9	0.8	0.5	0.6	0.7	0.6	0.8	0.8	0.7	0.9	1.1
Total	1.0	1.0	1.0	1.0	1.0	1.0	1.0	1.0	1.0	1.0	1.0	1.0	1.0	1.0	1.0	1.0	1.0	1.0
Exports to EC12																		
Food products	0.7	0.7	0.3	0.4	0.3	0.1	1.3	1.2	2.1	0.3	0.3	0.1	0.3	0.3	0.3	6.2	4.7	5.0
Pulp and paper	1.7	1.7	1.9	11.9	12.4	12.2	5.3	3.5	3.0	6.7	6.1	5.7	0.2	0.3	0.6	0.1	0.3	0.4
Wood products	6.0	5.3	4.0	13.2	14.2	10.6	0.5	0.9	0.9	4.6	6.2	4.9	0.2	0.4	0.6	0.5	0.9	1.4
Ferrous metals	2.0	1.5	1.9	0.2	0.4	1.6	1.8	1.7	2.0	1.0	1.2	2.1	0.1	0.2	0.5	0.1	0.2	0.5
Aluminium	2.6	1.2	1.8	0.0	0.2	0.2	8.5	12.4	18.0	0.1	0.4	0.8	1.3	1.0	1.4	0.1	0.3	0.8
Non-metallic minerals	2.4	1.6	1.2	0.1	0.1	0.2	0.2	0.2	0.3	0.4	0.4	0.4	2.0	1.2	2.4	0.3	0.5	0.4
Chemicals	0.3	0.3	0.7	0.1	0.2	0.3	1.2	0.7	0.9	0.4	0.4	0.6	2.3	2.3	1.7	0.3	0.5	0.6
Machinery	0.7	1.1	1.2	0.1	0.2	0.3	0.3	0.4	0.5	0.8	0.9	1.0	2.1	1.8	1.5	0.5	0.9	0.8
Transport equipment	0.2	0.2	0.3	0.0	0.3	0.2	0.5	1.9	0.4	0.8	1.1	1.1	0.0	0.1	0.1	0.1	0.3	0.3
Textiles and leather	0.9	1.3	1.4	0.1	0.5	0.7	0.4	0.4	0.5	0.3	0.3	0.4	1.0	1.0	1.2	0.3	0.7	0.9
Clothing	2.2	1.2	1.3	0.0	0.7	0.6	0.4	0.2	0.2	0.4	0.3	0.2	1.3	0.5	0.5	0.3	0.4	0.6
Other	0.7	0.9	0.9	0.1	0.3	0.4	0.7	0.7	0.7	0.8	0.7	0.6	0.6	0.9	0.8	0.5	0.8	1.1
Total	1.0	1.0	1.0	1.0	1.0	1.0	1.0	1.0	1.0	1.0	1.0	1.0	1.0	1.0	1.0	1.0	1.0	1.0
Exports to EFTA[c]																		
Food products	0.5	0.4	0.9	1.2	0.6	0.4	2.7	3.3	5.3	0.3	0.6	0.7	0.2	0.1	0.3	4.0	4.3	3.9
Pulp and paper	2.3	2.3	2.1	9.3	4.9	4.6	1.3	1.2	1.9	3.6	3.4	3.0	0.6	1.1	1.1	0.6	0.7	0.7
Wood products	3.5	3.8	3.5	15.9	4.4	3.8	1.5	1.2	1.5	2.9	3.4	3.5	0.2	0.4	0.6	1.7	1.3	1.4
Ferrous metals	2.7	1.6	1.8	1.0	1.1	1.4	1.2	1.5	1.5	1.0	1.1	1.5	0.2	0.3	0.6	0.5	0.5	0.8
Aluminium	2.2	1.0	2.0	0.2	0.7	0.4	5.9	7.2	8.3	1.0	2.0	0.8	3.1	3.2	1.9	0.4	1.1	0.6
Non-metallic minerals	2.0	0.8	1.4	1.0	0.5	0.5	0.3	0.3	0.6	0.4	0.3	1.0	0.5	0.5	0.5	1.0	0.6	0.8
Chemicals	0.5	0.4	0.7	0.5	0.4	0.5	1.7	1.3	1.4	0.5	0.7	0.8	1.9	1.5	1.4	0.8	0.6	0.8
Machinery	0.8	0.8	0.8	0.6	0.7	0.9	0.5	0.7	0.6	1.0	1.0	0.9	1.7	1.3	1.3	0.9	0.9	0.9
Transport equipment	0.2	0.4	0.4	0.4	1.1	1.2	0.9	0.8	0.6	2.4	1.5	1.0	0.0	0.1	0.1	0.7	0.3	0.9
Textiles and leather	1.7	2.3	1.7	1.1	0.8	0.8	0.7	0.7	0.7	0.4	0.6	0.6	2.0	2.5	2.2	0.7	1.2	0.2
Clothing	1.9	2.0	1.5	0.6	4.2	1.5	1.0	0.4	0.2	0.9	0.9	0.6	1.0	1.2	0.4	2.4	2.5	1.6
Other	0.8	1.0	1.1	0.7	0.7	0.8	0.7	1.1	0.9	0.6	0.8	1.0	0.6	0.8	0.9	0.9	1.1	2.0
Total	1.0	1.0	1.0	1.0	1.0	1.0	1.0	1.0	1.0	1.0	1.0	1.0	1.0	1.0	1.0	1.0	1.0	1.0

Source: As for table 6.1.

[a] The share of a given product in each country's exports, relative to the share of the same product in OECD's exports.
[b] Excluding oil and oil products.
[c] Austria, Finland, Iceland, Norway, Sweden and Switzerland.

In the period that followed the free trade agreements with the EC, the six countries' specialization often increased in products where they had a comparative advantage prior to the agreement. This applies to Austria (pulp and paper, ferrous metals, aluminium, textiles and clothing), Norway (food, ferrous metals, aluminium), Sweden (ferrous metals) and Denmark (food). There were some cases where previous comparative advantages declined (pulp, paper and wood in Finland, pulp and paper in Norway and Sweden, machinery and chemicals in Switzerland) but new comparative advantages also emerged (ferrous metals in Finland, wood products in Denmark). Specialization in chemicals and machinery tended to increase (although not in Switzerland), but remained relatively low.

To some extent these developments are what might have been "expected" from trade liberalization: in a significant number of cases, the countries increasingly specialized in products for which they had a comparative advantage. This happened first in exports to EFTA and later in trade with the EC. But there were also cases of new comparative advantages emerging.

Factors underlying comparative advantages

In those cases where traditional comparative advantages were reinforced, the countries' specialization is likely to reflect differences in relative factor endowments, including natural resources.[753] In fact, one is dealing here with comparative advantages that are apparent in the commodity composition of a country's exports, which is assumed to reflect both relative cost and non-price factors. As far as costs are concerned, international differences are supposed to be determined by differences in the relative endowment of production factors.

However, there has been increased specialization in goods where no comparative advantage was apparent in the early 1960s, particularly in chemicals and machinery. The emergence of these comparative advantages calls for other interpretations.

One possible explanation may be related to technological factors.[754] According to the "product cycle" and "technological gap" theories, comparative advantage in products using new technologies will tend to be held by the technologically more advanced countries; but other countries may be able to exploit a comparative advantage in "mature" products for which the technology has become standardized.[755] This may have been the case for the countries considered here.

In the above account, the emphasis is on the standardization of technologies over time. But standardized technologies are often used in large scale production which, in turn, tends to involve standardized goods. This leads to another possible explanation for changes in comparative advantage, namely Drèze's "hypothesis of standardization".[756] The argument is that a small domestic market may inhibit the production of differentiated goods; but small countries may reap the benefit of scale economies by becoming competitive in the production of internationally standardized goods. The increased "specialization" of some of the countries analysed here in certain goods (e.g. metals and chemicals) may be related to such a process.

Another account, also stressing economies of scale, maintains that expanding markets (which may be associated with trade liberalization) lead to a "disintegration" or increasing separability of production processes into more and more specialized stages, or to a growing division of labour within each industrial activity. This generates inter-firm and international trade in intermediate goods.[757] In the trade statistics, this phenomenon often appears as the simultaneous export and import of the "same good", a phenomenon that has been labelled "intra-industry" trade.

In fact, it has been shown that intra-industry trade has increased in the Nordic countries, most markedly in chemicals and machinery.[758] This suggests that the hypothesis of the "disintegration" of production processes across international borders may also explain the emerging comparative advantage of the six countries in machinery and transport equipment.[759]

Finally, there is the possibility of increased trade in consumer goods as a result of overlapping demand patterns among different countries. According to Linder, manufactured trade between two countries will increase as the demand patterns of the two countries overlap: a product which meets the demand of the "majority" in one country may meet the demand of the "minority" in the other.[760]

In short, the liberalization of trade seems to have led to a more rational division of labour across national borders. In some cases, traditional comparative advantages, probably related to relative factor endowments, were reinforced. In others, new comparative

---

[753] Note, however, that some difficulties arise when a third factor is introduced into the Heckscher-Ohlin framework. See B. Balassa, *loc.cit.*, 1985, p.101.

[754] In the factor proportions model, technology is assumed to be given and equally available to all producers.

[755] See, *inter alia* R. Vernon, "International Investment and International Trade in the Product Cycle", *Quarterly Journal of Economics*, 1966.

[756] J. Drèze, "Les exportations intra-CEE en 1958 et la position Belge", *Recherches Economiques de Louvain*, 1961.

[757] For a detailed discussion of this issue, see P.B.W. Rayment, "Intra-industry specialization and the foreign trade of industrial countries", in S.F. Frowen (ed.), *Controlling Industrial Economies*, London, Macmillan, 1983.

[758] J. Fagerberg, "Diffusion of Technology, Structural Change and Intra-Industry Trade: the Case of the Nordic Countries 1961-1982" in J.O. Andersson (ed.), *Nordic Studies on Intra-Industry Trade*, Aabo Academy Press, Aabo, 1987.

[759] The French Renault, for example, produces motors for Swedish Volvo, while Volvo imports Renault cars into Scandinavia.

[760] S.B. Linder, *An Essay on Trade and Transformation*, Uppsala, Almqvist and Wiksells, 1961.

advantages emerged. The six countries may have taken advantage of an enlarged market to reap scale economies and to acquire comparative advantages in goods for which technologies are internationally standardized (e.g., chemicals, metal products); they may also have increasingly exported intermediate goods, a reflection of trade liberalization resulting in increased international complementarity on the supply side.

(ii) Structure and export performance

The previous sections examined the geographical and product structures of exports in terms of summary statistics. In this section the focus shifts to the impact of these structures on export performance. A country's share of the world market may fall because it exports mainly to markets that are growing at a relatively low rate; it may also decline because the country's exports are dominated by "low growth" products. The issue is discussed here by means of a "constant market share" (CMS) analysis of export developments.

This approach has been frequently employed since it was first suggested by Tyszynski in 1951.[761] In a version that has been developed by Fagerberg and Sollie,[762] the change in a country's share of world imports is decomposed into five parts:

1. The *change in micro-shares,* i.e., the change in the country's shares of individual product markets;[763]

2. The *commodity composition effect,* i.e., the change in the country's share of world imports arising from changes in their commodity composition;

3. The *market composition effect, i.e,* the change in the country's share of world imports originating in changes in their market composition;

4. The *commodity adaptation effect,* i.e., the degree to which the country has succeeded[764] in adapting the commodity composition of its exports to the changes in the commodity composition of world imports; and

5. The *market adaptation effect,* i.e., the degree to which the country has succeeded in adjusting to changes in the market composition of world imports.

The last four components are related to changes in demand patterns and to the capacity of supply to adjust to the conditions of demand; the first represents the change in market shares that cannot be ascribed to demand, reflecting supply conditions and/or the impact of trade policies. Thus, the effects of trade liberalization are expected to show up primarily in the latter, together with the impact of supply conditions.[765]

(a) Aggregate results

In table 6.6, the changes in each country's share of the world market between 1961 and 1973 and between 1973 and 1985 are decomposed into the five effects listed above.

The results indicate that export structures had a significant and often negative impact on market shares, but that supply factors and/or trade policies (reflected in the changes in micro-shares) also played an important, and sometimes dominant role.

In the first period, *1961 to 1973,* there were considerable differences among the countries: the Swiss and Norwegian shares of the world market increased by about 7 and 2 per cent, respectively; those of Finland, Denmark and Sweden fell by some 27 per cent, 13 and 4 per cent; the Austrian share declined slightly.

All countries except Finland increased their *micro-shares* (strongly in the case of Norway, but marginally in Switzerland); in Finland there were significant losses. On the other hand, the total *composition and adaptation* effects were negative in all countries except Switzerland (where the commodity composition effect was large and positive). In Austria and Sweden the commodity composition effect was positive, as was the commodity adaptation effect in Finland and Norway (although it was quite small in the latter); these effects, however, were outweighed by the negative impact of other components. In Denmark all the composition and adaptation effects were negative.

Between 1973 and 1985, the market shares of Austria and Finland in world imports rose markedly, while those of Norway, Sweden and Denmark fell dramatically. In all countries except Denmark, these changes followed those in *micro-shares.* The negative *composition and adaptation effects* were larger than in the previous period, especially in Finland, Austria and Norway. Switzerland and Sweden continued to record commodity composition gains, but these were not suf-

---

[761] H.Tyszynski, "World trade in manufactured commodities, 1899-1950", *The Manchester School,* 19, 1951.

[762] J. Fagerberg and G. Sollie, "The method of constant market shares analysis reconsidered", *Applied Economics,* 19, 1987.

[763] For each market, the micro-shares are aggregated using as weights the commodity composition of that market's imports for the world market the market shares are aggregated using as weights the market composition of world imports.

[764] Note that a commodity adaptation effect equal to zero does not indicate the absence of adaptation, but that the country adapted at the same pace as the average of all the other exporting countries. The same applies to the market adaptation effect.

[765] The "constant market share" analysis was conducted for total exports, but the aggregate results were broken down by markets and products. (See Appendix, section (i) to this paper for the methodology). These computations were made at the University of Aalborg, on data from the University's data bank. However, the latter are less comprehensive than the United Nations' COMTRADE data, which were used in the previous section. For this reason, the periods, as well as the market and commodity breakdown used here are slightly different from those in that section.

TABLE 6.6

A CMS decomposition of changes in market share, 1961-1973 and 1973-1985
(Percentages)

	Austria	Finland	Norway	Sweden	Switzerland	Denmark
			1961-1973			
Change in market share	-0.93	-26.70	1.94	-3.65	6.86	-13.20
of which:						
Commodity composition	4.75	-9.46	-2.56	5.69	22.39	-2.92
Market composition	-0.52	-8.35	-7.93	-5.51	0.26	-9.68
Commodity adaptation	-4.09	3.75	0.65	-2.93	-14.10	-2.26
Market adaptation	-4.16	-0.78	-3.51	-2.43	-1.90	-0.02
Total composition and adaptation	-4.02	-14.84	-13.35	-5.18	6.65	-14.88
Micro-share changes	3.09	-11.90	15.30	1.42	0.17	1.71
			1973-1985			
Change in market share	6.78	9.87	-32.00	-22.00	-1.39	-12.30
of which:						
Commodity composition	-2.72	-10.10	-9.26	1.01	12.42	-10.40
Market composition	-7.28	-7.99	-7.62	-8.28	-3.33	-6.30
Commodity adaptation	-2.84	-5.79	-0.07	-2.31	-9.47	-5.11
Market adaptation	-2.52	-0.07	0.88	2.80	-2.41	-1.32
Total composition and adaptation	-15.36	-23.95	-16.07	-6.78	-2.79	-23.13
Micro-share changes	22.14	33.86	-15.90	-15.20	1.39	10.86

Sources: Calculations carried out at the University of Aalborg, Denmark.

ficient to offset the negative composition/adaptation effects.

(b) A breakdown by markets

Table 6.7 shows the decomposition of the CMS results by market. (The "rest of the world" is a residual, which includes some markets — eastern Europe, the Soviet Union, Japan — that were treated separately in the previous section.)

In *1961-1973* all countries lost market share in the EC6 but gained in the present day EFTA. Austria, Switzerland and Sweden also gained in EC3, but Finland, Denmark and Norway lost shares. Finland, Norway, Denmark and Switzerland lost shares in North America, while Austria, Finland and Denmark lost in the "rest of the world".

During this period, which corresponds to the early years of EFTA, all countries lost *micro-shares* in EC6, but gained in the original EFTA. Switzerland, Sweden and Norway registered losses in North America; Austria, Norway, Denmark and, especially, Finland lost in the "rest of the world". As mentioned above, the changes in micro-shares capture the effects of changes in supply conditions and/or trade policies. The regional distribution of these changes in 1961-1973 (gains in EFTA, losses in other markets, particularly in EC6) suggests that the impact of the formation of EFTA was significant.

The *adaptation effects* were largely negative (except in Finland). The *composition effects*, however, varied: Finland and Norway incurred losses in practically all markets; Austria and Switzerland, made significant gains, particularly in EC6 and in North America; Sweden and Denmark also had composition gains in these two markets, but these were offset by losses elsewhere.

Between 1973 and 1985, i.e., the period following Danish membership of the EC and when the FTAs with the EC were implemented, all countries lost market share in EFTA and in the countries that joined the EC in 1973. Austria, Switzerland, Finland and Denmark gained in EC6, but Norway and Sweden lost. Except for Norway, all countries gained share in North America. Austria, Finland and Denmark also gained in the "rest of the world".

The direction and size of the *changes in micro-shares* differed from country to country. Finland gained in all markets except EC3, particularly in the "rest of the world".[766] Austria and Denmark made substantial gains in EC6 and in the "rest of the world", which more than offset its losses in the original EFTA. Switzerland also increased its micro-share in EC6, while Norway and Sweden lost considerably in most markets.

To some extent, these changes in micro-shares reflect the impact of freeing trade with the EC: all countries except Norway had micro-share gains in the EC6 and most had losses in EFTA and its former members. But some features suggest the presence of other factors. Austria, Finland and Denmark made significant gains in micro-shares in the non-European markets, while Norway and Sweden had losses in most markets. This suggests that supply factors may have had a significant impact — negative in Norway and Sweden, positive in the others. (For Finland and Austria, exports to eastern markets were also helped by higher oil prices.)

---

[766] This was probably due to increased trade with the Soviet Union under bilateral agreement: as Finland imports oil from the USSR, the increase in oil prices led to a rise in Soviet imports from Finland.

TABLE 6.7

A CMS decomposition of changes in market share, by market, 1961-1973 and 1973-1985
(Percentage)

	1961-1973						1973-1985					
	EC6	EC3	EFTA	North America	Rest of the world	Total	EC6	EC3	EFTA	North America	Rest of the world	Total
Austria												
Change in market share	-10.00	6.11	7.21	1.02	-5.24	-0.93	12.47	-4.56	-6.94	0.78	5.03	6.78
of which:												
Composition effects	6.85	0.10	-1.96	1.72	-2.48	4.23	-8.90	-1.28	-3.67	2.76	1.10	-10.00
adaptation effects	-3.44	-1.74	-0.84	-1.05	-1.19	-8.25	-3.45	0.17	0.66	-1.10	-1.65	-5.36
Micro-share change	-13.40	7.76	10.01	0.34	-1.57	3.09	24.82	-3.45	-3.93	-0.89	5.59	22.14
Finland												
Change in market share	-13.50	-6.40	9.07	-0.23	-15.60	-26.70	1.20	-8.48	-2.22	3.73	15.64	9.87
of which:												
Composition effects	-0.95	-10.17	-1.43	-1.54	-3.71	-17.81	-5.48	-9.21	-4.22	1.51	-0.73	-18.09
adaptation effects	0.51	1.49	-0.31	-0.63	1.90	2.97	-1.47	2.21	-3.52	0.00	-3.07	-5.86
Micro-share change	-13.10	2.27	10.81	1.95	-13.80	-11.90	8.15	-1.48	5.51	2.24	19.44	33.86
Norway												
Change in market share	-0.03	-3.47	5.51	-2.62	2.54	1.94	-6.99	-11.30	-8.08	-1.44	-4.19	-32.00
of which:												
Composition effects	0.63	-8.65	-1.58	-2.46	1.57	-10.49	-5.14	-6.85	-5.50	2.03	-1.42	-16.88
adaptation effects	-0.50	-2.19	-2.58	0.19	2.22	-2.86	1.27	2.56	1.58	-1.18	-3.42	0.81
Micro-share change	-0.16	7.38	9.67	-0.35	-1.25	15.30	-3.12	-7.00	-4.17	-2.28	0.65	-15.90
Sweden												
Change in market share	-9.17	0.59	2.26	1.39	1.17	-3.75	-5.54	-11.40	-6.07	5.08	-4.01	-22.00
of which:												
Composition effects	0.96	-3.22	-1.48	4.28	-0.35	0.18	-5.86	-4.61	-2.40	4.58	1.02	-7.27
adaptation effects	-1.02	-0.74	-1.28	-2.35	0.04	-5.36	-0.05	0.71	-0.24	0.15	-0.07	0.49
Micro-share change	-9.11	4.56	5.02	-0.53	1.48	1.42	0.37	-7.51	-3.43	0.35	-4.96	-15.20
Switzerland												
Change in market share	-3.69	3.25	1.90	-0.46	5.87	6.86	4.95	0.26	-3.73	2.91	-5.78	-1.39
of which:												
Composition effects	14.67	2.46	-0.28	3.96	1.84	22.65	-2.07	0.87	-1.11	7.01	4.39	9.09
adaptation effects	-7.29	-3.77	-0.83	-2.28	-1.77	-16.00	-3.47	-3.53	0.01	-2.32	-2.55	-11.88
Micro-share change	-11.10	4.53	3.01	-2.13	5.80	0.17	10.50	2.92	-2.64	-1.78	-7.61	1.39
Denmark												
Change in market share	-4.41	-9.29	2.98	-0.30	-2.16	-13.20	0.34	-8.63	-7.31	1.76	1.57	-12.30
of which:												
Composition effects	5.37	-16.39	-1.50	0.54	-0.63	-12.60	-7.15	-7.17	-5.21	2.42	0.40	-16.70
adaptation effects	-1.73	1.13	-1.57	-0.92	0.81	-2.28	-4.08	0.16	1.30	-1.89	-1.91	-6.43
Micro-share change	-8.05	5.97	6.06	0.07	-2.34	1.71	11.58	-1.63	-3.41	1.24	3.08	10.86

Source: As for table 6.6.

In all countries except Switzerland the negative *composition effects* were due to the west European markets. In Switzerland, Austria, Finland and Denmark the negative *adaptation effects* originated mostly in EC6 and the "rest of the world".

(c) A decomposition by products

The breakdown of the CMS analysis by products is shown in table 6.8.

Until the early 1970s the six countries generally lost shares in traditional, resource intensive goods (food, pulp and paper, ferrous metals) and gained in more "modern" products (chemicals, machinery, transport equipment, clothing and "other goods").

To a large extent, these developments reflect *changes in micro shares*. In Austria and Denmark, the total micro-share gain was largely due to machinery, textiles and "other goods"; in Norway – and to a lesser extent in Sweden – the increases were spread over more products, including traditional exports, such as aluminium in Norway and wood products in Sweden; in Switzerland, losses in machinery, clothing and food were offset by gains elsewhere, particularly in "other goods"; in Finland, the large micro-share losses were due to pulp, paper and wood products.

The negative *composition effects* were frequently located in the traditional, resource intensive goods, while the negative *adaptation effects* were more frequent in "modern" products. This suggests that the export structures, particularly of Sweden and Switzerland, adapted to world patterns relatively slowly.

Between 1973 and 1985 there were larger inter-country differences: the market share gains of Austria and Finland were mostly in machinery, chemicals, transport equipment, and "other goods"; the losses in Denmark were concentrated in food products, while in Norway and Sweden they affected all goods except chemicals; Switzerland recorded significant losses in machinery, chemicals and textiles. The *changes in micro-shares* tended to follow this pattern, except in Denmark.

TABLE 6.8

A CMS decomposition of changes in market share, by product, 1961-1973 and 1973-1985
(Percentage changes)

	Food products	Pulp & paper	Wood products	Ferrous metals	Aluminium	Chemicals	Machinery	Transport equipment	Textiles & leather	Clothing	Other	Total
1961-1973												
Austria												
Change in market share	-0.8	-1.6	-3.7	-8.9	-1.2	2.1	9.7	0.4	0.7	1.3	1.1	-0.9
of which:												
Composition effects	2.1	-1.1	-1.9	-0.3	-0.2	1.2	3.5	2.4	-2.6	2.9	-1.8	4.1
Adaptation effects	-1.2	-0.4	-0.6	-0.8	-0.0	0.0	1.7	-1.9	-3.2	-1.4	-0.3	-8.3
Micro-share change	-1.7	-0.1	-1.2	-7.8	-1.0	0.9	4.5	-0.1	6.5	-0.2	3.2	3.1
Finland												
Change in market share	-1.0	-22.9	-19.0	0.9	0.2	1.1	2.8	1.6	1.3	3.7	4.5	-26.7
of which:												
Composition effects	-1.1	-10.5	-8.5	-0.2	0.0	0.1	-0.3	4.0	-0.6	0.0	-0.8	-17.8
Adaptation effects	0.5	2.6	3.7	0.0	0.0	0.1	0.6	-3.1	-0.9	0.8	-1.3	3.0
Micro-share change	-0.4	-15.0	-14.2	1.1	0.2	1.0	2.5	0.7	2.8	2.9	6.6	-11.9
Norway												
Change in market share	-3.6	-8.7	1.3	-1.1	0.8	-1.7	6.4	10.0	-0.7	0.0	-0.7	1.9
of which:												
Composition effects	-2.2	-5.3	-0.3	0.4	-2.7	-1.9	1.3	5.1	-1.4	0.7	-4.1	-10.5
Adaptation effects	0.4	1.9	-0.7	-2.8	0.1	-0.8	0.0	1.3	-0.6	-0.5	-1.3	-2.9
Micro-share change	-1.8	-5.3	2.3	1.3	3.4	1.0	5.1	3.6	1.3	-0.2	4.7	15.3
Sweden												
Change in market share	-1.2	-6.7	-1.0	-5.5	0.3	1.2	3.6	3.3	-0.2	0.3	2.2	-3.8
of which:												
Composition effects	-0.8	-4.3	-1.7	-4.4	0.0	1.0	5.4	4.8	-0.7	0.6	0.4	0.2
Adaptation effects	0.3	0.4	-0.6	0.6	-0.1	-0.4	-2.4	-1.2	-0.4	-0.3	-1.2	-5.4
Micro-share change	-0.7	-2.8	1.3	-1.7	0.4	0.6	0.6	-0.3	0.9	0.0	3.0	1.4
Switzerland												
Change in market share	-0.8	0.4	0.1	0.4	0.0	4.0	1.2	0.2	-3.2	-0.5	5.0	6.9
of which:												
Composition effects	0.9	0.1	-0.1	0.0	0.1	5.4	14.2	0.6	-3.2	2.5	2.1	22.7
Adaptation effects	-0.8	-0.1	0.0	0.0	-0.2	-2.0	-6.4	-0.4	-1.5	-1.8	-2.8	-16.0
Micro-share change	-0.9	0.4	0.2	0.4	0.1	0.6	-6.6	0.0	1.5	-1.2	5.7	0.2
Denmark												
Change in market share	-21.3	0.3	-0.1	0.3	0.1	0.7	3.5	0.6	0.2	1.0	1.7	-13.2
of which:												
Composition effects	-17.2	0.0	-0.3	-0.1	0.0	1.3	2.4	1.5	-1.6	0.8	0.6	-12.6
Adaptation effects	2.2	0.0	-0.1	0.0	-0.1	-0.5	0.1	-0.1	-1.3	-0.1	-2.5	-2.3
Micro-share change	-6.4	0.3	0.3	0.4	0.1	-0.1	1.0	-0.8	3.0	0.3	3.5	1.7
1973-1985												
Austria												
Change in market share	0.1	0.7	-4.3	0.1	0.7	4.4	3.9	1.8	-3.0	0.2	2.3	6.8
of which:												
Composition effects	-1.2	-0.4	-3.8	-3.2	0.2	1.1	1.3	-0.1	-4.4	0.2	0.2	-10.0
Adaptation effects	-1.0	-0.2	0.1	-0.9	0.0	0.4	-0.6	-0.1	-0.5	-0.2	-2.2	-5.4
Micro-share change	2.3	1.3	-0.6	4.2	0.5	2.9	3.2	2.0	1.9	0.2	4.3	22.1
Finland												
Change in market share	0.0	-1.8	-7.8	2.6	0.0	3.9	9.2	3.0	-0.4	-0.9	2.0	9.8
of which:												
Composition effects	-0.5	-1.9	-9.2	-1.2	0.0	0.3	-0.6	-3.0	-2.0	0.2	-0.3	-18.1
Adaptation effects	-0.2	-0.6	2.0	-1.6	0.0	0.2	1.2	-6.2	-0.2	-0.1	-0.4	-5.8
Micro-share change	0.7	0.7	-0.6	5.4	0.0	3.4	8.6	12.2	1.8	-1.0	2.7	33.9
Norway												
Change in market share	-6.0	-4.0	-1.6	-2.5	-2.1	1.7	-2.1	-6.4	-1.9	-0.3	-6.8	-32.0
of which:												
Composition effects	-2.8	-0.8	-1.3	-1.4	0.9	0.3	-0.3	-8.2	-1.3	0.1	-2.0	-16.9
Adaptation effects	0.6	0.3	0.7	-1.6	-0.5	0.4	0.7	-0.4	0.4	-0.1	0.3	0.8
Micro-share change	-3.8	-3.5	-1.0	0.5	-2.5	1.0	-2.5	2.2	-1.0	-0.3	-5.1	-15.9
Sweden												
Change in market share	-0.4	-5.5	-4.3	-5.3	0.0	1.4	-3.0	-1.2	-0.9	-0.7	-2.1	-22.0
of which:												
Composition effects	-0.6	-1.1	-4.8	-4.3	0.0	0.8	4.1	-1.0	-0.9	0.2	0.3	-7.3
Adaptation effects	-0.2	0.2	1.1	1.5	0.0	0.1	-2.5	1.5	-0.1	-0.2	-0.8	0.5
Micro-share change	0.4	-4.6	-0.6	-2.5	0.0	0.5	-4.5	-1.7	0.1	-0.7	-1.6	-15.2
Switzerland												
Change in market share	-0.5	0.3	-0.1	0.3	0.0	-1.5	-7.5	0.7	-2.4	-0.4	9.5	-1.4
of which:												
Composition effects	-0.2	0.0	-0.3	-0.2	0.2	4.3	7.0	-0.1	-2.9	0.2	1.1	9.1
Adaptation effects	-0.2	-0.1	-0.2	-0.6	-0.1	-1.2	-5.9	0.0	-0.3	-0.1	-3.3	-11.9
Micro-share change	-0.1	0.4	0.4	1.1	-0.1	-4.5	-8.6	0.8	0.8	-0.5	11.7	1.4
Denmark												
Change in market share	012.1	0.2	0.2	0.2	0.2	1.7	-1.2	-1.4	-1.0	-0.3	1.3	-12.3
of which:												
Composition effects	-14.3	0.0	-0.5	-0.5	0.0	1.2	0.8	-2.3	-1.8	0.4	0.4	-16.7
Adaptation effects	-3.3	-0.1	-0.5	-0.4	0.0	-0.2	-0.1	0.5	-0.3	-0.3	-1.7	-6.4
Micro-share change	5.6	0.3	1.2	1.1	0.2	0.7	-2.0	0.4	1.1	-0.4	2.6	10.9

Source: As for table 6.6.

The *composition effects* continued to be negative in traditional/resource intensive goods and became so in transport equipment. The *adaptation effects* were negative for most products in Austria, Finland, Denmark and Switzerland, and marginal in Norway and Sweden (except for a negative contribution of machinery in Sweden).

These findings, especially the changes in microshares, support the suggestion made above that, in 1973-1985, factors other than trade policies (e.g., supply conditions) significantly influenced the export performance of some of the countries under review: they contributed negatively in Norway and Sweden, and positively in Austria, Finland and Denmark.

6.3 ASSESSING THE EFFECTS OF INTEGRATION

In the previous section the purpose was to estimate the impact of export structures on export performance. It was found that the pattern of exports did have an important influence, but that other factors (trade policies and/or supply conditions) were equally or even more important. The CMS method, however, does not allow a distinction to be made between the effects of trade policies and of supply factors. In this section an attempt is made to identify the effects of past trade liberalization.

(i) The effects of past trade liberalization

A proper measurement of the effects of free trade would require that all factors affecting trade flows other than liberalization be "held constant". This requirement is impossible to fulfil; and thus any attempt to estimate these effects involves "strong" assumptions and the results must be interpreted with judicious reserve.

(a) Aspects of methodology

Following the work of Viner and Meade on customs unions, several trade analysts have tried to estimate the "static" effects of trade liberalization.[767] These effects are obtained by comparing the final (post-liberalization) situation with the one that would have prevailed had tariffs and quotas not been abolished. Most of these estimates are based on post-liberalization observations, in contrast to those that are made prior to the liberalization of trade on the basis of "independent" parameters.

To determine the effects of liberalization, the first step is to calculate the trade flows that would have occurred in the absence of trade liberalization. These hypothetical estimates are then compared with actual trade flows, the difference being interpreted as the impact of freer trade. This implies a *ceteris paribus* assumption which, in practice, is unlikely to hold.[768] Thus, the estimates obtained, which are assumed to represent the effects of eliminating tariffs and quotas, often contain the effects of other factors, including those of integration-induced growth.[769]

Several methods have been used to construct the hypothetical trade flows. This is not the place to survey different methodologies, which are extensively described in the literature, but it should be noted that they often refer to "import effects". These are obtained by comparing actual post-liberalization imports with those estimated on the basis of some pre-integration observations, e.g., for import/demand ratios.[770] In this case, the export effects have to be computed as the sum of import effects in the free trade partners. This approach, however, does not take into account the effects on exports to other markets.

To avoid this shortcoming, a somewhat different method was used here. The hypothetical export values, i.e., those that would have occurred in the absence of free trade, were computed *on the basis of constant pre-integration trade intensity coefficients*.[771] As mentioned in section 6.2 above, these coefficients are less sensitive to demand and supply factors than simple shares, the changes in their value reflecting to a large extent the effects of trade policies. Other factors affect the value of the trade intensity coefficients. Thus, the assumption that variations in their value reflect largely changes in trade policies involves also limitations of the type described above concerning the estimation of integration effects. Still, given their relative stability, these ratios appear to be more adequate to such a purpose than other trade variables.[772]

---

[767] See, *inter alia* J. Viner, *The Customs Union Issue*, Carnegie Endowment for International Peace, London, 1950; J.E. Meade, *Theory of Customs Union*, North Holland, Amsterdam, 1955; B. Balassa, "Trade Creation and Trade Diversion in the European Common Market", *The Economic Journal*, vol.LXXVII, No.305, March 1967; M.E. Kreinin, "Trade Creation and Diversion by the EEC and EFTA" *Economia Internazionale*, vol.XXII, No.2, May 1969 and *Trade Relations of the EEC – an Empirical Investigation*, Praeger Publishers Inc., New York, 1974; EFTA Secretariat, *The Effects of EFTA on the Economies of Member States*, Geneva, 1969 and *The Effects of EFTA on the EEC, 1959-1967*, Geneva 1972; W. Ch. Sawyer and R.L. Sprinkle, "EC Enlargement and US Exports – An Analysis of Trade Effects", *Journal of World Trade*, vol.22, No.1, 1988; United Nations Economic Commission for Europe, "The effects of west European integration on imports of manufactures from eastern and southern Europe", *The Economic Survey of Europe in 1988-1989*, New York, 1989.

[768] In order to "isolate" the integration effects from the effects of other factors, some analysts have "normalized" the developments in the integration area by those in a country that was not involved in the integration process (M.E. Kreinin, 1974, *op.cit.*). The difficulty of finding a country to serve as an adequate norm has led to results that are far from conclusive.

[769] It has been shown that the long-term growth effects of integration may counteract the diversion effects that are usually associated with the liberalization of trade in a given area. See M.E. Kreinin, 1974, *op.cit.* In particular with respect to the effects of the EC-Internal Market, it has been emphasized that the dynamic effects are likely to be more far reaching than the classic static effects of integration.

[770] See, *inter alia*, EFTA Secretariat (1969 and 1972) and the United Nations Secretariat (1989), *op.cit.*

[771] See Appendix to this paper, section (ii).

[772] A previous study by the ECE secretariat (see *Economic Bulletin for Europe*, vol.24, No.2, New York, 1973) has shown that these structural coefficients " ... remain fairly stable over time when trade policies remain unchanged, whilst they show significant trends when trade policies are themselves undergoing substantial changes. In particular, the impact of policies aimed at the creation of regional groupings in western Europe is reflected quite clearly in the trends of the corresponding structural coefficients".

The hypothetical exports were calculated for 1972 and 1985 on the basis of the trade intensity coefficients for each country's exports to each market in 1963 and 1972, respectively.

For 1972, the difference between actual exports and those computed on the basis of 1963 coefficients is assumed to capture the effects of the formation of the EC and EFTA; for 1985, the difference in relation to the values calculated from the 1972 coefficients is assumed to indicate the effects of the Free Trade Agreements between the six countries and the EC (in Denmark it shows the effects of EC membership).

(b) The estimated effects by markets

The estimated effects of past trade liberalization are presented in table 6.9 and chart 6.2. These results are to be interpreted against the "expected" effects of integration discussed above, keeping in mind the "strong" assumptions involved in their computation.

It was mentioned in section 6.2 that the strengthening of trade inside a free trade area may occur at the expense of trade with non-member countries. Furthermore, the formation of separate free trade areas may reduce the export opportunities of the members of a free trade area with respect to exports to the other trading group.

Thus, other things being equal, the formation of EFTA is likely to have led to an increase in the six countries' exports to the other EFTA members, probably at the expense of exports to other countries, including those in EC6. In addition, the six countries' exports to EC6 may have been affected further by the diversion effects that its formation probably had on its imports from other countries, including those in EFTA. After 1973, i.e,. in the wake of the FTAs between the non-members and the EC, the countries' exports to EC6 probably recovered, an increase that may have occurred at the cost of exports to other partners. Some of these developments are reflected in the estimates in table 6.9 and chart 6.2.

In 1972, *when the effects of the formation of the EC6 and EFTA had become apparent,* the six countries' exports to the initial EFTA members were clearly higher than could have been anticipated on the basis of the 1963 "trade intensity coefficients", while exports to EC6 were much less than expected. In Denmark and Finland there was also some diversion of exports to the countries that had joined the EC in 1973. It is worth noting that in all countries except Finland, the net effect of the creation of EFTA and the EC was either minor (Norway) or negative. This means that the trade creation effects of the formation of EFTA were insufficient to outweigh the trade diversion effects of the formation of the EC6 on the six countries' exports to the Community.

Exports to eastern Europe and the Soviet Union were generally lower than those computed on the basis of the 1963 coefficients. In Finland, Norway, and Switzerland there was also some diversion of exports to North America. On the other hand, there was an "unexpected" positive effect on exports to the "rest of the world" and to Japan. Except for Sweden and Austria, exports to southern Europe were also higher than those computed from the 1963 coefficients.[773]

In 1985, a year when the effects of the FTAs (and of Danish membership of the EC) were most likely to have been visible, exports to EC6 were much larger than those projected on the basis of the 1972 coefficients, a difference that arose partly from a decline in exports to the countries that became EC members in 1973 and, except for Norway and Sweden, to the remaining EFTA members. Nevertheless, in all countries except Finland the net EC9-EFTA effect was positive in the period 1972-1987. The effect was larger in Switzerland, Austria and Norway than in Denmark, the new EC member.

Exports to eastern Europe and the Soviet Union continued to be diverted, except for those from Austria and Finland. As mentioned above, exports from these two countries are likely to have been stimulated by the rise in oil prices: since they imported oil from eastern Europe and the Soviet Union, increased oil prices led to a significant growth in their exports to eastern markets.[774]

Some diversion also occurred in exports from Austria and Norway to North America and in exports from Finland, Norway, Sweden and Switzerland to southern Europe. Exports to the "rest of the world" and to Japan, on the other hand, continued to grow faster than expected (except for Switzerland).

In short, the liberalization of trade in western Europe over the past three decades appears to have had a considerable impact on the exports of the six countries reviewed here. After the formation of the EC and EFTA, the countries' exports to other EFTA members strengthened, sometimes the expense of trade with the other region. For most of the countries considered here, the net EC-EFTA effect was negative, suggesting that the negative impact of the creation of the EC on the EC's imports from EFTA more than offset the positive effects of the formation of EFTA. However, following the FTAs with the EC, there was a significant increase in exports to the Community, an increase which more than offset some weakening in exports to the original EFTA members: except in Finland, the net EC-EFTA effect was positive and, in some cases, was even larger than the trade benefit that Denmark obtained by joining the EC.

Section 6.2(ii) noted that the changes in microshares may have been due in part to supply factors and/or trade policies, but that the CMS method did not

---

[773] The group "southern Europe" consists here of Portugal, Spain and Greece. The first was a founding member of EFTA while the other two were not members of any free trade area. Thus, it is difficult to say what the "expected" results for this group should be.

[774] This shows that part of the export developments ascribed here to trade liberalization may well have been due to other factors.

TABLE 6.9

The estimated effects of trade liberalization on the six countries' exports, by market, 1963-1972 and 1972-1985

A: Million US dollars   B: As percentage of exports

	Austria		Finland		Norway		Sweden		Switzerland		Denmark	
	A	B	A	B	A	B	A	B	A	B	A	B
1963-1972												
EC6	-650	-16.8	-366	-12.4	-218	-6.8	-868	-10.0	-722	-10.5	-406	-9.6
EC3	204	5.3	-1	-0.0	125	3.9	433	5.0	162	2.4	-47	-1.1
Southern Europe	-8	-0.2	18	0.6	75	2.4	-14	-0.2	-17	0.2	16	0.4
EFTA	309	8.0	533	18.1	123	3.9	258	3.0	219	3.2	339	8.0
Eastern Europe and the Soviet Union	-179	-4.6	-238	-8.1	-66	-2.1	-63	-0.7	103	1.5	-79	-1.9
North America	44	1.1	-7	-0.2	-91	-2.9	148	1.7	-84	-1.2	68	1.6
Japan	12	0.3	5	0.2	14	0.5	30	0.3	16	0.2	-19	-0.5
Rest of the world	71	1.8	16	0.5	86	2.7	166	1.9	236	3.4	154	3.6
Total	-198	-5.1	-39	-1.3	49	1.5	90	1.0	-87	-1.3	27	0.6
Memorandum item:												
EC9 + EFTA	-137	-3.5	167	5.7	31	1.0	-177	-2.0	-341	-4.9	-113	-2.7
1972-1985												
EC6	2388	14.1	157	1.2	571	6.5	1460	5.0	2301	8.5	1487	9.5
EC3	-729	-4.3	-1057	-8.1	-668	-7.6	-2005	-6.9	-60	-0.2	-1225	-7.8
Southern Europe	97	0.6	-50	-0.4	-134	-1.5	-122	-0.4	-275	-1.0	54	0.3
EFTA	-741	-4.4	-221	-1.7	446	5.1	758	2.6	-542	-2.0	-253	-1.6
Eastern Europe and the Soviet Union	103	0.6	1484	11.4	-39	-0.5	-140	-0.5	-178	-0.7	-139	-0.9
North America	-71	-0.4	247	1.9	-99	-1.1	1437	5.0	219	0.8	294	1.9
Japan	44	0.3	132	1.0	159	1.8	146	0.5	20	0.1	357	2.3
Rest of the world	539	3.2	437	3.3	444	5.1	124	0.4	-233	-0.9	465	3.0
Total	1629	9.7	1128	8.6	680	7.8	1658	5.7	1253	4.6	1040	6.6
Memorandum item:												
EC9 + EFTA	918	5.4	-1121	-8.6	349	4.0	212	0.7	1700	6.3	9	0.1

Sources: As for table 6.1.

allow a separation of the two. In this section an attempt has been made to identify the effects of trade liberalization. Consequently, a comparison between the two sets of estimates was used to throw some light on the possible impact of supply factors.

In most cases the micro-share changes were in the same direction as the estimated effects of integration, suggesting that the changes in those shares were, to a large extent, the result of trade policies. But there are cases where the differences between the two changes are appreciable.

Up to the early 1970s, the integration effects were minor, but Austria and Norway made sizeable gains in micro-shares, while in Finland losses were much larger than the integration effects. This implies that other (supply) factors were important for export performance, positively so in the two first countries and negatively in Finland.

From the early 1970s to the mid-1980s, the most striking cases are those of Norway and Sweden. These two countries had considerable losses in micro-shares, while the effects of trade liberalization were significantly positive. This suggests that supply constraints (including a deterioration in relative competitiveness) more than offset the positive impact of trade liberalization on exports. In Austria and Finland, in contrast, favourable supply conditions appear to have amplified the positive effects of integration.

(ii) Possible effects of 1992

While trade in industrial goods inside western Europe is now virtually free of tariffs and quotas, a number of barriers continue to prevent complete integration of the west European market. The implementation of the European Community's White Paper of 1985 intends to correct this situation by removing all physical, technical and fiscal barriers to the free movement of goods, services, labour and capital among the member States.

With respect to *physical barriers* the purpose is to eliminate all border controls; as for the *technical barriers,* the goal is to abolish not only the traditional technical regulations, but also restrictions on competition for public purchases, distorting state subsidies and restraints on labour and capital movements; the elimination of *fiscal barriers* mainly focuses on the harmonization of indirect tax rates.

This programme requires a higher degree of policy co-ordination than some EFTA member States want at present (although Austria has applied for EC membership). Nevertheless, the EFTA members are trying to develop with the EC a number of arrangements designed to create an enlarged European market, the "European Economic Space" of the 12 plus the 6.

CHART 6.2
The estimated effects of trade liberalization on exports of the six countries, by market
(Per cent of end-year exports)
A: 1963-1972

EC3 = Denmark, Ireland and UK   EFT = EFTA   ROW = Rest of the World
SE = Southern Europe   JAP = Japan   EE7 = Eastern Europe and USSR
NA = North America   TOT = TOTAL   E9F = EC9 and EFTA

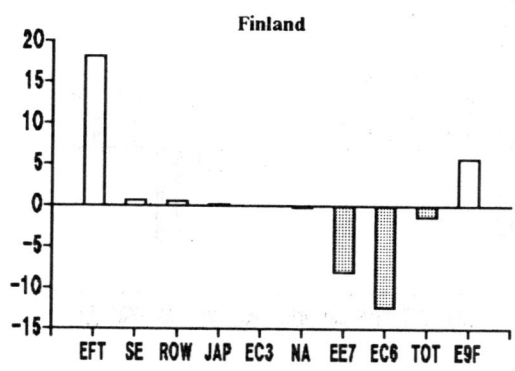
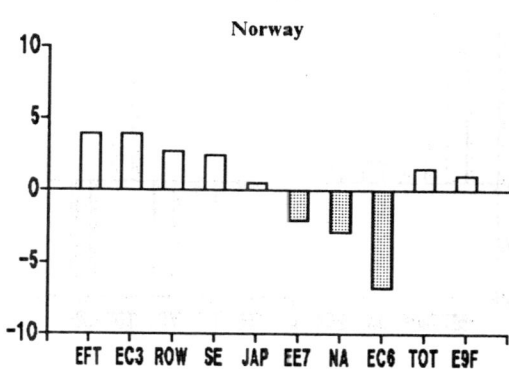
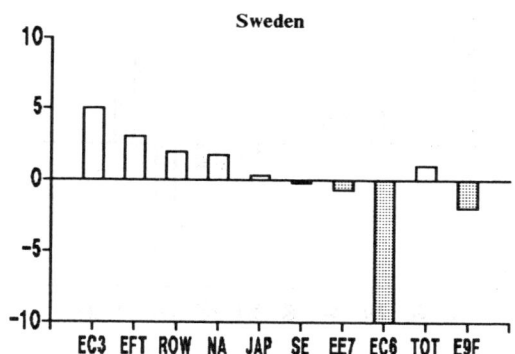
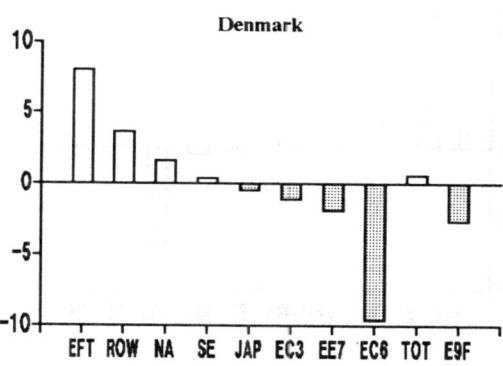
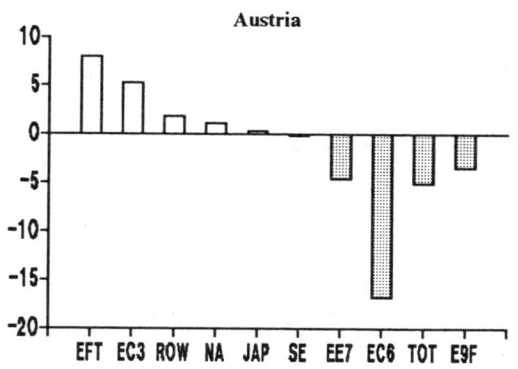
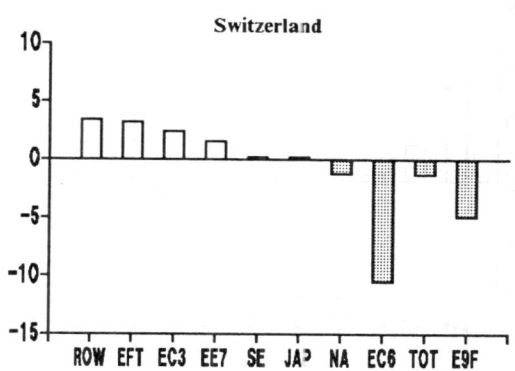

CHART 6.2 (continued)
The estimated effects of trade liberalization on exports of the six countries, by market
(Per cent of end-year exports)
B: 1972-1985

EC3 = Denmark, Ireland and UK   EFT = EFTA   ROW = Rest of the World
SE = Southern Europe   JAP = Japan   EE7 = Eastern Europe and USSR
NA = North America   TOT = TOTAL   E9F = EC9 and EFTA

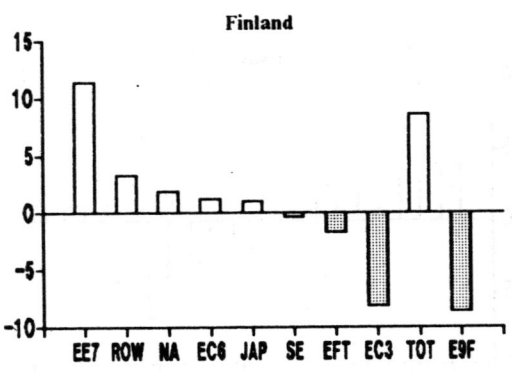
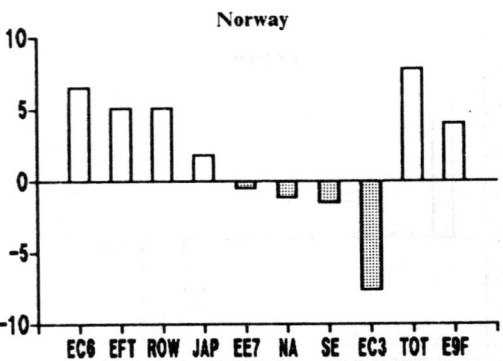
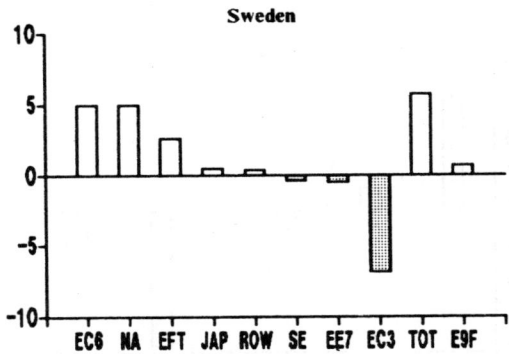
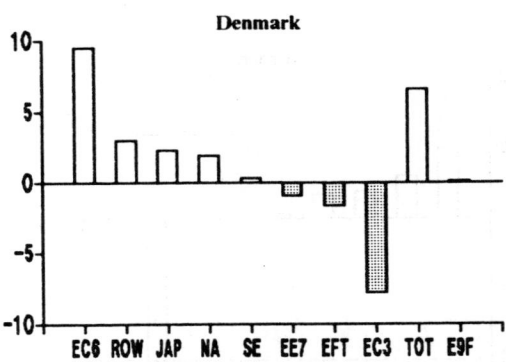
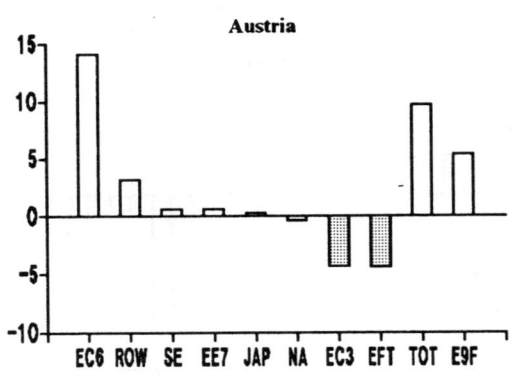
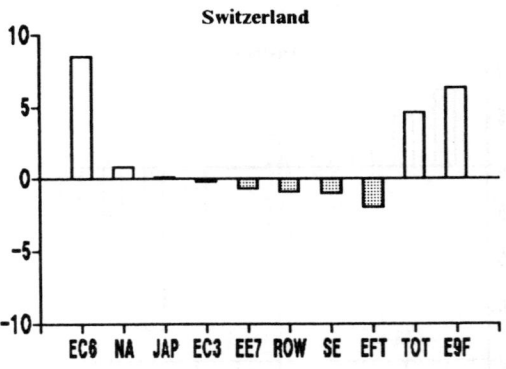

Source: As for table 6.9.

As far as *trade in goods* is concerned, the possible effects of the EC's programme for 1992 mainly concern the impact of removing *technical barriers*. The elimination of technical barriers to trade in goods entails, for the countries involved, two main consequences: a reduction in costs and an increase in competition.

With respect to *cost reduction,* several estimates have been made of the "size" of the costs associated with the technical obstacles to be abolished.[775] They point to total direct costs of identifiable barriers at about 3.5 per cent of industrial value added in the Community, or 8 per cent of the value of intra-Community trade. This includes the costs of border controls, which the EFTA members may not be willing to eliminate. If these were excluded, the costs of technical impediments would be about 2.7 per cent of the Community's value added, or 6.2 per cent of intra-EC trade.

The effects of eliminating these costs are comparable to those of a tariff cut. In fact, if they amount to 6-8 per cent of trade values, then they are close to the average MFN tariff that the EFTA countries faced in the EC market before the FTAs of 1973.[776] As was shown above, the elimination of these tariffs had a considerable positive impact on the six countries' exports, even if increased exports to the EC involved some diversion from the original EFTA members. If the technical barriers are removed by both the EC and EFTA, the positive effects will apply to both markets, in which case they may well be larger than those resulting from the FTAs. In addition, other costs will be reduced, insofar as increased competition will eliminate high-cost producers and allow a better exploitation of economies of scale.

However, the incidence of the obstacles to be removed varies from sector to sector and the impact of removing the technical barriers will ultimately depend on the importance of the sectors concerned. The Commission of the European Communities has estimated the following sectors as being, at present, particularly affected by such barriers: food processing, electrical and mechanical engineering (power generating, telecommunications, office and data processing equipment), construction materials (non-metallic minerals, metal products), chemicals (particularly pharmaceutical products), motor vehicles, precision and medical equipment.[777]

The products where public procurement is most important are energy products (public purchases amounting to 16 per cent of oil sales), transport equipment other than motor vehicles (8 per cent), electrical goods (4 per cent) and chemicals (3 per cent).

Some of the goods subject to technical barriers are defined in terms of very large product groups (e.g., mechanical and electrical engineering, transport equipment other than motor vehicles) and it would be misleading to assess the effects of the elimination of technical barriers on such a broad basis.

Table 6.10 shows the share of these goods in the countries' exports to the EC12 and to EFTA in 1987. In most cases, they represent 20 per cent or more of the countries' exports. Extreme cases are Denmark, where the proportion is nearly 45 per cent (mainly reflecting the large share of food products) and Finland, where it is less than 8 per cent (Finnish exports are dominated by pulp, paper and wood products, which are not much affected by technical barriers to trade).

Technical barriers often lead to a considerable degree of non-competitive market segmentation. Thus, the economic gains of eliminating them are primarily those associated with *increased competition*. This means that any direct trade effects of completing the EC-Internal Market (or of enlarging the European market) are likely to be less significant as compared with the dynamic long-term benefits of open competition. These gains have been grouped into four categories:[778]

1. Reduction in costs due to a better exploitation of several kinds of economies of scale;

2. Improved efficiency in enterprises, rationalization of industrial structures and the setting of prices closer to costs;

3. Adjustments between industries resulting from the full play of comparative advantages; and

4. A flow of innovations, new processes and new products, stimulated by the dynamics of the internal market.

These effects are difficult to quantify. Nevertheless, combining estimates based on different techniques of micro- and macro-economic analysis, the Commission of the EC itself has concluded that "the potential gains ... could be about large enough to make the difference between a disappointing and a very satisfactory economic performance for the Community economy as a whole".

The FTAs between the EC and the EFTA allowed the six countries under review, which have relatively small domestic markets, to benefit from an enlarged market and the greater opportunity to exploit economies of scale. The completion of a European internal market should facilitate further the standardization of technologies and products and, effectively, will lead to a further extension of the size of the market. This, in turn, may lead to a further "disintegration" of pro-

---

[775] See the Commission of the European Communities, "The Economics of 1992", *European Economy*, No. 35, March 1988.

[776] See United Nations Economic Commission for Europe, *Economic Survey of Europe in 1988-1989*, New York, 1989, section 2.5.

[777] Commission of the European Communities, *loc.cit.*

[778] The Commission of the European Communities, *op.cit.*

TABLE 6.10

The share of selected products in exports to the EC12 and to EFTA, 1987

(Percentages)

	Austria		Finland		Norway		Sweden		Switzerland		Denmark	
	EC12	EFTA	EC12	EFTA	EC12	EFTA	EC12	EFTA	EC12	EFTA	EC12	EFTA
Fish	0.0	0.0	0.0	0.1	13.2	7.4	0.3	0.4	0.0	0.0	10.3	3.8
Other food	2.2	1.6	0.7	0.8	0.7	2.8	0.5	0.9	1.8	0.5	22.6	3.6
Non-metallic minerals	2.6	3.3	1.1	1.2	0.7	1.5	1.0	2.3	5.3	1.2	0.9	1.8
Pharmaceutical products	1.3	1.1	0.2	0.4	0.6	1.1	1.6	1.6	5.7	5.1	2.6	3.1
Office machinery	0.8	0.5	1.3	1.9	2.5	2.3	3.7	2.2	1.1	0.8	1.1	1.3
Power generating machinery	6.0	0.7	0.6	0.7	0.6	0.5	2.2	2.1	0.9	0.8	0.7	0.5
Scientific equipment	2.1	2.8	1.4	1.2	1.5	1.8	2.4	2.2	10.0	9.1	3.6	3.0
Telecommunication equipment	0.8	0.5	0.6	2.5	0.9	2.0	2.7	2.7	0.7	1.3	1.6	2.8
Motor vehicles	4.1	4.6	1.6	11.5	1.7	6.3	13.1	10.9	1.2	0.9	1.5	2.0
Total	19.9	15.1	7.5	20.3	22.4	25.7	27.5	25.3	26.7	19.7	44.9	21.9

Sources: As for table 6.1.

duction processes across national borders, each country specializing in those activities for which it has a comparative advantage.

(iii) Conclusions

The effects of past trade liberalization may throw some light on possible consequences of further west European integration. This study has looked into the impact of free trade on the exports of west European countries that are not members of the EC, namely Austria, Finland, Norway, Sweden and Switzerland. Denmark, which became an EC-member in 1973, was included for purposes of comparison.

Other things being equal, the formation of EFTA appears to have increased the six countries' exports to the members of this group, probably at the cost of exports to other countries, including those in EC6. In addition, the six countries' exports to the EC6 may have also been affected by the diversion of EC imports away from non-EC members. After 1973, in the wake of the FTAs between the six countries and the EC, the countries' exports to the Community recovered at the cost of exports to other partners, including those in EFTA.

The main purpose of this study was to assess the extent to which the regional and product patterns of exports from the six countries followed the trends expected on the basis of standard customs union theory. An attempt was also made to quantify the impact of export structure on trade performance and to estimate the effects of past trade liberalization.

It was found that, to a considerable extent, changes in the regional patterns of the six countries' exports were in line with the "expected" effects of integration. Up to the early 1970s, reflecting the formation of two separate trade entities, there was a strengthening of exports to EFTA countries, mainly at the expense of exports to EC6. From 1972 to 1987 there was a recovery in exports to EC6, largely at the cost of exports to the countries that had joined the EC in 1973, particularly the United Kingdom. In most cases, exports to eastern markets and to North America weakened, while exports to Japan and to the "rest of the world" were not significantly affected.

The liberalization of trade appears to have led to a more rational division of labour across borders. On the one hand, some countries specialized further in goods in which they had already a "revealed" comparative advantage. This is apparent first in exports to EFTA and, from 1972, in exports to the EC. On the other hand, and particularly in the EC market, the six countries increasingly specialized in products such as machinery and chemicals where they had no comparative advantage in the early 1960s.

The latter development suggests that the six countries benefited from the opportunity offered by an enlarged west European market to better exploit different types of economies of scale. Thus, they may have benefited from increased opportunities to exploit standardized technologies and/or products (e.g. chemicals, metal products); and they may have also increased their exports of intermediate goods, a reflection of liberalization leading to higher levels of intra-industry trade in complementary inputs.

The product and market patterns of exports had a significant negative impact on export performance, but trade policies and/or supply factors were sometimes equally or more important. Trade policies appear to have had a significant impact: until the early 1970s, all countries lost micro-shares in EC6 while they gained in EFTA; in 1973-1985 all countries except Norway gained in EC6, while most of them lost in EFTA and its former members. But in some cases, and particularly from 1973, supply factors seem to have counteracted the effects of trade liberalization: this was clearly so for Norway and Sweden.

Past trade liberalization led to *sizeable integration effects*. By 1972, when the effects of the formation of the EC and EFTA would have begun to materialize, the six countries' exports to EFTA were well above the levels that could have been expected on the basis of 1963 trade structures. This increase, however, mirrored a decline in exports to other countries, particularly to EC6 members. Exports to the EC6 were probably also affected by the trade diversion effects of the creation of the EC6 on the latter's imports from EFTA. For most of the six countries, the net EC-EFTA effect was negative.

In 1985, when the Free Trade Agreements with the EC had probably began to take effect, exports to the EC6 greatly exceeded the values projected on the basis of the 1972 trade structures. To some extent, this occurred at the cost of exports to the countries that had joined the EC in 1973 and, except for Norway and Sweden, to the remaining EFTA countries. Nevertheless, in all countries except Finland, the net EC-EFTA effect in the latter period was positive and, in most cases, relatively large.

The liberalization of trade in western Europe seems to have caused some diversion of trade from the eastern markets (although not for Switzerland before 1972 and for Austria and Finland since 1973) and, in some cases, of trade with North America. On the other hand, exports to Japan and to "the rest of the world" tended to be above the levels estimated on the basis of constant trade structures.

These estimates support the hypothesis that, in some cases, *supply factors may have reversed the effects of integration:* up to the early 1970s, these effects were minor or negative, while some countries made sizeable gains in micro-shares (Austria and Norway); from then to the mid-1980s the effects of integration were positive, although some countries had large micro-share losses (Norway and Sweden).

The analysis of the impact of trade liberalization in the past was used as a basis for assessing the possible effects of completing the EC-Internal Market. As far as trade in goods is concerned, this implies the *elimination of technical barriers to trade,* with two main consequences: a reduction in costs and an increase in competition. The effects of removing these barriers may be comparable to the benefits of the FTAs between the EC and the six countries. Moreover, *if the barriers are removed by both the EC and EFTA, the positive effects could be even larger than those resulting from the FTAs.*

The elimination of technical barriers should lead to *increased international competition.* The dynamic long-term benefits of open competition have been estimated to be much more far-reaching than the direct effects of cost reduction. In particular, the creation of an internal European market will further the standardization of technologies and products and lead to increased "disintegration" of production processes across borders, each country specializing in those areas where its has greater comparative advantage. *This process will benefit especially the small non-EC member countries, where the size of the domestic market tends to hamper the full exploitation of economies of scale and, more generally, of national comparative advantages.*

APPENDIX

(i) A note on the CMS analysis

This appendix outlines the CMS method developed by Fagerberg and Sollie (1987) and shows how it was applied for the purpose of this study.

Let commodities and markets be denoted by i and j respectively. A country's exports of commodity i to market j is denoted by X_{ij}; the total imports of market j of commodity i by M_{ij}, and the total imports of market j of all commodities by M_j (M is world imports). Let

$$a_{ij} = X_{ij}/M_{ij}, \quad b_{ij} = M_{ij}/M_j \quad \text{and} \quad C_j = M_j/M$$

The market share of a country's exports in market j and the world market, S_j and S respectively, may then be written:

$$S_j = \sum_i a_{ij} b_{ij}$$

$$S = \sum_j c_j \sum_i a_{ij} b_{ij}$$

Let superscripts 1,0 denote two points in time and define the change in the market share for exports, dS:

$$dS = S^1 - S^0$$

As shown in Fagerberg and Sollie (1987), this change may be decomposed into five effects:

— Market share
— Commodity composition
— Commodity adaptation
— Market composition
— Market adaptation

An interpretation of the various effects is given in section 6.2 of this study.

A similar type of analysis may also be carried out for each market separately. In this case the last two effects disappear. However, in many cases it is more convenient and interesting to calculate the contribution of each single market to each of the five effects listed above than to carry out a separate CMS analysis for each market. To see how this may be done, consider the matrix in Appendix table 6.1 which shows markets in the columns and effects in the rows. Each effect can be summed over all markets (the total is given in the column on the far right). For each market the bottom row shows the sums over all effects (this gives the total contribution of each market to the total change in market share).

The first three rows of each column present a CMS analysis for that specific market multiplied by the weight of that market in world imports. If divided by this weight (C_j) the results would be identical to a separate CMS analysis of that specific market. The next two rows give the contribution to the total change in market share from a change in the weight of the market. Each column sum gives the contribution of that specific market to the change in "world market share".

In the case of a region the analysis may be expanded further by taking into account the fact that the market composition of a country's exports to a region may result in an export performance above or below what the weight of that region in world trade would indicate. Define

$$c_j = M_j/M = (M_j/M_r)/(M_r/M) = r_j c_r,$$

where M_r is total imports of all markets in the region from the world, r_j the share of market j in the total imports of all countries in the region and c_r the share of the region in world imports. Then

$$dc_j = c_r dr_j + (r_j dc_r + dr_j dc_r).$$

By substituting this into (4) and (5) the following is obtained:

(4) Market composition effect:

$$\sum_{j=1}^{m} dc_j s_j = \underbrace{\sum_{j=1}^{m} (c_r dr_j s_j)}_{(4a)} + \underbrace{\sum_{j=1}^{m} [(r_j + dr_j) dc_r s_j]}_{(4b)}$$

(5) Market adaptation effect:

$$\sum_{j=1}^{m} dc_j ds_j = \underbrace{\sum_{j=1}^{m} (c_r dr_j ds_j)}_{(5a)} + \underbrace{\sum_{j=1}^{m} [(r_j + dr_j) dc_r ds_j]}_{(5b)}$$

In both cases effect *(a)* is the "within-region" effect while effect *(b)* is the "regional effect". To illustrate: Norwegian exports to EC countries may be hampered because Norwegian exports are concentrated on the slowest growing members of the community *(4a)* and/or because the imports of the EC countries as a whole grow slower than world trade *(4b)*.

(ii) The method used to estimate the effects of integration

To estimate the "static" effects of past trade liberalization, the first step was to compute the hypothetical level of exports that would have occurred in the absence of free trade; these estimates were then compared with

APPENDIX TABLE 6.1

A market decomposition of the CMS analysis

Effect	Markets	Individual markets $j = 1..l..m..n$	Individual regions $\Sigma(1..m)$	The world $\Sigma(1..n)$
1.	Market share effect	$c_j \sum_i b_{ij} da_{ij}$	$\sum_{j=1}^{m} c_j \sum_i b_{ij} da_{ij}$	$\sum_{j=1}^{n} c_j \sum_i b_{ij} da_{ij}$
2.	Commodity composition effect	$c_j \sum_i a_{ij} db_{ij}$	$\sum_{j=1}^{m} c_j \sum_i a_{ij} db_{ij}$	$\sum_{j=1}^{n} c_j \sum_i a_{ij} db_{ij}$
3.	Commodity adaptation effect	$c_j \sum_i da_{ij} db_{ij}$	$\sum_{j=1}^{m} c_j \sum_i da_{ij} db_{ij}$	$\sum_{j=1}^{n} c_j \sum_i da_{ij} db_{ij}$
4.	Market composition effect	$dc_j \sum_i a_{ij} b_{ij}$	$\sum_{j=1}^{m} dc_j \sum_i a_{ij} b_{ij}$	$\sum_{j=1}^{n} dc_j \sum_i a_{ij} b_{ij}$
5.	Market adaptation effect	$dc_j \sum_i d(a_{ij} b_{ij})$	$\sum_{j=1}^{m} dc_j \sum_i d(a_{ij} b_{ij})$	$\sum_{j=1}^{n} dc_j \sum_i d(a_{ij} b_{ij})$
6.	Total effect (1-5)	$c_j dS_j + dc_j(S_j + dS_j)$	$\sum_{j=1}^{m}[c_j dS_j + dc_j(S_j + dS_j)]$	dS

the actual flows, the difference between the two values being interpreted as the effect of trade liberalization.

The *hypothetical exports* for 1972 and 1985 were computed on the basis of the *actual* "trade intensity coefficients" (TICs) in 1963 and 1972 respectively. The difference between actual and hypothetical exports in 1972 is assumed to capture the effects of the formation of the EC and EFTA; the difference between the two magnitudes in 1987 is assumed to reflect the effects of the 1973 free trade agreements between the selected countries and the European Community.

The intensity coefficient (T_{ij}) for exports from country i to market j is defined as the share of market j in country i's exports, relative to the share of the same market in world exports. Thus:

$$T_{ij} = (X_{ij}/X_{i.}) / (X_{.j}/X_{..}) \qquad (1)$$

where

X_{ij} = exports of i to j
$X_{i.}$ = i's total exports
$X_{.j}$ = world exports to j
$X_{..}$ = total world exports

It follows that

$$X_{ij} = T_{ij} Z_{ij}, \text{ where } Z_{ij} = (X_{.j}/X_{..})X_{i.} \qquad (2)$$

and that *changes* in X_{ij} (shown as ΔX_{ij} below) may be computed as:

$$\Delta X_{ij} = T_{ij} \Delta Z_{ij} + \Delta T_{ij} Z_{ij} + \Delta T_{ij} \Delta Z_{ij} \qquad (3)$$

Assuming a constant T_{ij}, the hypothetical change in exports from i to j, $\Delta^* X_{ij}$, are given by

$$\begin{aligned}\Delta^* X_{ij} &= T_{ij} \Delta Z_{ij} \\ &= T_{ij}[(X_{.j}/X_{..}) \Delta X_{i.} + \Delta(X_{.j}/X_{..}) X_{i.} \\ &\quad + \Delta(X_{.j}/X_{..}) \Delta X_{i.}]\end{aligned} \qquad (4)$$

The first term gives the change in i's exports to j arising from the increase in i's total exports; the second stands for the rise in i's exports to j resulting from the increase in market j's share in total world exports; and the last component is the interaction of the first two terms.

The effects of integration (E) are assumed to be the difference between the actual rise in exports from i to j and that estimated on the basis of a constant T_{ij}:

$$E = \Delta X_{ij} - \Delta^* X_{ij} \qquad (5)$$

For a commodity k the approach is the same, with the trade flows and "intensity coefficients" referring to i's exports to j of product k.

The "trade intensity coefficients" are *relative trade shares*. They are less sensitive to demand and supply factors than the simple trade shares that are commonly used in the analysis of trade structures. Changes in the coefficients are assumed to be due to changes in "economic distance", especially those arising from changes in trade policies.

Chapter 7

EUROPE'S TRADE IN ENGINEERING GOODS: SPECIALIZATION AND TECHNOLOGY

This is a study of changes in the structure of trade in engineering goods with emphasis on the role of human skills and technology in determining patterns of national comparative advantage. The main focus is on the market economies of western Europe, North America, Japan and the newly industrialized economies of Asia. Eastern Europe and the Soviet Union are also included, although the analysis of their specialization patterns is necessarily confined to their trade with the west.

7.1 INTRODUCTION

(i) General background

The elimination by 1992 of all existing non-tariff barriers to create a unified "internal market" within the European Community is generally expected to have favourable effects on aggregate GNP and employment growth for the twelve member countries.[779] These macro-economic consequences derive essentially from the micro-economic effects of barrier elimination, i.e., lower production costs, increased competition and greater efficiency in production. Examples of existing barriers to transactions among the EC members are the costs of complying with customs formalities, different national technical standards and norms, national quotas, subsidies and public sector procurement policies. Basically, all these various national rules and procedures involve a segmentation of markets which adds to costs, reduces competition from firms outside the Community and introduces an excessive amount of X-inefficiency into the production process. In contrast, a larger, more homogeneous market will allow a better exploitation of economies of scale; unit costs will decline and price competitiveness will increase. The integration of markets also provides firms with a larger sales basis for amortizing the very high equipment and development costs for products at the frontiers of technology.

In principle the elimination of the existing barriers allows for comparative advantage, based on relative cost and price differences, to play a larger role in shaping the international division of labour between the various countries in the Community. This affects not only sales of final goods but also intermediate products. Relocation of production to areas within the Community providing relative cost advantages (such as low wage costs) will therefore continue to play a major role.[780] In general, the consequences of the larger internal market tend not only to intensify competition between the firms in the various member countries of the Community but also to improve the competitive position of these firms *vis-à-vis* producers in non-member countries: imports of goods from the latter may be replaced by supplies from firms located within the Community,[781] and the ensuing efficiency gains should also strengthen the position of Community firms in other world markets.

It is appropriate to recall in this connection that the last two decades or so have seen important changes in the structure of world trade in manufactures, with Japan and the Asian newly industrialized economies (the NIEs) capturing substantial parts of the world market largely at the expense of producers in western Europe and the United States. These changes in market shares have sharpened the focus of economic policy on the the ability of European and US producers to meet these challenges both in home and overseas markets. In the United States, the issue of competitiveness has gained heightened importance against the back-

---

[779] For a comprehensive review, see "The economics of 1992", *European Economy*, No.35, Commission of the European Communities, March 1988. For a shorter review see Michel Catinat, "Les conditions de réussite du grand marché intérieur", *Économie et Statistique*, No.217-218, Janvier-février 1989, pp.97-115.

[780] Horst Siebert, "Perspektiven zur Vollendung des europäischen Binnenmarktes", *Kyklos*, Vol.42, 1989, Fasc.2, p.191.

[781] See Paul Krugman, *EFTA and 1992*, Occasional Paper No.23, Geneva, June 1988, pp.11-13.

ground of a persistent and large trade deficit, which is widely seen as a symptom of the declining competitive strength of the US manufacturing sector. An issue which has been attracting a lot of attention in this context is the ability of US firms to compete in the area of so-called high technology-intensive goods.

Over the last decade or so technology considerations have been given increasing importance in discussions of international trade and competitiveness. This has to do *inter alia* with the important role of technical change and innovation in determining patterns of comparative advantage between countries and the rapid diffusion over the last decade or so of micro-electronics, computers and information technology into virtually all sectors of economic activity. Broadly speaking, these new technologies are regarded as having strategic importance in shaping the future structure of industrial activity.

The process of west European economic integration will necessarily have effects on the economies of eastern Europe, which are themselves in the process of carrying out major economic reforms. One leitmotif of these reforms is the need to become much more involved in the international division of labour. The opening up of the eastern economies will entail domestic firms having to face external competition from western producers in what, hitherto, have been predominantly captive markets inside the CMEA area. However, the development of closer economic ties with the market economies also provides eastern companies with considerable opportunities to exploit their existing and developing comparative advantages on a broader, even global scale.

Against this background it is useful to inquire more deeply into the nature of the factors which determine the international exchange of industrial goods. Moreover, the consequences of economic integration may be gauged more reliably when both the nature and determinants of existing trade between countries are better understood. In this connection it is appropriate to recall that the traditional textbook approach to international trade is not very helpful in disentangling the complex issues involved because it mainly applies to North-South flows rather than North-North trade. This is so because traditional trade theory stresses the role of different factor endowments as the major determinant of international trade flows - but by far the largest part of international trade in manufactured goods is between the industrialized countries, which are characterized by relatively similar endowments with regard to human skills and physical capital.

The present study focuses on international trade in engineering goods.[782] Engineering industries occupy a major place in the manufacturing sectors of the industrialized market economies, accounting on average for some 45 per cent of total output. The industry produces a vast array of heterogeneous goods ranging from relatively simple metal products, such as nails and screws, to complex machinery, motor vehicles and highly sophisticated goods such as aircraft, microcircuits, robots and computers. In fact, all investment goods, which are the carriers of technical progress, originate in the engineering industries, as do consumer goods such as washing machines, refrigerators, colour television sets and watches. Together with the chemical sector the engineering industries are the major source of high technology-intensive goods.[783]

In addition, the engineering sector includes a large number of products which are likely to be particularly affected by completion of the European Community's Internal Market; this is because of the relatively great importance of economies of scale for production and R&D[784] (e.g., motor vehicles, aircraft, computers) and the existence of pervasive technical barriers. According to business surveys, trade in motor vehicles, electrical and non-electrical machinery, telecommunications apparatus, public and commercial transport equipment, suffers particularly from technical barriers, most often from differing safety regulations or, as in the case of telecommuncations, from discrimination in public sector procurement and differences in national standards which limit product compatibility.[785]

All these various factors suggest that it is worthwhile and interesting to analyse the changing pattern of international trade in engineering goods, to compare the different patterns of national comparative advantage in the various product groups and to assess the role of human skills and technology in determining trade and specialization patterns.

The main focus of the study is on the different patterns of performance and specialization among the market economies of the ECE region, Japan and the four Asian NIEs.[786] To extend the analysis of specialization patterns to the individual east European countries would be particularly interesting but, unfortunately, data are only available in the required detail for a relatively small subset of the foreign trade

---

[782] This study is one of a series by the ECE secretariat on intra-European trade in manufactures in general and engineering goods in particular. See "Aspects of Intra-west European trade in manufactures, 1962-1985", United Nations Economic Commission for Europe, *Economic Survey of Europe in 1987-1988*, New York, 1899, pp.78-98; "The effects of west European integration on imports of manufactures from eastern and southern Europe", United Nations Economic Commission for Europe, *Economic Survey of Europe in 1988-1989*, New York, 1989, pp.64-86; "Eastern imports of machinery and equipment 1960-1985", Economic Commission for Europe, *Economic Bulletin for Europe*, vol.38, No.4, (1986) Pergamon Press for the United Nations, pp.605-663; "World imports of engineering goods, 1961-1985", Economic Commission for Europe, *Economic Bulletin for Europe*, vol.39, No.4 (1987), Pergamon Press for the United Nations, pp.769-795; "East-west trade in investment goods, 1970-1987", *Economic Bulletin for Europe* vol.41, New York, 1989.

[783] For the precise definition of engineering goods employed in this study see the Statistical appendices to this chapter, which provide also the country coverage of regional aggregates, statistical sources, etc.

[784] See Cliff Pratten, *A Survey of Economies of Scale*, Economic Papers No.67, Commission of the European Communities, October 1988.

[785] See "The Economics of 1992", *loc. cit.*, p.51 and P. Buigues, F. Ilzkovitz, *Les enjeux sectoriels du marché interieur*, Document II/335/88-FR, Commission des Communautés Européennes.

[786] Hong Kong, Republic of Korea, Singapore and Taiwan, Province of China.

conducted by these countries. It is well known that the bulk of their trade takes place inside the CMEA area and statistical data on these transactions are hard to obtain. Moreover, the factors which determine these intra-group flows differ significantly from those governing their trade with market economies and from the factors that determine trade among market economies themselves. It is therefore clear that an analysis of the specialization patterns prevailing in the eastern countries would have to take all these special factors into account — a task which is beyond the scope of the present study. However, in order to set the eastern countries into a broad perspective, all the indicators derived for the individual market economies have also been calculated for the aggregate of the six east European countries and for the Soviet Union, although the underlying data refer only to their trade with the developed market economies and a group of 20 developing countries.

(ii) Structure of the study

The study is divided into three parts. Section 7.2 looks at the aggregate of world trade in engineering goods and provides an overview of its regional structure in the period 1970-1987. The purpose is to show how the regional map of trade in engineering goods has evolved over time and to identify the major participants. There is also a brief examination of regional trade links. Section 7.3 is concerned with measuring the detailed inter-industry specialization patterns of individual countries in engineering goods trade. The objective is to identify those commodity groups in which countries have a comparative advantage, to examine how this pattern has been changing over time and to see how countries differ with regard to their specializations. There is also an attempt to identify the role of some "systematic" factors, such as world market size in differential specialization patterns and to examine whether changes in individual country specialization are characterized by an underlying general trend. Section 7.4 then moves on to the examination of trade in terms of its technology-intensity. Industrialized countries have similar relative factor endowments in terms of human and physical capital, and differential trade performances may therefore depend much more on factors like economies of scale, technology and innovativeness. It is the technology factor and in general the overall innovativeness of firms which has been at the centre of recent economic policy debates. The study looks at the relative importance of four groups of technology-intensity (high, advanced, medium and low) in trade, and examines the relative specialization of countries in each of these areas. Section 7.5 summarizes the findings and presents some conclusions.

7.2 STRUCTURAL FEATURES OF ENGINEERING GOODS TRADE

This section provides a broad overview of changes in the regional pattern of trade in engineering goods in the period 1970-1987. It looks at the relative importance of engineering goods in total trade in manufactures, examines changes in the shares of individual countries in world exports and imports, and concludes with an analysis of the trade links between the main regions.

(i) Importance of engineering goods in total trade of manufactures

Over the last two decades the value of world trade in engineering goods has been growing at a rate similar to that for total manufactures. For 1970-1980 the two growth rates were identical, but since 1980 engineering goods exports have tended to rise somewhat faster than other manufactures (table 7.2.1). Overall, there has been a sharp slow-down in the growth of trade in value terms in the 1980s, although in volume terms the deceleration is much less pronounced.[787]

Given these similar growth rates, the share of engineering goods in world trade of manufactures has remained very stable over time. Between 1970 and 1980 they accounted for some 54 per cent of all trade flows, a share which has since risen slightly. In 1987 slightly more than 56 per cent of all manufactured exports were engineering goods (table 7.2.2).

The relative importance of engineering goods in exports varies considerably between the various regions and there have been some conspicuous changes over time.

In 1987 the greatest relative export specialization on engineering goods was in Japan, where they accounted for about 80 per cent of all exports of manufactures. Indeed, there has been a remarkable shift in Japan's export pattern towards engineering goods over the last two decades: in 1970 the share of engineering goods was 54 per cent, somewhat less than the average for the developed market economies. There is a similar degree of reliance on engineering goods in North America, where their share in total exports of manufactures varied between 68 and 70 per cent between 1970 and 1987. In contrast to Japan and North America the importance of engineering goods in western Europe is much less with a relatively stable average share of about 52 per cent. The share is still lower for south European countries (about 37 per cent on average) which, in 1987, was about the same as the average for the developing countries. However, the data display clearly the strong shift towards engineering goods which have taken place in the LDCs: since 1970 the share of engineering goods has doubled. This trend is even more pronounced for the four Asian NIEs where about 45 per cent of all manufactured exports in 1987 were engineering goods, compared with only 21.5 per cent in 1970.

It is noteworthy that there is no significant difference between the developed market economies and the eastern countries with regard to the relative importance of trade in engineering goods. The aggregate figure conceals, however, that the manufactures exports of the Soviet Union are more strongly dominated by this product group than is the case, on average, for the east European countries (table 7.2.2).

The country data in Appendix table 7.1[788] display some interesting variation in the relative role of engineering goods exports within western Europe.[789] Traditionally the Federal Republic of Germany and Sweden show the strongest concentration on engineering goods, which accounted for some 60 per cent of all exports of manufactures in 1987. The corresponding share was somewhat less in the United Kingdom (55 per cent) and

TABLE 7.2.1

Changes in world exports of engineering goods and total manufactures
(Average annual growth rates)

	Engineering goods	Total manufactures		
	Values	Values	Volume	Unit values [a]
1970-1980	19.1	19.1	6.9	11.4
1980-1987	7.3	6.7	4.8	1.8
1970-1987	14.1	13.8	6.1	7.3

Source: ECE secretariat based on COMTRADE data base.

[a] Market economies only.

---

[787] Volume data for world trade in manufactures are derived by deflating nominal trade data with a unit value index. Such an index, however, is available for total manufactured products, but not for the subgroup of engineering goods. It should be noted that changes in unit values over the last two decades reflect to a large extent the widely fluctuating exchange rate of the US dollar. Thus, the large dollar depreciations of 1972-1973 and of 1977-1979 added significantly to the rise in average unit values in dollars. Conversely, the rather low unit value growth of the 1980s reflects, apart from the overall low inflation rate, also the strong appreciation of the dollar since 1981. In a similar vein, the recent depreciation of the dollar has added to unit value growth. The overall implication of these exchange rate fluctuations is that estimates of trade volume growth are surrounded by a wider margin of uncertainty and should be regarded with some caution. See, e.g., GATT, *International Trade 1985-86*, Geneva, 1986, p.137.

[788] The Appendix tables are placed at the end of this chapter.

[789] These data are not available, unfortunately, for the individual east European countries.

TABLE 7.2.2

The share of engineering goods in total trade of manufactured products
(Percentages)

	Exports			Imports		
	1970	1980	1987	1970	1980	1987
Developed market economies	55.8	55.8	59.4	51.4	50.5	54.8
Western Europe	52.1	50.8	52.2	48.4	47.2	51.2
North America	68.4	66.2	70.2	58.3	60.9	65.0
Japan	54.0	69.6	79.0	50.5	39.4	36.5
Eastern countries (7)	55.2	60.7	57.4	53.6	55.1	56.4
Developing countries	18.0	33.5	38.6	55.0	58.1	56.1
World	53.9	54.1	56.4	52.4	52.8	55.2
Memorandum item:						
EC (9)	52.9	51.9	53.4	46.8	46.2	50.4
EFTA (6)	50.5	48.8	51.2	50.2	48.3	52.2
Southern Europe	35.6	37.5	37.4	57.1	55.8	56.4
Eastern Europe (6)	53.4	58.4	54.4	54.0	57.6	58.2
Soviet Union	56.7	65.1	63.2	53.2	52.6	54.8
Four Asian NIEs	21.5	37.7	44.9	47.8	54.9	53.5

Source: ECE secretariat based on COMTRADE data base.

TABLE 7.2.3

Regional shares of world trade in engineering goods
(Percentages)

	Exports				Imports			
	1970	1980	1985	1987	1970	1980	1985	1987
Developed market economies	88.5	86.2	83.6	83.9	68.4	63.5	70.2	74.2
Western Europe	53.8	51.7	42.9	48.5	42.4	41.0	35.3	42.3
North America	24.7	19.3	20.9	16.7	20.5	17.4	30.5	26.7
Japan	9.5	14.7	19.4	18.3	2.4	1.8	2.0	2.1
Eastern countries (7)	9.8	8.1	7.6	6.4	10.0	8.0	7.5	6.4
Developing countries	1.7	5.7	8.8	9.7	21.6	28.6	22.2	19.4
World	100.0	100.0	100.0	100.0	100.0	100.0	100.0	100.0
Memorandum item:								
EC (9)	45.3	43.2	34.9	39.7	29.6	30.6	26.5	32.0
EFTA (6)	7.4	6.8	6.0	6.8	8.4	6.9	5.9	7.4
Southern Europe	1.1	1.8	2.0	2.0	4.5	3.4	2.8	3.9
Eastern Europe (6)	6.9	5.9	5.7	4.6	5.5	4.2	3.2	3.1
Soviet Union	2.8	2.1	1.8	1.7	4.5	3.7	4.3	3.3
Four Asian NIEs	0.9	3.6	5.6	5.7	2.6	4.6	5.7	5.8

Source: ECE secretariat based on COMTRADE data base.

Ireland, where there was a large rise in the share of engineering goods from about 30 per cent in 1970 to 57.5 per cent in 1987. In France, Norway and Switzerland the share was about 50-52 per cent while in the most of the other west European countries it is in the range of 40 to 45 per cent. Among the four largest of the west European economies, Italy has the relatively weakest concentration on engineering goods. The relative importance of engineering goods exports in 1987 was still relatively low in Greece (7 per cent), Turkey (19 per cent) and Portugal (24 per cent).

Looking at changes over time, it is clear that there have been significant shifts towards engineering goods since 1970 in Ireland, Austria, Belgium and Turkey.[790]

In contrast to the export pattern there is in general relatively little variation in the importance of engineering goods in imports (table 7.2.2). The most conspicuous feature of table 7.2.2 is the large fall in the relative share of engineering goods imports in Japan's imports of manufactures, from about 50 per cent in 1970 to only 36.5 per cent in 1987. This is the by far lowest share among all the countries and regions considered here. It is also in striking contrast to the rising — albeit small — or stable share of engineering goods in total manufactured imports elsewhere. In 1987 nearly two thirds of all imports of manufactures in the United States were engineering goods, compared with 53 per cent in 1970 (Appendix table 7.1). Within western Europe the increase in the relative importance of engineering goods imports was most pronounced in the United Kingdom (a rise from about 44 to 54 per cent between 1970 and 1987).

---

[790] It is noteworthy that in Turkey engineering goods accounted for only 5 per cent of all manufactured exports in 1970.

(ii) Changes in the regional and country pattern of exports and imports

(a) Exports

The most striking development in the regional trade patterns for engineering goods has been the emergence of Japan as a major exporter in 1987. The other striking change is the strong advance of the four Asian NIEs (table 7.2.3). Between 1970 and 1987, Japan's share of total world exports of engineering goods nearly doubled from 9.5 per cent to 18.3 per cent. Over the same period the share of the four Asian NIEs increased from about 1 per cent to nearly 6 per cent. This is the major factor behind the increase in the share of the aggregate developing countries over the last two decades.[791] The mirror image of these changes are the lower world market shares for western Europe, North America, the east European countries and the Soviet Union.

Within western Europe, the fall in world market share is largely accounted for by the European Community. Between 1970 and 1987 the share of the Community fell by some 5.5 percentage points, compared with only 0.5 percentage points for the EFTA countries. In contrast, the share of southern Europe in world exports rose from 1.1 to 2 per cent between 1970 and 1987. In the most recent period, 1980-1987, a similar pattern emerges, with the share of EFTA and southern Europe remaining stable and that of the Community falling.[792]

It is noteworthy that the share of the four Asian NIEs in world exports in 1987 was only about 1 percentage point below the shares recorded for EFTA and the eastern countries, respectively. Indeed, the Asian NIEs exported more engineering goods to the world in 1987 than the six eastern European countries combined, which accounted for only about 4.5 per cent of the world market, compared with some 7 per cent in 1970.[793]

Although western Europe's share of world exports is now lower than in 1970 and 1980, it still remains the largest regional exporter of engineering goods, with a share of 48.5 per cent in 1987. The bulk of this — about 40 percentage points — is accounted for by the European Community. The relative strength of the Community in engineering goods exports may be gauged from the fact that its share is only slightly below the combined shares of Japan, North America and the four Asian NIEs (40.7 per cent) in 1987. But in 1970 the Community's share was some 10 percentage points higher than the combined share of these three regions.

Table 7.2.4 shows the twelve largest individual exporters of engineering goods in 1987. It can be seen that the difference in world market shares between the two leading countries — Japan and the Federal Republic of Germany — is only small (1.5 percentage points). The table displays clearly the declining role of the United States which in 1970 was still the leading exporter with a world market share of about 19.5 per cent.

The market for engineering goods exports is dominated by a relatively small number of countries. The above-mentioned three leading exporters combined have accounted for somewhat less than half of the world market over the whole period 1970-1987. The importance of the other countries is much less. Thus in 1987, France, Italy and the United Kingdom combined had a world market share of the same size as the Federal Republic of Germany. The concentration of engineering goods exports is quite high, with twelve countries accounting for about 80 per cent of the world market (table 7.2.4). The rapid advance of the Asian NIEs is illustrated by the appearance of the Republic of Korea in the list of the twelve largest exporters in 1987: its market share is larger than that of the Soviet Union.[794]

(b) Imports

Western Europe has traditionally been the largest market for engineering goods (table 7.2.3). In 1987 its share of world imports was about 42 per cent, the same as in 1970. The bulk of this (32 percentage points) is accounted for by the European Community. About a quarter of all shipments of engineering goods went to North America, whose importance as a market rose strongly after 1980. This reflects the combined effects of the rapid growth of domestic demand in the United States after the 1981/82 recession and the strong appreciation of the US dollar which stimulated imports.[795]

---

[791] In fact, a considerable part of the rising share of the "other" LDCs is accounted for by other Asian countries, i.e., the second generation of NIEs emerging in Asia, notably Malaysia, Thailand and, to a more limited extent, Indonesia and the Philippines.

[792] It should be recalled that these are nominal world market shares which reflect the combined effect of differential changes in export volumes, domestic prices and exchange rates. The conversion of trade values in national currency units into a common denominator, e.g., the US dollar, occasionally leads to large shifts in world market shares which may not necessarily reflect corresponding changes in competitiveness. Thus between 1980 and 1985 the US dollar appreciated strongly vis-à-vis the west European currencies but not against the Yen. Although its relative importance is difficult to determine, this goes some way towards explaining the decline of the world market share of the Community between these two years. In fact, over this period the world market share of the Community declined from 43 per cent to 35 per cent, whereas Japan's share rose from about 15 per cent to 19.5 per cent. However, since 1985 the Community has regained world market shares (an increase by nearly 4 percentage points, whereas Japan's relative share fell by 1 percentage point).

[793] Note that there is some uncertainty about the relative size of total eastern trade owing to the method of valuing intra-group trade flows, which account for some 80 per cent of total eastern trade in engineering goods. Intra-group trade flows have been derived by converting transferable rouble values to US dollars at the official exchange rate. These intra-group trade prices are known, however, to differ often significantly from world market prices. Moreover, the official dollar exchange rate deviates from the rate that would prevail if the conversion rate were determined in the foreign exchange market. Consequently, the eastern trade values should be regarded as approximations. For a more detailed presentation of these problems see Economic Commission for Europe Economic Bulletin for Europe, vol.37, No.4, Pergamon Press for the United Nations, December 1985, pp.404-405.

[794] The market shares for the other west European countries are not shown here. The highest shares among these countries in 1987 is for Austria (1.1 per cent) and Spain (1.2 per cent). For the other smaller countries the world export market shares are all below 1 per cent.

[795] In 1985 North America accounted for about 30 per cent of all world imports of engineering goods, a share which had fallen to some 27 per cent in 1987. These value figures tend to exaggerate the growth of imports in North America after 1980 because of the dollar appreciation.

TABLE 7.2.4

Major twelve exporters of engineering goods [a]
(World market shares, per cent)

	1970	1980	1987
Japan	9.5	14.7	18.3
Germany, Fed.Rep. of	17.9	16.7	16.8
United States	19.4	16.2	12.7
Total 3 countries	**46.8**	**47.6**	**47.8**
France	6.5	7.3	6.0
United Kingdom	8.9	7.7	5.6
Italy	5.6	5.1	4.9
Canada	5.4	3.1	4.0
Total 7 countries	**73.0**	**70.8**	**68.3**
Belgium	2.8	2.7	2.6
Netherlands	2.8	2.5	2.4
Switzerland	2.5	2.4	2.3
Sweden	3.0	2.4	2.3
Republic of Korea	0.1	0.8	2.0
Total 12 countries	**84.2**	**81.6**	**79.9**

Source: ECE secretariat based on COMTRADE data base.

[a] Based on ranking in 1987.

TABLE 7.2.5

Major twelve importers of engineering goods [a]
(World market shares, per cent)

	1970	1980	1987
United States	13.1	12.3	21.2
Germany, Fed.Rep. of	6.7	7.2	7.8
United Kingdom	4.2	6.0	6.5
Total 3 countries	**24.0**	**25.5**	**35.5**
France	5.6	5.8	6.1
Canada	7.4	5.1	5.5
Italy	3.5	3.9	4.1
Soviet Union	4.5	3.7	3.3
Total 7 countries	**45.0**	**44.0**	**50.4**
Netherlands	4.2	3.1	3.2
Belgium	3.4	3.2	2.8
Japan	2.4	2.0	2.1
Spain	1.4	1.2	2.0
Switzerland	2.1	1.8	2.0
Total 12 countries	**58.5**	**55.3**	**62.6**

Source: ECE secretariat based on COMTRADE data base.

[a] Based on ranking in 1987.

The main counterpart to this change after 1980 has been the declining share of the developing countries from about 29 per cent in 1980 to 19 per cent in 1987 — somewhat below their share in 1970. There is also a notable decline in the share of the eastern countries in world imports of engineering goods, from 10 per cent in 1970 to about 6.5 per cent in 1987. This contrasts with the rising share of the Asian NIEs which rivalled the importance of the eastern countries as markets for engineering goods in 1987. The share of the Asian NIEs in world imports exceeded the share of the six east European countries combined in 1987.

The most striking feature of table 7.2.3, however, is the very low share of Japan in world imports of engineering goods. Over the whole period examined here it hardly exceeded 2 per cent, which is in stark contrast to Japan's leading role Japan as an exporter. In fact, Japan's share of world imports is broadly the same as that of Spain and Switzerland (table 7.2.5). Indeed, the persistently very low import share, in conjunction with its rise to the position of the world's leading exporter of engineering goods, shows that "as far as participation in international trade is concerned" Japan is an "outlier".[796] The fact, that the Japanese market for manufactures and, more specifically, for engineering goods is much more difficult to penetrate than the markets of the other industrialized countries can also be inferred from the ratios of imports to apparent consumption, which are considerably lower than in the other major countries (table 7.2.6). Apart from differences in national preferences for imported goods, the importance of which is difficult to assess, this general resistance of the Japanese markets to foreign products is probably to a large extent the result of specific formal and informal trade barriers which hinder imports into Japan.[797]

In comparison with exports, the concentration of imports is much less pronounced (table 7.2.5). The three largest importers have a combined market share of 35.5 per cent, compared with some 48 per cent taken by the three largest countries in world exports. Similarly, the twelve largest importers in 1987 took about 63 per cent of all imports, while the twelve largest exporters accounted for some 80 per cent of the world market.

By far the largest individual market for engineering goods is the United States, followed by the Federal Republic of Germany and the United Kingdom. Six of the seven largest exporters are also among the seven largest importers, the exception being Japan.

(iii) Inter- and intra-regional trade flows of engineering goods

While aggregate market shares show the overall importance of various regions and countries in world trade, they conceal striking differences in the geographical pattern of their trade. It is therefore interesting to look at the distribution of regional exports by area of destination and the corresponding distribution of imports by area of origin and to assess the relative intensity of intra-regional versus inter-regional trade flows.

---

[796] See Bela Balassa, "Japan's Trade Policies", *Weltwirtschaftliches Archiv*, Band 122, Heft 4, 1986, pp.745-790.

[797] See Bela Balassa, *loc.cit.* for a more general review. The view that Japan's economy is highly protective, however, has also been challenged. Based on a cross-country analysis of trade patterns it has been argued that when proper adjustments are made "for the differing quantity and quality of Japanese labor, capital and natural resource endowments, and distance from trading partners ... the Japanese share of manufactures in total imports is comparable to European and American experiences", See Gary Saxonhouse, "The Micro- and Macro-economics of Foreign Sales to Japan", in William R. Cline (ed.), *Trade Policy in the 1980s*, Washington, D.C., 1983, p.294.

TABLE 7.2.6

Market penetration ratios: 1986
(Percentage shares)

ISIC		Japan	United States	Germany Fed.Rep. of	France	Italy	United Kingdom	Canada
381	Metal products except machinery	0.8	6.0	14.1	28.6	18.6	18.2	18.1
382	Non-electrical machinery, n.e.s.	3.7	19.0	49.1	35.4	44.6	52.9	70.6
383	Electrical machinery, n.e.s.	2.4	20.9	52.8	32.6	29.6	41.2	48.2
384	Transport equipment	3.1	22.9	42.3	30.8	35.5	56.8	71.5
385	Measuring and control equipment	6.6	20.3	55.5	85.2	95.5	71.8	24.6
3	Total manufacturing	4.1	14.3	35.5	25.1	26.7	32.4	32.0

Source: OECD Compatible Trade and Production Data Base, tape.

Note: The market penetration ratio is defined as the percentage share of imports in apparent total domestic consumption (production plus imports less exports) of the corresponding product group.

(a) Exports

Table 7.2.7 shows the geographical distribution of the exports of the major trading regions in 1987. It can be seen that there is a conspicuous contrast between the relative importance of intra-regional and inter-regional flows. Thus, nearly 66 per cent of all west European exports of engineering goods are intra-regional, with the bulk of the remainder going to North America (about 12 per cent) and the developing countries. The eastern countries combined receive only 3 per cent of west European exports. In fact, exports to the NIEs significantly exceed those to the six eastern European countries in 1987. Only about 1.5 per cent of all west European exports went to Japan.

About 47 per cent of all Community exports go to other member countries. Intra-area trade is much less marked for EFTA (15 per cent) and southern Europe (6 per cent). Indeed, it is the Community which provides the largest market for these two regions: in 1987 44 per cent of EFTA's engineering goods exports were shipped to the Community and for the south European countries the figure was 57 per cent.

Canada provides the single largest market for US exports of engineering goods. Its share in 1987 was about 26 per cent, somewhat more than that taken by the European Community and approximately the same as that of the developing countries (excluding the Asian NIEs). Indeed, the US is much more reliant on exports to third world countries than are western Europe and Japan.

Indeed, Japan is strongly oriented towards the US market, which has a share of about 41 per cent in its total exports. About 22 per cent of Japan's exports are shipped to western Europe but trade links with the Asian NIEs are also quite strong. These four countries accounted for 14 per cent of all Japanese exports in 1987, only slightly less than the developing countries combined.

The Asian NIEs are also strongly oriented towards the United States, which accounted in 1987 for about 45 per cent of all shipments. In contrast, only 5.6 per cent of their exports went to Japan. Western Europe and the developing countries are roughly equal in importance as markets for the NIEs, with a share of about 17 to 18 per cent of all exports.

The six eastern European countries combined shipped more than half of their exports to the Soviet Union in 1987, and another 30 per cent was accounted for by trade among themselves. Thus, more than 80 per cent of all east European exports remained within the eastern trading area. These figures do not include shipments to the Asian centrally planned economies: accordingly, the importance of other markets for east European exports is much smaller. Seven per cent of all exports in 1987 went to western Europe and 9.5 per cent to developing countries. The importance of other regions is negligible.

About half of all the Soviet Union's exports go to eastern Europe and about 44 per cent to developing countries.[798] As is the case for the east European countries, only 7 per cent of Soviet exports go to western Europe, while trade relations with North America and Japan are virtually non-existent.

(b) Imports

The geographical pattern of imports by origin has some strong similarities with that for exports as regards the importance of intra-area flows in western Europe and for the eastern countries. But there are some additional features that deserve mention (table 7.2.8).

Again western Europe is noteworthy for the importance of intra-area shipments, which in 1987 accounted for about 72 per cent of all imports. Japan and the United States each had a market share of about 10 per cent. The importance of the Asian NIEs is much less: only a little more than 3 per cent of west European imports originated in these countries — although this is still much more than the share (only 1 per cent) of the Soviet Union and the six east European countries combined.[799]

---

[798] Approximately 15 percentage points of this is accounted for by exports to the Asian CPEs.

[799] It should be recalled that these data exclude the trade between the Federal Republic of Germany and the German Democratic Republic.

TABLE 7.2.7
Origin and destination of engineering goods exports, 1987
(Percentage shares)

Exporter	EC (9)	EFTA (6)	Southern Europe	Western Europe	United States	North America	Japan	Other DMEs	DMEs	Eastern Europe	Soviet Union	Eastern Countries	Asian NIEs	Rest of World	World
EC (9)	47.4	11.7	7.0	66.2	10.9	12.0	1.4	2.4	82.0	1.2	0.9	2.2	2.1	13.7	100.0
EFTA (6)	44.1	14.9	4.6	63.7	10.7	12.2	1.6	2.0	79.4	2.6	3.3	5.8	3.2	11.5	100.0
Southern Europe	57.2	4.7	5.6	67.4	4.3	4.8	0.1	0.9	73.3	3.9	7.1	11.0	0.5	15.2	100.0
Western Europe	47.4	11.9	6.6	65.9	10.6	11.8	1.4	2.3	81.3	1.5	1.5	3.0	2.2	13.4	100.0
United States	23.1	3.0	2.0	28.1	..	26.2	6.8	4.7	65.8	0.1	0.1	0.3	8.0	25.9	100.0
North America	18.4	2.4	1.6	22.5	21.7	41.6	5.3	3.7	73.0	0.1	0.1	0.2	6.2	20.5	100.0
Japan	16.7	3.5	1.5	21.7	40.8	43.5	..	3.7	68.8	0.3	0.5	0.8	14.0	16.4	100.0
Other DMEs	14.3	1.7	1.1	17.2	26.2	27.2	2.9	16.1	63.3	0.1	0.1	0.2	4.3	32.3	100.0
DMEs	34.8	8.1	4.5	47.4	19.5	24.7	1.9	2.9	76.9	1.0	1.0	2.0	5.6	15.6	100.0
Eastern Europe	3.9	1.2	1.9	7.0	0.4	0.5	..	0.1	7.6	29.6	53.2	82.9	0.1	9.5	100.0
Soviet Union	3.0	1.8	1.7	6.5	0.1	0.1	0.1	0.1	6.7	49.3	..	49.3	0.1	43.9	100.0
Eastern countries	3.6	1.3	1.9	6.9	0.3	0.4	..	0.1	7.4	35.2	38.3	76.8	0.1	19.1	100.0
Asian NIEs	14.8	2.0	1.3	18.1	45.4	47.9	5.6	2.5	74.1	0.1	..	0.1	8.5	17.4	100.0
Rest of World	16.8	1.2	0.7	18.7	29.0	30.8	0.9	2.7	51.2	0.7	1.1	1.8	11.3	35.7	100.0
World	30.7	7.0	3.9	41.6	20.3	24.9	1.9	7.2	71.0	3.0	3.2	6.2	5.8	17.1	100.0

Source: ECE secretariat based on COMTRADE data base.

TABLE 7.2.8

Origin and destination of engineering goods imports, 1987
(Percentage shares)

Importer	EC (9)	EFTA (6)	Southern Europe	Western Europe	United States	North America	Japan	Other DMEs	DMEs	Eastern Europe	Soviet Union	Eastern Countries	Asian NIEs	Rest of World	World
EC (9)	58.1	9.4	3.6	71.1	10.4	10.9	10.5	0.3	92.7	0.5	0.2	0.7	3.5	3.1	100.0
EFTA (6)	62.0	12.7	1.2	75.8	8.1	8.5	11.1	0.1	95.5	0.7	0.4	1.1	2.3	1.0	100.0
Southern Europe	65.1	7.2	3.1	75.4	7.2	7.5	9.5	0.2	92.6	2.3	0.8	3.1	3.3	1.0	100.0
Western Europe	59.4	9.8	3.1	72.3	9.7	10.1	10.5	0.3	93.2	0.7	0.3	1.0	3.3	2.6	100.0
United States	20.3	3.3	0.5	24.1	..	16.2	37.0	0.6	77.9	0.1	..	0.1	14.0	8.1	100.0
North America	17.7	3.0	0.4	21.0	15.8	28.7	31.2	0.5	81.5	0.1	..	0.1	11.6	6.8	100.0
Japan	28.2	5.2	0.1	33.6	46.7	47.5	..	1.0	82.0	0.1	0.1	0.1	15.4	2.4	100.0
Other DMEs	29.6	5.4	0.6	35.7	23.7	24.6	26.4	3.8	90.4	0.1	..	0.2	7.1	2.3	100.0
DMEs	42.6	7.1	2.0	51.7	13.4	18.3	18.1	0.5	88.6	0.5	0.2	0.6	6.7	4.1	100.0
Eastern Europe	15.8	5.7	2.5	24.1	0.6	0.7	1.5	..	26.4	43.7	28.4	72.1	0.1	1.4	100.0
Soviet Union	11.4	6.7	4.3	22.5	0.4	0.5	2.8	..	25.8	72.2	..	72.2	..	1.9	100.0
Eastern countries	13.6	6.2	3.5	23.3	0.5	0.6	2.2	..	26.1	58.5	13.6	72.2	0.1	1.7	100.0
Asian NIEs	13.5	3.5	0.2	17.2	18.0	18.3	42.7	0.4	78.6	..	..	0.1	9.9	11.4	100.0
Rest of World	31.3	4.5	1.7	37.5	19.0	19.7	17.3	1.6	75.4	2.4	4.4	6.8	5.8	12.0	100.0
World	37.3	6.4	1.9	45.6	13.8	17.4	18.4	4.2	82.0	4.3	1.7	6.0	6.3	5.7	100.0

Source: ECE secretariat based on COMTRADE data base.

Japan was the largest foreign supplier of engineering goods in the United States, with an import share of 37 per cent in 1987. This compares with shares of 24 per cent for western Europe and 14 per cent for the four Asian NIEs. This pattern is roughly paralleled in the geographical structure of Japanese imports. About 45 per cent of the — very small — Japanese imports of engineering goods originate in the United States, 33 per cent in western Europe and 15 per cent in the Asian NIEs.

The major source of imports into the Asian NIEs is Japan which accounts for 43 per cent of the total. The importance of the United States is much lower (18 per cent) and is only slightly higher than that of western Europe. This is in contrast to the export structure of the NIEs, where the major market is the United States and Japan is of relatively small importance.

For the seven eastern countries, 72 per cent of all their imports are from one another. The remainder is largely accounted for by western Europe.

(c) Trade intensity coefficients

The relative importance of intra- and inter-regional trade flows can be explained by the interaction of the "trade potential" of the regions involved on the one hand, and "resistance" factors on the other. In general, trade potential may be measured by the GNP of the exporting and importing regions. Trade resistance factors include, for example, the geographical distance between potential trading partners, membership of a preferential trading area, the degree of complementarity between export and import patterns, non-tariff barriers such as quotas and voluntary export restraints and so on. An analysis of the spatial distribution of a region's trade flows in terms of these variables is well beyond the scope of the present study.[800] Instead, the overall strength of intra- and inter-regional trade is brought out with the use of trade intensity coefficients. The coefficients themselves do not of course reveal anything about the various underlying structural factors which account for differences in the intensity of trade between regions and countries, but they do provide a useful starting point for a more detailed discussion of the relative importance of such factors in determining bilateral trade flows.

This analysis takes the absolute bilateral trade flows between two regions or countries, say the United States and Japan, as given, and asks to what extent the share of US exports going to Japan deviates from the share of Japan in total world imports.

The trade intensity coefficients is defined as:

(1) $T_{ij} = (X_{ij}/X_{i.}) / (X_{.j}/X_{..})$,

where X_{ij} denotes the exports of region i to region j, $X_{i.}$ are total exports of region i, $X_{.j}$ represents total imports of country j, and $X_{..}$ is total world imports (exports). The first term on the right hand side of the equation measures the share of region j in total exports from region i, and the second term the relative share of region j in total world imports.[801] If the index is equal to unity then the importance of region j in exports of region i is equal to the importance of region j in total world imports, i.e., it is equal to the average importance of region j for all exporters. In a similar vein an index greater than unity indicates that trade links between region i and j exceed the average intensity, while conversely an index lower than unity points to trade links which are weaker than average. Because trade intensity coefficients tend to be relatively stable over time, they have been employed to project bilateral trade flows.[802]

Trade intensity coefficients for 1987 are depicted in table 7.2.9. All the intra-regional trade flows in western Europe are clearly greater than unity, with the exception of the export orientation of the south European countries towards EFTA.[803] The aggregate west European export intensity with other regions is not particularly strong: all indices are below unity. The average export coefficient with eastern countries is about 0.5, the same as for exports to the United States. It is noteworthy that the trade links between EFTA and the eastern countries are more intensive than between the Community and the east; this partly reflects bilateral trade agreements. Southern Europe also shows intensity coefficients with regard to the eastern countries which clearly exceed unity: this is largely the result of the relatively strong ties between Yugoslavia and the other socialist countries.

The coefficients also bring out quite clearly the above average intensity of trade flows between Japan, the United States and the four Asian NIEs. Note also the strong intensity of trade between the developing countries and the United States.

A salient feature of table 7.2.9 is the very high coefficients for trade among the eastern countries.[804] Thus, the value of the intensity coefficient for east European exports to the USSR (and vice versa) is more than 16, indicating that the flow of engineering goods in either direction is more than 15 times greater than expected on the basis of the shares of the two regions in world imports. For trade between the six east European

---

[800] The explanation of bilateral trade flows in terms of the above-mentioned variables is the purpose of so-called "gravity models".

[801] See Ippei Yamazawa, "Structural Changes in World Trade Flows", *Hitotsubashi Journal of Economics*, Vol.11, No.2, 1971, pp.11-21; Peter Drysdale and Ross Garnaut, "Trade Intensities and the Analysis of Bilateral Trade Flows in a Many-Country World: A Survey", *Hitotsubashi Journal of Economics*, Vol.22, No.2, 1982, pp.62-84.

[802] See United Nations Economic Commission for Europe, *Economic Bulletin for Europe*, vol.22, No.1, New York, 1971, pp.51, ("Note on the Projection of the Matrices of International Trade"). For a recent application pertaining to intra-CMEA trade see Juliusz Kotynski, "On some probability techniques of forecasting the distribution of trade" (applied to the intra-CMEA trade pattern), Foreign Trade Research Institute, Warsaw 1989.

[803] Note that the export intensity of region i with respect to region j is the same as the import intensity of region j with respect to region i.

[804] This feature is not limited to trade in engineering goods, but is characteristic of total eastern trade. See "The changing intensity of east-west trade, 1955-1984", Economic Commission for Europe *Economic Bulletin for Europe*, vol.37, No.4, Pergamon Press for the United Nations, 1985, pp.371-406.

TABLE 7.2.9

Trade intensity coefficients for engineering goods trade, 1987 and 1970

	EC (9)	EFTA (6)	Southern Europe	Western Europe	United States	North America	Japan	Asian NIEs	Eastern Europe	Soviet Union	Eastern countries	Rest of World [a]	World
Exporters, 1987													
EC (9)	1.55	1.68	1.79	1.59	0.54	0.48	0.74	0.37	0.41	0.29	0.35	0.80	1.00
EFTA (6)	1.44	2.14	1.17	1.53	0.53	0.49	0.83	0.56	0.86	1.01	0.94	0.68	1.00
Southern Europe	1.86	0.67	1.42	1.62	0.21	0.19	0.06	0.10	1.31	2.21	1.78	0.89	1.00
Western Europe	1.54	1.70	1.69	1.58	0.52	0.47	0.72	0.39	0.51	0.47	0.49	0.79	1.00
United States	0.75	0.42	0.51	0.68	..	1.05	3.57	1.40	0.05	0.04	0.04	1.52	1.00
North America	0.60	0.35	0.42	0.54	1.07	1.67	2.77	1.08	0.04	0.03	0.04	1.20	1.00
Japan	0.54	0.51	0.37	0.52	2.01	1.75	..	2.43	0.09	0.16	0.12	0.96	1.00
Asian NIEs	0.48	0.29	0.34	0.44	2.23	1.93	2.94	1.47	0.02	..	0.01	1.02	1.00
Eastern Europe	0.13	0.17	0.49	0.17	0.02	0.02	0.02	0.01	9.96	16.47	13.35	0.56	1.00
Soviet Union	0.10	0.26	0.44	0.16	..	..	0.03	0.01	16.59	..	7.95	2.57	1.00
Eastern countries	0.12	0.19	0.48	0.16	0.02	0.02	0.03	0.01	11.82	11.85	12.38	1.12	1.00
Rest of world [a]	0.55	0.18	0.17	0.45	1.43	1.24	0.45	1.96	0.25	0.33	0.29	2.09	1.00
World	1.00	1.00	1.00	1.00	1.00	1.00	1.00	1.00	1.00	1.00	1.00	1.00	1.00
Exporters, 1970													
EC (9)	1.49	1.49	1.36	1.47	0.69	0.54	0.60	0.49	0.41	0.34	0.38	0.83	1.00
EFTA (6)	1.31	2.33	1.25	1.51	0.63	0.53	0.93	0.73	0.75	0.88	0.81	0.63	1.00
Southern Europe	0.94	0.55	1.26	0.90	0.48	0.34	0.21	0.10	1.58	2.06	1.80	1.82	1.00
Western Europe	1.45	1.58	1.34	1.47	0.68	0.54	0.63	0.52	0.48	0.45	0.46	0.82	1.00
United States	0.81	0.45	0.66	0.72	..	1.38	3.16	1.19	0.03	0.06	0.04	1.35	1.00
North America	0.67	0.37	0.55	0.59	1.40	2.02	2.50	0.95	0.02	0.04	0.03	1.13	1.00
Japan	0.34	0.45	0.76	0.40	2.52	1.86	..	4.40	0.05	0.28	0.16	1.44	1.00
Asian NIEs	0.32	0.10	0.09	0.25	3.59	2.49	2.63	3.15	..	..	..	1.28	1.00
Eastern Europe	0.12	0.13	0.72	0.18	0.02	0.02	0.12	0.04	6.77	10.48	8.43	0.54	1.00
Soviet Union	0.06	0.12	0.52	0.12	..	..	0.10	0.04	9.76	..	5.39	2.12	1.00
Eastern countries	0.10	0.13	0.66	0.17	0.02	0.02	0.12	0.04	7.62	7.50	7.56	0.99	1.00
Rest of world [a]	0.73	0.13	0.57	0.59	1.35	0.93	0.42	2.38	0.05	0.04	0.04	2.39	1.00
World	1.00	1.00	1.00	1.00	1.00	1.00	1.00	1.00	1.00	1.00	1.00	1.00	1.00

Source: ECE secretariat based on COMTRADE data base.

Note: The trade intensity coefficients is defined as: $T_{ij} = (X_{ij}/X_{i.}) / (X_{.j}/X_{..})$, where X_{ij} denotes the exports of region i to region j, $X_{i.}$ are total exports of region i, $X_{.j}$ represents total imports of country j, and $X_{..}$ is total world imports (exports).

[a] Developing countries only.

countries the intensity coefficient is 10, which compares with 1.55 as the value for the coefficient of intra-Community trade.

Overall the coefficients in table 7.2.9 indicate the limited involvement of the eastern countries in the international division of labour, *inter alia* a consequence of their autarkic policies with the CMEA and lack of competitiveness.[805]

Viewed in a longer-term perspective the trade intensity coefficients show a high degree of stability: regions which showed above average trade intensity in bilateral trade in 1987 also did so in 1970. Thus, the intra-trade coefficients for western Europe have changed only slightly over this period: for intra-Community trade the coefficient has remained virtually unchanged between 1970 and 1987. Although not directly related, this is consistent with findings that the process of European integration has not resulted, on average, in "trade diversion".[806] The exception is the strong rise in southern Europe's export intensity with the European Community, from 0.94 in 1970 to 1.86 in 1987. This shows clearly that southern Europe's economic ties with the Community have been considerably strengthened over the last two decades or so — a process that was stimulated by bilateral trade agreements and, more recently, by the full membership of Greece, Spain and Portugal in the Community.[807] The counterpart to this process has been a marked decline in the export intensity coefficients of southern Europe with the developing countries.

Although the intensity coefficients for intra-eastern trade were already very high in 1970 there has been no tendency for them to decline thereafter. Instead, the average coefficient of the six eastern European countries combined for exports of engineering goods to the USSR rose from 10.5 in 1970 to 16.5 in 1987. Conversely, the coefficient for Soviet exports to eastern Europe rose from 9.8 to 16.6.

It is also noteworthy that the intensity coefficients for exports from Japan and the NIEs, respectively, to the United States have fallen between 1970 and 1987. In contrast, there were slight increases in the coefficients for trade flows from the United States to Japan and the NIEs, respectively.

---

[805] See Economic Commission for Europe, *Economic Bulletin of Europe*, vol.37, No.4, Pergamon Press for the United Nations, 1985, pp.379-382 for a more general discussion of the possible reasons for these high intensity coefficients in intra-eastern trade.

[806] See Alexis Jacquemin and André Sapir, "European Integration or World Integration?", *Weltwirtschaftliches Archiv*, Band 124, Heft 1, 1988, pp.127-139. For an analysis of the effects of west European integration on imports of manufactures from eastern Europe and southern Europe see United Nations Economic Commission for Europe, *Economic Survey of Europe in 1988-1989*, New York, 1989, section 2.5 .

[807] In the secretariat study mentioned in the preceding footnote it was estimated that "EC imports from eastern Europe and Yugoslavia may have been diverted in favour of southern Europe" and that this possible diversion of imports was mainly concentrated on textiles and machinery, *op.cit*, p.83.

7.3 INTER-INDUSTRY SPECIALIZATION IN ENGINEERING GOODS TRADE

This section examines the pattern and changes over time of revealed comparative advantage in the engineering industries of the ECE region, Japan and the Asian NIEs. Broadly speaking, the prevailing patterns of specialization and their changes over time are an important element in any assessment of the overall involvement of a country in the international division of labour and in the identification of areas of strength and weakness.

(i) Some theoretical considerations

Traditionally trade theory explains the flow of goods from one country to another in terms of the existing differences in relative factor endowments on the one hand and the relative factor requirements of production processes on the other. Since the 1960s, however, a number of alternative theoretical approaches have been developed: some of these have concentrated on differentiating factor inputs more carefully, while others have shifted attention to other determinants of international trade such as the demand for differentiated products, the role of economies of scale, technical change and so on. Thus, perceptions of the various factors which determine trade and specialization patterns have changed considerably in recent years.

The traditional theory postulates that a country will tend to export those products which make relatively intensive use of the factor input with which the country is relatively abundantly endowed.[808] Conversely, it will import those products which make heavy use of the input which is relatively scarce in the domestic market. In its original formulation this approach (the Heckscher-Ohlin model) considered only two inputs, viz. aggregate physical capital on the one hand and aggregate labour on the other: subsequently, neo-factor proportions theories stressed the role of differentiated labour skills, or, put differently, the role of the human capital stock as a prime determinant of international specialization. The neo-technology hypothesis, a rival approach, states that inter-country differences in comparative advantage are the result of the varying abilities of countries to innovate new products.

In a more general way, theoretical approaches which point to the role of innovation start from the observation that the bulk of trade in manufactures is between the advanced countries themselves which have similar relative factor endowments. In other words, a substantial portion of world trade does not fit neatly into the traditional factor proportions framework. This suggests that differences in relative factor endowments cannot be the only major cause of international trade.

One line of reasoning is, then, that trade reflects different rates of technical change in the various countries.[809] These models operate in a framework of imperfect competition where the innovator can exploit a temporary monopolistic position. An important factor in this process are dynamic economies of scale, defined as a firm's accumulated know-how of past experience in the production of a given product.[810] This sort of trade therefore reflects mainly the gap between the technologically advanced country and its followers. For the latter, this technology-gap trade may be a sort of moving target: in the process of imitating the technology leader they are able to close the gap in existing older product areas, but meanwhile the leader has opened up new gaps in other industries or product fields.

This sort of process is also reflected in the so-called product cycle hypothesis,[811] which shows how the comparative advantage for new products shifts gradually from the innovating country (the technological leader) first to other advanced countries and ultimately to developing countries as products mature over time and become highly standardized. This shifting comparative advantage can also be viewed as a process whereby the aging of a product is accompanied by a decline in its technology intensity, which in turn determines changes over time in the pattern of specialization in manufactured goods.[812]

Other models emphasize the role of increasing returns to scale as a major driving force behind the inter-

---

[808] This is the "weak" formulation of the theorem. The Heckscher-Ohlin prediction follows necessarily from its assumptions only if factor abundance is defined in terms of relative factor prices.

[809] See M.V. Posner, "International Trade and Technical Change", *Oxford Economic Papers*, New Series, Vol.13, No.3, 1961, pp.323-341. and G.C. Hufbauer, *Synthetic Materials and the Theory of International Trade*, London, Duckworth, 1966.

[810] See M.V. Posner, *loc.cit.*, pp.328-329.

[811] See R. Vernon, "International Investment and International Trade in the Product Cycle", *The Quarterly Journal of Economics*, Vol.LXXX, 1966, pp.190-207 and S. Hirsch, *Location of Industry and International Competitiveness*, Oxford, Clovenden Press, 1967.

[812] See e.g. A. Aquino, "Changes over time in the pattern of comparative advantage in manufactured goods", *European Economic Review*, Vol.15, 1981, pp.41-62 for an empirical examination of this hypothesis.

national division of labour.[813] Basically the argument is that the existence of economies of scale leads firms to specialize in more or less narrow product areas. This results in cross-border flows of goods even if the relative factor endowments and technologies are similar among countries. In a similar vein, the exploitation of economies of scale in conjunction with the demand for differentiated products may be used to explain one of the most striking phenomena of post-war trade, namely the considerable exchange of similar products between advanced countries, the so-called intra-industry trade.[814] Thus foreign trade plays a dual role: it extends the range of products available in the domestic market; and, at the same time, it allows firms to exploit scale economies by extending the market beyond domestic boundaries.

The many theoretical approaches towards explaining the pattern of international trade have provided many insights into particular aspects of trade. Attempts to discriminate empirically between alternative trade theories have, however, generally been inconclusive, *inter alia* because of the high degree of multicollinearity between the various explanatory variables, which, in turn, makes it difficult to quantify their respective roles.[815]

In a more general way, however, the interdependence between, say, the human capital factor, technology and the innovative strength of a country make tests which treat these factors as rivals look somewhat artificial.[816] These various hypotheses put forward to explain patterns of international trade and specializations may be better regarded as complementary rather than competitive. It is therefore no surprise that empirical research has found some truth in all of these theories, but none of them has "sufficiently commanding power to dispose exclusively of rival claimants."[817] In fact, it is still true that "no one theory monopolizes the explanation of international trade".[818]

(ii) Measuring specialization patterns

The analysis of specialization patterns prevailing in the engineering industries of the economies of the ECE region, Japan and the NIEs is conducted on the basis of trade data for 29 product groups, corresponding to the three-digit level of the SITC, Rev.1. These three-digit groups have been generally assumed to represent "industries" and in that sense the analysis below pertains to "inter-industry" specialization patterns.[819] Specialization patterns are measured here on the basis of an index proposed by Balassa.[820] This index compares the relative share of a commodity group in a country's total exports of manufactures to the corresponding share of that commodity group in total world exports of manufactures:

$$(2) \quad RCA = (X_{ij}/X_{.j}) / (X_{i.}/X_{..})$$
$$= (X_{ij}/X_{i.}) / (X_{.j}/X_{..}),$$

where X_{ij} are exports of product group i by country j, $X_{.j}$ are total manufactured exports of country j, $X_{i.}$ are the world exports of commodity group i and $X_{..}$ are the total world exports of manufactures.

It can be seen from equation (2) above that this index corresponds to a "relative" or "normalized" world market share. Country j's share in the world exports of commodity i is normalized by the share of country j in total world exports of manufactures. An index value greater than unity indicates that the share of commodity i in country j's exports is larger than the average share of this commodity in the exports of all countries taken together. Accordingly, country j is said to be relatively specialized in that particular commodity group.[821] In

---

[813] For a general overview see E. Helpman and P.R. Krugman, *Market Structure and Foreign Trade. Increasing Returns, Imperfect Competition, and the International Economy*, Cambridge, Massachusetts, 1985.

[814] This could also give rise to a view where the inter-industry specialization observed at the more aggregate broad commodity group level might still be explained in terms of the overall similarity between a country's relative factor endowments on the one hand and the relative factor requirements for the different commodity groups on the other, but where the specialization within these groups — the intra-branch specialization — is driven by the exploitation of increasing returns to scale. See E. Helpman and P.R. Krugman, *op.cit.*, p.131. For a general survey see D. Greenaway and C.R. Milner, *The Economics of Intra-Industry Trade*, Oxford, Basil Blackwell, 1986.

[815] See e.g., G.C. Hufbauer, "The Impact of National Characteristics and Technology on the Commodity Composition of Trade in Manufactured Goods", in R. Vernon (ed.), *The Technology Factor in International Trade*, Universities National Bureau Conference Series No.22, New York-London, 1970, pp.145-231, and R. Vernon, "The Technology Factor in a World Trade Matrix", in R. Vernon (ed.), *op.cit.*, pp.233-272. For an extensive analysis of the role of relative factor intensities and the technology factor in engineering goods specialization see L. Ohlsson, *Engineering Trade Specialization of Sweden and other Industrial Countries*, Studies in International Economics: Volume 6, Amsterdam, 1980.

[816] See H.G. Johnson, "Technological Change and Comparative Advantage: An Advanced Country's Viewpoint", *Journal of World Trade Law*, Vol.9, 1975, No.1, p.3. "Every blind man who touches a part of the elephant learns some of the truth about it — but not the whole truth; and only the rare unfortunate is unlucky enough to be caught in generalizing about the elephant from an unrepresentative hand-hold on the tip of its tail".

[817] See H.G. Johnson, *ibid*, p.3.

[818] See G.C. Hufbauer, *loc.cit*. p.194. In a similar vein Ohlsson summarizes his study on engineering goods trade with the statement that "no single theory can offer more than a minor contribution to explaining any country's trade specialization in a given year". L. Ohlsson, *op.cit.*, p.188.

[819] As noted above a substantial part of trade between countries consists of the exchange of similar products, the so-called intra-industry trade. If a country exports and at the same time also imports goods allocated to the same SITC group, then it is defined as "intra-industry" trade. One way of measuring the importance of intra-industry trade is to compare the degree of similarity between a country's total manufactured exports and imports, respectively at the three-digit SITC level, with each group corresponding to an "industry". But these calculations have also been carried out for trade data corresponding to the four-digit and five-digit SITC level.

[820] See Bela Balassa, "'Revealed' Comparative Advantage Revisited: An Analysis of Relative Export Shares of the Industrial Countries, 1953-1971", *The Manchester School of Economic and Social Studies*, Volume XLV, December 1977, pp.327-344.

[821] In the following the terms "industry", "product groups" and "commodity groups" are used interchangeably.

other words, the export pattern "revealed" that that country has a comparative advantage in this area. Conversely, an index value smaller than unity is often described as a comparative disadvantage. This simple dichotomy may, however, be questioned. The very fact that a country is able to export a given good (leaving aside the extreme cases of dumping and excessive subsidization) must reflect an existing comparative advantage, independently of whether the RCA index associated with these export values is greater or smaller than unity. Hence an index value less than unity is better interpreted as reflecting an activity for which a country's specialization is not particularly pronounced relative to other domestic activities characterized by an RCA index which is greater than unity.

Essentially what this index measures is the degree of inter-industry specialization in exports of engineering goods. It is, of course, possible to measure in a similar way the corresponding pattern of import specialization.

Before looking at the results of the corresponding calculations it is important to recall the basic underlying assumption, namely that the strength and changes of a country's product specialization − i.e., the degree of international competitiveness − can be gauged from the corresponding trade flows. Clearly, this is not a perfect indicator. The observed pattern of trade reflects the impact of factors like tariffs and protective measures, such as quotas and voluntary export restraints, which can cause substantial distortions of trade flows and thus prevent an inherent comparative advantage from "revealing" itself. Also, a relatively good trade performance may occasionally not reflect an underlying competitive strength but be mainly the result of large government subsidies. Exchange rate fluctuations and differential inflation rates can also have a sizeable impact on trade flows.

It should be noted that the specialization measure employed here is derived form export data only. Alternatively, relative export-import ratios for each commodity group are often used.[822] However, these latter ratios are likely to be more influenced by the above-mentioned potential distortive factors than a purely export based measure. To illustrate, from section 7.2 above it is known that Japan has for various reasons a much more closed market for engineering goods than the other countries. Any measure of comparative advantage based on export-import ratios will therefore most likely tend to overstate the relative strength of the Japanese industry in many of the engineering product groups. Another example are the voluntary restraint agreements which exist for Japanese cars in, say, France and Italy; consequently this will tend to overstate the competitiveness of the motor car industries in these two countries when measured on the basis of export-import ratios.

Moreover, specialization indices which take imports into account bear a close resemblance to measures of intra-industry trade. As such, they are less suited to gauge a country's RCA in a specific product group, because the resulting "net" specialization or relative "trade overlap" may simply reflect the demand for differentiated products or trade in intermediate goods falling under the same SITC heading as the final output.

(iii) A comparison of specialization patterns

RCA indices calculated for three years, 1970, 1980 and 1987, for the various product groups and countries are given in Appendix tables 7.2 to 7.5. In addition to the absolute values of the index, the ranking of the product indices within each country is also shown. This allows easier identification of each product group within the hierarchy of specialization in each country.

It should be noted that the "norm structure" of world exports has been approximated by the sum of the exports of the developed market economies, 20 developing market economies and the exports of the seven eastern countries to the two former country groups.[823]

Table 7.3.1 provides a synopsis of the pattern of country specialization by indicating all those sectors for which a country recorded an RCA greater than unity in either 1980 or 1987. As some of the RCA indices are only slightly above unity, suggesting that the comparative advantage is relatively weak, all product groups for which the RCA is relatively strong − 1.25 of higher − have been highlighted. The synoptic tables show a great diversity in country specialization, but they also reveal interesting similarities.

(a) Seven major countries

Looking at the seven major exporters of engineering goods it can be seen that they all show a relatively strong concentration of specialization in mechanical engineering (non-electrical machinery), although there is significant variation with regard to the product groups for which the RCA indexes are greater than unity. France is the only country which does not have any strong specialization in mechanical engineering, and Canada has only one strong comparative advantage in this sector. Only the United States, Japan and the United Kingdom had a strong comparative advantage in office machines and computers (SITC 714) in 1987 − Italy has lost a specialization in this area maintained in 1980. The Federal Republic of Germany, Italy and Japan are all strongly specialized in metalworking machinery. Japan's specialization in this product group has been on a rising trend since 1980.[824] Among the seven major countries the Federal Republic of Germany shows the strongest specialization in the production of industrial machinery (SITC 715-719).

Electrical machinery and apparatus is mainly the domain of the United States and Japan, the pattern of

---

822 These are calculated by dividing the share of a product in a country's total exports of manufactures by the corresponding share in total imports.

823 For the country coverage of these groups see the Statistical appendix to this study.

824 Developments in metalworking machinery are discussed in somewhat more detail in a special section below.

TABLE 7.3.1a
The pattern of specialization in engineering goods exports

△ : Weak specialization
● : Strong specialization

SITC	PRODUCT GROUP	SKI	USA 1980	USA 1987	Japan 1980	Japan 1987	FRG 1980	FRG 1987	France 1980	France 1987	Italy 1980	Italy 1987	UK 1980	UK 1987	Canada 1980	Canada 1987
69	Metal products n.e.s.															
691	Finished structural parts				△			△	●	△	●	●	△			●
692	Metal containers	*						△	●	△	△	△	●	●		
693	Wire products				△			△	△	△	△	●			●	●
694	Nails, screws, nuts	*			●		△	△			●	●			●	△
695	Hand tools						●	●								
696	Cutlery		●	△	△	●							△			
697	Household equipment								△		●	●				
698	Manufactures of metals						△	●	△	△	●	●				
71	Non-electrical machinery															
711	Power generating machinery	*	●	●					△				●	●	●	●
712	Agricultural machinery	*	●	△				△			●	●	●	●	●	△
714	Office machines	*	●	●	●						△		●	●	△	
715	Metalworking machinery	*			△	●	●	●			●	●				
717	Textiles machinery				△	△	●	●			●	●				
718	Machines for special industry	*	●	●			△	●					●	●		
719	Non-electrical machinery, n.e.s.	*	△				●	●	△		●	●	△			
72	Electrical machinery															
722	Electrical power machinery	*			△	△	●	△	△	△			△			
723	Equipment for distrib. electricity		●		●				△		△					
724	Telecom. apparatus	*			●	●										
725	Domestic electrical equipment				△		△		△		●	●				
726	Medical electric apparatus	*	●	●			△		●	●						
729	Other electrical machinery n.e.s.		●	●	△	●							△			
891.1	Phonographs, etc...				●	●									●	△
73	Transport equipment															
731	Railway vehicles	*			●	△			●	●					●	●
732	Road motor vehicles	*			●	●	●	●	△	△					●	●
733	Other road vehicles				●	●	△	△	●	△	●	●				
734	Aircraft	*	●	●						●			△	△	△	●
735	Ships and boats	*			●	●								●		
86	Instruments, etc...															
861	Instruments	*	△	△	●	●	△	△					△	△		
864	Watches and clocks				●	●										

Source: ECE secretariat based on Comtrade data base.

Note: SKI = Skill-intensitive (*)

TABLE 7.3.1b
The pattern of specialization in engineering goods exports

△ : Weak specialization
● : Strong specialization

SITC	PRODUCT GROUP	SKI	Austria 1980 1987	Belgium 1980 1987	Denmark 1980 1987	Finland 1980 1987	Ireland 1980 1987	Netherlands 1980 1987	Norway 1980 1987	Sweden 1980 1987	Switzerland 1980 1987
69	Metal products n.e.s.										
691	Finished structural parts		● ●	●	● ●	● ●		● ●	△	●	
692	Metal containers	*	● ●	● ●	● ●		△	● ●	△ ●	△	
693	Wire products		△ ●	● ●			●		● ●		
694	Nails, screws, nuts	*	△								● ●
695	Hand tools		● ●				●	△		● ●	● ●
696	Cutlery					△		△			● ●
697	Household equipment				● ●		●	△	● △		
698	Manufactures of metals		● ●		● ●		● ●	△	● ●	△ △	△
71	Non-electrical machinery										
711	Power generating machinery	*	●							△	
712	Agricultural machinery	*		△	● ●	●			△ ●		
714	Office machines	*					● ●			△	
715	Metalworking machinery	*	△ △								● ●
717	Textiles machinery										● ●
718	Machines for special industry	*	△ ●		● ●	△ ●				● ●	△ ●
719	Non-electrical machinery, n.e.s.	*	● ●		● ●	△				● ●	● ●
72	Electrical machinery										
722	Electrical power machinery	*	● ●		△ △		△			△	● ●
723	Equipment for distrib. electricity		● ●			● ●	● ●	△		△	
724	Telecom. apparatus	*			△	△		●		● △	
725	Domestic electrical equipment		● ●		● ●		● ●	△	△ △	● △	
726	Medical electric apparatus	*			● ●			● ●		●	
729	Other electrical machinery n.e.s.							△ △		·	● △
891.1	Phonographs, etc...		●								
73	Transport equipment										
731	Railway vehicles	*				●					
732	Road motor vehicles	*		△ ●						△ ●	
733	Other road vehicles		● △		● ●		△	△ △		△	
734	Aircraft	*									
735	Ships and boats	*			● ●	● ●		● △	● ●	●	
86	Instruments, etc...										
861	Instruments	*			● ●		● ●	● ●			● ●
864	Watches and clocks										● ●

Source: ECE secretariat based on Comtrade data base.
Note: SKI = Skill-intensive (*)

TABLE 7.3.1c

The pattern of specialization in engineering goods exports

△: Weak specialization
●: Strong specialization

SITC	PRODUCT GROUP	SKI	Greece 1980 1987	Portugal 1980 1987	Spain 1980 1987	Turkey 1980 1987	Yugoslavia 1980 1987	Hong Kong 1980 1987	Singapore 1980 1987	Republic of Korea 1980 1987	Taiwan 1980 1987
69	Metal products n.e.s.										
691	Finished structural parts				●		● ●			△ ●	
692	Metal containers	*	● ●	● ●	● △		● ●		△		
693	Wire products		● △	●	● ●		●			● ●	△ ●
694	Nails, screws, nuts	*			△ ●		● ●			● ●	● ●
695	Hand tools				● ●	●	● ●				● ●
696	Cutlery		● ●	●	● ●	△		● ●		● ●	● ●
697	Household equipment		●	● ●	● ●	● ●	△ ●	● ●		● ●	● ●
698	Manufactures of metals		△ △		△		△ △	△			● ●
71	Non-electrical machinery										
711	Power generating machinery	*									
712	Agricultural machinery	*					△ ●				
714	Office machines	*						●	●		△
715	Metalworking machinery	*			● △		△ ●				
717	Textiles machinery					●					
718	Machines for special industry	*					△		△		
719	Non-electrical machinery, n.e.s.	*									
72	Electrical machinery										
722	Electrical power machinery	*					△ ●	●	● ●		△
723	Equipment for distrib. electricity		● ●	●	△ △	●	● ●				
724	Telecom. apparatus	*	△					● ●	● ●	● ●	● ●
725	Domestic electrical equipment			● ●	●		● ●	● ●	● ●	●	● ●
726	Medical electric apparatus	*									
729	Other electrical machinery n.e.s.								● ●	△ ●	△
891.1	Phonographs, etc...							△	● ●	● ●	●
73	Transport equipment										
731	Railway vehicles	*	●	●			● ●			● ●	
732	Road motor vehicles	*			△ ●						
733	Other road vehicles						● ●				● ●
734	Aircraft	*									
735	Ships and boats	*			●		● ●		● ●	● ●	
86	Instruments, etc...										
861	Instruments	*									
864	Watches and clocks							● ●	●	● △	●

Source: ECE secretariat based on Comtrade data base.

Note: SKI = Skill-intensive (*)

TABLE 7.3.1d

The pattern of specialization in engineering goods exports

△ : Weak specialization
● : Strong specialization

SITC	PRODUCT GROUP	SKI	Eastern Europe 1980	Eastern Europe 1987	USSR 1980	USSR 1987	Eastern countries 1980	Eastern countries 1987
69	Metal products n.e.s.							
691	Finished structural parts							
692	Metal containers	*	△		●			
693	Wire products		△	●				△
694	Nails, screws, nuts	*	●	●			●	●
695	Hand tools		△					
696	Cutlery							
697	Household equipment		△	●				●
698	Manufactures of metals							
71	Non-electrical machinery							
711	Power generating machinery	*						
712	Agricultural machinery	*	●	●		●	△	●
714	Office machines	*						
715	Metalworking machinery	*	●	●	●	●	●	●
717	textiles machinery							
718	Machines for special industry	*						
719	Non-electrical machinery, n.e.s.	*						
72	Electrical machinery							
722	Electrical power machinery	*						
723	Equipment for distrib. electricity			●				△
724	Telecom. apparatus	*						
725	Domestic electrical equipment		△	●				●
726	Medical electric apparatus	*						
729	Other electrical machinery n.e.s.							
891.1	Phonographs, etc...							
73	Transport equipment							
731	Railway vehicles	*	●	●		●	●	●
732	Road motor vehicles	*						
733	Other road vehicles							
734	Aircraft	*						
735	Ships and boats	*	●		●		●	
86	Instruments, etc...							
861	Instruments	*						
864	Watches and clocks							

Source: ECE secretariat based on Comtrade data base.

Note: SKI = Skill-intensive (*)

specialization of the four major west European countries in this area being rather sparse. In this sector, in 1987, the Federal Republic had a strong advantage only for electrical medical apparatus, while Italy was strong in the relatively low-skilled group of "domestic electrical equipment", including items such as refrigerators and washing machines. It is noteworthy that only Japan among the seven large countries has a strong specialization in telecommunications equipment. The Japanese position is also very strong with regard to phonographs and gramophones (SITC 891.1).

Among the products under transport equipment, only Japan, the Federal Republic of Germany and Canada show a strong specialization in road motor vehicles, whereas the French specialization is relatively weak. In fact, France has a much stronger specialization in railway vehicles and aircraft. For the latter group also the United Kingdom shows a weak comparative advantage.[825] Canada and the United States reveal a strong specialization in aircraft in 1987. In fact, this is a traditional strong point of the United States: the RCA index for aircraft has been the highest of all 29 product groups in 1970, 1980 and 1987 (see Appendix tables 7.2 to 7.4).

The United States, Japan, the Federal Republic of Germany and the United Kingdom all have a revealed comparative advantage for precision instruments (SITC 861), but only the RCA values for Japan signal a relatively strong specialization. Japan is also the only one among the group of seven which has a strong position in watches and clocks.

Neither in 1980 nor in 1987 does the United States show any specialization in the more standardized, unskilled labour-intensive products included in SITC 69 (Metal products n.e.s.). Over the same period there is a conspicuous decline in Japan's specialization in these products: the number of the RCAs greater than unity declined from four to one. In contrast, the Federal Republic of Germany, France and, notably, Italy are still extensively specialized in this area.

There is thus some overlap in the patterns of comparative advantage among the seven major countries, but the dominant feature is diversity of specialization. An interesting feature is the overall weakness of the four major west European countries in electrical engineering, notably telecommunications apparatus. This may be to a large extent explained by specific national policies pursued in this area, which have aimed at fostering "national champions". One of its consequences was the lack of an agreement on European-wide standards, which means that markets are generally too small to allow for significant economies of scale and this reduces price competitiveness in the world market.[826] Japan has extended its specialization from its traditional areas of electrical machinery and transport towards mechanical engineering, thus increasingly competing with western Europe and the United States.

A striking feature is the relatively low degree of specialization of France in engineering goods. There are only two strong points (railway vehicles and aircraft) in 1987, with the remaining RCAs all relatively weak.

(b) The nine smaller west European countries

A similar pattern of diversity exists for the specialization of the nine smaller west European countries (table 7.4.1b). A common feature is that the products of SITC 69 (metal products n.e.s.) form a clear specialization cluster. As noted above, this is a product group characterized by low skill-intensity and for which economies of scale are not very important.

Under non-electrical machinery the strong comparative advantage of Switzerland in machinery production (SITC 715 to 719) is noteworthy, the range of strong specialization being similar to that of the Federal Republic of Germany. It is the only one of the nine smaller countries with a very strong specialization in metalworking and textile machinery. Austria, Denmark, Finland and Sweden — together with Switzerland — have strong comparative advantages in machines for special industries (SITC 718) and the heterogeneous group of machinery n.e.s. (SITC 719). Agricultural machinery (SITC 712) has been a traditional strong point in Denmark and more recently also in Finland and Norway. It is noteworthy that Ireland is the only small country with a strong specialization in office machinery and computers (SITC 714).

In electrical machinery, five of the nine countries (Austria, Denmark, Ireland, Norway and Sweden) show a specialization in domestic electrical equipment while electrical power machinery is a strong point only in Austria and Switzerland. Three countries show a comparative advantage in telecommunications equipment in 1987, namely Denmark, Finland and Sweden. The Netherlands had a strong specialization in this area in 1980, but by 1987 the RCA index had fallen below unity. The degree of specialization in this product group has also weakened in Sweden between 1980 and 1987, whereas neither Denmark nor Finland were specialized in this sector in 1980.

In transport only two of the smaller countries show a strong specialization in road motor vehicles (Belgium and Sweden), while all the Nordic countries (except Sweden) together with the Netherlands are strongly specialized in ships and boats.

Precision instruments etc. (SITC 861) is a point of common strength in Denmark, Ireland, the Netherlands and Switzerland. The latter, not surprisingly, was the only one with a very strong specialization in watches and clocks.[827]

---

[825] This specialization may reflect partly the division of labour between countries participating in the European Airbus project.

[826] See, e.g., "EC seeks to end parochialism in telecommunications", *Financial Times*, 11 July 1988 and "Who turned out the lights?", *The Economist*, 4 February 1988, p.74.

[827] In 1987 the RCA index for watches and clocks for Switzerland was 11.0, the highest value of all the groups in all the countries covered here.

(c) Southern Europe

The five south European countries have their strong points concentrated in the area of standardized, unskilled labour-intensive products, which generally fall into metal products n.e.s.(SITC 69), equipment for distributing electricity (SITC 723) and domestic electrical equipment such as washing machines and refrigerators (SITC 725). Spain and Yugoslavia are the only south European countries with a specialization in metalworking machinery. Turkey shows a remarkable strength in textile and leather machinery. Yugoslavia is also relatively specialized in transport equipment (railway vehicles, other road vehicles and ships and boats), but only Spain has an RCA index greater than unity in road motor vehicles.

It is interesting to compare briefly the south European patterns of specialization with those of the four Asian NIEs. Both regions have broadly similar relative factor endowments in terms of human capital — a dominance of low-skilled labour — and as such are potentially competing for products characterized by high labour-intensive manufacturing, which are being relocated to low-wage countries. It can be seen from table 7.3.1c that there is some overlap in specialization with regard to metal products n.e.s. (SITC 69) and domestic electrical equipment (SITC 725). However, none of the Asian NIEs specializes in equipment for distributing electricity, as all the south European countries do. In contrast, all the NIEs have a strong specialization in telecommunications apparatus and, partly, in office machines and computers, both areas where southern Europe is completely unspecialized. Hong Kong and the Republic of Korea also have a strong comparative advantage in watches and clocks, whereas Singapore and Taiwan, Province of China have lost the comparative advantage they had in this group in 1980. Finally, it is noteworthy that in 1980 all four NIEs had a comparative advantage in phonographs and gramophones etc. but only two had retained this in 1987 (the Republic of Korea and Singapore). This is also an area where none of the south European countries reveals a comparative advantage.

(d) Eastern countries

Although in principle similar specialization indices can be calculated for the eastern countries, any such attempt is confronted with two major practical problems. First, the data can in general be compiled in the necessary detail only for their trade with the market economies. Even aggregate data on exports of manufactures are not easily available. Even if the necessary data for intra-area trade were available, the valuation problems complicate the aggregation of intra- and extra-area trade flows.[828]

Second, there is the general problem of interpretation of these specialization indices for eastern countries, notably when calculated on data for intra-area trade. The underlying assumption behind the construction of RCA indices for market economies is that the revealed pattern of specialization reflects the outcome of a market process leading to an efficient allocation of resources. In other words, the RCA indices are proxies for competitiveness. Given the distortions in the price structure of the eastern countries, the problems of exchange rate determination and the fact that specializations are not the outcome of a market process but of decisions taken by national governments possibly agreed upon within the CMEA, such RCA indices would have to be interpreted in a different manner than those for the market economies.[829] On the other hand, limiting the calculations to trade with countries outside the CMEA does focus on that part of the foreign trade of eastern countries that is directly exposed to international competition. It is therefore interesting to identify the product areas in which these countries specialize in their trade with the "rest of the world". As trade with the market economies is only a relatively small subset of their total exports, it cannot be excluded that the resulting indices provide a somewhat distorted picture of their underlying specialization profile in comparison with the indices for individual market economies. However, the aggregation of the data for the six individual countries may partly compensate for that possibility.

Looking at table 7.3.1d it can be seen[830] that the six east European countries combined had a number of strong points in 1987 in the group of mainly low skill-intensive products, such as domestic electrical equipment, equipment for distributing electricity, wire products, nails and screws, etc. In addition, they also had strongly specialized in skill-intensive products groups (metalworking machinery, agricultural machinery and railway equipment). There are no other specializations within transport equipment in 1987; in fact, for ships and boats, which had been a strong point in 1980, the index was below unity. It is noteworthy that although metalworking machinery remains an area of comparative advantage, the specialization index fell sharply from 2.4 in 1980 to 1.5 in 1987. On the whole the specialization pattern of the six east European countries strongly resembles the average pattern for southern Europe, particularly as regards the specialization in domestic electrical equipment, equipment for distributing electricity and some of the metal products. But there are also differences: agricultural machinery is a weak point in southern Europe, as is textile and leather machinery in eastern Europe.

The indices for the Soviet Union reveal four areas of specialization in 1987. These are metal containers, agricultural machinery, metalworking machinery and

---

[828] See footnote 793.

[829] On this point see W. Bienkowski, "The Applicability of Western Measurement Methods to Assess East European Competitiveness", *Comparative Economic Studies*, Vol.XXX, No.3, Fall 1988, pp.33-50. The author notes that a "positive RCA index for Polish ship exports reflects a specialization decision made at the CMEA level, without necessarily having Polish comparative advantage in mind". p.44).

[830] The values of the RCA indices are shown in Appendix table 7.5.

railway equipment. Note that the last three groups are also areas where eastern Europe is specialized.

(iv) Recent trends in specialization patterns

The previous section was limited to product groups for which countries revealed a comparative advantage in either 1980 or 1987. This highlighted the country specialization patterns and their relative strength but did not characterize the underlying dynamics of changes in RCA indices.

Table 7.3.2 provides a summary of the changes in RCA indices between 1980 and 1987 by at least 0.2 points. Smaller changes than this are assumed to reflect mainly statistical noise. In addition, table 7.3.2 shows changes in RCA values by at least 0.5 index points.

There are a number of conspicuous features in table 7.3.1. First, the number of product groups for which there are significant changes in each country present a striking contrast between Japan on the one hand and the Federal Republic of Germany on the other (table 7.3.2a). Among the seven major countries the number of significant changes is largest (17) in Japan and smallest (only 2) in the Federal Republic of Germany.[831] In the other five countries the number of significant changes ranges from 8 in France and Italy to 12 in the United States.

The United States shows declining specialization indices in some products of SITC 69 and in mechanical engineering (agricultural machinery, office machines and machines for special industries). In contrast, there are significant increases for equipment for distributing electricity, medical apparatus and aircraft.

Japan's areas of increasing specialization are concentrated in non-electrical machinery (notably office machines and computers, but also metal working machinery) and in some parts of electrical engineering (medical apparatus). In contrast, the significant declines are mainly in the area of standardized products in SITC 69 and SITC 723. There is also a relatively strong decline in the RCA index for phonographs, but this group still has the highest RCA value of all the 29 engineering groups in Japan.

The RCA of the four major west European countries improved notably for agricultural machinery (France, Italy and the United Kingdom), but there was a strong decline in the Italian index for office machines. France shows an increasing specialization in railway vehicles and – together with Italy – in aircraft, while in the United Kingdom the largest rise in RCA was recorded for ships and boats.[832]

For the other countries the following features are prominent. Overall, the pattern of comparative advantage of the nine smaller west European countries is not shifting away from the relatively low-skilled product groups in SITC 69 (table 7.3.2b). The main feature is an increase in the RCA index, notably for Belgium, Denmark, the Netherlands and Switzerland.

Several countries show significantly rising specialization indices for products of mechanical engineering, but there is no common pattern with regard to the individual commodity groups. An exception to this is agricultural machinery (SITC 712) and machines for special industries (SITC 718), for which the RCA indices rose in five and six, respectively, of the nine countries.

Electrical machinery is noteworthy for the paucity of significantly rising RCA indices. The main exception is Finland, where there was a considerable strengthening of its comparative advantage in telecommunications equipment. In contrast, there was a weakening of Dutch and Swedish specialization in this group. Five out of the nine countries show declining specialization for domestic electrical equipment. Finally, Denmark, Finland and Norway were able to increase their specialization in electrical medical apparatus (SITC 726).

Among the south European countries there was a strengthening of Yugoslavia's comparative advantage in metal products and non-electrical machinery (table 7.3.2c). For the other countries there was no pervasive increase in specialization indices. Indeed, in Greece and Spain the general tendency was one of declining indices, notably in metal products n.e.s. Among the common features is the increasing specialization in equipment for distributing electricity in Spain, Portugal and Turkey. The latter country also strengthened its specialization in some metal products and especially in textiles machinery.

The most common feature among the four Asian NIEs is the general decline of the RCA indices for watches and clocks (table 7.3.2c). In contrast, the competitive position for office machinery and computers has improved significantly, with the exception of Hong Kong. None of the countries shows a significant change in its comparative advantage in non-electrical machinery other than office machines. Within electrical machinery only the Republic of Korea reveals an increasing specialization, for telecommunications apparatus. Electrical power machinery are areas of increasing specialization in Hong Kong and Singapore, while Taiwan, Province of China and the Republic of Korea show increasing strength for domestic electrical equipment. There is increasing specialization of the Republic of Korea in road motor vehicles which – as in Singapore – is accompanied by a declining specialization for ships and boats.

In eastern Europe there was a marked increase in the specialization index for agricultural machinery and for household equipment. As already noted above, there was a strong decline in the index for metalworking

---

[831] The overall stability in the specialization pattern of the Federal Republic of Germany is also illustrated by the fact that the number of significant changes is the smallest of all the 25 countries covered here.

[832] Shipbuilding is a classical example of how RCA indices may on occasion provide a distorted picture of a country's underlying comparative advantage. This sector receives heavy subsidies in many countries and the level of and changes in the RCA indices for ships and boats should be interpreted with care.

TABLE 7.3.2a

Recent trends in RCA - indices: 1980-1987

++ (− −) : Increase (Decrease) of more than 0.5 points
+ (−)   : Increase (Decrease) of 0.2 - 0.5 points

SITC	PRODUCT GROUP	SKI	USA	Japan	FRG	France	Italy	U K	Canada
69	Metal products n.e.s.								
691	Finished structural parts		−	− −		−	−	−	+
692	Metal containers	*		−	+				
693	Wire products		−	− −			+		+ +
694	Nails, screws, nuts	*		− −					
695	Hand tools		−						
696	Cutlery			− −					−
697	Household equipment		−						+
698	Manufactures of metals								
71	Non-electrical machinery								
711	Power generating machinery	*		+		+		−	+
712	Agricultural machinery	*		+		+	+	+	− −
714	Office machines	*		+ +			− −		−
715	Metalworking machinery	*	+			−			
717	Textiles machinery					−		+	−
718	Machines for special industry	*	− −		+				−
719	Non-electrical machinery, n.e.s.	*	−			−	+		
72	Electrical machinery								
722	Electrical power machinery	*							
723	Equipment for distrib. electricity		+ +	− −			−	−	
724	Telecom. apparatus	*							
725	Domestic electrical equipment								
726	Medical electric apparatus	*	+	+					−
729	Other electrical machinery n.e.s.			+					
891.1	Phonographs, etc...		−	− −					− −
73	Transport equipment								
731	Railway vehicles	*		−		+ +		−	−
732	Road motor vehicles	*				−			
733	Other road vehicles					−	−	−	
734	Aircraft	*	+ +			+ +	+	−	
735	Ships and boats	*		−				+ +	−
86	Instruments, etc...								
861	Instruments	*							
864	Watches and clocks			−					

Source: ECE/DEAP based on Appendix tables.

Note: SKI = Skill-intensitive (*)

TABLE 7.3.2b
Recent trends in RCA - indices: 1980-1987

++ (− −) : Increase (Decrease) of more than 0.5 points
+ (−) : Increase (Decrease) of 0.2 - 0.5 points

SITC	PRODUCT GROUP	SKI	Austria	Belgium	Denmark	Finland	Ireland	Netherlands	Norway	Sweden	Switzerland
69	Metal products n.e.s.										
691	Finished structural parts		+	++	++	++		++	+	++	+
692	Metal containers	*		++	+		−		++	+	+
693	Wire products					++	+		− −		
694	Nails, screws, nuts	*							−		+
695	Hand tools						+	+		−	+
696	Cutlery		−			−	−				++
697	Household equipment		−		−		− −		−		
698	Manufactures of metals		+		+		− −		+		+
71	Non-electrical machinery										
711	Power generating machinery	*	++						−		−
712	Agricultural machinery	*		+	+	++	−	+	+		
714	Office machines	*				++				− −	
715	Metalworking machinery	*									++
717	Textiles machinery	−	+								− −
718	Machines for special industry	*	+			++	−	+	+	+	+
719	Non-electrical machinery, n.e.s.	*				+					+
72	Electrical machinery										
722	Electrical power machinery	*				+	−			+	
723	Equipment for distrib. electricity		+			− −	++	−		−	+
724	Telecom. apparatus	*				++		− −		−	
725	Domestic electrical equipment				− −		−		−	−	−
726	Medical electric apparatus	*		−	++	+		−	++	− −	
729	Other electrical machinery n.e.s.				−						
891.1	Phonographs, etc...		++		−				−		
73	Transport equipment										
731	Railway vehicles	*			+	++	−		+		+
732	Road motor vehicles	*		+			−				
733	Other road vehicles				+	+			−		
734	Aircraft	*							+	+	
735	Ships and boats	*		−	++	− −		−	++	− −	
86	Instruments, etc...										
861	Instruments	*					−	+			−
864	Watches and clocks										++

Source: ECE/DEAP based on Appendix tables.
Note: SKI = Skill-intensive (*)

TABLE 7.3.2c

Recent trends in RCA - indices: 1980-1987

++ (− −) : Increase (Decrease) of more than 0.5 points
+ (−) : Increase (Decrease) of 0.2 - 0.5 points

SITC	PRODUCT GROUP	SKI	Greece	Portugal	Spain	Turkey	Yugoslavia	Hong Kong	Singapore	Republic of Korea	Taiwan
69	Metal products n.e.s.						−				
691	Finished structural parts		−	−	− −		+ +			+ +	+
692	Metal containers	*	− −		− −	+		+ +	−	+	−
693	Wire products		− −	− −	−		+ +		−	− −	+
694	Nails, screws, nuts	*				+ +					+ +
695	Hand tools					+ +	+				+
696	Cutlery			+ +		− −				− −	
697	Household equipment		− −			− −	+ +				+ +
698	Manufactures of metals		−			+			−		+
71	Non-electrical machinery										
711	Power generating machinery	*		+ +	+		−				
712	Agricultural machinery	*					+ +				
714	Office machines	*		−				−	+ +	+ +	+ +
715	Metalworking machinery	*			−		+ +				
717	Textiles machinery					+ +					−
718	Machines for special industry	*					+ +		− −		
719	Non-electrical machinery, n.e.s.	*				+	+				−
72	Electrical machinery										
722	Electrical power machinery	*					+	+ +	+ +		+
723	Equipment for distrib. electricity		− −	+ +	+	+ +	−	+			−
724	Telecom. apparatus	*		−					− −	+ +	− −
725	Domestic electrical equipment		−			− −	−		−	+ +	+ +
726	Medical electric apparatus	*					−				
729	Other electrical machinery n.e.s.			−					−	− −	−
891.1	Phonographs, etc...			+				−		+ +	− −
73	Transport equipment										
731	Railway vehicles	*	+	− −	− −						−
732	Road motor vehicles	*			+	−				+	
733	Other road vehicles		− −							+	+ +
734	Aircraft	*	+	−					−	−	
735	Ships and boats	*			−		− −			− −	− −
86	Instruments, etc...										
861	Instruments	*	−					+			
864	Watches and clocks			−				− −	− −	− −	− −

Source: ECE/DEAP based on Appendix tables.
Note: SKI = Skill-intensive (*)

TABLE 7.3.2d

Recent trends in RCA - indices: 1980 - 1987

+ + (− −): Increase (Decrease) of more than 0.5 points
+ (−): Increase (Decrease) of 0.2 - 0.5 points

SITC	PRODUCT GROUP	SKI	Eastern Europe	USSR	Eastern countries
69	Metal products n.e.s.				
691	Finished structural parts		−		+
692	Metal containers	*	− −	+ +	
693	Wire products		+		+
694	Nails, screws, nuts	*			
695	Hand tools		−		
696	Cutlery		+		+
697	Household equipment		+ +	+	+ +
698	Manufactures of metals				
71	Non-electrical machinery				
711	Power generating machinery	*		−	−
712	Agricultural machinery	*	+	+ +	+ +
714	Office machines	*			
715	Metalworking machinery	*	− −	+ +	−
717	Textiles machinery		−		
718	Machines for special industry	*		+	
719	Non-electrical machinery, n.e.s.	*			
72	Electrical machinery				
722	Electrical power machinery	*			
723	Equipment for distribution electricity		+	.	+
724	Telecom. apparatus	*		+	
725	Domestic electrical equipment		+	+ +	+
726	Medical electrical apparatus	*			
729	Other electrical machinery n.e.s.				
891.1	Phonographs, etc...				
73	Transport equipment				
731	Railway vehicles	*	+	+ +	+ +
732	Road motor vehicles	*		+	
733	Other road vehicles				
734	Aircraft	*		−	
735	Ships and boats	*	−	− −	− −
86	Instruments, etc...				
861	Instruments	*			
864	Watches and clocks				

Source: ECE/DEAP based on Appendix tables.
Note: SKI = Skill-intensitive (*)

machinery. The other changes in table 7.3.2d are much less pronounced.

The most striking feature in the changing pattern of comparative advantage in the Soviet Union is the strongly rising specialization in railway equipment, agricultural machinery, metal containers and metalworking machinery. Indeed, the changes in the indices are very large, as can be seen from the data in table 7.3.2d. It is noteworthy that the Soviet Union was only specialized in one of these four areas (metalworking machinery) in 1980. Table 7.3.2d also reveals a strong rise in the specialization index for domestic electrical equipment, although the index was still lower than unity (0.82) in 1987. There is also a significant rise in the index for telecommunications apparatus from 0.1 in 1980 to 0.4 in 1987 but it is clear from these data that the Soviet Union is still a long way to go to before establishing a significant specialization in this area.

(v) A brief digression: Country specialization in machine-tools

The analysis of patterns of revealed comparative above was limited to the three-digit SITC product groups. Although an examination of specialization patterns at a more disaggregated classification of commodities would yield additional interesting insights into the diversity of comparative advantage such an exercise is beyond the scope of the present study. There is, however, one particular product group at the four-digit SITC-level which merits an exception, namely, machine tools for working metals (SITC 715.1).

The share of this product group in world exports of engineering goods was less than 2 per cent in 1987, about the same as the share of machine-tools in total manufacturing output. Nevertheless, this figure is highly misleading when it comes to judging the strategic importance of this sector, which can be regarded as the "spider in the industrial web".[833] Indeed, the machine-tool industry plays a key role in the diffusion of technological advances in many industrial sectors. This implies that machine-tools have a major impact on the productive efficiency and competitiveness in other manufacturing sectors. Against this background the need has been emphasized to maintain a leading role in machine tool development to avoid excessive dependence on imports for the latest technology.[834] It is also noteworthy that machine tools are important in weapons production, an area where maintaining a technological lead and domestic supply is frequently regarded as a matter of national security.[835]

The machine-tool industry itself has undergone substantial change as a result of recent advances in micro-electronics. Indeed, the introduction and application of electronic control can be regarded as "the most important technical change affecting the machine-tool industry since the 1970s".[836] Industrial robots and computer numerical controls (CNC) machine tools have entered a period of rapid diffusion in the industrialized countries, a reflection of the fact that the competitiveness of both machine-tool producers and users is now crucially dependent on these technologies. Related developments are the growing use of computer-aided design and manufacture (CAD-CAM) together with the so-called advanced flexible manufacturing systems (FMS).[837] It is in the area of CNC machine tools and industrial robots that Japanese firms have gained considerable ground in world markets, although more recently west European firms have been able to catch up.[838]

The advance of Japan in the market for machine-tools is clearly reflected in the dramatic rise of the relevant specialization index from 0.4 in 1970 to 1.6 in 1987 (table 7.3.3). Among the west European countries machine tools have been traditionally a strong specialization of the Federal Republic of Germany, Italy and Switzerland. In the first two countries the RCA values for 1987 are both somewhat below those for 1980 and 1970, suggesting a slight deterioration of the overall competitive position over this period.

The steep fall of the RCA values of the United Kingdom between 1970 and 1987 illustrates a significant loss in international competitiveness in machine-tools.[839] In contrast, France has never been specialized in machine-tools, but its already weak position in 1970 deteriorated further, as illustrated by the declining RCA index between 1970 and 1987. A similar trend can be observed for the United States.

---

833 See Peter O'Brien, *Machine tools : Growing internationalisation in a small firm industry*, The Economist Intelligence Unit, Multinational Business, No.4, 1987, p.23.

834 For the United States see "The Competitive Status of the US Machine Tool Industry: A Study of the Influences in Determining International Industrial Competitive Advantage", prepared by the Machine Tool Panel, Committee on Technology and International Economic and Trade Issues of the Office of the Foreign Secretary, National Academy on Engineering and the Commission of Engineering and Technical Systems, National Research Council, National Academy Press, Washington, D.C. 1983. For the European Community see "The foreign trade of the Community, the United States of America and Japan", *European Economy*, No.16, July 1983, pp.107-117.

835 See "The Competitive Status of the U.S. Machine Tool Industry... ", *loc.cit.*, p.7.

836 E. Sciberras and B.D. Payne, *Machine Tool Industry, Technical Change and International Competitiveness*, London, 1985.

837 See, e.g., Economic Commission for Europe, *Recent Trends in Flexible Manufacturing*, United Nations, New York, 1986 and E.-J. Horn, H. Klodt and C. Saunders, "Advanced machine tools: production, diffusion and trade", in *Europe and the New Technologies. Six Case Studies in Innovation and Adjustment*, ed. M. Sharp. Ithaca, New York, 1986, pp.46-86.

838 A detailed analysis of these developments goes far beyond the scope of this study. See, e.g., E.J. Horn et. al., *op. cit.*

839 It has been noted elsewhere that in the 1960s the United Kingdom was ahead of its European competitors in both knowledge and the use of NC technlogy. "The virtual collapse of this advantage ... is sad testimony of the deep-rooted ills of the British economy ... it illustrates the British ability to grasp highly technical, highly sophisticated new technologies, but their abject failure to diffuse them more widely..." see: E.-J. Horn, H. Klodt and C. Saunders, *loc.cit.*, p.80.

TABLE 7.3.3

Machine tools (SITC, Rev.1: 715.1)
(Percentages)

	1970	1980	1987
Panel A: World export market shares [a]			
Germany, Fed.Rep. of	32.8	28.1	26.5
Japan	4.3	14.9	24.5
Switzerland	2.5	2.4	11.7
Italy	9.1	8.7	8.5
United States	14.5	8.3	5.4
Total 5 countries	69.9	68.9	76.6
France	5.5	5.3	2.3
Taiwan	0.1	1.8	2.3
Belgium	1.6	1.4	2.2
Spain	1.3	2.3	1.8
Sweden	2.1	1.9	1.6
Austria	1.0	1.4	1.6
Yugoslavia	0.3	0.7	1.4
Total 12 countries	81.8	83.7	89.8
Memorandum items:			
EC (9)	60.8	52.1	45.2
EFTA (6)	12.3	12.3	15.1
Southern Europe	1.7	3.2	3.4
Four Asian NIEs	0.2	2.4	3.1
Eastern Europe (6)	3.8	3.3	1.6
Soviet Union	1.1	0.7	0.4
Panel B: Indices of revealed comparative advantage [b]			
United States	0.86	0.59	0.47
Japan	0.40	1.21	1.61
Germany, Fed.Rep. of	1.85	1.72	1.55
France	0.71	0.65	0.32
Italy	1.09	1.32	1.25
United Kingdom	1.40	0.84	0.63
Austria	0.75	0.93	1.00
Belgium	0.32	0.31	0.53
Denmark	0.62	0.66	0.53
Sweden	0.69	0.77	0.64
Switzerland	3.40	3.33	4.20
Spain	1.69	1.56	1.12
Yugoslavia	0.51	1.12	2.40
Taiwan	0.16	0.99	0.98
Memorandum items:			
Eastern Europe (6)	2.96	2.72	1.72
Soviet Union	3.40	1.41	1.46

Source: ECE secretariat based on COMTRADE data base.

Note: Data for eastern countries cover only exports to DMEs and 20 developing countries. See Statistical appendices.

[a] Based on rankings in 1987.
[b] Only countries with an RCA-value of at least 0.5 in any of the relevant years are shown.

Among the other countries only Spain and Yugoslavia reveal a specialization in machine-tools, although the Spanish RCA values suggest a declining competitiveness after 1980. Austria is a border case, with a specialization index of unity in 1987, only slightly higher than in 1980.

Machine tools do not play an important role in the overall export performance of the Asian NIEs: only Taiwan, Province of China shows a relatively strong specialization in machine tools with an RCA index of just below unity.[840]

Finally, it is noticeable that the specialization index for machine-tools has fallen sharply in eastern Europe although the region as a whole continues to maintain a relatively strong specialization for this product group. The same holds for the Soviet Union, where the index declined from 3.4 in 1970 to 1.4 in 1980, but remained stable thereafter.

(vi) A statistical analysis of RCA patterns

The focus in the preceding section was on the specific strengths and weaknesses of individual countries in the engineering sector, as indicated by RCA indices. In this section there is an examination − using relatively simple statistical indicators − of some *general* characteristics of RCA patterns. Do large countries systematically show more specializations than smaller countries? How diversified is the RCA pattern of individual countries and how has this changed over time? Has the overall hierarchy of specialization undergone significant changes? Do large countries tend to specialize more in product groups that have a relatively large share of world exports of engineering goods and vice versa? How different are the specializations of the three major countries from each other and what is the "distance" between the specialization pattern of the "big three" and the other countries? And finally, is there a systematic pattern of RCA changes over time, i.e., is there a pervasive specialization trend?

(a) Specialization patterns and the size of the domestic market

A factor which is now recognized to have considerable importance in the context of international competitiveness is the ability to exploit economies of scale.[841] Basically, the assumption is that, for a given product, firms operating in a larger market may more fully exploit economies of scale and, consequently, become more competitive *vis-à-vis* firms operating in a smaller market with a correspondingly reduced plant size. Thus it has often been argued that the higher labour productivity and lower unit costs of US firms relative to their west European counterparts, is a consequence of the exploitation of economies of scale made possible by the size of the US market. It is therefore interesting to examine briefly to what extent the specialization patterns for engineering goods reflect the relative domestic market size of the individual countries. This is done by looking at two indicators, namely, the total number of product groups in which a country has an RCA index greater than unity on the one hand, and the degree of diversification of revealed comparative advantage, on the other. These two indicators may be related to each other since, it may be surmised, the existence of a large domestic market allows firms to exploit economies of scale for a wider range of products than is possible for

---

[840] The RCA value for the Republic of Korea was only 0.11 in 1987, 0.27 for Singapore and 0.06 for Hong Kong.

[841] Economies of scale are generally defined as reductions in unit costs resulting from an increase in the quantity of output produced by a firm.

companies in smaller countries. In a similar vein, it might also be expected that the size of the domestic market is an important determinant of the diversification of a country's export structure and, correspondingly, its pattern of comparative advantage.[842] Thus, it might be expected that smaller countries will tend to develop a strong specialization in a few sectors while larger countries will show a more even distribution of RCA indices.

Table 7.3.4 shows the total number of product groups per country for which the specialization index takes on a value greater than unity, together with a breakdown of the specializations for skill-intensive and unskilled-intensive product groups, respectively.

In 1987 (table 7.3.4) the largest number of specialized sectors is for the Federal Republic of Germany (17), followed, somewhat surprisingly, by Yugoslavia (16).[843] Japan and Austria had a revealed comparative advantage for 15 product groups, followed by Denmark with 14. Italy, Switzerland and Republic of Korea are specialized in 12 out of 29 product groups, followed by the Netherlands, Sweden, Spain and Taiwan, Province of China (each with 11) and France (10). The United States has the same number of specialized sectors (9) as Canada, the United Kingdom and Finland. The number of engineering specializations is relatively low in Belgium,[844] Portugal, Greece and Turkey.

In general, the number of specializations in skill-intensive products is greater than for unskilled-intensive groups in the seven major countries, with the exception of Italy. Among the smaller countries this is also true for Denmark, Finland and Sweden, whereas in the Netherlands and Ireland the large majority of specializations is in unskilled intensive products. In the south European countries (with the exception of Yugoslavia) the sometimes very low number of total specializations are predominantly in relatively unskilled activities. Turkey has no specialization in skill-intensive products.

The total number of specializations generally remained fairly stable between 1970 and 1987. The most striking change occurred in the United Kingdom, where the number of specialized product groups fell from 16 in 1970 to 9 in 1987, the decline, however, being located entirely in unskilled labour-intensive products. In Japan, the number of specialized product groups has doubled from five to ten between 1970 and 1987, and this was accompanied after 1980 by a strong shift away from unskilled labour-intensive products. The Federal Republic of Germany and France increased their specialization in skill-intensive products between 1970 and 1987, while it declined in the United States.

Among the smaller countries, skill-intensive products account for all of the increase in the number of specializations in Austria and Finland; in the others the distribution between the two skill groups did not change very much between 1970 and 1987. Among the Asian NIEs, there was a conspicuous increase in the number of specialized sectors in Republic of Korea, from only two in 1970 to 11 in 1980. Whereas in 1970 this country had no specialization in the group of skill-intensive goods, by 1987 it had a comparative advantage in four of them. There was a similar development in Taiwan, Province of China.

The data in table 7.3.4 do not suggest a strong and systematic influence of the domestic market size on the number of specialized product groups. The only clear feature is the low degree of representation of some of the south European countries in the field of skill-intensive products. Apart from that, the overall pattern is blurred and does not point to any clear relationship: many of the smaller countries have as many or more specializations than the larger countries both in total and in the skill-intensive groups.

Thus it appears that the size of the domestic market may not be an important hindrance to firms specializing in a given product group. Indeed, the data suggest that firms in smaller countries overcome the limitations of the domestic market by exporting, which in turn allows them to achieve the necessary economies of scale and become competitive in the world market. Although it is not visible at the level of commodity aggregation employed in the present study, such competitiveness is often achieved by specialization in intermediate goods.[845]

What about the relative comparative advantage of countries in the production of skill-intensive goods? Table 7.3.5 shows that in 1987 only a handful of countries possessed such a global specialization. This was the case for the United States, Japan, the Federal Republic of Germany, Canada, Ireland, Sweden and

---

[842] "It can be expected that large countries will tend to have a more diversified export structure, mainly because their large domestic markets permit the exploitation of economies of scale in a wide range of industries." See Bela Balassa, "'Revealed' Comparative Advantage Revisited ... ", *loc.cit.*, p.337.

[843] The large number of specializations shown for Yugoslavia is somewhat unexpected. On closer inspection it appears that this may be a "captive" market effect rather than a reflection of broadly based economic strength. In contrast to the market economies, Yugoslavia's exports are heavily oriented towards the eastern countries. Thus, in 1987 about 48 per cent of Yugoslavia's engineering goods exports were shipped to these markets. It is striking that out of the 16 specializations in 1987 only three are accounted for by product groups where exports to the developed market economies account for more than half of all shipments. These are SITC groups 697, 725 and 733, i.e., household equipment of base metals, domestic electrical equipment and road vehicles other than motor vehicles. A similar pattern emerges for the other years, too. This suggests that eastern and developing countries may provide Yugoslav firms with an outlet for goods which would have difficulties in meeting western standards of quality and technical sophistication.

[844] Note that in 1987 Belgium had the smallest number of product specializations in engineering goods among the nine smaller west European countries. Of the five specializations, three were for skill-intensive products. This relatively low degree of representation in skill-intensive products agrees with other findings suggesting that Belgium is relatively well endowed with physical capital but that human capital is a scarce factor. It has been claimed, however, that this does not reflect an inherent weakness in skill-intensive goods but is rather the result of a bias in public policy in favour of physical capital to the detriment of human capital. See P.K.M. Tharakan, J. Waelbroeck, "Has Human Capital become a Scarce Factor in Belgium?" in *Cahiers Economiques de Bruxelles*, No.118, 1988, pp.159-171.

[845] See also Cliff Pratten, *A Survey of Economies of Scale*, Economic Papers No.67, October 1988, Commission of the European Communities, p.39: "Easy access and close proximity to a large market provides firms with advantages for developing products and marketing. Firms in relatively small countries may circumvent their small market by exporting, and protecting their position in foreign markets by investment. They may also tend to specialize in producing intermediate goods for the sale to other firms to avoid a marketing disadvantage for production costs. Such specialization can be self-reinforcing".

TABLE 7.3.4

Country specialization in engineering goods exports
(Number of specialized product groups)

	Skill-intensive			Unskilled-intensive			Total		
	1970	1980	1987	1970	1980	1987	1970	1980	1987
Seven major countries									
Germany, Fed.Rep. of	7	8	10	7	6	7	14	14	17
United States	10	8	7	2	1	2	12	9	9
Japan	5	9	10	7	9	5	12	18	15
France	4	5	6	5	7	4	9	12	10
Italy	5	6	5	6	8	7	11	14	12
United Kingdom	8	9	8	8	2	1	16	11	9
Canada	5	8	6	2	1	3	7	9	9
Nine smaller countries									
Austria	4	5	7	8	7	8	12	12	15
Belgium	2	2	3	1	1	2	3	3	5
Denmark	9	8	9	4	5	5	13	13	14
Finland	2	2	6	3	3	3	5	5	9
Ireland	3	4	2	5	4	5	8	8	7
Netherlands	5	5	4	7	5	7	12	10	11
Norway	2	3	4	5	4	4	7	7	8
Sweden	7	7	7	2	5	4	9	12	11
Switzerland	6	6	6	4	5	6	10	11	12
Southern Europe									
Greece	1	1	1	2	5	3	3	6	4
Portugal	2	3	1	5	3	4	7	6	5
Spain	5	6	4	9	7	7	14	13	11
Turkey	-	-	-	2	3	4	2	3	4
Yugoslavia	5	7	8	8	7	8	13	14	16
Asian NIEs									
Hong Kong	1	3	2	5	5	4	6	8	6
Singapore	3	5	4	5	4	3	8	9	7
Republic of Korea	-	5	4	2	6	8	2	11	12
Taiwan	1	2	4	4	11	7	5	13	11
Eastern countries									
Eastern Europe (6)	3	6	4	5	4	4	8	10	8
Soviet Union	5	2	4	3	-	-	8	2	4

Source: ECE secretariat based on COMTRADE data base.
Note: The total number of product groups is 29.

Singapore. The United Kingdom shows an index greater than unity only for 1970 and 1980, whereas in France the index was just below unity in all three years. Italy is noteworthy for its declining average specialization in skill-intensive goods. For the majority of the smaller countries the specialization index is clearly below unity in all the years shown without in general any strong upward trend discernible between 1980 and 1987: the major exceptions to this are Finland, Spain and the Republic of Korea. The eastern economies are also clearly not specialized in skill-intensive engineering products.

Is there any pattern with regard to the overall degree of diversification in countries' specialization patterns? Table 7.3.6 shows for each country the coefficients of variation of the RCA indices for each of the years 1970, 1980 and 1987. (The smaller the coefficient the greater the degree of diversification in the overall specialization pattern in engineering goods exports.)

The coefficients conform in general to expectations, although there are some striking exceptions. The greatest diversification in the specialization pattern is in the Federal Republic of Germany and France, but it is also very high in other large countries such as Japan, Italy and the United Kingdom. In contrast, the smaller countries such as Norway, Switzerland, the Netherlands, Greece, Turkey and Portugal have the largest coefficients of variation. However, these data also suggest that there is no simple association between domestic market size and the degree of export diversification. Thus, smaller countries such as Austria, Denmark, the Netherlands, Sweden and Spain have roughly the same degree of export diversification as the United Kingdom, Italy and Japan and their coefficients of variation are even smaller than those of Canada and the United States.

It is noteworthy that in the large majority of countries the specialization patterns have tended to become more diversified over time, as suggested by the declining coefficients of variation between 1970 and 1987. In the United States (1980-1987), Italy and the United Kingdom, however, the tendency was for a decline in export diversification. In the Federal Republic of Germany export diversification narrowed only slightly between 1970 and 1987, but in all three years the coefficient of variation was the lowest of all the countries.

TABLE 7.3.5

Indices of revealed comparative advantage: skill-intensive engineering goods

	1970	1980	1987
Seven major countries			
United States	1.37	1.32	1.31
Japan	0.96	1.29	1.38
Germany, Fed.Rep. of	1.11	1.13	1.11
France	0.94	0.99	0.95
Italy	0.87	0.81	0.76
United Kingdom	1.07	1.07	0.99
Canada	1.41	1.25	1.37
Nine smaller countries			
Austria	0.58	0.68	0.72
Belgium	0.61	0.69	0.76
Denmark	1.03	0.96	0.85
Finland	0.52	0.54	0.71
Ireland	0.46	0.79	1.07
Netherlands	0.65	0.69	0.67
Norway	0.92	0.86	0.97
Sweden	1.17	1.15	1.12
Switzerland	0.66	0.71	0.68
Southern Europe			
Greece	0.10	0.11	0.08
Portugal	0.25	0.40	0.37
Spain	0.74	0.78	0.88
Turkey	0.03	0.21	0.18
Yugoslavia	0.73	0.75	0.70
Four Asian NIEs			
Hong Kong	0.17	0.32	0.41
Republic of Korea	0.10	0.42	0.61
Singapore	0.72	0.95	1.09
Taiwan	0.41	0.48	0.55
Eastern countries			
Eastern Europe	0.57	0.57	0.41
Soviet Union	0.66	0.55	0.63

Source: ECE secretariat based on COMTRADE data base.

Note: For the definition of skill-intensive goods, see Statistical appendices.

TABLE 7.3.6

Diversification of comparative advantage
(Coefficients of variation of RCA indices)

	1970	1980	1987
Seven major countries			
United States	0.75	0.74	0.96
Japan	0.82	0.72	0.67
Germany, Fed.Rep. of	0.36	0.35	0.34
France	0.45	0.35	0.40
Italy	0.72	0.61	0.65
United Kingdom	0.38	0.43	0.59
Canada	1.00	0.89	0.96
Nine smaller countries			
Austria	0.66	0.63	0.63
Belgium	1.00	0.70	0.87
Denmark	0.84	0.68	0.75
Finland	1.42	1.20	1.01
Ireland	1.11	1.06	1.49
Netherlands	0.68	0.60	0.64
Norway	1.95	1.88	2.37
Sweden	0.72	0.70	0.67
Switzerland	2.36	1.55	1.53
Southern Europe			
Greece	2.00	1.72	1.74
Portugal	1.22	0.72	1.20
Spain	1.02	0.75	0.65
Turkey	2.29	1.67	1.86
Yugoslavia	1.24	0.92	0.84
Asian NIEs			
Hong Kong	1.59	2.23	2.20
Singapore	1.50	1.08	1.08
Republic of Korea	2.16	1.21	1.01
Taiwan	1.45	0.92	1.11
Eastern countries			
Eastern Europe	0.65	0.74	0.79
Soviet Union	1.03	0.92	1.66

Source: ECE secretariat based on data in Appendix tables 2.4.2-2.4.5.

(b) Specialization patterns: The role of world market size

If relative domestic market size does not bear a close association to the specialization patterns of individual countries in engineering goods, it may be more appropriate to inquire whether the size of the relevant world markets for the various product groups is a more important influence on national specializations. Again the hypothesis is based on the exploitation of economies of scale: the larger the world market the greater the potential economies of scale for any one country although firms in large countries might be in a better starting position to exploit these potential benefits because of the initial cost advantages from their larger domestic market.

Table 7.3.7 shows the Spearman rank correlation coefficients between a country's share of world exports in 29 product groups and the corresponding RCA index, in 1970, 1980 and 1987.

The large majority of coefficients is very small and not statistically significant: this is particularly so for the four large west European countries. World market size and national specialization patterns do not, in general, appear to be associated.

There was, however, a clear and highly significant tendency for the United States and Japan (in 1987) to specialize in product groups with large world markets. For the United States this is so in all three years examined, but for Japan only in 1987. The changes in the correlation coefficient for Japan between 1970 and 1987 are noteworthy for they suggest that the Japanese specialization pattern has moved away from relatively unimportant products to those which yield considerable gains from scale and long production runs. In 1970, the RCA pattern for Japan was still negatively correlated with the size of the world markets for the various commodity groups.[846]

For some of the smaller countries there is a negative association between world market size and the specialization hierarchy. In 1987 this was the case for the Netherlands and the south European countries (except Portugal) and two of the Asian NIEs (Republic of Korea and Taiwan, Province of China). In striking

---

[846] Note that world markets are measured here on the basis of export data. It would in principle be more appropriate to measure world market size by total consumption. However, these data are not available for detailed commodity groups.

contrast, there is a positive and statistically significant association in Singapore.

(c) Specialization patterns: The overlap among the three major exporters

World exports of engineering goods are dominated by three countries, namely, Japan, the Federal Republic of Germany and the United States. Their combined share in total world exports of engineering goods over the last two decades averaged some 47 per cent (see table 7.3.7). The most noticeable feature of developments in the world market for engineering goods over this period has been the dramatic expansion of Japanese exports which has propelled this country to the top of the export league in 1987. More recently, the Asian NIEs have become increasingly involved in trade in engineering goods and have begun to challenge the the developed market economies in areas where the latter have well-established comparative advantages.[847] It is therefore interesting to examine whether this change in the world map of engineering goods exports has been accompanied by greater similarity in the inter-industry specialization patterns of the three major countries. The question also arises as to whether smaller countries, such as the Asian NIEs, are following in the footsteps of the three major countries.

Table 7.3.8 shows, for 1970, 1980 and 1987, the rank correlation coefficients between the RCA indices of the three major exporters (the Federal Republic of Germany, Japan and the United States) and those of 24 other countries.
The data underline that there was no significant association at all between the specialization hierarchies of Japan, on the one hand, and the United States and the Federal Republic of Germany on the other, in 1987 (chart 7.3.1). This contrasts with the situation in 1970 and 1980 when there was a statistically significant and negative association between the US and Japanese specialization patterns. Given the stability of the RCA rankings for the United States, in contrast with Japan's,[848] this means that there has been a clear tendency for changes in Japan's revealed comparative advantage to reverse the negative association prevailing in 1980. However, these changes were not large enough to lead to a positive association between the two specialization patterns until 1987. There was also a significant negative association between the RCA pattern of the Federal Republic of Germany and Japan in 1970, but it was much weaker than that between the US and Japan and by 1980 it was longer significant. In general the difference between the engineering specialization patterns of Japan and the Federal Republic has changed only slightly over the period examined here. There was

TABLE 7.3.7

Correlations between world market shares in engineering goods exports and the RCA index in each country
(Spearman rank correlation coefficients)

	1970	1980	1987
Germany, Fed.Rep. of	-0.03	0.03	-0.07
United States	0.57*	0.53*	0.49*
Japan	-0.33**	-0.03	0.46*
France	-0.13	-0.12	-0.13
Italy	-0.03	-0.24	-0.28
United Kingdom	-0.03	0.32	0.28
Canada	0.24	0.18	0.09
Austria	-0.49*	0.18	-0.10
Belgium	-0.25	-0.10	-0.21
Denmark	0.04	0.01	-0.15
Finland	-0.24	-0.12	-0.23
Ireland	-0.35**	-0.02	-0.06
Netherlands	-0.25	-0.16	-0.33**
Norway	-0.25	-0.07	-0.20
Sweden	0.17	0.28	0.27
Switzerland	0.04	-0.09	-0.18
Greece	-0.10	-0.40	-0.59*
Portugal	-0.33**	-0.23	-0.15
Spain	-0.33**	-0.50*	-0.38**
Turkey	-0.40	-0.23	-0.35**
Yugoslavia	-0.37**	-0.30	-0.37**
Hong Kong	-0.11	-0.15	-0.06
Singapore	0.12	0.35**	0.42**
Republic of Korea	0.01	-0.40**	-0.36**
Taiwan	0.27	-0.43**	-0.33**
Eastern Europe (6)	-0.56*	-0.36**	-0.57*
Soviet Union	0.02	0.37**	0.04

Source: ECE secretariat based on COMTRADE data base.

Note: * = significant at 1 per cent, ** = significant at 5 per cent (one-tailed test).

no significant relationship between the US and German RCA patterns in any of the three years for which the calculations made.

What about the association between the RCA pattern of the three major countries on the one hand and the remaining 21 countries on the other? In 1987 the correlation coefficients between the specialization pattern of Japan and those of west European countries are generally negative although the relationship is strong and statistically significant for France, Italy, Norway and Turkey. There is also a weaker (although still significant) association for some other countries (Austria, Belgium, Spain and Yugoslavia).

There is no significant relationship in 1987 between the US specialization pattern and those of most other countries. The only exception for western Europe is the United Kingdom with a rather strong positive association. In contrast, the Republic of Korea and Taiwan, Province of China show significant negative correlation coefficients when compared with the United States.

---

[847] This concerns notably relatively labour-intensive products within electrical engineering such as batteries and accumulators, parts for electrical machinery but also mechanical engineering products such as pumps, heating and cooling equipment, etc. For a more detailed overview see, e.g., W. Ochel, "Die asiatischen Schwellenländer - eine Gefahr für die deutsche Investitionsgüterindustrie?" *Ifo-schnelldienst*, 28/1984, 37. Jahrgang, pp.3-14 and H.-G. Vieweg, " Wettbewerbsposition der asiatischen Schwellenländer als Anbieter von Erzeugnissen des Maschinenbaus", *Ifo-schnelldient*, 20/1989, 42. Jahrgang, pp.13-21.

[848] The Spearman rank correlation coefficient between the US RCA pattern in 1980 and 1987 is very high (0.93) and statistically significant at the 1 per cent level. The same result is obtained for the Federal Republic of Germany. In contrast, for Japan the corresponding coefficient is only 0.33, which indicates a large shift in the Japanese RCA hierarchy between 1980 and 1987. Note that the coefficient for Japan is still significant at the 5 per cent level. It should also be noted that the high degree of stability in the inter-industry specialization patterns of the United States and the Federal Republic of Germany may conceal considerable variations in the specialization indices *within* the individual commodity groups.

TABLE 7.3.8

Rank correlation coefficients between RCA indices of three major countries
and the corresponding RCA indices of 25 countries

	1970 a			1980 b			1987 c		
	Germany Fed.Rep. of	Japan	United States	Germany Fed.Rep. of	Japan	United States	Germany Fed.Rep. of	Japan	United States
Germany, Fed. Rep. of............	1.00	-0.33**	0.11	1.00	-0.21	0.19	1.00	-0.18	0.07
Japan.................................	-0.30**	1.00	-0.70*	-0.21	1.00	-0.63*	-0.18	1.00	-0.13
United States......................	0.11	-0.70*	1.00	0.19	-0.63*	1.00	0.07	-0.13	1.00
France................................	0.04	-0.21	0.18	0.14	-0.25	0.11	0.02	-0.56*	0.26
Italy...................................	0.38	-0.30	-0.04	0.40**	0.35**	-0.17	0.49*	-0.57*	-0.19
United Kingdom..................	0.26	-0.23	0.13	0.11	-0.51*	0.59*	-0.06	-0.17	0.51*
Canada...............................	-0.25	-0.31	0.54*	-0.25	-0.01	0.29	0.13	-0.31**	0.27
Austria...............................	0.25	-0.13	-0.22	0.46*	-0.31**	-	0.34**	0.38**	-0.06
Belgium..............................	-0.05	0.22	-0.16	0.22	-0.20	-0.02	0.33**	-0.31**	-0.11
Denmark............................	0.14	-0.15	-0.06	0.16	-0.35**	-0.10	0.17	-0.26	0.06
Finland..............................	0.04	0.25	-0.38**	0.10	-0.07	-0.09	0.06	-0.23	0.11
Ireland...............................	-0.16	-0.48*	-0.37**	0.13	-0.18	0.16	-0.07	-0.31**	0.15
Netherlands........................	-0.10	0.27	-0.16	-	-0.08	-0.02	0.13	-0.27	-0.02
Norway..............................	-0.20	0.27	-0.42**	-0.12	-0.21	-0.14	-0.08	-0.52*	0.19
Sweden...............................	0.20	-0.21	0.19	0.38**	-0.14	0.31	0.40**	-0.22	0.27
Switzerland........................	0.53*	-0.10	0.09	0.45*	0.01	-0.06	0.52*	-0.07	-0.17
Greece................................	-0.27	0.21	-0.42	0.15	0.06	-0.45*	0.05	-0.57	-0.28
Portugal.............................	0.10	0.36**	-0.31	-0.15	0.02	-0.09	-0.10	-0.14	-0.16
Spain..................................	0.14	0.29	-0.47*	0.161	-0.03	-0.36**	0.26	-0.43**	-0.21
Turkey................................	0.29	-0.27	-0.11	-0.17	-0.29	0.06	0.33**	-0.55*	-0.19
Yugoslavia..........................	-0.12	0.27	-0.48*	0.13	-0.11	-0.18	0.14	-0.36**	-0.21
Hong Kong........................	-0.21	0.32	-0.29	-0.29	0.13	-0.29	-0.21	0.11	-0.26
Republic of Korea...............	-0.45*	0.33	-	-0.57*	0.54*	-0.59*	-0.58*	0.16*	-0.58*
Singapore...........................	-0.14	0.13	-0.15	-0.43**	0.18	-0.06	-0.44*	0.27	0.05
Taiwan...............................	0.08	0.42**	-0.36	-0.13	0.47*	-0.68*	-0.07	0.06	-0.50*
Memorandum items:									
Eastern Europe (6)..............	0.44**	0.17	-0.35	0.18	-0.04	-0.22	0.16	-0.42**	-0.26
Soviet Union	-0.08	-0.11	-	0.04	-0.05	0.24	0.15	-0.02	-0.03

Source: ECE secretariat based on data in Appendix tables.

Note: Asterisks after the correlation coefficient denote the significance level: * = 1 per cent, ** = 5 per cent.

a Calculations are based on RCA-values for 29 product groups, except for Canada (28), Greece (27), Ireland (28), Turkey (20), Hong Kong (24), Republic of Korea (27), Taiwan (28).
b As for a above but with the following exceptions: Turkey (22), Hong Kong (27).
c As for a above with the exception of Turkey (28 groups).

The specialization pattern of the Federal Republic of Germany is most closely matched by Switzerland and Italy in 1987. The other positive and significant coefficients (for Austria, Belgium, Sweden, Turkey) are much weaker. Among the Asian NIEs, two countries (the Republic of Korea and Taiwan, Province of China) show a significant negative correlation with the German specialization pattern.

The above results suggest that the specialization patterns of the three major countries are generally complementary, both among themselves and in relation to most other countries. In 1987, there was no significant overlap. This does not exclude, of course, intensive competing specializations in individual product groups. If it is recalled that this great diversity in specialization patterns was found for relatively broad commodity groups, then this suggests much more widespread possibilities for complementary *intra-branch* product specializations.[849] In fact, this appears to be a major factor behind the rapid growth of intra-industry trade in the post-war period.[850]

(d) Changes in specialization over time

A previous study of changes in specialization patterns in the engineering industries of 14 industrialized countries detected a conspicuous "negative specialization trend".[851] It was found, using regression analysis, that over the period 1964-1970 changes in the special-

---

[849] The argument that intra-industry trade consists for the most part of complementary goods rather than close substitutes was advanced in P.B.W. Rayment, "Intra-Industry Specialization and the Foreign Trade of Industrial Countries", in Stephen F. Frowen (ed.) *Controlling Industrial Economies*, London, Macmillan, 1983. See also Richard Pomfret, "On the Division of Labour and International Trade", or, Adam Smith's "Explanation of Intra Industry Trade", *Journal of Economic Studies*, Vol.13, No.4, 1986, pp.55-62.

[850] Consequently, the hypothesis, which is not tested here, is that the probability of significant correlations between the specialization patterns of the various countries at a more detailed of commodity breakdown than employed here is quite small. Lennart Ohlsson, who correlated *changes* in specialization indices between the three countries above and 14 industrial countries for 106 engineering product groups for the period 1964-1970 found that "Practically, all coefficients are small. Therefore the specialization change of a large country has not tended to affect very much the specialization of any other, single country." L. Ohlsson, *Engineering Trade Specialization of Sweden and other Industrial Countries*. Studies in International Economics, Amsterdam, 1980, p.199 and table 9:3 on p.200.

[851] L. Ohlsson, *op.cit.*, chapter 9.

CHART 7.3.1

Diversity of specialization patterns: RCA indices, by SITC groups, in 1987 for Japan, USA and the Federal Republic of Germany

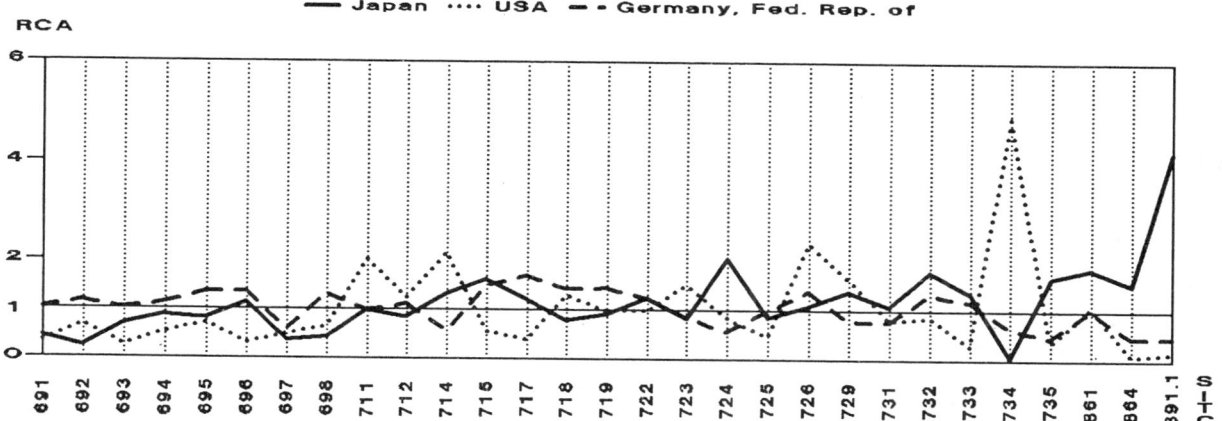

Source: ECE secretariat based on COMTRADE data base.

ization index in each country were negatively related to the level of the index in 1964. This means that product groups with a high specialization index in the base period experienced declines in their RCA values, and vice versa. In order to establish whether Ohlsson's finding reflected the peculiarities of the latter half of the 1960s, or a more persistent and pervasive trend, a regression analysis was carried out for the period 1970-1987 and for the two sub-periods 1970-1980 and 1980-1987. The results, presented in Appendix table 7.6, show that there was indeed a pervasive negative specialization trend in the engineering industries in the majority of countries over the period 1970-1987 (see also chart 7.3.2). The exceptions to this common pattern are the United States and Norway, although the positive slope coefficient is significant only for the latter country; Canada, where the estimated coefficient is negative, but not significant; and the Asian NIEs, where a negative trend exists only for Singapore.

A similar negative trend is also pervasive in the sub-period 1970-1980,[852] but in the period 1980-1987 the phenomenon appears to have considerably weakened. In the latter period there was a significant negative specialization trend only in Greece, Japan, Spain, Sweden, Turkey and three of the four Asian NIEs (the exception is Taiwan, Province of China, but the slope coefficient for Hong Kong is very small).

These results tend to corroborate Ohlsson's finding of a pervasive negative specialization trend — at least in the long run. The open question is why this phenomenon is less apparent in 1980-1987. One reason may be the relative shortness of the observation period. However, this question can only be answered once the underlying factors behind the negative trend are understood.

A purely agnostic explanation would be that there is no reason for changes in specialization indices to be unidirectional. The nature of a country's involvement in the international division of labour changes over time, among other things, with the emergence of new competitors, changes in technology and shifts in the pattern of international demand. All these entail changes in specialization patterns both within and among countries. Although these factors may explain general changes in a country's specialization over time, it cannot account for the pervasiveness of the negative trend in countries as different as, say, Japan on the one hand and Portugal and Spain on the other.

In theory the negative specialization trend could be consistent with the product-cycle hypothesis, where comparative advantages shift from the technological leaders to less developed countries as products mature over time and become — together with the production technology — more standardized. However, it is difficult to argue in terms of the product-cycle theory when discussing changes in specialization patterns at the rather high level of commodity aggregation used in this study. The question that arises is why, within these broad commodity groups, there are no new products emerging which would maintain the *aggregate* specialization index at its high level. (The United States in this context is a puzzling exception to the general case.)

Also, in terms of the neo-factor proportions theory or, alternatively, the neo-technology hypothesis, such a negative specialization trend is not easy to explain, unless it is assumed that within the individual countries there have been significant shifts in relative factor endowments. Although such a possibility cannot be excluded it is unlikely that this should have occurred systematically in so many countries.

---

[852] Note that there is now a significant negative relationship for Canada, but again not for the United States and Norway. Greece is noteworthy for a significant positive specialization trend over this period.

CHART 7.3.2

Changes in RCA indices 1970-1987 in relation to RCA indices in 1970

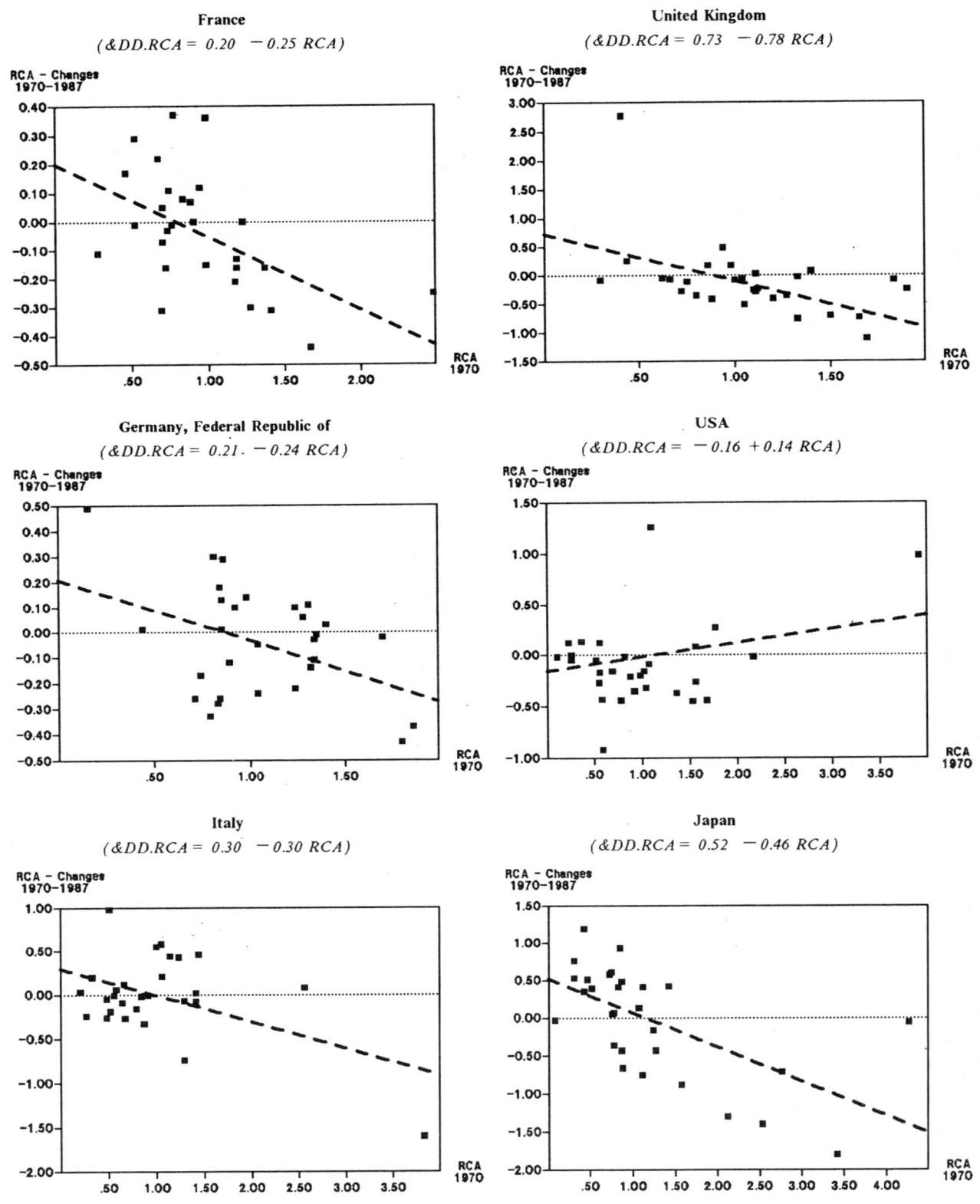

Source: Appendix table 7.6.

The forces which lead to higher intra-industry trade (product differentiation, exploitation of economies of scale, competition in imperfect markets) could also be major factors behind the pervasive negative specialization trends.[853] Basically this would imply that over time intra-industry trade leads to a flattening of a country's specialization profile. As an increasing number of countries engage in the exchange of similar goods the export pattern of any given country becomes more similar to the average world pattern. Consequently, strong specializations will tend to be reduced and product groups for which specialization was relatively low will tend to rise over time.

A detailed examination of this hypothesis is beyond the scope of this note, but the plausibility of this explanation may be judged by looking at an alternative measure of specialization which captures the effect of intra-industry specialization, viz. export-import ratios. This measure compares the share of a given product group in a country's total exports of manufactures to its corresponding share in total imports. This is tantamount to normalizing the export-import ratio for a given product group by the export-import ratio for total manufactures.[854] The rationale is that if the factors which work towards increasing intra-industry trade are also responsible for the negative specialization trend then this phenomenon should be even more pronounced for a specialization measure which takes imports explicitly into account. Trend equations were therefore estimated for the export-import ratios and the results are given in Appendix table 7.7. For the whole period 1970-1987 there is again a pervasive and generally strong negative specialization trend. There are, however, a few conspicuous deviations from the pattern observed previously for the relative export world market shares: there is now a significant negative trend for the United States, but not for the Federal Republic of Germany and France. And for Norway there is a swing from a positive to a negative trend. Also all of the Asian NIEs have significant negative slope coefficients when relative export-import ratios are used.

For the sub-period 1980-1987 the negative trend is more pervasive than was the case for the pure export measure. Again there is no negative trend for the Federal Republic, and for France and Switzerland there is even a significant positive coefficient. The other countries for which there is no negative specialization trend over the period 1980-1987 are Denmark, Finland and Yugoslavia, Singapore and the Republic of Korea.

Overall, the results are therefore somewhat mixed and do not point to a clear-cut conclusion. Broadly speaking they tend to support the hypothesis that increasing intra-industry trade — or the underlying causes of this trade — may be partly responsible for the negative specialization trend, but they also suggest that this may not be the whole story. Some of the findings remain somewhat puzzling, notably the change in the estimation results for the Federal Republic of Germany, France and the United States, when moving from one specialization measure to the other. On the whole therefore any explanation of the negative specialization trend can only be partial and tentative. Further analysis is required to gauge the influence of systematic factors such as intra-industry trade on changes in specialization over time. Also it should be recalled that the examination of specialization trends was carried out here for engineering goods only and at a relatively high level of aggregation, viz. 29 commodity groups. It would be useful to extend the analysis further, not only to a finer level of commodity detail but also to the whole range of manufactured products.

---

[853] See also L. Ohlsson, *op.cit.*, pp.203-205.

[854] The measure is defined as $(X_{ij}/M_{ij}) / (X_i./M_i.)$, where X_{ij} (M_{ij}) denotes country i's exports (imports) of product j and $X_i.$ ($M_i.$) are country i's total exports (imports) of manufactures.

7.4 ENGINEERING GOODS TRADE BY GROUP OF TECHNOLOGY INTENSITY

(i) General background

In the last decade or so there has been an increased interest in the role of technology as a determinant of a country's international competitiveness. In this context, the so-called high-technology industries or goods have become a major concern of policy makers and analysts. There are various factors which help to explain this renewed focus on the role of technology in international trade. To some extent it is associated with the penetration of the new technologies (micro-electronics, computer and telecommunications technology) into virtually all industries and services, and the perception that these are strategic technologies with a decisive influence on the future structure and competitiveness of industry in general in all countries. An overly high degree of dependence on foreign supplies may call into question the ability of firms to exploit profitable production outlets to the same extent as its competitors abroad and, in a more general way, may risk making the direction and pace of technical change in an economy excessively dependent on foreign producers.[855] An important role is also played by specific economic characteristics of high technology-intensive goods, such as very high R&D and fixed capital costs, which make the exploitation of economies of scale of primordial importance and ensure that competition takes on a global dimension, because the world market can only support a small number of competitors. More graphically, this is sometimes seen as a sort of "race", where being first is considered to be of strategic importance in enabling a firm to capture a large part of the generally substantial profits that these markets can provide.

All this has led some writers and policy makers to stress the potential importance of industrial policies aimed at nurturing these technologies (industrial targeting), thereby creating a comparative advantage for a country at the expense of competitors abroad. This in turn might lead to retaliatory policies by other governments in order to "level the playing field". In practice two types of strategic trade policies can be distinguished, namely profit-shifting subsidy policies and strategic infant-industry protection policies. Both types are partly overlapping and involve the use of policy tools such as import protection, export and production subsidies and tax incentives. The economic implications of this sort of "activist" or strategic trade policy are far reaching but at the same time also highly ambiguous. The results of theoretical models vary strongly with changes in the assumptions for example about the behaviour of other competitors or governments. In addition there are difficult problems of political economy involved when it comes to identifying the sectors to be targeted and evaluating the opportunity cost of an alternative allocation of scarce resources. Also the record of governments in "picking winners" is not too impressive. It has been argued that the presence of imperfect competition even strengthens the case for promoting free trade but at the same time calls for the "need to structure the rules of the game that prevents a process of unilateral strategies and counterstrategies leading to ruinous industrial policy, mutually destructive trade wars and suboptimal outcomes".[856] A further element is the overall change in the economic environment since the 1970s with the United States no longer by far the predominant force at many technological frontiers. More fundamentally, however, all this points to the fact that technological advance is a major vehicle for maintaining or improving competitiveness and, thus, standards of living in high-wage industrialized countries.

(a) Technology and competitiveness

The concern about technological performance in general and of high-technology industries in particular derives from the crucial role that technical change, innovation and human skills play in the long run development of industrial competitiveness in the advanced economies. The theoretical background to this is provided by the product life cycle theory, which argues that advanced countries benefit from the temporary monopoly provided by the introduction of new products and processes but that over time, as the technology matures, the locus of production will shift to other, generally low-wage countries that are less advanced. Therefore, in order to maintain their real income levels, the advanced industrialized countries are forced to generate a continuous stream of new products. In other words, innovations are at the heart of endeavours to maintain or improve competitive positions in domestic markets and abroad. "Like Alice and the Red Queen,

---

[855] For the United States see "An Assessment of US Competitiveness in High Technology Industries", US Department of Commerce, International Trade Administration, February 1983. For the European Community see Commission of the European Communities, "The Competitiveness of the Community Industry", Luxembourg 1982, and ----, "Improving Competitiveness and Industrial Structures in the Community", COM (86) 40 final, Brussels, 25 February 1986.

[856] See A. Jacquemin, "International and Multinational Strategic Behaviour", *Kyklos*, Vol.42, 1989, No.4, p.511. For a detailed overview of the role and importance of strategic trade policy see also Richard Baldwin, "Evaluating Strategic Trade Policies", *Aussenwirtschaft,*, 43. Jahrgang (1988), Heft I/II, pp.207-230. Paul Krugman (ed.), *Strategic Trade Policy and the New International Economics*, Cambridge, Massachusetts, 1986 and Rachel McCulloch, *The Challenge to US Leadership in High-Technology Industries (Can the United States maintain its lead? Should it try?)*, Working Paper No.2513, National Bureau of Economic Research, Cambridge, Massachusetts, February 1988; Horst Siebert, "Strategische Handelspolitik. Theoretische Ansätze und wirtschaftspolitische Empfehlungen", *Aussenwirtschaft*, 43 Jahrgang, (1988), Heft IV, pp.549-584.

the developed region must keep running to stay in the same place".[857] Moreover, with the increasing integration of the world economy — the so-called "globalization" of markets — technological innovations have increasingly important ramifications which alter significantly the relative competitive positions of the advanced countries themselves. Thus, international competition may be seen to operate at three different levels. Because a country cannot be at the technological frontier in all product fields, it faces, first, competition from "above", i.e., from the technologically leading countries; at the second level there is competition from countries that have broadly the same relative position in the technology hierarchy, and at the third level there is competition from "below", originating in the efforts of the newly industrializing countries to "catch up" with the more advanced countries.

Consequently, those advanced countries which fall relatively behind in exploiting new technologies will be "caught in the middle", i.e., they run the risk of being "trapped between the NIEs at the one end and the innovation high-performers at the other."[858] In other words, countries not advancing with the technological frontier may face a situation where their overall competitiveness is endangered both on grounds of innovation and — given lower wage cost in the NIEs — on price.

The nature of competition among the major trading regions has undergone significant changes since the 1970s. As already mentioned, the United States is no longer, as it was in the 1950s and 1960s, the predominant force at all the various technological frontiers. West European countries and Japan have been progressively closing the gap in many fields.[859] Of great significance in this context has been the changing economic environment in western Europe, with the increasing integration and enlargement of the European Community and, in a more general way, the emergence of a west European economic space. This had allowed west European producers to offset some of the potential advantages which US firms have obtained from their larger domestic market. This catching-up process has probably reduced the importance of "technology gap" trade between the advanced countries in favour of two-way trade in high technology-intensive goods.[860]

The technological challenges to the established leader over the last two decades or so has given rise to American fears of losing its global economic leadership and becoming dependent on foreign supplies for strategic high-technology products;[861] others are more sanguine and have pointed to the benefits that the US economy can obtain from trade at more balanced technology levels.[862] It is evident that with the emergence of multinational corporations, the growing number of international joint research projects and the growing importance of international subcontracting, the ability to design and produce technology-intensive goods is spreading rapidly not only among advanced countries[863] but also to the developing countries; the economic success of the NIEs and the emergence of a group of second-tier NIEs attests to that. Broadly speaking the closing of the technology gap means that the location of movements in the technological frontier is no longer confined to the United States but has become a process exposed to international competition.

(b) Basic economic features of high technology-intensive industries

What economists have in mind when they use the term "technology-intensity" is the relative importance of the investment in knowledge that is embodied in a good or in a production process. High technology-intensive goods are therefore those where this investment amounts to a substantial part of total costs of production. Usually, technology-intensity is gauged by measuring the relative importance of R&D expenditures in total costs or by looking at the share of scientific employees and engineers in the total employment of a firm or industry.

By their very nature, high technology-intensive industries are those where technical change occurs at a higher speed than in other fields of economic activity. At the same time these are often "leading" sectors, "in that they tend to drive and mould economic progress across a broad front".[864] The classical examples of this are the wide-ranging economic consequences of the steam engine, railways and aircraft. The last decade or so has seen the drastic ramifications of technical progress in the electronics industry, viz., computers, semiconductors and telecommunications.

---

[857] See Paul Krugman, "A Model of Innovation, Technology Transfer, and the World Distribution of Income", *Journal of Political Economy*, vol.87, No.21, 1979, p.262. Essentially, what this means is that the proprietary knowledge that lies at the heart of all innovations must be "renewed" because it diffuses to other firms and competitors, which limits the time for which this knowledge can generate revenues. As such, this points to a common characteristic of proprietary knowledge and physical assets: the economic equivalent of the diffusion process is the depreciation and wearing out of production equipment. See S. Hirsch, S. Kalish and S. Katznelson, "Effects of Knowledge and Service Intensities on Domestic and Export Performance", *Weltwirtschaftliches Archiv*, Band 124, Heft 2, 1988, p.230.

[858] See Henry Ergas, *Why Do Some Countries Innovate More Than Others?* CEPS Papers No.5, Centre for European Policy Studies, Brusels, 1984, p.33.

[859] See Nathan Rosenberg, *Inside the Black Box: Technology and economics*,. Cambridge, 1982, ch.12: "US technological leadership and foreign competition: De te fabula narratur?", pp.280.

[860] See Raymond Vernon, "Technology's Effects on International Trade: A Look Ahead", in Herbert Giersch (ed.), *Emerging Technologies: Consequences for Economic Growth, Structural Change, and Employment*, Tübingen, 1982, pp.157-160.

[861] See "An Assessment of US Competitiveness in High Technology Industries", *op.cit.* and James Botkin et. al., *Global stakes: The Future of High Technology in America*, Cambridge, Massachusetts, 1982.

[862] See Nathan Rosenberg, *op.cit.*, p 281 and Rachel McCulloch, *op.cit.*

[863] See Richard R. Nelson, *High Technology Policies, A Five-Nation Comparison*, American Enterprise Institute for Public Policy Research, Washington and London, 1984.

[864] See R. Nelson, *op.cit.*, p.1.

High technology-intensive industries are often claimed to generate significant spillover or external effects, i.e., the innovations benefit not only the high-tech sectors themselves but also lead to product or process innovations in other more or less related industrial activities. These inter-industry spillover effects may occur when a firm buys intermediate inputs or processing equipment from the technologically leading sectors or when an innovation in one sector provides the basis for a product or process innovation in another. In general, the knowledge embodied in new products, is so to speak, transferred to other firms operating downstream, and these, in turn, may derive important competitive gains to the extent that they are able to exploit these externalities before other competitors follow in their footsteps.

While this is not controversial, the argument becomes more strained, however, when it comes to asserting the strategic role of a strong *domestic* high-technology sector in order to reap more benefits from these potential interindustry spillovers than competitors in other countries. This is often the rationale employed by high-technology firms to demand from governments temporary protection in the form of subsidies, import restraints and export promotion schemes. Governments, in turn, quote these alleged effects to defend their, often considerable, financial involvement in high technology areas.[865] The argument that high technology-intensive industries are of strategic importance to high-wage countries hinges essentially on the relative importance of national versus international inter-industry spillover effects.[866] Thus, if these spillovers were, in general, to spread more quickly within domestic boundaries than across national frontiers, and if they were significant, then it would be difficult to deny high technology-intensive industries a strategic role in the determination of competitiveness.

Ultimately, of course, this is an empirical question. It may be argued that, for the reasons mentioned above, the period during which a firm can exploit an innovative lead for a given product has become shorter and shorter.[867] On the other hand, it may be that the learning curve effects and domestic externalities are so important that a country wishing to remain at the forefront of technical progress cannot do so by relying on high-tech imports. Thus it has been surmised that if the United States were to lose "its ability to compete effectively in semiconductors, it may lose its ability to innovate in both the semiconductor industry and in related electronic industries and its ability to diffuse electronics-based product and process innovations in a whole variety of actual and potential user industries".[868] Unfortunately, this whole issue is clouded by the lack of adequate quantitative evidence regarding the extent of domestic versus cross-boundary interindustry spillovers. The relative importance of the two is unclear and therefore the "question of whether high-technology or leading industries are strategic should be regarded as open".[869]

Besides this aspect of external or spillover effects, however, there are other features which shape the distinctive economic nature of high technology-intensive goods. First, the importance of R&D expenditure in total costs means that increasing returns to scale are an important characteristic of the production process: the fixed cost nature of R&D expenditures implies that the larger the number of products over which a firm can spread these costs, the higher, *ceteris paribus*, will be the profits. Put differently, once the know-how for the production of a particular good has been established, it is available to the firm at no additional cost and can be used to produce in principle an indefinite number of goods.[870]

In practice, however, the often considerable development costs are compounded by the fact that the market size is generally limited and on occasion can be quite small, as is the case of the commercial aircraft industry.[871] Significant economies of scale can therefore in general only be reaped at the world market level, i.e., by orienting the whole development and production process from the very beginning to meet the exigencies of the international market. This need for export-orientation is only slightly more important for firms in smaller economies[872] than for firms with a relatively large, domestic markets, although the latter may provide a more advantageous starting position.

The importance of achieving significant economies of scale has been intensified by steeply rising investment expenditures, a consequence of the increasing complexity of production equipment required to produce high technology-intensive goods.[873] It appears that in high technology-intensive industries the link between product and process innovation is a very close one, a relationship which has been especially strong in the field

---

[865] A case in point is government co-financing of space technology, although the alleged civil sector spin-offs appear to be by far outweighed by the expected military value of new products and processes.

[866] See R. Nelson, *op.cit.*; Paul Krugman, "Technology-intensive goods", *loc.cit.*, pp.195-196.

[867] See Richard R. Nelson, *op.cit.*, p.75 and R. McCulloch, *op.cit*, p.35.

[868] See M. Borrus, L.D. Tyson, J. Zysman, "Creating Advantage: How Government Policies Shape International Trade in the Semiconductor Industry" in P. Krugman (ed.), *op.cit.*, p.93.

[869] See R. Nelson, *op.cit.*, p.4.

[870] See Paul Krugman, "Technology-intensive goods", in J.M. Finger and A. Olechowski (eds.), *The Uruguay Round, A Handbook on the Multilateral Trade Negotiations*, The World Bank, Washington, D.C., 1988, p.191.

[871] See N. Rosenberg, *op.cit.*, p.285.

[872] H. Luukkanen, "The Finnish High-Tech Industry Takes Off", *Economic Review*, Kansallis-Osake-Pankki, 1987-2, p.13.

[873] High fixed capital and R&D costs act as a barrier to entry and are a major reason for imperfect competition in these markets.

of electronics.[874] A major example of this are the dramatic changes that have taken place in the semiconductor or integrated-circuit industry as regards the declining costs and steeply rising performance of integrated circuits, which lie at the heart of electronic equipment. These developments would not have been possible without mastering the complexity of the underlying process technology, which enabled the industry to move rapidly from the introduction of the integrated circuit in 1962 to the large-scale integrated (LSI) circuit designs and more recently to so-called very large-scale integration (VLSI), which puts entire electronic subsystems onto the structure of a chip.[875] As a consequence of this increasing complexity, however, there has been a steep rise in the cost of processing equipment,[876] which requires large-scale production in order to recover high R&D and fixed investment costs. Another strategy adopted by the industry has been "to integrate forward into systems production".[877] The pressure to achieve economies of scale is, of course, considerably enhanced if the fall in unit costs is accompanied by a similar decline in unit prices, as has been the case for semiconductors and personal computers.

All these various factors explain the considerably higher risks faced by technology-intensive industries as compared with mature industries. These risks are not only inherent in the very nature of the R&D process, but they stem mainly from the considerable time span between the marketing of a new product and the period when the break-even point is finally attained. In a more general way, these risks arise from the uncertain future that firms must face in the market and the negative impact which rapid technical change itself may have on the length of the product life cycle and on the cost efficiency of the equipment originally designed for producing the new good.[878]

One consequence of the rapidly rising R&D and fixed capital costs in the high technology sector is that the number of firms with sales sufficiently large to amortize these costs has been declining. As a result there has been an increasing tendency towards mergers and alliances within and across national boundaries.

This process has been particularly pronounced in western Europe, partly as a reaction to the intensifying competitive pressures emanating from Japan and the United States, where firms have the advantage of a larger, more homogeneous domestic market.[879] The numerous joint international production and research projects that have been set up, mainly under the auspices of the European Community in the fields of micro-electronics and information (ESPRIT), telecommunications (RACE), biotechnology (BAP) and semiconductors (JESSI), attest to this strategy.[880] A prominent example of joining forces is provided by the European Airbus programme.

Another consequence of the need for large-scale production to take advantage of economies of scale has been the emergence of common standards for individual high-technology products, notably in the field of information technology and telecommunication. International standards are tantamount to an increase in market size, i.e., the potential sales on which a firm can base its product development and investment strategy. It should be noted that one way to promote these standards is the collaboration of firms from different countries. The lack of truly European-wide standards has led to fragmented markets for many products which have not allowed European companies to exploit economies of scale to the same extent as their competitors in Japan and the United States, with negative repercussions on competitiveness. The elaboration of common standards is therefore an important element in the move towards completion of the Internal Market in 1992: "Failure to achieve a genuine industrial common market becomes increasingly serious since the research, development and commercialization costs of the new technologies, in order to have a realistic prospect of being internationally competitive, require the background of a home market of continental proportions".[881]

(c) Not everything is 'high-tech'

Despite the recent focus on high technology-intensive goods and their importance for the overall

---

[874] N. Rosenberg, op.cit., p.287.

[875] N. Rosenberg and W. E. Steinmueller, "The economic implications of the VLSI revolution", in N. Rosenberg, Inside the Black Box, op.cit., p.180, and M. Borrus et. al., op.cit., pp.94-96.

[876] According to Rosenberg the "cost of a wafer fabrication plant has increased from $2 million in 1970 to $50 million in 1979". See N. Rosenberg, op.cit., p.181. A more recent estimate now puts the costs of a new chip-production line at about $150 million. See The Economist, 18 February 1989, p.74.

[877] M. Borrus et. al., p.96.

[878] R. McCulloch, op.cit., pp.22-23; N. Rosenberg and W. Steinmueller state that in the semiconductor industry "the rapid continuing pace of technical progress makes it extremely risky to build large plants in order to exploit economies of scale. This is so because, by the time the plant becomes available for volume production it may prove already to be obsolete". loc.cit., p.182. It has been estimated that processes for chip designs and chip making presently "become obsolete two to three years after they come off the drawing board". The Economist, 18 February 1989.

[879] "Co-operative ventures have become so fashionable in certain parts of the high-technology sector that they are now the norm rather than the exception, seen virtually as an indicator of a company's determination to expand. They have affected almost every part of the western European region." Financial Times, 13 April 1988, Section III, "Collaboration. A change in attitudes", p.2.

[880] ESPRIT = European Strategic Programme for Research and Development in Information Technology; RACE = R&D in Advanced Communications-technologies in Europe; BAP = Biotechnology in Europe; JESSI = Joint European Semiconductor Silicon.

[881] "Completing the Internal Market", White Paper from the Commission to the European Council (Milan, 28-29 June 1985), Commission of the European Communities, COM(85) 310 final, Brussels, 14 June 1985, pp.17-18. It should be noted that different national standards are a technical barrier to trade which is of importance not only in high technology industries. An example is the different health and safety standards for engineering machinery in general, which the European Community is trying to harmonize in the proposed engineering machinery directive. See "Machinery rules spark EC power struggle", Financial Times, 13 June 1988.

pace of technical change and economic growth, it is important to remember that a country's competitiveness is determined by the interplay of several factors, of which technology is but one. Thus, better organizational and marketing skills may well make a significant difference in performance of two firms in different countries with equal level of technology embodied in their products or production processes. It is also clear from even a cursory look at world trade patterns in manufactured goods that a country need not necessarily excel in high technology-intensive goods to record a foreign trade surplus. Indeed, a country may develop special skills in combining mature and leading technologies. It is in the very nature of the international division of labour that countries specialize in different products and that the pattern of specialization itself undergoes continuous change over time. Also, by definition, not all countries can specialize in high technology-intensive goods.

It is built into the very concept of technology-intensive goods that the particular products to which this description applies are changing as the technology matures. Thus, at the time of their first appearance on the market it was certainly the case that automobiles were regarded as "high-tech" — but today that is no longer the case. Nevertheless, the motor-car industry still occupies an important place in world trade of manufactures and, in particular, of engineering goods. Against this background it is appropriate to examine not only the role of high-technology-intensive engineering goods in international trade but also the importance of goods that require lower levels of human skill and R&D in their production.

(ii) Measuring technology intensity

As mentioned above, "technology-intensity" refers to the relative importance of investment in knowledge that is embodied in a particular product. The proxy variable employed to measure technology-intensity is the share of R&D expenditures in total sales.[882] Basically, the procedure is to compile R&D expenditure data for industries or product groups and to relate them to total sales or gross output value. This then allows industries or products to be ranked by level of R&D intensity. The criterion used here pertains to the direct expenditures on R&D made by the final producer of the good in question. It may be objected that this leaves out the investment in knowledge embodied in the intermediate inputs purchased from other sectors. There is thus the possibility that the intensities calculated on the basis of total (i.e., direct plus indirect) R&D costs may differ significantly from those based on direct costs alone.[883] However, the available evidence suggests that these alternative ways of gauging technology-intensity do not lead to significant differences in the rankings of product groups by R&D-intensity.[884] Another difficulty is that the knowledge embodied in a good is the result of a cumulative process of research that often extends over several years, even decades: for example, it took nearly two decades of development, from when the first micro-circuits were available in the 1950s, to arrive at the personal computer.[885] The R&D expenditure data used for classifying goods generally pertain to a single year and therefore capture only the marginal investment in knowledge. A more satisfactory measure of technology-intensity would require long time series for R&D expenditures, but unfortunately these not do exist for detailed product groups.

A further problem arises from the fact that the basic data on R&D and sales are generally only available at a relatively high level of commodity aggregation. Thus the data underlying this study refer to 31 product groups of US manufacturing industry.[886] This is, however, a level of detail at which the degree of homogeneity of products with regard to R&D intensity within each commodity group may be quite large. Put differently, there is the inevitable problem of categorical aggregation i.e., it cannot be excluded that a product group which is ranked as "high" technology-intensive also contains items which are of lower technology-intensity, and vice versa.[887] This should be borne in mind when interpreting the findings reported below.

A further complication arises because of the disintegration of production processes across national boundaries. Product development, design, production of parts, and the assembly of the final good are different stages in the production process which often do not take place within the same country. The knowledge- and skill-intensity of these various stages, however, differ considerably. Often the low skilled, labour-intensive

---

882 Alternatively, the share of scientists and engineers in total employment of a branch has also been employed as a proxy variable. But employment captures only a part of total R&D input costs, leaving out e.g. expenditures for materials and equipment. This may be of particular relevance when it comes to examining the importance of firm size for innovative activity because there is evidence that total R&D costs increase with firm size much faster than R&D employment, thus tending to overestimate the propensity to invest in knowledge in small companies. See Luc L.G. Soete, "Firm Size and Inventive Activity. The Evidence Reconsidered", *European Economic Review*, Vol 12, 1979, pp.319-340.

883 See Lester A. Davis, *Technology Intensity of US Output and Trade*, Office of Trade and Investment Analysis, US Department of Commerce, July 1982.

884 See L.A. Davis, *op.cit*. In fact, it can be seen from the data compiled by Davis that the product groups defined there as "high-tech" are the same under both criteria, i.e., the direct expenditure approach and the total expenditure approach. Moreover, the rankings of *all* product groups in terms of their total and direct R&D intensities, respectively, is very similar. The Spearman rank correlation coefficient for the corresponding rankings of 30 product groups is 0.95, which is highly significant. (The maximum value in case of identical rankings is unity and the critical value at the 1 per cent significance level is only 0.43.) These comparisons are based on data published in L.A. Davis, *op.cit.*, table 2, p.20.

885 See B. Jovanovic and R. Rob, "The Growth and Diffusion of Knowledge", *Review of Economic Studies*, Vol.56, 1989, pp.569-570. It has also been reported that "Japanese manufacturers have spent about 20 years and $900 million developing HDTV production equipment and television sets". See "US Chip Makers to Work with Japan on Parts for HDTV", *International Herald Tribune*, 10 November 1989, p.17.

886 See the Statistical appendix to this study for more details.

887 See also Regina Kelly, *The Impact of Technological Innovation on International Trade Patterns*, Office of International Economic Research, US Department of Commerce, December 1977.

part of producing a more or less complex final good is shifted from the advanced industrialized countries to low-wage countries (e.g., the Asian NIEs and southern Europe). Typically, this relocation of activities abroad is carried out by multinational corporations. As the technology classification does not discriminate between the various stages of the production process, low-wage countries may therefore appear to have a relatively large share of high-tech products in their total exports. In general, this does not reflect a capacity of these countries to produce high-tech products *sui generis* but rather the fact that they have a comparative advantage – based on labour costs – as a locus of *production* for certain stages of the whole production process that leads to a final commodity, which in its entirety is classified as high-tech.[888]

It is also assumed that the level of technology embodied in a given product group is broadly comparable between countries. However, this may not always be the case. As noted above, the product groups for which the basic R&D data are available are not homogeneous with regard to technology-intensity and firms in one country may specialize on the more sophisticated products within a given commodity group, while companies in another country may concentrate on less sophisticated, more standardized goods within the same industry.

There is, furthermore, the problem of the stability of the technology classification over time. The allocation of products to a given technology group is kept constant to allow comparisons over time. But as products move through their life-cycle, from the initial innovation to standardized, mature goods, the technology-intensity will tend to decline. On the other hand, process and product innovations can raise the technology intensity of a given product group, with new high-tech products gaining importance relative to older, standardized goods of lower technology-intensity. An illustration of both cases is the television receiver which over time has turned into a mature, homogeneous good. However, with the emergence of High-Definition TV (HDTV), the technology-intensity of the sector is likely to rise significantly. A similar development has occurred recently for the product group of gramophones and sound reproducers with the introduction of compact discs and compact disc players.

It is clear from the preceding remarks that the analysis of international trade according to its technology-intensity is fraught with methodological and conceptual problems. Unfortunately, there is no way to solve these issues in a generally satisfying manner. The implication of all this is that the findings reported below should be approached with a good common sense. Neither the available R&D data nor the international trade data allow a detailed classification of commodities according to the level of technology-intensity. This section, therefore, can only provide a rough breakdown of trade in engineering goods into product groups that *on average* differ significantly as to the relative importance of investment in knowledge and the pace of technical innovation.

For the purposes of this study internationally traded goods were divided into four groups according to their relative technology-intensity: product groups with an R&D-intensity substantially above the average for manufacturing industry (by at least a factor of three) are classified as *highly technology intensive* or high-tech, while products with an R&D intensity of at least 10 per cent above but less than three times the manufacturing average are termed *advanced technology*. Product groups with an R&D-intensity falling within the range of 10 per cent above and below the manufacturing average are labelled *medium technology* intensive and the remainder is categorized as *low technology* intensive.[889]

(iii) **Trade in engineering goods by group of technology-intensity**

This section summarizes engineering goods trade broken down into the above-mentioned four groups of technology-intensity. Four different aspects are considered: the relative importance of the four groups in total trade, the relative importance of individual countries in world exports of each group, the "technology" structure of trade balances in engineering goods and finally, the revealed comparative advantage of countries in each group.

(a) Composition of trade by group of technology-intensity

Chart 7.4.1 shows that between 1970 and 1980 the technology composition of world trade in engineering goods was relatively stable. High technology-intensive goods accounted for some 18 to 20 per cent of all exports, and advanced technology goods for about 15 per cent. Medium and low technology goods accounted for some two thirds of all engineering goods trade, with an emerging tendency for the share of low-tech to decline.

Between 1980 and 1987 the differences in the growth rates of the four groups became much more pronounced, *inter alia*, a reflection of the soaring demand for electronic office equipment (computers) and telecommunications apparatus, which are the core of the high-tech goods originating in the engineering industries. As a consequence, the share of high technology-intensive goods rose to one quarter of total exports in 1987. This strong growth did not occur for advanced technology goods: indeed, their share of the total declined slightly, from 15 per cent to 14.2 per cent. Relative decline, however, was most pronounced for low technology intensive goods, which declined in importance from 37 per cent in 1980 to 30 per cent in 1987. In contrast, the share of medium technology-

---

[888] On the general question of the heterogeneity of product classifications with respect to factor intensity, see J.M. Finger, "Trade Overlap and Inter-Industry Trade", *Economic Inquiry*, Vol.12, December 1975 and P.W.B. Rayment, "The Homogeneity of Manufacturing Industries with respect to Factor Intensity: the case of the United Kingdom", *Oxford Bulletin of Economics and Statistics*, Vol.38, August 1976.

[889] For the detailed product list see the Statistical appendix.

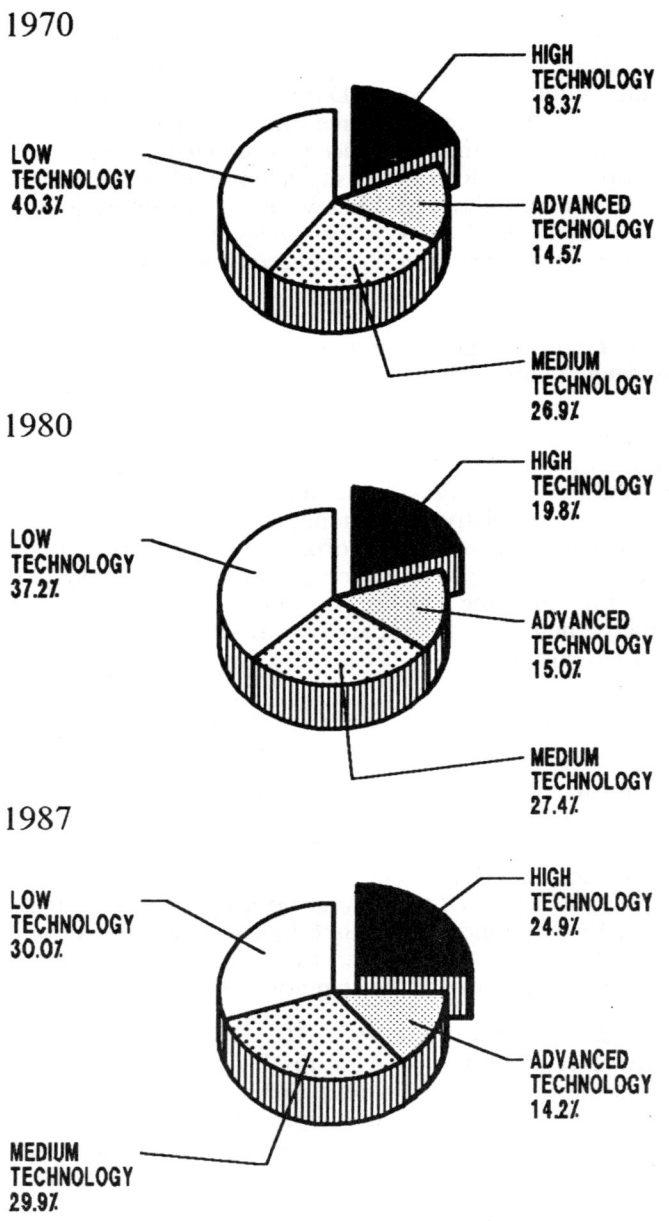

CHART 7.4.1
World exports of engineering goods, by group of technology intensity

Source: ECE secretariat based on COMTRADE data base.

technology-intensive goods together accounted for 60 per cent of world exports of engineering goods in 1987. This is less than in 1970 (67 per cent), but it illustrates the fact that international trade is far from being dominated by the exchange of highly sophisticated goods.

In the corresponding pattern of trade for regions and countries there is both stability and change (table 7.4.1 and Appendix tables 7.8 and 7.9). The United States has traditionally relied much more on exports of high technology-intensive goods than west Europe and Japan: nearly 44 per cent of all US exports of engineering goods fall into that category, compared with about 18 per cent for western Europe and 25 per cent for Japan. It is also noteworthy that the share of high-tech goods in total exports has been on a strong upward trend in the United States and Japan, while it has risen only moderately, on average, in western Europe. But in some west European countries, there have been large increases of high-tech exports, notably in Ireland, France, the United Kingdom, Austria, Norway and Finland.

Appendix table 7.8 shows that the variation among west European countries with regard to the share of high technology-intensive exports has always been considerable. In 1987 the shares ranged from 70.6 per cent in Ireland to 2.5 per cent in Turkey. The very high share for Ireland is largely a reflection of the assembly of electronic products organized by US and Japanese firms to supply the European and Middle East market.

A striking feature of the data in table 7.4.1 is the rather low share of high technology-intensive goods in the total engineering exports of the Federal Republic of Germany. This share, which was only 11.5 per cent in 1987 and has hardly changed since 1970, is the lowest among the four major western European economies. The rather low degree of specialization of the Federal Republic of Germany in the area of high-tech commodities is somewhat surprising since the ratio of R&D to GDP does not differ significantly between the United States, Japan and the Federal Republic of Germany.[890] Of course these similar ratios conceal large differences in the absolute sums actually spent on R&D: in 1985, the business sector in the United States spent $78.3 billion on R&D, compared with $26.8 billion in Japan and $14.6 billion in the Federal Republic of Germany.[891]

There are only a few countries among the developed market economies for which the share of the high and advanced technology-intensive groups combined is close to or above 50 per cent. Among the larger countries this is the case only for the United States (60.8 per cent) and the United Kingdom (48.5 per cent). For the smaller countries this holds notably for Ireland (79.6 per cent), Switzerland (51.3 per cent) and, to a much lesser extent, the Netherlands (45.4 per cent).

intensive goods climbed to nearly 30 per cent, an increase of 2.5 percentage points. The medium and low

---

[890] In 1985, the R&D/GDP ratio was 2.7 per cent for the Federal Republic and 2.8 per cent for Japan and the United States. In France and the United Kingdom this ratio was lower at 2.3 per cent, while in Italy it was only 1.1 per cent. See *Main Science and Technology Indicators 1982-88*, No.1, OECD, Paris, 1988, table 3.

[891] See OECD, *op.cit.*, table 14. Note that the data are expressed in current purchasing power parities.

TABLE 7.4.1

Composition of engineering goods trade, by group of technology intensity
(Percentages)

	Exports					Imports				
	HT	AT	MT	LT	Total	HT	AT	MT	LT	Total
EC9										
1970	14.4	15.1	27.8	42.7	100	22.0	16.3	22.7	39.0	100
1980	16.4	15.6	26.9	40.2	100	24.3	14.6	27.2	34.0	100
1987	19.0	14.3	28.7	35.8	100	26.8	14.8	29.0	29.5	100
EFTA (6)										
1970	17.5	16.9	12.5	53.2	100	14.6	15.7	23.1	46.6	100
1980	15.7	19.4	14.2	50.1	100	16.8	16.2	24.1	42.1	100
1987	17.7	20.0	16.5	45.9	100	20.6	14.7	25.7	38.7	100
Southern Europe										
1970	7.6	13.5	11.5	67.5	100	14.4	14.4	16.5	54.7	100
1980	8.6	13.6	29.4	48.4	100	15.8	16.6	18.7	48.9	100
1987	9.3	12.6	37.0	41.1	100	19.0	16.1	26.8	38.1	100
Western Europe										
1970	14.7	15.3	25.3	44.6	100	19.7	16.0	22.1	42.2	100
1980	16.1	16.1	25.3	41.8	100	22.3	15.1	25.9	36.6	100
1987	18.4	15.1	27.3	37.5	100	25.0	14.9	28.2	31.8	100
United States										
1970	31.5	15.6	20.9	32.1	100	14.0	11.4	51.0	25.5	100
1980	32.8	17.8	18.7	30.8	100	22.2	11.5	43.5	22.8	100
1987	43.8	17.0	19.2	20.0	100	24.7	11.8	43.3	20.1	100
Japan										
1970	13.8	9.1	31.8	45.4	100	37.9	23.8	5.8	32.6	100
1980	16.4	10.7	40.7	32.3	100	39.3	21.5	8.7	30.9	100
1987	25.5	12.3	40.6	21.5	100	41.1	19.6	15.4	24.0	100
Eastern countries										
1970	8.8	23.2	16.0	52.0	100	7.3	23.9	6.2	62.6	100
1980	8.4	19.7	23.7	48.1	100	6.0	24.1	8.1	58.3	100
1987	7.8	16.6	27.5	48.0	100	7.1	23.7	7.3	58.2	100
Four Asian NIEs										
1970	37.8	13.0	18.8	30.3	100	19.0	17.4	14.1	49.6	100
1980	35.8	8.7	21.6	33.9	100	33.1	17.0	11.4	38.5	100
1987	41.4	9.4	22.1	27.0	100	39.4	17.9	11.8	31.0	100
Sixteen LDCs										
1970	26.3	10.6	17.9	43.9	100	13.2	16.2	19.1	51.0	100
1980	28.2	15.9	27.0	28.5	100	14.2	16.5	22.2	46.8	100
1987	57.2	10.6	12.7	19.3	100	22.2	17.8	18.8	41.0	100
World										
1970	18.3	14.5	26.9	40.3	100	18.0	15.8	27.3	38.9	100
1980	19.8	15.0	27.4	37.2	100	21.4	15.2	27.4	35.8	100
1987	24.9	14.2	29.9	30.0	100	25.4	14.6	30.5	29.3	100

Source: ECE secretariat based on COMTRADE data base.

Note: HT = high technology, AT = advanced technology, MT = medium technology, LT = low technology. Some relatively large discrepancies between the sum of components and the total are due to the fact that it has not been possible to allocate all products to one of the four groups because of confidentiality restrictions in the underlying national statistics.

At the other end of scale the number of countries for which low technology-intensive goods accounted for about half or more of all exports is surprisingly large. Among the larger economies this holds only for Italy; it is more common among the smaller countries. Such a pattern is not unexpected for Greece, Turkey and Yugoslavia, but it also prevails in Austria, Denmark, Finland, Norway and Switzerland.

For the eastern countries combined high technology-intensive products accounted in 1987 for some 8 per cent of their exports to the world, and advanced technology-intensive goods for about 16.5 per cent. Thus, 75 per cent of all eastern exports are of medium (27.5 per cent) or low (48 per cent) technology-intensity. This average pattern conceals a much higher share of the the medium intensity group in the Soviet Union, which accounted for nearly half (49.4 per cent) of all exports. Virtually all of these flows are concentrated in one commodity group (road motor vehicles), which in 1987 had a share of 45.5 per cent in all Soviet engineering goods exports, compared with 30.9 per cent in 1980. In 1970 the share was as low as 13 per cent.[892] In contrast to the Soviet Union, the exports of the six east European countries combined is characterized by the predominance of low technology-intensive goods: in 1987 the share of this group was about 55 per cent, broadly the same as in 1970 (Appendix table 7.8).

Finally it is interesting to look at the technology content of the exports of the four Asian NIEs and the

---

[892] It should be recalled that the data pertaining to the eastern countries exclude intra-area trade.

aggregate of sixteen developing countries. The relatively high concentration on high technology-intensive goods largely reflects the internationalization of the electronics industry which has enabled some of the Asian developing countries to play an important role as "offshore" production or assembly units of multinational companies. But increasingly these countries have also nurtured their own independent producers.[893] The Asian NIEs display considerable differences in the technology composition of their exports. High-tech goods were dominating the exports of the Republic of Korea and Taiwan, Province of China in 1970 with shares of about 60 per cent, but in 1980 and 1987 these had fallen to some 30 per cent. Broadly the opposite trend occurred in Hong Kong and Singapore. The Republic of Korea is noteworthy for a considerable shift towards medium technology-intensive goods, which in 1987 accounted for 35 per cent of all engineering goods exports compared with only 8 per cent in 1970 and 21 per cent in 1987.[894]

A striking feature of table 7.4.1 is that for the group of 16 developing countries the share of high-tech goods in total exports in 1987 amounted to 57 per cent. This very high figure, however, is largely accounted for by products such as semiconductor devices and electronic micro-circuits falling under SITC heading 729.3 (thermionic etc. valves and tubes, photocells and transistors). In 1987 this product group alone accounted for 72.4 per cent of all high technology intensive exports from this group of developing countries.[895] An open question, which cannot be examined here in more detail, is to what extent this high share reflects the labour-intensive assembly of electronic products. However, it has been pointed out, notably with regard to chip assembly, that the nature of these activities in the developing countries has been changing over time and can no longer be simply characterized as low-skill, labour-intensive as was the case over the 1970s. The pattern of factor use has become more complex as a result of strongly rising capital-intensity in the semi-conductor industry and the introduction of new technologies to automate assembly.[896] Nevertheless, the most important reason for the location of the assembly of electronic components and of sub-assemblies in the Asian countries are the lower wage costs for all types of labour (including skilled engineers) in comparison with the developed economies. Another factor is that the social legislation in the Asian countries allows much more flexibility with regard to multi-shift works and longer working weeks. This allows considerable increases in capital productivity and reduces unit costs to competitive levels, thereby absorbing the very high costs of processing equipment.[897]

Compared with exports, the structure of *imports* (table 7.4.1 and Appendix table 7.9) does not differ very much between the United States and western Europe as regards the relative importance of high technology goods. In both regions this group accounted for one quarter of all engineering goods imports in 1987. There is a pronounced difference, however, in the development of this share over time. Since 1970, the United States has experienced a significant shift in its imports towards high-technology goods. Most of this change took place between 1970 and 1980, when the share of technology-intensive goods rose from 14 to 22.2 per cent of total imports. In western Europe the importance of this product group was already much higher in 1970 (about 20 per cent) and the subsequent increase was correspondingly smaller.

Against the rising share of high technology-intensive goods in the United States' imports there has been the decline in the importance of medium technology-intensive goods, although in 1987 they still accounted for the bulk (43.3 per cent) of all imports. In western Europe the corresponding share in 1987 was much lower — at 28 per cent — but it has been rising since 1970. The increase in the combined shares of high and medium technology-intensive goods has its counterpart in a large decline in the importance of low technology-intensive goods from 42 per cent in 1970 to 32 per cent in 1987.

Among the larger economies, Japan is the only country where high technology-intensive goods predominate the overall pattern of imports. In 1987, the share of this group was some 41 per cent, which is much the same as in 1970 (38 per cent). A similarly large share among the individual west European countries exists only in Ireland, where the relative importance of this product group rose from 19 per cent in 1980 to 44 per cent in 1987. This rapid growth reflects the increasing importance of Ireland as an assembly site for multinational companies in the electronics sector which has entailed a large increase in imports of components. A similar development also explains the importance of high-technology goods in the import structure of the Asian NIEs.

The import structure of the eastern countries bears some strong resemblances to the corresponding export pattern described above, but there are also some marked differences. As on the export side, the share of high technology goods in imports is rather small and has hardly changed over time: in 1987 this product group accounted for about 7 per cent of all imports of

---

[893] For a general overview see D. Ernst, "Automation and the Worldwide Restructuring of the Electronics Industry: Strategic Implications for Developing Countries", *World Development*, Vol.13, No.3, p.335, and R. Kaplinski, *Micro-electronics and employment revisited. A review.*, International Labour Office, Geneva, 1987.

[894] But see below, section 7.4(ii), on the intra-group variance of technological intensity. The Republic of Korea's shift from high to medium technology goods in reality is probably a shift from low to medium.

[895] This corresponds to about 41 per cent of all engineering goods exports of these countries in 1987, an example of the very strong product concentration occurring in the specialization patterns of developing countries. Moreover, virtually all these exports of SITC 729.3 are concentrated in Malaysia (82.1 per cent) and Thailand (17.6 per cent).

[896] See also D. Ernst, *loc.cit.*, p.335.

[897] See D. Ernst, *op.cit.*, p.346.

engineering goods. Less than a quarter of all engineering goods imports fall into the second category, viz. advanced technology-intensive goods. Medium technology-intensive goods are as equally unimportant as high technology-intensive goods in total imports, *inter alia* a reflection of the virtual absence of western car exports to eastern countries. About 60 per cent of all goods imported by the eastern countries over the period 1970 to 1987 were low technology-intensive goods.

Although a discussion of the technology transfer from the west to the east through normal trade channels is outside the scope of this note, the above data nevertheless provoke some reflections on the matter. First, the data suggest that western exports of high technology-intensive goods to the east are much less important than western exports to the rest of the world.[898] The proportions are somewhat different for the second group, viz. advanced technology-intensive goods, which have a higher share in western exports to the east (24 per cent) than in western exports to the world (about 15 per cent). It thus appears that transfer of technology through trade channels has mainly taken place in the area of advanced technology-intensive goods.[899]

These figures require two comments. First, trade figures do not provide a complete picture of the transfer of technology between countries. Indeed, trade is only one of several channels, and looking only at trade data probably exaggerates the relative importance of knowledge transfer from the west to the east relative to the corresponding transfers from the west to other regions, but notably to other western countries. The reason for this is that a considerable part of this knowledge transfer takes place in other communication channels, for example, technical literature, the exchange of views between technical experts and the regular interchanges between the producer and user of new technologies. All these channels are probably of a greater importance for technology transfer between western countries than between the west and the east.[900] Second, any claim that an easier access of eastern countries to the most advanced western technology would have significantly improved their overall economic performance and competitiveness overlooks the fundamental problems these countries have encountered in efficiently applying the technologies available to them. "In other words, when advanced machinery of a known productive capacity fails to live up to expectations in its new environment, the rigidities within the enterprise, the sector and the surrounding economic milieu are called into question."[901] Imports of technology cannot provide a quick fix for an economy in need of systemic reform.[902] The basic presumption is that the potentially favourable effects of a substantially larger inflow of western technology would have evaporated quickly under the impact of the inefficiencies inherent in the adminstrative allocation of resources.

(b) Trade balances by group of technology-intensity

Trade is one of the major channels by which a country is linked to the world economy. The overall trade balance is a major element of the current account, which in a way measures the net outcome of the interacting differential comparative advantages and disadvantages in the various sectors of an economy.

As noted in section 7.2(i) above, engineering goods account in general for more than half of manufactured goods trade in the various countries and therefore play an important role in determining the overall trade balance for manufactured goods. It is therefore of interest to examine the overall trade balances for engineering goods in terms of the four groups of technology intensity.

The relevant data for 1970, 1980 and 1987 are shown in table 7.4.2. It can be seen that the structure of the trade balances in terms of the differing technology-intensities varies markedly between countries and, in some cases, has changed considerably over time. There are only five countries with a positive trade balance in all three years examined, namely, Japan, the Federal Republic of Germany, Italy, Sweden and Switzerland. In 1987 this group is enlarged by Ireland, the Republic of Korea and Taiwan, Province of China.

In 1970 and 1980 the United States had a relatively large trade surplus in high, advanced and low technology-intensive goods, which was partly offset by a deficit in medium technology products. By 1987 this pattern had changed dramatically. There was a large overall trade deficit ($79.25 billion) on account of a swing in the balances for advanced and low technology-intensive goods, a soaring deficit for medium technology-intensive goods and a dwindling surplus for high-tech products. The US trade surplus in 1970 and 1980 was due to its performance in high and advanced technology-intensive goods, the deficit in medium technology goods being roughly offset by the surplus in low-tech products. In 1987, the high and advanced technology groups combined generated only

---

[898] The share of high technology-intensive goods in world exports of the developed market economies was 23.5 per cent in 1987. This compares with a share of this product group in eastern imports (which are mainly originating in the DMEs) of 7.1 per cent.

[899] It is well known that western countries have restricted or prohibited the shipments of certain high-tech products to the countries of eastern Europe and the Soviet Union within the COCOM (Coordinating Committee for Multilateral Export Controls). Western export restrictions have certainly limited the access of eastern countries to high-tech commodities. The quantitative impact of these policies on the overall economic performance of eastern countries is, however, not measured here.

[900] See also A. Lenz and K. Stiltner, *Quantification of Western Exports of High-technology Products to Communist Countries through 1983*, Office of Trade and Investment Analysis, International Trade Administration, US Department of Commerce. May 1985, p.8.

[901] Steven W. Popper, *East European Reliance on Technology Imports from the West*, The Rand Corporation, August 1988, p.44. See also Economic Commission for Europe, "East-west trade in investment goods, 1970-1987", *Economic Bulletin for Europe*, vol.41, No.3, Pergamon Press for the United Nations, 1989.

[902] *Ibid.*

TABLE 7.4.2

Balance of trade in engineering, by class of technology intensity
(Billion US dollars)

	1970					1980					1987				
	HT	AT	MT	LT	Total Engineering	HT	AT	MT	LT	Total Engineering	HT	AT	MT	LT	Total Engineering
Seven major countries															
United States	4.35	1.58	-2.50	3.24	6.67	15.04	8.51	-13.55	12.70	22.72	3.61	-3.11	-63.69	-16.19	-79.25
Japan	0.43	0.31	2.93	3.61	7.29	9.93	6.94	33.89	24.41	75.16	36.39	17.61	67.90	32.81	154.71
Germany, Fed.Rep. of	0.53	1.98	3.69	5.37	11.57	0.50	9.60	19.45	24.09	55.37	-3.69	11.65	35.14	35.70	87.00
France	-0.12	-0.02	0.93	0.26	1.05	-0.57	1.57	4.25	3.33	8.58	-0.20	0.19	1.07	-1.19	-0.11
Italy	0.02	0.02	0.62	1.39	2.05	-0.98	0.27	-1.27	8.83	6.85	-2.54	-0.22	-3.10	14.01	8.14
United Kingdom	0.24	0.73	1.85	2.02	4.83	0.79	3.37	-0.31	6.46	10.31	-1.24	0.81	-7.44	0.63	-7.24
Canada	-0.28	-0.54	0.11	-1.15	-1.86	-3.19	-2.10	-2.04	-4.60	-11.58	-5.65	-2.05	-0.47	-6.64	-13.89
Nine smaller countries															
Austria	-0.09	-0.00	-0.23	-0.08	-0.41	-0.61	-0.15	-1.47	-0.14	-2.45	-1.16	0.56	-1.90	0.02	-2.50
Belgium	-0.22	-0.20	0.11	-0.24	-0.55	-1.03	-0.89	0.24	-1.04	-2.72	-1.39	-2.02	1.97	-1.04	-2.47
Denmark	-0.19	-0.04	-0.25	0.04	-0.43	-0.42	0.06	-0.39	0.73	-0.02	-0.87	0.11	-1.32	0.55	-1.53
Finland	-0.11	-0.11	-0.22	-0.11	-0.55	-0.66	-0.42	-0.79	0.00	-1.86	-0.97	-0.40	-1.09	0.25	-2.20
Ireland	-0.03	-0.05	-0.12	-0.20	-0.40	0.23	-0.20	-0.69	-0.96	-1.61	1.90	-0.11	-0.67	-0.38	0.75
Netherlands	0.00	-0.20	-0.70	-0.42	-1.31	-0.40	-0.51	-2.19	-0.96	-3.47	-1.09	-0.75	-4.36	-1.43	-7.63
Norway	-0.14	-0.14	-0.17	-0.38	-0.83	-0.71	-0.51	-0.86	-1.06	-3.13	-1.45	-0.75	-1.62	-2.39	-6.23
Sweden	0.02	-0.11	0.18	0.47	0.56	0.20	-0.04	1.52	1.65	3.34	-0.05	-0.02	2.14	1.63	3.70
Switzerland	0.43	0.33	-0.51	0.24	0.48	1.20	2.29	-2.53	2.39	3.34	0.82	3.23	-4.59	3.56	3.01
Southern Europe															
Greece	-0.08	-0.07	-0.13	-0.70	-0.98	-0.27	-0.33	-0.64	-2.54	-3.78	-0.42	-0.32	-0.90	-1.70	-3.33
Portugal	-0.04	-0.06	-0.14	-0.19	-0.43	-0.13	-0.29	-0.55	-0.82	-1.79	-0.48	-0.26	-1.27	-1.19	-3.19
Spain	-0.27	-0.20	-0.07	-0.29	-0.83	-1.51	-0.47	0.85	0.33	-0.79	-3.05	-1.85	-0.30	-2.39	-7.59
Turkey	-0.04	-0.09	-0.05	-0.23	-0.40	-0.06	-0.41	-0.13	-0.78	-1.38	-0.83	-0.83	-0.32	-1.23	-3.21
Yugoslavia	-0.11	-0.07	-0.22	-0.24	-0.64	-0.30	-0.39	-0.18	-0.90	-1.76	-0.44	-0.25	-0.02	0.33	-0.37
Asian NIEs															
Hong Kong	-0.11	-0.07	-0.04	-0.11	-0.33	-0.90	-0.53	-0.21	-1.03	-2.67	-2.85	-1.18	-1.56	-2.30	-7.89
Singapore	-0.04	-0.10	-0.06	-0.28	-0.48	-0.61	-0.64	0.19	-1.49	-2.55	0.84	-1.13	0.41	-1.42	-1.30
Republic of Korea	-0.04	-0.11	-0.06	-0.37	-0.58	-0.33	-0.87	0.61	-0.40	-0.98	0.94	-2.59	5.35	-0.46	3.24
Taiwan	0.03	-0.05	-0.04	-0.26	-0.32	0.34	-0.73	0.81	-0.40	0.02	2.09	0.17	1.48	1.91	5.67
Eastern countries															
Eastern Europe	-0.07	-0.13	0.01	-0.51	-0.70	-0.28	-0.84	0.09	-2.08	-3.31	-0.36	-1.15	-0.00	-2.27	-3.99
Soviet Union	-0.04	-0.29	-0.03	-0.67	-1.03	-0.15	-1.56	-0.06	-3.71	-5.77	-0.37	-1.76	0.23	-4.52	-6.79

Source: ECE secretariat based on COMTRADE data base.

Notes: As for table 7.4.1.

a minor surplus of $0.5 billion, while the deficit for the two other groups amounted to about $80 billion.

Japan had a positive trade balance in all four product groups in all three years displayed in table 7.4.2, but the technology structure of the aggregate balance has changed considerably. In 1970 and 1980 the bulk of the Japanese trade surplus in engineering goods was due to medium and low technology-intensive goods. The relative importance of the first group remained broadly stable, accounting for some 40 to 45 per cent of the Japanese surplus in engineering goods, but the surplus in low technology goods fell from nearly half of the total trade surplus in 1970 to only 21 per cent in 1987. The obverse of this decline is the rapidly growing trade surplus in high and advanced technology-intensive goods, with a particularly large increase for the first group between 1980 and 1987. In 1970 and 1980 the trade surplus in high technology-intensive goods accounted for about 6 per cent and 13 per cent, respectively, of the overall trade surplus. In 1987 this figure had risen to nearly one quarter.

Most of the traditional surplus of the Federal Republic of Germany in engineering goods trade is due to medium and low technology goods, although there is also a surplus in advanced technology goods. Net exports for high-tech goods were very small in 1970 and 1980. However, in 1987 there was a deficit, nearly as large as that for the three other major west European economies combined.[903]

French trade in engineering goods in 1987 was broadly balanced, with small surpluses in advanced and medium level products offset by small deficits in the other two groups. The interesting feature here is the marked deterioration in the net trade position since 1980, when there was a large strong surplus. The surpluses in advanced and medium technology-intensive goods were greatly reduced and the low-tech balance moved into deficit.

The major factor behind the positive net exports of Italy in all three years is the structural surplus for low technology-intensive goods, which offset by far the deficits in the other groups in 1980 and 1987.[904] The considerable deterioration in the UK trade balance for engineering goods between 1980 and 1987 is largely due to the strongly rising deficit for medium-technology goods in combination with a markedly reduced surplus for low and advanced technology goods. Also the positive, although small surplus in high technology goods in 1980 turned into a deficit in 1987.

In general, the trade balances of the nine smaller west European countries in engineering goods, were in deficit in all four product groups. Only Sweden and Switzerland are traditional surplus countries in engineering goods. Also Ireland was in surplus in 1987 on account of the burgeoning exports of high-technology goods. Although the latter group contributes to the overall surplus, the main sources of Switzerland's trade surplus are advanced and low technology-intensive goods, there being a considerable deficit in the medium group. In contrast, Sweden's trade surplus in engineering goods is generated in the two lower technology-intensity groups with the high and advanced technology groups being broadly balanced.

Trade deficits in all the four technology groups is a more pronounced feature of the five south European countries (table 7.4.1). Yugoslavia had a surplus in low technology goods in 1987 but this was insufficient to offset the deficit in the other three groups. The same holds for Spain which in 1980 had surpluses in medium and low technology goods, but a relatively large deficit in high-tech products.

The six east European countries combined and the Soviet Union were also in overall deficit in engineering goods trade with the world in all three years examined here. This aggregate deficit is mainly due to low technology-intensive goods, although the deficit for advanced technology goods is also considerable. There is also a deficit in high-technology goods, but this is relatively small, since neither exports nor imports of these goods play an important role in the trade of the eastern countries. The Soviet Union had a surplus of about $230 million in medium technology goods in 1987; largely, as mentioned above, on account of its exports of road motor vehicles.

Finally, it is interesting to look at the trade balances for the four Asian NIEs for they illustrate how the shifting patterns of specializations in engineering industries within these countries is mirrored in the composition of the overall trade balances by group of technology intensity. In 1970 and 1980 the general feature was an overall trade deficit, the emerging surpluses in medium technology goods being insufficient to offset the deficit in the three other groups. (The exception is Taiwan, Province of China which was more or less in balanced trade account, with surpluses for high and medium-level goods offsetting deficits in the two other groups.) By 1987, both the Republic of Korea and Taiwan, Province of China, had large trade surpluses in engineering goods, although the underlying "technology structure" differed considerably between the two countries. The major factor behind this swing in the trade balance is the large export surplus in medium technology goods, in conjunction with a swing in the balance of high-tech trade from deficit in 1980 to surplus in 1987 (table 7.4.2). The changes in Taiwan, Province of China are equally impressive: between 1980 and 1987, the surpluses in high and medium technology trade rose considerably and the balances for the other two groups has moved from deficit to surplus,

---

[903] However, there is some uncertainty about the Federal Republic's deficit since there is a relatively large discrepancy between the sum of the balances for the four product groups ($78.8 billion) and the total balance ($87 billion). This is due to the fact that exports from the Federal Republic of Germany cannot be completely allocated to the four separate technology groups because of confidentiality restrictions in the national statistics. This means that the absolute and relative importance of the four groups cannot be precisely determined. It is nevertheless clear from the magnitudes involved that the main sources of the trade surplus are the medium and low technology-intensive groups.

[904] In 1980 Italy had a small trade surplus in advanced technology-intensive goods.

the swing being most pronounced for low technology-intensive goods.

(c) World export market shares

Section 7.2 above included an overview of the main changes in national and regional shares of total world trade in engineering goods. This is now amplified with a brief analysis of the relative importance of different countries and regions in world exports of each of the four different groups of technology-intensity of engineering goods.[905]

It can be seen from table 7.4.3 and the Appendix table 7.10 that the individual country and regional shares sometimes differ significantly from one technology group to the other. Thus in 1987 the United States had nearly a quarter of the high technology-intensive segment of the export market, but accounted for only 9 per cent of the world exports of medium and low technology goods. The Federal Republic of Germany's world market shares ranged in 1987 from 8.5 per cent of high technology-intensive goods in 1987 to 21.5 per cent of the low technology market, a category where the Federal Republic is the largest world exporter. Japan easily dominates the market for medium technology goods with a share of about 27 per cent in 1987. In contrast, Japan's world market share of low technology goods was much lower at only 14 per cent, while its share of high technology goods was just over 20 per cent.

Although the United States still accounted for a quarter of world exports of high technology goods in 1987, its position had considerably weakened since 1970, when its share was about 37 per cent. Several of the west European countries also experienced declining market shares in the high-tech group. This is notably the case for the Federal Republic of Germany, the United Kingdom, Italy, the Netherlands Sweden and Switzerland, although it can be seen from Apppendix table 7.10 that for some countries these changes only occurred after 1980. In contrast, France has maintained a broadly stable share of the market for high technology goods, while Ireland's share increased from only 0.3 per cent in 1970 to about 2 per cent in 1980.[906] The major counterparts to the declining market shares of the United States and western Europe in high-tech goods have been the large increases of Japan and the four Asian NIEs. Japan accounted for about 8 per cent of this market in 1970 but for more than 20 per cent in 1987, which is fairly close to the share of the United States. For the Asian NIEs the corresponding increase in share over the same period was from 2 per cent to 10.5 per cent. Thus, the combined share of Japan and the NIEs in world exports of high technology goods in 1987 was only slightly less than that of the European Community (including intra-trade).

The declining role of the United States in world exports of engineering goods is evident to broadly the same extent in all four technology groups, with market shares falling by some 7 to 8 percentage points between 1970 and 1987 (see table 7.4.3). There have been similarly large declines in the shares of the European Community, except in low technology goods where there was little change. The EFTA countries did rather better on average, maintaining their shares of the world market in all groups, except high technology.

The market shares of the south European countries edged upward in all four technology groups, but these changes were almost entirely due to Spain. p. The market shares of the eastern countries are small and, except in medium technology, they all fell between 1970 and 1987.[907] Japan and the Asian NIEs have increased their market shares in all four technology groups. The Japanese export thrust is noteworthy not only in high-technology but also in the advanced and medium technology groups. In contrast, Japan's share of low technology goods rose only modestly, from 12 per cent in 1970 to 14.4 per cent in 1987.

In marked contrast to its relatively modest role in the markets for high technology goods, the Federal Republic of Germany has large market shares, of around 20 per cent, in the other three groups. In 1987 the Federal Republic was the largest exporter of advanced and low technology-intensive goods. Japan, in turn, was by far the largest exporter of medium technology goods with a market share in 1987 of about 27.5 per cent (compared with 12.5 per cent in 1970).

The French export performance was quite different in the two periods 1970-1980 and 1980-1987. During the first period France gained market share in the advanced, medium and low technology-intensive goods, but the export drive lost momentum after 1980: by 1987 shares in medium and low technology goods were well below those in 1970 while the share of advanced technology-intensive goods had fallen back to the level in 1970.

With the exception of the high-tech market, the market shares of the United Kingdom continued to decline after 1980. There was a striking fall in the market share of medium technology-intensive goods, from about 10 per cent in 1970 to only 4 per cent in 1987.

Among the smaller countries Switzerland is noteworthy for maintaining its relatively strong representation in the market for advanced technology goods with a share of about 5 per cent.

---

[905] The market shares reported in this section are not directly comparable with those reported in section 7.2(i) above. World exports are defined as the sum of exports of developed market economies and 20 developing countries plus the exports of the seven eastern countries to these two aforementioned groups of countries.

[906] Note that Austria, Finland and Norway also slightly increased their world export shares, although their overall involvement in world trade in this product group is rather low.

[907] Recall that these data exclude intra-area trade.

TABLE 7.4.3

World export market shares for engineering goods exports, by group of technology intensity
(Percentages)

	1970	1980	1987		1970	1980	1987
A: High technology-intensive goods [a]				**C: Medium technology-intensive goods** [a]			
United States	36.7	29.2	24.5	Japan	12.5	23.7	27.3
Japan	7.9	13.2	20.6	Germany, Fed.Rep. of	21.2	19.8	20.9
Germany, Fed.Rep. of	11.9	11.6	8.5	Canada	12.8	6.9	9.3
United Kingdom	9.4	11.3	7.7	United States	16.7	12.0	9.0
France	6.7	6.1	6.6	France	8.3	8.8	6.7
Italy	4.4	3.6	3.5	United Kingdom	9.7	5.8	3.8
Total 6 countries	77.0	75.0	71.4	Total 6 countries	81.2	77.0	77.4
Memorandum items:				*Memorandum items:*			
EC (9)	39.5	39.0	33.0	EC (9)	51.8	46.0	41.9
EFTA (6)	7.8	5.8	5.3	EFTA (6)	3.8	3.8	4.1
Southern Europe	0.5	0.9	0.8	Southern Europe	0.5	2.1	2.7
Eastern countries [b]	0.5	0.4	0.2	Eastern countries [b]	0.6	0.8	0.5
Four Asian NIEs	2.0	7.0	10.5	Four Asian NIEs	0.7	3.1	4.7
Sixteen LDCs	0.5	2.0	2.1	Sixteen LDCs	0.2	1.4	0.4
B: Advanced technology-intensive goods [a]				**D: Low technology-intensive goods** [a]			
Germany, Fed.Rep. of	22.7	20.0	19.2	Germany, Fed.Rep. of	21.3	19.0	21.5
Japan	6.6	11.3	17.5	Japan	11.8	13.8	14.4
United States	23.0	20.8	16.7	Italy	7.3	7.8	9.3
United Kingdom	11.0	10.0	7.6	United States	17.0	14.6	9.3
France	7.0	8.4	7.0	United Kingdom	9.6	8.3	6.9
Switzerland	5.0	4.9	4.9	France	6.8	8.1	6.5
Total 6 countries	75.3	75.4	72.9	Total 6 countries	73.8	71.6	67.9
Memorandum items:				*Memorandum items:*			
EC (9)	52.4	48.9	44.2	EC (9)	53.0	50.6	52.1
EFTA (6)	9.5	9.5	10.5	EFTA (6)	10.8	9.9	11.4
Southern Europe	1.1	1.8	1.9	Southern Europe	2.0	2.5	3.0
Eastern countries [b]	1.6	1.2	0.7	Eastern countries [b]	1.3	1.2	0.9
Four Asian NIEs	0.9	1.2	4.2	Four Asian NIEs	0.7	3.5	5.7
Sixteen LDCs	0.2	1.5	0.7	Sixteen LDCs	0.3	1.1	0.6

Source: ECE secretariat based on COMTRADE data base.

Note: See Appendix table 7.10 for data for all individual countries.

[a] Major six countries for each group based on rankings in 1987.
[b] Limited coverage; see text.

(d) Revealed comparative advantage by group of technology intensity

In a similar vein to section 7.3 it is possible to calculate indices of revealed comparative advantage for each of the four groups of technology-intensive goods (see table 2.4.21). As this are indices for quite broad commodity groupings they have to be seen as reflecting "average" specialization patterns and — in a much more qualified sense than those presented in section 7.3 for products at the three-digit level of the SITC. Thus, an RCA index of less than unity for, say, high technology-intensive goods, means that "on average" a country is not strongly specialized in these products — but this average pattern may, nevertheless, conceal strong comparative advantages for some individual products within each of the four aggregates. The indices given here can only provide, therefore, a rough classification of national patterns of specialization according to technology intensity.

Table 7.4.4 shows that only six countries had, on average, a comparative advantage in high technology-intensive goods in 1987. These are the United States, Japan, the United Kingdom, Ireland, Hong Kong and Singapore. Nevertheless, France, the Netherlands and Switzerland had RCA values of around 0.9, indicating a relatively strong presence of high technology goods in exports. The most striking feature of table 2.4.21 is the very low value of the index (0.5) for the Federal Republic of Germany, a clear indication that this country is not strongly specialized in high technology-intensive goods.

The United States' revealed comparative advantage in high-tech goods has remained fairly stable,[908] while the changes in the index for Japan indicate a marked shift towards skill- and highly knowledge-intensive industries. In 1970 the Japanese specialization index for high technology goods was only 0.75 only slightly above that of the Federal Republic of Germany; by 1987, the Japanese index had risen to 1.41. In striking contrast, the RCA index for high-tech goods for the

---

[908] Whereas the declining world market shares suggest a deterioration in US competitiveness this is not the case for the RCA indices. The explanantion is that the RCA indices are *relative* world market shares: the decline in the world market share for high technology-intensive goods was accompanied by a similar fall in the share for all manufactured goods. Consequently, the RCA index has remained stable.

TABLE 7.4.4

Indices of revealed comparative advantage, by class of technology intensity

	1970				1980				1987			
	HT	AT	MT	LT	HT	AT	MT	LT	HT	AT	MT	LT
Seven major countries												
United States	2.18	1.37	0.99	1.01	2.07	1.48	0.85	1.03	2.18	1.48	0.79	0.82
Japan	0.75	0.63	1.18	1.12	1.06	0.92	1.91	1.12	1.41	1.20	1.87	0.99
Germany, Fed.Rep. of	0.67	1.28	1.20	1.20	0.71	1.22	1.21	1.16	0.50	1.12	1.22	1.26
France	0.86	0.90	1.07	0.88	0.75	1.02	1.07	0.99	0.92	0.97	0.93	0.90
Italy	0.67	0.81	0.85	1.12	0.55	0.71	0.70	1.18	0.51	0.68	0.53	1.38
United Kingdom	1.02	1.20	1.06	1.05	1.37	1.21	0.71	1.00	1.20	1.19	0.59	1.07
Canada	0.94	0.90	2.64	0.52	0.65	0.72	2.24	0.60	0.55	0.79	2.50	0.52
Nine smaller countries												
Austria	0.22	1.01	0.38	1.01	0.24	0.92	0.41	1.14	0.36	1.38	0.42	1.30
Belgium	0.31	0.38	1.02	0.55	0.36	0.42	1.12	0.57	0.32	0.37	1.30	0.61
Denmark	0.53	1.23	0.33	1.64	0.58	1.06	0.42	1.54	0.55	1.03	0.30	1.62
Finland	0.07	0.22	0.18	1.03	0.16	0.44	0.25	1.03	0.34	0.64	0.38	1.23
Ireland	1.27	0.12	0.11	0.62	1.88	0.65	0.31	0.69	2.84	0.63	0.05	0.63
Netherlands	1.21	0.83	0.36	0.85	0.89	0.73	0.39	0.86	0.87	0.78	0.37	0.94
Norway	0.22	0.44	0.25	1.72	0.39	0.75	0.24	1.52	0.50	0.74	0.27	1.94
Sweden	0.86	0.87	0.92	1.39	0.77	1.00	1.09	1.27	0.70	0.97	1.11	1.28
Switzerland	1.72	1.85	0.06	1.08	1.20	1.82	0.07	1.21	0.87	1.77	0.07	1.40
Southern Europe												
Greece	0.21	0.09	0.02	0.14	0.08	0.12	0.05	0.43	0.07	0.12	0.01	0.28
Portugal	0.34	0.23	0.23	0.42	0.64	0.32	0.42	0.41	0.24	0.51	0.44	0.51
Spain	0.31	0.73	0.40	1.31	0.29	0.64	1.03	0.97	0.36	0.62	1.33	0.90
Turkey	0.00	0.00	0.05	0.21	0.03	0.13	0.47	0.20	0.03	0.24	0.11	0.85
Yugoslavia	0.20	0.82	0.23	1.48	0.28	1.02	0.55	1.26	0.15	0.97	0.52	1.45
Asian NIEs												
Hong Kong	0.42	0.34	0.36	0.22	1.61	0.19	0.46	0.37	1.33	0.50	0.23	0.43
Singapore	0.86	1.10	0.77	0.84	2.15	0.83	0.92	0.96	2.67	1.07	0.64	0.75
Republic of Korea	0.66	0.15	0.06	0.12	0.78	0.26	0.42	0.64	0.98	0.26	0.90	0.73
Taiwan	1.60	0.22	0.06	0.32	0.97	0.47	0.54	0.65	0.97	0.57	0.39	0.84
Eastern countries												
Eastern Europe	0.26	1.00	0.36	0.79	0.20	0.78	0.44	0.81	0.14	0.58	0.29	0.81
Soviet Union	0.41	0.91	0.38	0.77	0.31	0.53	0.54	0.40	0.18	0.44	0.89	0.55

Source: ECE secretariat based on COMTRADE data base.

Note: Product groups: HT = high technology, AT = advanced technology, MT = medium technology, LT = low technology.

Federal Republic of Germany in 1987 had fallen below its level in 1970. Two of the smaller west European countries, the Netherlands and Switzerland, also appear to have lost an earlier comparative advantage in high technology-intensive goods.

There are some contrasts and similarities between the country patterns of specialization in high and advanced technology-intensive goods. As in the high-tech group, the United States' specialization in advanced technology goods has also remained strong and stable. In Japan the RCA in advanced-tech has risen strongly, from below unity in 1970 to well above it in 1987. Among the four large west European countries only the Federal Republic of Germany and the United Kingdom show a specialization in advanced technology-intensive goods. France had a weak specialization in 1980, but not in 1970 and 1987.[909] Among the smaller countries only Austria, Denmark and especially Switzerland were specialized in advanced technology goods.

In medium-technology goods only Japan, the Federal Republic of Germany and Canada have maintained their relative specialization. For France this was the case in 1970 and 1980, but not in 1987; the index for the United Kingdom exceed unity in 1970, but not in the other years. Among the smaller countries only Belgium, Spain and Sweden have indices greater than unity for these goods.

In low technology-intensive goods a number of the smaller west European countries have a relatively strong specialization (Austria, Denmark, Finland, Norway, Sweden and Switzerland). Among the south European countries only Yugoslavia presently shows a strong specialization in this group although the index for Turkey has been rising strongly since 1970.

Among the larger countries the Federal Republic of Germany, Italy and the United Kingdom (except in 1980) have maintained their specialization in this product group, but in the United States and Japan the indices had fallen below unity by 1987.

---

[909] It is striking how small the variance of the RCA indices is for France in 1987, all being around 0.9, but none exceeding unity. This reflects the broad diversification of French exports.

7.5 CONCLUSIONS

The aim of this present study was to provide some insights into the nature of international trade in engineering goods. One reason for doing this is the relative paucity of comparative studies of the trade of industrialized countries. Such an analysis is also timely in the light of current discussions about the likely effects of the completion of the EC's "Internal Market" on countries and firms inside and outside the Community. The purpose here has not so much been to estimate these likely effects but rather to add to the empirical stock of knowledge on trade and specialization patterns which would be helpful in such an analysis.

The present study has highlighted the changing role of individual countries and regions in world trade in engineering goods and given a rough idea of the diversity of relative product specialization within Europe and elsewhere. Given the aggregate nature of the data, there is a danger that strong generalizations from the results oversimplify what is in reality a more complex phenomenon. Nevertheless, a few salient findings merit attention.

Japan's rapid expansion of engineering exports is clearly demonstrated by the data compiled here, as is the strong advance of the Asian NIEs. The brunt of this expansion has been borne by the United States, but western Europe has also lost considerable market share. There is, however, significant variation among the individual countries. In general the EFTA countries have defended their market shares better than the Community, and within the Community it is France and the United Kingdom that largely account for the declining share of the Community in world exports. In a similar vein much of the aggregate (favourable) change for southern Europe is due to developments in Spain. The declining role of eastern Europe and the Soviet Union in engineering goods trade is evident.

The analysis of regional trade flows underlines the notion of a west European economic space: intra-area flows clearly dominate flows to other regions. In a similar way, North America, Japan and the NIEs form a region. Nevertheless, economic ties between the two groups remain relatively strong. A third, quite separate, economic region consists of the seven eastern countries. The trade intensity coefficients reveal the very weak integration of these countries in the international division of labour. The current economic problems facing these countries and their attempts at radical reform largely derive from the systemic problems with administrative management.

The examination of specialization patterns, based on data for 29 engineering product groups, revealed both continuity as well as conspicuous changes in the comparative advantage of the various countries. There exists some overlapping of national comparative advantages, but the more striking feature is the large diversity of specialization patterns. This was illustrated by the low degree of correlation between the RCA patterns of the three major economies (United States, Japan, and the Federal Republic of Germany), both among themselves and with other countries. These broad differences in inter-industry specialization most likely conceal a still greater diversification of specializations *within* these 29 product groups.

A striking result of the analysis was that western and eastern Europe are not, on average, highly specialized in skill-intensive engineering goods as a group. RCA indices were larger than unity (in 1987) only for the Federal Republic of Germany, Ireland Sweden, and also for Canada, the United States, Japan and Singapore. In fact, the data reveal clearly that Japan has followed a more or less deliberate policy to seek its comparative advantage in skill-intensive products. This shift is much less pronounced for the NIEs, but a similar underlying trend is clearly visible.

In general, west European countries failed to show particular strength in product groups which occupy a large share of world exports of engineering goods. There is a significant correlation between the national specialization indices and the size of the world market for different products only for the United States and Japan. Again, the results point to a significant shift in Japan's specialization pattern towards products with potential for large economies of scale. These results partly reflect the relatively weak comparative advantages of western Europe in the global markets for office equipment and telecommunications apparatus. These are typical areas in which technical barriers and public procurement policies have hindered intra-European trade flows and reduced the intensity of competition between firms in the individual European countries.[910] This is potentially a major area where competitive procurement could lead to a significant increase in market size and correspondingly allow for a much better exploitation of economies of scale. The creation of a single market is expected to halt the decline of traditional comparative advantage of the Community member countries in this area.[911]

---

[910] On the difficulties of deregulating the European telecommunications industry, see "Oh what a tangled web we weave", *The Economist*, 28 October 1989, p.87.

[911] It has been pointed out that more competitive public procurement, apart from the perceived micro- and macro-economic effects, has a "symbolic value". Increasing competition between firms is a major mechanism underlying the positive growth effects of the single market — and the opening up of public pro-

According to the product cycle theory, industrialized countries have to specialize increasingly in knowledge-intensive goods as they lose comparative advantage at the lower end of the technology scale. On this count, western Europe's performance has not been particularly good: market shares at the upper end of the spectrum (high and advanced technology) have been lost and relative specialization has been an exception rather than the rule. The market for high technology goods is clearly dominated by the United States and Japan; and there is a large gap between the market shares of these two countries and those of the three major west European countries. The aggregate export share of the European Community is considerable, but this includes intra-trade and thus exaggerates the European position relative to Japan and the United States.

It is noteworthy that western Europe has only been able to maintain market shares in low technology-intensive goods. It is significant that of all four technology groups this is the one were Japan's market share is smallest and has risen the least.

The fact that west European countries have continued to specialize extensively in low technology, low skill-intensive goods may be a signal of future structural adjustment problems, notably for the high-wage countries. Competition in this area is largely based on price, and therefore both developing countries and the south European countries should be able to increase their market shares in the years ahead as production is relocated to these areas. This is also a range of products where the eastern countries, given their relatively low wage levels, could find it profitable to seek their comparative advantage when reorienting exports to western markets. In general, the availability of a relatively large pool of skilled workers in combination with low wage costs will make these countries natural competitors not only with southern Europe but also with the the NIEs. In a dynamic, medium-term perspective, there is no reason why this competition should be limited to the lower end of the technology spectrum. In fact, the eastern countries have a number of potential advantages including geographical proximity, which could eventually increase the attractiveness to west European firms of sub-contracting and and other joint operations across the technology spectrum.

---

curement would therefore have a considerable demonstration effect which gives a credibility bonus to government policies aiming at a single market. See *The Economics of 1992*, op.cit., p.160.

STATISTICAL APPENDICES

(A) Definitions

(i) Commodity groupings

All commodity groups are defined for data classified according to the SITC Rev. 1 (see *Standard International Trade Classification Revised*, Statistical Papers, series M, no.34, United Nations, New York, 1961).

Engineering goods comprise:

SITC 7: Machinery and transport equipment
69: Manufactures of metal, n.e.s.
861: Scientific, medical, optical, measuring and controlling instruments and apparatus
864: Watches and clocks
891.1: Phonographs (gramophones), tape recorders and other sound records and producers

Manufactured goods comprise sections 5 to 8 of the SITC Rev 1, excluding division 68 (non-ferrous metals).

(ii) Regional aggregates

(a) Developed market economies (DMEs)

1. EC 9: Belgium, Luxembourg, Denmark, France, Federal Republic of Germany, Ireland, Italy, Netherlands, United Kingdom
2. EFTA 6: Austria, Finland, Iceland, Norway, Sweden, Switzerland
3. Southern Europe: Greece, Portugal, Spain, Turkey, Yugoslavia
4. Western Europe: 1 + 2 + 3
5. North America: Canada, United States
6. Japan
7. Other DMEs: Australia, Israel, South Africa, New Zealand
8. Total DMEs: 4 + 5 + 6 + 7

(b) Eastern countries

1. Eastern Europe: Bulgaria, Czechoslovakia, German Democratic Republic, Hungary, Poland, Romania
2. USSR
3. Total eastern countries: 1 + 2

(c) Developing Countries

1. LDC (I): All countries other than (a) and (b)
2. LDC (II) countries: Argentina, Brazil, Chile, Colombia, Uruguay, Algeria, Cameroon, Egypt, Jordan, Oman, Saudi Arabia, Tunisia, Hong Kong, Indonesia, Malaysia, Philippines, Singapore, Republic of Korea, Taiwan Province of China, Thailand (20 countries)
3. Four Asian NIEs: Hong Kong, Singapore, Republic of Korea, Taiwan, Province of China

(B) List of 29 engineering commodity groups

SITC, Rev. 1	Description
691	Finished structural parts and structures, n.e.s.
692	Metal containers for storage and transport
693	Wire products (excluding electric) and fencing grills
694	Nails, screws, nuts, bolts, rivets and similar articles of iron, steel or copper
695	Tools for use in the hand or in machines
696	Cutlery
697	Household equipment of base materials
698	Manufactures of metal, n.e.s.
711	Power generating machinery
712	Agricultural machinery and implements
714	Office machines
715	Metalworking machinery
717	Textiles and leather machinery
718	Machines for special industries
719	Machinery and appliances (other than electrical) and machine parts, n.e.s.
722	Electrical power machinery and switchgear
723	Equipment for distributing electricity
724	Telecommunications apparatus
725	Domestic electrical equipment
726	Electric apparatus for medical purposes and radiological apparatus
729	Other electrical machinery apparatus
731	Railway vehicles
732	Road motor vehicles
733	Road vehicles other than motor vehicles
734	Aircraft
735	Ships and boats
861	Scientific, medical, optical, measuring and controlling instruments and apparatus
864	Watches and clocks
891.1	Phonographs, gramophones, tape recorders and other sound recorders and reproducers

(C) Classification of engineering goods by technology intensity

The proxy used for measuring the degree of technology intensity of a given product group is R & D expenditure as a percentage of total sales. The basic data came from an earlier study pertaining to the US manufacturing industry.[912] The average R & D intensity for the US manufacturing sector was calculated there to be 2.36 per cent. For the purposes of the present study four product groups are being distinguished:

Commodity group	R & D intensity (RDI)	Comments
1. Hi-tech (HT)	more than 7.1 per cent	More than three times the manufacturing average.
2. Advanced technology (AT)	$2.6 \leq RDI < 7.1$	More than 10 per cent above manufacturing average but less than three times the manufacturing average.
3. Medium technology (MT)	$2.1 \leq RDI < 2.6$	Within a range of 10 per cent around the average.
4. Low technology (LT)	$RDI < 2.1$ per cent	--

A list of engineering goods falling into each of these four groups is given below. The allocation is largely based on the R & D intensity data provided in the US study with a few adjustments made by the secretariat.

GROUP 1: High technology

SITC, Rev. 1
- 711.4 : Aircraft engines
- 714 : Office machines
- 719.63: Weighing machinery and weights therefor
- 724.9 : Telecommunication equipment, n.e.s.
- 729.3 : Electron and proton accelerations
- 729.7 : Thermonic etc, valves and tubes, photocells, transistors, etc.
- 734 : Aircraft
- 861.1 : Optical elements
- 861.2 : Spectacles and spectacle frames
- 861.3 : Binoculars, microscopes and other optical instruments
- 861.4 : Photographic cameras
- 861.5 : Cinematographic cameras
- 861.6 : Photographic and cinematographic apparatus, n.e.s.
- 861.7 : Medical instruments, n.e.s.
- 864 : Clocks and watches

GROUP 2: Advanced technology

- 711.3 : Steam engines
- 711.5 : Internal combustion engines, other than for aircraft
- 711.6 : Gas turbines, other than for aircraft
- 711.7 : Nuclear reactors
- 711.8 : Engines, n.e.s.
- 715.1 : Machine tools for working metals
- 722 : Electrical power machinery and switchgear
- 726 : Electrical apparatus for medical purposes and radiological apparatus
- 729.5 : Electrical measuring and controlling instruments and apparatus
- 729.9 : Electrical machinery and apparatus, n.e.s.
- 861.8 : Meters and counters, non-electric
- 861.9 : Measuring, controlling and scientific instruments, n.e.s.

GROUP 3: Medium technology

- 712 : Agricultural machinery
- 724.1 : Television broadcast receivers
- 724.2 : Radio broadcast receivers
- 732.1 : Passenger motor cars
- 732.2 : Buses
- 732.3 : Lorries and trucks
- 732.5 : Road tractors
- 732.6 : Chassis with engines mounted for passenger motor cars
- 732.7 : Other chassis with engines mounted
- 732.8 : Bodies, chassis, frames and other parts of motor vehicles
- 891.1 : Phonographs (grammophones), tape recorders, etc.

GROUP 4: Low technology

- 69 : Manufactures of metal, n.e.s.
- 711.1 : Steam generating boilers
- 711.2 : Boiler house plant
- 715.2 : Metalworking machinery, other than machine tools
- 717 : Textile and leather machinery
- 718.1 : Paper mill and pulp mill machinery
- 718.2 : Printing and bookbinding machinery
- 718.3 : Food-processing machines
- 718.4 : Construction and mining machinery
- 718.5 : Mineral crushing and moulding machinery
- 719.1 : Heating and cooling equipment
- 719.2 : Pumps and centrifuges
- 719.3 : Mechanical handling equipment
- 719.4 : Domestic appliances, non-electrical
- 719.5 : Powered tools, n.e.s.
- 719.61: Calendering machines etc.
- 719.62: Machines for cleaning or filling of bottles
- 719.64: Spraying machinery
- 719.65: Automatic vending machines
- 719.66: Railway and tramway truck fixtures and fittings etc.
- 719.7 : Ball, roller or needle-roller bearings
- 719.8 : Machinery and mechanical appliances, n.e.s.
- 719.9 : Parts and accessories of machinery, n.e.s.
- 723.1 : Insulated wire and cable
- 723.2 : Electrical insulating equipment
- 725 : Domestic electrical equipment
- 729.1 : Batteries and accumulators
- 729.2 : Electric lamps
- 729.4 : Automotive electrical equipment
- 729.6 : Electro-mechanical hand-tools
- 731 : Railway vehicles
- 732.4 : Special purpose lorries, trucks and vans

---

[912] See Regina Kelly, *Alternative Measurements of Technology-Intensive Trade*, Staff Economic Report, Office of Economic Research, US Department of Commerce, September 1976, and, by the same author, *The Impact of Technological Innovation on International Trade Patterns*, Staff Economic Report, Industry and Trade Administration, US Department of Commerce, December 1977.

732.9 : Motorcycles, motorized cycles and their parts
733 : Road vehicles other than motor vehicles
735 : Ships and boats

(D) Statistical Sources and Explanatory Notes

(i) List of sources

(A) United Nations Statistical Office, COMTRADE data base

(B) *1982 Yearbook of International Trade Statistics*, volume I, United Nations, New York, 1984 (Special table B)

(C) *Monthly Bulletin of Statistics*, vol.XLIII, no.5, May 1988, United Nations, New York, (Special table C)

(D) *Monthly Bulletin of Statistics*, vol.XLIII, no.6, June 1989, United Nations, New York, (Special table E)

(E) *Monthly Bulletin of Statistics*, vol.XL, no.12. December 1986, United Nations, New York (Special table C)

(ii) Notes

(a) Table 7.2.1-7.2.5 (aggregate trade data)

Aggregates for the world were calculated as the sum of exports of developed market economies, centrally planned economies and developing countries (see Appendix A above for definition of the regions).

Data for *DMEs* were directly extracted from the UNSO COMTRADE data base.

Aggregate trade data on the *centrally planned economies* were compiled mainly from trade matrices available in sources (B) and (C). Note that engineering goods exclude SITC 696 (cutlery) and SITC 697 (household equipment of base metals) but include SITC 892 (Sanitary, plumbing, testing and lighting fixtures and fittings). Trade data on SITC 861 and 864 are not available in (B) and (C). Exports and imports for these two commodity groups were approximated by trade flows to and from developed market economies and 24 developing countries (LDC II and four Asian NIEs — see above Appendix A), hence excluding notably intra-CMEA trade. Data for SITC 861 and 864 were directly extracted from (A) on the basis of mirror statistics.

Note that the aggregate engineering trade data for eastern Europe (6) and the USSR do not add up to the total engineering trade flows for the centrally planned economies. The *small* discrepancy is explained by the fact that the trade matrices in (B) and (C) do not disaggregate SITC 691-696, 698,812 into the trade conducted by eastern Europe (6) and the USSR, respectively. Consequently for eastern Europe and the USSR, trade in SITC 69 and 861, 864 was approximated by the trade with the DMEs and the group of 20 developing countries (LDC II).

Trade data for the *aggregate* of developing countries were compiled from the same sources and following the same procedures as for the *total* centrally planned economies described above. From 1985, published UN data include Yugoslavia in the group of developing countries, whereas in this study Yugoslavia is classified as developed market economy. The data from sources (B) and (C) were accordingly adjusted by the secretariat.

(b) Tables 7.2.7-7.2.9

The data on engineering goods trade by origin and destination were compiled from the following sources:

Region	Source
1. Developed market economies	(A)
2. Centrally planned economies	
(a) trade with DMEs	(A) (mirror statistics)
(b) trade with CMEs	(B),(C) (covers only SITC 7)
(c) trade with NIEs	(A) (mirror statistics)
(d) trade with R.O.W.	(B) (C) (covers only SITC 7)
3. 4 Asian NIEs	(A)
4. Other developing countries	
(a) trade with DMEs, NIEs	(A) (mirror statistics)
(b) trade with CPEs	(B), (C) (covers only SITC 7)
(c) trade with other developing countries	(B) (C) (covers only SITC 7)

(c) All other tables (detailed commodity statistics)

For all countries detailed commodity trade data were directly extracted from the UNSO COMTRADE data base. Note that data pertaining to the centrally planned economies cover only trade with the developed market economies and the group of 20 developing countries (LDC II and the Asian NIEs). These detailed trade data for the 29 product groups of engineering goods are in general not available for intra-CMEA trade.

APPENDIX TABLE 7.1

The share of engineering goods in total trade of manufactures
(Percentages)

	Exports			Imports		
	1970	1980	1987	1970	1980	1987
France	50.6	52.2	52.5	50.4	46.6	50.9
Germany	60.6	59.9	62.0	42.3	42.8	47.9
Italy	50.2	45.8	45.6	50.0	51.6	52.8
United Kingdom	58.0	55.1	55.2	43.6	48.7	53.9
Austria	37.8	40.7	46.2	51.4	49.5	51.7
Belgium	33.0	35.5	40.4	50.3	45.0	47.5
Denmark	55.7	52.0	40.3	46.5	42.9	48.3
Finland	27.5	29.8	37.8	53.1	54.7	57.1
Ireland	30.3	43.9	57.5	49.6	49.3	52.4
Netherlands	42.3	40.4	41.4	48.8	44.6	49.4
Norway	47.0	44.4	50.8	56.3	50.7	55.9
Sweden	59.2	58.1	59.0	50.8	51.4	56.9
Switzerland	56.2	52.9	52.3	44.5	41.8	45.7
Greece	6.3	11.2	7.0	69.8	64.0	45.8
Portugal	17.9	23.9	23.9	52.2	53.6	54.8
Spain	43.3	43.0	48.5	54.2	55.8	61.7
Turkey	5.4	12.4	18.9	58.7	45.3	52.3
Yugoslavia	44.2	44.7	44.0	53.8	54.9	52.0
Canada	66.4	59.2	67.8	69.9	71.5	72.7
United States	69.0	67.7	71.0	53.4	57.3	63.2

Source: ECE secretariat based on COMTRADE data base.

APPENDIX TABLE 7.2

Indices of revealed comparative advantage in engineering goods, by SITC groups, 1970

	EC														EFTA						
	Belgium		Denmark		France		Germany, Fed.Rep. of		Ireland		Italy		Nether-lands		United Kingdom		Austria		Finland		Norway		Sweden		Switzer-land	
SITC	Value	Rank	Value	Rank	Value	Rank	Value	Rank	Value	Rank	Value	Rank	Value	Rank	Value	Rank	Value	Rank	Value	Rank	Value	Rank	Value	Rank	Value	Rank
691	0.94	5	0.56	19	1.41	3	0.84	21	1.33	6	1.41	5	1.58	4	1.27	9	1.64	5	1.45	4	0.85	9	0.87	16	0.41	21
692	1.27	2	2.55	3	1.67	2	0.86	18	2.22	4	1.29	7	1.31	8	1.40	6	0.82	18	0.67	7	1.09	6	0.59	23	0.40	22
693	3.77	1	0.35	26	1.18	8	0.92	16	1.05	8	0.51	24	0.54	23	1.20	10	1.00	13	1.71	3	1.92	2	0.65	21	0.21	25
694	0.81	7	0.43	22	0.70	22	0.98	15	2.57	3	1.00	12	0.91	14	0.66	25	0.83	17	0.13	21	0.60	15	0.90	15	2.49	4
695	0.47	18	0.73	16	0.76	18	1.35	5	0.35	18	0.88	14	0.65	19	1.12	11	1.56	6	0.16	19	0.27	21	3.10	1	1.36	7
696	0.12	28	0.37	24	0.52	27	1.24	12	0.89	9	0.84	16	1.41	5	1.65	4	0.96	14	0.57	10	0.40	19	0.40	25	0.68	15
697	0.68	13	2.14	4	1.17	9	0.84	22	1.98	5	2.56	2	0.89	16	0.80	22	1.14	11	0.65	8	1.47	5	0.83	18	0.55	16
698	0.71	12	1.28	10	0.94	13	1.34	6	0.77	12	1.05	11	1.00	13	1.11	12	1.57	7	0.60	9	1.68	4	0.93	12	0.91	11
711	0.31	23	1.05	13	0.77	17	0.85	20	0.02	28	0.58	21	0.58	21	1.83	2	0.84	15	0.11	23	0.45	17	0.75	20	0.08	26
712	0.83	6	1.95	5	0.83	16	0.81	24	0.25	20	1.14	9	0.47	24	1.90	1	0.47	23	0.35	14	0.70	13	0.98	10	0.08	26
714	0.19	26	0.40	23	0.98	12	0.83	23	0.42	17	1.29	6	0.77	17	0.94	19	0.10	28	0.03	26	0.14	24	1.31	7	0.54	17
715	0.39	21	0.54	20	0.69	24	1.86	1	0.02	27	1.41	4	0.26	27	1.10	14	0.81	19	0.03	27	0.09	26	0.78	19	2.94	3
717	0.47	17	0.61	17	0.72	21	1.70	3	0.13	23	1.44	3	0.36	25	1.33	8	0.43	24	0.26	17	0.07	27	0.36	26	4.14	2
718	0.56	15	1.38	9	0.88	15	1.31	9	0.10	24	0.91	13	0.57	22	1.33	7	0.83	16	1.13	5	0.48	16	1.28	9	1.01	10
719	0.46	19	1.92	6	0.90	14	1.40	4	0.55	15	1.23	8	0.72	18	1.04	16	1.06	12	0.67	6	0.74	11	1.51	5	1.13	8
722	0.71	11	1.73	8	1.22	6	1.34	7	0.44	16	0.79	17	0.91	15	1.00	17	1.36	10	0.39	13	0.65	14	0.92	14	1.81	5
723	0.71	10	0.61	18	1.27	5	0.85	19	0.84	10	0.66	19	1.11	12	1.50	5	1.89	3	1.89	2	0.76	10	0.85	17	0.51	18
724	0.73	8	1.14	12	0.46	28	0.74	26	0.65	14	0.67	18	1.22	9	0.75	23	0.70	21	0.55	11	0.70	12	1.57	4	0.33	24
725	0.22	25	3.73	1	0.67	25	1.04	13	3.57	1	3.83	1	1.34	7	0.88	20	1.76	4	0.50	12	1.75	3	1.40	6	0.46	19
726	0.54	16	1.20	11	0.73	20	1.80	2	0.21	21	0.52	23	3.37	1	0.44	27	1.45	9	0.33	15	0.43	18	2.30	3	0.85	12
729	0.41	20	0.83	15	0.98	11	1.04	14	1.07	7	0.64	20	2.18	2	0.98	18	0.78	20	0.15	20	0.28	20	0.50	24	1.02	9
731	0.68	14	0.35	25	2.48	1	0.89	17	0.13	22	0.48	25	0.27	26	0.62	26	1.59	6	0.21	18	0.06	28	1.29	8	0.43	20
732	1.01	3	0.10	28	1.18	7	1.28	10	0.04	26	0.87	15	0.23	28	1.05	15	0.20	26	0.09	24	0.10	25	0.95	11	0.02	28
733	0.73	9	1.91	7	1.37	4	1.32	8	0.70	13	1.06	10	1.22	10	1.69	3	2.17	2	0.30	16	0.92	8	0.93	13	0.33	23
734	0.24	24	0.05	29	0.98	10	0.16	29	0.32	19	0.33	27	0.64	20	0.86	21	0.11	27	0.01	29	0.14	23	0.21	27	0.06	27
735	0.34	22	3.45	2	0.52	26	0.44	28	0.78	11	0.21	29	1.39	6	0.41	28	0.23	25	4.17	1	10.5	1	3.04	2	0.01	29
861	0.17	27	0.89	14	0.74	19	1.24	11	3.47	2	0.56	22	1.20	11	1.11	13	0.51	22	0.11	22	0.19	22	0.62	22	1.61	6
864	0.04	29	0.13	27	0.70	23	0.79	25	0.08	25	0.48	26	0.07	29	0.30	29	0.08	29	0.02	28	0.04	29	0.06	28	20.7	1
891.1	0.96	4	0.50	21	0.28	29	0.71	27	..	..	0.27	28	2.07	3	0.72	24	2.94	1	0.03	25	1.04	7	0.04	29	0.70	14

(Table continued.)

APPENDIX TABLE 7.2 (continued)
Indices of revealed comparative advantage in engineering goods, by SITC groups, 1970

	Southern Europe								United States		Canada		Japan		Four Asian NIEs						
	Turkey		Greece		Portugal		Spain		Yugoslavia								Hong Kong		Republic of Korea		Singapore		Taiwan	
SITC	Value	Rank	Value	Rank	Value	Rank	Value	Rank	Value	Rank	Value	Rank	Value	Rank	Value	Rank	Value	Rank	Value	Rank	Value	Rank	Value	Rank
691	0.01	17	0.15	11	0.28	15	1.20	12	2.25	7	0.78	17	1.04	7	0.87	14	0.09	13	0.15	12	0.76	11	0.11	20
692	0.03	12	2.88	1	1.86	2	1.76	5	1.99	8	0.56	22	0.48	13	0.88	13	0.20	11	0.03	20	8.15	1	0.03	25
693	..	..	1.75	2	0.90	9	3.14	4	1.19	12	0.26	27	0.23	20	1.57	6	0.05	18	0.84	3	1.15	7	0.53	11
694	0.03	10	..	25	0.50	13	0.90	15	2.49	6	0.69	18	0.95	8	2.12	5	0.44	7	0.03	22	0.57	16	0.58	10
695	0.27	5	0.01	22	1.11	7	1.62	7	1.05	13	1.04	11	0.29	19	0.76	20	0.17	12	0.09	15	0.69	13	0.39	13
696	0.02	13	0.63	4	1.16	6	1.27	11	0.08	26	0.26	26	0.13	25	2.53	4	1.69	4	3.36	1	0.58	15	2.51	2
697	2.15	2	1.12	3	3.26	1	4.52	1	3.39	3	0.37	25	0.20	22	1.11	11	3.67	1	0.32	7	1.48	5	2.06	3
698	0.29	4	0.16	10	1.20	5	1.02	13	1.31	11	0.88	15	0.61	11	0.78	18	1.11	6	0.14	13	1.08	8	0.61	9
711	..	..	..	23	0.06	25	0.31	25	0.57	16	1.77	3	2.27	2	0.47	24	..	24	0.11	14	0.80	10	0.01	27
712	0.01	16	0.03	17	0.12	21	0.34	22	0.59	14	1.68	4	1.43	5	0.31	28	..	..	..	..	0.04	29	0.07	22
714	..	..	..	..	0.28	16	0.60	16	0.03	27	2.17	2	0.61	12	0.73	22	0.08	14	0.21	8	1.23	6	0.80	8
715	0.37	3	0.01	21	0.17	17	1.46	8	0.49	18	0.92	14	0.20	23	0.43	26	0.05	16	0.02	24	0.15	25	0.22	17
717	0.04	9	0.02	20	0.15	18	1.34	9	0.21	21	0.56	21	0.18	24	1.07	12	0.06	15	0.09	16	0.31	23	0.50	12
718	0.03	11	0.03	15	0.11	22	0.50	18	0.17	23	1.36	6	0.47	15	0.43	25	0.01	21	0.02	23	1.79	3	0.08	21
719	..	..	0.05	15	0.29	14	0.56	17	0.43	19	1.36	8	0.42	16	0.52	23	0.05	17	0.03	21	0.48	19	0.12	19
722	0.01	14	0.28	7	0.58	12	1.01	14	1.77	9	1.07	10	0.34	17	0.83	17	0.03	19	0.38	4	0.62	14	0.32	14
723	0.15	6	0.22	8	1.48	3	1.33	10	7.26	1	0.59	19	1.48	3	1.27	8	0.01	20	0.05	17	0.35	22	0.88	6
724	0.01	15	0.42	5	1.22	4	0.37	21	0.57	15	0.82	16	0.90	9	2.76	3	1.86	2	0.32	6	0.96	9	4.33	1
725	2.54	1	0.22	9	0.05	26	1.72	6	1.43	10	0.52	24	0.23	21	0.78	19	0.35	8	0.01	26	0.56	17	0.30	15
726	..	..	..	27	0.03	27	0.23	26	0.21	20	1.10	9	0.48	14	0.31	27	..	..	0.02	25	0.14	26	..	..
729	0.11	7	0.11	13	0.69	11	0.40	20	0.51	17	1.56	5	0.67	10	0.75	21	1.60	5	1.57	2	2.99	2	0.81	7
731	..	..	..	..	0.95	8	3.92	3	2.92	5	0.98	13	1.30	6	1.24	9	..	..	..	..	0.13	27	0.02	26
732	0.06	8	0.02	19	0.06	24	0.47	19	0.19	22	1.02	12	3.14	1	0.85	16	..	..	..	27	0.75	12	0.06	23
733	0.01	19	0.02	18	0.71	10	0.33	24	3.28	4	0.55	23	0.31	18	0.87	15	..	23	0.04	18	0.30	24	1.16	4
734	..	..	0.33	6	0.01	29	0.05	29	0.10	25	3.91	1	1.45	4	0.08	29	..	..	0.34	5	0.08	28	..	28
735	0.01	18	0.12	12	0.12	20	4.23	2	6.15	2	0.23	28	0.10	27	3.42	2	0.25	10	0.17	10	0.52	18	0.03	24
861	..	20	0.06	14	0.14	19	0.34	23	0.14	24	1.53	7	0.12	26	1.42	7	0.30	9	0.16	11	0.40	21	0.19	18
864	..	..	..	24	0.07	23	0.08	28	..	..	0.11	29	0.06	28	1.12	10	1.76	3	0.03	19	1.71	4	0.30	16
8911	..	..	..	26	0.01	28	0.18	27	..	28	0.58	20	..	..	4.27	1	..	22	0.19	9	0.41	20	1.11	5

Source: ECE secretariat based on COMTRADE data base.

APPENDIX TABLE 7.3
Indices of revealed comparative advantage in engineering goods, by SITC groups, 1980

	EC															EFTA							
	Belgium		Denmark		France		Germany, Fed.Rep. of		Ireland		Italy		Netherlands		United Kingdom		Austria		Finland		Norway		Sweden		Switzerland	
SITC	Value	Rank	Value	Rank	Value	Rank	Value	Rank	Value	Rank	Value	Rank	Value	Rank	Value	Rank	Value	Rank	Value	Rank	Value	Rank	Value	Rank	Value	Rank
691	0.87	5	1.55	8	1.40	3	0.87	19	0.53	17	1.82	3	1.37	4	1.14	8	1.63	3	1.93	3	0.80	11	0.74	19	0.68	14
692	1.76	2	2.00	6	1.38	4	0.94	15	1.01	8	1.21	11	1.33	5	1.36	4	1.60	4	0.66	11	1.21	6	0.81	18	0.63	15
693	2.16	1	0.37	23	1.19	7	0.85	21	0.70	12	1.07	12	0.74	19	0.77	20	1.20	10	0.69	10	2.26	2	0.43	25	0.26	25
694	0.61	14	0.84	16	0.75	20	1.07	14	0.54	15	1.40	7	0.86	14	0.66	23	1.00	13	0.32	17	0.52	17	0.94	14	2.76	4
695	0.51	17	0.68	17	0.87	17	1.29	7	1.00	9	0.71	18	0.75	17	0.94	15	1.69	2	0.30	18	0.38	21	3.57	1	1.79	6
696	0.08	29	0.22	26	0.72	21	1.19	10	0.54	16	0.72	15	0.98	11	1.02	10	0.50	21	1.08	5	0.26	23	0.27	26	1.32	8
697	0.70	11	1.66	7	1.07	10	0.68	25	1.45	6	2.60	1	0.91	13	0.54	26	0.78	17	0.54	15	1.56	4	0.55	24	0.53	19
698	0.84	6	1.32	12	1.09	9	1.20	9	2.05	3	1.52	5	0.91	12	0.99	13	2.06	1	0.75	7	1.57	3	1.06	11	0.90	12
711	0.42	19	0.60	20	0.93	14	0.92	18	0.26	24	0.67	20	0.52	23	2.02	2	0.51	20	0.25	21	0.72	13	1.00	13	0.79	13
712	0.80	7	2.17	2	0.63	25	0.93	16	0.41	20	1.36	8	0.59	21	1.42	3	0.80	16	0.61	13	1.04	7	0.93	15	0.16	26
714	0.28	23	0.35	24	0.88	15	0.74	23	4.61	1	1.07	13	0.75	16	1.25	6	0.22	25	0.18	23	0.62	15	1.18	10	0.32	23
715	0.40	20	0.62	19	0.64	24	1.67	2	0.28	22	1.33	10	0.26	24	0.89	18	1.06	11	0.18	22	0.16	25	0.84	17	2.93	3
717	0.70	12	0.51	22	0.62	26	1.68	1	0.27	23	1.47	6	0.46	24	0.91	17	0.48	22	0.10	26	0.15	26	0.57	21	5.45	2
718	0.70	10	1.32	11	0.96	13	1.11	13	0.59	14	0.72	16	0.57	22	1.30	5	1.04	12	1.19	4	0.56	16	1.41	6	1.01	11
719	0.43	18	2.06	5	1.01	11	1.38	4	0.62	13	1.36	9	0.78	15	1.09	9	1.26	9	0.87	6	0.97	8	1.49	5	1.27	10
722	0.56	15	1.07	13	1.28	5	1.30	6	1.13	7	0.68	19	0.74	18	1.01	11	1.34	7	0.56	14	0.79	12	0.86	16	1.84	5
723	0.66	13	0.54	21	1.12	8	0.92	17	1.73	5	1.02	14	1.16	8	1.00	12	1.42	5	3.07	2	0.82	10	1.18	9	0.62	17
724	0.90	4	0.98	14	0.52	28	0.73	24	0.70	11	0.41	25	1.42	2	0.58	24	0.56	19	0.72	8	0.68	14	1.56	3	0.40	22
725	0.27	24	2.72	1	1.01	12	1.15	12	2.02	4	1.85	2	1.17	7	0.58	25	1.38	6	0.30	19	1.37	5	1.74	2	0.49	20
726	0.79	9	2.11	3	0.67	22	1.38	3	0.25	26	0.42	24	2.84	1	0.52	27	0.60	18	0.61	12	0.30	22	0.56	23	0.55	18
729	0.40	21	0.86	15	0.87	16	0.86	20	0.78	10	0.52	22	1.14	10	0.97	14	0.83	15	0.34	16	0.45	19	0.57	22	1.31	9
731	0.26	26	0.21	27	1.71	1	0.77	22	0.44	19	0.46	23	0.13	28	0.80	19	0.15	27	0.12	25	0.05	28	1.19	8	0.62	16
732	1.16	3	0.20	28	1.23	6	1.32	5	0.28	21	0.71	17	0.33	26	0.69	22	0.38	23	0.16	24	0.17	24	1.01	12	0.05	28
733	0.79	8	1.36	10	1.46	2	1.21	8	0.52	18	1.57	4	1.14	9	0.91	16	1.33	8	0.70	9	0.92	9	1.01	7	0.42	27
734	0.23	27	0.32	25	0.79	18	0.64	26	0.12	29	0.27	27	0.66	20	2.13	1	0.04	29	0.04	28	0.07	27	0.04	28	0.12	27
735	0.26	25	2.09	4	0.66	23	0.34	28	0.19	28	0.30	26	1.38	3	0.75	21	0.17	26	3.50	1	10.8	1	1.50	4	0.04	29
861	0.33	22	1.39	9	0.76	19	1.17	11	2.32	2	0.52	21	1.31	6	1.24	7	0.91	14	0.26	20	0.49	18	0.71	20	1.73	7
864	0.09	28	0.12	29	0.62	27	0.46	27	0.24	27	0.26	28	0.13	29	0.23	29	0.06	28	0.02	29	0.03	29	0.05	27	11	1
891.1	0.55	16	0.66	18	0.13	29	0.30	29	0.25	25	0.14	29	0.43	25	0.45	28	0.35	24	0.07	27	0.41	20	0.03	29	0.28	2

(Table continued.)

APPENDIX TABLE 7.3 (continued)
Indices of revealed comparative advantage in engineering goods, by SITC groups, 1980

	Southern Europe											United States		Canada		Japan		Four Asian NIEs						
	Turkey		Greece		Portugal		Spain		Yugo-slavia									Hong Kong		Republic of Korea		Singa-pore		Taiwan	
SITC	Value	Rank	Value	Rank	Value	Rank	Value	Rank	Value	Rank	Value	Rank	Value	Rank	Value	Rank	Value	Rank	Value	Rank	Value	Rank	Value	Rank
691	0.40	5	0.77	7	0.55	13	1.31	9	1.55	7	0.70	19	0.90	11	1.04	17	0.05	20	1.20	10	0.48	22	0.10	23
692	0.14	12	4.48	1	1.59	3	1.72	5	1.61	5	0.74	16	0.42	18	0.55	28	0.21	15	0.12	24	1.09	9	0.46	20
693	..	..	3.01	4	1.54	4	2.61	2	0.77	16	0.47	24	1.56	5	1.21	12	0.03	23	3.12	3	0.56	18	1.13	11
694	0.04	20	0.15	13	0.15	22	1.23	11	1.54	8	0.58	21	1.33	6	1.37	10	0.39	12	1.68	7	0.52	19	1.92	6
695	0.16	9	0.23	12	0.73	10	1.41	8	1.58	6	0.95	11	0.43	17	0.76	20	0.56	11	0.32	18	0.59	16	1.58	8
696	1.20	3	3.37	2	0.88	7	1.80	4	0.15	26	0.43	25	0.26	24	1.66	7	1.69	5	0.32	1	0.51	21	2.41	4
697	2.82	1	1.93	5	1.93	1	3.28	1	1.02	14	0.55	22	0.16	28	0.70	23	3.66	3	4.79	1	0.51	20	3.22	2
698	0.20	8	0.76	8	1.04	6	0.97	14	1.12	12	0.76	14	0.63	12	0.60	26	1.08	7	3.10	4	0.69	13	1.29	10
711	0.23	7	0.01	24	0.06	26	0.53	20	0.97	15	1.93	5	1.30	7	0.76	21	..	..	0.17	22	0.58	17	0.05	26
712	0.39	6	0.02	23	0.14	23	0.50	22	1.17	11	1.83	6	1.96	4	0.62	24	0.05	21	0.02	29	0.09	28	0.02	28
714	..	..	..	..	0.50	16	0.51	21	0.10	27	2.38	2	1.04	9	0.74	22	..	27	0.22	20	0.68	14	0.49	19
715	0.09	16	0.02	22	0.17	21	1.43	6	1.04	13	0.71	17	0.49	15	1.21	13	1.25	6	0.16	23	0.39	24	0.88	16
717	0.07	18	0.03	21	0.30	18	0.84	15	0.59	20	0.52	23	0.21	26	1.11	14	0.04	22	0.21	21	0.32	25	1.07	12
718	0.10	15	0.04	19	0.03	27	0.58	18	0.40	24	1.94	4	0.91	10	0.61	25	0.10	17	0.04	27	1.27	8	0.08	25
719	0.06	19	0.12	14	0.25	19	0.70	16	0.77	18	1.22	8	0.48	16	0.81	19	0.01	24	0.10	25	0.71	11	0.22	22
722	0.13	13	0.30	10	0.75	8	0.56	19	1.53	9	0.99	10	0.38	20	1.10	15	0.07	18	0.42	15	1.36	7	0.72	17
723	0.15	11	3.34	3	0.74	9	1.21	12	4.98	1	0.71	18	0.56	13	1.42	8	0.36	13	0.74	12	0.63	15	0.96	14
724	0.16	10	0.25	11	1.13	5	0.32	24	0.51	22	0.75	15	0.36	22	2.23	3	0.26	14	2.02	6	4.66	1	3.50	1
725	1.42	2	0.61	9	0.07	25	1.43	7	2.56	3	0.67	20	0.22	25	1.03	18	2.35	4	0.50	14	1.54	6	1.34	9
726	..	..	0.01	25	0.01	28	0.27	25	0.77	17	2.12	3	0.35	23	0.59	27	3.72	2	0.03	28	0.11	27	0.05	27
729	0.09	17	0.04	18	0.68	12	0.45	23	0.60	19	1.79	7	0.41	19	1.04	16	0.78	9	1.12	11	3.95	2	1.07	13
731	..	..	..	29	1.60	2	2.20	3	1.48	10	0.85	12	2.92	1	1.40	9	..	25	4.24	2	0.04	29	0.90	15
732	0.51	4	0.06	17	0.30	17	1.19	13	0.52	21	0.83	13	2.45	2	1.87	5	..	26	0.06	26	0.19	26	0.08	24
733	0.10	14	1.14	6	0.23	20	0.62	17	2.15	4	0.39	26	0.14	29	1.35	11	0.07	19	0.26	19	0.46	23	2.96	3
734	..	..	..	27	0.55	14	0.25	27	0.27	25	3.65	1	1.12	8	0.03	29	..	..	0.34	17	0.70	12	..	29
735	..	..	0.09	16	0.53	15	1.25	10	3.44	2	0.38	27	0.51	14	2.70	2	0.12	16	2.79	5	3.40	3	0.46	21
861	..	21	0.11	15	0.69	11	0.26	26	0.44	23	1.02	9	0.38	21	1.80	6	0.67	10	0.35	16	0.78	10	0.55	18
864	..	22	..	..	0.10	24	0.13	28	0.05	28	0.13	29	0.19	27	1.95	4	13.3	1	1.63	8	1.58	5	1.66	7
891.1	..	..	0.03	20	..	29	0.07	29	..	29	0.36	28	2.15	3	5.00	1	1.05	8	1.37	9	1.93	4	2.00	5

Source: ECE secretariat based on COMTRADE data base.

APPENDIX TABLE 7.4
Indices of revealed comparative advantage in engineering goods, by SITC groups, 1987

	EC									EFTA			
	Belgium	Denmark	France	Germany, Fed.Rep. of	Ireland	Italy	Netherlands	United Kingdom	Austria	Finland	Norway	Sweden	Switzerland
SITC	Value Rank	Value Rank	Value Rank	Value Rank	Value Rank	Value Rank	Value Rank	Value Rank	Value Rank	Value Rank	Value Rank	Value Rank	Value Rank
691	1.51 3	2.75 3	1.09 7	1.02 15	0.62 13	1.43 9	2.79 1	0.92 12	1.96 2	2.84 3	1.15 7	1.40 4	0.98 14
692	2.67 1	2.47 5	1.23 3	1.15 12	0.68 9	1.22 12	1.47 4	1.48 4	1.63 6	0.81 12	1.84 2	1.15 7	1.00 13
693	2.29 2	0.42 24	1.05 9	1.02 17	1.37 6	1.49 8	0.93 12	0.80 18	1.34 10	0.75 14	1.60 4	0.25 27	0.28 23
694	0.52 14	0.82 15	0.76 21	1.12 13	0.47 15	1.55 7	0.84 17	0.59 22	1.06 15	0.22 25	0.30 23	0.86 17	3.11 4
695	0.46 16	0.73 17	0.75 22	1.34 6	1.41 5	0.87 14	1.09 8	0.89 14	1.82 5	0.38 18	0.50 19	3.33 1	2.03 5
696	0.15 27	0.29 26	0.81 20	1.34 7	0.29 19	0.82 15	1.11 7	0.92 11	0.31 23	0.86 11	0.23 25	0.32 26	1.87 6
697	0.76 9	1.31 11	0.96 12	0.58 24	0.65 10	2.64 1	1.03 9	0.45 27	0.55 22	0.46 15	1.24 6	0.64 21	0.51 18
698	0.69 12	1.54 9	1.06 8	1.31 9	1.35 7	1.63 3	1.01 11	0.84 16	2.36 1	0.64 16	1.80 3	1.05 11	1.11 12
711	0.25 25	0.55 20	1.14 6	0.98 19	0.30 18	0.64 17	0.52 22	1.75 2	1.84 4	0.43 17	0.52 18	1.06 10	0.44 21
712	1.01 5	2.54 4	0.91 14	1.11 14	0.21 20	1.57 6	0.92 14	1.66 3	0.93 16	1.29 6	1.36 5	0.97 13	0.18 26
714	0.38 19	0.39 25	0.83 18	0.56 26	6.49 1	0.55 19	0.93 13	1.42 5	0.18 27	0.30 22	0.67 15	0.67 20	0.19 25
715	0.58 13	0.49 22	0.38 28	1.48 2	0.15 23	1.33 10	0.26 27	0.85 15	1.17 13	0.27 24	0.15 26	0.73 19	3.71 3
717	0.72 11	0.54 21	0.56 26	1.68 1	0.14 24	1.90 3	0.50 23	0.56 24	0.69 19	0.09 27	0.12 28	0.53 22	4.29 2
718	0.80 7	1.48 10	0.95 13	1.42 4	0.35 17	0.90 13	0.87 15	1.30 6	1.35 9	1.99 4	0.96 9	1.80 2	1.50 9
719	0.45 18	1.94 7	0.90 15	1.43 3	0.59 14	1.66 4	0.81 18	0.99 10	1.39 8	1.14 8	0.84 12	1.46 3	1.50 8
722	0.46 15	1.04 14	1.23 4	1.23 10	0.93 8	0.63 18	0.61 21	0.92 13	1.30 11	0.79 13	0.67 14	1.08 9	1.76 7
723	0.79 8	0.74 16	0.96 11	0.86 20	2.43 2	0.78 16	0.76 19	0.80 17	1.87 3	1.96 5	0.96 10	0.96 14	0.86 16
724	0.73 10	1.06 13	0.63 24	0.57 25	0.64 11	0.40 25	0.65 20	0.64 20	0.64 20	1.22 7	0.73 13	1.22 6	0.38 22
725	0.28 24	2.04 6	0.88 16	0.99 18	1.61 4	2.19 2	0.86 16	0.47 26	1.26 12	0.34 20	1.05 8	1.13 8	0.54 17
726	0.35 21	2.83 1	0.70 23	1.37 5	0.10 26	0.33 26	2.43 2	0.71 19	0.61 21	0.98 10	0.87 11	0.95 15	0.50 19
729	0.33 22	0.64 18	0.83 19	0.80 21	0.63 12	0.54 22	1.02 10	1.16 7	0.86 17	0.31 21	0.36 22	0.42 24	1.14 11
731	0.29 23	0.55 19	2.23 1	0.77 22	0.18 21	0.44 24	0.18 28	0.57 23	0.26 25	3.67 1	0.39 20	0.49 23	0.93 15
732	1.37 4	0.16 27	1.02 10	1.33 8	0.04 29	0.54 24	0.34 25	0.54 25	0.30 24	0.29 23	0.25 24	1.25 5	0.06 28
733	0.81 6	1.62 8	1.21 5	1.17 11	0.36 16	1.27 11	1.12 6	0.63 21	1.14 14	1.11 9	0.58 16	0.86 16	0.44 20
734	0.22 26	0.14 28	1.34 2	0.65 23	0.12 25	0.54 23	0.47 24	1.04 9	0.06 29	0.17 26	0.39 21	0.39 25	0.28 24
735	0.07 29	2.79 2	0.51 27	0.45 29	0.16 22	0.24 27	1.18 5	3.18 1	0.22 26	2.93 2	16.70 1	1.00 12	0.02 29
861	0.37 20	1.29 12	0.85 17	1.02 16	2.04 3	0.55 20	1.55 3	1.13 8	0.76 18	0.34 19	0.57 17	0.81 18	1.41 10
864	0.12 28	0.13 29	0.63 25	0.46 27	0.05 28	0.22 28	0.12 29	0.22 29	0.07 28	0.03 29	0.07 29	0.07 28	11.80 1
891.1	0.45 17	0.44 23	0.17 29	0.45 28	0.06 27	0.03 29	0.32 26	0.45 28	1.54 7	0.08 28	0.13 27	0.05 29	0.17 27

(Table continued.)

Statistical appendices

APPENDIX TABLE 7.4 (continued)

Indices of revealed comparative advantage in engineering goods, by SITC groups, 1987

	Southern Europe														Four Asian NIEs							
	Turkey		Greece		Portugal		Spain		Yugo-slavia		United States		Canada		Japan		Hong Kong		Republic of Korea		Singa-pore		Taiwan	
SITC	Value	Rank	Value	Rank	Value	Rank	Value	Rank	Value	Rank	Value	Rank	Value	Rank	Value	Rank	Value	Rank	Value	Rank	Value	Rank	Value	Rank
691	0.49	10	0.31	9	0.31	19	0.70	16	2.20	5	0.34	24	1.33	5	0.43	25	0.07	18	1.86	9	0.35	23	0.32	22
692	0.66	7	1.68	3	1.50	3	1.17	9	1.50	11	0.68	16	0.58	13	0.23	28	0.97	7	0.49	17	0.65	12	0.23	23
693	0.57	8	1.18	4	0.56	11	2.30	1	1.54	10	0.26	27	2.19	3	0.69	24	0.02	24	2.52	6	0.35	21	1.39	9
694	0.87	5	0.09	17	0.12	25	1.29	7	1.44	13	0.53	19	1.23	7	0.87	18	0.31	15	1.54	10	0.67	11	2.90	3
695	1.78	3	0.26	11	0.59	10	1.28	8	1.85	7	0.72	15	0.33	20	0.81	22	0.49	12	0.26	22	0.55	16	2.05	6
696	0.66	6	3.31	1	1.48	4	1.64	2	0.13	25	0.31	25	0.05	28	1.12	13	1.67	5	3.87	2	0.44	19	2.53	4
697	1.41	4	0.78	5	1.80	2	1.63	3	1.68	9	0.50	20	0.43	17	0.36	27	3.48	2	3.16	3	0.35	22	5.08	2
698	0.41	12	0.41	7	1.05	5	1.14	10	1.05	16	0.66	17	0.63	12	0.42	26	0.84	10	0.56	16	0.60	15	1.69	8
711	0.23	15	0.02	25	0.80	6	0.73	14	0.64	18	2.03	4	1.67	4	0.98	16	0.03	22	0.29	21	0.44	18	0.03	27
712	0.46	11	0.08	18	0.06	28	0.44	21	1.72	8	1.24	8	1.18	8	0.84	20	0.00	29	0.13	25	0.03	29	0.13	24
714	0.01	26	0.01	28	0.16	22	0.62	17	0.05	27	2.15	3	0.67	11	1.31	10	0.92	8	0.73	15	3.56	2	1.24	10
715	0.13	18	0.03	23	0.15	23	1.10	11	2.17	6	0.57	18	0.32	21	1.61	6	0.06	19	0.10	26	0.24	25	0.84	15
717	5.27	1	0.07	19	0.33	17	0.85	13	0.59	19	0.39	22	0.20	25	1.20	12	0.25	16	0.18	24	0.31	24	0.87	13
718	0.07	23	0.06	21	0.13	24	0.49	20	1.06	15	1.30	7	0.68	10	0.78	23	0.03	23	0.06	28	0.62	13	0.12	25
719	0.50	9	0.14	15	0.32	18	0.72	15	1.00	17	0.99	10	0.46	15	0.91	17	0.16	17	0.22	23	0.78	9	0.35	21
722	0.37	13	0.32	8	0.61	9	0.49	19	1.35	14	0.98	11	0.30	22	1.24	11	1.29	6	0.41	19	2.26	4	1.11	11
723	5.03	2	2.11	2	3.55	1	1.50	5	4.65	1	1.51	6	0.47	14	0.83	21	0.47	13	0.73	14	0.73	10	0.95	12
724	0.14	17	0.10	16	0.70	7	0.23	27	0.36	22	0.84	13	0.36	19	2.05	2	2.17	4	2.54	5	3.83	1	2.36	5
725	0.32	14	0.23	13	0.36	15	1.47	6	2.35	3	0.47	21	0.22	24	0.84	19	3.46	3	2.40	7	1.49	6	1.91	7
726	0.00	27	0.02	26	0.03	29	0.35	25	0.35	23	2.36	2	0.13	26	1.08	15	0.05	20	0.03	29	0.19	26	0.00	29
729	0.07	22	0.07	20	0.43	12	0.42	22	0.57	20	1.64	5	0.41	18	1.37	8	0.44	14	1.26	11	2.91	3	0.76	16
731	0.00	28	0.24	12	0.33	16	0.53	18	1.44	12	0.79	14	2.49	2	1.08	14	0.00	27	4.09	1	0.03	28	0.53	19
732	0.10	20	0.01	29	0.36	14	1.53	4	0.50	21	0.86	12	2.83	1	1.78	4	0.00	26	0.47	18	0.06	27	0.10	26
733	0.11	19	0.48	6	0.42	13	0.36	24	2.29	4	0.28	26	0.22	23	1.34	9	0.01	25	0.84	13	0.37	20	5.32	1
734	..	..	0.27	10	0.06	27	0.37	23	0.12	26	4.89	1	1.30	6	0.05	29	0.00	28	0.08	27	0.47	17	0.00	28
735	0.09	21	0.15	14	0.64	8	0.99	12	2.86	2	0.35	23	0.11	27	1.66	5	0.05	21	2.20	8	1.46	7	0.47	20
861	0.14	16	0.05	22	0.30	20	0.27	26	0.31	24	1.08	9	0.43	16	1.84	3	0.88	9	0.37	20	0.62	14	0.59	18
864	0.01	25	0.01	27	0.07	26	0.18	28	0.04	28	0.09	29	0.02	29	1.53	7	12.2	1	1.01	12	0.97	8	0.85	14
8911	0.02	24	0.02	24	0.28	21	0.03	29	0.02	29	0.15	28	1.18	9	4.21	1	0.69	11	2.75	4	2.09	5	0.66	17

Source: ECE secretariat based on COMTRADE data base.

APPENDIX TABLE 7.5

Indices of revealed comparative advantages in engineering goods, by SITC groups: Eastern Europe and the Soviet Union

SITC	1970 Eastern Europe Value	1970 Eastern Europe Rank	1970 Soviet Union Value	1970 Soviet Union Rank	1980 Eastern Europe Value	1980 Eastern Europe Rank	1980 Soviet Union Value	1980 Soviet Union Rank	1987 Eastern Europe Value	1987 Eastern Europe Rank	1987 Soviet Union Value	1987 Soviet Union Rank
691	0.84	14	1.93	3	0.79	15	0.29	10	1.00	9	0.38	13
692	0.67	17	1.85	4	1.20	7	0.22	15	0.64	15	1.86	4
693	1.79	2	1.07	8	1.01	10	0.10	25	1.45	7	0.05	26
694	1.44	4	0.16	24	1.92	3	0.15	18	1.67	4	0.04	27
695	1.09	7	0.74	10	1.14	8	0.27	14	0.94	10	0.39	12
696	0.91	13	0.24	20	0.40	22	0.07	26	0.62	17	0.19	19
697	1.27	6	0.33	17	1.07	9	0.13	21	1.67	3	0.35	14
698	0.65	18	0.17	23	0.55	17	0.11	22	0.72	14	0.15	23
711	0.27	26	0.60	13	0.43	21	0.86	4	0.31	22	0.43	10
712	0.79	15	0.86	9	1.37	5	0.72	6	1.82	2	2.38	2
714	0.34	24	0.03	28	0.25	24	0.02	28	0.07	28	0.04	28
715	2.58	1	3.00	1	2.36	2	1.34	2	1.51	6	2.05	3
717	1.08	8	0.10	26	0.80	14	0.13	20	0.55	19	0.16	22
718	0.56	21	1.35	6	0.59	16	0.29	11	0.63	16	0.49	8
719	0.64	19	0.63	12	0.53	18	0.27	13	0.55	18	0.45	9
722	0.92	12	0.53	14	0.90	13	0.51	9	0.80	13	0.34	15
723	1.00	9	0.21	21	1.00	11	0.06	27	1.31	8	0.20	18
724	0.23	27	0.30	19	0.20	26	0.10	24	0.18	26	0.40	11
725	0.39	22	0.09	27	1.21	6	0.16	17	1.55	5	0.82	7
726	0.96	10	0.18	22	0.23	25	0.13	19	0.21	24	0.06	25
729	0.61	20	0.30	18	0.43	20	0.17	16	0.39	20	0.17	21
731	1.60	3	1.07	7	2.43	1	0.96	3	2.79	1	5.67	1
732	0.34	23	0.36	16	0.39	23	0.59	7	0.24	23	0.99	5
733	1.28	5	0.14	25	0.90	12	0.11	23	0.84	12	0.18	20
734	0.04	29	0.38	15	0.05	29	0.54	8	0.13	27	0.08	24
735	0.93	11	1.56	5	1.38	4	1.76	1	0.92	11	0.30	16
861	0.73	16	0.66	11	0.47	19	0.29	12	0.35	21	0.24	17
864	0.28	25	2.02	2	0.18	27	0.85	5	0.19	25	0.98	6
8911	0.20	28	0.03	29	0.14	28	0.02	29	0.06	29	0.00	29

Source: ECE secretariat based on COMTRADE data base.

Note: In this study indices of revealed comparative advantage have been calculated as the ratio (A/B) of two commodity shares, viz. the percentage share of a given commodity group in total manufactured exports of a country (A) divided by the corresponding share in "world" exports of manufactures (B). For the Soviet Union and eastern Europe the data underlying the numerator (A) of this ratio cover only exports to the developed market economies and 20 developing countries. Because of this limited coverage the above indices are not directly comparable to the indices for the other countries shown in Appendix tables 7.2 to 7.4.

APPENDIX TABLE 7.6

Changes in specialization patterns: Regression analysis

Equation: $\Delta RCA = A + B\ RCA$

	\multicolumn{4}{c	}{1980/1970}	\multicolumn{4}{c	}{1987/1980}	\multicolumn{4}{c}{1987/1970}
	dgf	A	B	R^2	dgf	A	B	R^2	dgf	A	B	R^2
Japan	27	0.294 (2.19)***	-0.168 (1.91)***	0.12	27	0.183 (1.71)***	-0.244 (3.59)*	0.32	27	0.515 (3.01)*	-0.464 (4.14)*	0.39
United States	27	0.073 (0.84)	-0.040 (0.59)	0.01	27	-0.216 (2.05)***	0.159 (1.96)***	0.12	27	-0.164 (1.27)	0.145 (1.41)	0.07
Germany, Federal Republic of	27	0.144 (1.61)	-0.191 (2.39)**	0.18	27	0.077 (0.31)	-0.056 (0.80)	0.02	27	0.214 (1.92)***	-0.238 (2.40)**	0.18
France	27	0.266 (3.73)*	-0.305 (4.46)*	0.42	27	0.064 (0.56)	-0.083 (0.71)	0.02	27	0.197 (2.42)***	-0.247 (3.15)*	0.27
Italy	27	0.335 (2.84)*	-0.362 (3.77)*	0.34	27	-0.008 (0.10)	0.035 (0.48)	0.01	27	0.303 (2.30)**	-0.303 (2.82)*	0.23
United Kingdom	27	0.330 (1.80)*	-0.402 (2.50)*	0.19	27	-0.358 (1.47)	-0.377 (1.63)	0.09	27	0.728 (2.42)**	-0.781 (2.96)*	0.25
Canada	26	0.293 (2.11)**	-0.309 (2.25)**	0.16	27	0.023 (0.24)	-0.100 (1.17)	0.05	26	0.207 (1.49)	-0.229 (1.66)	0.10
Austria	27	0.494 (2.93)*	-0.630 (4.60)*	0.44	27	0.165 (1.30)	-0.026 (0.21)	0.002	27	0.448 (2.52)**	-0.448 (3.09)*	0.26
Belgium	27	0.242 (3.95)*	-0.410 (6.29)*	0.59	27	-0.105 (1.44)	0.239 (2.54)*	0.19	27	0.224 (2.10)**	-0.314 (2.75)*	0.22
Denmark	27	0.316 (2.90)*	-0.339 (4.58)*	0.44	27	-0.002 (0.02)	0.094 (1.01)	0.04	27	0.413 (2.31)**	-0.339 (2.79)*	0.22
Finland	27	0.167 (2.03)***	-0.119 (1.47)	0.07	27	0.417 (2.38)**	-0.273 (1.66)	0.09	27	0.523 (3.06)*	-0.333 (2.00)***	0.13
Ireland	26	0.604 (2.63)**	-0.653 (3.75)*	0.25	27	-0.281 (2.54)***	0.261 (3.03)*	0.25	26	0.657 (2.02) ?	-0.762 (3.10)*	0.27
Netherlands	27	0.240 (2.41)**	-0.356 (4.35)*	0.41	27	0.136 (1.03)	-0.116 (0.91)	0.03	27	0.366 (2.40)*	-0.449 (3.58)*	0.32
Norway	27	0.040 (0.86)	0.015 (0.69)	0.02	27	-0.305 (2.95)*	0.520 (10.99)*	0.82	27	-0.245 (2.00)*	0.544 (9.44)*	0.77
Sweden	27	0.151 (1.34)	-0.205 (2.30)**	0.16	27	0.124 (1.40)	-0.174 (2.32)**	0.17	27	0.329 (2.22)**	-0.421 (3.60)*	0.32
Switzerland	27	0.518 (3.81)*	-0.456 (13.56)*	0.87	27	0.054 (0.65)	0.029 (0.90)	0.03	27	0.562 (4.50)*	-0.426 (13.73)*	0.87
Greece	25	0.265 (1.59)	0.588 (2.49)*	0.20	25	0.045 (0.59)	-0.464 (8.71)*	0.74	25	0.250 (1.73)***	-0.365 (1.79)***	0.11
Portugal	27	0.223 (2.95)*	-0.387 (4.79)*	0.46	27	0.226 (1.25)	-0.366 (1.61)	0.09	27	0.186 (1.43)	-0.312 (2.25)**	0.16
Spain	27	0.383 (3.51)*	-0.474 (7.47)*	0.67	27	0.269 (2.53)**	-0.424 (5.07)*	0.49	27	0.559 (4.51)*	-0.755 (10.47)*	0.80
Turkey	18	0.168 (1.66)	-0.221 (1.64)	0.13	20	0.875 (2.37)***	-0.99 (2.01)***	0.17	18	0.901	-0.849	0.14
Yugoslavia	26	0.422 (3.70)*	-0.465 (9.39)*	0.77	27	0.183 (1.70)	-0.093 (1.36)	0.06	26	0.571 (4.15)*	-0.514 (8.58)*	0.74

Source: ECE secretariat based on COMTRADE data base.

Notes: dgf = Degrees of freedom. Figures in brackets below parameter estimates are t-statistics. Significance levels for intercept (A) based on a two-tailed test. * = 1 per cent, ** = 5 per cent, *** = 10 per cent. Significance levels for slope (B) based on a one-tailed test. * = 1 per cent, ** = 2.5 per cent, *** = 5 per cent. For the definition of RCA (revealed comparative advantage), see text.

APPENDIX TABLE 7.7

Changes in specialization patterns: Regression analysis

Equation: $\Delta RESP = A + B\,RESP$

	1980/1970				1987/1980				1987/1970			
	dgf	A	B	R^2	dgf	A	B	R^2	dgf	A	B	R^2
Japan	27	0.508 (0.70)	-0.011 (0.07)	0.0002	27	1.36 (3.17)*	-0.704 (9.35)*	0.76	27	1.200 (2.71)*	-0.611 (6.43)*	0.60
USA	27	0.520 (2.23)*	-0.45 (4.93)*	0.47	27	0.015 (0.07)	-0.20 (1.73)***	0.10	27	0.135 (0.67)	-0.398 (5.09)*	0.49
Germany, Federal Republic of	27	0.150 (0.69)	-0.114 (0.70)	0.02	27	-0.019 (0.15)	-0.004 (0.96)	0.0001	27	0.150 (0.51)	-0.131 (0.68)	0.02
France	27	0.355 (3.59)*	-0.284 (4.70)*	0.45	27	-0.408 (1.90)***	0.339 (2.38)**	0.17	27	-0.099 (0.64)	0.094 (1.01)	0.04
Italy	27	0.075 (0.13)	0.097 (0.36)	0.005	27	0.757 (4.40)*	-0.570 (10.18)*	0.79	27	0.343 (1.64)	-0.235 (2.33)**	0.17
United Kingdom	27	0.507 (2.32)**	-0.493 (5.23)*	0.50	27	0.714 (4.12)*	-0.686 (6.93)*	0.64	27	1.01 (5.41)*	-0.910 (11.39)*	0.83
Canada	26	0.274 (0.84)	-0.037 (0.14)	0.0007	27	0.093 (0.53)	-0.270 (3.16)*	0.27	26	0.393 (1.21)	-0.392 (1.63)	0.09
Austria	27	0.355 (2.27)**	-0.524 (6.33)*	0.60	27	0.535 (3.57)*	-0.551 (4.82)*	0.46	27	0.648 (4.36)*	-0.753 (9.57)*	0.77
Belgium	27	0.532 (8.18)*	-0.640 (20.21)*	0.94	27	0.265 (3.44)*	-0.317 (4.72)*	0.45	27	0.650 (8.04)*	-0.776 (19.69)*	0.93
Denmark	27	0.410 (3.06)*	-0.320 (4.47)*	0.43	27	-0.218 (1.11)	0.176 (1.50)	0.08	27	0.379 (1.42)	-0.290 (2.03)***	0.13
Finland	27	-0.012 (0.15)	0.300 (4.04)*	0.38	27	0.245 (1.21)	-0.089 (0.65)	0.02	27	0.201 (0.97)	0.233 (1.27)	0.06
Ireland	26	0.630 (3.64)*	-0.715 (4.84)*	0.47	27	0.220 (1.77)***	-0.453 (3.92)*	0.36	26	0.475 (3.53)*	-0.721 (6.30)*	0.60
Netherlands	27	0.501 (6.96)*	-0.584 (15.05)*	0.89	27	0.147 (2.38)***	-0.194 (3.73)*	0.34	27	0.551 (7.53)***	-0.665 (16.86)*	0.91
Norway	27	0.084 (0.32)	0.001 (0.002)	-	27	0.213 (3.50)*	-0.339 (7.20)*	0.66	27	0.386 (1.88)***	-0.493 (2.26)**	0.16
Sweden	27	0.180 (1.850)***	0.066 (3.61)*	0.32	27	0.400 (3.41)	-0.501 (5.54)*	0.53	27	0.533 (4.12)*	-0.658 (7.45)*	0.67
Switzerland	27	0.551 (5.27)*	-0.415 (13.11)*	0.86	27	-0.158 (2.30)	0.172 (5.79)*	0.55	27	0.484 (3.72)*	-0.311 (7.90)**	0.70
Greece	25	0.522 (1.94)***	0.458 (2.37)**	0.18	27	0.246 (1.08)	-0.691 (7.58)*	0.68	25	0.555 (2.03)***	-0.859 (4.36)*	0.43
Portugal	27	0.400 (0.69)	0.756 (1.36)	0.06	27	0.424 (4.04)*	-0.830 (23.87)*	0.95	27	0.255 (2.29)**	-0.372 (3.47)*	0.31
Spain	27	0.605 (1.79)***	-0.554 (5.28)*	0.51	27	0.560 (2.39)**	-0.615 (6.09)*	0.58	27	0.301 (2.40)**	-0.588 (15.13)*	0.89
Turkey												
Yugoslavia	26	0.289 (1.02)	0.01 (0.07)	0.0002	27	0.161 (0.33)	0.011 (0.06)	0.0001	26	-0.095 (0.24)	0.401 (2.34)**	0.17

Source: ECE secretariat based on COMTRADE data base.

Notes: dgf = Degrees of freedom. Figures in brackets below parameter estimates are t-statistics. Significance levels for intercept (A) based on a two-tailed test. * = 1 per cent, ** = 5 per cent, *** = 10 per cent. Significance levels for slope (B) based on a one-tailed test. * = 1 per cent, ** = 2.5 per cent, *** = 5 per cent. The index of relative export-import specialization (RESP) is defined as the ratio of two shares, viz. the share of product group i in total manufactured exports of a country divided by the corresponding share in total manufactured imports.

APPENDIX TABLE 7.8
Composition of engineering goods exports by group of technology intensity
(Percentages)

	1970					1980					1987				
	HT	AT	MT	LT	Total Engineering	HT	AT	MT	LT	Total Engineering	HT	AT	MT	LT	Total Engineering
Seven major countries															
United States	31.47	15.57	20.92	32.05	100.00	32.79	17.76	18.67	30.77	100.00	43.75	17.00	19.18	19.96	100.00
Japan	13.76	9.11	31.78	45.35	100.00	16.35	10.66	40.71	32.28	100.00	25.53	12.33	40.62	21.52	100.00
Germany, Fed.Rep. of	11.06	16.63	28.87	43.44	100.00	12.64	16.57	30.02	38.98	100.00	11.47	14.70	33.85	34.88	100.00
France	16.91	13.97	30.82	38.21	100.00	15.39	15.93	30.41	38.25	100.00	24.91	15.03	30.34	29.66	100.00
Italy	13.34	12.73	24.81	49.12	100.00	12.90	12.57	22.55	51.99	100.00	16.02	12.04	19.95	51.99	100.00
United Kingdom	17.56	16.22	26.67	39.55	100.00	26.57	17.78	18.99	36.67	100.00	30.97	17.53	18.21	33.30	100.00
Canada	14.07	10.70	58.13	17.10	100.00	11.69	9.90	56.07	20.42	100.00	11.49	9.49	63.27	13.32	100.00
Nine smaller countries															
Austria	5.82	20.99	14.77	58.42	100.00	6.33	18.32	14.96	56.63	100.00	11.15	24.22	15.78	48.63	100.00
Belgium	9.48	9.02	45.09	36.41	100.00	10.94	9.66	46.79	32.62	100.00	11.27	7.38	55.38	25.94	100.00
Denmark	9.49	17.41	8.68	64.43	100.00	11.90	16.59	11.90	59.61	100.00	15.90	17.03	10.61	56.47	100.00
Finland	2.56	6.22	9.34	81.88	100.00	5.61	11.93	12.61	69.85	100.00	12.74	13.84	17.35	56.07	100.00
Ireland	41.65	3.01	5.42	44.65	100.00	45.78	12.09	10.32	31.81	100.00	70.58	8.95	1.55	18.92	100.00
Netherlands	28.43	15.37	12.42	43.78	100.00	23.83	14.84	14.26	43.04	100.00	30.15	15.27	15.30	39.28	100.00
Norway	4.73	7.37	7.82	80.08	100.00	9.35	13.78	7.97	68.91	100.00	14.00	11.86	9.14	65.67	100.00
Sweden	14.46	11.54	22.69	51.31	100.00	14.26	13.99	27.70	44.05	100.00	16.90	13.44	32.27	37.39	100.00
Switzerland	30.52	25.91	1.45	42.11	100.00	24.28	27.92	1.95	45.85	100.00	23.79	27.56	2.40	46.25	100.00
Southern Europe															
Greece	33.45	11.07	4.88	50.59	100.00	7.19	8.75	6.55	77.51	100.00	14.16	14.13	2.90	68.81	100.00
Portugal	19.21	9.98	18.88	51.93	100.00	28.73	10.96	25.73	34.58	100.00	14.22	17.40	31.59	36.80	100.00
Spain	7.16	13.34	13.39	66.11	100.00	7.11	12.06	35.57	45.25	100.00	10.64	10.3	47.04	31.97	100.00
Turkey	0.46	0.60	13.69	85.29	100.00	2.83	8.56	55.75	32.85	100.00	2.51	10.35	10.14	77.00	100.00
Yugoslavia	4.51	14.59	7.55	73.35	100.00	6.67	18.44	18.06	56.83	100.00	4.91	17.93	20.18	56.97	100.00
Asian NIEs															
Hong Kong	24.57	15.61	30.82	29.00	100.00	51.91	4.67	20.71	22.71	100.00	55.15	11.73	11.52	21.59	100.00
Singapore	18.27	18.52	23.95	39.26	100.00	36.61	10.72	21.72	30.95	100.00	53.92	12.27	15.60	18.21	100.00
Republic of Korea	58.88	10.45	8.20	22.47	100.00	28.24	7.16	20.95	43.64	100.00	31.63	4.83	35.07	28.47	100.00
Taiwan	62.11	6.66	3.41	27.31	100.00	29.34	10.81	22.56	37.29	100.00	34.94	11.65	16.97	36.45	100.00
Eastern countries															
Eastern Europe	7.90	23.69	15.84	52.55	100.00	6.68	20.17	20.77	52.27	100.00	7.58	18.33	19.52	54.33	100.00
Soviet Union	12.15	21.39	16.51	49.94	100.00	14.14	18.07	33.77	33.99	100.00	8.38	11.64	49.43	30.54	100.00

Source: ECE secretariat based on COMTRADE data base.

Note: Product groups: HT = high technology, AT = advanced technology, MT = medium technology, LT = low technology.

APPENDIX TABLE 7.9

Composition of engineering goods imports by group of technology intensity
(Percentages)

	1970				1980				1987			
	HT	AT	MT	LT	Total Engineering	HT	AT	MT	LT	Total Engineering	HT	AT	MT	LT	Total Engineering
Seven major countries													
United States	14.03	11.41	51.03	23.53	100.00	22.20	11.52	43.47	22.80	100.00	24.67	11.84	43.34	20.14	100.00
Japan	37.85	23.84	5.75	32.57	100.00	39.29	21.15	8.70	30.86	100.00	41.06	19.64	15.35	23.95	100.00
Germany, Fed.Rep. of	22.55	15.82	23.50	38.14	100.00	28.21	15.54	23.25	32.97	100.00	29.99	16.24	26.14	27.63	100.00
France	22.34	16.90	19.90	40.86	100.00	20.99	15.34	25.54	38.11	100.00	25.22	14.66	28.42	31.67	100.00
Italy	20.77	19.65	21.58	37.99	100.00	21.04	15.13	34.82	29.01	100.00	25.93	15.12	32.12	26.82	100.00
United Kingdom	32.34	17.63	13.15	36.88	100.00	32.17	13.37	25.49	28.97	100.00	29.33	14.12	28.21	28.33	100.00
Canada	14.35	15.34	41.76	28.55	100.00	17.89	13.14	41.00	27.97	100.00	19.29	10.89	47.29	22.53	100.00
Nine smaller countries													
Austria	11.37	14.29	28.43	45.92	100.00	11.83	14.76	28.20	41.62	100.00	17.70	15.50	26.99	39.45	100.00
Belgium	14.43	13.57	34.41	37.58	100.00	14.90	13.04	38.60	33.46	100.00	15.33	14.11	43.16	27.40	100.00
Denmark	20.08	14.77	23.43	41.72	100.00	20.71	15.32	20.05	43.91	100.00	23.01	12.83	23.68	40.48	100.00
Finland	12.39	13.76	27.05	46.79	100.00	17.17	16.03	24.16	42.70	100.00	21.00	14.98	25.92	38.10	100.00
Ireland	14.02	11.31	25.10	49.51	100.00	19.14	12.11	24.64	44.10	100.00	44.22	12.29	14.60	28.89	100.00
Netherlands	19.21	15.41	25.47	39.91	100.00	21.50	14.82	23.53	40.15	100.00	26.21	13.91	25.71	34.18	100.00
Norway	11.71	12.71	15.20	60.38	100.00	16.55	15.11	18.56	49.78	100.00	19.57	11.94	19.24	49.25	100.00
Sweden	17.03	18.59	20.64	43.74	100.00	16.86	18.74	22.05	42.34	100.00	20.67	16.31	27.01	36.02	100.00
Switzerland	17.03	16.21	26.52	40.24	100.00	20.62	15.32	26.18	37.88	100.00	23.26	14.95	26.89	34.89	100.00
Southern Europe													
Greece	8.63	7.50	12.88	70.99	100.00	7.05	8.77	16.28	67.90	100.00	12.68	9.88	25.22	52.22	100.00
Portugal	11.84	12.68	29.97	45.51	100.00	13.85	14.55	29.31	42.29	100.00	14.69	11.38	36.88	37.05	100.00
Spain	22.73	19.55	10.17	47.56	100.00	27.26	17.23	19.87	35.64	100.00	22.22	15.86	30.12	31.79	100.00
Turkey	9.87	21.32	11.45	57.36	100.00	4.43	28.18	12.20	55.19	100.00	19.27	21.38	9.95	49.40	100.00
Yugoslavia	11.87	12.54	23.06	52.54	100.00	10.54	19.78	15.06	54.62	100.00	14.65	22.28	18.81	44.26	100.00
Asian NIEs													
Hong Kong	28.54	19.19	20.90	31.38	100.00	44.97	10.47	15.78	28.78	100.00	45.86	13.30	15.56	25.29	100.00
Singapore	11.82	19.92	16.12	52.15	100.00	32.64	15.23	12.67	39.46	100.00	43.41	18.88	11.43	26.29	100.00
Republic of Korea	12.59	17.61	10.89	58.91	100.00	29.14	21.40	6.31	43.16	100.00	32.15	22.03	8.67	37.14	100.00
Taiwan	23.65	12.11	7.54	56.5	100.00	23.95	22.72	9.64	43.87	100.00	33.58	17.38	10.83	38.21	100.00
Eastern countries													
Eastern Europe	9.17	20.78	7.38	62.39	100.00	7.50	22.61	9.76	57.21	100.00	8.32	23.79	9.46	55.65	100.00
Soviet Union	5.04	27.46	4.75	62.74	100.00	4.41	25.53	6.38	59.33	100.00	5.97	23.55	5.28	60.63	100.00

Source: ECE secretariat based on COMTRADE data base.

Note: Product groups: HT = high technology, AT = advanced technology, MT = medium technology, LT = low technology.

APPENDIX TABLE 7.10

Engineering goods exports: World market shares by group of technology intensity
(Percentages)

	1970				1980				1987			
	HT	AT	MT	LT	Total Engineering	HT	AT	MT	LT	Total Engineering	HT	AT	MT	LT	Total Engineering

	HT	AT	MT	LT	Total Eng.	HT	AT	MT	LT	Total Eng.	HT	AT	MT	LT	Total Eng.
Seven major countries															
United States	36.69	22.99	16.65	16.99	21.38	29.18	20.84	12.00	14.55	17.61	24.54	16.74	8.95	9.27	13.94
Japan	7.90	6.62	12.46	11.84	10.53	13.16	11.32	23.67	13.81	15.93	20.61	17.47	27.27	14.38	20.06
Germany, Fed.Rep. of	11.93	22.69	21.24	21.30	19.76	11.56	19.99	19.84	18.95	18.11	8.52	19.17	20.92	21.46	18.47
France	6.65	6.95	8.27	6.83	7.21	6.14	8.39	8.77	8.12	7.90	6.59	6.98	6.68	6.50	6.58
Italy	4.36	5.26	5.53	7.29	5.99	3.62	4.65	4.57	7.75	5.55	3.48	4.59	3.60	9.34	5.40
United Kingdom	9.38	10.97	9.73	9.61	9.80	11.29	9.96	5.83	8.28	8.41	7.71	7.66	3.77	6.87	6.19
Canada	4.55	4.38	12.83	2.51	5.93	1.98	2.21	6.86	1.84	3.35	2.03	2.94	9.28	1.94	4.38
Nine smaller countries															
Austria	0.30	1.37	0.52	1.37	0.94	0.35	1.34	0.60	1.67	1.10	0.56	2.14	0.66	2.03	1.25
Belgium	1.60	1.93	5.20	2.80	3.10	1.62	1.89	5.01	2.57	2.93	1.29	1.49	5.29	2.46	2.85
Denmark	0.56	1.29	0.35	1.71	1.07	0.53	0.98	0.38	1.41	0.88	0.54	1.01	0.30	1.58	0.84
Finland	0.06	0.20	0.16	0.93	0.46	0.16	0.44	0.25	1.03	0.55	0.36	0.68	0.41	1.31	0.70
Ireland	0.27	0.02	0.02	0.13	0.12	0.87	0.30	0.14	0.32	0.37	1.94	0.43	0.04	0.43	0.68
Netherlands	4.71	3.23	1.40	3.30	3.04	3.33	2.73	1.44	3.19	2.76	3.21	2.86	1.36	3.47	2.65
Norway	0.18	0.35	0.20	1.38	0.69	0.23	0.45	0.14	0.90	0.49	0.27	0.40	0.14	1.04	0.47
Sweden	2.57	2.60	2.76	4.15	3.26	1.87	2.42	2.63	3.07	2.60	1.69	2.37	2.69	3.10	2.49
Switzerland	4.65	5.00	0.15	2.92	2.79	3.22	4.88	0.19	3.23	2.62	2.42	4.93	0.20	3.90	2.53
Southern Europe															
Greece	0.03	0.01	0.00	0.02	0.02	0.02	0.03	0.01	0.11	0.05	0.02	0.03	0.00	0.06	0.03
Portugal	0.12	0.08	0.08	0.15	0.12	0.21	0.11	0.14	0.14	0.15	0.11	0.25	0.21	0.25	0.20
Spain	0.23	0.55	0.30	0.99	0.60	0.43	0.96	1.55	1.46	1.20	0.58	0.98	2.12	1.44	1.35
Turkey	0.00	0.00	0.00	0.01	0.00	0.00	0.01	0.04	0.02	0.02	0.01	0.11	0.05	0.38	0.15
Yugoslavia	0.12	0.49	0.14	0.88	0.48	0.18	0.67	0.36	0.83	0.54	0.09	0.57	0.30	0.85	0.45
Asian NIEs															
Hong Kong	0.48	0.39	0.41	0.26	0.36	2.12	0.25	0.61	0.49	0.81	2.10	0.78	0.36	0.68	0.95
Singapore	0.22	0.28	0.19	0.21	0.22	1.96	0.76	0.84	0.88	1.06	3.32	1.33	0.80	0.93	1.53
Republic of Korea	0.25	0.06	0.02	0.04	0.08	1.23	0.41	0.66	1.01	0.86	2.80	0.75	2.59	2.09	2.20
Taiwan	1.03	0.14	0.04	0.21	0.30	1.70	0.83	0.95	1.15	1.15	2.29	1.34	0.92	1.98	1.63
Eastern countries															
Eastern Europe	0.34	1.29	0.47	1.03	0.79	0.24	0.94	0.53	0.99	0.70	0.13	0.55	0.28	0.77	0.43
Soviet Union	0.13	0.30	0.12	0.25	0.20	0.15	0.25	0.26	0.19	0.21	0.05	0.13	0.26	0.16	0.15
Sixteen LDCs	0.45	0.23	0.21	0.34	0.31	2.01	1.50	1.39	1.08	1.41	2.13	0.69	0.38	0.59	0.93

Source: ECE secretariat based on COMTRADE data base.

Notes: Product groups: HT = high technology, AT = advanced technology, MT = medium technology, LT = low technology. World exports are defined as the sum of exports of developed market economies and 20 developing countries plus the exports of the seven eastern countries to these aforementioned groups of countries. See the statistical notes at the end of this study for more details.

Statistical appendices

INTRODUCTORY NOTE

For the user's convenience, as well as to lighten the text, the *Economic Survey of Europe* includes a set of appendix tables showing annual changes in main economic indicators over a longer period (1970-1989). The data are presented in three sections, following the structure of the text: *Appendix A* provides macro-economic indicators for the ECE market economies, *Appendix B* does the same for the ECE centrally planned economies, and *Appendix C* collates time series on world trade and the development of foreign trade of the ECE economies.

Except where otherwise stated, time series reflect levels or changes in *real* terms, i.e. at constant prices in case of series measured in value terms.

Data were compiled from international (United Nations, OECD, CMEA) or national statistical sources, as indicated in the notes to individual tables.

Regional aggregations are ECE secretariat calculations, based on 1980 US dollar weights in the case of the market economies (unless stated otherwise) and on CMEA estimates of relative per-capita levels in the case of the centrally planned economies.

All figures for 1989 are preliminary estimates, based on data available in the first weeks of March 1989.

Appendix A. Western Europe and North America

Data for this section were compiled from national and international [913] statistical sources, as indicated in the notes to individual tables. Volume figures underlying the data in tables A.1-A.6 reflect data at constant prices of the following years: Greece (1970); Yugoslavia (1972); Austria (1976 up to 1983 and in 1983 prices from 1984); Portugal (1977); Denmark, France, Federal Republic of Germany, Italy, Netherlands, Norway, Spain, Switzerland (1980); Canada (1981); Turkey, United States (1982); Belgium, Finland, Ireland, Sweden and U.K. (1985).

---

[913] UN, OECD, EUROSTAT, IMF.

APPENDIX TABLE A.1

Gross domestic product
(Annual percentage change)

	1970	1971	1972	1973	1974	1975	1976	1977	1978	1979	1980	1981	1982	1983	1984	1985	1986	1987	1988	1989
France	5.7	4.8	4.4	5.4	3.1	-0.3	4.2	3.2	3.4	3.2	1.6	1.2	2.5	0.7	1.3	1.9	2.3	1.9	3.5	3.3
Germany, Fed.Rep. of	5.1	2.9	4.2	4.7	0.3	-1.6	5.4	3.0	2.9	4.2	1.4	0.2	-0.6	1.5	2.8	2.0	2.3	1.8	3.7	3.6
Italy	5.3	1.6	2.7	7.1	5.4	-2.7	6.6	3.4	3.7	6.0	4.2	1.0	0.3	1.1	3.0	2.6	2.5	3.0	3.9	3.4
United Kingdom [a]	1.8	1.4	3.0	5.9	-1.5	-1.9	2.0	2.8	3.4	3.0	-2.9	-1.3	2.2	3.3	2.8	3.5	3.1	4.8	4.5	2.4
Total 4 countries	4.6	2.8	3.7	5.6	1.6	-1.5	4.6	3.1	3.3	4.0	1.0	0.3	1.0	1.6	2.4	2.4	2.5	2.7	3.9	3.2
Austria	7.1	5.1	6.2	4.9	3.9	-0.4	4.6	4.4	0.5	4.7	3.0	-0.1	1.1	2.2	1.3	2.5	1.1	1.9	4.2	4.0
Belgium	6.7	3.7	5.4	6.0	4.2	-1.4	5.7	0.6	2.9	2.2	4.1	-0.9	1.5	0.4	2.1	0.9	1.8	2.0	4.3	4.5
Denmark	2.0	2.7	5.3	3.6	-0.9	-0.7	6.5	1.6	1.5	3.5	-0.4	-0.9	3.0	2.5	4.4	4.3	3.6	-0.6	-0.2	1.2
Finland	7.5	2.1	7.6	6.7	3.0	1.2	1.2	0.1	2.2	7.3	5.3	1.6	3.6	3.0	3.1	3.3	2.1	4.0	5.2	5.0
Ireland	3.5	3.4	6.4	4.7	4.3	3.7	1.4	8.2	7.2	3.1	3.1	3.3	2.3	-0.2	4.4	2.3	-0.3	4.9	3.7	5.7
Netherlands	5.7	4.2	3.3	4.7	4.0	-0.1	5.1	2.3	2.5	2.4	0.9	-0.7	-1.4	1.4	3.1	2.7	2.0	1.1	2.8	4.2
Norway	2.0	4.6	5.2	4.1	5.2	4.2	6.8	3.6	4.5	5.1	4.2	0.9	0.3	4.6	5.7	5.4	4.2	3.4	1.1	2.3
Sweden	7.2	0.9	2.3	4.0	3.2	2.6	1.1	-1.6	1.8	3.8	2.3	-	1.1	1.8	4.0	2.2	2.3	2.9	2.3	2.0
Switzerland	6.4	4.1	3.2	3.0	1.5	-7.3	-1.4	2.4	0.4	2.5	4.6	1.4	-0.9	1.0	1.8	3.7	2.9	2.0	3.0	3.0
Total 9 countries	5.8	3.4	4.3	4.5	3.1	-0.5	3.5	1.6	2.1	3.4	2.7	0.1	0.7	1.7	3.1	2.8	2.3	2.1	2.9	3.4
Total western Europe	4.9	3.0	3.9	5.3	2.0	-1.3	4.3	2.7	3.0	3.9	1.4	0.2	0.9	1.6	2.6	2.5	2.5	2.6	3.6	3.3
Greece	8.0	7.1	8.9	7.3	-3.6	6.1	6.4	3.4	6.7	3.7	1.8	0.1	0.4	0.4	2.8	3.1	0.8	-0.1	4.0	2.3
Portugal	9.1	6.6	8.0	11.2	1.1	-4.3	6.9	5.6	3.2	5.8	4.9	1.3	2.1	-0.2	-1.8	3.0	4.1	4.6	4.2	4.8
Spain	4.1	5.0	8.1	7.9	5.7	1.1	3.0	3.3	1.8	0.2	1.5	-0.2	1.2	1.8	1.8	2.3	3.3	5.5	5.0	4.9
Turkey	4.9	9.1	6.6	4.4	8.5	7.5	8.7	4.3	2.8	-0.9	-0.7	4.4	5.0	3.7	5.9	5.1	8.2	7.4	3.4	1.1
Yugoslavia [b]	5.6	8.1	4.2	5.0	8.5	3.6	3.9	8.0	6.9	7.0	2.2	1.5	0.7	-1.2	2.0	0.5	3.6	-1.1	-1.7	0.8
Total southern Europe	5.1	6.2	7.4	7.1	5.3	2.5	4.5	4.3	3.2	1.7	1.5	0.8	1.7	1.4	2.3	2.6	4.0	4.3	3.6	3.4
Total Europe	4.9	3.3	4.3	5.5	2.3	-0.9	4.3	2.9	3.0	3.6	1.5	0.3	1.0	1.6	2.6	2.5	2.6	2.7	3.6	3.3
United States	-0.3	2.7	4.9	4.9	-0.7	-1.0	4.8	4.6	5.2	2.1	-0.2	2.0	-2.5	3.7	7.0	3.6	2.9	3.8	4.4	3.0
Canada	2.6	5.8	5.7	7.7	4.4	2.6	6.2	3.6	4.6	3.9	1.5	3.7	-3.2	3.2	6.3	4.8	3.1	4.5	5.0	2.8
North America	-0.1	2.9	5.0	5.1	-0.3	-0.7	4.9	4.5	5.1	2.2	-0.0	2.1	-2.5	3.7	6.9	3.7	3.0	3.9	4.5	3.0
Total above	4.5	4.1	6.0	5.4	1.2	-0.8	4.6	3.6	4.0	3.0	0.8	1.1	-0.6	2.5	4.5	3.0	2.8	3.2	4.0	3.1

Sources: National statistics. Data are calculated at 1980 exchange rates.
[a] Output measure at factor cost.
[b] Gross material product.

Appendix A. Western Europe and North America

APPENDIX TABLE A.2
Private consumption
(Annual percentage change)

	1970	1971	1972	1973	1974	1975	1976	1977	1978	1979	1980	1981	1982	1983	1984	1985	1986	1987	1988	1989
France	4.3	4.9	4.9	5.3	1.2	2.8	4.9	2.7	3.7	3.0	1.2	2.1	3.5	0.9	1.1	2.4	3.7	2.7	2.8	2.5
Germany, Fed.Rep. of	7.6	5.2	4.5	3.1	0.7	3.2	3.7	4.3	3.8	3.6	1.2	-0.5	-1.3	1.7	1.5	1.4	3.4	3.5	2.7	1.6
Italy	8.4	3.5	3.7	6.9	3.7	0.3	5.2	4.1	3.4	7.3	5.6	1.4	1.3	0.6	2.1	3.1	3.8	3.9	3.8	3.4
United Kingdom	2.8	3.1	6.1	5.1	-1.5	-0.5	0.3	-0.5	5.6	4.2	-	0.7	1.0	4.3	1.8	3.7	5.5	6.1	6.9	3.7
Total 4 countries	5.6	4.3	4.8	4.8	0.8	1.7	3.5	2.7	4.1	4.3	1.8	0.8	1.0	1.9	1.6	2.5	4.0	4.0	3.9	2.7
Austria	4.2	6.7	6.1	5.4	3.0	3.2	4.5	5.7	-1.6	4.6	1.5	0.4	1.3	5.3	-0.3	2.4	1.6	3.0	3.0	3.7
Belgium	6.4	4.7	6.2	7.8	2.7	0.6	4.9	2.4	2.5	4.8	1.9	-0.9	1.4	-1.6	1.1	2.0	2.7	2.9	2.4	3.4
Denmark	3.5	-0.8	1.7	4.8	-2.9	3.7	7.9	1.1	0.7	1.4	-3.7	-2.3	1.4	2.6	3.4	5.0	5.7	-1.7	-1.7	-0.5
Finland	7.6	1.7	8.4	5.9	1.8	3.1	1.8	-1.2	2.5	5.5	2.0	1.2	4.7	2.6	2.7	3.2	4.1	5.7	5.0	4.0
Ireland	2.9	3.2	5.1	7.2	1.6	-2.7	2.8	6.8	9.1	4.4	0.4	1.7	-7.1	0.9	1.1	3.7	2.5	2.5	3.2	5.2
Netherlands	7.4	3.3	3.5	4.0	3.7	3.3	5.3	4.6	4.3	3.0	-	-2.5	-1.2	1.5	0.9	2.5	2.7	3.1	1.2	3.5
Norway	-0.0	4.6	2.9	2.9	3.9	5.1	6.1	6.9	-1.6	3.2	2.3	1.1	1.8	1.5	2.7	10.4	5.6	-0.8	-2.3	-1.7
Sweden	6.5	-0.1	3.3	2.4	3.5	2.8	4.2	-1.1	-0.7	2.4	-0.9	-0.5	0.7	-2.2	1.7	2.8	5.2	4.6	2.5	1.2
Switzerland	5.4	4.8	5.4	2.8	-0.5	-2.9	1.1	3.0	2.2	1.3	2.6	0.4	-	1.7	1.6	1.4	2.8	2.1	2.2	2.5
Total 9 countries	5.6	3.1	4.5	4.5	2.0	1.8	4.4	2.8	1.8	3.2	1.0	-0.6	0.5	0.8	1.5	3.1	3.5	2.6	1.7	2.5
Total western Europe	5.6	4.0	4.8	4.8	1.1	1.7	3.7	2.7	3.5	4.0	1.6	0.5	0.9	1.6	1.5	2.7	3.9	3.7	3.4	2.6
Greece	8.8	5.6	7.0	7.6	0.7	5.5	5.3	4.6	5.7	2.6	0.2	2.0	3.9	0.3	1.7	3.9	0.3	0.9	3.7	3.0
Portugal	2.6	12.7	4.0	12.0	9.7	-0.9	3.5	0.6	-2.4	-0.2	3.8	2.8	1.7	-1.3	-3.7	0.5	4.8	6.8	6.5	3.8
Spain	4.2	4.9	8.3	8.0	5.2	2.4	4.7	2.5	1.3	1.2	1.3	-0.6	0.2	0.3	-0.4	2.4	3.6	5.5	4.5	5.5
Turkey	2.2	13.5	6.4	0.2	9.0	7.7	10.1	6.7	-3.9	-3.1	-5.2	0.6	4.2	5.0	7.2	1.2	11.5	6.5	2.6	3.1
Yugoslavia	14.6	8.3	4.6	2.7	7.3	3.4	4.4	7.0	7.0	5.6	0.7	-1.0	-0.1	-1.7	-1.0	-	4.5	0.3	-1.3	1.0
Total southern Europe	5.3	7.3	7.1	6.3	5.9	3.5	5.6	3.9	1.2	1.0	0.1	-	1.3	0.8	0.9	1.9	4.9	4.7	3.5	4.2
Total Europe	5.5	4.3	5.0	4.9	1.7	1.9	3.9	2.9	3.2	3.6	1.5	0.4	0.9	1.5	1.5	2.6	4.0	3.8	3.4	2.8
United States	2.4	3.1	5.4	4.2	-0.9	2.3	5.4	4.4	4.1	2.2	-0.2	1.2	1.3	4.6	4.8	4.7	3.9	2.8	3.4	2.7
Canada	2.0	5.9	7.5	7.5	5.8	4.7	6.5	3.2	3.4	2.9	2.2	2.3	-2.6	3.4	4.6	5.2	4.2	4.9	4.3	3.9
North America	2.4	3.3	5.5	4.4	-0.4	2.5	5.5	4.3	4.0	2.3	-	1.3	1.0	4.6	4.8	4.7	3.9	2.9	3.4	2.8
Total above	4.1	3.8	5.2	4.7	0.7	2.2	4.6	3.6	3.6	3.0	0.8	0.8	1.0	2.9	3.0	3.6	4.0	3.4	3.4	2.8

Sources: National statistics. Data are calculated at 1980 exchange rates.

APPENDIX TABLE A.3
Public consumption
(Annual percentage change)

	1970	1971	1972	1973	1974	1975	1976	1977	1978	1979	1980	1981	1982	1983	1984	1985	1986	1987	1988	1989
France	4.2	3.9	3.5	3.4	1.2	4.4	4.2	2.4	5.2	3.0	2.5	3.1	3.8	2.1	1.2	2.3	1.7	3.0	2.3	2.4
Germany, Fed.Rep. of	4.4	5.1	4.2	5.0	4.0	3.7	1.5	1.4	3.8	3.4	2.6	1.8	-0.8	0.2	2.4	2.1	2.6	1.5	2.2	-0.8
Italy	4.4	5.2	5.1	2.6	2.5	2.5	2.3	2.8	3.5	3.0	2.1	2.7	2.9	2.9	2.5	3.5	2.9	3.6	3.0	2.4
United Kingdom	1.7	2.9	4.2	4.3	1.9	5.6	1.2	-1.7	2.3	2.2	1.6	0.2	0.8	2.0	1.0	-0.0	1.9	1.1	0.4	-0.3
Total 4 countries	3.6	4.3	4.2	4.0	2.5	4.2	2.2	1.0	3.7	2.9	2.2	1.9	1.3	1.6	1.8	1.8	2.2	2.1	1.9	0.7
Austria	3.3	3.3	4.1	3.0	5.7	4.0	4.3	3.6	3.8	3.2	2.5	2.0	2.3	2.3	0.6	1.9	1.7	0.4	0.7	1.0
Belgium	10.8	5.9	5.9	5.3	3.8	4.7	4.0	2.7	5.9	2.7	1.6	0.3	-1.6	-0.2	0.1	2.6	1.4	1.3	-0.7	-0.6
Denmark	6.9	5.5	5.7	4.0	3.5	2.0	4.5	2.4	6.2	5.9	4.3	2.6	3.1	-0.0	-0.4	2.5	0.5	2.5	-0.9	-0.5
Finland	5.4	5.8	7.8	5.6	4.5	6.9	5.7	4.2	4.1	3.8	4.2	4.3	3.5	3.7	2.8	5.2	3.1	4.5	2.5	3.4
Ireland	7.5	8.7	7.5	6.7	7.6	6.5	2.6	2.1	7.9	4.6	7.1	0.3	3.2	-0.4	-0.7	1.6	2.4	-3.8	-4.3	-2.5
Netherlands	6.0	4.4	0.8	0.8	2.2	4.1	4.1	3.4	3.9	2.8	0.6	2.0	0.7	1.2	-0.7	1.4	2.2	2.0	-0.1	1.2
Norway	6.3	6.0	4.5	5.5	4.0	6.4	7.4	4.9	5.3	3.5	5.4	6.1	3.9	4.6	2.4	3.4	2.2	4.5	0.1	2.1
Sweden	20.1	2.5	2.6	2.9	2.9	4.5	3.5	3.0	3.2	4.8	2.3	2.3	1.0	0.8	2.3	2.4	1.5	1.3	1.0	1.2
Switzerland	4.8	5.8	2.9	2.4	1.6	0.7	2.7	0.5	2.0	1.1	0.9	2.5	1.1	3.9	1.2	3.3	3.7	1.8	3.2	3.6
Total 9 countries	9.5	4.5	3.7	3.3	3.3	4.1	4.1	3.0	4.3	3.6	2.1	2.4	1.4	1.5	0.9	2.5	1.9	1.9	0.5	1.2
Total western Europe	5.0	4.3	4.0	3.9	2.7	4.2	2.7	1.5	3.9	3.1	2.2	2.0	1.3	1.5	1.5	2.0	2.1	2.0	1.6	0.8
Greece	5.9	4.9	5.7	6.8	12.1	11.9	5.1	6.5	3.5	5.8	0.2	6.8	2.3	2.7	3.0	3.2	-0.6	1.8	5.6	5.0
Portugal	7.0	6.4	8.6	7.8	17.3	6.6	7.0	11.8	3.1	6.4	7.9	5.6	3.8	3.9	0.3	6.4	7.2	2.0	4.5	2.7
Spain	5.2	4.7	5.5	6.7	8.2	5.3	5.3	4.1	5.5	4.2	4.4	1.9	4.9	3.9	2.9	4.6	5.7	8.7	5.0	5.5
Turkey	3.6	6.1	7.3	10.3	9.9	13.4	10.8	3.2	9.9	1.7	8.8	0.9	2.0	1.7	-	8.4	6.5	5.0	2.1	0.3
Yugoslavia	9.3	-0.1	5.1	4.1	7.3	9.3	9.5	7.4	6.5	4.5	-1.0	-4.8	-0.7	-5.1	-0.2	2.0	4.6	-1.5	0.1	-1.0
Total southern Europe	5.7	4.4	5.9	6.9	9.4	7.6	6.6	5.2	5.8	4.3	4.0	1.8	3.5	2.5	2.0	4.8	5.1	5.9	4.2	4.0
Total Europe	4.8	4.4	4.2	4.0	3.1	4.4	3.0	1.7	4.0	3.2	2.2	2.0	1.5	1.6	1.6	2.2	2.4	2.3	1.8	1.1
United States	-3.1	-1.1	0.7	-0.9	1.4	1.3	-0.1	1.5	2.5	0.8	1.9	1.5	1.9	1.1	4.4	7.9	4.2	2.7	0.4	2.6
Canada	9.4	4.4	2.7	5.8	5.6	6.5	2.0	4.6	1.7	0.6	2.8	2.5	2.4	1.4	1.2	3.2	1.7	0.7	3.1	2.3
North America	-2.4	-0.7	0.9	-0.4	1.7	1.8	0.1	1.8	2.5	0.8	2.0	1.6	1.9	1.2	4.1	7.5	4.0	2.5	0.6	2.6
Total above	0.9	1.7	2.5	1.8	2.4	3.1	1.6	1.8	3.3	2.1	2.1	1.8	1.7	1.4	2.8	4.7	3.1	2.4	1.2	1.8

Sources: National statistics. Data are calculated at 1980 exchange rates.

APPENDIX TABLE A.4
Gross domestic fixed capital formation
(Annual percentage change)

	1970	1971	1972	1973	1974	1975	1976	1977	1978	1979	1980	1981	1982	1983	1984	1985	1986	1987	1988	1989
France	4.6	7.3	6.0	8.5	1.3	-6.4	3.3	-1.8	2.1	3.1	2.6	-1.9	-1.4	-3.6	-2.6	3.2	3.3	3.7	7.8	5.4
Germany, Fed.Rep. of	9.4	6.1	2.7	-0.3	-9.6	-5.3	3.6	3.6	4.7	7.2	2.8	-4.8	-5.3	3.2	0.8	0.1	3.3	2.2	5.9	7.9
Italy	3.0	0.2	1.3	8.8	2.0	-7.3	-	1.8	0.6	5.7	8.7	-3.2	-5.2	-0.9	4.5	1.4	1.6	6.8	4.9	5.4
United Kingdom	2.5	1.8	-0.2	6.5	-2.4	-2.0	1.7	-1.8	3.0	2.8	-5.4	-9.6	5.4	5.0	8.6	3.9	2.1	8.5	13.7	5.2
Total 4 countries	5.5	4.4	2.8	5.0	-2.9	-5.4	2.4	0.6	2.8	4.9	2.4	-4.4	-2.4	0.7	1.9	1.9	2.7	4.7	7.8	6.2
Austria	9.8	13.8	12.1	0.3	4.0	-5.0	3.8	5.2	-3.8	3.6	3.6	-2.1	-7.1	-1.1	2.4	5.0	3.4	2.9	5.8	6.5
Belgium	9.1	-2.0	2.9	7.0	7.4	-1.8	3.8	0.1	2.6	-2.6	4.6	-15.9	-2.0	-4.5	1.8	0.6	4.4	5.2	16.0	14.1
Denmark	2.2	1.9	9.3	3.5	-8.9	-12.4	17.1	-2.4	1.1	-0.4	-12.6	-19.2	7.1	1.9	12.9	12.6	17.1	-7.4	-4.8	-1.5
Finland	12.5	3.8	6.5	8.5	3.5	5.9	-8.8	-3.5	-6.9	3.0	10.4	2.2	4.4	4.1	-2.1	2.9	-	5.4	9.8	12.6
Ireland	0.3	8.8	7.4	16.2	-11.6	-2.6	13.6	4.1	18.9	13.6	-3.2	7.3	-3.3	-9.0	-1.4	-8.3	-2.0	-1.9	-1.7	11.2
Netherlands	7.5	1.5	-2.3	4.2	-4.0	-4.4	-2.2	9.7	2.5	-1.7	-0.9	-10.4	-4.1	2.1	5.2	7.0	7.4	0.7	9.7	6.9
Norway	14.9	18.8	-4.1	13.6	5.1	11.9	10.1	3.6	-11.2	-5.0	-1.5	17.9	-11.0	5.8	10.9	-21.0	23.9	-0.5	1.9	-4.3
Sweden	10.2	-0.6	4.2	2.7	-3.0	3.1	1.9	-2.9	-6.8	4.5	3.4	-5.8	-0.3	1.9	6.0	7.3	0.7	7.6	6.4	5.6
Switzerland	8.9	9.9	5.0	2.9	-4.3	-13.6	-10.5	1.6	6.1	5.1	9.9	2.4	-2.5	4.1	4.1	5.3	7.9	7.4	6.9	5.3
Total 9 countries	8.7	4.6	3.5	4.9	-1.1	-3.0	0.9	2.2	-0.8	1.0	1.8	-4.4	-2.7	1.3	4.7	2.5	6.9	2.9	6.9	6.3
Total western Europe	6.3	4.5	3.0	5.0	-2.5	-4.8	1.9	1.0	1.9	3.9	2.2	-4.4	-2.5	0.8	2.6	2.1	3.8	4.3	7.5	6.2
Greece	-1.4	14.0	15.4	7.7	-25.6	0.2	6.8	7.8	6.0	8.8	-6.5	-7.5	-1.9	-1.3	-5.7	5.2	-6.2	-7.9	10.1	8.4
Portugal	11.5	9.8	13.5	9.5	-7.0	-11.3	0.8	12.0	6.5	-2.0	8.6	5.5	1.7	-6.9	-17.0	-3.4	10.9	20.2	16.0	11.5
Spain	3.0	-2.9	15.8	14.3	6.6	-3.9	-2.0	-0.2	-2.3	-4.5	1.3	-3.3	0.5	-2.5	-5.8	4.1	10.0	14.6	14.0	14.6
Turkey	13.5	-5.0	14.8	13.2	10.7	24.7	17.7	3.9	-10.0	-3.6	-10.0	1.7	3.5	3.0	0.1	16.8	11.1	5.6	-1.3	-3.4
Yugoslavia	12.8	4.6	1.8	4.2	9.1	9.7	8.1	9.5	10.5	6.4	-5.9	-9.8	-5.5	-9.7	-9.6	-3.7	3.5	-5.1	-5.8	0.5
Total southern Europe	5.7	0.5	13.0	11.5	3.2	1.1	3.1	3.4	0.1	-0.9	-2.0	-3.7	-0.4	-3.4	-6.5	4.3	7.9	8.8	8.7	9.5
Total Europe	6.2	3.5	3.9	5.7	-1.8	-4.1	2.1	1.3	1.7	3.3	1.7	-4.3	-2.3	0.3	1.5	2.3	4.2	4.8	7.7	6.6
United States	-3.1	7.1	11.0	8.4	-6.8	-11.6	8.9	14.1	9.8	3.7	-7.9	1.1	-9.6	8.2	16.8	5.3	1.0	2.6	5.8	1.8
Canada	-0.1	8.8	3.9	8.4	6.0	5.8	4.8	2.3	2.4	7.4	8.2	10.6	-11.0	-0.7	2.1	9.5	5.7	11.7	13.2	8.5
North America	-2.8	7.2	10.3	8.4	-5.6	-9.8	8.4	12.7	9.0	4.1	-6.2	2.2	-9.7	7.0	15.1	5.8	1.5	3.6	6.7	2.6
Total above	3.0	4.8	6.1	6.7	-3.2	-6.2	4.3	5.4	4.5	3.6	-1.4	-1.8	-5.3	2.9	6.9	3.8	3.0	4.3	7.3	4.9

Sources: National statistics. Data are calculated at 1980 exchange rates.

APPENDIX TABLE A.5

Volume of exports of goods and services
(Annual percentage change)

	1970	1971	1972	1973	1974	1975	1976	1977	1978	1979	1980	1981	1982	1983	1984	1985	1986	1987	1988	1989
France	16.1	9.2	12.0	10.8	8.8	-1.7	8.2	7.4	5.9	7.5	2.7	3.7	-1.7	3.7	7.0	1.9	-1.1	3.0	6.7	8.4
Germany, Fed.Rep. of	5.8	6.3	7.1	10.6	12.3	-6.8	9.7	3.9	3.2	4.3	5.1	7.7	3.4	-0.8	8.0	7.0	-0.5	0.4	5.6	9.4
Italy	-2.5	6.8	9.3	4.1	7.0	1.6	10.5	9.9	9.0	8.5	-8.7	7.6	-1.1	2.4	7.3	3.9	3.8	3.3	5.9	6.1
United Kingdom	5.2	7.0	1.1	11.9	7.3	-2.8	9.1	6.9	1.9	3.8	0.2	-0.7	0.8	2.2	6.5	5.9	4.2	5.1	0.8	4.7
Total 4 countries	6.3	7.2	6.8	10.0	9.5	-3.4	9.3	6.3	4.4	5.6	1.0	4.6	0.9	1.4	7.3	5.1	1.1	2.6	4.7	7.5
Austria	16.4	5.9	9.2	2.2	10.7	-2.4	11.1	4.6	6.0	10.8	5.8	3.8	1.9	3.3	6.6	6.9	-2.7	2.4	8.8	10.9
Belgium	10.9	6.3	10.0	14.4	6.8	-8.9	11.7	12.7	3.4	7.1	3.3	3.1	2.1	3.2	5.7	1.3	5.4	7.1	8.2	8.4
Denmark	5.6	5.6	5.6	7.8	3.5	-1.8	4.1	4.1	1.2	8.4	5.2	8.2	2.5	4.9	3.5	5.0	-	4.8	6.7	6.2
Finland	8.7	-1.3	14.5	7.3	-0.6	14.0	12.8	15.7	8.9	8.8	8.4	4.9	-1.1	2.5	5.4	1.2	1.3	2.6	3.9	1.7
Ireland	4.4	4.1	3.6	10.9	0.7	7.2	8.1	14.0	12.3	6.5	6.4	2.0	5.5	10.5	16.6	6.6	2.9	13.4	8.7	9.5
Netherlands	11.9	10.7	10.0	12.1	2.6	-3.1	9.9	-1.8	3.3	7.4	1.5	1.5	-0.0	3.5	7.3	5.5	2.9	4.1	7.7	6.2
Norway	0.1	1.1	14.1	8.3	0.7	3.1	11.3	3.6	8.4	2.6	2.1	1.4	-0.1	7.6	8.2	10.7	1.6	3.5	4.8	12.1
Sweden	1.0	4.8	5.9	13.7	5.3	-9.3	4.3	1.5	7.8	6.1	-0.5	2.0	5.7	9.9	6.9	1.4	3.2	3.9	3.3	4.0
Switzerland	6.8	3.9	6.4	7.9	1.0	-6.6	9.3	9.7	3.7	2.5	5.1	4.6	-2.9	1.1	6.3	8.3	0.4	1.7	5.2	6.1
Total 9 countries	8.1	6.1	8.9	10.6	3.8	-5.2	8.9	5.2	4.8	6.5	3.3	3.0	1.2	4.4	6.7	4.7	2.4	4.6	6.7	7.3
Total western Europe	7.0	6.7	7.6	10.2	7.3	-4.1	9.2	5.9	4.5	5.9	1.8	4.0	1.0	2.5	7.1	4.9	1.6	3.3	5.5	7.4
Greece	12.4	11.9	22.9	23.4	0.1	10.6	16.4	1.8	16.4	6.7	6.9	-5.9	-7.2	8.0	16.9	1.3	14.0	15.9	7.7	4.0
Portugal	-1.6	9.9	18.5	4.2	15.7	15.6	-	5.9	10.0	32.5	5.7	-4.0	6.2	13.4	10.8	7.1	7.7	10.8	7.1	13.0
Spain	17.5	13.0	12.2	9.0	0.8	-1.4	10.1	8.5	10.7	6.4	0.6	8.4	4.8	10.1	11.7	2.7	1.3	5.9	6.3	4.3
Turkey	14.3	15.5	14.6	26.2	11.0	-1.1	37.5	21.8	12.9	12.3	7.4	62.2	36.9	14.6	20.4	11.3	-0.6	26.0	17.2	5.0
Yugoslavia	3.3	3.7	17.6	6.8	1.0	-1.3	9.3	-3.1	-2.4	14.9	7.5	12.0	18.5	-4.4	6.4	7.9	-2.6	0.5	4.9	4.9
Total southern Europe	10.9	10.6	15.1	10.3	-2.3	-1.8	11.8	2.2	8.8	8.8	3.6	9.5	2.2	8.5	12.5	5.0	2.3	9.7	8.2	5.4
Total Europe	8.0	7.0	8.2	10.2	6.7	-3.9	9.3	5.7	4.8	6.1	2.0	4.3	1.1	2.9	7.5	4.9	1.6	3.8	5.7	7.3
United States	9.3	-	8.5	21.6	9.9	-0.7	5.0	1.5	9.3	8.3	10.1	-0.4	-8.8	-2.7	6.1	2.9	11.9	15.0	17.7	10.9
Canada	8.7	5.2	7.8	10.6	-2.0	-6.8	10.6	8.9	13.6	5.0	2.7	4.4	-2.2	6.4	17.7	6.0	3.9	6.5	9.5	-0.7
North America	9.2	1.3	8.3	18.7	7.1	-2.0	6.1	3.1	10.3	7.6	8.4	0.7	-7.3	-0.5	9.1	3.7	9.7	12.8	15.7	8.1
Total above	8.3	5.7	8.2	12.0	6.8	-3.5	8.6	5.1	6.0	6.4	3.5	3.5	-0.9	2.2	7.8	4.7	3.4	5.9	8.1	7.5

Sources: National statistics. Data are calculated at 1980 exchange rates.

APPENDIX TABLE A.6
Volume of imports of goods and services
(Annual percentage change)

	1970	1971	1972	1973	1974	1975	1976	1977	1978	1979	1980	1981	1982	1983	1984	1985	1986	1987	1988	1989
France	6.3	6.3	13.2	14.2	1.9	-9.7	17.4	0.1	3.0	10.1	2.5	-2.1	2.6	-2.7	2.7	4.5	7.0	7.7	8.1	7.1
Germany, Fed.Rep. of	14.9	10.5	6.0	4.3	1.4	0.3	11.1	2.9	6.3	9.8	3.8	-2.9	-1.5	1.8	5.7	3.4	3.1	4.1	5.9	6.9
Italy	12.4	2.7	9.8	9.3	2.2	12.6	14.1	1.7	4.8	11.7	2.9	-3.7	-0.7	-1.8	11.3	4.6	4.6	10.1	7.2	8.1
United Kingdom	4.9	5.3	9.8	12.0	0.9	-7.0	4.7	1.5	3.9	9.7	-3.4	-2.8	4.9	6.5	9.8	2.5	6.8	7.6	12.4	9.2
Total 4 countries	9.8	6.8	9.2	9.5	1.5	-6.3	11.5	1.7	4.6	10.2	1.7	-2.8	1.1	1.1	6.9	3.7	5.2	6.9	8.3	7.8
Austria	16.9	5.8	11.1	6.2	6.9	-4.6	17.4	8.0	-1.3	11.8	6.4	-1.5	-3.3	5.7	9.9	6.2	-1.2	4.7	10.0	9.6
Belgium	12.2	5.3	8.4	19.4	7.5	-9.8	11.0	15.4	3.7	9.1	0.3	-2.7	0.9	-1.1	6.0	1.0	7.4	9.3	8.3	8.7
Denmark	9.3	-0.7	1.5	12.8	-3.8	-4.8	15.6	-	0.1	5.0	-6.8	-1.7	3.8	1.8	5.5	8.1	6.8	-2.2	1.2	4.0
Finland	20.3	-0.6	4.2	13.0	6.7	0.6	-2.0	-1.5	-3.7	18.4	8.3	-4.7	2.5	3.0	1.0	6.8	3.1	9.0	11.5	9.6
Ireland	2.3	4.7	5.1	19.0	-2.3	10.2	14.7	13.3	15.7	13.9	-4.5	1.7	-3.1	4.7	9.9	3.2	5.6	5.0	3.9	10.0
Netherlands	14.7	6.1	4.8	11.0	-0.8	-4.1	10.1	2.9	6.3	6.0	-0.4	-5.9	1.1	3.9	5.0	6.5	3.6	6.1	7.1	6.5
Norway	13.6	6.4	-1.0	14.5	4.7	7.0	12.3	3.4	13.5	-0.7	3.2	1.5	3.7	-0.0	9.5	6.5	9.9	-6.6	-2.7	-0.3
Sweden	21.9	-3.3	4.0	6.9	9.9	-3.5	9.0	-3.8	-5.5	11.6	0.4	-5.8	3.4	0.8	5.4	7.8	4.7	7.2	5.8	6.0
Switzerland	13.9	6.2	7.3	6.5	-1.0	15.4	13.1	9.3	10.9	6.9	7.2	-1.3	-2.6	4.4	7.1	5.1	7.1	5.5	5.4	6.4
Total 9 countries	14.6	3.8	5.4	11.7	3.0	-5.8	11.1	5.4	2.2	8.0	1.6	-3.0	0.8	2.1	6.3	5.2	5.3	5.3	6.3	6.9
Total western Europe	11.5	5.7	7.8	10.3	2.1	-6.1	11.4	3.0	3.7	9.4	1.7	-2.8	1.0	1.5	6.6	4.2	5.2	6.3	7.5	7.5
Greece	6.2	7.6	15.4	32.2	16.3	6.3	6.1	8.0	7.2	7.2	-8.0	3.6	7.0	6.6	0.2	12.8	3.8	16.5	6.5	9.0
Portugal	0.9	14.5	12.0	12.7	4.8	25.2	3.4	12.0	-0.2	12.1	7.8	2.5	3.7	-6.3	-4.6	1.0	16.4	26.4	17.3	12.0
Spain	7.0	0.6	24.7	16.4	7.7	-1.1	10.1	-4.7	-0.7	11.5	3.8	-4.2	3.9	-0.6	-1.0	6.2	16.5	20.4	15.2	15.8
Turkey	22.0	9.7	19.0	0.6	18.3	26.1	32.1	-3.4	31.8	14.1	-0.4	12.5	13.0	18.6	15.5	7.8	13.1	17.4	5.0	5.5
Yugoslavia	27.8	9.2	-6.5	16.4	14.4	-5.6	-3.2	12.5	4.5	18.7	-7.2	-1.5	16.7	14.8	2.5	2.6	6.6	-6.9	-0.9	13.2
Total southern Europe	12.3	6.2	14.5	15.3	7.0	-1.2	10.1	1.2	-4.8	9.1	0.2	-0.3	1.2	-0.4	1.8	6.1	12.9	16.6	11.0	12.5
Total Europe	11.9	5.7	8.4	10.7	2.5	-5.7	11.3	2.9	3.0	9.4	1.5	-2.7	1.0	1.4	6.3	4.4	5.8	7.1	7.8	7.9
United States	4.2	6.8	12.1	10.9	-3.5	10.5	19.7	12.0	5.7	1.3	-8.2	2.1	-2.4	12.1	23.0	5.2	12.5	6.3	5.1	5.2
Canada	-1.7	7.2	13.8	14.7	11.1	-3.3	8.6	1.7	7.4	11.4	4.9	8.5	15.2	9.0	17.1	8.7	7.1	9.0	13.9	7.8
North America	3.2	6.9	12.4	11.5	-1.1	-9.1	17.5	10.1	6.0	3.0	-5.7	3.4	-5.2	11.5	21.9	5.8	11.5	6.8	6.7	5.7
Total above	9.7	6.0	9.4	10.9	1.6	-6.5	12.6	4.6	3.8	7.7	-0.4	-1.3	-0.5	3.7	10.2	4.8	7.4	7.0	7.5	7.3

Sources: National statistics. Data are calculated at 1980 exchange rates.

APPENDIX TABLE A.7
Current account balances
(Million US dollars)

	1970	1971	1972	1973	1974	1975	1976	1977	1978	1979	1980	1981	1982	1983	1984	1985	1986	1987	1988	1989
France	-199	161	-417	1421	-3857	2743	-3373	-408	7064	5142	-4208	-4811	-12082	-5166	-876	-35	2426	-4446	-3549	-3300
Germany, Fed.Rep. of	850	940	1160	5190	10630	4420	3720	3980	9160	-5650	-13890	-3310	4980	5400	9750	16980	39850	45630	48640	52700
Italy	799	1622	2056	-2465	-8004	-525	-2841	2487	6252	5503	-9957	-9700	-6388	1381	-2501	-3540	2912	-1663	-5446	-11700
United Kingdom	1985	2719	508	-2419	-7481	-3417	-1683	-209	1858	-875	7520	14500	8041	5831	2608	4765	158	-6422	-26115	-34110
Total 4 countries	3435	5442	3307	1727	-8712	3221	-4177	5850	24334	4120	-20535	-3321	-5449	7446	8981	18170	45346	33099	13530	3590
Austria	-75	-91	-157	-254	-203	-231	-1119	-2200	-706	-1141	-1725	-1464	641	246	-264	-273	86	-429	-458	1
Belgium	717	643	1296	1337	774	181	435	-554	-823	-3080	-4931	-4168	-2594	-495	-55	669	3055	2794	3379	3500
Denmark	-544	-425	-63	-476	-980	-490	-1914	-1722	-1502	-2965	-2466	-1875	-2259	-1176	-1637	-2728	-4490	-3002	-1765	-1300
Finland	-240	-339	-117	-389	-1210	-2143	-1117	-105	674	-169	-1410	-385	-763	-935	-10	-766	-731	-1812	-2997	-4200
Ireland	-198	-200	-150	-254	-688	-124	-428	-522	-849	-2100	-2132	-2617	-1934	-1217	-1038	-688	-677	375	651	500
Netherlands	-588	-230	1184	2419	3039	2373	3450	1231	-1208	215	-1036	3696	4487	4969	6571	4027	3620	3489	5246	5000
Norway	-242	-526	-59	-365	-1118	-2478	-3746	-5034	-2103	-1044	1098	2177	662	1986	2919	3052	-4545	-4151	-3678	2000
Sweden	-265	352	567	1429	-552	-342	-1648	-2181	-251	-2414	-4404	-2847	-3440	-1034	246	-1608	62	-1247	-2549	-5000
Switzerland	72	82	220	280	173	2288	3133	3395	3723	1282	-1544	1456	3928	1209	6152	6039	4654	6280	8326	5000
Total 9 countries	-1363	-734	2721	3727	-765	-966	-2954	-7692	-3045	-11416	-18550	-6027	-1272	3553	12884	7724	1034	2297	6155	5501
Total western Europe	2072	4708	6028	5454	-9477	2255	-7131	-1842	21289	-7296	-39085	-9348	-6721	10999	21865	25894	46380	35396	19685	9091
Greece	-422	-344	-400	-1189	-1143	-877	-929	-1075	-955	-1886	-2209	-2408	-1892	-1878	-2132	-3276	-1676	-1223	-958	-2500
Portugal	63	271	354	341	-830	-755	-1282	-957	-463	-54	-1064	-2605	-3250	-1004	-514	410	1144	640	-629	-1000
Spain	79	856	581	585	-3233	-3514	-4292	-2133	1634	1128	-5173	-4989	-4245	-2746	2018	2851	3965	-233	-3784	-11600
Turkey	-44	43	212	660	-561	-1648	-2029	-3138	-1266	-1413	-3409	-1916	-935	-1898	-1407	-1030	-1528	-982	1503	800
Yugoslavia	-372	-395	431	502	-951	-625	186	-1329	-1273	-3659	-2317	-959	-473	275	478	833	1100	1248	2487	2300
Total southern Europe	-696	431	1178	899	-6718	-7419	-8346	-8632	-2323	-5884	-14172	-12877	-10795	-7251	-1557	-212	3005	-550	-1381	-12000
Total Europe	1376	5139	7206	6353	-16195	-5164	-15477	-10474	18966	-13180	-53257	-22225	-17516	3748	20308	25682	49385	34846	18304	-2909
United States	2330	-1450	-5780	7070	1920	18130	4170	-14490	-15450	-970	1840	6300	-6650	-44180	-104220	-112740	-132590	-143090	-126150	-105880
Canada	1008	363	-278	305	-1324	-4571	-4152	-4101	-4285	-4138	-967	-5110	2231	2487	1995	-1470	-7600	-7060	-8330	-14000
North America	3338	-1087	-6058	7375	596	13559	18	-18591	-19735	-5108	873	1190	-4419	-41693	-102225	-114210	-140190	-150150	-134480	-119880
Total above	4714	4052	1148	13728	-15599	8395	-15459	-29065	-769	-18288	-52384	-21035	-21935	-37945	-81917	-88528	-90805	-115304	-116176	-122789
Japan	1970	5797	6624	-136	-4693	-682	3680	10918	16534	-8754	-10746	4770	6850	20799	35003	49169	85845	87015	79590	57000

Sources: IMF, *International Financial Statistics*, March 1990; national statistics (Portugal 1970, 1971) and secretariat estimates for 1989 based on the above mentioned sources and OECD, *Economic Outlook*, No. 46, December 1989.

Appendix A. Western Europe and North America

APPENDIX TABLE A.8
Industrial production
(Annual percentage change)

	1970	1971	1972	1973	1974	1975	1976	1977	1978	1979	1980	1981	1982	1983	1984	1985	1986	1987	1988	1989[a]
France	5.6	6.7	5.0	7.1	2.2	-7.6	9.4	1.1	2.1	5.2	-	-2.0	-	0.7	-	1.0	0.9	1.9	4.6	4.5
Germany, Fed.Rep. of	6.0	0.8	3.6	6.2	-1.6	-6.2	6.9	2.5	-1.0	5.1	-	-1.9	-3.2	0.7	3.0	4.5	2.0	0.4	3.6	5.0
Italy	6.6	-0.5	4.9	9.8	3.9	-8.8	11.6	-	2.0	6.6	5.2	-2.2	-3.1	-2.4	3.4	1.3	4.1	2.6	6.9	2.5
United Kingdom	0.4	-0.5	1.8	9.0	-2.0	-5.4	3.4	5.1	2.9	3.9	-6.7	-3.2	1.7	4.1	0.2	5.4	2.1	3.6	3.6	1.0
Total 4 countries	4.7	1.5	3.7	7.7	0.2	-6.8	7.6	2.3	1.1	5.1	-0.5	-2.2	-1.5	0.6	1.8	3.3	2.2	1.9	4.5	3.5
Austria	8.6	5.9	8.1	3.7	5.5	-6.3	6.6	3.8	2.1	7.7	2.7	-1.6	-0.8	1.0	5.3	4.5	1.1	1.0	4.4	5.5
Belgium	2.9	1.7	7.7	6.0	4.0	-9.8	7.7	0.4	2.4	4.5	-1.2	-2.7	-	1.9	2.4	2.6	0.8	2.2	5.7	3.0
Denmark	..	..	..	..	..	..	..	..	..	..	..	..	..	..	..	..	..	..	..	..
Finland	10.2	5.6	8.8	6.5	4.5	-1.4	-	1.5	4.3	11.1	7.5	2.3	1.1	3.4	4.3	4.2	1.7	5.1	4.0	3.0
Ireland	3.4	3.9	4.5	10.6	1.6	-4.0	8.8	8.0	7.8	7.8	-4.8	5.4	-0.7	7.9	9.9	3.5	3.2	9.8	10.9	12.5
Netherlands	9.2	5.6	5.3	6.3	6.0	-5.6	8.3	-	1.1	3.3	-	-2.1	-4.3	2.2	4.4	5.3	-	1.0	-	5.0
Norway	4.3	4.2	8.0	5.6	3.5	5.1	6.5	-	10.6	6.8	5.1	-	-	8.5	6.7	5.3	3.5	7.5	5.1	16.5
Sweden[b]	5.1	1.2	2.4	7.1	4.4	-2.1	-2.2	-5.5	-1.2	7.1	-1.1	-1.1	-2.2	4.6	6.6	3.1	-	2.1	2.0	3.0
Switzerland	8.7	2.3	2.2	5.5	1.0	12.4	-	5.9	-	2.2	5.4	-1.0	-3.1	-1.1	3.3	5.3	4.0	1.0	6.7	3.0
Total 9 countries[c]	6.9	3.5	5.3	6.0	4.0	-5.8	4.0	0.9	2.2	5.4	1.9	-1.0	-1.8	2.8	4.8	4.3	1.5	2.7	4.0	5.7
Total western Europe[c]	5.1	1.9	4.0	7.4	0.9	-6.6	6.8	2.0	1.3	5.2	-	-2.0	-1.5	1.1	2.4	3.5	2.1	2.1	4.4	3.9
Greece	10.4	11.3	14.1	15.3	-1.6	4.4	10.6	2.0	7.5	6.1	1.0	0.8	1.0	-0.3	2.3	3.3	-1.0	-1.5	5.1	1.5
Portugal	6.4	7.7	12.9	11.8	2.8	-4.9	3.3	13.2	6.8	7.2	5.5	2.4	7.7	3.5	2.5	0.7	6.1	2.4	6.2	4.5
Spain	10.5	2.9	16.1	14.9	9.4	-8.8	5.1	5.3	2.3	0.7	1.3	-1.0	-1.1	2.7	0.9	1.9	3.1	4.6	3.1	5.0
Turkey	..	..	..	..	..	..	..	..	..	..	..	..	..	..	..	..	..	..	..	..
Yugoslavia	7.5	9.3	8.5	5.9	11.1	5.0	3.2	10.8	8.3	9.0	3.5	3.4	..	1.1	5.4	3.1	4.0	1.0	-1.0	2.0
Total southern Europe[d]	9.5	5.3	13.9	12.8	8.4	-4.7	5.0	6.8	4.4	3.7	2.1	0.5	-	2.1	2.4	2.3	3.3	2.9	2.4	3.9
Total Europe[e]	5.4	2.1	4.8	7.8	1.6	-6.4	6.7	2.4	1.6	5.0	0.2	-1.7	-1.4	1.2	2.4	3.4	2.2	2.1	4.2	3.9
United States	-3.1	1.7	9.2	8.4	-0.4	-8.9	10.7	5.9	6.6	3.9	-1.9	2.2	-7.1	6.0	11.4	1.6	1.1	3.8	5.7	3.5
Canada	-1.6	5.7	8.8	11.9	1.9	-7.3	6.7	3.4	3.4	4.8	-3.4	2.1	-9.9	6.5	12.2	5.4	-0.1	5.7	6.2	1.0
North America	-3.0	2.0	9.2	8.7	-0.2	-8.7	10.4	5.7	6.3	4.0	-2.0	2.2	-7.3	6.0	11.5	1.9	1.0	3.9	5.8	3.3
Total above[e]	0.9	2.1	7.1	8.3	0.6	-7.7	8.6	4.2	4.2	4.5	-1.0	0.4	-4.7	3.8	7.4	2.5	1.5	3.1	5.1	3.6

Sources: OECD, *Main Economic Indicators*, Paris (monthly), and national statistics. Data for France, Finland, Norway and Sweden for 1970-1984, as well as for the Netherlands, Switzerland and Yugoslavia for 1970-1989 are calculated from rounded index numbers (1985 = 100). National data are aggregated by means of weights derived from GDP originating in industry, expressed at 1985 US dollar exchange rates.

[a] Country data rounded to the nearest 0.5 percentage point.
[b] Refers to mining and manufacturing only.
[c] Excluding Denmark.
[d] Excluding Turkey.
[e] Excluding Denmark and Turkey.

APPENDIX TABLE A.9
Consumer prices [a]
(Annual percentage change)

	1970	1971	1972	1973	1974	1975	1976	1977	1978	1979	1980	1981	1982	1983	1984	1985	1986	1987	1988	1989
France	5.2	5.5	6.2	7.3	13.7	11.8	9.6	9.4	9.1	10.8	13.6	13.4	11.8	9.6	7.4	5.8	2.5	3.3	2.8	3.6
Germany, Fed.Rep. of	3.3	5.4	5.5	7.0	7.0	5.9	4.3	3.7	2.7	4.1	5.5	6.3	5.2	3.3	2.4	2.0	-0.1	0.2	1.3	2.8
Italy	4.9	4.8	5.8	10.8	19.1	17.0	16.8	17.0	12.1	14.8	21.2	17.8	16.5	14.6	10.8	9.2	5.9	4.7	5.0	6.6
United Kingdom	6.4	9.4	7.1	9.1	16.0	24.2	16.5	15.8	8.3	13.4	18.0	11.9	8.6	4.6	5.0	6.1	3.4	4.1	4.9	7.8
Total 4 countries	4.8	6.2	6.1	8.2	13.0	13.5	10.6	10.3	7.4	9.9	13.2	11.5	9.8	7.3	5.8	5.2	2.4	2.7	3.1	4.8
Austria	4.4	4.7	6.3	7.6	9.5	8.4	7.3	5.5	3.6	3.7	6.3	6.8	5.4	3.3	5.7	3.2	1.7	1.4	2.0	2.5
Belgium	3.9	4.3	5.4	6.9	12.7	12.8	9.2	7.1	4.5	4.5	6.6	8.2	8.2	7.7	6.3	4.9	1.3	1.6	1.1	3.2
Denmark	6.5	5.8	6.6	9.3	15.2	9.6	9.0	11.1	10.1	9.6	12.3	6.8	5.4	3.3	5.6	3.2	1.7	4.0	4.6	4.8
Finland	2.7	6.1	7.4	11.4	17.8	17.4	14.4	12.5	7.7	7.1	11.7	12.2	9.6	8.3	7.1	5.9	2.9	4.1	5.1	6.6
Ireland	8.2	9.0	8.6	11.4	17.0	20.9	18.0	13.6	7.6	13.2	18.2	20.4	17.1	10.5	8.6	5.4	3.8	3.2	2.1	4.0
Netherlands	3.6	7.5	7.8	8.0	9.6	10.2	8.8	6.7	4.1	4.2	6.5	6.7	5.7	2.8	3.2	2.3	0.3	-0.2	0.7	1.1
Norway	10.7	6.0	7.2	7.6	9.4	11.6	9.2	9.0	8.2	4.8	10.9	13.6	11.3	8.4	6.3	5.7	7.2	8.7	6.7	4.6
Sweden	7.0	7.4	6.0	6.8	9.9	9.8	10.3	11.4	10.0	7.2	13.7	12.1	8.6	9.0	8.0	7.4	4.2	4.2	5.8	6.4
Switzerland	3.6	6.6	6.7	8.7	9.8	6.7	1.7	1.3	1.0	3.6	4.1	6.5	5.6	3.0	3.0	3.4	0.7	1.5	1.8	3.2
Total 9 countries	4.9	6.3	6.7	8.1	11.3	10.7	8.6	7.6	5.5	5.4	8.6	8.8	7.3	5.5	5.4	4.3	2.0	2.3	2.8	3.6
Total western Europe	4.8	6.2	6.2	8.2	12.6	12.8	10.1	9.6	6.9	8.8	12.1	10.9	9.2	6.9	5.7	5.0	2.3	2.6	3.1	4.5
Greece	2.9	3.0	4.3	15.5	26.9	13.4	13.3	12.1	12.6	19.0	24.9	24.5	21.0	20.2	18.5	19.3	23.0	16.4	13.5	13.7
Portugal [b,c]	6.4	11.9	10.7	12.9	25.1	15.3	21.0	27.4	22.0	24.2	16.6	20.0	22.4	25.5	29.3	19.2	11.8	9.4	9.6	12.6
Spain	5.6	8.3	8.3	11.4	15.7	16.9	14.9	24.5	19.8	15.7	15.5	14.5	14.4	12.2	11.3	8.8	8.7	5.3	4.8	6.8
Turkey [d]	8.1	16.3	12.9	16.6	18.7	20.1	15.3	28.4	49.5	56.5	116.6	35.9	27.1	31.4	48.4	44.9	34.6	38.9	75.4	69.6
Yugoslavia	10.6	15.6	16.6	19.7	21.1	24.3	11.7	14.9	14.3	20.6	30.2	40.9	32.3	42.9	50.0	60.0	87.5	126.7	194.1	1252.0
Total southern Europe	6.4	10.3	9.8	13.8	18.6	17.9	14.8	22.9	23.3	23.8	34.8	22.7	19.9	20.9	24.1	22.9	24.6	27.6	41.5	176.5
Total Europe	5.0	6.7	6.7	8.8	13.3	13.5	10.7	11.2	8.9	10.6	14.8	12.3	10.5	8.6	7.9	7.1	5.0	5.6	7.7	25.1
United States [e]	5.9	4.3	3.3	6.2	11.0	9.1	5.8	6.4	7.6	11.3	13.5	10.3	6.2	3.2	4.3	3.6	1.9	3.7	4.1	4.8
Canada	3.3	2.9	4.7	7.7	10.9	10.8	7.5	7.9	8.8	9.2	10.2	12.5	10.8	5.8	4.3	4.0	4.1	4.4	4.1	5.0
North America	5.7	4.2	3.4	6.3	11.0	9.3	5.9	6.6	7.7	11.1	13.3	10.5	6.5	3.4	4.3	3.6	2.0	3.7	4.1	4.8
Total above	5.3	5.5	5.1	7.7	12.2	11.5	8.5	9.1	8.3	10.9	14.1	11.4	8.6	6.2	6.3	5.5	3.6	4.7	6.0	15.7

Source: National statistics. Regional aggregates were obtained from time series in annual percentage change form, with weights taken from OECD *National Accounts*. (Private final consumption expenditure in US dollars for 1980 at current prices and exchange rates.)

[a] Cost-of-living index for the Federal Republic of Germany and Yugoslavia, retail price index for United Kingdom.
[b] 1970-1976, Lisbon.
[c] Break in series after 1975.
[d] 1970-1982, Ankara; 1983 and thereafter, total urban areas.
[e] 1970-1978, urban wage earners and clerical workers; 1979 and thereafter, all urban consumers.

APPENDIX TABLE A.10

Average hourly earnings in manufacturing
(Annual percentage change)

	1970	1971	1972	1973	1974	1975	1976	1977	1978	1979	1980	1981	1982	1983	1984	1985	1986	1987	1988
France [a]	10.8	11.2	11.1	14.5	19.6	17.3	14.0	12.7	12.9	13.0	15.1	14.5	15.2	11.2	7.7	5.8	4.3	3.2	3.2
Germany, Fed.Rep. of	13.8	10.8	8.9	10.7	10.6	8.0	6.4	7.6	5.0	5.5	6.3	5.3	4.9	3.4	2.3	4.5	3.5	4.2	4.3
Italy [a]	22.4	13.4	10.2	24.4	22.4	26.6	20.8	27.9	16.2	19.0	18.5	23.1	17.1	19.6	11.4	10.9	4.8	6.4	6.1
United Kingdom [b]	13.1	10.9	12.9	13.0	16.8	26.3	16.6	10.3	14.4	15.7	17.4	13.4	11.2	8.9	8.8	9.1	7.7	8.0	8.5
Total 4 countries	14.9	11.5	10.6	15.0	16.5	18.3	13.5	13.7	11.3	12.4	13.4	12.9	11.1	9.8	6.9	7.2	4.9	5.4	5.4
Austria [c]	9.4	13.7	11.6	12.7	15.9	13.3	9.1	8.5	5.7	5.8	7.9	6.2	6.1	4.5	5.0	6.1	4.5	3.1	3.8
Belgium [d]	15.0	13.0	11.5	17.2	20.6	19.5	12.2	9.1	6.7	7.8	8.7	10.7	6.0	4.5	5.4	3.1	2.0	2.0	1.0
Denmark [e]	12.4	14.1	12.3	14.1	19.6	22.4	11.5	9.1	10.8	11.1	11.1	9.0	10.1	6.7	5.0	4.9	5.0	9.1	7.1
Finland	11.1	15.6	14.1	16.6	22.4	21.3	14.8	8.8	7.5	11.4	12.8	12.8	10.5	9.6	10.3	7.6	6.1	6.8	8.7
Ireland	11.1	20.0	16.7	14.3	25.0	25.0	16.0	20.7	14.3	15.0	21.7	16.1	15.1	11.5	10.4	8.6	7.5	5.9	5.4
Netherlands [a]	8.3	10.3	14.0	14.3	17.9	12.1	9.5	7.4	5.7	4.3	4.2	3.0	6.8	2.7	0.9	5.3	1.7	1.5	1.3
Norway [f]	10.0	13.6	8.0	11.1	16.7	20.0	14.3	12.5	7.4	3.4	8.3	10.8	9.7	8.9	8.1	7.5	10.0	16.4	5.5
Sweden [e]	15.6	5.3	15.6	8.8	10.2	14.9	19.3	6.8	7.7	8.2	8.7	11.1	7.1	8.4	9.3	7.5	7.4	6.4	8.0
Switzerland [g]	6.2	9.7	9.0	9.2	13.9	7.4	1.6	1.7	3.4	2.1	5.2	5.1	6.2	6.8	1.8	3.6	4.1	2.8	3.6
Total 9 countries	10.9	11.6	12.4	12.8	16.9	15.5	11.2	7.8	6.7	6.8	8.3	8.3	7.6	6.3	5.4	5.6	4.7	4.8	4.5
Total western Europe	14.0	11.5	11.0	14.5	16.5	17.7	13.0	12.4	10.4	11.2	12.3	12.0	10.4	9.1	6.6	6.9	4.9	5.2	5.3
Greece	6.1	8.7	9.3	16.0	26.8	24.4	27.3	21.4	23.5	23.8	26.9	24.2	34.1	20.0	25.8	20.5	13.0	9.7	17.7
Portugal [h]	29.4	13.6	18.0	16.9	50.7	51.0	22.9	19.2	15.2	21.1	26.2	20.0	20.6	18.6	18.8	21.1	16.8	14.0	11.3
Spain [i]	13.2	15.0	15.9	20.0	27.1	31.1	30.0	29.3	27.5	23.9	15.3	24.7	15.9	15.0	11.7	10.0	10.9	7.6	6.5
Turkey	..	..	..	..	..	..	..	..	..	..	..	..	..	..	..	..	..	..	..
Yugoslavia	16.3	22.3	16.1	19.3	27.8	22.4	14.2	17.9	19.1	20.7	24.2	37.0	27.7	27.5	45.3	76.9	105.4	105.0	171.2
Total southern Europe [i]	16.2	16.8	15.7	18.8	31.1	30.4	22.8	22.7	22.1	22.3	21.5	28.4	22.8	20.6	26.5	37.2	46.4	44.2	68.2
Total Europe [j]	14.4	12.4	11.8	15.3	19.2	20.0	14.8	14.3	12.5	13.2	14.0	14.9	12.6	11.2	10.2	12.3	12.3	12.2	16.6
United States	5.1	6.6	7.0	7.3	7.9	9.3	8.1	8.8	8.7	8.5	8.5	10.0	6.2	4.0	4.0	3.8	2.0	1.9	2.7
Canada	9.2	8.0	7.4	9.2	12.7	17.2	12.8	11.4	7.8	8.3	9.8	12.1	11.5	4.0	4.7	4.4	3.1	2.4	5.0
North America	5.4	6.7	7.0	7.4	8.3	10.0	8.5	9.0	8.7	8.5	8.7	10.2	6.7	4.0	4.1	3.9	2.1	1.9	2.9
Total above [j]	10.9	10.2	10.0	12.3	15.0	16.1	12.3	12.2	11.0	11.4	11.9	13.1	10.3	8.4	7.8	9.1	8.4	8.2	11.3

Sources: National statistics; OECD, *Economic Outlook – Historical Statistics, 1960-1986*, Paris; OECD, *Main economic indicators*, No. 2, 1989, Paris. National data in annual percentage change form are aggregated by means of weights derived from manufacturing employment in 1985.

[a] Wage rates.
[b] Weekly earnings of all employees in Great Britain.
[c] Monthly earnings in mining and manufacturing.
[d] Includes transport.
[e] Includes mining.
[f] Males only.
[g] Data refers to workers who had accidents during the relevant period.
[h] Daily earnings; for 1970-1973, wage bill for all activities.
[i] Refers to all activities.
[j] Excluding Turkey.

APPENDIX TABLE A.11
Total employment
(Annual percentage change)

	1970	1971	1972	1973	1974	1975	1976	1977	1978	1979	1980	1981	1982	1983	1984	1985	1986	1987	1988	1989
France	1.5	0.5	0.6	1.4	0.9	-0.9	0.8	0.8	0.4	0.1	0.1	-0.6	0.2	-0.4	-0.9	-0.3	0.1	0.2	0.6	1.2
Germany, Fed.Rep. of	1.3	0.6	-0.2	0.7	-1.3	-2.8	-0.8	-0.2	0.6	1.4	1.1	-0.7	-1.7	-1.5	0.1	0.7	1.0	0.8	0.6	1.3
Italy [a]	0.2	1.0	0.5	1.5	1.9	-3.7	0.7	0.5	0.7	1.0	0.8	-0.0	0.6	0.6	0.4	0.9	0.8	0.6	1.4	1.0
United Kingdom [b]	-0.4	-0.9	-0.1	2.3	0.3	-0.4	-0.8	0.1	0.6	1.5	-0.3	-3.9	-1.8	-1.2	2.6	1.2	0.1	2.1	3.2	1.8
Total 4 countries	0.6	0.3	0.2	1.5	0.3	-1.9	-0.1	0.3	0.6	1.0	0.4	-1.4	-0.8	-0.7	0.6	0.6	0.5	1.0	1.5	1.3
Austria	0.4	1.1	0.7	1.7	0.9	-0.5	0.6	0.9	0.2	0.7	0.4	0.1	-1.2	-0.8	0.1	0.2	0.4	-0.0	0.6	1.4
Belgium [b]	1.8	0.9	-0.1	1.3	1.4	-1.3	-0.7	-0.1	-0.0	1.3	-0.1	-2.0	-1.4	-1.0	0.1	0.7	1.0	0.4	1.5	1.0
Denmark	0.7	0.8	0.8	1.0	-1.4	-1.0	2.5	1.0	2.4	0.8	-1.6	2.5	-1.2	0.9	-0.1	2.3	3.0	0.8	-0.3	-0.7
Finland	2.1	-0.6	1.0	2.0	0.4	-0.4	-1.9	-1.9	-1.1	2.2	2.9	1.0	0.7	0.4	0.3	-0.2	-0.5	0.2	-0.0	1.3
Ireland [c]	-1.2	-0.4	0.3	1.4	1.4	-0.8	-0.8	1.8	2.5	3.2	1.0	-0.9	-	-1.9	-1.9	-2.2	0.2	-0.1	1.0	-0.1
Netherlands [d]	1.1	0.5	-0.9	0.1	0.2	-0.7	-0.0	0.2	0.7	1.3	0.7	-1.5	-2.5	-0.1	-0.1	1.5	2.0	1.4	1.3	1.6
Norway [d,e]	1.5	0.9	1.1	0.7	1.3	1.9	3.3	2.6	1.8	1.5	2.3	1.0	0.2	-0.4	0.6	2.7	3.1	2.0	-0.8	-3.1
Sweden	2.0	-0.2	0.3	0.4	2.0	2.0	0.4	0.2	0.4	1.5	1.1	0.2	-0.2	0.2	0.8	1.0	0.6	0.8	1.4	1.5
Switzerland	1.5	1.8	1.4	1.0	-0.1	-4.8	-3.0	0.4	1.0	1.1	2.3	1.3	-0.7	-1.3	-0.2	0.9	1.5	1.2	1.2	1.2
Total 9 countries	1.3	0.6	0.4	0.9	0.7	-0.7	-0.1	0.4	0.7	1.3	0.9	-	-0.9	-0.7	0.1	1.0	1.3	0.8	0.8	0.8
Total western Europe	0.7	0.3	0.2	1.4	0.4	-1.7	-0.1	0.3	0.6	1.1	0.5	-1.1	-0.8	-0.7	0.5	0.7	0.7	0.9	1.3	1.2
Greece	-0.1	0.3	0.5	1.0	0.1	0.1	2.3	-5.0	6.6	0.6	1.3	4.9	-0.8	1.0	0.3	1.0	0.3	-0.1	1.1	0.7
Portugal	-0.7	-0.3	-0.6	-0.8	-0.8	-1.4	0.2	-0.1	-0.3	2.2	2.5	-0.3	-0.0	4.8	-2.6	-0.5	0.2	2.6	2.6	2.2
Spain	1.0	1.2	2.3	-0.5	0.7	-1.6	-1.9	-0.7	-1.7	-1.6	-3.0	-2.9	-1.0	-0.7	-2.9	-0.9	2.4	4.9	3.5	4.0
Turkey	-0.3	2.1	2.3	1.7	1.6	1.7	2.3	1.9	1.0	0.1	-0.1	0.9	2.0	1.8	2.5	2.3	3.1	3.0	1.4	1.1
Yugoslavia [f]	3.9	4.8	4.3	2.4	5.0	5.5	3.6	4.5	4.5	4.3	3.2	2.9	2.3	2.0	2.1	2.5	2.9	2.1	0.2	0.1
Total southern Europe	0.6	1.6	2.0	0.7	1.3	0.5	0.9	0.5	1.0	0.4	-0.1	0.3	0.7	1.3	0.2	1.0	2.3	3.0	1.9	1.8
Total Europe	0.7	0.6	0.6	1.2	0.6	-1.2	0.1	0.4	0.7	0.9	0.4	-0.7	-0.4	-0.2	0.4	0.8	1.1	1.5	1.5	1.4
United States [a]	-0.8	-0.4	2.5	4.3	1.6	-2.1	2.8	3.5	5.0	3.2	0.2	0.9	-1.6	1.0	4.9	2.4	1.7	2.9	2.9	2.0
Canada	1.0	2.3	2.9	4.9	4.1	1.7	2.0	1.8	3.5	4.0	3.0	2.7	-3.4	0.5	2.4	2.6	2.7	2.9	3.2	2.0
North America	-0.6	-0.2	2.5	4.4	1.8	-1.7	2.7	3.3	4.9	3.3	0.5	1.1	-1.8	1.0	4.6	2.4	1.8	2.9	2.9	2.0
Total above	0.2	0.3	1.3	2.3	1.1	-1.4	1.1	1.5	2.3	1.9	0.4	-0.0	-1.0	0.3	2.1	1.5	1.4	2.0	2.1	1.6

Sources: National statistics: OECD, *National accounts*, detailed tables, vol. II., 1975-1987, Paris; OECD, *Labour force statistics 1967-1987*, Paris;; *Quarterly labour force statistics*, No. 4. 1989. Paris; ECE secretariat estimates. National data are aggregated by adding the annual data on persons engaged taken from the national accounts statistics, where available. Otherwise the data refer to annual labour force surveys.

[a] Refers to full-time equivalent data.
[b] June of each year.
[c] April of each year.
[d] Man-years.
[e] Break in series after 1986.
[f] Socialist sector.

APPENDIX TABLE A.12
Annual unemployment rates
(Percentage of total labour force)

	1970	1971	1972	1973	1974	1975	1976	1977	1978	1979	1980	1981	1982	1983	1984	1985	1986	1987	1988	1989
France	2.5	2.7	2.8	2.7	2.8	4.0	4.4	4.9	5.2	5.9	6.3	7.4	8.1	8.3	9.7	10.2	10.4	10.5	10.0	9.5
Germany, Fed.Rep. of	0.8	0.9	0.8	0.8	1.6	3.6	3.7	3.6	3.5	3.2	3.0	4.4	6.1	8.0	7.1	7.2	6.4	6.2	6.1	5.6
Italy	5.3	5.3	6.3	6.2	5.3	5.8	6.6	7.0	7.1	7.6	7.5	7.8	8.4	8.8	9.3	9.6	10.5	11.2	11.3	11.4
United Kingdom	3.0	3.6	4.0	3.0	2.9	4.3	5.6	6.0	5.9	5.0	6.4	9.8	11.3	12.4	11.7	11.2	11.2	10.2	8.3	6.4
Total 4 countries	2.8	3.0	3.4	3.1	3.1	4.4	5.0	5.3	5.4	5.3	5.7	7.3	8.5	9.4	9.4	9.5	9.5	9.4	8.8	8.0
Austria	1.1	1.0	1.0	0.9	1.1	1.5	1.5	1.4	1.7	1.7	1.5	2.1	3.1	3.7	3.8	3.6	3.1	3.8	3.6	3.3
Belgium	2.1	2.1	2.7	2.7	3.0	5.0	6.4	7.4	7.9	8.2	8.8	10.8	12.6	12.1	12.1	11.3	11.2	11.0	9.9	9.0
Denmark	1.3	1.6	1.6	1.0	2.3	5.3	5.3	6.4	7.3	6.2	7.0	9.2	9.8	10.4	10.1	9.0	7.8	7.8	8.6	9.4
Finland	1.9	2.2	2.5	2.3	1.7	2.2	3.8	5.8	7.2	5.9	4.6	4.8	5.3	5.4	5.2	5.0	5.3	5.0	4.5	3.5
Ireland	5.8	5.5	6.2	5.7	5.3	7.3	9.0	8.8	8.2	7.1	7.3	9.9	11.4	14.0	15.5	17.4	17.4	17.5	16.7	16.2
Netherlands	1.0	1.3	2.2	2.2	2.7	5.2	5.5	5.3	5.3	5.4	6.0	8.5	11.4	12.0	11.8	10.6	9.9	9.6	9.5	9.3
Norway	1.6	1.5	1.6	1.5	1.5	2.3	1.7	1.4	1.8	2.0	1.6	2.0	2.6	3.4	3.1	2.6	2.0	2.1	3.2	4.9
Sweden	1.2	2.1	2.2	2.0	1.6	1.3	1.3	1.4	1.8	1.7	1.6	2.1	2.6	2.9	2.6	2.4	2.2	1.9	1.6	1.4
Switzerland	-	-	-	-	-	0.3	0.7	0.4	0.3	0.3	0.2	0.2	0.4	0.8	1.0	0.8	0.8	0.8	0.7	0.6
Total 9 countries	1.4	1.7	2.0	1.9	2.0	3.3	3.7	4.1	4.4	4.2	4.3	5.6	6.8	7.2	7.2	6.7	6.3	6.3	6.1	5.9
Total western Europe	2.5	2.7	3.1	2.8	2.8	4.1	4.7	5.0	5.1	5.1	5.4	6.9	8.1	8.9	8.9	8.9	8.8	8.7	8.2	7.6
Greece	4.2	3.1	2.1	2.0	2.1	2.3	1.9	1.7	1.8	1.9	2.8	4.0	5.8	7.8	8.1	7.8	7.4	7.5	7.7	7.8
Portugal	2.2	2.1	2.1	2.2	1.8	3.5	5.8	7.1	7.9	8.2	8.0	7.7	7.5	10.2	10.5	10.4	10.2	8.5	7.0	6.6
Spain	0.9	1.2	2.1	2.2	2.3	3.8	4.6	5.2	7.0	8.6	11.5	14.3	16.4	18.2	20.1	21.5	21.0	20.5	19.5	17.0
Turkey	7.8	7.8	7.6	7.9	8.4	8.7	7.9	7.5	7.8	9.7	11.6	11.6	12.3	12.1	11.8	11.3	10.5	9.5	9.8	10.7
Yugoslavia	7.7	6.7	7.0	8.1	9.0	10.2	11.4	11.9	12.0	11.9	11.9	11.9	12.4	12.8	13.3	13.8	14.1	13.6	14.1	14.7
Total southern Europe	5.1	4.9	5.1	5.4	5.8	6.7	7.0	7.3	8.0	9.1	10.7	11.5	12.6	13.5	14.0	14.3	13.9	13.1	12.9	12.7
Total Europe	3.2	3.3	3.6	3.5	3.6	4.8	5.4	5.6	5.9	6.2	6.8	8.2	9.3	10.2	10.3	10.4	10.2	9.9	9.5	9.0
United States	4.8	5.8	5.5	4.8	5.5	8.3	7.6	6.9	6.0	5.8	7.0	7.5	9.5	9.5	7.4	7.1	6.9	6.1	5.4	5.2
Canada	5.6	6.1	6.2	5.5	5.3	6.9	7.1	8.0	8.3	7.4	7.4	7.5	10.9	11.8	11.2	10.4	9.5	8.8	7.7	7.5
North America	4.9	5.8	5.6	4.9	5.5	8.2	7.6	7.0	6.2	6.0	7.0	7.5	9.6	9.7	7.8	7.4	7.2	6.4	5.6	5.4
Total above	3.9	4.3	4.4	4.1	4.4	6.2	6.3	6.2	6.0	6.1	6.9	7.9	9.4	10.0	9.3	9.2	9.0	8.5	7.9	7.5

Sources: OECD, *Labour force statistics 1966-1986* Paris, OECD, *Quarterly labour force statistics*, No. 4, 1989. Paris; *Main economic indicators*, No. 2, 1989. Paris; Yugoslavia: ILO *Yearbook of Labour Statistics 1988*, Geneva; ECE secretariat estimates. National data are aggregated from annual figures on the number of unemployed and total labour force, and the rates have been calculated as percentages of the total labour force.

Note: Comparisons with previous years are limited due to changes in methodology in the Federal Reublic of Germany, (1984), United Kingdom (1984), Italy (1983), Belgium (1983), Netherlands (1983), Portugal (1983), Finland (1982) and Norway (1980).

Appendix B. Eastern Europe and Soviet Union

Data for this section were compiled from national and international [913] statistical sources, as indicated in the notes to individual tables. Volume figures underlying the data in tables B.1-B.2, B.8-B.9, B.11 and B.14 reflect data at constant prices of the following years: Bulgaria, 1982; Czechoslovakia, 1977; German Democratic Republic, 1985; Hungary, 1981; Poland, 1982; Romania, 1977; Soviet Union, 1973.

---

[913] CMEA, UN, IMF.

APPENDIX TABLE B.1
Net material product
(Annual percentage change)

	1970	1971	1972	1973	1974	1975	1976	1977	1978	1979	1980	1981	1982	1983	1984	1985	1986	1987	1988	1989
Bulgaria	7.1	6.9	7.7	8.1	7.6	8.8	6.5	6.3	5.6	6.6	5.7	5.0	4.2	3.0	4.6	1.8	5.3	5.1	2.4	-0.4
Czechoslovakia	5.7	5.5	5.7	5.2	5.9	6.2	4.1	4.2	4.1	3.1	2.9	-0.1	0.2	2.3	3.5	3.0	2.6	2.1	2.4	1.3
German Dem. Rep.	5.6	4.4	5.7	5.6	6.5	4.9	3.5	5.1	3.7	4.0	4.4	4.8	2.6	4.6	5.5	5.2	4.3	3.3	2.8	2.0
Hungary	4.9	5.9	6.2	7.0	5.9	6.1	3.0	7.1	4.0	1.2	-0.9	2.5	2.6	0.3	2.5	-1.4	0.9	4.1	0.3	-2.0*
Poland	5.2	8.1	10.6	10.8	10.5	9.0	6.8	5.0	3.0	-2.3	-6.0	-12.0	-5.5	6.0	5.6	3.4	4.9	1.9	4.9	-
Romania	6.8	13.5	10.0	10.7	12.4	9.8	11.2	8.6	7.6	6.2	2.8	2.2	2.7	3.7	7.7	5.9	7.3	4.8	3.2	..
Eastern Europe	5.7	7.3	8.1	8.3	8.6	7.6	6.1	5.7	4.3	2.0	0.1	-1.9	0.1	3.9	5.3	3.7	4.6	3.2	3.1	0.5 [a]
Soviet Union	9.0	5.6	3.9	8.9	5.5	4.4	5.9	4.5	5.1	2.2	3.9	3.3	3.9	4.2	2.9	1.6	2.3	1.6	4.4	2.4
Eastern Europe and the Soviet Union	8.0	6.1	5.1	8.7	6.5	5.4	5.9	4.9	4.9	2.1	2.7	1.7	2.8	4.1	3.6	2.2	3.0	2.1	4.0	1.8

Sources: ECE secretariat Common Data Base, derived from national or CMEA statistics. National data are aggregated by means of 1981 weights based on CMEA investigations.

[a] Excluding Romania.

APPENDIX TABLE B.2

Net material product used for domestic consumption and accumulation
(Annual percentage change)

	1970	1971	1972	1973	1974	1975	1976	1977	1978	1979	1980	1981	1982	1983	1984	1985	1986	1987	1988	1989
Bulgaria [a]																				
Total	3.7	1.6	9.8	9.0	11.8	11.1	0.3	5.2	0.2	3.5	5.1	7.7	1.9	1.2	5.2	2.3	8.4	0.4	3.7	..
Consumption	5.6	7.4	6.3	6.6	7.1	7.7	6.0	4.0	3.6	3.0	3.6	5.3	3.7	2.9	4.9	3.3	3.6	4.6	3.6	..
Accumulation	-0.6	-11.5	21.0	16.0	24.2	18.7	-11.5	8.9	-9.3	5.0	9.5	14.8	-3.3	-3.6	6.2	-0.8	23.8	-10.7	4.1	..
Czechoslovakia																				
Total	5.0	4.9	5.7	7.3	8.1	4.5	3.1	1.6	2.7	1.1	2.7	-3.4	-1.6	0.6	1.2	3.2	4.9	2.8	1.9	2.1
Consumption	1.9	6.6	5.2	5.8	6.1	3.0	3.3	3.7	3.7	0.9	1.0	2.6	-1.1	2.8	3.0	2.8	3.4	3.6	4.3	..
Accumulation	16.7	-0.6	7.7	12.2	14.3	9.2	2.5	-4.5	-0.5	1.8	8.2	-21.7	-3.6	-8.0	-6.6	5.4	12.2	-1.1	-9.8	..
German Dem. Rep.																				
Total [b]	8.4	3.4	5.8	6.3	6.5	2.6	6.3	5.1	0.8	1.1	5.1	1.1	-3.4	-	3.4	4.8	4.3	4.1	3.6	..
Consumption [c]	4.4	5.0	6.1	5.1	6.7	5.4	5.1	4.6	3.2	3.3	3.0	2.3	1.4	0.1	3.8	4.5	4.4	3.6	3.8	..
Accumulation [c]	17.3	-2.0	2.5	10.3	5.3	-1.9	9.5	6.2	-5.3	-5.0	11.4	-2.4	-17.6	-0.5	2.0	5.8	3.8	6.1	2.6	..
Hungary																				
Total	11.8	11.3	-3.7	2.0	12.7	6.4	1.3	6.0	9.2	-5.8	-1.7	0.7	-1.1	-2.8	-0.6	-0.6	3.9	3.0	-3.4	-3
Consumption	8.4	5.4	3.1	3.7	6.9	4.7	2.2	5.0	4.3	3.3	0.2	3.0	1.4	0.6	0.9	1.2	2.0	3.1	-3.5	..
Accumulation	23.6	30.4	-21.4	-3.8	34.2	11.5	-1.4	9.1	24.0	-28.9	-8.7	-8.6	-12.4	-20.4	-11.3	-15.0	21.4	2.7	-2.5	..
Poland																				
Total	5.0	9.8	12.5	14.3	12.0	9.5	6.5	2.2	0.5	-3.7	-6.0	-10.5	-10.5	5.6	5.0	3.8	5.0	1.8	4.7	-
Consumption	4.1	7.7	9.1	8.1	7.4	11.1	8.8	6.8	1.7	3.1	2.1	-4.6	-11.5	5.8	4.4	2.9	4.8	2.8	2.9	..
Accumulation	7.4	15.2	20.9	27.8	20.5	7.0	2.4	-6.5	-2.0	-19.2	-29.6	-27.6	-6.6	4.9	7.3	7.2	5.4	-2.4	12.8	..
Romania																				
Total	..	..	..	..	..	..	12.3	6.8	9.6	5.5	0.8	-6.5	-1.5	2.2	2.8	4.8	..	..	..	..
Consumption	..	..	..	..	..	..	8.8	7.8	9.4	6.3	3.4	3.0	-1.3	0.7	5.9	7.4	..	..	..	..
Accumulation	..	..	..	..	..	..	18.9	5.1	10.1	3.9	-3.7	-24.5	-2.0	6.0	-4.7	-0.2	..	..	..	..
Eastern Europe																				
Total	6.5 [d]	6.7 [d]	7.3 [d]	9.2 [d]	10.0 [d]	6.8 [d]	6.0	3.9	3.2	-0.2	-0.3	-4.2	-4.2	1.8	3.2	3.6	5.0 [d]	2.5 [d]	3.0 [d]	..
Consumption	4.3	6.5	6.7	6.3	6.9	-2.3	6.4	5.7	3.8	3.3	2.2	0.4	-3.4	2.6	4.0	3.9	4.0	3.3	2.8	..
Accumulation	13.5	6.8	5.8	15.0	17.1	6.8	5.7	1.1	2.8	-7.8	-4.7	-15.8	-7.8	-1.3	-1.2	2.1	10.3	-0.4	2.1	..
Soviet Union																				
Total	11.2 [e]	5.1 [e]	3.5 [e]	7.7 [e]	4.1 [d]	4.2 [d]	5.0	3.5	4.5	2.0	3.9	3.2	3.5	3.6	2.0	1.8	1.6	0.7	4.6	..
Consumption	7.5	5.8	5.8	5.1	4.8	5.5	4.3	4.0	4.6	4.5	6.0	4.0	1.2	3.2	..	..	..	..	..	..
Accumulation	21.3	3.4	-2.1	14.4	0.5	-1.4	6.6	3.3	5.2	-2.9	-0.6	0.9	11.0	5.0	..	..	..	..	..	..
Eastern Europe and Soviet Union																				
Total	9.9 [d]	5.6 [d]	4.6 [d]	8.1 [d]	5.8 [d]	5.0 [d]	5.3	3.6	4.0	1.3	2.5	0.8	1.2	3.1	2.3	2.3	3.5 [d]	1.2 [d]	4.2 [d]	..
Consumption	6.6	6.0	6.1	5.5	5.4	-2.2	5.0	4.5	4.3	4.1	4.7	2.8	-0.3	3.0	..	..	..	..	..	..
Accumulation	19.5	4.2	-0.3	14.6	4.6	0.8	6.3	2.6	4.4	-4.5	-1.9	-4.3	5.9	3.5	..	..	..	..	..	..

Sources: ECE secretariat Common Data Base, derived from national or CMEA statistics. National data are aggregated by means of 1981 weights based on CMEA investigations.

[a] Calculated from absolute volume figures at 1962 prices.
[b] Calculated from rounded index numbers (1950 = 100).
[c] Calculated from rounded index numbers (1970 = 100).
[d] Excluding Romania.
[e] Nominal.

APPENDIX TABLE B.3

Monthly nominal wages [a]
(In national currencies)

	1970	1971	1972	1973	1974	1975	1976	1977	1978	1979	1980	1981	1982	1983	1984	1985	1986	1987	1988	1989
Bulgaria [b]	124	127	131	139	142	146	148	151	157	165	182	192	197	199	207	214	225	234	246	266
Czechoslovakia	1937	2009	2091	2161	2232	2304	2369	2444	2517	2579	2637	2677	2738	2789	2837	2883	2927	2985	3054	3218
German Dem. Rep. [c]	750	779	808	835	860	889	920	947	977	1006	1021	1046	1066	1080	1102	1130	1170	1233	1269	1315
Hungary [d]	2139	2239	2342	2512	2682	2881	3042	3288	3567	3785	4014	4267	4542	4761	5342	5866	6291	6808	8817	10440
Poland [e]	2235	2358	2509	2798	3185	3913	4281	4596	4887	5327	6040	7689[f]	11631[f]	14475[f]	16838[f]	20005[f]	24095[f]	29184[f]	53090	205000
Romania [g]	1289	1308	1332	1389	1478	1595	1712	1818	2011	2108	2238	2340	2525	2601	2773	2827	2855	2872	2946	..
Soviet Union [b]	122	126	130	135	141	146	151	155	160	163	169	173	177	181	185	190	196	203	220	240

Source: National statistics.

a Gross remuneration of full-time workers and employees in the socialist sector (without co-operative farmers).
b Before deductions for taxation.
c In six sectors of the material sphere.
d State sector only; without bonuses and compensation for price rises. 1988: not comparable with previous years.
e Excluding bonuses.
f Including compensations for price rises.
g Total economy; net remuneration, including bonuses.

APPENDIX TABLE B.4

Money incomes of population and volume of retail trade [a]
(Annual percentage change)

	1970	1971	1972	1973	1974	1975	1976	1977	1978	1979	1980	1981	1982	1983	1984	1985	1986	1987	1988	1989
Bulgaria																				
Money incomes (nominal)	..	6.6	6.5	8.8	9.1	7.9	7.2	3.1	3.1	2.4	2.9	4.6	4.6	2.4	2.8	3.2	3.5	3.9	2.0	0.3
Retail trade turnover (real) [b]	7.8																			
Czechoslovakia																				
Money incomes (nominal)	4.6	5.5	6.0	6.4	4.6	3.7	4.9	4.5	3.5	3.6	4.0	2.6	4.3	3.1	2.6	3.2	3.2	3.3	4.1	3.3
Retail trade turnover (real)	1.3	5.5	5.2	5.9	6.8	2.6	2.7	2.2	3.7	-0.3	-0.7	1.4	-1.7	2.2	2.1	2.3	1.7	2.9	4.7	2.3
German Dem. Rep.																				
Money incomes (nominal)	3.1	3.4	6.2	6.3	5.1	3.8	3.7	5.5	3.6	3.0	2.5	3.1	2.8	2.3	3.9	4.0	5.6	4.7	3.9	3.0
Retail trade turnover (real) [c]	4.6	3.5	6.6	6.6	6.5	3.5	4.6	4.6	3.4	3.2	4.0	2.3	1.0	0.7	4.2	4.0	4.1	3.6	3.9	1.5
Hungary																				
Money incomes (nominal)	10.2	7.8	7.2	9.6	10.1	9.7	6.1	9.8	7.9	8.6	9.2	8.1	7.3	8.5	9.2	9.2	8.1	8.4	14.0	20.0
Retail trade turnover (real)	12.3	7.4	3.2	5.8	9.7	5.2	1.4	6.2	3.9	1.8	0.1	3.5	1.2	0.3	0.2	2.0	3.7	5.3	-6.5	-2.3
Poland																				
Money incomes (nominal)	..	10.4	13.6	14.2	14.8	13.5	12.1	12.3	8.9	9.9	12.1	31.1	64.9	23.0	18.3	23.3	19.2	26.0	83.2	267.0
Retail trade turnover (real)	3.7	9.3	13.1	8.9	8.8	11.8	8.6	8.4	0.2	1.6	-0.4	-4.4	-15.0	7.3	5.0	3.1	5.7	5.0	5.2	-7.1
Romania																				
Money incomes (nominal) [d]	..	8.9	6.1	7.1	9.4	..	9.8	8.5	12.1	5.9	8.4	6.4	9.5	5.1	5.5	4.0	3.6	0.5	..	..
Retail trade turnover (real)	8.9					8.4	5.5	6.3	10.1	5.0	5.4	2.7	-3.9	-2.0	4.0	2.2	2.3	2.8	..	..
Soviet Union																				
Money incomes (nominal) [e]	6.9	6.0	6.2	6.1	6.6	6.3	5.9	4.4	5.1	3.9	5.5	3.9	4.2	4.0	3.1	3.8	4.3	3.8	9.2	12.9
Retail trade turnover (real) [b]	7.5	6.7	6.5	5.2	5.9	7.0	4.6	4.8	3.9	3.8	5.8	4.3	-0.1	2.8	4.7	1.9	0.4	0.9	4.9	7.6

Sources: National statistics and ECE secretariat estimates.

[a] Calculated from sales turnover figures (including public catering) by means of deflation with official retail price indices.
[b] State and co-operative sector only.
[c] Without sales in canteens of enterprises and institutions.
[d] Socialist sector only.
[e] Secretariat estimates for 1970-1987.

APPENDIX TABLE B.5
Real wages and per capita real incomes
(Annual percentage change)

	1970	1971	1972	1973	1974	1975	1976	1977	1978	1979	1980	1981	1982	1983	1984	1985	1986	1987	1988	1989
Bulgaria																				
Real wages	6.1	2.2	3.5	6.1	1.5	2.8	0.9	1.8	2.3	0.4	-3.2	4.8	2.5	-0.1	3.2	1.4	1.6	4.3	3.7	-1.2
Real incomes	4.9	4.3	7.0	8.7	3.3	5.3	4.5	0.7	1.2	2.8	3.5	5.8	4.2	2.6	3.0	2.9	2.8	4.0	3.4	-2.4
Czechoslovakia																				
Real wages	1.3	4.1	4.5	3.2	2.9	2.6	1.9	1.8	1.4	-0.5	-1.1	0.6	-2.3	0.7	0.8	0.3	1.1	1.9	2.1	3.8
Real incomes	..	6.2	6.5	5.2	3.1	2.8	3.9	2.4	0.7	-0.2	0.1	1.7	-	1.5	2.5	2.3	2.6	3.6 [a]	3.7 [a]	1.6
German Dem. Rep.																				
Real wages	4.7	3.6	4.2	3.9	3.4	3.4	3.5	3.0	3.3	2.7	1.1	2.2	1.9	1.3	2.0	2.6	3.5	5.4	2.9	1.6
Real incomes	3.3	4.2	6.7	6.3	6.3	4.8	5.0	6.1	4.2	3.4	2.8	4.4	4.1	2.4	5.1	5.2	5.7	4.6	4.1	..
Hungary																				
Real wages	4.9	2.6	1.7	3.8	4.8	3.5	0.6	4.0	3.7	-2.5	-2.8	1.7	-0.4	-2.3	3.6	2.6	1.9	-0.4	11.9 [b]	1.2
Real incomes	7.0	4.2	3.4	4.6	6.2	4.3	0.9	4.8	2.9	-0.1	0.4	2.9	0.9	1.1	1.0	1.9	2.4	0.7	-0.9	2.0
Poland																				
Real wages	1.6	5.7	6.4	8.7	6.6	19.3	4.5	2.4	-2.2	2.2	3.9	2.4	-24.9	1.2	0.5	3.8	2.7	-3.5	14.4	9.1
Real incomes	4.0	8.7	11.8	9.7	5.0	9.0	5.6	6.2	-0.5	2.5	0.8	3.3	-18.0	0.3	1.8	6.0	1.7	0.8	13.2	..
Romania																				
Real wages	7.9	0.9	1.8	3.6	5.3	7.7	6.6	5.7	8.8	2.8	3.9	2.5	-7.8	-2.3	5.7	2.3	1.1	0.6	..	..
Real incomes	..	11.8	5.8	4.8	6.1	5.8	8.5	3.5	8.0	2.9	2.8	1.5	..	..	..	..	..	..	..	..
Soviet Union																				
Real wages	4.4	3.2	3.4	3.6	4.6	3.3	3.8	2.5	2.3	0.7	2.7	0.7	-0.6	1.1	3.8	2.2	0.9	1.8	5.9	6.7
Real incomes [c]	5.6	4.5	3.8	5.1	4.0	4.4	3.7	3.5	3.0	2.9	3.7	3.3	0.2	2.0	2.8	2.4	2.6	2.0	3.2	..

Sources: Appendix tables B.3 and B.6 (real wages); national statistics (per capita real incomes).

[a] Real money incomes.
[b] Not comparable with previous years, due to changes in personal incomes taxation.
[c] Material consumption of the population.

APPENDIX TABLE B.6

Consumer prices
(Annual percentage change)

	1970	1971	1972	1973	1974	1975	1976	1977	1978	1979	1980	1981	1982	1983	1984	1985	1986	1987	1988	1989
Bulgaria [a]	-0.4	-0.1	-	0.2	0.5	0.3	0.3	0.4	1.5	4.5	14.0	0.4	0.3	1.4	0.7	1.7	3.5	-	1.3	9.2
Czechoslovakia [b]	1.7	-0.4	-0.4	0.2	0.4	0.6	0.9	1.4	1.5	3.0	3.4	0.9	4.7	1.1	0.9	1.3	0.4	0.1	0.2	1.5
German Dem. Rep. [c]	-0.1	0.4	-0.5	-0.6	-0.4	-	-	-0.1	-0.1	0.3	0.4	0.2	-	-	-	-0.1	-	-	-	2.0
Hungary	1.3	2.0	2.8	3.3	1.8	3.8	5.0	3.9	4.6	8.9	9.1	4.6	6.9	7.3	8.3	7.0	5.3	8.6	15.7	17.0
Poland [d]	1.2	-0.2	-	2.6	6.8	3.0	4.7	4.9	8.7	6.7	9.1	24.4	101.5	23.0	15.8	14.4	17.3	25.5	59.0	254.0
Romania [a]	0.1	0.6	-	0.7	1.1	0.2	0.7	0.5	1.6	2.0	2.1	2.0	17.0[e]	5.5[e]	0.9[e]	-0.4[e]	-0.1[e]	..	..	..
Soviet Union [a,f]	-	-	-	-	-	-	-	-	0.7	1.4	0.7	1.4	3.4	0.7	-1.3	0.7	2.0	1.9	2.3	2.3

Sources: National statistics.

[a] Retail prices in the state sector.
[b] Cost of living index for workers and employees.
[c] Including fees and charges of various kinds (1985 weights).
[d] Cost of living index for workers and employees in the socialist sector.
[e] IMF, *International Financial Statistics*.
[f] Including public catering; based on rounded index numbers; 1970-1987: approved "list price" changes only.

APPENDIX TABLE B.7

Dwellings constructed
(Thousands)

	1970	1971	1972	1973	1974	1975	1976	1977	1978	1979	1980	1981	1982	1983	1984	1985	1986	1987	1988	1989
Bulgaria	45.7	48.9	46.5	54.2	44.1	57.2	67.6	75.9	67.8	66.2	74.3	71.4	68.2	69.7	68.9	64.9	56.0	63.6	62.9	38.8
Czechoslovakia	112.1	107.4	115.6	118.6	129.0	144.7	132.5	134.8	129.3	122.7	128.9	95.4	101.8	95.7	91.9	104.5	78.7	79.6	82.9	88.2
German Dem. Rep. [a]	65.8	65.0	69.6	80.7	88.3	96.0	103.1	106.8	111.9	117.4	120.2	125.7	122.4	122.6	121.7	99.0	101.0	91.0	93.5	83.4
Hungary	80.3	75.3	90.2	85.2	87.8	99.6	93.9	93.4	88.2	88.2	89.1	77.0	75.6	74.2	70.4	72.5	69.4	57.2	50.6	51.5
Poland	194.2	190.6	205.5	227.1	249.8	248.1	263.5	266.1	283.6	278.0	217.1	187.0	186.1	195.8	195.9	189.6	185.0	191.4	189.6	149.8
Romania	159.2	147.0	136.0	149.1	154.3	165.4	139.4	145.0	166.8	191.6	197.8	161.4	161.2	146.6	131.9	105.6	108.1	110.4	104.2	..
Eastern Europe	657.2	634.2	663.3	715.0	753.4	810.9	800.0	822.1	847.5	864.1	827.4	717.9	715.3	704.7	680.7	636.1	598.2	593.3	583.7	..
Soviet Union	2266.0	2256.0	2233.0	2276.0	2231.0	2228.0	2113.0	2111.0	2080.0	1932.0	2004.0	1997.0	2002.0	2030.0	2008.0	1991.0	2100.0	2265.0	2230.0	2200.0
Eastern Europe and the Soviet Union	2923.2	2890.2	2896.3	2991.0	2984.4	3038.9	2913.0	2933.1	2927.5	2796.1	2831.4	2714.9	2717.3	2734.7	2688.7	2627.1	2698.2	2858.3	2813.7	..

Sources: National statistics.

[a] Revised data from 1985 onwards.

APPENDIX TABLE B.8
Total gross investment
(Annual percentage change)

	1970	1971	1972	1973	1974	1975	1976	1977	1978	1979	1980	1981	1982	1983	1984	1985	1986	1987	1988	1989
Bulgaria [a]																				
Total	10.6	1.7	10.0	6.9	7.8	17.3	0.6	14.2	0.6	-2.2	7.5	10.5	3.6	0.7	0.3	8.6	8.0	7.2	2.4	-7.7
Material sphere	7.0	0.4	8.7	6.7	7.8	19.8	-1.3	16.0	0.4	-1.6	5.4	12.2	2.8	-0.9	2.0	10.6	5.6	11.3	..	..
Non-material sphere	24.0	6.7	13.2	7.2	7.8	10.2	6.6	8.9	1.3	-4.0	14.3	5.3	6.1	5.3	-3.7	3.8	13.6	-2.5	..	..
Czechoslovakia																				
Total	5.8	5.7	8.9	9.0	9.1	8.3	4.4	5.7	4.1	1.8	1.4	-4.6	-2.3	0.6	-4.2	5.4	1.4	4.4	4.1	2.1
Material sphere	-	4.9	6.2	14.4	9.0	7.7	5.8	6.7	4.8	3.8	2.5	-2.1	-2.1	0.6	-3.9	6.0	2.2	5.7	4.2	..
Non-material sphere	20.0	7.0	13.2	0.9	9.2	9.2	2.1	3.9	2.9	-2.0	-0.5	-9.5	-2.6	0.4	-5.0	4.1	-0.2	1.5	3.8	..
German Democratic Republic																				
Total	6.8	1.7	5.0	8.4	5.4	4.6	7.3	5.3	2.8	1.2	0.1	2.4	-5.1	-0.3	-4.9	3.4	5.3	8.0	8.2	-4.0*
Material sphere	9.0	0.5	3.6	8.1	4.7	4.4	7.8	4.4	1.7	1.3	0.7	1.9	-5.1	0.1	-5.8	3.3	6.9	9.3	9.4	..
Non-material sphere	-1.0	6.8	11.1	9.6	8.1	5.4	5.5	8.8	6.8	0.9	-1.8	4.3	-5.1	-1.8	-1.7	3.5	0.1	3.3	3.7	..
Hungary																				
Total	16.9	10.6	-1.1	3.2	10.9	11.5	-	12.2	4.8	0.8	-5.5	-4.7	-1.6	-3.4	-3.7	-3.0	6.5	9.8	-7.2	-2.0
Material sphere	15.0	8.6	-3.6	1.6	9.1	15.1	1.1	14.3	6.4	-	-7.8	-5.0	-2.6	-4.9	-5.4	-2.4	0.6	10.2	-7.6	..
Non-material sphere	29.0	16.4	6.8	10.0	8.6	8.0	-2.1	9.1	0.9	3.9	-0.3	-5.4	-1.1	2.7	1.5	-2.2	5.8	2.2	-7.0	..
Poland																				
Total	4.0	7.4	23.0	25.4	22.3	10.7	1.0	3.1	2.1	-7.9	-12.3	-22.3	-12.1	9.4	11.4	6.0	5.1	4.2	5.4	-2.0
Material sphere	3.0	9.6	26.0	26.5	23.3	16.1	0.2	1.6	-0.1	-11.2	-12.8	-23.5	-15.3	8.2	13.8	6.7	5.8	4.2	5.6	..
Non-material sphere	8.0	1.4	16.0	19.9	19.8	7.4	4.1	8.6	9.7	2.3	-11.0	-19.9	-5.7	11.4	7.2	4.6	3.7	4.3	5.1	..
Romania [a]																				
Total	11.6	10.5	10.4	8.2	13.4	15.1	8.5	11.7	16.0	4.1	3.0	-7.1	-3.1	2.4	6.0	1.6	1.2	0.9	-1.3	..
Material sphere	10.0	12.2	10.4	8.2	12.0	13.8	9.3	13.4	17.0	3.9	3.4	-6.6	-3.2	4.8	7.5	1.7	0.3	-3.8	..	..
Non-material sphere	20.0	2.1	9.3	8.1	19.3	21.2	5.2	4.4	11.0	5.2	1.1	-9.4	-2.6	-8.6	-2.3	1.4	6.3	13.5	..	..
Eastern Europe																				
Total	8.0	6.4	11.1	12.5	13.4	10.8	3.9	7.3	5.7	-1.0	-2.2	-7.2	-4.4	2.3	2.2	3.9	3.9	4.7	2.6	-2.7 [b]
Material sphere	7.0	6.5	10.4	13.3	13.0	12.6	4.0	7.5	5.4	-1.6	-2.0	-6.6	-4.9	2.4	2.8	4.4	3.4	4.2	..	..
Non-material sphere	13.0	5.1	12.3	10.7	14.1	10.2	4.0	7.1	7.1	1.7	-2.8	-8.9	-2.9	1.7	0.4	3.1	4.4	4.6	..	..
Soviet Union [c]																				
Total	11.4	7.2	7.0	4.6	7.0	8.6	4.3	3.5	5.8	0.7	2.2	3.7	3.5	5.6	1.9	3.0	8.3	5.7	6.2	0.6
Material sphere	13.0	8.5	8.6	6.5	7.8	9.3	5.0	3.5	7.1	0.7	2.5	3.5	3.3	5.3	1.3	2.6	7.5	4.0	6.2	..
Non-material sphere	8.0	4.4	3.7	0.1	5.4	6.7	3.0	4.1	3.1	1.0	1.8	4.6	4.6	6.9	3.6	4.0	10.6	9.5	6.2	..
Eastern Europe and the Soviet Union																				
Total	10.4	6.9	8.2	6.9	8.9	9.3	4.2	4.7	5.7	0.1	0.8	0.3	1.2	4.7	2.0	3.2	7.1	5.4	5.3	-0.1
Material sphere	11.0	7.9	9.1	8.5	9.4	10.3	4.7	4.8	6.5	-0.1	1.0	0.4	0.9	4.5	1.7	3.1	6.4	4.0	..	..
Non-material sphere	10.0	4.6	5.9	3.1	8.0	7.8	3.3	5.1	4.5	1.2	0.2	0.1	2.4	5.4	2.7	3.8	9.0	8.3	..	..

Sources: ECE secretariat Common Data Base, derived from national or CMEA statistics; *Statisticheskii ezhegodnik stran-chlenov SEV 1972* (CMEA statistical yearbook 1972), p.137; and plan fulfilment reports. National data are aggregated by means of 1975 weights based on CMEA investigations.

[a] At current prices in 1984-1989.
[b] Excluding Romania.
[c] Calculated from absolute volume figures at 1984 prices.

APPENDIX TABLE B.9

Total gross fixed assets [a]
(Annual percentage change)

	1970	1971	1972	1973	1974	1975	1976	1977	1978	1979	1980	1981	1982	1983	1984	1985	1986	1987	1988
Bulgaria [b]																			
Total	8.6	7.3	7.6	7.4	8.7	8.6	7.8	20.8	7.2	6.9	7.1	5.4	7.9	7.4	5.4	6.4	5.4	7.4	6.1
Material sphere	10.5	8.3	8.2	7.8	11.0	9.4	7.6	8.5	7.6	7.3	8.2	7.3	8.3	7.2	5.2	6.2	5.2	7.8	..
Non-material sphere	5.8	5.5	6.5	6.6	4.1	6.9	8.0	8.1	6.3	6.0	5.8	7.4	6.9	8.0	5.9	6.9	5.9	6.5	..
Czechoslovakia																			
Total	5.2	4.9	4.9	5.5	5.6	6.1	6.2	5.4	5.6	5.3	5.4	5.6	4.7	4.5	4.7	4.7	4.4	3.7	4.1
Material sphere	4.7	5.4	5.2	6.0	5.8	6.6	6.7	6.1	6.1	6.0	5.9	6.5	5.0	4.7	5.2	5.5	4.7	4.2	4.6
Non-material sphere	3.9	4.4	4.5	4.9	5.5	5.5	5.5	4.4	5.1	4.5	4.6	4.4	4.3	4.1	4.1	3.6	4.0	3.0	3.3
German Democratic Republic [c]																			
Total	4.7	5.1	4.8	5.2	5.4	6.5	5.3	4.9	4.9	4.7	5.0	4.5	4.8	4.6	4.1	4.3	4.0	3.5	3.7
Material sphere	5.6	5.8	5.2	5.5	5.5	6.8	5.2	4.9	5.0	4.8	5.3	4.5	4.8	4.3	3.9	4.4	4.2	3.8	4.1
Non-material sphere	1.7	3.5	3.8	4.6	5.1	5.7	5.6	4.7	4.7	4.3	4.2	4.6	4.8	5.2	4.4	3.9	3.4	2.7	3.0
Hungary																			
Total	5.9	5.8	6.0	5.7	5.5	6.6	6.0	5.3	5.5	5.5	5.1	3.8	4.3	4.3	3.2	3.3	3.8	3.2	..
Material sphere	5.0	6.9	6.7	6.6	6.1	7.3	6.4	5.6	6.0	5.9	5.1	3.8	4.2	4.3	2.7	3.0	3.7	3.0	..
Non-material sphere	..	..	..	..	..	..	5.5	4.7	4.6	4.9	5.2	3.9	4.4	4.4	3.6	4.0	4.0	3.7	..
Poland																			
Total	5.0	2.9	5.2	5.8	7.8	7.6	7.3	7.5	6.7	6.2	4.4	3.3	1.9	2.5	2.4	2.7	2.5	3.8	2.5
Material sphere	6.9	4.5	7.2	7.9	10.6	9.7	9.8	9.8	8.6	6.4	5.1	3.5	1.8	2.6	2.8	3.0	2.1	3.2	2.6
Non-material sphere	3.1	0.9	2.5	2.9	3.6	4.3	3.5	4.2	4.2	4.4	3.1	3.1	2.1	2.4	2.0	2.3	1.6	4.7	2.4
Romania [b]																			
Total	9.1	9.2	8.2	8.8	10.4	11.7	10.1	9.7	8.7	8.7	8.5	8.3	8.6	8.5	9.0	7.0	7.0	6.4	..
Material sphere	10.9	12.0	9.8	10.6	12.5	14.4	12.0	10.7	10.1	9.2	9.2	8.8	9.4	9.1	10.1	7.7	7.7	7.0	..
Non-material sphere	5.2	4.0	4.8	4.6	5.3	5.8	5.5	6.7	5.6	6.6	6.2	6.4	6.6	6.2	6.3	4.7	4.8	4.2	..
Soviet Union																			
Total	8.2	7.9	8.1	8.0	7.8	7.6	7.1	6.8	7.0	6.5	6.4	6.3	6.3	6.2	5.8	5.5	5.2	4.9	4.7
Material sphere	8.8	8.7	8.0	8.3	9.8	8.6	7.8	7.4	7.7	7.0	7.1	6.9	6.8	6.6	6.1	5.6	5.2	4.8	4.4
Non-material sphere	6.7	7.9	7.0	7.1	4.2	6.4	5.8	5.9	5.5	5.6	5.2	5.1	5.3	5.5	5.2	5.1	5.5	5.1	5.2

Sources: ECE secretariat Common Data Base, derived from national and CMEA statistics.

[a] At replacement values in constant prices; end-year basis.
[b] At prices of time of installation.
[c] At annual averages basis.

APPENDIX TABLE B.10
Employment [a]
(Annual percentage change)

	1970	1971	1972	1973	1974	1975	1976	1977	1978	1979	1980	1981	1982	1983	1984	1985	1986	1987	1988	1989
Bulgaria																				
Total*	0.9	0.9	1.3	-	1.0	0.4	0.2	-0.6	0.2	0.9	0.7	1.3	0.7	0.1	-	-0.1	0.5	-	..	..
Material sphere	0.3	0.9	0.7	-0.7	0.4	-0.5	-0.5	-0.6	0.1	0.8	0.1	1.2	0.6	0.1	-0.5	-0.3	0.2	-0.1	..	-2.8
Non-material sphere	5.4	0.9	5.1	4.3	4.5	5.3	3.8	-0.4	1.1	1.4	3.3	2.1	1.3	0.1	2.3	1.1	1.6	0.6	..	..
Czechoslovakia																				
Total	1.1	0.3	0.1	0.5	1.0	0.8	0.5	0.8	0.9	1.0	1.0	0.7	0.4	0.4	0.9	1.0	1.3	0.6	0.6	0.4
Material sphere	1.1	0.4	-0.4	0.4	0.7	0.4	-	0.3	0.6	0.6	0.4	0.3	0.1	0.4	0.7	0.6	1.0	0.5	-	-
Non-material sphere	1.0	-	1.9	1.0	2.2	1.9	2.0	2.4	2.1	2.4	3.0	1.7	1.3	0.5	1.7	2.0	2.3	1.0	2.4	..
German Dem. Rep. [b,c,d]																				
Total	0.2	0.5	0.1	0.5	0.6	0.5	1.0	0.8	0.8	0.7	0.4	0.5	0.6	0.7	0.5	0.2	-	0.2	0.3	..
Material sphere	-0.1	0.1	-0.3	0.1	0.3	0.3	0.8	0.6	0.6	0.4	0.2	0.2	0.2	0.4	0.3	0.1	-0.2	-0.1	0.2	..
Non-material sphere	1.7	2.6	1.6	2.4	1.8	1.6	1.8	1.7	1.7	2.1	1.2	1.7	2.0	1.9	1.3	0.9	0.8	1.2	0.7	..
Hungary [b,e]																				
Total	1.2	0.6	0.5	0.3	0.2	0.2	-	-0.2	-	-	-0.7	-0.7	-0.4	-0.6	-0.6	-0.5	-0.3	-0.5	0.6	..
Material sphere	1.1	0.3	0.2	-0.1	-0.3	-0.3	-0.6	-0.7	-0.3	-0.5	-1.2	-1.1	-0.8	-0.4	-0.5	-1.2	-1.3	-1.3	-1.6	-1
Non-material sphere	2.3	2.3	2.4	2.7	3.0	2.9	2.8	1.8	1.4	2.5	1.9	1.1	0.9	-1.4	-0.1	2.7	4.0	2.8	2.8	..
Poland																				
Total	1.2	2.0	2.6	2.3	2.0	1.7	0.3	1.3	0.4	0.8	0.3	0.8	-2.9	-0.3	0.3	1.0	0.6	0.2	-0.6	..
Material sphere	2.0	1.4	2.3	1.9	1.7	1.9	-	1.2	0.1	0.5	-0.1	0.2	-3.1	-0.8	-0.3	0.5	0.3	-	-1.1	..
Non-material sphere	-3.1	5.7	4.5	4.5	3.4	0.4	1.9	2.0	2.0	2.5	2.3	4.0	-2.1	2.4	3.0	3.0	1.7	-1.1	1.4	-1
Romania																				
Total	-0.4	0.3	-	-0.1	0.4	0.8	0.4	0.2	0.6	0.4	0.1	-0.3	0.7	0.6	0.1	0.7	0.8	0.5	0.4	..
Material sphere	-0.4	-0.1	-0.4	-0.2	-	0.4	-0.2	0.2	0.3	-0.2	0.3	-0.6	0.5	0.7	-	0.5	0.7	0.7	0.6	..
Non-material sphere	-0.9	2.9	3.0	0.1	3.1	3.6	5.0	0.7	2.5	3.8	-1.3	2.0	1.7	-0.2	0.8	1.6	..	..	..	..
Eastern Europe																				
Total	0.7	1.0	1.0	0.9	1.1	1.0	0.4	0.6	0.5	0.7	0.3	0.5	-0.7	0.1	0.3	0.6	..	..	..	..
Material sphere	0.8	0.6	0.6	0.6	0.7	0.8	-	0.5	0.2	0.3	-	-	-0.9	-0.1	-	0.2	..	..	..	..
Non-material sphere	-	2.9	3.1	2.7	2.9	2.0	2.6	1.6	1.9	2.5	1.7	2.5	0.3	1.0	1.7	2.1	..	..	..	..
Soviet Union [f]																				
Total	1.7	2.0	2.0	1.9	1.9	1.6	1.4	1.5	1.6	1.3	1.2	0.9	0.9	0.6	0.6	0.6	0.5	-0.2	-1.6	-1
Material sphere	1.3	1.6	1.5	1.5	1.6	1.2	1.5	1.2	1.3	0.8	0.8	0.7	0.7	0.5	0.4	0.3	0.5	-0.3	-2.7	0.1
Non-material sphere	3.4	3.5	3.5	3.4	3.0	3.0	1.1	2.5	2.7	2.9	2.6	1.8	1.3	1.1	1.3	1.5	0.5	0.2	2.0	..
Eastern Europe																				
and the Soviet Union																				
Total	1.4	1.7	1.7	1.6	1.6	1.4	1.1	1.2	1.3	1.1	0.9	0.8	0.4	0.5	0.5	0.6	..	..	..	..
Material sphere	1.1	1.3	1.2	1.2	1.3	1.1	1.0	1.0	0.9	0.6	0.6	0.5	0.2	0.3	0.2	0.3	..	..	..	..
Non-material sphere	2.5	3.4	3.4	3.2	3.0	2.7	1.5	2.3	2.5	2.8	2.4	2.0	1.0	1.1	1.4	1.7	..	..	..	..

Sources: ECE secretariat Common Data Base, derived from national statistics.

[a] Annual averages.
[b] Economically active population.
[c] 30 September of each year.
[d] Including apprentices.
[e] Mid-year estimates.
[f] Workers and *kolkhoz* members engaged in the collective sector.

APPENDIX TABLE B.11

Gross industrial production
(Annual percentage change)

	1971	1970	1972	1973	1974	1975	1976	1977	1978	1979	1980	1981	1982	1983	1984	1985	1986	1987	1988	1989
Bulgaria [a]	9.6	9.1	9.1	9.0	8.1	9.6	6.8	6.8	6.9	5.4	4.2	5.4	4.6	4.3	4.2	3.2	4.0	4.2	5.0	2.2
Czechoslovakia	8.5	6.9	6.6	6.8	6.2	7.0	5.5	5.6	5.0	3.7	3.5	2.1	1.1	2.8	4.0	3.5	3.2	2.5	2.1	1.0
German Dem. Rep.	6.7	5.7	6.0	6.7	7.2	6.4	5.9	4.8	4.8	4.6	4.7	4.7	3.1	4.1	4.2	4.4	3.7	3.1	3.2	2.3
Hungary	7.9	6.7	5.2	7.0	8.4	4.7	4.5	5.7	5.4	3.1	-1.7	2.4	2.5	1.2	3.2	0.7	1.9	3.5	-0.7	-2.0
Poland	8.1	7.9	10.7	11.2	11.4	10.9	9.3	6.9	4.9	2.7	-	-10.8	-2.1	6.4	5.2	4.5	4.7	3.4	5.3	-2.0
Romania	12.1	11.6	11.8	14.7	14.6	12.0	11.4	12.6	9.0	8.1	6.5	2.6	1.1	4.7	6.7	4.9	7.7	4.5	3.6	..
Eastern Europe	8.4	7.6	8.3	9.3	9.4	8.8	7.7	7.0	5.7	4.5	3.0	-0.5	1.2	4.4	4.8	4.1	4.6	3.5	3.5	0.3 [b]
Soviet Union [c]	8.5	7.7	6.5	7.5	8.0	7.6	4.8	5.7	4.8	3.4	3.6	3.4	2.9	4.2	4.1	3.4	4.4	3.8	3.9	1.7
Eastern Europe and the Soviet Union	8.5	7.7	7.0	8.0	8.4	7.9	5.6	6.1	5.1	3.7	3.4	2.3	2.4	4.3	4.3	3.6	4.4	3.7	3.8	1.3

Sources: ECE secretariat Common Data Base, derived from national or CMEA statistics. National data are aggregated by means of 1965 weights based on CMEA investigations.

[a] Based on rounded index numbers (1956 = 100).
[b] Excluding Romania.
[c] Based on rounded index numbers (1940 = 100).

APPENDIX TABLE B.12

Industry: Gross investments, gross fixed assets and employment
(Annual percentage change)

	1970	1971	1972	1973	1974	1975	1976	1977	1978	1979	1980	1981	1982	1983	1984	1985	1986	1987	1988
Bulgaria																			
Investment [a]	5.0	-0.9	2.7	7.8	1.1	18.5	1.7	17.8	1.2	-0.2	9.0	10.6	10.1	-2.8	4.3	12.2	11.7	8.6	..
Gross fixed assets	..	6.8	9.3	9.2	12.9	8.9	6.7	9.7	8.6	8.2	10.2	8.1	9.8	7.5	5.7	7.1	6.1	10.4	..
Employment	1.1	3.8	2.6	1.8	2.9	2.3	1.3	0.6	1.4	1.8	1.5	2.8	2.4	1.4	0.8	0.5	1.3	1.3	..
Czechoslovakia																			
Investment	5.0	4.7	3.2	15.5	7.8	5.0	8.4	7.3	3.2	6.6	3.6	-1.4	-4.4	-3.0	-4.8	6.5	1.6	10.1	6.7
Gross fixed assets	..	5.3	5.0	5.7	5.7	6.3	6.9	6.2	5.6	5.9	5.9	6.7	5.2	4.6	5.2	5.8	4.8	4.3	4.8
Employment	1.2	0.2	0.8	0.9	0.4	0.7	0.1	0.5	0.8	0.6	0.5	0.6	0.4	0.5	0.4	0.5	1.4	0.6	0.4
German Democratic Republic																			
Investment	13.0	3.6	7.6	10.1	-1.0	1.3	8.3	6.5	5.5	3.2	4.0	2.7	-1.4	3.6	-7.4	2.4	5.5	12.8	9.0
Gross fixed assets	..	5.8	5.6	5.9	6.2	8.0	5.1	4.8	5.1	4.7	5.6	4.6	5.4	4.8	4.3	5.2	4.9	4.1	4.5
Employment	0.1	0.4	0.7	0.8	0.1	-	0.9	0.7	0.7	0.6	0.1	0.5	0.3	0.3	0.4	0.2	-0.5	-0.3	0.1
Hungary																			
Investment	9.0	11.3	0.6	-0.2	9.3	10.8	8.0	23.3	3.3	-1.8	-11.5	-8.1	0.2	-2.5	-2.2	-0.2	-6.3	5.4	-7.0
Gross fixed assets	..	8.4	8.1	7.4	7.2	9.9	6.6	7.3	9.1	8.1	6.4	4.3	4.9	5.7	4.7	3.3	5.7	3.7	..
Employment	0.1	-0.4	0.6	1.1	0.4	-0.8	-1.3	-1.0	-0.9	-1.6	-2.3	-2.3	-2.1	-2.2	-1.2	-0.3	-0.4	-1.3	..
Poland																			
Investment	1.0	10.4	34.6	26.7	22.2	17.0	2.3	-2.4	-4.7	-15.4	-13.9	-27.2	-12.9	6.2	13.7	9.9	6.8	4.8	4.5
Gross fixed assets	..	6.3	8.9	9.4	13.8	11.1	10.6	12.3	9.6	6.2	4.6	3.4	2.4	2.8	3.0	3.4	2.3	4.1	2.6
Employment	1.9	3.0	3.9	2.9	2.4	2.6	0.2	1.0	-0.2	-0.1	0.1	-0.2	-4.7	-0.1	0.7	0.3	-2.0	0.2	-0.3
Romania																			
Investment [b]	4.0	12.9	15.0	13.8	9.4	10.7	4.9	16.3	20.4	7.4	2.6	-5.8	-9.6	5.5	11.1	-2.8	4.7	-6.9	..
Gross fixed assets	..	13.0	10.6	12.0	14.3	15.6	11.9	10.6	10.0	9.5	9.8	9.2	9.7	9.1	9.6	7.6	8.7	7.2	..
Employment	4.3	6.6	5.6	6.9	7.1	5.3	3.8	4.1	2.6	3.9	3.2	2.0	2.1	1.7	-0.2	1.7	..	..	..
Eastern Europe																			
Employment	1.4	2.1	2.5	2.4	2.1	1.8	0.8	1.1	0.7	0.8	0.6	0.5	-0.9	0.4	0.3	0.5	..	..	..
Soviet Union																			
Investment [a]	13.0	5.2	7.1	5.5	7.1	9.3	4.7	4.5	4.9	0.2	4.3	4.0	2.8	5.5	3.7	4.4	8.4	5.7	5.9
Gross fixed assets	..	9.4	7.5	8.7	8.3	9.1	8.1	7.0	7.9	7.1	7.8	7.0	6.9	6.8	6.6	6.0	5.5	4.3	4.9
Employment	1.4	1.4	1.3	1.3	1.7	1.9	2.2	1.7	1.7	1.3	1.1	0.9	1.0	0.6	0.3	0.4	0.3	-0.2	-2.0
Eastern Europe and the Soviet Union																			
Employment	1.4	1.6	1.7	1.7	1.8	1.8	1.8	1.5	1.3	1.2	0.9	0.8	0.4	0.5	0.3	0.4	..	..	..

Sources: ECE secretariat Common Data Base, derived from national or CMEA statistics; *Statisticheskii ezhegodnik stran-chlenov SEV 1972* (CMEA statistical yearbook 1972), p.143; and plan fulfilment reports.
[a] At current prices in 1984-1988.
[b] Calculated from absolute volume figures at 1984 prices.

APPENDIX TABLE B.13

Gross agricultural output
(Annual percentage change)

	1970	1971	1972	1973	1974	1975	1976	1977	1978	1979	1980	1981	1982	1983	1984	1985	1986	1987	1988	1989
Bulgaria [a]																				
Total	3.9	1.9	5.6	1.3	-1.5	7.5	4.1	-4.7	4.3	6.1	-4.6	5.9	5.2	-7.2	7.0	-12.3	11.7	-5.1	-0.1	0.4
Crop	2.3	-0.3	8.5	0.2	-7.5	7.8	5.6	-9.5	4.5	5.6	-8.7	10.2	7.9	-17.4	14.4	-22.5	22.7	-8.8	-0.3	4.1
Animal	6.9	6.1	1.4	3.1	7.4	7.3	2.0	2.0	4.0	6.5	0.3	2.2	2.6	3.0	1.1	-2.9	3.7	-1.9	0.4	-2.6
Czechoslovakia																				
Total	1.3	2.0	4.3	3.8	2.2	-1.0	-3.2	9.4	2.1	-3.3	4.8	-2.5	4.4	4.2	4.4	-1.6	0.6	0.9	2.9	1.1
Crop	-4.5	0.4	4.5	4.0	1.5	-2.6	-8.2	16.8	1.7	-7.2	6.2	-5.3	13.9	2.8	6.1	-4.1	-2.5	1.8	4.0	0.2
Animal	6.3	3.3	4.1	3.6	2.7	0.2	0.5	4.3	2.4	-0.3	3.9	-0.5	-2.0	5.4	3.1	0.4	2.9	0.3	2.1	1.7
German Dem. Rep.																				
Total	4.1	-0.3	10.0	-0.3	7.2	-2.5	-5.0	7.1	1.1	3.1	0.7	1.6	-4.0	4.1	7.7	3.2	-	0.1	-2.9*	1.5*
Crop	10.5	-5.9	18.3	-7.8	8.8	-9.6	-12.5	20.9	-	5.3	-3.7	1.9	1.7	1.2	11.6	6.0	-3.7	-0.8	-6.3	2.4*
Animal	-	4.0	4.4	5.3	6.1	2.2	-0.6	-0.1	1.7	1.8	3.5	1.5	-7.4	6.0	4.9	2.2	3.0	-0.9	-	..
Hungary																				
Total	-5.7	7.6	2.6	6.3	3.2	3.7	-2.7	10.9	1.1	-1.5	4.6	2.0	7.3	-2.7	2.9	-5.5	2.4	-2.0	4.3	-.2
Crop	-16.4	9.5	5.8	7.8	0.5	4.7	-7.1	12.3	-1.5	-3.2	7.6	1.6	9.4	-7.5	4.9	-5.4	3.7	-5.5	7.5	-.2
Animal	10.4	5.5	-1.0	4.5	6.4	2.5	2.7	9.6	3.7	0.1	1.9	2.4	5.3	2.2	1.0	-5.6	1.1	1.5	1.5	-.2
Poland																				
Total	2.2	3.6	8.4	7.3	1.6	-2.1	-1.1	1.4	4.1	-1.5	-10.7	3.8	-2.8	3.3	5.7	0.7	5.0	-2.3	1.2	2.0
Crop	4.3	1.1	7.8	6.5	-0.7	-3.0	5.0	-7.2	5.4	-3.7	-15.2	18.9	-2.5	5.9	7.4	-2.0	6.3	-2.0	-0.3	.4
Animal	-1.1	6.6	9.0	8.2	4.2	-1.0	-8.7	13.7	2.6	1.3	-5.6	-8.9	-3.2	0.4	3.7	4.0	3.2	-2.7	3.2	-.1
Romania																				
Total	-4.9	18.9	9.5	0.7	1.1	3.2	17.3	-0.9	2.6	5.5	-4.3	-0.9	7.6	-1.6	13.3	0.1	12.8	2.3	2.9	..
Crop	-11.8	26.3	7.6	-3.2	0.7	-	22.0	-5.0	0.3	6.2	-6.1	0.6	12.8	-5.1	20.3	-1.5	19.9	-0.2	2.9	..
Animal	5.4	8.9	12.5	7.7	1.4	6.7	11.5	5.6	5.6	4.8	-2.3	-2.8	0.2	3.7	4.4	2.5	2.8	3.3	2.9	..
Eastern Europe																				
Total	0.5	5.1	7.4	4.0	2.4	0.2	1.1	3.3	2.8	0.8	-3.7	1.8	1.6	0.9	7.0	-1.1	5.3	-0.8	1.4	1.0 [b]
Crop	-1.1	3.9	8.7	2.0	0.8	-1.8	1.9	1.4	2.3	-0.4	-6.0	6.7	5.0	-1.0	10.3	-2.9	6.8	-1.9	0.9	2.2 [b]
Animal	2.8	5.9	6.4	6.3	4.3	1.9	-0.8	7.4	3.2	2.1	-1.2	-2.9	-1.5	3.0	3.4	1.1	2.9	-0.3	2.0	..
Soviet Union																				
Total	10.3	1.1	-4.1	16.1	-2.7	-5.3	6.5	4.0	2.7	-3.1	-1.9	-1.0	5.5	6.2	-0.1	0.1	5.3	-0.6	1.7	0.8
Crop	11.8	-1.3	-7.7	27.1	-10.0	-10.5	18.4	-1.8	5.0	-5.9	-2.3	-2.4	9.2	6.0	-1.9	-1.0	6.2	-2.7*	-1.4	0.2
Animal	8.7	3.5	-0.6	6.1	5.2	-2.5	-2.4	9.4	0.8	-0.7	-1.6	0.1	2.6	6.3	1.4	1.0	4.6	1.5*	4.1	.1
Eastern Europe and the Soviet Union																				
Total	7.0	2.4	-0.4	11.9	-1.1	-3.5	4.6	3.8	2.7	-1.8	-2.5	-0.1	4.2	4.4	2.2	-0.3	5.3	-0.7	1.6	0.8
Crop	7.6	0.3	-2.5	18.3	-6.7	-7.6	12.7	-0.8	4.1	-4.2	-3.5	0.5	7.8	3.7	1.9	-1.6	6.4	-2.4	-0.6	..
Animal	6.7	4.3	1.7	6.2	4.9	-0.9	-1.8	8.7	1.7	0.3	-1.4	-1.0	1.1	5.1	2.0	1.0	4.0	0.7	3.4	..

Sources: ECE secretariat Common Data Base, derived from national or CMEA statistics. National data are aggregated by means of 1965 weights for total agricultural output based on CMEA investigations.

[a] Based on index numbers (1939=100).
[b] Excluding Romania.

APPENDIX TABLE B.14

Agriculture: Gross investments, gross fixed assets and employment
(Annual percentage change)

	1970	1971	1972	1973	1974	1975	1976	1977	1978	1979	1980	1981	1982	1983	1984	1985	1986	1987	1988
Bulgaria																			
Investment [a]	6.0	3.7	11.5	3.8	17.1	5.1	1.4	10.9	-9.8	-1.7	6.9	10.7	-18.6	1.6	2.6	8.0	-12.1	13.0	..
Gross fixed assets	..	6.6	6.3	6.4	-0.4	14.5	7.3	6.6	4.7	4.5	5.3	5.3	5.0	5.1	2.6	3.5	4.4	3.8	..
Employment	-4.1	-4.2	-2.0	-4.1	-3.5	-6.3	-4.9	-4.0	-2.6	-0.1	-1.8	-1.5	-2.8	-3.1	-3.2	-2.5	-2.0	-3.5	..
Czechoslovakia																			
Investment	-5.0	5.8	9.0	18.5	10.0	13.1	-0.5	6.3	8.0	-6.6	-3.2	5.0	4.6	12.7	1.6	7.8	3.0	-1.5	0.4
Gross fixed assets	..	5.4	5.4	5.5	6.3	6.8	7.2	6.4	6.8	6.3	6.0	6.1	5.3	5.6	5.8	6.4	5.4	5.2	5.4
Employment	-0.9	-1.5	-6.2	-3.0	-0.8	-2.2	-2.1	-2.3	-1.9	-0.7	-0.2	-0.0	-0.8	-1.4	0.9	0.5	-0.5	-0.9	-1.6
German Democratic Republic																			
Investment	-1.0	2.3	-2.6	4.8	9.1	0.8	2.8	3.5	-3.2	-3.9	-1.1	2.6	-7.5	-9.4	-10.8	-5.7	5.8	8.6	9.1
Gross fixed assets	..	5.6	4.8	5.6	4.3	4.2	4.8	5.1	5.0	5.4	4.9	4.9	4.3	4.0	3.6	3.2	2.9	3.0	3.1
Employment	-3.3	-2.4	-3.7	-1.9	-1.4	-0.8	-1.4	-0.5	0.5	-0.2	0.3	0.4	0.6	1.5	2.3	0.7	0.5	0.1	0.1
Hungary																			
Investment	26.0	-	-13.3	-	7.7	14.3	-5.7	8.8	9.5	-2.0	-11.2	8.0	-1.0	-15.4	-7.2	-7.0	6.9	21.4	-22.5
Gross fixed assets	..	9.3	8.6	8.6	6.9	7.0	5.8	5.9	5.8	5.6	4.3	4.3	4.3	3.4	0.5	2.1	1.7	2.5	..
Employment	-1.7	-2.3	-2.5	-3.4	-3.7	-2.6	-1.9	-1.5	-0.5	0.6	0.2	-0.5	-0.0	-0.3	-2.2	-4.1	-4.6	-3.9	..
Poland																			
Investment	3.0	4.7	14.9	17.1	18.0	16.1	2.0	12.9	5.9	-3.6	-17.2	-12.5	-15.3	5.6	4.6	-1.9	0.4	3.6	3.5
Gross fixed assets	..	2.9	4.2	5.2	6.1	6.4	7.0	7.2	7.0	6.5	5.7	4.0	1.9	2.0	2.6	2.4	1.6	2.1	2.1
Employment	-0.3	-0.3	-1.4	-1.8	-1.6	1.4	-0.4	1.4	-0.2	1.7	0.2	1.1	-0.5	-2.2	-1.9	-0.1	-1.2	-0.7	-2.6
Romania																			
Investment [a]	25.0	10.9	2.4	0.4	8.9	13.9	12.2	12.1	11.4	-1.7	4.4	10.0	-1.8	8.6	9.2	10.7	-3.2	-2.4	..
Gross fixed assets	..	10.0	9.1	9.2	9.2	10.5	7.6	10.6	6.9	7.0	5.6	8.8	10.1	9.9	9.2	8.6	7.5	7.1	..
Employment	-3.6	-4.4	-4.9	-4.4	-4.3	-4.5	-4.7	-4.1	-4.1	-5.2	-4.6	-2.7	-1.0	0.3	0.8	-	-0.2	..	..
Eastern Europe																			
Employment	-2.1	-2.4	-3.2	-3.1	-2.7	-1.9	-2.4	-1.3	-1.6	-0.8	-1.3	-0.4	-0.7	-1.1	-0.8	-0.5	-1.1	..	..
Soviet Union																			
Investment [b]	12.0	14.4	9.2	10.1	8.5	9.1	4.2	2.6	4.6	1.6	1.6	2.6	1.6	3.5	-2.8	1.3	6.4	2.3	6.3
Gross fixed assets	..	7.5	10.5	8.7	11.7	9.2	7.8	7.8	7.7	6.7	6.7	6.7	7.1	5.9	5.2	4.3	4.4	4.2	2.9
Employment	-1.5	-0.7	-0.6	0.5	0.1	-1.3	0.4	-0.7	-0.2	-1.1	-0.5	-0.5	0.4	0.2	0.2	-0.7	-1.0	-1.5	-4.2
Eastern Europe and the Soviet Union																			
Employment	-1.7	-1.3	-1.5	-0.8	-0.9	-1.5	-0.6	-0.9	-0.6	-1.0	-0.8	-0.5	-	-0.2	-0.2	-0.6	-1.0	..	..

Sources: ECE secretariat Common Data Base, derived from national or CMEA statistics; *Statisticheskii ezhegodnik stran-chlenov SEV 1972* (CMEA statistical yearbook 1972), p.143.

[a] At current prices in 1984-1988.
[b] Calculated from absolute volume figures at 1984 prices.

APPENDIX TABLE B.15

Export and import volumes
(Annual percentage change)

	1970	1971	1972	1973	1974	1975	1976	1977	1978	1979	1980	1981	1982	1983	1984	1985	1986	1987	1988	1989
Bulgaria																				
Exports	8.7	8.0	11.6	9.6	8.3	12.4	13.4	14.3	10.7	13.7	12.2	8.3	11.4	4.5	4.7	7.4	-3.7	1.8	2.0	-9.5*
Imports	4.7	13.3	13.3	10.7	21.9	12.6	-2.3	5.3	7.1	2.1	4.1	9.3	3.1	5.2	2.2	10.5	3.9	-1.4	6.0	-9.3*
Czechoslovakia																				
Exports	20.7	8.4	7.7	3.5	5.0	6.8	7.5	9.1	7.1	3.2	4.7	0.5	5.8	5.9	9.6	2.6	1.2	3.4	3.2	-3.1*
Imports	15.9	5.9	4.1	9.8	10.9	1.9	3.4	7.1	3.6	2.2	-1.6	-6.9	2.9	2.1	0.3	4.6	2.7	4.3	2.9	2.6*
German Dem. Rep.																				
Exports	8.8	10.3	11.9	7.4	8.4	7.2	5.8	4.2	7.4	8.9	3.6	8.4	5.4	10.6	2.1	2.1	0.5	-0.7	1.0	1.7*
Imports	15.9	2.0	7.6	13.1	8.7	5.0	11.1	4.6	-0.2	6.5	5.1	-1.3	-4.7	5.3	3.6	3.1	4.7	3.4	3.3	2.8*
Hungary																				
Exports	7.6	7.6	19.3	12.5	3.5	4.8	8.2	12.6	1.5	12.5	1.0	2.6	7.3	9.4	5.8	-0.3	-2.2	4.0	5.1	–
Imports	27.1	17.3	-5.1	2.9	17.5	5.7	3.9	8.5	12.5	-3.3	-1.1	0.1	-0.1	3.9	0.1	1.1	2.1	3.3	-2.0	1.0
Poland																				
Exports	10.1	6.5	15.2	11.0	12.8	8.3	5.3	7.0	5.7	6.8	-4.2	-19.0	8.7	10.3	9.5	1.3	4.9	4.8	9.1	-0.7
Imports	10.4	13.8	22.1	22.7	14.1	5.0	10.2	0.2	1.6	-1.2	-1.9	-16.9	-13.7	5.2	8.6	7.9	4.9	4.5	9.4	-0.7
Romania[a]																				
Exports	3.9	9.8	4.7	18.8	2.2	3.5	11.1	7.3	5.2	5.7	1.2	11.3	-8.3	3.2	15.9	0.3	0.2	-4.3	7.4	-8.2[b]
Imports	8.2	3.1	10.5	10.7	13.4	-3.7	11.5	8.4	17.2	6.8	2.0	-7.2	-22.4	-3.8	10.5	8.5	18.3	-6.3	5.8	0.8[b]
Eastern Europe																				
Exports	10.6	8.7	11.1	9.4	7.0	7.1	7.8	8.0	6.5	7.9	3.0	2.4	5.0	7.7	6.9	2.4	0.3	1.2	3.9	-2.4
Imports	14.0	7.5	8.2	12.2	13.0	4.3	6.7	5.2	5.0	2.7	1.4	-4.1	-4.9	3.5	3.5	5.5	5.3	1.8	3.0	0.8
Soviet Union																				
Exports	6.1	3.2	2.7	14.4	2.6	2.5	8.6	10.6	3.4	0.6	1.6	1.9	4.5	3.3	2.5	-4.3	10.0	3.3	4.8	-0.3*
Imports	7.8	5.9	17.2	14.6	1.0	14.8	7.0	0.9	13.3	1.1	7.5	6.4	9.7	4.0	4.4	4.7	-6.0	-1.6	4.0	7.1*
Eastern Europe and the Soviet Union																				
Exports	7.9	5.4	6.2	12.2	4.5	4.5	8.2	9.5	4.7	3.8	2.3	2.2	4.8	5.3	4.6	-1.1	5.1	2.3	4.4	-1.3
Imports	11.4	6.8	11.8	13.2	7.9	8.5	6.8	3.4	8.4	2.0	4.0	0.5	1.9	3.8	4.0	5.1	-0.3	0.2	3.5	3.7

Sources: ECE secretariat Common Data Base, derived from national or CMEA statistics. National data are aggregated by means of weights calculated from 1985 US dollar trade shares.

[a] ECE secretariat estimates.
[b] January-September.

APPENDIX TABLE B.16
Energy production: Electricity, coal and crude oil
(Billion kWh, million tons)

	1970	1971	1972	1973	1974	1975	1976	1977	1978	1979	1980	1981	1982	1983	1984	1985	1986	1987	1988	1989
Bulgaria																				
Electricity	19.5	21.0	22.3	22.0	22.8	25.2	27.7	29.7	31.5	32.5	34.8	37.0	40.5	42.6	44.7	41.6	41.8	43.5	45.0	44.3
Coal	29.3	27.0	27.3	26.8	24.3	27.8	25.5	25.2	25.8	28.2	30.2	29.2	32.2	32.4	32.4	30.9	35.2	36.8	34.1	34.3
Oil	0.3	0.3	0.2	0.2	0.1	0.1	0.1	..	..	..	..	..	..	..	..	..	..	..	..	..
Czechoslovakia																				
Electricity	45.2	47.2	51.4	53.5	56.0	59.3	62.7	66.5	69.1	68.1	72.7	73.5	74.7	76.3	78.4	80.6	84.8	85.8	87.4	89.3
Coal	109.5	113.0	112.9	109.0	110.1	114.4	117.7	121.2	123.2	124.7	123.1	122.8	124.6	127.4	129.3	126.6	126.4	126.1	123.5	117.4
Oil	0.2	0.2	0.2	0.2	0.1	0.1	0.1	0.1	0.1	0.1	0.1	0.1	0.1	0.1	0.1	0.1	0.1	0.1	0.1	0.1
German Dem. Rep.																				
Electricity	67.6	69.4	72.8	76.9	80.3	84.5	89.1	92.0	96.0	96.8	98.8	100.7	102.9	104.9	110.1	113.8	115.3	114.2	118.3	119.0
Coal	261.6	263.7	249.2	247.0	244.1	247.2	247.4	254.1	253.3	256.1	258.1	266.7	276.0	278.0	296.3	312.2	311.3	309.0	310.3	301.0
Oil	0.1	0.1	0.1	0.1	0.1	0.1	0.1	0.1	0.1	0.1	0.1	-	-	..	..	..	..	..	..	..
Hungary																				
Electricity	14.5	15.0	16.3	17.6	19.0	20.5	22.0	23.4	25.6	24.5	23.9	24.3	24.7	25.7	26.2	26.7	28.0	29.7	29.2	29.6
Coal	27.8	27.4	25.8	26.8	25.8	24.9	25.3	25.5	25.7	25.7	25.7	25.9	26.1	25.2	25.0	24.0	23.1	22.8	20.9	20.2
Oil [a]	1.9	2.0	2.0	2.0	2.0	2.0	2.1	2.2	2.2	2.0	2.0	2.0	2.0	2.0	2.0	2.0	2.0	1.9	1.9	2.0
Poland																				
Electricity	64.5	69.9	76.5	84.3	91.6	97.2	104.1	109.4	115.6	117.5	121.9	115.0	117.6	125.8	134.8	137.7	140.3	145.8	144.3	145.0
Coal	172.9	180.0	188.9	195.8	201.8	211.5	218.6	226.9	233.6	239.0	230.0	198.6	227.0	233.6	242.0	249.4	259.3	266.2	266.5	249.8
Oil	0.4	0.4	0.3	0.4	0.5	0.6	0.5	0.4	0.4	0.3	0.3	0.3	0.2	0.2	0.2	0.2	0.2	0.2	0.2	0.2
Romania																				
Electricity	35.1	39.5	43.4	46.8	49.1	53.7	58.3	59.9	64.3	64.9	67.5	70.1	68.9	70.3	71.6	71.8	75.5	74.1	75.3	..
Coal	20.5	20.6	23.2	24.9	26.9	27.1	25.8	26.8	29.3	32.8	35.2	36.9	37.9	44.5	44.3	46.6	47.5	51.5	58.8	..
Oil	13.4	13.8	14.1	14.3	14.5	14.6	14.7	14.6	13.7	12.3	11.5	11.6	11.7	11.6	11.5	10.7	10.1	9.5	9.4	..
Eastern Europe																				
Electricity	246.5	262.0	282.7	301.1	318.8	340.4	364.1	380.8	401.9	404.3	419.6	420.6	429.3	445.7	465.8	472.3	485.7	493.1	499.5	502.4 [b]
Coal	621.6	631.7	627.3	630.3	633.0	652.9	660.3	679.5	690.9	706.4	702.3	680.3	723.7	741.1	769.3	789.7	802.9	812.5	814.1	781.5 [b]
Oil	16.4	16.7	17.0	17.1	17.4	17.5	17.6	17.4	16.5	14.9	14.0	14.1	14.1	13.9	13.7	13.0	12.4	11.7	11.7	11.7 [b]
Soviet Union																				
Electricity	740.9	800.4	857.4	914.6	975.8	1038.6	1111.4	1150.1	1202.0	1238.2	1293.9	1326.0	1367.1	1418.1	1492.6	1544.0	1599.0	1665.0	1705.0	1722.0
Coal	577.5	591.5	603.6	614.7	630.6	644.9	654.4	663.3	664.4	657.6	652.9	637.8	647.3	641.6	634.6	647.8	672.7	680.3	691.5	663.8
Oil	353.0	371.8	393.8	421.4	450.6	490.8	519.7	545.8	571.5	585.6	603.2	608.8	612.6	616.3	612.7	595.3	614.8	624.2	624.3	607.0
Eastern Europe and Soviet Union																				
Electricity	987.4	1062.4	1140.2	1215.7	1294.5	1379.0	1475.5	1530.9	1603.9	1642.5	1713.5	1746.6	1796.4	1863.8	1958.4	2016.4	2084.7	2158.1	2204.5	2224.4 [b]
Coal	1199.1	1223.2	1230.9	1245.0	1263.5	1297.8	1314.7	1342.8	1355.3	1364.0	1355.1	1318.1	1371.1	1382.7	1403.9	1437.4	1475.6	1492.8	1505.6	1445.3 [b]
Oil	369.4	388.5	410.8	438.5	468.0	508.3	537.3	563.2	588.0	600.4	617.2	622.9	626.7	630.2	626.5	608.3	627.2	635.9	636.0	618.7 [b]

Source: Statisticheskii ezhegodnik stran-chlenov SEV (CMEA statistical yearbook), various issues, and ECE secretariat estimates.

[a] Excluding gas condensate.
[b] Assuming unchanged output in Romania.

APPENDIX TABLE B.17

Steel production
(Million tons)

	1970	1971	1972	1973	1974	1975	1976	1977	1978	1979	1980	1981	1982	1983	1984	1985	1986	1987	1988	1989
Bulgaria	1.8	1.9	2.1	2.2	2.2	2.3	2.5	2.6	2.5	2.5	2.6	2.5	2.6	2.8	2.9	2.9	3.0	3.0	2.8	2.9
Czechoslovakia	11.5	12.1	12.7	13.2	13.6	14.3	14.7	15.1	15.3	14.8	15.2	15.3	15.0	15.0	14.8	15.0	15.1	15.4	15.3	15.5
German Dem. Rep.	5.1	5.4	5.7	5.9	6.2	6.5	6.7	6.8	7.0	7.0	7.3	7.5	7.2	7.2	7.6	7.9	8.0	8.2	8.1	7.8
Hungary	3.1	3.1	3.3	3.3	3.5	3.7	3.7	3.7	3.9	3.9	3.8	3.6	3.7	3.6	3.8	3.6	3.7	3.6	3.6	3.3
Poland	11.8	12.7	13.4	14.1	14.6	15.0	15.6	17.8	19.3	19.2	19.5	15.7	14.7	16.2	16.5	16.1	17.1	17.1	16.9	15.1
Romania	6.5	6.8	7.4	8.2	8.8	9.5	10.7	11.5	11.8	12.9	13.2	13.0	13.1	12.6	14.4	13.8	14.3	13.9	14.3	..
Eastern Europe	39.7	42.0	44.6	46.8	48.9	51.3	53.9	57.5	59.7	60.4	61.5	57.6	56.2	57.5	60.0	59.4	61.2	61.4	61.0	..
Soviet Union	115.9	120.7	125.6	131.5	136.2	141.3	144.8	146.7	151.5	149.1	147.9	148.4	147.2	152.5	154.2	154.7	163.5	161.9	163.0	160.0
Eastern Europe and the Soviet Union	155.6	162.6	170.3	178.3	185.1	192.6	198.7	204.2	211.1	209.5	209.5	206.0	203.4	210.0	214.2	214.1	221.7	223.2	224.0	..

Source: National statistics.

Appendix B. Eastern Europe and Soviet Union

APPENDIX TABLE B.18

Grain production [a]

(Million tons)

	1970	1971	1972	1973	1974	1975	1976	1977	1978	1979	1980	1981	1982	1983	1984	1985	1986	1987	1988	1989
Bulgaria																				
Total	6.9	7.2	8.2	7.4	6.7	7.8	8.6	7.7	7.6	8.4	7.7	8.5	10.1	8.0	9.3	5.5	8.6	7.4	7.9	9.8
Wheat	3.0	3.1	3.6	3.3	2.9	2.8	3.5	3.4	3.5	3.4	3.8	4.4	4.9	3.6	4.8	3.1	4.3	4.1	4.7	..
Maize	2.4	2.5	3.0	2.6	1.6	2.8	3.0	2.5	2.2	3.2	2.3	2.4	3.4	3.1	3.0	1.3	2.8	1.9	1.6	..
Czechoslovakia																				
Total	7.3	8.9	8.7	9.7	10.5	9.4	9.2	10.5	11.1	9.3	10.9	9.5	10.4	11.2	12.2	12.0	11.0	12.0	12.2	12.3
Wheat	3.2	3.9	4.0	4.6	5.1	4.2	4.8	5.2	5.6	3.7	5.4	4.3	4.6	5.8	6.2	6.0	5.3	6.2	6.5	..
Maize	0.5	0.5	0.6	0.6	0.6	0.8	0.5	0.8	0.6	0.9	0.7	0.7	0.9	0.7	0.9	1.0	1.0	1.2	1.0	..
German Democratic Republic																				
Total	6.5	7.8	8.6	8.6	9.8	9.0	8.2	8.8	9.9	9.0	9.7	8.9	10.1	10.2	11.4	11.7	11.8	11.3	9.9	10.9
Wheat	2.1	2.5	2.7	2.9	3.2	2.7	2.7	2.9	3.1	3.1	3.1	2.9	2.7	3.5	3.9	3.9	4.2	4.0	3.7	..
Maize	-	-	-	-	-	-	-	-	-	-	-	-	-	-	-	-	-	-	-	..
Hungary																				
Total	7.8	10.0	10.9	11.8	12.6	12.4	11.5	12.4	13.5	12.2	14.2	13.0	15.1	13.9	15.9	15.0	14.5	14.4	15.0	15.0
Wheat	2.7	3.9	4.1	4.5	5.0	4.0	5.1	5.3	5.7	3.7	6.1	4.6	5.8	6.0	7.4	6.6	5.8	5.7	7.0	..
Maize	4.1	4.7	5.6	6.0	6.2	7.2	5.1	6.0	6.7	7.4	6.7	7.0	8.0	6.4	6.7	6.8	7.3	7.2	6.3	..
Poland																				
Total	16.6	20.2	20.7	22.2	23.3	19.8	21.1	19.6	21.8	17.6	18.5	19.9	21.4	22.4	24.8	24.2	25.5	26.6	25.1	27.6
Wheat	4.6	5.5	5.1	5.8	6.4	5.2	5.7	5.3	6.0	4.2	4.2	4.2	4.5	5.2	6.0	6.5	7.5	7.9	7.6	..
Maize	-	-	-	-	-	0.1	0.2	0.2	0.1	0.2	0.1	0.1	0.1	0.1	0.1	0.1	0.1	0.1	0.2	..
Romania																				
Total	10.9	14.8	17.1	14.0	13.7	15.4	19.9	18.7	19.1	19.4	20.3	20.1	22.5	19.8	23.9	23.3	30.7	32.1	32.6	..
Wheat	3.4	5.6	6.0	5.5	5.0	4.9	6.8	6.5	6.3	4.7	6.5	5.3	6.5	5.3	7.6	5.7	7.4	9.7	-	..
Maize	6.5	7.8	9.8	7.4	7.4	9.2	11.6	10.1	10.2	12.4	11.2	11.9	12.6	12.0	13.3	15.2	20.2	18.4	-	..
Eastern Europe																				
Total	56.0	68.8	74.3	73.6	76.5	73.8	78.5	77.6	83.0	75.8	81.3	80.1	89.6	85.5	97.6	91.7	102.1	103.8	102.6	..
Wheat	19.0	24.4	25.6	26.6	27.6	23.8	28.7	28.7	30.2	22.8	29.1	25.9	29.0	29.4	35.9	31.8	34.5	37.8	-	..
Maize	13.5	15.6	19.0	16.6	15.9	20.2	20.5	19.7	19.8	24.2	20.9	22.1	25.0	22.3	24.0	24.5	31.4	28.8	-	..
Soviet Union																				
Total	186.8	181.2	168.2	222.5	195.7	140.1	223.8	195.7	237.4	179.3	189.1	158.2	186.8	192.2	172.6	191.7	210.1	211.4	195.1	211.1
Wheat	99.7	98.8	86.0	109.8	83.9	66.2	96.9	92.2	120.9	90.3	98.2	81.1	84.3	77.5	68.6	78.1	92.3	83.3	84.4	..
Maize	9.4	8.6	9.8	13.2	12.1	7.3	10.1	11.0	8.9	8.4	9.5	9.4	14.7	13.3	13.6	14.4	12.5	14.8	16.0	..
Eastern Europe and the Soviet Union																				
Total	242.8	250.0	242.5	296.1	272.2	213.9	302.3	273.4	320.4	255.1	270.4	238.3	276.4	277.7	270.2	283.4	312.2	315.2	297.7	..
Wheat	118.8	123.2	111.6	136.4	111.5	90.1	125.6	120.8	151.2	113.1	127.2	107.0	113.3	106.9	104.6	109.9	126.8	121.1	-	..
Maize	23.0	24.2	28.9	29.8	28.0	27.5	30.6	30.6	28.7	32.6	30.3	31.5	39.7	35.6	37.5	38.9	43.9	43.6	-	..

Sources: ECE secretariat Common Data Base, derived from national and CMEA statistics; plan fulfilment reports for 1989.

[a] Including pulses.

APPENDIX TABLE B.19

Saving deposits of the population
(Billions of national currency units)

	1970	1971	1972	1973	1974	1975	1976	1977	1978	1979	1980	1981	1982	1983	1984	1985	1986	1987	1988	1989
Bulgaria	3.9	4.5	5.2	6.1	6.9	7.6	8.2	8.6	8.9	9.6	10.3	10.9	11.8	12.8	13.5	15.6	16.2	17.1	18.4	19.0
Czechoslovakia	63.5	73.8	85.5	98.5	107.2	115.8	126.1	137.0	143.2	147.8	155.9	165.1	177.6	190.7	203.7	218.9	234.9	251.7	265.6	277.7
German Dem. Rep.	52.1	55.7	60.0	65.1	70.2	75.3	80.2	86.1	92.0	97.0	99.7	103.0	107.6	113.2	118.7	124.6	132.3	141.9	151.6	160.0
Hungary [a]	42.1	48.4	54.5	62.0	70.8	81.3	92.9	107.5	124.9	135.8	145.3	160.1	175.7	194.2	216.1 [b]	241.5 [b]	276.6 [b]	297.7 [b]	328.9 [b]	364.7
Poland [c]	114.8	133.6	166.5	209.7	260.5	302.8	334.1	370.6	409.0	456.6	492.9	664.7	866.9	1058.2	1237.3	1667.2	2091.1	2482.3	3695.4	3266.6
Romania	..	..	..	35.5	40.8	47.4	55.0	64.3	80.1	89.6	101.4	114.6	118.2	127.8	138.9	153.2	167.3	266.9	296.7	..
Soviet Union	46.7	53.4	60.9	68.8	79.1	91.2	103.2	116.8	131.3	146.4	157.0	166.0	174.3	186.9	202.1	220.8	242.8	266.9	296.7	337.0

Sources: National statistics (Czechoslovakia, German Democratic Republic, Hungary, Poland); International Monetary Fund, *International Financial Statistics* (Romania); *Statisticheskii ezhegodnik stran-chlenov SEV* (CMEA statistical yearbook), various years (for Bulgaria and the Soviet Union).

[a] Since 1986 without convertible currency deposits.
[b] Including bonds and other types of new saving facilities.
[c] Excluding current accounts.

Appendix C. International trade and payments.

Data for this section were compiled from international [914] and national statistical sources, as indicated in the notes to individual tables. Regional aggregates for tables C.2-C.3 were obtained by means of weights representing 1985 shares in the US dollar value of trade.

---

[914] United Nations COMTRADE data base, IMF, IBRD, OECD, BIS.

APPENDIX TABLE C.1

World trade: Value, by region
(Billion US dollars)

	1970	1971	1972	1973	1974	1975	1976	1977	1978	1979	1980	1981	1982	1983	1984	1985	1986	1987	1988	1989 [a]
Exports																				
Developed market economies	216.8	242.6	288.9	393.0	528.9	564.2	628.0	712.9	854.8	1048.7	1237.7	1221.0	1156.2	1142.9	1219.1	1261.8	1474.0	1721.6	1968.2	1542.0
North America	59.4	61.9	70.4	97.3	133.9	142.9	157.4	166.7	194.3	244.7	293.3	311.4	287.7	282.4	314.2	309.8	317.4	352.0	440.2	362.0
Western Europe [b]	131.9	149.4	180.3	246.0	322.7	348.0	383.4	443.1	535.4	667.4	771.5	713.7	685.1	669.1	684.3	721.8	888.0	1066.7	1182.0	913.5
Southern Europe	6.2	7.2	9.1	12.7	16.7	17.4	19.9	22.0	26.9	34.3	42.4	44.4	45.0	44.4	50.9	53.1	57.9	71.7	81.1	61.9
Japan	19.3	24.1	29.1	37.0	55.5	55.8	67.3	81.1	98.2	102.3	130.4	151.5	138.4	147.0	169.7	177.2	210.8	231.3	264.9	204.6
Developing market economies	52.5	61.1	71.4	107.1	228.3	212.5	257.6	290.3	306.5	434.3	559.0	550.5	481.8	447.0	462.9	443.7	405.6	496.3	573.8	363.5
Oil-exporting countries [c]	17.9	23.3	26.7	40.5	131.3	120.9	146.7	159.3	155.6	237.6	303.4	280.8	224.5	180.8	166.1	154.2	111.7	126.7	128.6	96.5
Non-oil developing countries	34.6	37.9	44.7	66.6	97.0	91.6	110.9	131.0	150.9	196.7	255.6	269.7	257.3	266.3	296.7	289.5	294.0	369.6	445.2	267.0
Eastern Europe and Soviet Union	31.0	33.8	40.2	52.6	65.6	78.5	85.4	99.5	113.8	136.8	157.4	158.9	166.8	175.1	177.8	174.3	192.2	211.0	218.9	134.0
Eastern Europe	18.2	20.0	24.7	31.4	38.2	45.2	48.2	54.3	61.4	72.1	80.9	79.5	79.8	83.7	86.6	87.5	95.2	103.4	108.4	56.2
Soviet Union	12.8	13.8	15.5	21.3	27.4	33.3	37.2	45.2	52.4	64.7	76.5	79.4	87.0	91.4	91.2	86.8	96.9	107.6	110.5	77.7
Total above	300.3	337.6	400.4	552.7	822.8	855.1	971.1	1102.7	1275.1	1619.8	1954.1	1930.4	1804.8	1765.0	1859.8	1879.9	2071.9	2428.9	2760.8	2039.5
Memorandum item																				
ECE region	228.5	252.3	299.9	408.6	539.0	586.8	646.2	731.3	870.4	1083.2	1264.7	1228.4	1184.6	1171.0	1227.2	1259.0	1455.5	1701.4	1922.2	1471.3
Imports																				
Developed market economies	227.5	252.8	302.3	414.6	593.1	596.7	687.0	779.7	898.6	1153.2	1384.0	1311.8	1228.2	1211.5	1322.4	1356.9	1534.7	1817.6	2050.5	1622.3
North America	56.6	64.8	78.9	97.9	145.1	142.0	172.7	202.5	232.3	278.9	319.5	343.4	313.0	334.7	424.2	433.1	467.4	517.0	571.7	456.4
Western Europe [b]	139.8	154.8	183.3	255.5	350.4	359.0	409.2	461.0	540.0	705.0	846.3	750.1	711.0	682.1	693.2	722.1	861.0	1046.5	1173.3	915.6
Southern Europe	12.1	13.3	16.2	22.8	35.6	37.9	40.3	44.9	46.4	59.5	76.8	75.5	73.3	68.3	68.9	71.2	78.8	103.0	118.1	96.2
Japan	18.9	19.8	23.9	38.4	61.9	57.9	64.9	71.3	79.9	109.8	141.3	142.9	131.5	126.4	136.2	130.5	127.6	151.0	187.4	154.1
Developing market economies	51.9	58.7	63.6	89.3	147.3	169.6	185.0	222.4	268.2	317.9	427.4	489.5	453.2	426.8	426.5	405.4	392.6	436.7	545.4	433.7
Oil-exporting countries [c]	9.6	11.2	13.8	19.9	32.1	50.9	63.1	83.8	94.6	98.0	131.4	158.0	160.3	144.5	125.8	105.2	93.0	90.4	99.8	65.0
Non-oil developing countries	42.3	47.6	49.8	69.4	115.1	118.7	121.9	138.6	174.0	219.9	296.0	331.5	293.0	282.3	300.7	300.3	299.6	346.2	445.6	368.7
Eastern Europe and Soviet Union	30.3	32.8	40.6	53.3	67.8	88.2	92.6	101.5	118.9	135.0	155.2	155.1	153.1	157.9	159.7	165.6	183.4	195.2	206.0	152.0
Eastern Europe	18.5	20.3	24.4	32.4	43.0	51.2	54.4	60.6	68.2	77.3	86.6	82.1	75.4	77.7	79.6	82.6	94.5	99.2	98.9	69.3
Soviet Union	11.7	12.5	16.2	20.9	24.8	36.9	38.1	40.9	50.7	57.8	68.5	73.2	77.7	80.2	80.1	82.9	88.9	95.9	107.1	82.7
Total above	309.6	344.4	406.4	557.2	808.2	854.5	964.6	1103.7	1286.2	1606.1	1966.6	1956.6	1835.1	1796.2	1908.7	1927.9	2110.7	2449.4	2801.9	2208.1
Memorandum item																				
ECE region	238.8	265.8	319.0	429.6	599.0	627.0	714.7	809.9	937.6	1178.4	1397.8	1324.2	1250.4	1243.0	1346.0	1391.9	1590.6	1861.7	2069.2	1620.2

Sources: IMF, *International Financial Statistics*, March 1990 and ECE secretariat calculations, based on national publications for the European centrally planned economies.

[a] January-September.
[b] Austria, Belgium-Luxembourg, Denmark, Finland, France, the Federal Republic of Germany, Ireland, Italy, the Netherlands, Norway, Sweden, Switzerland and the United Kingdom.
[c] OPEC members, except Ecuador and Gabon, plus Oman.

APPENDIX TABLE C.2

World trade: Volume change, by region
(Annual percentage change)

	1970	1971	1972	1973	1974	1975	1976	1977	1978	1979	1980	1981	1982	1983	1984	1985	1986	1987	1988	1989
Exports																				
Developed market economies	10.4	5.6	8.7	13.4	8.3	-4.3	11.2	4.5	6.6	6.1	4.8	2.4	-2.0	2.3	9.5	3.9	1.6	5.5	8.2	7.3
North America	8.8	0.5	9.1	20.4	5.6	-3.2	5.3	1.8	11.4	7.2	7.5	-2.0	-8.6	-3.0	9.9	-0.2	1.7	10.4	15.4	7.7
Western Europe	10.4	6.2	8.6	11.2	8.1	-5.7	12.5	5.1	5.4	6.6	0.9	2.8	0.9	3.2	7.4	5.4	2.4	4.4	6.3	7.5
Southern Europe [a]	12.3	8.4	17.0	11.7	3.0	-2.1	14.0	3.3	7.8	7.0	8.7	6.7	6.8	5.6	15.0	6.9	-3.1	8.3	2.5	6.0
Japan	15.8	18.3	6.4	6.8	20.5	-0.2	21.1	8.6	0.7	0.2	17.1	10.7	-2.3	8.7	15.8	4.9	-0.6	0.4	4.4	5.8
Developing economies [b]	9.6	7.0	12.1	8.3	1.5	-8.7	13.9	2.6	0.6	5.1	-9.0	-5.5	-6.7	1.7	6.9	0.6	8.9	11.1	11.0	6.6
Oil-exporting countries [c]	18.1	10.2	4.6	8.9	2.1	-14.0	13.4	0.4	-4.2	2.8	-15.8	-13.9	-14.9	-5.2	0.3	-5.0	11.3	1.5	11.6	5.9
Non-oil developing countries	5.0	4.9	17.0	8.0	0.3	-	14.6	5.1	6.3	9.3	2.1	4.7	1.8	6.8	11.8	4.2	8.0	15.0	10.7	6.8
Eastern Europe and Soviet Union	7.9	5.4	6.2	12.2	4.5	4.5	8.2	9.5	4.7	3.8	2.3	2.2	4.8	5.3	4.6	-1.1	5.1	2.3	4.4	-1.3
Eastern Europe	10.6	8.7	11.1	9.4	7.0	7.1	7.8	8.0	6.5	7.9	3.0	2.4	5.0	7.7	6.9	2.4	0.3	1.2	3.9	-2.4
Soviet Union	6.1	3.2	2.7	14.4	2.6	2.5	8.6	10.6	3.4	0.6	1.6	1.9	4.5	3.3	2.5	-4.3	10.0	3.3	4.8	-0.3
Total above	10.0	5.9	9.3	12.1	6.3	-4.6	11.6	4.5	4.9	5.6	1.2	0.5	-2.5	2.4	8.4	2.7	3.7	6.5	8.5	6.3
Memorandum item																				
ECE region	9.8	4.8	8.7	13.6	6.8	-3.5	10.2	4.8	6.9	6.4	3.0	1.7	-0.7	2.1	8.0	3.2	2.4	5.7	8.1	6.2
Imports																				
Developed market economies	9.7	5.3	10.7	12.0	0.8	-6.4	12.9	3.7	5.8	7.5	-1.7	-2.3	-1.2	4.5	11.6	5.8	8.2	6.6	7.4	8.5
North America	2.0	9.0	14.1	7.0	1.1	-6.4	13.2	8.4	8.8	2.3	-6.8	2.7	-7.9	10.5	22.9	8.3	11.1	3.8	6.2	7.5
Western Europe	12.1	4.7	8.2	11.2	0.6	-5.8	14.2	1.8	5.1	9.4	1.1	-4.6	2.1	2.5	6.4	5.4	5.7	6.8	7.3	7.6
Southern Europe [a]	11.2	4.2	13.1	12.7	4.4	-1.5	6.5	1.9	-4.1	9.2	3.9	-3.5	-0.4	2.0	7.6	6.8	12.1	17.2	7.1	15.8
Japan	18.7	-0.4	13.9	30.6	-0.7	-12.2	8.9	2.5	6.6	11.4	-5.1	-2.2	-0.6	1.2	10.5	-	10.5	9.0	16.6	7.5
Developing economies [b]	8.8	8.8	3.9	14.0	18.4	6.5	5.7	10.9	6.3	2.0	9.3	8.0	-3.7	-2.8	2.6	-0.6	-4.4	5.7	10.2	8.7
Oil-exporting countries [c]	6.6	11.5	13.4	18.5	26.8	45.2	23.6	22.4	0.3	-10.2	17.2	22.7	-0.9	-11.9	-7.8	-10.6	-20.7	-8.3	3.4	5.1
Non-oil developing countries	9.2	8.4	2.3	13.0	16.8	-1.6	0.7	6.9	8.8	6.4	6.8	2.2	-4.4	1.8	7.0	3.2	1.6	9.8	11.9	9.5
Eastern Europe and Soviet Union	11.4	6.8	11.8	13.2	7.9	8.5	6.8	3.4	8.4	2.0	4.0	0.5	1.9	3.8	4.0	5.1	-0.3	0.2	3.5	3.7
Eastern Europe	14.0	7.5	8.2	12.2	13.0	4.3	6.7	5.2	5.0	2.7	1.4	-4.1	-4.9	3.5	3.5	5.5	5.3	1.8	3.0	0.8
Soviet Union	7.8	5.9	17.2	14.6	1.0	14.8	7.0	0.9	13.3	1.1	7.5	6.4	9.7	4.0	4.4	4.7	-6.0	-1.6	4.0	7.1
Total above	9.7	6.2	9.3	12.5	5.3	-2.3	10.8	5.3	6.1	5.8	1.2	0.2	-1.5	2.8	8.9	4.3	4.7	5.8	7.7	8.1
Memorandum item																				
ECE region	8.8	6.2	10.7	10.2	1.8	-4.1	12.6	4.0	6.2	6.3	-0.9	-1.7	-1.2	5.1	11.3	6.3	7.0	5.6	6.5	7.4

Sources: IMF, *International Financial Statistics*, March 1990 for the developed market economies; IMF, *IFS Supplement on Trade Statistics* (Supplement Series No.15) and *World Economic Outlook*, October 1989 for developing countries; ECE secretariat calculations, based on national sources for the European centrally planned economies. For market economies and eastern Europe, weights for aggregations are US dollar trade shares in 1985.

[a] Includes ECE, OECD or World Bank estimates for certain sub-periods for Portugal, Turkey and Yugoslavia.
[b] IMF definitions for developing countries.
[c] OPEC members, except Ecuador and Gabon, plus Oman.

APPENDIX TABLE C.3
Western Europe and North America: Trade volume change
(Annual percentage change [a])

	1970	1971	1972	1973	1974	1975	1976	1977	1978	1979	1980	1981	1981	1983	1984	1985	1986	1987	1988	1989
Exports																				
France	15.9	8.4	14.1	10.2	9.6	-4.2	9.1	6.5	6.1	10.0	2.1	2.9	-2.9	3.4	5.4	2.7	0.5	3.7	8.7	8.9
Germany, Fed.Rep. of	14.7	4.1	6.4	13.9	11.0	-11.2	18.6	3.9	3.2	4.9	1.7	6.6	3.3	-0.3	9.1	5.9	1.3	3.0	7.4	7.8
Italy	8.0	7.9	12.5	1.1	7.7	3.7	11.7	7.6	10.8	7.8	-7.9	4.2	0.5	3.6	6.5	7.5	1.8	2.0	6.0	9.3
United Kingdom	2.5	7.0	1.2	12.8	5.3	-2.2	8.6	8.4	2.8	3.7	0.8	-1.3	3.3	2.2	8.4	5.8	3.8	5.2	1.1	6.3
Total 4 countries	10.7	6.3	7.7	10.7	8.9	-5.3	13.0	6.1	5.0	6.3	-0.1	3.6	1.4	1.7	7.7	5.4	1.8	3.5	6.0	8.0
Austria	7.7	3.5	11.8	7.8	12.4	-7.0	15.7	3.0	10.3	13.0	4.7	5.2	1.1	4.6	9.4	7.8	0.8	2.5	12.1	13.0
Belgium	11.4	10.2	13.0	13.1	1.4	-7.1	13.8	5.4	2.6	6.3	2.4	-	1.1	4.5	4.3	4.2	8.0	8.3	8.5	8.5
Denmark	6.8	4.3	8.2	5.7	7.1	-3.3	3.4	5.0	6.3	10.4	6.8	3.8	1.2	8.4	6.7	4.2	-	2.0	5.9	6.5
Finland	8.0	-3.7	13.5	8.5	-	-17.2	17.0	9.7	7.4	9.6	8.7	3.4	-2.2	3.4	9.9	-	-1.0	3.0	-1.0	4.8
Ireland	8.1	7.1	6.3	9.3	5.7	7.8	3.8	17.6	10.4	8.2	7.7	0.8	7.3	12.0	18.4	6.5	4.0	14.2	7.0	10.0
Netherlands	11.9	8.5	9.8	12.5	14.3	-5.6	13.2	-1.3	3.9	7.6	1.2	1.2	-1.1	4.7	5.6	5.3	3.0	5.8	7.3	4.4
Norway	5.3	2.5	12.2	10.9	-	3.9	15.1	-3.3	22.0	5.6	6.6	-2.5	-1.3	12.8	9.1	4.2	2.0	13.7	6.5	15.0
Sweden	13.3	3.9	7.5	17.5	6.0	-9.9	4.7	1.5	7.4	8.2	-2.5	1.3	2.6	12.5	7.8	3.1	3.0	3.9	2.8	-0.9
Switzerland	6.1	3.8	5.6	10.5	4.8	-7.6	11.5	11.8	3.9	2.5	2.5	3.6	-3.5	-	7.2	12.4	2.0	1.0	7.0	5.1
Total 9 countries	9.9	6.0	10.0	11.9	6.7	-6.3	11.7	3.4	6.0	7.3	2.7	1.4	-0.0	6.0	7.0	5.2	3.4	6.0	6.7	6.6
Total western Europe	10.4	6.2	8.6	11.2	8.1	-5.7	12.5	5.1	5.4	6.6	0.9	2.8	0.9	3.2	7.4	5.4	2.4	4.4	6.3	7.5
United States	8.5	-1.0	8.9	23.9	8.6	-2.1	3.5	-0.2	11.8	8.9	10.0	-3.2	-11.0	-6.3	6.8	-2.0	-0.4	13.0	18.0	11.4
Canada	9.9	5.3	9.6	10.6	-3.8	-7.2	12.0	8.9	10.0	1.8	-1.2	2.7	0.1	7.7	18.5	4.2	6.9	4.8	9.4	-1.7
Total above	9.9	4.3	8.7	14.2	7.2	-4.8	10.0	4.0	7.3	6.8	3.1	1.1	-2.4	1.2	8.2	3.6	2.2	6.2	9.1	7.6
Imports																				
France	6.6	7.5	14.0	13.7	4.3	-7.1	20.8	0.8	5.2	11.7	6.2	-3.3	3.6	-1.9	2.3	4.1	3.3	7.1	6.7	7.7
Germany, Fed.Rep. of	18.4	8.3	6.4	5.5	-3.9	-0.3	17.8	2.3	6.8	7.5	2.8	-5.0	1.4	3.9	5.3	4.2	6.1	5.5	6.6	7.2
Italy	15.6	0.3	11.0	11.2	-5.5	-10.7	15.6	-0.4	7.5	13.1	-6.6	-6.6	-	8.6	9.0	8.8	4.5	9.5	6.9	10.6
United Kingdom	4.8	3.8	9.8	13.7	0.4	-8.7	6.6	1.7	6.8	8.5	-3.9	-3.9	5.9	2.7	10.7	3.6	6.9	6.9	13.6	9.2
Total 4 countries	11.9	5.4	9.6	10.3	-1.4	-5.9	15.4	1.3	6.5	9.7	1.2	-4.7	2.6	2.7	6.5	4.9	5.3	6.9	8.4	8.5
Austria	18.3	8.6	14.4	10.5	2.6	-6.6	22.9	9.8	-1.6	10.6	6.4	-4.2	-1.2	6.2	8.7	5.6	3.0	5.1	8.3	12.5
Belgium	10.0	9.1	8.3	16.9	1.3	-5.2	13.7	3.6	3.5	6.7	1.1	-4.2	1.1	-1.1	5.4	3.1	11.0	7.2	10.0	10.3
Denmark	9.7	-4.4	4.6	20.6	-7.3	-6.6	19.7	-2.4	4.8	5.7	-8.7	-4.8	2.5	6.1	6.9	7.5	-1.0	5.1	-1.0	0.7
Finland	21.1	-1.4	4.4	12.7	7.5	-	-3.5	-8.4	-5.3	19.4	11.6	-6.3	1.1	3.3	-	6.4	6.0	13.2	-0.8	7.0
Ireland	3.3	5.2	6.1	20.2	-1.9	-13.4	15.1	12.8	14.7	14.3	-4.4	2.1	-3.5	3.2	10.5	3.3	3.0	6.2	4.7	11.9
Netherlands	13.2	3.3	3.2	10.9	8.5	-5.2	12.3	1.2	6.0	6.8	-2.1	-7.6	1.2	2.3	5.7	7.5	4.0	6.7	6.3	4.3
Norway	12.8	1.9	-	13.0	8.2	-	10.6	8.2	-11.4	5.7	10.8	-3.7	3.8	-3.7	12.7	12.4	15.0	-1.7	-9.7	-7.5
Sweden	11.5	-3.4	5.4	8.5	15.6	2.7	5.3	-3.8	-5.2	15.1	2.4	-7.0	6.3	3.5	4.5	8.7	4.0	7.7	4.5	2.6
Switzerland	14.3	5.4	6.8	6.3	-1.5	-18.2	14.8	9.7	10.3	9.3	2.4	3.6	-2.3	3.5	8.0	5.3	9.0	6.4	6.8	5.5
Total 9 countries	12.5	3.4	5.8	12.7	4.2	-5.6	12.2	2.6	2.7	8.9	1.0	-4.4	1.1	2.1	6.3	6.3	6.4	6.4	5.3	5.9
Total western Europe	12.1	4.7	8.2	11.2	0.6	-5.8	14.2	1.8	5.1	9.4	1.1	-4.6	2.1	2.5	6.4	5.4	5.7	6.8	7.3	7.6
United States	3.2	8.8	13.4	4.7	-1.4	-12.0	21.8	10.7	10.3	0.1	-7.1	2.6	-5.1	10.4	24.0	8.7	10.5	2.6	3.8	6.3
Canada	-3.1	9.9	16.9	16.1	10.1	11.9	-8.9	0.5	3.2	11.2	-5.7	2.8	-18.1	11.1	18.6	6.6	13.7	8.9	15.8	12.0
Total above	8.6	6.1	10.2	9.7	0.8	-6.0	13.9	4.0	6.4	6.9	-1.6	-2.2	-1.3	5.1	12.0	6.4	7.7	5.6	6.8	7.6

Source: IMF, *International Financial Statistics*, March 1990. 1989 data are provisional estimates for most countries based on national, and OECD statistics. National data are aggregated by means of weights derived from 1985 US dollar trade shares.

[a] Calculated from rounded index numbers (1985 = 100) for Belgium, Denmark, Finland, Netherlands, Norway, Sweden and Switzerland. Comparisons with the previous year are limited due to changes in methodology in France (1973, 1975, 1986), Italy (1970, 1980), United Kingdom (1970, 1973), Austria (1979,1988), Belgium (1974), Denmark (1971, 1974, 1985), Finland (1970, 1977), Greece (1977), Ireland (1975), Norway (1970, 1980), Sweden (1975, 1983), Switzerland (1979 imports only, 1988) and Canada (1981).

APPENDIX TABLE C.4
Eastern Europe and Soviet Union: Exports by main directions, 1970-1989
(Value, billion US dollars)

	1970	1971	1972	1973	1974	1975	1976	1977	1978	1979	1980	1981	1982	1983	1984	1985	1986	1987	1988	1989 [a]
Bulgaria																				
World	2.00	2.18	2.63	3.24	3.84	4.69	5.38	6.35	7.45	8.86	10.39	10.70	11.44	12.14	12.86	13.31	14.14	15.86	17.29	16.02
ECE-East	1.51	1.64	2.01	2.46	2.73	3.50	4.10	4.81	5.51	6.18	6.90	6.95	7.75	8.87	9.30	9.82	11.26	12.64	13.92	13.30
ECE-West	0.32	0.34	0.39	0.48	0.55	0.55	0.69	0.75	0.87	1.54	1.92	1.70	1.53	1.48	1.49	1.39	1.10	1.18	1.25	1.32
Other	0.17	0.20	0.22	0.30	0.55	0.64	0.59	0.79	1.07	1.14	1.57	2.05	2.16	1.78	2.08	2.11	1.78	2.03	2.12	1.40
Czechoslovakia																				
World	3.79	4.18	4.92	5.99	7.03	8.36	9.03	10.27	11.75	13.19	14.93	14.91	15.64	16.50	17.20	17.47	20.30	22.99	14.83	14.40
ECE-East	2.43	2.66	3.26	3.89	4.27	5.47	6.18	6.95	7.95	8.69	9.46	9.60	10.42	11.19	11.85	12.28	14.55	16.87	8.45	7.70
ECE-West	0.92	1.00	1.12	1.51	1.98	1.97	1.98	2.30	2.57	3.15	3.82	3.53	3.51	3.53	3.57	3.39	3.78	4.16	4.58	5.02
Other	0.43	0.52	0.54	0.60	0.78	0.92	0.87	1.02	1.23	1.35	1.64	1.77	1.71	1.78	1.78	1.80	1.96	1.96	1.80	1.68
German Democratic Republic																				
World	4.65	5.18	6.32	7.74	9.05	10.44	11.75	12.55	14.04	16.17	18.59	20.67	22.53	24.53	25.41	25.78	28.71	31.20	16.62	17.33
ECE-East	3.13	3.50	4.39	5.20	5.60	6.84	7.46	8.29	9.21	10.30	11.05	12.20	12.90	14.27	15.09	15.38	17.38	19.20	7.44	7.40
ECE-West	1.16	1.30	1.56	2.09	2.89	2.86	3.41	3.33	3.71	4.58	5.86	6.68	7.49	8.27	8.43	8.43	9.25	9.71	7.55*	8.65*
Other	0.36	0.37	0.37	0.45	0.56	0.74	0.87	0.93	1.12	1.29	1.68	1.79	2.14	1.99	1.89	1.97	2.08	2.29	1.63*	1.28*
Hungary																				
World	2.32	2.50	3.29	4.37	5.13	6.06	4.93	5.82	6.35	7.93	8.61	8.73	8.86	8.77	8.62	8.47	9.17	9.58	10.00	9.83
ECE-East	1.44	1.62	2.15	2.80	3.22	4.10	2.73	3.25	3.45	4.14	4.33	4.65	4.62	4.32	4.17	4.43	4.95	4.79	4.46	3.90
ECE-West	0.69	0.68	0.89	1.26	1.49	1.45	1.68	1.97	2.22	2.91	3.27	2.90	2.93	3.19	3.28	2.90	3.19	3.74	4.30	4.85
Other	0.19	0.20	0.24	0.31	0.42	0.52	0.52	0.60	0.68	0.88	1.01	1.18	1.31	1.25	1.17	1.13	1.04	1.05	1.24	1.09
Poland																				
World	3.55	3.87	4.93	6.35	8.32	10.29	11.02	12.27	13.77	16.22	17.02	13.29	11.22	11.58	11.76	11.49	12.07	12.21	13.96	12.86
ECE-East	2.13	2.29	2.97	3.67	4.38	5.82	6.25	6.99	7.90	9.25	8.90	7.41	5.51	5.84	5.68	5.53	5.56	5.03	5.68	4.51
ECE-West	1.09	1.24	1.60	2.28	3.17	3.49	3.76	4.13	4.66	5.42	6.21	4.22	3.99	4.17	4.54	4.50	4.55	5.51	6.55	6.80
Other	0.33	0.34	0.35	0.40	0.77	0.98	1.01	1.15	1.21	1.54	1.91	1.66	1.71	1.57	1.54	1.46	1.96	1.67	1.73	1.55
Romania																				
World	1.85	2.10	2.60	3.67	4.87	5.34	6.14	7.02	8.05	9.72	11.40	11.18	10.12	10.16	10.72	10.99	10.84	11.54 [a]	12.63 [a]	11.34 [a]
ECE-East	0.92	1.00	1.23	1.65	1.75	2.04	2.33	2.92	3.29	3.48	4.24	3.35	3.24	3.42	3.08	3.94	4.48	4.90 [a]	5.16 [a]	4.59 [a]
ECE-West	0.66	0.79	0.97	1.42	2.22	2.03	2.40	2.37	2.95	3.93	4.39	4.16	3.48	3.77	4.20	3.92	3.88	4.24 [a]	4.47 [a]	4.27 [a]
Other	0.27	0.31	0.40	0.60	0.90	1.27	1.40	1.73	1.81	2.31	2.77	3.67	3.40	2.98	3.44	3.13	2.48	2.40 [a]	3.01 [a]	2.49 [a]
Eastern Europe																				
World	18.16	20.02	24.70	31.35	38.24	45.18	48.25	54.28	61.42	72.10	80.94	79.47	79.81	83.68	86.58	87.52	95.24	103.37	85.21	81.79
ECE-East	11.56	12.71	16.02	19.66	21.96	27.77	29.05	33.21	37.31	42.05	44.89	44.16	44.43	47.92	49.17	51.38	58.19	63.43	45.05	41.40
ECE-West	4.84	5.35	6.55	9.05	12.30	12.34	13.93	14.85	16.98	21.53	25.47	23.20	22.93	24.41	25.50	24.53	25.75	28.55	28.64	30.90
Other	1.75	1.95	2.13	2.65	3.98	5.07	5.27	6.22	7.13	8.52	10.57	12.12	12.44	11.35	11.90	11.61	11.30	11.39	11.52	9.48
Soviet Union																				
World	12.80	13.81	15.47	21.26	27.36	33.29	37.17	45.18	52.38	64.71	76.50	79.39	86.97	91.38	91.20	86.78	96.94	107.62	110.50	108.44
ECE-East	6.76	7.24	8.17	9.93	11.48	16.44	17.38	20.74	24.88	28.29	32.24	33.78	36.21	39.24	39.72	40.63	50.97	54.28	54.00	50.39
ECE-West	2.78	3.16	3.44	5.62	9.24	9.63	11.68	13.55	14.47	21.78	28.13	27.49	29.55	30.20	30.06	25.61	21.23	25.69	27.24	29.29
Other	3.26	3.41	3.86	5.71	6.64	7.22	8.11	10.89	13.03	14.64	16.13	18.12	21.21	21.94	21.42	20.53	24.75	27.65	29.26	28.75
Eastern Europe and Soviet Union																				
World	30.96	33.82	40.16	52.62	65.60	78.47	85.41	99.47	113.79	136.81	157.44	158.86	166.78	175.06	177.77	174.29	192.18	210.99	195.72	190.23
ECE-East	18.32	19.95	24.19	29.59	33.44	44.21	46.43	53.96	62.19	70.34	77.13	77.94	80.64	87.16	88.89	92.00	109.15	117.72	99.05	91.80
ECE-West	7.62	8.51	9.98	14.67	21.54	21.98	25.61	28.41	31.45	43.31	53.60	50.69	52.49	54.61	55.56	50.15	46.98	54.24	55.89	60.20
Other	5.01	5.36	5.99	8.36	10.62	12.28	13.37	17.11	20.16	23.16	26.70	30.23	33.65	33.30	33.32	32.14	36.05	39.04	40.77	38.24

Source: Secretariat of the United Nations Economic Commission for Europe, based on national foreign trade statistics. Partner country groupings: ECE-East — east European member countries of CMEA and the Soviet Union; ECE-West — ECE market economies and Japan; Other — all remaining countries.

Note: Substantial discontinuities in the value series are indicated by '||'. These usually relate to large changes in the rouble/dollar cross rate (reductions in the relative valuation of rouble exports). Such changes were introduced by Hungary in 1976, Romania in 1981, Poland in 1982, and Czechoslovakia and the German Democratic Republic (together with other data revisions) in 1989 with application to the trade data from 1988.

[a] ECE secretariat estimates in the absence of national data.

APPENDIX TABLE C.5
Eastern Europe and Soviet Union: Imports by main directions, 1970-1989
(Value, billion US dollars)

	1970	1971	1972	1973	1974	1975	1976	1977	1978	1979	1980	1981	1982	1983	1984	1985	1986	1987	1988	1989 [a]
Bulgaria																				
World	1.83	2.12	2.57	3.21	4.33	5.40	5.63	6.39	7.62	8.51	9.67	10.80	11.54	12.29	12.72	13.63	15.20	16.16	16.71	14.89
ECE-East	1.33	1.57	1.97	2.40	2.83	3.71	4.13	4.91	5.96	6.59	7.29	7.76	8.56	9.41	9.72	10.04	11.27	12.43	12.32	10.00
ECE-West	0.38	0.39	0.43	0.56	1.07	1.35	1.12	1.08	1.20	1.42	1.79	2.29	2.04	1.86	1.91	2.20	2.49	2.59	2.74	2.64
Other	0.13	0.16	0.17	0.24	0.43	0.34	0.37	0.41	0.47	0.50	0.59	0.75	0.95	1.02	1.09	1.39	1.44	1.14	1.64	1.44
Czechoslovakia																				
World	3.70	4.01	4.67	6.07	7.51	9.09	9.70	11.15	12.57	14.25	15.18	14.67	15.45	16.37	17.13	17.55	20.91	23.24	14.55	14.24
ECE-East	2.33	2.54	3.04	3.81	4.41	5.85	6.30	7.31	8.43	9.39	9.83	9.79	10.82	11.92	12.82	13.09	15.55	17.20	8.15	7.75
ECE-West	1.01	1.12	1.22	1.69	2.34	2.52	2.68	2.87	3.23	3.84	4.21	3.80	3.59	3.39	3.14	3.22	3.90	4.59	4.95	4.87
Other	0.35	0.34	0.41	0.57	0.76	0.71	0.72	0.97	0.91	1.02	1.14	1.08	1.04	1.06	1.16	1.24	1.46	1.45	1.45	1.62
German Democratic Republic																				
World	4.92	5.09	6.07	8.07	9.94	11.71	13.62	14.92	15.48	17.35	20.29	20.93	20.95	22.27	23.42	23.96	28.49	30.27	17.41	17.33
ECE-East	3.19	3.23	3.71	4.81	5.40	7.09	7.97	9.28	9.52	9.82	11.27	12.60	12.97	13.38	14.25	14.80	17.49	18.74	7.39	7.40
ECE-West	1.43	1.55	2.09	2.88	3.75	3.91	4.86	4.64	4.92	6.48	7.49	7.14	6.72	7.42	7.56	7.57	9.15	9.94	8.95*	8.65*
Other	0.30	0.30	0.27	0.38	0.79	0.70	0.79	1.01	1.04	1.06	1.54	1.20	1.27	1.47	1.61	1.60	1.85	1.58	1.07*	1.28*
Hungary																				
World	2.51	2.99	3.15	3.88	5.58	7.15	5.53	6.52	7.94	8.68	9.19	9.16	8.87	8.55	8.13	8.18	9.59	9.86	9.37	9.08
ECE-East	1.56	1.88	1.98	2.33	3.00	4.48	2.81	3.23	3.86	4.33	4.31	4.30	4.33	4.12	3.91	4.04	4.87	4.66	4.10	3.54
ECE-West	0.72	0.89	0.93	1.21	2.05	2.03	2.09	2.52	3.20	3.46	3.88	3.93	3.48	3.41	3.12	3.41	3.87	4.23	4.34	4.77
Other	0.22	0.22	0.25	0.34	0.53	0.64	0.64	0.77	0.88	0.89	1.01	0.93	1.06	1.21	1.10	0.73	0.85	0.96	0.93	0.77
Poland																				
World	3.61	4.04	5.33	7.76	10.49	12.55	13.88	14.63	15.70	17.55	19.12	15.53	10.25	10.60	10.65	10.84	11.21	10.85	12.24	11.30
ECE-East	2.36	2.58	3.08	3.81	4.40	5.45	6.20	7.25	8.06	8.99	10.09	9.59	5.98	6.25	6.11	5.87	6.09	4.93	4.95	3.66
ECE-West	0.98	1.18	1.89	3.49	5.41	6.31	6.92	6.44	6.52	6.87	6.92	4.72	3.35	3.29	3.42	3.82	4.08	4.62	5.89	6.30
Other	0.27	0.28	0.35	0.46	0.68	0.78	0.75	0.94	1.12	1.68	2.11	1.22	0.92	1.06	1.12	1.14	1.04	1.30	1.41	1.34
Romania																				
World	1.96	2.10	2.62	3.44	5.14	5.34	6.10	7.02	8.88	10.92	13.20	10.98	8.32	7.64	7.56	8.48	9.13	8.85	8.25	8.39 [a]
ECE-East	0.94	0.97	1.17	1.37	1.64	1.97	2.42	2.92	3.27	3.69	4.04	3.44	3.08	3.28	2.89	3.63	4.84	4.93	4.82	5.07 [a]
ECE-West	0.81	0.89	1.14	1.57	2.64	2.39	2.32	2.65	3.56	4.07	4.35	3.63	2.05	1.48	1.62	1.61	1.66	1.30 [a]	1.23 [a]	1.24 [a]
Other	0.21	0.25	0.31	0.50	0.87	0.99	1.36	1.45	2.06	3.15	4.79	3.91	3.20	2.88	3.05	3.24	2.64	2.62 [a]	2.20 [a]	2.08 [a]
Eastern Europe																				
World	18.52	20.34	24.41	32.42	42.98	51.24	54.45	60.62	68.20	77.26	86.65	82.06	75.38	77.72	79.60	82.64	94.54	99.22	78.53	75.68
ECE-East	11.71	12.77	14.95	18.53	21.67	28.56	29.82	34.88	39.10	42.82	46.83	47.48	45.73	48.35	49.70	51.46	60.11	62.89	41.72	37.77
ECE-West	5.33	6.03	7.70	11.40	17.26	18.51	20.00	20.20	22.63	26.14	28.64	25.51	21.22	20.67	20.77	21.83	25.15	27.30	28.10	29.61
Other	1.48	1.55	1.76	2.49	4.05	4.17	4.63	5.54	6.46	8.31	11.18	9.08	8.43	8.70	9.12	9.35	9.27	9.03	8.70	8.30
Soviet Union																				
World	11.73	12.48	16.16	20.91	24.85	36.94	38.11	40.89	50.74	57.78	68.53	73.16	77.67	80.21	80.15	82.91	88.85	95.93	107.09	114.47
ECE-East	6.63	7.26	9.34	10.89	11.35	15.67	16.22	18.82	24.63	26.67	29.43	29.40	33.49	37.05	37.41	39.50	47.26	54.19	57.96	55.83
ECE-West	3.02	3.11	4.46	6.37	8.61	14.10	14.98	14.26	17.33	21.23	25.70	28.24	28.98	27.65	26.89	26.51	25.60	24.70	29.83	33.53
Other	2.08	2.12	2.36	3.66	4.89	7.17	6.91	7.80	8.78	9.89	13.40	15.52	15.21	15.50	15.85	16.91	15.99	17.04	19.31	23.11
Eastern Europe and Soviet Union																				
World	30.25	32.82	40.57	53.34	67.83	88.18	92.56	101.51	118.94	135.05	155.18	155.23	153.06	157.93	159.75	165.55	183.39	195.16	185.62	190.15
ECE-East	18.35	20.03	24.29	29.42	33.02	44.23	46.04	53.70	63.74	69.49	76.26	76.88	79.22	85.40	87.11	90.96	107.37	117.08	99.68	93.59
ECE-West	8.35	9.13	12.15	17.77	25.87	32.60	34.98	34.46	39.96	47.36	54.34	53.74	50.20	48.32	47.66	48.34	50.75	52.00	58.06	65.14
Other	3.56	3.66	4.13	6.15	8.94	11.34	11.54	13.34	15.24	18.19	24.58	24.61	23.64	24.20	24.98	26.25	25.27	26.07	27.88	31.42

Source: Secretariat of the United Nations Economic Commission for Europe, based on national foreign trade statistics. Partner country groupings: ECE-East — east European member countries of CMEA and the Soviet Union; ECE-West — ECE market economies and Japan; Other — all remaining countries.

Note: Substantial discontinuities in the value series are indicated by ‖. These usually relate to large changes in the rouble/dollar cross rate (reductions in the relative valuation of rouble imports). Such changes were introduced by Hungary in 1976, Romania in 1981, Poland in 1982, and Czechoslovakia and the German Democratic Republic (together with other data revisions) in 1989 with application to the trade data from 1988.

[a] ECE secretariat estimates in the absence of national data.

Appendix C. International trade and payments

APPENDIX TABLE C.6

East-west trade: Value of western exports, by country of origin
(Million US dollars)

	1970	1971	1972	1973	1974	1975	1976	1977	1978	1979	1980	1981	1982	1983	1984	1985	1986	1987	1988	1989 [c]
Austria	368	387	457	627	1078	1279	1287	1419	1671	1998	2108	1808	1743	1868	1907	1885	2165	2447	2644	2910
Belgium-Luxembourg	171	184	269	498	821	847	792	761	851	1058	1308	1107	908	1091	934	1056	1027	1065	1029	1103
Denmark	114	141	140	189	265	294	268	271	319	354	371	270	213	213	262	294	394	336	478	649
Finland	361	329	449	530	899	1313	1505	1707	1754	1811	2814	3707	3756	3460	2768	3159	3540	3371	3481	3515
France	647	731	950	1307	1604	2602	2733	2782	2919	4032	4643	3906	2811	3331	2959	2909	2751	3089	3354	3819
Germany, Fed. Rep. of [a]	1296	1528	2199	3753	5563	6458	6247	6648	7715	8693	9443	7587	7526	7719	7105	7315	9033	9904	11181	13081
Greece	15	86	117	166	240	261	288	338	389	359	520	343	333	318	278	320	274	275	275	581
Iceland	15	16	22	24	41	41	41	62	49	64	83	71	58	60	71	64	60	65	78	82
Ireland	8	6	8	12	31	34	20	29	38	72	111	75	63	81	49	67	107	88	91	94
Italy	702	741	781	984	1647	2167	1960	2271	2413	2637	2728	2469	2446	2710	2475	2631	2879	3595	3569	4036
Netherlands	210	251	354	496	755	793	763	816	942	1145	1420	1386	994	1078	840	907	1058	1300	1249	1492
Norway	61	62	95	139	198	254	275	276	319	246	266	262	211	219	163	162	173	222	262	292
Portugal	8	6	8	11	20	43	83	81	75	96	91	84	86	79	85	91	77	90	90	123
Spain	68	65	121	115	202	256	303	285	355	548	546	787	428	516	584	730	495	544	516	701
Sweden	338	310	328	524	786	1095	1033	944	985	1177	1195	1035	814	699	749	775	819	915	1032	1134
Switzerland	210	214	285	427	598	744	794	885	1069	1069	1063	852	811	774	751	861	1133	1490	1694	1679
Turkey	84	81	87	101	145	122	167	174	324	301	481	320	312	228	261	302	284	314	314	430
United Kingdom	596	591	654	763	992	1293	1178	1457	1872	2049	2628	2028	1505	1434	1747	1527	1708	1831	2128	2282
Yugoslavia	538	670	785	968	1452	1871	2029	1904	2328	2663	3976	5348	5355	4551	4674	5208	4876	3869	4207	3662
Western Europe [b]	6561	7116	9028	12758	18756	23360	23460	25009	28665	32948	38707	35912	32999	33148	30913	32983	36312	38957	41790	41667
Canada	133	166	350	371	162	600	786	546	743	991	1773	1893	2035	1678	1883	1367	1131	750	1170	730
United States	352	382	817	1797	1428	2778	3497	2531	3665	5661	3843	4255	3585	2879	4167	3207	1960	2190	3637	5244
North America	485	548	1167	2168	1590	3378	4284	3077	4408	6652	5616	6148	5620	4557	6049	4575	3091	2940	4807	5974
Japan	447	536	736	810	1674	2198	2799	2669	3197	3265	3584	4012	4472	3564	3007	3314	3831	3280	3905	3696
Developed market economies [b]	7493	8201	10931	15737	22020	28936	30543	30755	36270	42865	47907	46072	43092	41269	39970	40872	43234	45177	50503	51337

Sources: United Nations commodity trade data (COMTRADE); 1988: ECE secretariat estimates for Greece, Portugal and the German Democratic Republic.

[a] Excluding trade between the Federal Republic of Germany and the German Democratic Republic.
[b] Including trade between the Federal Republic of Germany and the German Democratic Republic. Data cover reported balances (f.o.b.-f.o.b.) with six east European countries (Bulgaria, Czechoslovakia, German Democratic Republic, Hungary, Poland, Romania) and the Soviet Union.
[c] Extrapolations based on data for January-September.

APPENDIX TABLE C.7
East-west trade: Value of western imports, by country of destination
(Million US dollars)

	1970	1971	1972	1973	1974	1975	1976	1977	1978	1979	1980	1981	1982	1983	1984	1985	1986	1987	1988	1989 [a]
Austria	322	369	428	578	844	920	1053	1209	1346	1707	2294	2403	2088	1936	2174	2113	2133	2113	2213	2286
Belgium-Luxembourg	170	208	256	375	538	581	559	684	785	1010	1569	1415	1798	1488	2176	1630	1500	1800	1818	1698
Denmark	138	131	150	258	397	494	541	458	528	713	792	567	631	577	667	641	607	597	584	610
Finland	397	469	466	616	1414	1470	1504	1674	1677	2463	3636	3592	3541	3497	3107	2977	2646	3129	2812	2999
France	425	535	667	941	1253	1616	1901	2119	2449	3142	5075	4835	3994	3850	3657	3610	4146	4287	4578	4577
Germany, Fed. Rep., of [b]	1033	1188	1442	2181	2862	3084	3880	4331	5434	7722	8267	7312	7485	7341	8029	7803	8079	8522	8748	9743
Greece	91	92	112	161	175	243	359	345	584	523	536	518	469	423	720	690	471	553	588	702
Iceland	15	18	21	26	65	55	59	68	63	95	101	87	88	84	85	72	66	83	80	79
Ireland	29	33	39	50	91	87	87	114	127	184	137	107	123	129	139	144	173	177	166	192
Italy	733	799	1005	1354	1767	1781	2298	2425	2606	3451	4887	4398	4817	4876	5668	4550	4428	4744	5198	5929
Netherlands	201	239	295	416	610	750	888	986	1148	1711	2167	2505	3096	3162	2746	2928	1763	2149	1940	2270
Norway	80	160	132	174	221	243	334	385	311	387	362	389	563	472	489	393	350	433	565	649
Portugal	8	20	18	26	32	76	150	150	121	189	204	249	116	114	91	94	94	95	95	111
Spain	60	57	121	176	307	426	396	322	352	519	724	809	815	819	846	666	583	1196	1459	1691
Sweden	308	313	334	473	779	1018	1056	1063	1009	1646	1596	1255	1507	1681	1460	1449	1182	1610	1641	1698
Switzerland	130	138	155	240	353	334	484	583	819	1099	1369	1191	1115	973	907	849	804	711	666	710
Turkey	102	101	146	157	230	218	283	298	335	536	711	756	381	697	828	511	712	737	866	1161
United Kingdom	550	563	620	813	1048	1394	1758	2060	2140	2777	2747	1540	1832	1827	2242	1926	2123	2675	2709	2840
Yugoslavia	540	716	726	1060	1553	1691	1971	2320	2577	3169	4048	4437	4384	4049	3537	3535	3437	3372	3271	2920
Western Europe [c]	5877	6816	7879	11069	15797	17838	21107	23300	26361	35551	44289	41042	41579	40691	42287	39198	38451	42703	43867	42866
Canada	65	79	101	131	183	154	183	176	189	252	225	227	155	162	200	180	206	236	447	470
United States	226	223	320	526	890	729	864	915	1254	1354	1413	1596	1105	1404	2242	2013	1956	2024	2280	2354
North America	290	302	421	657	1073	882	1047	1091	1443	1606	1638	1824	1261	1566	2442	2194	2161	2260	2727	2824
Japan	494	488	589	1061	1493	1213	1217	1466	1480	1984	1901	1586	1401	1525	1620	1459	1778	2335	3030	3193
Developed market economies [c]	6660	7605	8889	12787	18363	19934	23371	25858	29284	39141	47828	44451	44241	43781	46350	42851	42391	47298	49624	48884

Sources: As for Appendix table C.6. Data cover reported balances (f.o.b.-f.o.b.) with six east European countries (Bulgaria, Czechoslovakia, German Democratic Republic, Hungary, Poland, Romania) and the Soviet Union.

[a] Extrapolations based on data for January-September.
[b] Excluding trade between the Federal Republic of Germany and the German Democratic Republic.
[c] Including trade between the Federal Republic of Germany and the German Democratic Republic.

Appendix C. International trade and payments

APPENDIX TABLE C.8

East-west trade: Western trade balances by western country
(Million US dollars)

	1970	1971	1972	1973	1974	1975	1976	1977	1978	1979	1980	1981	1982	1983	1984	1985	1986	1987	1988	1989[a]
Austria	46	18	30	49	234	360	233	210	325	292	-186	-595	-345	-68	-267	-228	32	335	431	624
Belgium-Luxembourg	1	-25	13	123	283	266	233	77	66	48	-261	-309	-891	-397	-1242	-574	473	-735	-789	-595
Denmark	-24	10	-10	-69	-132	-200	-273	-187	-210	-358	-422	-297	-418	-364	-405	-347	-214	-261	-106	38
Finland	-36	-139	-17	-86	-516	-157		33	78	-652	-821	115	214	-37	-339	182	894	241	670	516
France	223	195	283	366	351	986	832	664	471	890	-432	-929	-1183	-518	-698	-701	-1395	-1199	-1224	-758
Germany, Fed. Rep. of[b]	264	339	757	1573	2701	3375	2367	2316	2281	971	1177	275	41	378	-924	-488	954	1381	2433	3339
Greece	15	-7	6	5	65	19	-71	-7	-196	-163	-16	-175	-137	-105	-442	-370	-197	-278	-313	-121
Iceland		-2	1	-2	-24	-14	-18	-6	-13	-31	-18	-16	-31	-24	-15	-8	-6	-18	-2	3
Ireland	-21	-27	-31	-38	-60	-54	-67	-84	-88	-112	-27	-32	-61	-48	-90	-78	-66	-89	-75	-98
Italy	-31	-58	-224	-370	-120	386	-338	-154	-193	-813	-2159	-1929	-2372	-2166	-3192	-1919	-1549	-1149	-1629	-1893
Netherlands	9	12	60	79	144	43	-126	-170	-206	-566	-747	-1119	-2102	-2085	-1906	-2021	-705	-849	-691	-778
Norway	-19	-98	-38	-34	-23	11	-59	-109	8	-141	-96	-127	-352	-253	-326	-231	-178	-212	-303	-356
Portugal		-14	-11	-15	-12	-33	-67	-69	-47	-93	-112	-165	-30	-35	-6	-2	-17	-5	-5	12
Spain	8	8		-61	-105	-170	-94	-37	3	28	-178	-21	-387	-303	-261	65	-88	-651	-942	-990
Sweden	30	-2	-6	51	7	77	-22	-119	-24	-469	-401	-220	-693	-983	-711	-674	-363	-696	-608	-564
Switzerland	80	76	130	188	245	410	310	302	250	-30	-306	-338	-304	-200	-156	12	329	779	1029	969
Turkey	-18	-20	-59	-55	-84	-95	-116	-123	-11	-235	-230	-436	-69	-469	-567	-209	-429	-423	-552	-731
United Kingdom	46	28	34	-50	-56	-102	-580	-603	-268	-728	-120	489	-327	-393	-495	-399	-415	-844	-581	-558
Yugoslavia	-1	-46	59	-92	-102	180	58	-415	-250	-506	-72	911	971	502	1136	1673	1439	497	936	742
Western Europe[c]	684	301	1149	1689	2959	5522	2353	1709	2304	-2603	-5581	-5130	-8580	-7543	-11374	-6216	-2139	-3746	-2076	-1200
Canada	68	87	249	240	-21	446	603	369	554	740	1548	1666	1880	1517	1683	1187	925	514	723	259
United States	127	160	497	1271	538	2050	2633	1616	2411	4307	2429	2659	2480	1474	1924	1194	4	166	1357	2891
North America	195	246	746	1512	517	2496	3236	1986	2965	5046	3977	4325	4360	2991	3607	2381	929	680	2080	3150
Japan	-47	48	147	-251	181	985	1582	1203	1717	1281	1683	2426	3071	2039	1387	1855	2053	945	876	503
Developed market economies[c]	832	595	2042	2950	3658	9002	7172	4897	6986	3724	79	1621	-1149	-2513	-6380	-1979	843	-2121	879	2453

Sources: As for Appendix table C.6. Data cover reported balances (f.o.b.-f.o.b.) with six east European countries (Bulgaria, Czechoslovakia, German Democratic Republic, Hungary, Poland, Romania) and the Soviet Union.

[a] Extrapolations based on data for January-September.
[b] Excluding trade between the Federal Republic of Germany and the German Democratic Republic.
[c] Including trade between the Federal Republic of Germany and the German Democratic Republic.

APPENDIX TABLE C.9

East-west trade: Western exports, imports and balances by eastern country
(Million US dollars)

	1970	1971	1972	1973	1974	1975	1976	1977	1978	1979	1980	1981	1982	1983	1984	1985	1986	1987	1988	1989[a]
Western exports to:																				
Bulgaria	349	352	384	537	914	1154	1003	943	1147	1308	1710	1967	1641	1680	1573	1984	2320	2475	2495	2420
Czechoslovakia	865	1026	1119	1462	1914	2101	2295	2251	2565	3067	3375	2851	2773	2560	2424	2617	3123	3699	3976	3888
German Dem. Rep.	1144	1275	1626	1955	2541	2910	3181	3282	4004	5225	5719	5273	4692	5041	4422	4496	5686	7003	7270	3598
Hungary	671	800	884	1164	1879	1913	1904	2406	3105	3134	3468	3461	3139	2856	2784	3079	3711	4111	4153	4943
Poland	922	1114	1746	3233	4669	5593	5633	5145	5725	6210	6670	4469	3385	3115	3227	3455	3678	4252	5139	6605
Romania	728	787	1038	1432	2157	2091	2104	2395	3082	3881	4016	3108	1771	1366	1453	1512	1763	1338	1248	1157
Eastern Europe	4680	5353	6798	9782	14074	15763	16120	16421	19628	22825	24958	21129	17403	16618	15884	17142	20282	22878	24282	22611
Soviet Union	2813	2847	4133	5954	7946	13173	14422	14334	16642	20040	22949	24943	25690	24650	24086	23730	22952	22299	26221	28726
Total	7493	8201	10931	15737	22020	28936	30543	30755	36270	42865	47907	46072	43092	41269	39970	40872	43234	45177	50503	51337
Western imports (f.o.b.) from:																				
Bulgaria	247	268	290	387	463	428	522	556	635	973	1084	948	894	783	803	786	808	831	843	920
Czechoslovakia	808	910	1025	1374	1704	1826	1900	2079	2391	3042	3546	3181	3107	3106	3189	3036	3493	3840	4056	4289
German Dem. Rep.	988	1142	1312	1749	2302	2534	2753	3046	3509	4351	5383	5182	5399	5390	5299	5166	5868	6512	6861	3038
Hungary	541	604	813	1119	1376	1287	1484	1792	2069	2635	2920	2626	2429	2507	2720	2770	3130	3796	4209	4701
Poland	1032	1197	1490	2117	2820	3182	3611	3852	4330	5036	5471	3634	3392	3400	4032	4073	4350	5062	5805	6297
Romania	543	624	796	1137	1620	1677	2060	1979	2401	3259	3466	3517	2576	2750	3686	3453	3639	4067	4095	3920
Eastern Europe	4159	4745	5726	7883	10285	10934	12330	13304	15335	19295	21870	19087	17796	17936	19729	19284	21288	24109	25869	23166
Soviet Union	2501	2860	3163	4904	8078	9000	11041	12554	13949	19846	25958	25364	26444	25845	26621	23567	21103	23189	23754	25718
Total	6660	7605	8889	12787	18363	19934	23371	25858	29284	39141	47828	44451	44241	43781	46350	42851	42391	47298	49624	48884
Western balances with:																				
Bulgaria	103	84	94	150	451	726	481	386	512	335	625	1019	748	897	770	1198	1513	1644	1652	1500
Czechoslovakia	58	117	94	88	210	276	396	172	175	25	-171	-330	-334	-546	-765	-419	-371	-141	-80	-401
German Dem. Rep.	156	132	314	206	239	376	428	237	495	874	336	90	-707	-349	-877	-671	-182	491	409	559
Hungary	130	196	72	44	503	625	420	614	1036	499	549	835	711	349	64	309	581	315	-56	241
Poland	-110	-84	256	1116	1849	2411	2022	1293	1395	1175	1200	836	-7	-285	-804	-618	-671	-810	-666	309
Romania	185	163	242	295	538	415	44	416	680	623	549	-408	-805	-1384	-2233	-1941	-1876	-2730	-2847	-2763
Eastern Europe	521	608	1072	1899	3790	4829	3790	3118	4293	3530	3088	2042	-394	-1318	-3845	-2142	-1006	-1231	-1588	-555
Soviet Union	311	-13	970	1050	-132	4173	3382	1780	2693	193	-3009	-421	-755	-1195	-2535	163	1850	-890	2467	3008
Total	832	595	2042	2950	3658	9002	7172	4897	6986	3724	79	1621	-1149	-2513	-6380	-1979	843	-2121	879	2453

Sources: As for Appendix table C.6.

[a] Extrapolations based on data for January-September.

Appendix C. International trade and payments 415

APPENDIX TABLE C.10
Eastern Europe and the Soviet Union: Balance of payments in convertible currencies
(Billion US dollars)

	1970	1971	1972	1973	1974	1975	1976	1977	1978	1979	1980	1981	1982	1983	1984	1985	1986	1987	1988	1989
Bulgaria [a]																				
Merchandise export	0.4	0.5	0.6	0.7	1.0	1.0	1.1	1.4	1.7	2.4	3.2	3.5	3.4	2.9	3.3	3.2	2.5	2.9	2.9	2.3
Merchandise import	0.5	0.5	0.6	0.7	1.4	1.6	1.4	1.3	1.5	1.7	2.2	2.8	2.7	2.6	2.7	3.3	3.6	3.3	4.1	3.7
Balance	.	.	.	.	-0.4	-0.5	-0.2	.	0.2	0.7	1.0	0.7	0.7	0.3	0.6	-0.1	-1.1	-0.4	-1.2	-1.4
Invisibles	.	.	.	.	-0.1	-0.1	-0.1	-0.1	-0.1	-0.1	-0.1	.	.	0.1	0.1	0.1	-0.1	-0.1	-0.1	-0.3
Current account	.	.	.	-0.1	-0.4	-0.6	-0.3	-0.1	0.1	0.6	0.9	0.6	0.7	0.5	0.7	.	-1.2	-0.5	-1.3	-1.7
Czechoslovakia [a]																				
Merchandise export	1.3	1.4	1.5	2.0	2.6	2.7	2.7	3.1	3.5	4.1	5.1	4.9	4.7	4.9	4.8	4.6	5.1	5.3	5.7	6.1
Merchandise import	1.2	1.4	1.5	2.1	2.9	3.1	3.2	3.6	3.9	4.5	5.0	4.6	4.3	4.1	3.9	4.0	4.7	5.4	5.9	5.8
Balance	.	.	.	-0.2	-0.3	-0.4	-0.6	-0.5	-0.4	-0.4	0.1	0.3	0.4	0.8	0.9	0.7	0.4	-0.1	-0.1	0.3
Invisibles	.	.	.	.	.	.	.	-0.1	-0.2	-0.2	-0.3	-0.4	-0.3	-0.3	-0.2	0.2	-0.2	-0.1	-0.2	-0.3
Current account	.	.	.	-0.2	-0.3	-0.4	-0.6	-0.6	-0.5	-0.6	-0.3	.	0.1	0.5	0.7	0.5	0.2	-0.2	-0.3	0.0
German Democratic Republic [a]																				
Merchandise export	1.3	1.4	1.6	2.2	3.0	2.9	3.5	3.4	3.7	4.3	5.7	7.1	8.3	9.0	9.1	9.1	9.6	9.7	8.7	9.6
Merchandise import	1.5	1.6	2.1	2.9	4.0	4.0	5.1	4.8	4.7	6.1	7.4	7.1	6.8	7.7	8.1	8.0	9.2	9.4	9.8	10.5
Balance	-0.3	-0.2	-0.4	-0.7	-1.0	-1.0	-1.5	-1.4	-1.0	-1.8	-1.7	.	1.5	1.3	1.0	1.1	0.4	0.3	-1.0	-0.9
Invisibles	0.2	0.2	0.2	0.3	0.1	0.2	0.3	0.3	0.3	0.5	0.1	-0.4	-0.3	-0.1	.	.	0.2	0.6	0.5	0.2
Current account	-0.1	.	-0.2	-0.5	-0.9	-0.8	-1.3	-1.1	-0.7	-1.3	-1.6	-0.4	1.1	1.2	0.9	1.1	0.6	0.9	-0.6	-0.7
Hungary																				
Merchandise export	0.6	0.6	0.9	1.5	2.1	2.2	2.3	2.7	3.2	4.1	4.9	4.9	4.8	4.8	4.9	4.2	4.2	5.0	5.5	6.7
Merchandise import	0.7	0.8	0.9	1.4	2.5	2.5	2.5	3.0	4.0	4.2	4.6	4.4	4.2	4.1	4.0	4.1	4.7	5.0	5.0	6.1
Balance	-0.1	-0.2	-0.1	0.1	-0.4	-0.3	-0.2	-0.4	-0.8	-0.2	0.3	0.4	0.7	0.8	0.9	0.1	-0.5	.	0.5	0.6
Invisibles	.	-0.1	-0.2	-0.1	-0.1	-0.2	-0.2	-0.4	-0.5	-0.7	-0.6	-1.2	-1.0	-0.7	-0.8	-1.0	-1.0	-0.9	-1.3	-2.0
Current account	-0.1	-0.3	-0.1	.	-0.5	-0.5	-0.4	-0.8	-1.2	-0.8	-0.4	-0.7	-0.3	0.1	0.1	-0.8	-1.5	-0.9	-0.8	-1.4
Poland																				
Merchandise export	1.1	1.3	1.6	2.3	3.5	4.1	4.3	4.7	5.3	5.9	7.2	5.5	5.0	5.4	5.8	5.8	6.2	6.9	7.9	8.1
Merchandise import	1.0	1.1	1.8	3.6	5.6	6.9	7.0	6.6	7.4	8.0	8.1	6.2	4.6	4.3	4.4	4.6	5.1	5.9	7.0	8.0
Balance	0.1	0.2	-0.2	-1.3	-2.1	-2.8	-2.7	-1.9	-2.1	-2.1	-0.9	-0.8	0.4	1.1	1.5	1.2	1.1	1.0	0.9	0.1
Invisibles	0.1	0.1	0.2	0.2	-0.1	-0.2	-0.1	-0.3	-0.4	-1.0	-1.7	-2.4	-2.6	-2.3	-2.2	-1.7	-1.7	-1.4	-1.5	2.0
Current account	0.3	0.3	.	-1.1	-2.1	-3.0	-2.8	-2.1	-2.4	-3.1	-2.7	-3.1	-2.2	-1.2	-0.7	-0.5	-0.6	-0.4	-0.6	-1.9
Romania																				
Merchandise export	0.7	0.8	1.1	1.7	2.6	2.8	3.4	3.7	4.0	5.4	6.5	7.2	6.2	6.2	6.9	6.3	6.0	6.3	7.2	6.6
Merchandise import	0.8	0.9	1.1	1.7	2.9	2.9	3.3	3.8	4.6	6.5	8.0	7.0	4.7	4.6	4.7	4.8	4.0	4.0	3.2	3.0
Balance	-0.1	-0.1	-0.1	-0.1	-0.2	-0.1	0.1	-0.1	-0.6	-1.2	-1.5	0.2	1.5	1.7	2.2	1.4	1.9	2.4	3.9	3.0
Invisibles	-0.1	-0.1	-0.1	-0.1	-0.2	-0.1	-0.1	-0.1	-0.2	-0.5	-0.9	-1.0	-0.9	-0.8	-0.6	-0.5	-0.5	-0.2	-0.1	0.0
Current account	-0.2	-0.1	-0.2	-0.2	-0.5	-0.3	-0.1	-0.3	-0.8	-1.7	-2.4	-0.8	0.7	0.9	1.5	0.9	1.4	2.1	3.8	3.7
Eastern Europe																				
Merchandise export	5.4	6.0	7.3	10.2	14.7	15.8	17.4	18.9	21.4	26.2	32.5	33.1	32.5	33.3	34.8	33.2	33.6	36.2	37.9	39.5
Merchandise import	5.7	6.3	8.0	12.4	19.3	21.0	22.4	23.2	26.0	31.1	35.3	32.1	27.4	27.3	27.8	28.8	31.3	32.9	34.9	37.1
Balance	-0.4	-0.3	-0.7	-2.2	-4.5	-5.2	-5.1	-4.2	-4.6	-4.9	-2.8	0.9	5.1	5.9	7.0	4.4	2.3	3.3	3.0	2.4
Invisibles	.	0.2	0.2	0.2	-0.2	-0.4	-0.3	-0.7	-1.0	-2.1	-3.6	-5.4	-5.0	-3.9	-3.8	-3.2	-3.2	-2.2	-2.8	-4.5
Current account	-0.4	-0.1	-0.5	-2.0	-4.8	-5.6	-5.4	-5.0	-5.6	-6.9	-6.4	-4.5	0.1	2.0	3.2	1.2	-0.9	1.1	0.3	-2.0
Soviet Union [a]																				
Merchandise export	4.8	5.1	5.7	9.5	13.6	14.2	16.6	20.7	22.8	30.9	38.2	39.1	43.4	44.2	43.3	36.9	34.6	40.8	42.7	45.1
Merchandise import	4.3	4.6	6.2	9.0	12.0	18.7	19.3	18.8	21.8	26.7	34.8	39.9	39.1	38.0	36.6	36.2	33.3	32.7	39.2	47.4
Balance	0.4	0.5	-0.4	0.5	1.6	-4.5	-2.7	1.9	0.9	4.2	3.4	-0.7	4.3	6.2	6.7	0.7	1.4	8.1	3.5	-2.3
Invisibles	0.5	0.3	0.3	0.6	0.7	0.3	0.1	.	1.0	0.1	-0.4	-0.9	-0.7	-0.4	.	-0.1	-0.5	-0.3	-0.4	-0.9
Current account	0.9	0.8	-0.2	1.1	2.4	-4.2	-2.6	1.9	1.0	4.3	3.0	-1.6	3.6	5.8	6.7	0.6	0.9	7.8	3.1	-3.2
Eastern Europe and the Soviet Union																				
Merchandise export	10.1	11.1	13.1	19.7	28.3	30.0	33.9	39.7	44.2	57.2	70.7	72.2	75.8	77.5	78.2	70.1	68.2	77.0	80.6	84.7
Merchandise import	10.1	10.9	14.2	21.4	31.3	39.7	41.7	42.0	47.8	57.8	70.1	72.0	66.4	65.3	64.5	65.0	64.6	65.6	74.1	84.5
Balance [b]	0.1	0.2	-1.1	-1.7	-2.9	-9.7	-7.8	-2.4	-3.7	-0.7	0.6	0.2	9.4	12.2	13.7	5.2	3.7	11.4	6.5	0.1
Invisibles	0.4	0.4	0.4	0.7	0.3	-0.3	-0.4	-1.0	-1.3	-2.4	-4.5	-7.0	-6.3	-4.7	-4.1	-3.7	-4.0	-2.8	-3.5	-5.7
Current account	0.5	0.7	-0.7	-1.0	-2.6	-10.0	-8.2	-3.4	-5.0	-3.1	-3.9	-6.8	3.1	7.5	9.6	1.5	-0.3	8.6	3.0	-5.5

Sources: ECE secretariat Common Data Base, derived from national and international statistics and ECE Secretariat estimates. Hungary (1970-1981), Poland (1976-1980), Romania (1970-1986): IMF *Balance of Payments Statistics*, and *International Financial Statistics*; National Bank of Hungary (1982-1988, revised data), National Bank of Poland (merchandise trade 1970-1981; cash *plus* clearing transactions: 1981-1989).

[a] Trade with all developed and developing market economies (non-socialist countries *plus* Yugoslavia) based upon national foreign trade statistics.
[b] Includes estimated net interest payments of the CMEA banks.

APPENDIX TABLE C.11

Eastern Europe and the Soviet Union: Gross debt, assets and net debt in convertible currencies
(Billion US dollars)

	1970	1971	1972	1973	1974	1975	1976	1977	1978	1979	1980	1981	1982	1983	1984	1985	1986	1987	1988	1989
Gross debt																				
Bulgaria	0.7	0.8	1.0	1.1	1.8	2.7	3.3	3.8	4.4	4.6	3.6	3.2	2.8	2.4	2.1	3.5	4.9	6.2	7.7	9.0
Czechoslovakia	0.3	0.4	0.6	0.7	1.0	1.0	1.7	2.4	3.0	3.8	4.5	4.1	3.7	3.5	3.1	3.3	3.9	5.1	5.2	5.0
German Democratic Republic	1.1	1.4	1.5	2.2	3.2	5.2	6.0	7.5	9.3	11.1	13.6	14.4	12.6	12.1	11.6	13.6	16.1	19.1	20.2	20.6
Hungary	1.0	1.5	1.9	2.3	3.1	3.9	4.5	5.2	7.6	8.3	9.1	8.7	10.2	10.7	11.0	14.0	16.9	19.6	19.6	20.6
Poland	1.2	1.1	1.2	2.6	5.2	8.4	12.1	14.9	18.6	23.7	24.1	25.9	26.3	26.4	26.9	29.3	33.5	39.2	39.2	39.9
Romania	1.0	1.2	1.2	1.6	2.6	2.9	2.9	3.6	5.1	7.2	9.6	10.2	9.8	8.9	7.2	6.6	6.4	5.7	3.1	1.4
Eastern Europe	5.1	6.4	7.5	10.4	16.9	24.2	30.6	37.5	48.0	58.7	64.6	66.4	65.4	64.0	61.9	70.3	81.7	94.9	95.0	96.5
Soviet Union	1.6	2.6	4.2	6.0	8.1	15.4	20.9	22.7	24.4	26.1	25.2	29.0	28.4	26.9	25.6	31.4	37.4	40.2	41.7	50.6
Eastern Europe and the Soviet Union	6.7	9.0	11.7	16.4	25.0	39.5	51.5	60.2	72.4	84.8	89.7	95.4	93.8	90.9	87.5	101.6	119.0	135.1	136.8	147.1
Assets: With BIS-reporting banks [a]																				
Bulgaria	-	-	0.1	-	0.3	0.4	0.4	0.5	0.6	0.7	0.8	0.8	1.0	1.2	1.4	2.1	1.4	1.1	1.8	1.3
Czechoslovakia	0.3	0.3	0.5	0.5	0.4	0.4	0.4	0.5	0.6	1.0	1.3	1.1	0.7	0.9	1.0	1.0	1.2	1.6	1.7	1.9
German Democratic Republic	0.2	0.2	0.3	0.3	0.5	1.6	0.8	0.9	1.3	2.0	2.0	2.2	1.9	3.4	4.5	6.5	7.5	9.0	9.5	9.6
Hungary	0.2	0.2	0.3	0.6	0.6	0.9	1.2	1.1	0.9	1.2	1.4	0.9	0.7	1.3	1.5	2.3	2.1	1.5	1.4	1.1
Poland	0.3	0.4	0.4	0.6	0.5	0.6	0.8	0.4	0.8	1.2	0.7	0.3	1.0	1.2	1.6	1.6	1.7	3.0	3.6	3.4
Romania	-	-	-	0.1	0.2	1.5	0.4	0.2	0.8	0.3	0.3	0.3	0.3	0.5	0.6	0.4	0.6	1.4	0.8	1.5
Eastern Europe	1.1	1.2	1.7	1.8	2.6	5.4	4.1	3.6	4.6	6.4	6.4	6.0	5.6	8.6	10.7	13.9	14.5	17.6	18.8	18.8
Soviet Union	1.0	1.2	1.9	2.6	3.5	3.1	4.7	4.4	6.1	8.8	8.6	8.5	10.0	10.9	11.3	13.1	14.8	14.1	15.3	14.2
Eastern Europe and the Soviet Union	2.1	2.4	3.5	4.4	6.1	8.5	8.8	8.0	10.7	15.2	14.9	14.4	15.6	19.5	22.1	26.9	29.4	31.7	34.0	33.0
Assets: International reserves [b]																				
Hungary	..	0.6	0.8	1.2	1.4	1.5	1.5	1.5	2.1	2.1	2.4	2.0	1.2	1.9	2.6	3.5	3.6	2.5	2.2	..
Romania	..	..	..	0.3	0.3	0.6	0.7	0.4	0.5	0.7	0.5	0.5	0.6	0.7	0.8	0.3	0.7	0.7	..	..
Assets: Total assets [c]																				
Hungary	0.6	0.8	1.0	1.5	1.7	2.0	2.3	2.4	3.1	3.3	3.7	3.2	2.8	3.7	4.8	6.7	7.3	6.8	6.3	5.7
Romania	..	..	..	..	..	..	..	..	..	2.0	1.7	1.9	2.3	2.9	3.6	3.0	3.1	3.2	..	..
Net debt (reflecting assets with BIS-reporting reserves)																				
Bulgaria	0.6	0.7	0.9	1.0	1.4	2.3	2.9	3.3	3.8	3.9	2.9	2.4	1.9	1.2	0.7	1.4	3.5	5.1	5.9	7.7
Czechoslovakia	-	0.1	0.1	0.2	0.6	0.7	1.3	1.9	2.3	2.8	3.3	3.0	3.0	2.6	2.1	2.3	2.7	3.5	3.5	3.1
German Democratic Republic	0.9	1.2	1.2	1.9	2.6	3.6	5.2	6.6	8.0	9.2	11.6	12.3	10.7	8.7	7.1	7.1	8.6	10.1	10.7	11.0
Hungary	0.8	1.3	1.5	2.0	2.5	3.0	3.3	4.1	6.7	7.1	7.7	7.8	9.5	9.4	9.4	11.7	14.8	18.1	18.2	19.5
Poland	0.9	0.7	0.8	2.0	4.7	7.7	11.3	14.5	17.7	22.6	23.5	25.1	25.3	25.2	25.4	27.7	31.8	36.2	35.6	36.5
Romania	1.0	1.2	1.2	1.5	2.4	1.4	2.4	3.4	4.8	6.9	9.3	9.9	9.5	8.4	6.6	5.8	4.3	4.3	2.3	-0.1
Eastern Europe	4.0	5.2	5.8	8.6	14.3	18.8	26.5	33.9	43.4	52.3	58.2	60.5	59.8	55.5	51.2	56.4	67.1	77.3	76.3	77.7
Soviet Union	0.6	1.4	2.3	3.4	4.6	12.2	16.1	18.3	18.3	17.3	16.6	20.5	18.4	16.0	14.2	18.3	22.5	26.1	26.5	36.4
Eastern Europe and the Soviet Union	4.6	6.6	8.2	12.0	18.8	31.0	42.7	52.2	61.7	69.6	74.8	81.0	78.2	71.4	65.4	74.7	89.7	103.4	102.7	114.2
Net debt (reflecting international reserves)																				
Hungary	..	0.9	1.1	1.1	1.7	2.4	3.1	3.7	5.5	6.2	6.6	6.7	9.0	8.9	8.4	10.4	13.3	17.1	17.4	..
Romania	..	..	..	1.3	2.3	2.2	2.1	3.2	4.5	6.5	9.1	9.6	9.2	8.2	6.4	6.3	5.7	5.0 [d]	..	..
Net debt (reflecting total assets)																				
Hungary	0.4	0.7	0.9	0.8	1.4	1.9	2.3	2.9	4.5	5.2	5.4	5.5	4.9	4.6	4.1	5.0	7.8	10.9	11.1	15.0
Romania	..	..	..	..	..	..	..	..	..	5.2	7.8	8.2	7.5	6.0	3.6	3.6	3.3	2.5	..	..

Sources: ECE secretariat Common Data Base, derived from national and international statistics and ECE secretariat estimates. Hungary (revised data 1982-1988); Poland, Romania (1970-1986): national statistics; Bulgaria, Czechoslovakia, German Democratic Republic and the Soviet Union (including CMEA banks): BIS/OECD *Statistics on External Indebtedness: Bank and Trade-Related Non-Bank External Claims on Individual Borrowing Countries and Territories*, Paris and Basle (adjusted here to include gross claims of the Federal Republic of Germany *vis-à-vis* the German Democratic Republic arising from clearing exchanges). For these four countries data reflect convertible currency debt *vis-à-vis* reporting institutions only and thus exclude any claims of developing countries.

[a] 1989 figures are end-September.
[b] International reserves including gold. Hungarian gold reserves at national valuation: $275/oz (1982-1985); $320/oz (1986-1989.) Romania's gold reserves valued at SDR 35/oz.
[c] International reserves *plus* other assets (mainly trade credits). The concept of total assets ("claims from deliveries on credit") used by Romania to calculate its net debt appears to differ from the definitions used here, since international reserves seem to be excluded.
[d] End-June.